Lecture Notes in Computer Science   **9233**

Commenced Publication in 1973
Founding and Former Series Editors:
Gerhard Goos, Juris Hartmanis, and Jan van Leeuwen

Advanced Research in Computing and Software Science

Subline of Lecture Notes in Computer Science

More information about this series at http://www.springer.com/series/7407

Jesper Larsson Träff · Sascha Hunold
Francesco Versaci (Eds.)

Euro-Par 2015: Parallel Processing

21st International Conference
on Parallel and Distributed Computing
Vienna, Austria, August 24–28, 2015
Proceedings

 Springer

Editors
Jesper Larsson Träff
Vienna University of Technology
Vienna
Austria

Francesco Versaci
Vienna University of Technology
Vienna
Austria

Sascha Hunold
Vienna University of Technology
Vienna
Austria

ISSN 0302-9743   ISSN 1611-3349   (electronic)
Lecture Notes in Computer Science
ISBN 978-3-662-48095-3   ISBN 978-3-662-48096-0   (eBook)
DOI 10.1007/978-3-662-48096-0

Library of Congress Control Number: 2015945134

LNCS Sublibrary: SL1 – Theoretical Computer Science and General Issues

Springer Heidelberg New York Dordrecht London

Printed on acid-free paper

Springer-Verlag GmbH Berlin Heidelberg is part of Springer Science+Business Media
(www.springer.com)

Preface

Euro-Par is an annual, international conference on European ground, covering all aspects of parallel and distributed processing, ranging from theory to practice, from small to the largest parallel and distributed systems and infrastructures, from fundamental computational problems to full-fledged applications, from architecture, compiler, language and interface design and implementation to tools, support infrastructures, and application performance aspects. Euro-Par has a unique organization into topics capturing all these different aspects and has proven an excellent forum for focused technical discussions within a large, broad, and diverse audience. The Euro-Par conference itself is complemented by a workshop program, where workshops dedicated to more specialized themes, to cross-cutting issues, and to upcoming trends and paradigms can be easily and conveniently organized with little administrative overhead. The Euro-Par topics are relatively stable but have evolved over the years to adequately reflect the state of the field, often in reaction to thematic developments initiated by previous workshops.

Euro-Par's ambition is to be the first choice for presenting solid (European) research in all areas of parallel and distributed computing as covered by the Euro-Par topics. The target audience includes researchers, scientists and students from universities, academic research institutions, research laboratories, development centers, and also companies and industrial organizations with an often vital interest in parallel and distributed computing. With its wide spectrum, Euro-Par fosters interaction between different people and personalities and between different areas and approaches in parallel and distributed computing.

Euro-Par 2015 was the 21th conference in the Euro-Par series, and was organized in Vienna, Austria, by the Vienna University of Technology (TU Wien), Faculty of Informatics, Research Group for Parallel Computing. Previous Euro-Par conferences took place in Stockholm (1995), Lyon (1996), Passau (1997), Southampton (1998), Toulouse (1999), Munich (2000), Manchester (2001), Paderborn (2002), Klagenfurt (2003), Pisa (2004), Lisbon (2005), Dresden (2006), Rennes (2007), Las Palmas (2008), Delft (2009), Ischia (2010), Bordeaux (2011), Rhodes (2012), Aachen (2013), and Porto (2014). In 2016, the conference will be held in Grenoble. General information on the Euro-Par conference series and organization is available at http://www.europar.org.

Euro-Par 2015 was organized into 13 topics, each with its own topic Program Committee consisting of a global chair, a local chair, and at least two additional members. Topics that received a larger number of submissions had additional members, such that each topic member had the responsibility to solicit reviews for about five papers. With this organization, the aim of Euro-Par is that each submitted paper receives at least four reviews, that each paper is actually reviewed by at least one topic committee member, and that papers receive reviews from different communities and groups. For Euro-Par 2015, topic committee members hailed from 17 different countries.

The Euro-Par 2015 Call-for-Papers attracted 190 full-paper submissions, representing 37 countries. The topic committees made sure that all papers were reviewed according to the Euro-Par standards. A total of 772 paper reviews were collected over an eight-week review period, giving an average of 4.1 review reports per paper. Based on the reviews and discussions among the reviewers and topic committee members, 51 papers were selected for presentation at the conference. Of the 51 accepted papers, two were accepted with distinction. Topic 11 attracted few papers and unfortunately none could be accepted. The accepted papers represent contributions from 21 countries from all continents, resulting in an acceptance rate of 27 %. The final decisions on acceptance or rejection of the submitted papers were made at a general Program Committee meeting with physical presence of the conference co-chairs, the local (in some cases global) chairs of the topics, and additional representatives from the Euro-Par Steering Committee. An effort was made to handle potential conflicts of interest at this large meeting in a proper way.

The conference program was organized into parallel sessions roughly following the topics. The two distinguished papers that were presented at separate sessions were:

- Shahar Timnat, Maurice Herlihy and Erez Petrank: "A Practical Transactional Memory Interface".
- Leyuan Wang, Sean Baxter and John Owens: "Fast Parallel Suffix Array on the GPU".

In addition to the paper presentations, Euro-Par 2015 was very pleased to present three renowned invited speakers who gave keynote presentations on new developments and perspectives in their respective areas. These were:

- Michel Raynal (IRISA, University of Rennes, France),
- Mateo Valero (UPC Barcelona, Spain), and
- Christian Scheideler (University of Paderborn, Germany).

The program also included a panel discussion on "The Future of Parallel, Distributed and High-Performance Computing, in Europe", which was moderated by Raffaele Tripiccione, University of Ferrara, Italy, and took place before the conference dinner.

The workshop program of Euro-Par 2015 on the Monday and Tuesday before the main conference included the following workshops:

1. Big Data management in Clouds (BigDataCloud)
2. Parallel and Distributed Computing Education for Undergraduate Students (Euro-EDUPAR)
3. Algorithms, Models, and Tools for Parallel Computing on Heterogeneous Platforms (HeteroPar)
4. Large-Scale Distributed Virtual Environments (LSDVE)
5. On-chip Memory Hierarchies and Interconnects: Organization, management and implementation (OMHI)
6. Parallel and Distributed Agent-Based Simulations (PADABS)
7. Performance Engineering for Large-scale Graph Analytics (PELGA)
8. Reproducibility in Parallel computing (REPPAR)
9. Resiliency in high-performance computing with clouds, grids, and clusters (Resilience)
10. Runtime and Operating Systems for the Many-core Era (ROME)

11. UnConventional High-Performance Computing (UCHPC)
12. Virtualization in High-Performance Cloud Computing (VHPC)

Workshop papers will be published in a separate, post-conference proceedings volume.

The success and relevance of Euro-Par are first and foremost due to the researchers, who submit their contributions to the conference. We hereby warmly thank all contributors of submitted papers, and hope that also those whose contributions were not accepted for presentation this time will feel encouraged by the feedback to continue their work and consider Euro-Par in the future as a relevant venue. Reviewing papers, preparing feedback, and partaking in the discussions is a serious and considerable effort. We expressly thank all topic committee members and all reviewers for their work, especially all topic chairs for always being available and overseeing the reviewing process.

Euro-Par is largely financed by the participants' fees. A small number of institutional and industrial sponsors contributed to the conference, and we deeply thank them all. These contributions are essential for maintaining the modest conference fees, which are a significant factor in making it possible for students to attend the conference. Their names and logos appear on the Euro-Par 2015 website at http://www.europar2015.org. We point out that sponsors have no influence on the conference program or any other aspects of the Euro-Par organization.

This year, 15 special student scholarships consisting in free registrations for the conference and workshops were available and financed by the Euro-Par fund. There was a lot of interest in these scholarships, and we thank the Euro-Par Steering Committee for facilitating this support.

Euro-Par is a large conference and its organization depends on the work of many individuals and organizations. We thank all members of the local organization team, especially Christine Kamper and Margret Steinbuch. Vienna University of Technology (TU Wien) provided lecture halls and seminar rooms at reasonable costs, and supported us with the logistics. We are grateful for that. The Euro-Par Steering Committee, especially the chair Christian Lengauer and the vice-chair Luc Bougé, provided reliable guidance and support throughout the whole organizational phase going back to 2013. We acknowledge the trust put in us to organize the 2015 edition of Euro-Par.

Lastly, we thank all participants who attended the conference and the workshops and contributed to a productive meeting. It was a pleasure to organize and host Euro-Par 2015 in Vienna. We hope that everybody enjoyed the technical program, the social events, and the city of Vienna.

August 2015

Jesper Larsson Träff
Sascha Hunold
Francesco Versaci

Organization

Euro-Par Steering Committee

Chair

Christian Lengauer · University of Passau, Germany

Vice-Chair

Luc Bougé · ENS Rennes, France

European Representatives

Marco Danelutto	University of Pisa, Italy
Emmanuel Jeannot	LaBRI-Inria, Bordeaux, France
Christos Kaklamanis	Computer Technology Institute, Greece
Paul Kelly	Imperial College, UK
Thomas Ludwig	University of Hamburg, Germany
Emilio Luque	Autonomous University of Barcelona, Spain
Tomàs Margalef	Autonomous University of Barcelona, Spain
Wolfgang Nagel	Dresden University of Technology, Germany
Rizos Sakellariou	University of Manchester, UK
Fernando Silva	University of Porto, Portugal
Henk Sips	Delft University of Technology, The Netherlands
Domenico Talia	University of Calabria, Italy
Felix Wolf	Technische Universität Darmstadt, Germany

Honorary Members

Ron Perrott	Oxford e-Research Centre, UK
Karl Dieter Reinartz	University of Erlangen-Nuremberg, Germany

Observers

Jesper Larsson Träff	Vienna University of Technology, Austria
Denis Trystram	Grenoble Institute of Technology, France

Euro-Par 2015 Organization

Chair

Jesper Larsson Träff · Vienna University of Technology, Austria

Proceedings

Francesco Versaci · Vienna University of Technology, Austria

Workshops

Sascha Hunold   Vienna University of Technology, Austria

Local Organization

Christine Kamper   Vienna University of Technology, Austria
Margret Steinbuch   Vienna University of Technology, Austria

Program Committee

Topic 1: Support Tools and Environments

Chair

Rosa Badia   Barcelona Supercomputing Center, Spain

Local Chair

Karl Fürlinger   LMU Munich, Germany

Members

Todd Gamblin   Lawrence Livermore National Laboratory, USA
Nathan R. Tallent   Pacific Northwest National Laboratory, USA
Marios D. Dikaiakos   University of Cyprus, Cyprus
Brian Wylie   Forschungszentrum Jülich, Germany
Thilo Kielmann   Vrije Universiteit Amsterdam, The Netherlands
Matthias S. Mueller   RWTH Aachen, Germany

Topic 2: Performance Modeling, Prediction, and Evaluation

Chair

Felix Wolf   Technische Universität Darmstadt, Germany

Local Chair

Marian Vajteršic   University of Salzburg, Austria

Members

Laura Carrington   San Diego Supercomputer Center, USA
Frédéric Suter   IN2P3 Computing Center, France
Miquel Pericàs   Chalmers University of Technology, Sweden

Topic 3: Scheduling and Load Balancing

Chair

Denis Trystram   Grenoble Institute of Technology, France

Local Chair

Hans Kellerer   Graz University of Technology, Austria

Members

Henri Casanova   University of Hawai'i, USA
Vitus Leung   Sandia National Laboratories, USA
Giorgio Lucarelli   LIG Grenoble, France
Ariel Oleksiak   Poznan Supercomputing Center, Poland
Natasha Shakhlevich   University of Leeds, UK
Leonel Sousa   University of Lisbon, Portugal

Topic 4: Architecture and Compilers

Chair

Franz Franchetti   Carnegie Mellon University, USA

Local Chair

Jens Knoop   Vienna University of Technology, Austria

Members

Markus Schordan   Lawrence Livermore National Laboratory, USA
Louis-Noël Pouchet   University of California, Los Angeles, USA
Sid Touati   Inria, France

Topic 5: Parallel and Distributed Data Management

Chair

André Brinkmann   University of Mainz, Germany

Local Chair

Harald Kosch   University of Passau, Germany

Members

Gabriel Antoniu   Inria Rennes, France
Veronika Sonigo   FEMTO-ST, Besançon, France

Topic 6: Grid, Cluster and Cloud Computing

Chair

Frédéric Desprez   Inria, France

Local Chair

Radu Prodan   University of Innsbruck, Austria

Members

Adrien Lebre   Inria, France
Helge Meinhard   CERN, Switzerland
Rizos Sakellariou   University of Manchester, UK
Uwe Schwiegelshohn   TU Dortmund University, Germany
Domenico Talia   University of Calabria, Italy
Ramin Yahyapour   Georg-August University of Göttingen, Germany

Topic 7: Distributed Systems and Algorithms

Chair

André Schiper   EPFL, Switzerland

Local Chair

Josef Widder   Vienna University of Technology, Austria

Members

Antonio Casimiro   University of Lisbon, Portugal
Christof Fetzer   Dresden University of Technology, Germany
Marta Patino-Martinez   Technical University of Madrid, Spain
Pierre Sens   LIP6/Inria Paris Rocquencourt, France

Topic 8: Parallel and Distributed Programming, Interfaces and Languages

Chair

Bill Gropp   University of Illinois at Urbana-Champaign, USA

Local Chair

Erwin Laure   KTH Royal Institute of Technology, Sweden

Members

Keshav Pingali   The University of Texas at Austin, USA
Rajeev Thakur   Argonne National Laboratory, USA
Michael Gerndt   Technische Universität München (TUM), Germany

Topic 9: Multi- and Many-core Programming

Chair

Marco Aldinucci   University of Turin, Italy

Local Chair

Siegfried Benkner   University of Vienna, Austria

Members

Hans Vandierendonck   Queen's University Belfast, UK
Franscisco De Sande   Universidad de La Laguna, Spain
Antoniu Pop   University of Manchester, UK
Massimo Torquati   University of Pisa, Italy
Samuel Thibault   Inria Bordeaux, France
Massimiliano Meneghin   Autodesk Research, Toronto, Canada
José Daniel García   Charles III University of Madrid, Spain

Topic 10: Theory and Algorithms for Parallel Computation

Chair

Peter Sanders   Karlsruhe Institute of Technology, Germany

Local Chair

Robert Elsässer   University of Salzburg, Austria

Members

Leah Epstein   University of Haifa, Israel
Pierre Fraigniaud   Paris Diderot University - Paris 7, France
Geppino Pucci   University of Padua, Italy

Topic 11: Communication, Routing and Networks

Chair

Torsten Hoefler   ETH Zurich, Switzerland

Local Chair

Holger Fröning   Heidelberg University, Germany

Members

Mondrian Nüssle   Extoll GmbH, Germany
Federico Silla   Technical University of Valencia, Spain
Mitch Gusat   IBM Zurich, Switzerland
Tor Skeie   University of Oslo, Norway

Topic 12: Numerical Methods and Applications

Chair

Paolo Bientinesi	RWTH Aachen, Germany

Local Chair

Wilfried Gansterer	University of Vienna, Austria

Members

Daniel Ruprecht	Università della Svizzera italiana, Lugano, Switzerland
Xavier Vasseur	CERFACS, France

Topic 13: Accelerator Computing

Chair

Jörg Keller	University of Hagen, Germany

Local Chair

Andreas Steininger	Vienna University of Technology, Austria

Members

Lee Howes	Qualcomm, USA
Michael Klemm	Intel, Germany
Naoya Maruyama	RIKEN, Japan
Norbert Eicker	Jülich Supercomputing Centre, Germany
Erik Saule	UNC Charlotte, USA
Benedict Gaster	University of the West of England, UK

Euro-Par 2015 Reviewers

Euro-Par is grateful to all reviewers for their willingness and their effort in providing good feedback to authors and topic committees. All external reviewers are listed and hereby thanked.

Ashwin Aji	Enes Bajrovic
Goetz Alefeld	Tomáš Balyo
Pedro Alonso	Gergö Barany
Andreea Simona Anghel	Denis Barthou
Peter Arbenz	Ezio Bartocci
Rohit Atre	Andreas Beckmann
Guillaume Aupy	Shajulin Benedict
Eduard Ayguadé	Nadia Bennani
Michael Bader	Fatih Berber

Tobias Grosser
Armin Größlinger
João F.D. Guerreiro
Carla Guillen
Jens Gustedt
Stefan Guthe
Mary Hall
Jeff Hammond
Frank Hannig
Stuart Hawkins
Thomas Herault
Marc-André Hermanns
Fabien Hermenier
Ruben Hoeksma
Matthias Hofmann
Andreas Hollmann
Dan Holmes
Tetsuya Hoshino
Derek Hower
Zia Ul Huda
Andra-Ecaterina Hugo
Maxime Hugues
Udo Hönig
Shadi Ibrahim
Kamran Idrees
Hisham Ihshaish
Aleksandar Ilic
Guillaume Iooss
Christian Iwainsky
Jeremie Jakubowicz
Andreas Janecek
Matthias Janetschek
Mateusz Jarus
Ernesto Jiménez
Pavel Jiranek
Mark Joshi
Dominik Kaaser
Imed Kacem
Rashid Kaleem
Boda Kang
Lars Karlsson
Kostas Katrinis
Kamer Kaya
Jörg Keller
Martin Keller-Ressel
Christoph Kessler

Michael Knobloch
Joanna Kolodziej
Martin Kong
Xi Kong
Anthony Kougkas
Alessandro Kraemer
Andreas Krall
Lidia Kuan
Jean-Yves L'Excellent
Stefan Lankes
Johan Larsson
Laurent Lefèvre
Dimitrios Letsios
Xiaoming Li
Chunhua Liao
Mulugeta Libsie
Calvin Lin
Pei-Hung Lin
Torsten Linss
Jack Liu
Drazen Lucanin
Matthias Maiterth
Saeed Maleki
Andrew Mallinson
Valerio Mariani
Artur Mariano
Stefano Markidis
Fabrizio Marozzo
Paulo Martins
Carlo Mastroianni
Roland Mathà
Eduard Mehofer
Dirk Meister
Gabriele Mencagli
Christopher Menke
Ludovic Métivier
Ulrich Meyer
Henning Meyerhenke
Samuel Midiff
Antoine Miné
Claudia Misale
Svetislav Momcilovic
Hans Moritsch
Karen Murphy
Claudio Márquez
Lars Nagel

Raymond Namyst

Alberto Nannarelli

Lorenzo Naranjo

Wahid Nasri

Emanuele Natale

Barry L. Nelson

Ulrich Neumerkel

Nuno Neves

Jean-Marc Nicod

Boyana Norris

Lucas Nussbaum

Yury Oleynik

Stephane Operto

Anne-Cécile Orgerie

Vitaly Osipov

Simon Ostermann

David Ozog

Dario Pacciarelli

Sreepathi Pai

Ardavan Pedram

Hung Pei-Lin

Anh Huy Phan

Jean-Marc Pierson

Ilia Pietri

Rene-Edouard Plessix

Sabri Pllana

Antoniu Pop

Andreas Prell

Ronald Rahaman

Abtin Rahimian

Cristian Ramon-Cortés

Lawrence Rauchwerger

Veronika Rehn-Sonigo

Paul Renaud-Goud

Ruymán Reyes

Admilson Ribeiro

David Richards

Ángel Rodríguez-Rozas

Sascha Roloff

Thomas Ropars

Barry Rountree

Alban Rousset

Jonathan Rouzaud-Cornabas

Karl Rupp

Krzysztof Rzadca

Jean-Charles Régin

P. Sadayappan

Rizos Sakellariou

Debasmita Samaddar

Abdoulaye Samake

Luis Miguel Sánchez

Peter Sanders

Martin Sandrieser

Ahmet Erdem Sarıyüce

Mitsuhisa Sato

Erik Saule

Christian Scheideler

Olaf Schenk

Wolfram Schiffmann

Stephan Schlagkamp

Dirk Schmidl

Oliver Schmitt

Stefan Schuh

Christian Schulz

Martin Schulz

R. Oguz Selvitopi

Sangmin Seo

Marc Sergent

Aamer Shah

Jun Shirako

Min Si

Albert Sidelnik

Mikhail Smelyanskiy

Steven Smith

Chrystalla Sofokleous

Rafael Sotomayor

Jochen Speck

Paul Springer

Luka Stanisic

Josef Strnadel

Michelle Strout

Jiawen Sun

Petter Svärd

Tim Süß

Andrei Tchernykh

Marc Tchiboukdjian

Thomas Toifl

Fabio Tordini

Ennio Torre

Guy Tremblay

Demetris Trihinas

Horst Trinker

Euro-Par 2015 Invited Talks

Concurrent Systems: Hybrid Object Implementations and Abortable Objects

Michel Raynal, IRISA, University of Rennes, France

As they allow processes to communicate and synchronize, concurrent objects are, de facto, the most important objects of concurrent programming. The talk will present and illustrate two important notions associated with such objects. The first one, which is related to their implementation, is the notion of a hybrid implementation. The second one, which is related to their definition, is the notion of an abortable object.

Roughly speaking, a hybrid implementation of a concurrent object is such that the algorithms implementing its operations do not use locks in "good circumstances", those being defined statically or dynamically. In particular the use of locks must be prevented in concurrency-free execution patterns.

The notion of an abortable object is related to the object definition itself. It addresses the case where, in practice, conflicts are rare. So the idea is here to allow a process that invokes an object operation, to return a predefined default value (abort) in specific circumstances, namely in the presence of concurrency. To illustrate this, the talk will present a non-blocking implementation of an abortable stack (non-blocking means here that, in the presence of concurrency, at least one stack operation does not return abort).

Runtime Aware Architectures

Mateo Valero, UPC Barcelona, Spain

In the last few years, the traditional ways to keep the increase of hardware performance to the rate predicted by the Moore's Law have vanished. When unicores were the norm, hardware design was decoupled from the software stack thanks to a well defined Instruction Set Architecture (ISA). This simple interface allowed developing applications without worrying too much about the underlying hardware, while hardware designers were able to aggressively exploit instruction-level parallelism (ILP) in superscalar processors. With the irruption of multi-cores and parallel applications, this simple interface started to leak. As a consequence, the role of decoupling again applications from the hardware was moved to the runtime system. Efficiently using the underlying hardware from this runtime without exposing its complexities to the application has been the target of very active and prolific research in the last years.

Current multi-cores are designed as simple symmetric multiprocessors (SMP) on a chip. However, we believe that this is not enough to overcome all the problems that multi-cores already have to face. It is our position that the runtime has to drive the design of future multi-cores to overcome the restrictions in terms of power, memory, programmability and resilience that multi-cores have. In this talk, we introduce a first approach towards a Runtime-Aware Architecture (RAA), a massively parallel architecture designed from the runtime's perspective.

Self-stabilizing Distributed Data Structures

Christian Scheideler, University of Paderborn, Germany

Once a distributed system becomes large enough, faults are not the exception but the rule. Proactive strategies that aim at protecting a distributed system from becoming corrupted can only protect a system up to a certain point, which is nicely demonstrated by the CAP-Theorem and other impossibility results. So also reactive strategies, which aim at recovering from corruptions, should be considered. A standard approach to obtain systems that are able to recover from any kind of faults is self-stabilization. However, previous research has mostly focused on the case that there are no more faults or other changes to the system (due to pending requests) during self-stabilization. So it is not clear for many of the proposed solutions how well the system would be able to serve requests while it is self-stabilizing. In my presentation I will address this issue for the specific case of self-stabilizing distributed data structures that are managed by a large distributed system that does not just allow changes to the data but also to the set of its members, and I will present our newest results in this area.

Euro-Par 2015 Topics Overview

Topic 1: Support Tools and Environments

Rosa Badia, Karl Fürlinger, Todd Gamblin, Nathan R. Tallent,
Marios D. Dikaiakos, Brian Wylie, Thilo Kielmann, Matthias S. Mueller

Despite an impressive body of research, parallel and distributed programming remains a complex task prone to subtle software issues that can affect both the correctness and the performance of applications. The topic on support tools and environments focuses on tools and techniques to help tackling that complexity. Contributions were sought to address any of the many challenges of parallel and distributed programming related to programmability, portability, correctness, reliability, scalability, efficiency, performance and energy consumption. The aim was to bring together tool designers, developers, and users to share their concerns, ideas, solutions, and products for a wide range of parallel platforms. Contributions with solid theoretical foundations and with strong experimental validations on production-level parallel and distributed systems were especially valued, as were submissions that detailed novel program development tools and environments addressing the expected complexity of exascale systems.

Concrete topics of interest included debugging and correctness tools, hybrid shared memory and message passing tools, instrumentation and monitoring tools and techniques, program development tools, programming environments, interoperable tool environments, integration of tools, compilers and operating systems, performance and reliability analysis (manual and automatic), energy efficiency and savings tools, performance and code structure visualization, testing and analysis tools, computational steering, tool infrastructure and scalability, tool evaluations and comparisons in production environments, tools for extremescale systems, tools for code modernization, tools for homogeneous and heterogeneous multi/many-core processors, and tools and environments for clusters, clouds, and grids.

Two papers were selected for presentation.

Topic 2: Performance Modeling, Prediction, and Evaluation

Felix Wolf, Marian Vajteršic, Laura Carrington, Frédéric Suter, Miquel Pericàs

In recent years, a range of novel methods and tools have been developed for the evaluation, design, and modeling of parallel and distributed systems and applications. At the same time, the term "performance" has broadened to include scalability and energy efficiency, as well as to touch on reliability and robustness in addition to the classic resource-oriented notions.

The aim of the topic was to reach researchers working on different aspects of performance modeling, evaluation, and prediction, be it for systems or for applications running on the whole range of parallel and distributed systems (multi-core and heterogeneous architectures, HPC systems, grid and cloud contexts etc.), and to help bring together current theory and practice. Submissions were sought on novel research in all areas of performance modeling, prediction and evaluation, more concretely on advanced simulation techniques and tools, measurement, benchmarking, and tracing, workload modeling, verification and validation of performance models, performance visualization, power consumption modeling and prediction, performance-driven code optimization, and performance modeling and simulation of emerging exascale systems.

Three papers were selected for presentation.

Topic 3: Scheduling and Load Balancing

Denis Trystram, Hans Kellerer, Henri Casanova, Vitus Leung, Giorgio Lucarelli, Ariel Oleksiak, Natasha Shakhlevich, Leonel Sousa

Parallel and distributed systems are becoming more complex and powerful, but are still not fully exploited. Scheduling and load balancing issues remain crucial for more efficient and transparent use. At the application level, the mapping of applications onto the underlying computing platforms, and the development of dynamic algorithms able to adapt to the particular characteristics and actual utilization of the systems are of particular relevance. At the system level, areas of interest include the support for modern multi-core and many-core architectures, huge data centers, and virtual systems like cloud infrastructures.

The topic covered aspects related to scheduling and load balancing, ranging from theoretical foundations for modeling and designing efficient and robust strategies to experimental studies, applications and practical tools. This applies to multi-core processors, servers, heterogeneous systems, HPC systems, as well as to distributed systems, such as computational grids, clouds and global computing platforms. Concrete areas of interest included theoretical foundations of scheduling algorithms, robustness of scheduling algorithms, multi-objective scheduling, decentralized or hierarchical scheduling, scheduling at extreme scale, on-line scheduling, scheduling algorithms for homogeneous or heterogeneous platforms, resource management and awareness, energy-efficient scheduling, power-aware and thermal-aware methods in scheduling and load balancing, performance models for scheduling and load balancing, evaluation and analysis of load balancing and scheduling techniques, implementation issues for scheduling, workload characterization and modeling, workflow and job scheduling, and concurrent workflow scheduling.

Eleven papers were selected for presentation.

Topic 4: Architecture and Compilers

Franz Franchetti, Jens Knoop, Markus Schordan, Louis-Noël Pouchet, Sid Touati

The topic dealt with architecture design, languages, and compilation for parallel high performance systems. The areas of interest ranged from microprocessors to large-scale parallel machines (including multi-/many-core, possibly heterogeneous, architectures); from general-purpose to specialized hardware platforms (e.g., graphic coprocessors, low-power embedded systems); and from architecture design to compiler technology and language design.

On the compilation side, topics of interest included programmer productivity issues, concurrent and/or sequential language aspects, program analysis, program transformation, automatic discovery and/or management of parallelism at all levels, auto-tuning and feedback directed compilation, and the interaction between the compiler and the system at large. On the architecture side, the scope spanned system architectures, processor micro-architecture, memory hierarchy, and multi-threading, architectural support for parallelism, and the impact of emerging hardware technologies. Concretely, submissions were sought to deal with compiling for multi-threaded and multi-core and heterogeneous processors and architectures, compiling for emerging architectures (low-power embedded systems, reconfigurable hardware, processors in memory, graphics processors), iterative, just-in-time, feedback-oriented, dynamic, and machine-learning-based compilation, static analysis and interaction between static and dynamic analysis, compiler, run-time, and architectural support for dynamic adaptation, programmer productivity tools and analysis, program transformation systems, high-level programming models and tools for multi- and many-core and for heterogeneous architectures, interaction between compiler, runtime system, hardware, and operating system, parallel computer architecture design (ILP, DLP, multi-threaded, and multi-core processors), power-performance efficient designs, software and hardware fault-tolerance techniques, memory hierarchy, emerging memory technologies, and stacked memories, and application-specific, reconfigurable and embedded parallel systems.

Three papers were selected for presentation.

Topic 5: Parallel and Distributed Data Management

André Brinkmann, Harald Kosch, Gabriel Antoniu, Veronika Sonigo

The proliferation of extremely large and heterogeneous data sets poses complex requirements for both cloud and high-performance computing environments, ranging from the integration and management of data to complex data analytics. In addition, managing diverse data requires solutions that integrate different data management paradigms. Thus, data-intensive applications require new approaches and efficient techniques to perform such tasks on locally stored or geographically dispersed data to cope with this data explosion and heterogeneity.

An important issue is the design of highly scalable distributed data platforms offering consistency levels and programming models that can simplify the development of complex, big-data applications, with the ultimate goal of shielding programmers from sources of complexity like concurrency, distribution, and failures. The understanding of applications and storage systems, leading to these scalable data platforms, must be based on empirical evidence.

It is still necessary to improve the provisioning, staging, manipulation, continuous maintenance, and monitoring of data hosted in distributed and heterogeneous systems. This includes the interaction between object storage systems, key-value stores, and parallel file systems with batch-systems and middleware environments. The issue of self-tuning is also of paramount importance for distributed data platforms, which aim to minimize the infrastructure's operational costs or to provide quality-of-service levels by elastically adapting their scale to match dynamic shifts of the workload. Interestingly, these problems can be approached using inter-disciplinary methodologies, such as machine learning, analytical modelling, and control theory. The parallel and concurrent execution at all levels remains key to enable the development of scalable and effective data-intensive applications.

The topic sought papers on all aspects of distributed and parallel data management and data-intensive applications, with a focus on concurrency, parallelism, and distributed processing aspects. Concretely, submissions were encouraged on parallel, replicated, and highly-available distributed databases, distributed and parallel transaction and query processing over homogeneous and heterogeneous management paradigms, parallel and distributed information retrieval, middleware for processing large-scale data, management of parallel and distributed data sources, data-intensive clouds, grids and peer-to-peer systems, empirical evaluation of storage systems, integration of large datasets on parallel systems, internet-scale data-intensive applications, sensor-network data management, mobile data management, cloud- and HPC-based storage architectures and file systems, parallel data streaming and data stream mining, NoSQL data management and analysis (key value, graph management, etc.), parallel and distributed knowledge discovery and data mining, algorithms for security and privacy in data management, and new storage hierarchies in distributed data systems, e.g., based on Flash- and NVRAM-technologies.

Two papers were selected for presentation.

Topic 6: Grid, Cluster and Cloud Computing

Frédéric Desprez, Radu Prodan, Adrien Lebre, Helge Meinhard, Rizos Sakellariou, Uwe Schwiegelshohn, Domenico Talia, Ramin Yahyapour

Heterogeneous Distributed Computing (HDC) systems (e.g., grids, clouds) have changed the IT landscape with respect to the ways in which we access and manage IT infrastructures. The use of computing resources accessible remotely in a seamless way has become essential for many applications in various areas. These technologies provide easy-to-use and on-demand access to large-scale infrastructures and have stimulated much research involving both academia and industry.

Although significant progress has been made in the design, deployment, operation and use of such infrastructures, many research challenges remain to achieve the goal of user-friendly, efficient, and reliable HDC systems. Research issues cover many areas of computer science to address the fundamental capabilities and services that are required in a heterogeneous environment, such as adaptability, scalability, reliability and security, and to support applications as diverse as ubiquitous local services, enterprise-scale virtual organizations, and internet-scale distributed supercomputing. Research on these specific systems greatly benefits from interactions with the many related areas of computer science also represented at Euro-Par. Submissions were sought on HDC systems middleware, HDC systems-enabled applications and platforms, interoperability and portability, resource/service/information discovery, power management in cluster systems, aggregation and federation of clouds, resource management and scheduling, efficient energy usage of resources, programming models, tools, and algorithms for HDC systems, dependability, adaptability, and scalability, security and privacy for HDC systems, workflow management, automated or autonomic management of resources and applications, Quality-of-Service and Service-Level-Agreement in HDC systems, use of grid and cloud computing for HPC applications, scalability and elasticity of applications and algorithms, and faults and failure management in clusters, grids and clouds.

Two papers were selected for presentation.

Topic 7: Distributed Systems and Algorithms

André Schiper, Josef Widder, Antonio Casimiro, Christof Fetzer,
Marta Patino-Martinez, Pierre Sens

Parallel computing is heavily dependent on and interacting with the developments and challenges for distributed systems, such as asynchrony, failures, malicious and selfish behavior, load balancing, long latencies, network partitions, disconnected operations, distributed computing models and concurrent data structures, and heterogeneity. The topic on distributed systems and algorithms provided a forum for both theoretical and practical research, of interest to both academia and industry, on distributed systems, distributed computing, distributed algorithms and data structures, and parallel processing on distributed systems. Concretely, contributions were sought on design and practice of distributed algorithms and data structures, analysis of the behavior of distributed algorithms and systems, self-organized and self-adjusting distributed systems, distributed fault tolerance, resource and service discovery, resource sharing in distributed systems, collaborative computing, modeling of distributed environments, scalability, concurrency and performance of distributed systems, transactional memory, distributed operating systems, and system support for parallelism.

Two papers were selected for presentation.

Topic 8: Parallel and Distributed Programming, Interfaces and Languages

Bill Gropp, Erwin Laure, Keshav Pingali, Rajeev Thakur, Michael Gerndt

Developing parallel or distributed applications is a difficult task, which requires adequate programming abstractions and models, efficient design tools, parallelization techniques and practices, efficient and effective parallel languages, interfaces, libraries and frameworks, backed up by solid practical and experimental validation. The topic provided a forum for presentation of new results and practical experience in this domain. It emphasized research that facilitates the design and development of high-performance, correct, portable, and scalable parallel programs via adequate parallel and distributed programming model, interface and language support. Contributions were especially sought on assessing programming abstractions, models and methods for usability, performance prediction, scalability, self-adaptation, rapid prototyping and fault-tolerance, as needed, for instance, in dynamic heterogeneous parallel and distributed infrastructures. Therefore, authors were urged to include quantitative evaluations to substantiate their claims. Concrete themes included: programming models, languages and libraries for parallel and distributed applications, programming paradigms and techniques for novel infrastructures like accelerators, exascale systems and clouds, design, implementation, performance analysis and performance portability of programming models across parallel and distributed platforms, programming models and techniques for heterogeneity, self-adaptation and fault tolerance, programming tools for application design, implementation, and performance-tuning, application case-studies for benchmarking and comparative studies of parallel programming models, domain-specific libraries and languages, and parallel and distributed programming productivity, usability, and component-based parallel programming.

Two papers were selected for presentation.

Topic 9: Multi- and Many-core Programming

Marco Aldinucci, Siegfried Benkner, Hans Vandierendonck, Franscisco De Sande, Antoniu Pop, Massimo Torquati, Samuel Thibault, Massimiliano Meneghin, José Daniel García

Modern homogeneous and heterogeneous multi-core and many-core architectures are now part of the high-end and mainstream computing scene and can offer impressive performance for many applications. This architecture trend has been driven by the need to reduce power consumption, increase processor utilization, and deal with the memory-processor speed gap. However, the complexity of these new architectures has created several programming challenges, and achieving performance on these systems is often a difficult task. The topic on multi- and many-core programming explores productive programming of multi- and manycore systems, as well as stand-alone systems with large numbers of cores like GPUs and various types of accelerators; this can also include hybrid and heterogeneous systems with different types of multi-core processors. It focuses on novel research and solutions in the form of programming models, algorithms, languages, compilers, libraries, runtime and analysis tools to increase the programmability of multi-core, many-core, and heterogeneous systems in the context of general-purpose parallel computing, including HPC.

Concretely, submissions were sought to deal with programming techniques, models, frameworks and languages, advances in algorithms and data structures, lock-free algorithms, transactional memories, compiler optimizations and techniques, libraries and runtime systems, tools for discovering and understanding parallelism, performance and scalability, innovative applications and case studies, and hardware support for programming models and runtime systems.

Six papers were selected for presentation, one as distinguished paper.

Topic 10: Theory and Algorithms for Parallel Computation

Peter Sanders, Robert Elsässer, Leah Epstein, Pierre Fraigniaud, Geppino Pucci

Parallelism permeates all levels of current computing systems. Hence, most performance critical applications now need efficient and scalable parallel algorithms at their heart. This is currently causing a renaissance in the study of parallel algorithms and their underlying machine models and theoretical foundations. High quality, original papers were solicited, which contribute new results on parallel algorithms, computational models, and their theoretical foundations. Concrete themes included parallel algorithms for graphs, geometrical data, strings etc., parallel data structures, parallel streaming algorithms, communication algorithms for networks, parallel memory hierarchies, communication-efficient algorithms, algorithms for GPUs and accelerators, exascale algorithms, energy-efficient parallel algorithms, fault-tolerant parallel algorithms, algorithmic challenges arising from concrete applications, algorithms and models for big-data parallel processing, foundations, models, and emerging paradigms for parallel, distributed, multiprocessor and network computation, parallel complexity theory, and lower bounds for parallel computation.

Three papers were selected for presentation.

Topic 11: Communication, Routing and Networks

Torsten Hoefler, Holger Fröning, Mondrian Nüssle, Federico Silla, Mitch Gusat, Tor Skeie

The topic on communication, routing and networks is dedicated to communication issues in scalable compute and storage systems, such as tightly-coupled parallel computers, clusters, and networks of workstations, including hierarchical and hybrid designs featuring several levels of possibly different interconnects. All aspects of communication in modern compute and storage systems were of interest, including advances in the design, implementation, and evaluation of interconnection networks, network interfaces, system and storage area networks, on-chip interconnects, communication protocols and interfaces, routing and communication algorithms, communication interfaces, and communication aspects of parallel and distributed algorithms. Papers were sought to present significant, original work in theory or practice on aspects of performance, reliability and availability, power consumption and heat dissipation, cost, scalability, and management. Industrial case studies were also welcome. Concrete themes included communication modeling of parallel and distributed algorithms, communication interfaces, collective communication and synchronization support, multi-level heterogeneous communication systems, lightweight and user-level communication protocols, on-chip and power-efficient interconnects, routing algorithms, congestion management, performance modeling and evaluation of routing algorithms and implementations, network performance evaluation and analysis, I/O architectures and storage area networks, interconnection networks, switch architectures, network adapters, and software-defined networking.

The topic received few submissions, and no papers were selected for presentation.

Topic 12: Numerical Methods and Applications

Paolo Bientinesi, Wilfried Gansterer, Daniel Ruprecht, Xavier Vasseur

The solution of large-scale problems in Computational Science and Engineering requires accurate, robust, and efficient numerical algorithms and software that can exploit the potential of modern computer architectures. Such algorithms provide the means to further the development of existing applications, and the building blocks to prototype new methodologies. Ultimately, the objective is to relieve users from issues related to numerical methods and from implementation aspects strongly influenced by the computing environment.

The topic provided a forum for discussing recent developments in the design and implementation of parallel and distributed numerical algorithms and software. The focus was on fundamental algorithmic concepts, efficient implementations on modern parallel architectures (e.g., multi-core and hybrid platforms, multi-GPU systems), design and prototyping of scientific simulation software, performance analysis of numerical methods, and application studies. Concretely, submissions were sought on dense and sparse linear algebra, discrete algorithms in scientific computing, combinatorial scientific computing, solvers (PDE, ODE, DAE), tensor decompositions and contractions, low-rank approximations, methods for uncertainty quantification, differential, integral, and differential algebraic equations, non-linear systems, optimization, transforms (wavelets, FFTs, etc.), and large-scale parallel applications and workflows.

Five papers were selected for presentation.

Topic 13: Accelerator Computing

Jörg Keller, Andreas Steininger, Lee Howes, Michael Klemm, Naoya Maruyama, Norbert Eicker, Erik Saule, Benedict Gaster

Hardware accelerators of many different kinds offer a potential for achieving massive performance in applications that can leverage their high degree of parallelism and customization. Examples include graphics processors (GPUs), many-core devices, as well as more custom devices and customizable FPGA-based systems and streaming dataflow architectures. The research challenge for the topic on accelerators was to explore new avenues for actually realizing this potential. Submissions were encouraged in all areas related to accelerators: architectures, algorithms, languages, compilers, libraries, runtime systems, coordination of accelerators and CPUs, and debugging and profiling tools. Application-related submissions that contribute new insights into fundamental problems or solution approaches in this domain were also welcomed.

Concrete themes included new accelerator architectures, languages, compilers, and runtime environments for accelerator programming, programming techniques for clusters of accelerators, tools for debugging, profiling, and optimizing programs on accelerators, hybrid and heterogeneous computing with several, possibly different types of accelerators, parallel algorithms for accelerators, applications benefitting from acceleration, models and benchmarks for accelerators, manual optimization and auto-tuning, and library support for accelerators.

Ten papers were selected for presentation, one as distinguished paper.

Contents

Architecture and Compilers

Parallel and Distributed Data Management

Grid, Cluster and Cloud Computing

Distributed Systems and Algorithms

Parallel and Distributed Programming, Interfaces and Languages

Multi- and Many-core Programming

Theory and Algorithms for Parallel Computation

Numerical Methods and Applications

Accelerator Computing

Invited Papers

Concurrent Systems: Hybrid Object Implementations and Abortable Objects

Michel Raynal[1,2,3]($\boxtimes$)

[1] Institut Universitaire de France, Paris, France
[2] IRISA, Université de Rennes, Rennes, France
[3] Department of Computing, Polytechnic University, Hong Kong, China
raynal@irisa.fr

Abstract. As they allow processes to communicate and synchronize, concurrent objects are, de facto, the most important objects of concurrent programming. This paper presents and illustrates two important notions associated with concurrent objects. The first one, which is related to their implementation, is the notion of a hybrid implementation. The second one, which is related to their definition, is the notion of an abortable object.

1 Introduction

Concurrent Objects: On the Classical Side. An *object* is a (passive) computing entity providing processes with operations. Only these operations are visible from outside the object. Said differently, the internal representation, of an object remains invisible to the processes. Hence, an object is an abstraction. An object is defined by a specification, which states the properties defining all its correct behaviors. Those are usually captured by the set of the allowed sequences on operation invocations. It appears that the object notion was introduced a long time ago (it seems that its very first appearance dates back in 1967, in the language SIMULA 67 [21]).

The first object, specific to the domain of concurrent programming, seems to be the *semaphore* [3,9]. It is a counting object whose value has to never become negative. Hence, processes can decrease and increase it as long they maintain invariant the fact that it remains non-negative. Then, more sophisticated object constructs have been introduced to cope with concurrent objects, such the concept of a *monitor* [4,20]. In nearly all cases, these language constructs reduce concurrency to sequential computing (they basically ensure that the object operations are executed in mutual exclusion).

Concurrent Objects: The World is Changing. Concurrency in multiprocessors (e.g., multicore) is *real* concurrency. It follows that the concurrency concepts and techniques used to cope with multiplexing or interrupt handling are no longer appropriate, and must be revisited to address the new computing world. As expressed in [15]: "Changes in technology can have far-reaching effects on theory. [...] After decades of being respected but not taken seriously, research

© Springer-Verlag Berlin Heidelberg 2015
J.L. Träff et al. (Eds.): Euro-Par 2015, LNCS 9233, pp. 3–15, 2015.
DOI: 10.1007/978-3-662-48096-0_1

on multiprocessor algorithms and data structures is going mainstream" (see also [18, 29, 34]).

Among the most important concepts that have been introduced there is the notion of progress conditions suited to systems where processes are asynchronous and can fail by crashing. These notions are obstruction-freedom [16], non-blocking [19], and wait-freedom [14]. This has motivated researchers to re-think the implementation of concurrent data structures to exploit the benefit of new architectures (e.g. [2, 7, 8, 26, 27, 35, 36] to cite a few).

Concurrent Objects: The Topics Addressed in the Paper. This paper first defines (Sect. 2) basic computing models, which allow us to reason on concurrent objects. Their main characteristics lies in the hardware operations the processes can use, the asynchrony of the processes, and the fact that failures can occur or not.

Then the paper presents the notion of a hybrid implementation of a concurrent object (Sect. 3). Roughly speaking, a hybrid implementation is such that the algorithms implementing the object operations do not use locks in "good circumstances", those being defined statically or dynamically. It follows that in concurrency-free patterns, locks are not used.

Finally (Sect. 4), the paper considers the notion of an abortable object, and illustrates it with a non-blocking abortable stack. An abortable object allows operations to return a default value $\bot$ when operation invocations are concurrent.

The paper is an introductory paper to concurrent objects, addressing hybrid implementation and abortable objects, which are only two facets of concurrent objects. The reader will find more developments on concurrent programming objects in [18, 29, 33].

2   Computing Models, Objects, and Progress Conditions

2.1   Basic Read/Write Model and Enriched Models

Basic Read/Write Model. The basic read/write model consists of n sequential asynchronous deterministic processes, denoted $p_1, ..., p_n$, which communicate by reading and writing atomic registers only.

Asynchronous means each process proceeds to its own speed, which is not known by other processes, and can be arbitrary and vary with time. *Deterministic* means that the behavior of a process is entirely determined from its initial state, the algorithm it executes, and the sequence of values read from atomic registers. *Atomic* means that, for each register, the read and write operations appear as if they had been invoked sequentially, each abstracted as a point of the time line occurring between its start and its end [19, 23].

This computation model, where there are no failures, is denoted $\mathcal{ARW}_n$.

Crash Failures. The most common failures studied in multicore distributed computing are process crash failures and Byzantine failures. Here we consider only process crash failures. Such a failure occurs when a process halts unexpectedly. Before crashing it executes correctly its algorithm, and after it crashed, a process remains crashed forever.

Let t be the maximal number of processes that may crash; t is a model parameter and the corresponding model is called t-*resilient* model. The asynchronous read/write model in which all processes, except one, may crash is called *wait-free* model. Hence, "wait-free model" is synonym of "$(n-1)$-resilient model".

This crash-prone computation model is denoted $\mathcal{ARW}_n[\emptyset]$. When enriched with hardware-provided objects of some type $TYPE$ (whose aim is to allow processes to communicate), the corresponding system model is denoted $\mathcal{ARW}_n[TYPE]$.

Enriched Model. While, from a computability point of view, $\mathcal{ARW}_n[\emptyset]$ has the same power as a Turing machine, this is no longer the case for $\mathcal{ARW}_{n,t}[\emptyset]$ which is strictly weaker than $\mathcal{ARW}_n[\emptyset]$ as soon as only even one process may crash (i.e., for any $t > 0$) [10,14,17,25,30,33].

The situation is different as soon as processes can use hardware-provided synchronization objects stronger than atomic read/write registers, such as test&set objects, compare&swap objects, or LL/SC objects, to cite a few. The crash-prone computation model, enriched with objects of type $TYPE$, is denoted $\mathcal{ARW}_{n,t}[TYPE]$.

It was shown by Herlihy [14] that the computability power of such objects can be measured with the notion of a *consensus number*. The greater this number, the stronger the object. An infinite hierarchy of objects suited to the wait-free model has been exhibited, where it is shown that the consensus number of registers is 1, the one of test&set objects is 2, while the one of compare&swap or LL/SC objects is infinite. Hence, the model $\mathcal{ARW}_{n,n-1}[\text{Compare\&swap}]$ is computationally stronger than $\mathcal{ARW}_{n,n-1}[\text{Test\&set}]$, which itself is stronger than $\mathcal{ARW}_{n,n-1}[\emptyset]$ (see, e.g., [14,29]).

2.2   Concurrent Objects

Definition. A *concurrent* object (sometimes also called *shared* object) is an object that can be accessed by several processes, simultaneously or not.

We consider here the subset of concurrent objects defined by a sequential specification on total operations. An operation is *total* if it always returns a result, whatever the state of the object (e.g., the operation remove() applied to an empty queue is not allowed to wait until an element is added to the queue; it must always terminate, for example returning the control value *empty*). *Sequential specification* means that the correct behaviors of an object can be expressed by traces on its operation invocations.

One-Shot vs Multi-shot. An object is *one-shot* if it has only one operation and each process is allowed to invoke this operation at most once. Otherwise, the object is *multi-shot*. As an example, a consensus object is one-shot, while a set object or a stack are multi-shot objects.

Consistency Condition. The most familiar consistency condition considered for concurrent objects is *atomicity* [23], also called *linearizability* [19]. It states that it must be possible to totally order the operations issued on each object in such a way that (a) this total order respects the occurrence order of non-concurrent operations, and (b) the resulting sequence of operations belongs to the specification of the object.

An important property of linearizability, which motivates its practical consideration, lies in its *composability* dimension (also called *locality*) [19], namely, linearizable objects compose for free. This means that if we have two linearizable objects $O1$ and $O2$ (whose implementations are independent) then the composed object $\langle O1, O2 \rangle$ is also linearizable, and this is obtained for free, i.e., without additional implementation cost. (Intuitively, this comes from the fact that linearizability respects the occurrence order of non-concurrent operations).

It is important to notice that other consistency conditions such as *sequential consistency* [22] (or non-strict serializability encountered in databases [28]) are not composable. This means that, to obtain a sequentially consistent composed object $\langle O1, O2 \rangle$ from two sequentially consistent objects $O1$ and $O2$, the implementation of both $O1$ and $O2$ has to be modified, each one must cooperate with the other one to ensure that the composite object is sequentially consistent [29].

2.3   Progress Conditions for Object Operations

Classical Progress Conditions. The classical progress conditions encountered in the implementation of concurrent objects are *deadlock-freedom* and *starvation-freedom*. The first one captures the point of view of the object (service), namely, if processes concurrently invoke operations, at least one process succeeds. The second one captures the point of view of the processes (clients), namely, if any process invokes an operation, it eventually executes it. These progress conditions are usually implemented with locking mechanisms. Trivially, starvation-freedom ⇒ deadlock-freedom.

Locks in the Presence of Failures. It is important to notice that locks cannot be used in the system model $\mathcal{ARW}_{n,t}[\emptyset]$. This is due to the following reason. If a process p obtains a lock on an object and crashes before unlocking it, due to asynchrony, no other process can distinguish the case where p crashes and the case where p is slow. Hence, in an asynchronous crash-prone system, locks may prevent processes from progressing.

Progress Conditions Suited to Net Effect of Asynchrony and Process Crashes. Three progress conditions have been proposed to cope with the net effect of asynchrony and process crashes. Actually, a process crash can be seen as if the corresponding process was pausing during a "very" long period of time, during which the non-faulty processes must progress despite its absence of progress.

Obstruction-Freedom [16] is the weakest progress conditions (from a progress point of view). It states that a non-faulty process, that invokes an object operation, is required to terminate it, if it executes alone during a "long enough" period. ("Long enough" means it has enough time to terminate its operation, without being bothered by other processes). Hence, obstruction-freedom allows concurrent operations to never terminate.

Non-blocking is a stronger progress condition [19]. It states that, whatever the concurrency among operation invocations, at least one of the concurrent invocations terminate. As one can see, this is nothing else than deadlock-freedom in a context where locks are forbidden (also called mutex-free context).

Finally, *wait-freedom* is the strongest progress condition [14]. It requires that, until it possibly crashes, and whatever the behavior of the other processes, all the operations issued by a process terminate.

Trivially, wait-freedom $\Rightarrow$ non-blocking $\Rightarrow$ obstruction-freedom. Of course, the previous three mutex-free progress conditions remain meaningful in the classical failure system model $\mathcal{ARW}_n[\emptyset]$.

Where is the Difficulty. As previously indicated, locks cannot be used when one has to cope with asynchrony and failures. Hence, *mutex-free* solutions have to be found [29].

The main difficulty when one wants to implement a concurrent object whose operations have to satisfy one of obstruction-freedom, non-blocking, or wait-freedom, comes from the fact that there is no way to prevent several processes to simultaneously access the internal representation of the object. This is true even for the weak obstruction-freedom progress condition. As a simple example, let us consider two processes that, invoking the operation $S.\mathsf{pop}()$ on a stack S, access simultaneously its internal representation, and then one of them pauses during a long enough period that allows the other process to terminate. Both the returned values must be correct.

According to the high level object that has to be built, solving this issue may require basic objects whose computational power is stronger than read/write registers. In some cases, the power required is the one provided by the most powerful objects (such as compare&swap) when considering the consensus number hierarchy.

3 Hybrid Implementation of a Concurrent Object

3.1 The Notion of a Hybrid Implementation of a Concurrent Object

Definition. The idea that underlies the notion of a hybrid implementation is that locks are expensive, and consequently their use must be prevented in some circumstances.

Given a concurrent object O, an *hybrid implementation* of O is an implementation that merges lock-based code and mutex-free code in the implementation of the operations of O. This notion has been introduced in an explicit way in [29]. As locks can be used, these implementations are for failure-free systems. (Said differently, this means that, in the presence of failures, the system may stop progressing in configurations where a process crashes while holding a lock.)

Static Hybrid vs Dynamic Hybrid Implementation. Two types of hybrid implementations can be distinguished.

- *Static* hybrid implementation. In this case, the operations on the object are statically divided into subsets: the ones whose implementation can use locks, and the others whose implementation cannot use locks.
- *Dynamic* hybrid implementation. In this case, whatever the operation, its implementation cannot use locks in "favorable circumstances". Those are defined according to the object, the context in which it is used, the aplication features, etc.

3.2 Example 1: Static Hybrid Implementation of a Set Object

Set Object A concurrent set object S is defined by three operations:

- $S.\mathsf{add}(v)$ adds v to the set S and returns `true` if v was not in the set. Otherwise it returns `false`.
- $S.\mathsf{remove}(v)$ suppresses v from the set S and returns `true` if v was in the set. Otherwise it returns `false`.
- $S.\mathsf{contain}(v)$ returns `true` if v belongs to the set. Otherwise it returns `false`.

In a lot of applications using a set object, the number of invocations of $S.\mathsf{contain}()$ outperforms the number of invocations of $S.\mathsf{add}()$ and $S.\mathsf{remove}()$. This is, for example, the case of dictionary-like objects. In such a context, for efficiency reasons, we want to have an implementation of $S.\mathsf{contain}()$ that (a) is mutex-free (it does not use locks), and (b) always terminates. Said more compactly, the algorithm implementing $S.\mathsf{contain}()$ has to be wait-free. Differently, the algorithms implementing the operations $S.\mathsf{add}()$ and $S.\mathsf{remove}()$ may use locks. These operations are required to be only deadlock-free. Moreover, to allow them to be as concurrent as possible, a lock is associated with each element of the set, and a process can simultaneously hold locks on at most two elements.

An hybrid implementation of such a concurrent set has been proposed in [13] and proved correct in [6] (see also [29] for a pedagogical presentation). This implementation is list-based. It assumes that the elements of the set are totally ordered, they have a smallest element and a greatest element, and there is finite number of elements between any two elements.

3.3 Example 2:
Dynamic Hybrid Implementation of a Double-Ended Queue

A dynamic hybrid implementation of a double-ended queue (in short, dequeue) is presented in [16]. The "favorable circumstances" are when there is no concurrency. The main difficulty that this implementation has to solve occurs when a process started executing an operation in a no-concurrency context (hence it uses no lock) and, while it is executing its operation, another process issue a conflicting operation. This implementation considers the enriched system model $\mathcal{ARW}_n[\text{Compare\&swap}]$. A version of it, suited to the system model $\mathcal{ARW}_n[\text{LL}/\text{SC}]$ is described in [29,34].

Due to page limitation, the reader will consult [16,29] for a full presentation of these implementations.

3.4   Example 3:
Dynamic Hybrid Implementation of a Consensus Object

Binary Consensus Object. Such an object C is a one-shot object that provides the processes with a single operation denoted C.propose() ans returns a value, called "decided value". Only the values 0 and 1 can be proposed. The object is defined by the following properties.

- Validity. A decided value is a proposed value.
- Agreement. No two processes decide different values.
- Termination. If a process invokes C.propose(), it decides a value.

Favorable Circumstances. Here "favorable circumstances" concern two different cases. The first is when all the processes that invoke C.propose(), propose the same value. The second is when an invocation of propose() executes in a concurrency-free context.

When a favorable circumstance occurs, no lock has to be used. This means that an invocation of propose(v) is allowed to use an underlying lock only if (a) the other value $(1 - v)$ was previously or is currently proposed, and (b) there are concurrent invocations. Hence, from a lock point of view, the notion of conflict is related to both concurrency and proposed values.

Dynamic Hybrid Implementation: Internal Representation of the Object. The implementation that follows is from [34]. The internal representation of the consensus object is made up of the following atomic read/write registers, plus a lock:

- $PROPOSED[0..1]$, which is an array of two Boolean registers, both initialized to *false*. The atomic register $PROPOSED[v]$ is set to *true* to indicate that a process has proposed value v.
- $DECIDED$, which is an atomic register whose domain is $\{\bot, 0, 1\}$. Initialized to $\bot$, it is eventually set to the value that is decided and never the value which is not decided.
- AUX, which is an atomic register whose domain and initial value are the same as for $DECIDED$.
- $LOCK$, which is a starvation-free lock used to solve conflicts (if any).

Dynamic Hybrid Implementation: Algorithm. This algorithm is described in Fig. 1. A process decides when it executes the statement return(val), where val is the value it decides.

When a process p invokes propose(v), it first indicates that v was proposed, and writes it into AUX if this register is still equal to $\bot$ (line 01). Let us notice that, if several processes proposing different values concurrently read $\bot$ from AUX, each writes its proposed value in AUX.

Then, process p checks if the other binary value $(1 - v)$ was proposed by another process (line 02). If it is not the case, p writes v into $DECIDED$ (line 03), and assuming that no other process has written a different value into $DECIDED$

```
operation C.propose(v) is
(01)  PROPOSED[v] ← true; if (AUX = ⊥) then AUX ← v end if;
(02)  if (¬PROPOSED[1 − v])
(03)     then DECIDED ← v
(04)     else if (DECIDED = ⊥)
(05)         then LOCK.acquire_lock();
(06)             if (DECIDED = ⊥) then DECIDED ← AUX end if;
(07)             LOCK.release_lock()
(08)         end if;
(09)  end if;
(10)  return(DECIDED)
end operation.
```

Fig. 1. A dynamic hybrid implementation of a binary consensus object in $\mathcal{ARW}_n$ [LOCK] [34]

in the meantime, it decides the value stored in $DECIDED$ (line 10). If the other value was proposed there is a conflict. Process p then decides the value kept in $DECIDED$ if there is one (lines 04 and 10). If there is no decided value, the conflict is solved with the help of the lock (lines 05–07). Process p assigns the current value of AUX to $DECIDED$ if that register was still equal to $\perp$ when it read it (lines 06) and p finally decides the value kept in $DECIDED$. Proofs can be found in [29, 34].

4   Abortable Concurrent Objects

4.1   The Notion of a Concurrent Abortable Object

In practice, conflicts are rare in a lot of applications. So the idea is here, not only to forbid locks at the implementation level, but, at the semantics/interface level, allow a process, that invokes an object operation, to return a predefined default value $\perp$ (abort) in specific circumstances, namely in the presence of concurrency[1].

Hence, the meaning of $\perp$ is "the operation has not been executed because the invocation occurred in a concurrency context". Moreover, if we do not consider the operation invocations that return $\perp$, an abortable object behaves as described by its sequential specification.

---

[1] In some sense, the origin of abortable objects can be found in Lamport's fast mutex algorithm [24]. This paper presents a mutual exclusion algorithm which allows a process to take a *fast path* to access the critical section when there is no concurrency. This fast path requires only five accesses to atomic read/write registers, and is consequently independent of the total number of processes. When there is concurrency, the number of accesses to atomic read/write registers is $O(n)$. This algorithm was the starting point of the design of *time-adaptive* algorithms. The time complexity of such an algorithm A is $O(f(d)) \leq O(f(n))$, where $d \in [1..n]$ is the concurrency degree at the time where the object operation implemented by A is executed.

This notion of an abortable object, introduced in [12, 29], has not to be confused with a close (but different) notion introduced in [1]. In this paper, when an operation returns $\perp$, the invoking process learns that its call occurred in a concurrency context, but it does know if the operation was executed or not.

4.2 Example: A Non-blocking Abortable Stack in $\mathcal{ARW}_{n,n-1}$[Compare&swap]

The implementation of a non-blocking abortable stack presented below is from [32]. It is based on compare&swap objects.

Compare&swap Object and the ABA Problem. A compare&swap object X is an atomic register that can be read, and can be written by a hardware-provided operation called compare&swap(). This operation is a conditional write, which has two input parameters (denoted *old* and *new*), and returns a Boolean value. Its effect can be described as follows:

> X.compare&swap(old, new) is
>> if ($X = old$) then $X \leftarrow new$; return($true$) else return($false$) end if.

When using compare&swap(), a process p_i usually does the following. It first reads the atomic register X (obtaining its current value a), then executes statements (possibly involving accesses to the shared memory) and finally updates X to a new value c only if X has not been modified by another process since it was read by p_i. To that end, p_i invokes X.compare&swap(a, c).

Unfortunately, the fact that this invocation returns $true$ to p_i does not allow p_i to conclude that X has not been modified since the last time it read it. This is because, between the read of X and the invocation X.compare&swap(a, c) both issued by p_i, X could have been updated twice, first by a process p_j that successfully invoked X.compare&swap(a, b), and then by another process p_k that successfully invoked X.compare&swap(b, a), thereby restoring the value a to X. This is called the ABA problem.

This problem can be solved by associating sequence numbers with each value that is written (see [29]). Hence, in the previous scenario, the read of X by p_i would have returned a pair $\langle a, sn \rangle$. Then, $X = \langle a, sn+2 \rangle$ after the the successful invocations issued by p_j and p_k. Hence, the X.compare&swap($\langle a, sn \rangle, c$) cannot be successful.

Abortable Stack: Operations. The stack operations are denoted push(v) (where v is the value to be added at the top of the stack) and pop(). The stack is a bounded stack: it can contain at most k values. If the stack is full, push(v) returns the control value *full*, otherwise v is added at the top of the stack and the control value *done* is returned. The operation pop() returns the value that is at the top of the stack (and suppresses it from the stack), or the control value *empty* if the stack is empty. Both operations may return $\perp$ in the presence of concurrency.

Non-blocking Abortable Stack. As the stack must be non-blocking, even in the presence of concurrency, at least one operation does not return $\perp$.

Non-blocking Abortable Stack: Internal Representation. The stack is implemented with an atomic register denoted TOP and an array of $k+1$ atomic registers denoted $STACK[0..k]$. These registers can be read and can be modified only by using the compare&swap() primitive.

- TOP has three fields that contain an index (to address an entry of $STACK$), a value, and a counter. It is initialized to $\langle 0, \perp, 0 \rangle$.
- Each atomic register $STACK[x]$ has two fields: the field $STACK[x].val$, which contains a value, and the field $STACK[x].sn$, which contains a sequence number (used to prevent the ABA problem as far as $STACK[x]$ is concerned). $STACK[0]$ is a dummy entry initialized to $\langle \perp, -1 \rangle$. Its first field always contains the default value $\perp$. As far as the other entries are concerned, $STACK[x]$ ($1 \leq x \leq k$) is initialized to $\langle \perp, 0 \rangle$.

The array $STACK$ is used to store the contents of the stack, and the register TOP is used to store the index and the value of the element at the top of the stack. The contents of TOP and $STACK[x]$ are modified with the help of the conditional write operation compare&swap() (which, with the help of sequence numbers, is used to prevent erroneous modifications of the stack internal presentation).

A Non-blocking Abortable Stack: The Algorithm. The implementation is *lazy* in the sense that a stack operation assigns its new value to TOP and leaves the corresponding effective modification of $STACK$ to the next stack operation. Hence, while on the one hand a stack operation is lazy, on the other hand it has to help terminate the previous stack operation (as far as the internal representation of the stack is concerned) (Fig. 2).

When a process p_i invokes push(v), it first reads the content of TOP (which contains the last operation on the stack) and stores its three fields in its local variables *index*, *value*, and *seqnb* (line 01).

Then, p_i calls the internal procedure help(*index*, *value*, *seqnb*) to help terminate the previous stack operation (line 02). That stack operation (be it a push() or a pop()) is required to write the pair $\langle value, seqnb \rangle$ into $STACK[index]$. To that end, p_i invokes $STACK[index]$.compare&swap.(old, new) with the appropriate values *old* and *new* so that the write is executed only if not yet done (lines 15–16).

After its help (which was successful if not yet done by another stack operation) to move the content of TOP into $STACK[index]$, p_i returns *full* if the stack is full (line 03). If the stack is not full, it tries to modify TOP so that it registers its push operation. This invocation of TOP.compare&swap() (line 06) succeeds if no other process modified TOP since it was read by p_i at line 01. If it succeeds, TOP takes its new value and push(v) returns the control value *done* (line 06). Otherwise, p_i returns $\perp$ (line 07).

The triple of values to be written in TOP at line 06 is computed at lines 04–05. Process p_i first computes the last sequence number sn_of_next used in $STACK[index + 1]$ and then defines the new triple, namely $newtop = \langle index + 1, v, sn\_of\_next + 1 \rangle$, to be written first in TOP and, later, in $STACK[index + 1]$

```
operation push(v) is
(01)    (index, value, seqnb) ← TOP;
(02)    help(index, value, seqnb);
(03)    if (index = k) then return(full) end if;
(04)    sn_of_next ← STACK[index + 1].sn;
(05)    newtop ← ⟨index + 1, v, sn_of_next + 1⟩;
(06)    if TOP.compare&swap(⟨index, value, seqnb⟩, newtop)
(07)            then return(done) else return(⊥) end if
end operation.

operation pop() is
(08)    (index, value, seqnb) ← TOP;
(09)    help(index, value, seqnb);
(10)    if (index = 0) then return(empty) end if;
(11)    belowtop ← STACK[index − 1];
(12)    newtop ← ⟨index − 1, belowtop.val, belowtop.sn + 1⟩;
(13)    if TOP.compare&swap(⟨index, value, seqnb⟩, newtop)
(14)            then return(value) else return(⊥) end if
end operation.

internal procedure help(index, value, seqnb):
(15)    stacktop ← STACK[index].val;
(16)    STACK[index].compare&swap(⟨stacktop, seqnb − 1⟩, ⟨value, seqnb⟩)
end procedure.
```

Fig. 2. A non-blocking abortable stack in $\mathcal{ARW}_{n,n-1}$[Compare&swap] [32]

thanks to the help provided by the next stack operation ($sn\_of\_next + 1$ is used to prevent the ABA problem).

5   Conclusion

Considering concurrent objects, the aim of this paper was to present the notion of an hybrid implementation of such objects, and the notion of an abortable object. To this end, it first introduced fundamental notions associated with concurrent objects (namely, consistency conditions and progress conditions). Then, after having defined the notions of an hybrid implementation and an abortable object, it illustrated them with appropriate examples.

The reader interested in concurrent programming can consult the following textbooks devoted to concurrent objects, where are presented concurrency-related concepts, algorithms, techniques, and numerous object implementations [18,29,33] (parts of this paper are from [29]). A more general and sophisticated notion, related to concurrent objects, is the one of a *universal construction* for concurrent objects. This important topic, focusing on *universality in the presence of concurrency, asynchrony and process crash failures*, introduced in [14], is addressed in the previous textbooks, and in [5,11,31].

References

1. Aguilera, M.K., Frolund, S., Hadzilacos, V., Horn, S.L., Toueg, S.: Abortable and query-abortable objects and their efficient implementation. In: Proceedings of 26th ACM Symposium on Principles of Distributed Computing (PODC 2007), pp. 23–32. ACM Press (2007)
2. Afek, Y., Attiya, H., Dolev, D., Gafni, E., Merritt, M., Shavit, N.: Atomic snapshots of shared memory. J. ACM **40**(4), 873–890 (1993)
3. Hansen, P.B.: The Architecture of Concurrent Programs. Prentice Hall, Upper Saddle River (1977)
4. Hansen, P.B. (ed.): The Origin of Concurrent Programming, p. 534. Springer, New York (2002)
5. Capdevielle, C., Johnen, C., Milani, A.: Solo-fast universal constructions for deterministic abortable objects. In: Kuhn, F. (ed.) DISC 2014. LNCS, vol. 8784, pp. 288–302. Springer, Heidelberg (2014)
6. Colvin, R., Groves, L., Luchangco, V., Moir, M.: Formal verification of a lazy concurrent list-based set algorithm. In: Ball, T., Jones, R.B. (eds.) CAV 2006. LNCS, vol. 4144, pp. 475–488. Springer, Heidelberg (2006)
7. Crain, T., Gramoli, V., Raynal, M.: A contention-friendly binary search tree. In: Wolf, F., Mohr, B., an Mey, D. (eds.) Euro-Par 2013. LNCS, vol. 8097, pp. 229–240. Springer, Heidelberg (2013)
8. Crain, T., Gramoli, V., Raynal, M.: No hot spot non-blocking skip list. In: Proceedings of 33rd International Conference on Distributed Computing Systems (ICDCS 2013), pp. 196–205. IEEE Press (2013)
9. Dijkstra, E.W.D.: Cooperating sequential processes. In: Genuys, F. (ed.) Programming Languages, pp. 43–112. Academic Press, New York (1968)
10. Fischer, M.J., Lynch, N.A., Paterson, M.S.: Impossibility of distributed consensus with one faulty process. J. ACM **32**(2), 374–382 (1985)
11. Gafni, E., Guerraoui, R.: Generalized universality. In: Katoen, J.-P., König, B. (eds.) CONCUR 2011. LNCS, vol. 6901, pp. 17–27. Springer, Heidelberg (2011)
12. Hadzilacos, V., Toueg, S.: On deterministic abortable objects. In: Proceedings of 32nd ACM Symposium on Principles of Distributed Computing (PODC 2013), pp. 4–12. ACM Press (2013)
13. Heller, S., Herlihy, M.P., Luchangco, V., Moir, M., Scherer, W.I.I.I., Shavit, N.: A lazy concurrent list-based algorithm. Parallel Process. Lett. **17**(4), 411–424 (2007)
14. Herlihy, M.P.: Wait-free synchronization. ACM Trans. Program. Lang. Syst. **13**(1), 124–149 (1991)
15. Herlihy, M.P., Luchangco, V.: Distributed computing and the multicore revolution. ACM SIGACT News **39**(1), 62–72 (2008)
16. Herlihy, M.P., Luchangco, V., Moir, M.: Obstruction-free synchronization: double-ended queues as an example. In: Proceedings of 23th International IEEE Conference on Distributed Computing Systems (ICDCS 2003), pp. 522–529. IEEE Press (2003)
17. Herlihy, M.P., Rajsbaum, S., Raynal, M.: Power and limits of distributed computing shared memory models. Theor. Comput. Sci. **509**, 3–24 (2013)
18. Herlihy, M., Shavit, N.: The Art of Multiprocessor Programming, p. 508. Morgan Kaufmann, Burlington (2008). ISBN 978-0-12-370591-4
19. Herlihy, M.P., Wing, J.M.: Linearizability: a correctness condition for concurrent objects. ACM Trans. Program. Lang. Syst. **12**(3), 463–492 (1990)

20. Hoare, C.A.R.: Monitors: an operating system structuring concept. Commun. ACM **17**(10), 549–557 (1974)
21. https://en.wikipedia.org/wiki/Simula
22. Lamport, L.: How to make a multiprocessor computer that correctly executes multiprocess programs. IEEE Trans. Comput. C **28**(9), 690–691 (1979)
23. Lamport, L.: On interprocess communication. Part I: basic formalism. Distrib. Comput. **1**(2), 77–85 (1986)
24. Lamport, L.: Fast mutual exclusion. ACM Trans. Comput. Syst. **5**(1), 1–11 (1987)
25. Loui, M., Abu-Amara, H.: Memory Requirements for Agreement among Unreliable Asynchronous Processes. Advances in Computing Research, pp. 163–183. JAI Press, Greenwich (1987)
26. Michael, M.M., Scott, M.L.: Simple, fast and practical blocking and non-blocking concurrent queue algorithms. In: Proceedings of 15th International ACM Symposium on Principles of Distributed Computing (PODC 1996), pp. 267–275. ACM Press (1996)
27. Moir, M., Nussbaum, D., Shalev, O., Shavit, N.: Using elimination to implement scalable and lock-free FIFO queues. In: Proceedings of 17th ACM Symposium on Parallelism in Algorithms and Architectures (SPAA 2005), pp. 253–262. ACM Press (2005)
28. Papadimitriou, C.H.: The serializability of concurrent database updates. J. ACM **26**(4), 631–653 (1979)
29. Raynal, M.: Concurrent Programming: Algorithms, Principles, and Foundations, p. 530. Springer, Heidelberg (2013). ISBN 978-3-642-32026-2
30. Raynal, M.: What can be computed in a distributed system? In: Bensalem, S., Lakhneck, Y., Legay, A. (eds.) From Programs to Systems. LNCS, vol. 8415, pp. 209–224. Springer, Heidelberg (2014)
31. Raynal, M., Stainer, J., Taubenfeld, G.: Distributed universality. In: Aguilera, M.K., Querzoni, L., Shapiro, M. (eds.) OPODIS 2014. LNCS, vol. 8878, pp. 469–484. Springer, Heidelberg (2014)
32. Shafiei, N.: Non-blocking array-based algorithms for stacks and queues. In: Garg, V., Wattenhofer, R., Kothapalli, K. (eds.) ICDCN 2009. LNCS, vol. 5408, pp. 55–66. Springer, Heidelberg (2008)
33. Taubenfeld, G.: SynchroNization Algorithms and Concurrent Programming, p. 423. Pearson Education/Prentice Hall, Upper Saddle Rive (2006). ISBN 0-131-97259-6
34. Taubenfeld, G.: Contention-sensitive data structures and algorithms. In: Keidar, I. (ed.) DISC 2009. LNCS, vol. 5805, pp. 157–171. Springer, Heidelberg (2009)
35. Tsigas, Ph., Zhang, Y.: A simple, fast and scalable non-blocking concurrent FIFO queue for shared memory multiprocessor systems. In: Proceedings of 13th ACM Symposium on Parallelism in Algorithms and Architectures (SPAA 2001), pp. 134–143. ACM Press (2001)
36. Valois, J.D.: Implementing lock-free queues. In: Proceedings of 7th International Conference on Parallel and Distributed Computing Systems (PDCS 1994), pp. 64–69. IEEE Press (1994)

Runtime-Aware Architectures

Marc Casas[⊠], Miquel Moreto, Lluc Alvarez, Emilio Castillo,
Dimitrios Chasapis, Timothy Hayes, Luc Jaulmes, Oscar Palomar,
Osman Unsal, Adrian Cristal, Eduard Ayguade, Jesus Labarta,
and Mateo Valero

Barcelona Supercomputing Center (BSC),
Universitat Politècnica de Catalunya (UPC), Barcelona, Spain
marc.casas@bsc.es

Abstract. In the last few years, the traditional ways to keep the increase
of hardware performance to the rate predicted by the Moore's Law have
vanished. When uni-cores were the norm, hardware design was decoupled
from the software stack thanks to a well defined Instruction Set Architecture (ISA). This simple interface allowed developing applications without worrying too much about the underlying hardware, while hardware
designers were able to aggressively exploit instruction-level parallelism
(ILP) in superscalar processors. Current multi-cores are designed as simple symmetric multiprocessors (SMP) on a chip. However, we believe that
this is not enough to overcome all the problems that multi-cores face.
The runtime system of the parallel programming model has to drive
the design of future multi-cores to overcome the restrictions in terms of
power, memory, programmability and resilience that multi-cores have. In
the paper, we introduce an approach towards a Runtime-Aware Architecture (RAA), a massively parallel architecture designed from the runtime's perspective.

1 Introduction and Motivation

In uni-core processors Instruction Level Parallelism (ILP) and Data Level Parallelism (DLP) are exploited to maximize the number of instructions executed per
cycle. The most important designs devoted to exploit ILP are superscalar and
Very Long Instruction Word (VLIW) processors. VLIW requires to statically
figure out dependencies between instructions and to schedule them accordingly.
However, since compilers do not do good a job obtaining optimal schedulings,
VLIW is not successful in exploiting the maximal ILP of workloads. Superscalar processors handle the increasing memory latencies, the so called Memory
Wall [25], by using Out of Order (OoO) and speculative executions [11]. Also,
improvements like prefetching, to fetch data from main memory in advance,
memory hierarchies, to exploit temporal and spatial locality, and reorder buffers,
to expose more instructions to the hardware, have been extensively used. DLP
is typically expressed at the software layer in an explicit way and it consists of a
parallel operation on multiple data performed by multiple independent instructions, or by multiple independent threads. In uniprocessors, the Instruction Set

© Springer-Verlag Berlin Heidelberg 2015
J.L. Träff et al. (Eds.): Euro-Par 2015, LNCS 9233, pp. 16–27, 2015.
DOI: 10.1007/978-3-662-48096-0_2

Architecture (ISA) is typically in charge of decoupling the high level application source code and the underlying hardware. In this context, new architecture ideas are applied at the pipeline level. In the left hand side of Fig. 1 we represent the ISA role in decoupling the application and the hardware and the way new architectural designs impact the pipeline.

Besides the problems associated with the Memory Wall, traditionally useful ways to increase hardware performance at the Moore's Law rate do not work anymore. For instance, the processor clock frequency is stagnated because the power per unit of area (power density) can not be dissipated once a certain frequency threshold is reached. That problem is called the Power Wall. Indeed, a study made by the International Technology Roadmap for Semiconductors expects the frequency to increase by 5 % every year for the next 15 years [12]. Therefore, further performance increases are expected to come from larger concurrency levels rather than higher frequencies. Indeed, to deal with the stagnation of the processor clock frequency, multi-core devices started to be on the market over a decade ago. By exploiting Task Level Parallelism (TLP) multi-core devices may achieve significant performance gains. While some aspects of the Memory and Power Walls may be aggravated: The memory bandwidth per operation and the ratio cache storage/operation remain stable or decrease in multi-cores. These challenges related to memory hierarchy issues constitute a new Memory Wall.

Also, there is a trend towards more heterogeneous multi-core systems, which might have processors with different ISA's connected through deep and complex memory hierarchies. To move data across these memory hierarchies while issues like Non-Uniform Memory Access (NUMA) or sharp power budgets are properly handled is going to be a major challenge in future multi-core machines. The Programmability Wall [7] concept is commonly use to categorize the above mentioned data management and programmability issues.

As the voltage scales up with respect to the transistor threshold voltage, the sensitivity of circuit delays to transistor parameter variations increases remarkably, which implies that processor faults will become more frequent in future designs. Additionally, future designs are expected to have more hardware components than today machines, which only makes the fault prevalence problem more dramatic. Therefore, in addition to the current challenges in parallelism, memory and power management, we are moving towards a Reliability Wall.

Since the irruption of multi-cores and parallel applications it is not possible to write high-level code in a completely hardware oblivious way anymore. An option is to transfer the role of decoupling applications from the hardware to the runtime system, that is, to let the runtime layer be in charge of efficiently using the underlying hardware without exposing its complexities to the application. In fact, the collaboration between the heterogeneous parallel hardware and the runtime layer seems appropriated to keep the programmability hardship that we are anticipating within acceptable levels while dealing with the Memory, Power and Reliability Walls.

However, this is not enough to overcome all the problems that multi-cores already have to face. To properly take advantage of their potential, tight hardware-software collaboration is required. The runtime has to drive the

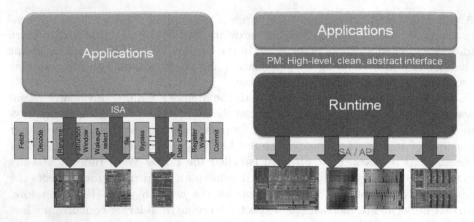

Fig. 1. Left: Decoupling the hardware and the software layers in uniprocessors. Right: The runtime drives the hardware design in multiprocessors. We call this approach a Runtime-Aware Architecture (RAA) design.

design of hardware components to overcome the challenges of the above mentioned walls. We envision a Runtime-Aware Architecture (RAA) [23], a holistic approach where the parallel architecture is partially implemented as a software runtime management layer whose activity is supported by specific hardware components specially designed with this purpose. In the right hand side of Fig. 1 we display the RAA concept in a schematic way. In this architecture, TLP and DLP are managed by the runtime and are transparent to the programmer. The idea is to have a task-based representation of parallel programs and handle the tasks in the same way as superscalar processors manage ILP, by means of a Task Dependency Graph (TDG), which can be built at runtime or statically. In this context, the runtime drives the design of new architecture components to support activities like the construction of the TDG [9], among other things.

In the next sections, we describe some illustrative examples of techniques that allow alleviating the challenges arisen from the Memory, Power, Resilience and Programmability Walls. These examples show how an adequate hardware-software co-designed system can significantly improve performance and energy consumption. Section 2 presents a hybrid memory approach that combines scratchpads and caches to deal with the Memory Wall. Section 3 shows how task criticality and hardware reconfiguration can reduce energy consumption. We also highlight the importance of vector processors in that same section. Next, Sect. 4 describes how the asynchrony provided by the OmpSs programming model [8], a forerunner of OpenMP, combined with fine grain error detection techniques can be efficiently combined to mitigate the Resilience Wall. Section 5 provides some examples to illustrate how to deal with the Programmability Wall. Finally, Sect. 6 presents the related work and Sect. 7 summarizes the main findings of this work.

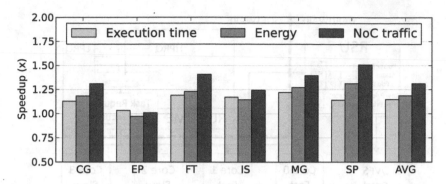

Fig. 2. Performance, energy and NoC traffic speedup of the hybrid memory hierarchy on a 64-core processor with respect to a cache-only system.

2   Memory Wall

The increasing number of cores in shared memory manycore architectures causes important power and scalability problems in the memory hierarchy. One solution is to introduce ScratchPad Memories (SPM) alongside the caches, forming a hybrid memory hierarchy. SPMs are more power-efficient than caches and they do not generate coherence traffic, but they suffer from poor programmability. A good way to hide the programmability difficulties to the programmer is to give the compiler the responsibility of generating code to manage the scratchpad memories but, unfortunately, compilers do not succeed in generating this code in the presence of random memory accesses with unknown aliasing hazards.

We propose a hardware/software co-designed coherence protocol that allows the compiler to always generate code to manage the SPMs of hybrid memory hierarchies, even if it encounters memory aliasing hazards between strided and random memory references [1]. On the software side, the proposed solution consists on simple modifications to the compiler analysis so that it can classify memory references in three categories: strided memory references, random memory references that do not alias with strided ones, and random memory references with potential aliases. The compiler then transforms the code for the strided memory references to map them to the SPMs using tiling software caches, while for the random memory references that do not alias with strided ones it generates memory instructions that are served by the cache hierarchy. For the random memory references with possible aliasing hazards, the compiler generates a special form of memory instruction that gives the hardware the responsibility to decide what memory is used to serve them. On the hardware side, a coherence protocol is proposed so that the architecture can serve memory accesses with aliasing hazards with the valid copy of the data. For this purpose the hybrid memory hierarchy is extended with a set of directories and filters that track what part of the data set is mapped and not mapped to the SPMs. These new elements are consulted at the execution of memory accesses with unknown aliases,

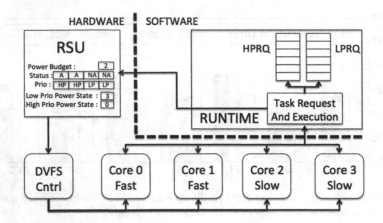

Fig. 3. Runtime Support Unit (RSU) to accelerate critical tasks in the application.

so all memory accesses can be correctly and efficiently served by the appropriate memory component avoiding thus coherence hazards.

As shown in Fig. 2, the proposed system achieves significant speedups in terms of performance, energy and NoC traffic for several NAS benchmarks. Average improvements reach 14.7%, 18.5% and 31.2%, respectively. Reduced execution time combined with more energy-efficient accesses to the hybrid memory hierarchy lead to the energy reductions. Even for benchmarks with minimal accesses to the SPM (as in the case of EP) performance, and NoC traffic are not degraded. With respect to the EP's energy consumption, there is a very minor increase, below 5%, due to the extra hardware components of the hybrid hierarchy, which consume some static power and do not contribute, in the case of EP, to the reduction of the total execution time.

3   Power Wall

3.1   Exploiting Task Criticality

Task-based data-flow programming models' intrinsic information and execution mechanisms can be exploited to open new performance gains or power savings opportunities. Such programming models overcome the performance of widely used threading approaches when running on heterogeneous many-cores. Furthermore, task criticality information can be exploited to optimize execution time or energy consumption. A task is considered critical if it belongs to the critical path of the Task Dependency Graph. Consequently, critical tasks can be run in faster or accelerated cores while non critical tasks can be scheduled to slow cores without affecting the final performance and reducing overall energy consumption. Moreover, task criticality can be simply annotated by the programmer and exploited to reconfigure the hardware by using DVFS, achieving improvements over static scheduling approaches that reach 6.6% and 20.0% in terms of performance and EDP respectively on a simulated 32-core processory.

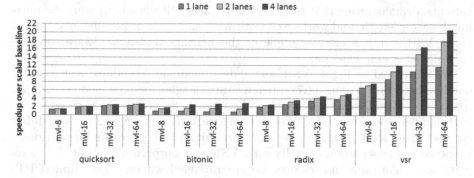

Fig. 4. Speedup over a scalar baseline for different vectorized sorting algorithms. Different maximum vector lengths (MVL) and lanes are considered.

The cost of reconfiguring the hardware with a software-only solution rises with the number of cores. Therefore, novel architectural support is proposed to reduce these overheads on future many-core systems. Figure 3 illustrates such hardware support to build a runtime-aware architecture. The runtime system is in charge of informing the Runtime Support Unit (RSU) of the criticality of each running task. Based on this information and the available power budget, the RSU decides the frequency of each core, which can be seen as a criticality-aware turbo boost mechanism. Consequently, this hardware support minimally extends hardware structures already present in current processors, which allows further improvements in performance with negligible hardware overhead. The proposed solution, which goes from the source code to the hardware level passing through the runtime and the operating system, shows the need for a multi-layer approach to optimally exploit the heterogeneity of future many-core systems.

3.2 Vector Processors

Due to their energy efficiency, SIMD extensions are ubiquitous in modern microprocessors and expected to grow in width and functionality in future generations. After extensive analysis on three diverse sorting algorithms in the context of future SIMD support, we learn that all of the algorithms suffer from bottlenecks and scalability problems due to the irregularity of the DLP and the limitations of a standard SIMD instruction set. Based on these findings we propose VSR sort [10], a novel way to efficiently vectorize the radix sort algorithm. To enable this algorithm in a SIMD architecture we define two new instructions: vector prior instances (VPI) and vector last unique (VLU). VPI uses a single vector register as input, processes it serially and outputs another vector register as a result. Each element of the output asserts exactly how many instances of a value in the corresponding element of the input register have been seen before. VLU also uses a single vector register as input but produces a vector mask as a result that marks the last instance of any particular value found. We provide a suitable hardware proposal that includes both serial and parallel variants, demonstrating that the algorithm scales well when increasing the maximum vector length, and works well both with and without parallel lockstepped lanes. VSR sort is a clear example of the benefits that a hardware/software co-designed system can offer.

As illustrated in Fig. 4, VSR sort shows maximum speedups over a scalar baseline between 7.9x and 11.7x when a simple single-lane pipelined vector approach is used, and maximum speedups between 14.9x and 20.6x when as few as four parallel lanes are used. Next, we compare VSR sort with three very different vectorized sorting algorithms: quicksort, bitonic mergesort and a previously proposed implementation of radix sort. VSR sort outperforms all of the aforementioned algorithms and achieves a comparatively low Cycles Per Tuple (CPT) without strictly requiring parallel lanes. It has a complexity of $O(k \cdot n)$ meaning that this CPT will remain constant as the input size increases, a highly-desirable property of a sorting algorithm. The k factor is significantly improved over the original vectorized radix sort as well as the constant performance factor. Its dominant memory access pattern is unit-stride which helps maximise the utilisation of the available memory bandwidth. Unlike the previous vectorized radix sort, VSR sort does not replicate its internal bookkeeping structures which consequently allows them to be larger and reduces the number of necessary passes of the algorithm. On average VSR sort performs 3.4x better than the next-best vectorized sorting algorithm when run on the same hardware configuration.

4   Reliability Wall

Relying on error detection techniques already available in commodity hardware, we develop algorithmic-level error correction techniques for Detected and Uncorrected Errors (DUE) in iterative solvers. When a data loss or corruption is detected, we use simple algorithmic redundancies that are not applicable under coarser grain error models without paying prohibitive overheads. By using this straightforward relations existing in the solver it is possible to interpolate the lost data and manage to recover it. This forward recovery scheme has better performance than backwards recoveries such as checkpointing and rollback. We are also able to avoid sacrificing convergence rate altogether thanks to the exactitude of the recovered data, allowing the solver to continue, which is better in the long run.

Furthermore, we can lever the asynchrony of task-based programming models to perform our recoveries' interpolations simultaneously with the normal workload of the solver. This allows to reduce the overheads of our recovery technique, and is done with virtually no burden on the programmer thanks to the programming model, by scheduling the recoveries in tasks that are placed out of the critical path of the solver.

Figure 5 illustrates these behaviours, for a single error scenario where the Conjugate Gradient (CG) method for the matrix thermal2 is disturbed by a DUE around 30s. The lightblue checkpointing scheme incurs a significant overhead when rolling back, and the restart method, in green, has a slower convergence

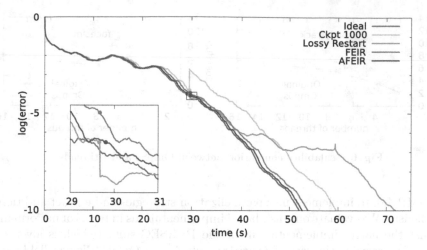

Fig. 5. CG execution example with a single error occurring at the same time for all implemented mechanisms.

afterwards, when compared to the ideal baseline, in red, which has no fault injected nor resilience mechanism. Our recovery technique, in purple, shows a convergence time close to the ideal baseline, and its asynchronous counterpart, in blue, displays an even smaller overhead.

5 Programmability Wall

Task-based models are used to program parallel shared memory machines, offering an alternative to other models like POSIX threads. They allow the programmer to easily describe parallel work as asynchronous tasks. Task-based models are coupled with a runtime system which in its simplest form takes the burden of thread management from the programmer. Such runtime systems offer additional functionality, such as load balancing or tracking data dependencies between different tasks, ensuring their correct order of execution. To allow data dependence tracking by the runtime system, task-based models often offer syntactic tools to the programmer to express data-flow relations between tasks [2,8,13,22,24]. The OpenMP standard has recently adopted tasks and data-flow extensions to its syntax [18], allowing dynamic tracking of dependencies during execution.

Studies on how effective this emerging programming model is in terms of performance have been done in the context of HPC [3,20,22]. Since there is an increasing interest, driven by technological trends, in parallel workloads that go beyond the traditional HPC applications, the importance of understanding how task parallelism can be effectively adopted in application domains like search engines, multimedia or finantial analytics is growing. To answer this question we consider a large subset (10 out of 13 applications) of the PARSEC benchmark suite [5] and we use the OmpSs programming model [8], which is a forerunner of

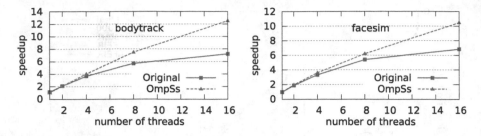

Fig. 6. Scalability comparion between OmpSs and Pthreads.

OpenMP 4.0, to implement new parallelization strategies and extract additional parallelism. We evaluate our task-based implementations in terms of performance against the native implementations of the PARSEC suite (which is always in Pthreads, except in the case of `freqmine`, which uses OpenMP's parallel loops). In some cases, for example when the applications use pipeline parallelism, we extract additional parallelism executing asynchronously I/O intensive sequential stages and overlapping them with computation intensive parallel regions. In these cases we improve the scalability of the applications. Figure 6 shows the scalability comparison between OmpSs and Pthreads versions for `bodytrack` and `facesim` on a 16-core machine. Both applications improve significantly their scalability over the original code, reaching a scaling factor of 12 and 10, respectively, when running with 16 cores.

To evaluate the usability of task-parallel models we study how compact and expressive the code is, compared to Pthreads/OpenMP. By measuring the lines of code, we observe that OmpSs' syntax is less verbose than Pthreads, for most benchmarks. In general, applications that have pipeline parallelism can greatly reduce the lines of code of the application, since simple data-flow relations can replace user implemented queuing and thread management systems.

6   Related Work

Some previous work has been devoted to many-core architectures with a single global address space where parallel work is expressed in terms of a taskcentric bulk-synchronous model using hardware support [14]. The execution paradigm of this approach is based on tasks, like the one presented in this paper. However, this previous approach assummes the mapping of the tasks to the functional units of the processor to be specified in the application binary, significantly reducing its flexibility. Other approaches propose architectures composed of multiple processor types and a set of user-managed direct memory access (DMA) engines that let the runtime scheduler overlap data transfer and computation [21]. The runtime system automatically allocates tasks on the heterogeneous cores and schedules the data transfers through the DMA engines. The programming model suggested by this approach supports highly parallel applications and specialized accelerator processors. The Runtime-Aware Architecture presented in this paper includes these ideas and incorporates new ones (resilience, hardware support for frequency reconfiguration, etc.) to achieve a more general and robust design.

Other many-core proposals with separate execution units for runtime and application code, application-managed on-chip memory and direct physical addressing, a hierarchical on-chip network and a codelet-based execution model [6] have been suggested to reduce energy consumption and increase performance. Hardware techniques to accelerate dynamic task scheduling on scalable CMPs have also been suggested [15]. They consist in relatively simple hardware that can be placed far from the cores. While our proposal also aims to support task scheduling, it incorporates many more innovations like runtime-based hybrid memory designs or hardware support for reconfiguration, to mention just two.

Our research group has experience on runtime system techniques to enable optimizations like software prefetching [4] or overlapping communication and computation [17]. More recently, approaches derived from our initial work aim to exploit the runtime system information to either reduce cache coherence traffic [16] or enable software prefetching mechanisms [19]. The Runtime-Aware Architecture presented in this paper gathers all these previous experiences and provides a holistic view that integrates not only the memory system but also all the hardware components to ride again on the Moore's Law.

7 Conclusions

Our approach towards Runtime-Aware Architectures offers a single solution to fix most of the problems other approaches have: handling parallelism, the Memory Wall, the Power Wall, the Programmability Wall, and the upcoming Reliability Wall. The approach presented in this paper is applicable to a wide range of application domains from mobile up to supercomputers and its main feature consists in hardware components specifically designed to support the activity of a runtime system that handles task-parallelism plus control and data dependences. Further, we envision a hardware-software codesign approach where the parallel architecture has a software layer composed by a runtime system whose activity is supported by hardware components specifically designed for that purpose.

Altogether, this novel approach towards future parallel architectures is the way to ensure continued performance improvements by exploiting a tight collaboration between the hardware and the software without sacrificing programmability. All in all, the integrated solution proposed by this paper aims to get us out of the hardship in terms of hardware design and programmability that computers have turned into, once more riding on Moore's Law.

Acknowledgments. This work has been partially supported by the European Research Council under the European Union's 7th FP, ERC Grant Agreement number 321253, by the Spanish Ministry of Science and Innovation under grant TIN2012-34557 and by the HiPEAC Network of Excellence. M. Moreto has been partially supported by the Ministry of Economy and Competitiveness under Juan de la Cierva postdoctoral fellowship number JCI- 2012-15047, and M. Casas is supported by the Secretary for

Universities and Research of the Ministry of Economy and Knowledge of the Government of Catalonia and the Co-fund programme of the Marie Curie Actions of the 7th R&D Framework Programme of the European Union (Contract 2013 BP_B 00243).

References

1. Alvarez, L., Vilanova, L., Moreto, M., Casas, M., Gonzàlez, M., Martorell, X., Navarro, N., Ayguadé, E., Valero, M.: Coherence protocol for transparent management of scratchpad memories in shared memory manycore architectures. In: International Symposium on Computer Architecture (ISCA), pp. 720–732 (2015)
2. Ayguadé, E., Copty, N., Duran, A., Hoeflinger, J., Lin, Y., Massaioli, F., Teruel, X., Unnikrishnan, P., Zhang, G.: The design of OpenMP tasks. IEEE Trans. Parallel Distrib. Syst. **20**(3), 404–418 (2009)
3. Ayguadé, E., Duran, A., Hoeflinger, J., Massaioli, F., Teruel, X.: An experimental evaluation of the new OpenMP tasking model. In: LCPC, pp. 63–77 (2007)
4. Bellens, P., Perez, J.M., Badia, R.M., Labarta, J.: CellSs: a programming model for the cell B.E. architecture. In: Supercomputing (SC) (2006)
5. Bienia, C.: Benchmarking Modern Multiprocessors. Ph.D. thesis, Princeton University, January 2011
6. Carter, N.P., Agrawal, A., Borkar, S., Cledat, R., David, H., Dunning, D., Fryman, J.B., Ganev, I., Golliver, R.A., Knauerhase, R.C., Lethin, R., Meister, B., Mishra, A.K., Pinfold, W.R., Teller, J., Torrellas, J., Vasilache, N., Venkatesh, G., Xu, J.: Runnemede: An architecture for ubiquitous high-performance computing. In: International Symposium on High Performance Computer Architecture (HPCA), pp. 198–209 (2013)
7. Chapman, B.: The multicore programming challenge. In: International Conference on Advanced Parallel Processing Technologies (APPT), pp. 3–3 (2007)
8. Duran, A., Ayguadé, E., Badia, R.M., Labarta, J., Martinell, L., Martorell, X., Planas, J.: OmpSs: a proposal for programming heterogeneous multi-core architectures. Parall. Proc. Lett. **21**(2), 173–193 (2011)
9. Etsion, Y., Cabarcas, F., Rico, A., Ramírez, A., Badia, R.M., Ayguadé, E., Labarta, J., Valero, M.: Task superscalar: An out-of-order task pipeline. In: MICRO, pp. 89–100 (2010)
10. Hayes, T., Palomar, O., Unsal, O.S., Cristal, A., Valero, M.: VSR sort: A novel vectorised sorting algorithm & architecture extensions for future microprocessors. In: International Symposium on High Performance Computer Architecture (HPCA), pp. 26–38 (2015)
11. Hennessy, J.L., Patterson, D.A.: Computer Architecture - A Quantitative Approach, 5th edn. Morgan Kaufmann, San Francisco (2012)
12. International technology roadmap for semiconductors (ITRS) (2011)
13. Jenista, J.C., Eom, Yh, Demsky, B.C.: OoOJava: Software out-of-order execution. SIGPLAN Not. **46**(8), 57–68 (2011)
14. Kelm, J.H., Johnson, D.R., Johnson, M.R., Crago, N.C., Tuohy, W., Mahesri, A., Lumetta, S.S., Frank, M.I., Patel, S.J.: Rigel: An architecture and scalable programming interface for a 1000-core accelerator. In: ISCA 09, pp. 140–151
15. Kumar, S., Hughes, C.J., Nguyen, A.: Carbon: Architectural support for fine-grained parallelism on chip multiprocessors. In: International Symposium on Computer Architecture (ISCA), pp. 162–173 (2007)

16. Manivannan, M., Stenstrom, P.: Runtime-guided cache coherence optimizations in multi-core architectures. In: International Parallel and Distributed Processing Symposium (IPDPS), pp. 625–636 (2014)
17. Marjanović, V., Labarta, J., Ayguadé, E., Valero, M.: Overlapping communication and computation by using a hybrid mpi/smpss approach. In: Proceedings of the 24th ACM International Conference on Supercomputing, ICS 2010, pp. 5–16. ACM, New York (2010)
18. OpenMP Architecture Review Board: OpenMP application program interface version 4.0, July 2013. http://www.openmp.org/mp-documents/OpenMP4.0.0.pdf
19. Papaefstathiou, V., Katevenis, M.G., Nikolopoulos, D.S., Pnevmatikatos, D.: Prefetching and cache management using task lifetimes. In: International Conference on Supercomputing (ICS), pp. 325–334 (2013)
20. Podobas, A., Brorsson, M.: A comparison of some recent task-based parallel programming models. In: Multiprog (2010)
21. Ramírez, A., Cabarcas, F., Juurlink, B.H.H., Alvarez, M., Sánchez, F., Azevedo, A., Meenderinck, C., Ciobanu, C.B., Isaza, S., Gaydadjiev, G.: The SARC architecture. IEEE Micro **30**(5), 16–29 (2010)
22. Tzenakis, G., Papatriantafyllou, A., Kesapides, J., Pratikakis, P., Vandierendonck, H., Nikolopoulos, D.S.: BDDT: Block-level dynamic dependence analysis for deterministic task-based parallelism. SIGPLAN Not. **47**(8), 301–302 (2012)
23. Valero, M., Moreto, M., Casas, M., Ayguade, E., Labarta, J.: Runtime-aware architectures: A first approach. Int. J. Supercomputing Front. Innovations **1**(1), 29–44 (2014)
24. Vandierendonck, H., Tzenakis, G., Nikolopoulos, D.: A unified scheduler for recursive and task dataflow parallelism. In: International Conference on Parallel Architectures and Compilation Techniques (PACT), pp. 1–11, October 2011
25. Wulf, W.A., McKee, S.A.: Hitting the memory wall: Implications of the obvious. SIGARCH Comput. Archit. News **23**(1), 20–24 (1995)

Support Tools and Environments

MPI Thread-Level Checking
for MPI+OpenMP Applications

Emmanuelle Saillard[1]([⊠]), Patrick Carribault[1], and Denis Barthou[2]

[1] CEA, DAM, DIF, F-91297 Arpajon, France
emmanuelle.saillard.ocre@cea.fr
[2] Bordeaux Institute of Technology, LaBRI / INRIA, Bordeaux, France

Abstract. MPI is the most widely used parallel programming model. But the reducing amount of memory per compute core tends to push MPI to be mixed with shared-memory approaches like OpenMP. In such cases, the interoperability of those two models is challenging. The MPI 2.0 standard defines the so-called thread level to indicate how MPI will interact with threads. But even if hybrid programs are more common, there is still a lack in debugging tools and more precisely in thread level compliance. To fill this gap, we propose a static analysis to verify the thread-level required by an application. This work extends PARCOACH, a GCC plugin focused on the detection of MPI collective errors in MPI and MPI+OpenMP programs. We validated our analysis on computational benchmarks and applications and measured a low overhead.

Keywords: Static verification · OpenMP · MPI · MPI thread level

1 Introduction

To address the challenges of exascale systems, MPI evolves to be mixed with shared-memory approaches like OpenMP. E. Lusk and A. Chan report for instance some successful use cases of OpenMP threads exploiting multiple cores per node with MPI communicating among the nodes [11]. But combining models does not facilitate the debugging task and requires special care for MPI calls [4]. Indeed, in an MPI+OpenMP program, not only the correctness of MPI should be ensured but also the multi-threaded model should not interfere with MPI. As an example, within a process, the same communicator may not be concurrently used by two different MPI collective calls. This means MPI collective operations may not be called by multiple parallel threads. The MPI-2 standard defines four thread-safety levels to indicate how MPI should interact with threads. According to the MPI standard, *it is the user responsibility to prevent races when threads within the same application post conflicting communication calls* ([17], p. 482). This should be checked above all for the fully multithreaded case (MPI_THREAD_MULTIPLE). This paper presents a static analysis to verify MPI Thread-level compliance required by an MPI+OpenMP application.

Figure 1 illustrates some of the possible issues related to MPI communications in a multithreaded context through three examples. MPI_Allreduce in

© Springer-Verlag Berlin Heidelberg 2015
J.L. Träff et al. (Eds.): Euro-Par 2015, LNCS 9233, pp. 31–42, 2015.
DOI: 10.1007/978-3-662-48096-0_3

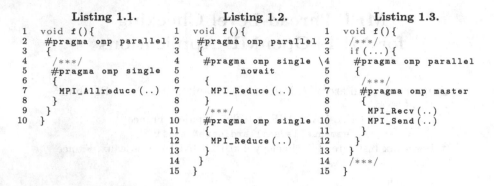

Fig. 1. MPI+OpenMP examples showing different uses of MPI calls.

Listing 1.1 is called in a **single** block, **MPI_THREAD_SERIALIZED** then corresponds to the minimum level of compliance. However if the function f is called itself in a parallel construct, the collective is then executed in a nested parallel region, possibly leading to more than one concurrent call to this collective. This erroneous situation always occurs unless only one thread is created in the first parallel region or in both regions. Listing 1.2 illustrates a more complex case: two **MPI_Reduce**s are executed in **single** constructs in the same OpenMP parallel region. As the first construct contains a **nowait** clause, both **MPI_Reduce** can be executed concurrently by different threads. This requires a thread-level equal to **MPI_THREAD_MULTIPLE**, assuming the communicators used by the two collectives are different. If they are identical, the code is incorrect. In Listing 1.3, function f is compliant with the **MPI_THREAD_FUNNELED** level. However, if the master directive is replaced by a single directive, the **MPI_THREAD_SERIALIZED** level is the minimum thread-level required. Thus, these examples illustrate the difficulty for a developer to ensure that MPI calls are correctly placed inside an hybrid MPI+OpenMP application whatever the required thread-level support.

This paper proposes a static analysis that helps the application developer to check which thread-level support is required for a specific code. For this purpose, we suppose the programs are SPMD (Single Program Multiple Data) MPI programs. It means that every MPI rank calls the same functions in the same order. This covers a large amount of scientific simulation applications for High-Performance Computing. We integrated our analysis in the GCC plugin PARCOACH [13,14] and we designed it to be compatible with other dynamic tools. Our paper makes the following contributions:

- Analysis to check the conformance of MPI+OpenMP codes with any MPI thread level (including **MPI_THREAD_MULTIPLE** level) defined in the MPI-2 standard and code transformation to verify the non-compliance at runtime.
- Full implementation inside a production compiler (GCC).
- Experimental results on multiple benchmarks and production applications.
- Functional integration with existing dynamic debugging tools (our approach is designed to be complementary to existing dynamic PMPI-based debugging tools like MUST [6]).

This paper is organized as follows: Sect. 2 summarizes the related work on debugging of MPI and hybrid MPI+OpenMP applications, focusing on MPI thread-level compliance. Section 3 describes the basis of our approach. Then Sect. 4 exposes our static analysis detecting the thread-level compliance. Section 5 illustrates our approach on experimental results and finally Sect. 6 concludes.

2   Related Work

As most HPC applications are parallelized with MPI, a lot of work has been done to help programmers to debug MPI applications (TASS [15], DAMPI [21], MPI-CHECK [10], Intel Message Checker [2], Marmot [9], Umpire [20], MUST [6], MPICH [3]). Existing tools, static or dynamic, are able to detect the line in the source code where an error occured but rarely the line responsible for this situation. Although the compile-time offers the possibility to detect and correct possible errors earlier than at runtime, few tools rely on purely static analysis because of the combinatory aspect of methods used. We have developed in previous work a GCC plugin named PARCOACH [13,14], to statically detect MPI collective errors in MPI and MPI+OpenMP programs. It combines compile-time code analysis with an instrumentation to prevent the application from deadlocking. This approach avoids systematic instrumentation, highlights conditionals that can lead to a deadlock and issues warnings with precise information.

One of the MPI challenges is its interoperability with other programming models. Even if it is now possible to profile and visualize profiles and traces for MPI+OpenMP programs, debugging tools especially those detecting thread levels compliance are practically non-existent. To our knowledge, Marmot [5] is the only tool that provides a support for detecting violations in MPI+OpenMP programs. Marmot uses the MPI profiling interface (PMPI) to introduce artificial data races only occuring when some constraints are violated and detect them with the Intel Thread Checker tool. The authors define five restrictions for hybrid MPI applications based on the definition of the thread levels mentioned in the MPI standard. The fifth restriction is the non-violation to the provided thread level. However, as Marmot only relies on profiling, it may find for one run that the program is non compliant to a given thread level, and for another run find its compliance (so defining a compliance per run). The same happens for bugs, where detection may require many runs in a profile-only approach. On the contrary, PARCOACH finds statically the possible non-compliance of the code, pinpointing non-compliant code fragments and situations. The runtime instrumentation only checks whether these situations occur.

3   Analysis of the Multithreaded Context

Our static analysis verifies the thread-level compliance of hybrid applications. The analysis proposed does not depend on one particular run and finds all possible situations of non-compliance to a given thread level. As it is conservative, it can be complemented by an instrumentation phase that checks the occurence of these situations. An essential part of the static analysis consist in determining the multithreaded context in which MPI calls (Point-to-point and collectives) are performed. The method described in this section computes a parallelism word to characterize this context in each point of the function analyzed.

3.1 Parallelism Words Construction

The analysis operates on the code represented as an intermediate-code form. We consider the program is represented as a *control-flow graph* (CFG), built in almost all compilers. The compile-time verification then consists in a static analysis of the CFG for each function of a program. The CFG is defined as a directed graph with artificial entry and exit nodes. Each node corresponds to a *basic block* and has a set of successors and predecessors. The CFG is augmented to highlight nodes containing MPI calls (collectives and P2P). As for the GCC compiler, OpenMP directives are put into separate basic blocks. Hence new nodes are added for explicit and implicit thread barriers. For sake of clarity, implicit thread barriers at the end of parallel regions are denoted by **end parallel**.

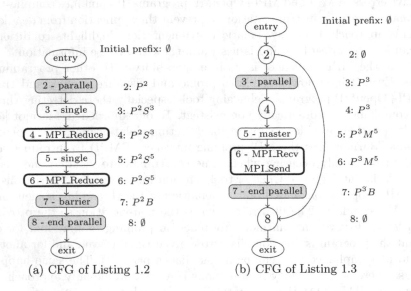

(a) CFG of Listing 1.2   (b) CFG of Listing 1.3

Fig. 2. Control Flow Graph and parallelism words of Listings 1.2 and 1.3

To highlight the thread context in which an MPI call is performed, we extend the notion of parallelism words defined in [14], taking into account the needs of a thread level compliance analysis. The *parallelism word* of a basic block is the sequence of OpenMP parallel constructs (pragma **parallel**, **single**, ...) surrounding this block and the barriers traversed from the beginning of a function to the block. Parallel regions containing the block are denoted by P^i, with i the id of the basic block with the OpenMP construct. Similarly, regions executed by the master thread are denoted by M^i and other single threaded regions are denoted S^i. Finally, barrier corresponds to B. OpenMP defines a perfectly-nested parallelism, thus the control flow has no impact on the parallelism word. Each node (basic block) n is associated to a parallelism word denoted $pw[n]$. With a depth-first search starting at the entry node, each node then sets its parallelism word depending on its predecessor and the OpenMP directives it contains. P is added when a parallel region is encountered, S is added when a single, section or task region is traversed, M is added when a master construct is traversed and B is added when an implicit or explicit thread barrier is met. Figure 2 shows examples of CFG with their associated parallelism words.

3.2 Parallelism Words Analysis

The automaton Fig. 3 defines the possible parallelism words. Nestings forbidden by the OpenMP specification (SS, MS,...) are not considered by the automaton. If the target obtains such forbidden nested regions, our analysis returns the error message: *invalid state, error*. The language of accepted parallelism words will depend on the specified thread level. As we check each function independently, the level of parallelism in which a function is called is unknown. To provide an accurate picture of the level of thread parallelism in which function occurrence is called, the statistics on the NAS Parallel Benchmarks multizone (NASPB-MZ) using class B [18] have been collected and are shown in Table 1 per thread, in each process. We notice that functions are mainly called within one level of multithreading. Thus to consider all possible initial conditions, each callsite is instrumented in order to capture the initial parallelism word of each function. This word corresponds to a prefix P_i for all basic blocks of the called function and defines an initial state in Automaton Fig. 3 (all states are possible initial states). The user can choose the initial state at compile-time.

Table 1. Level of threads parallelism at function entries for NASPB-MZ

Benchmark	# function calls	# calls in state 0,2,3	# calls in state 1,4	# calls in state 5,6
BT-MZ	396,918,403	45,379	396,873,024	0
SP-MZ	15,479,425	116,161	15,363,264	0
LU-MZ	3,017,513	40,745	2,976,768	0

The following section describes the analysis checking the thread-level compliance based on the parallelism words of the basic blocks containing MPI communications.

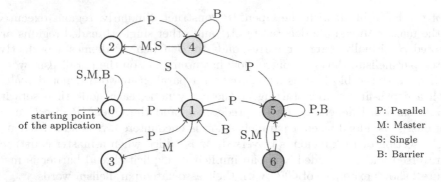

Fig. 3. Automaton of possible parallelism words. Nodes 0, 2 and 3 correspond to code executed by the master thread or a single thread. Nodes 1 and 4 correspond to code executed in a parallel region, and 5 and 6 to code executed in nested parallel region.

4   Thread-Level Compliance Checking

This section describes how the non-compliance of thread levels can be detected at compile-time. For that purpose we use parallelism words introduced in the previous section to check the placement of MPI calls within a process.

4.1   Static Analysis and Interface to Dynamic Checkings

For each possible thread level we define a language of valid parallelism words based on the automaton Fig. 3. For a given basic block, its parallelism word consists in the prefix (obtained from the callsite of the function or user-defined) and the word computed from previous analysis. The analysis verifies if nodes containing MPI calls (P2P and collectives) are associated with an accepted word. Thread barriers can be safely ignored as they do not influence the level of thread parallelism. In case of the detection of a possible error, a warning related to the initial level with the name of the call is returned to the programmer. Algorithm 1 takes as input the CFG and the language L of correct parallelism words and outputs the sets S and S_{ipw}. These sets respectively contain the nodes violating the input language and the nodes that dominate these nodes before the execution/control flow changes. This set will be given as one of the input parameters of the dynamic analysis. In the algorithm, line 5, the node u corresponds to the node preceeding n in the CFG and that is the immediate successor of a control flow node (with two successors) or of a pragma node (changing the parallelism word). The nodes in the set S_{ipw} correspond to execution points where compliance should be tested at runtime, in order to handle possible false-positives detected statically. A unique parallelism word is computed at runtime and updated after each OpenMP construct. Compared to the compile-time parallelism words, parallel regions created with only one thread correspond to the parallelism word ϵ. This implies that such region has no impact on the current multithreaded context.

The insertion of such computations and checks can be conducted in tools such as MUST [6], Marmot [9] or following the techniques proposed in [12].

Algorithm 1. Detection of *parallelism words* for multithreaded regions

1: **function** MULTITHREADED_REGIONS($G = (V, E), L$)   ▷ G: CFG, L: language
2:       $S_{ipw} \leftarrow \emptyset$, $S \leftarrow \emptyset$
3:       **for** *each* $n \in V | n$ contains a MPI call **do**
4:             **if** $pw[n] \notin L$ **then**
5:                   $u \leftarrow$ Node that dominates n before execution/control flow changement
6:                   $S \leftarrow S \cup \{n\}$, $S_{ipw} \leftarrow S_{ipw} \cup u$
7:             **end if**
8:       **end for**
9:       Output nodes in S as warnings
10: **end function**

4.2   MPI_THREAD_SINGLE

By setting the MPI_THREAD_SINGLE level, the user ensures only one thread will execute MPI calls ([17], p. 486). This means all MPI calls should be performed outside multi-threaded regions. Thus all nodes of the CFG containing a MPI call must be associated with an empty parallelism word. The language L of accepted parallelism words is then defined by $L = \{\epsilon\}$. Algorithm 1 with $L = \{\epsilon\}$ returns the non-compliant MPI calls (set S).

4.3   MPI_THREAD_FUNNELED

The use of MPI_THREAD_FUNNELED level means the process may be multi-threaded but the application must ensure that only the thread that initialized MPI can make MPI calls ([17], p. 486). For this level, State 3 in Automaton Fig. 3 is the accepting state and the language $L = (PB^*M)^+$ describes the accepted words. With Algorithm 1 and L, our analysis detects MPI calls that are not executed in a master region.

4.4   MPI_THREAD_SERIALIZED

The MPI_THREAD_SERIALIZED level means the process may be multi-threaded but only one thread at a time can perform MPI calls ([17]). The accepting states in Automaton Fig. 3 are states 2 and 3. Thus, the language $L = (PB^*S | PB^*M)^*$ describes the accepted words. This language contains parallelism words ending by S or M without a repeated sequence of P. Critical sections and locks are not supported here and is part of our future work.

To verify the compliance of this level, Algorithm 1 is used to make sure all MPI calls are performed in a monothreaded context. Different MPI calls in the same monothreaded region are sequentially performed as only one thread executes it. However, calls in different monothreaded regions may be called simultaneously if monothreaded regions are executed in parallel (no thread synchronization between monothreaded regions). Special care is requested for MPI collective operations. All MPI processes should execute the same sequence of MPI collective operations in a deterministic way. That means there is a total order between MPI collective calls. Algorithm 2 shows the detection of concurrent calls. It takes as input the CFG and outputs two sets: S and S_{cc}. When nodes containing a MPI call with the same number of B are detected these nodes are put in the set S and the nodes that begin the monothreaded regions are put in the set S_{cc} for the dynamic analysis. A warning is issued for nodes in S.

Algorithm 2. Detection of potential concurrent calls

1: **function** CONCURRENT_CALLS($G = (V, E)$)   ▷ G: CFG
2:     $S_{cc} \leftarrow \emptyset$, $S \leftarrow \emptyset$
3:     Remove loop back edges
4:     **if** $\exists \, u, v \in$ nodes in concurrent monothreaded regions **then**
5:         $i, j \leftarrow$ nodes immediate successors of nodes creating monothreaded regions
6:         $S \leftarrow S \cup \{u, v\}$, $S_{cc} \leftarrow S_{cc} \cup \{i, j\}$
7:     **end if**
8:     Output nodes in S as warnings
9: **end function**

To dynamically verify the total order of MPI collective sequences in each MPI process, validation functions are inserted in nodes in the sets S_{ipw} and S_{cc} generated by Algorithms 1 and 2: CC_{ipw} and CC_{cc}. Function CC_{ipw} detects incorrect execution parallelism words and Function CC_{cc} detects concurrent collective calls. In Fig. 2, nodes 4 and 6 have the same number of thread barriers in their parallelism words (node 4: P^2S^3, node 6: P^2S^5) so the collective operations involved are potential concurrent collective calls. Indeed, the nowait clause remove the implicit barrier at the end of the first single region. The algorithm outputs a warning for collective calls located nodes 4 and 6 ($S = \{4, 6\}$) and flags nodes 4 and 6 for dynamic checks ($S_{cc} = \{4, 6\}$). CC_{cc} functions are then inserted in nodes 4 and 6.

4.5   MPI_THREAD_MULTIPLE

This level is the least restrictive level. It enables multiple threads to call MPI with no restriction ([17], p. 486). However MPI calls should be thread safe, meaning that when two concurrently running threads make MPI calls, the outcome will be as if the calls executed sequentially in some order. The verification of this level follows the same analyses as for the MPI_THREAD_SERIALIZED level.

5 Experimental Results

This section is intended to show the impact of our analysis on the compilation time. For that purpose we present experimental results obtained on the NAS Parallel benchmarks multizone (NAS-MZ v3.2) using class B [18], five MPI+OpenMP Coral benchmarks [19] (AMG2013, LULESH, HACC, SNAP, miniFE) and a production test case named HERA [8], which is a large multiphysics 2D/3D AMR hydrocode platform. To highlight the functionality of our analysis, we created a microbenchmark suite called BenchError containing five hybrid programs that violate thread level constraints (coll_single, coll_funneled, coll_serialized, p2p_multiple) and contain MPI collective (coll_deadlock) errors. All compilation experiments were conducted on the Tera-100 supercomputer (peak performance of 1.2 PFlops) and computed with BullxMPI 1.1.16.5.

5.1 Functionnalities of the Analysis

We extended PARCOACH, a GCC plugin located in the middle end of the compilation chain after the CFG generation and before OpenMP directives transformation. Hence the plugin is language independent allowing the verification of programs written in C, C++ and Fortran. Our analysis is therefore simple to deploy in existing environment as it does not modify the whole compilation chain. The analysis issues warnings at compile-time with potential error information (lines of MPI calls, line where the dynamic check is inserted,...). The following example shows what a user can read on *stderr* when compiling the program coll_serialized corresponding to Listing 1.2.

```
in function 'f':
Warning: PARCOACH: possible non-compliance of MPI_THREAD_SERIALIZED level. Potential concurrent
coll. calls within a process : MPI_Reduce 1.11 may be called simultaneously with MPI_Reduce 1.6
PARCOACH: Minimum thread-level required: MPI_THREAD_MULTIPLE
PARCOACH inserted a check after the single directive 1.4 | the single directive 1.9
```

In this example, **MPI_Reduce** calls were done on different communicators. As our analysis does not check communicators, both single regions are instrumented to check if the non-compliance of the thread level is confirmed at runtime. In comparison, the error message returned by Marmot at runtime is the following: Marmot finds that the code should be executed within the **MPI_THREAD_FUNNELED** thread level whereas PARCOACH finds the level **MPI_THREAD_MULTIPLE**. The reason comes from the fact that Marmot detects conformance w.r.t. one execution, and in particular to one parallel schedule. During the execution monitored by Marmot, the **single** constructs are executed by the master thread leading to a serialized sequence of these constructs. However, from a conformance point of view, this is incorrect and the thread level **MPI_THREAD_MULTIPLE** as analyzed by PARCOACH should be chosen.

5.2 Static Analysis Results

Table 2 shows the language and the number of lines of each benchmark we tested. The 4th and 5th columns depict the thread level provided (level actually returned to the user, might be lower than the desired level, depending on the MPI implementation) and the minimum thread level required by the application (thread-level the user should use). The last column displays the compliance our analysis returned. Our analysis was able to find the thread-level non-compliance in our microbenchmark suite. Notice that the MPI_THREAD_MULTIPLE level was not supported by the MPI implementation we used. For each benchmark, the overhead obtained at compile-time (serial compilation) is presented Fig. 4. This overhead is acceptable as it does not exceed 6 %.

Table 2. Compliance results

Benchmark	Language	Lines of code	Thread level provided	Thread level required	Compliant
BT-MZ || SP-MZ	Fortran	6,779 || 4,862	SINGLE	SINGLE	yes
LU-MZ	Fortran	6,542	SINGLE	SINGLE	yes
AMG2013 || LULESH	C	75,000 || 5,000	SINGLE	SINGLE	yes
miniFE || HACC	C++	50,000 || 35,000	SINGLE	SINGLE	yes
SNAP	Fortran	3,000	SINGLE	SINGLE	yes
HERA	C++	500,000	SERIALIZED	SERIALIZED	yes
coll_single	C	29	SINGLE	FUNNELED	no
coll_funneled	C	36	FUNNELED	SERIALIZED	no
coll_serialized	C	47	SERIALIZED	MULTIPLE	no
coll_deadlock	C	38	FUNNELED	FUNNELED	yes
p2p_multiple	C	45	SERIALIZED	MULTIPLE	no

PARCOACH issues warnings for potential MPI collective errors within an MPI process and between processes. The type of each potential error is specified (collective mismatch, concurrent calls in an MPI process,...) with the names

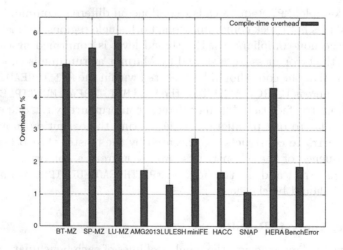

Fig. 4. Overhead of average compilation time

and lines in the source code of MPI collective calls involved. Table 3 shows the number of static MPI collective calls and the number of nodes in the set S found by PARCOACH (Algorithms 1 and 2 of our analysis). The 4th column depicts the percentage of the benchmarks functions instrumented. We notice a good impact of the static analysis on the selective instrumentation. The two last columns give the number of expected errors and the number of errors actually found.

Table 3. Debugging results

Benchmark	# collective calls	# nodes in S	% instrumented functions	# expected errors	# errors found
BT-MZ || SP-MZ	15 || 15	7 || 7	8,57 % || 8,57 %	0 || 0	0 || 0
LU-MZ	20	7	8,82 %	0	0
AMG2013	86	75	13.33 %	0	0
LULESH || miniFE	3 || 4	1 || 6	1.44 % || 2.56 %	0 || 0	0 || 0
HACC || SNAP	26 || 9	11 || 13	1.41 % || 10 %	0 || 0	0 || 0
HERA	574	375	<1 %	0	0
coll_single || coll_funneled	1 || 1	1 || 1	100 % || 100 %	1 || 1	1 || 1
coll_serialized	2	2	100 %	1	1
coll_deadlock	1	1	100 %	1	1
p2p_multiple	0	2	100 %	1	1

6 Conclusion and Future Work

Augmenting MPI applications with OpenMP constructs is one possible approach to face exascale systems. But the development of such hybrid applications requires effective debugging methods to assist programers. In this paper, we presented a compiler analysis to verify the MPI thread-level compliance of C/C++ and Fortran MPI+OpenMP codes. The analysis proposed finds the right MPI thread level to be used and identifies code fragments that may prevent conformance to a given level. We have shown a small impact on compilation-time with an overhead lower than 6 %. For future work, our analysis could be extended to include critical sections and locks. Furthermore, it could be integrated into existing tools like Marmot or MUST to cover other errors like calls arguments (e.g., communicators) or to report warnings concerning the execution path responsible for bugs related to thread-level MPI compliance.

References

1. Chiang, W.-F., Szubzda, G., Gopalakrishnan, G., Thakur, R.: Dynamic verification of hybrid programs. In: Keller, R., Gabriel, E., Resch, M., Dongarra, J. (eds.) EuroMPI 2010. LNCS, vol. 6305, pp. 298–301. Springer, Heidelberg (2010)

2. DeSouza, J., Kuhn, B., de Supinski, B.R., Samofalov, V., Zheltov, S., Bratanov, S.: Automated, scalable debugging of MPI programs with intel message checker. In: SE-HPCS 2005, pp. 78–82. ACM (2005)
3. Falzone, C., Chan, A., Lusk, E., Gropp, W.: A portable method for finding user errors in the usage of MPI collective operations. IJHPCA **21**(2), 155–165 (2007)
4. Gropp, W., Thakur, R.: Thread safety in an MPI implementation: requirements and analysis. Parallel Comput. **33**(9), 595–604 (2007)
5. Hilbrich, T., Müller, M.S., Krammer, B.: Detection of violations to the MPI standard in hybrid OpenMP/MPI applications. In: Eigenmann, R., de Supinski, B.R. (eds.) IWOMP 2008. LNCS, vol. 5004, pp. 26–35. Springer, Heidelberg (2008)
6. Hilbrich, T., de Supinski, B.R., Hänsel, F., Müller, M.S., Schulz, M., Nagel, W.E.: Runtime MPI collective checking with tree-based overlay networks. In: EuroMPI, pp. 129–134 (2013)
7. Hilbrich, T., Protze, J., de Supinski, B.R.d., Schulz, M., Müller, M.S., Nagel, W.E.: Intralayer communication for tree-based overlay networks. In: International Conference on Parallel Processing, pp. 995–1003 (2013)
8. Jourdren, H.: HERA: a hydrodynamic AMR platform for multi-physics simulations. In: Plewa, T., Linde, T., Gregory Weirs, V. (eds.) Adaptive Mesh Refinement - Theory and Applications, vol. 41, pp. 283–294. Springer, Heidelberg (2003)
9. Krammer, B., Bidmon, K., Müller, M.S., Resch, M.M.: MARMOT: an MPI analysis and checking tool. In: PARCO. Advances in Parallel Computing, vol. 13, pp. 493–500. Elsevier (2003)
10. Luecke, G.R., Chen, H., Coyle, J., Hoekstra, J., Kraeva, M., Zou, Y.: MPI-CHECK: a tool for checking Fortran 90 MPI programs. Concurrency Comput. Pract. Experience **15**(2), 93–100 (2003)
11. Lusk, E.R., Chan, A.: Early experiments with the OpenMP/MPI hybrid programming model. In: Eigenmann, R., de Supinski, B.R. (eds.) IWOMP 2008. LNCS, vol. 5004, pp. 36–47. Springer, Heidelberg (2008)
12. Saillard, E., Carribault, P., Barthou, D.: Combining static and dynamic validation of MPI collective communications. In: EuroMPI, pp. 117–122. ACM (2013)
13. Saillard, E., Carribault, P., Barthou, D.: PARCOACH: combining static and dynamic validation of MPI collective communications. IJHPCA **28**, 425–434 (2014)
14. Saillard, E., Carribault, P., Barthou, D.: Static/Dynamic validation of MPI collective communications in multi-threaded context. In: PPoPP. ACM (2015)
15. Siegel, S., Zirkel, T.: Automatic formal verification of MPI based parallel programs. In: PPoPP. pp. 309–310 (2011)
16. Smith, L., Bull, M.: Development of mixed mode MPI/OpenMP applications. Sci. Program. **9**(2,3), 83–98 (2001)
17. Message Passing Interface Forum. http://www.mpi-forum.org/docs/docs.html
18. NASPB site: http://www.nas.nasa.gov/software/NPB
19. CORAL site: https://asc.llnl.gov/CORAL-benchmarks/
20. Vetter, J.S., de Supinski, B.R.: Dynamic software testing of MPI applications with Umpire. In: ACM/IEEE Conference on Supercomputing (2000)
21. Vo, A., Aananthakrishnan, S., Gopalakrishnan, G., de Supinski, B.R.d., Schulz, M., Bronevetsky, G.: A scalable and distributed dynamic formal verifier for MPI programs. In: ACM/IEEE SC 2010, pp. 1–10 (2010)
22. Wolff, M., Jaouen, S., Jourdren, H.: High-order dimensionally split lagrange-remap schemes for ideal magnetohydrodynamics. In: Discrete and Continuous Dynamical Systems Series S. NMCF (2009)

Event-Action Mappings for Parallel Tools Infrastructures

Tobias Hilbrich[1,4]($\boxtimes$), Martin Schulz[2,4], Holger Brunst[1,4], Joachim Protze[3,4],
Bronis R. de Supinski[2,4], and Matthias S. Müller[3,4]

[1] Technische Universität Dresden, 01062 Dresden, Germany
{tobias.hilbrich,holger.brunst}@tu-dresden.de
[2] Lawrence Livermore National Laboratory, Livermore, CA 94551, USA
{schulzm,bronis}@llnl.gov
[3] RWTH Aachen University, 52056 Aachen, Germany
[4] JARA – High-Performance Computing, 52062 Aachen, Germany
{protze,mueller}@rz.rwth-aachen.de

Abstract. The development of applications for High Performance Computing (HPC) systems is a challenging task. Development steps such as optimization, tuning, porting, and debugging often motivate the use of tools, many of which operate at application runtime. Current trends in the HPC community, such as increasing compute core counts and the advent of new programming paradigms challenge the development of applications, as well as the development of runtime tools. Parallel tools infrastructures can help to simplify the development and adaption of runtime tools by reducing development time and increasing applicability. They can provide reusable tool components, communication services, and abstractions for scalable tools, which preserve lessons learned from existing tools projects.

This paper defines an abstraction for a highly integrated infrastructure, which we implement in a prototype that targets MPI applications. Our abstraction enables an incorporation of common tasks such as instrumentation, i.e., observing application behavior, with existing concepts for tool communication, while at the same time enabling scalability. A formal description of our abstraction allows us to highlight its design and to differentiate it from alternatives, so tool developers have a clear understanding of the high-level approach that our infrastructure follows. Existing prototype tools that are based on this infrastructure demonstrate applicability at 1,024 and 16,384 processes respectively.

1 Introduction

The development of efficient applications for todays and future High Performance Computing (HPC) systems is a challenging process that involves important steps such as debugging and performance optimization. Tools play a critical role in aiding developers during these steps. Increasing HPC system size, in terms of parallel processing elements, primarily impacts runtime tools, i.e., tools that operate while an application is running on an HPC system. Additionally, deeper

© Springer-Verlag Berlin Heidelberg 2015
J.L. Träff et al. (Eds.): Euro-Par 2015, LNCS 9233, pp. 43–54, 2015.
DOI: 10.1007/978-3-662-48096-0_4

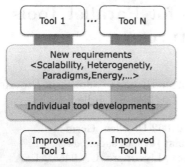 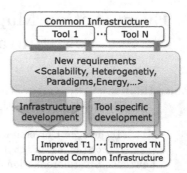

(a) With stand-alone tools each tools requires large development efforts to adapt to new requirements.

(b) With a tools infrastructure, a single development effort can adapt the infrastructure, adaptions of individual tools require a small effort.

Fig. 1. Tool development with a common tools infrastructure can drastically simplify the adaption of tools to novel requirements.

system hierarchies for parallelization, caused by hybrid parallelization schemes, e.g., by adding threading models or targeting accelerators such as GPGPUs, impact tools since they must be able to track system execution across these hierarchies. Future systems of an exascale level are likely to add further challenges on the development environment. In order to be widely applicable, portable and future-proof, tools must both be able to handle the increasing scale, adapt to changes in parallelization paradigms, and be capable to deal with limitations on individual systems without loosing their portability.

Tool development efforts that implement all components of a tool themselves are challenged by these trends, since addressing them requires tremendous effort from tool developers. Figure 1(a) illustrates this situation. Each tool must individually be adapted for the wide range of new requirements that novel HPC systems and advancements in parallel programming yield. One way to reduce this dramatic development cost, which is finding increased adoption in the tools community, is the use of tool infrastructures and frameworks, which can provide many types of common functionality to tool developers, as well as basic portability layers across platforms and programming paradigms. The use of such common functionality decreases development efforts, since it allows tool developers to reuse adaptions across multiple tools. Figure 1(b) illustrates this situation: The tool infrastructure needs to be adapted for new requirements, tool specific adaptions can require drastically reduced effort then. Benefit increases with the number of tools that adopt an infrastructure.

Following this motivation, we present an abstraction that enables a highly integrated tools infrastructure. The goal of this abstraction is to maximize the amount of common functionality that the infrastructure provides and to minimize tool specific implementation. As Fig. 1(b) illustrates, fulfilling this goal directly reduces the development effort to adapt tools to new requirements.

Naturally, wide adoption of a tools infrastructure does not only depends on the features and capabilities of an infrastructure, but also on a multitude of strategic considerations. Thus, we try not to solely promote a specific infrastructure, but focus on describing an abstraction that enables highly integrated tools development. Existing or novel infrastructures can utilize our concepts, at the same time we provide an open source prototype implementation called GTI [4]. Our contributions include:

- A high-level abstraction that enables quick prototyping and efficient tool development;
- Event-flow definitions that define the meaning of our abstraction for both its usage and implementation; and
- A comparison to existing tools infrastructures to highlight how we achieve a high degree of integration.

Section 2 summarizes related work. We then detail our tools infrastructure abstraction in Sect. 3. Section 4 compares our abstraction to existing infrastructures to highlight the increased degree of integration that we achieve with our abstraction. Finally, we shortly present existing tools that use our abstraction in Sect. 5.

2   Related Work

We classify runtime tool developments for HPC systems into: (1) developments that largely use a custom-made implementations; (2) developments that reuse existing components; and (3) developments with parallel tools infrastructures.

Efforts such as the development of Score-P [6] largely employ custom-made source code. Motivations include highest performance requirements, lack of existing components, or redesign efforts. Usually, such developments reuse little existing source code and must cope with trends in HPC by themselves, in order to remain applicable. In practice this can increase development costs and is only suitable for large efforts with significant developer support for maintenance.

Component-based developments reuse existing packages to implement parts of the tool. This can be compared to using support libraries, such as solvers or I/O libraries, in application code. Examples include instrumentation services, wrapper generators, tracing libraries, and stack tracing utilities. Existing components for common types of tool functionality allow developers to reuse lessons learned from other developers. As an example, if a developer improves the scalability of a component, other developers that use the same component can reuse this improvement.

Tool development with parallel tools infrastructures or frameworks, called *tools infrastructures* in the following, provide wider-ranging services for the development of tools and is similar to developing applications in larger frameworks that provide the basic workflow and only require the addition of the actual application components, often in the form of plugins. Examples include P^nMPI [8] as an infrastructure that combines and connects multiple MPI tools; OCM [10] as

Table 1. Tool infrastructure comparison.

	Abstraction	Instrumentation	Topology	Means of Communication	Component Migratability	Component Dependencies
OCM	Event-Action	✓	Centralized		✗	✗
P^nMPI	Modules	✓	None	MPI	✓	✗
MRNet	Filters	✗	TBON	TCP sockets	✗	✗
STCI	Filters	✗	TBON	MPI subsystem	✗	✗
CBTF	Dataflow	✗	TBON	MRNet (extensible)	✓	✓
Proposed (GTI)	Distrib. Event-Action	✓	Layers	Flexible	✓	✓

an early online tools infrastructure; STCI [2], and MRNet [7] as infrastructures that provide Tree Based Overlay Network (TBON) services; and CBTF [3] and GTI [4] that target a development with a higher degree of integration. TBON services such as provided by STCI, MRNet, CBTF, and GTI are important since they enable tool scalability. The TBON concept uses a hierarchy of processing nodes that allows tools to condense information as it progresses towards the root of the hierarchy. Aggregations and filters on all hierarchy layers provide a step-by-step means to condense information. TBON-based tools such as STAT [1] and Allinea DDT operate for applications that run on close to, or even more than, one million compute cores.

The mentioned infrastructures differ in the depth of their integration and in whether they provide TBON services or not. Table 1 compares these approaches. P^nMPI and OCM provide no TBON services, which is a common requirement for scalable tools. However, in both cases TBON functionality could be added as an extension leveraging an existing TBON infrastructure. OCM uses event-action mappings that relate to the analysis-hook mappings that we subsequently present, but it considers no distributed and hierarchical processing. The infrastructures STCI [2] and MRNet [7] focus on providing TBON services and allow tool developers to specify *modules* as tool components. The modules run on the TBON nodes to aggregate or filter information. However, these infrastructures lack a deeper integration, e.g., they provide no instrumentation systems, components can not be used on the leaves or the root of the TBON, and no dependency tracking ensures that dependent components are present. Thus, tool developers must provide several common tool components themselves. CBTF and GTI provide such a deep integration and combine it with TBON services. In the following we present the abstraction behind GTI, while our previous publication [4] focused on an implementation of this abstraction. Section 4 compares MRNet—due to its wide usage—with CBTF and GTI in more detail.

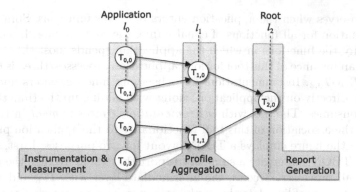

Fig. 2. Illustration of a tool layout and analyses for a profiling tool.

3   A Mapping-Based Tools Infrastructure

We base our abstraction for parallel tool development on the notion of:

Events: Occurrences of information that the runtime tool must know about, and
Analyses: The types of processing that need to take place upon perceiving
events.

The following examples show how both events and analyses map to common
steps in well-known types of tools:

- Tracing tools for performance analysis store information on a function invocation (event) into a trace buffer, from where they are processed (analysis);
- A debugging tool retrieves a stack trace (analysis) due to a request from the
graphical user interface (event); or
- A runtime correctness tool for MPI analyzes whether send and receive datatypes
match (analysis) when a pair of send and receive operations is observed (events).

These examples highlight that events and analyses can represent the activities
of a wide range of runtime tools. Following this notion, tool developers can create
their tools by solely focusing on the two fundamental questions:

*(1) What activities must the tool implement and (2) which events trigger
them?*

The first identifies the analyses of the tool and the second its events and their
source. We follow this approach and let developers then specify *mappings* as the
relation between events and analyses. This approach allows tool developers to
specify the workings of their tool in a high level abstraction. In comparison to
existing infrastructure approaches, this allows us to increase the amount of tool
functionality that an infrastructure can implement.

We illustrate our abstraction with an example, a simplified profiling tool
that creates basic execution profiles and maps them to source code regions.
Irrespective of the parallel programming paradigm of the target application,

the tool observes when the application enters or leaves functions. Summarizing this information for all functions of equal name, the tool provides basic profiles that identify the functions in which the application spends most time. Figure 2 illustrates an instance of this tool for four application processes/threads depicted as nodes $T_{0,0}$–$T_{0,3}$. Instrumentation, i.e., observing function enters and leaves, takes place directly on the application, along with adding up the time that each function consumes. The box with *instrumentation &measurement* in the figure illustrates the association of this tool functionality to the application processes. The tool in the figure employs a TBON layout for two purposes: First, the root $T_{2,0}$ of the TBON can create a summary report that could average the profiling data from all processes. Second, the intermediate layer with $T_{1,0}$ and $T_{1,1}$ aids in averaging the profiling data, by applying a step-wise aggregation of the data. Consequently, specific analyses can run on different levels of a TBON layout and a mapping can specify this relation. Additionally, events must travel through the TBON layout from their origin to the analyses that are interested in them.

By specifying the tool functionality in these terms, instead of hard-coding the tool functionality and the tool layout, we allow the infrastructure to handle event instrumentation, of spawning the tool layout, and of handling event communication. This results in the desired deep integration that minimizes the amount of functionality that individual tools must implement.

3.1   Terms and Abstraction

The tool infrastructure abstraction that we propose extends *events* and *analysis* with *layers*, *places*, *mappings*, *hooks*, and an *event-flow*. We formally define these terms to concisely present our abstraction and to simplify comparison and adoption. Figure 3 showcases how our abstraction represents the aforementioned profiling tool.

Analyses. Represent available tool actions. A selection from these analyses makes up the overall functionality of a *tool instance*, i.e., of a running representation of a tool. We use a set A to specify the available analyses. For the profiling tool, we have A={enter, leave, finalize, printProfile}, where enter/leave observes when the application enters/leaves a function, finalize triggers creation and forwarding of the profiling data before the application exits, and printProfile writes the resulting profiling data into a file for investigation.

The example analyses highlight a need for dependencies: Both the enter and the leave analysis must be used together and they require the finalize analysis to forward their results. We provide analysis dependencies $depends : A \rightarrow \mathcal{P}(A)$ for this purpose[1]. In our example, dependencies include $depends$(enter)={leave, finalize} and so forth. If a tool consists of a large number of fine-grained analyses, dependencies ensure that all analyses can operate correctly. This feature facilitates effective component reuse.

---

[1] The power set $\mathcal{P}(A)$ of A is the set of all subsets of A.

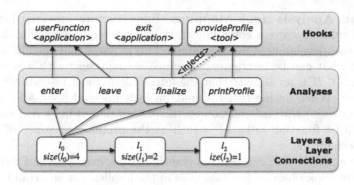

Fig. 3. Illustration of our mapping-based abstraction for the profiling tool example from Fig. 2.

Layers and Places. Figure 2 illustrates a possible layout for the example tool. Our abstraction defines such layouts with a set of *layers* $L = \{l_0, l_1, \ldots\}$. We use a specifically marked layer l_0 as the layer that consists of the application processes. We then use the remaining layers to build a hierarchy of layers as in a TBON layout. The layers both specify the hierarchy layers and they enable that distinct layers can execute distinct analyses, as Fig. 2 illustrates. Formally, a *layer tree* $\mathcal{L} = (L, E_{\mathcal{L}} \subseteq L \times L)$ connects the layers to indicate which layers send information to which other layers. This forwarding represents a *towards-root* direction for scalable tools that apply event aggregation. In our example we have $L = \{l_0, l_1, l_2\}$ and $E_{\mathcal{L}} = \{(l_0, l_1), (l_1, l_2)\}$. The lower third of Fig. 3 illustrates this layer tree.

Further, we use a size function to associate how many *places* each layer uses. Where a place represents an application process/thread or a tool process/thread. Thus, $T_{1,0}$, $T_{1,1}$, and $T_{2,0}$ in Fig. 2 could be tool owned processes and $T_{0,0}$–$T_{0,3}$ could be MPI processes.

We use connection rules to create a *tool topology graph* $\mathcal{T} = (P, E_{\mathcal{T}})$ from a layer tree and the size function, i.e., to create the layout in Fig. 2 from the layer tree in Fig. 3 (bottom). This graph uses the set of all places $P = \{T_{i,j} : l_i \in L \text{ and } 0 \le j < \text{size}(l_i)\}$ as its node set. A connection rule then connects places of connected layers to create the set of arcs $E_{\mathcal{T}} \subseteq P \times P$.

Layer-Analysis-Mapping. A *layer-analysis-mapping* specifies which analyses each layer executes. Formally, the function $m_{L,A} : L \to \mathcal{P}(A)$ specifies this mapping. Figure 2 illustrates the association for the example tool, which could use $m_{L,A}(l_0)=\{\text{enter,leave, finalize}\}$, $m_{L,A}(l_1) = \emptyset$, and $m_{L,A}(l_2)=\{\text{printProfile}\}$. Figure 3 illustrates $m_{L,A}$ with arrows between layers and analyses. Based on the layer-analysis mapping, the tool infrastructure can compute dependent analyses according to *depends*.

Hooks and Analysis-Hook-Mapping. Infrastructure provided instrumentation and automatic event communication is a key requirement for the deeply integrated tool development that we target. This requires that the infrastructure is aware of what can be instrumented, which we represent with a set of *hooks* H. A hook $h \in H$ is an activity that the infrastructure can instrument in order to observe it. When during tool runtime, an instrumented hook h is triggered, we create an *event* with information on the observation of hook h. Examples of hooks could be function calls, APIs such as the profiling interface of MPI, or callback mechanisms.

For the example case, we use H={userFunction, exit, provideProfile}. The userFunction hook observes function calls of the application and could rely on a compiler-based instrumentation of the application. The exit hook observes when the application attempts to exit. When it is triggered, it must pass the profiling data to the printProfile analysis. To do so, an analysis can simply trigger a hook itself, i.e., analyses can inject events with hooks. The hook provideProfile is used in this manner and implements part of the tool functionality, rather than to observe application activities. With the provideProfile hook, the finalize analysis can inject an event that carries this data. Any analysis that is interested in the data, e.g., printProfile, can then observe it. Figure 3 (top) illustrates these hooks and highlights that the first two hooks serve for application activities, while the third hook implements part of the tool functionality.

The above example illustrates a notion of *an analysis is interested in events of a hook*. We use *analysis-hook-mappings* $m_{A,H} : A \rightarrow \mathcal{P}(H)$ towards this end. The enter and leave analyses must observe the userFunction hook, i.e., $m_{A,H}$(enter)={userFunction} and $m_{A,H}$(leave)={userFunction}. Additionally, the finalize analysis must observe the exit hook, while the printProfile analysis must observe the provideProfile hook. Figure 3 illustrates these mappings with arrows between the analyses and hooks.

Event-Flow. The previous specifications detail how we can represent a tool in the terms of a deeply integrated abstraction. However, we associated no semantics, yet. For a given tool specification, we use *event-flow* definitions to define the workflow within the tool. These definitions use a mapping $execute : P \rightarrow \mathcal{P}(A)$ that represents the final layer-analysis mapping, e.g., to correctly consider module dependencies. The first event-flow definition specifies which analyses a place must trigger when it observes or receives an event for a hook:

Event-Flow 1 (Trigger) *A place $T \in P$ that observes or receives an event for a hook h must trigger an analysis $a \in$ execute(T) exactly if $h \in m_{A,H}(a)$.*

The definition requires that when a place receives or observes an event, it triggers any analysis that is mapped to the hook that created the event.

The remaining event flow definitions depend on *communication directions*. As in the previous examples, events can travel towards higher hierarchy layers, e.g., towards a root place. We call this the *primary direction*, which we cover in the following. The opposite direction is called the *broadcast direction* and distributes information from a root towards application places. The function $dir : H \rightarrow \{primary, broadcast\}$ assigns a communication direction with each hook to specify the direction that events of this hook use. In the example, all hooks use the primary direction.

For the primary communication direction, the hierarchies of places, as illustrated in Fig. 2, determine which events are forwarded to a place. A place T must perceive events that are directly triggered on T and any event that a predecessor in the tool topology graph perceives. As an example, in the figure, $T_{0,0}$ perceives its own events only, whereas $T_{1,1}$ must perceive events from itself, $T_{0,2}$, and $T_{0,3}$. To minimize tool overhead, a place perceives only events for hooks to which some of its analyses are mapped or for which a descendant in the tool topology graph must perceive. The relation $requiresInformation \subseteq P \times H$ formally defines the hooks whose events a place must observe as $(T, h) \in requiresInformation$ exactly if $\exists T' \in \{T\} \cup successors(T, \mathcal{T})$ and $a \in A$:

$$ a \in execute(T'), \ h \in m_{A,H}(a), \text{ and } dir(h) = \text{primary}. $$

The relation includes pairs of a place and a hook if the place itself or a direct successor of the place executes at least one analysis that is mapped to the respective hook[2]. This relation directly allows us to define what hooks a place must instrument, i.e., observe, and towards which places a place forwards events along the primary communication direction:

Event-Flow 2 (Observe) *A place $T \in P$ must observe (i.e., instrument) a hook $h \in H$ exactly if $(T, h) \in$ requiresInformation.*

Event-Flow 3 (Forward) *A place $T \in P$ must forward an event of hook h, which it observes or receives from another place, to a direct successor $T' \in P$ exactly if $(T', h) \in$ requiresInformation (with $(T, T') \in E_{\mathcal{T}}$).*

In the profiling tool example, these definitions require that places $T_{0,0}$–$T_{0,3}$ observe the provideProfile hook, even though no analysis mapping assigns these places an analysis that is mapped to this hook. This results from place $T_{2,0}$ executing the analysis printProfile, which is mapped to provideProfile, while $T_{2,0}$ is a successor of $T_{0,0}$–$T_{0,3}$ in the tool topology graph.

These three event-flow definitions formally define the workings of a tool that follows our abstraction.

3.2 Event-Aggregation

Our abstraction allows integration of event aggregation with so called *aggregation analyses* $A_{\text{agg}} \subseteq A$. These analyses have all properties of regular analyses, but they try to replace their input events with a single/few events. Hooks serve to inject the new events and return values of the aggregation enable the removal of the input events. Adaptions of the above event flow definitions can formalize this notion.

---

[2] $successors(T, \mathcal{T})$ is the set of successor places of T in the tool topology graph $\mathcal{T}$.

4   Infrastructure Comparison

In the following we compare our abstraction with MRNet [7] as a widely used infrastructure for TBON-based tools and with CBTF [3] as a further highly integrated infrastructure.

An MRNet-based tool consists of back-end code running on the application processes, front-end code running on the root of the TBON, and module code that runs on the intermediate layers of the TBON. The modules are managed by MRNet—much like analyses in our abstractions—and get triggered when events of interest occur. Front-end and back-end code, however, are directly provided by the tool developer and use a specific MRNet API. If a tool developer wants to migrate tool functionality that is implemented as part of the front-end/back-end code to a module, or vice versa, then an adaption of the API in use or a redesign of that code is necessary. This imposes unnecessary restrictions on the use of available pieces of a tool implementation. Our abstraction uses a single concept to provide tool functionality instead, which are analyses. Migrating analyses between any hierarchy layers requires no adaptions as we note in Table 1.

Instrumentation services for MRNet-based tools reside in the back-end code. The infrastructure provides no services for the instrumentation of an application. Our abstraction incorporates instrumentation directly into the infrastructure to provide it to the tool developer directly. Portable instrumentation is often challenging for tools, thus our approach simplifies tool development. A further differentiation is the analysis dependency system that we integrate in our abstraction. MRNet has no such notion and tool developers can consequentially create nonfunctional tool instances if they are not careful.

The Component Based Tool Framework (CBTF) [3] is closely related to our efforts and is younger than the GTI implementation that realized our abstraction. Few studies on the applicability and scalability of CBTF are available, so we focus on a high-level comparison. As opposed to our event-action mappings, CBTF uses a dataflow-programming paradigm. A CBTF tool consists of components that could be compared to our analyses. Rather than using analysis-hook mappings, CBTF connects components towards a component network. The output of a component then forms the input of connected components. For scalability, CBTF allows component networks to employ MRNet to apply hierarchical aggregations or filters. Both approaches achieve a deeply integrated tool development and should support similar ranges of tools. A key differentiation is that CBTF lacks instrumentation services, which challenges portable tool development. An integration of such functionality would require a mapping of instrumentation sources to CBTF components, much as in our proposed abstraction.

5   Tools Enabled by Our Abstraction

The tools infrastructure GTI implements our abstraction and extends it with additions for practicality [4]. This includes a packaging of multiple tool analyses into so called *modules* that provide data sharing between closely related analyses. The runtime correctness tool MUST [5] and the trace-based online performance analysis prototype OTFX-GTI [9] are both based on GTI and demonstrate applicability to multiple compute systems at up to 16,384 and 1,024 processes respectively. Both tools focus on MPI applications and use a TBON layout in their standard configurations. MUST uses a total of 358 analyses (in 59 GTI modules) and OTFX-GTI uses 168 analyses (in 20 GTI modules). Large numbers of these analyses (276 and 126 respectively) execute on the application layer. This situation highlights that with abstractions such as MRNet, which provides no concept for tool components on the application layer, a large portion of the tool functionality might not be as reusable. Whereas our abstraction enables component reuse on all hierarchy layers of the tool.

6   Conclusions

Development of HPC tools must consider increasing system scale and the rise of novel parallel programming paradigms. Developing portable tools that handle these challenges well is time consuming and often requires similar solutions across tools. Tool infrastructures can provide common tool services to wide ranges of tools. Such that development investments into the infrastructure can benefit all tools that utilize them. In such a situation, the total development effort that is needed to adapt tools to new requirements could be drastically reduced.

We extend upon TBON-oriented tools infrastructures with a mapping-based abstraction. This abstraction allows tool developers to implement their overall tool as fine-grained analyses. The abstraction carefully connects the concept of tool hierarchies with a high-level thinking in terms of events and analyses. This targets a deeply integrated development that lets the infrastructure provide as much functionality as possible. If we compare our approach with existing infrastructures we see increased opportunity for component reuse, as well as simplified development for tool developers. The infrastructure CBTF, which follows similar goals as our approach, compares closely, but lacks portable support for instrumentation.

If deeply integrated tools infrastructures receive widespread use, tool development could be drastically simplified. Developers could reuse valuable lessons learned that are embedded in a repository of existing tool components. A large community could then maintain these modules to adapt them to ongoing trends in HPC. Developing a novel tool becomes a reuse of existing modules with an addition of tool specific modules, towards reduced time to solution. Experience with tools that are based on our abstraction are promising and enable tools that operate for 1,024 and 16,384 application processes respectively.

Acknowledgments. We thank the ASC Tri-Labs for their friendly support. Part of this work was performed under the auspices of the U.S. Department of Energy by Lawrence Livermore National Laboratory under Contract DE-AC52-07NA27344. (LLNL-PROC-670945). This work has been supported by the CRESTA project that has received funding from the European Community's Seventh Framework Programme (ICT-2011.9.13) under Grant Agreement no. 287703.

References

1. Arnold, D.C., Ahn, D.H., de Supinski, B.R., Lee, G.L., Miller, B.P., Schulz, M.: Stack trace analysis for large scale debugging. In: Proceedings of the 2010 IEEE 21th International Parallel and Distributed Processing Symposium. IPDPS 2007. IEEE Computer Society, Los Alamitos (2007)
2. Buntinas, D., Bosilca, G., Graham, R.L., Vallée, G., Watson, G.R.: A scalable tools communications infrastructure. In: Proceedings of the 2008 22nd International Symposium on High Performance Computing Systems and Applications, HPCS 2008, pp. 33–39. IEEE Computer Society, Washington, DC (2008)
3. Galarowicz, J.: Project Final Report: Building a Community Infrastructure for Scalable On-Line Performance Analysis Tools around Open—SpeedShop. Technical report, Krell Institute (2014)
4. Hilbrich, T., Müller, M.S., de Supinski, B.R., Schulz, M., Nagel, W.E.: GTI: A generic tools infrastructure for event-based tools in parallel systems. In: Proceedings of the 2012 IEEE 26th International Parallel and Distributed Processing Symposium, IPDPS 2012, pp. 1364–1375, Washington, DC (2012)
5. Hilbrich, T., de Supinski, B.R., Nagel, W.E., Protze, J., Baier, C., Müller, M.S.: Distributed wait state tracking for runtime mpi deadlock detection. In: International Conference for High Performance Computing, Networking, Storage and Analysis, SC 2013, pp. 16:1–16:12. ACM, New York (2013)
6. Knüpfer, A., Rössel, C., an Mey, D., Biersdorff, S., Diethelm, K., Eschweiler, D., Geimer, M., Gerndt, M., Lorenz, D., Malony, A., Nagel, W.E., Oleynik, Y., Philippen, P., Saviankou, P., Schmidl, D., Shende, S., Tschüter, R., Wagner, M., Wesarg, B., Wolf, F.: Score-P: a joint performance measurement run-time infrastructure for periscope, scalasca, TAU, and vampir. Tools for High Performance Computing 2011, pp. 79–91. Springer, Heidelberg (2012)
7. Roth, P.C., Arnold, D.C., Miller, B.P.: MRNet: A software-based multicast/reduction network for scalable tools. In: Proceedings of the 2003 ACM/IEEE Conference on Supercomputing, SC 2003, ACM, New York (2003)
8. Schulz, M., de Supinski, B.R.: PNMPI Tools: A whole lot greater than the sum of their parts. In: Proceedings of the 2007 ACM/IEEE Conference on Supercomputing, SC 2007, pp. 30:1–30:10. ACM, New York (2007)
9. Wagner, M., Hilbrich, T., Brunst, H.: Online performance analysis: an event-based workflow design towards exascale. In: To appear. In: The 16th IEEE International Conference on High Performance Computing and Communications, HPCC 2014 (2014)
10. Wismüller, R., Trinitis, J., Ludwig, T.: OCM-A monitoring system for interoperable tools. In: Proceedings of the 2nd SIGMETRICS Symposium on Parallel and Distributed Tools SPDT 1998, pp. 1–9. ACM Press (1998)

Performance Modeling, Prediction and Evaluation

Low-Overhead Detection of Memory Access Patterns and Their Time Evolution

Harald Servat[1,2]($\boxtimes$), Germán Llort[1,2], Juan González[1], Judit Giménez[1,2], and Jesús Labarta[1,2]

[1] Computer Sciences Department - Barcelona Supercomputing Center,
c/Jordi Girona 1-3, 08034 Barcelona, Catalunya, Spain
harald.servat@bsc.es
[2] Computer Architecture Department - Universitat Politècnica de Catalunya,
c/Jordi Girona 31, 08034 Barcelona, Catalunya, Spain

Abstract. We present a performance analysis tool that reports the temporal evolution of the memory access patterns of in-production applications in order to help analysts understand the accesses to the application data structures. This information is captured using the Precise Event Based Sampling (PEBS) mechanism from the recent Intel processors, and it is correlated with the source code and the nature of the performance bottlenecks if any. Consequently, this tool gives a complete approach to allow analysts to unveil the application behavior better, and to lead them to improvements while taking the most benefit from the system's characteristics. We apply the tool to two optimized parallel applications and provide detailed insight of their memory access behavior, thus demonstrating the usefulness of the tool.

Keywords: Performance analysis · Address sampling · Data-object analysis · Sampling · Instrumentation

1 Introduction

The memory hierarchy is becoming more and more sophisticated as the processors evolve generation after generation. Its advances respond not only to address the speed divergence between the processor and the memory outside the chip, but also to reduce the energy dissipated by the data movement. Processor manufacturers have typically organized the memory hierarchy in different *strata* to exploit the temporal and spatial localities of reference. The memory hierarchy ranges from the extremely fast but tiny and power-hungry registers to the slow but huge and less energy-consuming DRAM, including multiple cache levels. Still, some processor researchers and manufacturers are looking for opportunities to extend the memory hierarchy to improve the application execution in terms of performance and energy. Their research consider additional integration directions so that the memory hierarchy adds layers as scratchpad memories, stacked 3D DRAM [12], and even non-volatile RAM [24].

© Springer-Verlag Berlin Heidelberg 2015
J.L. Träff et al. (Eds.): Euro-Par 2015, LNCS 9233, pp. 57–69, 2015.
DOI: 10.1007/978-3-662-48096-0_5

When it comes to performance analysis, traditional performance analysis tools (e.g. gprof [9], Scalasca [25], TAU [20], HPCToolkit [23] and Periscope [7]) have naturally associated performance metrics to syntactical application components such as routines, loops, and even statements. Despite this association has proven valuable and has helped understanding and improving applications, the impact of the memory hierarchy makes necessary to explore the performance from the data perspective, also. A study from this point of view includes, but it is not limited to, unveil which application variables are referenced the most and their access cost, detect memory streams to help prefetch mechanisms, calculate reuse distances, and even identify the cache organization that may improve the execution behavior. To this end, two mechanisms have emerged to address this type of studies. On the one hand, there exists instruction-based instrumentation that monitors load/store instructions and decodes them to capture the referenced addresses. While this approach accurately correlates code statements with data references, it imposes a severe expense, daunting the analysis with large data collections and/or time-consuming analysis; thus not being practical for long in-production executions. On the other hand, several processors have enhanced their Performance Monitoring Unit (PMU) to sample instructions based on a user specified period and associate them with data such as the referenced address. These mechanisms help on delimiting the amount of data captured and the overhead imposed. However, the results obtained are statistical approximations that may require sufficiently long runs so that the results approximate the actual distribution, yet highly volatile metrics may be missed.

The framework described in [18,19] addresses the latter issue and provides accurate and instantaneous performance metrics even using coarse grain sampling and minimal instrumentation. This framework smartly combines sampled and instrumented data by taking benefit of the repetitiveness from the applications. In this paper, we extend this framework by incorporating the application address space perspective to unveil the access patterns and the locality of reference to the application data structures. Such an extension relies on the address sampling mechanisms offered by the PMU extension known as PEBS [4] and to minimize the overhead we use large sampling periods. The result of this enhancement is a framework that provides complete support to gain insight of the application behavior, including the application syntactical level, its data structure organization, and its memory hierarchy usage and achieved performance.

The organization of this paper is as follows: Sect. 2 contextualizes our mechanism with respect to previous existing tools. Section 3 introduces the framework used as the basis for our mechanism and the hardware support for the address sampling. Then Sect. 4 describes the extension applied to the framework and exemplifies its results. Section 5 explores the behavior of two applications to demonstrate the usefulness of the resulting framework. Finally, Sect. 6 draws some conclusions and discusses possible future research trends.

2   Related Work

This section describes earlier approaches related to performance analysis tools that have focused to some extent on the analysis of data structures and the efficiency achieved while accessing to them. We divide this research into two groups depending on the mechanism used to capture the addresses referenced by the load/store instructions.

The first group includes tools that instrument the application instructions to obtain the referenced addresses. MemSpy [13] is a prototype tool to profile applications on a system simulator that introduces the notion of data-oriented, in addition to code oriented, performance tuning. This tool instruments every memory reference from an application run and leverage the references to a memory simulator that calculates statistics such as cache hits, cache misses, *etc* according to a given cache organization. SLO [1] suggests for locality optimizations by analyzing the application reuse paths to find the root causes of poor data locality. This tool extends the GCC compiler to capture the application's memory accesses, function calls, and loops in order to track data reuses, and then it analyzes the reused paths to suggest code loop transformations. MACPO [17] captures memory traces and computes metrics for the memory access behavior of source-level data structures. The tool uses PerfExpert [3] to identify code regions with memory-related inefficiencies, then employs the LLVM compiler to instrument the memory references, and, finally, it calculates several reuse factors and the number of data streams in a loop nest. Tareador [22] is a tool that estimates how much parallelism can be achieved in a task-based data-flow programming model. The tool employs dynamic instrumentation to monitor the memory accesses of delimited regions of code in order to determine whether they can simultaneously run without data race conditions, and then it simulates the application execution based on this outcome. Peña *et al.* have designed an emulator based data-oriented profiling tool to analyze actual program executions in an emulated system equipped with a DRAM-based memory system only [16]. They also use dynamic instrumentation to monitor the memory references in order to detect which memory structures are the most referenced. With this setup, they estimate the CPU stall cycles incurred by the different memory objects to decide their optimal object placement in heterogeneous memory system.

The second group consists of tools that take benefit of hardware mechanisms to sample addresses referenced when processor counter overflows occur and estimate the accesses weight from the sample count. The Sun ONE Studio analysis tool has been extended in [10] by incorporating memory system behavior in the context of the application's data space. This extension brings the analyst independent and uncorrelated views that rank program counters and data objects according to hardware counter metrics, as well as, shows metrics for each element in data object structures. HPCToolkit has been recently extended to support data-centric profiling of parallel programs [11]. In contrast to the previous tool, HPCToolkit provides a graphical user interface that presents data- and code-centric metrics in a single panel, easing the correlation between the two. Giménez *et al.* use PEBS to monitor load instructions that access addresses within memory regions delimited by user-specified data objects and focusing on those that surpass a given latency [8]. Then, they associate the memory behavior with several semantic attributes, including the application context which is shown through the MemAxes visualization tool.

Our proposal belongs to the second group and its main difference from existing tools relies on the ability to report time-based memory access patterns, in addition to source code profiles and performance bottlenecks. The inclusion of the temporal analysis allows time-based studies such as detection of simultaneous memory streams, ordering accesses to the memory hierarchy, and even, code reordering. This data is captured using two independent monitoring tools that are configured to collect data sparsely. While one of the tools capture information regarding the performance bottlenecks, their nature and their association with the code; the other tool samples the references to the process address space.

3   Background

3.1   The Basic Framework

The framework described in [18,19] generates reports of the performance along time for computing regions from trace-files containing instrumented and sampled data. The computing regions can be manually delimited using instrumentation or automatically detected by the framework after the execution based on their performance characteristics. In the latter case, a computing region is defined as the user code in between successive parallel programming calls (such as MPI or OpenMP). These regions are automatically grouped according to their performance metrics (typically number of instructions and instruction rate) through a density-based clustering algorithm. Then, the framework applies a mechanism named folding that combines coarse grain sampled and instrumented information to provide detailed performance metrics within a computing region. In the context of the folding process, the samples are gathered from the computing into a synthetic region by preserving their relative time within their original region so that the sampled information determines how the performance evolves within the region. Consequently, the folded samples represent the progression in shorter periods of time no matter the monitoring sampling frequency, and also, the longer the runs the more samples get mapped into the synthetic instance. The framework has shown mean differences up to 5 % when comparing results obtained sampling frequencies that are two orders of magnitude more frequent (50×10^3 cycles *vs* 10^6 cycles).

3.2   Capturing the Referenced Addresses

The Precision Event Based Sampling (PEBS), and similarly the Instruction Based Sampling (IBS [5]), are respective extensions to the Intel's and AMD's PMU component that allow monitoring instructions at a user-configurable sampling period. These mechanisms periodically choose an instruction from those that enter into the processor pipeline. Then, the selected instruction is tagged, and it is monitored as it progresses through the pipeline while annotating any event caused by the instruction. When the instruction completes, the processor generates a record containing the instruction address, its associated events and the machine state (without time-stamp), and then the record is written into a previously allocated buffer. Every time the buffer gets full, the processor invokes an interrupt service routine provided by a profiler that collects the generated records. Since instructions are reported at the retirement stage, these mechanisms exclude contributions from speculative execution. For the particular case of load instructions, PEBS collects data such as, but are not limited to: the linear address[1] referenced, the layer of the memory hierarchy that served the reference, and how many cycles did it take to reach the processor. These monitoring mechanisms report linear addresses from the process address space but do not provide information with respect to the physical addresses, thus they do not help understanding memory migrations.

4 Enhancement of the Framework

This section describes the integration of the sampled memory references into the aforementioned framework to display the time evolution of the memory access patterns in addition to other performance metrics. We also provide an example on how to use the output of this framework by applying it to a slightly modified version of a well-known benchmark.

4.1 Capturing Referenced Addresses

The first enhancement involves collecting the referenced addresses during the application execution so that the framework can later display them in the report. We use the Extrae[2] instrumentation package to generate the input for the original framework. Extrae uses PAPI [2] to capture hardware performance metrics, but PAPI does not capture the PEBS generated information[3]. perf [15], on the other hand, is a tool that uses the performance counters subsystem in Linux, and since Linux kernel version 3.11 it benefits from PEBS or IBS to collect memory references from either load or store instructions, but not both at the same time. This tool allocates a 1-entry buffer to store the memory references and then samples the application at a user defined period. Thus, each time the processor reaches the period, it generates a memory reference record, and then perf captures this record and associates a time-stamp to it. This way, perf is capable of generating timestamped trace-files containing sampled memory references even though neither PEBS nor IBS capture a timestamp.

Our approach relies on combining the results of these two monitoring tools when applied on an optimized application binary with debugging information in the same run, as depicted in Fig. 1. In this context, perf collects a time-stamped sequence of references while Extrae collects performance counters and

---

[1] Linear addresses also refer to logical addresses in x86-64 architectures as segmentation is generally disabled thus creating a flat 64-bit space, according to Sects. 3.3.4 and 3.4.2.1 from Intel®64 and IA-32 Architectures Software Developers Manual.

[2] http://www.bsc.es/paraver - Last accessed June, 2015.

[3] As of PAPI 5.4.0.

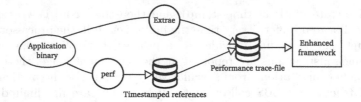

Fig. 1. Combination of two monitoring tools to generate a single trace-file that includes hardware counter performance metrics, call-stack references and data references.

call-stack references, and then a post-process combines them into a single trace-file. Both tools must use the same timing source in order to correlate the data captured. The perf tool uses low-level kernel timing routines and Extrae uses the Posix compliant high precision clock routines by default. Thus, we have adopted a kernel module that exposes the low-level timing routines[4] to the user-space applications, yet there are other possibilities to achieve this goal. After generating the trace-file, we extend the folding mechanism to apply to the memory reference samples and to collocate all the metrics (source code, memory references and node-level performance [such as MIPS rate and L1D miss ratio per instruction]) in one report per region.

4.2   Associating Addresses with Data Structures

When exploring the address space, it is convenient to map the address space to the application data structures in order to let the analyst match the generated results with the application code and also to explore their pattern access type. For that reason, Extrae has been extended to capture the base address and the size of the static variables, as well as, of the dynamically allocated variables. With respect to the static variables, the instrumentation package explores the symbols within application binary image using the binutils library[5] in order to acquire their name, starting address and size. Regarding the dynamic variables, we instrument the `malloc` family related routines and capture their input parameters and output results to determine the starting address and size. As dynamically allocated variables do not have a name, the tool collects their allocation call-stack reference to identify them. Since applications may contain lots of variables, Extrae ignores those smaller than a specified threshold (that defaults to 1 MiB). Finally, it is worth to mention that some languages (such as C and C++) allow declaring local (stack) variables within code blocks that can only be referenced by the inner block statements. While these references are captured by the perf tool, Extrae cannot track their creation; so, their references may appear on the resulting plot but do not have an associated variable name.

---

[4] https://lkml.org/lkml/2013/3/14/523.

[5] http://www.gnu.org/software/binutils. Last accessed June, 2015.

4.3   Practical Example

We have applied this framework to a modified version of the Stream benchmark [14] in order to show the usability of the described framework when exploring the load references. Since Stream accesses to statically allocated variables through ordered linear accesses, we have modified the code so that: (1) the c array is no longer a static variable but allocated by `malloc` and (2) the `scale` kernel loads data from pseudo-random indices from the c array. Due to modification (2), `scale` executes additional instructions and exposes lesser locality of reference, thus we have reduced the loop trip count in this kernel to $N/8$ to compensate its duration. The resulting code looks like:

```
for i := 1 to NITERS do                                    ! main loop
    for j := 1 to N do c[j] := a[j];  od                   ! Copy
    for j := 1 to N/8 do b[j] := s * c[random(j)];  od     ! Scale
    for j := 1 to N do c[j] := a[j] + b[j];  od            ! Add
    for j := 1 to N do a[j] := b[j] + s * c[j];  od        ! Triad
od
```

We have instrumented the loop body, compiled it using the GNU suite v4.8.1, and then, we have monitored the execution of the resulting binary on an Intel Core i7 2760QM running at 2.40 GHz and executing Linux 3.11. With respect to the monitoring, the Extrae package has sampled the application at 20 Hz and the perf tool has sampled the application every 250k load instructions, resulting in an overhead below 5 %.

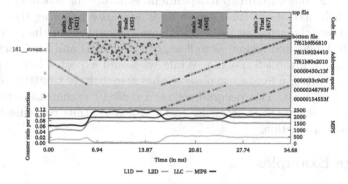

Fig. 2. Analysis of the modified Stream benchmark. Triple correlation time-lines for the main iteration: source code, addresses referenced and performance.

Figure 2 shows the result of the extended framework. The Figure consists of three plots: (1) source code references (top), (2) address space load references (middle), and (3) performance metrics (bottom). In the source code profile each color indicates the active routine (identified by a label of the form X >Y [n], where Y and X refer to the active routine and its ancestor, and n indicates the most observed line). Additionally, the purple dots represent a time-based profile of the sampled code lines where the top (bottom) of the plot represents the begin (end) of the container source file. This plot indicates that the application progresses through four routines and that most of the activity observed of each of these routines occurs in a tiny amount of lines. The second plot shows the address space. On this plot, the background color alternates showing the space used by the variables (either static or dynamically allocated), and the left and right Y-axes show the name of the variables referenced and the address space, respectively. The dots show a time-based profile of the addresses referenced through load instructions and their color indicate the time to solve the reference based on a gradient that ranges from green to blue referring to low and high values, respectively. We want to outline several phenomena observed in this plot. First, as expected, the access pattern in the `Scale` routine to the variable allocated in line 181 of the file `stream.c` (formerly `c`) shows a randomized access pattern with most of the references in blue (meaning high latency). The straight lines formed by the references in the rest of the routines denote that they progressively advance and thus expose spatial locality, and also the greenish color indicates that these references take less time to be served. Second, the `Copy` routine accesses to the array `a` downwards despite the loop is written so that the loop index goes upwards. This effect occurs because the compiler has replaced the loop by a call to `memcpy` (from glibc 2.14) that reverses the loop traversal, unrolls the loop body and uses SSSE3 vector instructions. A linear regression analysis indicates that approximately each instruction references five addresses in `Copy` and since SSSE3 vector instructions may load up to 16 bytes, this translates into a 31.25 % vector efficiency. Finally, the instructions within routines `Add` and `Triad` reference two addresses per variable in average, the loaded data comes from two independent variables (or streams) simultaneously, and their accesses go from low to high addresses honoring the code. The third plot shows the achieved instruction rate (referenced on the right Y-axis) within the instrumented region, as well as, the L1D, L2D and LLC cache misses per instruction (on the left Y-axis). While we would expect a large cache miss ratio per instruction in `Scale`, we observe that they behave similarly to the rest of the kernel routines. This occurs because `random()` executes instructions to compute its results without accessing to the memory, thus reducing the cache miss ratio per instruction.

5 Usage Examples

We have applied the extended framework to two parallel applications to demonstrate its usefulness. Table 1 provides details of the application, execution and monitoring characteristics. With respect to the systems, we have used a Core i7 system that includes the kernel module that allows the two monitoring mechanisms use the same clock source. Since the system only has four cores and we do not want to overload the system, we have used an additional Xeon system to execute the remaining processes that do not fit on the former machine. The Core i7 system has three levels of cache with a line size of 64 bytes: level 1 are two 8-way 32 KiB caches for instructions and data, level 2 consists of a 8-way unified 256 KiB cache, and level 3 is a 12-way unified 6,144 KiB cache.

Regarding the applications, each has been executed twice: the first execution captures information regarding the load references, while the second run collects

Table 1. Applications analyzed.

	CGPOP	BigDFT 1.7.5.13
# Processes	24	21
Processor type	Intel Core i7-2760QM @ 2.40 GHz	
	Intel Xeon E5-2620v2 @ 2.10 GHz (*max*: 2.60 GHz)	
Application size	6 Klines	496 Klines
	20 files	769 files
Compiler	GNU compiler suite 4.8.1	
Compiler flags	-O3 -g	-O2 -g
MPI implementation	OpenMPI v1.6.5	
Sampling period	20 ms	
Data sampling period	10^6 load, store instructions	

store references. The resulting plots are shown side-by-side for comparison purposes. Regarding the collecting, Extrae has been used to monitor MPI activity and it has sampled using a period coarser than the gprof sampling frequency (10 *vs* 20 ms). perf has been instructed to sample memory references every 10^6 load (or store) instructions. These coarse grain sampling frequencies ensured that the applications suffered a time dilation below 5 %.

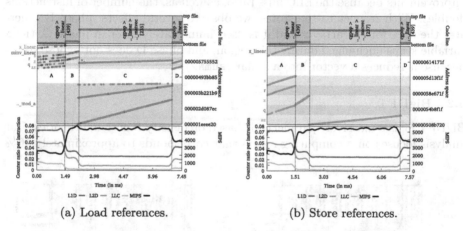

(a) Load references.   (b) Store references.

Fig. 3. Analysis of CGPOP mini-application.

5.1 CGPOP

CGPOP [21] is a proxy application of the Parallel Ocean Program application. POP is a three-dimensional ocean circulation model designed primarily for studying the ocean climate system and it is a component within the Community Earth System Model. Figure 3 shows the obtained plots depicting the load and store references for the most time-consuming region of this execution. Note that both plots have its own address space depending on the accessed variables and that the store memory references are shown in green because in this architecture the store instructions are inserted into a store buffer and these instructions are no longer under control of PEBS thus not having latency information for them. The Figure indicates that the region faces two routines: `pcg_chrongear_linear` (in red) and `matvec` (from the matrix module, in green), but we have also manually added labels (A-D) in the plot to ease the referencing. The latter routine takes most of the execution time within the region and also achieves the highest MIPS rate (above 5,000 MIPS). With respect to the load instructions within the data structures, we observe that phase C accesses to variables `z` and `a` (from the matrix module). The plot shows that the load references to variable `a` are partitioned into three disjoint portions that are accessed linear and simultaneously by the processor. The analysis of the source code shows that this variable represents a sparse row matrix that includes three arrays (one for double precision values and two for integer indices). When analyzing phase A, we observe that references require more time to be served (blue colored) and this is also related to the highest ratio of cache misses (1 out of every 14 instructions miss at L1D). The code in this phase loads data from six arrays (`x_linear`, `s`, `r`, `z`, `q` and `az`) and stores data to four arrays (`x_linear`, `s`, `r` and `q`). We have tested whether the code using an array of structures (AoS) improves the performance; however, our results indicate that using AoS does not offer performance improvements because the LLC miss ratio, as well as, the number of instructions doubles. With respect to the stores, we observe several effects: phase B generates the data for the array `z` and it is used immediately after in phase C, the `a` variable keeps unchanged during this region, and phase D does not expose stores because it reduces a vector into a scalar (`sumN2`).

5.2   BigDFT

BigDFT [6] is a massively parallel code based on density functional theories. Our analysis focuses on a computing region that corresponds to approximately 16 %

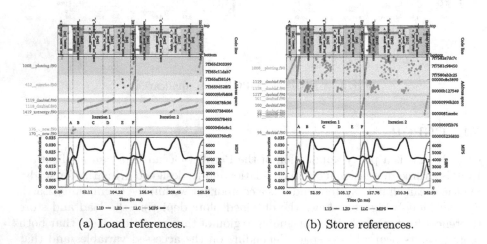

(a) Load references.   (b) Store references.

Fig. 4. Analysis of BigDFT.

of the total execution time, and Fig. 4 shows the outcome of the extended framework for this region. The results indicate that the region consists of two iterations at all levels (source code, references, and performance). We have added labels to identify the iterations, as well as, the phases (routines) within the iterations (A-F). The first thing we notice is that load references expose better spatial locality than the store references, and that phase E shows a random access behavior in the load references and these references take more time to be served. We also outline that phase A traverses completely the array allocated in `plotting.f90` (line 1,008) to store values on it, and that happens immediately after executing the `razero` routine (depicted in green) which may be redundant because there aren't loads in between.

This report also shows some insights on the chances of making this region parallel using a task-based programming model. For instance, phases B and D store data in the data allocated in `daubis.f90` (line 1,118) and this data is used in phases C and E, begetting true (RAW) dependencies between these pair of phases. Also, phases B and D load and store data from the region allocated in `daubis.f90` (line 1,119) causing true (RAW) and output (WAW) dependencies between these phases. Finally, phase F mainly depends on the data located by `plotting.f90` (line 1,008) which is written by phases C and E. Due to the described dependencies, only phases A and B might safely run in parallel.

6   Conclusions and Future Work

We have presented an extension to a framework that displays the memory access patterns of computing regions and their time evolution along the source code and the performance behavior. This extension relies on the ability of recent hardware mechanisms available in current processors to sample instructions based on a user-defined period and attributes to each sample several performance metrics, including the addresses referenced. This enhanced framework has proven valuable to give detailed insight regarding several optimized application binaries, such as detecting the most dominant data streams and their temporal evolution along computing regions. For instance, we have seen that the compiler has replaced the source code by a call in Stream, that CGPOP accesses multiple memory streams simultaneously, and that there may exist redundant work in BigDFT. All this information has been captured using minimal instrumentation and coarse grain sampling periods, thus keeping a low expense during the measurement.

We believe that there are research opportunities using these hardware memory sampling techniques. For instance, we consider using the outcome of this extended framework to capture the store access patterns and then search for those variables that are not used shortly. The access to these variables may benefit from non-temporal instructions because these instructions do not write data into the cache hierarchy, nor fetches the corresponding line; thus not polluting the cache hierarchy. Another direction would include studying data dependencies for porting an application to a task-based data-flow programming model using partial data. Finally, it would be valuable to extend the memory monitoring mechanism to multiplex in order to capture load and store references in one run.

Acknowledgments. We would like to thank Damien Caliste and Luigi Genovese for their insightful comments on BigDFT. We thankfully acknowledge the support of the *Comisión Interministerial de Ciencia y Tecnología* (CICYT) under contract No. TIN2012-34557 which has partially funded this work.

References

1. Beyls, K., D'Hollander, E.H.: Refactoring for data locality. IEEE Comput. **42**(2), 62–71 (2009). http://dx.doi.org/10.1109/MC.2009.57
2. Browne, S., Dongarra, J., Garner, N., Ho, G., Mucci, P.: A portable programming interface for performance evaluation on modern processors. Int. J. High Perform. Comput. Appl. **14**(3), 189–204 (2000). http://icl.cs.utk.edu/papi
3. Burtscher, M., et al.: PerfExpert: an easy-to-use performance diagnosis tool for HPC applications. In: Conference on High Performance Computing Networking, Storage and Analysis, pp. 1–11 (2010). http://dx.doi.org/10.1109/SC.2010.41
4. Corporation, I.: Intel 64 and IA-32 architectures software developer's manual. Volume 3B: System Programming Guide, Part 2, January 2015
5. Drongowski, P., et al.: Incorporating instruction-based sampling into AMD Code-Analyst. In: Performance Analysis of Systems Software, pp. 119–120 (2010)
6. Genovese, L., Neelov, A., Goedecker, S., Deutsch, T., Ghasemi, S.A., Willand, A., Caliste, D., Zilberberg, O., Rayson, M., Bergman, A., Schneider, R.: Daubechies wavelets as a basis set for density functional pseudopotential calculations. J. Chem. Phys. **129**(1), 014109 (2008)
7. Gerndt, M., Fürlinger, K., Kereku, E.: Periscope: advanced techniques for performance analysis. In: PARCO, pp. 15–26 (2005)
8. Giménez, A., et al.: Dissecting on-node memory access performance: a semantic approach. In: International Conference for High Performance Computing, Networking, Storage and Analysis, vol. 2014, pp. 166–176 (2014)
9. Graham, S.L., Kessler, P.B., Mckusick, M.K.: Gprof: a call graph execution profiler. In: SIGPLAN 1982: Proceedings of the 1982 SIGPLAN Symposium on Compiler Construction, pp. 120–126 (1982). http://doi.acm.org/10.1145/800230.806987
10. Itzkowitz, M., et al.: Memory profiling using hardware counters. In: SC 2003: Proceedings of the 2003 ACM/IEEE Conference on Supercomputing, p. 17 (2003)
11. Liu, X., Mellor-Crummey, J.M.: A data-centric profiler for parallel programs. In: International Conference for High Performance Computing, Networking, Storage and Analysis, SC 2013, pp. 28:1–28:12 (2013). http://doi.acm.org/10.1145/2503210.2503297
12. Loh, G.H.: 3D-stacked memory architectures for multi-core processors. In: 35th International Symposium on Computer Architecture, pp. 453–464 (2008). http://dx.doi.org/10.1109/ISCA.2008.15
13. Martonosi, M., Gupta, A., Anderson, T.E.: MemSpy: analyzing memory system bottlenecks in programs. In: SIGMETRICS, pp. 1–12 (1992). http://doi.acm.org/10.1145/133057.133079
14. McCalpin, J.D.: Memory bandwidth and machine balance in current high performance computers. In: IEEE Computer Society Technical Committee on Computer Architecture Newsletter, pp. 19–25 (1995)
15. de Melo, A.C.: The new linux "perf" tools. In: Linux Kongress (2010)
16. Peña, A.J., Balaji, P.: Toward the efficient use of multiple explicitly managed memory subsystems. In: 2014 IEEE International Conference on Cluster Computing, pp. 123–131 (2014)

17. Rane, A., Browne, J.: Enhancing performance optimization of multicore chips and multichip nodes with data structure metrics. In: International Conference on Parallel Architectures and Compilation Techniques, pp. 147–156 (2012). http://doi.acm.org/10.1145/2370816.2370838

18. Servat, H., et al.: Unveiling internal evolution of parallel application computation phases. In: ICPP, pp. 155–164 (2011)

19. Servat, H., et al.: Bio-inspired call-stack reconstruction for performance analysis. Technical report, UPC-DAC-RR-2014-20, Department of Computer Architecture, Universitat Politècnica de Catalunya (2014)

20. Shende, S.S., Malony, A.D.: The TAU parallel performance system. Int. J. High Perform. Comput. Appl. **20**(2), 287–311 (2006)

21. Stone, A., Dennis, J., Strout, M.M.: The CGPOP miniapp, version 1.0. Technical report, CS-11-103, Colorado State University (2011)

22. Subotic, V., Ferrer, R., Sancho, J.C., Labarta, J., Valero, M.: Quantifying the potential task-based dataflow parallelism in MPI applications. In: Jeannot, E., Namyst, R., Roman, J. (eds.) Euro-Par 2011, Part I. LNCS, vol. 6852, pp. 39–51. Springer, Heidelberg (2011)

23. Tallent, N., et al.: HPCToolkit: performance tools for scientific computing. J. Phys.: Conf. Ser. **125**(1), 012088 (2008)

24. Wang, C., et al.: NVMalloc: exposing an aggregate SSD store as a memory partition in extreme-scale machines. In: 26th IEEE International Parallel and Distributed Processing Symposium, pp. 957–968 (2012)

25. Wolf, F., et al.: Usage of the SCALASCA for scalable performance analysis of large-scale parallel applications. In: Tools for High Performance Computing, pp. 157–167 (2008)

Automatic On-Line Detection of MPI Application Structure with Event Flow Graphs

Xavier Aguilar[1]([✉]), Karl Fürlinger[2], and Erwin Laure[1]

[1] KTH Royal Institute of Technology, High Performance Computing
and Visualization Department (HPCViz) and Swedish e-Science Research Center
(SeRC), Lindstedvägen 5, 10044 Stockholm, Sweden
xaguilar@pdc.kth.se
[2] Computer Science Department, MNM Team, Ludwig-Maximilians-Universität
(LMU) Munich, Oettingenstr. 67, 80538 Munich, Germany

Abstract. The deployment of larger and larger HPC systems challenges the scalability of both applications and analysis tools. Performance analysis toolsets provide users with means to spot bottlenecks in their applications by either collecting aggregated statistics or generating lossless time-stamped traces. While obtaining detailed trace information is the best method to examine the behavior of an application in detail, it is infeasible at extreme scales due to the huge volume of data generated.

In this context, knowing the application structure, and particularly the nesting of loops in iterative applications is of great importance as it allows, among other things, to reduce the amount of data collected by focusing on important sections of the code.

In this paper we demonstrate how the loop nesting structure of an MPI application can be extracted on-line from its event flow graph without the need of any explicit source code instrumentation. We show how this knowledge on the application structure can be used to compute postmortem statistics as well as to reduce the amount of redundant data collected. To that end, we present a usage scenario where this structure information is utilized on-line (while the application runs) to intelligently collect fine-grained data for only a few iterations of an application, considerably reducing the amount of data gathered.

Keywords: Application structure detection · Flow graph analysis · Performance monitoring · Online analysis · Automatic loop detection

1 Introduction

Computer simulations are nowadays an important method of scientific discovery. By using computers, scientists can model processes that would be difficult or impossible to reproduce and study in a real-world scenario. Moreover, the deployment of larger and larger High Performance Computing (HPC) systems provides scientists with an opportunity to solve problems which could not be

J.L. Träff et al. (Eds.): Euro-Par 2015, LNCS 9233, pp. 70–81, 2015.
DOI: 10.1007/978-3-662-48096-0_6

tackled before. However, scientific applications have to be tuned and highly optimized to effectively use all the computational power provided by current HPC
infrastructures.

In our previous work we have explored the use of event flow graphs as a
novel method for MPI monitoring and analysis, demonstrating that graphs are
a good compressed representation of MPI event traces due to the iterative nature
of MPI parallel applications [1,8]. Event flow graphs retain the temporal order
of the events executed during the lifetime of a program without saving explicit
timestamps. Thus, graphs can be used to reconstruct the full ordered sequence
of events performed by the application.

In this paper we present how event flow graphs can be used beyond trace
compression and reconstruction. Our approach for automatic analysis of event
flow graphs sheds light on the inherent structure of parallel applications, for
instance, revealing the nesting loop structure present in the program.

Knowledge of the application structure can be very useful both for post-
mortem and for on-line performance analysis. On one hand, this structural
knowledge can be utilized to automatically generate reports that show the user
where and how time is spent among loops, and how the performance characteristics of those loops evolve over the lifetime of an application. This can be done
without the need of recompilation, access to the source code, or user involvement at all. On the other hand, knowing the structure of a program while it
runs can benefit how data is collected and aggregated. For instance, data can be
aggregated at a loop level instead of keeping every event, or redundant information can be reduced by keeping fine-grained data for a few loop iterations only.
Furthermore, this structural knowledge can also be used, for example, to help a
dynamic runtime system with its decision making process, or to feed an external
monitoring tool that decides the grain of the performance data collected.

The contributions of this paper include:

- We develop a simple mechanism to extract the structure of applications with
  very low overhead and without the need to have access to the source code.
- We present a real usage scenario in which the structure of an application is
  detected automatically while the application runs to intelligently select the
  performance data collected.
- We demonstrate that the overall performance behavior of an iterative MPI
  application is still captured with our approach by selecting only a few representative iterations.

The remainder of this paper is organized as follows: Sect. 2 provides
background on our previous work on event flow graphs. Section 3 describes
the mechanisms implemented for application structure detection, and its on-line
application. Section 4 presents a real usage scenario where the on-line detection
of an application's structure is used to intelligently select the amount of performance data generated. Section 5 surveys related work. Finally, Sects. 6 and 7
discuss future work and conclusion, respectively.

2   Background: IPM and Event Flow Graphs

The work presented in this paper builds on top of the Integrated Performance Monitoring (IPM) tool [13]. In [1,8], IPM was extended to capture and generate event flow graphs of MPI parallel applications. Upon program termination, IPM generates for each MPI process a weighted directed graph in which nodes are the different[1] MPI calls performed by that process, and edges are the transitions between those calls. In other words, edges are the computational parts between two MPI calls. Therefore, event flow graphs keep the temporal order of the events performed by the application. In addition, metrics such as timers and hardware counters can be associated with the nodes and edges of the graph, increasing thereby the usability of such graphs.

3   Automatic Analysis of Event Flow Graphs

3.1   Loops in Event Flow Graphs

It is commonly accepted conventional wisdom that the vast majority of HPC scientific parallel codes are iterative and spend most of their time in loops. These scientific applications are usually composed of a large outer loop, which controls the simulation time-steps, and which contains several inner loops with different nesting levels. Since most of the application time is spent in loops, they become one of the main targets when analyzing and optimizing programs.

Most MPI parallel programs contain MPI operations in some of their loops, as data needs to be shared among processes across loop iterations. In those cases, the generated event flow graphs will contain cycles. Thus, by detecting those cycles, we are detecting the actual loops that drive the simulation process in the application. Loops without MPI calls are not detected with this approach, however, their behavior gets captured in the edges of the graph as these loops are just pure computational parts between two MPI calls.

Figure 1 shows the basic cycle shapes that can appear in our event flow graphs. Each one of the loops is accompanied with a source code example that generates such a loop structure. Calls to A, B, C and D represent any MPI routine. As can be seen in the picture, loops can range from single node cycles, through several nesting structures, to cycles with multiple tails. In addition, all these basic loop structures can be combined to form more complex ones. At the moment, our work focuses in reducible loops [23], that is, loops with just one entry point. Formally, given a loop L with header h (h dominates all the nodes in the loop L) and an edge $< u, v >$, if $u \notin L$ and $v \in L - \{h\}$, then v is a re-entry point and the loop is irreducible.

Irreducibility in our event flow graphs can be caused by two different factors: the application's source code structure, and the event signatures used for the

---

[1] What constitutes different MPI calls for recording our event flow graphs is governed by a configurable event signature in IPM. The signature usually consists of the name of the call and its call site and can optionally also include the communication partner rank and the transfer size.

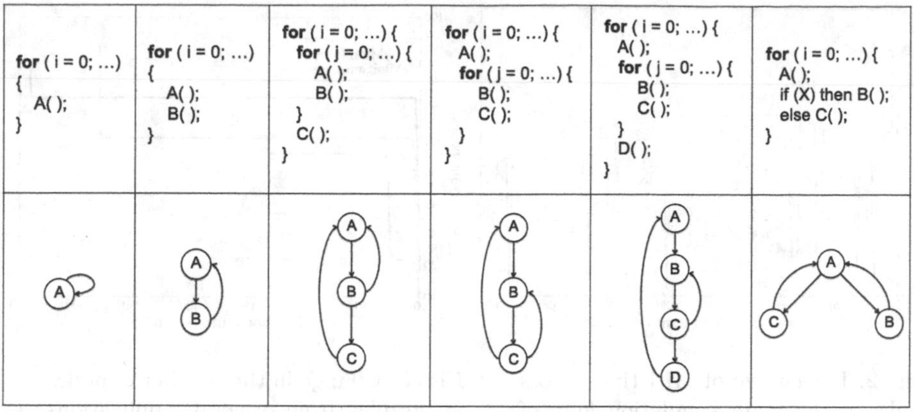

for (i = 0; ...) { A( ); }	for (i = 0; ...) { A( ); B( ); }	for (i = 0; ...) { for (j = 0; ...) { A( ); B( ); } C( ); }	for (i = 0; ...) { A( ); for (j = 0; ...) { B( ); C( ); } }	for (i = 0; ...) { A( ); for (j = 0; ...) { B( ); C( ); } D( ); }	for (i = 0; ...) { A( ); if (X) then B( ); else C( ); }

Fig. 1. Different cycle shapes in event flow graphs.

nodes of the graph. Irreducibility caused by unstructured programming (e.g., the use of goto), however, is nowadays rare and will become even rarer in the future due to the adoption of more structured programming practices [22]. On the other hand, irreducibility caused by the event signature used can always be solved by changing the signature. If transfer size is used in the signature for example, one single MPI call in the source code can be translated into different nodes in the graph if such a call has different transfer sizes at runtime. Thereby, generating sometimes irreducible cycles. However, this situation is also rare, and the graph usually becomes reducible again by using the call name and call site as event signature, because then each graph node maps exclusively to only one MPI call in the source code.

Algorithms for graph cycle detection have been studied and used in the field of compilers for years [12,20,21]. Our framework for graph analysis implements the algorithm from [24]. This algorithm traverses the graph using a depth-first search (DFS) and runs in almost linear time. It does not require any complicated data structures as other cycle detection algorithms, and thus, it is much easier to implement. After running the algorithm, loop header nodes (entry node in a graph cycle) are identified and all loop nodes are labeled with their corresponding header. If multi-entry loops (irreducible loops) are found, the graph is marked as irreducible and the process ends.

Once nodes have been labeled, our framework knows for every graph node to which loop it belongs, which loops are outermost, which are nested, etc. Thereby, our analysis tool can provide detailed exclusive and inclusive loop metrics such as percentage of MPI time over total loop time. Figure 2 shows the percentage of MPI time across ranks in the main simulation loop for MiniFE, a finite-element code. The MPI time is the inclusive total time for this outermost loop, that is, the time for its nested loops is also included. The picture shows that MiniFE suffers of imbalance in this loop as some processes spend around 20 % of their time in MPI whereas some others less than 5 %. It is important to

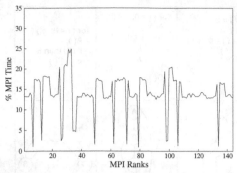
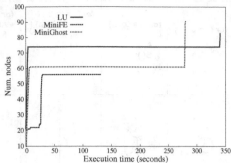

Fig. 2. Percentage of MPI time across ranks in the main simulation loop of MiniFE.

Fig. 3. Change in the number of nodes in graphs from several applications during their execution time.

remark that the statistics on loops provided by our approach are automatically obtained without any user involvement or source code modification. Our solution utilizes the PMPI interface to intercept MPI calls, and the libunwind library to determine their call sites.

The use of event flow graphs together with automatic loop detection opens many possibilities for post-mortem performance analysis of MPI parallel applications. However, this topic is out of the scope of this article. More details in the use of graphs for visual performance analysis of MPI applications can be found in [2].

3.2   Runtime Loop Detection

The previous section has focused on the automatic post-mortem analysis of graphs to detect the structure of an application, however, our mechanism can also be used in real-time while applications run.

In order to minimize the amount of overhead introduced into the application, our on-line loop detection mechanism is performed only once when the application has reached a stable state. The application is considered stable when it enters into an iterative phase in which its performance behavior presents minor fluctuations. Most scientific applications arrive into this state when they start executing their main simulation loop, which is executed for most of the running time. In our case, this situation is reflected in the number of nodes in the event flow graph. In other words, once the application reaches an iterative stable state, the number of nodes in the graph does not change since the same MPI calls are repeated over and over again. Figure 3 shows the number of nodes in the graph during application execution for one process of different MPI applications. It can be seen, for instance with MiniGhost, that after some short initialization time, the number of nodes in the graph does not change during most of the execution time since the application has entered its stable state. At the end of its execution, the number of nodes in the graph increases again as the application exits the main loop and performs some new MPI calls before finalizing. However, these

Table 1. Overhead introduced by IPM over total application running time.

Metrics	MiniGhost	MiniFE	GTC	MiniMD	BT	LU
Ranks	96	144	64	192	144	128
% Overhead	0.9 %	0.65 %	1.06 %	1.10 %	0.81 %	1.2 %

new final nodes represent a minimal percentage over the total running time, and thus, they are not important for performance analysis purposes.

To detect when an application becomes stable, IPM checks at regular intervals if the graph has changed since the last time it was checked. When the graph remains the same for a certain number of times, the graph is considered stable and the loop detection mechanisms are triggered. This graph sampling interval used by IPM as well as the number of times the graph has to remain identical are configured by the user.

4 Experiments

In this section we demonstrate the ability of our system to automatically identify the structure of an application while it runs. Moreover, we demonstrate how this knowledge can be used to reduce the amount of tracing data collected by only keeping information from a few representative iterations.

To this end, we run six different applications that represent typical scientific codes: MiniGhost, MiniFE and MiniMD from the Mantevo project [17]; BT and LU from the NAS Benchmarks [4]; and the GTC code [15]. The applications were run in a Cray XE6 machine with 2 twelve-core AMD MagnyCours CPUs at 2.1 GHz per node. The nodes had a total of 32 GB DDR3 memory and were interconnected through a Cray Gemini network. The benchmarks were compiled using Intel 12.1.5.

4.1 Overhead

Table 1 shows for each benchmark the percentage of overhead introduced by IPM over the total application running time. This overhead includes intercepting every MPI call, building the graph, and detecting the cycles in it. As can be seen in the table, the applications are not perturbed much since the overhead is very small, being always under 2 %. In addition, this overhead does not increase with the number of cores used as the graph creation and structure detection mechanism are performed locally without any inter-process communication required.

4.2 Usage Scenario

Collecting fine-grained information with tracing tools avoids the loss of microscopic information that can occur with other summarization methods such as

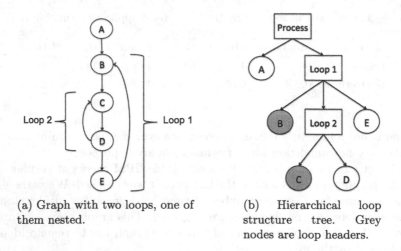

(a) Graph with two loops, one of them nested.

(b) Hierarchical loop structure tree. Grey nodes are loop headers.

Fig. 4. Event flow graph and its hierarchical tree representation after loop detection.

profiling. However, detailed trace-based analysis for the whole lifetime of an application is infeasible due to the scalability problems caused by the amount of data generated.

Nevertheless, most MPI scientific applications are usually iterative algorithms that repeat the same operations over time as the simulation evolves. Given this iterative nature, applications exhibit a similar performance behavior across iterations during their lifetime. Thus, keeping information on only a few iterations of such a stable region should be sufficient to capture the overall application behavior.

By means of detecting the application structure, we aim to identify at runtime the repetitive pattern of the program, thereby, collecting information on a few representative iterations only. This process works as follows. First, the corresponding event flow graphs are built when the application reaches a stable state. In other words, when the number of graph nodes remains stable and does not change. Once the event flow graph has been built for each process, each graph is analyzed to automatically detect and label its cycles. Then, IPM creates for each graph one tree that depicts the hierarchical relation of the loops detected. The root of the tree represents the process and every internal tree node corresponds to a loop or an event in such a process. If two loops are nested, they will be parent and child in the tree. These trees model naturally the hierarchical relations among loops and allow IPM to check easily, among other things, if an event belong to a certain loop, if a loop is nested within another, or if two loops are nested within the same loop. Figure 4 presents an event flow graph with two loops and how this information would be represented within IPM after the loop detection.

As previously stated, the loop detection mechanisms are triggered once the application enters into a stable state, that is, when the application starts iterating over its main simulation loop. Therefore, in order to monitor some iterations of

Table 2. Size comparisons between full traces and traces with 10 selected iterations.

Metric	MiniGhost	MiniFE	GTC	MiniMD	BT	LU
Ranks	96	144	64	192	144	128
Total iterations	60	200	200	2000	250	300
Total trace size	26 MB	77 MB	48 MB	555 MB	717 MB	7.7 GB
10 iterations size	4.4 MB	4.1 MB	1.3 MB	788 KB	29 MB	267 MB
% reduced	83 %	94.7 %	97.3 %	99.8 %	96 %	96.53 %

that main loop, IPM only has to wait for the event that is the loop header of the current outermost loop being executed. In other words, an event that is the header of a loop that hangs from the root of the constructed tree. Once this event is intercepted, IPM starts the tracing to collect detailed information for a certain number of iterations defined by the user. Afterwards, IPM stops the tracing and the application continues its execution normally.

Table 2 shows a comparison of sizes between a full trace and a trace with a few selected iterations for our various test applications. The table contains the number of processes used, the total number of iterations for the full test case, the total trace size for the full test, the trace size when tracing automatically only 10 iterations, and the percentage of trace size reduction achieved. As can be observed in the table, by keeping information on only a few iterations, we can reduce the final trace size up to several orders of magnitude.

The current approach leaves room for some improvements though. For instance, IPM could take into account some loop performance metrics before turning on the tracing. Checking metrics such as instructions per cycle (IPC) across iterations of the outermost loop could guarantee even more that the application has reached its stable state. At the moment, the loop detection mechanism and the selective tracing are triggered only once during the whole lifetime of the application. Therefore, in cases where applications have several phases or various outermost loops, our methodology will trace only one of them. It is planned in our future work to solve this issue by triggering the selective tracing few times during the execution, as well as providing the possibility to trigger the loop detection explicitly with an API.

Although tracing just a few iterations provides detailed information while reducing the amount of data collected, it always comes with an inevitable data loss. Specially in punctual variations between iterations. Therefore, we performed several experiments to measure the quality of our results, that is, we examined how representative from the overall execution are the iterations automatically selected by IPM. With that in mind, we used the CrayPat performance tool to collect several statistics about the most important functions in MiniGhost. Then we computed the same statistics from the reduced trace that contained only 10 iterations. Those statistics are the percentage of time spent in each call, and the average of instructions and cycles per call. Table 3 compares the measurements obtained with Craypat for the whole run with the measurements obtained from

Table 3. Statistics per call for the most relevant functions in MiniGhost.

Function name	CrayPat			IPM Trace		
	Time %	Kinstr	KCycles	Time %	Kinstr	KCycles
MG_BSPMA_DIAGS	5.70 %	401,476	558,737	5.42 %	394,140	552,064
MG_STENCIL_3D27PT	80.8 %	120,886	199,126	79 %	120,864	199,397
MG_ALLREDUCE_SUM	12.10 %	14,052	29,822	12.96 %	14,432	29,818

the automatically reduced trace. As can be seen in the table, the differences
are very small (always under 2 %) and could be explained due to the different
overheads introduced by both tools, or by small variances between executions
or even across iterations. In any case, the results demonstrate that the trace
containing only a few selected iterations is representative of the overall behavior
of the application.

5   Related Work

Detection and analysis of parallel application structure is the topic of several related works. The ScalaTrace [18] framework provides on-the-fly lossless
trace compression of MPI communication traces by detecting loops, or repeat-
ing events, and encoding them using RSDs [11]. Our approach differs in the fact
that whereas ScalaTrace detects loops for trace compression, our on-line loop
detection has more general purposes, from statistic aggregation to data filtering.
Our solution is highly customizable, allowing the generation of compressed full
traces and small uncompressed fine-grained traces.

The work of Gonzalez et al. [9,10] works on two-dimensional hardware counter
data derived from computational bursts, and employs a density based clustering approach to identify the SPMD structure of the application. Although this
approach allows to reduce the size of traces by collecting only relevant information from a few iterations, it has no precise control over which part of the
code corresponds to a certain traced region. In contrast, our approach provides
fine-grained precision in delimiting loops within the application. In addition, the
use of burst clustering demands a more complex parallel software infrastructure
to be used in an on-line scenario [16].

The work of Casas et al. [6,7] utilizes spectral analysis techniques such as
wavelets to unveil the inner structure of parallel programs in performance traces.
Thereby, generating sub-traces that only contain a few representative iterations.
In addition, the tool can also find regions within the trace that are not usable
due to tool perturbation, e.g. flushing of tracing buffers to disk. Although this is
a good approach that helps the user to focus in relevant parts of the application
while reducing the trace size, it still requires the whole original post-mortem
trace. In contrast, our approach can be performed on-line while the application runs.

An approach that puts more focus on the communication structure is followed by [3,19]. Repeated communication patterns are here first identified locally (on a single process) and then grown globally by using string processing techniques such as n-gram detection and suffix trees. The work of Alawneh et al. [3] further attempts to group repeated patterns into homogeneous phases using information theory concepts.

AutomaDeD [5,14] has similarities to our approach in that the application execution is also represented as a set of states and the transitions between them. However, AutomaDeD focuses on debugging and only records transition propabilities between the states to create a Semi-Markov Model (SMM) of the application execution. In contrast, our event flow graphs record the actual program execution, allowing us to reproduce exactly the full sequence of events ordered in time.

6   Future Work

Our current implementation captures information from several consecutive iterations only once during the lifetime of an application. Nevertheless, this mechanism can be easily extended to acquire information with more advanced strategies. For instance, every time a certain condition such as the variation of a particular performance parameter is fulfilled. IPM could keep track of metrics such as instructions per cycle (IPC) on an iteration basis, and then trigger the tracing every time there is a noticeable change of such a metric. Thereby, if an application degrades during a long job we can have fine-grained snapshots at several points in time. Furthermore, we want to extend the iteration selection mechanism in order to automatically detect when an application has irregular loop behavior or combined repetitive loop patterns. That is, the sequence of events executed by the application is not regular and it changes from time to time regarding current loop iteration, program state, or simulation phase. Our current solution for selective tracing generates always a fixed number of consecutive iterations, therefore, we can lose irregular loop patterns if their frequency of appearance is smaller than the fixed number of iterations traced.

In the present work, we have shown how we discover the structure of an application across the time dimension, that is, detecting patterns (loops) in the sequence of events performed by each process. However, our ongoing work is also directed towards investigating the structure of applications across the process dimension. We are studying the utilization of graphs to build a process signature that could be clustered to detect processes with the same program behavior. Thereby, we could reduce even more the amount of data collected as only data from a few representative tasks could be kept.

Our current event flow graphs are focused in pure MPI applications, however, with the increase in the number of cores within computer nodes, hybrid approaches such as MPI+OpenMP or MPI+PGAS are becoming more usual. Thus, we want to provide our graphs with extensions to model such situations, for instance, having new graph nodes that represent OpenMP regions, or PGAS operations. Moreover, we want to study the utilization of graphs with non-iterative applications, for instance, recursive codes or applications with task-based parallelism.

7   Conclusion

This paper presents the use of event flow graphs together with cycle detection algorithms to automatically detect the loop nesting structure of MPI parallel applications. This loop structure can be extracted from any MPI program without recompilation or modification of the source code.

We demonstrate how our work can be used, for instance, to automatically compute post-mortem statistics that help users to better understand their applications, e.g., the distribution of time across loops, or the percentage of MPI time spent in a certain loop. Nevertheless, the greatest strength of our structure detection approach is that it can be performed with very low overhead while the application runs. To that end, we present a test case where the structure of a stencil code is extracted on-line while the program runs to intelligently filter the performance data collected. By knowing the loop structure of an application, our framework traces automatically only a small fraction of representative iterations, reducing considerably the amount of data collected while keeping the overall performance behavior of the application. Furthermore, the overhead introduced by our mechanism is very small, being always under 2 % in our experiments.

References

1. Aguilar, X., Fürlinger, K., Laure, E.: MPI trace compression using event flow graphs. In: Silva, F., Dutra, I., Santos Costa, V. (eds.) Euro-Par 2014 Parallel Processing. LNCS, vol. 8632, pp. 1–12. Springer, Heidelberg (2014)
2. Aguilar, X., Fürlinger, K., Laure, E.: Visual MPI performance analysis using event flow graphs. Procedia Comput. Sci. **51**, 1353–1362 (2015). International Conference On Computational Science, ICCS 2015 Computational Science at the Gates of Nature
3. Alawneh, L., Hamou-Lhadj, A.: Identifying computational phases from inter-process communication traces of HPC applications. In: 2012 IEEE 20th International Conference on Program Comprehension (ICPC), June 2012, pp. 133–142 (2012)
4. Bailey, D.H., Barszcz, E., Barton, J.T., Browning, D.S., Carter, R.L., Dagum, L., Fatoohi, R.A., Frederickson, P.O., Lasinski, T.A., Schreiber, R.S., et al.: The NAS parallel benchmarks. Int. J. High Perform. Comput. Appl. **5**(3), 63–73 (1991)
5. Bronevetsky, G., Laguna, I., Bagchi, S., de Supinski, B.R., Ahn, D.H., Schulz, M.: AutomaDeD: automata-based debugging for dissimilar parallel tasks. In: Proceedings of the 2010 IEEE/IFIP International Conference on Dependable Systems and Networks, DSN 2010, Chicago, IL, USA, 28 June - 1 July 2010, pp. 231–240 (2010)
6. Casas, M., Badia, R.M., Labarta, J.: Automatic structure extraction from MPI applications tracefiles. In: Kermarrec, A.-M., Bougé, L., Priol, T. (eds.) Euro-Par 2007. LNCS, vol. 4641, pp. 3–12. Springer, Heidelberg (2007)

7. Casas, M., Badia, R.M., Labarta, J.: Automatic phase detection and structure extraction of MPI applications. Int. J. High Perform. Comput. Appl. **24**(3), 335–360 (2010)
8. Fürlinger, K., Skinner, D.: Capturing and visualizing event flow graphs of MPI applications. In: Lin, H.-X., Alexander, M., Forsell, M., Knüpfer, A., Prodan, R., Sousa, L., Streit, A. (eds.) Euro-Par 2009. LNCS, vol. 6043, pp. 218–227. Springer, Heidelberg (2010)
9. Gonzalez, J., Gimenez, J., Labarta, J.: Automatic detection of parallel applications computation phases. In: IEEE International Symposium on Parallel Distributed Processing, IPDPS 2009, May 2009, pp. 1–11 (2009)
10. Gonzalez, J., Huck, K., Gimenez, J., Labarta, J.: Automatic refinement of parallel applications structure detection. In: 2012 IEEE 26th International Parallel and Distributed Processing Symposium Workshops Ph.D. Forum (IPDPSW), May 2012, pp. 1680–1687 (2012)
11. Havlak, P., Kennedy, K.: An implementation of interprocedural bounded regular section analysis. IEEE Trans. Parallel Distrib. Syst. **2**, 350–360 (1991)
12. Havlak, P.: Nesting of reducible and irreducible loops. ACM Trans. Program. Lang. Syst. (TOPLAS) **19**(4), 557–567 (1997)
13. IPM WWW site: http://www.ipm2.org
14. Laguna, I., Gamblin, T., de Supinski, B.R., Bagchi, S., Bronevetsky, G., Anh, D.H., Schulz, M., Rountree, B.: Large scale debugging of parallel tasks with AutomaDeD. In: Proceedings of 2011 International Conference for High Performance Computing, Networking, Storage and Analysis, SC 2011, pp. 50:1–50:10. ACM, New York (2011)
15. Lin, Z., Hahm, T.S., Lee, W., Tang, W.M., White, R.B.: Turbulent transport reduction by zonal flows: Massively parallel simulations. Science **281**(5384), 1835–1837 (1998)
16. Llort, G., Gonzalez, J., Servat, H., Gimenez, J., Labarta, J.: On-line detection of large-scale parallel application's structure. In: 2010 IEEE International Symposium on Parallel & Distributed Processing (IPDPS), pp. 1–10. IEEE (2010)
17. Mantevo Project: http://mantevo.org
18. Noeth, M., Ratn, P., Mueller, F., Schulz, M., de Supinski, B.R.: ScalaTrace: scalable compression and replay of communication traces for high-performance computing. J. Parallel Distrib. Comput. **69**(8), 696–710 (2009)
19. Preissl, R., Kockerbauer, T., Schulz, M., Kranzlmuller, D., Supinski, B., Quinlan, D.: Detecting patterns in MPI communication traces. In: 37th International Conference on Parallel Processing, 2008. ICPP 2008, September 2008, pp. 230–237 (2008)
20. Ramalingam, G.: Identifying loops in almost linear time. ACM Trans. Program. Lang. Syst. (TOPLAS) **21**(2), 175–188 (1999)
21. Sreedhar, V.C., Gao, G.R., Lee, Y.F.: Identifying loops using DJ graphs. ACM Trans. Program. Lang. Syst. (TOPLAS) **18**(6), 649–658 (1996)
22. Stanier, J., Watson, D.: A study of irreducibility in C programs. Softw. Pract. Experience **42**(1), 117–130 (2012)
23. Tarjan, R.: Testing flow graph reducibility. In: Proceedings of the Fifth Annual ACM Symposium on Theory of Computing, pp. 96–107. ACM (1973)
24. Wei, T., Mao, J., Zou, W., Chen, Y.: A new algorithm for identifying loops in decompilation. In: Riis Nielson, H., Filé, G. (eds.) SAS 2007. LNCS, vol. 4634, pp. 170–183. Springer, Heidelberg (2007)

Online Automated Reliability Classification of Queueing Models for Streaming Processing Using Support Vector Machines

Jonathan C. Beard$^{(\boxtimes)}$, Cooper Epstein, and Roger D. Chamberlain

Department of Computer Science and Engineering, Washington University
in St. Louis, St. Louis, Missouri
{jbeard,epsteinc,roger}@wustl.edu

Abstract. When do you trust a performance model? More specifically, when can a particular model be used for a specific application? Once a stochastic model is selected, its parameters must be determined. This involves instrumentation, data collection, and finally interpretation; which are very time consuming. Even when done correctly, the results hold for only the conditions under which the system was characterized. For modern, dynamic stream processing systems, this is far too slow if a model-based approach to performance tuning is to be considered. This work demonstrates the use of a Support Vector Machine (SVM) to determine if a stochastic queueing model is usable or not for a particular queueing station within a streaming application. When combined with methods for online service rate approximation, our SVM approach can select models while the application is executing (online). The method is tested on a variety of hardware and software platforms. The technique is shown to be highly effective for determining the applicability of $M/M/1$ and $M/D/1$ queueing models to stream processing applications.

1 Introduction

Stochastic modeling is essential to the optimization of performant stream processing systems. Successful application of a stochastic queueing model often requires knowledge of many factors that are unknowable without extensive application and hardware characterization. Extensive characterization, is however quite expensive (both in time and effort) when considering streaming applications of any appreciable size. Complicating matters further is that each streaming application could require that multiple models be selected in order to fully model its performance; each with its own assumptions and parameters that must be quantified before use. Even when modeling assumptions are verified offline, often they are broken by unpredictable behavior that can occur during execution.

R.D. Chamberlain—This work was supported by Exegy, Inc. Washington Univ. and R. Chamberlain receive income based on the license of technology by the university to Exegy, Inc.

© Springer-Verlag Berlin Heidelberg 2015
J.L. Träff et al. (Eds.): Euro-Par 2015, LNCS 9233, pp. 82–93, 2015.
DOI: 10.1007/978-3-662-48096-0_7

This paper proposes a machine learning method for classifying the reliability of stochastic queueing models for stream processing systems.

Stream processing is a compute paradigm that views an application as a set of compute kernels connected via communications links or "streams" (example shown in Fig. 1). Stream processing is increasingly used by multi-disciplinary fields with names such as computational-x and x-informatics (e.g., biology, astrophysics) where the focus is on safe and fast parallelism of a specific application. Many of these applications involve real-time or latency sensitive big data processing necessitating usage of many parallel kernels on several compute cores. Intrinsically stream processing comes with a high communications cost and infrastructure overhead. Optimizing or reducing the communication within a streaming application is often a non-trivial task, however it is central to the widespread adoption of stream processing techniques.

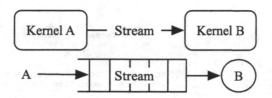

Fig. 1. The top image is an example of a simple streaming system with two compute kernels (labeled A & B). Each kernel could be assigned to any number of compute resources depending on the platform (e.g., processor core, graphics engine). The bottom image is the resulting queue with arrival process A (emanating from compute kernel A) and server B. For more complex systems this becomes a queueing network.

Streams allocated within a streaming application can be modeled as a stochastic queueing network for which there are well understood relationships between input arrival rates, computational service rates, queue occupancies, etc., in the steady state. Understanding the streaming application's queueing network is essential to its optimization. Streaming systems such as RaftLib [4], can spawn tens to hundreds of queues; each potentially with a unique environment and characteristics to model. Hand selection of performance models for these applications is clearly impractical. Offline modeling attempts are often thwarted by dynamic characteristics present within the system that were not included in the model. This paper outlines what is perhaps an easier route. Utilizing 76 features easily extracted from a system along with a streaming approximation of non-blocking service rate, we show that a Support Vector Machine (SVM) can identify where a model can and cannot be used. Results are shown that demonstrate that this model is generalizable in trained form to multiple operating systems and hardware types. In addition to testing the trained model on micro-benchmark data, two full streaming applications are utilized: matrix multiplication and Rabin-Karp string search.

2   Methodology

For most stream processing systems (including RaftLib) the queues between compute kernels are directly implied as a result of application construction. In order to use models for optimizing the queues within a stream processing application the service rate must be determined. Work from Beard and Chamberlain [3] enables the online determination of mean service rates for kernels. Working under the assumption that accurate determination of service distributions will be too expensive to be practical, we instead learn the applicability of two distinct queueing models based on features (shown in Fig. 2) that are knowable during execution with low overhead. Once trained, the parameters are supplied to a SVM which will label each parameter combination as being "usable" or "not" for the stochastic queuing model (in our case the $M/D/1$ and $M/M/1$ models) for which the SVM is trained.

Fig. 2. Word cloud depicting features used for machine learning process with the font size representing the significance of the feature as determined by [8].

A SVM is a method to separate a multi-dimensional set of data into two classes by a separating hyperplane. It works by maximizing the margin between the hyperplane and the support vectors closest to the plane. The theory behind these are covered by relevant texts on the subject [10,15]. An SVM labels an observation with a learned class label based on the solution to Eq. (1) [5,9] (the dual form is given, $\mathbf{e}$ is a vector of ones of length l, Q is an $l \times l$ matrix defined by $Q_{i,j} \leftarrow y_i y_j K(x_i, x_j)$ K is a kernel function, specific symbolic names match those of [6]). A common parameter selected to optimize the performance of the SVM is the penalty parameter, C, discussed further in Sect. 2.2.

$$\min_{\boldsymbol{\alpha}} \quad \tfrac{1}{2}\boldsymbol{\alpha}^T \mathbf{Q}\boldsymbol{\alpha} - \mathbf{e}^T \boldsymbol{\alpha}$$
$$\text{subject to} \quad 0 \leq \alpha_i \leq C, i = 1, \ldots, l, \tag{1}$$

$$K(x,y) = e^{-\gamma \|x-y\|^2}, y > 0. \tag{2}$$

A Radial Basis Function (RBF, [13], Eq. (2)) is used to map attributes to features. The parameter γ is optimized separately in order to maximize the performance of the SVM/Kernel combination. This work does not seek to add new techniques to SVM or machine learning theory, rather it is focused on expanding the application of SVMs to judging the reliability of stochastic performance models for streaming systems.

The stochastic mean queue occupancy models under consideration by our SVM are intended for systems at steady state. We apply these models to non-steady state applications with steady state behavior over small periods of time (i.e., they have multi-phase distributions). Applications whose behavior is too erratic to have any steady state behavior over any period of time are not good candidates for these models or our method. When testing the SVM we will test with applications that do exhibit steady state behavior and we discuss how this changes for applications whose distributions are more variable. Architectural features of a specific platform such as cache size are used as features for this work. As such we assume that we can find them either via literature search or directly by querying the hardware. Platforms where this information is unknown are avoided, however a surfeit of such platforms exists (see Table 1).

Implicit within most stochastic queueing models (save for the circumstance of a deterministic queue) is that $\rho < 1$ to obtain a finite queue. In this work, it is expected that the SVM should be able to find this relationship based upon the training process. It is shown in Sect. 3 that this is indeed the case. If deciding on a queueing model were as simple as selecting one class for $\rho \geq 1$ and another for $\rho < 1$ then the method described in this paper would be relatively inconsequential. However we also assume that the SVM is not explicitly told what the actual service process distributions are of the compute kernels modulating data arrival and service so this relationship is not quite so binary. It is also shown in the results that training the SVM with broader distributions slightly decreases the overall classification accuracy while increasing the generalizability of the trained SVM.

In order to train and test the SVM we use a set of micro-benchmark and full benchmark streaming applications (described below). All are authored using the RaftLib library in C++ and compiled using g++ using the -O1 optimization flag.

A micro-benchmark (with the topology shown in Fig. 1) has the advantage of having a known underlying service distribution for both compute kernels A and B. A synthetic workload for each compute kernel is composed of a simple busy-wait loop whose looping is dependent on a random number generator (either Exponential, Gaussian, Deterministic, or a mixture of multiple random distributions are produced). Simple workloads similar to those used within the real applications also constitute up to 5 % of the micro-benchmark loop workloads. Data exiting the servers are limited to one 8-byte item per firing.

Dense matrix multiply ($C = AB$) is a staple of many computational tasks. Our implementation divides the operation into a series of dot-product operations. Matrix rows and columns are streamed to n parallel dot-product kernels (see Fig. 3 for the topology). The result is streamed to a reducer kernel (at right)

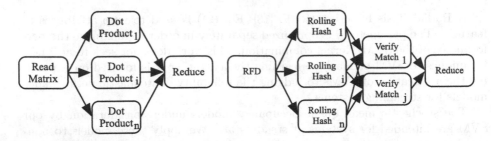

Fig. 3. Matrix multiply application (left image). The first kernel reads both matrices to be multiplied and streams the data to an arbitrary (n) number of dot product kernels. The final kernel reduces the input from the dot to a multiplied matrix. Rabin-Karp matching algorithm (right image). The first compute kernel (RFD, at left) reads the file to be searched, hashes the patterns to search and distributes the data to n "rolling-hash" kernel(s). Next are $j, j \leq n$ verification kernel(s) to guard against matches due to hash collision. The final kernel (at right) is a reducer which consolidates all the results.

which re-forms the output matrix, C. This application differs from the micro-benchmark in that it uses data read from disk and performs multiple operations on it. As with the micro-benchmark, it has the advantage of having a continuous output stream from both the matrix read and dot-product operations. The data set used is a single matrix (10000×10000) of single precision floating point numbers produced by a uniform random number generator.

The Rabin-Karp [12] algorithm is classically used to search a text for a set of patterns. The implementation divides the text amongst n parallel rolling-hash functions whose output is streamed to j parallel verification kernels. The final kernel simply reduces the output from the verification kernel(s), returning the byte position of each match (see Fig. 3). The data set for our tests is 2 GB of the phrase "foobar."

2.1   Data Collection and Hardware

Using benchmarking the applications enumerated above, we were able to collect a variety of features from each platform using a myriad of methods ranging from system calls through architecture-specific methods. Service rate is also used, which is approximated online via methods [3]. The number of features utilized prohibit their complete enumeration, however some of the more pertinent ones include: service rate, instruction set architecture, cache hierarchy sizes, operating system (OS) and version, scheduler, and main memory available (further enumerated in Fig. 2).

To collect mean queue occupancy, a separate monitor thread is used for each queue to sample the occupancy over the course of the application. For both real and synthetic applications, the service times of compute kernels are verified via monitoring the arrival and departure rate of data from each kernel with a non-blocking infinite queue (implemented by ignoring the read and write pointers).

All timing is performed using the POSIX.1–2001 `clock_gettime()` function with a real time system clock using the setup described in [2].

Relying on measurements from only one hardware type or operating system would undoubtedly bias any classification algorithm. To reduce the chance of bias for one particular platform, empirical data are collected from platforms with the processors and operating systems listed in Table 1. For all tests either the Linux or Apple OS X versions of the completely fair scheduler are used. To unbias the results further, task parallel sections of each application are replicated varying numbers of times (up to $2x$ the number of physical processor cores available). Application kernels are run "un-pinned." That is, the compute core which each executes on is assigned by the operating system and not by the user. Presumably more stable results could be obtained by "pinning" each compute kernel to dedicated cores, however this is not a realistic environment for many platforms. Micro-benchmark data are collected from all of the platforms in Table 1, Matrix multiply and Rabin-Karp Search data are collected from platforms 2, 8, 10, and 15.

In all, approximately 45,000 observations were made for the micro-benchmark application. This data is divided using a uniform random process into two sets with a 20/80 split. The set with 20 % of the data is used for training the SVM and the 80 % is set aside as a testing set. To give an idea of the range with which the SVM is trained, the micro-benchmark training set has the following specifications: approximately 8,200 observations, server utilization ranges from close to zero to greater than one and distributions vary widely (a randomized mix of Gaussian, Deterministic and the model's expected Exponential Distribution as well as some mixture distributions). For each of the other two applications, the SVM trained exclusively on the training micro-benchmark data (same training set as above) is used, with classification results reported in Sect. 3.

2.2 SVM and Training

Before the SVM can be trained as to which set of attributes to assign to a class, a label must be provided. Our two classes are "use" and "don't use" which are encoded as a binary one and zero respectively. The SVM is trained to identify one stochastic model at a time (i.e., either "use" or "don't use" for $M/M/1$ or $M/D/1$ but not both at the same time). In order to label the dataset as to which queueing model to use, a fixed difference is used. If the actual observed queue occupancy is within $n \leftarrow 5$ items, then the model is deemed acceptable otherwise false. A percentage based function for l shows a similar trend. After sampled mean queue occupancy is used for labeling purposes, it is removed from the data set presented to the SVM.

Feature selection is a very hot topic of research [11]. There are several methods that could be used including (but not limited to) Pearson correlation coefficients, Fisher information criterion score [8], Kolmogorov-Smirnov statistic [7]. Our selected feature set has a total of 35 linearly independent variables. The rest of the features exhibit weak non-linear dependence between variables. Extensive cross-validation followed by evaluating the Fisher information criterion score

Table 1. Summary of processor types and operating systems used for both the micro-benchmark and application data collection.

Platform	Processor type	OS	Kernel version
P_1	Intel Xeon CPU E5-2650	Linux	2.6.32
P_2	Quad-Core AMD Opteron 2376	Linux	2.6.32
P_3	Intel Xeon X5472	Darwin (OS X)	13.1.0
P_4	Dual-Core AMD Opteron 2218	Linux	2.6.32
P_5	ARM1176JZF-S	Linux	3.10.37
P_6	Dual-Core AMD Opteron 2222 SE	Linux	3.0.27
P_7	IBM Power PC 970	Linux	3.13.0
P_8	Six-Core AMD Opteron 2431	Linux	3.0.27
P_9	Intel Xeon E5345	Linux	2.6.32
P_{10}	Intel Xeon CPU E3-1225	Linux	3.13.9
P_{11}	Dual Core AMD Opteron 875	Linux	2.6.32
P_{12}	AMD Opteron 6136	Linux	2.6.32
P_{13}	ARM Cortex-A9	Linux	3.3.0
P_{14}	Intel Core i5 M540	Darwin (OS X)	13.1.0
P_{15}	AMD Opteron 6272	Linux	2.6.32
P_{16}	Six-Core AMD Opteron 2435	Linux	3.0.27
P_{17}	Dual Core AMD Opteron 280	Linux	2.6.32
P_{18}	Quad-Core AMD Opteron 2387	Linux	2.6.32
P_{19}	Dual-Core AMD Opteron 2220	Linux	2.6.32
P_{20}	Dual-Core AMD Opteron 8214	Linux	2.6.32

showed that the training data relied extensively on 67 of our candidate features. Most notably the variables that indicated the type of processor, operating system kernel version and cache size ranked highest followed closely by amount of main memory and total number of processes on the system. During the training phase we noted that despite the Fisher information criteria results, the additional 9 features provided a significant increase in correct classification, therefore we decided to include all 76 as opposed to the reduced set selected via statistical feature selection.

For all data sets (and all attributes contained in each set) the values are linearly scaled in the range $[-1000, 1000]$ (see [14]). This causes a slight loss of information, however it does prevent extreme values from biasing the training process and reduces the precision necessary for the representation. Once all the data are scaled, there are a few SVM specific parameters that must be optimized in order to maximize classification performance (γ and C). We use a branch and bound search for the best parameters for both the RBF Kernel ($\gamma \leftarrow 4$) and for the penalty parameter ($C \leftarrow 32768$). The branch and bound search is performed by training and cross-validating the SVM using various values of γ and C for the training data set discussed above. The SVM framework utilized in this work is sourced from LIBSVM [6].

3   Results

To evaluate how effective a SVM is for model reliability classification we'll compare the class label predicted by the SVM compared to that of ground truth as determined by the labeling process. If the queueing model is usable and the predicted class is "use" then we have a true positive (TP). Consequently the rest of the error types true negative (TN), false positive (FP) and false negative (FN) follow this pattern.

The micro-benchmark data ($\text{Micro}_{\text{test}}$) consists of queues whose servers have widely varying distributions and server utilizations. Utilization ranges from close to zero through greater than one (i.e., the queues are always full). As enumerated in Fig. 4, the SVM correctly predicts (TP or TN) 88.1 % of the test instances for the $M/M/1$ model and 83.4 % for the $M/D/1$ model. Overall these results are quite good compared to manual selection [1]. Not only do these results improve upon manual mean queue occupancy predictions, they are actually faster since the user doesn't have to evaluate the service time and arrival process distributions, and they can be done online while the application is executing.

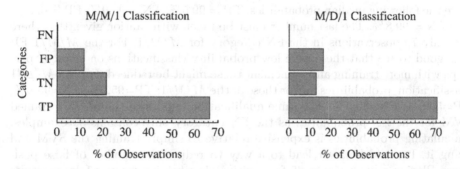

Fig. 4. Summary of overall classification rate by error category. In general the correct classification is quite high $TP + TN > 83 \%$ in all cases.

Server utilization (ρ) is a classic and simple test to divine if a mean queue length model is suitable. At high ρ it is assumed that the $M/M/1$ and $M/D/1$ models can diverge widely from reality. It is therefore assumed that our SVM should be able to discern this intuition from its training without being given the logic via human intervention. Figure 5 shows a box and whisker plot for the error types separated by ρ. As expected the middle ρ ranges offer the most true positive results. Also expected is the correlation between high ρ and true negatives. Slightly unexpected was the relationship between ρ and false positives.

M/M/1 Classification

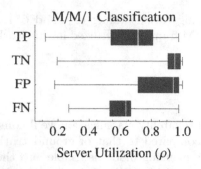

M/D/1 Classification

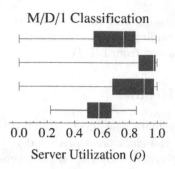

Fig. 5. Summary of true positive (TP), true negative (TN), false positive (FP), false negative (FN) classifications for the $M/M/1$ (left) and $M/D/1$ (right) queueing models for the microbenchmark's single queue by server utilization ρ demonstrating empirically that the SVM can recognize the instability of these models at high ρ.

Directly addressing the performance and confidence of the SVM is the probability of class assignment. Given the high numbers of TP and TN it would be useful to know how confident the SVM is in placing each of these feature sets into a category. Probability estimates are not directly provided by the SVM, however there are a variety of methods which can generate a probability of class assignment [16]. We use the median class assignment probability for each error category as it is a bit more robust to outliers than the mean. For the $M/M/1$ model we have the following median probabilities: TP = 99.5 %, TN = 99.9 %, FP = 62.4 % and FN = 99.8 %. The last number must be taken with caution given that there are only 79 observations in the FN category for $M/M/1$. For the $M/M/1$ FP it is good to see that these were low probability classifications on average, perhaps with more training and refinement these might be reduced. For the $M/D/1$ classification, probabilities mirror those of the $M/M/1$: TP=95.9 %, TN=95.8 %, FP=50.9 %, FN=85.3 %. The same qualification applies to the $M/D/1$ trained SVM for the FN probabilities as the FN category only contains 39 examples. Calculating probabilities is expensive relative to simply training the SVM and using it. It could however lead to a way to reduce the number of false positives. Placing a limit of $p = .65$ for positive classification reduces false positives by an additional 95 % for the micro-benchmark data. Post processing based on probability has the benefit of moving this method from slightly conservative to very conservative if high precision is required, albeit at a slight increase in computational cost.

The full application results are consistent with those of the micro-benchmark applications. Each application is run with a varying number of compute kernels with its queue occupancies sampled as described in Sect. 2.1. Table 2 breaks the application results into categories by model and application. Due to the processor configuration and high data rates with this application all examples are tested with a high server utilization. One trend that is not surprising is the lack of true positives within Table 2. The application as designed has very high throughput, consequently all servers are highly utilized. In these cases (ρ close to 1), it is expected that neither of these models is usable. As is the case for the micro-benchmark data, the overall correct classification rates are high for both applications and models tested.

Table 2. % SVM classification rate for application data.

Application	Model	TP	TN	FP	FN	Correct classification
Matrix multiply	$M/M/1$	17.1%	75.2%	5.4%	2.4%	92.3%
Matrix multiply	$M/D/1$	5.4%	83.9%	4.6%	6.1%	89.3%
Rabin-Karp	$M/M/1$	0.0%	86.0%	14.0%	0.0%	86.0%
Rabin-Karp	$M/D/1$	0.0%	87.4%	12.6%	0.0%	87.4%

One potential pitfall of this method is the training process. What would happen if the model is trained with too few distributions and configurations. To test this a set of the training data from a single distribution (the Exponential) is labeled in order to train another SVM explicitly for the $M/M/1$ model. We then apply this to two differing test sets. The first is data drawn from an exponential distribution and the second is data drawn from many distributions (training data is excluded from all test sets). The resulting classification rates are shown in Table 3. Two trends are apparent: specifically training with a single distribution increases the accuracy when attempting to classify for only the distribution for which the model was trained, and conversely lack of training diversity increases the frequency of false positives when attempting use the SVM to classify models with distributional assumptions that it have not been trained for. Unlike the false positives seen in prior sets, these are high confidence predictions that post processing for classification probability will not significantly improve. One thing is clear, training with as many service rate distributions as possible and as many configurations tends to improve the generalizability of the SVM for our application.

Table 3. % for SVM predictions with SVM trained only with servers having an exponential distribution and tested as indicated.

Dist	# obs	Model	TP	TN	FP	FN	Correct classification
Exp.	3249	$M/M/1$	53.0%	31.2%	15.7%	0.1%	84.2%
Many	6297	$M/M/1$	55.8%	0.0%	44.2%	0.0%	55.8%

Our method is currently only applicable to queues with sufficient steady state behavior. To show what happens when a local steady state is not reached we will use the Rabin-Karp string searching kernel and change the packet to be extremely large proportionate to the size of the data set. This results in fewer data packets sent from the source kernel to the "rolling-hash" kernel and no steady state. The resulting observed queue occupancies are much lower than what is calculated by either queueing model. Applying an $M/M/1$ mean queue occupancy model to this application will still result in a queue which is sized for the mean potential occupancy. Table 4 shows the result of attempting to evaluate the SVM against a queue that has not reached steady state. As a consequence of the streaming streaming service rate approximation method, it is knowable when the application has reached at least a local steady state and this condition can generally be avoided.

Table 4. % for SVM evaluated against a Rabin-Karp string search algorithm that has not reached steady state.

Model	#obs	TP	TN	FP	FN	Correct classification
$M/M/1$	120	21.6 %	41.5 %	20.7 %	16.2 %	63.1 %
$M/D/1$	120	11.1 %	44.4 %	44.4 %	0.0 %	55.5 %

4 Conclusions and Future Work

We have shown a proof of concept for using a SVM to classify a stochastic queuing model's reliability for a particular queue within a streaming application that is usable online. This enables fast online modeling and re-optimization of stream processing systems. Across multiple hardware types, operating systems, and applications it has been shown to produce fairly good reliability estimates for both the $M/M/1$ and $M/D/1$ stochastic queueing models.

This work chose to ignore the actual distribution of each compute kernel. What would happen if we knew the underlying distribution of the service and arrival process for each compute kernel in the system? Manually determining the distributions of each compute kernel and retraining the SVM with this knowledge for the $M/M/1$ model we arrive at a 96.6 % correct classification rate. This works just as well for the $M/D/1$ model where we observed 96.4 % of the queues being correctly classified as either "use" or "don't use." One obvious path for future work is faster and lower overhead process distribution estimation. Mathematically this can be done with the method of moments, what is left is an engineering challenge.

Empirical data could also be seen as a weakness of our approach since it is obviously finite in its coverage of the combinatorial plethora of possible configurations. We trained our SVM using as wide a variety of configurations as possible, however the permutations of possible application configurations are quite high. Other combinations of applications could provide slightly differing results. Our choices of attributes is limited to what the hardware and operating system could provide. Omniscient knowledge of the system would obviously be helpful, it is possible that future platforms will provide more robust identification and monitoring features which could improve the training and classification process.

In conclusion we have demonstrated an automated way to classify the reliability of stochastic queueing models for streaming systems. We have shown that it can be done, and that in many cases it works quite well for the applications and configurations tested. There are several avenues for future work to improve upon what is demonstrated here ranging from improved instrumentation to improved kernel functions.

References

1. Beard, J.C., Chamberlain, R.D.: Analysis of a simple approach to modeling performance for streaming data applications. In: Proceedings of IEEE International Symposium on Modelling, Analysis and Simulation of Computer and Telecommunication Systems, August 2013, pp. 345–349 (2013)
2. Beard, J.C., Chamberlain, R.D.: Use of a levy distribution for modeling best case execution time variation. In: Horváth, A., Wolter, K. (eds.) EPEW 2014. LNCS, vol. 8721, pp. 74–88. Springer, Heidelberg (2014)
3. Beard, J.C., Chamberlain, R.D.: Run time approximation of non-blocking service rates for streaming systems. arXiv preprint (2015). arXiv:1504.00591v2
4. Beard, J.C., Li, P., Chamberlain, R.D.: RaftLib: a C++ template library for high performance stream parallel processing. In: Proceedings of 6th International Workshop on Programming Models and Applications for Multicores and Manycores, February 2015, pp. 96–105 (2015)
5. Boser, B.E., Guyon, I.M., Vapnik, V.N.: A training algorithm for optimal margin classifiers. In: Proceedings of 5th Workshop on Computational Learning Theory, pp. 144–152 (1992)
6. Chang, C.C., Lin, C.J.: LIBSVM: a library for support vector machines. ACM Trans. Intell. Syst. Technol. **2**, 27:1–27:27 (2011)
7. Chapelle, O., Vapnik, V., Bousquet, O., Mukherjee, S.: Choosing multiple parameters for support vector machines. Mach. Learn. **46**(1–3), 131–159 (2002)
8. Chen, Y.W., Lin, C.J.: Combining SVMs with various feature selection strategies. In: Guyon, I., Nikravesh, M., Gunn, S., Zadeh, L.A. (eds.) Feature Extraction, pp. 315–324. Springer, Heidelberg (2006)
9. Cortes, C., Vapnik, V.: Support-vector networks. Mach. Learn. **20**(3), 273–297 (1995)
10. Cristianini, N., Shawe-Taylor, J.: An Introduction to Support Vector Machines and Other Kernel-based Learning Methods. Cambridge University Press, Cambridge, UK (2000)
11. Guyon, I., Elisseeff, A.: An introduction to variable and feature selection. J. Mach. Learn. Res. **3**, 1157–1182 (2003)
12. Karp, R.M., Rabin, M.O.: Efficient randomized pattern-matching algorithms. IBM J. Res. Dev. **31**(2), 249–260 (1987)
13. Schölkopf, B., Smola, A.J.: Learning with Kernels: Support Vector Machines, Regularization, Optimization, and Beyond. MIT Press, Cambridge, MA (2002)
14. Tax, D.M., Duin, R.P.: Support vector data description. Mach. Learn. **54**(1), 45–66 (2004)
15. Vapnik, V.N., Vapnik, V.: Statistical Learning Theory, vol. 2. Wiley, New York (1998)
16. Wu, T.F., Lin, C.J., Weng, R.C.: Probability estimates for multi-class classification by pairwise coupling. J. Mach. Learn. Res. **5**, 975–1005 (2004)

Scheduling and Load Balancing

A Duplicate-Free State-Space Model for Optimal Task Scheduling

Michael Orr[✉] and Oliver Sinnen

Department of Electrical and Computer Engineering, University of Auckland,
Auckland, New Zealand
morr010@aucklanduni.ac.nz

Abstract. The problem of task scheduling with communication delays $(P|prec, c_{ij}|C_{\max})$ is NP-hard, and therefore solutions are often found using a heuristic method. However, an optimal schedule can be very useful in applications such as time critical systems, or as a baseline for the evaluation of heuristics. Branch-and-bound algorithms such as A* have previously been shown to be a promising approach to the optimal solving of this problem, using a state-space model which we refer to as exhaustive list scheduling. However, this model suffers from the possibility of producing high numbers of duplicate states. In this paper we define a new state-space model in which we divide the problem into two distinct subproblems: first we decide the allocations of all tasks to processors, and then we order the tasks on their allocated processors to produce a complete schedule. This two-phase state-space model offers no potential for the production of duplicates. An empirical evaluation shows that the use of this new state-space model leads to a marked reduction in the number of states considered by an A* search in many cases, particularly for task graphs with a high communication-to-computation ratio. With additional refinement, and the development of specialised pruning techniques, the performance of this state-space model could be improved.

1 Introduction

In order to use the full potential of a multiprocessor system in speeding up task execution, efficient schedules are required. In this work, we address the classic problem of task scheduling with communication delays, known as $P|prec, c_{ij}|C_{\max}$ using the $\alpha|\beta|\gamma$ notation [11]. The problem involves a set of tasks, with associated precedence constraints and communication delays, which must be scheduled such that the overall finish time (schedule length) is minimised. The optimal solving of this problem is well known to be NP-hard [7], so that the amount of work required grows exponentially as the number of tasks is increased. For this reason, many heuristic approaches have been developed, trading solution quality for reduced computation time [3,5,9,12]. Unfortunately, the relative quality of these approximate solutions cannot be guaranteed, as no α-approximation scheme for the problem is known [2].

Although the NP-hardness of the problem usually discourages optimal solving, an optimal schedule can give a significant advantage in time critical systems

© Springer-Verlag Berlin Heidelberg 2015
J.L. Träff et al. (Eds.): Euro-Par 2015, LNCS 9233, pp. 97–108, 2015.
DOI: 10.1007/978-3-662-48096-0_8

or applications where a single schedule is reused many times. Optimal solutions are also necessary in order to evaluate the effectiveness of a heuristic scheduling method. Branch-and-bound algorithms have previously shown promise in efficiently finding optimal solutions to this problem [8], but the state-space model used, exhaustive list scheduling (ELS), was prone to the production of duplicate states. This paper presents a new state-space model, in which the task scheduling problem is tackled in two distinct phases: first allocation, and then ordering. The two-phase state-space model (abbreviated AO) does not allow for the possibility of duplicate states.

In Sect. 2, background information is given, including an explanation of the task scheduling model, an overview of branch-and-bound algorithms, and a description of the ELS model. Section 3 describes the new AO model, and how a branch-and-bound search is conducted through it. Section 4 explains how the new model was evaluated by comparison with the old one, and presents the results. Finally, Sect. 5 gives the conclusions of the paper and outlines possible further avenues of study.

2   Background

2.1   Task Scheduling Model

The specific problem that we address here is the scheduling of a task graph $G = \{V, E, w, c\}$ on a set of processors P. G is a directed acyclic graph wherein each node $n \in V$ represents a task, and each edge $e_{ij} \in E$ represents a required communication from task n_i to task n_j. The computation cost of a task $n \in V$ is given by its positive weight $w(n)$, and the communication cost of an edge $e_{ij} \in E$ is given by the non-negative weight $c(e_{ij})$. The target parallel system for our schedule consists of a finite number of homogeneous processors, represented by P. Each processor is dedicated, meaning that no executing task may be preempted. We assume a fully connected communication subsystem, such that each pair of processors $p_i, p_j \in P$ is connected by an identical communication link. Communications are performed concurrently and without contention. Local communication (from p_i to p_i) has zero cost.

Our aim is to produce a schedule $S = \{proc, t_s\}$, where $proc(n)$ allocates the task to a processor in P, and $t_s(n)$ assigns it a start time on this processor. For a schedule to be valid, it must fulfill two conditions for all tasks in G. The Processor Constraint requires that only one task is executed by a processor at any one time. The Precedence Constraint requires that a task n may only be executed once all of its predecessors have finished execution, and all required data has been communicated to $proc(n)$. The goal of optimal task scheduling is to find such a schedule S for which the total execution time or schedule length $sl(S)$ is the lowest possible.

It is useful to define the concept of node levels for a task graph [9]. For a task n, the top level $tl(n)$ is the length of the longest path in the task graph that ends with n. This does not include the weight of n, or any communication costs.

Similarly, the bottom level $bl(n)$ is the length of the longest path beginning with n, excluding communication costs. The weight of n is included in $bl(n)$.

2.2 Branch-and-Bound

The term branch-and-bound refers to a family of search algorithms which are widely used for the solving of combinatorial optimisation problems. They do this by implicitly enumerating all solutions to a problem, simultaneously finding an optimal solution and proving its optimality [1]. A search tree is constructed in which each node (usually referred to as a state) represents a partial solution to the problem. From the partial solution represented by a state s, some set of operations is applied to produce new partial solutions which are closer to a complete solution. In this way we define the children of s, and thereby *branch*. Each state must also be *bounded*: we evaluate each state s using a cost function f, such that $f(s)$ is a lower bound on the cost of any solution that can be reached from s. Using these bounds, we can guide our search away from unpromising partial solutions and therefore remove large subsets of the potential solutions from the need to be fully examined.

A* is a particularly popular variant of branch-and-bound which uses a best-first search approach [4]. A* has the interesting property that it is optimally efficient; using the same cost function f, no search algorithm could find an optimal solution while examining fewer states. To achieve this property, it is necessary that the cost function f provides an underestimate. That is, it must be the case that $f(s) \leq f^*(s)$, where $f^*(s)$ is the true lowest cost of a complete solution in the subtree rooted at s. A cost function with this property is said to be *admissable*.

2.3 Exhaustive List Scheduling

Previous branch-and-bound approaches to optimal task scheduling have used a state-space model that is inspired by list scheduling algorithms [8]. States are partial schedules in which some subset of the tasks in the problem instance have been assigned to a processor and given a start time. At each branching step, successors are created by putting every possible ready task (tasks for which all parents are already scheduled) on every possible processor at the earliest possible start time. In this way, the search space demonstrates every possible sequence of decisions that a list scheduling algorithm could make. This branch-and-bound strategy can therefore be described as exhaustive list scheduling.

Branch-and-bound works most efficiently when the subtrees produced when branching are entirely disjoint. Another way of stating this is that there is only one possible path from the root of the tree to any given state, and therefore there is only one way in which a search can create this state. When this is not the case, a large amount of work can be wasted: the same state could be expanded, and its subtree subsequently explored, mulitple times. Avoiding this requires doing work to detect duplicate states, such as keeping a set of already created states with which all new states must be compared. This process increases the algorithm's need for both time and memory.

Unfortunately, the ELS strategy creates a lot of potential for duplicated states [10]. This stems from two main sources: firstly, since the processors are homogeneous, any permutation of the processors in a schedule represents an entirely equivalent schedule. This means that for each truly unique complete schedule, there will be $|P|!$ equivalent complete schedules in the state space. This makes it very important to use some strategy of processor normalisation when branching, such that these equivalent states cannot be produced. The other source of duplicate states is more difficult to deal with. When tasks are independent of each other, the order in which they are selected for scheduling can be changed without affecting the resulting schedule. This means there is more than one path to the corresponding state, and therefore a potential duplicate. The only way to avoid these duplicates is to enforce a particular sequence onto these scheduling decisions. Under the ELS strategy, however, no method is apparent in which this could be achieved while also allowing all possible legitimate schedules to be produced.

3　Duplicate-Free State-Space Model

Both sources of duplicate states can be eliminated by adopting a new state-space model (AO), in which the two dimensions of task scheduling are dealt with separately. Rather than making all decisions about a task's placement simultaneously, the search proceeds in two stages. In the first stage, we decide for each task the processor to which it will be assigned. We refer to this as the allocation phase. The second stage of the search, beginning after all tasks are allocated, decides the start times of each task. Given that each processor has a known set of tasks allocated to it, this is equivalent to deciding on an ordering for each set. Therefore, we refer to this as the ordering phase. Once the allocation phase has determined the tasks' positions in space, and the ordering phase has determined the tasks' positions in time, a complete schedule is produced. Essentially, we divide the problem of task scheduling into two distinct subproblems, each of which can be solved separately using distinct methods.

3.1　Allocation

In the allocation phase, we wish to allocate each task to a processor. Since the processors in our task scheduling problem are homogeneous, the exact processor on which a task is placed is unimportant. What matters is the way the tasks are grouped on the processors. The problem of task allocation is therefore equivalent to the problem of producing a partition of a set. A partition of a set X is a set of non-overlapping subsets of X, such that the union of the subsets is equal to X. In other words, the set of all partitions of X represents all possible ways of grouping the elements of X. Applying this to our task scheduling problem, we find all possible ways in which tasks could be grouped on processors. In the allocation phase, we are therefore searching for an optimal partition of the set V, consisting of all tasks in our task graph. The search is conducted by constructing a series of partial partitions of V. A partial partition A of V is defined as a partition of a set V', $V' \subset V$ [6]. At each level of the search we expand the subset V' by adding one additional task, until $V' = V$ and all tasks are allocated. At each stage, the task n selected can be placed into any existing set $a \in A$, or alternatively, a new set can be added to A containing only n.

A search using this method has the potential to produce every possible partition of V, and there is only one possible path to each partition. In this way, we remove the first source of duplicates: there is no possibility of producing allocations that differ from each other only by the permutation of processors. If we are allocating tasks to a finite number of processors, we simply limit the number of sets allowed in a partial partition to the same number. This has no effect other than to reduce the search space by disregarding partitions consisting of a larger number of sets (Fig. 1).

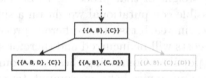

Fig. 1. Branching in the allocation state-space with a maximum of two processors

Allocation Heuristic. In order to guide our branch-and-bound search towards an optimal partition, we need a heuristic by which to determine f-values for each state s. In the case of allocation, there are two crucial types of information we can obtain from a partial partition A which allow us to determine a lower bound for the length of a resulting schedule. The first, and simplest, is the total computational weight of the tasks in each grouping. Even without waiting for communication, each processor must take at least the sum of the computation times of its assigned tasks to finish. The length of the overall schedule must therefore be at least as long as the time needed for the most heavily loaded processor to perform its computations:

$$f_{load}(s) = \max_{a \in A} \left\{ \sum_{n \in a} w(n) \right\}$$

The second bound derives from our knowledge of which communication costs must be incurred, and is obtained from the length of the allocated critical path of the task graph; that is, the longest path through the task graph given the particular set of allocations. The critical path as calculated only includes the weights of edges for which both tasks have been allocated. If two tasks are allocated to the same processor, an edge between them is considered to have a length of zero and does not extend the critical path. However, if they are allocated to different processors, the communication cost is incurred and the length of the critical path may increase. The allocated critical path represents the longest sequence of computations and communications that we know must occur given this allocation. Therefore, again, the resulting schedule must be at least as long:

$$f_{\text{acp}}(s) = \max_{n \in V'} \{tl_a(n) + bl(n)\}$$

Since we want the tightest bound possible, the maximum of these two bounds is taken as the final f-value:

$$f_{\text{alloc}}(s) = \max\{f_{\text{load}}(s), f_{\text{acp}}(s)\}$$

By their nature, these two bounds oppose each other; lowering one is likely to increase the other. The shortest possible allocated critical path can be trivially obtained simply by allocating all tasks to the same processor, but this will cause the total computational weight of that processor to be the maximum possible. Likewise, the lowest possible computational weight on a single processor can be achieved simply by allocating each task to a different processor, but this means that all communication costs will be incurred and therefore the allocated critical path will be the longest possible. Combining these two bounds guides the search to find the best possible compromise between computational load-balancing and the elimination of communication costs.

3.2   Ordering

In the ordering phase, we begin with a complete allocation, and our aim is to produce a complete schedule S. After giving an arbitrary ordering to both the sets in A and the processors in P, we can define the processor allocation in S such that $n \in a_i \implies proc(n) = p_i$. Our remaining task is to determine the optimal start time for each task. Given a particular ordering of the tasks $n \in p_i$, the best start time for each task is trivial to obtain, as it is simply the earliest it is possible for that task to start. To complete our schedule we therefore only need to determine an ordering for each set of tasks $p_i \in P$. Our search could proceed by enumerating all possible permutations of the tasks within their processors.However, it is likely that many of the possible permutations do not describe a valid schedule. This will occur if any task is placed in order after one of its descendants (or before one of its ancestors).

In order to produce only valid orderings, an approach inspired by list scheduling is taken. In this variant, however, each processor p_i is considered separately, with a local ready list $R(p_i)$. Initially, a task $n \in p_i$ is said to be locally ready if it has no predecessors also on p_i. At each step we can select a task $n \in R(p_i)$ and place it next in order on p_i. Those tasks which have been selected and placed in order are called *ordered,* while those which have not are called *unordered.* In general, a task $n \in p_i$ belongs to $R(p_i)$ if it has no unordered predecessors also on p_i. After a task n has been ordered, each of its descendants on p_i must be checked to see if this condition has now been met, in which case they will be added to $R(p_i)$. Following this process to the end, we can produce any possible valid ordering of the tasks on p_i.

Producing a full schedule requires that this process be completed for all processors in P. At each level of the search, we can select a processor $p_i \in P$ and order one of its tasks. The order in which processors are selected can be decided arbitrarily; however, in order to avoid duplication, it must be fixed by some scheme such that the processor selected can be determined solely by the depth of the current state. The simplest method to achieve this is to proceed through the processors in order: first order all the tasks on p_1, then all the tasks on p_2, and so on to p_n. Another method is to alternate between the processors in a round-robin fashion. Unlike in exhaustive list scheduling, tasks are not guaranteed to be placed into the schedule in topological order. When a task is ordered, its predecessors on other processors may still be unordered, and therefore their start times may not be known. During the ordering process, therefore, a task n may only be given an *estimated earliest start time* $eest(n)$. For all unordered tasks, $eest(n) = tl_a(n)$. For ordered tasks, we first define $prev(n)$ as the task ordered immediately before n. We also define the estimated data ready time $edrt(n_j) = max_{n_i \in parents(n_j)} \{eest(n_i) + w(n_i) + c(e_{ij})\}$. Where $prev(n)$ does not exist, $eest(n) = edrt(n)$. Otherwise, $eest(n) = max(eest(prev(n)) + w(prev(n)), edrt(n))$.

In this way, we have solved the problem of duplicates arising from making the same decisions in a different order. By allocating each task to a processor ahead of time, and enforcing a strict order on the processors, it is no longer possible for these situations to arise. Where before we might have placed task B on p_2 and then task A on p_1, we now must always place task A on p_1 and then task B on p_2. Unfortunately, in a small number of cases, the combination of valid local orders for all processors produces an overall schedule with an invalid global ordering. Consider a partial schedule as a graph in which there is a directed edge from each task to the one placed in order after it, and also where interprocessor communications occur. For invalid states, this graph will display a cycle. In our implementation, such states cause the f-value of a state to be increased indefinitely; they are therefore detected and removed from consideration once the f-value reaches an upper bound (e.g., the sequential schedule length).

Ordering Heuristic. The heuristic for determining f-values in the ordering stage follows a similar pattern to that for allocation. As we assign estimated start times to tasks, it is possible that we introduce idle time to a processor in which it will not be executing any task. The difference between the heuristics for allocation and ordering lies in the incorporation of these idle times. For each state s, the current estimated finish time of a processor p_i is the latest estimated finish time of any task $n \in p_i$ which has so far been ordered. This estimated finish time must include both the full computation time of each task already ordered on p_i, as well as any idle time incurred between tasks.

With this in mind, we define our two bounds like so: first, the latest estimated start time of any task already ordered, plus the allocated bottom level of that task. We refer to this as the partially scheduled critical path, as it corresponds to the allocated critical path through our task graph, but with the addition of the now known idle times:

$$f_{\mathrm{scp}}(s) = \max_{n \in ordered(s)} \{eest(n) + bl_{\mathrm{a}}(n)\}$$

Second, the latest finish time of any processor in the partial schedule, plus the total computational weight of all tasks allocated to that processor which are not yet scheduled:

$$f_{\mathrm{ordered-load}}(s) = \max_{p \in P} \left\{ t_{\mathrm{f}}(p) + \sum_{n \in p \cap unordered(s)} w(n) \right\}$$

Again, this corresponds to the total computational load on a processor with the addition of now known idle times. To obtain the tightest possible bound, the maximum of these bounds is taken as the final f-value:

$$f_{\mathrm{order}}(s) = \max\{f_{\mathrm{scp}}(s), f_{\mathrm{ordered-load}}(s)\}.$$

3.3   Combined State-Space

Solving a task scheduling problem instance requires both the allocation and ordering subproblems to be solved in conjunction. To produce a combined state-space, we begin with the allocation search tree, S_{A}. The leaves of this tree represent every possible distinct allocation of tasks in G to processors in P. Say that leaf l_i represents allocation a_i. We produce the ordering search tree S_{O_i} using a_i. The leaves of S_{O_i} represent every distinct complete schedule of G which is consistent with a_i. For each leaf l_{a_i}, we set the root of tree S_{O_i} as its child. The result is a tree S_{AO}, the leaves of which represent every distinct complete schedule of G on the processors in P (Fig. 2).

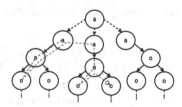

Fig. 2. A possible search path through the combined state space

A branch-and-bound search conducted on this state-space will begin by searching the allocation state-space. Each allocation state representing a complete allocation has one child state, which is an initial ordering state with this allocation. When considering the allocation subproblem in isolation, we define the optimal allocation as that which has the smallest possible lower bound on the length of a schedule resulting from it. Unfortunately, these lower bounds cannot be exact and therefore it is not guaranteed that the allocation with the smallest lower bound will actually produce the shortest possible schedule. This means that in the combined state-space, a number of complete allocations may be investigated by the search, having their possible orderings evaluated. The tighter the bound which can be calculated, the more quickly the search is likely to be guided toward a truly optimal allocation.

A search of this state-space model is theoretically able to benefit from several pruning techniques already developed for ELS. Namely, these are identical task pruning, equivalent schedule pruning, fixed order pruning and heuristic list scheduling [10].

4   Evaluation

4.1   Experimental Methodology

The AO model was evaluated empirically by comparison with ELS. The evaluation was performed by running branch-and-bound searches on a diverse set of task graphs using each state-space model. Task graphs were chosen that differed by the following attributes: graph structure, the number of tasks, and the communication-to-computation ratio (CCR). Almost 500 task graphs with unique combinations of these attributes were selected. An optimal schedule was found for each task graph using 2, 4, and 8 processors, once each for each state-space model. Searches were performed using the A* search algorithm. Pruning techniques were applied to each state-space model that could take advantage of them. Common to both state space models were identical task pruning, equivalent schedule pruning, and heuristic list scheduling. With ELS, additional pruning techniques were applied: processor normalisation, fixed order pruning, and the use of a closed list.

The implementations were built with the Java programming language. An existing implementation of ELS was used as the basis for an AO implementation, with code for common procedures shared wherever possible. Notably, the basic implementation of the A* search algorithm is shared, with the implementations differing only by how the children of a search node are created. The implementations of commonly applicable pruning techniques are also shared. All tests were run on a Linux (Ubuntu 12.04) machine with 64 processing cores and 256 GB of RAM. The Java environment was version 1.7, running on the OpenJDK 64-Bit Server JVM. Tests were single-threaded, so only one core was utilised by our code, but the JVM's concurrent garbage collector could potentially have benefited from all 64 cores. For all tests, the JVM was given a maximum heap size of 192 GB. A new JVM instance was started for every search, to minimise the possibility of previous searches influencing the performance of later searches due to garbage collection and JIT compilation.

The dependent variable measured was the number of states created in the course of a search. States created includes states which are removed from consideration immediately after their creation by pruning techniques. The number of states created by a search is considered as a more reliable metric for evaluating the performance of a search algorithm, as it can be made deterministic and relies only on the details of the algorithm itself. The time taken for a search to complete is extremely dependent on the environment in which the program is run, as it can vary greatly based on the processing speed of the hardware.

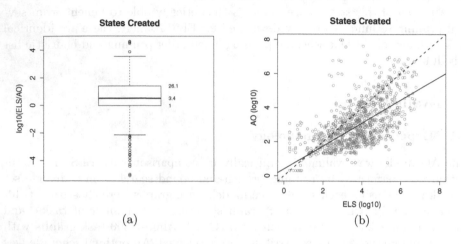

(a)   (b)

Fig. 3. Overall comparison between state-space models

4.2 Results

The overall results, presented in Fig. 3, show that AO performs better than ELS in the majority of cases. Data is displayed on a $\log_{10}$ scale both because of its extreme range, and so that positive (>1) and negative (<1) IFs have equal weighting on the axis. The improvement factor (IF) for a particular problem instance is determined by dividing a particular metric for a search with ELS by the same metric for a search with the AO model. Figure 3a shows that the lower quartile IF for the overall dataset was zero; AO performed better than ELS in roughly 75 % of cases. As indicated by the median, in roughly 50 % of cases AO performed at least 3.4 times better than ELS. At its best, the AO model led to a reduction in the number of states created by a factor of more than 10^4. On the other hand, at its worst, almost 10^5 times more states were created. In Fig. 3b we see a direct case-by-case comparison of the performance of the two models. The central dotted line represents equal performance. Cases above this line are those where AO performed worse, while those below are those where it performed better. The solid regression line shows the average improvement of AO increasing with the number of states created by ELS. This plot therefore shows us that cases where AO's performance was worse were more often smaller, less difficult problem instances. Of the variables surveyed, the one with the most dramatic impact on the relative performance of the state-space models was the communication-to-computation ratio. Figure 4 shows a clear trend towards better performance for the AO model as the CCR increases.

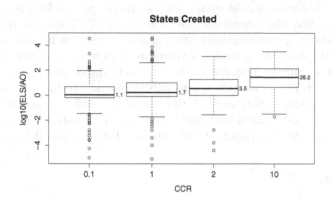

Fig. 4. Comparison by CCR

The results indicate that the new AO model is generally superior to the more mature ELS model, with an increased advantage in certain classes of scheduling problem. Most obviously, these are problems in which communication costs dominate and have a large influence on the optimal solution. By deciding the allocation of tasks first, a search using the AO model very quickly determines the entire set of communication costs which will be incurred. Allocations which incur very large communication costs are likely to be quickly ruled out, and knowledge of all the communication costs can be used in the calculation of f-values throughout the ordering stage. It is likely that ELS performed better on 25 % of cases, despite the duplicates, because the pruning techniques used were specifically developed for it and therefore benefited it much more. It may also be the case that the f-value calculations used by ELS provide tighter bounds than those so far developed for AO, in the case of low communication costs.

5   Conclusions

Previous attempts at optimal task scheduling through branch-and-bound methods have used a state-space model which we refer to as exhaustive list scheduling. This state-space model is limited by its high potential for producing duplicate states. In this paper, we have described a new state-space model which approaches the problem of task scheduling with communication delays in two distinct phases: allocation, and ordering. In the allocation phase, we assign each task to a processor by searching through all possible groupings of tasks. In the ordering phase, with an allocation already decided, we assign a start time to each task by investigating each possible ordering of the tasks on their processors. Using a priority ordering on processors, and thereby fixing the sequence in which independent tasks must be scheduled, we are able to avoid the production of any duplicate states.

An experimental evaluation shows that in roughly 75 % of problem instances, the new AO state-space model significantly outperforms the ELS model. This is most evident when scheduling task graphs with high CCRs, most likely because information about communication costs is able to be used earlier and more extensively. The AO state-space model is therefore a promising avenue for optimal task scheduling. Further research is likely to yield improvements to the heuristics used in each phase, as well as specialised pruning techniques which could greatly improve the performance of the model. In addition, a parallel search implementation using this model could have much potential, since the lack of duplicates eliminates the possibility of collisions between parallel searches.

References

1. Bundy, A., Wallen, L.: Branch-and-bound algorithms. In: Bundy, A., Wallen, L. (eds.) Catalogue of Artificial Intelligence Tools, pp. 12–12. Symbolic Computation, Heidelberg (1984)
2. Drozdowski, M.: Scheduling for Parallel Processing, 1st edn. Springer Publishing Company, Incorporated (2009)
3. Hagras, T., Janecek, J.: A high performance, low complexity algorithm for compile-time task scheduling in heterogeneous systems. Parallel Comput. **31**(7), 653–670 (2005)
4. Hart, P.E., Nilsson, N.J., Raphael, B.: A formal basis for the heuristic determination of minimum cost paths. IEEE Trans. Syst. Sci. Cybern. **4**(2), 100–107 (1968)
5. Hwang, J.J., Chow, Y.C., Anger, F.D., Lee, C.Y.: Scheduling precedence graphs in systems with interprocessor communication times. SIAM J. Comput. **18**(2), 244–257 (1989)
6. Ronse, C.: Closures on partial partitions from closures on sets. Math. Slovaca **63**(5), 959–978 (2013). http://dx.doi.org/10.2478/s12175-013-0147-9
7. Sarkar, V.: Partitioning and Scheduling Parallel Programs for Multiprocessors. MIT press, Cambridge (1989)
8. Shahul, A.Z.S., Sinnen, O.: Scheduling task graphs optimally with A*. J. Supercomputing **51**(3), 310–332 (2010)
9. Sinnen, O.: Task Scheduling for Parallel Systems (Wiley Series on Parallel and Distributed Computing). Wiley-Interscience, Hoboken (2007)
10. Sinnen, O.: Reducing the solution space of optimal task scheduling. Comput. Oper. Res. **43**, 201–214 (2014). http://www.sciencedirect.com/science/article/pii/S0305054813002542
11. Veltman, B., Lageweg, B., Lenstra, J.K.: Multiprocessor scheduling with communication delays. Parallel Comput. **16**(2), 173–182 (1990)
12. Yang, T., Gerasoulis, A.: List scheduling with and without communication delays. Parallel Comput. **19**(12), 1321–1344 (1993). http://www.sciencedirect.com/science/article/pii/016781919390079Z

On the Heterogeneity Bias of Cost Matrices When Assessing Scheduling Algorithms

Louis-Claude Canon[✉] and Laurent Philippe

FEMTO-ST/CNRS – Université de Franche-Comté/UBFC, 25000 Besançon, France
{louis-claude.canon,laurent.philippe}@univ-fcomte.fr

Abstract. Assessing the performance of scheduling heuristics through simulation requires to generate synthetic instances of tasks and machines with well-identified properties. Carefully controlling these properties is mandatory to avoid any bias. We consider the scheduling problem consisting of allocating independent sequential tasks on unrelated processors while minimizing the maximum execution time. In this problem, the instance is a cost matrix that specifies the execution cost of any task on any machine. This paper proposes a measure for quantifying the heterogeneity properties of a cost matrix. An analysis of two classical methods used in the literature reveals a bias in previous studies. A new method is proposed to generate instances with given heterogeneity properties and it is shown that they have a significant impact on several heuristics.

1 Introduction

Leveraging the parallelism of multi-core distributed platforms involves to efficiently schedule applications on several machines [19]. Current studies on performance evaluation can be divided into several categories: formal analysis, experiments, simulations, etc. In the case of simulations, a scheduling strategy is tested in a virtual environment with a given workload. Synthetic instances of workload allow a more general evaluation than specific traces. They are particularly useful for sensitivity analysis [21], which consists in assessing the impact of the instance properties on the algorithms. The lack of control on the instance properties, however, makes it difficult to confront the results of independent studies. For instance, although many papers have compared several scheduling heuristics [9,10,13,20], predicting their performance is still an issue. These problems can be tackled by carefully controlling the instance properties.

We consider the scheduling problem noted $R||C_{\max}$ in $\alpha|\beta|\gamma$ notation [17]. It consists in scheduling n independent sequential tasks on m unrelated machines to minimize the latest task completion time. All tasks are available simultaneously and preemption is not possible. The instance is a *cost matrix* where each element $e_{i,j} \in \mathbb{N}$ is the execution cost of task i on machine j.

This paper provides the following contributions[1]: a statistical description of the use of the range-based and CVB methods in the literature (Sect. 3); a study

---

[1] These results are also available in the companion research report [11].

© Springer-Verlag Berlin Heidelberg 2015
J.L. Träff et al. (Eds.): Euro-Par 2015, LNCS 9233, pp. 109–121, 2015.
DOI: 10.1007/978-3-662-48096-0_9

of how to quantify the heterogeneity properties of a cost matrix (Sect. 4); a formal analysis of the range-based and CVB methods and the identification of a bias that impacts several studies (Sect. 4); a new method with control over heterogeneity properties (Sect. 5); and, an assessment[2] of the impact of these properties on several heuristics (Sect. 6).

2   Related Work

The concept of heterogeneity was first introduced in the context of cost matrix by Armstrong [8]. He described the *heterogeneity quadrant* in which cost matrices are divided into four categories depending on their heterogeneity properties regarding tasks and processors: low/low, low/high, high/low, and high/high. However, no method for generating such matrices was proposed.

The range-based and CVB methods were proposed to fill this gap in [5] and then in [6,7]. However, task and machine heterogeneities were not formally defined and analyzed. The methods were assumed to generate matrices with the expected properties and only validated through some examples.

The limits of these methods were later acknowledged in [4], which proposed to consider the average coefficient of variation[3], skewness and kurtosis of the costs for each task and for each machine. The proposed scheme (based on decision trees) uses these additional information to predict heuristic performance. Despite a wide experimentation plan, the study lacks discussion and interpretation on the relative importance of the considered measures. Additionally, no formal analysis was provided. The exhibited decision trees suggest that the average coefficient of variation plays a significant role, which supports the current work.

The MPH (Machine Performance Homogeneity) is introduced in [3] for capturing the heterogeneity between the machines, while its counterpart for the tasks, the TDH (Task Difficulty Homogeneity), appears in [2]. We discuss them more extensively in Sect. 4. In addition, the TMA (Task-Machine Affinity) is also defined in [3]: it quantifies the specialisation of the system (i.e., whether some machines are particularly efficient for some specific tasks). Although the three measures are applied to a real benchmark, no method is proposed for generating matrices with given MPH, TDH and TMA.

Friese et al. [14] present a method for adding tasks in a given cost matrix while preserving some statistical properties on each column (mean, coefficient of variation, skewness and kurtosis). It ignores the properties on each row however.

A method for generating matrices with varying affinity (similar to the TMA) is proposed in [1]. Khemka et al. [18] propose a method for changing the TMA of an existing matrix while keeping the same MPH and TDS. TMA is mentioned to be related to the correlation. Investigating the correlation properties is left for future work. There is also another field of studies dedicated to the generation of matrices with given correlation and covariance matrices [15].

---

[2] Computations have been performed on the supercomputer facilities of the Mésocentre de calcul de Franche-Comté.

[3] Ratio of the standard deviation to the mean.

3   Matrix Generations Methods

3.1   Range-Based and CVB Methods

The most used methods for generating cost matrices are the range-based and the CVB (Coefficient of Variation Based) methods [5–7].

The range-based method generates n vectors of m values that follow a uniform distribution in the range $[1, R_{mach}]$. Each line is then multiplied by a random value that follows a uniform distribution in the range $[1, R_{task}]$.

The CVB method is based on the same principle except it uses parameters that are distinct from the underlying distribution parameters. In particular, it requires two coefficients of variation (V_{task} for the tasks and V_{mach} for the machines) and one mean (μ_{task} for the tasks). The random values follow a gamma distribution whose parameters are computed such that the provided CV (Coefficient of Variation) and mean are respected.

Proposition 1. *When used with parameters V_{task}, V_{mach} and μ_{task}, the CVB method generates costs with expected value μ_{task} and coefficient of variation $\sqrt{V_{task}^2 V_{mach}^2 + V_{task}^2 + V_{mach}^2}$.*

Proof. Each cost is the product of a random variable that follows a gamma law with mean μ_{task} and CV V_{task} and a random variable that follows a gamma law with mean 1 and CV V_{mach}. Therefore, the expected value of the costs is the product of the expected values of both distributions, namely μ_{task}.

The standard deviation of the product of two random variables with means μ_1 and μ_2, and standard deviations σ_1 and σ_2 is $\sqrt{\sigma_1^2 \sigma_2^2 + \mu_1^2 \sigma_2^2 + \sigma_1^2 \mu_2^2}$. With a similar argument as for the expected value we can derive the CV of the costs. □

To obtain the CV of the costs with the range-based method, we can replace V_{task} by the CV of the first uniform law, $\frac{\sqrt{12}}{6} \frac{R_{task}-1}{R_{task}+1}$, and V_{mach} by the CV of the second uniform law, $\frac{\sqrt{12}}{6} \frac{R_{mach}-1}{R_{mach}+1}$. This CV remains close to a constant except for low values of R_{task} and R_{mach}. For instance, it is around 0.86 when $R_{task} = R_{mach} = 100$ and the asymptotic value is $\frac{\sqrt{7}}{2} \approx 0.88$ when both R_{task} and R_{mach} are large. This is not well-suited to control the heterogeneity of the resulting cost matrix. Also, the asymmetry of this method may lead to different heterogeneity properties for the tasks and for the machines.

3.2   Consistency Extension

Both the previous methods produce cost matrices that may not be representative of realistic settings. For instance, the costs of a given task is not correlated to the costs of another task, which may often be the case in practice. The consistency extension consists in reordering the costs in the generated matrix to have an instance that is closer to the uniform case. Specifically, the rows of a submatrix of an rows and bm columns are sorted. Thus, a machine that is faster for a given task than another machine will likely be also faster for another task. Inconsistent matrices have $a = b = 0$ while consistent matrices have $a = b = 1$ (other matrices are either called semiconsistent or partially consistent).

3.3   Usage in the Literature

We covered the English articles that cite at least one of the references in which the methods were initially presented [5–7] and that were freely available. For each reference, we extracted all the distinct sets of parameters. However, the size was ignored because we only consider asymptotic properties (see Sect. 4.2).

Some data were not specifically provided. The parameters that could be directly inferred from the article or from similar works are mostly related to missing parameters for the consistency extension (the ones from the cited article were taken). Otherwise, they are treated as missing values. Some articles lack enough information, which prevented any parameter extraction.

On the 160 analysed articles, 78 provide exploitable information on the cost matrix instances. The rest consists of 40 articles with no description, but which refer to instances described in other articles and 42 articles with unclear descriptions or approaches that do not fit the current study. The extracted data are available in [11, Appendix B] and summarized below. While most articles fail to precisely describe the used method, only the range and CV parameters are crucial for reproducing similar instances. In the end, 342 sets of parameters were extracted in 78 articles for a total of 210 unique settings: 37 for the range-based method and 173 for the CVB one.

Figure 1 depicts the values used with both methods. Although there is no clear agreement on which precise parameters are the most relevant, there are some common tendencies. Values for low heterogeneity are usually 10 and 100 for the range-based method and .1, .25 and .3 for the CVB method. Values for high heterogeneity are usually 100, 1e3, 3e3 and 1e5 for the range-based method and .3, .35, .4, .5, .6, .7, .9, 1 and 2 for the CVB method.

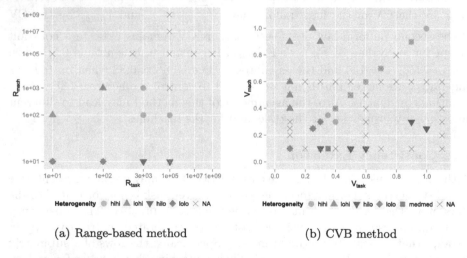

(a) Range-based method   (b) CVB method

Fig. 1. Parameters used in the literature. Three points are not shown for the CVB method: $(1.4, 0.4)$, $(1.8, 0.4)$ and $(0.1, 2)$

4 Heterogeneity Measures

Assessing the impact of heterogeneity on heuristic performance requires a method for quantifying the heterogeneity of the generated cost matrices.

4.1 TDH and MPH

The closest related measures are the TDH (Task Difficulty Homogeneity) and the MPH (Machine Performance Homogeneity) [2,3]. The TDH computation consists in computing the difficulty of each task (noted $TD[i]$), sorting all the $TD[i]$ in ascending order and averaging all the ratios between successive $TD[i]$. The measure lies in the interval $(0, 1]$: if it is one, then tasks are all similar; if it is close to zero, then the task heterogeneity is large. The MPH computation is analogous, but for the machine.

These measures have two major shortcomings. First, they are not intuitive (they require to invert costs, to order sums and to average ratios). Also, they do not rely on classical statistical measures, which makes deriving formal results more difficult. Another notable problem is that the resulting values depend on the size of the matrix. In particular, it is close to one when the matrix is large (even if it is generated with the same parameters and has, intuitively, the same characteristics). For instance, if we consider only one machine, the following matrices (cost vectors in this case) have the same TDH: $[1, 2]$ and $[0.125, 0.25, 0.5, 1, 2, 4]$. The second vector, however, seems more heterogeneous. As another example, let the minimum TD be 1 and the maximum TD be 100. The TDH is always greater than 0.60 when there are 10 tasks and it is always greater than 0.95 when there are 100 tasks [11, Proposition 1]. This measure is thus relevant only for comparing small cost matrices with similar sizes.

4.2 Intuitive Measures of Heterogeneity

Assuming that the mean of each row represents a task weight, the task heterogeneity may be defined as the CV (Coefficient of Variation) of the means of the rows (noted $V\mu_{task}$). Analogously, the machine heterogeneity may be measured as the CV of the means of the columns (noted $V\mu_{mach}$).

These measures of task and machine heterogeneity has been criticized for small instances [2]. It is argued that the MPH is better than the CV as it is less sensible to outliers. However, we consider asymptotic properties for large matrices in this work because we expect them to hold for small instances. Moreover, in the case of outliers, the CV can be replaced by the quartile coefficient of dispersion, which is a similar standard statistical measure but is more difficult to formally analyse. Finally, the decision trees in [4] suggest that varying this measure has an impact on the heuristics performance and is thus significant.

4.3 Coherence with the Uniform Model

The previous measures do not only rely on intuition, they are also consistent with the expectation when we consider the uniform model. In this model, the cost of executing a task i on a machine j is given by the product of the task weight, w_i, and the inverse of the machine speed, b_j. The concept of task and machine heterogeneity is easy to grasp in the uniform model: it is given by the statistical dispersion of the weights and the speeds, respectively. We assume that the CV of the weights, noted CV_{task}, is a relevant measure of the task heterogeneity. Analogously, the CV of the speeds, noted CV_{mach}, represents the machine heterogeneity.

It is possible to convert an instance of the uniform model in the unrelated model because this last model is more general. The cost matrix is generated by combining both vectors $\{w_i\}_{1 \leq i \leq n}$ and $\{b_j\}_{1 \leq j \leq m}$ such that $e_{i,j} = w_i b_j$. As we know the heterogeneity properties of a uniform instance, we expect our proposed measures for the unrelated model to be consistent when applied on the converted instance, which is indeed the case [11, Proposition 2].

4.4   Heterogeneity of the Range-Based and CVB Methods

We analyse the asymptotic heterogeneity properties of the CVB method with the proposed measures depending on the parameters V_{task} and V_{mach}. An estimator T converges to θ when the expected value of T tends to θ as the number of samples (n and m in our case) tends to ∞.

Proposition 2. *The measure $V\mu_{task}$ of a cost matrix generated using the CVB method with the parameters V_{task} and V_{mach} converges to V_{task} as $n \to \infty$ and $m \to \infty$.*

Proof. This proof assumes that the mean of a set of n samples (called the sample mean) of a random variable with mean μ and standard deviation σ is a random variable with mean μ and standard deviation $\frac{\sigma}{\sqrt{n}}$. Moreover, the CV of a set of n samples (called the sample CV) of a random variable with CV V converges to V as $n \to \infty$.

Let μ_i be the sample mean of the costs on line i. This row is the product of a random variable that follows a distribution with mean μ_{task} and CV V_{task} and m values that follow a distribution with mean one and CV V_{mach}. μ_i is thus also the product of the first random variable and the sample mean of the other m values, which follows a random variable with mean one and CV $\frac{V_{mach}}{\sqrt{m}}$. Therefore, the mean of μ_i is μ_{task} and its CV is $\sqrt{V_{task}^2 \frac{V_{mach}^2}{m} + \frac{V_{mach}^2}{m} + V_{task}^2}$, which tends to V_{task} as $m \to \infty$. Then, the sample CV of all μ_i tends to V_{task} as $n \to \infty$ and $m \to \infty$. $\square$

We can also show that $V\mu_{mach}$ converges to $a\sqrt{b}V_{mach}$ as n and $m \to \infty$. Although more technical, the proof is analogous and provided in [11, Proposition 6].

These formal results can be extended to the range-based method by replacing V_{task} by the CV of the first random variable ($\frac{\sqrt{12}}{6} \frac{R_{task}-1}{R_{task}+1}$) and V_{mach} by the CV of the second one ($\frac{\sqrt{12}}{6} \frac{R_{mach}-1}{R_{mach}+1}$). Indeed, the proofs only use the mean and the CV of the random underlying distributions.

In the case of complete consistency (i.e., when $a = b = 1$), $V\mu_{task} = V_{task}$ and $V\mu_{mach} = V_{mach}$, which supports the proposed heterogeneity measures. This special case is due to the fact that consistent cost matrices are closer to uniform instances than inconsistent ones.

The main issue of the CVB method is related to the impact of the consistency parameters on the heterogeneity properties. It biases comparisons of scheduling methods when cost matrices are used with different consistency settings because these matrices will also have different heterogeneity properties. The range-based method presents an even stronger bias as both V_{task} and V_{mach} tends to $\frac{\sqrt{12}}{6}$ as R_{task} and $R_{mach} \to \infty$ (the heterogeneity properties are thus often similar).

4.5   Task and Machine Heterogeneity in Previous Studies

For each of the instances summarized in Sect. 3, we computed both heterogeneity measures using the previous analysis and the input parameters: R_{task}, R_{mach}, V_{task}, V_{mach}, a and b.

Figure 2 depicts the values for the measures proposed above. The range-based method has a clear bias because many heterogeneity properties have never been obtained. Also, the consistency parameters invalidate the claimed properties of the cost matrices relatively to the heterogeneity quadrant: some *hihi* instances have the same machine heterogeneity as *lolo* instances.

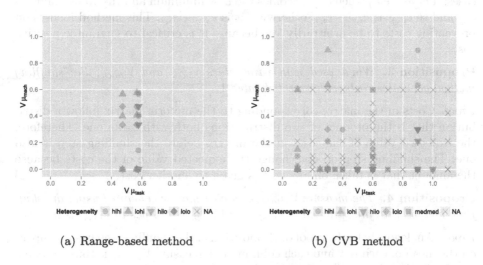

(a) Range-based method   (b) CVB method

Fig. 2. Heterogeneity properties ($V\mu_{task}$ and $V\mu_{mach}$) of cost matrices used in the literature. Two points are not shown for the CVB method: $(1.4, 0)$ and $(1.8, 0)$.

This analysis is also consistent with the observation made in [3] about the fact that the range-based and CVB methods do not cover the entire range of possible values for the MPH.

5   Controlling the Heterogeneity

We are interested in generating cost matrices that have specific heterogeneity properties according to the measures introduced in Sect. 4. We propose a method that alters a cost matrix generated from uniform instances for which we control the task and machine heterogeneities. This cost matrices have specific properties in terms of consistency and correlation between each row and each column, and the proposed method introduces some randomness in the matrix by shuffling the costs. It first generates the task weights, $\{w_i\}_{1 \le i \le n}$, with a gamma distribution with mean one and CV V_{task}, and then the inverse of the machine speeds, $\{b_j\}_{1 \le j \le m}$, with a gamma distribution with mean one and CV V_{mach}. The corresponding matrix is computed such that $e_{i,j} = w_i b_j$ before starting the shuffling part. For each cost $e_{i,j}$, another cost $e_{i',j'}$ is selected on a different row and column. The same amount is then removed from these costs and is added to two other costs, $e_{i,j'}$ and $e_{i',j}$ (one that is on the same row as the first cost and on the same column as the second, and another one that is on the same row as the second cost and on the same column as the first). This step preserves the mean of each row and the mean of each column. The heterogeneity properties remain thus the same. The transfered amount is the largest value (in absolute) such that no cost among the four considered costs becomes lower than the minimum one among them (this prevents costs to be arbitrarily low). For instance, if $e_{i,j}$ is the minimum cost (i.e., $e_{i,j} = \min(e_{i,j}, e_{i',j}, e_{i,j'}, e_{i',j'})$), there are two cases: if $e_{i,j'} < e_{i',j}$, then $e_{i,j'}$ becomes the new minimum and the added value to $e_{i,j}$ and to $e_{i',j'}$ is $e_{i,j'} - e_{i,j}$; otherwise, it is $e_{i',j} - e_{i,j}$. This method focuses on preventing costs to be arbitrarily low because it is critical to guarantee positive costs.

Proposition 3. *When used with parameters V_{task} and V_{mach}, the shuffling method generates costs with expected value 1.*

Proof. Costs in the matrix corresponding to the uniform matrix follow a distribution that is the product of two distributions both with mean one. Therefore, the expected value of the costs in the matrix before the shuffling step is also one. The shuffling step do not change the expected value of the costs because the amount that is taken on any cost is given to another cost.   □

Proposition 4. *The measure $V\mu_{task}$ of a cost matrix generated using the shuffling method with the parameters V_{task} and V_{mach} converges to V_{task} as $n \to \infty$.*

Proof. Analogously to the proof of Proposition 3, the shuffling step has no impact on the mean of each row and each column. The measure $V\mu_{task}$ is thus the same for the final cost matrix as for the intermediate matrix that corresponds to a uniform instance.

The sample CV of the sample means of all rows in this intermediate matrix is equal to the sample CV of the vector $\{w_i\}_{1 \le i \le n}$. This last sample CV tends to V_{task} as $n \to \infty$.   □

An analogous proof relying on the symmetry of the shuffling method shows that $V\mu_{mach}$ converges to V_{mach} as $m \to \infty$.

6   Impact on Scheduling Heuristics

This section assesses the impact of the heterogeneity properties defined in Sect. 4 on the performance of some classic heuristics. Our intention is not to find the best heuristic but rather to show the impact of the cost matrix generation method on the performance results. We use classical heuristics from the literature summarized in Table 1. These heuristics are described in [11, Appendix C].

Table 1. Summary of the scheduling heuristics for the $R||C_{\max}$ problem

Name	Ref.	Complexity	Remark
Min-min	[10]	n^2m	Earliest finish time
Max-min	[10]	n^2m	Earliest finish time of largest task
GA	[10]	–	Genetic Algorithm
Suff	[12]	n^2m	Task that will suffer most first
HLPT	[16]	$nm + n\log(n)$	Heterogeneous version of LPT
BalSuff	[11]	–	Reconsider allocation on sufferage

   Cost matrices are generated with the shuffling method using $V\mu_{task}$ and $V\mu_{proc}$, each with 30 values exponentially distributed in $[0.001, 10]$. For each pair of parameters, 100 cost matrices are generated with $n = 100$ tasks and $m = 30$ machines. For each scenario, we compute the makespan of each heuristics. We only consider the relative difference from the reference makespan: $|C - C_{\min}|/C_{\min}$ where C is the makespan of a given heuristic and $C_{\min}$ the best makespan we obtained (a genetic algorithm initialized with all the solutions obtained by the other algorithms). The closer to zero, the better the performance.

   The results presented on Fig. 3 is a heat map of the relative performance for each algorithm. On each figure, we use a logarithmic scale on both axises: the x-axis gives the heterogeneity value for the tasks ($V\mu_{task}$) while the y-axis gives the heterogeneity value for the machines ($V\mu_{mach}$). The bottom-left area represents almost homogeneous instances, while the top-right area is the most heterogeneous one. The heterogeneity values covered by the range-based and CVB methods in the literature are represented with dark rectangles on each sub-figure. Contour lines correspond to the levels in the legend.

   Figure 4 plots the best heuristic depending on the heterogeneity properties. Contour lines show the number of heuristics which performance is closer to the best heuristic than 0.001. For instance, there are at least four heuristics whose relative performances are almost equivalent when task heterogeneity is high. When several heuristics are equivalent for a given tile, the appearing heuristic is the one that is the best the least often. The dark rectangles correspond to the properties covered by the range-based and CVB methods in the literature.

   The settings cover a large part of the possible instances for the $R||C_{\max}$ problem. Some areas on the figures may be associated to specific scheduling

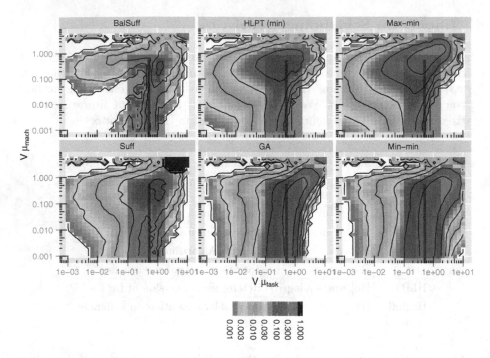

Fig. 3. Heuristic performance relatively to the best case with the shuffling method. Values below 0.001 are shown in white and values above 1 are shown in black.

problems: the $Q|p_i = p|C_{\max}$ problem (top-left area), the $P|p_i = p|C_{\max}$ problem (bottom-left area) and the $P||C_{\max}$ problem (bottom-right area). While the first two problems can be solved in polynomial time, the last problem is NP-complete.

The heat maps suggest that the area where the heterogeneity values are between 0.1 and 1 is more challenging for most heuristics (areas in purple on the heat maps are 30 % far from the reference). This is confirmed by Fig. 4 where the best heuristic is often far from the second best with these settings. Oppositely, many heuristics are close to the best one when the task heterogeneity is low or high, or when the machine heterogeneity is high. On one hand, execution costs are quite similar when the coefficient of variation is below 0.1. A non-optimal allocation will thus have a lower impact than with higher heterogeneity. On the other hand, most execution costs are close to zero when the coefficient of variation is higher than 1 and bad allocations may be easy to avoid because there are few allocations that are extremely critical while most of them are not. It is thus easier to generate a reasonable schedule. When the machine heterogeneity is low (with medium task heterogeneity), there is often a single best heuristic. This suggests that these settings leads to difficult instances. As mentioned above, this is close to the $P||C_{\max}$ problem. We may conclude that dealing with heterogeneous tasks is more difficult than with heterogeneous machines, which is also supported by the asymmetry of the heat maps.

The range-based and CVB generation methods used in the literature could not provide these results due to two factors: the heterogeneity properties of the generated instances have a limited coverage (shown by the dark rectangles) and the erroneous claimed properties of these matrices prevent an unbiased analysis.

This study focuses on the impact of two measures, $V\mu_{task}$ and $V\mu_{proc}$, on the performance of several heuristics. There are however many other properties that could be measured. If we consider the skewness and the kurtosis as in [4], we can think of 4×4 measures for the lines and as many for the columns. The main limitation of this study is to ignore the effect of all these possible measures.

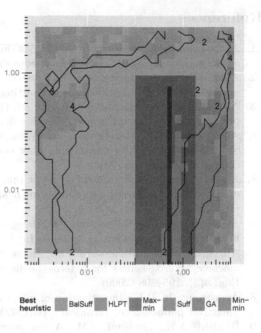

Fig. 4. Best heuristic in the average case

Another limitation is related to the effect of outliers. For large instances, the law of large number applies and the measures proposed in Sect. 4 correspond to the characteristics of the cost matrices. However, for small instances, we suggest to switch to robust measures such as the median, the interquartile range and the quartile coefficient of dispersion instead of the mean, the standard deviation and the CV, respectively.

7 Conclusion

This study shows that the methods used in the literature for generating cost matrices are biased: the claimed heterogeneity properties of these instances are invalidated by the measures we proposed to quantify them. We also show that the range of instances that has been used are restricted. It is specifically the case for the range-based method that covers only a minor fraction of all the possible settings in terms of heterogeneity. By providing a new cost matrix generation method we show that heuristics for the $R||C_{max}$ problem have interesting behavior outside this restriction.

In addition to all the possible measures mentioned in Sect. 6, we plan to analyse other properties, in particular the correlation. It would also be interesting to see if the conclusions hold for some variations of the $R||C_{max}$ problem such as considering arrival times or online scheduling.

References

1. Al-Qawasmeh, A., Pasricha, S., Maciejewski, A., Siegel, H.: Power and thermal-aware workload allocation in heterogeneous data centers. TC **64**(2), 477–491 (2013)
2. Al-Qawasmeh, A., Maciejewski, A., Roberts, R.G., Siegel, H.: Characterizing task-machine affinity in heterogeneous computing environments. In: IPDPSW (2011)
3. Al-Qawasmeh, A., Maciejewski, A., Siegel, H.: Characterizing heterogeneous computing environments using singular value decomposition. In: IPDPSW (2010)
4. Al-Qawasmeh, A., Maciejewski, A., Wang, H., Smith, J., Siegel, H., Potter, J.: Statistical measures for quantifying task and machine heterogeneities. J. Supercomput. **57**(1), 34–50 (2011)
5. Ali, S.: A comparative study of dynamic mapping heuristics for a class of independent tasks onto heterogeneous computing systems. Ph.D. thesis, Purdue University (1999)
6. Ali, S., Siegel, H., Maheswaran, M., Hensgen, D.: Task execution time modeling for heterogeneous computing systems. In: HCW, pp. 185–199. IEEE (2000)
7. Ali, S., Siegel, H., Maheswaran, M., Hensgen, D., Ali, S.: Representing task and machine heterogeneities for heterogeneous computing systems. Tamkang J. Sci. Eng. **3**(3), 195–208 (2000)
8. Armstrong, Jr. R.K.: Investigation of effect of different run-time distributions on SmartNet performance. Technical report, DTIC Document (1997)
9. Bardsiri, A.K., Hashemi, S.M.: A comparative study on seven static mapping heuristics for grid scheduling problem. IJSEIA **6**(4), 247–256 (2012)
10. Braun, T.D., Siegel, H., Beck, N., Bölöni, L.L., Maheswaran, M., et al.: A comparison of eleven static heuristics for mapping a class of independent tasks onto heterogeneous distributed computing systems. JPDC **61**(6), 810–837 (2001)
11. Canon, L.C., Philippe, L.: On the heterogeneity bias of cost matrices when assessing scheduling algorithms. Technical report, FEMTO-ST, February 2015
12. Casanova, H., Legrand, A., Zagorodnov, D., Berman, F.: Heuristics for scheduling parameter sweep applications in grid environments. In: HCW, pp. 349–363 (2000)
13. Diaz, C.O., Pecero, J.E., Bouvry, P.: Scalable, low complexity, and fast greedy scheduling heuristics for highly heterogeneous distributed computing systems. J. Supercomput. **67**(3), 837–853 (2014)
14. Friese, R., Khemka, B., Maciejewski, A., Siegel, H.J., Koenig, G., et al.: An analysis framework for investigating the trade-offs between system performance and energy consumption in a heterogeneous computing environment. In: IPDPSW (2013)
15. Ghosh, S., Henderson, S.G.: Behavior of the norta method for correlated random vector generation as the dimension increases. ACM TOMACS **13**(3), 276–294 (2003)
16. Graham, R.L.: Bounds on multiprocessing timing anomalies. J. Appl. Math. **17**(2), 416–429 (1969)
17. Graham, R.L., Lawler, E.L., Lenstra, J.K., Kan, A.H.G.R.: Optimization and approximation in deterministic sequencing and scheduling: a survey. Ann. Discrete Math. **5**, 287–326 (1979)
18. Khemka, B., Friese, R., Pasricha, S., Maciejewski, A., Siegel, H., et al.: Utility maximizing dynamic resource management in an oversubscribed energy-constrained heterogeneous computing system. In: Sustainable Computing: Informatics and Systems (2014)
19. Leung, J.Y.T. (ed.): Handbook of Scheduling: Algorithms, Models, and Performance Analysis. Chapman & Hall/CCR, London (2004)

20. Luo, P., Lü, K., Shi, Z.: A revisit of fast greedy heuristics for mapping a class of independent tasks onto heterogeneous computing systems. JPDC **67**(6), 695–714 (2007)
21. Saltelli, A., Chan, K., Scott, E.M.: Sensitivity analysis. Wiley, New York (2009)

Hardware Round-Robin Scheduler
for Single-ISA Asymmetric Multi-core

Nikola Markovic[1,2]([⊠]), Daniel Nemirovsky[1,2], Veljko Milutinovic[4],
Osman Unsal[1], Mateo Valero[1,2], and Adrian Cristal[1,2,3]

[1] Barcelona Supercomputing Center (BSC), Barcelona, Spain
{nikola.markovic,daniel.nemirovsky,osman.unsal,
mateo.valero,adrian.cristal}@bsc.es
[2] Department of Computer Architecture,
Universitat Politecnica de Catalunya (UPC), Barcelona, Spain
[3] Spanish National Research Council (IIIA-CSIC), Barcelona, Spain
[4] School of Electrical Engineering (ETF), Univeristy of Belgrade, Belgrade, Serbia
vm@etf.bg.ac.rs

Abstract. As thread level parallelism in applications has continued to
expand, so has relevant research on heterogeneous CMPs. Nowadays
multi-threaded workloads running on CMPs are common case, but as the
quantity of these workloads increase and as heterogeneous CMPs become
more diverse, thread scheduling within an operating system will become
ever more critical to maintaining efficient performance and system utilization. As a consequence, the operating system will require increasingly larger amounts of CPU time to schedule these threads effectively.
Instead of perpetuating the trend of performing complex thread scheduling to the software, we propose a simple yet effective mechanism that
can easily be implemented in hardware which outperforms the typical
Linux OS scheduler as well as Fairness scheduler. Our approach fairly
redistributes running hardware threads across available cores within OS
scheduling quantum. It achieves an average speed up of 37.7 percent and
16.5 percent respectively compared to the Linux OS scheduler and state-
of-the-art Fairness scheduling when running a multi-threaded application
workloads.

Keywords: Hardware · Thread · Scheduling

1 Introduction

The relentless push in technology scaling driven by Moore's law has resulted in
more transistors packed into a very small area. Computer architects responded
by integrating many cores on the same die. Chip multiprocessors, or CMPs for
short, are now the most common way to build high-performance microprocessors, for a variety of reasons. Large uniprocessors are no longer scaling in performance, because it is only possible to extract a limited amount of parallelism
from a typical instruction stream using conventional superscalar instruction issue

© Springer-Verlag Berlin Heidelberg 2015
J.L. Träff et al. (Eds.): Euro-Par 2015, LNCS 9233, pp. 122–134, 2015.
DOI: 10.1007/978-3-662-48096-0_10

techniques. In addition, one cannot simply ratchet up the clock speed on today's processors, or the power budget will become prohibitive. Compounding these problems is the simple fact that with the immense numbers of transistors available on today's microprocessor chips, it is too costly to design and debug ever-larger processors every year or two.

CMPs avoid these problems by filling up a processor die with multiple, relatively simpler processor cores instead of one huge core. The exact size of a CMP's cores can vary from very simple pipelines to moderately complex super-scalar processors, but once a core has been selected the CMP's performance can easily scale across silicon process generations simply by stamping down more copies of the hard-to-design, high-speed processor core in each successive chip generation. In addition, parallel code execution, obtained by spreading multiple threads of execution across the various cores, can achieve significantly higher performance than would be possible using only a single core. While parallel threads are already common in many useful workloads, there are still important workloads that are hard to divide into parallel threads. The low inter-processor communication latency between the cores in a CMP helps make a much wider range of applications viable candidates for parallel execution than was possible with traditional, multi-chip multiprocessors; nevertheless, limited parallelism in key applications is the main factor limiting acceptance of CMPs in some types of systems. Nowadays, chip multiprocessors (CMPs) may be symmetric (SCMP), consisting of many cores of the same type, or asymmetric (ACMP), where cores may differ from one another with respect to their functionality and/or performance [5,13]. As is shown by a number of recent studies ACMPs are likely to outperform SCMPs for a fixed budget (area or power or both) [11,15]. Since it is well known that different workloads have different resource requirements, the benefits of ACMPs are intuitive.

The need for a scheduling algorithm arises from the requirement for CMP and ACMP systems to perform multitasking (executing more than one process or thread at a time). Scheduling is the method by which threads, processes or data flows are given access to system resources (e.g. processor time). This is usually done to load balance and share system resources effectively or to achieve a target quality of service. Parallel applications relying on multiple threads must be efficiently managed and dispatched for execution if the parallelism is to be properly exploited. Thus, dynamic thread scheduling techniques are of paramount importance in ACMP designs since they can make or break performance benefits derived from the asymmetric hardware or parallel software. Several thread scheduling methods have been proposed and applied to ACMPs. Most of these make use of online or offline profiling as well as sampling or estimation techniques to determine the optimum thread to core mapping (in relation to performance and/or power) whenever a specific event is detected or scheduling time quantum is completed [1,9,19] among others. Though these scheduling techniques include certain performance or energy efficiency gains, their broad application remains stifled due to scalability limitations, runtime overheads, and additional hardware requirements and complexities. Our goal is to develop a scheduling policy that can be used as a foundation upon which to build practical and scalable hardware scheduling designs in order to increase the performance capabilities of ACMPs.

This paper provides the following **contributions**:

- We propose a Hardware Round-Robin Scheduling (HRRS) policy which is influenced by Fairness Scheduling techniques thereby reducing thread serialization and improving parallel thread performance.
- We analyze and evaluate the performance of the HRRS policy on an ACMP and show that it lowers total execution time by 37.7 percent and 16.5 percent respectively compared to the state-of-the-art Linux OS scheduler and Fairness scheduler when running a multi-threaded application workloads.

2   Motivation

The exciting rise of asymmetric multi-core processors (ACMPs) has fostered a critical reevaluation of the traditional scheduling mechanisms in order to take full advantage of the new hardware resources in relation to the increasingly common thread level parallelism as well as in meeting certain system performance and power requisites. The operating system scheduler module orchestrates critical execution time junctures, selecting which jobs to be admitted next into the system and the next process to run. A technique known as fair-share scheduling is used by computer operating systems where CPU usage is equitably divided between system users or groups, in contrast to equal distribution among processes. The Linux OS scheduler, based on a fair-share scheduler strategy, is a process scheduler which was merged into the 2.6.23 release of the Linux kernel as its default scheduler [8]. It handles CPU resource allocation for executing processes aimed at maximizing overall CPU utilization as well as interactive performance. Operating systems may feature up to three distinct types of schedulers, a long-term scheduler (also known as an admission scheduler or high-level scheduler), a mid-term or medium-term scheduler and a short-term or CPU scheduler. The names suggest the relative frequency with which these functions are performed.

The third type of scheduler, the primary focus of this work, is the short-term commonly referred to as the CPU scheduler. It is responsible for determining which of the ready processes (loaded into the memory by the other schedulers) should be sent for execution and on which computational core. This decision takes place periodically at interrupt points caused principally by the clock, I/O events, or OS system level calls. In relation to the long and short-term schedulers, the short-term scheduler must make scheduling decisions much more frequently. Furthermore, the short-term scheduler can be preemptive or non-preemptive based on its ability to force processes off the CPU. The preemptive method depends on a programmable interval timer that invokes a kernel level interrupt handler which implements the scheduling algorithm. A key function involved in the CPU-scheduling decision is the dispatcher which gives control of the CPU to the process selected. This function involves the context switching, changing to user mode, and jumping to the proper location of a program once it is restarted.

The actual time it takes for the dispatcher to perform its job stopping one process and starting another is known as the dispatch latency typically requiring several thousands of cycles [12]. Since the dispatcher needs to analyze the program counter values, fetch instructions, and load data into the registers of the CPU every time a process switch occurs, minimizing the dispatcher latency should be a primary objective. Moreover, it is also important to avoid unnecessary context switches due to the fact that the processor remains idle for a period of time during context switches.

It has been shown by Van Craeynest et al. [18], that in a asymmetric multi-core system, a round robin scheduler using threads pinned to cores produces no speedup compared to a lighter symmetric multi-core system for most multithreaded benchmarks. This behavior is caused by barrier-synchronized multi-threaded workloads since the execution progress is limited by the slowest thread which has little meaning in a symmetric system, but is significant for asymmetric systems since the thread pinned to the simplest core will be the weakest link that all other threads will have to wait for at every barrier. Work-stealing workloads, in contrast, allows for idle large cores to steal work that would normally be run on the small cores so that the execution time isn't as constrained.

Therefore, in asymmetric multi-core systems, guaranteeing fairness is fundamental for improving performance of multithreaded workloads. Fairness, as defined by giving each software thread equal execution time on each core or allowing each thread to make equal progress, enables all threads to reach the barriers simultaneously, and has been sown to provide average performance improvements of 14 percent (and up to 25 percent) compared with a pinned scheduler [18] for the system configuration we are using.

3   Hardware Round-Robin Scheduling

In the previous section we have noted the importance and the impact scheduling fairness may have on the potential speedup that can be achieved from the parallelization of multi-threaded applications and multiprocess workloads on single-ISA asymmetric multi-cores. In the next two subsections we describe the proposed Hardware Round-Robin Scheduling (HRRS) policy and discuss its hardware implementation.

3.1   HRRS Algorithm

Figure 1 is used to illustrate the inner workings of the HRRS approach, we will assume a system composed of an x86 ACMP hardware containing one large out-of-order (OoO) core and three smaller and identical in-order cores. The operating system is provided an abstracted homogeneous hardware view comprised of four identical logical cores, which correlate to four identical hardware threads. The OS scheduler maps threads to the logical cores which enables the OS scheduling policies and implementation to be left unmodified. While the OS scheduler maps threads to the logical cores at every software-quantum or other interrupts, the

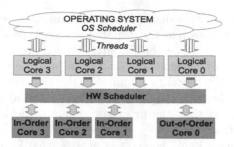

Fig. 1. HRRS scheduling - All logical cores (which correlate to hardware threads) are the same while the large physical core is represented by Core 0 and the small physical cores are shown as Cores 1,2 and 3

HRRS in turn maps the threads running on the logical cores to the physical cores as shown in Fig. 2 at every hardware-quantum. In essence, the HRRS can be viewed as mapping the logical cores that the OS sees and schedules threads onto, to the physical cores of the underlying hardware which actually execute the threads. Furthermore, the HRRS algorithm must produce a new scheduling scheme after every hardware-quantum of time passes (as opposed to the software-quantum which invokes the OS scheduler). In order to minimize the amount of overhead in implementing the scheduling policy, the HRRS algorithm determines the next scheduling scheme to apply before the beginning of the next hardware-quantum. The defining characteristic of the HRRS algorithm is that it evenly rotates threads (scheduled onto the logical cores by the OS scheduler) running on the physical cores after every hardware-quantum. The OS scheduler, on the other hand, is triggered at every software-quantum which happens much less frequently than that of the hardware-quantum. Additionally, the HRRS algorithm does not need to take into account whether the OS scheduler has activated and swapped one of the currently executing threads on a logical core for another thread from its ready queue. In such cases, the thread context of the thread being swapped out must be saved and replaced by the context of the new thread chosen by the OS to be executed all of which is performed by the triggered OS scheduler routine. Consequentially, the HRRS scheduling policy guarantees that a thread will not occupy a large physical core for more than one hardware-quantum unless it is the only runnable thread at the end of the hardware-quantum.

The Fundamental Difference. Between the HRRS and Fairness-aware scheduler algorithms [18] is the way in which the threads are selected to be mapped onto the physical cores. In both approaches, a thread running on one of the smaller physical cores is swapped with the thread running on the large physical core after a given time quantum. However, while Fairness-aware scheduling strives at achieving fairness by guaranteeing even progress using specific heuristic for each software thread, it does not necessarily enforce swaps of threads between large and small core every scheduling quantum but prefers to leave threads to run on the same physical core. In contrast, the HRRS policy runs each logical core,

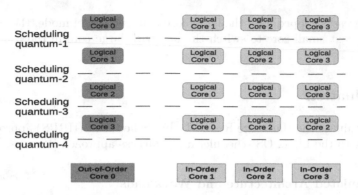

Fig. 2. An example of the HRRS scheduling logical cores on actual physical cores at every hardware-scheduling quantum. At the beginning logical core 0 is running on the large physical core while logical cores 2, 3 and 4 are running on small physical cores. After a first hardware scheduling quantum, Logical core 1 will be moved to large physical core and logical core 0 will be moved to a small physical core.

hardware thread, on each physical core type for a specified amount of time. After every quantum, the HRRS triggers a swap between the thread running on the large core with one executing on a small core that is chosen using a round-robin selection algorithm.

3.2 Hardware Implementation

Hardware Round-Robin Scheduling leaves the operating system level scheduling untouched and it maintains a consistent view of the underlying hardware. The hardware is able to provide the abstraction of a symmetric hardware to software while dynamically rescheduling threads among the cores in an asymmetric multi-core system [14]. Both of these approaches (HRRS and Fairness approach [18]) may also be implemented at the OS level by extending the OS scheduler but the advantage of a hardware approach, in addition to minimizing scheduling overheads, is that it provides a finer level of granularity for the scheduling quanta and requires no changes to the OS code [19].

HRRS has hardware additions which include a bit on every core to signal if the core is executing kernel or user code and a separate unit with vector that holds all of the bits, one counter and one decoder to facilitate round-robin mechanism. The size of these depends on the number of the cores in the system. For instance, for four core system we need 2-bit counter. Unlike to some of the other dynamic schedulers [7], the HRRS scheduling technique does not facilitate hardware overheads in order to be able to store and restore the architecture state in the cores. It utilizes the x86 hardware context switching mechanism, called Hardware Task Switching in the CPU manuals [6]. In the case that large core is in the kernel mode (handling an interrupt etc.) HRRS scheduler will wait until it returns to user mode to mark rescheduling, while if the small core that isto have its thread swapped with the large core is in the kernel mode, the scheduler will chose next small core to switch threads with large core in the round-robin fashion.

4   Evaluation

Here we evaluate the Hardware Round-Robin Scheduling (HRRS) approach and compare it to the Linux OS scheduler and Fairness approach [18].

4.1   Simulated Architecture and Workloads

For conducting the simulation experiments in this paper we have used Sniper [2], a parallel, hardware-validated, x86-64 multi-core simulator capable of running both multi-program and multi-threaded applications. We configured the simulator to model an ACMP made up of one large core and three small cores respectively. The differences between the core types lie in the pipeline complexity (out-of-order for large, in-order for small). In order to isolate the causes of potential performance differences, the clock frequency (2.6 GHz), issue width (4-wide), number of available thread contexts (one hardware context per core), and cache sizes are the same for both core types. We assume a cache hierarchy with separate and private 32 KB L1 instruction and data caches, private 256 KB L2 caches, and a shared 4 MB L3 last-level cache (LLC). All the caches employ a LRU replacement policy and we assume the memory controllers are on-chip. Similar to the work in [18], we utilize a conservative hardware-quantum of 1 ms and a software-quantum of 4 ms even though it is typically upwards of this range.

We use the SPLASH-2 [20] benchmarks in our experiments. The SPLASH-2 benchmarks are designed to represent multi-threaded applications in order to evaluate hardware architectures when running several thread contexts. All applications are run from start to finish. We run each benchmark on the four simulated cores with each core capable of executing one hardware thread context at a time. We evaluate single multi-threaded application workloads running an equal number of threads per application as the number of available hardware contexts, i.e., maximum number of threads, which is a common practice for running non-I/O-intensive applications [7]. For example, when we run one multi-threaded application on a system simulated with 4 cores, we use 4 threads for that application.

4.2   Performance Evaluation

Implementing dynamic scheduling requires the migration of workloads between different cores. This leads to overheads incurred by context switches and the loading of the working-sets into the private caches of the destination cores. A context switch incurs a fixed cost for storing and restoring the architecture state (at most a few kilobytes) [12] for which we presume a fixed 1,000 cycle penalty. Our simulations also take into account the warming of the cache hierarchy needed after a

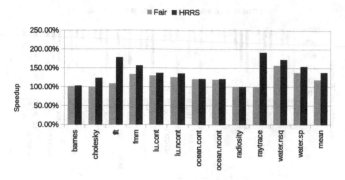

Fig. 3. Net Speedup comparison of the HRRS and Fairness scheduler normalized to Linux OS scheduler for the SPLASH-2 benchmark suite running on four cores (1 OoO + 3 InO)

context switch. The study [19] has shown the total migration execution time overhead to be less than 1.5 percent across different types of single-threaded workloads, ranging form memory-intensive to compute-intensive, for a 4 MB shared LLC using a 1ms hardware-quantum.

Figure 3 shows the speedup of the HRRS scheme over the hardware implementation of the Fairness scheduler on four core system running multi-threaded application workloads. The results are scaled to a Linux OS scheduler where the operating system has a notion of the underlying hardware. Under the Linux OS scheme, in the case of a symmetric CMP, the operating system pins individual threads to each of the cores in a round-robin fashion until all threads are assigned. The threads are then selected to be executed in a round-robin fashion on the respective core that they are pinned to (when there are more than one thread assigned per core). When using Linux OS scheduler threads on an asymmetric CMP, the operating system does not necessarily pin the threads to the cores, nor does it tend to swap the threads running on the large core with those on the small core at every scheduling quantum until threads pinned to the lagre core are all stalled or finished its execution. Rather, the OS scheduler tries to ensure quality-of-service for the threads. This reflects the current practice in contemporary operating system schedulers, as exemplified in the Linux 2.6 kernel [8]. The average speedups of HRRS over the Fairness and Linux OS scheduler when running the Splash2 workloads are 16.5 percent and 37.7 percent respectively on a four core system.

A key element driving these performance benefits comes from the redistribution of the workloads amongst the cores. Figure 4 shows per benchmark LLC access distribution between large core and small cores, while total number of the LLC accesses grows up by only up to 1.5 percent for Fair and HRRS schedulers compared to Linux OS scheduler. The HRRS scheme produces a higher proportion of LLC accesses originating from the large core. Fundamentally, the large core can better support the extra burden of LLC cache accesses since the large out-of-order instruction window allows for a greater quantity of instructions to be processes concurrently, which enables it to hide the additional latency caused by the extra

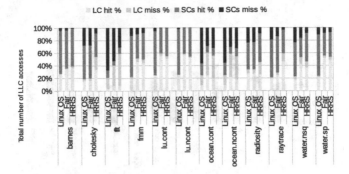

Fig. 4. The LLC cache accesses breakdown for the large and small cores of the Linux OS, Fairness and HRRS scheduler for the SPLASH-2 benchmark

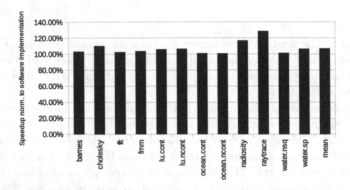

Fig. 5. Speedup of the hardware over the software implementation (baseline) for the HRRS scheduler, where scheduling quanta are 1 ms and 4 ms for hardware and software implementations respectively

cache accesses and still, even after including overheads from the context swap, outperform the small cores in thread execution time. This hit/miss ratio and considerable change in total number of LLC accesses between large and small cores are clearly noticeable with cholesky and raytrace benchmarks which have the highest performance gains.

Hardware vs. Software Implementation. Hardware Round-Robin Scheduling leaves the operating system level scheduling untouched and it maintains a consistent view of the underlying hardware. The hardware is able to provide the abstraction of a symmetric hardware to software while dynamically rescheduling threads among the cores in an asymmetric multi-core system [14]. Figure 5 represents the speedup that a hardware implementation, with a scheduling quantum of 1 ms, has over a software implementation (baseline), with a scheduling quantum of the 4 ms, for the HRRS scheduler. We can see that a hardware implementation results in an average speedup of 6.98 percent over a software implementation for the HRRS scheduler.

5 Related Work

Due to possible performance and efficiency gains, there has been increasing interest in heterogeneous multi-core architectures, and various scheduling proposals have been presented. An ACMP which consists of multiple cores of the same ISA but of different sizes was proposed by Kumar et al. in [10]. Their process consists of sampling for and choosing the core that will execute in the most power efficient manner each time a new phase or program is detected. This work was later expanded to maximize performance of multithreaded applications [11].

Similar work by Becchi [1] consists of an ACMP that includes two distinct core sizes where thread to core assignment is managed by initiating a mandatory swap of threads between two different sized cores in order to measure the corresponding performance ratio. Based on this ratio, the threads are then scheduled to their core that will maximize the system performance. This work has given insight into ratio based ACMP scheduling techniques but is limited as the number of distinct core types used increases. Other work in this area has been done by Saez et al. [16] who use a utility factor, defined as the ratio of L1 miss latency compared to a baseline ACMP configuration (only small cores), with the aim of optimizing the performance of both single and multithreaded workloads. Likewise, Koufaty et al. [9] determine optimal thread to ACMP core mapping using a biasing method estimated by the quantity of external memory stalls and internal pipeline stalls. Another approach is detailed in the work by Srinivasan et al. [17] who propose a formula based ACMP thread to core scheduling method which is used to estimate and compare thread performance on individual cores. With respect to microarchitectural differences, Chen et al. [3] chose to implement their ACMP with cores consisting of separate branch predictor, issue width, and L1 cache sizes that together with their scheduling method, achieve throughput and energy efficiency improvements.

6 Future Work

When considering an LLC cache for many-core processors, an popular option gaining traction in the industry is to distribute the cache into separate blocks, therefore appearing as unified rather than being physically unified. This is a similar approach to that taken by the IBM Power8 architecture [4] where each core has an 8 MB low-latency LLC cache and a high-speed cache-coherent ring is used to connect all of the cores. Thus joined, the LLC cache blocks can be viewed as a shared 96 MB cache with a nonuniform latency. Access to the local 8 MB LLC is speedy, but access to remote LLC cache blocks will require additional cycles to traverse the ring. By comparison, a large unified LLC cache would have a constant access time slower than the local cache but faster than remote blocks. The IBM design keeps hot data in the CPUs local LLC, reducing the average LLC latency.

In a many-core processor with this kind of distributed LLC cache configuration, a latency problem may arise due to frequent context switches among cores being connected to a different LLC cache segments. Therefore, the HRRS scheduling heuristic many need to be adjusted to account for the added latencies of the LLC and moreover can be tuned to allow for the scheduling of threads to be such as to take advantage of the distribution of cache blocks. Perhaps it may become viable to not only swap threads from large to small cores but also from small to small depending on which LLC segments their data sets are located. Furthermore, it would be beneficial to implement the HRRS scheme on an FPGA in order to gauge the feasibility of the design as well as raise the level of accuracy concerning the latency overheads.

7 Conclusion

In this paper we have presented the Hardware Round-Robin Scheduler (HRRS). Our work is influenced by the rise of many core processors, particularly the asymmetric core multi-processors (ACMPs) and their dependence on dynamic schedulers such as the commodity Linux OS CPU scheduler in order to achieve fair and balanced performance between active threads. Our initial objective was to achieve these performance benefits from running parallel workloads on ACMPs without the need for substantial hardware extensions, sampling, or runtime overheads. Incorporating minimal hardware additions, our HRRS policy promotes a balanced distribution of execution time for threads per core type. We have shown that HRRS provides greater opportunity for all threads to share time running on the more efficient large core, selected via a round-robin algorithm, which produces generous performance benefits even after including scheduler and context swap overheads as well as latencies arising from the additional cache accesses needed for loading the working data sets. By using the HRRS policy on an ACMP, we got a total execution time speedup of 37.7 percent and 16.5 percent respectively compared to the state-of-the-art Linux OS scheduler and Fairness scheduler when running a multi-threaded application workloads (Splash2).

Acknowledgment. Nikola Markovic is supported through a doctoral scholarship by the Universitat Politecnica de Catalunya (UPC). Additional support is provided by the CICYT (Spanish National Science Foundation) project TIN2012-34557. We would also like to thank to all reviewers for their comments and suggestions.

References

1. Becchi, M., Crowley, P.: Dynamic thread assignment on heterogeneous multiprocessor architectures. J. Instr.-Level Parallelism **10**, 1–26 (2008)
2. Carlson, T.E., Heirman, W., Eeckhout, L.: Sniper: exploring the level of abstraction for scalable and accurate parallel multi-core simulation. In: Proceedings of the International Conference for High Performance Computing, Networking, Storage and Analysis, pp. 1–12 (2011)

3. Chen, J., John, L. K.: Efficient program scheduling for heterogeneous multi-core processors. In: Proceedings of the Annual Design Automation Conference, pp. 927–930 (2009)
4. Fluhr, E.J. et al.: IBM STG, POWER8TM: a 12-core server-class processor in 22nm SOI with 7.6Tb/s off-chip bandwidth. In: Proceedings of the IEEE International Solid-State Circuits Conference on Digest of Technical Papers, pp. 96–97 (2014)
5. Greenhalgh, P.: big.LITTLE Processing with ARM Cortex-A15 & Cortex-A7 (2011). www.arm.com/files/downloads/bigLITTLE_Final_Final.pdf
6. Intel Corp.: Intel 64 and ia-32 architectures developers manual (2015). http://www.intel.com/content/www/us/en/architecture-and-technology/64-ia-32-architectures-software-developer-manual-325462.html
7. Joao, J., Suleman, M.A., Mutlu, O., Patt, Y.: Utility-based acceleration of multi-threaded applications on asymmetric CMPs. In: Proceedings of the Annual International Symposium on Computer Architecture, pp. 154–165 (2013)
8. Jones, M.T.: Inside the Linux 2.6 Completely Fair Scheduler (2009). http://www.ibm.com/developerworks/library/l-completely-fair-scheduler/l-completely-fair-scheduler-pdf.pdf
9. Koufaty, D., Reddy, D., Hahn, S.: Bias scheduling in heterogeneous multi-core architectures. In: Proceedings of the 5th European Conference on Computer Systems, pp. 125–138 (2010)
10. Kumar, R., Farkas, K., Jouppi, N., Ranganathan, P., Tullsen, D.: Single-ISA heterogeneous multi-core architectures: the potential for processor power reduction. In: Proceedings of the Annual IEEE/ACM International Symposium on Microarchitecture, p. 81 (2003)
11. Kumar, R., Tullsen, D., Ranganathan, P., Jouppi, N., Farkas, K.: Single-ISA heterogeneous multi-core architectures for multithreaded workload performance. In: Proceedings of the Annual International Symposium on Computer Architecture, p. 64 (2004)
12. Li, C., Ding, C., Shen, K.: Quantifying the cost of context switch. In: Proceedings of the Workshop on Experimental Computer Science, p. 2-es (2007)
13. NVIDIA: Variable SMP: A Multi Core CPU Architecture for Low Power and High Performance (2011). http://www.nvidia.com
14. NVIDIA: Tegra 3 (Kal-El) Quad-Core Mobile Processor (2011). http://www.nvidia.com/object/tegra-3-processor.html
15. Rodrigues, R., Annamalai, A., Koren, I., Kundu, S., Khan, O.: Performance per watt benefits of dynamic core morphing in asymmetric multicores. In: Proceedings of the International Conference on Parallel Architectures and Compilation Techniques, pp. 121–130 (2011)
16. Saez, J.C., Prieto, M., Fedorova, A., Blagodurov, S.: A comprehensive scheduler for asymmetric multicore systems. In: Proceedings of the 5th European Conference on Computer Systems, pp. 139–152 (2010)
17. Srinivasan, S., Zhao, L., Illikkal, R., Iyer, R.: Efficient interaction between OS and architecture in heterogeneous platforms. SIGOPS Oper. Syst. Rev. **45**(1), 62–72 (2011)
18. Van Craeynest, K., Akram, S., Heirman, W., Jaleel, A., Eeckhout, L.: Fairness-aware scheduling on single-ISA heterogeneous multi-cores. In: Proceedings of the International Conference on Parallel Architectures Compilation Techniques, pp. 177–187 (2013)

19. Van Craeynest, K., Jaleel, A., Eeckhout, L., Narvaez, P., Emer, J.: Scheduling heterogeneous multi-cores through performance impact estimation (PIE). In: Proceedings of the Annual International Symposium on Computer Architecture, pp. 213–224 (2012)
20. Woo, S., Ohara, M., Torrie, E., Singh, J., Gupta, A.: The SPLASH-2 programs: characterization and methodological considerations. In: Proceedings of the Annual International Symposium on Computer Architecture, pp. 24–36 (1995)

Moody Scheduling for Speculative Parallelization

Alvaro Estebanez[1], Diego R. Llanos[1]([✉]), David Orden[2], and Belen Palop[1]

[1] Dpto. Informática, Universidad de Valladolid,
Campus Miguel Delibes, 47011 Valladolid, Spain
{alvaro,diego,bpalop}@infor.uva.es
[2] Dpto. Física y Matemáticas, Universidad de Alcalá,
Alcalá de Henares, Madrid, Spain
david.orden@uah.es

Abstract. Scheduling is one of the factors that most directly affect performance in Thread-Level Speculation (TLS). Since loops may present dependences that cannot be predicted before runtime, finding a good chunk size is not a simple task. The most used mechanism, Fixed-Size Chunking (FSC), requires many "dry-runs" to set the optimal chunk size. If the loop does not present dependence violations at runtime, scheduling only needs to deal with load balancing issues. For loops where the general pattern of dependences is known, as is the case with Randomized Incremental Algorithms, specialized mechanisms have been designed to maximize performance. To make TLS available to a wider community, a general scheduling algorithm that does not require a-priori knowledge of the expected pattern of dependences nor previous dry-runs to adjust any parameter is needed. In this paper, we present an algorithm that estimates at runtime the best size of the next chunk to be scheduled. This algorithm takes advantage of our previous knowledge in the design and test of other scheduling mechanisms, and it has a solid mathematical basis. The result is a method that, using information of the execution of the previous chunks, decides the size of the next chunk to be scheduled. Our experimental results show that the use of the proposed scheduling function compares or even increases the performance that can be obtained by FSC, greatly reducing the need of a costly and careful search for the best fixed chunk size.

Keywords: Thread-level speculation · Speculative parallelization ·
Speculative multithreading · Scheduling

1 Introduction

Thread-Level Speculation (TLS) [4,18,20] is the most promising technique for automatic extraction of parallelism of irregular loops. With TLS, loops that can not be analyzed at compile time are optimistically executed in parallel. A hardware or software mechanism ensures that all threads access to shared data according to sequential semantics. A *dependence violation* appears when

© Springer-Verlag Berlin Heidelberg 2015
J.L. Träff et al. (Eds.): Euro-Par 2015, LNCS 9233, pp. 135–146, 2015.
DOI: 10.1007/978-3-662-48096-0_11

one thread incorrectly consumes a datum that has not been generated by a predecessor yet. In the presence of such a violation, earlier software-only speculative solutions (see, e.g. [10, 20]) interrupt the speculative execution and re-execute the loop serially. Subsequent approaches [5, 7, 21] squash only the offending thread and its successors, re-starting them with the correct data values. More sophisticate solutions [9, 15, 22] squash only the offending thread and subsequent threads that have actually consumed any value from it.

It is easy to see that frequent squashes adversely affect the performance of a TLS framework. One way to reduce the cost of a squash is to assign smaller subsets (called *chunks*) of iterations to each thread, reducing both the amount of work being discarded in the case of a squash, and the probability of occurrence of a dependence violation. However, smaller chunks also imply more frequent commit operations and a higher scheduling overhead. Therefore, a correct choice of the chunk sizes is critical for speculation performance. Most scheduling methods proposed so far in the literature deal with independent blocks of iterations, and were not designed to take into account the cost of re-executing threads in the context of a speculative execution.

A widely used mechanism to solve this problem is to choose a fixed, optimum size by trial and error. This method, called Fixed-Size Chunking [12] requires many dry-runs to find an acceptable value. Moreover, a particular size found for one application is of little use for another one, or even for a different input set of the same application.

In this work we address the general problem of scheduling chunks of iterations for their speculative execution, regardless of the number of dependence violations that may actually appear. We have found that the pattern of dependence violations heavily depends on the application. Therefore, a scheduling strategy that is able to dynamically adapt the size of chunks at runtime is very desirable.

In this paper, we introduce a scheduling method, called *Moody Scheduling*, that tries to predict, at runtime, the best chunk size for the next chunk to be scheduled. To do so, we rely on the number of re-executions of the previous chunks, not only by using the mean of the last re-executions, but also their tendency. With this method, we are able to (a) provide a general solution that does not need an in-depth study of the dependence violation pattern, and (b) greatly reduce the need of repetitive executions to tune the scheduling mechanism used.

The rest of the paper is organized as follows. Section 2 reviews some of the existent scheduling alternatives currently used with TLS. Section 3 introduces the main aspects of our proposal. Section 4 describes the function from a mathematical point of view. Section 5 explores two different uses for our Moody Scheduling. Section 6 gives some experimental results, comparing the new algorithm with FSC, while Sect. 7 concludes this paper.

2   Related Work

Since the size of the chunk assigned to each processor directly affects performance in TLS, numerous algorithms have been proposed to give a solution to this problem. The simplest one, called Fixed-Size Chunking (FSC), was initially proposed by Kruskal and Weiss [12]. With this mechanism, each thread is assigned a constant number of iterations. Finding the right constant needs several dry-runs on each particular input set for each parallelized loop. When no dependence violations arise at runtime, this technique is perfectly adequate. The only remaining concern is to achieve a good load balance when the last iterations are being scheduled. Some examples of mechanisms that implement load-balancing techniques can be found in [11] or [23].

There are solutions based on compile-time dependence analysis [19,25]. In these approaches, scheduling decisions are taken by reviewing the possible dependence pattern that can arise, so an in-depth analysis of the loop is needed.

Other approaches rely on the *expected* dependence pattern of the loop to be parallelized. In particular, for Randomized Incremental Algorithms, where dependences tend to accumulate in the first iterations of the loop, two methods have been shown to improve performance. The first one, called Meseta [16], divides the execution in three stages. In the first one, chunks of increasing sizes are scheduled, aiming to compensate for possible dependence violations, until a lower bound of the probability of finding a dependence is reached. From then on, a second stage applies FSC to execute most of the remaining iterations. A third stage gradually decreases the chunk size, aiming to achieve a better load balancing.

The second mechanism is called Just-In-Time (JIT) Scheduling [17]. This method also focuses on randomized incremental algorithms, where dependences are more likely to appear during the execution of the first chunks. JIT Scheduling defines different logarithmic-based functions that issue chunks of increasing size, and relies on runtime information to modulate these functions according to the number of dependence violations that effectively appear.

Kulkarni et al. [13] also discussed the importance of scheduling strategies in TLS. These authors defined a schedule through three steps, i.e., three design choices that specify the behavior of a schedule, namely *clustering*, *labeling* and *ordering*. They tested several strategies for each defined module, using their Galois framework. Their results show that each application analyzed was closely linked to a different scheduling strategy.

In summary, we can conclude that proposed solutions so far either depend on the expected dependency pattern of the loop to be speculatively executed, or require a big number of training experiments to be tuned, as in the case of FSC. In this paper we present a new mechanism that issues chunks of different sizes, by taking into account the actual occurrence of dependence violations, without using any prior knowledge about their distribution.

3   Moody Scheduling: Design Guidelines

Our main purpose is to design a scheduling function that is able to predict the best size for the following chunk to be issued at runtime, without the need of a knowledge of the underlying problem. In order to decide the size of the

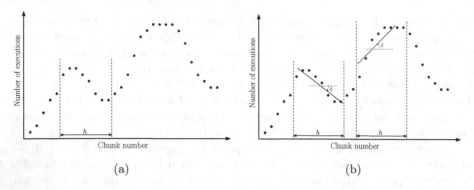

Fig. 1. (a) A possible execution profile for a given loop, and (b) an example of the use of linear regression to measure the tendency of the last h chunks. Recall that the y-axis does not represent the chunk size, but the number of re-executions for each chunk.

next chunk to be scheduled, we will use the number of times that the last h chunks have been squashed and re-executed due to dependence violations. As an example, Fig. 1(a) shows, for each scheduled chunk (x-axis), the number of times it has been executed so far (y-axis).

Given the number of executions of the last h chunks (regardless whether they were already committed or not), we will consider two parameters. The first one is the average number of executions of the last h chunks, which we call meanH and whose value is, at least, 1. The second one is the *tendency* of these re-executions. This value, which we call d, lies in the interval $(-1, 1)$ and determines if the number of executions is decreasing ($d < 0$), increasing ($d > 0$), or remaining unchanged ($d = 0$). As we will see, d depends on the angle δ between the linear regression line for the last h chunks and the horizontal axis (see Fig. 1(b)).

The size of the following chunk to be scheduled will depend on these two parameters. We will first present an informal description of the idea. The following section shows the mathematical background and the implementation details.

1. If the tendency of re-executions is decreasing (d close to -1):
   (a) If meanH is very low (close to 1), we will (optimistically) set the chunk size to the maximum size suitable for this problem. We will call this maximum value maxChunkSize.
   (b) If meanH is between the minimum value (1) and an *acceptable* value (that we call accMeanH), we will (optimistically) increase the chunk size.
   (c) If meanH is between accMeanH and an upper limit (that we call maxMeanH), we will keep the same chunk size, with the aim that its execution will help to further reduce meanH.
   (d) If meanH is higher than maxMeanH, we set the size of the following chunk to 1.
2. If the tendency of re-executions is stable (d close to 0):
   (a) If meanH is very low (close to 1), then we will (optimistically) issue a larger chunk size.

(b) If meanH is acceptable (close to accMeanH), then we will keep the same chunk size.
(c) If meanH is between accMeanH and maxMeanH, then we will (pessimistically) decrease the chunk size.
(d) If meanH is higher than maxMeanH, we set the size of the following chunk to 1.

3. If the tendency of re-executions is increasing (d close to 1):
   (a) If meanH is very low (close to 1), then we propose to keep the same chunk size, waiting for the next data to confirm if meanH really gets larger.
   (b) If meanH is acceptable (close to accMeanH), then we decrease the chunk size, intending to reduce the number of executions.
   (c) If meanH is close to (or higher than) maxMeanH, then we propose a chunk of size 1 intending to minimize the number of re-executions.

The last question is what size we should use to issue the first chunk, where there is no past history to rely on. As we will see in Sect. 6, setting this inital value to 1 leads to a good performance in all the applications considered.

Table 1 summarizes the behavior of our scheduling mechanism. Using this approach, given the current lastChunkSize and a pair of values (d, meanH) our function will use the guidelines described above to propose a value for nextChunkSize. The following section discusses the implementation details.

Table 1. Changes on the following chunk sized according to d and meanH parameters

	meanH $\approx$ 1	meanH $\approx$ accMeanH	meanH $\approx$ maxMeanH	meanH $>$ maxMeanH
$d \to -1$	$\uparrow$	$\nearrow$	$=$	1
$d \approx 0$	$\swarrow$	$=$	$\searrow$	1
$d \to 1$	$=$	$\searrow$	1	1

4 Moody Scheduling Function Definition

After the informal description presented above, the following step is to define a function that determines the value for nextChunkSize using the current value of lastChunkSize, together with d and meanH. In order to obtain the value of δ, we compute the regression line defined by the last h points in our execution window (see Fig. 1(b)).

The main problem with the intuitive behavior described above is that its straightforward implementation (with nested if...then constructs) leads to a discontinuous function. This is not a desirable situation, since the behavior of the scheduling function would drastically change for very similar situations.

Instead, we define a bidimensional function that, for a given value of meanH and d, returns the size of the next chunk to be scheduled. Figure 2(a) shows a 3D

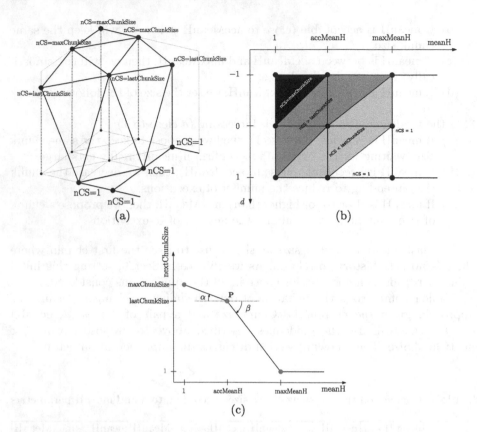

Fig. 2. (a) 3D representation of the Moody Scheduling function, that returns a value for nextChunkSize (nCS) provided the current lastChunkSize and depending on d and meanH; (b) 2D representation that connects our function with the intuitive behavior described in Sect. 3; (c) Intersection of the graphic of nextChunkSize (d, meanH) with $d = 0$.

representation of the Moody Scheduling function proposed. Figure 2(b) shows its projection onto a horizontal plane, using the same grey scale as in Table 1.

To properly define this scheduling function, several parameters should be set. The value of d is calculated by measuring the angle δ of the tendency with respect to the horizontal axis. This angle lies in $(-\pi/2, \pi/2)$. Our growth tendency $d \in (-1, 1)$ will be given by $d = \frac{\delta}{\pi/2}$.

The following parameter to be defined is accMeanH, that is, the highest value of meanH considered to be acceptable. We initially set accMeanH = 2, considering that, on average, we will accept that chunks have to be reexecuted at most once.

There are two remaining parameters: maxChunkSize and maxMeanH, whose values depend on the slopes of the graphic of the bidimensional scheduling function as follows. If we fix $d = 0$ in the scheduling function, we obtain the plot depicted in Fig. 2(c). In this case, we can define two angles, α and β (see figure). The angle α represents how optimistically the chunk size is going to be increased. The higher the value for α, the most optimistic the scheduling function will be. Analogously, β represents how pessimistically the chunk size is going to be decreased. If we fix the value for these two angles, the value of maxChunkSize is determined by the intersection between the segment from P with angle α, and the vertical line defined by meanH $= 1$. Analogously, the value for maxMeanH is determined by the intersection between the segment from P with angle β, and the horizontal line defined by nextChunkSize $= 1$. In the case that lastChunkSize $= 1$, β will be 0. On the other hand, $\alpha \neq 0$ as long as accMeanH will never be set to 1.

The nine particular points defined by meanH $\in \{1, \text{accMeanH}, \text{maxMeanH}\}$ and $d \in \{-1, 0, 1\}$ are defined by the values described above. Given that the call to nextChunkSize(d, meanH) will return maxChunkSize for the three points $(-1, 1)$, $(-1, \text{accMeanH})$, and $(0, 1)$, the function will also return maxChunkSize to all points inside this triangle. Analogously, for all points inside the triangle with vertices $(1, \text{accMeanH})$, $(1, \text{maxMeanH})$, and $(0, \text{maxMeanH})$, the function will return 1. Notice that points on the diagonals $(1, 1)$ to $(0, \text{accMeanH})$, and from there to $(-1, \text{maxMeanH})$ will return lastChunkSize. These three facts provide a natural triangulation for the space in Fig. 2(b).

5   Dynamic and Adaptive Implementations

If no dependences arose during the parallel execution, the size of the following chunk would be calculated only once, that is, just before issuing its execution. Otherwise, if the execution of the chunk fails, it gives the runtime system an opportunity to adjust its calculation by calling the scheduling function with updated runtime information. As it happens in [17], this leads to two different ways to use the scheduling function:

- To calculate the size of the following chunk only the first time this particular chunk will be issued. Subsequent re-executions will keep the same size. See Fig. 3(a).
- To re-calculate the size of the following chunk each time the chunk is scheduled. This solution is called *adaptive scheduling* in [17]. See Fig. 3(b).

The advantage of adaptive over dynamic scheduling is that the first calculation of the chunk size may rely on incomplete information, since some or all of the previous chunks are still being executed, and therefore they may suffer additional squashes. Adaptive scheduling will always reconsider the situation using updated data. Naturally, this comes at the cost of additional calls to the scheduling function.

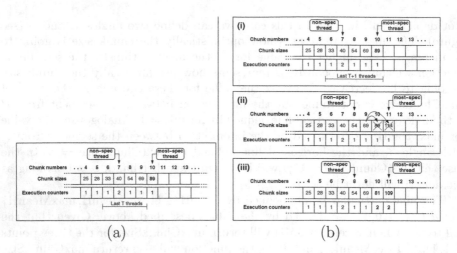

Fig. 3. (a) Dynamic Moody Scheduling. The size for the following chunk to be executed (#10) is calculated once (89 iterations). Its size will be preserved regardless of the number of re-executions of this chunk. (b) Adaptive Moody Scheduling. (i) Size of chunk #10 is calculated with the Moody Scheduling function (89 iterations). (ii) Chunk #9 issues a squash operation. (iii) Squashed threads recalculate in program order the new sizes of the chunks to be executed, using the new values of the execution counters.

6   Experimental Evaluation

We have used ATLaS, a software-based TLS framework [1,8], to execute in parallel four different applications that present non-analyzable loops with and without dependences among iterations.

The first benchmark used is TREE from [2]. This application spends a large fraction of its sequential execution time on a loop that can not be automatically parallelized by state-of-the-art compilers because it has dependence structures that are either too complicated to be analyzed at compile time or dependent on the input data.

We consider three additional applications that present loops with dependences. The first one is the 2-Dimensional Convex Hull (2D-Hull), an incremental randomized algorithm due to Clarkson et al. [6]. The algorithm computes the convex hull (smallest enclosing convex polygon) of a set of two-dimensional points in the plane. We have tested this application using three different input sets: Disc and Square, that are composed of points uniformly distributed inside a disc and a square, and Kuzmin, that is composed of points that follow a Kuzmin distribution [3].

The second application, called the 2-Dimensional Minimum Enclosing Circle (2D-MEC) [24], finds the smallest enclosing circle containing a given set of points in the plane. The construction is also incremental. In this case, a dependence violation forces not only an update of the current solution, but the recalculation of the entire enclosing ball. This fact produces devastating effects when the benchmark is speculatively parallelized.

Table 2. Characteristics of the algorithms and input sizes used

Algorithm	Input set description	Loop parallelized	Loop time as % of total time	Iterations per invocation	% of dependence violations	FSC chunk size used (iterations)
TREE	Off-axis parab. collision	accel_10	94	4 096	0	100
2D-Hull	Kuzmin, 10M points	Main loop	99	9 999 997	0.0008	11 000
2D-Hull	Square, 10M points	Main loop	99	9 999 997	0.0032	3 000
2D-Hull	Disc, 10M points	Main loop	99	9 999 997	0.021	1 250
2D-MEC	Disc, 10M points	Inner loop	99	Changes dynamically	0.009	1 800
Delaunay	100K points	Main loop	99	95 000	0.5	2

The last benchmark is the Delaunay triangulation [14] of a two-dimensional set of points. We have used an input set of 100 K points. Table 2 summarizes the characteristics of each application considered.

Experiments were carried out on a 64-processor server, equipped with four 16-core AMD Opteron 6376 processors at 2.3 GHz and 256 GB of RAM, which runs Ubuntu 12.04.3 LTS. All threads had exclusive access to the processors during the execution of the experiments, and we used wall-clock times in our measurements. Applications were compiled with gcc. Times shown below represent the time spent in the execution of the main loop of the application. The time needed to read the input set and the time needed to output the results have not been taken into account.

Figure 4 shows the relative performance of the mentioned applications when executed with the ATLaS speculative parallelization framework [1] and three different scheduling mechanisms: Adaptive Moody Scheduling, Dynamic Moody Scheduling and Fixed-Size Chunking (FSC).

The plots show the performance obtained when an optimum chunk size is used for FSC (a choice that required more than 20 experiments per application) and for Moody Scheduling, whose choice of parameters required less than five experiments in all cases. In the case of Moody Scheduling, we have used a value of 2 for accMeanH, $\beta = \frac{\pi}{4}$, and a value for h (the size of the window to be considered) equal to twice the number of processors for all applications. Regarding α, we have used values $\in (\frac{\pi}{20}, \frac{\pi}{6})$, depending on whether the application is known to produce dependence violations at runtime.

Furthermore, Moody Scheduling turns out to be competitive even without any tuning: If we set to 1 the initial chunk size, its performance reaches 88.3 % of the best FSC on geometric average. Meanwhile, the performance of FSC with chunk size 1 drops almost to zero (except for Delaunay, when the best chunk size for FSC is 2).

Regarding 2D-Hull (Fig. 4(a), (b), and (c)), the results for the Disc and Square input sets show that our scheduling method leads to a better performance than FSC. For the Disc input set, the highest speedup (2.17×) is achieved with 32 processors and the Dynamic version. For the Square input set, the biggest speedup (6.81×) is achieved with the Dynamic version and 40 processors. Finally, the performance figures when processing the Kuzmin input set are similar for all the scheduling alternatives. The best performance (11.11×) is achieved with 56 processors and the Adaptive version. The two remaining applications lead

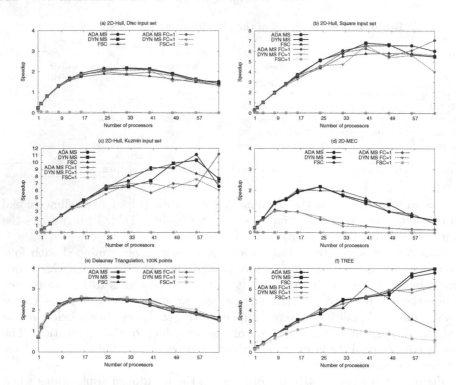

Fig. 4. Performance comparison for 2D-Hull with Disc, Square, and Kuzmin input sets, and 2D-MEC, Delaunay, and TREE benchmarks. Note the extremely poor performance of FSC when the chunk size is set to 1.

to similar performance results with all the scheduling mechanisms considered. The 2D Smallest Enclosing Circle (Fig. 4(d)) achieved a speedup of 2.18× with 24 processors and the Dynamic version. The Delaunay triangulation (Fig. 4(e)) achieved a speedup of 2.58× using the Adaptive version. Finally, Fig. 4(f) shows the speedup of TREE. This benchmark gained with the use of our scheduling method: With 40 processors, FSC approach achieved its speedup peak, while the Adaptive version continued improving its performance even with the maximum of available processors. It is interesting to note that, for TREE, both the Dynamic and Adaptive mechanisms are equivalent: As long as no squashes are issued, the size for each new chunk is calculated only once. The best performance in this benchmark (7.96×) is obtained with the Adaptive version and 64 processors.

Regarding the relative performance of FSC and Moody Scheduling, both strategies lead to similar performance figures for all applications, with the exception of the TREE benchmark, where Moody Scheduling is clearly better. The main difference between them is that the choice of the optimum block size in FSC required a prior, extensive testing (more than 20 runs per benchmark), while the Moody Scheduling self-tuning mechanism leads to competitive results right from the beginning. Moreover, the results obtained for the TREE application show that, contrary to intuition, our self-tuning mechanism leads to better results than FSC even without dependence violations, despite the higher computing cost added by the runtime calls to the Moody Scheduling function. Regarding which approach is better, Dynamic or Adaptive, it seems to depend on the application. Therefore, we will keep both of them in the ATLaS framework.

7   Conclusions

This work addresses an important problem for speculative parallelism: How to compute the size of the following chunk of iterations to be scheduled. We have found that most of the existent solutions are highly dependent on the particular application to parallelize, and they require many executions of the problem to obtain the scheduling parameters. Our new method, Moody Scheduling, automatically calculates an adequate size for the next chunk of iterations to be scheduled, and can be tuned further by making slight changes to its parameters, namely α, β, h, and accMeanH. Our scheduling method can be used as a general approach that avoids most of the 'dry-runs' required to arrive to scheduling parameters in other methods. Results show that execution times are similar (or better) to those obtained with a carefully-tuned FSC execution. Moody Scheduling just needs from the user to decide how optimistic, and pessimistic, the TLS system will be when it schedules the following chunk of iterations.

Acknowledgments. The authors would like to thank the anonymous referees for their comments. This research is partly supported by Castilla-Leon (VA172A12-2), MICINN (Spain) and the European Union FEDER (MOGECOPP project TIN2011-25639, HomProg-HetSys project, TIN2014-58876-P, CAPAP-H5 network TIN2014-53522-REDT), Madrid Regional Government through the TIGRE5-CM program (S2013/ICE-2919), and by the MICINN Project MTM2011-22792. Belen Palop is partially supported by MINECO MTM2012-30951.

References

1. Aldea, S., Estebanez, A., Llanos, D.R., Gonzalez-Escribano, A.: An OpenMP extension that supports thread-level speculation. IEEE Trans. Parallel Distrib. Syst. (2015, to appear)
2. Barnes, J.E.: Institute for Astronomy, University of Hawaii. ftp://ftp.ifa.hawaii.edu/pub/barnes/treecode/
3. Blelloch, G.E., Miller, G.L., Hardwick, J.C., Talmor, D.: Design and implementation of a practical parallel delaunay algorithm. Algorithmica **24**(3), 243–269 (1999)
4. Cintra, M., Llanos, D.R.: Toward efficient and robust software speculative parallelization on multiprocessors. In: Proceedings of the PPoPP 2003, pp. 13–24. ACM (2003)
5. Cintra, M., Llanos, D.R.: Design space exploration of a software speculative parallelization scheme. IEEE Trans. Parallel Distrib. Syst. **16**(6), 562–576 (2005)
6. Clarkson, K.L., Mehlhorn, K., Seidel, R.: Four results on randomized incremental constructions. Comput. Geom. Theor. Appl. **3**(4), 185–212 (1993)

7. Dang, F.H., Yu, H., Rauchwerger, L.: The R-LRPD test: speculative parallelization of partially parallel loops. In: Proceedings of the 16th IPDPS, pp. 20–29. IEEE Computer Society (2002)
8. Estebanez, A., Llanos, D., Gonzalez-Escribano, A.: New data structures to handle speculative parallelization at runtime. International Journal of Parallel Programming pp. 1–20 (2015)
9. García-Yágüez, A., Llanos, D.R., Gonzalez-Escribano, A.: Squashing alternatives for software-based speculative parallelization. IEEE Trans. Comput. **63**(7), 1826–1839 (2014)
10. Gupta, M., Nim, R.: Techniques for speculative run-time parallelization of loops. In: Proceedings of the ICS 1998, pp. 1–12. IEEE Computer Society (1998)
11. Hagerup, T.: Allocating independent tasks to parallel processors: an experimental study. J. Parallel Distrib. Comput. **47**(2), 185–197 (1997)
12. Kruskal, C., Weiss, A.: Allocating independent subtasks on parallel processors. IEEE Trans. SE- Softw. Eng. **11**(10), 1001–1016 (1985)
13. Kulkarni, M., Carribault, P., Pingali, K., Ramanarayanan, G., Walter, B., Bala, K., Chew, L.P.: Scheduling strategies for optimistic parallel execution of irregular programs. In: Proceedings of the 20th SPAA, pp. 217–228. ACM (2008)
14. Lee, D., Schachter, B.: Two algorithms for constructing a delaunay triangulation. Int. J. Comput. Inf. Sci. **9**(3), 219–242 (1980)
15. Li, X.F., Du, Z., Yang, C., Lim, C.C., Ngai, T.F.: Speculative parallel threading architecture and compilation. In: Proceedings of the ICPPW 2005, pp. 285–294. IEEE Computer Society (2005)
16. Llanos, D.R., Orden, D., Palop, B.: Meseta: a new scheduling strategy for speculative parallelization of randomized incremental algorithms. In: HPSEC-05 Workshop (ICPP 2005), pp. 121–128. IEEE Computer Society, Oslo, June 2005
17. Llanos, D.R., Orden, D., Palop, B.: Just-in-time scheduling for loop-based speculative parallelization. In: PDP 2008, pp. 334–342 (2008)
18. Oancea, C.E., Mycroft, A., Harris, T.: A lightweight in-place implementation for software thread-level speculation. In: Proceedings of the SPAA 2009, pp. 223–232. ACM (2009)
19. Ottoni, G., August, D.: Global multi-threaded instruction scheduling. In: Proceedings of the MICRO 40, pp. 56–68. IEEE Computer Society, Washington, DC, USA (2007)
20. Rauchwerger, L., Padua, D.: The LRPD test: speculative run-time parallelization of loops with privatization and reduction parallelization. In: Proceedings of the PLDI 1995, pp. 218–232. ACM (1995)
21. Rundberg, P., Stenström, P.: An all-software thread-level data dependence speculation system for multiprocessors. J. Instr.-Level Parallelism **2001**(3), 1–26 (2001)
22. Tian, C., Feng, M., Gupta, R.: Speculative parallelization using state separation and multiple value prediction. In: Proceedings of the 2010 International Symposium on Memory Management, ISMM 2010, pp. 63–72. ACM, New York (2010)
23. Tzen, T.H., Ni, L.M.: Trapezoid self-scheduling: a pratical scheduling scheme for parallel compilers. IEEE Trans. Parallel Distrib. Syst. **4**(1), 87–98 (1993)
24. Welzl, E.: Smallest enclosing disks (balls and ellipsoids). In: Maurer, H.A. (ed.) New Results and New Trends in Computer Science. LNCS, vol. 555, pp. 359–370. Springer, Heidelberg (1991)
25. Zhai, A., Steffan, J.G., Colohan, C.B., Mowry, T.C.: Compiler and hardware support for reducing the synchronization of speculative threads. ACM Trans. Archit. Code Optim. **5**(1), 3–33 (2008)

Allocating Jobs with Periodic Demand Variations

Olivier Beaumont[1,2], Ikbel Belaid[1,2], Lionel Eyraud-Dubois[1,2],
and Juan-Angel Lorenzo-del-Castillo[1,2]([⊠])

[1] Inria Bordeaux – Sud-Ouest, Talence, France
[2] University of Bordeaux, Bordeaux, France
juan-angel.lorenzo-del-castillo@inria.fr

Abstract. In the context of service hosting in large-scale datacenters, we consider the problem faced by a provider for allocating services to machines. Based on an analysis of a public Google trace corresponding to the use of a production cluster over a long period, we propose a model where long-running services experience demand variations with a periodic (daily) pattern and we prove that services following this model acknowledge for most of the overall CPU demand. This leads to an allocation problem where the classical Bin-Packing issue is augmented with the possibility to co-locate jobs whose peaks occur at different times of the day, which is bound to be more efficient than the usual approach that consist in over-provisioning for the maximum demand. In this paper, we provide a mathematical framework to analyze the packing of services exhibiting daily patterns and whose peaks occur at different times. We propose a sophisticated SOCP (Second Order Cone Program) formulation for this problem and we analyze how this modified packing constraint changes the behavior of standard packing heuristics (such as Best-Fit or First-Fit Decreasing). We show that taking periodicity of demand into account allows for a substantial improvement on machine utilization in the context of large-scale, state-of-the-art production datacenters.

1 Introduction

The Cloud paradigm provides an illusion of infinite elasticity and seamless provisioning of IT resources. However, as providers keep scaling their infrastructures year after year, the efficient allocation of services in *Platform-as-a-Service* (PaaS) becomes crucial.

We concentrate on the case of a Cloud platform in which several independent services, typically virtualized as Virtual Machines (VMs) or lightweight containers, are serving user queries and need to be allocated onto physical machines (PMs) [1,17]. We consider the static case where a set of *dominant* services define the overall resource usage of the physical platform, which has proved to be commonplace in large datacenters [3]. In this context, mapping services with heterogeneous computing demands onto PMs is amenable to a multi-dimensional Bin-Packing problem (each dimension corresponding to a different kind of resource,

© Springer-Verlag Berlin Heidelberg 2015
J.L. Träff et al. (Eds.): Euro-Par 2015, LNCS 9233, pp. 147–158, 2015.
DOI: 10.1007/978-3-662-48096-0_12

memory, CPU, disk, bandwidth,...). Indeed, on the infrastructure side, each physical machine presents a given computing capacity (*i.e.* the number of Flops it can process during one time-unit), a memory capacity and a failure rate (*i.e.* the probability that the machine will fail during the next time period). On the client side, each service has a set of requirements along the same dimensions (memory and CPU footprints) and a reliability requirement that has been negotiated typically through an SLA [8].

In this work, we consider a specific feature of CPU demand that arises in the context of service allocation. Based on the analysis of a large cluster trace provided by Google, we demonstrate in Sect. 3 that many services representing most of the overall CPU demand exhibit daily patterns and their demand can be modeled as a set of sinusoids, each comprising a constant component, an amplitude and a phase. Under this premise, the contribution of this paper is threefold. First, we propose and advocate a novel model for jobs with time-varying resource demands and we define the associated packing problem. This model can be used to aggregate onto the same physical machines more resources than it would be possible based on their maximal demands only, taking advantage of the fact that different phases for different services imply that peak demands do not occur simultaneously. Second, we show the benefits of antagonistic job aggregation, and how this can be used to improve the system performance. Third, we propose several algorithms for packing jobs with periodic demands on the hosting platform. The first one is based on a Second Order Cone Program (SOCP) formulation [11] whereas the others are adaptations of classical greedy packing heuristics.

The remaining of this paper is organized as follows. We discuss some related works in Sect. 2. In Sect. 3, we characterize the periodic behavior of some of the jobs in a cluster usage trace provided by Google. In Sect. 4, we formulate the optimization problem using Complex Analysis and we prove that it can be expressed as a SOCP (*Second Order Cone Program*). In Sect. 5, we propose several packing heuristics, whose performance is analyzed and validated on a realistic trace in Sect. 6. Finally, conclusions are drawn in Sect. 7.

2 Related Works

In order to deal with resource allocation problems arising in the context of Clouds, several sophisticated techniques have been developed in order to optimally allocate user services onto PMs, either to achieve good load-balancing [4,7] or to minimize energy consumption [5]. Most of the approaches in this domain are based on offline [9] and online [10] variants of Bin-Packing strategies.

In this paper, we concentrate on the allocation of jobs that last for a long time and whose CPU demands exhibit periodic patterns. Some other work deal with allocating jobs whose demands varies over time, either with predictable (static) or unknown (dynamic) behavior. In the static case which is the focus of this present work, historical average resource utilization is typically used as input to an algorithm that maps services to physical machines. Therefore, the mapping is done off-line. In contrast, dynamic allocation schemes are implemented on shorter timescales. Dynamic allocation leverages the ability to perform run-time migrations of jobs and to recompute resource allocation amongst services.

A dynamic migration algorithm *Measure Forecast Remap* is introduced in [6], where highly variable workloads are forecast over intervals shorter than the time scale of demand variability to ensure dynamic minimization of the number of required machines. Based on stochastic vector packing model, the static scheme proposed in [14] makes use of customers' periodic access patterns in web server farms to assign each customer to a server so as to minimize the total number of required servers. In this latter work, the variable demand is analyzed at a different time scale to extract probability distributions that are independent of time. Then, *stream-packing* heuristics are employed to select the most complementary jobs to be packed in the same server. Urgaonkar et al. [15] rely on on-line application profiling to demonstrate the feasibility and benefits of overbooking resources in shared platforms to guide the application placement onto dedicated resources while providing performance guarantees at runtime. A new mechanism for dynamic resource management in cluster-based network servers [2], called cluster reserve, allows performance isolation between service classes and provides a minimal amount of resources, irrespective of the load imposed by other requests. In contrast to these other directions, our work focuses on a part of the workload which exhibits deterministic periodic variability. In this context, dynamic resource management is unnecessary: the migration cost can be avoided by using periodicity-aware static approaches for service allocation. Still, above mentioned approaches can be used in order to allocate at runtime all the tasks that do not exhibit daily sinusoidal patterns in their demand. Nevertheless, we will prove that the overall weight of such services in terms of CPU demand makes it useful to design specific allocation algorithms for them.

3   Periodicity Analysis

When considering efficient allocations, it is important to categorize how services are correlated in order to schedule them efficiently. Indeed, if many services reach their (say, CPU) peak demand at the same time (*i.e.* high positive correlation), the stress on the platform and on the resource allocation algorithm will be much higher. In this case, it seems reasonable to place those services on different physical machines to avoid machine starvation. On the other hand, if peaks are spread on a large enough time-frame, this will allow for some slack in the allocation algorithm to provide efficient placements by co-allocating jobs whose peaks happen at different times, hence resulting in a more efficient average resource utilization.

Our periodicity analysis is based on the study of a usage trace released by Google from one of its production clusters [16]. The workload consists in a massive number of jobs, which can be further divided into *tasks*, being each task assigned to a single physical machine. The data are collected from 12583 machines, span a time of 29 days and provide exhaustive profiling information on 5 min monitoring intervals. Each job belongs to a priority group, namely (in order of decreasing importance) *Infrastructure, Monitoring, Normal Production, Other* and *Gratis (free)* [12,13]. The scheduler generally gives preference to resource demands from higher priority tasks over tasks belonging to lower priority groups, to the point of evicting the latter ones if needed.

Given the thorough information contained in the trace, one of the main difficulties is related to the time needed to validate any assumption based on these data. To simplify this process without loss of accuracy, we proposed in [3] an extraction of the information from a subset of jobs that we defined as *dominant*, *i.e.* jobs which account for most of platform usage at any time.

In this work, we have restricted our study to dominant jobs in the *Normal Production* class, given that they represent standard production utilization in the datacenter and last for long enough to allow periodicity correlation. In addition, considering only one priority class avoids issues due to the fact that hosts have finite capacity. Indeed, this finite capacity implies that when the resource demand of one job increases, another job with lower priority may end up using fewer resources (or even getting evicted by the scheduler) even if its actual demand remained invariable.

The spectral analysis of the *Normal Production*, dominant jobs that run during the whole trace allowed us to quantify the main components of their CPU demand, namely the amplitude, phase, frequency and background noise. Table 1 provides the averaged ratios between the jobs' components' amplitudes and their constant part. The residual noise is about 6 % of the average CPU demand for a large part of the jobs, which can be used as a threshold: any pattern with an amplitude significantly larger can be identified as a relevant component. Attending to the percentile variation, we conclude that very few jobs exhibit hourly patterns, more than half of the jobs show very strong daily patterns, and only two thirds have significant daily patterns. Weekly patterns are not as strong, but they are still significant for about half of the jobs.

Regarding pattern synchronization, we observed that all jobs with a weekly pattern show the same behavior: 5 days of high usage followed by 2 days of lower usage. For the daily patterns, we analyzed jobs with an amplitude of, at least, 10 % of the mean. Half of the jobs show a phase difference below 60 degrees (*i.e.* their peaks are within 4 hours from each other). Furthermore, 90 % of the jobs exhibit a phase difference below 120 degrees (peaks are at most 8 hours apart). This shows that the jobs' behavior is clearly correlated by this daily pattern.

Table 1. Ratios amplitude/mean part for long-running, dominant jobs [3]. Each row shows the mean, standard deviation, and different percentiles of such ratios.

Stats	Ratio of Amplitude to mean				
	Hourly	Daily	Weekly	Long term	Noise
Mean	0.057	0.267	0.148	0.154	0.100
Std	0.246	0.232	0.127	0.161	0.154
Min	0.001	0.006	0.011	0.001	0.012
25 %	0.004	0.052	0.076	0.051	0.036
50 %	0.007	0.268	0.106	0.102	0.058
75 %	0.009	0.376	0.196	0.196	0.072
Max	1.612	1.075	0.669	1.149	0.836

4   Packing of Jobs with Periodic Demands

4.1   Notations and Problem Formulation

Let us assume that the cloud platform we consider consists of M homogeneous nodes $M_1, \ldots, M_k, \ldots, M_M$ and let us denote the processing capacity of a node by C. For the sake of simplicity and in order to focus on issues related to the aggregation of periodic demands, we will concentrate on CPU demands only.

The tasks of a job (corresponding to a service in the trace) can run on any node, and job J_j is split into N_j tasks denoted by $T_{j,1}, \ldots, T_{j,l}, \ldots, T_{j,N_j}$, who share the same characteristics in terms of CPU demand.

In turn, platform nodes are allowed to run several tasks, provided that at any time step, their capacity is not exceeded. We assume that the set of tasks running on a node does not change over time, what is a realistic assumption for dominant *Normal Production* jobs, as shown in Sect. 3, and we model the instantaneous demand at time t of task $T_{j,l}$, which does not depend on l, as

$$W_j(t) = C_j + \rho_j \sin\left(2\pi \frac{t}{P_j} + \phi_j\right),$$

where C_j denotes the average of CPU demand of Task $T_{j,l}$, ρ_j denotes its maximal amplitude with respect to C_j, P_j denotes the period of its pattern and ϕ_j denotes its phase. As noticed in Sect. 3, one can concentrate in this context on jobs that exhibit daily patterns and we will therefore assume in what follows that $\forall j, P_j = P$, where P denotes a daytime.

In this context, our aim is to provide a static packing for the set of tasks $T_{j,l}$ such that at any step and on any resource, capacity constraints are not exceeded and such that the number of required nodes is minimized. More specifically, our goal is to take advantage of daily variations in order to obtain an efficient packing of tasks. Indeed, most packing strategies are based on the maximal demand of each task, what corresponds to $C_j + \rho_j$ for a task of job j. Taking advantage of the fact that all tasks do not achieve their peak demand at the same time in the day, it is possible to pack more tasks, and therefore to use fewer nodes whilst packing statically all the tasks.

Let us consider several tasks $T_{j,l}$ clustered together on node M_k. Knowing that all the jobs have the same period P, the constraint stating that the capacity of M_k is not exceeded at any time

$$\forall t, k, \quad \sum_{j,l:T_{j,l} \in M_k} W_j(t) \leq C, \text{ becomes}$$

$$\Longleftrightarrow \forall t, k, \quad \sum_{j,l:T_{j,l} \in M_k} C_j + \sum_{j,l:T_{j,l} \in M_k} \rho_j \sin(2\pi t/P + \phi_j) \leq C$$

$$\Longleftrightarrow \forall t, k, \quad \sum_{j,l:T_{j,l} \in M_k} C_j + \text{Im}\left(\sum_{j,l:T_{j,l} \in M_k} \rho_j \exp(2i\pi t/P)\exp(i\phi_j)\right) \leq C$$

$$\Longleftrightarrow \forall t, k, \quad \sum_{j,l:T_{j,l}\in M_k} C_j + \mathrm{Im}\left((\exp(2i\pi t/P))\left(\sum_{j,l:T_{j,l}\in M_k} \rho_j \exp(i\phi_j)\right)\right) \leq C$$

$$\Longleftrightarrow \forall k, \quad \sum_{j,l:T_{j,l}\in M_k} C_j + \|\sum_{j,l:T_{j,l}\in M_k} \rho_j \exp(i\phi_j)\| \leq C,$$

where $Im(z)$ denotes the imaginary part of complex number z, i is the imaginary unit satisfying $i^2 = -1$ and $\|z\|$ denotes the modulus of z.

Note that in the last expression, the constraint does not involve t anymore, and that all above complex analysis derivations are equivalences, such that this last expression exactly states that the capacity constraint is never exceeded at any time step. In order to design exact solutions and heuristics, we will use the following formulation,

$$\forall k, \quad \sum_{j,l:T_{j,l}\in M_k} C_j + \sqrt{(\sum_{j,l:T_{j,l}\in M_k} \rho_j \cos(\phi_j))^2 + (\sum_{j,l:T_{j,l}\in M_k} \rho_j \sin(\phi_j))^2} \leq C \quad (1)$$

4.2 Quadratic Formulation

From this modified packing constraint (1), we propose a quadratically constrained programming (QCP) formulation of our problem. This formulation uses two types of variables:

Integer variables $X_{j,k}$ representing the number of tasks of job j allocated on the node M_k,

Boolean variables Y_k representing whether node M_k is used.

With these variables, the formulation is the following:

$$\text{Minimize} \sum_k Y_k$$

$$\forall j \in J, \quad \sum_{k\in M} X_{j,k} = N_j \qquad (2)$$

$$\forall k \in M, \quad (\sum_{j\in J} X_{j,k}\rho_j \cos(\phi_j))^2 + (\sum_{j\in J} X_{j,k}\rho_j \sin(\phi_j))^2 \leq (C\, Y_k - \sum_{j\in J} X_{j,k}\, C_j)^2$$

$$(3)$$

$$\forall k \in M, \quad C\, Y_k - \sum_{j\in J} X_{j,k}\, C_j \geq 0 \qquad (4)$$

In this formulation, constraint (2) ensures that all instances of all jobs are allocated. Tasks belonging to the same job could co-exist in the same node. Constraints (3) and (4) are a quadratic reformulation of Eq. (1), ensuring that an unused node does not contribute any resource to the platform. Due to the nature of this constraint, this formulation can be expressed as a Second Order Cone Program, and can thus benefit from efficient general purpose solvers [11] for convex optimization. However, on real-size instances with thousands of machines, this formulation can not be solved in reasonable time with integer and boolean values. Relaxing the problem by allowing rational variables makes it possible to obtain a lower bound on the necessary number of resources in reasonable time.

5 Packing Heuristics

5.1 Complexity and Lower Bound

The optimization problem that consists in packing tasks with periodic demands into nodes is clearly NP-Complete, since it is amenable to classical Bin-Packing problems [9,10] in its most simplified setting where $\forall j$, $\rho_j = 0$, *i.e.* the case when demands do not change over time. The SOCP formulation proposed in Sect. 4.2 can be used to solve the optimization problem, but its use is in practice restricted to small cases. On the other hand, the relaxation of this SOCP where variables can take rational values (including the $X_{j,l}$'s) can be solved in reasonable time. This solution is not feasible in general but it provides a lower bound on the number of necessary nodes that will be used in order to evaluate the quality of the heuristics we propose.

5.2 Notations

In order to describe the algorithms, we will consider that tasks are sorted by decreasing values of C_j, as usual when designing packing heuristics. Other possible choices would include sorting tasks by decreasing values of $C_j + \rho_j$ and will be discussed in Sect. 6.2. Let us assume that tasks $T_{j,l}$ have been assigned to node M_k. Then, the load of node M_k will be represented, following the analysis performed in Sect. 4, by the triplet $S_k = (C_k, x_k, y_k)$, where

$$C_k = \sum_{j,l:T_{j,l}\in M_k} C_j, \ x_k = \sum_{j,l:T_{j,l}\in M_k} \rho_j \cos(\phi_j), \ y_k = \sum_{j,l:T_{j,l}\in M_k} \rho_j \sin(\phi_j).$$

The maximal load of node M_k at any time step t is therefore given by

$$\mathcal{L}(M_k) = C_k + \sqrt{x_k^2 + y_k^2}$$

and becomes $\mathcal{L}(M_k, T_{j,l}) = C_k + C_j + \sqrt{(x_k + \rho_j \cos(\phi_j))^2 + (y_k + \rho_j \sin(\phi_j))^2}$ when one task $T_{j,l}$ of job J_j is added to M_k.

5.3 Heuristics

We propose the following set of heuristics, adapted from classical efficient greedy Bin-Packing algorithms to the case of tasks exhibiting daily patterns.

– First-Fit Decreasing $\mathcal{FFD}$ is a greedy algorithm in which tasks are considered by decreasing values of C_j. At any step, task $T_{j,l}$ (from job J_j) is allocated to the node with the smallest index and such that $\mathcal{L}(M_k, T_{j,l}) \leq C$. If no such node exists, then a new node is added to the system to hold the task.

- Best-Fit Decreasing $\mathcal{BFD}$ is a greedy algorithm in which tasks are considered by decreasing values of C_j. At any step, task $T_{j,l}$ (from job J_j) is allocated to the node M_k such that $\mathcal{L}(M_k, T_{j,l})$ is maximized (while remaining below C). Note that contrarily to what happens in classical $\mathcal{BFD}$, the size that is considered is the size after the allocation. If no such node exists, then a new node is added to the system to hold the task.
- In Min-Max $\mathcal{MM}(M)$, the target number of nodes is fixed to M a priori. Then, $\mathcal{MM}$ is a greedy algorithm where tasks are considered by decreasing values of C_j. At any step, task $T_{j,l}$ (from job J_j) is allocated to the node M_k such that $\mathcal{L}(M_k, T_{j,l})$ is minimized, in order to balance the load between the different nodes. The allocation may fail if M is to small. In $\mathcal{MM}$, the best number of nodes is found using dichotomic search.
- Min-Max-Module $\mathcal{MMM}$ is similar to $\mathcal{MM}$, except that tasks are represented using their maximal demand over time $C_j + \rho_j$ only. Hence, in this case, the problem is reduced to the classical bin packing. This is typically what happens when one neglects the possibility to take advantage of the fact that peak demands do not occur at the same time for all jobs.

6   Experimental Evaluation

6.1   Simulated Data

We perform a set of experiments with synthetic data in order to assess the influence of the parameters on the performance of the different heuristics. In all the experiments, we display the ratio between the number of nodes using the heuristics described in Sect. 5 against the lower bound on the number of necessary nodes described in Sect. 5.1.

In the following, we set the capacity of the nodes to 20 and we consider the following parameters:

- CPU footprint of the tasks: we consider the case of Big Tasks (where C_j is chosen uniformly at random in $[0, 10]$) and Small Tasks (where C_j is chosen uniformly at random in $[0, 1]$).
- Daytime amplitude: we consider the case of Large Daytime Amplitude (where ρ_j is chosen uniformly at random in $[0, C_j]$) and Small Daytime Amplitude (where ρ_j is chosen uniformly at random in $[0, C_j/2]$).
- Size of the Jobs: we consider the case of Large Jobs (where the number of identical tasks of the job is set to 10) and Small Jobs, which consist in a single task.

In all cases, the phase of each job is chosen uniformly at random in $[0, 2\pi]$. In all the experiments, in order to perform a fair comparison, the expected value of the lower bound is set to 250, so that there are 10 times more tasks in the case of Small Tasks with respect to the case of Big Tasks. We performed other experiments with different number of jobs and tasks, but the results showed very little sensitivity to these parameters and were excluded from the paper in order to save space.

Results for the eight possible combinations (Small or Big tasks/Small or Big amplitude/Small or Big jobs) are displayed in Fig. 1.

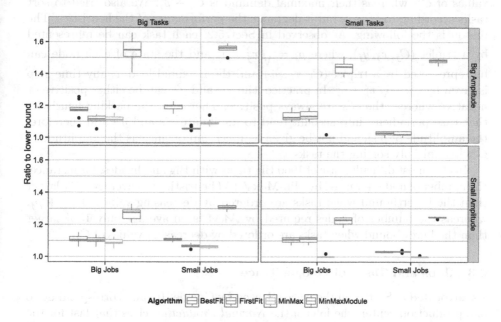

Fig. 1. Performance of the heuristics on synthetic data

The first conclusion that can be drawn is that failing to take periodic demand variations leads to a large waste of resources. Indeed, the performance of Min-Max-Module $\mathcal{MMM}$ is consistently far from the lower bound, by 50 % in the case of Big Amplitudes and by 25 % in the case of Small Amplitudes.

The second conclusion is that when the tasks are Small, so that each node holds a few tens of tasks, Min-Max $\mathcal{MM}$ performs extremely well and is always at most within 1 % of the lower bound. The results of Min-Max $\mathcal{MM}$ slightly degrade when tasks get Big. Indeed, in this case, the number of tasks per node is relatively small (a few units) and greedy heuristics fail to achieve close to optimal performance. Nevertheless, the number of nodes required by $\mathcal{MM}$ always stays within 20 % of the lower bound, and this lower bound is certainly underestimated, especially in the case of Big Tasks.

In the case of Big Tasks, it happens that First-Fit Decreasing $\mathcal{FFD}$ outperforms Min-Max $\mathcal{MM}$. Indeed, $\mathcal{FFD}$ is an efficient heuristic for classical Bin-Packing problems. On the other hand, it tends to pack together on the same node tasks whose characteristics are close in terms of C_j. In the case of Big Jobs consisting in several identical tasks, then $\mathcal{FFD}$ packs together tasks that achieve their peak demand at the same time and therefore fails to take full benefit of their periodic behavior.

6.2 Task Ordering

Note that in all the heuristics described in Sect. 5, tasks are sorted by decreasing values of C_j, whereas their maximal demand is $C_j + \rho_j$. We also tried to sort tasks according to $C_j + \rho_j$ but it degrades the performance of the heuristics. The reason is the following. As observed in Sect. 5.2, each task can be represented by a triplet (C_j, x_j, y_j), where $\rho_j = \sqrt{x_j^2 + y_j^2}$ and the state of each node can be represented by a triplet (C_k, x_k, y_k) and the maximal load at any time step is given by $C_k + \sqrt{x_k^2 + y_k^2}$. In practice, the x's and y's can be either positive or negative whereas the C's are always positive. Therefore, the packing heuristics that take periodicity into account tend to annihilate x's and y's and therefore, the amplitude of ρ should not be given as much importance as the amplitude of C when initially sorting the tasks.

In the (most difficult) case of 1000 Big tasks with Big amplitudes, for instance, the number of nodes required by Min-Max $\mathcal{MM}$ heuristic is on average 30 % larger than the lower bound when tasks are ordered by decreasing values of $C_j + \rho_j$, whereas the number of nodes required by $\mathcal{MM}$ is on average only 15 % larger than the lower bound when tasks are ordered by decreasing values of C_j.

6.3 Jobs and Tasks of Google Trace

As advocated in Sect. 3, in the trace released by Google [16] and corresponding to one production center, the jobs of the *Normal Production* class that last for the duration of the trace and that exhibit strong daily patterns count for about 50 % of the overall load. In this paper, we concentrate on this set of jobs, and we prove that their characteristics make them suitable for the design of efficient resource allocation algorithms, which take into account both their periodic nature and the fact that they do not all reach their peak values at the same time step.

Of course, since this set of jobs accounts for half of the overall demand, it is also crucial to design more dynamic strategies for the rest of the jobs. These jobs typically correspond to the *Gratis (free)* class [12,13] and can be allocated at runtime and then migrated to other nodes when the load of a node becomes too high so that the QoS (Quality of Service) of the *Normal Production* class cannot be enforced. Nevertheless, this important problem, addressed in the papers mentioned in Sect. 2, is out of the scope of this paper.

Following the classification of Sect. 3, we have extracted 89 jobs corresponding to a total of 22600 tasks. The largest job (in terms of tasks) consists in 1608 tasks. The largest job (in terms of CPU demand) corresponds to the capacity of 184 nodes at its peak demand. A capacity equivalent to 2198 nodes would be required if all jobs reached their peak demand at the same instant. On the other hand, the overall peak demand for the whole set of jobs is equivalent to the capacity of 2090 nodes.

Therefore, there exists a potential improvement on the number of required nodes of 5 %, what should be considered as large in the context of an actual production center. The results achieved by the different heuristics are displayed in Table 2.

Table 2. Number of nodes required per heuristic.

	First-Fit $\mathcal{FFD}$	Best-Fit $\mathcal{BFD}$	Min-Max $\mathcal{MM}$	Min-Max-Module $\mathcal{MMM}$
Number of nodes	2181	2182	2114	2226

It can be observed that the results of $\mathcal{MM}$ are extremely good on this actual dataset. Indeed, the number of required machines is only 1.1 % higher than the lower bound (2090 nodes), whereas $\mathcal{MMM}$, the equivalent heuristic that does not benefit from daily patterns, requires 6.5 % more machines than the lower bound. This result proves that there is clear interest to take benefit of daily patterns on an actual dataset.

7   Conclusions

This paper assesses the impact of designing efficient resource allocation algorithms for jobs that exhibit daily periodic sinusoidal patterns. First, we demonstrate that in a trace of a production cluster released by Google, those jobs actually represent a significant part of the workload. Then, we present a novel model of periodic jobs with variable resource demand in shared hosting platforms. We prove that the job aggregation problem, where the objective is to minimize the number of nodes, can be formulated as a SOCP, what enables us to solve it exactly in reasonable time, at least for small instances. We argue that provisioning resources solely based on the maximal demand of tasks, as showed by Min-Max-Module heuristic, results in larger number of nodes. On the other hand, resource provisioning based on an antagonistic job aggregation, as illustrated by the Min-Max heuristic, can yield gains that significantly decrease the number of required nodes. As future work, we plan to extend job aggregation strategies to provide performance guarantees for other resources like memory, disk, network bandwidth, etc. Our future research plans include refining the suggested second order cone program to more efficient mathematical programming relying on *column generation* algorithm. This algorithm is proved to be efficient for solving larger programs as it generates only variables which have the potential to improve the objective function. At last, in order to deal with larger classes of problems, it is crucial to understand how to mix the (close to optimal) strategies used to schedule long-running high priority job classes and the dynamic resource allocation strategies that are used for short and low priority classes.

References

1. Armbrust, M., Fox, A., Griffith, R., Joseph, A., Katz, R., Konwinski, A., Lee, G., Patterson, D., Rabkin, A., Stoica, I., et al.: Above the clouds: a berkeley view of cloud computing, University of California, Berkeley (2009)

2. Aron, M., Druschel, P., Zwaenepoel, W.: Cluster reserves: a mechanism for resource management in cluster-based network servers. In: Proceedings of the ACM SIG-METRICS Conference, pp. 90–101 (2000)
3. Beaumont, O., Eyraud-Dubois, L., Lorenzo-del Castillo, J.A.: Analyzing real cluster data for formulating allocation algorithms in cloud platforms. In: 2014 IEEE 26th International Symposium on Computer Architecture and High Performance Computing (SBAC-PAD), pp. 302–309 (2014)
4. Beaumont, O., Eyraud-Dubois, L., Rejeb, H., Thraves, C.: Heterogeneous resource allocation under degree constraints. In: IEEE Transactions on Parallel and Distributed Systems (2012)
5. Beloglazov, A., Buyya, R.: Energy efficient allocation of virtual machines in cloud data centers. In: IEEE/ACM International Conference on Cluster, Cloud and Grid Computing, pp. 577–578. IEEE (2010)
6. Bobroff, N., Kochut, A., Beaty, K.: Dynamic placement of virtual machines for managing SLA violations. In: 10th IFIP/IEEE International Symposium on Integrated Network Management, IM 2007, pp. 119–128 (2007)
7. Calheiros, R., Buyya, R., De Rose, C.: A heuristic for mapping virtual machines and links in emulation testbeds. In: Proceedings of International Conference on Parallel Processing (ICPP), pp. 518–525. IEEE (2009)
8. Cirne, W., Frachtenberg, E.: Web-scale job scheduling. In: Cirne, W., Desai, N., Frachtenberg, E., Schwiegelshohn, U. (eds.) JSSPP 2012. LNCS, vol. 7698, pp. 1–15. Springer, Heidelberg (2013)
9. Garey, M.R., Johnson, D.S.: Computers and Intractability, a Guide to the Theory of NP-Completeness. W.H. Freeman and Company, San Francisco (1979)
10. Hochbaum, D.: Approximation Algorithms for NP-hard Problems. PWS Publishing Company, Boston (1997)
11. Mittelmann, H.D.: An independent benchmarking of SDP and SOCP solvers. Math. Program. **95**(2), 407–430 (2003)
12. Reiss, C., Tumanov, A., Ganger, G.R., Katz, R.H., Kozuch, M.A.: Towards understanding heterogeneous clouds at scale: google trace analysis. Technical report, Carnegie Mellon University, April 2012
13. Reiss, C., Wilkes, J., Hellerstein, J.L.: Google cluster-usage traces: format + schema. Technical report, Google Inc., Mountain View, CA, USA (2011). Revised 20 March 2012. http://code.google.com/p/googleclusterdata/wiki/TraceVersion2
14. Shahabuddin, J., Chrungoo, A., Gupta, V., Juneja, S., Kapoor, S., Kumar, A.: Stream-packing: resource allocation in web server farms with a QoS guarantee. In: Monien, B., Prasanna, V.K., Vajapeyam, S. (eds.) HiPC 2001. LNCS, vol. 2228, pp. 182–191. Springer, Heidelberg (2001)
15. Urgaonkar, B., Shenoy, P., Roscoe, T.: Resource overbooking and application profiling in shared hosting platforms. In: SIGOPS Operating Systems Review, vol. 36(SI), pp. 239–254 (2002). http://doi.acm.org/10.1145/844128.844151
16. Wilkes, J.: More google cluster data. Google research blog (2011). http://googleresearch.blogspot.com/2011/11/more-google-cluster-data.html
17. Zhang, Q., Cheng, L., Boutaba, R.: Cloud computing: state-of-the-art and research challenges. J. Internet Serv. Appl. **1**(1), 7–18 (2010)

A Multi–level Hypergraph Partitioning Algorithm Using Rough Set Clustering

Foad Lotfifar and Matthew Johnson[✉]

School of Engineering and Computing Sciences, Durham University, Durham, UK
{foad.lotfifar,matthew.johnson2}@durham.ac.uk

Abstract. The hypergraph partitioning problem has many applications in scientific computing and provides a more accurate inter-processor communication model for distributed systems than the equivalent graph problem. In this paper, we propose a sequential multi-level hypergraph partitioning algorithm. The algorithm makes novel use of the technique of rough set clustering in categorising the vertices of the hypergraph. The algorithm treats hyperedges as features of the hypergraph and tries to discard unimportant hyperedges to make better clustering decisions. It also focuses on the trade-off to be made between local vertex matching decisions (which have low cost in terms of the space required and time taken) and global decisions (which can be of better quality but have greater costs). The algorithm is evaluated and compared to state-of-the-art algorithms on a range of benchmarks. The results show that it generates better partition quality.

1 Introduction

A hypergraph is a pair: a set of vertices and a set of hyperedges. Each hyperedge is a subset of the vertex set (there is no restriction on its size). The *hypergraph partitioning problem* asks, roughly speaking, for a partition of the vertex set such that the vertices are evenly distributed amongst the parts and the number of hyperedges that intersect multiple parts is minimised. A tool to solve this probem is called a *partitioner*. Hypergraph partitioning has applications in many areas of computer science such as data mining and image processing.

The hypergraph partitioning problem is a generalisation of the graph partitioning problem (in which the edges of a graph are subsets of the vertex set of size two contrasting with hyperedges whose size is unbounded), and provides a more natural way of representing the relationships between objects inherent in many problems [14]. The removal of the constraint on edge size, however, increases the practical difficulty of partitioning [13]. As both the graph and hypergraph variants of the partitioning problem are NP-hard [12], a number of heuristic algorithms have been proposed [10,17]. In this paper, we propose and evaluate a new algorithm.

Our serial *Feature Extraction Hypergraph Partitioning (FEHG)* algorithm is of a type known as multi-level. It has three distinct phases: coarsening, initial partitioning and uncoarsening. During coarsening vertices are merged to obtain

© Springer-Verlag Berlin Heidelberg 2015
J.L. Träff et al. (Eds.): Euro-Par 2015, LNCS 9233, pp. 159–170, 2015.
DOI: 10.1007/978-3-662-48096-0_13

hypergraphs with progressively smaller vertex sets. After the coarsening stage, the partitioning problem is solved on the smaller hypergraph obtained in the initial partitioning. During uncoarsening, the coarsening stage is reversed and the solution obtained on the small hypergraph is used to provide a solution on the input hypergraph. We describe some of the problems of multi-level partitioning that motivate our study:

1. Heuristics for multi-level hypergraph partitioning focus on finding highly-connected clusters of vertices that can be merged to form a coarser hypergraph. This requires a metric of similarity, the evaluation of which requires the recognition of "similar" vertices. As the mean and standard deviation of vertex degrees are usually high (and so the similarity of pairs of vertices is typically low), it is often a problem to define and measure the similarity [9].
2. There can be redundancy in modelling scientific problems with hypergraphs and it is desirable to remove it. In [13], an attempt to reduce the storage overhead of saving and processing hypergraphs is presented, but the strategy can increase either the storage requirement or the running time in some cases.
3. Decision making for matching vertices (that will be merged) is usually done locally. Global decisions are avoided due to their high cost and complexity though they give better results [21]. All proposed heuristics reduce the search domain and try to find the vertices to be matched using some degree of randomness. This degrades the quality of the partitioning by increasing the possibility of getting stuck in a local minimum. A better trade-off is needed between the low cost of local decisions and the high quality of global ones.

Highlights of our contribution:

- We propose a new serial multi-level hypergraph partitioning algorithm which gives significant quality improvements over state-of-the-art algorithms.
- We use rough set based clustering techniques for removing redundant attributes while partitioning and so make better clustering decisions.
- We provide a trade-off between global and local clustering methods by calculating sets of core vertices (a global decision) and then traversing these cores one at a time to find best matchings between vertices (a local decision).
- We show that solely relying on a vertex similarity metric can result in major degradation of the partitioning quality for some hypergraphs and different coarsening methods should be considered.

In the next section, we briefly review partitioning algorithms and software tools. In Sect. 3, we give a technical introduction to the Hypergraph Partitioning Problem. In Sect. 4 we introduce FEHG. In Sect. 5 we evaluate the algorithm and report results of a simulation comparing FEHG to state-of-the-art algorithms. Finally in Sect. 6, we conclude with comments on ongoing and future work.

2   Related Work

We provide a brief review of algorithms, tools, and applications of hypergraph partitioning; the reader is referred to [21] for an extensive survey. We note that, in general, there is no partitioner recognized to perform well for all types of hypergraphs as there are always trade-offs such as those between quality and speed [21]. Partitioning algorithms can be serial [4,16] or parallel [8], iterative move-based [10] or multi-level [5], static [22] or dynamic [5], recursive [8] or direct [1], and finally they can work directly on hypergraphs [16] or model them as graphs and use graph partitioning algorithms [17].

Few software tools are available for hypergraph partitioning and there is no unified framework for hypergraph processing. One popular tool designed for VLSI circuit partitioning is *hMetis*[1] [16]. The algorithms are based on multi-level partitioning schemes and support recursive bisectioning (*shmetis*, *hmetis*), and direct *k–way* partitioning (*kmetis*). Examples of tools that are designed for specific applications are *MLPart*[2] and *Mondriaan*[3], designed for VLSI circuit partitioning and rectangular sparse matrix-vector multiplications, respectively. The emphasis of *MLPart* is on simplicity of design and *Mondriaan* uses the idea of 2D matrix partitioning to enhance performance [22]. *PaToH*[4] [4] is a multi-level recursive bipartitioning tool designed for serial hypergraph partitioning. It supports agglomerative (vertex clusters are formed one at a time) and hierarchical (several clusters of vertices can be formed simultaneously) clustering algorithms. *Zoltan*[5] [8] is developed for parallel applications. Its library includes a range of tools for problems such as dynamic load balancing and graph and hypergraph colouring and partitioning. Both static and dynamic hypergraph partitioning are supported as are multi-criteria load balancing and processor heterogeneity.

There are a wide range of applications for hypergraph partitioning (see, for example, [20]) including classifying gene expression data, replication management in distributed databases [6] and high dimensional data clustering [15].

3   Definitions

3.1   Hypergraph Partitioning

A hypergraph $H = (V, E)$ is a pair consisting of a finite set of vertices V, with size $|V| = n$ and a multi–set $E \subseteq 2^n$ of hyperedges with size $|E| = m$. For a hyperedge $e \in E$ and vertex v, we say e contains v, or is incident to v, if $v \in e$; this is represented by $e \triangleright v$. The degree of a vertex is the number of distinct incident hyperedges and the size of a hyperedge $|e|$ is the number of vertices it contains. The hypergraph is simply a graph if every hyperedge has size two.

Definition 1. *Let k be a non–negative integer and let $H = (V, E)$ be a hypergraph. A* **k–way partitioning** *of H is a collection of sets $\Pi = \{P_1, P_2, \cdots, P_k\}$ such that $\cup_{i=1}^k P_i = V$, and $\forall P_i, P_j \subset V$, $1 \leqslant i \neq j \leqslant k$, we have $P_i \neq \emptyset$, $P_i \cap P_j = \emptyset$.*

---

[1] http://glaros.dtc.umn.edu/gkhome/metis/hmetis/overview.
[2] http://vlsicad.ucsd.edu/GSRC/bookshelf/Slots/Partitioning/MLPart/.
[3] http://www.staff.science.uu.nl/~bisse101/Mondriaan/mondriaan.html.
[4] http://bmi.osu.edu/umit/software.html.
[5] http://www.cs.sandia.gov/zoltan/.

We say that $v \in V$ is *assigned* to a part $P \in \Pi$ if $v \in P$. Let $\omega \colon V \mapsto \mathbb{N}$ and $\gamma \colon E \mapsto \mathbb{N}$ be weight functions for the vertices and hyperedges. The weight of P is defined as $\omega(P) = \sum_{v \in P} \omega(v)$. A hyperedge $e \in E$ is said to be connected to P if $e \cap P \neq \emptyset$. The *connectivity degree* of e is the number of parts connected to e and is denoted by $\lambda_e(H, \Pi)$. A hyperedge is cut if it connects to more than one part. We define the *cost* of a partition Π of H as

$$\sum_{e \in E} (\gamma(e) \cdot (\lambda_e(H, \Pi) - 1)).$$

The *connectivity objective* is to find a partition Π of low cost. Let W_{ave} be the average weight of the parts: that is $W_{\text{ave}} = \sum_{v \in V} \omega(v)/k$. The *balancing requirement* asks that all parts of the partition have similar weight: that is, given *imbalance tolerance* $\epsilon \in (0,1)$, it is required that

$$W_{\text{ave}} \cdot (1 - \epsilon) \leqslant \omega(P) \leqslant W_{\text{ave}} \cdot (1 + \epsilon), \ \forall P \in \Pi. \tag{1}$$

The *hypergraph partitioning problem* is finding a minimum cost partition Π of H that satisfies the balancing requirement.

3.2   Rough Set Clustering

Rough set theory was introduced by Pawlak in 1991 as an approach to understanding fuzzy and uncertain knowledge [19]. It provides a mathematical tool to discover hidden patterns in data; it can be used, for example, for feature selection, data reduction, pattern extraction. It can deal efficiently with large data sets [2] by extracting global information that resides in the data.

Definition 2. *Let $\mathbb{U}$ be a non-empty finite set of objects (called the universe). Let $\mathbf{A}$ be a non-empty finite set of attributes. Let $\mathbf{V}$ be a multi-set of attribute values such that $\mathbf{V}_a \in \mathbf{V}$ is a set of values for each $a \in \mathbf{A}$. Let $\mathcal{F}$ be a mapping function such that $\mathcal{F}(u, a) \mapsto \mathbf{V}_a, \forall(a, u) \in \mathbf{A} \times \mathbb{U}$. Then $\mathfrak{I} = (\mathbb{U}, \mathbf{A}, \mathbf{V}, \mathcal{F})$ is called an* **information system**.

For any $\mathbf{B} \subseteq \mathbf{A}$ there is an associated equivalence relation denoted $\text{IND}(\mathbf{B})$ and called a *B-Indiscernibility* relation:

$$\text{IND}(\mathbf{B}) = \left\{ (u, v) \in \mathbb{U}^2 \mid \forall b \in \mathbf{B}, \ \mathcal{F}(u, b) = \mathcal{F}(v, b) \right\}. \tag{2}$$

When $(u, v) \in \text{IND}(\mathbf{B})$, it is said that u and v are indiscernible under B and this is represented as $u\mathcal{R}v$. Furthermore, the equivalence class of u with respect to B is $[u]_{\mathbf{B}} = \{v \in \mathbb{U} \mid u\mathcal{R}v\}$. The equivalence relation provides a partitioning of the universe and it is represented as $\mathbb{U}/\text{IND}(\mathbf{B})$ or simply $\mathbb{U}/\text{IND}$. Thus, for every $X \in \mathbb{U}$, and with respect to $\mathbf{B} \subseteq \mathbf{A}$, a $\mathbf{B}$-*lower* and $\mathbf{B}$-*upper* approximation can be defined for X, by, respectively, $\underline{\mathbf{B}X} = \{x \mid [x]_{\mathbf{B}} \subseteq X\}$ and $\overline{\mathbf{B}X} = \{x \mid [x]_{\mathbf{B}} \cap X \neq \emptyset\}$. $\underline{\mathbf{B}X}$ contains objects that belong to X with certainty and $\overline{\mathbf{B}X}$ contains objects that possibly belong to X. We describe a hypergraph $H = (V, E)$ with an information system $\mathcal{I}_H = (V, E, \mathbf{V}, \mathcal{F})$ such that $\mathbf{V}_e \in [0, 1], \forall e \in E$ and the mapping function is defined as:

$$\mathcal{F}(v, e) = \frac{f(e)}{\sum_{\forall e' \triangleright v} \gamma(e')}, \text{ where } f(e) = \gamma(e) \text{ if } e \triangleright v \text{ and is otherwise } 0.$$

3.3   Hyperedge Connectivity Graph

We use rough set clustering in our algorithm to make better clustering decisions in hypergraphs. We will need a measure of *similarity* of a pair of hyperedges, a function $sim(\cdot)$. Different similarity measures, such as *Jaccard Index* or *Cosine Measure*, can be used. Similarity is scaled according to the weight of hyperedges: for two $e_i, e_j \in E$ the scaling factor is $\frac{\gamma(e_i)+\gamma(e_j)}{2\times\max_{e\in E}(\gamma(e))}$.

Definition 3. *For a given similarity threshold* $s \in (0,1)$, *the* **Hyperedge Connectivity Graph** *(HCG) of a hypergraph* $H = (V, E)$ *is a graph* $\mathcal{G}^s(\mathcal{V}, \mathcal{E})$ *where* $\mathcal{V} = E$ *and two vertices* $v_i, v_j \in \mathcal{V}$ *are adjacent if, for the corresponding hyperedges* $e_i, e_j \in E$ *we have* $sim(e_i, e_j) \geqslant s$.

We discuss the importance of the choosing the similarity threshold in Sect. 5.

4   The Algorithm

The proposed algorithm is a recursive multi–level algorithm composed of coarsening, initial partitioning and uncoarsening phases.

4.1   The Coarsening

The process of coarsening involves finding a sequence of hypergraphs $H = (V, E)$, $H^1 = (V^1, E^1), \ldots, H^c = (V^c, E^c)$ such that each hypergraph has fewer vertices than its predecessor and the coarsest hypergraph H^c has fewer vertices than a predefined threshold. We say H^i is the hypergraph found at the ith level of coarsening. The compression ratio of successive levels i, j is defined as $\frac{|V^i|}{|V^j|}$. We use vertex matching to match a pair of vertices and merge them to form a coarser vertex. The best pair is chosen using the *Weighted Jaccard Index* defined by:

$$J(u,v) = \frac{\sum_{\{e \triangleright v \,\wedge\, e \triangleright u\}} \gamma(e)}{\sum_{\{e \triangleright v \,\vee\, e \triangleright u\}} \gamma(e)}, \quad v, u \in V, \text{and } \forall e \in E. \tag{3}$$

This is similar to *non-weighted jaccard index* in *PaToH* which is called *Scaled Heavy Connectivity Matching*. The algorithm first constructs *HCG* graph defined above. by traversing H using Breadth-First Search (the graph itself does not need to be saved). A partition E^R of the hyperedges of H is then obtained where each part contains hyperedges that belong to the same connected component of HCG. The size and weight of each $e_R \in E^R$ is the number of hyperedges it contains and the sum of their weights, respectively. If we represent a hypergraph with an information system, a reduced information system $\mathcal{I}_H^R(V, E^R, \mathbf{V}^R, \mathcal{F}^R)$ is constructed based on E^R. A vertex is incident to $e_R \in E^R$ if at least one of its incident edges $e \in H$ is in e_R. In addition $\mathbf{V}_{e_R}^R \subseteq \mathbb{N}, \forall e_R \in E^R$ and the mapping function is defined as:

$$\mathcal{F}^R(v, e_R) = |\{e \triangleright v \,\wedge\, e \in e_R, \forall e \in E \}|. \tag{4}$$

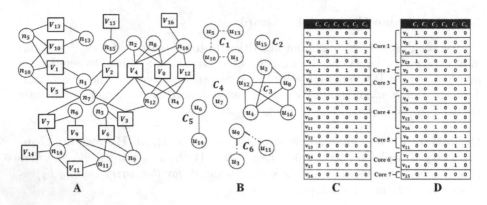

Fig. 1. An example of the coarsening procedure. (a) The sample hypergraph. (b) *HCG* using *weighted jaccard index* in (3) and similarity threshold $s = 0.5$. (c) The reduced information system, and (d) Remaining attributes after removing superfluous attributes for clustering threshold $c = 0.5$.

The next step is to remove superfluous attributes from E^R. A clustering threshold $c \in [0,1]$ is defined and the mapping function of (4) is transformed to:

$$\mathcal{F}^f(v, e_R) = \begin{cases} 1, & \text{if } \frac{\mathcal{F}^R(v, e_R)}{|\{e \triangleright v, \forall e \in E\}|} \geq c \\ 0, & \text{otherwise.} \end{cases} \tag{5}$$

At this point we have a reduced information system $\mathcal{I}^f$ and we use this to find clusters of vertices using rough set clustering techniques. Using the indiscernibility relation defined in (2), the equivalence relation between vertices (Sect. 3.2), and the mapping function $\mathcal{F}^f$ of (5), $\mathbb{U}/\text{IND}(E^R)$ provides a partitioning of the vertex set V. The parts are called the cores of the hypergraph. Cores of unit size as well as vertices whose $\mathcal{F}^f(v, e_R) = 0, \forall e_R \in E^R$ are categorised as non–core vertices and they will be processed after core vertices. The cores are visited one at a time and they are searched locally to find the best matching pairs according to (3). The larger the mean vertex degree in the hypergraph is, the larger denominator we get in (5) and this makes it difficult to choose a clustering threshold. As a result, large mean vertex degrees produce more cores of unit size and this causes the number of vertices that belong to cores to be small compared to $|V|$.

To maintain a certain compression ratio between two successive levels of the coarsening, we perform a random matching of the non–core vertices. An example of the coarsening procedure is given in Fig. 1.

4.2 Initial Partitioning and Uncoarsening

In the initial partitioning phase, a bipartitioning on the coarsest hypergraph H^c is found using a number of algorithms. An output is selected to be projected back to the original hypergraph: if many outputs fulfill the balancing requirement then the one with lowest cost is chosen else it is the output that comes closest to

Table 1. Tested hypergraphs and their specifications

Hypergraph	Description	Rows	Columns	Non-zeros	Structure[a]	NSC[b]
CNR–2000	Small web crawl of Italian CNR domain	325,557	325,557	3,216,152	USYM	100,977
AS–22JULY06	Internet routers	22,963	22,963	96,872	SYM	1
CELEGANSNEURAL	Neural Network of Nematode C. Elegans	297	297	2,345	USYM	57
NETSCIENCE	Co-authorship of scientists in Network Theory	1,589	1,589	5,484	SYM	396
PGPGIANTCOMPO	Largest connected component in graph of PGP users	10,680	10,680	48,632	SYM	1
GUPTA1	Linear Programming matrix $(A \times A^T)$	31,802	31,802	2,164,210	SYM	1
MARK3JAC120	Jacobian from MULTIMOD Mark3	54,929	54,929	322,483	USYM	1,921
NOTREDAME	Barabasi's web page network of nd.edu	325,729	325,729	929,849	USYM	231,666
PATENTS–MAIN	Pajek network: mainNBER US Patent Citations	240,547	240,547	560,943	USYM	240,547
STD1–JAC3	Chemical process simulation	21,982	21,982	1,455,374	USYM	1
COND–MAT–2005	Collaboration network, www.arxiv.org	40,421	40,421	351,382	SYM	1,798

[a] NSC stands for the number of strongly connected components.
[b] SYM stands for symmetric and USYM stands for unsymmetric.

meeting the balancing requirement. The algorithms used are random partitioning (randomly assign vertices to parts), linear partitioning (linearly assign vertices to parts), and a modification of the *FM* algorithm [10]. During uncoarsening, we try to refine the quality of the partitioning by moving the vertices across the partition boundary. A vertex is on the boundary if at least one of its incident edges is cut by the bipartitioning. The FM algorithm and its variants have been shown to be successful for the refinement process [8,16] and we use a modified version of FM or *Boundary FM* algorithm.

5   Evaluation

We have compared our algorithm (*FEHG*) with *PHG* (the Zoltan hypergraph partitioner) [8], *hMetis* [16], and *PaToH* [4]. These algorithms achieve k-way partitioning by recursive bipartitioning. The evaluated hypergraphs listed in Table 1 are from the University of Florida Sparse Matrix Collection [7]. They are from a variety of applications with different specifications and include both symmetric and non–symmetric instances, and hypergraphs with different numbers of strongly connected components, etc. Each matrix in the table is treated as a hypergraph. We use the column-net model where each row of the matrix corresponds to a vertex and each column corresponds to a hyperedge [8]. The weights of vertices and hyperedges are set to unity. The evaluated tools have different input parameters that can be selected by the user. For our case, we use default settings for the comparison: *shmetis* is the default partitioner selected for *hMetis*, *PaToH* is initialised by setting SBProbType parameter to PATOH_SUGPARAM_DEFAULT, and the coarsening algorithm for *PHG* is set to *agglomerative*. All of them use a variation of *FM* for the refinement and uncoarsening phase.

FEHG has two input parameters: the *similarity threshold* to construct *HCG*, and the clustering threshold from (5). The values chosen for these parameters can have a large impact on the quality of the partitioning. We describe how calculate the similarity threshold when the *Jaccard Index* is used for measuring the similarity between hyperedges.

The Clustering Coefficient (CC) is a graph theory measure determined by the degree to which a node clusters with other nodes of the graph or hypergraph. Different methods for finding CC in hypergraphs have been proposed [18]. Given a hypergraph $H = (V, E)$, we define CC for a hyperedge $e \in E$ as:

$$
CC(e) = \begin{cases} \dfrac{\sum_{\{e' \cap e \neq \emptyset\}} \left(\left(1 - \frac{(|e|-1) - |e \cap e'|}{|e|-1} \right) \cdot \gamma(e') \right)}{\sum_{\{v \in e\}} \sum_{\{e'' \rhd v\}} \gamma(e'')}, \ \forall e', e'' \in E \backslash e, & \text{if } |e| > 1 \\ 0, & \text{otherwise.} \end{cases} \tag{6}
$$

The CC of the hypergraph is calculated as the average CC over all hyperedges. We calculate CC at the start of the algorithm. As the structure of the hypergraph changes at each level of coarsening, we readjust its value instead of recalculation. As proposed in [11] to analyse Facebook social networks and theoretically investigated in [3] on sparse random intersection graphs, the clustering of nodes in hypergraphs is inversely correlated with average vertex degree. Based on this, we readjust CC's value according to the variation of average vertex degree from one level of the coarsening to the next. Finally, CC value of the hypergraph is set as the similarity threshold at each coarsening level.

Figure 2a depicts the variation of *similarity threshold* for each coarsening level of a tested graph CNR–2000. Both the readjusted value and the actual value are shown. The readjusted value provides a lower bound for the actual value and it is about 50 % of its value from the third iteration onward which is sufficient for feature reduction. In Fig. 2b, the percentage of the edges whose clustering coefficients are at least equal to the *similarity threshold* along with normalised variation of edge size and its standard deviation (STD) is represented. As the partitioner gets close to the coarsest hypergraph we have small average size of hyperedges (2.09) and small average vertex degrees (2.47) but larger vertex degree standard deviation (14.33); most of the vertices share very few hyperedges so clustering decisions are difficult. As we see, the automatic readjustment still catches the possible similarities. In general we achieve a cut size 50 for CNR–2000.

In our evaluation we found that variation of the similarity threshold has higher impact on the quality of the partitioning than the clustering threshold. The reason is that hyperedges with higher CC value are more likely to cluster with others and they get higher coefficient in (4) and tend to be included in the final reduced information system in (5). This reduces the effects of clustering threshold variations. Therefore, we remove each $e_R \in E^R$ of unit size (refer to Sect. 4.1) and we set the clustering threshold to 0 in (5) for the others. For example, edge partitions C_2 and C_4 are removed from the table in Fig. 1c. For all

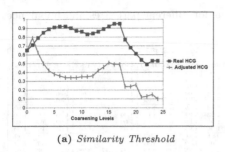

(a) *Similarity Threshold*

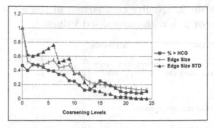

(b) Change *vs.* edge size and its STD

Fig. 2. (a) Readjusted *similarity threshold s* for the test hypergraph CNR–2000 according to (6) compared to its recalculation at each coarsening level. (b) The percentage of the hyperedges whose CC is more than s and comparison to normalised edge size edge and its standard deviation (STD).

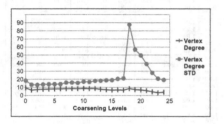

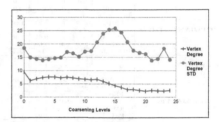

Fig. 3. Variation of vertex degree and its standard deviation when *FEHG* makes extra effort for achieving maximum vertex similarity matching vs normal matching

tested hypergraphs, the algorithms are each run 20 times and the average and best cut sizes are reported. Simulations are done with 2 % imbalance tolerance in (1) and the number of parts are $\{2, 4, 8, 16, 32\}$. The final imbalance achieved by the algorithms are not reported because the balancing requirement was always met by all algorithms. The simulation results as well as standard deviation from the average cut are reported in Table 2. The latter could be used as a measure of the robustness of the algorithms specifically when they give close partitioning quality. The values are normalised with the best cut generated among all algorithms except the standard deviation. According to the results, *FEHG* performs very well compared to *Zoltan* and *hMetis* and it is competitive with *PaToH*. For example in Noterdame and Patents-Main, FEHG achieves a superior quality improvement compared to *Zoltan* and *hMetis*. In another simulation, we investigate whether relying only on a vertex similarity metric is enough to achieve better partition quality. When two vertices are matched, we refer to their similarity degree as the *roughness* of the match and it is calculated using (3). Matching pairs of vertices with higher similarity degree at each level of coarsening means higher average roughness of the matched vertices in that level. According to the algorithms that investigate vertex similarity metrics, an algorithm would be better if it yields higher average roughness for levels of coarsening compared to the others [21]. Furthermore, the decision about the vertex similarity is made locally in those algorithms without collecting global information. In *FEHG*, we refer to

Table 2. Quality comparison of the algorithms for different part sizes and imbalance factor 2 % with normalised values.

Graph	Algorithm	Number of Parts														
		2			4			8			16			32		
		AVE	STD	BEST	AVE	STD	BEST	AVE	STD	BEST	AVE	STD	BEST	AVE	STD	BEST
AS-22JULY06	FEHG	1.11	34	1.00	1.02	32	1.00	1.04	25	1.01	1.01	30	1.00	1.01	28	1.03
	PHG	2.90	86	2.46	1.77	92	1.56	1.64	78	1.36	1.43	87	1.34	1.37	90	1.32
	hMetis	1.34	0	1.95	1.19	7	1.30	1.16	12	1.18	1.04	23	1.06	1.09	27	1.04
	PaToH	1.00	4	1.43	1.00	16	1.03	1.00	20	1.00	1.00	37	1.00	1.00	43	1.00
	Best Value	136	–	93	355	–	319	629	–	599	1051	–	995	1591	–	1529
CELEGANSNEURAL	FEHG	1.00	2	1.00	1.09	9	1.00	1.10	15	1.06	1.11	16	1.08	1.07	17	1.03
	PHG	1.07	6	1.00	1.04	8	1.03	1.02	9	1.00	1.06	12	1.00	1.00	18	1.00
	hMetis	1.17	0	1.21	1.00	5	1.05	1.00	0	1.04	1.00	2	1.02	1.00	6	1.00
	PaToH	1.01	0	1.04	1.00	0	1.06	1.03	0	1.07	1.03	0	1.06	1.05	0	1.05
	Best Value	79	–	77	195	–	184	354	–	342	548	–	536	773	–	769
CNR-2000	FEHG	1.37	63	1.00	1.71	131	1.07	1.59	226	1.41	1.53	218	1.45	1.63	217	1.51
	PHG	35.88	552	45.62	12.48	760	9.17	5.73	569	4.84	3.54	477	2.98	2.42	530	2.02
	hMetis	12.19	74	18.82	8.24	163	8.43	5.08	240	4.71	3.46	238	3.29	2.66	231	2.50
	PaToH	1.00	3	1.71	1.00	37	1.00	1.00	48	1.00	1.00	62	1.00	1.00	85	1.00
	Best Value	81	–	45	244	–	202	569	–	509	1014	–	911	1927	–	1830
COND-MAT-2005	FEHG	1.00	28	1.00	1.00	58	1.00	1.00	87	1.00	1.01	88	1.02	1.01	82	1.00
	PHG	1.17	37	1.17	1.11	84	1.10	1.05	94	1.05	1.03	112	1.03	1.02	105	1.01
	hMetis	1.05	14	1.07	1.11	75	1.12	1.11	81	1.12	1.11	129	1.10	1.01	122	1.01
	PaToH	1.02	39	1.02	1.03	193	1.03	1.00	98	1.00	1.00	153	1.10	1.00	178	1.00
	Best Value	2134	–	2087	5057	–	4951	8609	–	8485	12370	–	12150	16270	–	16150
NETSCIENCE*	FEHG	0.0	0	0.0	0.0	0	0.0	2.00	1	1.50	1.50	2	1.00	2.08	2	1.81
	PHG	0.0	0	0.0	0.0	0	0.0	1.50	1	1.00	1.40	2	1.00	1.87	2	1.5
	hMetis	2.0	0	2.0	5.0	0	5.0	4.22	1	3.50	1.75	0	1.75	1.99	2	1.87
	PaToH	0.0	0	0.0	0.0	0	0.0	1.00	0	1.00	1.00	0	1.00	1.00	0	1.00
	Best Value	0	–	0	0	–	0	2	–	2	8	–	8	16	–	16
PGPGIANTCOMPO	FEHG	2.12	8	1.27	1.00	23	1.00	1.04	18	1.00	1.00	16	1.00	1.00	18	1.00
	PHG	13.23	48	1.83	1.44	65	1.04	1.25	45	1.04	1.02	53	1.00	1.08	46	1.00
	hMetis	9.7	3	9.61	1.46	11	1.71	1.04	13	1.40	1.31	24	1.40	1.26	25	1.27
	PaToH	1.00	0	1.00	1.04	0	1.27	1.00	7	1.04	1.02	2	1.15	1.08	5	1.06
	Best Value	18	–	18	242	–	200	419	–	400	695	–	617	956	–	930
GUPTA1	FEHG	1.00	60	1.00	1.00	55	1.00	1.00	80	1.00	1.00	115	1.00	1.00	15	1.00
	PHG	1.58	67	1.45	1.31	146	1.24	1.15	204	1.04	1.07	253	1.04	1.09	58	1.05
	hMetis	1.73	2	1.82	1.61	10	1.69	1.58	58	1.64	1.60	137	1.57	1.51	643	1.48
	PaToH	1.22	32	1.17	1.08	43	1.09	1.04	84	1.05	1.05	95	1.07	1.08	120	1.09
	Best Value	486	–	462	1466	–	1384	3077	–	2893	5342	–	5134	8965	–	8519
MARK3JAC120	FEHG	1.01	6	1.01	1.02	18	1.01	1.01	23	1.00	1.00	83	1.00	1.06	132	1.07
	PHG	1.00	4	1.01	1.02	15	1.02	1.02	27	1.00	1.00	53	1.00	1.72	106	1.78
	hMetis	1.00	13	1.00	1.00	15	1.02	1.00	29	1.00	1.30	217	1.00	4.20	214	1.78
	PaToH	1.00	0	1.02	1.00	11	1.00	1.00	17	1.00	1.26	248	1.20	1.00	267	1.00
	Best Value	408	–	400	1229	–	1202	2856	–	2835	6317	–	6245	3142	–	2944
NOTREDAME*	FEHG	0	0	0	1.00	9	1.00	1.12	40	1.12	1.09	116	1.03	1.06	119	1.07
	PHG	4326	0	4326	158.56	124	288.69	13.82	67	16.78	2.09	75	3.06	1.72	78	1.78
	hMetis	880	84	707	67.92	65	129.92	10.98	108	12.65	3.36	143	3.37	2.23	129	2.30
	Patoh	24	1	22	1.90	8	3.31	1.00	27	1.00	1.00	52	1.00	1.00	62	1.00
	Best Value	0	–	0	27	–	13	316	–	259	1577	–	1484	3142	–	2944
PATENTS-MAIN	FEHG	1.20	180	1.00	1.03	275	1.01	1.05	270	1.03	1.00	327	1.00	1.00	342	1.00
	PHG	12.49	1286	13.19	2.52	1736	2.30	1.79	1749	1.65	1.42	1575	1.38	1.23	1602	1.18
	hMetis	2.38	36	2.77	1.16	70	1.24	1.26	115	1.43	1.26	161	1.31	1.21	231	1.22
	PaToH	1.00	70	1.02	1.00	145	1.00	1.00	217	1.00	1.00	220	1.00	1.01	306	1.00
	Best Value	643	–	528	3490	–	3198	6451	–	6096	11322	–	10640	16927	–	16460
STD1-JAC3	FEHG	1.01	260	1.03	1.00	246	1.03	1.00	424	1.00	1.00	549	1.00	1.00	557	1.00
	PHG	1.15	227	1.08	1.16	377	1.10	1.18	748	1.13	1.28	768	1.35	1.33	801	1.29
	hMetis	1.05	105	1.00	1.52	1649	1.03	1.54	2057	1.23	1.70	2330	1.53	1.71	2995	1.51
	Patoh	1.00	125	1.00	1.08	506	1.00	1.16	700	1.14	1.00	827	1.26	1.30	945	1.29
	Best Value	1490	–	1371	3735	–	3333	7616	–	6167	13254	–	11710	22242	–	21200

* When the minimum cut for the average or best cases are zero, the values shown are actual cut values rather than normalised values.

the average roughness of core vertices as core roughness. We consider two scenarios for our test while we find a pair match for non–core vertices: in the first one, a match is allowed for a non–core vertex if the roughness of the match is at least equal to the core roughness. In the second scenario we allow non–core vertex to be matched to any vertex as long as the roughness of the match is greater than zero. In the first scenario, the emphasis is on finding vertices with higher similarity as is the case for similarity metric based methods and it guarantees higher average roughness compared to the second scenario during levels of coarsening. The test is done on the hypergraphs and the result for CNR-2000 is reported in Fig. 3. According to the results, the first scenario causes high fluctuations of vertex degree standard deviations while the second scenario produces a smooth change. We achieve average cuts of 490 and 110 for CNR–2000 for the first and second scenarios, respectively.

The agglomerative clustering of *Zoltan* and *hMetis* give 25.54 and 8.89 times worse quality. *PaToH* also produces good average quality of 81 using absorption clustering using pins and hyperedge clustering. The variations in vertex degree or its standard deviation causes problems for clustering algorithms, making it hard to make good clustering decisions because of the increased conflicts between local and global decisions. Consequently, finding vertices with higher similarity for matching can not be relied on for every hypergraph and it does not always gives a better partitioning cut. In addition, gathering some global information before making clustering decisions can give a major quality improvement and decreases the unexpectedness of the partitioning cut as depicted in Table 2.

6   Conclusions and Future Work

We have proposed a multi–level hypergraph partitioning algorithm based on feature extraction and attribute reduction using rough set clustering techniques. The algorithm clusters hyperedges using different similarity metrics and a similarity threshold and tries to removes less important hyperedges. An automated calculation of this similarity threshold is proposed. The hypergraph is then transformed into a reduced information system. Employing the idea of Rough Set clustering, the algorithm calculates the partitioning of the objects in the reduced information system based on indispensability relations and core sets of vertices with globally high similarities. Then cores are searched locally for vertex matchings. Evaluating the algorithm in comparison to the state-of-the-art algorithms has shown improvements in quality of the partitioning for tested hypergraphs. Future work is to implement parallel versions of the algorithm. Using a special distribution of vertices and hyperedges among processors and the ideas of rough set theory, we are focusing on proposing a scalable partitioner.

Acknowledgments. This work is supported by the EU FP7 Marie Curie Initial Training Network "SCALUS — Scaling by means of Ubiquitous Storage" under grant agreement No.238808. We thank the Efficient Computing and Storage Group at Johannes Gutenberg Universität Mainz, Germany for their help and support.

References

1. Aykanat, C., Cambazoglu, B.B., Uar, B.: Multi-level direct K-way hypergraph partitioning with multiple constraints and fixed vertices. J. Parallel Distrib. Comput. **68**(5), 609–625 (2008)
2. Bazan, J., Szczuka, M.S., Wojna, A., Wojnarski, M.: On the evolution of rough set exploration system. In: Tsumoto, S., Słowiński, R., Komorowski, J., Grzymała-Busse, J.W. (eds.) RSCTC 2004. LNCS (LNAI), vol. 3066, pp. 592–601. Springer, Heidelberg (2004)
3. Bloznelis, M., et al.: Degree and clustering coefficient in sparse random intersection graphs. Ann. Appl. Probab. **23**(3), 1254–1289 (2013)

4. Catalyurek, U.V., Aykanat, C.: Hypergraph-partitioning-based decomposition for parallel sparse-matrix vector multiplication. IEEE Trans. Parallel Distrib. Syst. 10(7), 673–693 (1999)
5. Catalyurek, U., Boman, E., Devine, K., Bozdag, D., Heaphy, R., Riesen, L.: Hypergraph-based dynamic load balancing for adaptive scientific computations. In: Parallel and Distributed Processing Symposium (IPDPS 2007), pp. 1–11 (2007)
6. Curino, C., Jones, E., Zhang, Y., Madden, S.: Schism: a workload-driven approach to database replication and partitioning. Proc. VLDB Endow. 3(1–2), 48–57 (2010)
7. Davis, T.A., Hu, Y.: The university of florida sparse matrix collection. ACM Trans. Math. Softw. 38(1), 1 (2011)
8. Devine, K.D., Boman, E.G., Heaphy, R.T., Bisseling, R.H., Catalyurek, U.V.: Parallel hypergraph partitioning for scientific computing. In: Proceedings of 20th International Parallel and Distributed Processing Symposium (IPDPS 2006). IEEE (2006)
9. Ertöz, L., Steinbach, M., Kumar, V.: Finding clusters of different sizes, shapes, and densities in noisy, high dimensional data. In: SDM, pp. 47–58. SIAM (2003)
10. Fiduccia, C.M., Mattheyses, R.M.: A linear-time heuristic for improving network partitions. In: 19th Conference on Design Automation, pp. 175–181. IEEE (1982)
11. Foudalis, I., Jain, K., Papadimitriou, C., Sideri, M.: Modeling social networks through user background and behavior. In: Frieze, A., Horn, P., Prałat, P. (eds.) WAW 2011. LNCS, vol. 6732, pp. 85–102. Springer, Heidelberg (2011)
12. Garey, M.R., Johnson, D.S.: Computers and Intractability, vol. 29. W.H. Freeman, New York (2002)
13. Heintz, B., Chandra, A.: Beyond graphs: toward scalable hypergraph analysis systems. SIGMETRICS Perform. Eval. Rev. 41(4), 94–97 (2014)
14. Hendrickson, B., Kolda, T.G.: Graph partitioning models for parallel computing. Parallel Comput. 26(12), 1519–1534 (2000)
15. Hu, T., Liu, C., Tang, Y., Sun, J., Xiong, H., Sung, S.Y.: High-dimensional clustering: a clique-based hypergraph partitioning framework. Knowl. Inf. Syst. 39(1), 61–88 (2014)
16. Karypis, G., Aggarwal, R., Kumar, V., Shekhar, S.: Multilevel hypergraph partitioning: applications in vlsi domain. In: IEEE Transactions on Very Large Scale Integration (VLSI) Systems, vol. 7, no. 1, pp. 69–79 (1999)
17. Kayaaslan, E., Pinar, A., Çatalyrek, Ü., Aykanat, C.: Partitioning hypergraphs in scientific computing applications through vertex separators on graphs. SIAM J. Sci. Comput. 34(2), A970–A992 (2012)
18. Latapy, M., Magnien, C., Vecchio, N.D.: Basic notions for the analysis of large two-mode networks. Soc. Netw. 30(1), 31–48 (2008)
19. Pawlak, Z.: Rough Sets: Theoretical Aspects of Reasoning about Data. Kluwer Academic Publishers, Norwell (1991)
20. Tian, Z., Hwang, T., Kuang, R.: A hypergraph-based learning algorithm for classifying gene expression and arrayCGH data with prior knowledge. Bioinformatics 25(21), 2831–2838 (2009)
21. Trifunovic, A.: Parallel algorithms for hypergraph partitioning. Ph.D. thesis, University of London (2006)
22. Vastenhouw, B., Bisseling, R.H.: A two-dimensional data distribution method for parallel sparse matrix-vector multiplication. SIAM Rev. 47(1), 67–95 (2005)

Non-preemptive Throughput Maximization for Speed-Scaling with Power-Down

Eric Angel[1], Evripidis Bampis[2], Vincent Chau[3(✉)], and Nguyen Kim Thang[1]

[1] IBISC, Université d'Évry Val d'Essonne, Évry, France
[2] Sorbonne Universités, UPMC Univ Paris 06, UMR 7606, LIP6, Paris, France
[3] Department of Computer Science, City University of Hong Kong,
Kowloon Tong, Hong Kong
vincchau@cityu.edu.hk

Abstract. We consider the problem of scheduling a set of n jobs on a single processor. Each job is characterized by its release date r_j, its deadline d_j and its processing volume p_j. The processor can vary its speed and can switch into a sleep state in order to reduce its energy consumption. No energy is consumed in this state, but a fixed amount of energy, equal to L, is required for a transition from the sleep state to the active state. Here, we study the *throughput maximization* version of the problem where we are given a budget of energy E and our goal is to determine a feasible schedule maximizing the number of jobs that are executed between their respective release dates and deadlines without preemption. We first consider the case in which jobs have agreeable deadlines, i.e. for every pair of jobs i and j, one has $r_i \leq r_j$ if and only if $d_i \leq d_j$. Then we consider the case where the jobs have arbitrary release dates and deadlines, but the same processing volume. We propose polynomial-time algorithms for both cases.

1 Introduction

Power management aims to reduce the energy consumption in computer systems while maintaining a good level of performance. One of the mechanisms used to save energy is speed-scaling where the processor is capable to vary its speed dynamically. The faster the processor runs, the more it consumes energy. Another mechanism for energy savings is the power-down mechanism, in which we have to decide whether to put the system into the sleep state when it is idle, or maintain it in the active state. No energy is consumed during the sleep state, but a fixed amount of energy is required to wake up the system.

More formally, we are given a set of n jobs. Each job is characterized by its release date r_j, its deadline d_j and its processing volume p_j. We are also given one processor which can vary its speed and can switch into the sleep state in

Research partially supported by a grant from City University of Hong Kong (Proj. 9231168 and 9041897), by FMJH program Gaspard Monge in Optimization and Operations Research and by EDF and by the project ALGONOW, co-financed by the European Union (European Social Fund - ESF).

J.L. Träff et al. (Eds.): Euro-Par 2015, LNCS 9233, pp. 171–182, 2015.
DOI: 10.1007/978-3-662-48096-0_14

order to reduce the energy consumption. No energy is consumed in this state, but a fixed amount of energy is required for transitioning the system from the sleep state to the active one which is equal to L. The processor can execute at most one job at each time during the active state. We measure the processor's speed in units of executed work per unit of time. If $s(t)$ denotes the speed of the processor at time t, then the total amount of work executed by the processor during an interval of time $[t, t')$ is equal to $\int_t^{t'} s(u)du$. Specifically, at any time t, the power consumption of the processor is $P(t) = s(t)^\alpha + \gamma$, where $\alpha > 1$ is a constant and γ is the energy leakage. We are given an energy budget E and the goal is to find a feasible schedule maximizing the number of jobs that are executed between their release dates and their deadlines and respecting the energy budget.

Related Works

A series of papers have studied *energy minimization* for the speed-scaling model, the power-down model and the combined speed-scaling and power-down model.

Speed-Scaling. The energy minimization problem of scheduling n jobs with release dates and deadlines on a single processor that can vary its speed dynamically and where the preemption of the jobs is allowed has been first studied in the seminal paper by Yao et al. [22]. The time complexity for general instances has been improved in [15,20], while for jobs with agreeable deadlines in [16,21]. For the non-preemptive energy minimization problem, Antoniadis and Huang [7] showed its NP-hardness in the strong sense and they proposed a polynomial time approximation algorithm. This result has been improved recently in [9,14].

Power-Down. Baptiste [10] showed that the problem is polynomially solvable for the power-down model when the processor's speed is fixed by introducing $O(n^7)$ time algorithm. Later on, Baptiste et al. [11] improved the time complexity of this algorithm to $O(n^5)$. When the jobs have agreeable deadline (a formal definition is given below), an $O(n^2)$ exact algorithm has been proposed by Angel et al. [3]. Finally, Chrobak et al. [13] proposed a 2-approximation algorithm of complexity $O(n^2 \log n)$.

Speed-Scaling and Power-Down. Irani et al. [17] introduced a model incorporating both mechanisms, i.e. speed-scaling and power-down, and proposed a 2-approximation algorithm for the speed-scaling with power-down model. Recently, Albers et al. [1] proved that the speed-scaling problem with power down is NP-hard and provided a 4/3-approximation algorithm for the preemptive case, while Bampis et al. [8] showed that when jobs have agreeable deadlines, the problem can be solved in $O(n^3)$ time.

The most relevant works in the *throughput maximization* version of this problem but only for the speed scaling settings are [4,5,19]. Li [19] has considered throughput maximization when there is an upper bound in the processor's speed and he proposed a greedy algorithm which leads to a 3-approximation for the throughput and a constant approximation ratio for the energy consumption. Angel et al. studied the throughput maximization problem in [5]. They proposed a polynomial time algorithm that solves optimally the single-processor problem for agreeable instances. More recently in [4], the authors proved that there is a pseudo-polynomial time algorithm for solving optimally the preemptive throughput maximization problem with arbitrary release dates and deadlines as well as arbitrary processing volumes. For the weighted version, the problem is NP-hard even for instances in which all the jobs have common release dates and deadlines.

Our Contributions

We consider the non-preemptive throughput maximization problem for the speed-scaling and power-down model. Notice that this problem is at least as hard as the energy minimization version since we can make a binary search in the energy budget in order to find the minimum energy consumption for all jobs with respect to the accuracy of the search. Since the non-preemptive general case is strongly NP-hard [7] for the speed-scaling settings, then it is also for the combined model. Indeed, the decision version is to ask whether there exists a non-preemptive schedule that have a cost less than some value, and if so, we could construct a solution of the same cost for the 3-partition. Here, we prove that the problem can be solved in polynomial time for two special cases of instances. First, we consider instances where jobs have agreeable deadlines, i.e. such that for every pair of jobs $i < j$, one has $r_i \leq r_j$ if and only if $d_i \leq d_j$. Intuitively, in an instance with agreeable deadlines a later released job also has a later deadline. We propose a $O(n^{11})$ time algorithm to solve this case. Then we consider the case where jobs have arbitrary release dates and deadlines, but have the same processing volume, i.e. $p_j = p \ \forall j$. We first prove that the complexity time remains the same as for the speed scaling case, and improve the time complexity of the energy minimization variant to $O(n^{19})$. These families of instances have received a lot of attention in the literature (see for instance [2,16]).

2 Preliminaries

In this paper, we consider schedules without preemption. Without loss of generality, we assume that all parameters of the problem such as release dates, deadlines and processing volumes of jobs are integers. We rename jobs in non-decreasing order of their deadlines, i.e. $d_1 \leq d_2 \leq \ldots \leq d_n$. We denote by $r_{\min} := \min_{1 \leq j \leq n} r_j$ the minimum release date. Define Ω as the set of release dates and deadlines, i.e. $\Omega := \{r_j | j = 1, \ldots, n\} \cup \{d_j | j = 1, \ldots, n\}$.

We refer to the energy cost of the processor induced by the speed as dynamic energy and to the energy induced by the leakage and the wake-up cost as static energy.

We call an EDF (Earliest Deadlines First) schedule, a schedule in which at any time, the job with the smallest deadline among the available jobs is scheduled first.

We give some simple observations on non-preemptive scheduling with the objective of maximizing throughput under the energy constraint. First, it is well known that due to the convexity of the power function $P(s) := s^{\alpha} + \gamma$, each job runs at a constant speed during its whole execution in an optimal schedule. This follows from Jensen's Inequality.

We first define the critical speed that minimizes the energy consumption of a single job. This shows that we do not scheduled every job at the lowest speed as possible.

Definition 1. *[17] Let $s^\star := \arg\min_s \frac{P(s)}{s}$ be the critical speed.*

Definition 2. *We define a block of jobs with respect to a schedule as the maximal interval when the processor is in the working state (ON-state). The processor is in the sleep state (OFF-state) before and after this block.*

Definition 3. *(Fig. 1) [8] We define the prefix (resp. suffix) of a block of jobs with respect to a schedule as the maximal subset of continuous scheduled jobs at the beginning (resp. at the end) of the block and such that the processor runs at speed $s^\star$.*

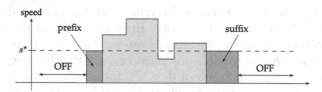

Fig. 1. Illustration of Definition 3

Remark 1. The prefix and suffix of a block of jobs can be empty.

Proposition 1. *[8] The processor speed is at least $s^\star$ at the beginning and at the end of a continuous block of jobs.*

Proof. Let S be an optimal schedule and suppose that there is a block B of jobs such that the processor speed is strictly lower than $s^\star$ at the beginning of the block (prefix). Let j be the first job of B. Job j is therefore scheduled with a speed $s < s^\star$ and let $\ell(j)$ be its execution length. The energy consumption of job j is $\ell(j) \cdot P(s)$. Then we can increase the processor speed from s to $s^\star$ for this job, the length of the job b will decrease to $\frac{\ell(j) \cdot s}{s^\star}$, by shifting to the right its starting time without changing its finishing time, the overall schedule will remain feasible, and its energy consumption will decrease. Indeed, the new energy consumption of job j is $P(s^\star) \cdot \frac{\ell(j) \cdot s}{s^\star}$, and one has $\ell(j) \cdot P(s) > P(s^\star)\frac{\ell(j) \cdot s}{s^\star}$ which follows immediately from the definition of the critical speed. □

3 Agreeable Deadlines Jobs

We study in this part instances in which jobs have agreeable deadlines, i.e. for every pair of jobs i and j, one has $r_i \le r_j$ if and only if $d_i \le d_j$.

Proposition 2. *There exists an optimal solution in which jobs are scheduled according to the EDF order and without preemption.*

Proof. We prove this proposition in two part. The first part is to prove that jobs are scheduled in EDF order. Then we prove that the schedule can be transform into a non-preemptive schedule. Let $\mathcal{O}$ be an optimal schedule in which there exists two consecutive piece of jobs $j' < j$ such that job j is scheduled before job j' with $d_{j'} \leq d_j$. Let a (resp. b) be the starting time (resp. completion time) of job j (resp. job j') in $\mathcal{O}$. Then, we have necessarily $r_{j'} \leq r_j \leq a < b \leq d_{j'} \leq d_j$. The execution of jobs j and j' can be swapped in the time interval $[a, b)$. Thus we obtain a feasible schedule $\mathcal{O}'$ in which job j' is scheduled before job j with the same energy consumption. Once we obtain a schedule in which jobs are in the EDF order, we may have a same job into several pieces. If the processor is at sleep state between two pieces, then we can merge the second piece with the first one by shifting the piece to the left. The energy's consumption does not increase. Similarly, if the processor is on active state between the two pieces, then we can shift the second piece to the left without increasing the energy's consumption. □

Definition 4. *Define $Y(i, j, a, b, u)$ as the minimum energy consumption of a T-schedule T such that:*

– $T \subseteq \{i, \ldots, j\}$ *and* $|T| = u$ *where T is the set of jobs scheduled in T,*
– *the jobs of T are entirely scheduled in $[a, b)$,*
– *the processor is in working state (ON-state) during $[a, b)$.*

Remark 2. By convention, $\{i, i - 1\}$ is an empty set.

The energy consumption of a schedule corresponding to $Y(i, j, a, b, u)$ is exactly the minimum combined dynamic and static energy. Note that $Y(i, j, a, b, u)$ could be computed with the algorithm proposed in [5]. Note that by applying this algorithm, we obtain a non-preemptive schedule.

Definition 5. *Define $X(i, j, a, b, u)$ as the minimum energy consumption of a T-schedule T such that:*

– $T \subseteq \{i, \ldots, j\}$ *and* $|T| = u$ *where T is the set of jobs scheduled in T,*
– *during interval $[a, b)$, there is exactly one sub-interval where the processor is in sleep state. Otherwise, the processor executes jobs in T with speed (exactly) s^*.*

By definition, the energy consumption of the schedule is $((a' - a) + (b - b'))P(s^\star) + L$ where $[a', b') \subseteq [a, b)$ is the interval during which the processor is in sleep state. Note that the processor needs to be waken up once, which costs L. Intuitively, $X(i, j, a, b, u)$ represents the energy consumption during an interval which consists of a prefix and a suffix and a sleep-state interval. Since the speed is fixed in the definition of $X(.)$, we show how to compute the minimum energy consumption with classical scheduling algorithm.

Definition 6. *We define $C(i, j, a, b, u)$ (resp. $S(i, j, a, b, u)$) as the minimum length of a schedule starting at time a (resp. ending at time b), such that there are exactly u jobs among $\{i, \dots, j\}$ which are scheduled, and such that all these jobs are scheduled in $[a, b)$ with the speed s^*. If no such schedule exists, then the length is infinity.*

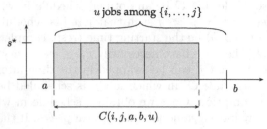

Fig. 2. Illustration of the definition of $C(i, j, a, b, u)$ in Definition 6

Proposition 3. *The values $C(i, j, a, b, u)$ and $S(i, j, a, b, u)$ can be computed in polynomial time.*

Proof. This can be done by setting:

- the processing time of each job k, $i \leq k \leq j$, to p_k / s^*,
- the release date r_k of a job k to $\max\{r_k, a\}$ for $i \leq k \leq j$,
- the deadline d_k of a job k to $\min\{d_k, b\}$ for $i \leq k \leq j$.

Note that with these modifications, we still have an agreeable instance. Finally, we solve this problem with the algorithm proposed in [18]. Indeed, in the classical scheduling problem, the throughput maximization can be reduced to the minimum makespan problem [12], so $C(i, j, a, b, u)$ is computed correctly and in time $O(n \log n)$ if all parameters i, j, a, b, u are set.

Similarly, $S(i, j, a, b, u)$ is the minimum length of a schedule finishing at time b, such that there are exactly u jobs among $\{i, \dots, j\}$ which are scheduled, and such that all these jobs are scheduled in $[a, b)$ with the speed s^*. This value can be computed in a similar way as $C(.)$ values and by reversing the schedule. More formally, we set b as the starting time of the schedule. Then, for each job k with $i \leq k \leq j$:

- if $r_k \leq b$, we set $d_k^* := b + (b - r_k) = 2b - r_k$;
- if $d_k \leq b$, we set $r_k^* := b + (b - d_k) = 2b - d_k$.

Finally, we solve the minimum makespan problem with the modified jobs with the same algorithm as previously. Thus, it computes the values $S(i, j, a, b, \ell)$ correctly and in time $O(n \log n)$ if all parameters i, j, a, b, u are set. $\qquad \square$

Proposition 4. *It holds that*

$$X(i, j, a, b, u) = L + P(s^*) \cdot \min_{\substack{i-1 \leq k \leq j \\ 0 \leq \ell \leq u \\ C := C(i,k,a,b,\ell) \\ S := S(k+1,j,a,b,u-\ell) \\ C+S \leq b-a}} \left\{ \begin{array}{c} C(i, k, a, b, \ell) \\ + S(k+1, j, a, b, u - \ell) \end{array} \right\}$$

Proof. The energy consumption depends on the length of the period that the processor is in working state with a speed s^*, and the above computation returns a feasible schedule minimizing this length.   □

Definition 7. *For* $0 \leq u \leq n$, *define* $E(i, j, a, b, u)$ *the minimum energy consumption of a* T-*schedule* T *such that:*

$- T \subset \{i, \ldots, j\}$ *and* $|T| = u$ *where* T *is the set of jobs scheduled in* T,
$-$ *the jobs of* T *are entirely scheduled in* $[a, b)$.

The objective function is $\max\{u \mid E(1, n, 0, d_n, u) \leq E\}$.

Proposition 5. *One has*

$$
E(i, j, a, b, u) = \min \left\{
\begin{array}{l}
Y(i, j, a, b, u) \\
\min\limits_{\substack{a_1, b_1 \\ 0 \leq u_1, u_2 \leq u \\ i \leq i', j' \leq j \\ i' - 1 \leq j'}}
\left\{
\begin{array}{l}
Y(i, i' - 1, a, a_1, u_1) \\
+ X(i', j', a_1, b_1, u_2) \\
+ E(j' + 1, j, b_1, b, u - u_1 - u_2)
\end{array}
\right\}
\end{array}
\right\}
$$

$E(i, j, a, b, u) = +\infty, \quad u > j - i + 1$
$E(i, i - 1, a, b, u) = 0 \; \forall i$

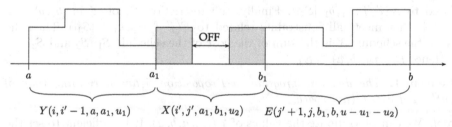

Fig. 3. Illustration of Proposition 5

Proof. (See Fig. 3) Let $E' := \min\{E'_1, E'_2\}$ be the right hand side of the equation. The first case is when the processor is never idle during the interval $[a, b)$ and the second is when there is at least one idle period.

We first prove that $E(i, j, s, t, u) \leq E'$.

If the processor is never idle, then we can build the schedule associated with $Y(i, j, s, t, u)$ from s to t. Since this schedule respects all the constraints associated with $E(i, j, s, t, u)$ it shows that $E(i, j, s, t, u) \leq Y(i, j, s, t, u) = E'_1$.

Suppose now that there is at least one idle period in the schedule. Let a schedule S_1 that realizes $Y(i, i' - 1, a, a_1, u_1)$, a schedule S_2 that realizes $X(i', j', a_1, b_1, u_2)$ and a schedule S_3 that realizes $E(j' + 1, j, b_1, b, u - u_1 - u_2)$. We can build a schedule with S_1 from a to a_1, with S_2 from a_1 to b_1 and with S_3 from b_1 to b. Moreover, the sets of jobs $\{i, \ldots, i' - 1\}, \{i', \ldots, j'\}, \{j' + 1, \ldots, j\}$ do not intersect. So this is a feasible schedule, and its cost is E'_2. Hence $E(i, j, a, b, u) \leq E'_2$.

We now prove that $E' \leq E(i, j, a, b, u)$.

The first case is that the processor is never idle in a solution. Obviously, we have $E' = Y(i, j, a, b, u)$.

Suppose now that there is at least one idle period in the schedule corresponding to $E(i, j, a, b, u)$. We denote by $\mathcal{X}$ the schedule that realizes $E(i, j, a, b, u)$ in which the first starting time a_1 of the first suffix block is maximal and the first completion time b_1 of the first prefix block is minimal. We split $\mathcal{X}$ into three sub-schedules $\mathcal{S}_1 \subseteq \{i, i' - 1\}$, $\mathcal{S}_2 \subseteq \{i', j'\}$ and $\mathcal{S}_3 \subseteq \{j' + 1, j\}$ according to the set of jobs executed into those three sub-schedules. Let a' (resp. b') be the completion time (resp. starting time) of the first suffix (resp. prefix) block. We have $a_1 \leq a' < b' \leq b_1$. We claim that we have the following properties:

– the processor execute always something in $[a_1, a')$
– the processor execute always something in $[b', b_1)$

Suppose that the processor does not execute a job at time a'' with $a_1 \leq a'' \leq a'$, then we can take $a_1 := a''$ and we have a contradiction with the fact that a_1 was maximal and we have another job j'. A similar argument can be applied for the value of b_1.

Then the restriction $\mathcal{S}_1$ of $\mathcal{X}$ in $[a, a_1)$ is a schedule that meets all constraints related to $Y(i, i' - 1, a, a_1, |\mathcal{S}_1|)$ and its cost is greater than $Y(i, i' - 1, a, a_1, |\mathcal{S}_1|)$. Similarly, the restriction $\mathcal{S}_2$ of $\mathcal{X}$ in $[a_1, b_1)$ is a schedule that meets all constraints related to $X(i', j', a_1, b_1, |\mathcal{S}_2|)$. Finally, the restriction $\mathcal{S}_3$ of $\mathcal{X}$ in $[b_1, b)$ is a schedule that meets all constraints related to $E(j' + 1, j, b_1, b, |\mathcal{S}_3|)$. Then the cost of the schedule $\mathcal{X}$ is the sum of the cost of the schedule $\mathcal{S}_1$, $\mathcal{S}_2$ and $\mathcal{S}_3$.

Hence $E(i, j, a, b, u) \geq E_2'$.   □

Theorem 1. *The dynamic program in Proposition 5 has a running time of $O(n^{11})$ and uses $O(n^5)$ space.*

Proof. We can precompute the values of $Y(i, j, a, b, u)$. It is sufficient to set the value of i and compute with the algorithm in [5]. Since it is also a dynamic programming, it will compute the other values of $Y(i, j, a, b, u)$. Then the table $Y(i, j, a, b, u)$ can be computed in time $O(n \times n^6 \log V \log n)$ where V is the total processing volume, i.e. $V = \sum_j p_j$.

We can also precompute the values of $X(i, j, a, b, u)$. By setting the values i, j, a, b, u, we have to minimize over the values k and ℓ. Once all the values are set, the algorithm needs $O(n \log n)$ to compute (twice) the minimum makespan. Finally the table $X(i, j, a, b, u)$ can be computed in time $O(n^8 \log n)$ and has size $O(n^5)$.

Finally, the table $E(i, j, a, b, u)$ has size $O(n^5)$. We have to minimize over the values $a_1, b_1, u_1, u_2, i', j'$ where we pick already computed values. Then the overall time complexity is $O(n^{11})$.   □

4   Equal Processing Volume

In this section, we assume that $p_j = p$ for every job j, and we extend the result in [6] to the model with speed-scaling and power-down. Although the results in [6] solve the multiprocessor case, we focus here on the single processor case but our result can be easily extended to the multiprocessor case when the number of processors is a given constant. Moreover, we do not just consider dates, but vector of dates in order to divide a schedule into two sub-schedules. We first define the set of relevant dates for our problem.

Definition 8. *Let* $\Theta_{a,b} := \{a + \ell \cdot \frac{b-a}{k} \mid k = 1, \ldots, n \text{ and } \ell = 0, \ldots, k \text{ and } a \leq b\}$. *Moreover,* $\Theta := \bigcup \{\Theta_{a,b} | a, b \in \Omega\} \cup \{a \pm \ell \cdot \frac{p}{s^*} \mid a \in \Omega \text{ and } \ell = 1, \ldots, n\}$.

The following lemma gives an observation on the structure of an optimal schedule.

Lemma 1. *There exists an optimal schedule in which the starting time and completion time of each job belong to the set* Θ.

Proof. Let $\mathcal{O}$ be an optimal schedule. $\mathcal{O}$ can be partitioned into successive blocks of jobs where the blocks are separated by idle-time periods. Consider a block B and decompose B into maximal sub-blocks $B_1, \ldots, B_k$ such that all the jobs executed inside a sub-block B_ℓ are scheduled with the same common speed s_ℓ for $1 \leq \ell \leq k$.

The first part of this proof comes from [6] where the the starting and completion times of each job in any sub-blocks $B_2, \ldots, B_{k-1}$ belong to $\Theta_{a,b}$ for some $a \in \Omega$ and $b \in \Omega$.

Finally, thanks to Proposition 1, the speed of sub-block B_1 and B_k are at least s^*. If the speed of the processor during the sub-block B_1 is equal to s^*, then the starting time of the sub-block B_1 is at a distance $h \cdot \frac{p}{s^*}$ from the completion time of B_1 (which is a date in Ω). Thus the starting time of B_1 is in Θ. Note that there are h jobs in B_1 and each job has its starting time and completion time in $\{a \pm \ell \cdot \frac{p}{s^*} \mid a \in \Omega \text{ and } \ell = 1, \ldots, n\}$. If the speed of the processor during the sub-block B_1 is strictly larger to s^*, then the starting time of the sub-block B_1 is necessary a release date, otherwise, we can decrease the speed and the energy consumption as well.

Similarly, the completion time of the sub-block B_k is either a deadline, either at a distance $h \cdot \frac{p}{s^*}$ from the starting time of the sub-block B_k for some value $h = 1, \ldots, n$.   □

Using Lemma 1 we can assume that each job is processed at some speed which belongs to the following set.

Definition 9. *Let* $\Lambda := \{\frac{\ell \cdot p}{b-a} \mid \ell = 1, \ldots, n \text{ and } a, b \in \Omega \text{ and } a < b\} \cup \{s^*\}$ *be the set of different speeds.*

Definition 10. *Let* $J(k, a, b) := \{j | j \leq k \text{ and } a \leq r_j < b\}$ *be the set of jobs among the k first ones w.r.t. the EDF order, whose release dates are within a and b.*

Definition 11. *For* $0 \leq u \leq n$, *define* $E_k(a, t, b, u)$ *as the minimum energy consumption of a non-preemptive schedule S such that*

– $S \subseteq J(k, a, b)$ and $|S| = u$ where S is the set of jobs scheduled in S,
– it is idle during interval $[a, t]$.

Note that $E_k(a, t, b, u) := \infty$ if no such schedule S exists.

Proposition 6. (Fig. 4) One has

$$E_0(a, t, b, 0) = \gamma(t - a) + \min\{L, \gamma(b - t)\}$$
$$E_0(a, t, b, u) = +\infty \ \forall u \neq 0$$

$$E_k(a, t, b, u) = \min \begin{cases} E_{k-1}(a, t, b, u) \\ \min\limits_{\substack{a', t' \in \Theta \\ s \in \Lambda \\ t' = a' + p/s \\ r_k \leq a' < t' \leq d_k \\ 0 \leq u' \leq u - 1}} \left\{ \begin{array}{l} E_{k-1}(a, t, a', u') + p \cdot s^{\alpha - 1} \\ + E_{k-1}(a', t', b, u - u' - 1) \end{array} \right\} \end{cases}$$

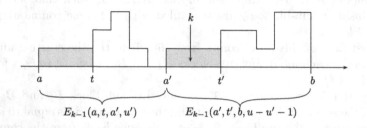

$$\underbrace{}_{E_{k-1}(a, t, a', u')} \quad \underbrace{}_{E_{k-1}(a', t', b, u - u' - 1)}$$

Fig. 4. Illustration of Proposition 6

The main difference with [6] lies in the initialization of the table where we consider the energy consumption of idle periods since there is no jobs scheduled at these moments. The proof of the dynamic program is the same as for the speed-scaling model.

Theorem 2. The dynamic program in Proposition 6 has a running time of $O(n^{21})$.

Proof. The objective function is $\max\{u \mid E_n(r_{\min}, r_{\min}, d_n, u) \leq E\}$. The values of $E_k(.)$ are stored in a multi-dimensional array of size $O(|\Theta|^2 |\Lambda| n^2) = O(n^{13})$. Each value need $O(|\Lambda| |\Theta| \ W)$ time to be computed thanks to Proposition 6. Thus we have a total running time of $O(|\Theta|^3 |\Lambda|^2 n^3)$. This leads to an overall time complexity $O(n^{21})$.   □

Corollary 1. The minimization energy version of the problem can be solved in time $O(n^{19})$.

Proof. In the minimization energy variant, we have to schedule every job. Then it is not necessary to guess how many jobs are scheduled in each part. We have to redefine the definition of $E_k(a, t, b, u)$ into $E_k(a, t, b)$ where we have to schedule every jobs in $\{j \leq k \mid a \leq r_j < b\}$. Moreover, we don't need to guess the value of u' in the dynamic program. By adapting the dynamic program in Proposition 6, we decrease by $O(n)$ the size of the table, and by $O(n)$ the time complexity to compute one value of the table. Therefore, the energy minimization variant has a complexity of $O(n^{19})$. □

5 Concluding Remarks

Maximizing throughput is one of the most important problems in scheduling theory. In the last years, an increasing interest has been devoted to this problem in the energy-aware setting. While the problem is closely related to the energy minimization problem, throughput maximization seems harder to tackle. For instance, while a polynomial time algorithm is known for the preemptive energy minimization problem for the single-processor case, the complexity of the throughput maximization problem remains still open. Only recently, a pseudo-polynomial time algorithm appeared in the literature showing that the problem is not strongly NP-hard [4], but the question of whether the problem is solvable in polynomial time or not remains open. For the speed-scaling with power-down model, the question is even more challenging. While a polynomial time algorithm existed for instances with agreeable deadlines, no results were known for the throughput maximization problem.

References

1. Albers, S., Antoniadis, A.: Race to idle: new algorithms for speed scaling with a sleep state. In: SODA, pp. 1266–1285. SIAM (2012)
2. Albers, S., Müller, F., Schmelzer, S.: Speed scaling on parallel processors. In: SPAA, pp. 289–298. ACM (2007)
3. Angel, E., Bampis, E., Chau, V.: Low complexity scheduling algorithms minimizing the energy for tasks with agreeable deadlines. Discrete Appl. Math. **175**, 1–10 (2014)
4. Angel, E., Bampis, E., Chau, V.: Throughput maximization in the speed-scaling setting. In: STACS. LIPIcs vol. 25, pp. 53–62 (2014)
5. Angel, E., Bampis, E., Chau, V., Letsios, D.: Throughput maximization for speed-scaling with agreeable deadlines. In: Chan, T.-H.H., Lau, L.C., Trevisan, L. (eds.) TAMC 2013. LNCS, vol. 7876, pp. 10–19. Springer, Heidelberg (2013)
6. Angel, E., Bampis, E., Chau, V., Thang, N.K.: Throughput maximization in multiprocessor speed-scaling. In: Ahn, H.-K., Shin, C.-S. (eds.) ISAAC 2014. LNCS, vol. 8889, pp. 247–258. Springer, Heidelberg (2014)
7. Antoniadis, A., Huang, C.C.: Non-preemptive speed scaling. J. Sched. **16**(4), 385–394 (2013)
8. Bampis, E., Dürr, C., Kacem, F., Milis, I.: Speed scaling with power down scheduling for agreeable deadlines. Sustain. Comput. Inf. Syst. **2**(4), 184–189 (2012)
9. Bampis, E., Kononov, A., Letsios, D., Lucarelli, G., Sviridenko, M.: Energy efficient scheduling and routing via randomized rounding. In: FSTTCS. LIPIcs, vol. 24, pp. 449–460 (2013)

10. Baptiste, P.: Scheduling unit tasks to minimize the number of idle periods: a polynomial time algorithm for offline dynamic power management. In: SODA, pp. 364–367. ACM Press (2006)
11. Baptiste, P., Chrobak, M., Dürr, C.: Polynomial-time algorithms for minimum energy scheduling. ACM Trans. Algorithms 8(3), 26 (2012)
12. Brucker, P.: Scheduling Algorithms, 5th edn. Springer Publishing Company, Incorporated, Heidelberg (2010)
13. Chrobak, M., Feige, U., Hajiaghayi, M.T., Khanna, S., Li, F., Naor, S.: A greedy approximation algorithm for minimum-gap scheduling. In: Spirakis, P.G., Serna, M. (eds.) CIAC 2013. LNCS, vol. 7878, pp. 97–109. Springer, Heidelberg (2013)
14. Cohen-Addad, V., Li, Z., Mathieu, C., Milis, I.: Energy-efficient algorithms for non-preemptive speed-scaling. In: Bampis, E., Svensson, O. (eds.) WAOA 2014. LNCS, vol. 8952, pp. 107–118. Springer, Heidelberg (2015)
15. Gaujal, B., Navet, N.: Dynamic voltage scaling under EDF revisited. Real-Time Syst. 37(1), 77–97 (2007)
16. Gaujal, B., Navet, N., Walsh, C.: Shortest-path algorithms for real-time scheduling of FIFO tasks with minimal energy use. ACM Trans. Embed. Comput. Syst. 4(4), 907–933 (2005)
17. Irani, S., Shukla, S.K., Gupta, R.: Algorithms for power savings. ACM Trans. Algorithms 3(4) (2007). Article No 41
18. Kise, H., Ibaraki, T., Mine, H.: A solvable case of the one-machine scheduling problem with ready and due times. Oper. Res. 26(1), 121–126 (1978)
19. Li, M.: Approximation algorithms for variable voltage processors: Min energy, max throughput and online heuristics. Theor. Comput. Sci. 412(32), 4074–4080 (2011)
20. Li, M., Yao, F.F.: An efficient algorithm for computing optimal discrete voltage schedules. In: Jedrzejowicz, J., Szepietowski, A. (eds.) MFCS 2005. LNCS, vol. 3618, pp. 652–663. Springer, Heidelberg (2005)
21. Wu, W., Li, M., Chen, E.: Min-energy scheduling for aligned jobs in accelerate model. Theor. Comput. Sci. 412(12–14), 1122–1139 (2011)
22. Yao, F.F., Demers, A.J., Shenker, S.: A scheduling model for reduced CPU energy. In: FOCS, pp. 374–382. IEEE Computer Society (1995)

Scheduling Tasks from Selfish Multi-tasks Agents

Johanne Cohen[1] and Fanny Pascual[2]([⊠])

[1] LRI-CNRS, Université Paris Sud, bât 650, 91400 Orsay, France
johanne.cohen@lri.fr
[2] Sorbonne Universités, Université Pierre et Marie Curie (Univ. Paris 06), CNRS,
LIP6 UMR 7606, 4 place Jussieu, 75005 Paris, France
fanny.pascual@lip6.fr

Abstract. We are interested in scheduling tasks from several selfish agents on a set of parallel identical machines. A coordination mechanism consists in giving a scheduling policy to each machine. Given these policies, each agent chooses the machines on which she assigns her tasks, and her aim is to minimize the average completion times of her tasks. The aim of the system (social cost) is to minimize the average completion time of all the tasks. We focus on coordination mechanisms inducing Nash equilibria, and on the performance of such mechanisms. When the machines do not know the owners of the tasks, the classical coordination mecanisms used for single-task agents do not work anymore and we give necessary conditions to obtain coordination mechanisms that induce Nash equilibria. When each machine is able to know the owner of each task it has to schedule, we give coordination mechanisms which always induce Nash equilibria.

1 Introduction

Among the most fundamental problems in algorithmic game theory are scheduling and load balancing problems. Since the seminal paper by Koutsoupias and Papadimitriou [16], these problems have been of growing interest [21]. Indeed, besides their conceptual simplicity, these problems are central in distributed environments where some machines are shared between selfish users, and where the users decide on which machines they will assign their tasks. In such environments, coordination mechanisms have been introduced by Christodoulou *et al.* [7] in order to obtain socially desirable solutions despite the selfishness of the agents. A *coordination mechanism* is a set of scheduling policies, one for each machine. A scheduling mechanism for a machine M_i takes as input a set of tasks assigned to machine M_i along with their processing times. The output is a schedule of the tasks on M_i. The aim is to design a coordination mechanism such that for each instance (set of tasks) there exists a Nash equilibrium (a schedule where no agent has incentive to change the assignement of her tasks).

When a coordination mechanism always induces Nash equilibria, it is useful to measure the quality of the Nash equilibria induced, which is usually done

© Springer-Verlag Berlin Heidelberg 2015
J.L. Träff et al. (Eds.): Euro-Par 2015, LNCS 9233, pp. 183–195, 2015.
DOI: 10.1007/978-3-662-48096-0_15

using the price of anarchy [16]. The *price of anarchy* is defined as the maximal value, over all the instances, of the ratio between the social cost in the worst Nash and the social cost in an optimal solution.

Starting from the seminal paper of Christodoulou *et al.* [7], coordination mechanisms have been extensively studied for single tasks agents [3,4,6,9,11,13–15]. In these papers, each agent owns *a single* task, and her aim is to minimize the completion time of her task. The social cost is either the largest completion time of a task or the average completion time of the tasks. The coordination mechanism studied are often the ones which schedule the tasks in order of non decreasing lengths (ShortestFirst policy), in order of non increasing lengths (LongestFirst policy), or in a random order; for identical machines [7,14], related machines [13], or unrelated machines [3,4,9,11]. These coordination mechanisms usually induce pure Nash equilibria, and the aim is to measure their price of anarchy.

In our setting, each agent may own *several* tasks, and her aim is to minimize the average completion time of her tasks. We study the existence and the quality of coordination mechanisms for this extension of this classical game. The social cost that we consider is the sum of the completion times of all the tasks.

Most of the papers dealing with multi-task selfish agents sharing machines are interested by designing centralized fair solutions (see [2] for a recent survey). In these models, the agents cannot choose themself the machines on which their tasks will be scheduled. Starting from the seminal paper [20], some papers (e.g. [5,8,12]) consider a set of agents owing each one a set of tasks but also a set of machines. The aim is to design a centralized algorithm which assigns all the tasks to all the machines in a way which minimizes the overall makespan whilst ensuring that the cost of each agent is not increased compared to the solution where each agent schedules her own tasks on her own machines.

There is, up to our knowledge, only one paper which deals with coordination mechanisms with multi-tasks agents. In this paper, Abed et al. [1] consider that each agent owns several tasks, each task having a length and a weight. The machines are unrelated, and each agent aims at minimizing the weighted completion time of her tasks, whereas the social cost is the sum of agents' costs. The main difference to our paper is that the authors do not consider Nash equilibria but a superclass of Nash equilibria: they consider that a schedule is stable (they call such a schedule a *weak Nash equilibrium*) if no agent may decreases her cost by moving *exactly one* of her task to a different machine. They show that when the policies of the machines order the tasks according to their length to weight ratio, then there exists a weak Nash equilibrium, and that the price of anarchy (with respect to weak Nash equilibrium) is 4. They extend this policy by introducing some delays between tasks, and they show that the price of anarchy of this new coordination mecanism is about 2.6.

We now describe precisely the problem studied and the notions used in this paper.

Model. We consider a set of K selfish agents $\{A_1, \ldots, A_K\}$, each agent A_i owning a set of n_i tasks. When we only consider two agents, these agents will be called A and B; the set of tasks of agent A will be $\{a_1, a_2, \ldots, a_{n_A}\}$, and the set of tasks of agent B will be $\{b_1, b_2, \ldots, b_{n_B}\}$. Each task has a unique identification number and an arbitrary processing time (length). It cannot be preempted. The agents share a set of $m \geq 2$ identical parallel machines $\{M_1, \ldots, M_m\}$. Each machine M_i has a public *policy*, which is an algorithm which returns a schedule (on M_i) of the tasks assigned to M_i. This policy may introduce idle times between the tasks. However, since we consider a totally decentralized setting, the policy of M_i depends only on the tasks assigned to M_i: it cannot be a function of the tasks assigned to the other machines. A set of policies, one for each machine, is called a *coordination mechanism*. We consider two models. In the first one, the machines cannot distinguish the tasks of one agent from the tasks of another agent: a machine is only aware of the length and identification number of the tasks it has to schedule. In the second one, the machines know the owner of each task.

Knowing the policies of the machines, the set of the tasks of the other agents and the strategies of the other agents, each agent chooses, for each of her tasks, on which machine it will be scheduled. The *strategy* of each agent is thus an assignment to a machine of each of her tasks. The aim of each agent is to minimize the average completion time of her tasks. This is equivalent to minimize the sum of completion times of her tasks: in the sequel the cost of each agent is thus the sum of the completion times of her tasks. A schedule is a (pure) *Nash equilibrium* if no agent can decrease the sum of completion times of her tasks by changing her assignment. In this paper, we focus on coordination mechanisms which always induce pure Nash equilibria (i.e., coordination mechanism such that, for each instance, there exists at least one pure Nash equilibrium). A game always has a mixed Nash equilibrium [19], but pure Nash equilibria are more natural and are the only possible solutions in some settings.

Our Contribution. In Sect. 2, we consider that the machines do not know the owners of the tasks. We show that if all the machines use the same deterministic policy then this policy necessarily have to introduce some idle times between the tasks in order to induce Nash equilibria. Moreover the price of anarchy of such a coordination mechanism is at least 2. In Sect. 3, we show that there exists coordination mechanisms which induce Nash equilibria when the machines are able to know the owner of each task. In particular, we introduce a simple and fair coordination mechanism which has a bounded price of anarchy if the number of agents is small. We conclude this paper in Sect. 4.

2 Properties of Coordination Mechanisms in Which the Machines Do Not Know the Owners of Their Tasks

We consider in this section that the machines are not able to detect the owner of the tasks they have to schedule. We will focus on coordination mechanisms with deterministic identical policies. Given two tasks i and j, we note $i \prec j$ if and only if task i is scheduled before task j when a machine has only these two tasks to schedule.

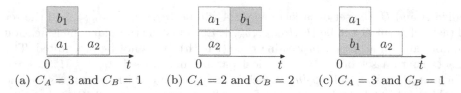

(a) $C_A = 3$ and $C_B = 1$ (b) $C_A = 2$ and $C_B = 2$ (c) $C_A = 3$ and $C_B = 1$

Fig. 1. Instance with no pure Nash equilibrium when all the machines have the same deterministic policy without idle times. C_A (resp. C_B) is the cost of agent A (resp. B).

Proposition 1. *If all the machines have the same deterministic policy, and if this policy does not introduce idle times between the tasks, then the coordination mechanism does not always induce a pure Nash equilibrium.*

Proof. We provide a instance without pure Nash equilibrium. This instance, depicted in Fig. 1, consists in two machines and two agents A and B. Agent A has two tasks a_1 and a_2, each of length 1, while B has one task b_1 of length 1. We consider tasks a_1, a_2, and b_1 such that $a_1 \prec b_1$ and $b_1 \prec a_2$. Note that given three tasks i, j, k, and any deterministic policy, there always exists a permutation of the tasks such that $i \prec j$ and $j \prec k$. The configuration which consists of three tasks on the same machine is not a Nash equilibrium since b_1 would have incentive to move on the idle machine. The other configurations are represented in Fig. 1 and are also not Nash equilibria: in Fig. 1(a) Agent A can decrease her cost by assigning task a_1 to M_1; in Fig. 1(b) Agent B has incentive to move her task; in Fig. 1(c) Agent A has incentive to exchange the assignment of her two tasks a_1 and a_2.   □

Note that the classical policies LongestFirst and ShortestFirst have this property, and thus they do not always induce pure Nash equilibria (contrary to the case where each agent has only one task [14]). Moreover, the move of only two tasks is needed to show this result. Abed et al. [1] show that when multi-tasks agents are able to move only one task to improve their cost, then the ShortestFirst policy is stable (for each instance there exist a schedule where the agents cannot improve their costs by moving at most one of their tasks). If the agents are able to move at most two tasks to compute their best response, then Proposition 1 shows that there exists instances without stable schedules.

Note also that this result does not depend on the social cost considered, and is thus valid for any social cost.

Proposition 2. *Consider a coordination mechanism in which all the machines have the same deterministic policy which is not based on identification numbers[1]. If this coordination mechanism always induces a pure Nash equilibrium, then its price of anarchy is larger than or equal to 2.*

---

[1] The schedule is constructed by considering only the lengths of the tasks to schedule. Identification numbers are used thereafter to break the ties only, i.e. to assign each task to a slot of its length in the constructed schedule.

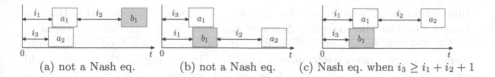

(a) not a Nash eq.   (b) not a Nash eq.   (c) Nash eq. when $i_3 \geq i_1 + i_2 + 1$

Fig. 2. Different configurations where both machines have the same deterministic policy having idle times.

Proof. Let us consider the following instance, with two machines and two agents: Agent A owns two tasks a_1 and a_2, and Agent B owns one task b_1. We consider that these three tasks are all of length one, and are such that $a_1 \prec b_1$ and $b_1 \prec a_2$. Let i_1 (resp. i_2) be the length of the idle time before the first (resp. second) task when a machine schedules two tasks of length 1. Let i_3 be the length of the idle time before the first task when a machine schedules one task of length 1. We proceed by cases analysis. There are four possible schedules. We show that if one of these schedules is a Nash equilibrium then the price of anarchy is at least 2.

- Schedule 1: *Tasks a_1 and b_1 are on the same machine (w.l.o.g. on M_1); task a_2 is alone on M_2.* Figure 2(a) shows this configuration. The completion time of b_1 is $i_1 + i_2 + 2$. If this task would jump on M_2, then its completion time would be $i_1 + 1$: this task has incentive to change machine (because $i_1 + i_2 + 2 > i_1 + 1$). Thus, this schedule is not a Nash equilibrium.
- Schedule 2: *Tasks b_1 and a_2 are on the same machine (w.l.o.g. on M_2); task a_1 is alone (on M_1).* This configuration is depicted in Fig. 2(b). The completion time of all the tasks of Agent A is $i_1 + i_2 + i_3 + 3$. If Agent A moves task a_2 on M_1 and a_1 on M_2, then the sum of completion times of her tasks will be $i_1 + i_3 + 2$. Since $i_1 + i_2 + i_3 + 3 > i_1 + i_3 + 2$, Agent A has incentive to move her tasks, and this schedule is thus not a Nash equilibrium.
- Schedule 3: *Tasks a_1 and a_2 are on the same machine (w.l.o.g. on M_1); task b_1 is alone (on M_2).* Figure 2(c) shows this configuration. Let us focus on Agent A. The completion time of the tasks of Agent A is $2i_1 + i_2 + 3$ in this schedule. If Agent A would place task a_1 on M_2 and task a_2 on M_1, then the sum of completion times of her tasks would be $i_3 + i_1 + 2$. Thus this schedule is a Nash equilibrium only if $2i_1 + i_2 + 3 \leq i_1 + i_3 + 2$, i.e. if $i_3 \geq i_1 + i_2 + 1$. Thus $i_3 \geq 1$ is a necessary condition for schedule 3 to be a Nash equilibrium. Let us thus consider any policy where $i_3 \geq 1$, and let us consider an instance which consists of only one task of length 1. The completion time of this task is at least 2, whereas the optimal completion time would be 1. Therefore the price of anarchy of a coordination mechanism using such a policy is at least 2.
- Schedule 4: *The three tasks are on the same machine (w.l.o.g. on M_1).* Let us denote this schedule by $\mathcal{S}$. Let us consider that $\mathcal{S}$ is a Nash equilibrium, and that the price of anarchy of the coordination mechanism is smaller than 2. This implies that $i_3 < 1$, otherwise an instance with only one task of length 1 would have a sum of completion times larger than 2, whereas the optimum is 1. Thus task b_1 has to be scheduled first in $\mathcal{S}$, otherwise its completion

time would be at least 2 and this task would decrease its completion time by jumping on the idle machine: $\mathcal{S}$ would not be a Nash equilibrium. Tasks a_1 and a_2 are thus on second and third positions. Since $\mathcal{S}$ is a Nash equilibrium, Agent A has no incentive to move a_2 on M_2. By moving a_2, this agent would let a_1 and b_1 on one machine (a_1 is scheduled first since $a_1 \prec b_1$), and a_2 alone on the other machine. Let us denote by $C_i^{(j)}$ the completion time of the ith task when there are j tasks of length 1 on a machine. Thus we have:

$$C_2^{(3)} + C_3^{(3)} \leq C_1^{(1)} + C_1^{(2)} \tag{1}$$

We saw that $i_3 < 1$, so $C_1^{(1)} < 2$. Moreover, since $C_2^{(3)} \geq 2$, we get: $C_3^{(3)} < C_1^{(2)}$. We now show that with these hypothesis on the policies, there is an instance in which there is no Nash equilibrium.

Let us consider the following instance: three tasks of length 1: a_1', a_2' (belonging to Agent A), and b_1' (belonging to Agent B), such that, when they are together on one machine a_1' is scheduled first. The schedule where the three tasks are together is not a Nash equilibrium, since b_1' has a completion time larger than or equal to 2, whereas it would get a completion time smaller than 2 by going on the other machine. The schedule where b_1' is alone on a machine is also not a Nash equilibrium. Indeed, in this schedule the sum of completion times of a_1' and a_2' is $C_1^{(2)} + C_2^{(2)} \geq 2C_1^{(2)} > 2C_3^{(3)}$, whereas by going with b_1', tasks a_1' and a_2' would have a sum of completion times smaller than $2C_3^{(3)}$: Agent A has incentive to move her tasks. The last possible configuration is when b_1' is with one task of A, the other task of A being on the other machine. In this case the sum of the completion times of the tasks of A is larger than or equal to $C_1^{(1)} + C_1^{(2)} \geq C_2^{(3)} + C_3^{(3)}$ by Eq. 1. By going with b_1', the sum of completion times of A's tasks would be at most $C_1^{(3)} + C_3^{(3)} < C_2^{(3)} + C_3^{(3)}$: these tasks again have incentive to move. Therefore there is no Nash equilibrium in this instance, if we assume that the price of anarchy of the coordination mechanism is smaller than 2.   □

We studied the case where the owners of the tasks are not known by the machines: the results are rather negative since we gave strong necessary conditions to get coordination mechanisms which always induce Nash equilibria. Let us now show that the results are more positive if the machines are able to know the owners of the tasks.

3   Coordination Mechanisms in Which the Machines Know the Owners of Their Tasks

If the identification numbers (IDs) of the owners of the tasks are used only to break the ties between the tasks of the same length, then we can extend Proposition 1: in this case, if all the machines have the same deterministic policy, and if this policy does not introduce idle times between the tasks, then the coordination mechanism does not always induce a pure Nash equilibrium[2]. Thus the coordination mechanism which considers the tasks with the ShortestFirst policy and breaks the ties with the IDs of the agents does not always induce Nash equilibria. Since the IDs of the agents should not be considered only to break the ties, let us now consider coordination mechanisms which make a more intensive use of these IDs.

Let us first introduce a simple coordination mechanism, called PRIOSPT: each machine schedules the tasks of the same agent together, considering the agents by increasing order of their ID. In other words, each machine schedules the tasks of Agent A_1, and then the tasks of Agent A_2, and so forth. The tasks of a same agent are scheduled with the ShortestFirst policy. This coordination mechanism induces a Nash equilibrium, since each agent A_i has assigned her tasks in order to minimize her cost given the tasks of higher priority agents, and the tasks of lower priority agents will be scheduled after the tasks of A_i and thus will not change the cost of A_i. Note that this coordination mechanism induces Nash equilibria which can be reached in a polynomial time. Indeed, it has been shown [17,18] that the SPT list algorithm[3] is optimal for the minimization of the sum of the completion times, even if some machines are not available at time 0. Each agent will thus use this polynomial time algorithm to schedule her tasks, given the schedule obtained with the tasks of the higher priority agents.

However, this coordination has two main drawbacks: it is unfair (the lower is the ID of an agent, the higher is her priority), and its price of anarchy is unbounded: consider for example an instance where Agent A_1 has m very large tasks, and Agent A_2 has a lot of tiny tasks. Let us now introduce a new coordination mechanism which is fair with the agents and which has a bounded price of anarchy. This coordination mechanism, that we call EQUALPRIOSPT, works if the number of agents is known and smaller than or equal to the number of machines, which is realistic in many situations, like the one studies in [12], where a few organizations (universities, associations, etc.) share a set of machines.

The idea of EQUALPRIOSPT is the following one: for each agent A_i, there are $\lfloor \frac{m}{K} \rfloor$ (or $\lfloor \frac{m}{K} \rfloor + 1$) machines on which the tasks of A_i are scheduled first (from the smallest one to the largest one). On these machines, once the tasks of A_i have been scheduled, the tasks of $A_{1+(i \bmod K)}$ are scheduled, from the smallest one to the largest one, and then the tasks of $A_{1+((i+1) \mod K)}$, etc. The latest tasks to be scheduled are the tasks of A_{i-1} (or A_K if $i = 1$).

More formally, to each agent $A_i \in \{A_1, \ldots, A_K\}$, we associate a priority list $L_i = (A_{1+(i \bmod K)}, A_{1+((i+1) \bmod K)}, \ldots, A_{1+((i+K-2) \bmod K)})$ (e.g. the priority list of A_3 is $(A_4, A_5, A_6, A_1, A_2)$ when there are 6 agents). Let q and r be the

---

[2] The proof is the same as the one of Proposition 1, except that the three considered tasks i, j and k are not of length 1 but of length $1 - \varepsilon$, 1 and $1 + \varepsilon$ for a small value of ε. For any deterministic policy, there always exists a permutation of the tasks such that $i \prec j$ and $j \prec k$. Tasks i and k are the ones of Agent A, and task j is the one of Agent B.

[3] The *SPT list algorithm* considers the tasks in non-decreasing order of their lengths, and assigns each task to a machine, as soon as a machine is available (idle).

two positive integers such that $m = qK + r$. For $0 \le i \le K - 1$, machine M_{iq+1} to machine $M_{(i+1)q}$ schedule the tasks of agent A_{i+1} first (using the ShortestFirst policy). If $r \ne 0$, then for $1 \le i \le r$ machine M_{Kq+i} schedules the tasks of agent A_i first (using the ShortestFirst policy). Let M_j be one of the machines which schedule first the tasks of A_i. Once M_j has scheduled the tasks of agent A_i, it schedules the tasks of the other agents in the order of the priority list L_i. The tasks belonging to a same agent are scheduled with the ShortestFirst policy.

Proposition 3. EQUALPRIOSPT *induces a pure Nash equilibrium, and this equilibrium can be reached in* $O(nK)$, *where* $n = \sum_{i=1}^{K} n_i$ *is the number of tasks.*

Proof. We give a constructive proof: we provide a polynomial time algorithm which takes as input an instance of the game (m machines and a set of tasks belonging to K agents), and which returns a Nash equilibrium of this instance. In this algorithm, we say that an agent is *fixed* or not (once an agent is fixed, her tasks won't be moved anymore). We will also say that each agent *owns*, at each step of the algorithm, a set of machines. This algorithm is the following one:

- No agent is fixed. For each agent $A_j \in \{A_1, \ldots, A_K\}$, the machines owned by A_j are the ones on which A_j has the highest priority. Each agent A_j schedules her tasks using the SPT list algorithm on the machines she owns.
- For i from 1 to K:
  - For each agent $A_j \in \{A_1, \ldots, A_K\}$, let D_i^j be the smallest date at which a machine is idle among the machines owned by A_j. Let $D_i = \min_{j \in \{1,\ldots,K\}} \{D_i^j\}$. Let A_{x_i} be an agent such that $D_i^j = D_i$.
  - Agent A_{x_i} is now *fixed* (and will remain fixed in the sequel).
  - Let A_{y_i} be the first agent, among the agents which are not fixed, in the priority list L_{x_i}. Add to the set of machines owned by A_{y_i} the machines previously owned by A_{x_i}. Remove from the schedule all the tasks of A_{y_i} which are started after time D_i, and schedule them again using the SPT list algorithm on the machines that A_{y_i} currently owns (on these machines, the tasks starting before D_i are not moved - note that it includes all the tasks of the agents other than A_{y_i}).

At each step (iteration) one agent is fixed (her tasks won't move anymore) and the only tasks which are moved are the one of a single agent A_{y_i}: the SPT list algorithm used to schedule them takes time $O(n_{y_i}) \subset O(n)$ (once the tasks have been sorted for each agent - which takes time $O(n \log n)$). There are K steps so this algorithm runs in $O(nK)$. Let us now prove the following property: *at the end of each iteration i of this algorithm, the agents which are fixed do not have incentive to move their tasks.* The proof is by induction on i.

- This is true when $i = 1$: all the tasks of the only fixed agent, A_{x_1}, start at the latest at time D_i, whereas the first idle time on a machine is D_i. Moreover, A_{x_1} used the SPT list algorithm to schedule her tasks on the machines she owns: this minimizes her sum of completion times.

– Let $i > 1$. Let us now consider that the property is true for each iteration $j < i$, and let us show that it is also true for iteration i. Agent A_{x_i}, which has been fixed at iteration i, has not incentive to move her tasks since all her tasks starts at the latest at time D_i, whereas the first idle time on a machine is D_i. Before this date, all the machines which are not owned by A_{x_i} schedule tasks which have a higher priority than A_{x_i} (otherwise by construction, some tasks of A_{x_i} would have been scheduled instead of the tasks of a lower priority agent). Furthermore, the tasks of A_{x_i} have been scheduled with the SPT list algorithm: this minimizes the cost of A_{x_i}. Likewise, each agent A_{x_j} fixed at a given iteration $j < i$ has not incentive to move her tasks. Indeed, by induction, she had no incentive to move her tasks at the time at which she has been fixed, D_j, and, by construction, the schedule of the tasks scheduled before time D_j does not change after this time.

We have proved that the agents which are fixed do not have incentive to move their tasks once they are fixed. Since at the end of the execution of the algorithm all the agents are fixed, no agent has incentive to move her tasks, and the schedule obtained is thus a Nash equilibrium.   □

Let us now show that, contrarily to the coordination mechanism PrioSPT, the price of anarchy of EqualPrioSPT is bounded.

Lemma 1. *Let q and m be two positive integers such that $q < m$. The sum of the completion times of a set of tasks scheduled with the SPT list algorithm on q machines is smaller than or equal to $\frac{m}{q}$ times the sum of completion times of the same tasks scheduled with the SPT list algorithm on m machines.*

Proof. An $OPT_\sum$ schedule is a schedule in which the sum of completion times of the tasks is minimized. A schedule obtained by executing the SPT list algorithm (we will call such a schedule a SPT schedule) is thus an $OPT_\sum$ schedule. Conway *et al.* [10] show that an $OPT_\sum$ schedule of x tasks on m machines can be described as follows. W.l.o.g., we assume that $\ell_1 \geq \ell_2 \geq \cdots \geq \ell_x$, where ℓ_i is the length of task i. We define the following sets: $\pi_1 = \{\ell_1, \ell_2, \ldots, \ell_m\}$, $\pi_2 = \{\ell_{m+1}, \ell_{m+2}, \ldots, \ell_{2m}\}, \ldots, \pi_k = \{\ell_{(k-1)m}, \ldots, \ell_x\}$, where $k = \lceil \frac{x}{m} \rceil$.

The set π_i is called the ith rank of the tasks. A $OPT_\sum$ schedule is a schedule obtained by scheduling the tasks rank by rank, in the order $\pi_k, \pi_{k-1}, \ldots, \pi_1$: the tasks of π_k are scheduled first, each one on a different machine, and the tasks of π_{k-1} are scheduled, also each one on a different machine, and so forth.

By this way, a task in π_i will be followed by $i - 1$ tasks on its machine, and thus it will be counted i times in the sum of the completion times of the tasks: this sum is $\sum_{j=1}^{x} C_j = \sum_{i=1}^{k} \sum_{j \in \pi_i} i\ell_j$.

Let us assume without loss of generality that the number of tasks x is divisible by the number of machines m. If it is not the case, then we can add dummy tasks of length 0. If there are m machines, then task ℓ_i will be in the set $\pi_{\lceil \frac{i}{m} \rceil}$ and thus it will be counted $\lceil \frac{i}{m} \rceil$ times in the sum of the completion times.

Let r_i be the rank of task ℓ_i in a SPT schedule for q machines. For $1 \leq i \leq x$, we have $r_i = \lceil \frac{i}{q} \rceil$, and thus $r_1 \leq r_2 \leq \cdots \leq r_x$.

We will focus on the tasks of rank j in the SPT schedule on m machines. In other words, we will focus on set $\pi_j = \{\ell_{(j-1)m+1}, \ldots, \ell_{jm}\}$. We will prove that

$$\sum_{i=(j-1)m+1}^{jm} r_i \ell_i \leq \frac{m}{q} \sum_{i=(j-1)m+1}^{jm} j\ell_i \qquad (2)$$

By definition, we have $r_{jm} = \lceil \frac{jm}{q} \rceil$. We can notice that if $r_{jm} = \frac{jm}{q}$, then Eq. (2) holds. Now, we assume that $jm = q(r_{jm} - 1) + \alpha$ where $q > \alpha > 1$. First, there are α tasks of this rank in π_j. So, we have

$$\sum_{i=jm+1-\alpha}^{jm} r_i \ell_i = r_{jm} \sum_{i=jm+1-\alpha}^{jm} \ell_i = \left(\frac{jm}{q} + \frac{q-\alpha}{q} \right) \sum_{i=jm+1-\alpha}^{jm} \ell_i \qquad (3)$$

Second, there are $m - \alpha$ tasks of rank at most $r_{jm} - 1$.

$$\sum_{i=(j-1)m+1}^{jm-\alpha} r_i \ell_i \leq (r_{jm} - 1) \sum_{i=(j-1)m+1}^{jm-\alpha} \ell_i = \left(\frac{jm-\alpha}{q} \right) \sum_{i=(j-1)m+1}^{jm-\alpha} \ell_i \qquad (4)$$

Third, we will find an upper bound of the following value $X = \sum_{i=jm+1-\alpha}^{jm}(q - \alpha)\ell_i - \sum_{i=(j-1)m+1}^{jm-\alpha} \alpha\ell_i$. Since $\ell_1 \geq \ell_2 \geq \cdots \geq \ell_x$, we get $\alpha(q-\alpha)\ell_{jm+1-\alpha} \geq (q-\alpha)\sum_{i=jm+1-\alpha}^{jm} \ell_i$ and $\sum_{i=(j-1)m+1}^{jm-\alpha} \alpha\ell_i \geq (m-\alpha)\alpha\ell_{jm+1-\alpha}$. By computation, we obtain $X \leq \alpha(q-m)\ell_{jm+1-\alpha}$. Since $q < m$, we get $X < 0$. From Eqs. (3) and (4), we obtain

$$\sum_{i=(j-1)m+1}^{jm} r_i \ell_i \leq \left(\frac{m}{q} \sum_{i=(j-1)m+1}^{jm} j\ell_i \right) \qquad (5)$$

Thus we have: $\sum_{j=1}^{k} \sum_{i \in \pi_j} j\ell_i \leq \frac{m}{q} \sum_{j=1}^{k} \sum_{i \in \pi_j} r_i \ell_i$. Hence the sum of completion times of the tasks scheduled on q machines is at most $\frac{m}{q}$ times larger than the sum of completion times of these tasks scheduled on m machines. $\qquad \square$

Proposition 4. *The price of anarchy of* EQUALPRIOSPT *is at most* $\frac{m}{\lceil m/K \rceil}$. *This bound is asymptotically tight.*

Proof. The proof is split into two parts. The first part gives an upper bound on the price of anarchy by finding a relationship between the sum of the completion times in a schedule induced by the EQUALPRIOSPT coordination mechanism and the sum of the completion times in an optimal schedule, obtained by using the SPT list algorithm. The second part provides a lower bound on the price of anarchy by giving an example. Let q and r be two integers such that $m = qK + r$.

First, we consider the schedule obtained when the tasks of each agent A_i (with $i \in \{1, \ldots, K\}$), are scheduled using the SPT list algorithm on the machines where A_i has the highest priority (there are q or $q + 1$ such machines). Let us denote this schedule by $\mathcal{S}$. In $\mathcal{S}$, the cost of each agent is larger than or equal to her cost in a Nash equilibrium (otherwise an agent would schedule her tasks with the SPT list algorithm on the machines where she has the highest priority and she would decreases her cost). Let us now show that the cost of the sum of completion times in $\mathcal{S}$ is at most $\frac{m}{\lceil m/K \rceil} OPT$, where OPT is the optimal sum of completion times. The sum of the completion times of a set of tasks scheduled with the SPT list algorithm on q machines is smaller than or equal to $\frac{m}{q}$ times the sum of completion times of the same tasks scheduled with the SPT list algorithm on m machines (Lemma 1). The SPT list algorithm minimizes the sum of completion times. Thus, the cost of Agent A_i in $\mathcal{S}$ is smaller than or equal to $\frac{m}{q}$ times its cost in any solution (including the optimal solution): the sum of the completion times in $\mathcal{S}$ is thus smaller than or equal to $\frac{m}{q} OPT$. Therefore, the price of anarchy of EQUALPRIOSPT is at most $\frac{m}{\lceil m/K \rceil}$ because $q = \lfloor \frac{m}{K} \rfloor$.

Let us now prove the lower bound by providing a particular instance: there are K agents and $m = K(2K + 4)$ machines. Thus $q = 2K + 4$. Agent A_1 has $qm\alpha$ tasks of length 1 and q tasks of length $m\alpha$ where α is an arbitrary integer larger than 1. For $2 \leq i \leq K$, Agent A_i has q tasks of length equal to $m\alpha$. By computation we get that the price of anarchy is at least $\frac{\alpha m}{(\alpha+1)q}$, which for large values of α tends towards to $\frac{m}{q}$. □

4 Conclusion and Future Work

We studied the existence of coordination mechanism for multi-tasks agents. Classical deterministic policies do not always induce pure Nash equilibria in this context. In order to get Nash equilibria, if the machines are not able to identify the owners of the tasks, then we have either to use non deterministic policies (but such policies may be not easy to use in practice); or different policies on the machines (but this may also not be very practical since it may not be easy to add a machine to the system whilst ensuring that the coordination mechanism still induce Nash equilibria); or we should use policies which introduce idle times between the tasks (in this case the price of anarchy is at least 2).

Thus, knowing the owner of each task in the case of multi-tasks agents is a very useful information. In this case there exists coordination mechanisms inducing Nash equilibria. In particular, we have introduced a very simple coordination mechanism which may be used when the number of agents is known and small compared to the number of machines: this mechanism is fair since all the agents are treated equitably, and its price of anarchy is about K (this corresponds to the best we may have for $K = 2$ agents in the case of deterministic identical policies when the owner of the tasks are not known). Note that Lemma 1, introduced to show this result, can also be useful in other contexts: it indeed allows to bound the deterioration of the sum of completion times of a set of tasks when the number of machines to schedule these tasks decreases.

This work is a first step towards the study of coordination mechanism with agents owning several tasks. The main remaining open problem consists in determining whether there exists a coordination mechanism which always induce Nash equilibria with multi-tasks agents when the machines do not know the owners of the tasks.

Acknowledgments. The work of the second author was supported by ANR grant ANR-14-CE24-0007 (project COCORICO).

References

1. Abed, F., Correa, J.R., Huang, C.-C.: Optimal coordination mechanisms for multi-job scheduling games. In: Schulz, A.S., Wagner, D. (eds.) ESA 2014. LNCS, vol. 8737, pp. 13–24. Springer, Heidelberg (2014)
2. Agnetis, A., Billaut, J.C., Gawiejnowicz, S., Pacciarelli, D., Soukhal, A.: Multiagent Scheduling - Models and Algorithms. Springer, Heidelberg (2014)
3. Azar, Y., Jain, K., Mirrokni, V.: (Almost) optimal coordination mechanisms for unrelated machine scheduling. In: SODA 2008, pp. 323–332. SIAM (2008)
4. Caragiannis, I.: Efficient coordination mechanisms for unrelated machine scheduling. Algorithmica **66**(3), 512–540 (2013)
5. Chakravorty, A., Gupta, N., Lawaria, N., Kumar, P., Sabharwal,Y.: Algorithms for the relaxed multiple-organization multiple-machine scheduling problem. In: HiPC 2013, pp. 30–38 (2013)
6. Christodoulou, G., Gourvès, L., Pascual, F.: Scheduling selfish tasks: about the performance of truthful algorithms. In: Lin, G. (ed.) COCOON 2007. LNCS, vol. 4598, pp. 187–197. Springer, Heidelberg (2007)
7. Christodoulou, G., Koutsoupias, E., Nanavati, A.: Coordination mechanisms. Theor. Comput. Sci. **410**(36), 3327–3336 (2009)
8. Cohen, J., Cordeiro, D., Trystram, D., Wagner, F.: Analysis of multi-organization scheduling algorithms. In: D'Ambra, P., Guarracino, M., Talia, D. (eds.) Euro-Par 2010, Part II. LNCS, vol. 6272, pp. 367–379. Springer, Heidelberg (2010)
9. Cole, R., Correa, J.R., Gkatzelis, V., Mirrokni, V., Olver, N.: Inner product spaces for MinSum coordination mechanisms. In: STOC 2011, pp. 539–548. ACM (2011)
10. Conway, R.W., Maxwell, W.L., Miller, L.W.: Theory of Scheduling. Addison-Wesley Publishing Company, Reading (1967)
11. Correa, J.R., Queyranne, M.: Efficiency of equilibria in restricted uniform machine scheduling with total weighted completion time as social cost. Naval Res. Logistics (NRL) **59**(5), 384–395 (2012)
12. Dutot, P.F., Pascual, F., Rzadca, K., Trystram, D.: Approximation algorithms for the multiorganization scheduling problem. IEEE Trans. Parallel Distrib. Syst. **22**(11), 1888–1895 (2011)
13. Hoeksma, R., Uetz, M.: The price of anarchy for minsum related machine scheduling. In: Solis-Oba, R., Persiano, G. (eds.) WAOA 2011. LNCS, vol. 7164, pp. 261–273. Springer, Heidelberg (2012)
14. Immorlica, N., Li, L.E., Mirrokni, V.S., Schulz, A.S.: Coordination mechanisms for selfish scheduling. Theor. Comput. Sci. **410**(17), 1589–1598 (2009)
15. Kollias, K.: Nonpreemptive coordination mechanisms for identical machines. Theory Comput. Syst. **53**(3), 424–440 (2013)
16. Koutsoupias, E., Papadimitriou, C.: Worst-case equilibria. In: Meinel, C., Tison, S. (eds.) STACS 1999. LNCS, vol. 1563, pp. 404–413. Springer, Heidelberg (1999)
17. Liman, S.: Scheduling with capacities and due-dates. Ph.D. thesis, University of Florida (1991)
18. Montreuil, B., Kaspi, M., Ramudhin, A.: Scheduling identical parallel processors with arbitrary initial available times. Université Laval, Faculté des sciences de l'administration (1992)

19. Nash, J.F.: Equilibrium points in n-person games. In: Proceedings of the National Academy of Sciences, vol. 36, no. 1, pp. 48–49 (1950)
20. Pascual, F., Rzadca, K., Trystram, D.: Cooperation in multi-organization scheduling. In: Kermarrec, A.-M., Bougé, L., Priol, T. (eds.) Euro-Par 2007. LNCS, vol. 4641, pp. 224–233. Springer, Heidelberg (2007)
21. Vöcking, B.: Selfish load balancing. In: Nisan, N., Roughgarden, T., Tardos, E., Vazirani, V.V. (eds.) Algorithmic Game Theory, pp. 517–542. Cambridge University Press, Cambridge (2007)

Locality and Balance for Communication-Aware Thread Mapping in Multicore Systems

Matthias Diener[1,2](✉), Eduardo H.M. Cruz[1], Marco A.Z. Alves[1],
Mohammad S. Alhakeem[2], Philippe O.A. Navaux[1], and Hans-Ulrich Heiß[2]

[1] Informatics Institute, Federal University of Rio Grande Do Sul, Porto Alegre, Brazil
{mdiener,ehmcruz,mazalves,navaux}@inf.ufrgs.br
[2] Communication and Operating Systems Group, Technische Universität Berlin,
Berlin, Germany
{alhakeem,hans-ulrich.heiss}@tu-berlin.de

Abstract. In multicore architectures, deciding where to execute the
threads of parallel applications is increasingly a significant challenge.
This thread mapping has a large impact on the application's performance
and energy consumption. Recent research in this area mostly focuses on
improving the locality of memory accesses and optimizing the use of
shared caches by mapping threads that frequently communicate with
each other to processing units that are closer to each other in the memory hierarchy. However, locality-based policies can lead to a substantial
performance reduction in some cases due to communication imbalance. In
this paper, we perform a comprehensive exploration of communication-
aware thread mapping policies in multicore architectures. We develop a
set of metrics to evaluate the communication behavior of parallel applications, and describe how these metrics can be used to favor locality-based
or balance-based mapping policies. Based on these metrics, we introduce
a novel mapping policy that combines locality and balance aspects and
achieves the highest overall improvements. We provide an experimental
evaluation of the performance gains using different mapping policies as
well as a detailed analysis of the sources of energy savings.

1 Introduction

Due to the rising parallelism in modern multicore architectures, deciding where
to execute each thread of a parallel application is becoming increasingly important to improve the application's performance as well as its energy consumption.
The assignment of threads to processing units (PUs), which is called *thread mapping*, can take into account several characteristics of the parallel application and
the underlying hardware architecture, such as utilization of PUs, contention on
functional units, memory usage or memory access patterns. Recent research in
this area mostly focuses on threads' memory accesses to shared data, which we
call *communication* between threads, and uses a thread mapping policy that
puts threads closer to each other in the memory hierarchy if they communicate
frequently. In this way, threads can make better use of shared caches, and the
overall memory access *locality* increases [2,9].

© Springer-Verlag Berlin Heidelberg 2015
J.L. Träff et al. (Eds.): Euro-Par 2015, LNCS 9233, pp. 196–208, 2015.
DOI: 10.1007/978-3-662-48096-0_16

However, these *communication-aware* mapping policies based on increasing locality can actually reduce the performance in some cases. We identify two conditions under which a locality-based policy has no improvements or is even detrimental to performance; when communication is imbalanced between threads, and when the ratio of communication to private data memory accesses is low. In such cases, it can be better to balance the communication or to scatter threads, such that there is less contention on caches or interconnections.

In this paper, we make the following contributions to the thread mapping problem: (1) We develop a set of metrics that are based on shared memory accesses and comprehensively represent the communication behavior of the threads in parallel applications. These metrics describe the structure and volume of communication. (2) We discuss which characteristics are suitable for each type of thread mapping, and introduce policies that optimize the mapping for each metric, as well as a policy that combines locality and balance. (3) We evaluate parallel applications in terms of the metrics and show the performance improvements of the different mapping policies. We also analyze the sources of performance improvements and energy savings by using a microarchitectural simulator.

2   Communication in Shared Memory

In parallel applications based on shared memory programming models, such as OpenMP and Pthreads, communication is *implicit* and is performed via memory accesses to shared memory areas. By observing accesses to memory addresses at the cache line granularity, we can define a *communication event* as two memory accesses from two different threads to the same cache line. With this definition, we create a *communication matrix* that represents the communication behavior of a parallel application by grouping the communication events [8,14].

In a communication matrix, the axes represent the thread IDs, while each cell in the matrix contains the number of communication events for the corresponding thread pair. For example, Fig. 1a shows a communication matrix for an application that consists of 5 threads. Figure 1b shows a visualization of this matrix, where darker matrix cells illustrate more communication. Based on the communication matrix, we introduce metrics to describe the communication behavior formally. Our goal is to determine the most appropriate mapping policy for a particular communication behavior depending on these metrics. Four metrics are presented: *heterogeneity* and *balance* describe the structure of communication, while *amount* and *ratio* describe the volume of communication.

Communication Heterogeneity. For policies that focus on improving the locality of communication, it is necessary to have groups of threads that communicate more within the group than with threads outside the group. Based on this intuition, a higher variation in the number of communication events for thread pairs in the communication matrix indicates opportunities to increase the overall locality. We refer to this variation as the *heterogeneity* of communication. We adapt previous work [6,10] to formulate the metric H_{Comm}, which evaluates

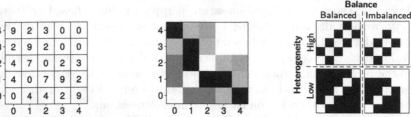

4-	9	2	3	0	0
3-	2	9	2	0	0
2-	4	7	0	2	3
1-	4	0	7	9	2
0-	0	4	4	2	9
	0	1	2	3	4

(a) Communication matrix. Axes show thread IDs. Cells contain the number of communication events.

(b) Visualization of the communication matrix (a). Darker cells indicate more communication.

(c) Communication matrices with different values for heterogeneity and balance.

Fig. 1. Communication behavior of a parallel application consisting of 5 threads.

this heterogeneity. As shown in (1), H_{Comm} is calculated by first normalizing the communication matrix M to its highest value, and then calculating the average variance of the number of communication events per thread. The max and var functions calculate the maximum and variance, respectively, and T represents the number of threads. A locality-based thread mapping policy is more suitable for higher values of H_{Comm}.

$$M_{norm} = \frac{M}{max(M)} \cdot 100, \qquad H_{Comm} = \frac{\sum_{i=1}^{T} var(M_{norm}[i][1...T])}{T} \qquad (1)$$

Communication Balance. For mapping policies that are based on balance, it is necessary to determine if some threads are performing more communication than others. To evaluate this property, we introduce the metric B_{Comm}, which we refer to as the *balance* of the threads' communication behavior. To calculate B_{Comm}, we first calculate the total amount of communication per thread in a *communication vector* $CommV$, where each element i of $CommV$ contains the number of communication events of thread i. Then, similar to traditional load balance [15], B_{Comm} is calculated by (2).

$$CommV[i] = \sum_{j=1}^{T} M[i][j], \quad B_{Comm} = \left(\frac{max(CommV)}{\sum_{i=1}^{T} CommV[i]/T} - 1 \right) \cdot 100\% \quad (2)$$

A value of B_{Comm} that is close to 0 indicates a highly balanced communication between threads, while higher values indicate more imbalance in the threads' communication behavior, suggesting that communication balance-based mapping policies are more beneficial. A comparison of communication matrices with different values of *heterogeneity* and *balance* is shown in Fig. 1c.

Communication Amount. Improvements according to a specific thread mapping policy depend on how much threads are communicating. We expect higher gains for parallel applications that communicate more. To describe the *amount* of communication, we introduce the A_{Comm} metric, defined as the average number of communication events per thread, which is calculated by (3).

$$A_{Comm} = \frac{\sum_{i=1}^{T} \sum_{j=1}^{T} M[i][j]}{T^2} \qquad (3)$$

Communication Ratio. The amount of communication itself is not sufficient to evaluate if an application is suitable for communication-aware thread mapping. If threads have much more memory accesses to private data than communication, a communication-aware mapping might not affect the overall memory access behavior. For this reason, we define the *communication ratio* metric R_{Comm}, which is the ratio of the communication accesses to the total number of memory accesses of the application threads. R_{Comm} is calculated by (4), where $AccV[i]$ is the number of memory accesses performed by thread i.

$$R_{Comm} = \frac{A_{Comm}}{\sum_{i=1}^{T} AccV[i]} \qquad (4)$$

3   Communication Behavior of the Benchmarks

In this section, we analyze the communication behavior of two sets of parallel applications in terms of the metrics introduced in the previous section.

3.1   Methodology of the Experiments

Benchmarks. We chose two parallel benchmark suites for the evaluation. *NAS-OMP* [11] is the OpenMP implementation of the NAS Parallel Benchmarks (NPB), which consists of 10 applications from the HPC domain. We use three input sizes for the characterization, W, A, and B (from smallest to largest), to show how the behavior changes with increasing input sizes. All applications were executed with 64 threads. *PARSEC* [3] is a suite of 13 benchmarks that focus on emerging workloads and are implemented using OpenMP and Pthreads. All benchmarks were executed with the *native* input size. The number of threads is different for each application, but most of them use 64 threads.

Profiling Environment. To characterize the benchmarks' communication behavior, we use a memory tracer based on our `numalize` technique [10], built with the Pin DBI tool [13]. We calculate the communication behavior in a simplified way to characterize the applications independently from a particular hardware architecture. We collect all memory accesses of the application's threads at a granularity of 64 byte-wide memory blocks and within time intervals of 10 ms. During each time interval, every time a memory block is accessed by a thread, we record a communication event between this thread and the other threads that have been involved in memory accesses to the same block since the beginning of the current time interval. By aggregating these events, we generate a communication matrix. Comparison with different time intervals, as well as a full cache simulator, showed that the detected behavior is stable in such a way that our characterization remains the same.

3.2   Results of the Communication Characterization

We begin with a discussion of several common types of communication matrices of the benchmarks, followed by an analysis of the metrics introduced in Sect. 2.

Communication Matrices. Figure 2 shows the communication matrices of selected benchmarks that represent the most common types of behavior. For the NAS-OMP benchmarks (LU and UA), we show the matrices of the *B* input. In LU, threads that are far apart communicate mostly with each other, e.g., the threads 0 and 53. UA has a nearest neighbor pattern, where neighboring threads perform most communication. In Blackscholes, thread 0 communicates with all other threads, indicating that communication is due to initialization or reduction of data. Ferret has a pipeline pattern, where one stage (threads 34–49) performs most of the communication of the application. Swaptions has an all-to-all pattern with similar amounts of communication for all threads.

From the communication matrices, it is possible to develop an idea of which applications can benefit from which type of mapping. In LU, UA, and Ferret, groups of threads perform substantial amounts of communication among themselves and only little communication with threads outside the group. Therefore, a locality-based policy can increase the overall locality by mapping threads that communicate closer to each other. Blackscholes and Swaptions can not benefit from such a policy, as no mapping can improve the overall locality. LU and Ferret can also benefit from a balance-based policy, as some threads perform very little communication, such as threads 53–63 of LU and threads 1–33 of Ferret.

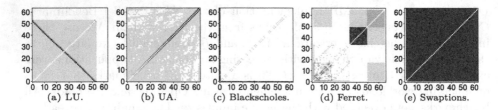

(a) LU.   (b) UA.   (c) Blackscholes.   (d) Ferret.   (e) Swaptions.

Fig. 2. Communication matrices of several parallel applications.

Communication Metrics. The values of the communication metrics introduced in Sect. 2 for the two benchmark suites are shown in Figs. 3 and 4.

All NAS-OMP applications except EP, FT, and IS have a high *heterogeneity*, indicating their suitability for locality-based mapping. In BT, LU, SP, and UA, the *heterogeneity* increases with larger input sizes. Evaluating the *communication balance* shows that only BT, LU, and SP are significantly imbalanced and show a suitability for balance-based policies. The reason for the imbalance of these applications is shown in Fig. 2a, as some of the threads are not communicating at all. This behavior changes with the input size: inputs *W* and *B* are imbalanced, while *A* is much more balanced. However, despite this communication imbalance, there is no significant load imbalance for these benchmarks according to our measurements, showing that the threads that communicate less

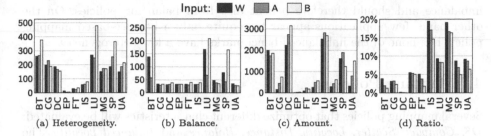

Fig. 3. Communication characteristics of the NAS-OMP benchmarks.

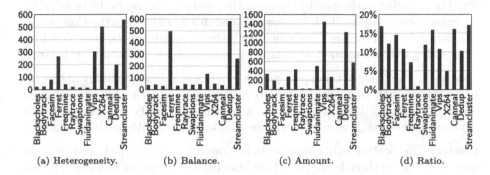

Fig. 4. Communication characteristics of the PARSEC benchmarks.

still perform substantial amounts of computation. For example, SP with the B input has a load balance of only 3.8, while the *communication balance* metric is much higher (16.5, higher values indicate a higher imbalance). The *communication amount* increases slightly with larger input sizes for most benchmarks. The *communication ratio* presented in Fig. 3d shows that with increasing input sizes, less communication in comparison to the total number of memory accesses is performed. This indicates that larger input sizes of NAS-OMP are less suitable for communication-aware thread mapping in most cases. Although DC has a high *amount* of communication, its *ratio* is very low.

Only a minority of the PARSEC benchmarks have a high *heterogeneity*, indicating that PARSEC applications are generally less suitable for locality-based thread mapping than those from NAS-OMP. Three PARSEC benchmarks, Ferret, Dedup, and Streamcluster, are significantly imbalanced. These three applications have a pipeline communication pattern, similar to the one shown in Fig. 2d. The load balance is again much lower than the *communication balance* (13.1 and 58.0 for Ferret, respectively). The *communication amount* differs widely between applications, but PARSEC benchmarks have a high *communication ratio* in general compared to NAS-OMP.

Summary. Summarizing our analysis, we find that a majority of the applications have a high heterogeneity and are therefore suitable for locality-based thread mapping. Some of these applications show varying degrees of communication imbalance and should therefore benefit also from balancing policies. On the other hand, few applications appear to require only a balance-based mapping policy, i.e., none of the imbalanced benchmarks have a low heterogeneity.

4 Mapping Policies

Several mapping policies that optimize different characteristics will be evaluated: *OS*, *Compact*, *Scatter*, *Locality*, *Distance*, *Balance* and *Balanced Locality*. The three last policies are introduced in this paper.

OS. The mapping performed by the operating system represents the baseline for our experiments. We use the Linux kernel, version 3.8, which uses the Completely Fair Scheduler (CFS) [18]. The scheduler focuses mostly on fairness and load balance [18], and has no means for improving communication locality or balance.

Compact. The Compact mapping performs a round-robin scheduling of threads to PUs such that neighboring threads are placed close to each other in the memory hierarchy. This mapping can increase the locality of communication behaviors where neighboring threads communicate frequently with each other.

Scatter. The Scatter policy represents the opposite of Compact. In this mapping, neighboring threads are placed far from each other in the hierarchy. In this way, performance can be improved for applications with little communication or a low communication ratio, by reducing competition for cache space. Compact and Scatter do not take the actual communication behavior into account.

Locality. The Locality policy optimizes the communication behavior by mapping threads that communicate frequently close to each other in the memory hierarchy. The mapping algorithm receives as input the communication matrix and a description of the memory hierarchy of the system, generated with hwloc [4]. It outputs a thread mapping that maximizes the overall locality of communication. Several algorithms have been proposed to calculate this mapping. We use the recently-proposed EagerMap algorithm [7] to calculate the Locality policy.

Distance. The Distance policy represents the opposite of Locality, placing threads that communicate far apart in the memory hierarchy. We calculate this mapping by inverting the communication matrix, subtracting each cell by the maximum value of the matrix. We then apply the same mapping algorithm as for the Locality mapping to the inverted matrix. This mapping can be useful when the heterogeneity is high, but the communication ratio is low, similar to the Scatter policy, but taking the actual communication behavior into account.

Balance. The Balance policy focuses on maximizing the communication balance for the application. The mapping algorithm receives the communication vector (introduced in Sect. 2) and the description of the memory hierarchy as input. The mapping is calculated by selecting the thread with the highest amount of communication that has not been mapped to a PU yet. This thread is then mapped to the PU which currently has the lowest amount of communication mapped to it. This process is repeated until all threads are mapped to a PU. This policy focuses only on balance and does not take locality into account.

Balanced Locality. The Balanced Locality policy focuses on increasing locality while still maintaining the balance of the communication. First, it maps threads that communicate frequently to nearby PUs, similar to the Locality policy. Second, for each level of the memory hierarchy, it keeps a similar amount of communication for each cache memory of that level. We model the memory hierarchy as a tree, where the leaves represent the PUs, and the other levels of the tree represent cache levels and their nodes represent specific cache memories. Our algorithm groups threads with high amounts of communication to the leaves of the tree, propagating this mapping to the parent nodes up to the root node. We add threads to the leaves until the amount of communication is higher than the average amount of communication per leaf. Summarizing, this policy maps threads that communicate frequently to close PUs whose amounts of communication are lower than the average amount of communication per PU.

Load Balance. We also evaluate the Load Balance of selected benchmarks to compare it to the *Communication Balance* metric introduced in Sect. 2. We use the number of executed instructions per thread as the metric for the load.

5   Performance Evaluation on a Real Machine

In this section, we evaluate the performance improvements that are achieved by the thread mapping policies proposed in the previous section on a real machine.

Methodology. We run the experiments on a 4-socket system consisting of 4 Intel Xeon X7550 processors, with 8 cores and 2-SMT each (64 processing units in total). Each core has private L1 and L2 caches, while the L3 cache is shared among all the cores of the same processor. The same benchmarks with the same number of threads and input sizes (NAS-OMP only with A and B) as in the previous sections were evaluated. For each mapping policy presented in Sect. 4, we show the average execution time of 10 runs. The OS mapping policy is our baseline, and results are presented in terms of performance gains over this policy. In all policies except OS, no thread migrations during execution were performed.

Results. Figure 5 shows the performance gains compared to the OS mapping. For NAS-OMP with the A input, most benchmarks profit from the Locality policy, as predicted by our analysis. With the A input, this policy never reduces performance. The Balanced Locality policy has similar results as Locality for all benchmarks except DC. For the benchmarks that have a nearest neighbor communication pattern, the Compact policy improves performance, but reduces it in some cases, such as LU. The Distance and Balance policies only show performance improvements close to the Locality policy for the DC benchmark, which benefits from a better balance due to its low communication ratio. The Scatter policy never results in significant performance gains and reduces it in many cases. On average, the Locality, Balanced Locality, and Compact policies show improvements of more than 12 %, the other policies gain less than 4 %.

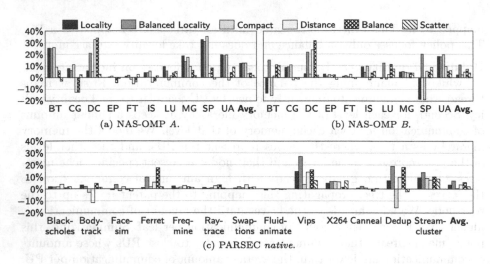

(a) NAS-OMP *A*.   (b) NAS-OMP *B*.

(c) PARSEC *native*.

Fig. 5. Performance improvements on the real machine compared to the OS mapping.

For the NAS-OMP benchmarks with the *B* input, the Locality policy reduces performance for the benchmarks that are imbalanced (BT, LU, and SP). On the other hand, Balanced Locality achieves the highest gains, proving that only taking locality into account is not sufficient for applications with this characteristic. The Load Balance policy (not shown in the figure) has improvements of less than 5 % for the 3 benchmarks, indicating that balancing the load is not as effective as balancing the communication in these cases. The other benchmarks show a similar behavior as the *A* input, with lower average gains. This echoes our discussion of the communication ratio, were we expected lower improvements when the ratio decreases. On average, Balanced Locality achieved the highest improvements, of 10.9 %. As several benchmarks benefit from balancing, the Balance policy has the second-highest improvements, of 7.3 %. The other policies gain less than 5 %.

As discussed in Sect. 3, the PARSEC benchmarks generally have lower metrics than the NAS-OMP benchmarks, which is reflected in the performance results. Five benchmarks (Ferret, Vips, X264, Dedup, and Streamcluster) benefit from communication-aware thread mapping. Most of them benefit from both the Locality and the Balance polices, but the Balanced Locality policy, which combines both, results in the highest improvements in most cases. The Compact, Distance, and Scatter policies do not improve performance consistently and result in performance losses in several cases. On average, Balanced Locality has again the highest gains of 6.7 %, followed by Balance (5.4 %) and Locality (3.4 %).

Summary. We conclude that increasing locality is the most important way to perform communication-aware thread mapping for most parallel applications. However, many applications can benefit from improving the balance of the communication, achieving higher performance gains and avoiding the performance reduction that a locality-based policy can cause. Simple mapping policies that do not take the communication behavior into account only improve performance in some cases and provide no consistent improvements over the OS.

6 Performance and Energy Consumption in a Simulator

Apart from performance, thread mapping can also improve the energy efficiency of parallel applications, for two main reasons. By reducing execution time, static energy consumption (leakage) will be reduced proportionally, since the processor is in a high power-consuming state for less time. Additionally, reducing the number of cache misses and traffic on the interconnections reduces the dynamic energy consumption, leading to a more energy-efficient execution. This section investigates the architectural impacts of thread mapping on the performance and energy consumption using a microarchitecture simulator.

Table 1. Parameters of the simulated machine.

Parameter	Value
System	2x 4-core processors; L1I/L1D cache per core; L2 cache shared between 2 cores
Execution cores	OoO; 1.8 GHz, 65 nm; 12 stages; 16 B fetch size; 96-entry ROB; PAs branch predictor
L1I/L1D caches	32 KB, 8-way, 64 B line size; LRU policy; 1 cycle; MOESI protocol; stride prefetch
L2 caches	2 MB, 8-way, 64 B line size; LRU policy; 4 cycles; stream prefetch
Interconnection	Cache line transfer: 2 cycles L2-to-L2; 32 cycles L2-to-DRAM
DRAM	DDR2 667 MHz (5-5-5); 8 DRAM banks/channel; 2 channels; 1 KB row buffer

Methodology. We use an in-house, cycle-accurate x86 processor simulator [1]. The execution statistics of the simulator are fed into McPAT [12] to calculate the energy consumption. Table 1 shows the simulation parameters. As benchmark, we chose SP from NAS-OMP, and run it with input W and 8 threads. We compare the Locality and Distance mappings in depth, which have the highest performance difference for this configuration of SP in the simulated machine.

Results. Figure 6 presents the results for execution time, performance statistics and energy consumption. The results are normalized to the values of the Distance mapping. Regarding the performance, the execution time was reduced by 10.1 %, caused by the reduction of the number of L2 cache misses (32.0 %) and a reduction of the number of DRAM accesses (39.9 %). The processor memory read time was reduced by 22.6 %. The higher data locality also led to a reduction of

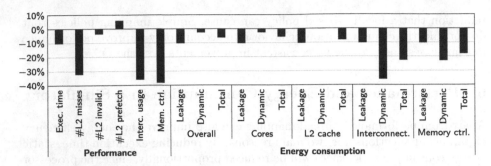

Fig. 6. Results of executing SP in the simulator, normalized to the Distance mapping.

the number of L2 invalidation messages and off-chip interconnection usage. The reduction of the interconnection traffic and L2 misses enabled the L2 prefetcher to issue 5.8 % more requests, which also contributed to the overall performance gains.

The more efficient execution also reduced energy consumption. Leakage was reduced by 10.1 % for all components, the same amount as the execution time. As expected, dynamic energy consumption was reduced less, by 2.4 % overall, leading to a total energy reduction of 6.1 %. Although there are reductions of the energy consumed by the cores and L2 caches, of 5.5 % and 8.0 % respectively, the extra prefetches reduced potential reductions of the L2 dynamic energy, which comprises 23.2 % of the total L2 energy. The highest energy reductions were achieved by the memory controller and the interconnections between the L2 caches, and between the processors and the main memory, with reductions of 17.9 % and 22.4 % respectively. The interconnection savings are caused by less off-chip searches, as well as less cache-to-cache and DRAM data transfers.

7   Related Work

Many techniques for thread mapping have been investigated previously, focusing on balance-based or locality-based policies. Most balance-based policies depend on characteristics of the parallel application and the underlying architecture, such as memory usage or core utilization. Sasaki et al. [16] develop a scheduling scheme for multi-threaded applications based on predicting the application scalability to balance the resource utilization. The Extended Lowest Load technique [17] uses a heuristic that is based on the amount of time spent by each core doing useful work to find the optimal target core for each thread. Pearce et al. [15] argue that the limitation in load balancing-based mapping policies is related to inaccurate load information. Depending on information about the work units of the application and dependencies between them, they develop load metrics and a cost model for re-correcting load imbalance.

In these approaches, locality issues and the communication behavior are not considered. On the other hand, policies that perform communication-aware mapping mostly focus on improving the locality of communication without evaluating balance. For parallel applications that communicate through MPI, most previous research focuses on methods to trace the messages and uses the information to perform a process mapping. MPIPP [5] is a framework for process mapping, consisting of a message tracer and mapping algorithm. Some papers evaluate process mapping for particular applications, such as the NAS-MPI benchmarks [14]. For applications that use OpenMP or Pthreads, most mapping solutions focus on analyzing memory accesses to map threads that communicate on shared caches, but do not address the balance issue [6,8].

8 Conclusions

Communication-aware thread mapping can improve the performance of parallel applications on multicore systems. In this paper, we introduced metrics to describe the communication behavior and determine if an application can benefit from mapping policies that focus on the locality or the balance of communication. We presented a mapping policy that increases locality while still maintaining the balance. Our evaluation on a real system showed that this policy can provide the highest improvements and avoids the performance losses that may occur using a pure locality-based policy. We also provided an in-depth analysis of performance and energy efficiency gains from thread mapping in a hardware simulator.

References

1. Alves, M.A.: Increasing energy efficiency of processor caches via line usage predictors. Ph.D. thesis, Federal University of Rio Grande do Sul (2014)
2. Barrow-Williams, N., Fensch, C., Moore, S.: A communication characterisation of Splash-2 and Parsec. In: International Symposium on Workload Characterization (2009)
3. Bienia, C., Kumar, S., Singh, J.P., Li, K.: The PARSEC benchmark suite: characterization and architectural implications. In: International Conference on Parallel Architectures and Compilation Techniques (2008)
4. Broquedis, F., Clet-Ortega, J., Moreaud, S., Furmento, N., Goglin, B., Mercier, G., Thibault, S., Namyst, R.: hwloc: a generic framework for managing hardware affinities in HPC applications. In: International Conference on Parallel, Distributed and Network-based Processing (2010)
5. Chen, H., Chen, W., Huang, J., Robert, B., Kuhn, H.: MPIPP: an automatic profile-guided parallel process placement toolset for SMP clusters and multiclusters. In: International Conference on Supercomputing (2006)
6. Cruz, E.H.M., Diener, M., Alves, M.A.Z., Navaux, P.O.A.: Dynamic thread mapping of shared memory applications by exploiting cache coherence protocols. J. Parallel Distrib. Comput. **74**(3), 2215–2228 (2014)
7. Cruz, E.H.M., Diener, M., Pilla, L.L., Navaux, P.O.A.: An efficient algorithm for communication-based task mapping. In: International Conference on Parallel, Distributed, and Network-Based Processing (2015)
8. Diener, M., Cruz, E.H.M., Navaux, P.O.A.: Communication-based mapping using shared pages. In: International Parallel and Distributed Processing Symposium (2013)

9. Diener, M., Cruz, E.H.M., Navaux, P.O.A., Busse, A., Heiß, H.U.: kMAF: automatic kernel-level management of thread and data affinity. In: International Conference on Parallel Architectures and Compilation Techniques (2014)
10. Diener, M., Cruz, E.H.M., Pilla, L.L., Dupros, F., Navaux, P.O.A.: Characterizing communication and page usage of parallel applications for thread and data mapping. Perform. Eval. **88–89**, 18–36 (2015)
11. Jin, H., Frumkin, M., Yan, J.: The OpenMP implementation of NAS parallel benchmarks and its performance. Technical report, October 1999
12. Li, S., Ahn, J.H., Strong, R.D., Brockman, J.B., Tullsen, D.M., Jouppi, N.P.: The McPAT framework for multicore and manycore architectures: simultaneously modeling power, area, and timing. ACM Trans. Archit. Code Optim. (TACO) **10**(1), 5 (2013)
13. Luk, C., Cohn, R., Muth, R., Patil, H.: Pin: building customized program analysis tools with dynamic instrumentation. In: SIGPLAN Conference on Programming Language Design and Implementation (2005)
14. Mercier, G., Clet-Ortega, J.: Towards an efficient process placement policy for MPI applications in multicore environments. In: Ropo, M., Westerholm, J., Dongarra, J. (eds.) PVM/MPI. LNCS, vol. 5759, pp. 104–115. Springer, Heidelberg (2009)
15. Pearce, O., Gamblin, T., de Supinski, B.R., Schulz, M., Amato, N.M.: Quantifying the effectiveness of load balance algorithms. In: Supercomputing (2012)
16. Sasaki, H., Tanimoto, T., Inoue, K., Nakamura, H.: Scalability-based manycore partitioning. In: International Conference on Parallel Architectures and Compilation Techniques (2012)
17. Tousimojarad, A., et al.: An efficient thread mapping strategy for multiprogramming on manycore processors. In: International Conference on Parallel Computing (2013)
18. Wong, C.S., Tan, I., Kumari, R.D., Wey, F.: Towards achieving fairness in the Linux scheduler. SIGOPS Oper. Syst. Rev. **42**(5), 34–43 (2008)

Priority Queues Are Not Good Concurrent Priority Schedulers

Andrew Lenharth[✉], Donald Nguyen, and Keshav Pingali

The University of Texas at Austin, Austin, USA
lenharth@ices.utexas.edu, {ddn,pingali}@cs.utexas.edu

Abstract. The need for priority scheduling arises in many algorithms. In these algorithms, there is a dynamic pool of lightweight, unordered tasks, and some execution orders are more efficient than others. Therefore, each task is given an application-specific priority that is a heuristic measure of its importance for early scheduling, and the runtime system schedules these tasks roughly in this order. Concurrent priority queues are not suitable for this purpose. We show that by exploiting the fact that algorithms amenable to priority scheduling are often robust to small deviations from a strict priority order, and by optimizing the scheduler for the cache hierarchy of current multicore and NUMA processors, we can implement concurrent priority schedulers that improve the end-to-end performance of complex irregular benchmarks by orders of magnitude compared to using state-of-the-art concurrent priority queues.

1 Introduction

The problem of *priority scheduling* is ubiquitous in computer systems, and it can be formulated abstractly as follows. There is a work-set W of tasks that must be executed by some number of processors. The time to execute a task may be unpredictable and may vary by task. When a task is executed, it may add new tasks to W. Tasks in W can be processed in any order; however, some orders may be more efficient than others—for example, the order may affect the time taken to process a given task, and it may even affect the total number of tasks created during the execution of the program. Therefore, each task has an associated integer called its *priority* that is an application-specific, heuristic measure of its relative importance for early scheduling. The problem of priority scheduling is to assign tasks to processors according to the specified order (priority) with the goal of minimizing the total execution time of the program.

In this paper, we focus on a particular instance of this problem that arises when implementing irregular graph algorithms such as single-source, shortest-path (sssp), preflow-push maxflow computation (pfp), Delaunay mesh generation and refinement, and betweenness-centrality (bc). Each task in such an algorithm is associated with a node called its *active node* [14] and it makes an update to a small region of the graph containing its active node, such as modifying node and edge data or adding and removing nodes and edges. Tasks that update disjoint regions of the graph can be executed in parallel.

© Springer-Verlag Berlin Heidelberg 2015
J.L. Träff et al. (Eds.): Euro-Par 2015, LNCS 9233, pp. 209–221, 2015.
DOI: 10.1007/978-3-662-48096-0_17

An important feature of many such algorithms is that although the semantics of the algorithm permit tasks to be performed in arbitrary order, some orders may be far more efficient than others. There are several reasons for this.

- The work-efficiency and even the asymptotic complexity of the program may depend on the schedule; sssp and preflow-push are well-known examples.
- Some schedules may exploit locality better than others. For example, in Delaunay mesh refinement, working on recently generated triangles has significant locality benefits. It may also be desirable to schedule tasks with overlapping working sets on the same core (affinity scheduling).
- In some algorithms such as the Metis graph partitioner [8], the quality of the result may depend on the schedule even if the asymptotic complexity does not.

Priority scheduling can be used to achieve the desired task execution order. For sssp, the priority of an active node is the length of the shortest known path from the source to that node; processing active nodes in increasing distance order, as is done by Dijkstra's algorithm, is good for work-efficiency. For pfp, each active node is associated with an integer called its height, which is a heuristic estimate of its distance from the sink in the residual graph; processing nodes in decreasing height order improves work-efficiency [4].

Priority scheduling for sequential programs is straightforward: use a priority queue. The priority of items is defined by a user-supplied *priority function* that encodes the less-than relation between items. There are many implementations of priority queues; one of the most commonly used representations is a heap.

For parallel programs, it is possible in principle to use a concurrent priority queue that uses either locks or lock-free approaches to synchronize insertions and removals from the priority queue. In this paper, we argue that concurrent priority queues are not good priority schedulers for parallel programs. Tasks in the parallel programming context may execute only a few hundred or thousand instructions; for example, sssp tasks take roughly 1,500 cycles (about 300 instructions) on the machines described in Sect. 4. Therefore, it is imperative that scheduling be a lightweight operation. In Sect. 2, we survey prior work that uses concurrent priority queues for priority scheduling. Using sssp, we show experimentally that parallel scaling is severely limited with these approaches.

To address these problems, we introduce a novel priority scheduler in Sect. 3. This *ordered-by-integer-metric* (**obim**) scheduler does not use priority queues and has much lower overhead than concurrent priority queues. Its efficiency comes from exploitation of two insights.

- **Exploiting priority inversion.** Algorithms that use priorities are often robust to some priority inversion. Although a substantial number of priority inversions can hurt work efficiency, we show that allowing a small number can dramatically reduce communication, synchronization, and coordination between threads.
- **Architecture-aware design.** The memory systems of multicores are hierarchical and communication between remote cores is expensive. The design of obim exploits the memory hierarchy to minimize and control coherence traffic.

In Sect. 4, we evaluate the end-to-end performance of seven irregular benchmarks that benefit from priority scheduling, using obim and concurrent priority queues on four multicore machines. For almost all machine/benchmark/input combinations, obim provides far superior performance; for some of them, the obim-based implementation is 50 times faster than a concurrent priority-queue-based implementation.

2 Prior Work on Concurrent Priority Scheduling

In this section, we evaluate the pros and cons of three different ways in which concurrent priority queues have been used in the literature to implement high-performance parallel sssp. Our conclusions apply to other irregular programs as well, but sssp is a good model problem because scheduling strategies for this problem have been studied extensively.

2.1 Schedulers Based on Priority Queues

We study three ways to use concurrent priority queues for parallel scheduling.

Heap: a central concurrent priority queue. There are many choices of concurrent priority queues, which we discuss below.

Sheap: a concurrent priority queue for each thread with work-stealing. New work created by a thread is always pushed to its own local priority queue, although it may get stolen later. Bertsekas et al. implemented one of the first parallel sssp programs using this approach [1].

Pheap: a concurrent priority queue for each thread, with logically partitioned data structures and owner-computes rule for task assignment. When a new task B is created, the owner-computes rule determines which priority queue to push the task on. This policy has been used by Tang et al. [17]; it was also mentioned in [1]. Work-stealing is usually not performed.

All of these require a concurrent priority queue. We used the concurrent priority queue from the Intel TBB library. We also evaluated a centralized priority scheduler based on a **concurrent skip-list** [15], but we found that the absolute performance of the TBB priority queue was substantially better, and although the concurrent skip-list scaled better than the TBB priority queue, it never caught up in absolute performance. Besides concurrent skip-lists, many other concurrent priority queues have been proposed [3,7,16]. These have various limitations such as being blocking, invalidation heavy, or supporting only bounded ranges which make them unsuitable for scheduling very small tasks on multi-processors with high remote-cache access latency.

Table 1. Number of iterations by type for sssp on machine m1 (Table 3) at 8 threads.

	Good	Bad	Empty
obim	671M	4.61M	74.6M
sheap	671M	96.3M	106M
pheap	671M	7.98M	721M
heap	671M	0	72.7M

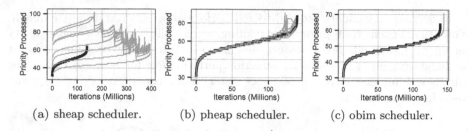

(a) sheap scheduler.   (b) pheap scheduler.   (c) obim scheduler.

Fig. 1. Priorities processed over time by different implementations. Each line corresponds to priority values processed be one thread. For reference, sequential heap is shown in black.

2.2   Priority Scheduling for Work Efficiency

For sssp, updates to the graph are called relaxations. Each node A has a label $d(A)$ that contains the length of the shortest known path to that node from the source. For edge $A \to B$ with weight $w(A, B)$, the relaxation operator updates $d(B)$ to $d(A)+w(A, B)$ if this value is less than the current value of $d(B)$. Initially, only the source is active. If the distance of a node is lowered by a relaxation, it becomes active in turn. We classify the relaxations into three categories called *good work*, *empty work*, and *bad work*.

- *Good* work: relaxation that lowers the distance value of a node to its final value.
- *Empty* work: attempted relaxation to a value higher than the current value.
- *Bad* work: relaxation of a label to a value greater than its final value.

Relaxations can be applied in any order but ordering them by the distance labels of the active nodes minimizes work. Dijkstra's algorithm [5] performs only good and empty work. It uses the priority queue to store pending updates to nodes and updates the node label in the graph only when the first (smallest) update to that node reaches the head of the priority queue. In contrast, asynchronous label-correcting algorithms perform relaxations in a random order and may perform a lot of bad work [13]. Table 1 shows the breakdown of the different types of work performed by different implementations on a machine with 8 cores. The input is described in Sect. 4. The amount of good work is the same for all implementations, but the amount of bad work and empty work differ. In particular, sheap performs a lot of bad work.

It is useful to characterize the instantaneous behaviors by plotting the priorities of the work processed by thread over time. Figure 1 shows this data using the total iterations executed as a proxy for time. In each graph, there is a line for each of the 8 threads; in addition, the priority of the work processed by a sequential implementation using a heap is superimposed in black.

Figure 1a shows that with sheap, threads quickly diverge from processing the globally earliest priority work. Threads eventually converge to processing the earlier priority work through work-stealing. Each of the drops in priorities processed corresponds to a thread stealing earlier priority work from another thread. Figure 1b shows that pheap is much better at keeping threads working on early priority work. This is because the graph is a random graph and thus fairly uniform, so the average earliest priority among t partitions (where t is the number of threads) is close to the earliest priority globally. This may not be true for non-random graphs, and the performance of pheap implementations will be poor for such graphs. Figure 1c shows that obim is successful in keeping all the threads working on the globally earliest priority work.

Although sheap performs poorly, priority scheduling using sheap may be a significant improvement over not using priorities at all. Using a *random* scheduler on the same input produces an runtime greater than several hours, while using sheap finishes in about 2 min (obim completes in 11 s).

Parallel Overheads: If work efficiency were the only concern, choosing a parallel scheduler would be easy: always pick the one that sticks closely to the ideal priority order. However, the end-to-end performance of a program depends also on the parallel overheads of the scheduler. The overhead costs of a parallel scheduler come from two sources: the sequential cost of performing a scheduling operation and the synchronization and communication cost from making the scheduler concurrent. We find the sequential performance of the heap-based variants are approximately 2x that of obim. Using a sampling profile, we find that at 8 threads, the costs are quite different. Obim scales essentially perfectly, the overhead per task is the same as the sequential result. The concurrent heap being a centralized data structure, however, scales extremely poorly, taking 14.5x more time for scheduling than it did serially. pheap takes 2x and sheap takes 5x more time than each did serially. As we saw in Table 1, sheap performs significantly more iterations also.

End-to-end performance of sssp: Figure 2 shows the end-to-end performance of the four implementations of sssp on a 24 core Intel Xeon. The baseline for speedup is a sequential implementation of sssp using the Intel TBB priority heap (which performed substantially better than the serial priority queue in *libstdc++*). The two factors discussed above—work efficiency of the algorithm and parallel overheads of the priority scheduler—limit the speed-up of the concurrent-priority-queue-based implementations to roughly 3 on 24 cores. In contrast, it can be seen the obim scheduler gives almost perfect speed-up.

2.3   Priority Scheduling for Output Quality

Priority scheduling is also useful for improving output quality in algorithms such as Metis, a multi-level graph partitioner, which uses a lowest-degree first heuristic for graph coarsening. Figure 3 shows the effect on the edge-cut, a measure of partition quality, from varying the scheduling policy in the coarsening phase. For comparison, *random* chooses nodes at random to match next, and *simple* implements a simple work-stealing scheduler. We see that obim provides consistent quality across thread counts, producing better results than random scheduling. Simple scheduling produces widely varying quality. In these tests, both simple and obim had similar runtimes.

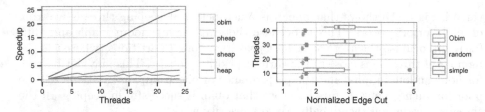

Fig. 2. Speed-up of sssp on 24 cores relative to best single threaded version.

Fig. 3. Metis-style quality results by scheduling heuristic and threads.

3 A Scalable Priority Scheduler

The design of obim exploits the observation that *algorithms that use priorities are robust to small amounts of priority inversion.* This observation is used to (i) enhance parallelism by allowing each thread to schedule work asynchronously, and (ii) minimize communication by using an approximate consensus protocol with communication matched to the memory system topology. A full discussion with pseudocode can be found in [10]. A simplified, high-level picture of obim is shown in Fig. 4. The obim scheduler is built out of *bags*, which are used

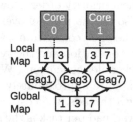

Fig. 4. Priority map in obim.

to hold tasks at the same priority level, and *priority maps*, which are used to hold a collection of bags at different priority levels.

3.1 Implementation of Bags

There is one bag per priority level in the entire system but it is implemented in a distributed, machine-topology-aware way as follows. For a given bag, each core has a data structure called a *chunk*, which is a ring-buffer that can contain 8–64 tasks (size chosen at compile time). In addition, each package has a list of chunks. When the chunk associated with a core becomes full, it is moved to the package-level list. When the chunk associated with a core becomes empty, the core probes its package-level list to obtain a chunk. If the package-level list is also empty, the core probes the lists of other packages to find work. To reduce traffic on the inter-package connection network, only one hungry core hunts for work in other packages on behalf of all hungry cores in a package.

3.2 Implementation of Priority Map

The priority map is also implemented in a distributed way by (i) a global map of priorities to bags, and (ii) an approximate copy of the global map within each thread. Each thread operates on its thread local map, synchronizing with the global map only when necessary, as explained next.

The thread-local map is implemented by a non-concurrent sorted vector of pairs. The implementation of the map is straight forward and not presented. Threads also maintain a version number representing the last version of the global map they synchronized with. Each thread also tracks the current priority it is working on and bag for that priority. This priority and bag are used by the thread for *pop* operations.

To minimize synchronization overhead, the global map uses a log-based structure which stores bag-priority pairs created by insert operations on the global map. Each insertion operation also updates a global version number, which corresponds to the length of the log. When a thread cannot find a bag for a particular priority using only its local map, it must synchronize with the global map and possibly create a new mapping there. A thread atomically appends a record to the log and increments the version number. The implementation ensures that the log can be appended in the presence of concurrent readers without requiring locks.

Push: A thread pushing a task uses its local map to find the bag to insert to. If its local map does not know if such a bag exists, the global map is consulted and if the bag is found, the local map is updated appropriately. If the priority of the pushed item is earlier than the current priority, the thread immediately updates its current working priority to operate on the earlier priority work.

Pop: To keep close to the ideal schedule, all threads must be working on early priority work. We adopt the heuristic that threads scan for earlier priority work only when they find that the bag they are working on is empty. Thus, if the bag for the current priority is not empty, a task from that bag is retrieved. Otherwise, when a bag is empty the thread scans the priority space looking for early priority work. We call this procedure *back-scan*.

Because a scan over the entire global map can be expensive, especially if there are many bags (which often happens with algorithms on high-diameter graphs), an approximate consensus heuristic is used to locally estimate the earliest priority work available and to prune the length of the back-scans, which we call *back-scan prevention*. Each thread makes available its estimate of the earliest priority work. When a thread needs to scan for work, it looks at this value for all threads that share the same package and uses the earliest priority it finds to start the scan for work. To propagate information between packages, in addition to scanning all the threads in its package, one leader thread per package will scan the other package leaders. This restriction allows most threads to incur only a small amount of local communication.

Once a thread has a starting point for a scan, it simply tries to pop work from each bag from the scan point onwards. The implementation ensures that attempting to pop from empty bags does not perform any writes to shared-memory, so popping from an empty bag, while not free, does not incur poor locality or communication. This *back-scan prevention* method is especially effective in many algorithms because it exploits the common structure of priority spaces. In most algorithms such as BFS, the priority space is populated monotonically: processing work at one priority will usually generate work at the same or later priority. Thus back-scan prevention can easily limit the scan to just a few bags.

Table 2. Obim variants used in evaluation.

Bag type	Backscan prevention	
	No	Yes
Centralized	cmn	cmb
Distributed	dmn	dmb (obim)

Table 3. Properties of machines used in the evaluation.

Label	Packages	Cores per Pkg	Speed (GHz)	L3 (MB)	Model (Xeon)
m2x4	2	4	2.93	8	X5570
m4x6	4	6	2.00	18	E7540
m4x10	4	10	2.27	24	E7-4860
numa8x4	8	4	1.87	18	E7520

3.3 Evaluation of OBIM Design Choices

To evaluate the obim design decisions, we implemented several de-optimized variants of the obim scheduler. Table 2 lists these variants, which focus on two main optimizations. These are (i) the use of distributed bags and (ii) back-scan prevention. Table 3 shows the four machines we used for the evaluation. The numa8x4 is an SGI Ultraviolet (strong NUMA). The other 3 machines are standard Intel Xeons with multiple packages connected by QPI.

We use three inputs which stress the priority scheduler in different ways. The first input is a large random graph, which has many work items and stresses the bag implementation. The second one is the USA road network, which is a smaller graph with a large diameter. It stresses the efficiency of the priority map implementation and the ability of the scheduler to find highest priority work efficiently. The third input is a scale-free rmat graph of 2^{27} nodes.

The bottom row of Fig. 5 shows the speedup of sssp for the small input for the four obim variants on the four machines. Speedup is relative to the best overall single-threaded execution time. The first conclusion is that the back-scan optimization is critical for performance: peak speedup goes from 2.5 (cmn and dmn) to 5 (cmb and dmb). Given the back-scan optimization (cmb and dmb), the second conclusion is that using distributed bags is also important for performance: without this optimization, speedup is never more than 5 on any machine. Without

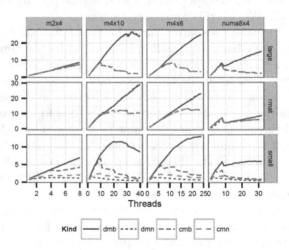

Fig. 5. Scaling of obim variants for sssp.

back-scan prevention, a distributed bag is less efficient than a centralized one on this high-diameter input because it is more efficient to check that a centralized bag is still empty than it is to perform this check on a distributed bag.

The top row of Fig. 5 shows the speedup of sssp for the large input. We see that for this input, back-scan prevention is almost irrelevant. However, distributed bags are even more important on this input than for the small input, pushing scaling from 8 to 25. The power-law graph (rmat) behaves similarly to the large graph. Machine m2x4 did not have enough RAM to load the rmat graph.

We investigated how the differences between variants manifest themselves at the architectural level through sample-based profiling using hardware counters. Briefly, back-scan prevention significantly reduces CPU cycles chiefly by reducing total instructions. The communication profiles with back-scan prevention (dmb) and without it (dmn) are similar at the L3 level. This shows (a) the amount of communication added to perform priority consensus is small, and (b) making sure that probing bags is write-free significantly reduces communication compared to trying to avoid checks using back-scan prevention. The former optimization is shared by both bag variants, and addition back-scan prevention does not change the L3 profile.

The second dimension we investigate is centralized versus distributed bags. There is little difference in total number of instructions executed between these two classes of implementations: we find no more than 6 % difference at 24 threads. However, we see that the centralized queues have more than twice the communication costs of the per-package queues.

4   Experimental Evaluation

We implemented seven applications on the four machines in Table 3, using obim and the three priority-queue-based schedulers. All the machines run Linux 2.6.32 with gcc 4.6. Processor affinity was used (and is necessary for the topology-aware

Table 4. Test programs and inputs

Name	Algorithm	Input
sssp	Single-Source Shortest-Path [13]	random constant average degree, 2^{26} nodes, 2^{28} edges
bfs	Breadth-first search	same as sssp
bp	Loopy Belief Propagation [6]	3SAT problem with 350 k clauses and 100 k variables
matching	Maximum Cardinality Bipartite Matching [12]	bipartite graph with 10^6 nodes and 10^8 edges from [12]
avi	Asynchronous Variational Integrator [11]	10×10 m neo-Hookean plate with 42000 elements
pfp	Pre-flow Push	R-MAT with 2^{22} nodes
bc	Betweenness Centrality [2]	USA road network

code). Each application was run on a large input graph and a small input graph; for lack of space, we only show the results for the large input graph.

We used the following seven applications from the Lonestar benchmark suite [9] in our study. The Lonestar suite publishes comparisons of these benchmarks to third party serial and parallel implementations, so we do not repeat these results here. Descriptions of the benchmarks can likewise be found published with Lonestar. Brief descriptions of the benchmark programs and inputs are given in Table 4.

4.1   End-to-End Performance

Figure 6 shows *speed-up* for large inputs, relative to the best serial times for these algorithms. First we see, for most applications, the obim scheduler gives the best performance *even on one thread.* This is due to the lower overheads of pushing and popping tasks with obim's bucketing scheme compared to a heap. The minor improvements in scheduling order of the heap do not make up for this overhead.

Second, at full scale, the obim scheduler is almost always substantially faster than all the priority-queue-based implementations for most applications and machines. For instance, at 24 threads on machine m4x6, on sssp with the large input, obim (4.4 s) is about 7 times faster than the partitioned heap schedulers (about 32 s) and 50 times faster than a concurrent heap (about 227 s). There are a few application/machine combinations such as avi for which obim is slower than the heap-based schedulers on one thread, but as the number of threads increase, the performance of obim surpasses that of other priority schedulers for almost all application/machine combinations.

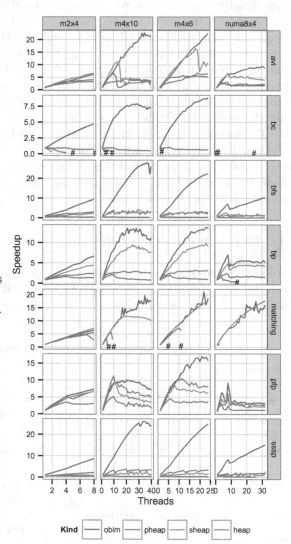

Fig. 6. Speedup. "#" indicate runs where runs timed out after ten minutes.

The results for numa8x4 show that on a machine with high NUMA penalty, obim doesn't scale much beyond one NUMA-node, although it does performs better than the other schedulers. Although all the machines are NUMA, the latency penalty on numa8x4 is significantly higher. We do not optimize for memory-bank locality in scheduling work, we only distribute the graph evenly between nodes. Graph partitioning and partitioning-aware scheduling must be applied in this case. We leave this for future work.

4.2 Differences in Application-Level Work

Figure 7 show how many iterations were executed with each scheduler for each application, input, and machine, relative to the best single-threaded scheduler. An important caveat is that the number of iterations is only a rough, though easily understood, proxy for the total amount of *useful* work as we discussed in Sect. 2.2.

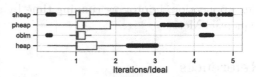

Fig. 7. Total iterations relative to best sequential scheduler for each combination. Outliers exist for pheap (28) and sheap (16).

First, we see sheap and pheap can perform many more iterations than obim. Extra iterations come from priority inversion. Second, the heap scheduler can sometimes generate more work than the serial heap scheduler. This is because in the parallel implementation, pushes and pops from different threads can get interleaved in a different order than in the sequential implementation. For a few benchmark/input/machine combinations, obim performs more iterations than the best single-threaded scheduler for that combination.

4.3 A Full Application: Metis

We also evaluated obim for parallelizing a complete application, the Metis graph partitioner [8]. Figure 8 shows the scaling of Metis as well as the scaling of the coarsening, initial partitioning, and refinement phases on m4x10 (Table 3). Creating 4 partitions of the USA road map takes roughly 35s with sequential Metis, 4s with our parallel Metis, and 2s with Mt-Metis, a hand-parallelized version of Metis from the University of Minnesota, while creating 1000 partitions takes roughly 38s, 5s and 7s

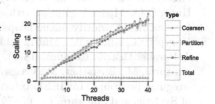

Fig. 8. Scaling of Metis for coarsening, initial partitioning, and refinement phases as well as total scaling.

respectively. The Mt-Metis program uses data structures optimized for graph partitioning while we use generic Galois data structures.

5   Conclusion

We presented a concurrent priority scheduler called the ordered-by-integer-metric (obim) scheduler, which (i) exploits the seemingly innocuous fact that algorithms amenable to priority scheduling are usually robust to small deviations from a strict priority schedule, and (ii) is optimized for the cache hierarchy of current multicore processors. Across a suite of seven complex, irregular benchmarks and four machines, we showed that implementations that use obim almost always outperformed implementations that used concurrent priority queues; for some benchmarks, end-to-end performance improved by a factor of 50. We also showed that obim could be used to successfully parallelize Metis, a complete and complex application, improving running time by roughly a factor of 10 compared to sequential Metis.

References

1. Bertsekas, D.P., Guerriero, F., Musmanno, R.: Parallel asynchronous label-correcting methods for shortest paths. J. Optim. Theory Appl. **88**(2), 297–320 (1996)
2. Brandes, U.: A faster algorithm for betweenness centrality. J. Math. Sociol. **25**(2), 163–177 (2001)
3. Bronson, N.G., Casper, J., Chafi, H., Olukotun, K.: A practical concurrent binary search tree. In: Proceedings of the 15th ACM SIGPLAN Symposium on Principles and Practice of Parallel Programming, pp. 257–268. ACM (2010)
4. Cherkassy, B.V., Goldberg, A.V.: On implementing push-relabel method for the maximum flow problem. In: Balas, E., Clausen, J. (eds.) IPCO 1995. LNCS, vol. 920, pp. 157–171. Springer, Heidelberg (1995)
5. Dijkstra, E.: A note on two problems in connexion with graphs. Numer. Math. **1**(1), 269–271 (1959)
6. Elidan, G., McGraw, I., Koller, D.: Residual belief propagation: informed scheduling for asynchronous message passing. In: Proceedings of the Twenty-Second Conference on Uncertainty in AI (2006)
7. Hunt, G.C., Michael, M.M., Parthasarathy, S., Scott, M.L.: An efficient algorithm for concurrent priority queue heaps. Inf. Process. Lett. **60**, 151–157 (1996)
8. Karypis, G., Kumar, V.: Multilevel k-way partitioning scheme for irregular graphs. J. Parallel Distrib. Comput. **48**(1), 96–129 (1998)
9. Kulkarni, M., Burtscher, M., Cascaval, C., Pingali, K.: Lonestar: a suite of parallel irregular programs. In: IEEE International Symposium on Performance Analysis of Systems and Software, pp. 65–76 (2009)
10. Lenharth, A., Nguyen, D., Pingali, K.: Priority queues are not good concurrent priority schedulers. Technical report 2056, University of Texas at Austin (2011)
11. Lew, A., Marsden, J.E., Ortiz, M., West, M.: Asynchronous variational integrators. Arch. Ration. Mech. Anal. **167**, 85–146 (2003)
12. Mehlhorn, K., Näher, S.: LEDA: A Platform for Combinatorial and Geometric Computing. Cambridge University Press, Cambridge (1999)
13. Meyer, U., Sanders, P.: Delta-stepping: a parallel single source shortest path algorithm. In: Proceedings of the European Symposium on Algorithms, pp. 393–404 (1998)

14. Pingali, K., Nguyen, D., Kulkarni, M., Burtscher, M., Hassaan, M.A., Kaleem, R., Lee, T.H., Lenharth, A., Manevich, R., Méndez-Lojo, M., Prountzos, D., Sui, X.: The TAO of parallelism in algorithms. In: Proceedings of the 32nd ACM SIG-PLAN Conference on Programming Language Design and Implementation, pp. 12–25 (2011)

15. Shavit, N., Lotan, I.: Skiplist-based concurrent priority queues. In: International Parallel and Distributed Processing Symposium/International Parallel Processing Symposium, pp. 263–268 (2000)

16. Shavit, N., Zemach, A.: Scalable concurrent priority queue algorithms. In: Proceedings of the Eighteenth Annual ACM Symposium on Principles of Distributed Computing, pp. 113–122 (1999)

17. Tang, Y., Zhang, Y., Chen, H.: A parallel shortest path algorithm based on graph-partitioning and iterative correcting. Comput. Syst. Sci. Eng. **24**(5), 155–161 (2009)

Load Balancing Prioritized Tasks via Work-Stealing

Shams Imam[✉] and Vivek Sarkar

Department of Computer Science, Rice University, Houston, USA
{shams,vsarkar}@rice.edu

Abstract. Work-stealing schedulers focus on minimizing overhead in task scheduling. Consequently, they avoid features, such as task priorities, which can add overhead to the implementation. Thus in such schedulers, low priority tasks may be scheduled earlier, delaying the execution of higher priority tasks and possibly increasing overall execution time.

In this paper, we develop a decentralized work-stealing scheduler that dynamically schedules fixed-priority tasks in a non-preemptive manner. We adhere, as closely as possible, to the priority order while scheduling tasks by accepting some overhead to preserve order. Our approach uses non-blocking operations, is workload independent, and we achieve performance even in the presence of fine-grained tasks. Experimental results show that the Java implementation of our scheduler performs favorably compared to other schedulers (priority and non-priority) available in the Java standard library.

Keywords: Work-stealing · Multi-level queue · Priority levels · Priority scheduling · Load balancing · Task-parallel programming

1 Introduction

Load balancing is an important component in improving the performance of parallel applications as it distributes the workload over all processors. Work-stealing algorithms [1] have been gaining popularity as the technology of choice for load-balancing of parallel tasks in multicores, especially for irregular and dynamic computations. Applications such as tree or graph search problems can benefit from attempting to execute tasks in a specific order. Assigning priorities to tasks can be a method to influence the execution ordering in the scheduling of tasks [18]. In fact, benchmarks such as branch-and-bound and single-source shortest path show that prioritization of tasks can reduce the total amount of work required compared to standard work-stealing execution order [17]. Soft real-time applications with time constraints can also use priorities to promote the execution of tasks, violations of these can allow the application to continue to operate, but with a degraded quality of results. Mainstream work-stealing schedulers do not support user-defined priorities in tasks and may schedule less important tasks earlier. This scheduling leads to increased execution time or degraded quality.

© Springer-Verlag Berlin Heidelberg 2015
J.L. Träff et al. (Eds.): Euro-Par 2015, LNCS 9233, pp. 222–234, 2015.
DOI: 10.1007/978-3-662-48096-0_18

The goal of priority scheduling is to assign tasks to processors in a way that optimizes overall performance metrics such as the total execution time [11]. Sequential implementations of priority scheduling are simple as they can use priority queue data structures, however, scalable and efficient parallel implementations can be comparatively more complex. Parallel implementations of priority scheduling tend to use shared concurrent priority queues. However, synchronization overheads cause such queues to not necessarily make efficient schedulers [11]. Other work-stealing priority schedulers guarantee priorities only in local scheduling via the use of priority queues per worker thread [17] and perform steals from victims once the worker becomes idle. Thus, these approaches do not adhere closely to global priorities while scheduling tasks trading off accuracy for reduced overhead. However, priority scheduling is primarily used to reduce the total amount of work done by an application. Using the priority order can curtail computation time by avoiding further exploration of a solution space or by causing the successful termination of the entire computation. Deviations from priority order may cause the application to end up doing more work.

In this paper, we develop a decentralized work-stealing scheduler that dynamically schedules fixed-priority tasks in a non-preemptive manner. We adapt a multi-level queue scheduling algorithm [13] where the tasks can be classified into priority classes and assign a separate container for each priority class. Our algorithm uses non-blocking operations and minimizes the number of compare-and-swap operations that each local worker thread performs. Furthermore, our workload independent approach extracts performance even in the presence of fine-grained tasks. Our approach relies on the unusual approach of performing steals even if the worker thread is not idle to adhere close to the priority order while scheduling. This strategy ensures that worker threads, in our scheduler, are executing tasks from the highest priority class. Thus, we minimize instances of priority inversion where low priority tasks are scheduled for execution even if higher priority tasks are available in the distributed work queue.

In summary, the contributions of this paper are as follows:

- We introduce our decentralized non-blocking algorithm for a work-stealing scheduler that respects global priorities.
- We present a lock-free implementation of our scheduler written using the standard Java library (JDK) and three work-stealing pool implementations.
- An empirical evaluation that shows our scheduler variants perform competitive to existing priority-based and non-priority-based schedulers available in the JDK.

2 Background

In the task parallel model, an application is usually decomposed into several independent and/or interdependent sets of cooperating parallel tasks. The tasks are stored in task pools, and worker threads are employed by the task scheduler to process the tasks. Scheduling deals with the problem of deciding which of the tasks from the work pool are allocated worker threads for execution. Efficient task scheduling improves resource utilization by automatically load-balancing tasks across worker threads, thereby enhancing the overall performance of the computation.

Load balancing is based on the idea of migration of excess load from heavily loaded workers to lightly loaded ones. Given perfect information, a static scheduling algorithm attempts to produce an optimal assignment of tasks to workers that ideally balances their loads. Such information, however, may be unavailable in irregular computations that generate non-uniform tasks. Such applications cannot rely on static load balancing and have to defer to dynamic schemes that redistribute the workload at runtime.

While dynamic load balancing is complex, its benefits outweigh its complexity. The main challenge of the scheduler is to deal with the dynamic load imbalance with minimal overhead while executing tasks on multiple workers. Conventional scheduling policies, such as work-sharing, are normally centralized and global in scope. The overhead of global synchronization that must be performed to maintain a consistent state limits the scalability of such schedulers. One of the simplest, yet best-performing, dynamic load balancing algorithms for shared-memory architectures is work-stealing.

2.1   Work-Stealing Schedulers

The work-stealing algorithm is an effective decentralized technique for scheduling parallel computations. The key observation is that there is no need to migrate tasks between the workers for load balancing if all threads have enough work. What makes work-stealing successful is that it employs a reactive asynchronous strategy [16]. When a worker runs out of local work, it (randomly) chooses a victim thread and asynchronously tries to steal some work from it. The attempt to load balance is receiver-initiated as the thief actively attempts to obtain available work. The asynchronous nature allows a thief to get some work without any involvement from the victim thread that may be busy processing user tasks. Thus, the idle workers eventually unburden the busy workers and load balance is achieved.

A key component of work-stealing is the use of double-ended queues by each worker thread [2,10]. Workers treat their own deques as a stack, pushing and popping tasks from the bottom, but treat the deque of another busy worker as a queue, stealing tasks only from the top, whenever they have no local tasks to execute. Worker threads process their own deques in a LIFO order processing local tasks, as long as they are available. Consequently, it may be the case that most tasks are consumed locally, and relatively few steals are required to address a load imbalance [9].

When a worker becomes idle, it transitions into a thief searching for available work from active workers. The thief attempts to steal tasks from its victim using FIFO order, i.e. from the opposite end from which the victim is working on its deque. Since the victim and thief operate on opposite ends of the deque, efficient algorithms can be implemented for the deque that minimize the need for synchronization [6]. On a successful steal, a thief pushes the stolen task onto its local deque, returns to the worker state, and continues to process its local tasks. If unsuccessful, the thief randomly searches for another victim and continues steal attempts until successful. This procedure repeats until all workers have exhausted their tasks and termination is detected.

Work-stealing schedulers focus on minimizing overhead in task creation and scheduling [1]. As a result, they avoid features, such as task priorities, which can add overhead to the implementation.

3 Priority Work-Stealing Algorithm

In this section, we provide the details of our work-stealing algorithm for scheduling tasks under global priority. We briefly describe the pool data structure and our overall technique before describing the algorithm.

3.1 Operations on Pool Data Structure

We generalize the data structure used to store tasks in a work-stealing algorithm as a *pool* – a container of ready tasks. Like the concurrent deque described by Arora et al. [1] in their work-stealing algorithm, the pool data structure is owned by a worker thread and supports the following methods:

- push operation: this method is executed only by the owner thread and always succeeds in storing a task into the pool.
- pop operation: this method is executed only by the owner thread and may return a special empty value if the pool is empty.
- steal operation: this method is executed only by the thief thread and method may return a special empty value if the pool is empty.

The pools support concurrent method invocations and may be implemented using any concurrent data structure. Concurrency can only occur between one invocation of push or pop in the owner thread and one or more executions of steal from thief threads. Each pushed task is extracted exactly once either by a call to pop or by a call to steal.

Note that we do not restrict the owner of the pool to use it as a stack (pushing and popping at the bottom) and victim to steal only from the top of the pool. Thus, pool implementations can also internally support priorities and can choose the appropriate task to return during the pop or steal operation. Our priority work-stealing scheduler (Sect. 3.3) which uses priority levels can be paired with any appropriate pool implementation to use specific execution orders. Thus depending on the application, a queue, a stack, or some other container data type can be used as the pool.

3.2 Work-Stealing with Global Priorities

We assume that tasks are assigned fixed priorities and our work-stealing algorithm schedules the highest priority task available globally in a non-preemptive manner. In non-preemptive priority scheduling, when a task starts execution, it executes to completion even if a higher priority task arrives at the ready pool. Since we expect fine-grained parallel programs; the iterations of the scheduler loop are expected to be frequent. Thus, a minor delay in the execution of a higher priority task is not a concern, and we do not expect major priority inversion issues despite the use of a non-preemptive scheduler.

Our algorithm is inspired from the Multi-Level Queue Scheduling (MLQS) algorithm [13] where tasks are partitioned into priority levels. Like MLQS, our scheme maintains a number of distinct pools, each assigned a different priority level. More than one task may be in a given pool and thus have the same priority. However, like work-stealing algorithms, the tasks need to be distributed across worker threads. Each worker thread maintains a local pool for each priority level; we avoid a fully shared task pool as it would require expensive synchronization for every access. Thus, the tasks of any given priority are potentially distributed across the pools in the different worker threads.

In MLQS, higher priority queues must be empty before tasks from lower priority queues are allowed to execute. Similarly, in our scheme higher priority pools from all worker threads must be empty before a worker thread executes a local task from a lower priority pool. This strategy requires the maintenance of a global data structure to track the availability of tasks in the different priority levels across all the workers. It also implies that worker threads will need to perform a steal even if they are not idle, i.e. their pools may not be empty.

The assumption with standard work-stealing algorithms is that stealing accesses are rare as they only occur when the local pool is empty. One strategy that works well under this assumption is the choice of a random victim. Since steals are concurrent operations, they are accompanied by synchronization overheads. To maintain scalability, a work-stealing algorithm needs to be careful with victim selection to minimize the number of failed steal attempts where the thief discovers that the victim has no work available. When performing a steal operation, a thief must also determine how much work to steal.

Our goal is to adhere, as closely as possible, to the priority order while scheduling tasks tolerating added overheads to preserve accuracy. We can neither predict the dynamic priorities of newly spawned tasks nor expect the highest priority tasks to be evenly balanced across workers. Hence, we expect steal attempts to be relatively more frequent than traditional work-stealing approaches and steal only one task from a carefully chosen victim. This avoids *ping-pong* effects where a task, being one of the highest priority ready tasks, moves back and forth between worker threads. This also minimizes failed steal attempts required by thieves to locate and steal work when highest priority tasks are available on a single worker thread's pool.

Starvation: Enforcing priorities means that high-priority processes will always be favored over low-priority ones, causing starvation for low priority tasks. One common method of ameliorating this situation is aging in which we gradually increment the priority of waiting tasks, ensuring that they will all eventually execute. As our benchmarks did not exhibit starvation, we do not address this issue further in this paper.

3.3   Priority Work-Stealing Algorithm

Our priority work stealing algorithm does not depend on synchrony for correctness, and it involves lock-free operations[1]. Each worker thread is guaranteed to make a locally optimal decision while making a best-effort at a globally optimal decision in scheduling a task. The local guarantee is achieved as a worker will not schedule a lower-priority task if there exists a higher-priority task in its pool(s). The lack of guarantee in global optimality is because the global data structure maintains a weakly consistent state of the availability of tasks in the different priority levels.

```
1  class WorkerThread {
2    def pushTask(priority, task) {
3      val level = priorityLevel(priority) // compute the level
4      myPools[level].push(task) // owner thread pushes local task
5      globalState.set(level, true) // update global state after populating pool
6    }
7    def run() {
8      while !stopped()
9        val task = findTask()
10       if task != EMPTY then task.run()
11         else yield()
12   }
13   private def findTask() {
14     // exhaustively search local and global pools, attempting steals
15     var level = globalState.nextAvailableLevel(0)
16     // Not shown: search lower level pools locally and...
17     // return if task found updating global data structure before returning
18     while level < priorityLevels()
19       // first search for a local task to execute
20       val localTask = myPools[level].pop()
21       if localTask != EMPTY then return localTask
22       // choose victim carefully and try to steal from there
23       for victimThread in threadClaimsTaskWithPriority(level)
24         val stolenTask = victimThread.steal(level)
25         if stolenTask != EMPTY then return stolenTask
26       // update global state, try and search again
27       globalState.set(level, false)
28       level = globalState.nextAvailableLevel(level)
29     // found no task to execute
30     return EMPTY
31 } }
```

Fig. 1. Simplified version of the non-blocking work-stealing algorithm that adheres, as closely as possible, to the global priorities of tasks. All worker threads execute the same scheduling loop. The heart of the algorithm is in findTask() which determines which task is scheduled next.

The scheduler operates as shown in Fig. 1. The pushTask operation (lines 2 to 6) finds and populates the local pool for a task with a specified priority. The important operation here is that the global data structure is updated after performing local updates to the pool (line 5). Each worker thread uses a scheduling loop (lines 7 to 12) which tries to find a task to execute and executes it until the scheduler is stopped. The heart of the algorithm lies in each iteration of the scheduling loop where each thread attempts to find a task to execute. The

---

[1] The pool implementation may involve locking in the pop, push, and steal operations.

worker tries to find the highest available priority level by querying a global data structure (line 15) implemented using atomic variables to store the full/empty state for each level. This global state can be out of sync with the state of the local pools, hence the thread attempts to find a local task with a higher priority (lower level index) and schedule the task if available (code not shown on line 16). If no such local task exists, we enter the loop on line 18. The worker then attempts to find a task from the local pool and returns if it finds such a task (lines 19 to 21). If no such task is found locally, the worker must now become a thief and attempt to find a similar priority task from sibling workers (lines 22 and 25). The worker queries global state to find the workers (potential victims) that claim to have a task with the specified priority level. The worker then iterates through each of these victims and attempts to asynchronously steal a task from them. Since steals are attempted from victims claiming to have tasks at the specified level, the number of failed steals should be relatively low and only fail during high contention for few highest priority tasks. If the steal attempt is successful, the worker executes the stolen task. Otherwise, the worker now realizes that the global state is out of sync as none of the victims could provide a task. The worker updates the global state to signal no tasks of the specified priority are available (line 27). The worker keeps looping until the global state returns an invalid index (line 28) signaling no global tasks are currently available to steal. The `findTask` method returns the special value `EMPTY` signaling no tasks are currently available to execute. The worker yields itself when it is unable to find a task to execute (line 11) and then resumes the scheduling loop.

4   Implementation

We briefly describe the Java-based implementation of our scheduler in this section. Our implementation has no third party dependencies; it relies on classes and data structures available in the Java standard library (JDK). Our implementation and the benchmarks are released open source online on GitHub at https://github.com/shamsmahmood/priorityworkstealing.

We have implemented three variants of unbounded pool data structures for use in our scheduler based on:

(a) lock-based implementation of THE protocol in Cilk's deque [6];
(b) wait-free array-based pool based on X10's concurrent deque [3]; and
(c) wait-free linked-list-based pool based on JDK's `ConcurrentLinkedQueue` [4].

Our scheduler is flexible in that it can be configured to use either of these implementations as its pool data structure in the worker threads. Table 1 summarizes the properties our priority work-stealing scheduler compared to other work-stealing schedulers.

Our scheduler's implementation is lock-free and uses the help-first policy for task scheduling as this strategy is favorable when stealing is frequent [7]. Under this policy, spawning a child task pushes it in the task pool and allows the parent task to continue execution past the spawn operation. The scheduler maintains

Table 1. Comparing our work-stealing algorithm with couple other algorithms in the literature.

Scheduler	Pool Type	When to steal from chosen victim	What to steal	What to pop
Work-Stealing without priority	Deque	Local deque is empty; victim chosen randomly	Oldest item by age	Newest item by age
Work-Stealing local priorities	Priority Queue	Local queue is empty; victim chosen randomly	Highest priority item	Highest priority item
Our Work-Stealing global priorities	Deque	Another worker (victim) has a higher priority level pool which is non-empty	Oldest item in pool by age	Newest item in pool
	Queue			Oldest item in pool

a fixed number of worker threads which are configured during initialization. All worker threads execute a scheduling loop similar to the one displayed in Fig. 1. During steal attempts, the victims are traversed in round-robin order starting at the previous successful victim.

Work-stealing schedulers do not enforce global prioritization since this could compromise scalability of the implementation [17]. A limiting factor for scalability of concurrent data structures is the number of global operations performed concurrently by the worker threads. We use atomic variables available in the JDK to implement the global state to reduce the risk of memory consistency errors and to minimize the cost of overheads from synchronization. We reduce the number of calls made to update the global state for a given priority level by identifying instances when the owning worker realizes a pool has transitioned to empty or non-empty states.

We allow tuning parameters like the number of worker threads and the kind of pool to use. We also allow arbitrary scalars ranges to be used as priority levels, there is no limit imposed on the size of the range. A default priority can be specified for tasks created without an explicit priority property. Tasks with invalid priorities are sanitized to meet the constraints of the allowable range for priorities.

5   Experimental Results

Our benchmarks were run on four eight-core IBM POWER7 processors running at 3.8 GHz each. Each node contains 256 GB of RAM and the software stack includes IBM Java SDK Version 1.7.0. Each benchmark ran using the same kernel where the user specifies priorities during task creation; only the task scheduler was changed to report the execution times. Each benchmark was configured to run using 32 worker threads; the arithmetic mean of the best fifty execution times (from the hundred and eighty iterations) are reported and error bars represent one standard deviation. Using the best execution time allows us to minimize the effects of JVM warm up, just-in-time compilation, and garbage collection.

We evaluated several different priority schedulers in the Java platform. We present empirical evaluation of our implementation using Cilk-like deques

(PWSTCD), X10-like deques (PWSTXD), and JDK's (PWSTJQ) priority queues
compared against: (a) JDK's work-stealing `ForkJoinPool` scheduler (FRKJPL)
[10] that does not support priorities; (b) custom implementation of a work-stealing
scheduler using local priority queues that steals only when local queues are empty
(WSTLPQ). (c) JDK's work-sharing `ThreadPool` scheduler that does not support
priorities (THRDPL); (d) JDK's `ThreadPool` scheduler with a thread-safe priority queue using `synchronized` statements (SYNCPQ); and (e) JDK's `ThreadPool`
scheduler using a concurrent queue (`PriorityBlockingQueue`) from the JDK
(PBLKQ). All the priority schedulers were configured to run with ten levels of priorities unless otherwise specified.

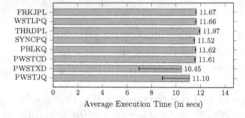

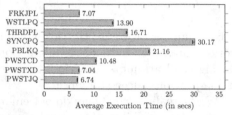

Fig. 2. Trapezoid - 800 thousand tasks   **Fig. 3.** Fibonacci - computing the 34th
to compute an area approximation.   term using recursive formula.

Micro-Benchmarks. The first two micro-benchmarks measure overheads in
the scheduler implementation, the rate at which tasks are processed. Almost all
variants perform similarly in the `Trapezoid` benchmark (Fig. 2), showing that
the scheduler implementations for all the variants are of equivalent quality. In
the `Fibonacci` benchmark, each parent task spawns two additional tasks with
random priorities. Thus, this benchmark measures the overheads from supporting priorities. As expected the SYNCPQ and PBLKQ variants perform the worst
due to overheads from a centralized queue implementation over the equivalent
non-priority version (THRDPL) as seen in Fig. 3. The WSTLPQ, despite having
a decentralized pool, also shows noticeable overheads compared to a non-priority
work-stealing scheduler using a similar victim selection strategy (FRKJPL). Our
scheduler implementation with queues and deques (PWSTJQ, PWSTCD, and
PWSTXD) performs close to FRKJPL.

Quality of Priority Scheduler Benchmarks. Next benchmark used is a variant of the `JGK ForkJoin` benchmark (Fig. 4) where equal numbers of tasks with
random priorities are created upfront on each worker. This synthetic benchmark
mimics applications that use priorities to ensure quality of results. The FRKJPL
and THRDPL do not support priorities and scheduled tasks with an average priority of 4.00 as expected. WSTLPQ, with a local priority queue, schedules its
local task to completion ignoring global priorities. Our decentralized implementations (PWSTJQ, PWSTCD, and PWSTXD) perform as well as a centralized
global priority queue variants (SYNCPQ and PBLKQ) which schedule the tasks

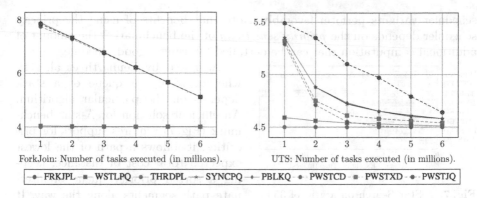

ForkJoin: Number of tasks executed (in millions).   UTS: Number of tasks executed (in millions).

→ FRKJPL ■ WSTLPQ ● THRDPL ─╳ SYNCPQ ◆ PBLKQ ● PWSTCD ■ PWSTXD ● PWSTJQ

Fig. 4. Y-axis represents average priority of tasks executed by scheduler, higher is better.

in perfect priority order. Next is the Unbalanced Tree Search (UTS) benchmark designed to help evaluate systems that require dynamic load balancing. In UTS, the nodes are assigned random priorities, tasks are spawned to process each node as it is discovered. SYNCPQ and PBLKQ with global priority queues and PWSTCD and PWSTXD with deque-based implementations report similar numbers. WSTLPQ, with local priority guarantees, reports priorities close to FRKJPL and THRDPL. PWSTJQ performs best, even outperforming the global priority queues due to a different traversal order. Along with results from Fig. 3, this shows that our scheduler performs scheduling close to global priorities but at a low overhead.

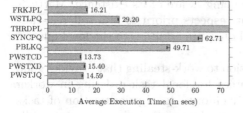

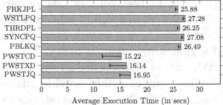

Fig. 5. NQueens: board size of 13, and cutoff after finding first 30 K solutions.

Fig. 6. Knapsack benchmark with 40 items and a sequential cutoff of 34.

Priority to Curtail Computation Benchmarks. Priority scheduling can be used to reduce the total amount of work done by an algorithm. In the NQueens benchmark (Fig. 5), priorities are used based on the number of queens placed on the board populated so far. Our scheduler using all three pools comfortably outperforms all the other variants except FRKJPL. The Knapsack benchmark (Fig. 6) has been ported from a Cilk implementation [5]. The computation can be reduced by pruning sub-trees that cannot produce a better solution than the best one found so far, this leads to an irregular computation. We can see the benefits of using priorities to guide computations in a depth-first manner as our scheduler variants perform favorably. Note that benefits of using the priority scheduler depends on the *priority-sensitivity* of the benchmark – the amount of additional computation that can be curtailed by using a good schedule.

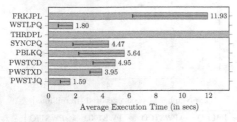

Fig. 7. A-Star Search on a grid of 350 × 350 × 350.

As noted by Lenharth et al. [11], whether to use a queue or a stack depends on the particular algorithm. An efficient solution for A-star benchmark (Fig. 7) requires support for priorities, it follows a path of the lowest expected total cost or distance, keeping a sorted priority queue of alternate path segments along the way. It benefits from the use of breadth-first traversal order via queues rather than deques. Hence the decentralized queued variants (WSTLPQ, PWSTJQ) perform better than dequed versions (PWSTCD and PWSTXD). One of the concerns with our approach is poor performance due to overheads from increased frequency of steals compared to standard work-stealing approaches. However, our experimental results in our benchmarks show that this is not the case.

6   Related Work

Lenharth et al. presented a chunk-based priority scheduler for unordered algorithms [11] that provide weak guarantees on the priority order of scheduled tasks. By their own admission, there are many cases where worker threads do not retrieve the highest priority task despite being aware of its existence. Mattheis et al. used a work-stealing scheduler that respects priorities in a soft real-time system [12]. Their approach uses a global queue in addition to the local queues, and a global-first stealing policy.

Wimmer et al. proposed a basic extension to work-stealing that provides good scalability, but can only provide guarantees for local task ordering in worker threads [17,18]. One of the strategies only enforces local prioritization of tasks and a worker only attempts a steal from a random victim when it becomes idle (i.e. only when the local work queue becomes empty). They also propose a ρ-relaxed priority data structure which guarantees that at most the latest k items added by each worker will be ignored, which implies that $W \times k$ items might be globally ignored during scheduling, W being the number of worker threads.

In Intel Thread Building Blocks (TBB), priority levels can be assigned to individual tasks or task groups [14]. In TBB, worker threads always attempt to execute tasks with highest priorities, while master threads execute any task they have started even if higher priority ones become available. Like TBB, we use non-preemptive scheduling; unlike TBB, our priority scheduler is decentralized and relies on work-stealing strategies for load balancing.

7 Summary

We have developed a priority-based lock-free work-stealing algorithm to work with multiple pool implementations to support priority scheduling of tasks. Our scheduler performs competitively with existing priority and non-priority schedulers in the JDK. We are exploring the idea of using a model similar to Tchiboukdjian et al. [15] to provide a theoretical analysis of our approach. Another area of future work is to integrate priorities for eureka-style computations [8].

Acknowledgments. We are very grateful to the anonymous reviewers, Suguman Bansal, Prasanth Chatarasi, Vivek Kumar, Sri Raj Paul, and Hamim Zafar for their suggestions to clarify the contents of the paper.

References

1. Arora, N.S., Blumofe, R.D., Plaxton, C.G.: Thread scheduling for multiprogrammed multiprocessors. In: SPAA 1998, pp. 119–129 (1998)
2. Blumofe, R.D., Leiserson, C.E.: Scheduling multithreaded computations by work stealing. J. ACM **46**(5), 720–748 (1999)
3. Charles, P., Grothoff, C., et al.: X10: an object-oriented approach to non-uniform cluster computing. SIGPLAN Not. **40**, 519–538 (2005)
4. ConcurrentLinkedQueue (Java Platform SE 8), May 2014. http://docs.oracle.com/javase/8/docs/api/java/util/concurrent/ConcurrentLinkedQueue.html
5. Frigo, M.: knapsack.cilk. http://courses.cs.tau.ac.il/368-4064/cilk-5.3.1/examples/knapsack.cilk
6. Frigo, M., Leiserson, C.E., Randall, K.H.: The implementation of the cilk-5 multithreaded language. SIGPLAN Not. **33**(5), 212–223 (1998)
7. Guo, Y., Barik, R., Raman, R., Sarkar, V.: Work-first and help-first scheduling policies for async-finish task parallelism. In: IPDPS 2009, pp. 1–12. IEEE Computer Society (2009)
8. Imam, S., Sarkar, V.: The Eureka Programming Model for speculative task parallelism. In: ECOOP 2015 (2015)
9. Kumar, V., Frampton, D., et al.: Work-stealing without the baggage. SIGPLAN Not. **47**(10), 297–314 (2012)
10. Lea, D.: A Java fork/join framework. In: Proceedings of Java Grande, pp. 36–43 (2000)
11. Lenharth, A., Nguyen, D., Pingali, K.: Priority Queues Are Not Good Concurrent Priority Schedulers. UT Austin, Department of CS, Technical report TR-11-39 (2011)
12. Mattheis, S., Schuele, T., Raabe, A., Henties, T., Gleim, U.: Work stealing strategies for parallel stream processing in soft real-time systems. In: Herkersdorf, A., Römer, K., Brinkschulte, U. (eds.) ARCS 2012. LNCS, vol. 7179, pp. 172–183. Springer, Heidelberg (2012)
13. Silberschatz, A., et al.: Operating System Concepts, 8th edn. Wiley Publishing, New York (2008)
14. Task and task group priorities in TBB, April 2011. https://software.intel.com/en-us/blogs/2011/04/01/task-and-task-group-priorities-in-tbb

15. Tchiboukdjian, M., Gast, N., Trystram, D.: Decentralized list scheduling. Ann. Oper. Res. **207**(1), 237–259 (2013)
16. Vyukov, D.: Task Scheduling Strategies, December 2010. http://www.1024cores. net/home/scalable-architecture/task-scheduling-strategies
17. Wimmer, M., Cederman, D., Träff, J.L., Tsigas, P.: Work-stealing with configurable scheduling strategies. In: PPoPP 2013, pp. 315–316 (2013)
18. Wimmer, M., Versaci, F., Träff, J.L., Cederman, D., Tsigas, P.: Data structures for task-based priority scheduling. In: PPoPP 2014, pp. 379–380 (2014)

Architecture and Compilers

Optimizing Task Parallelism
with Library-Semantics-Aware Compilation

Peter Thoman, Stefan Moosbrugger$^{(\boxtimes)}$, and Thomas Fahringer

University of Innsbruck, Innsbruck, Austria
{petert,stefanm,tf}@dps.uibk.ac.at

Abstract. With the spread of parallel architectures throughout all areas of computing, task-based parallelism is an increasingly commonly employed programming paradigm, due to its ease of use and potential scalability. Since C++11, the ISO C++ language standard library includes support for task parallelism. However, existing research and implementation work in task parallelism relies almost exclusively on runtime systems for achieving performance and scalability. We propose a combined compiler and runtime system approach that is aware of the parallel semantics of the C++11 standard library functions, and therefore capable of statically analyzing and optimizing their implementation, as well as automatically providing scheduling hints to the runtime system.

We have implemented this approach in an existing compiler and demonstrate its effectiveness by carrying out an empirical study across 9 task-parallel benchmarks. On a 32-core system, our method is, on average, 11.7 times faster than the best result for Clang and GCC C++11 library implementations, and 4.1 times faster than an OpenMP baseline.

1 Introduction

Task-based parallelism is one of the most fundamental parallel abstractions in common use today [11], with applications in areas ranging from embedded systems, over user-facing productivity software, to high performance computing clusters. In all of these fields, the C++ programming language is one of the first choices for performance-sensitive applications. The C++11 standard, which is now implemented in all the most widely-used C++ compilers, introduced several parallelism-related functions and classes in the standard library. One of the most interesting of these from both the perspective of an application developer and a library implementation is the **async** function template. It has the potential to express both coarse- and fine-grained task parallelism, and can serve as a building block for more complex and feature-rich parallel patterns.

While relatively easy to implement and use, achieving good efficiency with task parallelism can be challenging not only for application developers but also for runtime systems, particularly in the case of fine-grained tasks [5]. The *granularity* of tasks is defined by the length of the execution time of a single task between interactions with the runtime system, such as spawning new tasks.

© Springer-Verlag Berlin Heidelberg 2015
J.L. Träff et al. (Eds.): Euro-Par 2015, LNCS 9233, pp. 237–249, 2015.
DOI: 10.1007/978-3-662-48096-0_19

It has recently been demonstrated that the performance of fine-grained task-parallel programs written in C++11 is insufficient in all mainstream compilers and standard libraries [16].

In order to achieve high performance with fine-grained tasks, the overhead of interactions with the runtime system needs to be minimized, and both task distribution and communication need to be implemented in a scalable and efficient fashion. Previous work in this area has focused mostly on new libraries, dynamic optimization at runtime, or user-controlled tuning parameters. Conversely, we propose an approach that combines a *library-semantics-aware optimizing compiler* with a high-performance runtime system which is statically tuned by leveraging knowledge analytically derived at the compiler level. Our goal is to maximize the efficiency of task execution without requiring any additional effort or systems-level knowledge on part of the application programmer, and without introducing any tuning overhead at runtime.

We implemented our method within the Insieme compiler and runtime system [7], but its principles are equally applicable in any other framework. Our concrete contributions are the following:

- A library-semantics-aware compilation process, in which an existing compiler is enriched with the capability to comprehend C++11 standard library semantics, and thus recognize, analyze and optimize task-parallel programs written using these libraries.
- A set of analyses which statically determine several performance-relevant properties of task-parallel code regions, and a heuristic which automatically tunes various runtime system parameters based on these properties.
- An implementation of our approach within the Insieme system.
- Evaluation and analysis of the performance of our method on a set of 9 task-parallel benchmarks. We compare to existing C++11 implementations, as well as OpenMP versions of the benchmarks in order to provide a more optimized and mature performance baseline.

The remainder of this paper is structured as follows. In Sect. 2 we discuss some initial results that motivated our work. We then describe our library-semantics-aware compilation method in detail in Sect. 3, and our static analyses as well as the tuning heuristics derived from them in Sect. 4. The performance of our implementation is evaluated in Sect. 5, followed by an overview of related work in Sect. 6. Section 7 summarizes and concludes our findings.

2   Motivation

Our primary motivation for this work is the desire to be able to employ C++11 threading constructs as building blocks for task parallel programs. Clearly, this approach should offer significant advantages over third-party and homegrown solutions: it is easier to teach and read, thereby increasing programmer productivity, it can be more closely integrated and supported within a given compiler

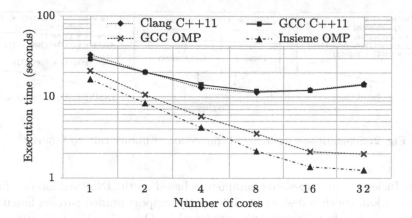

Fig. 1. Performance of the *pyramids* benchmark across APIs and compilers

and its associated runtime library, thereby potentially offering superior performance, and it is portable to any standard-conformant implementation of C++ without external dependencies.

However, the primary reason for parallelization is generally the desire to improve program performance. As Fig. 1 illustrates, both the performance and scalability of state-of-the-art C++11 compilers and runtime systems is insufficient to serve as a replacement for existing parallel languages. The figure depicts the execution time over varying degrees of parallelism for the *pyramids* benchmark from the INNCABS [16] C++11 benchmark suite, as well as an OpenMP implementation of the same benchmark provided for reference. The hardware and software setup for this test is the same as used for the evaluation in Sect. 5, where it is described in detail. At the maximum degree of parallelism of 32, the production-ready OpenMP implementation of GCC outperforms the C++11 versions generated by both GCC with libstdc++ and Clang with libc++ by a *factor of 7*, and the research OpenMP implementation in Insieme is a full order of magnitude faster.

While some degree of improvement of the C++11 results could be achieved purely at the library level, we believe that providing high efficiency rivaling existing parallel languages over several distinct task-parallel patterns without the overhead of runtime tuning requires the co-operation of a library-semantics-aware compiler with a high-performance runtime system.

3 Semantics-Aware Compilation

A fundamental issue with effectively implementing parallelism in mainstream compilers and languages is that it is often expressed by means of library function calls, opaque to the compiler and thus impossible for it to optimize. Furthermore, even parallelism expressed at the language (extension) level – e.g. using OpenMP constructs – is usually translated to internal library calls [3] before reaching the main compiler intermediate representation (IR), once again rendering important semantic information inaccessible to the compiler.

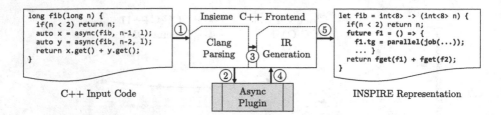

Fig. 2. Semantics-aware frontend conversion of library calls to INSPIRE

The Insieme source-to-source compiler is based on the INSPIRE intermediate representation, which is designed to inherently support unified parallel language semantics. It has been successfully employed in OpenMP [17], Cilk [19], and OpenCL [10] compilation. Detailing INSPIRE semantics is beyond the scope of this paper, a summary is provided by Jordan et al. [6].

In order to enable semantics-aware compilation, analysis, and optimization of C++11 task-parallel programs, we have extended the Insieme C++ frontend to (i) identify relevant C++11 thread support library calls and data types, (ii) analyze their suitability for direct semantic translation, and (iii) translate them to appropriate INSPIRE constructs.

Figure 2 provides a simplified overview of this conversion process, which we will now describe in more detail. The Insieme C++ frontend is based on Clang [13] and features a plugin system allowing multiple entry points for custom INSPIRE generation. For this work, we have created a *C++11 Async* plugin, resulting in the following frontend conversion process:

① The input program is parsed by Clang.
② For every language construct encountered, the Async plugin is invoked.
③ In case of the vast majority of language constructs, the plugin ignores them and they are passed directly to the default IR generation phase.
④ However, the relevant subset of suitable library calls and data structures are intercepted and converted appropriately, as detailed below.
⑤ Finally, the full INSPIRE representation including a semantically equivalent implementation of the library functions is generated.

Table 1 lists the most relevant subset of C++11 library functions and types the Async plugin acts upon, as well as their INSPIRE equivalent. Several implementation details – such as the management of the **valid** state of each **future** – are omitted for brevity. The same is true for the **future::wait** operation, as it is simply equivalent to a **future::get** operation ignoring its return value.

Focusing on the essentials, the conversion is relatively straightforward. Future type templates are converted to structures comprising the return value (of automatically deduced type **'a**) and a **threadgroup**, which is the fundamental INSPIRE type allowing operations on an asynchronously executing process. Async calls are converted to a call to a function which takes an arbitrary closure **() => 'a f** as its argument and returns a pointer to a future

Table 1. Semantic mapping of standard library constructs

C++11	INSPIRE
future<T>	let future = struct { 'a result; threadgroup tg; }
async(f)	(() => 'a f) -> ref<ref<future>> {
	ref<ref<future>> x = var.new(future);
	(*x)->tg = parallel(job { (*x)->result = f(); });
	return x; }
future::get()	(ref<ref<future>> f) -> 'a {
	merge((*f)->tg);
	auto var = (*f)->result;
	ref.delete(*f);
	return var; }

ref<ref<future>>. It allocates the new future structure on the heap, launches a new parallel job executing the closure f and storing its result in the future structure, and stores the result of this parallel call – a **threadgroup** – in the future structure as well. Finally, it returns a pointer to this new future structure. When **get** is invoked on a future, its associated threadgroup is first **merge**d to ensure that it has completed, the return value is stored, and the heap allocation for the future structure is freed.

The crucial feature of this conversion process is that, after it has completed, the entire parallel program semantics are expressed in pure INSPIRE. This uniformity allows the compiler core to perform analysis as it would on e.g. an OpenMP, Cilk or OpenCL program. Furthermore, it enables the compiler backend to generate code targeting the highly optimized Insieme runtime system, instead of relying on the implementation provided by a given C++11 standard library.

One important prerequisite during the conversion of **async** calls is checking the specification of the **std::launch** parameter. Our semantics-aware compilation applies if and only if this parameter is either (i) not supplied, thereby leaving the choice up to the compiler, or (ii) supplied and set to **async | deferred**. Other cases, that is settings of exclusively **async** or exclusively **deferred**, prescribe the desired behavior exactly, and leave little room for compiler- and runtime-level optimization. Therefore, the Async plugin forwards those cases directly to the default IR generation phase, maintaining their correctness.

4 Static Optimization and Compiler-Assisted Tuning

Library-semantics-aware compilation as described up to now is quite useful in and of itself, as it allows C++11 programs to automatically benefit from all backend and runtime optimization work carried out for any other parallel language

Listing 1. Common pattern of `async` and `future` usage

```
let mmul = (int l, int r, int t int b, ...) -> unit {
    auto f1 = async(mmul(l, 1+(r-1)/2, t, t+(b-t)/2, ...));
    auto f2 = async(mmul(1+(r-1)/2, r, t, t+(b-t)/2, ...));
    auto f3 = async(mmul(l, 1+(r-1)/2, t+(b-t)/2, b, ...));
    auto f4 = async(mmul(1+(r-1)/2, r, t+(b-t)/2, b, ...));
    ...
    f1.wait(); f2.wait(); f3.wait(); f4.wait();
    ... }
```

compiled to INSPIRE. However, its full set of advantages can only be leveraged in combination with static compiler-level optimization and analysis.

In this section, we will discuss both *static optimization*, which is always attempted by the compiler and invariably improves performance when applicable, as well as *feature analysis and tuning*, whereby compiler analysis is used to derive code features which determine runtime tuning parameters according to some heuristics.

Static Optimization. Listing 1 depicts a common pattern of async and future usage in parallel programs. While this particular example is highly simplified, the underlying pattern of launching a set of asynchronous tasks, and then waiting for their completion before returning from the current task is exceedingly common in real-world task-parallel applications, including most instances of divide-and-conquer and branch-and-bound algorithms. In fact, Cilk semantics – the original template for task-parallel programming – strictly proscribe this behavior.

The observation that this type of synchronization pattern is common is interesting from an optimization perspective, as synchronizing on the completion of all active child tasks can generally be implemented much more efficiently in a given parallel runtime library than waiting for each of them individually. Therefore, we have created a static optimization we call *synchronization coalescing* to optimize this type of pattern.

Algorithm 1 describes the synchronization coalescing transformation. First, on line 1 to 4, it is ensured that no `threadgroup` object is accessible outside of the current task T, as this might allow unknown synchronization and access patterns. This means that e.g. futures stored in global variables or moved outside the function cannot be optimized, but in practice we have not found this to be a significant limitation so far.

From line 5 to 12, all possible static control paths to `merge` calls are examined to ensure that the expected synchronization pattern is maintained. As this check is done on static control paths, repeated `parallel`/`merge` invocations within a loop are not optimized, but the common idiom of first launching a set of tasks in a loop and then waiting on their results in a new loop is captured.

If neither of the two safety checks prevents the optimization, starting from line 13 the code transformation is performed.

It is important to note that the actual implementation of this transformation benefits from the semantics-aware translation of library calls to the unified and inherently parallel INSPIRE representation in several important ways:

Algorithm 1. Synchronization coalescing

T	input/output task function

1: P of all **parallel** invocations in T.
2: **for all parallel** $p \in P$ **do**
3:    **if** the *threadgroup* $= p()$ is accessible outside T **then return**
4: **end for**
5: Determine the set M of all **merge** invocations in T.
6: **for all merge** $m \in M$ **do**
7:    Compute the set of all static execution paths F
       from the entry point of T to m.
8:    **for all** paths $f \in F$ **do**
9:       Reverse f and remove the first entry.
10:    **end for**
11:    **if** $\exists f \in F : f$ encounters a **merge** after a **parallel then return**
12: **end for**
13: Insert **merge_all** before the lexicographically first $m \in M$.
14: Remove all $m \in M$ from T.

1. There is no need to deal with slightly different variants of the same underlying operation individually – e.g. it is sufficient to process only **merge** calls rather than **future::get** *and* **future::wait** invocations, as both of these map to INSPIRE functions internally calling **merge**.
2. Existing tools for the analysis of parallel control and data flow in Insieme can be re-used directly, e.g. in the implementation of the safety checks, without requiring specific adaptation for C++11 **async**.
3. The resulting optimization is equally available and applicable to any other input language or library generating INSPIRE.

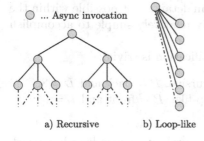

a) Recursive   b) Loop-like

Fig. 3. Parallel patterns

Table 2. Runtime system settings

Parameter	Possible values
Push position	$P = \{\text{front, back}\}$
Queue length	$L = 2^n$
	$n \in \mathbb{N}, n > 1$
Meaningful choices	$8, 16, 32, 64$

Feature Analysis and Tuning. As task parallelism is a versatile abstraction, it can model a variety of parallel patterns. Among those, two highly relevant ones for runtime system optimization are *recursive parallelism* and *loop-like parallelism*, both of which are illustrated in Fig. 3. The former occurs e.g. in divide-and-conquer and branch-and-bound algorithms, while the latter is common whenever lists or arrays are processed. The crucial difference between the two, which directly affects how they are most efficiently executed, is the fact that in recursive parallelism each task generally generates further sub-tasks, while this is not the case for loop-like parallelism.

Many task-parallel runtime systems offer tuning options, which can significantly influence the achieved performance. The same is true for the Insieme runtime system we employ. Two of its most relevant settings are listed in Table 2: *push position* and *queue length*. These describe, respectively, whether newly generated tasks are inserted at the front or the back of each work queue, and the number of full parallel tasks which will be generated before falling back to sequential execution (lazy task creation). These settings relate directly to the differences between recursive and loop parallelism: as recursively parallel tasks generate new tasks, long queues are not necessary to maintain good utilization, and newly generated tasks should be inserted at the back of the queue so that other workers have a chance to first steal large blocks of work (further up in the task tree). Conversely, for loop-like parallelism, longer queues are desireable to maintain enough available tasks for all workers to be utilized effectively, and new tasks should be inserted at the front of the queue to maintain cache locality on the local worker.

In a conventional runtime system or parallel library, these settings need to be taken care of by cautious selection of defaults, or, at best, by studying the behavior of the application at execution time and gradually converging towards an optimum. With library-semantics-aware compilation, we are able to classify applications at compile time by means of static analysis, and automatically choose appropriate runtime system settings based on this classification.

Currently, our classification is based on two relatively simple analyses: (i) a *recursion check* which determines whether a task function may invoke itself recursively, and (ii) a *loop check* which investigates the invocation context of a given parallel call to find out whether it occurs within any loop structure.

Describing these inter-procedural analyses in detail is not possible within the constraints of this paper, but they are actually relatively simple to accomplish within the Insieme infrastructure.

Based on the result of these analyses, classification is trivial:

1. if *recursion check* succeeded, classify as recursive, $P =$ back and $L = 8$;
2. else, if *loop check* succeeded, classify as loop-like, $P =$ front and $L = 64$;
3. else, use the defaults ($P =$ front and $L = 32$).

While the arguments for the choice of P and the relative queue length for each category were outlined above, the question for best choice of absolute value for L has not been fully solved. Our current selection for each category is based on empiric experience, with a more rigorous mechanism planned in future work.

5   Evaluation

We evaluate the effectiveness of our semantics-aware compilation approach on 9 task-parallel C++11 benchmarks from the INNCABS suite [16]. We have selected benchmarks for which equivalent OpenMP versions exist so as to provide an additional reference measurement. Relying exclusively on current C++11 library implementations as the sole point of comparison seems insufficient – as illustrated in Sect. 2, their performance is not competitive for fine-grained tasks.

Experimental Setup. Our evaluation platform is a quad-socket shared-memory system equipped with Intel Xeon E5-4650 processors, each offering 8 cores clocked at a nominal frequency of 2.7 GHz (up to 3.3 GHz with Turbo Boost). The software stack consists of Clang 3.4.2 using libc++ 3.4.2 and gcc 4.9.0 using libstdc++ 3.4.20, both with -O3 optimizations, on a Linux operating system with kernel version 2.6.32-431. The thread affinity for all benchmark runs was fixed using a fill-socket-first policy, and all reported numbers are medians over five runs.

Presentation. Due to a lack of space, we are unable to give a detailed account of all our results. In order to provide some more in-depth discussion as well as a comprehensive impression of the overall performance of our approach, we have decided to discuss the results of three individual benchmarks – each representative of a broader category – in detail, as well as provide a separate overview across the entire set of benchmarks. In all cases, we discuss 4 metrics:

cpp11 best defined as the best result obtained by either gcc or Clang using the highest-performing of the three available task launch policies available for async. This summarized metric maintains readability on the charts while presenting the state of the art in C++11 production compilers in the best possible light.

omp indicating the performance achieved by the OpenMP version of each benchmark compiled using gcc.

insieme our result using library-semantics-aware compilation in the Insieme infrastructure, without heuristic runtime tuning.

insieme opt the same as above, but with the inclusion of the compiler-assisted runtime tuning described in Sect. 4.

Alignment. The *alignment* benchmark is loop-like in structure, and features coarse-grained tasks. As Fig. 4 illustrates, its parallel scaling is reasonable with all tested technologies. However, it is worth noting in this context that the best C++11 version shows worse scaling than the other options, likely due to higher threading overhead. The *insieme* and *insieme opt* results are almost indistinguishable for up to 8 cores, with insieme opt scaling better beyond that. This fits perfectly with expectations, as the *alignment* benchmark is classified correctly by the compiler as loop-like, increasing the runtime system queue size which in turn improves utilization at higher degrees of parallelism.

While the log-log presentation in the chart hides it to some extent, the improvement achieved by our approach is tangible even in this coarse-grained case. At 32 cores, the *insieme opt* execution time is 47 % shorter than *cpp11 best*, 28 % better than *omp*, and an improvement of 21 % over *insieme*.

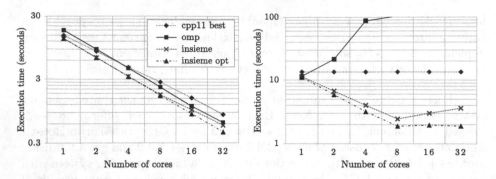

Fig. 4. *Alignment* benchmark results   **Fig. 5.** *Health* benchmark results

Health. This benchmark is recursive in structure, and features extremely fine-grained tasks. Therefore, as depicted in Fig. 5, the best C++11 result remains flat as the `deferred` launch policy – which is not parallel – is always the fastest. Even the OpenMP version suffers from slowdown, rather than speedup, with increasing thread counts, and its results for 8 or more threads are omitted for readability. The low-overhead Insieme runtime system and synchronization coalescing allow our system to achieve scaling up to 8 cores. Once again, the benchmark is correctly categorized by the compiler, with *insieme opt* scaling better and not suffering from the performance drop-off incurred by the base *insieme* version at 16 and 32. This is due to new tasks being pushed to the back of work queues, resulting in larger tasks being spread across all cores and preventing the severe overheads with higher core counts that affect all other versions.

Sort. This divide-and-conquer implementation of a mergesort is another example of recursive task parallelism, but its tasks are significantly more coarse-grained than those of *health*. Consequently, the OpenMP version performs much better. However, as seen in Fig. 6, the task granularity is still too low for either gcc or Clang to achieve any speedup in the C++11 code. One interesting artifact of note here is that the *omp* version is faster on a single core than any other option, likely due to differences in code generation between pure C and C++11. However, due to its better scaling, the C++11 version compiled and executed with the *insieme* framework catches up to and matches the *omp* version at 4, 8 and 16 cores. At the highest degree of parallelism, the OpenMP version hits a task scheduling wall while our implementation of C++11 continues to scale.

Overall. The boxplot in Fig. 7 provides a statistical overview of the results across the entire set of 9 benchmarks (*alignment, fib, floorplan, health, sort, sparselu, strassen, qap,* and *pyramids*). In order to allow for direct comparison across this diverse set of programs, it was created thusly: (i) select the best result across 1 to 32 cores for each benchmark and each of the four previously described versions, (ii) normalize these values to the sequential time for the C++11 version of each benchmark, and (iii) calculate the required quartiles and medians for the box

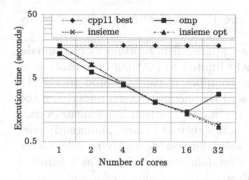

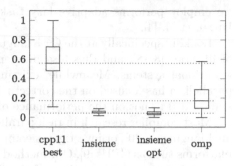

Fig. 6. *Sort* benchmark results   **Fig. 7.** Overview of results (32 cores)

plot across the 9 resulting benchmark values for each version. Horizontal lines were added at the median for *cpp11 best* and *omp*, and between the two median values for *insieme* and *insieme opt* to improve readability.

These results can be interpreted as follows: with 32 cores at its disposal, the best available C++11 implementation achieves, on average, a parallel speedup of 1.8 (the median is at 0.55) over the sequential version in this set of benchmarks. OpenMP fares better, with a median speedup of 5.9, while our implementation reaches 21.2 without and 23.8 with runtime tuning. In a direct comparison, our tuned results are on average 11.7 times as fast as the *cpp11 best* and 4.1 times as fast as the *omp* baseline.

Looking beyond median performance, it is interesting to note that there is no overlap between *cpp11 best* and *insieme* performance – that is, even at its worst our system performs on par with the best results possible on any of our chosen benchmarks for the existing C++11 implementations. Similarly, the worst cases for *omp* are still on par with the average for *cpp11 best*.

Finally, while *insieme opt* achieves superior median, upper and lower quartile performance than *insieme*, its upper limit is slightly higher. This is due to the *pyramids* benchmark, despite being correctly classified as recursive, performing better at default runtime settings. We believe that this is due to improved cache effectiveness with the default queuing order. We consider statically analyzing memory access patterns and taking them into account for runtime configuration an area for future work.

6   Related Work

There is a large body of existing work in optimizing task parallelism, with a particular focus on scheduling strategies [1,12] and alleviating task creation overhead [4,15]. What is common to all of these approaches is that they focus primarily on the runtime level, while we introduce a library-semantics-aware compiler component in order to generate more efficient parallel code, and to provide any given runtime system with static tuning information to use as an initial default. As such, our approach is orthogonal to and compatible with any further runtime-level adaptation and optimization – in fact the runtime system we employ performs adaptive lazy task creation similar to that described by Duran et al. [4].

Looking specifically at the C++ language, parallelism is primarily the domain of libraries [8,18], and thus also inherently limited to runtime optimization in traditional systems. Meanwhile, existing compiler research related to C++11 parallelism has focused on the correctness of the memory model underlying the standard [14], not on the performance of its library function implementations.

Most compiler research in task parallelism is related to novel, inherently parallel languages [20], or investigates compilation for specific highly-parallel target platforms such as GPUs [9]. Our method is fundamentally different, as it enriches a compiler with understanding of the library-level semantics of a widely-used mainstream language, improving its ability to analyze and optimize the implementation of these semantics. Liao et al. [2] performed one of the few existing investigations of semantics-aware compilation in parallel computing. However, their goal was improving the applicability of compiler autoparallelization by taking into account STL container semantics in the ROSE compiler framework. Conversely, we propose semantic analysis of programs which are already parallel, in order to more efficiently implement this explicit parallelism.

7   Conclusion

We have presented a *library-semantics-aware* compilation approach for C++11 tasks. It enables (i) static optimization of task parallelism by *synchronization coalescing*, (ii) executing C++11 programs on a highly optimized parallel runtime system without any user effort, and (iii) automatic tuning of runtime settings based on features derived by compiler analysis. Our system, implemented as an extension to the Insieme compiler, massively improves performance over existing implementations of C++11 parallelism across a range of 9 benchmarks, by a factor of 11.7 on average. Additionally, while compiling code using standard C++11 library constructs for parallelism, it matches and often exceeds the performance and scalability obtained by C/OpenMP programs.

Acknowledgments. This project was funded by the FWF Austrian Science Fund as part of the projects I 1523 "Energy-Aware Autotuning for Scientific Applications" and I 1079-N23 "Greener mobile systems by cross layer integrated energy management".

References

1. Augonnet, C., et al.: StarPU: a unified platform for task scheduling on heterogeneous multicore architectures. Concurrency Comput. Pract. Experience **23**(2), 187–198 (2011)
2. Liao, C., et al.: Semantic-aware automatic parallelization of modern applications using high-level abstractions. Int. J. Parallel Prog. **38**(5–6), 361–378 (2010)
3. Novillo, D.: OpenMP and automatic parallelization in GCC. In: Proceedings of the GCC Developers Summit. GNU (2006)

4. Duran, A., Corbalán, J., Ayguadé, E.: An adaptive cut-off for task parallelism. In: International Conference for High Performance Computing, Networking, Storage and Analysis, SC 2008, pp. 1–11. IEEE (2008)
5. Turner, D.N., Loidl, H.W., Hammond, K. (eds.): On the granularity of divide-and-conquer parallelism. Glasgow Workshop on Functional Programming, pp. 8–10. Springer, Heidelberg (1995)
6. Jordan, H., et al.: Inspire: the insieme parallel intermediate representation. In: 22nd International Conference on Parallel Architectures and Compilation Techniques (PACT), pp. 7–17. IEEE (2013)
7. Insieme Compiler and Runtime Infrastructure. http://insieme-compiler.org
8. Reinders, J.: Intel threading building blocks: outfitting C++ for multi-core processor parallelism. "O'Reilly Media, Inc." (2007)
9. Stratton, J.A., et al.: Efficient compilation of fine-grained SPMD-threaded programs for multicore CPUs. In: Proceedings of the 8th Annual IEEE/ACM International Symposium on Code Generation and Optimization, pp. 111–119. ACM (2010)
10. Kofler, K., et al.: An automatic input-sensitive approach for heterogeneous task partitioning. In: Proceedings of the 27th International ACM conference on International Conference on Supercomputing, pp. 149–160. ACM (2013)
11. Asanovic, K. et al.: The Landscape of Parallel Computing Research: A View from Berkeley. Technical report UCB/EECS-2006-183, EECS Department, University of California, Berkeley, 12 December 2006. http://www.eecs.berkeley.edu/Pubs/TechRpts/2006/EECS-2006-183.html
12. Lakshmanan, K., Kato, S., Rajkumar, R.: Scheduling parallel real-time tasks on multi-core processors. In: IEEE 31st Real-Time Systems Symposium (RTSS), pp. 259–268. IEEE (2010)
13. Lattner, C.: LLVM and Clang: Next generation compiler technology. In: The BSD Conference, pp. 1–2 (2008)
14. Batty, M., et al.: Clarifying and compiling C/C++ concurrency: from C++11 to POWER. In: Proceedings of the 39th Annual ACM SIGPLAN-SIGACT Symposium on Principles of Programming Languages, POPL 2012, pp. 509–520. ACM, New York (2012). http://doi.acm.org/10.1145/2103656.2103717
15. Mohr, E., Kranz, D.A., Halstead Jr., R.H.: Lazy task creation: a technique for increasing the granularity of parallel programs. IEEE Trans. Parallel Distrib. Syst. **2**(3), 264–280 (1991)
16. Thoman, P., Gschwandtner, P., Fahringer, T.: On the quality of implementation of the C++11 thread support library. In: 23rd Euromicro International Conference on Parallel, Distributed and Network-Based Processing (PDP). IEEE (2015, to appear)
17. Thoman, P., Jordan, H., Pellegrini, S., Fahringer, T.: Automatic OpenMP loop scheduling: a combined compiler and runtime approach. In: Chapman, B.M., Massaioli, F., Müller, M.S., Rorro, M. (eds.) IWOMP 2012. LNCS, vol. 7312, pp. 88–101. Springer, Heidelberg (2012)
18. An, P., et al.: STAPL: an adaptive, generic parallel C++ library. In: Dietz, H.G. (ed.) LCPC 2001. LNCS, vol. 2624. Springer, Heidelberg (2003)
19. Robert, D., Blumofe, et al.: Cilk: An Efficient Multithreaded Runtime System. SIGPLAN Not. **30**(8), 207–216 (1995). doi:10.1145/209937.209958
20. Armstrong, T.G., et al.: Compiler techniques for massively scalable implicit task parallelism. In: International Conference for High Performance Computing, Networking, Storage and Analysis, SC14, pp. 299–310. IEEE (2014)

Data Layout Optimization for Portable Performance

Kamal Sharma[1]([⊠]), Ian Karlin[2], Jeff Keasler[2], James R. McGraw[2],
and Vivek Sarkar[1]

[1] Rice University, Houston, TX, USA
{kamal.g.sharma,vsarkar}@rice.edu
[2] Lawrence Livermore National Laboratory, Livermore, CA, USA
{karlin1,keasler1,mcgraw1}@llnl.gov

Abstract. This paper describes a new approach to managing data layouts to optimize performance for array-intensive codes. Prior research has shown that changing data layouts (e.g., interleaving arrays) can improve performance. However, there have been two major reasons why such optimizations are not widely used in practice: (1) the challenge of selecting an optimized layout for a given computing platform, and (2) the cost of re-writing codes to use different layouts for different platforms. We describe a source-to-source code transformation process that enables the generation of different codes with different array interleavings from the same source program, controlled by data layout specifications that are defined separately from the program. Performance results for multicore versions of the benchmarks show significant benefits on four different computing platforms (up to 22.23× for IRSmk, up to 3.68× for SRAD and up to 1.82× for LULESH). We also developed a new optimization algorithm to recommend a good layout for a given source program and specific target machine characteristics. Our results show that the performance obtained using this algorithm achieves 78 %–95 % performance of the best manual layout on each platform for different benchmarks (IRSmk, SRAD, LULESH).

1 Introduction

As computing platforms increase in diversity, "portable performance" has become one of the most challenging problems for application developers. Achieving good performance on a specific platform often requires coding adjustments to fit a specific set of machine parameters e.g., number of cores, cache size, cache line size, number of registers, memory bandwidth, etc. Unfortunately, adjustments for one platform can impede performance on other platforms. This paper focuses on *data layout optimization*, which has been increasing in importance in recent years. Most programming languages require developers to make array-of-struct (AoS) or struct-of-array (SoA) decisions (or combinations thereof) early in development. For long-lived applications, the following challenge can be encountered repeatedly (and now with increasing frequency): what to do when a new

© Springer-Verlag Berlin Heidelberg 2015
J.L. Träff et al. (Eds.): Euro-Par 2015, LNCS 9233, pp. 250–262, 2015.
DOI: 10.1007/978-3-662-48096-0_20

parallel architecture is introduced with a memory and storage subsystem that would benefit from a different data structure layout in the program? This question is taking on a new urgency as proposals for exascale architectures increasingly include major changes in memory and storage structures. With current languages, a near-complete rewrite of an application is usually required, because each data access usually needs to be rewritten when the data layout is changed. Historically, developers of large codes avoid changing data layouts because it involves changing too many lines of code, the expected benefit of a specific change is difficult to predict, and whatever works well on one system may hurt on another. Our approach demonstrates how these obstacles can be overcome.

This paper is organized as follows. Section 2 describes a motivating example (IRSmk) and shows that changing array layouts can significantly impact performance on four different parallel platforms. Section 3 introduces our extensions to TALC, a source-to-source transformation tool. TALC enables the same program to be compiled and executed with different data layouts, without requiring any changes to the source code. Section 4 presents a new automatic optimization algorithm to recommend an optimized layout for a given source program and target machine. Section 5 presents a summary of empirical results obtained for three benchmarks (IRSmk, SRAD, LULESH) on four different multicore platforms: IBM POWER7, AMD APU, Intel Sandy Bridge, and IBM BG/Q. Section 5 also presents results from the automated layout algorithm that are very close to the hand tuned manual layouts. Finally, Sect. 6 summarizes related work, and Sect. 7 contains our conclusions and plans for future work.

2 Motivating Example

We use the IRSmk benchmark (a 27-point stencil loop kernel in the ASC Sequoia Benchmark Codes [2]) as a motivating example to illustrate the impact of data layouts on performance. IRSmk is an Implicit Radiation Solver for diffusion equations on a block-structured mesh. Figure 1 shows the main loop kernel of IRSmk. For simplicity, we do not consider arrays starting with the letter x as candidates for layout optimization, since they all alias to the same array with different offsets. We also ignore array b since it only occurs in a single write access. This leaves 27 arrays as candidates for layout optimization (dbl to ufr).

```
for ( kk = kmin ; kk < kmax ; kk++ ) {
  for ( jj = jmin ; jj < jmax ; jj++ ) {
    for ( ii = imin ; ii < imax ; ii++ ) {
      i   = ii + jj * jp + kk * kp ;
      b[i] =  dbl[i] * xdbl[i] + dbc[i] * xdbc[i] + dbr[i] * xdbr[i]
            + dcl[i] * xdcl[i] + dcc[i] * xdcc[i] + dcr[i] * xdcr[i]
            + dfl[i] * xdfl[i] + dfc[i] * xdfc[i] + dfr[i] * xdfr[i]
            + cbl[i] * xcbl[i] + cbc[i] * xcbc[i] + cbr[i] * xcbr[i]
            + ccl[i] * xccl[i] + ccc[i] * xccc[i] + ccr[i] * xccr[i]
            + cfl[i] * xcfl[i] + cfc[i] * xcfc[i] + cfr[i] * xcfr[i]
            + ubl[i] * xubl[i] + ubc[i] * xubc[i] + ubr[i] * xubr[i]
            + ucl[i] * xucl[i] + ucc[i] * xucc[i] + ucr[i] * xucr[i]
            + ufl[i] * xufl[i] + ufc[i] * xufc[i] + ufr[i] * xufr[i];
} } }
```

Fig. 1. IRSmk source code

Table 1. Performance improvement of different layouts relative to baseline 27×1 layout, for different platforms

Platform	27×1	9×3	3×9	1×27
IBM POWER7	1.00	4.66	4.66	4.71
AMD APU	1.00	1.26	1.38	1.40
Intel Sandy Bridge	1.00	1.06	1.10	1.10
IBM BG/Q	1.00	1.65	2.14	2.20

As a preview of results to come (with larger number of layouts), we look at four different array layouts here to illustrate the potential for performance gains on different platforms. The default layout is the one observed in Fig. 1, where the 27 arrays are stored separately (27×1). A simple rewrite can change the layout by interleaving[1] groups of three arrays, thus producing 9 arrays of structs where each structure contains 3 fields (9×3). Another rewrite can interleave 9 arrays each, producing three arrays (3×9). The final rewrite interleaves all 27 arrays into one array (1×27). We ran these four versions of IRSmk on four different platforms: IBM Power7, AMD APU, Intel Sandy Bridge, and the IBM BG/Q, using a problem size of 100^3 and all cores within a single node on each platform. The results are presented in Table 1. All examples show positive gains for all of the layout options. However, the performance improvement varies dramatically across different layouts and different platforms.

3   TALC Data Layout Framework

This section describes our extensions to the TALC Framework [14] to support user-specified and automatic data layouts, driven by a Meta file specification. The past framework had limited capabilities in terms of error checking, no automatic layout selection, did not take into consideration machine characteristics and profiled information, and explored limited platforms. TALC stands for Topologically-Aware Layout in C. TALC is a source-to-source compiler translation tool and accompanying runtime system that dramatically reduces the effort needed to experiment with different data layouts. Our extended version of TALC has been implemented in the latest version of the ROSE [4] compiler infrastructure. In the process of extending TALC, we have re-implemented its entire code, added new functionality for automated layouts and extended layout transformations [3]. Our new tool explores a wide range of layouts, considers platform characteristics and profile information and performs safety and error checking for different layouts.

Figure 2 shows our extended TALC framework. TALC can be configured to run in two modes: Automated Layout and User Specified Layout. For both these

---

[1] In this paper, we use array regrouping and interleaving interchangeably.

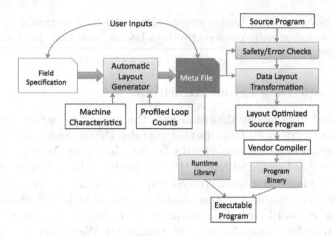

Fig. 2. Extended TALC framework

```
View node
{
    Field {x:d}
    Field {y:d}
    Field {z:d}
...
}
```

```
View node
{
    Field {x:d,y:d,z:d}
    Field {xd:d,yd:d,zd:d}
    Field {xdd:d,ydd:d,zdd:d}
    Field {fx:d,fy:d,fz:d}
}
```

Fig. 3. Sample field specification file   **Fig. 4.** Sample TALC meta file

modes, a user needs to provide some input to perform data layout transformations. In the Automated Layout mode, the user provides a *field specification*. A field specification file is a simple schema file, which specifies arrays that should be considered for transformation. The field specification file is necessary because it enables our tool to only transform the specified arrays (like the 27 arrays in the IRSmk example discussed in Sect. 2). Figure 3 shows a sample field specification file. The View keyword is used to specify a data layout. The field keyword specifies arrays considered for layout transformation. Each field has a type associated with it, specified by the : separator. In this example, d stands for the double data type. Specifying the data type helps with type checking array subscripts during layout transformations. Further details about our TALC tool along with a working example can be found in our technical report [18]. More information on the Automatic Data Layout Selection is provided in the next section.

4   Automatic Data Layout Selection

In this section, we describe the automatic data layout selection algorithm. The algorithm takes in a user-written field specification file which specifies arrays that should be considered for transformation, and uses a greedy optimization algorithm to automatically construct a data layout based on the input program and target architecture.

4.1 Automatic Data Layout Algorithm

Our automated data layout algorithm uses the cache-use factors and platform characteristics to produce a meta file that contains the recommended data layout. Algorithm 1 shows the automated data layout algorithm. More details can be found in the related technical report [18]. To begin with, each array in the field specification is placed in its own ArrayGroup. As a heuristic, we disallow arrays that occur in vectorizable loops as candidates for data layout transformation. This heuristic is used to avoid performance degradations that may result from data layout transformations breaking vectorization. We expect this heuristic to be relaxed in the future when processors have more flexible vector capabilities with respect to memory accesses, compared to today's processors. The algorithm compares all pairs of ArrayGroups to determine the profitability of merging each pair. We use Cache-Use Factor (CUF) as a cost metric to capture the possible cache impact of merging two or more array groups. This factor denotes cache usage efficiency across all the candidate loops in the program. The CUF metric helps limit the amount limit of merging performed by our greedy algorithm. The pair with the highest cache-use factor is merged to form a new group. This process is repeated until the best candidate pair for merging falls below the acceptable merge threshold. After the final grouping is determined, each group's arrays are sorted based on data type (largest data size to smallest data size), to better pack them. The final step performs cache line splitting i.e. split array groups based on cache line boundaries of an architecture, to further improve cache line utilization within a group.

The evaluation of the profitability of merging two candidate ArrayGroups considers two factors. The first consideration examines reads versus writes to an ArrayGroup. Our experimental results (Sect. 5) showed that grouping arrays written to frequently with arrays that are only read can decrease performance significantly. Our current heuristic prohibits creating a new merged ArrayGroup, if the number of write-only arrays is more than 2× the number of read and read-write arrays The second consideration for merging ArrayGroups computes the cache use factor for the proposed combination. If the cache use factor is greater than our established thresholds, the ArrayGroups are viable for merging. From our empirical results, we have chosen *Cache Use threshold* = 0.57 for our algorithm. A detailed analysis to study the effects of varying this threshold across architectures and benchmarks is a subject of future work.

5 Experimental Results

We ran a series of tests to evaluate the productivity and performance gains obtained by using TALC to perform layout transformations. In Sect. 5.1, we first

Algorithm 1. Automated Data Layout Algorithm

```
 1: procedure AUTODATALAYOUT(ArrayGroupList)
 2:     for loop L in the program do
 3:         if loop L is vectorizable (based on vector pragma or compiler analysis)
 4:             Remove arrays in loop from ArrayGroupList
 5:         end if
 6:     end for
 7:     IsMerge ← true
 8:     while IsMerge is true do
 9:         IsMerge ← false
10:         for pairs ∈ ArrayGroupList do
11:             if (pair writes) > 2*(pair reads+pair read/writes)
12:                 Ignore pair
13:             end if
14:             best pair ← pair with highest cache use factor
15:         end for
16:         if CUF resulting from merging best pair > threshold
17:             merge pair
18:             IsMerge ← true
19:         end if
20:     end while
21:     sortGroups(ArrayGroupList)
22:     splitCacheLine(ArrayGroupList)
23:     return ArrayGroupList
24: end procedure
```

describe our experimental methodology. We then provide a detailed discussion of performance results for user-specified layouts, obtained by evaluating a range of manual layouts on different architectures (Sect. 5.2). Finally, we present performance results obtained by using our automatic layout algorithm (Sect. 5.3).

5.1 Experimental Methodology

To show the impact of data layouts on performance we ran experiments using our three benchmark programs on four different platforms: *IBM Power7, AMD APU, Intel Sandy Bridge* and *IBM BG/Q. IBM Power7* represents a 32-core IBM Power 7 processor system (four eight-core 3.55 GHz processor, 32 KB L1 D-Cache per core, 256 KB L2 Cache, 32 MB L3 Cache) used with compiler options xlc-v11.1 -O3 -qsmp=omp -qthreaded -qhot -qtune=pwr7 -qarch=pwr7. *AMD APU* represents a 4-core AMD A10-5800K APU processor (quad-core 3.8 GHz processor, 16 KB L1 D-Cache per core, 4 MB L2 Cache) used with compiler options gcc-v4.7.2 -O3 -fopenmp. *Intel Sandy Bridge* represents a 16-core Intel E5-2670 Sandy Bridge CPU system (eight-core 2.6 GHz processor, 32 KB L1 D-Cache per core, 256 KB L2 Cache per core, 20 MB L3 Cache) used with compiler options icc-v12.1.5 -O3 -fast -parallel -openmp. *IBM BG/Q* represents a 16-core IBM PowerPC A2 system (1.6 GHz processor, 32 MB eDRAM L2 cache) used with compiler options gcc-v4.4.6 -O3 -fopenmp. For the *AMD APU*, we focused on the CPU and ignored the GPU. IRSmk and LULESH were both run in double precision, while SRAD was run in single precision. Specifically, we ran IRSmk on a problem based on a 100^3 mesh for 500 iterations. LULESH was run with a problem size = 90 (i.e. 90^3 elements and 91^3 nodes). SRAD was run for 200 iterations on a 4096^2 grid with the $x1$ and $y1$

speckle values set to 0, the $x2$ and $y2$ values set to 127 and lambda set to 0.5. We made minor changes to the original source program to conform to extended TALC framework specifications. These changes related to renaming the program variables and did not affect program execution in any way.

All of these benchmarks use OpenMP for parallelism. We use the default memory allocation scheme provided in these benchmarks and limited our experiments to one socket. Studying the Non Uniform Memory Access (NUMA) effects with data layouts will be part of future work. All benchmarks were run with varying thread counts on the four platforms. For this work, we only used the default memory allocation provided on these systems. For all codes, TALC enabled testing a range of layouts, 9 for IRSmk and 11 for LULESH and 5 for SRAD. To perform the layout transformations in IRSmk, between 56 and 272 (82%) lines of the original 330 lines of code were changed. For the LULESH the numbers are 98 to 477 (18%) lines of the original 2640. For SRAD the number are 11 to 39 (16%) lines of the original 239. By using TALC, we not only were able to automate these changes, but also eliminate the possibility of subtle bugs being introduced when these changes are performed manually (and repeated for different architectures).

5.2   User Specified Layout Results

For each benchmark, we conducted extensive experiments across different layouts on four architectures. However, due to space limitations, we limit the number of layouts presented here to the most interesting ones. For each test case, we report the speedup (which can be a slowdown, for *values* < 1) of each layout against the "base case" which is the original code, running with an equivalent number of threads. In some cases, for example IBM BG/Q for 2, 4 and 8 threads, we omit showing results for all thread counts because their results were similar to adjacent thread counts of 1 and 16. However, full details with results for all layouts can be found in [18].

IRSmk. The implicit radiation solver (IRS) [2] is a benchmark used as part of the procurement of the Sequoia system at LLNL. Figure 5a, d, g and j show the results obtained by running IRSmk with different thread counts on all nine layouts on each of the four platforms. IRSmk is a memory bound kernel whose performance is limited by memory bandwidth. However, we see that except for Sandy Bridge significant speedups occur at all thread counts due to data layouts.

The results of the best layout for IRS on all machines show performance of at least 70% of optimal and over 95% on Sandy Bridge. For Sandy Bridge, the execution time for the best layout is 3.05 s, for the AMD APU it is 10.04 s, for BG/Q it is 5.2 s and for the Power 7 it is 12.52 s. BG/Q performs slightly worse than other architectures due to in-order cores not hiding as much latency as the other processors, while the AMD APU could be hurt by less data in the x array staying in its smaller cache. Finally, all the processors might be limited in their handling of the unequal amount of read and write data in IRSmk.

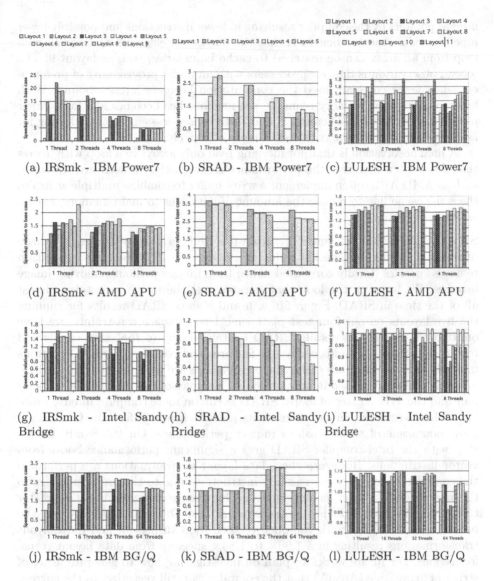

Fig. 5. Benchmark performance results on different platforms with varying threads.

On the Sandy Bridge, data layouts only sped up the computation by $1.11\times$. Since, the base case was already running at over 85 % of peak memory bandwidth. On the other processors, performance is significantly worse for the base case. A related trend is that improvements from data layouts are more significant at lower core counts. This implies two conclusions. First compute-bound codes also benefit from data layout transformations. In the case of Sandy Bridge where there are enough stream prefetchers for the base code and enough bandwidth to feed a few, but not, all, cores merging arrays reduces the number of registers used as pointers by the compiler resulting in fewer instructions and possibly fewer pipeline stalls. Another benefit is that the number of elements accessed in each loop from an array can be matched to cache boundaries, such as layout 9. The second observation is that for processors with an under provisioning of prefetchers when fewer cores are used the computation becomes latency-bound. With fewer cores to issue memory requests, the memory bus becomes idle for a larger percentage of the time. Therefore, bandwidth is used less efficiently, allowing for larger speedups when the core uses it more effectively.

A final observation is that not merging read only arrays in a loop with arrays that are written increases the performance significantly. Modern architectures, such as AMD APU, often implement a write buffer to combine multiple writes to the same cache line to reduce the amount of data sent to main memory, known as Write-Combining [1].

SRAD. The SRAD benchmark [7] from the Rodinia suite performs the image processing calculation speckle reducing anisotropic diffusion. The algorithm removes speckles (locally correlated noise) from images without removing image features. We focus on the loop that iterates over the image as it takes almost all of the time in SRAD. Figure 5b, e, h and k show SRAD results for running the five layouts on our four test platforms. Due to space constraints, we have omitted the five layout details. SRAD contains many of the same trends and results as IRSmk, but adds some new features and complexity. SRAD contains multiple loops so there are cases where two arrays are used together in one loop and only one array is used in another loop. Examples of this are the IN, IS loop pair and the JW, JE set of loops. SRAD is run on more compute intense problems where vectorization can increase its performance significantly. Our results show how some of these tensions impact performance. On the Sandy Bridge chip with the Intel compiler SRAD gets a significant performance boost from vector instructions. However, when data layout transformations are performed the compiler no longer vectorizes any instructions due to the use of pointers to the structures. The result is a performance hit from vectorization that is greater than the gain from data layout transformations. To confirm this we ran the base version of SRAD with compiler vectorization turned off and data layout transformations resulting in a 1.66× to 1.84× speedup from data layout transformations. For future work, we plan on investigating how to generate array of struct of array code (AoSoA) that the compiler can still vectorize. In the current tool, we ignore the array references where the loop has a vector pragma associated with it. Overall, performance gains on SRAD ranged from the minor 1.07× on most BG/Q thread counts to 3.68× on a single thread of an AMD APU.

LULESH. The largest application we focus on is the Livermore Unstructured Lagrange Explicit Shock Hydrodynamics (LULESH) mini-application [5]. LULESH solves the Sedov problem on a 3D hexahedral mesh. Different array sizes and the fact that they are used in various combinations throughout the loops in LULESH provide a larger search space for data layouts and tension for data layout transformations not found in the smaller benchmarks. The version of LULESH used in this study has undergone a variety of optimizations from the original published code, including aggressive loop fusion and elimination of temporary arrays [13]. Figure 5c, f, i and l show LULESH results for running the eleven layouts on our four test platforms. Due to space constraints, we have omitted the eleven layout details. We only show selected interesting thread counts (with the full data available in [18]).

Data layout transformations on LULESH were less profitable overall than for IRSmk. This is not surprising since LULESH is a larger application than IRSmk, and some arrays in LULESH are used together in certain places and not together in others. Therefore, combining them together will help and hurt performance simultaneously[2]. For example, layout 4 combines all four triples of x, y, z values together. Many of these triples are used together in many functions, but not all. However, most of the time layout 6 which leaves the triples separate is faster. A notable exception can be seen on Power7 for a single thread, which has the most cache, but the least bandwidth. It also suffers the most from not getting good prefetching as shown by the IRSmk results.

The most interesting result from LULESH is that in most cases it seems the code, not the hardware, is dictating the best data layout. On the AMD APU, Intel Sandy Bridge and BG/Q the list of the best layouts always includes 8 and 10 and usually, includes 2 and 3. However, the Power7 is an outlier with its best layout being 11 for all thread counts by a significant margin for the reasons explained above. For LULESH, as with IRSmk and SRAD, data layouts impacted the Sandy Bridge system the least with the largest speedup seen being only 1.02×. There are a few likely reasons for this. First, as with IRSmk, the Sandy Bridge architecture should be able to prefetch many streams at once. Also, in the case of bundling indirect accesses, the large re-order window of the Sandy Bridge might hide memory latency better than the other chips. Finally, the Intel compiler used on this platform was the best at generating SIMD instructions for some of the compute bound loops of LULESH. Some of the data transformations result in the compiler no longer generating SIMD instructions and, therefore, while data layouts save on data motion in memory-bound portions of the code they can sometimes hurt performance in the compute bound sections.

5.3   Automatic Data Layout Results

Table 2 shows the speedup of the best manual layout and the automated layout relative to the base layout. The results demonstrate that automated layouts can come close to the best manual layout in most cases. In one particular case, 8 Threads on Power7 for LULESH, automated layout improved performance as compared to manual layouts. For SRAD, automated results were close to the best manual results for Power7 and BG/Q. However, the results fell behind manual results for AMD APU and Sandy Bridge. In both cases, we suspect that the data layout transformation inadvertently disabled some compiler optimizations, especially vectorization in the case of Sandy Bridge. (All results in this section were obtained without enabling the vectorization test at the start of the automatic layout algorithm).

---

[2] This phenomenon motivates future work on redistributing data layouts across phases.

Table 2. Speedup of best manual layout (ML) and automated layout (AL) speedup relative to base layout

Benchmark	Power7-8Threads	AMD APU-4Threads	Sandy Bridge-8Threads	BG/Q-64Threads
IRSmk ML	4.70	1.46	1.11	2.20
IRSmk AL	4.67	1.43	1.10	2.08
LULESH ML	1.43	1.50	1.02	1.10
LULESH AL	1.58	1.46	0.96	1.07
SRAD ML	1.35	3.13	1.00	1.08
SRAD AL	1.20	2.55	0.46^a	0.98

[a]Assuming vector pragma is not specified. If vector pragma is specified then results is same as ML.

6 Related Work

Past research has proposed various data layout optimization techniques [6,8,9]. Here, we present a brief survey of past work, focusing on aspects that are most closely related to our work.

Zhang et al. [20] introduced a data layout framework that targets on-chip cache locality, specifically reducing shared cache conflicts while observing data patterns across threads. Using polyhedral analysis, their framework rearranges data layout tiles to reduce on-chip shared cache conflicts. However, their optimization currently works with single arrays. In contrast, our approach works on merging multiple arrays and operates at the element level rather than tiles. Henretty et al. [11] presented a data layout framework to optimize stencil operations on short-SIMD architectures. Their work specifically targets stream alignment conflicts on vector registers and uses a dimension transposition method (non-linear data layout optimization) to mitigate the conflicts. In comparison, our approach works for more general applications, not just stencil code. Also, our work did not specifically address the impact of data layout on vectorization. Ding and Kennedy [9] introduced a data-regrouping algorithm, which has similarities to our work on automatic selection of data layouts. Their compiler analysis merges multi-dimensional arrays based on a profitability cache analysis. Dynamic regrouping was also provided for layout optimization at runtime. Experimental results show significant improvement in cache and TLB hierarchy. However, their results were all obtained on uniprocessor systems and it is unclear how their approach works in the presence of data aliasing. Raman et al. [17] used data layout transformations to reduce false sharing and improve spatial locality in multi-threaded applications. They use an affinity based graph approach (similar to our approach) to select candidates. Inter-procedural aliasing issues arising due to pointers is not addressed in this work. Our work is intended to explore data layout transformations more broadly, not just for false sharing and spatial locality. Using polyhedral layout optimization, Lu et al. [15] developed a data layout optimization for future NUCA CMP architectures. Their work reduces shared cache conflict on such architectures. Simulation results show significant reductions in remote accesses. Finally, a number of papers, [10,12,16,19] have explored the integration of loop and data layout transformations. To the best of our knowledge, our work is the first to support both user-specified and automatic AoS data layout transformations, while allowing the user to provide a data layout specification file. Our results on the LULESH mini-application demonstrates the importance of data layout transformations on modern multicore processors.

7   Conclusions

This paper establishes the foundation for a new approach to supporting portable performance of scientific codes across HPC platforms. The upgraded TALC source-to-source transformation tool permits application developers to maintain one "neutral" data layout source code and explore architecture specific array layouts. The new automated portion of TALC can analyze the original source code based on platform characteristics and produces a new source code with new array data layouts ready to be compiled and run on that system. The results for the three test codes show that manual layouts improve performance by $1.10\times$ to $22.23\times$ for IRSmk, $1.00\times$ to $3.68\times$ for SRAD and $1.02\times$ to $1.82\times$ for LULESH with results varying with thread count and architecture. The automated algorithm achieves 95–99% of the best layout manual layout performance for IRSmk. For LULESH the automated approach achieves 90% of the best layout performance on all processors. For SRAD, automated results achieves 78% of best manual layout performance for all architectures except for Intel Sandybridge where layouts interfered with vectorization provided by Intel compiler.

Our future direction is to expand the flexibility of constraints on the original source code to include manipulation of multi-dimensional arrays. Finally, we also need to include enriched layouts (such as AoSoA) that reduce interference with vectorization. Another interesting direction to pursue is to develop specialized data layouts for accelerators such as GPU and Xeon Phi. We look forward to pursuing these challenges in the future.

Acknowledgments. We thank the anonymous reviewers for their feedback to improve the presentation of the paper. This work was prepared by LLNL under Contract DE-AC52-07NA27344 (LLNL-CONF-672056).

References

1. AMD64 Architecture Programmer's Manual Volume 2
2. ASC Sequoia Benchmark. https://asc.llnl.gov/sequoia/benchmarks/
3. Extended TALC Infrastructure. https://github.com/rose-compiler/edg4x-rose/tree/master/projects/TALCDataLayout
4. ROSE Compiler Infrastructure. http://rosecompiler.org/

5. Hydrodynamics Challenge Problem. Technical report LLNL-TR-490254, LLNL, July 2011. https://computation.llnl.gov/casc/ShockHydro

6. Calder, B., Krintz, C., John, S., Austin, T.: Cache-conscious data placement. In: ACM ASPLOS VIII, pp. 139–149 (1998)

7. Che, S., Boyer, M., Meng, J., Tarjan, D., Sheaffer, J.W., Lee, S.H., Skadron, K.: Rodinia: a benchmark suite for heterogeneous computing. In: IEEE IISWC (2009)

8. Chilimbi, T.M., Hill, M.D., Larus, J.R.: Cache-conscious structure layout. In: PLDI 1999, pp. 1–12 (1999)

9. Ding, C., Kennedy, K.: Inter-array data regrouping. In: Carter, L., Ferrante, J. (eds.) LCPC 1999. LNCS, vol. 1863, pp. 149–163. Springer, Heidelberg (2000)

10. Ding, C., Kennedy, K.: Improving effective bandwidth through compiler enhancement of global cache reuse. In: IEEE IPDPS 2001, p. 10, April 2001

11. Henretty, T., Stock, K., Pouchet, L.-N., Franchetti, F., Ramanujam, J., Sadayappan, P.: Data layout transformation for stencil computations on short-vector SIMD architectures. In: Knoop, J. (ed.) CC 2011. LNCS, vol. 6601, pp. 225–245. Springer, Heidelberg (2011)

12. Kandemir, M., Choudhary, A., Ramanujam, J., Banerjee, P.: A framework for inter-procedural locality optimization using both loop and data layout transformations. In: IEEE ICPP 1999, pp. 95–102 (1999)

13. Karlin, I., McGraw, J., Keasler, J., Still, C.: Tuning the LULESH mini-app for current and future hardware. In: NECDC 2012, December 2012

14. Keasler, J., Jones, T., Quinlan, D.: TALC: a simple C language extension for improved performance and code maintainability. In: 9th LCI International Conference on High-Performance Clustered Computing, April 2008

15. Lu, Q., Alias, C., Bondhugula, U., Henretty, T., Krishnamoorthy, S., Ramanujam, J., Rountev, A., Sadayappan, P., Chen, Y., Lin, H., Ngai, T.F.: Data layout transformation for enhancing data locality on NUCA chip multiprocessors. In: IEEE PACT 2009, pp. 348–357, September 2009

16. O'Boyle, M.F.P., Knijnenburg, P.M.W.: Efficient parallelization using combined loop and data transformations. In: PACT 1999, p. 283 (1999)

17. Raman, E., Hundt, R., Mannarswamy, S.: Structure layout optimization for multithreaded programs. In: IEEE CGO 2007, pp. 271–282 (2007)

18. Sharma, K., Karlin, I., Keasler, J., McGraw, J.R., Sarkar, V.: User-specified and automatic data layout selection for portable performance, April 2013. http://cohesion.rice.edu/engineering/computerscience/tr/TR_Download.cfm?SDID=307

19. Taylan Kandemir, M.: Improving whole-program locality using intra-procedural and inter-procedural transformations. J. Parallel Distrib. Comput. 65(5), 564–582 (2005)

20. Zhang, Y., Ding, W., Liu, J., Kandemir, M.: Optimizing data layouts for parallel computation on multicores. In: PACT 2011, pp. 143–154, October 2011

Automatic Data Layout Optimizations for GPUs

Klaus Kofler[1](✉), Biagio Cosenza[1,2], and Thomas Fahringer[1]

[1] DPS, University of Innsbruck, Innsbruck, Austria
{klaus,tf}@dps.uibk.ac.at
[2] AES, TU Berlin, Berlin, Germany
cosenza@tu-berlin.de

Abstract. Memory optimizations have became increasingly important in order to fully exploit the computational power of modern GPUs. The data arrangement has a big impact on the performance, and it is very hard for GPU programmers to identify a well-suited data layout. Classical data layout transformations include grouping together data fields that have similar access patterns, or transforming Array-of-Structures (AoS) to Structure-of-Arrays (SoA).

This paper presents an optimization infrastructure to automatically determine an improved data layout for OpenCL programs written in AoS layout. Our framework consists of two separate algorithms: The first one constructs a graph-based model, which is used to split the AoS input struct into several clusters of fields, based on hardware dependent parameters. The second algorithm selects a good per-cluster data layout (e.g., SoA, AoS or an intermediate layout) using a decision tree. Results show that the combination of both algorithms is able to deliver higher performance than the individual algorithms. The layouts proposed by our framework result in speedups of up to 2.22, 1.89 and 2.83 on an AMD FirePro S9000, NVIDIA GeForce GTX 480 and NVIDIA Tesla k20m, respectively, over different AoS sample programs, and up to 1.18 over a manually optimized program.

1 Introduction

With the advent of new massively parallel architectures such as GPUs, many research projects focus on memory optimizations. In order to exploit the properties of the memory hierarchy, a key aspect is to maximize the reuse of data.

In this context, **data layout transformation** represents a very interesting class of optimizations. Two typical examples are: organizing data with similar access patterns in structures or rearranging array of structures (AoS) as structure of arrays (SoA). Recent work extends the classical SoA layout by introducing AoSoA (Array of Structure of Array) [16], also called ASA [14]. In this paper we prefer the expression **tiled-AoS**, but we remark that all approaches exploit the same idea: mixing AoS and SoA in a unique data layout.

1.1 Motivation

In this work, we investigate an automatic memory optimization method that can be easily ported to different GPU architectures, using OpenCL as programming

© Springer-Verlag Berlin Heidelberg 2015
J.L. Träff et al. (Eds.): Euro-Par 2015, LNCS 9233, pp. 263–274, 2015.
DOI: 10.1007/978-3-662-48096-0_21

model. We combine together two different optimization strategies: we try to group together data fields with similar data access patterns and find the best data layout for each of these clusters.

Considering SAMPO [7] as an example, using a struct containing twelve fields. The number of possible ways to partition these twelve fields is equal to 4,213,597. Considering that this program has minimum run-time of 65 s on an AMD FirePro S9000, depending on the data layout, just evaluating all the possible partitions (i.e., clusters) would take more than eight years.

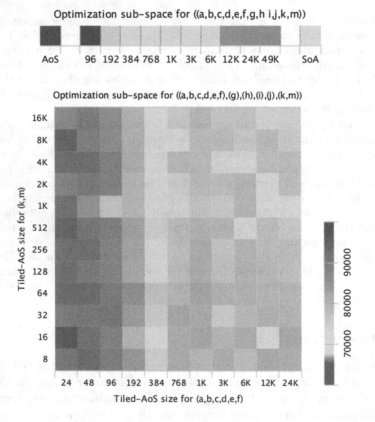

Fig. 1. Excerpt of SAMPO's optimization space. Execution times vary from 65 s (in red) to 104 s (in blue) (Color figure online).

The exploration of the whole search space, including both fields' clustering and data tiling (i.e., finding the best data layout for each of these clusters) would take more than 400 years.

Figure 1 shows a subset of the optimization space for SAMPO. The heat-map on top depicts all possible data tiling for the one-cluster grouping of all the twelve data fields. For this partition, the un-tiled AoS layout is slow (blue); by increasing the data tile-size the run-time decreases (shown in red), and with data tile-size bigger than 12 K it also outperforms the SoA layout. The lower heat-map shows the performance results while applying the specific data tiling suggested by our algorithm (Sect. 3.1). The fastest version of the shown optimization subspace is achieved when we use a tile-size of 16 for the smaller struct containing two fields, 24 for the bigger struct with six fields, and having the other fields in a SoA layout. This example program also shows that the best tile-size can be different within the same code and different clusters: when using only one cluster, the highest performance is achieved with large data tiles; however, different clustering delivers better performance with smaller data tiling sizes. This suggests that the optimal data tile-size highly depends on the size of the individual cluster.

Our work is the first approach which automatically tackles the two problems mentioned above. Our contributions are:

- A Kernel Data Layout Graph (*KDLG*) model extracted from an input OpenCL kernel; each vertex weight represents structure field's size and the edge weight expresses intra-data field memory distance.
- A two-phase algorithm: first, a *KDLG* partitioning algorithm — driven by a device-dependent graph model — splits the original graph into partitions with similar data access patterns; second, for each partition we exploit a data layout selection method — driven by a device-dependent layout calculation — selects the most suitable layout from AoS, SoA and tiled-AoS layouts.
- An evaluation of five OpenCL applications on three GPUs showing a speedup of up to 2.83.

2 Related Work

The problem of finding an optimal layout is not only NP-hard, but also hard to approximate [11]. Raman et al. [9] introduced a graph based model to optimize structure layout for multi-threaded programs. They developed a semi-automatic tool which produces layout transformations optimized for both false sharing and data locality. Our work uses a different graph based model encoding the variables memory distance and data structure size, in order to provide a completely automatic approach; we also support AoS, SoA and tiled-AoS layouts. Kendermi et al. [5] introduced an inter-procedural optimization framework using both loop optimizations and data layout transformation; our method does not apply to a single function only, but can span over multiple functions.

Data layout transformations such as SoA conversion have been described to be the core optimization techniques for scaling to massively threaded systems such as GPUs [13]. DL presented data layout transformations for heterogeneous computing [15]; DL supports AoS, SoA and ASTA and implements and automatic data marshaling framework to easily change data layout arrangements. Our work supports similar data layouts, but we provide an automatic approach for the layout selection. MATOG [16] introduces a DSL-like, library-based approach which optimizes GPU codes using either static and empirical profiling to adjust parameters or to change the kernel implementation. MATOG supports AoS, SoA and AoSoA with 32 threads (to match the warp size on CUDA) on multi-dimensional layouts and builds an application-dependent decision tree to select the best layout. Dymaxion [4] is an API that allows programmers to optimize memory mapping on heterogeneous platforms. It extends NVIDIA's CUDA API with a data index transformation and a latency hiding mechanism based on CUDA stream. Dymaxion C++ [3] further extends prior work. However, it does not relieve the programmer from selecting a good data layout.

3   Method

Our approach tries to answer two complex questions: (1) What is the best way to group data fields? (2) For each field cluster, what is the best data layout?

Once clusters have been identified, for each cluster we try to find the best possible layout within that cluster (i.e., *homogenous layout*). Our model supports AoS, SoA, as well as tiled-AoS with different tile-sizes.

In the next section we introduce a novel graph based model, where we encode data layout, field's size and field locality information. The presented two-step approach (1) identifies field partitions (i.e., clusters of fields) with high locality within intra-partition fields and (2) determines an efficient data layout for each partition.

3.1   Kernel Data Layout Graph Model

We define a Kernel Data Layout Graph ($KDLG$) as an undirected, complete graph whose nodes represent fields of the input *struct* (assumed to have AoS layout). The $KDLG$ has two labeling functions: σ for verteices, representing the field's data size; δ for edges, representing the memory distance (or inverse-affinity) between fields. Formally, a $KDLG$ is a quadruple defined as follows:

$$KDLG = (F, E, \sigma, \delta)$$

where F is the set of all fields of the struct, which corresponds to the set of nodes in the $KDLG$. $E = F^2 \setminus \{(x,x)|x \in F\}$ is the set of all edges $e = \{(f_1, f_2)|f_1, f_2 \in F\}$. The mapping function $\sigma : F \to \mathbb{N}$ returns the size of a field f in bytes, e.g., if f refers to a field of type *int*, then $\sigma(f) = 4$, according to the OpenCL specifications. $\delta : E \to \{\mathbb{N} \cup \infty\}$ returns the weight of an edge e. The mapping function $\delta((f_1, f_2))$ is defined as the *memory distance* between the two fields f_1 and f_2 by counting the number of unique memory locations, in bytes, touched by the program between the instruction where they are accessed.

We borrow the idea of memory distance from [9] and extend it with the actual data type size, which is important to distinguish different memory behaviors.

The $KDLG$ is based on an OpenCL kernel. The set F will have a vertex for each field defined in the structure, which is passed as an argument to the device kernel function. For each vertex f, the σ function returns the actual type's size in bytes of the corresponding field of f.

```
struct T {
    float a, b, c;
    double d;
};
__kernel fun(__global T *t) {
    float a, b, c;
    double d;
    int id = get_global_id(0);
    double sum = 0;
    for(int i=id; i<id+32; i++)
        sum += t[i].a * t[i].b;
    t[id].c = sum;
};
```

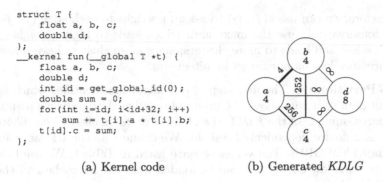

(a) Kernel code   (b) Generated *KDLG*

Fig. 2. A *KDLG* generated by a sample input data layout and kernel. Darker edges show fields that are closer in memory (smaller δ).

Figure 2b displays the *KDLG* generated from the code shown in Fig. 2a: The fields a and b are always accessed consecutively, therefore $\delta(a, b)$ is 4 bytes. c is accessed after the for loop with 32 iterations, therefore $\delta(c, b) = 252$ and $\delta(c, a) = 256$ bytes, resulting from the 32 iterations that access $2 \cdot 4$ bytes in each iteration. d is never accessed, therefore its distance from other fields is ∞.

Our graph based model unrolls all loops before starting the analysis. Therefore, it assumes that loop bounds are known at compile time. If not known, we use a OpenCL kernel specific loop size inference heuristic to have a good approximation (see Sect. 3.1). Our analysis focuses on global memory operations, as they are considerably slower than local and private memory operations

Let $MI(f)$ define the set of all global memory instructions (loads and stores) involving the data field f. Our distance function δ between two fields f_1 and f_2 is defined by taking into account the maximum-memory-distance path between the accessing instructions $i_1 \in MI(f_1)$ and $i_2 \in MI(f_2)$.

In order to calculate δ, we use a data flow analysis where each node of the control flow graph (CFG) consists of a single instruction. The function $\sigma(i)$ returns the number of bytes which are written to/read from the global memory in instruction i. We define IN and OUT as

$$IN_i[j] = \min_{x \in pred(j)} (OUT_i[x]) \qquad OUT_i[j] = \begin{cases} 0 & \text{if } i = j \\ IN_i[j] + \sigma(j) & \text{if } i \neq j \end{cases}$$

We define a instruction-memory distance function $MD(i_1, i_2)$ as

$$MD(i_1, i_2) = \max(OUT_{i_1}[i_2], OUT_{i_2}[i_1])$$

so that $MD(i_1, i_2) = MD(i_2, i_1)$. We calculate $\delta(f_1, f_2)$, the memory distance between the fields f_1 and f_2, as the maximum memory distance between all instructions in $MI(f_1)$ and $MI(f_2)$ as follows:

$$\delta(f_1, f_2) = \max \left(\max_{i \in MI(f_1), j \in MI(f_2)} MD(i, j) \right)$$

Therefore, we can use $\delta(f_1, f_2)$ to assign a weight to each edge $(f_1, f_2) \in E$.

We conservatively use the maximum, which leads to higher weights on the *KDLG*'s edges and leads to more clusters; since more clusters have a lower risk of performance loss on our target architectures.

KDLG Partitioning. The first step of our algorithm identifies which fields in the input data structure should be grouped together. Formally, we assume that a field partitioning C of the *KDLG* (i.e., field clusters) is *good* if $\forall e \in C | \delta(e) < \epsilon$, where ϵ is a device dependent threshold. We define ϵ as the L1 cache line size of the individual GPUs. The values of ϵ are listed in Table 1. We use this value as it is the smallest entity that can be loaded from the L1 cache and therefore should be loaded at once.

We propose a strategy based on Kruskal's Minimum-weight Spanning Tree (MST) algorithm [8] that extends the classical MST algorithm with an ϵ-based early termination criteria and multiple clusters of nodes (i.e., struct fields).

KDLG-PARTITIONING(F, E, δ, ϵ)

```
1   C = ∅
2   for each field f ∈ F
3       C = C ∪ {{f}}
4   E_ε = {e ∈ E : δ(e) < ε}
5   for each edge (f_1, f_2) ∈ E_ε
6       c_1 = {x ∈ C|f_1 ∈ x}
7       c_2 = {x ∈ C|f_2 ∈ x}
8       if c_1 ≠ c_2
9           C = (C ∖ {c_2, c_1}) ∪ {c_1 ∪ c_2}
10  return C
```

It takes as input a *KDLG*, previously computed from an input kernel, and a threshold ϵ. It starts by creating a partitioning with $|F|$ sets, each of which contains one field in F (lines 1–3). Line 4 initializes E_ϵ for all edges in E with a weight smaller then ϵ, according to the weighting function δ. The **for** loop in lines 5–9 checks, for each edge (f_1, f_2), whether the endpoints f_1 and f_2 belong to the same set. If they do, then the edge is discarded. Otherwise, the two sets are merged in line 9. The complexity of this algorithm is $\mathcal{O}(|E| \cdot |F|)$. Figure 3 shows three possible output partitions that can be generated from the graph seen in Fig. 2b using different ϵ values.

Loop Bounds Approximation. When generating the test data to select ϵ we use loops with a fixed number of iterations, in order to to accurately understand the memory distance between two memory accesses. In real world codes, the actual number of iterations is often not known at compile time. Therefore we use a heuristic that is specifically designed for OpenCL kernel codes. If the number of loop iterations are determined by compile-time constants, we use the actual number of iterations. If not, we apply a heuristic to approximate the number of iterations: When a loop performs one iteration for each OpenCL work-item [6] of the work-group [6], we estimate it has 256 iterations, as the work-group size

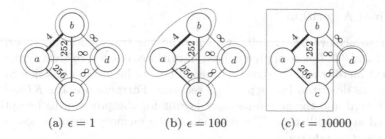

Fig. 3. Different output partitions using different ϵ values on a *KDLG*.

is usually in this range. When a loop performs one iteration for each work-item of the NDRange [6], we assume it will have $1 \cdot 10^6$ iterations. If the number of iterations is neither constant nor linked to the work-group size or NDRange, we estimate it to have $512 \cdot 10^3$ iterations. The estimation of loop bounds is not very sensitive: we only need to distinguish short loops, which may not completely flush the L1 cache, from long ones.

3.2 Per-Cluster Layout Selection

After KDLG-PARTITIONING, we assume that each field in the same cluster has similar memory behavior. Therefore, all the fields within a cluster should have the same data layout arrangement, e.g., tiled-AoS with a specific tile-size.

To understand what layout is best for a given cluster, we generate different kernels corresponding to a simple one-cluster *KDLG* where δ is roughly the same for each pair of fields. The kernel consists of a single for-loop with a constant number of iterations n. The value of n comprises all powers of two from 128 to 16384. We evaluated the performance of these kernels with different combinations of loop size n, number of structure fields m, and tile-size t.

From the results we derive a device-dependent function SELECT-TILESIZE $(\sigma(c))$ which returns the suggested layout for a cluster c, where $\sigma(c) = \sum_{f \in c} \sigma(f)$ and $\sigma(f)$ returns the size of the field f in bytes. SELECT-TILESIZE is implemented using a decision tree, constructed by the C5.0 algorithm [12]. $\sigma(c)$ is the only attribute the decision tree depends on. The potential target classes are AoS , SoA and all powers of two from 2^1 to 2^{15}. The performance measurements of the aforementioned kernels are used to generate the training data. For each kernel we create a training pattern for the fastest tile-size as well as all other tile-sizes that are less than 1% slower than the fastest one. These training patterns consist only of the size of the structure $\sigma(c)$, which is the only feature while the used tile-size acts as the target value. Generating training patterns not only for the fastest tile-size but for all which achieve at least 99% of it, as well as several training patterns for different structures with the same size, may lead to contradicting training patterns. However, our experiments demonstrated that the resulting decision tree is more accurate and less prone to overfitting. C5.0 was used with default settings; its run-time was about 1ms, depending on the input.

3.3 Final Algorithm

In order to achieve best results, we combine the two algorithms described in Sects. 3.1 and 3.2. Before applying these algorithms, one has to identify the device dependent factor ϵ and construct a decision tree to be used in function SELECT-TILESIZE, as described in the previous sections. Furthermore, the $KDLG$ graph is constructed and the actual memory layout for the program to be optimized is selected at compile time. The selection of the memory layout is described by the following pseudo code:

LAYOUTOPTIMIZE(F, E, δ, ϵ)
1   $L = \varnothing$
2   $C =$ KDLG-PARTITIONING(F, E, δ, ϵ)
3   **for** each cluster $c \in C$
4       $t =$ SELECT-TILESIZE$(\sigma(c))$
5       $L = L \cup \{(c, t)\}$
6   **return** L

Line 2 calls the KDLG-Partitioning algorithm and returns a set of clusters C in which the corresponding structure should be split. Then the decision tree determines an efficient tiling factor for each of these clusters and stores the resulting pair (cluster, tile-size) (line 3–5).

4 Experimental Results

To verify the validity of our approach we implemented a prototype of our framework and observed its performance on several OpenCL applications. The deployment of our system is split into two parts: A device dependent part which has to be performed once for each GPU (installation time), and a program dependent part, which is executed at the compile time of the program. These two parts are depicted in Fig. 4. The device dependent part consists of identifying the L1 cache line size to be used as ϵ and running a set of training programs to collect the information needed to build the decision tree as defined in Sect. 3.2. Collecting all the necessary data requires to run many benchmarks takes 196, 158 and 299 min on the FirePro, GeForce and Tesla, respectively. The program dependent part constructs a $KDLG$ graph for the structure to be optimized in the corresponding program. This graph is hardware independent. By combining the $KDLG$ graph with the hardware depended ϵ we split the struct into several clusters (Sect. 3.1). For each of these clusters we query the hardware dependent decision tree to obtain the tile-size to be used (Sect. 3.2).

To evaluate our framework we run different programs on three different GPUs. The test programs are listed in Table 2. In each program we focus on the structure with the most instances and try to optimize its layout. The result of our framework on five tested programs is shown in Table 2. The data layouts proposed by our system always reach at least the performance of the AoS data layout. In the following paragraphs we give more details about three example

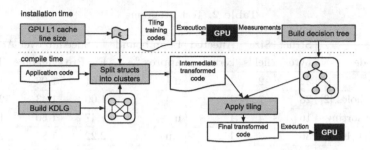

Fig. 4. Work-flow of our data layout optimization process.

Table 1. Properties determined using our algorithms

Hardware	ϵ	Decision tree
AMD FirePro S9000	64	≤ 20, > 48: ≤ 32 → 32, AoS; 16384; ≤ 12 → 512, 1024
NVIDIA GeForce GTX 480	128	≤ 12, ≤ 96 → SoA, 512; ≤ 8 → SoA, AoS
NVIDIA Tesla K20m	128	≤ 48, ≤ 96 → 32768, 16384; ≤ 20 → 8192, SoA

test cases. For all charts we use AoS as a baseline and report the speedup of four transformed versions: SoA, the version generated after applying the *KDLG* algorithm and splitting the structure if applicable, a tiled AoS version were we use the tile-size proposed by our hardware dependent decision tree-based algorithm, and the final result of our framework as described in Sect. 3.3.

The first test case that we used to evaluate our framework is N-body, which performs a direct summation of the forces of all particles on every other particle. The struct in the used implementation consists of two fields with a size of 16 bytes each. As those fields have a big memory distance, the *KDLG*-based algorithm will split those fields into separate structs. Therefore, the result after applying the *KDLG*-based optimization is the same as when using the SoA layout. Furthermore, applying our tiling algorithm after the *KDLG*-based algorithm has no effect. The speedup achieved is shown in Fig. 5a. It clearly shows that the tiled version of the program is not only slower than the one in SoA data layout, but also slower than our baseline implementation. This applies to all tile-sizes

Table 2. Test programs

Test codes	Struct bytes	Size fields	Affected kernels	Loop bound approx.[a]	Speedup over AoS		
					FirePro	GeForce	Tesla
N-body	32	2	1	n	1.01	1.06	1.01
BlackScholes [2]	28	7	1	–	1.00	1.43	2.83
Bitonic sorting	16	4	1	u	1.47	1.50	1.38
LavaMD [10]	36	3	1	c,u	2.22	1.89	2.07
SAMPO	48	12	9	w,u	2.19	1.59	1.96

[a]Used Loop bound approximations Sect. 3.1: loop over all work-items in the NDRange (n), over the work-group size (g), with constant boundaries (c), with unknown boundaries (u)

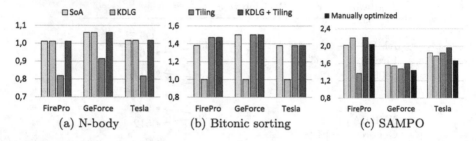

(a) N-body   (b) Bitonic sorting   (c) SAMPO

Fig. 5. Speedup over AoS implementation on two example applications using different data layouts.

we evaluated. However, since our framework uses a combination of two layout optimizations, it still correctly selects SoA, which is the data layout with the highest performance for this program on all tested GPUs.

Bitonic Sort [1] is a sorting algorithm optimized for massively parallel hardware such as GPUs. The implementation that we are using sorts a struct of four elements, where the first element acts as the sorting-key. As all elements are always moved together, the $KDLG$-based algorithm results in one single cluster for any $\epsilon \geq 4$. Therefore, the version generated by the $KDLG$-based algorithm is the same as AoS. The decision-tree-based tiling algorithm converts this layout into a tiled-AoS layout with a tile-size of 512 bytes for the FirePro and GeForce while it suggests to use SoA on the Tesla. The results can be found in Fig. 5b. It clearly shows that, although the $KDLG$-based algorithm fails to gain any improvement over AoS, the decision-tree-based algorithm as well as the combination of both algorithm exceeds the performance of the AoS based implementation by a factor of 1.38 to 1.5. Furthermore, it delivers performance that is comparable or superior than the one achieved by a SoA implementation.

SAMPO [7] is an agent-based mosquito point model in OpenCL, which is designed to simulate mosquito populations to understand how vector-borne illnesses (e.g., malaria) may spread. The version available online is already manually optimized for AMD GPUs. Therefore, we ported this version to a pure AoS layout, where each agent is represented by a single struct with twelve fields. The measurements are displayed in Fig. 5c. The results clearly show, that SoA yields a much better performance than AoS on all tested GPUs. Applying the *KDLG*-based algorithm already results in a speedup between 1.54 and 2.18 on the three tested GPUs, which is within ±10% of the SoA version. Applying tiling to the AoS implementation shows good results on the NVIDIA GPUs. Also the AMD GPU benefits from tiling, but it does not reach the performance of the SoA version or the version optimized with the *KDLG*-based algorithm. Applying tiling to the latter version further increases the performance on all evaluated GPUs and leads to a speedup over the AoS version of 2.19, 1.59 and 1.96 on the FirePro, GeForce and Tesla, respectively outperforming any other version we tested. Even the manually optimized implementation is outperformed by 7%, 10% and 18% on the FirePro, GeForce and Tesla, respectively.

5   Discussion

The results clearly show, that programs with AoS data layout are not well suited for GPUs. SoA delivers a much higher performance on all GPU/program combinations we tested. However, also SoA fails to achieve the maximum performance in some cases. We observed that a tiled-AoS can achieve results that are usually equal or better compared to the ones achieved with an SoA layout. But tiled-AoS is not suited for all programs. Similarly, splitting structures in several smaller ones based on a *KDLG* is beneficial for most programs. However, also this technique fails to improve the performance of some applications . Therefore, combining these two algorithms leads to much better overall results than each of them can achieve individually. This is underlined by the results of SAMPO, where the combination of both algorithms does not only outperform the results of each algorithm applied individually, but also leads to higher performance than obtained by both, a SoA layout and the manually optimized layout.

6   Conclusions

We presented a system to automatically determine an improved data layout for OpenCL programs. Our framework consists of two separate algorithms: The first one constructs a *KDLG*, which is used to split a given struct into several clusters based on the hardware dependent parameter ϵ. The second algorithm constructs a decision tree, which is used to determine the tile-size for a certain structure when converting it from AoS to tiled-AoS or SoA layouts.

The combination of both algorithms is crucial, as using only one of them often leads to no improvement over AoS. The layouts proposed by our framework result in speedups of up to 2.22, 1.89 and 2.83 on an AMD FirePro S9000, NVIDIA GeForce GTX 480 and NVIDIA Tesla k20m, respectively.

Acknowledgments. This project was funded by the FWF Austrian Science Fund as part of project I 1523 "Energy-Aware Autotuning for Scientific Applications" and by the Interreg IV Italy-Austria 5962-273 EN-ACT funded by ERDF and the province of Tirol.

References

1. Batcher, K.E.: Sorting networks and their applications. In: Proceedings of the Spring Joint Computer Conference, AFIPS 1968 (Spring), 30 April - 2 May 1968, pp. 307–314. ACM, New York (1968)
2. Black, F., Scholes, M.: The pricing of options and corporate liabilities. J. Polit. Econ. **81**, 637–654 (1973)
3. Che, S., Meng, J., Skadron, K.: Dymaxion++: a directive-based API to optimize data Layout and memory mapping for heterogeneous systems. In: AsHes 2014 (2014)
4. Che, S., Sheaffer, J.W., Skadron, K.: Dymaxion: optimizing memory access patterns for heterogeneous systems. In: SC 2011, pp. 13:1–13:11. ACM, New York (2011)
5. Kandemir, M., Choudhary, A., Ramanujam, J., Banerjee, P.: A framework for interprocedural locality optimization using both loop and data layout transformations. In: Proceedings of the International Conference on Parallel Processing, pp. 95–102 (1999)
6. Khronos Group: OpenCL 1.2 Specification, April 2012
7. Kofler, K., Davis, G., Gesing, S.: Sampo: an agent-based mosquito point model in opencl. In: ADS 2014, pp. 5:1–5:10. Society for Computer Simulation International, San Diego (2014)
8. Kruskal, J.B.: On the shortest spanning subtree of a graph and the traveling salesman problem. Proc. Am. Math. Soc. **7**(1), 48–50 (1956)
9. Raman, E., Hundt, R., Mannarswamy, S.: Structure layout optimization for multithreaded programs. In: CGO 2007, pp. 271–282. IEEE Computer Society, Washington (2007)
10. Rodinia: LavaMD, November 2014. http://www.cs.virginia.edu/~skadron/wiki/rodinia/index.php/LavaMD
11. Rubin, S., Bodík, R., Chilimbi, T.: An efficient profile-analysis framework for data-layout optimizations. In: POPL 2002, pp. 140–153. ACM, New York (2002)
12. RULEQUEST RESEARCH: Data mining tools see5 and c5.0, October 2014. https://www.rulequest.com/see5-info.html
13. Stratton, J.A., Rodrigues, C.I., Sung, I.J., Chang, L.W., Anssari, N., Liu, G.D., Hwu, W.W., Obeid, N.: Algorithm and data optimization techniques for scaling to massively threaded systems. IEEE Comput. **45**(8), 26–32 (2012)
14. Strzodka, R.: Data layout optimization for multi-valued containers in opencl. J. Parallel Distrib. Comput. **72**(9), 1073–1082 (2012)
15. Sung, I.J., Anssari, N., Stratton, J.A., Hwu, W.W.: Data layout transformation exploiting memory-level parallelism in structured grid many-core applications. Int. J. Parallel Program. **40**(1), 4–24 (2012)
16. Weber, N., Goesele, M.: Auto-tuning complex array layouts for gpus. In: Proceedings of Eurographics Symposium on Parallel Graphics and Visualization, EGPGV14, EG

Parallel and Distributed
Data Management

Performance Impacts with Reliable Parallel File Systems at Exascale Level

Ramon Nou[1](✉), Alberto Miranda[1], and Toni Cortes[1,2]

[1] Barcelona Supercomputing Center, Barcelona, Spain
ramon.nou@bsc.es
[2] Technical University of Catalonia, Barcelona, Spain

Abstract. The introduction of Exascale storage into production systems will lead to an increase on the number of storage servers needed by parallel file systems. In this scenario, parallel file system designers should move from the current replication configurations to the more space and energy efficient erasure-coded configurations between storage servers. Unfortunately, the current trends on energy efficiency are directed to creating less powerful clients, but a larger number of them (light-weight Exascale nodes), increasing the frequency of write requests and therefore creating more parity update requests. In this paper, we investigate RAID-5 and RAID-6 parity-based reliability organizations in Exascale storage systems. We propose two software mechanisms to improve the performance of write requests. The first mechanism reduces the number of operations to update a parity block, improving the performance of writes up to 200 %. The second mechanism allows applications to notify when reliability is needed by the data, delaying the parity calculation and improving the performance up to a 300 %. Using our proposals, traditional replication schemes can be replaced by reliability models like RAID-5 or RAID-6 without the expected performance loss.

1 Introduction

Nowadays, it seems clear that changes will need to be made to reliability planes in parallel file systems, once storage requirements reach into the Exascale orders of magnitude. Given the strong constraints on energy efficiency imposed on Exascale clusters [2,24,30], the current replication techniques used by parallel file systems (PFSs) to increase reliability and availability (where several copies of each datum are kept in independent storage nodes) can represent a huge penalty, since they multiply the investment and energy costs in the storage layer.

Parity based-reliability, where mathematical checksums are computed and stored to recover failed data, is a more suitable method in this scenario since it uses less storage resources than replication. As such, there is an increasing interest to support node-wide RAID-5/6 reliability schemes in current PFSs. For instance, Lustre [4] is planning to support file-level replication, and this technique can already be found in Gluster [13]. On the other hand, Panasas (with PanFS [20]) supports object/file level RAID configurations using triple parity

© Springer-Verlag Berlin Heidelberg 2015
J.L. Träff et al. (Eds.): Euro-Par 2015, LNCS 9233, pp. 277–288, 2015.
DOI: 10.1007/978-3-662-48096-0_22

data [21], and GPFS [27] also supports a similar configuration with the *declus-tered array* technique that can visualize all the JBOD disks individually [10].

In addition, there has been some interest on shifting the HPC cluster para-digm to include more energy efficient computing nodes. Currently, some projects (e.g. Montblanc [23], or Euroserver [11]) are attempting to create the next-generation supercomputers using mobile technology, moving away from the more standard and powerful nodes (i.e., x86 or PowerPC-based) to the more energy efficient ARM-based nodes, which usually have reduced performance capabili-ties. Thus, to account for this reduction in performance, the number of nodes needs to be increased to provide enough computing power and, as a result, there will be an undesired congestion on all I/O levels as more requests go through the I/O layer. Unfortunately, an increase in the number of I/O requests will also affect traditional parity-based reliability techniques. Increasing the number of data writes will accentuate the *partial stripes* and *small writes* problems [28] that typically affect these strategies: a small change to a datum will force the parity checksum to be recomputed and stored, which requires additional I/O operations as well as computation. Thus, introducing these node-wide reliabil-ity strategies into Exascale storage can cause a performance impact: updating a datum in RAID-5 requires four I/O requests (reading the original datum and the old parity and writing the new datum and the new parity) and six I/O requests in RAID-6 (due it uses two parity checksums). As we will show later, even though these additional requests can be distributed between storage servers to be processed in parallel, they can represent a loss of performance of up to 85 % for update operations when compared to storing raw data. In this situa-tion, it seems clear that optimizations over RAID parity calculations are needed to remove or alleviate this performance penalty and provide Exascale storage systems with alternatives for reliability. In this paper we propose a transparent (from the user perspective) I/O layer called the Write Cache Layer that reduces the number of parity updates for arbitrary reliability configurations. Finally, we also propose a novel method (Delayed Parity) that takes advantage of the collaboration between the PFS and the clients and, using this layer, allows appli-cations to delay parity computations. The analysis and design is evaluated with a simulator, using a write-only workload to focus on the issue that we are solving (read operations are not affected negatively).

The rest of the paper is organized as follows: In Sect. 2, we present the design of the Write Cache Layer. In Sect. 3, we describe the simulator and we evaluate our proposal. Section 4 describes related work. Finally, Sect. 5 states our conclu-sions and future work.

2   Partial Stripe Avoidance

In this section, we discuss the two strategies proposed to reduce the overhead of parity update operations. The first one (basic avoidance) actively reduces the number of read operations done on each write request, whereas the second one (delayed parity) delays the parity calculation until the application decides that it actually needs the reliability. These strategies are implemented within a new I/O layer called the Write Cache Layer (WCL) that sits on top the PFS' Object Storage Servers (OSSs) and directly communicates with them. More specifically, the WCL keeps all the metadata on parity blocks necessary to implement the proposed strategies, communicates with the PFS servers in order to allocate enough space to write full stripes and, whenever possible, transforms the different write access patterns into a series of non-overwriting I/O operations, so that our optimization techniques can be applied. Note that this transformation of access patterns can be done with already existing techniques (e.g. log file systems [25] or versioning [19]) that fall out of the scope of this paper. Also notice that the WCL only needs to take into account write operations to implement our proposed techniques and therefore read operations can follow through normally.

2.1 Basic Avoidance

Whenever stripes are rewritten, the PFS needs to read the original data blocks in order to be able to compute the new parity checksum. Our first proposal, the basic avoidance technique, reduces the number of data reads needed to write full stripes by avoiding these read operations of old data blocks. This is ensured because, as we have mentioned, the WCL can either detect a workload of non-overwriting writes (which should be the case of a big majority of HPC applications), or transform a mixed workload into a sequence of non-overwriting operations. To implement this mechanism, the WCL creates a *cache zone* or working zone using the available space in the storage devices connected to each OSS, and redirects all write operations to it (see Fig. 1.b). This effectively allows the WCL to treat all data writes as new data writes instead of updates, which allows to compute the parities based only on the new data written (i.e., avoiding the unnecessary reads of old data blocks). Once a stripe has been completely written and its parity checksums computed, the WCL simply moves (i.e., rewrites) the stripe back to its original placement into the OSS. With this technique the reads of old data are removed from the critical path of write operations, and are replaced with full-stripe reads (probably cached in the OSS) and writes that can happen out of the critical path. The WCL layer keeps the same reliability level as in the original system (e.g., RAID-5 or RAID-6) as it is built in top of the OSSs. This is a basic difference of this technique with buffering techniques.

In order to be able to support both sequential and non-sequential access patterns, the WCL keeps an in-memory data structure (a bitmap or interval tree) to manage the used space of the cache zone. This structure is used to be able to identify which blocks need to have their parity calculated and be able to send large chunks of full-stripe writes to the disk. The metadata included in this structure is made persistent in the OSSs storage, in order to guarantee that new versions of data blocks can be safely recovered in case of unexpected shutdowns.

Figure 1.a shows the parity update workflow of the basic avoidance technique when compared to vanilla RAID-5. The technique reduces the congestion in Data OSSs by removing one (or two in RAID-6) data reads, hence reducing the number of operations when writing new data by 25 % in RAID-5 and 16 % in RAID-6.

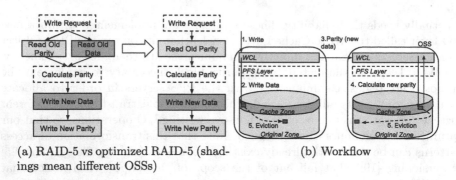

(a) RAID-5 vs optimized RAID-5 (shad-   (b) Workflow
ings mean different OSSs)

Fig. 1. Basic avoidance technique

Note that even though the WCL has been implemented without modifying the original PFS, better performance gains can be achieved and less control over errors (failures, concurrency) will need to be taken if the implementation is done directly inside the PFS (e.g. the in-memory bitmap would no longer be needed). We will assume in this paper that the WCL layer is persistent in the disk, to show the worst performance. We will also consider that the available storage space is enough to avoid forced evictions, to avoid interferences in the evaluation. These forced evictions and the space required depend on the randomness, in block position terms, of the workload.

2.2 Advanced Avoidance: Delayed Parity

One of the most used fault tolerance mechanism in HPC applications is check-pointing, an operation that stores the current status of all processes creating an opportunity to restore the application in case of failure. Due to the continuous writes needed to save the state, this particular operation issues many parity update requests to maintain the reliability. However, is such reliability really needed? Consider for instance that the system fails in the middle of the check-pointing: the application could recover using a previous checkpoint and delete the partial-checkpoint file, rendering the parity computations for the partial check-point useless. This also applies to long computations like matrix multiplications (e.g., MADCAP, on MADBench2 [8]). A failure in the middle of the computation would require it to be restarted again from the beginning, hence the partially stored data would be discarded and the parity calculations would become an avoidable overhead. We can envision a lot of HPC applications that could make use of such functionality, since reprocessing a chunk would be less costly than the cost over all the system to store *all the data* in a reliable way compared to doing it when the process completes.

Using this idea, we propose the START_DELAYED and END_DELAYED hints to mark this kind of candidate operations, delaying the parity calculations until all the writes are completed. When the WCL receives a START_DELAYED hint, redirects all write operations to the caching zone and disables the parity

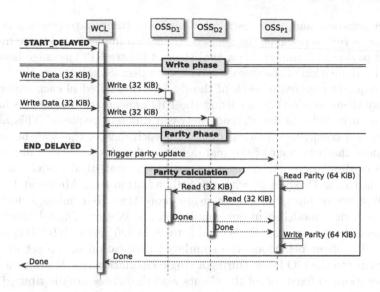

Fig. 2. Delayed Parity: Clients issue two writes and then the parity is calculated. The writes are aligned so they end at the same Parity OSS but at sequential positions. Due to this alignment, the parity calculation can be consolidated.

computations for this data. Once the corresponding END_DELAYED hint is received, the WCL computes the parities of all the full stripes affected by the hints, and moves (rewrites) the data to its original location in the OSS. As a result, the PFS can avoid using the Parity OSSs during the creation of the data and, when parities are calculated, it only needs to send them the consolidated writes.

Figure 2 shows a simplified sequence diagram for the delayed parity technique. In that example, 2 clients issue a 32 KiB write and then their parity is calculated. The writes are directed to different data OSS, but the same Parity OSS. Parity blocks are sequential, and hence parity updates can be consolidated.

The WCL supports synchronous parity calculations, but can also advance the calculation in the background to reduce time. However, advancing the calculation may generate extra work if the calculation is not needed (i.e., application cancellation or error in the client). In short, the delayed parity technique can be represented as a collective operation between all clients, but without increasing intermediate memory requirements since partial data will be written to disk. Failure in acquiring the END signal can be detected with timeouts.

3 Evaluation

Due to the large number of clients, servers and requests involved in Exascale computing clusters, we decided to evaluate the feasability of the proposed techniques using simulations. The simulation environment is created using the OMNet++ framework [29], a C++-based event simulation package targeted at simulating computer networks and other distributed systems. In order to create a network simulation as real as possible, the devised simulation implements Lustre message sizes and payloads, including the actual sizes of Lustre RPC message headers.

For the simulation of the storage devices, we decided to capture the individual I/O requests received by each of the devices configured in each experiment and replay them on a real device using the FIO benchmark, taking special consideration to include the interference between different requests. This allowed us to create a complete statistical model for each device, that can be used to approximate the behaviour of the real device under the conditions imposed by the network simulation. The decision to create this statistical model came after attempting to use DiskSim [6] with the SSD addition from Microsoft Research and finding severe limitations when using more than 64 combined devices at once. The devices modelled in our simulation are Western Digital Black Hard Disks (750 GB capacity, 7200 RPM) and Intel SSD 320 Series (160 GB capacity).

Regarding client behaviour, the simulated application uses a set of clients issuing writes to the I/O layer. During a single simulation run, the datum size of write operations is fixed for all the clients and the writes are distributed along a different file per application to avoid overwrites. Each client writes enough data to produce a statistically representative number of parity calculations. The behaviours of the applications simulated mimic that of the FLASH application [17], a computational tool for simulating and studying thermonuclear reactions, that periodically outputs large checkpoint files and smaller plot files. For the Delayed Parity evaluation, one process of each application acts as master issuing the new hints and all the clients wait until the parity is calculated.

Workloads with mixed block sizes were only tested with a low number of devices, as the cost of generating the statistical device model was too high (it is necessary to attempt all the possible combinations of request sizes, which grows exponentially). This is an important drawback of modelling the storage devices without a simulator. Nevertheless, we did not find significant differences between these simulated workloads in systems with the large number of clients targeted in the paper. The same also applies to different stripe sizes.

We decided to use this workload in order to concentrate on the effect of typical HPC writes over the proposed reliability techniques. Nevertheless, we also checked other workloads, which showed similar results. In particular, our preliminary results using mixed workloads (with reads and writes), showed improvements in the performance on read operations since the proposed techniques favoured a reduction of the overhead on the storage devices. Due to space limitations, we will not discuss these results further.

To assess the effectiveness of the novel strategies, we repeat each measurement with different seeds, that control how requests are mapped into each storage device. Each simulation run stops when we have a minimum of 1000 s of simulated time, other variables (BW, latency, etc.) are tracked to assess that the results are representative. In the following experimental results, RAID-0 represents the performance obtained from the OSSs when there are no parity calculations. STD-RAID represents a standard striped RAID with parity and

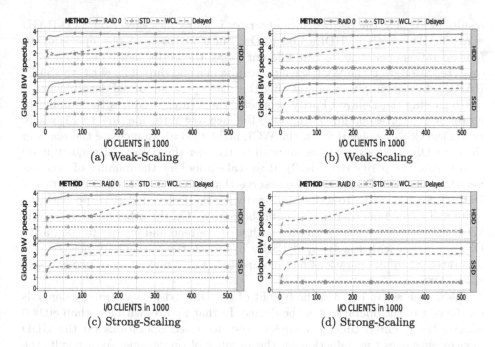

Fig. 3. RAID-5 (left) and RAID-6 (right) write bandwidth w.r.t. STD-RAID.

without optimizations. Finally, our two proposals are WCL and Delayed Parity. If not specified, the results are scaled relative to STD-RAID for each x-axis point. We use 512 OSSs in all the experiments with a stripe unit of 1 MiB and a width of 512 OSSs.

We measure the results in two different ways: using Weak-Scaling and using Strong-Scaling. Weak-Scaling means that the problem size increases with the number of clients and thus, regardless of the number of clients, each one will process the same amount of data (128 KiB per data write). Conversely, in Strong-Scaling the number of clients is increased, but the problem size is kept. Consequently, this increases the network and storage congestion due to I/Os when the number of clients increases, due to the higher number and smaller size of requests. In this scenario, the data writes grow from 8 KiB to 1 MiB according to the number of clients in the simulation. For all the scenarios, the data is partitioned to avoid overwrites according to their block size. We analyse the outcome of the new techniques using RAID-5 in Subsect. 3.1 and RAID-6 in Subsect. 3.2.

3.1   RAID-5 Results

This section describes the measured results of our simulations when reliability is implemented using RAID-5 (i.e., one parity checksum per stripe).

Weak-Scaling Results. Each client writes 128 KiB per write distributed along a file avoiding overwrites with other clients. As we can see on the simulation results in Fig. 3.a, the performance of writes is four times slower on STD-RAID w.r.t. RAID-0 both in HDDs and SSDs. Since we go from one operation to four operations per write to two different OSSs, the performance degradation is expected. Moreover, the WCL scenario results in a speedup of 2x w.r.t. the STD-RAID, achieved simply by eliminating the read operation of old data blocks.

Regarding the Delayed Parity proposal, the strategy reduces the number of writes on the corresponding Parity OSS for each row of the file ($m-1$ vs 1, where m are the OSSs involved) w.r.t. the WCL strategy, but we increase the reads in the data OSSs (0 vs $m-1$) as we need to transfer the data to the parity node to calculate the parity (see Fig. 2). If we take a look at the number of accesses per Data OSS and Parity OSS, we observe that only one access is needed to the Data OSS with WCL (to write) and two with the Delayed Parity approach (to write and to read in order to calculate the parity). On the other hand, using the WCL approach requires a parity for each write (a read and a write to the Parity OSS), whereas with the Delayed Parity approach the parity only needs to be generated when all operations have completed (i.e., a maximum of two accesses to the OSSs).

As we can see in Fig. 3.a, the benefit of the Delayed Parity strategy depends on the cost of the operations in the device. In that Figure, with less than 80,000 clients, the required time to complete the described operations on the HDD devices surpasses the reduction on the number of operations. As a result, the performance with Delayed Parity with a low number of clients is comparable to the WCL strategy, but without the reliability of RAID-5 (as the parity is calculated at the end). Despite this result, the general behaviour is for performance to grow up close to RAID-0, as we remove a big number of parity updates producing a higher throughput.

Apart from the results presented with a 128 KiB write size, if we fix the number of clients to 250 K and we check different block sizes, we can observe how the relative performance is stable using HDDs. However, using 4 KiB blocks with SSDs STD-RAID achieves a better performance, which means that the benefit of the other schemes is lower. The reason is that SSDs offer a better performance of parallel operations, and thus a reduction of them on 4 KiB block sizes does not produce the same improvement w.r.t. the STD-RAID.

Strong-Scaling Results. The experiments done with Strong-Scaling (see Fig. 3.c.) are similar to the Weak-Scaling ones. Specifically, we obtain the same results for RAID-0, STD-RAID and WCL, and thus the difference on block size (i.e., from 128 KiB for Weak-Scaling to 8 KiB for Strong-Scaling in the 500,000 client scenario) is not important at this scale.

Using the Delayed Parity technique, we observe performance improvements due to the fact that the number of parity updates is reduced greatly as the number of clients increases. For instance, with 250 K clients, we do not issue a parity update until all the clients of an application have stored their 16 KiB to the devices, which means that we go from 250 K parity updates (clients · appl. iterations) to 1.7 K parity updates ($\frac{clients}{clients\ per\ appl.}$ · appl. iterations).

Actually, the performance obtained differs when using HDD or SSD technology (as in Weak-Scaling). On HDDs, the Delayed Parity achieves less performance, thus it may be preferable to avoid using this strategy for a small number of clients.

3.2   RAID-6 Results

The complexity and variability of RAID-6 deployments make it more difficult to simulate than RAID-5. Using RAID-6 with two or more parity devices, where location and modification rules depend on the erasure codes used, adds too many variables into the evaluation. The position of the parity devices can modify the number of operations of each OSS and the network communication patterns, but in any situation, our proposal will always optimize them by removing the need to read the old data (because it is a new write). For this reason, in this experiments we have selected two horizontal parity devices per stripe for RAID-6.

Weak-Scaling Results. As we can observe in Fig. 3.b, we found that the STD-RAID performance of RAID-6 configurations is lower than for RAID-5 configurations and the improvement on performance using WCL is a bit lower (1.18x speedup). This happens because the strategy can only successfully avoid 16 % of the operations instead of the 25 % for RAID-5.

The Delayed Parity option offers a bigger performance boost on RAID-6 since we now have two parity devices, and we move from two parity updates per write to two parity updates per application iteration (START-END hint).

Strong-Scaling Results. For Strong-Scaling results with RAID-6 we obtain similar results to RAID-5 (see Fig. 3.d). Like with RAID-5 results, the block size is not important on the simulated scenarios for all the experiments except Delayed Parity. In that particular experiment, we can see the same performance loss found on RAID-5 with HDD devices. However, the performance improvement compared to the WCL proposal is bigger even with a lower number of clients since parity updates are more expensive in RAID-6 than in RAID-5. Thus, removing them (more precisely, grouping and delaying them) produces bigger improvements. In general, since the performance loss of STD-RAID w.r.t. RAID-0 is much higher for RAID-6, the potential gain of the Delayed Parity strategy is higher.

4   Related Work

RAID-5 and RAID-6 are redundant systems that provide a way to recover from a data loss using the remaining disks, so for RAID-5 we can recover using $n - 1$ disks and with RAID-6 we can recover using only $n - 2$ disks. RAID-6 can use a huge range of erasure codes offering different performance and recoverability values. One such example is *Reed-Solomon*, which maps to a polynomial equation so the missing data recovers using interpolation, therefore we can use extra devices to extend the recovery capabilities (for example 12 data disks using 4 redundant disks, will be able to recover any failed disk from 12 correct disks of the 15 available that are still working).

Node-Local Redundancy. Inside RAID-6 research at controller layer, we can find optimizations of the erasure codes as in *P-Code* [15] and *HDP-Code* [31], and optimizations of the erasure codes using specialized hardware (FPGAs and GPUs [5]) as in Gilroy [12] and Curry [9]. Moreover, we can find improvements with SSD RAIDs [22] taking into account the wear-levelling of the parity stripe. Directly related to the partial write on stripes problem, we found H-Code [32] with a performance improvement of 15.54 % and 22.17 % compared to *RDP* and *EVENODD* erasure codes. Finally, there are also patents that solve the problem in the hardware level as Lyons [18] and Baylor [1], reducing the reads and writes done at the controller level. Historically we also have parity logging to solve small writes problem as Stodolsky [28] proposes, we study the problem in distributed systems, RAID-6, and newer devices as SSDs. Our first proposal maintains the reliability of the original system using a small fraction of space of the devices, depending on the randomness of the workload and the cost of evictions, and reduces the number of operations issued to the devices.

Those proposals may not be fully usable or become inefficient at the storage server layer, as it involves network communication and bigger latencies. Despite of this, some of them may improve the performance due to the different parity layouts or calculations. Our work is transparent to the reliability configuration used and will improve their performance.

Distributed Redundancy. Inside distributed redundancy, with can find Ticker-TAIP [7] building a RAID system using the network as transport method. It can be seen as a preliminary approach to support RAID parity schemes over PFS, finally RAID-x [14] presents how to optimize it using a mirroring mechanism reducing the number of operations in small writes. On the PFS plane, GlusterFS supports mirroring schemes and some requests have been done to support RAID-5/6 schemes. Hadoop (HDFS [3]) supports file replication. Finally, PanFS supports file level RAID configurations using triple parity data [21].

Delayed Parity Calculation. About our delayed parity proposal, a similar approach is found in NetApp [16] where writes are buffered to issue an improved write operation. Also, at AFRAID [26] they move the parity calculation to idle periods to obtain a performance boost. The main difference of our proposal with the previous mentioned works is that the lower reliability mode is selected by the user (via hints) when he decides that the data is not useful until it is completed (i.e., check-pointing or partial results that will need to be recalculated). All writes are persisted to the disk, so it may recover from failures, at the same rate than the used PFS.

5   Conclusions and Future Work

Under Exascale constraints, reliability will be needed on the PFS layer if we want to keep the storage costs and the energy used under control. Especially, when we use a high number of clients the number of parity updates will increase.

We propose a transparent cache layer that is able to reduce the number of operations needed to update the parity on such environments. To do that, we ensure that the writes are not overwriting so we can drop the read of old data from the parity update workflow. This proposal improves the write performance of the standard workflow by a 1.18x to a 2x depending on the RAID level (6 or 5, respectively). Moreover, we show that applications gain substantial performance controlling the parity calculation as in the Delayed Parity Proposal. Using reliability oriented application hints, we can improve the write performance up to levels near a RAID-0. This behaviour is useful when partial data does not need to be reliable until all the data writing is finished, e.g. big partial matrices.

In this paper, we used simulation to predict the impact of these strategies. The implementation in existing file systems is non-trivial and out of scope of this paper; nevertheless this theoretical consideration steers the direction of a beneficial implementation in the future.

Acknowledgements. The research leading to these results has received funding from the European Community [FP7 / 2007–2013] Montblanc project under grant agreement 288777 and 610402, by the Spanish Ministry of Economy and Competitiveness under the TIN2012-34557 grant and by the Catalan Government under the 2014-SGR-1051 grant. Thanks to Julian Kunkel and André Brinkmann for their comments and corrections of this paper.

References

1. Baylor, S., Corbett, P., Park, C.: Efficient method for providing fault tolerance against double device failures in multiple device systems (1999). http://www.google.com/patents/US5862158, uS Patent 5,862,158
2. Bergman, K., et al.: Exascale computing study: technology challenges in achieving exascale systems. Technical report, DARPA (2008)
3. Borthakur, D.: Hadoop - HDFS Design (2014), apache
4. Braam, P.J., Zahir, R.: Lustre: A scalable, High Performance File System. Cluster File Systems Inc., Boulder (2002)
5. Brinkmann, A., Eschweiler, D.: A microdriver architecture for error correcting codes inside the linux kernel. In: SC (2009)
6. Bucy, J.S., Schindler, J., Schlosser, S.W., Ganger, G.R.: The disksim simulation environment version 4.0 reference manual. Parallel Data Laboratory (2008)
7. Cao, P., Lin, S.B., Venkataraman, S., Wilkes, J.: The tickertaip parallel raid architecture. ACM TOCS **12**(3), 236–269 (1994)
8. Carter, J., Borrill, J., Oliker, L.: Performance characteristics of a cosmology package on leading HPC architectures. In: Bougé, L., Prasanna, V.K. (eds.) HiPC 2004. LNCS, vol. 3296, pp. 176–188. Springer, Heidelberg (2004)
9. Curry, M.L., Skjellum, A., Ward, H.L., Brightwell, R.: Accelerating reed-solomon coding in RAID systems with GPUS. In: IPDPS, pp. 1–6 (2008)
10. Deenadhayalan, V.: GPFS Native RAID slides, LISA (2011)
11. Durand, Y., Carpenter, P., Adami, S., Bilas, A., Dutoit, D., Farcy, A., et al.: Euroserver: energy efficient node for european micro-servers. In: DSD (2014)
12. Gilroy, M., Irvine, J.: RAID 6 hardware acceleration. In: FPL, pp. 1–6 (2006)
13. Gluster: Glusterfs web page (2014). http://www.gluster.org/
14. Hwang, K., Jin, H., Ho, R.: Raid-x: a new distributed disk array for I/O-centric cluster computing. In: HPDC, pp. 279–286 (2000)

15. Jin, C., Jiang, H., Feng, D., Tian, L.: P-Code: A new RAID-6 code with optimal properties. In: SC, pp. 360–369 (2009)
16. Kleiman, S., Sundaram, R., Doucette, D., Strange, S., Viswanathan, S.: Method for writing contiguous arrays of stripes in a RAID storage system using mapped block writes (2007). http://www.google.com/patents/US7200715, uS Patent 7,200,715
17. Latham, R., Daley, C., Liao, W.K., Gao, K., Ross, R., Dubey, A., Choudhary, A., Choudhary, A.: A case study for scientific I/O: improving the FLASH astrophysics code. Comput. Sci. Discov. **5**(1), 015001 (2012)
18. Lyons, G.: Method and apparatus for improving sequential writes to RAID-6 devices (2000). http://www.google.com/patents/US6101615, uS Patent 6,101,615
19. Muniswamy-Reddy, K.K., Wright, C.P., Himmer, A., Zadok, E.: A versatile and user-oriented versioning file system. In: FAST (2004)
20. Nagle, D., Serenyi, D., Matthews, A.: The panasas activescale storage cluster: delivering scalable high bandwidth storage. In: SC (2004)
21. Panasas: PanFS RAID. https://www.panasas.com/products/panfs/PanFS_RAID
22. Park, K., Lee, D.H., Woo, Y., Lee, G., Lee, J.H., Kim, D.H.: Reliability and performance enhancement technique for SSD array storage system using RAID mechanism. In: ISCIT, pp. 140–145 (2009)
23. Rajovic, N., Carpenter, P.M., Gelado, I., Puzovic, N., Ramirez, A., Valero, M.: Supercomputing with commodity CPUs: are mobile SoCs ready for HPC? In: SC, pp. 40:1–40:12 (2013)
24. Rajovic, N., Vilanova, L., Villavieja, C., Puzovic, N., Ramirez, A.: The low power architecture approach towards exascale computing. J. Comput. Sci. **4**(6), 439–443 (2013)
25. Rosenblum, M., Ousterhout, J.K.: The design and implementation of a log-structured file system. ACM TOCS **10**(1), 26–52 (1992)
26. Savage, S., Wilkes, J.: AFRAID: a frequently redundant array of independent disks. In: USENIX ATC (1996)
27. Schmuck, F.B., Haskin, R.L.: GPFS: a shared-disk file system for large computing clusters. In: FAST (2002)
28. Stodolsky, D., Gibson, G., Holland, M.: Parity logging overcoming the small write problem in redundant disk arrays. ACM SIGARCH Comput. Archit. News **21**, 64–75 (1993)
29. Varga, A., et al.: The OMNeT++ discrete event simulation system. In: ESM, vol. 9, p. 185 (2001)
30. Villa, O., Johnson, D.R., O'Connor, M., Bolotin, E., Nellans, D., Luitjens, J., Sakharnykh, N., Wang, P., Micikevicius, P., Scudiero, A., et al.: Scaling the power wall: a path to exascale. In: SC (2014)
31. Wu, C., He, X., Wu, G., Wan, S., Liu, X., Cao, Q., Xie, C.: HDP code: a horizontal-diagonal parity code to optimize I/O load balancing in RAID-6. In: Dependable Systems and Networks (DSN), pp. 209–220 (2011)
32. Wu, C., Wan, S., He, X., Cao, Q., Xie, C.: H-Code: a hybrid MDS array code to optimize partial stripe writes in RAID-6. In: IPDPS, pp. 782–793 (2011)

Rapid Tomographic Image Reconstruction via Large-Scale Parallelization

Tekin Bicer[1]($\boxtimes$), Doga Gursoy[2], Rajkumar Kettimuthu[1],
Francesco De Carlo[2], Gagan Agrawal[3], and Ian T. Foster[1,4]

[1] Mathematics and Computer Science Division, Argonne National Laboratory,
Lemont, USA
{bicer,kettimut,foster}@anl.gov
[2] X-Ray Science Division, Argonne National Laboratory, Lemont, USA
{dgursoy,decarlo}@aps.anl.gov
[3] Department of Computer Science and Engineering, Ohio State University,
Columbus, OH, USA
agrawal@cse.ohio-state.edu
[4] Department of Computer Science, University of Chicago, Chicago, USA

Abstract. Synchrotron (x-ray) light sources permit investigation of the structure of matter at extremely small length and time scales. Advances in detector technologies enable increasingly complex experiments and more rapid data acquisition. However, analysis of the resulting data then becomes a bottleneck—preventing near-real-time error detection or experiment steering. We present here methods that leverage highly parallel computers to improve the performance of iterative tomographic image reconstruction applications. We apply these methods to the conventional per-slice parallelization approach and use them to implement a novel in-slice approach that can use many more processors. To address programmability, we implement the introduced methods in high-performance MapReduce-like computing middleware, which is further optimized for reconstruction operations. Experiments with four reconstruction algorithms and two large datasets show that our methods can scale up to 8 K cores on an IBM BG/Q supercomputer with almost perfect speedup and can reduce total reconstruction times for large datasets by more than 95.4 % on 32 K cores relative to 1 K cores. Moreover, the average reconstruction times are improved from ~2 h (256 cores) to ~1 min (32 K cores), thus enabling near-real-time use.

1 Introduction

As data volumes increase, research success in a growing number of fields depends on the ability to analyze the data rapidly. In scientific computing, this situation is true both for data generated by simulations and instruments. In the context of scientific instruments, for instance, techniques such as time-resolved microtomography can produce three or more dimensional data at rates of terabytes per day or more. Moreover, data generation rates are expected to increase with advances in detector technologies and experimental techniques.

J.L. Träff et al. (Eds.): Euro-Par 2015, LNCS 9233, pp. 289–302, 2015.
DOI: 10.1007/978-3-662-48096-0_23

The utility of such techniques is severely limited by the hours required to analyze the resulting large datasets [3,11]. Scientists often want *quasi-instant* feedback so that they can check results and adjust the experimental setup. For instance, the x-ray tomography systems available at the imaging beamlines of the Advanced Photon Source (APS, located at Argonne National Laboratory) are routinely used in materials science applications, where high-resolution and fast 3D imaging are instrumental in extracting valuable information. Quasi-instant feedback can help identify optimal experimental parameters (beamline condition and sample environment such as temperature and pressure) and accelerate the end-to-end scientific process.

In the absence of such quasi-real-time analysis, precious time on many expensive instruments is used less effectively. In this paper, we focus on improving the efficiency of tomographic image reconstruction, thus enhancing the turnaround time of scientific workflows. Specifically, we address the following issues: (1) how to enable efficient and parallel execution of tomographic reconstruction algorithms and (2) how to ease the rapid development of reconstruction codes.

With regard to the first issue, different parallel reconstruction algorithms have been proposed for multicore machines [1,14,17,23,24,26]. Although these works provide reasonable reconstruction times with small datasets, they typically have scalability limitations and are not suitable for high-resolution large datasets such as those generated at synchrotron x-ray light sources (e.g., APS). Another effort in the same direction is to use accelerators such as GPUs [5,16,19]. Accelerators can provide high computational througput and enable the use of compute-intensive algorithms that can operate on fewer projections (i.e., smaller datasets) [12,20,21]. However, these devices can accommodate only a small fraction of data and require repeated communication between host and device, which can limit the performance.

With regard to the second issue, we note that reconstruction algorithms might need to be developed according to different properties, including experimental setup and data acquisition; point of interests in reconstruction object; and total analysis or reconstruction time. These requirements result in various application-specific algorithms that are difficult to modify and maintain [8,9,18]. There are several frameworks that provide workflows and algorithms for tomographic reconstruction [7,22]; however, these typically provide limited support for easy implementation of reconstruction algorithms and parallelization of computation. The data-intensive computing community has also developed frameworks, such as Hadoop [2] and Spark [25], that ease the implementation of parallel algorithms. Although these frameworks show good scalability, they are not always suited for science applications that run on high-end clusters and supercomputers.

To address these issues, we make the following contributions. First, we introduce two parallelization techniques, `per-slice` and `in-slice`, for tomographic reconstruction algorithms. Our `in-slice` technique provides fine-grained high-performance parallelism using *replicated reconstruction objects*, which significantly improves the conventional `per-slice` approach. Second, we extend and

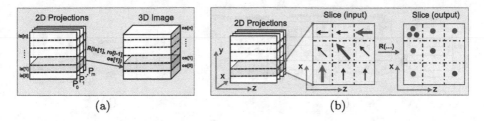

Fig. 1. Per-slice parallelization

optimize a MapReduce-like framework, MATE [13], to help implement these parallel methods efficiently. Third, we extensively evaluate the proposed methods and middleware-based implementations (for different reconstruction algorithms and real-world datasets). Our experimental results show that our middleware can scale almost linearly up to 8 K cores and can achieve execution times on 32 K cores that are $\geq 95.4\,\%$ less than those on 1 K cores. Moreover, the average reconstruction times are improved from ~2 h (256 cores) to ~1 min (32K cores). To the best of our knowledge, this is the first study that examines the parallelization of tomographic reconstruction algorithms at this scale.

2 Parallelization of Image Analysis and Reconstruction

In this section, we first discuss the organization of tomography datasets and reconstruction approach; then we present two parallelization techniques, `per-slice` and `in-slice`, for tomographic image reconstruction.

2.1 Tomography Datasets and Reconstruction

A tomography dataset is a set of 2D projections collected from different directions (θ) of a target sample. Each projection is a 2D array of floating-point numbers, each representing the line integrals of a ray, namely, a *ray-sum*. Therefore, a complete dataset is a 3D array in which the dimensions are projections, rows, and columns, respectively.

The tomographic reconstruction algorithms that we consider in this paper proceed in an iterative manner. At each iteration, rays are simulated according to the *ray-sum* values and reconstructed data from the previous iteration. Since rays in rows corresponding to different projections do not intersect, the reconstruction of individual rows (also referred to as *slices*) can proceed in parallel. We further discuss the tomographic image reconstruction and parallelization techniques in the following sections.

2.2 Per-slice Parallel Reconstruction

Figure 1(a) illustrates the per-slice parallelization technique. We name the slices in the tomography dataset $IS = \{is_0, is_1, ..., is_n\}$, and denote the reconstructed

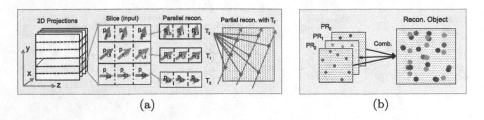

(a)   (b)

Fig. 2. In-slice parallelization

object generated at the ith iteration as ro_i. Then, we can define a function R that, for iteration $i + 1$, determines $ro_{i+1} = R(IS, ro_i)$ by computing each of n output slices os_j from the corresponding input slice is_j and from ro_i, and then setting $ro_{i+1} = \{os_0, os_1, ..., os_n\}$. Since there are no dependencies between slices, each slice can be processed independently.

Figure 1(b) shows a sample reconstruction operation. Each arrow represents a ray-sum value, with the direction of the arrow indicating the ray's θ. Simulating the propagation of the colored rays using the R function leads to the updates on the dotted cells in the output slice. Note that only the updates of the colored rays are shown in the figure. Typically, for each iteration, all rays in the projection (input) dataset are simulated for rapid convergence to the real 3D image. Although there are no dependencies between slices, different rays within a slice can update the same cell in the output slice, a situation that results in a race condition and limits the scalability of the per-slice parallelization technique.

2.3   In-slice Parallel Reconstruction

The per-slice technique can use only as much parallelism as there are slices in a dataset. Thus, for example, a dataset with 2,048 slices cannot be reconstructed with more than 2,048 parallel units (e.g. threads) and hence can take days to finish, depending on dataset size, reconstruction algorithm, and computational resources.

Our *in-slice* parallelization technique addresses this limitation by performing parallel reconstruction for each *ray*, therefore it significantly decreases the granularity of parallelism and increases the number of threads that can be applied. However, two obstacles must be addressed for in-slice parallelism: (1) different rays in the same slice may update the same cell at the same time (i.e., *race conditions* can occur); and (2) threads that operate on the same slice may need to synchronize in order to compute the correct output slice.

One way to address race conditions is to use mutexes. However, the use of mutexes can introduce significant overhead considering the many threads that must perform update operations on the same slice. An alternative approach is to replicate the assigned output slices (reconstruction objects) for each thread so that reconstruction operations can proceed independently. This approach avoids race conditions, and it achieves better performance than using (un)locks on individual reconstruction objects. Figure 2(a) illustrates how replication can be used for parallel reconstruction. First, each row in an input slice is assigned to a thread. Then, each thread simulates its assigned rays on the replicated reconstruction object. For example, in the figure, T_2 simulates rays $p_{2,*}$ and updates results on its own replica. Similarly, other threads perform the same operation on their own replicas.

We address the second issue by grouping and synchronizing threads according to their assigned slices. For example, Fig. 2(b) shows how replicas (PR_0, PR_1 and PR_2) from threads (T_0, T_1 and T_2) are combined in order to generate the correct reconstructed slice. The combination function used may vary depending on the reconstruction algorithm.

In-slice parallelization uses both replicas and combination operations to enable fine-grained parallelism and large-scale 3D reconstruction of tomographic images. However, these techniques require additional resources and introduce overheads that are not required in per-slice parallelization.

3   Our MapReduce-like Middleware

We next describe the processing structure of our middleware and the methods used to port the aforementioned parallelization techniques into this middleware.

Our middleware is built on top of MATE [13], a MapReduce-like middleware that supports *reduction-based processing structure* [4]. The MATE middleware has been specialized to have a *reconstruction object* similar to the reduction object. The processing structure of the middleware consists of three main phases: *local reconstruction* (specialization of local reduction), *partial combination*, and *global combination*. In this section, we first explain how data management and distribution are performed in our system. Then, we provide details about the processing structure of our middleware. Finally, we introduce **ordered-subsetting** feature and its implementation.

Data Organization and Distribution: Typically, tomography datasets are stored by using a scientific data format such as HDF5 [6]. Before beginning reconstruction, our middleware reads metadata information from the input dataset and allocates the resources required for the output dataset, setting the first dimension of the 3D reconstruction object to the number of slices and the other two dimensions to the number of columns. For instance, if the input dataset's dimensions are $360 \times 2048 \times 1024$ (where 360 is the number of projections and 2048 and 1024 are the number of slices and columns, respectively), then the reconstruction object's dimensions are $2048 \times 1024 \times 1024$.

Since the parallelization of reconstruction methods is based on slices, the data distribution partitions the input dataset along its second dimension and the 3D reconstruction object along its first dimension. For example, if the system has 128 processes, then the middleware partitions the input dataset and the reconstruction object into subsets of size $360 \times \mathbf{16} \times 1024$ and $\mathbf{16} \times 1024 \times 1024$, respectively, where in each case $\mathbf{16} = 2048/128$. It then assigns each portion of the input data and reconstruction object to a process. If there are more

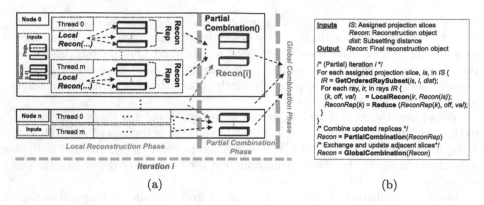

Fig. 3. (a) Execution flow of our middleware; (b) pseudocode for in-slice parallelization

reconstruction processes/threads than there are slices, then portions of the same slice can be distributed to multiple processes.

Reconstruction Object: With per-slice parallelization, our middleware creates a single output object (portion of reconstruction object) in each process and lets all the threads update it. Since each slice is an atomic unit in the per-slice parallelization, threads can perform direct updates.

With in-slice parallelization, however, direct update on output object is not a correct operation. Recall from Sect. 2.3 that each slice may be shared among several threads, thus introducing the potential for race conditions. Our middleware eliminates these race conditions by creating a replica of the output object for each thread, which we refer to as *ReconRep* in Fig. 3(a). For example, assume that the user sets the number of processes per node to 1 and the number of threads per process to 32. In the aforementioned example, our middleware will allocate a replica of the corresponding input slices ($16 \times 1024 \times 1024$) for each thread. Therefore, each thread can perform reconstruction on its own replica. This use of replicas provides the greatest reconstruction parallelization among the threads, but does require additional synchronization. We quantify the costs associated with this overhead in our experiments.

Local Reconstruction Phase: Local reconstruction corresponds to the mapping phase of the MapReduce processing structure. The user implements the reconstruction algorithms in the local reconstruction function (*LocalRecon* in Fig. 3(a)); our middleware applies this function to each assigned data chunk. Each data chunk can be a set of slices (for per-slice parallelization) or a subset of rays in a slice (for in-slice parallelization).

The local reconstruction function performs update operations using a 3-tuple, (sliceID, offset, value), where *sliceID* refers to the slice, *offset* is the data point on the slice, and *value* is the computed value. The usage of a 3-tuple is similar to (key, value) pairs in MapReduce, where key corresponds to sliceID and offset. Unlike MapReduce, however, the generated 3-tuple is being reduced/updated on replicas right after its generation.

Partial Combination Phase: After all the rays in the assigned data chunks are processed, the threads that are working on the same slices synchronize and combine their replicas by using a user-defined function (*PartialCombination()* in Fig. 3(a)). Although this phase resembles the *reduce* phase in the MapReduce processing structure, subtle yet important differences exist. First, there is no barrier between the local reconstruction and partial reconstruction phases; thus, idle time occurs only for the threads that need to synchronize. Second, the use of replicas eliminates the need for shuffling, grouping, and sorting operations used in MapReduce. This optimization has been shown to increase application performance significantly [13]. The partial combination is required only for the in-slice technique, since the per-slice technique does not need to use replicas.

Global Combination Phase: At the end of the partial combination phase, processes generate the slices of the 3D image. If the reconstruction algorithm uses neighboring slices, then the processes must exchange border slices. During the global combination phase, processes exchange these slices and then continue next iteration. This phase is required only for reconstruction algorithms that utilize neighboring slices.

Once all the iterations are completed, the final reconstruction object (*Recon[i]* in Fig. 3(a)) is generated. Our middleware, then, writes this reconstruction object using parallel HDF5.

Figure 3(b) gives **pseudocode** for the in-slice parallelization technique. Our middleware also supports **ordered-subsetting**, which lets users perform reconstruction using a subset of the rays in the assigned projection dataset. For example, assume that $PS_{is_i} = \{ps_0, ps_1, ..., ps_m\}$ are the projection rows in slice is_i. If the *GetOrderedRaySubset* function is called with $is = 0$, $i = 0$ and $dist = 2$ values, it sets $IR = \{ps_0, ps_2, ps_4, .., ps_m\}$. These projections' rows are then used for reconstruction. Here $dist$ is used for setting the distances between projections, and i is the current iteration. The iteration number determines the beginning index of the projection; that is, if $i = 1$ and $dist = 2$, then projections $IR = \{ps_1, ps_3, .., ps_{m-1}\}$ are processed.

While only a subset of the rays is processed in each iteration, the middleware varies the beginning index of the projection so that all rays are eventually processed. Ordered subsetting converges more rapidly to the 3D image than does the sequential approach. After the target rays are determined, they are iteratively reconstructed. Again, notice that the generated values are *reduced* in *ReconRep* right after the *LocalRecon* function. Once all assigned rays are processed, *Recon-Reps* from different threads are combined with *PartialCombination*. The *Recon* object, then, is updated with *GlobalCombine*.

4   Experimental Results

We evaluated our middleware's performance and scalability using four iterative reconstruction algorithms and two real world datasets.

The reconstruction algorithms are ported from TomoPy [10], a widely used tomographic data processing and image reconstruction library. Specifically, we used maximum likelihood expectation maximization (MLEM), simultaneous iterative reconstruction technique (SIRT), penalized maximum likelihood (PML), and accelerated PML reconstruction (APMLR). Among these algorithms, APMLR requires adjacent slices, whereas MLEM, SIRT, and PML can perform reconstruction using data points on the same slice (i.e., neighboring slices are not needed).

To evaluate our framework, we used two datasets, Seed and Hornby, from two different APS beamlines. Seed is acquired from a seed of *arabidopsis thaliana*, a flowering plant [9]. It consists of 720 projections, each with 2048 rows and 501 columns (i.e., 720 × 2048 × 501 single-precision floating-point numbers). Hornby is an x-ray microtomography data from a shale sample [15]. It includes 360 projections, each with 2,048 rows and 1,024 columns. The reconstructed 3D images from Seed and Hornby have dimensions 2048 × 501 × 501 and 2048 × 1024 × 1024, respectively.

We conducted our experiments on Mira, a 10-petaflops IBM Blue Gene/Q (BG/Q) supercomputer at the Argonne Leadership Computing Facility. Mira is equipped with 49,125 nodes, each with 16 cores (1600 MHz PowerPC A2) and 16 GB memory. The nodes have access to a GPFS file system that provides 24 PB of capacity and 240 GB/sec bandwidth. Moreover, the nodes are connected with a 5D torus proprietary network. [1]

4.1 Multithreaded Performance

We first evaluated the performance of our middleware when using different numbers of threads on a single node. In these experiments, we processed 64 slices (i.e., rows) of the Seed dataset using the MLEM and APMLR reconstruction algorithms.

The MLEM column in Fig. 4 shows the single-iteration reconstruction time (y-axis) for varying numbers of threads (x-axis). We observe the best performance with 32 threads, achieving a speedup of 18.76 relative to 1 thread.

The performance with 64 threads is slightly slower, presumably because of overheads resulting from insufficient resources. Each BG/Q node can provide hardware registers for up to four threads; thus, the maximum number of supported threads is 16 × 4 per node. Since these threads share the same resources, we observe a performance degradation after 32 threads.

The parallelization performance of APMLR follows the same trend as MLEM. Here, 32 threads provides the best performance, achieving 18.38 speedup. We

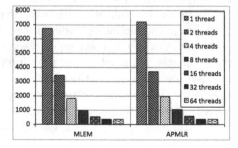

Fig. 4. Multithreaded reconstruction times (in sec) of the Seed dataset on a single BG/Q node.

[1] For more information, see https://www.alcf.anl.gov/mira.

observe, however, that the execution time of APMLR is slightly longer than that of MLEM. Although MLEM and APMLR use similar library functions from our middleware, APMLR performs additional computation and communication operations because of the use of adjacent slices, which introduces overhead during runtime.

4.2 Scalability

We next present the distributed-memory performance of our middleware. For these experiments, we used up to 2 K nodes (i.e., 32 K cores) and reconstructed both the Seed and Hornby datasets. We set the total number of iterations to 10.

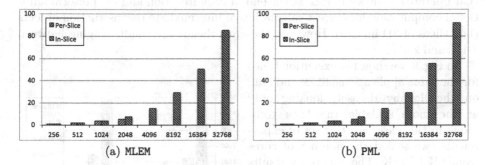

(a) MLEM   (b) PML

Fig. 5. Speedups achieved (y-axis) when reconstructing the Seed dataset on up to 32 K cores (x-axis). Speedups are calculated with 256-core per-slice configurations.

Figure 5 shows the speedups achieved for the MLEM and PML algorithms on the Seed dataset, when using the per-slice and in-slice parallelization techniques. For these experiments, we used the 256-core per-slice timings as the baseline for speedup calculations, and set the number of threads per core to 2, i.e., 32 threads per node.

Notice that the per-slice technique has results for only up to 2 K cores, while the in-slice technique has results for up to 32 K cores. This difference is because the per-slice technique can create at most one thread per slice and the Seed dataset has 2 K slices. Looking more closely, we see that per-slice performs similarly to in-slice on up to 1 K cores but less well on 2 K cores. We attribute this relative decline to the maximum 2 K threads that can be created by per-slice for Seed. Thus, per-slice has 16 threads per BG/Q node when running on 2 K cores—less than the 32 threads that we showed in Sect. 4.1 to provide the best CPU utilization.

If we compare the 256- and 1 K-core timings of per-slice, we see speedups of 3.99 and 3.98 for MLEM and PML, respectively. Since these speedups are close to the ideal (4×), we conclude that our middleware introduces negligible scalability overhead for these compute-intensive applications. The speedup for 2 K-core configuration is 5.18 for both MLEM and PML, relative to the 256-core configuration. The fact that the in-slice technique can scale to more than 2 K cores allows it to achieve far better reconstruction performance than does `per-slice`: at least 15.6× faster (on 32 K cores) than `per-slice` (on 2 K cores) for both `MLEM` and `PML`.

Looking more closely, we see that `in-slice` achieves almost linear speedup on up to 8 K cores. Beyond 8 K cores, however, the rate of speedup decreases. On 32 K cores, for example, we observe a speedup of 85.6 for `MLEM` and 91.9 for `PML` application relative to the times taken on 256 cores. We attribute these less-than-perfect speedups to the short execution times (~1 min.) with many threads; the time taken by I/O; and the serial computation.

A closer look at the data shows that on up to 1 K cores (in which both techniques utilize 32 threads per node), `per-slice` performs slightly better than `in-slice`. We attribute this difference to the need for `in-slice` to (1) synchronize threads that operate on the same slice at the end of each iteration and (2) perform additional computation for correct calculation of intermediate reconstruction objects (i.e., slices of 3D images). However, these overheads are small, ranging between 2.1 % and 2.5 %.

In Fig. 6, we show the execution times for the same applications, `MLEM` and `PML`, on the `Hornby` dataset, looking only at the more scalable `in-slice` technique in this case. For this set of experiments, we scaled the number of cores from 1 K to 32 K. The scalability results show a similar trend to that seen in the previous experiments: an almost linear speedup up to 8 K cores for both `MLEM` and `PML`, increasing more slowly subsequently because of increased I/O, synchronization, and communication costs. The execution times on 32 K vs. 1 K cores show

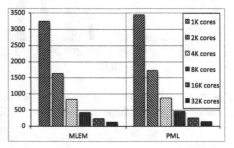

Fig. 6. Reconstruction times (in secs.) of `MLEM` and `PML` with the `Hornby` dataset using up to 32 K cores.

speedups of 24.22 and 25.5 for `MLEM` and `PML`, respectively.

Since `Hornby` is larger and thus computationally more demanding than `Seed`, we achieve better scalability than with the former dataset. Specifically, the speedups observed on 32 K relative to 1 K cores of `MLEM` and `PML` for `Seed` are 21.94 and 23.51, respectively: 7.8–9.5 % less than those achieved with `Hornby`.

In Fig. 7, we show the performance achieved when we repeat the same experiments with the `APMLR` reconstruction algorithm. The execution times (left y-axis) and speedups (right y-axis) are presented in Fig. 7(a). Similar to the previous experiments, speedups are close to linear for up to 8 K cores. Considering 32 K vs. 1K cores, the speedup of `APMLR` is 24.77, which decreases the execution time from over 1 h to less than 2.5 min. Note that the 1 h execution time is with 1 K cores; thus, the estimated execution time of the same application on a single BG/Q node (i.e., 16 cores) is more than 67 h.

In Fig. 7(b), we show the percentage times spent in five different activities for the experiments of Fig. 7(a): (1) `Reconstruction` time, encompassing reconstruction and update operations on replicas; (2) Intermediate computation, i.e.,

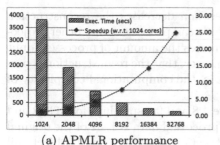
(a) APMLR performance

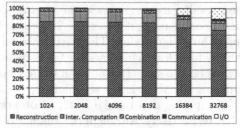
(b) APMLR reconstruction time breakdown: % time spent on different activities

Fig. 7. Performance achieved by the APMLR algorithm for the `Hornby` dataset, using up to 32 K cores.

`Inter. Computation`, in which intermediate matrices are calculated for reconstruction; (3) `Combination`, which is the sum of local and global combinations; (4) `Communication`, in which neighbors are updated; and (5) `I/O` time, in which data read and write operations are performed.

We see that `Reconstruction` dominates overall execution time for all core counts. The fraction of time spent in `I/O` increases as the number of cores grows; this result is not surprising since increasing the number of cores decreases per-core computation time and increases synchronization costs. `Communication` also does not scale well, since it requires constant time for updating neighbors. Moreover, the fraction of time spent in `Inter. Computation` and `Combination` remains roughly the same with increasing number of cores; the reason is that since these phases process data structures which are tightly coupled with the size of reconstruction objects, they show good parallelization performance.

4.3 Ordered-Subsetting Performance

In our next experiments, we evaluate the performance of the ordered-subsetting feature of our middleware. We apply the APMLR and SIRT reconstruction algorithms to the `Hornby` dataset with different distance parameters (d) on 4 K cores and for 10 iterations. In contrast to previous experiments, however, these are *partial iterations*; that is, only a portion of the assigned data is processed.

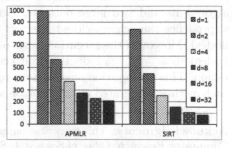

Figure 8 shows our results. We see that execution times improve with increasing distance configurations for both APMLR and SIRT algorithms. Since the amount of processed data directly affects

Fig. 8. Reconstruction times (in secs) of APMLR and SIRT using different distances. (`Hornby` dataset; # cores=4 K).

the overall execution times, the *partial iteration* decreases the reconstruction times. For example, if we set $d = 2$, then each thread processes every other projection in an assigned slice. This effectively decreases the amount of processed input data by half (for each iteration). We note, however, that the reconstruction is performed on the same (full) output data; that is, the computational complexity of updating the 3D object is still high.

Comparing $d = 1$ and $d = 32$, we observe 4.8 and 9.7 speedups for APMLR and SIRT, respectively. Although the amount of processed data is 1/32 of the original for $d = 32$ configuration, update and reconstruction operations on 3D object still involve significant computation. Moreover, the strided access to the input data degrades the data locality. These effects are more visible in the case of the APMLR application, in which reconstruction also requires additional synchronization and communication.

The main advantage of using ordered-subsetting is the high image quality that it achieves with only a small number of *full iterations*. For example, 10 partial iterations with ordered-subsetting (where $d = 2$) provide better image quality than do five full iterations without ordered-subsetting for SIRT (normal execution). Note that 10 partial iterations correspond to 5 full iterations where $d = 2$. The ordered-subsetting method is being used extensively to improve reconstruction times and 3D image quality [3].

5   Conclusion

We have described the design and implementation of parallelization methods for tomographic reconstruction algorithms on high-performance clusters. We presented two parallel reconstruction techniques: per-slice and in-slice. The in-slice technique, which provides fine-grained high-performance parallelism using *replicated reconstruction objects*, represents a significant improvement over the conventional per-slice approach. We integrated the per-slice and in-slice techniques in a lightweight MapReduce-like middleware and extended the middleware to make it easy to implement different reconstruction algorithms.

We evaluated the techniques and middleware using four reconstruction algorithms and two large datasets. Our results show that our reconstruction approaches can achieve close to perfect speedups on up to 8 K cores (512 BG/Q nodes). Moreover, the execution times of the 32K-core configurations (2 K BG/Q nodes) show $\geq 95.4\%$ reduction in execution time relative to a 1K-core configuration. This acceleration enables near-real-time reconstruction of large datasets, such as those generated at synchrotron x-ray light sources.

Acknowledgments. This work was supported by the Office of Advanced Scientific Computing Research, Office of Science, U.S. Department of Energy, under the contract DE-AC02-06CH11357 and the RAMSES project under the Next Generation Networking for Science Program.

References

1. Agulleiro, J., Fernandez, J.-J.: Fast tomographic reconstruction on multicore computers. Bioinformatics **27**(4), 582–583 (2011)
2. Apache software foundation. Apache Hadoop (2014). http://hadoop.apache.org. [Online Accessed January 2015]
3. Beister, M., Kolditz, D., Kalender, W.A.: Iterative reconstruction methods in X-ray CT. Physica Medica **28**(2), 94–108 (2012)
4. Bicer, T.: Supporting data-intensive scientific computing on bandwidth and space constrained environments. Ph.D. thesis, The Ohio State University (2014)
5. Chou, C.-Y., Chuo, Y.-Y., Hung, Y., Wang, W.: A fast forward projection using multithreads for multirays on GPUs in medical image reconstruction. Med. Phys. **38**(7), 4052–4065 (2011)
6. De Carlo, F., Gürsoy, D., Marone, F., Rivers, M., Parkinson, D.Y., Khan, F., Schwarz, N., Vine, D.J., Vogt, S., Gleber, S.-C., Narayanan, S., Newville, M., Lanzirotti, T., Sun, Y., Hong, Y.P., Jacobsen, C.: Scientific data exchange: a schema for HDF5-based storage of raw and analyzed data. J. Synchrotron Radiat. **21**(6), 1224–1230 (2014)
7. Deslippe, J., Essiari, A., Patton, S.J., Samak, T., Tull, C.E., Hexemer, A., Kumar, D., Parkinson, D., Stewart, P.: Workflow management for real-time analysis of light-source experiments. In: Proceedings of the 9th Workshop on Workflows in Support of Large-Scale Science, pp. 31–40. IEEE Press (2014)
8. Gürsoy, D., Biçer, T., Almer, J.D., Kettimuthu, R., Stock, S.R., De Carlo, F.: Maximum a posteriori estimation of crystallographic phases in X-ray diffraction tomography. Philos. Trans. Royal Soc. Lond. A: Math. Phys. Eng. Sci. **373**(2043), 20140392 (2015)
9. Gürsoy, D., Biçer, T., Lanzirotti, A., Newville, M.G., De Carlo, F.: Hyperspectral image reconstruction for X-ray fluorescence tomography. Opt. Express **23**(7), 9014–9023 (2015)
10. Gürsoy, D., De Carlo, F., Xiao, X., Jacobsen, C.: TomoPy: a framework for the analysis of synchrotron tomographic data. J. Synchrotron Radiat. **21**(5), 1188–1193 (2014)
11. Hsieh, J., Nett, B., Yu, Z., Sauer, K., Thibault, J.-B., Bouman, C.A.: Recent advances in CT image reconstruction. Curr. Radiol. Rep. **1**(1), 39–51 (2013)
12. Jang, B., Kaeli, D., Do, S., Pien, H.: Multi GPU implementation of iterative tomographic reconstruction algorithms. In: IEEE International Symposium on Biomedical Imaging: From Nano to Macro, ISBI 2009, pp. 185–188. IEEE (2009)
13. Jiang, W., Ravi, V.T., Agrawal, G.: A map-reduce system with an alternate API for multi-core environments. In: Proceedings of the 2010 10th IEEE/ACM International Conference on Cluster, Cloud and Grid Computing, CCGRID 2010, Washington, DC, USA, pp. 84–93. IEEE Computer Society (2010)
14. Jones, M., Yao, R., Bhole, C.: Hybrid MPI-OpenMP programming for parallel OSEM PET reconstruction. IEEE Trans. Nucl. Sci. **53**(5), 2752–2758 (2006)
15. Kanitpanyacharoen, W., Parkinson, D.Y., De Carlo, F., Marone, F., Stampanoni, M., Mokso, R., MacDowell, A., Wenk, H.-R.: A comparative study of X-ray tomographic microscopy on shales at different synchrotron facilities: ALS, APS and SLS. J. Synchrotron Radiat. **20**(1), 172–180 (2013)
16. Lee, D., Dinov, I., Dong, B., Gutman, B., Yanovsky, I., Toga, A.W.: CUDA optimization strategies for compute-and memory-bound neuroimaging algorithms. Comput. Methods Programs Biomed. **106**(3), 175–187 (2012)

17. Mohan, K., Venkatakrishnan, S., Gibbs, J., Gulsoy, E., Xiao, X., De Graef, M., Voorhees, P., Bouman, C.: TIMBIR: a method for time-space reconstruction from interlaced views. IEEE Trans. Comput. Imaging **PP**(99), 1 (2015)
18. Phatak, C., Gürsoy, D.: Iterative reconstruction of magnetic induction using lorentz transmission electron tomography. Ultramicroscopy **150**, 54–64 (2015)
19. Pratx, G., Chinn, G., Olcott, P., Levin, C.: Fast, accurate and shift-varying line projections for iterative reconstruction using the GPU. IEEE Trans. Med. Imaging **28**(3), 435–445 (2009)
20. Sidky, E.Y., Kao, C.-M., Pan, X.: Accurate image reconstruction from few-views and limited-angle data in divergent-beam CT. J. X-ray Sci. Technol. **14**(2), 119–139 (2006)
21. Stone, S.S., Haldar, J.P., Tsao, S.C., Hwu, W.-M., Sutton, B.P., Liang, Z.-P., et al.: Accelerating advanced MRI reconstructions on GPUs. J. Parallel Distrib. Comput. **68**(10), 1307–1318 (2008)
22. Thielemans, K., Tsoumpas, C., Mustafovic, S., Beisel, T., Aguiar, P., Dikaios, N., Jacobson, M.W.: Stir: software for tomographic image reconstruction release 2. Phys. Med. Biol. **57**(4), 867 (2012)
23. Treibig, J., Hager, G., Hofmann, H.G., Hornegger, J., Wellein, G.: Pushing the limits for medical image reconstruction on recent standard multicore processors. Int. J. High Perform. Comput. Appl. **27**(2), 162–177 (2012)
24. Wang, Y., De Carlo, F., Mancini, D.C., McNulty, I., Tieman, B., Bresnahan, J., Foster, I., Insley, J., Lane, P., von Laszewski, G., et al.: A high-throughput X-ray microtomography system at the advanced photon source. Rev. Sci. Instrum. **72**(4), 2062–2068 (2001)
25. Zaharia, M., Chowdhury, M., Franklin, M.J., Shenker, S., Stoica, I.: Spark: cluster computing with working sets. In: Proceedings of the 2nd USENIX Conference on Hot Topics in Cloud Computing, HotCloud 2010, Berkeley, CA, USA, p. 10. USENIX Association (2010)
26. Zeng, K., Bai, E., Wang, G.: A fast CT reconstruction scheme for a general multi-core PC. Int. J. Biomed. Imaging **2007**, 1 (2007)

Grid, Cluster and Cloud Computing

Software Consolidation as an Efficient Energy and Cost Saving Solution for a SaaS/PaaS Cloud Model

Alain Tchana[1]([✉]), Noel De Palma[2], Ibrahim Safieddine[2], Daniel Hagimont[1], Bruno Diot[3,4], and Nicolas Vuillerme[3,5]

[1] University of Toulouse, Toulouse, France
alain.tchana@enseeiht.fr
[2] University of Joseph Fourier, Grenoble, France
noelde.palma@imag.fr
[3] IDS, Montceau-les-mines, France
b.diot@ids-assistance.com, bruno.diot@agim.eu
[4] AGIM, Université Grenoble Alpes, Saint-Martin-d'Hères, France
[5] Institut Universitaire de France, Paris, France

Abstract. Virtual machines (VM) are used in cloud computing environments to isolate different software. Virtualization enables live migration, and thus dynamic VM consolidation. This possibility can be used to reduce power consumption in the cloud. However, consolidation in cloud environments is limited due to reliance on VMs, mainly due to their memory overhead. For instance, over a 4-month period in a real cloud located in Grenoble (France), we observed that 805 VMs used less than 12% of the CPU (of the active physical machines). This paper presents a solution introducing dynamic software consolidation. Software consolidation makes it possible to dynamically collocate several software applications on the same VM to reduce the number of VMs used. This approach can be combined with VM consolidation which collocates multiple VMs on a reduced number of physical machines. Software consolidation can be used in a private cloud to reduce power consumption, or by a client of a public cloud to reduce the number of VMs used, thus reducing costs. The evaluation was performed using both the SPECjms2007 benchmark and an enterprise LAMP benchmark on both a VMware private cloud and Amazon EC2 public cloud. The results show that our approach can reduce the energy consumed in our private cloud by about 40% and the charge for VMs on Amazon EC2 by about 40.5%.

Keywords: Cloud · Consolidation · Energy saving · Virtualization

1 Introduction

In recent years, cloud computing has emerged as one of the best solutions to host applications for companies or individual users. For these cloud customers (hereafter called clients), its pay-per-use model reduces the cost compared to

© Springer-Verlag Berlin Heidelberg 2015
J.L. Träff et al. (Eds.): Euro-Par 2015, LNCS 9233, pp. 305–316, 2015.
DOI: 10.1007/978-3-662-48096-0_24

using internal IT resources. For cloud providers (hereafter called providers) one of the main challenges is limiting power consumption in their data centers. In 2010, for example, data centers consumed approximately 1.1–1.5 % of the world's energy [14]. Power consumption can be minimized by limiting the number of active physical machines (PM) through sharing the same PM between several software applications and providing dynamic software consolidation (filling unused resources by grouping software). This helps to balance the variable workload due to the departure of some software.

In this paper, we considered a SaaS/PaaS-based cloud model (e.g. RightScale [5]). This type of cloud provides a fully customizable environment, allowing clients, e.g. companies, to focus on applications. The cloud provider offers a software catalogue. Clients can select an application and request its start in a virtualized data center. The data center may belong either to the cloud provider (private cloud), or be part of a public cloud; alternatively it can be a mixture of the two (hybrid cloud). The cloud provider is responsible for managing the clients' software (scalability, highly-available, failover, etc.) while efficiently managing resources to reduce data center costs: power consumption when relying on its own private cloud, or resource charged for when using a public cloud.

Advances in virtualization make transparent dynamic consolidation possible in the cloud. Based on this technology, the cloud runs each software application on a separate virtual machine (VM). Many studies [12,16,23] have described algorithms providing software consolidation through the consolidation of VMs. However, this approach is not sufficient since an infinite number of VMs cannot be packed into a single PM, even when the VMs are underused and the PM has sufficient computation power. Indeed, as argued by [20], VM packing is limited by memory. **In this paper, we therefore propose a solution consolidating software onto VMs. This solution is complementary to VM consolidation**. Rather than dedicating one VM to each software, we propose that the same VM be shared between several software applications. This will fill the gaps remaining inside the VM, as mentioned earlier. **This strategy also reduces the total number of VMs. This is very important in a commercial cloud to reduce the charge for VMs**.

Software consolidation raises two main challenges that need to be addressed:

- Software isolation. Isolation ensures that if a software application fails it does not compromise the execution of another software application, it also stops software from "stealing" the resources allocated to another application.
- Software migration. Migration involves moving software from its current node to another node without interrupting the service offered by the software, and while avoiding Service Level Agreement (SLA) violations on the migrated software.

In this paper we focus only on the live software migration and consolidation. For software isolation, we rely on Docker [2]. We present a solution to consolidate software on VMs (Sect. 2) based on a Constraints Programming (CP) solver. **The genericity of the solution allows the integration of a range of**

live software migration mechanisms since this operation is specific to software. We evaluated our approach using the SPECjms2007 benchmark [6] and an enterprise Internet application benchmark (Sect. 4) in the context of a SaaS offering messaging and Internet software on a private VMware cloud and on the Amazon EC2 cloud. These evaluations showed that: (1) our approach results in reduced power consumption and costs; and (2) the efficient live migration algorithms implemented for JMS messaging and Internet web servers are viable. For the specific workload assessed, our solution reduces the power consumption in our private cloud by about 40 % when software consolidation is combined with VM consolidation. Running the same workload on Amazon EC2 leads to a reduction in VMs charged of about 40.5 %. The paper ends by presenting related work in Sect. 5 and a conclusion is provided in Sect. 6.

2 Software Consolidation

Like VMs, software consolidation is an NP-hard [13] problem. We presents a solution that allows software consolidation for SaaS/PaaS platform.

2.1 Solution Overview

We focus on software consolidation and migration. VM placement at start time is part of the consolidation problem. Figure 1 presents the key components of the system studied. Applications are isolated within VMs using Docker containers [2]. *QuotaComputer* determines the amount of resources required by each application. *MonitoringEngine* is responsible for gathering statistics for both VM and software from all *MonitoringAgents*. The *ConsolidationManager* implements an online, reactive consolidation algorithm which acts as an infinite loop. It periodically:

1. Gets VMs and software status (quota consumption, which is an average of the most recent values) from the *MonitoringEngine*.
2. Checks if there are applications which need more resources and provides for them (relocation Algorithm 1).
3. Computes software assignment on VMs to minimize the number of VMs required to support all the software running. It also computes the reconfiguration plan (a set of software migrations) that must be performed for the ideal assignment to be achieved (Sect. 2.2).
4. And finally, runs (through the *LocalManager*) the reconfiguration plan.

At the end of each loop, VMs not running any software are terminated, either immediately in the case of a private cloud, or when its uptime is close to a multiple of Θ (the payment time unit) in a public cloud. In the latter case, a timer is started for each VM to be terminated so that it stops it before a new payment time unit starts. The timer is disabled when the VM is eligible to host a running application.

Before presenting our solution in detail, there follows a list of the notations used:

- $S = \{S_1, S_2, ..., S_m\}$ is the set of software types offered by the cloud.
- $\bar{S}_i = \{S_k, ...\}$ is the set of software, instances of which are collocate-able with an instance of S_i. This can be used to protect sensitive software from other potentially dangerous applications.
- For each VM vm_i, we consider three types of resources: cpu (vm_i^u), memory (vm_i^m) and IO bandwidth (vm_i^o).
- vm_i^γ is the cost of running the VM for a payment time unit Θ. This is considered when the SaaS/PaaS is placed on a public cloud.
- vm_i^{st} is the start time of vm_i.
- An instantiated VM is assigned an identifier (an integer). s_i^{vm} is the identifier of the VM running software s_i.
- $len(vm_i)$ is the number of applications on vm_i.
- Like VMware does for VMs, we consider two levels of resource reservation for a software: the minimum quota and the maximum quota. $s_i^{u_{min}}$ and $s_i^{u_{max}}$ are, respectively, the minimum and the maximum cpu (or memory or IO) quota. The software starts with $s_i^{*_{min}}$ and increases stepwise until it reaches $s_i^{*_{max}}$. $s_i^{*_{cur}}$ denotes the current quota. Note that * is u, m or o.
- s_i^T is the acceptable service degradation threshold defined at start time for software s_i. It corresponds to its SLA.

The relocation algorithm described in Algorithm 1, checks if the current resources available for each application are insufficient, excessive or sufficient. If not, the software acquires more resources within its maximum quota. This operation can cause the software to be relocated to another VM (an existing one or a new one). On the other hand, if the software is wasting resources, its quota is reduced; the algorithm includes a clause to avoid the frequent transitions (yo-yo effect). The choice of the destination VM (on which software is to be relocated) does not need to be optimal. Indeed, the consolidation manager will correct the placement. This will be discussed in the next section, where the formalization of the software placement problem as a Constraint Satisfaction Problem (CSP) [9] is presented.

2.2 Software Placement as a CSP

Definition: A CSP [9], C, is a set of constraints, L, acting on a set of variables, $\Delta = \{A_1, A_2, ..., A_n\}$, each of which has a finite domain of possible values, D_i. A solution to L is an instantiation of all of the variables in Δ such that all of the constraints in C are satisfied.

We used the ChocoCP library [19] to solve CSP. Choco aims to minimize or maximize the value of a single variable, while respecting a CSP definition. To do this, it uses an exhaustive search based on a depth-first search. We used two CSPs to resolve the consolidation problem. The first CSP was used to determine the minimum number of VMs n_{new} needed to run all software; we call this the *MinVMToUse* problem. But n_{new} can be provided by several configurations (software mapping onto VMs). Therefore, the second CSP chooses the appropriate configuration and generates the reconfiguration plan to reach that

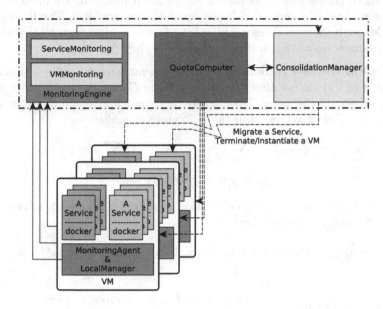

Fig. 1. Architecture of our software consolidation system

Algorithm 1. Software relocation

Begin

1: **for each** *software s_i of the SaaS/PaaS* **do**
2:      **for each** *resource type r (u, m, or o)* **do**
3:          **if** $s_i^{r^{cur}}$ *is insufficient and* $s_i^{r^{cur}} < s_i^{r^{max}}$ **then**
4:              Increase the quota of s_i
5:          **else**
6:              **if** $s_i^{r^{cur}}$ *is excessive and* $s_i^{r^{cur}} \neq s_i^{r^{min}}$ **then**
7:                  **if** *The last quota decrease time is enough to avoid yo − yo effect* **then**
8:                      Decrease the quota of s_i
9:                  **end if**
10:             **end if**
11:         **end if**
12:     **end for**
13:     **if** *The actual VM of s_i does not have enough resources for − the new quota* **then**
14:         DestinationVM← The Best-Fit VM which can host s_i with its new quota
15:         **if** *DestinationVM* == *NULL* **then**
16:             DestinationVM←Allocate a new VM
17:         **else**
18:             Disable any timer on DestinationVM
19:         **end if**
20:         Compute the docker container for s_i on DestinationVM
21:         *Migrate s_i to DestinationVM*
22:     **else**
23:         Update the docker container for s_i on its current VM
24:     **end if**
25: **end for**

End

configuration; this is called the *RightConfiguration* problem. We modeled these problems as a mixed-integer non-linear optimization problem. The inputs are a list of VMs with their total resources, a list of software (for each VM) with their current resource quota and status (service level they provide).

The *MinVMToUse* Problem. If no deployment request has been submitted, the number of VMs in use after application of the *ConsolidationManager* should decrease or remain the same. This should be done while avoiding resource over commitment. This is expressed in the following inequality:

$$\sum s_j^{u_{cur}} \leq vm_i^u \wedge \sum s_j^{m_{cur}} \leq vm_i^m \wedge \sum s_j^{o_{cur}} \leq vm_i^o, \qquad (1)$$

$$where \ s_j^{vm} = i, \ \forall \ VM \ vm_i$$

We also allow the user to specify collocation requirements for each software. The following equation expresses that:

$$| \ s_i^{vm} - s_j^{vm} \ | + Col(s_i, s_j) \neq 0, \ \forall \ couple \ of \ software \ (s_i, s_j), \ i \neq j \qquad (2)$$

$$where \ Col(s_i, s_j) = \begin{cases} 1 \ if \ s_i \ and \ s_j \ are \ collocate - able \\ 0 \ otherwise \end{cases}$$

The variable X minimizing the number of VMs is defined as follows:

$$X = \sum((len(vm_i) == 0)?0 : 1) \qquad (3)$$

Speeding Up the Consolidation Process. We improved the consolidation process to reduce the solver execution time. First, we reduced the search domain for X by bounding it. In the best case, the minimum number of VMs is the sum of the resource quotas needed by all the software divided by the resource capacity of the biggest VM (we choose the most restrictive resource type). In the worst case, there will be no consolidation. This improvement is formalized as follows:

$$max\left(\left\lceil \frac{\sum s_i^{u_{cur}}}{max(vm_j^u)} \right\rceil, \left\lceil \frac{\sum s_i^{m_{cur}}}{max(vm_j^m)} \right\rceil, \left\lceil \frac{\sum s_i^{o_{cur}}}{max(vm_j^o)} \right\rceil \right) \leq X \leq n, \qquad (4)$$

where n is the current number of VMs.

Second, some VMs or software may be equivalent in terms of resources or collocation constraints. If the resources offered by a VM, vm_i, are insufficient to host software s_j, then they are also insufficient to host any software s_k which has the same requirements. In addition, software s_j cannot be hosted by any other VM vm_k having the same characteristics as vm_i. With regard to the collocation constraint, if a VM, vm_i, runs software s_j which cannot be collocated with software s_k, then vm_i cannot host any software of the same type as s_k.

The *RightConfiguration* Problem. For correct configuration, the solver only considers configurations using the number of VMs determined by the first problem. The reconfiguration operation likely to affect the software SLA is live migration. The impact of this process could be a degradation of the service offered by the migrated software. Three factors affect live migration: network utilization, remaining computation power on both source and destination VM, and efficiency of the implementation of the live migration itself. Considering this, we call s_i^I the function calculating the impact of migrating software s_i for a given triplet of factors. Thus, if s_i^e represents the current service level provided by s_i before migration, then $s_i^e * s_i^I$ is the service level during migration. We define the cost of migrating a software s_i as $s_i^\Delta = s_i^e - s_i^e * s_i^I$. The correct configuration is the one minimizing K,

$$K = \sum s_i^\Delta, \ \forall \ software \ s_i \ to \ be \ migrated \tag{5}$$

while avoiding SLA violations:

$$s_i^e * s_i^I < s_i^T, \ \forall \ software \ s_i \ to \ be \ migrated \tag{6}$$

3   Use Cases

This work was conducted conjointly with two industrial groups: Scale Agent and Eolas. The former provides an implementation of the JMS specification, while the latter is a SaaS provider offering Internet services. We used our solution to manage a SaaS offering both a messaging service (such as IronMQ [3]) provided by Joram [4] software, and an Internet service based on a LAMP architecture.

Migrating a running software serving requests raises two main challenges that we had to address:

- (C1) Avoid loss of requests and state during migration.
- (C2) Make the migrated software available and accessible on the destination node after migration. This should be transparent for the clients.

Due to space limitation for this article, we present only the migration algorithm for the JMS server. Joram ensures that any message will reach its addressee within a configurable time window. We relied on this feature to complete the initial part of the first challenge (C1). For the second part of (C1), at runtime a Joram server keeps a persistence basis containing its entire state: processing messages, messages in transit, and processed messages. Therefore, a Joram server can be made available with the same state on the destination node by copying this basis from the source node to the destination node. With regard to (C2), in contrast to live migration of VMs, where the migrated VM keeps its IP address on the destination node, migrating software results in a new IP address (the IP address of the destination node). How can remote clients be transparently informed of this new address? In our system this is resolved by forcing clients to use the DNS name when dealing with the Joram servers. Thus, the accessibility of the migrated server is provided by (1) dynamically updating the DNS server and (2) rebinding the JMS client to the DNS server. This is transparent to the client because the JMS client is implemented to automatically resolve new addresses after several attempts.

Immediate copy of the persistence basis can have an important impact on the service offered by the migrated Joram server when this file is very large. To avoid this problem, we have optimized the algorithm to transmit the log file block by block to the destination node. This optimization was inspired by the copy-on-write mechanism used for live VM migration. We customized the Joram implementation to dynamically integrate and evolve its state at runtime when receiving new persistence information. A timer, which is triggered at the beginning of the migration process, ends the copy to limit the duration of the whole process. This optimization is currently being integrated into the official implementation of Joram on the OW2 [4] open source platform.

4   Evaluations

We evaluated our solution to show the benefits of software consolidation on top of VM consolidation. These benefits are shown in terms of energy and cost savings. The efficiency and scalability of CSP-based consolidation methods were evaluated in [10,12].

4.1   Testbed Overview

The cloud testbed integrates both a private and a public platform. Our private cloud is a part of the Eolas data center. It is composed of 8 DELL PowerEdge R510 equipped with Xeon E5645 2.40 Ghz processors (one with a 12-core CPU, and the others with 8-core CPU), 32 Gb memory and 2 NICs at 1 Gbps. They are connected through a gigabyte network switch. The virtualized layer is provided by VMware VCenter 5.1.0 (ESXi 5) with the VM consolidation module DRS/DPM [1] enabled: a PM for the VCenter, a PM with an NFS server to host VM images and user sessions, and 5 PMs as ESXi to host VMs. The last PM hosts our system (including the DNS server) and the agents simulating the Joram and web server users. The cloud provides a single type of VM: 1 vcpu running at 2.4 GHz and 1 Gb memory. The public cloud used was Amazon EC2 in the M1, medium VM, configuration.

SPECjms2007 [6] was used to bench the Joram servers. It includes seven interactions. Thus 7 Joram servers (7 VMs) are needed to run it. The second use case was based on real traces of the Internet service (LAMP) offered by the Eolas SaaS.

4.2   Power Saving in the Private Cloud

We simultaneously ran 15 SPECJms2007 and 6 LAMP scenarios (up to 37 VMs) in two situations. In the first situation (noted WSC (With Software Consolidation)) we ran the experiment with both software and VM consolidation enabled,

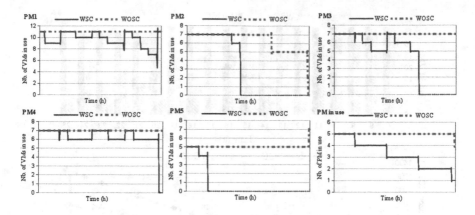

Fig. 2. Power saving in the private cloud: Utilization of PMs

while in the second situation (noted WOSC (WithOut Software Consolidation)) we disabled software consolidation (but maintained VM consolidation). The scenarios were configured to provide a varied workload over 30 h: a mix of constant, ascending and descending phases. Figure 2 presents (1) the occupancy (in terms of the number of VMs) of each PM in the private cloud, and (2) the number of PMs in use during the 25 h of observation. We see that the first situation results in 3 PMs (PM2, PM3 and PM5) being freed, while 1 PM (PM2) was freed in the second situation. Software consolidation accelerates VM consolidation. The bottom right curve in Fig. 2 shows that this improvement represents an approximately 40 % power saving with this particular workload.

4.3 Cost Saving in a Public Cloud

We repeated the previous experiments with VMs configured to run for an hour (before termination because they were empty) on Amazon EC2. We used M1, medium VMs instances, which are charged at $0.120 per VM per hour. Figure 3 presents the total number of VMs used over the 25 h of observation, and the total cost of the experiments. The number of VMs is seen to drastically decrease thanks to software consolidation, resulting in an approximate 40.5 % saving: from about $1300 (without software consolidation) to $800 (with software consolidation).

5 Related Work

Memory Footprint Improvements. Significant research has been devoted to improving workload consolidation in data centers. Some studies have investigated reducing the VM memory footprint to increase the VMs' consolidation, when a VM is dedicated to a single software. Among these, memory compression and memory over commitment ([8,15,22]) are very promising. In the same

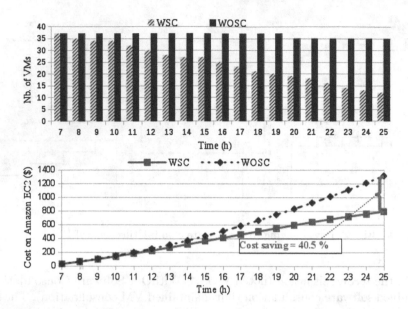

Fig. 3. Cost saving on Amazon EC2: (top) nb. of VMs per hour, (bottom) VMs charged

vein, [21] extends the VM ballooning technique to software to increase the density of software collocation on the same VM. [7] presented VSwapper, a guest-agnostic solution to reduce the effect of memory ballooning. Xen offers what it called "stub domain"[1]. This is a lightweight VM which requires very few memory (about 32 MB) for its execution. As our solution, all these works try do minimize the footprint of a VM in order to increase the number of VMs that can be collocated on top of the same physical machine. Therefore, they result to the same result as us in terms of energy saving. However, they do not minimize the total number of VMs as we do in order to reduce VMs charged for the clients when considering of a commercial cloud.

VM Consolidation Algorithms. In our previous work [23], we proposed a couple of this sort of VM relocation and collocation algorithms. [18] treats the VMs consolidation problem using a heuristic algorithm which minimizes the number of live migrations in the reconfiguration plan. An SLA-aware VMs consolidation system is presented in [11]. Like with our proposal, it formalizes the problem of minimizing the operating cost for a private cloud while also minimizing SLA violations for services offered by software. Our formalization can be extended by considering this work. [17] presents a VM consolidation strategy based on a predictive approach. Since the placement problem is NP-hard, it is not possible to develop a solution running within an acceptable time. [24] presents DejaVu, a consolidation system which takes into consideration the interference between

---

[1] http://wiki.xen.org/wiki/StubDom.

consolidated VMs. Based on hardware counters, it proposes a metric for characterizing workloads which are collocatable. In this paper, we do not focus on VM consolidation. We bring the same idea at software level (software within VMs). Therefore, any VM consolidation algorithm presented in this section can be applied to software consolidation. In this paper, we base on a solver to resolve the problem.

Software Consolidation. The main problem with previous solutions is that they are limited by the footprint of the VMs consolidated (they are all operating systems). Execution of a VM requires a set of minimum resources, even if the application it runs is idle. Thus, we propose a solution which dynamically packs software into VMs to effectively use the overall VM resources while respecting the individual requirements of the different software applications. With current knowledge, [10] is the only previous work that studies dynamic software consolidation on the same OS; however, it does not rely on VMs. [10] focuses on the MySQL database software and provides a live migration algorithm for that. This algorithm can be plugged into our framework. [10] (as well as Entropy [12]) describes a consolidation algorithm based on a CSP. Thus, no previous study has investigated software consolidation onto VMs. In this paper, we developed a working prototype and showed that it can achieve high VM utilization to provide cost and power-saving benefits.

6 Conclusion

In this paper we proposed a solution to consolidate software onto VMs to reduce power consumption in a private cloud and the number of VMs charged for in a public cloud. We focused on the algorithms for live migration and consolidation. Although the proposed solution can integrate other live software migration algorithms, we have provided a migration algorithm for JMS messaging. The consolidation algorithm is based on a Constraint Satisfaction Problem (CSP) approach. Evaluations with realistic benchmarks on a messaging and web applications SaaS cloud showed that our solution (1) reduces the power consumed by our industrial cloud partner by about 40 % when combined with VM consolidation, and (2) reduces the charge for VMs used on Amazon EC2 by about 40.5 %. Future work will include extended analysis of how best to coordinate software consolidation on VMs with VM consolidation on physical machines in order to further improve power gains.

Acknowledgment. This work was in part funded by IDS company, the French national program "Investissements d'Avenir IRT Nanoelec" ANR-10-AIRT-05 and Institut Universitaire de France.

References

1. Vmware distributed power management (DPM), Technical white paper (2010). http://www.vmware.com/files/pdf/DPM.pdf

2. Docker, June 2013. http://www.docker.com/
3. Ironmq: The message queue for the cloud, April 2013. http://www.iron.io/mq
4. Joram: Java (tm) open reliable asynchronous messaging, April 2013. http://joram.ow2.org/
5. Rightscale cloud management, April 2013. http://www.rightscale.com/
6. Specjms 2007, April 2013. http://www.spec.org/jms2007/
7. Amit, N., Tsafrir, D., Schuster, A.: Vswapper: a memory swapper for virtualized environments. In: ASPLOS, pp. 349–366 (2014)
8. Barker, S., Wood, T., Shenoy, P., Sitaraman, R.: An empirical study of memory sharing in virtual machines. In: USENIX ATC (2012)
9. Benhamou, F., Jussien, N., O'Sullivan, B. (eds.): Trends in Constraint Programming. ISTE, London (2007)
10. Curino, C., Jones, E.P.C., Madden, S., Balakrishnan, H.: Workload-aware database monitoring and consolidation. In: SIGMOD, pp. 313–324 (2011)
11. Goudarzi, H., Ghasemazar, M., Pedram, M.: Sla-based optimization of power and migration cost in cloud computing. In: CCGRID, pp. 172–179 (2012)
12. Hermenier, F., Lorca, X., Menaud, J.M., Muller, G., Lawall, J.: Entropy: a consolidation manager for clusters. In: VEE, pp. 41–50 (2009)
13. Karve, A., Kimbrel, T., Pacifici, G., Spreitzer, M., Steinder, M., Sviridenko, M., Tantawi, A.: Dynamic placement for clustered web applications. In: WWW, pp. 595–604 (2006)
14. Koomey, J.G.: Growth in Data Center Electricity Use 2005 to 2010. Analytics Press, Oakland (2011)
15. Liu, L., Chu, R., Zhu, Y., Zhang, P., Wang, L.: Dmss: a dynamic memory scheduling system in server consolidation environments. In: ISORC, pp. 70–75 (2011)
16. Lv, H., Dong, Y., Duan, J., Tian, K.: Virtualization challenges: a view from server consolidation perspective. In: VEE, pp. 15–26 (2012)
17. Mars, J., Tang, L., Hundt, R., Skadron, K., Soffa, M.L.: Bubble-up: increasing utilization in modern warehouse scale computers via sensible co-locations. In: MICRO, pp. 248–259 (2011)
18. Murtazaev, A., Oh, S.: Sercon: server consolidation algorithm using live migration of virtual machines for green computing. IETE TR **28**(3), 212–231 (2011)
19. Jussien, N., Rochart, G., Lorca, X.: The choco constraint programming solver. In: OSSICP, pp. 1–10 (2008)
20. Norris, C., Cohen, H.M., Cohen, B.: Leveraging ibm ex5 systems for breakthrough cost and density improvements in virtualized x86 environments. white paper, January 2011
21. Salomie, T.I., Alonso, G., Roscoe, T., Elphinstone, K.: Application level ballooning for efficient server consolidation. In: EuroSys, pp. 337–350 (2013)
22. Sharma, P., Kulkarni, P.: Singleton: system-wide page deduplication in virtual environments. In: HPDC, pp. 15–26 (2012)
23. Tchana, A., Tran, G.S., Broto, L., Palma, N.D.: Two levels autonomic resource management in virtualized iaas. FGCS **29**, 1319–1332 (2013)
24. Vasic, N., Novakovic, D., Miucin, S., Kostic, D., Bianchini, R.: Accelerating resource allocation in virtualized environments. In: ASPLOS (2012)

VMPlaceS: A Generic Tool to Investigate and Compare VM Placement Algorithms

Adrien Lebre[✉], Jonathan Pastor, and Mario Südholt

ASCOLA Research Group (Mines Nantes, Inria, LINA), Nantes, France
{adrien.lebre,jonathan.pastor,mario.sudholt}@inria.fr

Abstract. Advanced Virtual Machines placement policies are evaluated either using limited scale *in-vivo* experiments or ad hoc simulator techniques. These validation methodologies are unsatisfactory. First they do not model precisely enough real production platforms (size, workload representativeness, etc.). Second, they do not enable the fair comparison of different approaches.

To resolve these issues, we propose VMPlaceS, a dedicated simulation framework to perform in-depth investigations and fair comparisons of VM placement algorithms. Built on top of SimGrid, our framework provides programming support to ease the implementation of placement algorithms and runtime support dedicated to load injection and execution trace analysis. It supports a large set of parameters enabling researchers to design simulations representative of a large space of real-world scenarios. We also report on a comparison using VMPlaceS of three classes of placement algorithms: centralized, hierarchical and fully-distributed ones.

1 Introduction

Most of the popular Cloud Computing (CC) management systems [7,16,17], or IaaS toolkits [14], rely on elementary virtual machine (VM) placement policies that prevent them from maximizing the usage of CC resources while guaranteeing VM resource requirements as defined by Service Level Agreements (SLAs). Typically, a batch scheduling approach is used: VMs are statically allocated to physical machines according to user requests. Such static policies are clearly suboptimal, because users often overestimate their needs and the effective resource requirements of a VM may significantly vary during its lifetime [2].

An important impediment to the adoption of more advanced strategies such as dynamic consolidation, load balancing and other SLA-enforcing algorithms developed by the academic community [8,10,19,22,23] is related to the experimental processes used for their validation: most VM placement proposals have been evaluated either using ad hoc simulators or small *in-vivo* (*i.e.*, real-world) experiments. These methods are not accurate and not representative enough to (i) ensure their correctness on real platforms and (ii) perform fair comparisons between them. Analyzing proposals for VM placement on representative testbeds in terms of scalability, reliability and varying workload changes would

J.L. Träff et al. (Eds.): Euro-Par 2015, LNCS 9233, pp. 317–329, 2015.
DOI: 10.1007/978-3-662-48096-0_25

definitely be the most rigorous way to support their development for CC production infrastructures. However, *in-vivo* experiments, if they can be executed at all, are always expensive and tedious to perform (see [1] for a recent reference).

In this article, we propose VMPlaceS, a dedicated simulation framework to perform in-depth investigations of VM placement algorithms and compare them in a fair way. To cope with real conditions such as the increasing scale of modern data centers, as well as the workload dynamicity and elasticity characteristics that are specific to the CC paradigm, VMPlaceS allows users to study large-scale scenarios that involve thousands of VMs, each executing a specific workload that evolves during the simulation. To illustrate the relevance of VMPlaceS, we have implemented and analyzed three well-known approaches: Entropy [10], Snooze [8], and DVMS [19]. We chose these three systems as they represent three classes of placement algorithms: Entropy is an instance of a centralized model, Snooze of a hierarchical one and DVMS of a fully distributed one. Using VMPlaceS, we compare the scalability and reactivity (*i.e.*, the time to solve SLA violations) of the strategies — a contribution of its own. Our results also reveal the importance of the duration of the reconfiguration phase (*i.e.*, the step where VMs are relocated throughout the infrastructure) compared to the computation phase (*i.e.*, the step where the scheduler solves the VMPP). We believe that VMPlaceS will be beneficial to a large number of researchers in the field of CC as it enables them to analyze the main characteristics of a new proposal, allowing *in vivo* experiments to be restricted to placement mechanisms that have the potential to handle CC production infrastructures.

The rest of the article is organized as follow. Section 2 gives an overview of the SimGrid framework on which our proposal is built. Section 3 introduces VMPlaceS. Entropy, Snooze and DVMS are briefly presented in Sect. 4 and evaluated in Sect. 5. Sections 6 and 7 present, respectively, related work and a conclusion.

2   Simgrid, a Generic Toolkit to Build Simulators

SimGrid is a toolkit for the simulation of potentially complex algorithms executed on large-scale distributed systems [6]. To perform simulations, users develop a *program*, and define a *platform* and a *deployment* files. The *program* typically leverages SimGrid's MSG API that allows end users to create and execute SimGrid abstractions such as processes, tasks, VMs and network communications. The *platform* file provides the physical description of all resources that are the object of the simulation. The *deployment* file is used to launch the different SimGrid processes of the program on the simulated nodes. Finally, the simulation is orchestrated by the SimGrid engine that internally relies on a constraint solver to assign the CPU/network resources during the entire simulation.

We chose to base VMPlaceS on SimGrid since (i) the latter's relevance in terms of performance and validity has already been demonstrated [20] and (ii) because it has been recently extended to integrate VM abstractions and a live migration model [11]. In addition to enabling researchers to control VMs in the same manner as in the real world (*e.g.*, create/destroy VMs; start/shutdown, suspend/resume and migrate them), the live migration model provided by Sim-Grid is the only one that successfully determines correctly the time and the resulting network traffic of a migration by taking into account the competition arising in the presence of resource sharing and the memory refresh rate. These two capabilities were mandatory to build VMPlaceS.

3   VM Placement Simulator

The aim of VMPlaceS is twofold: (i) to relieve researchers of the burden of dealing with VM creations and workload fluctuations when they evaluate new VM placement algorithms and (ii) to offer the possibility to compare them.

Overview. VMPlaceS has been implemented in Java by leveraging the SimGrid MSG API. Although Java has an impact on the efficiency of SimGrid, we believe its use is acceptable because Java offers important benefits to researchers for the implementation of advanced scheduling strategies, notably concerning the ease of implementation of new strategies. As examples, we implemented the Snooze proposal in Java and the DVMS proposal using Scala and Java.

VMPlaceS performs a simulation in three phases, see Fig. 1: (i) initialization, (ii) injection and (iii) trace analysis. The initialization phase corresponds to the creation of the environment, the VMs and the generation of an event queue. The simulation is performed by at least two SimGrid processes, one executing the *injector*, the generic part of the framework which is in charge of injecting the events during the execution of the simulation, and a second one executing the to-be-simulated *scheduling algorithm*. The latter analyzes the collected traces in order to gather the

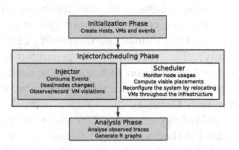

Fig. 1. VMPlaceS's Workflow Gray parts correspond to the generic code while the white one must be provided by end-users.

results of the simulation, notably by means of the generation of figures representing, *e.g.*, resource usage statistics.

Researchers develop their scheduling algorithm using the SimGrid MSG API and a more abstract interface that is provided by VMPlaceS and consists of the classes XHost, XVM and SimulatorManager. The two former classes respectively extend SimGrid's Host and VM abstractions while the latter controls the interactions between the different components of the simulator. Through these three classes users can inspect, at any time, the current state of the infrastructure (*i.e.*, the load of a host/VM, the number of VMs hosted on the whole infrastructure or on a particular host, check whether a host is overloaded, etc.).

Initialization Phase. VMPlaceS first creates n VMs and assigns them in a round-robin manner to the first p hosts defined in the platform file. The default platform file corresponds to a cluster of $h + s$ hosts, where h corresponds to the number of hosting nodes and s to the number of services nodes. The values n, h and s constitute input parameters of the simulations (specified in a Java property file). These hosts are organized in form of topologies, a cluster topology being the most common one. It is possible, however, to define more complex platforms to simulate, for instance, federated data center scenarios.

Each VM is created based on one of the predefined VM classes. A VM class corresponds to a template specifying the VM attributes and its memory footprint. It is defined in terms of five parameters: the number of cores nb_cpus, the size of the memory ramsize, the network bandwidth net_bw, the maximum bandwidth available mig_speed and the maximum memory update speed mem_speed available when the VM is consuming 100 % of its CPU resources. Available classes are defined in a text file that is modifyable by users. As pointed out in Sect. 2, the memory update speed is a critical parameter that governs the migration time as well as the amount of transferred data. VM classes provide means to simulate arbitrary kinds of workload (*e.g.*, memory-intensive ones).

All VMs start with a CPU consumption of 0 that will evolve during the simulation depending on the injected load as explained below. Once the creation and the assignment of VMs completed, VMPlaceS spawns at least two SimGrid processes, the *injector* and the launcher of the selected scheduler. At its start the *injector* creates an event queue that will be consumed during the second phase of the simulation. Currently, VMPlaceS supports *CPU load change* events (only). The event queue is generated in order to change the load of each VM every t seconds on average. t is a random variable that follows an exponential distribution with rate parameter λ_t while the CPU load of a VM evolves according to a Gaussian distribution defined by a given mean (μ) as well as a given standard deviation (σ). t, μ and σ are provided as input parameters of a simulation. Furthermore, each random process used in VMPlaceS is initialized with a seed that is defined in a configuration file. This way, we can ensure that different simulations are reproducible and may be used to establish fair comparisons.

Finally, we highlight that adding new events can be done by simply defining new event Java classes implementing the InjectorEvent interface and by adding the code in charge of generating the corresponding events that are then handled similarly to the *CPU Load* ones. As an example, the next release of VMPlaceS will integrate *node apparition/removal events* that will be used to simulate crashes.

Injector Phase. Once the VMs and the global event queue are ready, the evaluation of the scheduling mechanism can start. First, the injector process iteratively consumes the different events. Changing the load of a VM corresponds to the creation and the assignment of a new SimGrid task in the VM. This new task has a direct impact on the time that will be needed to migrate the VM as it increases or decreases the current CPU load and thus its memory update speed.

Based on the scheduler decisions, VMs will be suspended/resumed or relocated on the available hosts. Users must implement the algorithm in charge of solving the VMPP but also the code in charge of applying reconfiguration plans using methods from the `SimulatorManager` class. This step is essential as the reconfiguration cost is a key element of dynamic placement systems.

It is noteworthy that VMPlaceS invokes the execution of each scheduling solver, as a real implementation would do, to get the effective reconfiguration plan. That is, the computation time that is observed is not simulated but corresponds to the effective one, only the workload inside the VMs and the reconfiguration operations (*i.e.*, suspend/resume and migrate) are simulated in SimGrid.

Trace Analysis. The last step of VMPlaceS consists in analyzing the information that has been collected during the simulation. This analysis is done in two steps. First, VMPlaceS records several metrics related to the platform utilization using an extended version of SimGrid's TRACE module[1]. This way, visualization tools that have been developed by the SimGrid community, such as PajeNG [18], may be used with VMPlaceS. Furthermore, our extension enables the creation of a JSON trace file, which is used to represent resource usage by figures generated using the R statistical environment [3].

By default, VMPlaceS records the load of the VMs and hosts, the start and the duration of each violation of VM requirements in the system, the number of migrations, the number of times the scheduler mechanism has been invoked and the number of times it succeeds or fails to resolve non-viable configurations. The TRACE API is extensible in that as many variables as necessary can be created by users of our system, thus allowing researchers to instrument their own algorithm with specific variables that record other pieces of information.

4   Dynamic VMPP Algorithms

To illustrate the interest of VMPlaceS, we implemented three dynamic VM placement mechanisms: a centralized one based on the Entropy proposal [10], a hierarchical one based on Snooze [8], and a fully-distributed one based on DVMS [19].

These systems search for solutions to violations caused by overloaded nodes. A host is overloaded when its VMs try to consume more than 100 % of the CPU capacity of the host. In such a case, a resolution algorithm looks for a reconfiguration plan that can lead to a viable configuration. For the sake of simplicity, we chose to use the latest solver developed as part of the Entropy framework [9] as this resolution algorithm for all three systems. The Entropy solver evaluates different viable configurations until it reaches a predefined timeout. Once the timeout has been triggered, the algorithm returns the best solution among the ones it finds and applies the associated reconfiguration plan by invoking live migrations in the simulation world.

In the remainder of this section, we present an overview of the three systems.

---

[1] http://simgrid.gforge.inria.fr/simgrid/3.12/doc/tracing.html.

Entropy-Based Centralized Approach. The centralized placement mechanism consists in one single SimGrid process deployed on a service node. This process implements a simple loop that iteratively checks the viability of the current configuration by invoking the aforementioned VMPP solver with a pre-defined frequency. The resource usage is monitored through direct accesses to the states of the hosts and their respective VMs. We also monitor, for each iteration, whether the VMPP solver succeeds or fails. In the case of success, VMPlaceS records the number of migrations that have been performed, the time it took to apply the reconfiguration and whether the reconfiguration led to new violations.

Snooze-Based Hierarchical Approach. Snooze [8,21] harnesses a hierarchical architecture in order to support load balancing and fault tolerance, cf. Fig. 2. At the top, a *group leader (GL)* centralizes information about the whole cluster using summary data about *group managers (GMs)* that constitute the intermediate layer of the hierarchy. GMs manage a number of *local controllers (LCs)* that, in turn, manage the VMs assigned to nodes.

During execution, higher-level components periodically send heartbeats to lower-level ones; monitoring information, *e.g.*, about the system load, is also sent periodically in the opposite direction. In order to propagate information, Snooze relies on hardware support for multicast communication.

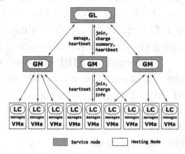

The implementation in VMPlaceS of the core architectural abstractions of Snooze leverages the XHOST, XVM and SimulatorManager while other mechanisms have been implemented using Simgrid's primitives and standard Java mecha-

Fig. 2. Snooze architecture

nisms. For instance, communication between Snooze actors is implemented based on Simgrid's primitives for, mainly asynchronous, event handling. The multicast capability that is used, *e.g.*, to relay heartbeats, is implemented as a dedicated service that manages a state to relay heartbeat events in a concurrent manner to all receivers. Finally, our Snooze simulation uses, as its original counterpart, a multi-threaded implementation (*i.e.*, based on multiple SimGrid processes) in order to optimize reactivity even for large groups of LCs (or GMs) that have to be managed by one GM (or GL).

DVMS-Based Distributed Approach. DVMS (Distributed Virtual Machine Scheduler) [19] enables the cooperative and fully-distributed placement of VMs. A DVMS agent is deployed on each node in order to manage the VMs on the node and collaborate with (the agents of) neighboring nodes. Agents are defined on top of an overlay communication network that defines the node-neighbor relation. We have implemented a simple unstructured overlay that enables the agents to collaborate by providing a link to a neighbor on the latter's request.

Figure 3 depicts the DVMS algorithm. When a node N_i detects that it cannot provide enough resources for its hosted VMs, an *Iterative Scheduling*

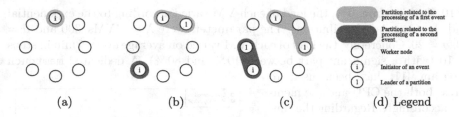

(a)   (b)   (c)   (d) Legend

Fig. 3. Processing two events simultaneously

Procedure (ISP) is started: it initiates a partition, reserving itself to solve the problem, see Fig. 3(a). Then, its closest neighbor is considered. If this neighbor, N_{i+1}, is already part of another partition, the next neighbor is considered. Otherwise, N_{i+1} joins the partition (see Fig. 3(b)) and becomes the partition leader.

The other nodes involved in the partition then send it information about their capacities and current load. The leader, in turn, starts a scheduling computation looking for a reconfiguration within the current partition. If no solution is found, the same algorithm is applied to the next node N_{i+2}. This approach constructs small partitions in a highly parallel manner (Fig. 3(c)), thus accelerating the scheduling process and reactivity.

Most of the DVMS code has been coded in SCALA leveraging the Java primitives of SimGrid for the communications between the different DVMS agents that have been implemented, in turn, using the abstractions of VMPlaceS.

5 Experiments

Two kinds of experiments have been performed to validate the relevance of VMPlaceS. The objective of the first one was to evaluate the accuracy of the returned results while the second was a concrete use-case of VMPlaceS, analyzing the three strategies introduced before.

5.1 Accuracy Evaluation

To validate the accuracy of VMPlaceS, we have implemented a dedicated version of our framework[2] on top of the Grid'5000 testbed and compared the execution of the Entropy strategy invoked every 60 s over a 3600 s period in both the simulated and the real world. Regarding the *in-vivo* conditions, experiments have been performed on top of the Graphene cluster (Intel Xeon X3440-4 CPU cores, 16 GB memory, a GbE NIC, Linux 3.2, Qemu 1.5 and SFQ network policy enabled) with 6 VMs per node. Each VM has been created using one of 8 VM predefined classes. The template was 1:1GB:1Gbps:1Gbps:X, where the memory update speed X was a value between 0 and 80 % of the migration bandwidth (1Gbps) in steps

---

[2] https://github.com/BeyondTheClouds/G5K-VMPlaceS.

of 10. Starting from 0 %, the load of each VM varied according to the exponential and the Gaussian distributions. The parameters were $\lambda = \#\text{VMs}/300$ and $\mu = 60$, $\sigma = 20$. Concretely, the load of each VM varied on average every 5 min in steps of 10 (with a significant part between 40 % and 80 %). A dedicated `memtouch`

program [11] has been used to stress both the CPU and the memory accordingly. Regarding the simulated executions, VMPlaceS has been configured to reflect the *in-vivo* conditions. In particular, we configured the network model of SimGrid in order to cope with the network performance of the Graphene servers that were allocated to our experiment (6 MBytes for the TCP gamma parameter and 0.88 for the bandwidth corrective simulation factor). Figure 4 shows the time to perform the two phases of the Entropy algorithm for each invocation when considering 32 PMs and 192 VMs through simulations (top) and in reality (bottom). Overall, we can see that simulation results successfully fol-

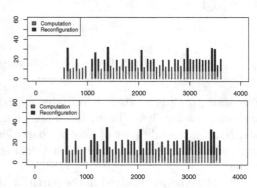

Fig. 4. Comparison between simulated (top) and *in-vivo* (bottom) Executions The Y-axis represents the duration of each Entropy invocation. It is divived into two parts: the time to look for a new configuration (the computation phase in red) and the time to relocate the VMs (the reconfugration phase in black). Both axis are in seconds (Color figure online).

lowed the in-vivo ones. During the first hundreds seconds, the cluster did not experience VM requirement violations because the loads of VM were still small (*i.e.*, Entropy simply validated that the current placement satisfied all VM requirements). At 540 s, Entropy started to detect non viable configurations and performed reconfigurations. Diving into details, the difference between the *simulated* and *in-vivo* reconfiguration time fluctuated between 6 % and 18 % (median was around 12 %). The worst case, *i.e.*, 18 %, was reached when multiple migrations were performed simultaneously on the same destination node. In this case and even if the SFQ network policy was enabled, we discovered that in the reality the throughput of migration traffic fluctuated when multiple migration sessions simultaneously shared the same destination node. We confirmed this point by analyzing TCP bandwidth sharing through `iperf` executions. We are currently investigating with the SimGrid core-developers how we can integrate this phenomenon into the live-migration model. However, as a migration lasts less than 15 s in average, we believe that the current simulation results are sufficiently accurate to capture performance trends of placement strategies.

5.2   Analysis of Entropy, Snooze and DVMS

As a validation of our approach (and a contribution by itself), we now provide simulation results comparing the Entropy, Snooze and DVMS strategies.

Experimental Conditions. Each simulation has been executed on a dedicated server, thus avoiding interferences between simulations and ensuring reproducibility between the different invocations. VMPlaceS has been configured to simulate a homogeneous infrastructure of PMs composed of 8 cores, 32 GB of RAM and 1 Gpbs Ethernet NIC. To enable a fair comparison between the three strategies, the scheduling resolver only considered 7 cores, *i.e.*, one was devoted to run the Snooze LC or the DVMS admin processes (a common experimental setup). Ten VMs have been initially launched on each simulated PM. Each VM relied on one of the VM classes described in the accuracy experiment and one set of load-change parameters has been used: $\lambda = \#\text{VMs}/300$, $\mu = 60$ and $\sigma = 20$. The stationary state was reached after 20 min of the simulated time with a global cluster load of 85 %. We have performed simulations over a period of 1800 s. The consolidation ratio, *i.e.*, the number of VMs per node, has been defined such that a sufficient number of violations is generated. We have discovered that below a global load of 75 %, few VM violations occurred under the selected Gaussian distribution we have chosen. This result is rather satisfactory as it can explained why most production DCs target a comparable load level.[3] Finally, infrastructures composed of 128, 256, 512 and 1024 PMs, hosting respectively 1280, 2560, 5120 and 10240 VMs have been investigated. For Entropy and Snooze that rely on service nodes, additional simulated PMs have been provided. For Snooze, one GM has been created per 32 LCs (*i.e.*, PMs). The solver has been invoked every 30 s for Entropy and Snooze.

General Analysis. Figure 5 presents on the left the cumulated violation time for each placement policy and on the right several tables that give more details by presenting the mean and the standard deviations of the duration of, respectively, the violations and the computation/reconfiguration phases. As anticipated, the centralized approach did not scale and even incurs an overhead in the largest scenario compared to a system that did not perform any dynamic scheduling. The more nodes Entropy has to monitor, the less efficient it is during both the computation and reconfiguration phases. This is to be expected for the computation phase (which tries to tackle an NP-complete problem). As to reconfiguration, the reconfiguration plan becomes more complex for large scenarios, including several migrations coming from and going to the same nodes. Such plans are not optimal as they increase the bottleneck effects at the network level of each involved PM. Such a simulated result is valuable as it confirms that reconfiguration plans should avoid such manipulations as much as possible. The results of the hierarchical approach are clearly better than the Entropy-based ones but worse than those using DVMS-based placement. However, diving into the details, we can see that both the time needed for the computation and reconfiguration are almost independent from the cluster size (around 3 s and 10 s) and not much worse than those of DVMS, especially for the reconfiguration phase, which is predominant. These results can be easily explained: the centralized policy addresses

---

[3] http://www.cloudscaling.com/blog/cloud-computing/amazons-ec2-generating-220m-annually/.

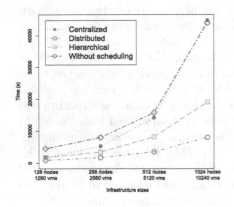

Infrastructure size	Duration of **violations** ($\mu \pm \sigma$)		
	Centralized	Hierarchical	Distributed
128 nodes	21.26 ± 13.55	21.07 ± 12.32	9.55 ± 2.57
256 nodes	40.09 ± 24.15	21.45 ± 12.10	9.58 ± 2.51
512 nodes	55.63 ± 42.26	24.54 ± 16.95	9.57 ± 2.67
1024 nodes	81.57 ± 86.59	29.01 ± 38.14	9.61 ± 2.54

Infrastructure size	Duration of **computations** ($\mu \pm \sigma$)		
	Centralized	Hierarchical	Distributed
128 nodes	3.76 ± 7.43	2.52 ± 4.63	0.29 ± 0.03
256 nodes	7.97 ± 15.03	2.65 ± 4.69	0.25 ± 0.02
512 nodes	15.71 ± 29.14	2.83 ± 4.98	0.21 ± 0.01
1024 nodes	26.41 ± 50.35	2.69 ± 4.92	0.14 ± 0.01

Infrastructure size	Duration of **reconfigurations** ($\mu \pm \sigma$)		
	Centralized	Hierarchical	Distributed
128 nodes	10.34 ± 1.70	10.02 ± 0.14	10.01 ± 0.11
256 nodes	10.26 ± 1.45	10.11 ± 0.83	10.01 ± 0.08
512 nodes	11.11 ± 3.23	10.28 ± 1.50	10.08 ± 0.82
1024 nodes	18.90 ± 7.57	10.30 ± 1.60	10.04 ± 0.63

Fig. 5. Scalability/Reactivity analysis of Entropy, Snooze and DVMS

the VMPP by considering all nodes at each invocation, while the hierarchical and the distributed algorithms divide the VMPP into sub problems, considering smaller numbers of nodes (32 PMs in Snooze and, on average, 4 in the case of DVMS). To clarify the influence of the group size on the performance of Snooze, *i.e.*, the ratio of LCs attached to one GM, we have performed additional simulations for varying group sizes. VMPlaceS has significantly facilitated this study as the corresponding simulations differ just by configuration parameters and do not require modifications to the code base.

Investigating Algorithm Variants. VMPlaceS facilitates the in-depth analysis of variants of placement algorithms. We have, for example, analyzed, as a first study of its kind, how the Snooze-based placement depends on the no. of LCs assigned to a GM. Figure 6 presents the simulated values obtained for scenarios with 2, 4, 8 and 32 LCs per GM for four infrastructure sizes. The overall performance (*i.e.*, cumulated violation time) shows that 2 LCs per GM result in significantly higher violation times. The relatively bad performance of the smallest group size can be explained in terms of the number of failures of the reconfiguration process, that is, overloading situations that are discovered but cannot be resolved due to a lack of resources (see tables on the right). Groups of 2 LCs per GM are clearly insufficient at our global load level (85 %). Failed reconfigurations are, however, already very rare in the case of 4 LCs per GM and do not occur at all for 8 and 32 LCs per GM. This is understandable because the load profile we evaluated rarely results in many LCs of a GM to be overloaded at once. Violations can therefore be resolved even in the case of a smaller number of LCs available for load distribution. Conversely, we can see that the duration of the computation phases decreases strongly along with the group size. It reaches a value close to the computation times of DVMS for a group size of 4-LCs per GM. We thus cannot minimize computation times and violation times by reducing the number of LCs because larger group sizes are necessary to resolve overload

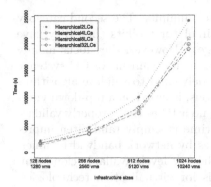

Infra. Size	No. of failed reconfigurations			
	2 LCs	4 LCs	8 LCs	32 LCs
128	19	0	0	0
256	29	0	0	0
512	83	1	0	0
1024	173	7	0	0

Infra. Size	Duration of the computations ($\mu \pm \sigma$)			
	2 LCs	4 LCs	8 LCs	32 LCs
128	0.16 ± 1.23	0.34 ± 1.81	0.58 ± 2.40	2.53 ± 4.62
256	0.18 ± 1.31	0.42 ± 1.99	0.66 ± 2.50	2.65 ± 4.69
512	0.15 ± 1.20	0.33 ± 1.78	0.67 ± 2.54	2.83 ± 4.98
1024	0.19 ± 1.37	0.42 ± 2.02	0.89 ± 2.90	2.69 ± 4.91

Fig. 6. Hierarchical placement: influence of varying group sizes

situations if the VM load gets higher. In contrast, DVMS resolves this trade-off by means of its automatic and dynamic choice of the partition size necessary to handle an overload situation. Once again, this information is valuable as it will help researchers to design new algorithms favoring the automatic discovery of the optimal subset of nodes capable to solve violations for given load profiles.

The study performed in this paper has allowed us to analyze several other variants and possible improvements (which we cannot present here for lack of space), such as a reactive approach to hierarchical placement instead of the periodical one used by Snooze, as well as more aggressive partitioning in the case of DVMS. VMPlaceS also provides additional metrics such as the overall count of migrations, the average duration of each migration ... These allow important properties, *e.g.*, the migration overhead, to be studied. All these variants can be easily studied and evaluated thanks to VMPlaceS.

Finally, we have succeeded to conduct DVMS simulations up to 8 K PMs/80 K VMs in a bit less than two days. We did not present these results in this paper because it was not possible to run a sufficient number of Snooze simulations at such a scale (the Snooze protocol being more complex). The time-consuming portions of the code are related to SimGrid internals such as `sleep` and `send/recv` calls. Hence, we are collaborating with SimGrid core developers in order to reduce the simulation time in such cases.

6   Related Work

Simulator toolkits that have been proposed to address CC concerns [4,5,12,13, 15] can be classified into two categories. The first corresponds to ad-hoc simulators that have been developed to address one particular concern. For instance, CReST [5] is a discrete event simulation toolkit built for Cloud provisioning algorithms. If ad-hoc simulators allow some characteristics of the behaviors of the system to be analyzed, they do not consider the implication of the different layers, which can lead to non-representative results. Moreover, most ad-hoc solutions are developed for one shot analyses. That is, there is no effort to release them as a complete and reusable tool for the scientific community. The second category [4,13,15] corresponds to more generic cloud simulator toolkits (*i.e.*, they have been designed to address multiple CC challenges). However, they focus mainly on the API and not on the model of the different mechanisms of CC systems. For instance, CloudSim [4], which has been widely used to validate algorithms and applications in different scientific publications, is based on a top-down viewpoint of cloud environments. That is, there are no articles that properly validate the different models it relies on: a migration time is simply (and often imprecisely) calculated by dividing VM memory sizes by network bandwidth values. In addition to be subject to inaccuracies at the low level, available cloud simulator toolkits often use oversimplified models for virtualization technologies, also leading to non-representative results. As highlighted throughout this article, we have chosen to build VMPlaceS on top of SimGrid in order to build a generic tool that benefits from the accuracy of its models related to virtualization abstractions [11].

7   Conclusion

We have presented VMPlaceS, a framework providing generic programming support for the definition of VM placement algorithms, execution support for their simulation at large scales, as well as new means for their trace-based analysis. We have validated its accuracy by comparing simulated and *in-vivo* executions of the Entropy strategy. We have also illustrated the relevance of VMPlaceS by evaluating and comparing algorithms representative of three different classes of virtualization environments: centralized, hierarchical and fully distributed placement algorithms. The corresponding experiments have provided the first systematic results comparing these algorithms in environments including up to one 1 K nodes and 10 K VMs.

A version of VMPlaceS is available on a public git repository[4]. We are in touch with the SimGrid core developers in order to improve our code with the ultimate objective of addressing infrastructures up to 100 K PMs and 1 Millions VMs. As future work, it would be valuable to add additional dimensions in order to simulate other workload variations stemming from network and HDD I/O changes. Moreover, we plan to provide a dedicated API to be able to provision and remove VMs during the execution of a simulation.

References

1. Barker, A., et al.: Academic cloud computing research. In: 6th USENIX Workshop on Hot Topics in Cloud Computing (HotCloud 2014), June 2014
2. Birke, R., et al.: Multi-resource characterization and their (in)dependencies in production datacenters. In: IEEE NOMS 2014, May 2014
3. Bloomfield, V.A.: Using R for Numerical Analysis in Science and Engineering. Chapman and Hall/CRC, Newyork (2014)

---

[4] http://beyondtheclouds.github.io/VMPlaceS/.

4. Calheiros, R.N., et al.: CloudSim: a toolkit for modeling and simulation of cloud computing environments and evaluation of resource provisioning algorithms. Softw. Pract. Experience **41**(1), 23–50 (2011)
5. Cartlidge, J., Cliff, D.: Comparison of cloud middleware protocols and subscription network topologies using CReST. In: CLOSER 2013, May 2013
6. Casanova, H., et al.: Versatile, scalable, and accurate simulation of distributed applications and platforms. Parallel Distrib. Comput. **74**(10), 2899–2917 (2014)
7. CloudStack, Open Source Cloud Computing. http://cloudstack.apache.org
8. Feller, E., et al.: Snooze: a scalable and autonomic virtual machine management framework for private clouds. In: IEEE CCGRID 2012, May 2012
9. Hermenier, F., Demassey, S., Lorca, X.: Bin repacking scheduling in virtualized datacenters. In: Lee, J. (ed.) CP 2011. LNCS, vol. 6876, pp. 27–41. Springer, Heidelberg (2011)
10. Hermenier, F., et al.: Entropy: a consolidation manager for clusters. In: VEE 2009: Virtual Execution Environments. ACM, New York (2009)
11. Hirofuchi, T., Lebre, A., Pouilloux, L.: Adding a live migration model into simgrid: one more step toward the simulation of infrastructure-as-a-service concerns. In: CloudCom 2013: Cloud Computing Technology and Science. IEEE (2013)
12. Iosup, A., Sonmez, O.O., Epema, D.H.J.: DGSIM: comparing grid resource management architectures through trace-based simulation. In: Luque, E., Margalef, T., Benítez, D. (eds.) Euro-Par 2008. LNCS, vol. 5168, pp. 13–25. Springer, Heidelberg (2008)
13. Kliazovich, D., et al.: Greencloud: a packet-level simulator of energy-aware cloud computing data centers. In: IEEE GlobeCom 2010, December 2010
14. Moreno-Vozmediano, R., et al.: IaaS cloud architecture: from virtualized datacenters to federated cloud infrastructures. Comput. J. **45**(12), 65–72 (2012)
15. Nunez, A., Vazquez-Poletti, J.L., et al.: iCanCloud: a flexible and scalable cloud infrastructure simulator. J. Grid Comput. **10**(1), 185–209 (2012)
16. Open Source Data Center Virtualization. http://www.opennebula.org
17. The Open Source, Open Standards Cloud. http://www.openstack.org
18. PajeNG - Trace Visualization Tool. https://github.com/schnorr/pajeng
19. Quesnel, F., Lebre, A., Südholt, M.: Cooperative and reactive scheduling in large-scale virtualized platforms with DVMS. Concurrency Comput. Pract. Experience **25**(12), 1643–1655 (2013)
20. Simgrid publications. http://simgrid.gforge.inria.fr/Publications.html
21. Snooze web site. http://snooze.inria.fr
22. Van, H.N., Tran, F., et al.: SLA-aware virtual resource management for cloud infrastructures. In: IEEE CIT 2009, October 2009
23. Wang, M., Meng, X., Zhang, L.: Consolidating virtual machines with dynamic bandwidth demand in data centers. In: IEEE INFOCOM 2011, April 2011

Distributed Systems and Algorithms

A Connectivity Model for Agreement in Dynamic Systems

Carlos Gómez-Calzado[1], Arnaud Casteigts[2],
Alberto Lafuente[1], and Mikel Larrea[1(✉)]

[1] University of the Basque Country UPV/EHU, Donostia - San Sebastián, Spain
{carlos.gomez,alberto.lafuente,mikel.larrea}@ehu.es
[2] LaBRI, University of Bordeaux, Bordeaux, France
arnaud.casteigts@labri.fr

Abstract. The consensus problem is a fundamental paradigm in distributed systems, because it captures the difficulty to solve other agreement problems. Many current systems evolve with time, e.g., due to node mobility, and consensus has been little studied in these systems so far. Specifically, it is not well established how to define an appropriate set of assumptions for consensus in dynamic distributed systems. This paper studies a hierarchy of three classes of time-varying graphs, and provides a solution for each class to the problem of Terminating Reliable Broadcast (TRB). The classes introduce increasingly stronger assumptions on timeliness, so that the trade-off between weakness versus implementability and efficiency can be analysed. Being TRB equivalent to consensus in synchronous systems, the paper extends this equivalence to dynamic systems.

1 Introduction

The consensus problem is a central paradigm in distributed systems, as it represents many agreement problems, e.g., leader election, atomic commitment and total-order broadcast. Solving consensus has attracted a lot of attention in dependable computing and has generated fundamental results. In this regard, it is known that in crash-prone asynchronous distributed systems it is impossible to solve consensus deterministically due to the impossibility of distinguishing between "slow" processes and crashed ones, a result known as FLP impossibility [8]. Alternatively, consensus can be easily solved in synchronous systems, where perfect failure detection can be implemented [5].

Most of the research on consensus has considered a static distributed system with permanent connectivity among nodes. In many current distributed systems,

Research supported by the Spanish Research Council, grant TIN2013-41123-P, the Basque Government, grant IT395-10, and the University of the Basque Country UPV/EHU, grant UFI11/45. Carlos Gómez-Calzado is recipient of a doctoral fellowship from the Basque Government. This work has been carried out during a research stay of Carlos Gómez-Calzado at the University of Bordeaux. The authors want to thank Antonio Fernández Anta for his valuable comments.

© Springer-Verlag Berlin Heidelberg 2015
J.L. Träff et al. (Eds.): Euro-Par 2015, LNCS 9233, pp. 333–345, 2015.
DOI: 10.1007/978-3-662-48096-0_26

however, these assumptions are not valid any more. Instead, these new systems exhibit a dynamic behavior, with nodes joining the system, leaving it or just moving, which implies uncertain connectivity conditions. Indeed, and unlike in classical static systems, these events are no longer considered incorrect or sporadic behaviors, but rather the natural dynamics of the system.

Clearly, even the synchrony assumptions of classical (static) models of distributed systems are not enough to solve agreement problems in dynamic systems. For example, having an upper bound on link latencies is pointless if the link is not available at the time of transmission of the message. Note however that the nodes could still communicate using an alternative path in the network. Thus, assumptions should consider the overall system connectivity, which encourages for a holistic approach to model dynamic distributed systems.

In recent years there was a rising interest in modeling dynamic distributed systems from the perspective of graph theory. In this regard, there exist several works that study the solvability of deterministic problems, including consensus, in highly-dynamic systems [2,3,7,11,12]. However, regarding consensus, none of them lowers the assumptions to the realm of *temporal* connectivity, i.e., not requiring that the graph be connected at every instant, but only that paths exist over time and space (temporal path, aka *journeys*). The time-varying graph formalism [4] (TVG, for short) provides a useful qualitative framework to model dynamic distributed systems. In this formalism, the dynamic network is represented as a graph, together with a presence function that tells whether a given edge is present at a given time and a latency function that tells how long it takes to cross a given edge at a given time. In [4], Casteigts et al. define a hierarchy of classes of dynamic networks, most of which are based on temporal connectivity concepts. Among them, the *recurrent connectivity* class requires that a journey exists between any two nodes infinitely often (that is, recurrently). Nevertheless, this class lacks the necessary timeliness (i.e. time bounds in communication) to describe the specific assumptions that are required by synchronous agreement algorithms, such as TRB, to terminate. One of the goals of our paper is to extend some of the existing TVG classes by introducing timeliness constraints, together with practical considerations, and analyze the impact of these new constraints on solving consensus.

Our Contribution. In this paper, we address timeliness in evolving systems (i.e., time-varying graphs, TVG) from a synchronous point of view, i.e., systems where the transmission delay of messages is bounded and the bound is known a priori by the processes. The resulting set of concepts and mechanisms makes it possible to describe system dynamics at different levels of abstraction and with a gradual set of assumptions.

We first formulate a very abstract property on the temporal connectivity of the TVG, namely, that the temporal diameter (i.e. maximum duration of a foremost journey) of a component in the TVG is always bounded by Δ. We refer to such a component as a Δ-*component*, and define the concept of correct process in terms of this component. We then specify a version of the Terminating

Reliable Broadcast problem (TRB) for Δ-components, which we relate to the ability of solving agreement at component level.

Although Δ-components are proven to be a sufficient concept at the most abstract level, they rely on non implementable communication patterns in message-passing systems. Indeed, the solution to TRB proposed in this abstract model relies on an oracle that provides the algorithm with instantaneous knowledge of the appearance of an edge. Unfortunately, this oracle does not have a straightforward implementation in terms of real processes and communication links. Therefore, we introduce a first constraint to force the existence of journeys whose edges presence duration is lower-bounded by some duration β (which holds a relation to the maximal latency of a link), thereby enabling repetitive communication attempts to succeed eventually. These journeys are called β-journeys and their existence makes it possible to implement the TRB algorithm without oracle. We then look at a further constrained class of TVG, inspired by the work of Fernández-Anta et al. [7], whereby the local appearance of the edge used by every next hop of (at least one of the possibly many) β-journeys also must be bounded by some duration α, yielding to the concept of (α, β)-journeys. The existence of recurrent (α, β)-journeys allows the nodes to stop sending a message α time after they receive it, which is much more efficient.

The rest of the paper is organized as follows. Section 2 introduces basic time-varying graph notations, used in Sect. 3 to define the abstract timely connectivity model based on Δ-components. In the same section we redefine the TRB problem with respect to Δ-components and give a solution to it. Then, in Sect. 4, we introduce β-journeys (and the corresponding β-components), which we show to be sufficient to implement an effective (i.e., oracle-free) version of the algorithm. We then define (α, β)-journeys and components, and discuss their advantages (and disadvantages) over β-journeys. In Sect. 5, we describe how consensus can be solved by using the TRB implementations introduced in Sects. 3 and 4. We finally conclude in Sect. 6 with open questions and future work.

2   Time-Varying Graphs

A recent framework called *time-varying graphs*, proposed by Casteigts et al. [4], aims to provide a precise formalism for describing dynamic networks. As usual, the entities of the system and the communication links between them are represented as a graph. More specifically, a time-varying graph (TVG, for short) is defined as a tuple $\mathcal{G} = (V, E, \mathcal{T}, \rho, \zeta)$, where:

- V is the set of communicating entities (or nodes, or processes, interchangeably).
- E is the set of edges (or links, interchangeably) that interconnect the nodes in V. In this work, all edges are undirected.
- $\mathcal{T}$ is the *lifetime* of $\mathcal{G}$, *i.e.* the interval of time over which the graph is defined. It is a subset of the temporal domain $\mathbb{T}$, itself being $\mathbb{N}$ or $\mathbb{R}^+$ depending on whether time is discrete or continuous (in this work, it is continuous).

For convenience, both endpoints of $\mathcal{T}$ are referred to as $\mathcal{T}^-$ and $\mathcal{T}^+$, the latter being possibly $+\infty$.

- $\rho : E \times \mathcal{T} \to \{true, false\}$, i.e., the *presence* function, indicates whether a given edge is present at a given time (i.e., $\rho(e, t) = true$ iff edge e is present at time t).
- $\zeta : E \times \mathcal{T} \to \mathbb{T}$, i.e., the *latency* function, indicates how long it takes to send a message across a given edge for a given emission time (assuming the edge is present at that time).

The kind of network we are addressing is possibly disconnected at every instant. Still, a form of communication can be achieved over time by means of *journeys* (a.k.a. *temporal path*). Formally, a journey $\mathcal{J} = \{((e_1, t_1), (e_2, t_2), \ldots, (e_k, t_k))\}$ is a sequence such that $(e_1, e_2, \ldots, e_k)$ is a valid path in the underlying graph (V, E), and (1) for every $i \in [1, k]$ edge e_i is present at time t_i long enough to send a message across (formally, $\rho(e_i, t_i + \delta) = true$ for all $\delta \in [0, \zeta(e_i, t_i)]$), and (2) the times when edges are crossed (we also say *activated*) and the corresponding latencies allow a sequential traversal (formally, $t_{i+1} \geq t_i + \zeta(e_i, t_i)$ for all $i \in [1, k)$). What makes this form of connectivity *temporal* is the fact that a journey can pause in between hops, e.g. if the next link is not yet available.

Given a journey $\mathcal{J}$, departure($\mathcal{J}$) and arrival($\mathcal{J}$) denote respectively its starting time t_1 and its ending time $t_k + \zeta(e_k, t_k)$. Journeys can be thought of as paths over time, having both a *topological length* k (i.e., the number of *hops*) and a *temporal length* (i.e., a duration) arrival($\mathcal{J}$)−departure($\mathcal{J}$) = $t_k + \zeta(e_k, t_k) - t_1$. Note that journeys describe *opportunities* of communication between an emitter and a receiver. $\mathcal{J}_{\mathcal{G}}^*$ is the set of all such opportunities over $\mathcal{G}$'s lifetime, while $\mathcal{J}_{(p,q)}^* \subseteq \mathcal{J}_{\mathcal{G}}^*$ are those journeys from p to q. A simplified way of denoting the existence of a journey between a process p and a process q, when the context of $\mathcal{G}$ is clear, is $p \rightsquigarrow q$. Finally, the graph is *temporally connected* if for every $p, q \in V, p \rightsquigarrow q$.

An induced sub-TVG $\mathcal{G}' \subseteq \mathcal{G}$ is obtained by restricting either the set of vertices $V' \subseteq V$ or the lifetime $\mathcal{T}' \subseteq \mathcal{T}$, resulting in the tuple $(V', E', \mathcal{T}', \rho', \zeta')$ such that:

- (V', E') is the subgraph of (V, E) induced (in the usual sense) by V'
- $\rho' : E' \times \mathcal{T}' \to \{true, false\}$ where $\rho'(e, t) = \rho(e, t)$
- $\zeta' : E' \times \mathcal{T}' \to \mathbb{T}$ where $\zeta'(e, t) = \zeta(e, t)$.

If only the lifetime is restricted, say to some interval $[t_a, t_b)$, then the resulting graph $\mathcal{G}'$ is called a *temporal* subgraph of $\mathcal{G}$ and denoted $\mathcal{G}_{[t_a, t_b)}$. The *temporal diameter* of a graph $\mathcal{G}$ at time t is the smallest duration d such that $\mathcal{G}_{[t, t+d)}$ is temporally connected.

Finally, following Bhadra and Ferreira in [1], we consider a temporal variant of connected components (hereafter, simply called *components*), which are maximal sets of nodes $V' \subseteq V$ such that $\forall p, q \in V', p \rightsquigarrow q$. Two variants are actually considered, whether the corresponding journeys can also use nodes that are in $V \setminus V'$ (*open* components) or not (*closed* components). Observe that a close component is equivalent to an induced sub-TVG being temporally connected.

3   A Timely Model for Dynamic Systems

This section focuses on the analysis of timeliness in dynamic systems at the most abstract level, i.e. considering only a general communication bound Δ for end-to-end communication. We first provide a set of definitions related to this bound, which leads to the formulation of a new class of TVGs that is a strict subset of Class 5 (*recurrent connectivity*) in [4]. We then specify a solution to the problem of Terminating Reliable Broadcast (TRB) in the corresponding context.

3.1   Definitions

We define the concept of bounded-time journey as follows:

Definition 1. *A journey $\mathcal{J}$ is a Δ-journey if and only if $arrival(\mathcal{J}) - departure(\mathcal{J}) \leq \Delta$.*

Based on Δ-journeys we define the concept of bounded-time component. Unlike components, we require here that connectivity also be recurrent by definition.

Definition 2. *A Δ-component in $\mathcal{G} = (V, E, \mathcal{T}, \rho, \zeta)$ is a set $V' \subseteq V$ such that for every t in $[\mathcal{T}^-, \mathcal{T}^+ - \Delta]$, for every p, q in V', there exists a Δ-journey from p to q in $\mathcal{G}_{[t,t+\Delta)}$.*

Similarly to components, Δ-components can be open or closed, depending on whether the Δ-journeys use nodes in $V \setminus V'$. Observe that, a graph behaving in an open way provides flexibility in mobility, and therefore, a model allowing open Δ-components is weaker (in the sense that it requires less assumption) than a model strictly based on closed Δ-components. Henceforth we assume that in our system model Δ-components are by default open.

Informally, Δ-components allow us to think about subsets of nodes behaving timely with each other. Hence, nodes in a Δ-component are also *timely connected*. We define the (parametrized) class of timely (and recurrently) connected TVGs $\mathcal{TC}(\Delta)$ as follows:

Definition 3. $\mathcal{G} \in \mathcal{TC}(\Delta) \iff V$ *is a Δ-component.*

3.2   Terminating Reliable Broadcast in $\mathcal{TC}(\Delta)$

According to [6], consensus is equivalent to Terminating Reliable Broadcast in static synchronous systems. We take this as a starting point and describe here a solution for TRB in the scope of a Δ-component.

We assume that processes know a global time. Processing times are negligible with respect to communication time. The system is composed by processes that can crash/recover, and leave/join the system. Processes that crash or leave the system, even if they recover or join again later, are by definition excluded from any Δ-component, however since we assume the existence of open Δ-components, they can punctually take part on various journeys.

Recall that a distributed system $\mathcal{G}$ may have several Δ-components. There may exist values of Δ for which a process belongs to different components, which are thus overlapping. However, since every component is *recurrently* connected, then overlapping components become naturally merged as the value for Δ increases, and transitively, there must exist a sufficiently large value of Δ such that all remaining components are disjoint. Henceforth, we consider Δ to be (an upper bound on) such a value.

We define now which processes are *correct* in terms of the classical terminology. In a classical partitioned system it can be considered that a process p behaves correctly in its partition, and incorrectly with respect to the other partitions in the system. Similarly, in our Δ-component based system a process p behaves correctly with respect to the Δ-component p belongs to, e.g. C. Hence, a member of a Δ-component C is by definition correct with respect to C. However p could still sporadically communicate timely with *some* processes in another Δ-component, C'. Obviously, we consider p incorrect with respect to C', but a message m from p received by some process in C' should either be delivered by all processes in C', or by none of them in order to hold the agreement property of reliable broadcast.

Thus, in $\mathcal{TC}(\Delta)$ a set of properties should be hold by a process *with respect to* a Δ-component in order to provide Δ-TRB:

- Δ-*Termination*: Every process in the same Δ-component eventually delivers some message.
- Δ-*Validity*: If a process in a Δ-component broadcasts a message m, then all processes in the same Δ-component eventually deliver m.
- Δ-*Agreement*: If a process in a Δ-component delivers a message m, then all processes in the same Δ-component eventually deliver m.
- Δ-*Integrity*: For any message m, every process in the same Δ-component delivers m at most once, and if it delivers $m \neq SF$ (*sender faulty*) then the sender(m) must have broadcast m.

As usual, the broadcast at time t_{init} of a message m is considered in the scope of m.

To guarantee the Δ-Agreement property we should correctly understand when a message m broadcast by $p \notin C$ should be delivered by all processes in C. If p has been able to propagate m to some process $q \in C$, then we assume that there exists a Δ-journey from p to q. Observe that this assumption is consistent with the fact that our model allows the existence of open Δ-components.

A solution to the TRB problem is described in Fig. 1 (see [9] for details). Informally, the distinguished process p_B Δ-TRBroadcasts a message m by sending m on all its active edges at time t_{init}. Whenever an edge in p_B's neighborhood appears[1], p_B also sends m on that edge. Every other process p, upon

---

[1] We assume here the existence of an abstract *oracle* to capture events of edge appearance. In the next section we will board the implementation of such an oracle.

To *Δ-TRBroadcast* a message m at time t_{init}:
if $p = p_B$ **then**
    for all *edge* $e = (p_B, -)$ s.t. $\rho(e, t_{init}) = true$ **do**
        send(m) on e at t_{init}

On appearance of $e = (p_B, -)$ at time $t \in [t_{init}, t_{init} + \Delta)$:
send(m) on e at t

On reception of a message m for the first time at time $t_{rec} \in [t_{init}, t_{init} + 2\Delta)$:
if $p \neq p_B$ **then**
    for all *edge* $e = (p, -)$ s.t. $\rho(e, t_{rec}) = true$ **do**
        send(m) on e at t_{rec}

On appearance of $e = (p, -)$ at time $t \in [t_{init}, t_{init} + 2\Delta)$:
if a message m has been previously received **then**
    send(m) on e at t

At time $t_{init} + 2\Delta$:
if a message m has been previously received **then**
    Δ-TRDeliver(m)
else
    Δ-TRDeliver(SF)

Fig. 1. Terminating Reliable Broadcast for $\mathcal{TC}(\Delta)$.

reception of m for the first time, forwards m on all its active edges, as well as upon the appearance of a new edge. Finally, at time $t_{init} + 2\Delta$ every process $p\Delta$-TRBdelivers either m (if m has been received) or SF.

We explain next why a time of 2Δ is necessary and sufficient to deliver m.

Observe that, since we are assuming that p_B could be not in C, p_B could not be able to communicate to all nodes in C in Δ time, (otherwise $p_B \in C$), thus, after m is resent by q, every process in C will receive m into a second Δ time interval. Henceforth the bound for a process in C to *TRDeliver* a message is 2Δ.

Theorem 1. *The specification in Fig. 1 satisfies the properties of Δ-TRB in $\mathcal{TC}(\Delta)$.*

4 Implementability of TRB

The specification of TRB provided in Fig. 1 relies on an "oracle" available at every process p, which informs p instantaneously upon appearance of a new edge in its neighbourhood. Such an abstraction has been recently used by Raynal et al. [13] to implement a broadcast algorithm for recurrent dynamic systems. However, a strict implementation of this oracle in a real system is far from being trivial, as we discuss now.

Observe that the only temporal assumption on Δ-journeys is that they satisfy a given upper-bound Δ in its temporal length, thus the duration of an edge may be as short as the latency of the message. In consequence, an implementation of this oracle should be able to allow the sending of a message at the very same time that the edge get activated, which is unrealistic since the oracle should be able to predict the behaviour of the links in a real network. Alternatively, an algorithm could continuously send message m along the whole time interval in the hope that one of the sending attempts will success in the appearance of an edge. Observe, however, that this iteration would require a period of time zero between two consecutive sends. In other words, the algorithm should be able to send an infinite number of messages per unit of time, which is impossible.

Therefore, additional assumptions should be introduced in order to provide an implementation for the above specification of TRB. Specifically we first propose an extra assumption that allow to maintain active the edge not only for communicating the message but also to detect its appearance.

4.1   (Lower)-Bounding the Edge Stability

We assume that the edge latency is bounded, i.e., there exist a bound on $\max\{\zeta(e,t) : t \in \mathcal{T}, e \in E\}$, that we call ζ_{MAX}. Additionally, we assume that edges are active at least β time. Let us call β-edge an edge that fulfils this bounded disposability. For this new model we define β-journeys as follows:

Definition 4. A β-journey $\mathcal{J} = \{((e_1, t_1), \ldots, (e_k, t_k))\}$ is a Δ-journey such that:

1. $\zeta_{MAX} < \beta \leq \Delta$.
2. $\forall i \in [1, k), e_i$ is a β-edge.
3. The times when edges are activated and their corresponding latencies allow a bounded sequential traversal (formally, $\forall i \in [1, k), t_{i+1} \geq t_i + \beta$).

We now define β-components as a subset of Δ-components that uses β-journeys. Formally:

Definition 5. A β-component is a Δ-component where a set $V' \subseteq V$ satisfies that $\forall t \in [\mathcal{T}^-, \mathcal{T}^+ - \Delta], V'$ is a β-journey based temporal component in $\mathcal{G}_{[t,t+\Delta)}$.

We define the parametrized timely connectivity class $\mathcal{TC}'(\beta)$ as follows:

Definition 6. $\mathcal{G} \in \mathcal{TC}'(\beta) \iff V$ is a β-component.

TRB in $\mathcal{TC}'(\beta)$

We give now a TRB algorithm for the $\mathcal{TC}'(\beta)$ model, which is shown in Fig. 2.

In the algorithm proposed in Fig. 2 a process p_B sends at time t_{init} a message m by Δ-TRBroadcasting it, and p_B keeps sending m each W time in order to assure the correct send of m by every β-journey. Observe that, according to the definition of β-edge, for a β-edge $e = (p, q)$ in a β-journey, if process p sends a message m on e each $W \leq \beta - \zeta_{MAX}$ time during Δ, q will receive m at least once (see [9] for the complete correctness proof). When a process p receives the

1   $W \leftarrow value \in (0, \beta - \zeta_{MAX}]$

2   **To Δ-*TRBroadcast* a message m at time t_{init}:**
3   **if** $p = p_B$ **then**
4   **while** $now() < t_{init} + \Delta$ **do**
5   send(m) to all
6   wait(W)

7   **On reception of a message m for the first time at time $t_{rec} \in [t_{init}, t_{init} + 2\Delta)$:**
8   Δ-TRDeliver(m)
9   **if** $p \neq p_B$ **then**
10   **while** $now() < t_{rec} + \Delta$ **do**
11   send(m) to all
12   wait(W)

13 **At time $t_{init} + 2\Delta$:**
14   **if** p has not Δ-*TRDelivered any message* **then**
15   Δ-TRDeliver(SF)

Fig. 2. Terminating Reliable Broadcast for $\mathcal{TC}'(\beta)$.

message m automatically Δ-TRDelivers m, and additionally, if $p \neq p_B$, p sends m each W time during Δ. Finally, if a process does not receive the message m, at time $t_{init} + 2\Delta$, it Δ-TRDelivers the special message SF.

Theorem 2. *The specification in Fig. 2 satisfies the properties of Δ-TRB in $\mathcal{TC}'(\beta)$.*

4.2   (Upper)-Bounding the Edge Appearance

Observe that, in the algorithm in Fig. 2 messages are forwarded during the whole Δ interval. This is necessary because the ending edge of a β-journey could be activated at a time as late as $t_{init} + \Delta - \beta$. It is apparent that more efficient implementations of a TRB algorithm in terms of number of messages could be envisaged if stronger connectivity assumptions are introduced in the model. Specifically, in this section we introduce an additional timely assumption on the appearance of edges.

We adopt the assumption of [7], where, besides β, a bound α on the appearance of links is defined. We define a new type of journey, that we call (α, β)-journey. Formally:

Definition 7. *A (α, β)-journey $\mathcal{J} = \{((e_1, t_1), \ldots, (e_k, t_k))\}$ is a β-journey such that:*

1. *The appearance of e_1 is bounded by α.*
2. *The appearance of the subsequent edges are also bounded by α. Formally, $t_{i+1} \leq t_i + \zeta(e_i, t_i) + \alpha$ for all $i \in [1, k)$.*

We define a (α, β)-component as follows:

Definition 8. *A (α, β) -component is a β-component where a set $V' \subseteq V$ satisfies that $\forall t \in [\mathcal{T}^-, \mathcal{T}^+ - \Delta], V'$ is a (α, β)-journey based temporal component in $\mathcal{G}_{[t,t+\Delta)}$.*

We define the parametrized timely connectivity class $\mathcal{TC}''(\alpha, \beta)$ as follows:

Definition 9. $\mathcal{G} \in \mathcal{TC}''(\alpha, \beta) \iff V$ *is a (α, β)-component.*

TRB in $\mathcal{TC}''(\alpha, \beta)$. The algorithm in Fig. 3, describes a TRB algorithm executable in a $\mathcal{TC}''(\alpha, \beta)$ dynamic system.

The new bound α, altogether with the latency bound β and ζ_{MAX}, allows to calculate global system bounds, namely the period W and a time to deliver Γ, strictly in terms of specific network parameters. In the algorithm proposed in Fig. 3 a process p_B Δ-TRBroadcast a message m at time t_{init} by sending each W time m until the time is strictly higher than $t_{init} + \alpha$, in order to assure the correct sending of m by every (α, β)-journey. When a process p receives the message m at time t_{rec} for the first time, automatically Δ-TRDelivers m and, additionally, if $p \neq p_B$, p sends m each W until the time is strictly higher than $t_{rec} + \alpha$. Finally, if any of the process in p does not receive the message m at time $t_{init} + \Gamma$, Δ-TRDelivers the special message SF denoting the sender failure.

A detailed explanation of how Γ is obtained can be found in the extended version of this paper [9]. It is important to note that in the TRB algorithm for $\mathcal{TC}''(\alpha, \beta)$, differently to the previous classes, processes need to known the network diameter, which is bounded by $|V| - 1$. This is a consequence of the fact of considering strictly local bounds in $\mathcal{TC}''(\alpha, \beta)$. Instead, both $\mathcal{TC}(\Delta)$ and $\mathcal{TC}'(\beta)$ rely on a system-wide bound, Δ.

Theorem 3. *The specification in Fig. 3 satisfies the properties of Δ-TRB in $\mathcal{TC}''(\alpha, \beta)$.*

4.3   Relating Timely Classes

We have defined a hierarchy of classes with increasingly stronger timely assumptions. Being $\mathcal{TC}(\Delta)$, $\mathcal{TC}'(\beta)$ and $\mathcal{TC}''(\alpha, \beta)$ the *parametrized* classes, we define now for each one the union of all its possible instances:

$$\mathcal{G} \in \mathcal{TC}^* \iff \exists \Delta \neq \infty : \mathcal{G} \in \mathcal{TC}(\Delta)$$

$$\mathcal{G} \in \mathcal{TC}'^* \iff \exists \beta \neq \infty : \mathcal{G} \in \mathcal{TC}'(\beta)$$

$$\mathcal{G} \in \mathcal{TC}''^* \iff \exists \alpha, \beta \neq \infty : \mathcal{G} \in \mathcal{TC}''(\alpha, \beta)$$

In spite of the different strength of the parametrized classes, we show in [9] that $\mathcal{TC}''^* \equiv \mathcal{TC}'^*$. Besides, $\mathcal{TC}'^* \subset \mathcal{TC}^*$ and $\mathcal{TC}''^* \subset \mathcal{TC}^*$.

```
1   W ← value ∈ (0, β − ζMAX]
2   Γ ← (⌈α/W⌉ + (|V| − 2)⌈(ζMAX+α)/W⌉)W + ζMAX
3   To Δ-TRBroadcast a message m at time tinit:
4       if p = pB then
5           send(m) to all
6           repeat
7               wait(W)
8               send(m) to all
9           until now() > tinit + α

10  On reception of a message m for the first time at time trec:
11      Δ-TRDeliver(m)
12      if p ≠ pB then
13          send(m) to all
14          repeat
15              wait(W)
16              send(m) to all
17          until now() > trec + α

18  At time tinit + Γ:
19      if p has not Δ-TRDelivered any message then
20          Δ-TRDeliver(SF)
```

Fig. 3. Terminating Reliable Broadcast for $\mathcal{TC}''(\alpha, \beta)$.

5   From Δ-TRB to Δ-Consensus in Dynamic Systems

In this section we analyse the equivalence between TRB and consensus, originally stated for synchronous static systems [6], in terms of a dynamic system as the one we have modelled.

In the previous sections we have presented three Δ-TRB algorithms in the scope of respectively Δ-, β- and (α, β)-components. We show now how the consensus problem can be reduced[2] to a Δ-TRB problem. We will refer as Δ-Consensus to this kind of consensus in the scope of Δ-components.

By the properties of Δ-TRB, it is straightforward to define the Δ-Consensus properties as follows:

- Δ-*Termination:* Every process in the Δ-component eventually decides.
- Δ-*Agreement:* Every process in the Δ-component decides the same value.
- Δ-*Validity:* The decided value is a proposed one.

Without loosing generality we focus here on Δ-Consensus using the Δ-TRB specification of Fig. 1 for the $\mathcal{TC}(\Delta)$ Class.

The resulting Δ-Consensus algorithm is shown in Fig. 4. Every process p holds a vector V_p initialized to ⊥. At time t_{init}, $|V|$ instances of Δ-TRB are started, one per process, being each process the sender in one instance. Every

---

[2] We say that a problem A can be reduced to a problem B if A can be solved using B.

1 Vector $V_p(i) \leftarrow \perp : i \in [0, |V|)$

2 **To Δ-Propose v at time t_{init}:**
3   Δ-TRBroadcast(v)

4 **On Δ-TRDeliver(m) by q:**
5      $V_p(q) \leftarrow m$

6 **At time $t_{init} + 2\Delta$:**
7   Δ-decide($V_p(\min(i : V_p(i) \neq SF))$)

Fig. 4. Δ-TRB based Δ-Consensus algorithm for $\mathcal{TC}(\Delta)$.

process p records in vector $V_p(q)$ the message m_q delivered from process q (or SF in case m_q has not been received on time). At time $t_{init} + 2\Delta$, p decides on the first non-SF value of V_p.

Note that solving consensus at system level would require a second Δ-TRB round to agree on the decision of the majority, provided that the temporal interval $[\mathcal{T}^-, \mathcal{T}^+]$ in which the Δ-component is defined covers both rounds. In other words, the stability of Δ-components must be temporally extended to solve consensus at system level.

6   Conclusions

In this paper we studied how to introduce timeliness in evolving systems so that the resolution of agreement problems (specifically consensus) is possible. On the basis of previous works, we have adopted the concept of journey or temporal path and have introduced the necessary timeliness (i.e., time bounds) to describe the specific assumptions that are required by an agreement algorithm to terminate and satisfy the consensus properties.

We have first proposed a general class, $\mathcal{TC}(\Delta)$, with a very abstract property on the temporal connectivity of the TVG to provide the necessary stability conditions, namely, that the temporal diameter of a recurrent component in the TVG is bounded. We refer to such a component as a Δ-component. To approach the consensus problem we have defined a TRB specification in terms of Δ-components, Δ-TRB. However, Δ-TRB is not implementable in $\mathcal{TC}(\Delta)$ by message-passing without zero processing time assumptions. Henceforth, by introducing increasingly stronger connectivity assumptions, we have provided two *implementable* connectivity classes, namely $\mathcal{TC}'(\beta)$ and $\mathcal{TC}''(\alpha, \beta)$, as well as two respective implementations of Δ-TRB in these classes. Finally, we have shown that consensus at Δ-component level is easily reduced to Δ-TRB.

An open issue is the search of the weakest connectivity class that allows to implement Δ-TRB (and henceforth consensus) in message-passing systems. Of additional interest is to extend the proposed classes to partially synchronous models. In this regard, in [10], leader election is implemented in a partially synchronous system with dynamic partitions that could be modelled as Δ-components.

References

1. Bhadra, S., Ferreira, A.: Complexity of connected components in evolving graphs and the computation of multicast trees in dynamic networks. In: Pierre, S., Barbeau, M., An, H.-C. (eds.) ADHOC-NOW 2003. LNCS, vol. 2865, pp. 259–270. Springer, Heidelberg (2003)
2. Biely, M., Robinson, P., Schmid, U.: Agreement in directed dynamic networks. In: Even, G., Halldórsson, M.M. (eds.) SIROCCO 2012. LNCS, vol. 7355, pp. 73–84. Springer, Heidelberg (2012)
3. Casteigts, A., Flocchini, P., Mans, B., Santoro, N.: Shortest, fastest, and fore-most broadcast in dynamic networks. Int. J. Found. Comput. Sci., World Scientific (Accepted January 2015, to appear)
4. Casteigts, A., Flocchini, P., Quattrociocchi, W., Santoro, N.: Time-varying graphs and dynamic networks. Int. J. Parallel Emergent Distrib. Syst. **27**(5), 387–408 (2012)
5. Chandra, T.D., Toueg, S.: Unreliable failure detectors for reliable distributed systems. J. ACM **43**(2), 225–267 (1996)
6. Feldman, P., Micali, S.: Optimal algorithms for byzantine agreement. In: Proceedings of the 20th Annual ACM Symposium on Theory of Computing, STOC 1998, pp. 148–161. ACM (1988)
7. Fernández-Anta, A., Milani, A., Mosteiro, M.A., Zaks, S.: Opportunistic information dissemination in mobile ad-hoc networks: The profit of global synchrony. Distrib. Comput. **25**(4), 279–296 (2012)
8. Fischer, M.J., Lynch, N.A., Paterson, M.: Impossibility of distributed consensus with one faulty process. J. ACM **32**(2), 374–382 (1985)
9. Gómez-Calzado, C., Casteigts, A., Lafuente, A., Larrea, M.: A Connectivity Model for Agreement in Dynamic Systems. Technical report EHU-KAT-IK-01-15, University of the Basque Country UPV/EHU, February 2015. http://www.sc.ehu.es/acwlaalm/research/EHU-KAT-IK-01-15.pdf
10. Gomez-Calzado, C., Lafuente, A., Larrea, M., Raynal, M.: Fault-tolerant leader election in mobile dynamic distributed systems. In: Proceedings of the 19th IEEE Pacific Rim International Symposium on Dependable Computing, PRDC 2013, pp. 78–87 (2013)
11. Kuhn, F., Lynch, N.A., Oshman, R.: Distributed computation in dynamic networks. In: Proceedings of the 42nd ACM Symposium on Theory of Computing, STOC 2010, Cambridge, Massachusetts, USA, 5–8 June 2010, pp. 513–522. ACM (2010)
12. Kuhn, F., Oshman, R.: Dynamic networks: models and algorithms. ACM SIGACT News **42**(1), 82–96 (2011)
13. Raynal, M., Stainer, J., Cao, J., Wu, W.: A simple broadcast algorithm for recurrent dynamic systems. In: Proceedings of the IEEE 28th International Conference on Advanced Information Networking and Applications, AINA 2014, pp. 933–939 (2014)

DFEP: Distributed Funding-Based Edge Partitioning

Alessio Guerrieri[✉] and Alberto Montresor

DISI, University of Trento, via Sommarive 9, Trento, Italy
{a.guerrieri,alberto.montresor}@unitn.it

Abstract. As graphs become bigger, the need to efficiently partition them becomes more pressing. Most graph partitioning algorithms subdivide the *vertex set* into partitions of similar size, trying to keep the number of cut edges as small as possible. An alternative approach divides the *edge set*, with the goal of obtaining more balanced partitions in presence of high-degree nodes, such as hubs in real world networks, that can be split between distinct partitions. We introduce DFEP, a distributed edge partitioning algorithm based on the metaphor of currency distribution. Each partition starts from a random edge and expands independently by spending currency to buy neighboring edges. After each iteration, smaller partitions receive an higher amount of currency to help them recover lost ground and reach a similar size to the other partitions. Simulation experiments show that DFEP is efficient and obtains consistently balanced partitions. Implementations on both Hadoop and Spark show the scalability of our approach.

1 Introduction

One of the latest trend in computer science is the emergence of the "big data" phenomena that concerns the retrieval, management and analysis of datasets of extremely large dimensions, coming from wildly different settings.

Although the collected data is often structured, several interesting datasets are unstructured and can be modeled as graphs. An obvious example is the World Wide Web, but there are many other examples such as social network topologies, biological systems or even road networks. While graph problems have been studied since before the birth of computer science, the sheer size of these datasets makes classic graph problems extremely difficult. Even solving the shortest path problem needs too many iterations to complete when the graph is too big to fit into memory. The big Internet players (such as Google, Yahoo and Facebook) have invested large amount of money in the development of novel distributed frameworks for the analysis of very large graphs and are working on novel solutions of many interesting classic problems in this new context [2,8].

The most common approach to cope with this huge amount of data using multiple processes or machines is to divide the graph into non-overlapping subsets, called *partitions*. Edges between vertices that have been assigned to distinct partitions, called *cut edges* in the literature, act as communication channels between the partitions themselves.

© Springer-Verlag Berlin Heidelberg 2015
J.L. Träff et al. (Eds.): Euro-Par 2015, LNCS 9233, pp. 346–358, 2015.
DOI: 10.1007/978-3-662-48096-0_27

When such partitions are assigned to a set of independent computing nodes (being them actual machines or virtual executors like processes and threads, or even mappers and reducers in the MapReduce model), their size matters: the largest of them must fit in the memory of a single computing entity. A common solution to the problem of optimizing the usage of memory in such cases is to compute partitions that have similar sizes. Dividing the vertex set in equal-sized partitions can still lead to an unbalanced subdivision, though: having the same amount of vertices does not imply having the same size, given the unknown distribution of their degrees and the potential high assortativity of some graphs.

In this paper we study a different approach: edges are partitioned into disjoint subsets, while vertices are associated to edges and thus may belong to multiple partitions at the same time. The advantage of such approach is that it makes possible to obtain well-balanced partitions, because the adjacency lists of high-degree nodes may be subdivided among multiple computing nodes. A good load balancing enables the use of a smaller number of computing units.

This type of partitioning can then be used by edge-centric programming models to speed up computation. For example, the Gather-Apply-Scatter model introduced by GraphLab [4] is executed independently on each edge in both the Gather and Scatter phase, and thus needs an efficient edge partitioning. Their system uses Powergraph [4], a one-pass greedy edge partitioning algorithm that can scale to huge graphs.

The main contribution of this paper is DFEP, a distributed graph partitioning algorithm that divides the edge set in partitions of similar size. The paper thoroughly evaluates DFEP, using both simulations and then implementation on top of both Hadoop and Spark, using the Amazon EC2 cloud. The experiments show that DFEP is efficient, scalable and obtains consistently good partitions.

2   Edge Partitioning

The task of subdividing a graph into partitions of similar size, or *partitioning*, is a classical problem in graph processing, and has many clear applications in both distributed and parallel graph algorithms. Most solutions, from Lin's and Kernighan's algorithm [6] in the 70's to more recent approaches [10], try to solve *vertex* partitioning. This approach, however, may lead to unbalanced partitions, because even if they end up having the same amount of vertices, an unbalanced distribution of edges may cause some subgraphs to be much larger than others. Approaching the problem from an edge perspective, thus, may bring us to interesting and practical results.

Given a graph $G = (V, E)$ and a parameter K, an *edge partitioning* of G subdivides all edges into a collection $E_1, \ldots, E_K$ of non-overlapping edge partitions:

$$E = \cup_{i=1}^{K} E_i \quad \forall i, j : i \neq j \Rightarrow E_i \cap E_j = \emptyset$$

The i-th partition is associated with a vertex set V_i, composed of the end points of its edges:

$$V_i = \{u : (u, v) \in E_i \vee (v, u) \in E_i\}$$

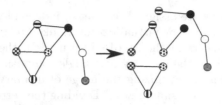

Fig. 1. Edge partitioning example: each edge appears in only one partition, while frontier vertices may appear in more than one partition

The edges of each partition, together with the associated vertices, form the subgraph $G_i = (V_i, E_i)$ of G, as illustrated in Fig. 1.

The *size* of a partition is proportional to the amount of edges and vertices $|E_i| + |V_i|$ belonging to it. Given that each edge $(u, v) \in E_i$ contributes with at most two vertices, $|V_i| = O(|E_i|)$ and the amount of memory needed to store a partition is strictly proportional to the number of its edges. This fact can be exploited to fairly distribute the load among machines. Vertices may be replicated among several partitions, in which case are called *frontier vertices*. We denote with $F_i \subseteq V_i$ the set of vertices that are frontier in the i-th partition.

3   Distributed Funding-Based Edge Partitioning

The properties that a "good" partitioning must possess are the following:

– **Balance:** partition sizes should be as close as possible to the average size $|E|/K$, where K is the number of partitions, to have a similar computational load in each partition. Our main goal is to minimize the size of the largest partition.
– **Communication Efficiency:** given that the amount of communication that crosses the border of a partition depends on the number of its frontier vertices, the total sum $\sum_{i=1}^{K} |F_i|$ must be reduced as much as possible.
– **Connectedness:** the subgraphs induced by the partitions should be as connected as possible. This is not a strict requirement and later in this section we illustrate a variant of our algorithm that relax it.

Balance is the main goal; it would be simple to just split the edges in K sets of size $\approx |E|/K$, but this could have severe implications on communication efficiency and connectedness. The approach proposed here is thus heuristic in nature and provides an approximate solution to the above requirements.

Since the purpose is to compute the edge partitioning as a preprocessing step to help the analysis of very large graphs, we need the edge partitioning algorithm to be distributed as well. As with most distributed algorithms, we are mostly interested in minimizing the amount of communication steps needed to complete the partitioning.

Ideally, a simple solution could work as follows: to compute K partitions, K edges are chosen at random and each partition grows around those edges.

Then, all partitions take control of the edges that are *neighbors* (i.e., they share one vertex) of those already in control and are not taken by other partitions. All partitions will incrementally get larger and larger until all edges have been taken. Unfortunately, this simple approach does not work well in practice, since the starting position may greatly influence the size of the partitions. A partition that starts from the center of the graph will have more space to expand than a partition that starts from the border and/or very close to another partition.

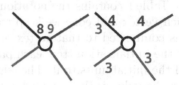

Fig. 2. Step 1

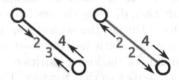

Fig. 3. Step 2

Table 1. Notation

$d(v)$	Degree of vertex v
$E(v)$	Edges incident on vertex v
$V(e)$	Vertices incident on edge e
$M_i[v]$	Units of partition i in vertex v
$M_i[e]$	Units of partition i in edge e
E_i	Edges bought by partition i
$owner[e]$	The partition that owns edge e

Algorithm 1. DFEP Init
Executed by the coordinator

> **foreach** *edge* $e \in E$ **do**
> $\quad owner[e] = \bot$
> **for** $i = 1$ to K **do**
> $\quad v \leftarrow random(V)$
> $\quad M_i[v] = |E|/K$

Algorithm 3. DFEP Step 2
Executed at each edge e

> $best = argmax_p(M_p(e))$
> **if** $owner[e] = \bot$ **and** $M_{best}(e) \geq 1$ **then**
> $\quad owner[e] = best$
> $\quad M_{best}[e] = M_{best}[e] - 1$
>
> **for** $i = 1$ to K **do**
> $\quad$ **if** $owner[e] = i$ **then**
> $\quad\quad$ **foreach** $v \in N(e)$ **do**
> $\quad\quad\quad M_i[v] = M_i[v] + M_i[e]/2$
> $\quad$ **else**
> $\quad\quad S = $ vertices that funded
> $\quad\quad$ partition i in e
> $\quad\quad$ **foreach** $v \in S$ **do**
> $\quad\quad\quad M_i[v] = M_i[v] + M_i[e]/|S|$
> $\quad M_i[e] = 0$

Algorithm 2. DFEP Step 1
Executed at each vertex v

> **for** $i = 1$ to K **do**
> $\quad$ **if** $M_i[v] > 0$ **then**
> $\quad\quad eligible = \emptyset$
> $\quad\quad$ **foreach** $e \in E(v)$ **do**
> $\quad\quad\quad$ **if** $owner[e] = \bot$ **or**
> $\quad\quad\quad owner[e] = i$ **then**
> $\quad\quad\quad\quad eligible = eligible \cup \{e\}$
>
> $\quad\quad$ **foreach** $e \in eligible$ **do**
> $\quad\quad\quad M_i[e] =$
> $\quad\quad\quad M_i[e] + (M_i[v]/|eligible|)$
> $\quad\quad M_i[v] = 0$

Algorithm 4. DFEP Step 3
Executed by the coordinator

> $AVG = \sum_{i \in [1...K]}(|E_i|)/K$
> **for** $i = 1$ to K **do**
> $\quad funding = min(10, AVG/E_i)$
> $\quad$ **foreach** $v \in V$ **do**
> $\quad\quad$ **if** $M_i(v) > 0$ **then**
> $\quad\quad\quad M_i(v) = M_i(v) + funding$

To overcome this limitation, we introduce DFEP (Distributed Funding-based Edge Partitioning), an algorithm based on concept of "buying" the edges through an amount of *funding* assigned to partitions. Initially, each partition is assigned the same amount of funding and an initial, randomly-selected vertex. The algorithm is then organized in a sequence of *rounds*. During each round, the partitions try to acquire the edges that are neighbors to those already taken, while a coordinator monitors the sizes of each partition and sends additional units of funding to the smaller ones, to help them overcome their slow start.

Table 1 contains the notation used in the pseudocode of the algorithm. For each vertex and edge we keep track of the amount of units that each partition has committed to that vertex or edge. Algorithm 1 presents the code executed at the initialization step: each partition chooses a vertex at random and assigns all the initial units to it. The edges are initialized as unassigned. Each round of the algorithm is then divided in three steps. In the first step (Algorithm 2), each vertex propagates the units of funding to the outgoing edges. For each partition, the vertex can move its funding only on edges that are free or owned by that partition, dividing the available units of funding equally among all these eligible edges. During the second step (Algorithm 3), each free edge is bought by the partition which has the most units committed in that edge and the units of funding of the losing partitions are sent back in equal parts to the vertices that contributed to that funding. The winning partition loses an unit of funding to pay for the edge and the remaining funding is divided in two equal parts and sent to the vertices composing the edge. In the third step (Algorithm 4), eachpartition receives an amount of funding inversely proportional to the number of edges it has already bought. This funding is distributed between all the vertices in which the partition has already committed a positive amount of funding. Two examples are illustrated in Figs. 2–3. The red and blue color represents partitions, while black edges are still free.

DFEP creates partitions that are connected subgraphs of the original graph, since currency cannot traverse an edge that has not been bought by that partition. It can be implemented in a distributed framework: both Step 1 and Step 2 are completely decentralized; Step 3, while centralized, needs an amount of computation that is only linear in the number of partitions.

In our implementation, the amount of initial funding is equal to what would be needed to buy an amount of edges equal to the optimal sized partition. A smaller quantity would not decrease the precision of the algorithm, but it would slow it down during the first rounds. The cap on the units of funding to be given to a small partition during each round (10 units in our implementation) avoids the over-funding of a small partition during the first rounds.

In a distributed setting the algorithm will follow the Bulk Synchronous Processing model: each machine receives a subset of the graph, executes Step 1 on each of its vertices independently, sends money to the correct edges (that may be on other machines), wait for the other machines to finish Step 1, and executes Step 2. Step 3 must be executed by a coordinator, but the amount of computation is minimal since the current sizes of the partitions can be computed via aggregated counting by the machines. Once the coordinator has computed the amount of funding for each partition, it can send this information to the machines that will apply it independently before Step 1 of the successive iteration. If the coordinator finds that all edges have been assigned, it will terminate the algorithm.

3.1 Variant: DFEPC

If the diameter is very large, there is the possibility that a poor starting vertex is chosen at the beginning of the round. A partition may be cut off from the rest of the graph, thus creating unbalanced partitions. A possible solution for this problem involves adding an additional dynamic, at the cost of losing the connectedness property.

A partition is called *poor* at round i if its size is less than $\frac{\mu}{p}$, with μ being the average size of partitions at round i and p being an additional parameter; otherwise, it is called *rich*. A poor partition can commit units on already bought edges that are owned by rich partitions and try to buy them. This addition to the algorithm allows small partitions to catch up to the bigger ones even if they have no free neighboring edges and results in more balanced partitions in graphs with larger diameter.

4   Results

We evaluated our algorithms with both simulations (experiments repeated 100 times) and actual implementations (experiments repeated 20 times. The metrics considered to evaluate DFEP in our simulation engine are the following:

- **Rounds**: the number of rounds executed by DFEP to complete the partitioning. This is a good measure of the amount of synchronization needed and can be a good indicator of the eventual running time in a real world scenario.
- **Balance**: Each partition should be as close as possible to the same size. To obtain a measure of the balance between the partitions we first normalize the sizes, so that a partition of size 1 represents a partition with exactly $|E|/K$ edges. We then measure the standard deviation of the normalized sizes.
- **Communication Costs**: Each partition will have to send a message for each of its frontier vertices, to share their state with the other partitions. We thus use the frontier nodes to estimate the communication costs: $M = \sum_{i=1}^{K} F_i$.

Since the simulation engine is not able to cope with larger datasets, we used different datasets for the experiments in the simulation engine and the real world experiments. For both types of datasets we list the size of the graphs, the diameter D, the clustering coefficient CC and the clustering coefficient RCC of a random graph with the same size.

The first four datasets in Table 2 have been used in the simulation engine. ASTROPH is a collaboration network in the astrophysics field, while EMAIL-ENRON is an email communication network from Enron. Both datasets are small-world, as shown by the small diameter. The USROADS dataset is a road networking the US, and thus is a good example of a large diameter network. Finally, WORDNET is a synonym network, with small diameter and very high clustering coefficient.

The three larger graphs are used in our implementation of DFEP on the Amazon EC2 cloud. DBLP is the co-authorship network from the DBLP archive, YOUTUBE is the friendship graph between the users of the service while AMAZON is a co-purchasing network of the products sold by the website.

All the networks have been taken from the SNAP graph library [7] and cleaned for our use, by making directed edges undirected and removing disconnected components.

Table 2. Datasets used in the simulation engine (1–4) and EC2 (5–7)

#	Name	$|V|$	$|E|$	D	CC	RCC
1	ASTROPH	17903	196972	14	1.34×10^{-1}	1.23×10^{-3}
2	EMAIL-ENRON	33696	180811	13	3.01×10^{-2}	3.19×10^{-4}
3	USROADS	126146	161950	617	1.45×10^{-2}	2.03×10^{-5}
4	WORDNET	75606	231622	14	7.12×10^{-2}	8.10×10^{-5}
5	DBLP	317080	1049866	21	1.28×10^{-1}	2.09×10^{-5}
6	YOUTUBE	1134890	2987624	20	2.08×10^{-3}	4.64×10^{-6}
7	AMAZON	400727	2349869	18	5.99×10^{-2}	2.93×10^{-5}

4.1 Simulations

Figure 4 shows the performance of the two versions of DFEP against the parameter K, in the ASTROPH and USROADS datasets. As expected, the larger the number of partitions, the larger is the variance between the sizes of those partitions and the amount of messages that will have to be sent across the network. The rounds needed to converge to a solution go down with the number of partitions, since it will take less time for the partitions to cover the entire graph.

The diameter of a graph is a strong indicator of how our proposed approach will behave. To test DFEP on graphs with similar characteristics but different diameter we followed a specific protocol: starting from the USROADS dataset (a graph with a very large diameter) we remapped random edges, thus decreasing the diameter. The remapping has been performed in such a way to keep the number of triangles as close as possible to the original graph, to avoid introducing bias in the experiment by radically changing the clustering coefficient.

Figure 5 shows that changing the diameter leads to completely different behaviors. The size of the largest partitions and the standard deviation of partitions size rise steeply with the growth of the diameter, since in a graph with higher diameter the starting vertices chosen by our algorithm affect more deeply the quality of the partitioning. As expected, the number of rounds needed by

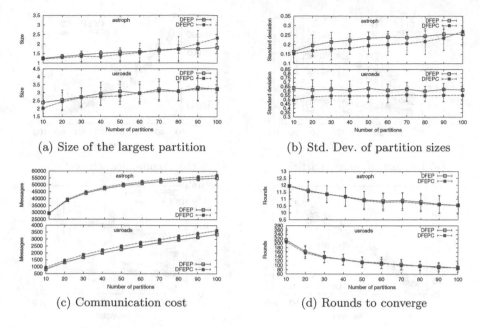

(a) Size of the largest partition

(b) Std. Dev. of partition sizes

(c) Communication cost

(d) Rounds to converge

Fig. 4. Behavior of DFEP and DFEPC with varying values of K

DFEP to compute the partitioning also rise linearly with the diameter. Since the partitions will be more interconnected, the amount of messages sent across the network will decrease steeply with a larger diameter. Our variant of DFEP is able to cope well also in case of graphs with large diameter.

Finally, we compare the two version of DFEP against JaBeJa [9] and Power-Graph [4]. Since JaBeJa is a vertex-partitioning algorithm, its output has been converted into an edge-partitioning.

PowerGraph processes the graph one edge at a time, assigning it to the best partition according to which partitions already contain the nodes of the current edge. The sequential version of the algorithm needs at each step complete knowledge of the choices of the previous iteration. The authors also illustrate a version called "Oblivious PowerGraph" in which each process behaves independently on a subset of the edges. The quality of the partitioning thus depends on the number of independent processes used. In our comparison, we used both the centralized version (labeled "PowerGraph") and the oblivious version (labeled "Oblivious PowerGraph"). In the oblivious version, we tested the algorithm by simulating two distinct processes.

Both PowerGraph versions create remarkably balanced partitions and are extremely fast, since they work in a single pass over the graph. On the downside, their partitions are less connected than DFEP and thus incur in more communication costs.

Figure 6 shows the experimental results over 100 samples, on the four different datasets. A pattern can be discerned: the algorithms have wildly different

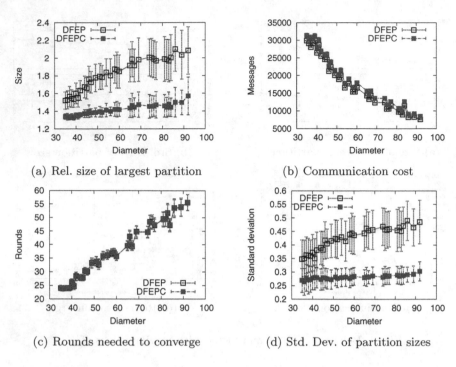

(a) Rel. size of largest partition   (b) Communication cost

(c) Rounds needed to converge   (d) Std. Dev. of partition sizes

Fig. 5. Behavior of DFEP and DFEPC with varying diameter ($K = 20$)

behaviors in the small world dataset than in the road network. In the small world datasets our approaches results in more balanced partitions, while needing less rounds to converge than JaBeJa. In the USROADS dataset JaBeJa creates more balanced partitions, but with a communication costs that is roughly ten times higher. This result shows the importance of creating partitions that are as much connected as possible. Powegraph instead gets balanced, but not very connected partitions in all cases. With the oblivious version of the algorithm the quality degrades, since the approach will obtain a partitioning of worse quality the higher the number of the processes that participate in the computation.

Since JaBeJa uses simulated annealing to improve the candidate solution, the number of round needed is mostly independent from the structure of the graph. As shown in Fig. 5 the number of rounds DFEP needs depend mostly from the graph diameter. Both versions of PowerGraph work in a single pass over the edge set, and therefore is a better choice if the amount of computation needed after the partitioning step is not large enough to warrant a more precise partitioning.

4.2 Experiments in EC2

DFEP has been implemented in both Apache Hadoop in the MapReduce model and in Spark/Graphx, and have been tested over the Amazon EC2 cloud. All the experiments have been repeated 20 times on *m1.medium* machines.

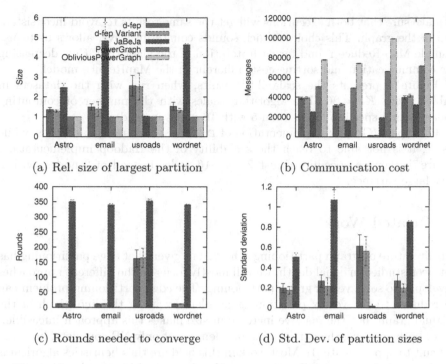

(a) Rel. size of largest partition

(b) Communication cost

(c) Rounds needed to converge

(d) Std. Dev. of partition sizes

Fig. 6. Comparison between DFEP, DFEPC, JaBeJa and PowerGraph ($K = 20$)

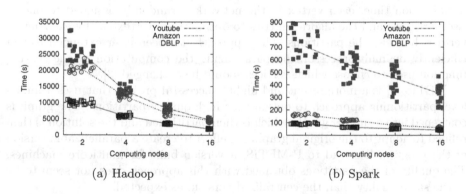

(a) Hadoop

(b) Spark

Fig. 7. Speedup of real implementation of DFEP in the amazon cloud

It was not possible to implement DFEP in Hadoop using a single Map-Reduce round for each iteration while keeping exactly the same structure as in the pseudocode. Each instance of the Map function is executed on a single vertex, which will output messages to its neighbor and a copy of itself. Each instance of the Reduce function will receive a vertex and all the funding sent by the neighbors on common edges. The part of the algorithm that should be executed on each edge is instead executed by both its neighboring vertices, with special care to make sure that both executions will get the same results to avoid inconsistencies in the graph. This choice, which sounds counterintuitive, allows us to use a single Map-Reduce round for each iteration of the algorithm, thus decreasing the communication and sorting costs inherent in the MapReduce model.

Figure 7a presents the scalability results, when run with the datasets in Table 2, with $K = 20$. The algorithm scales with the number of computing nodes, with a speedup larger than 5 with 16 nodes instead of 2.

Our Spark/Graphx implementation of DFEP is still unstable, and thus, while faster, it is not able to reach the scalability of the Hadoop implementation. Figure 7b shows a speedup of just 2 with 16 nodes instead of 2 nodes, with a very large variance.

5   Related Work

The literature on graph partitioning is huge, but given that edge partitioning has not been studied in equal depth, we will mostly focus on the different approaches developed to solve vertex graph partitioning. The edge partitioning problem can be reduced to the vertex partitioning problem by using the line graph of the original graph, but the massive increase in size makes this approach infeasible.

In both versions, the partitioning problem is not only NP-complete, but even difficult to approximate [1]. Most work in this field are thus heuristics algorithms with no guaranteed approximation rate. Kernighan and Lin developed the most well-known heuristic algorithm for binary graph partitioning in 1970 [6]. At initialization time, each vertex in the network is randomly assigned to one of two partitions and the algorithm tries to optimize the vertex cut by exchanging vertices between the partitions. This approach has been later extended to run efficiently on multiprocessors by parallelizing the computation of the scoring function used to choose which vertices should be exchanged [3].

METIS [5] is a more recent and highly successful project that uses a multi-level partitioning approach to obtain very high quality partitions. The graph is coarsened into a smaller graph, which is then partitioned and the solution is then refined to adapt to the original graph. An effort to create a parallelizable version of the program has lead to P-METIS, a version built for multicore machines. The quality of the partitions obtained with this approach does not seem to be of the same quality than the centralized version, as expected.

The presence of additional constraints has driven the research field towards more specialized algorithms. For example, in the streaming scenario it is infeasible to use the classical partitioning algorithm, since the data is continuously arriving. A greedy algorithm that assign each incoming vertex to a partition has been proposed [10] and computes partitions of only slightly less quality than most centralized algorithms.

The two algorithms selected for our comparison are JaBeJa [9] and Powergraph [4]. JaBeJa is a completely decentralized partitioning algorithm based on local and global exchanges. Each vertex in the graph is initially mapped to a random partition. At each iteration, it will try to exchange its mapping with one of its neighbor or with one of the random vertices obtained via a peer selection algorithm, if the exchange decreases the vertex cut size. An additional layer of simulated annealing decrease the likelihood of returning to a local minima. JaBeJa is similar in approach to Kernighan and Lin's algorithm, but moves the choices from the partition level to the vertex level, greatly increasing the possibility for parallelization.

Powergraph instead uses a greedy approach, processing and assigning each edge before moving to the next. It keeps in memory the current sizes of each partition and, for each vertex, the set of partitions that contain at least one edge of that vertex. If both endpoints of the current edge are already inside one common partition, the edge will be added to that partition. If they have no partition in common, the node with the most edges still to assign will choose one of its partitions. If only one node is already in a partition, the edge will be assigned to that partition. Otherwise, if both nodes are free, the edge will be assigned to the smallest partition. This heuristic can be run independently on N subsets of the edge set to parallelize the workload, at the cost of lower quality partitions.

6 Conclusions

This paper presented DFEP, an heuristic distributed edge partitioning algorithm based on a simple funding model. Our experimental results, obtained through simulation and through an actual deployment on an Amazon EC2 cluster, show that DFEP scales well and is able to obtain balanced partitions.

As future work, we are working on an efficient Spark implementation of DFEP, to allow us to partition larger graphs and analyze the scalability of our approach. We will study how does the algorithm behaves in presence of dynamism (such as addition and deletion of edges) and how to use external information about nodes and edges to obtain a better partitioning.

References

1. Andreev, K., Räcke, H.: Balanced graph partitioning. In: Proceedings of the 16th Annual ACM Symposium on Parallelism in Algorithms and Architectures, SPAA 2004, pp. 120–124. ACM (2004). doi:10.1145/1007912.1007931
2. Bialecki, A., Cafarella, M., Cutting, D., O'Malley, O.: Hadoop: a framework for running applications on large clusters built of commodity hardware. Wiki at (2005). http://lucene.apache.org/hadoop
3. Gilbert, J., Zmijewski, E.: A parallel graph partitioning algorithm for a message-passing multiprocessor. Int. J. Parallel Program. 16(6), 427–449 (1987)
4. Gonzalez, J.E., Low, Y., Gu, H., Bickson, D., Guestrin, C.: Powergraph: distributed graph-parallel computation on natural graphs. In: Proceedings of the 10th USENIX Symposium on Operating Systems Design and Implementation (OSDI), pp. 17–30 (2012)
5. Karypis, G., Kumar, V.: METIS: Unstructured graph partitioning and sparse matrix ordering system, version 2.0. Technical report, University of Minnesota (1995)

6. Kernighan, B., Lin, S.: An efficient heuristic procedure for partitioning graphs. Bell Syst. Tech. J. **49**(2), 291–307 (1970)
7. Leskovec, J.: Stanford large network dataset collection (2011). http://snap.stanford.edu/data/index.html
8. Malewicz, G., Austern, M., Bik, A., Dehnert, J., Horn, I., Leiser, N., Czajkowski, G.: Pregel: a system for large-scale graph processing. In: Proceedings of the 2010 International Conference on Management of Data, pp. 135–146. ACM (2010)
9. Rahimian, F., Payberah, A.H., Girdzijauskas, S., Jelasity, M., Haridi, S.: Ja-be-ja: a distributed algorithm for balanced graph partitioning. In: Proceedings of the 7th International Conference on Self-Adaptive and Self-Organizing Systems (SASO 2013), pp. 51–60. IEEE (2013)
10. Tsourakakis, C., Gkantsidis, C., Radunovic, B., Vojnovic, M.: Fennel: Streaming Graph Partitioning For Massive Scale Graphs. Microsoft Research, Cambridge (2012)

Parallel and Distributed Programming, Interfaces and Languages

PR-STM: Priority Rule Based Software Transactions for the GPU

Qi Shen, Craig Sharp$^{(\boxtimes)}$, William Blewitt, Gary Ushaw, and Graham Morgan

Newcastle University, Newcastle upon Tyne NE1 7RU, UK
{qi.shen1,craig.sharp,william.blewitt,
gary.ushaw,graham.morgan}@ncl.ac.uk

Abstract. In this paper we describe an implementation of a software transactional memory library for the GPU written in CUDA. We describe the implementation of our transaction mechanism which features both tentative and regular locking along with a contention management policy based on a simple, yet effective, static priority rule called Priority Rule Software Transactional Memory (*PR-STM*). We demonstrate competitive performance results in comparison with existing STMs for both the GPU and CPU. While GPU comparisons have been studied, to the best of our knowledge we are the first to provide results comparing GPU based STMs with a CPU based STM.

Keywords: Transactional memory · GPU · CUDA · Concurrency control · STM

1 Introduction

The availability of Graphics Processing Units (GPU) has recently expanded into the area of general purpose programming, giving rise to a new genre of applications known as General Purpose GPU [10] (hereafter GPGPU). The principle benefit of using the GPU is the relatively high degree of parallel computation available compared to the CPU. Furthermore, programming APIs, such as CUDA [13,14], have grown in sophistication with every new advancement in GPU design. As such, GPGPU programmers now have at their disposal tools to enable them to write complex and expressive applications which can leverage the power of modern GPUs.

As with multi-threaded applications on the CPU, GPGPU applications require synchronisation techniques to prevent corruption of shared data. As has long been experienced in the domain of CPU computing, correctly synchronising multiple threads is a difficult task to implement without introducing errors (such as deadlock and livelock) [7]. To compound matters, the high number of threads available on modern GPUs means that contention for shared data is an issue of greater potential significance than on the CPU where the number of threads is typically much lower.

© Springer-Verlag Berlin Heidelberg 2015
J.L. Träff et al. (Eds.): Euro-Par 2015, LNCS 9233, pp. 361–372, 2015.
DOI: 10.1007/978-3-662-48096-0_28

To address the difficulties of multi-threading on the CPU, significant progress has been made in providing Concurrency Control techniques to aid the concurrent programmer. One notable technique is Transactional Memory [8] (TM), which allows the execution of transactions in both Software [2,6] and Hardware [8,15]. TM provides an intuitive interface to aid programmers of multi-threaded programs. The TM system guarantees that programs are free of data inconsistency issues while handling the intricacies of thread coordination and contention management.

At the time of writing, implementing an efficient TM technique for the GPU remains an area with much potential for development. The work in this paper aims to contribute to that development by providing the following:

- An STM algorithm for the GPU based on a simple, yet effective, static priority rule. We demonstrate that our technique can out-perform a state-of-the-art STM technique for the GPU called *GPU-STM* [19];
- Benchmarked performance figures are provided, comparing *PR-STM* with both *GPU-STM* and a widely used STM technique for the CPU, namely *TinySTM* [3]. To our knowledge this is the first time that comparisons have been produced between STM techniques for the GPU and the CPU.

We have enhanced the benchmarking software to assess the performance of all three techniques with variation on the number of threads, transaction size and the granularity of lock coverage in addition to the impact of invisible reads.

Section 2 describes the implementation of our STM and Sect. 3 surveys related work. Section 4 describes our evaluation and, finally, Sect. 5 concludes the paper and discusses future work.

2   Implementation

2.1   Overview

The operation of the GPU differs considerably from the CPU and this must be taken into account when implementing transactional algorithms on the GPU. In addition to the high degree of threads available, groups of GPU threads execute as part of a 'warp'. Threads belonging to the same warp share the same instruction counter and thus execute the same instruction in a 'lock-step' fashion. In addition to the risk of high contention given the high number of threads, deadlock and livelock are possible because threads of the same warp cannot coordinate their accesses to locks as they can on the CPU (see Fig. 1(A)).

To prevent the possibility of deadlock and livelock, we use a 'lock stealing' algorithm which requires each thread be assigned a static priority. This allows a thread with priority n to steal a lock which is currently owned by any thread with a priority less than n (see Fig. 1(B)). As every thread has a unique priority, this addresses the possibility of deadlock because any thread can always determine its next action when encountering locked data. Livelock is also addressed as threads will never attempt to perpetually steal one another's locks.

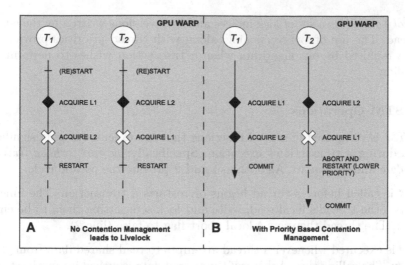

Fig. 1. Livelock and contention management in GPU transaction execution.

PR-STM implements a commit time locking approach where threads attempt to acquire locks at the end of their transactions. Before committing, threads first attempt to validate their transactions by tentatively 'pre-locking' shared data. Pre-locked data can be stolen based on the thread priority rule. If validation is successful the thread may commit its transaction. We implement invisible reads and threads maintain versions of the data they have accessed so that they can abort early if a conflict is detected. This has the benefit of reducing the costs of false conflict where a thread needlessly aborts when encountering data locked by a transaction which itself will abort in future.

2.2 Metadata

PR-STM consists of two types of metadata: a *global* metadata which is shared among all threads and a *local* metadata which is private to a single thread:

- *Global Lock Table.* A lock table is required which should be accessible to all GPU threads, hence it is located in global memory. Each word of shared data is hashable to a unique lock in the *global lock table*. To enhance the scalability of our system we can vary the number of words that are covered by a single lock. When the hashing function has a 1:1 configuration, for instance, every word of shared data has its own lock. While this configuration demands the most memory it minimises the chance of a false conflict based on shared locks. Each entry in the *global lock table* is an unsigned integer composed of version (11 bits), owner (19 bits), locked (1 bit) and pre-locked (1 bit);
- *Local Read Set* is a set of read entries each composed of a memory location, version and value read by the current thread;
- *Local Write Set* is a set of write entries recording the memory location and value written by the current thread;

– *Local Lock Set* is a set of lock indices and lock versions written by the current thread. The use of lock versioning, along with thread priorities provides the data required by our algorithm when a transaction wishes to perform lock stealing.

2.3   STM Operations

PR-STM is comprised of several functions that are executed during significant events during a transaction's execution. Specifically: *txStart*, *txRead*, *txWrite*, *txValidate* and *txCommit*. Algorithms 1 and 2 provide the pseudo code.

txStart is called before a thread begins or restarts a transaction. The function initialises the thread's local read, write and lock sets setting them to be empty (line 1). The thread then sets a local abort flag to false (line 2).

txRead is executed whenever a thread attempts to read shared data from global memory. The calling thread checks if the shared data is locked by another thread (line 3) and if so the thread aborts and restarts its transaction (line 10). If the data is not locked the thread checks to see if the data has already been added to its *local write set* (line 4) and if so, returns the stored value (line 5). If the data is not in the thread's *local write set* it retrieves the value from global memory (line 6) using an atomic read to ensure the value is up to date. The thread then adds the value read to its *local read set* along with the atomically read lock version corresponding to the shared data (lines 7–8) before it is returned.

txWrite records each write a thread wishes to make in its *local write set* . The thread first checks if the data is already locked and if so sets its abort flag to true indicating the transaction must abort and restart when the function returns (line 19). If the data is not locked the thread checks if the data is already in its *local write set* (line 14) and overwrites it. If the data has not been previously written the thread creates a new write set entry (lines 15–18).

txValidate is invoked before the transaction can commit. The thread attempts to lock all shared data that it intends to modify and performs validation of all the shared data it has read. The thread invokes *prelock* on all data read/written (line 20) to determine whether it has the highest priority value. Then the thread validates all the data in its read set by checking that their versions have not changed (lines 21–22). If validation is successful the thread will try to lock all data (line 23). If this is successful then the thread can now commit its transaction. If any of these steps fail, the transaction must abort.

txCommit is invoked only when a transaction has already successfully validated. The thread writes to all global shared data in its *local write set* (line 26) and executes a 'thread fence' (line 27). CUDA provides a thread fence function to ensure memory values modified before the fence can be seen by all other threads. Without a thread fence, the weak memory model of the GPU might cause a

Algorithm 1. PR-STM functions

```
   function txStart()
1  |   readSet ← writeSet ← lockTable ← ∅;
2  |   abort ← false;

   function txRead(Address addr)
3  |   if getLockBit(g_lock[hash(addr)]) = 0 then
4  |   |   if < addr, valWritten >∈ writeSet then
5  |   |   |   return valWritten ;
   |   |   else
6  |   |   |   value ← atomicRead(addr);
7  |   |   |   version ← getVersion(atomicRead(g_lock[hash(addr)]));
8  |   |   |   readSet ← readSet ∪ {< addr, value, version >};
9  |   |   |   return value;
   |   else
10 |   |   abort ← true;
11 |   |   return 0;

   function txWrite(Address addr, Value val)
12 |   if getLockBit(g_lock[hash(addr)]) = 0 then
13 |   |   if < addr, valWritten >∈ writeSet then
14 |   |   |   < addr, valWritten >←< addr, val >;
   |   |   else
15 |   |   |   idx ← hash(addr);
16 |   |   |   version ← getVersion(g_lock[idx]);
17 |   |   |   writeSet ← writeSet ∪ {< addr, val >};
18 |   |   |   lockSet ← lockSet ∪ {< idx, version >}};
   |   else
19 |   |   abort ← true;

   function txValidate()
20 |   if tryPreLock() = true then
21 |   |   for all< addr, value, version >∈ readSet do
22 |   |   |   if getVersion(g_lock[hash(addr)]) ≠ version then
   |   |   |   |   return false;

23 |   |   return tryLock();
   |   else
24 |   |   return false;

   function txCommit()
25 |   for all < addr, val >∈ writeSet do
26 |   |   *addr ← val;
27 |   _threadfence();
28 |   for all< idx, version >∈ lockSet do
29 |   |   if version < maxVersion then
30 |   |   |   setVersion(g_lock[idx], version + 1);
   |   |   else
31 |   |   |   setVersion(g_lock[idx], 0);
```

reordering of a thread's instructions, which could lead to inconsistent shared data. The thread fence ensures that modifications to shared data are visible to all threads before any locks are released. The thread then updates the version bit in the *global lock table* for each lock in its lock set. The version bit is either incremented (line 30) or reset (line 31) if the version value has reached the maximum value.

Algorithm 2. PR-STM functions

```
      function tryPreLock()
32       for all< idx, version >∈ lockSet do
33          repeat
34             tmpLockVal ← g_lock[idx];
35             if getVersion(tmpLockVal) ≠ version
36             or getLockBit(tmpLockVal) = 1
37             or(getPreLockBit(tmpLockVal) = 1 and
                  getOwner(tmpLockVal) < threadIdx) then
38                releaseLocks();
39                return false;

40             preLockVal ← calcPreLockedVal(version, threadIdx);
          until atomicCAS(g_lock+idx,tmpLockVal,preLockVal) = tmpLockVal;
41       return true;

      function tryLock()
42       for all< idx, version >∈ lockSet do
43          PreLockVal ← calcPreLockedVal(version, threadIdx);
44          FinalLockVal ← calcLockedVal(version);
45          if atomicCAS(g_lock+idx,PreLockVal,FinalLockVal) ≠ PreLockVal then
46             releaseLocks();
47             return false;

48       return true;

      function releaseLocks()
         for all idx ∈ PreLocked do
49          preLockVal ← calcPreLockedVal(version, threadIdx);
50          atomicCAS(g_lock+idx,preLockVal,preLockVal-1);

         for all idx ∈ Locked do
51          unLockVal ← calcUnlockVal(version);
52          g_lock[idx] ← unLockVal;
```

2.4 Contention Management Policy

In *PR-STM*, 32-bit memory words are used to represent locks. We use locks for both protecting shared data and implementing our priority rule policy. The various bits of each lock represent the following:

- The first 11 bits of a lock represent the current version of that lock. The version is incremented whenever an update transaction is successfully committed.
- Bits 12–30 represent the priority of whichever thread has currently pre-locked this lock (if such a thread exists). A lower value represents a higher priority.
- The 31st bit indicates whether this lock is pre-locked. Pre-locked locks may be stolen from threads with lower priorities and acquired by threads of higher priorities.
- The last bit represents whether the lock is currently locked. Once this bit is set, no other threads can acquire this lock.

Algorithm 2 (lines 32–52) shows three required handlers which are used to manage the locks:

tryPreLock is called whenever a thread attempts to pre-lock shared data. For each lock in its *local lock set*, the thread checks whether the lock versions are inconsistent (line 35) and whether the lock is unavailable (line 36). Finally, the thread checks whether the lock has been pre-locked by another thread with a higher priority (line 37). If any of these conditions are true, then the thread releases all locks it has previously pre-locked and aborts (line 39) otherwise the thread attempts to pre-lock the lock using an atomic Compare and Swap (CAS). If the CAS fails then another thread must have accessed the lock. The thread must then repeat lines 35–37 until it aborts or the CAS succeeds and it has the highest priority so far of all the threads attempting to pre lock this lock.

tryLock is called when a thread successfully pre-locks every lock in its *local lock set*. The thread attempts to lock each pre-locked lock (line 45). If any CAS fails then the lock has been stolen by a higher priority thread and the original thread must then release all locks and abort (lines 46–47).

releaseLocks is called when a thread commits or aborts. All pre-locked/locked locks are released. Pre-locked locks must be released by CAS (line 50) in case the lock has been stolen by another thread.

3 Related Work

Although STM research on the GPU is a recent research area at the time of writing, numerous implementations of software transactions for the GPU have been implemented. Cederman et al. [1], for instance, implemented the first STM on the GPU that works at the granularity of a thread-block (rather than the granularity of individual threads). By using a relatively coarse 'thread-block granularity', Cederman's technique avoids dependency violations between threads within a single block. Although this reduces contention due to the typically high thread numbers used on the GPU, it does not accommodate workloads more appropriate for STM execution.

Xu et al. have implemented an approach called GPUSTM [19] which, like *PR-STM*, operates at the granularity of the thread. GPUSTM implements an approach based on a combination of timestamp-based and value-based validation called 'hierarchical based validation'. Their validation technique requires that locks are sorted whenever transactional reading takes place to avoid the possibility of livelock. The static priority rule used by *PR-STM* on the other hand avoids the need to sort locks (our threads are effectively pre-sorted by their priorities instead).

Research has also been explored in providing Hardware Transactional Memory (HTM) for the GPU. In particular, Fung et al. [4,5] proposed a technique using value based validation like Xu's work but required significant modifications to the GPU architecture. Nasre et al. have also described generic modifications to improve the performance of morph algorithms with irregular access patterns [12], and [11] explored GPU techniques to speed up execution by reducing the usage of atomic operations.

More recently, Holey et al. have provided Lightweight Software Transactions for the GPU [9]. Three variations of STM design are described, namely: ESTM (eager), PSTM (pessimistic) and ISTM (invisible reads). ESTM updates shared memory during transaction execution while updating an undo log to remove those updates upon an abort. PSTM is a simpler version of ESTM which treats reads and writes in the same manner, hence PSTM is more effective where transactions regularly read and write to the same shared data. Like our approach, ISTM can represent invisible reads to reduce conflicts during a transaction. None of Holey's techniques allow for lock stealing based on thread priorities however. While Holey's work compares the performance of their algorithms with the CPU, they employ basic fine-grain and coarse-grain locking benchmarks. To our knowledge neither Holey's work, nor any of the other techniques described compare their performance with an actual STM implementation on the CPU.

4 Evaluation

In this section we present results from a series of benchmarks to demonstrate the performance of our system. We compare the performance of *PR-STM* against a recently developed STM system for the GPU called *GPU-STM* [19] and a widely used STM system for the CPU called *TinySTM* [3]. The tests were carried out on a desktop PC with Nvidia Fermi GPU (GeForce GTX 590) which has 16 SMs, operates at a clock frequency of 1225 MHz and has access to 1.5 GB of GDDR5 memory. All shared data and the *global lock table* are allocated in global memory, while all local meta-data is stored in local memory. The *global lock table* data accessed the L2 cache, while local memory accessed both the L1 and L2 caches. The CPU tests were carried out on 2 × dual-core 3.07 GHz Intel(R) processors with 16 GB of RAM. We used the Windows 7 Operating System. *TinySTM* used the Time Stamp Contention Management Policy [16] with the Eager Write Back configuration (with invisible reads).

The experiments use a benchmark called *bank* which accompanies *TinySTM*. A configurable array of bank accounts represents the shared data from which transactions withdraw and deposit funds. We allocated 10 MB of memory to create roughly 2.5 million accounts. We required many accounts to accommodate the presence of many more threads in the GPU. We found that this number of accounts allowed us to observe the effects of both low and high contention as we varied scenario parameters. We also added several adaptations to the base scenario, most notably the ability to vary the amount of shared data accessed within a transaction (i.e. the number of bank accounts). This allowed us to vary the likelihood of contention caused by longer transactions. We also implemented changes to the hashing function used in all three STM systems so that we could control the amount of shared data covered by a single lock to experiment with the degree of false-sharing. Finally, we included results where the number of threads are increased to observe the contention caused by high numbers of threads featured in GPU applications.

In the following graphs we present results where: (i) all threads perform update transactions (i.e. read and write operations) and (ii) 20 % of the threads in the scenario execute read-only transactions. This was included to observe the impact of invisible reads on the scenario. Each test lasted for 5 s and was executed 10 times with the average results presented.

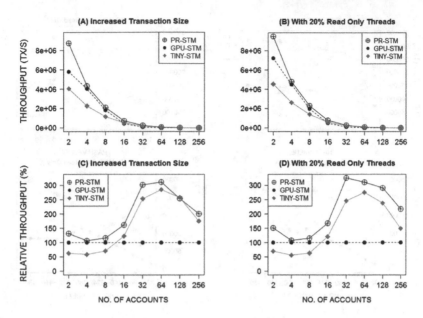

Fig. 2. Average throughput with increasing transaction size

4.1 Transaction Throughput

Figure 2 shows the degree of transaction throughput when the number of accounts accessed per transaction is increased. The number of threads used was kept constant at 512 threads for the GPU and 8 threads for the CPU. These values were used as they provided the best performance in each system. In Figs. 2(A) and (B), Y-axes show the number of transactions committed per second and X-axes show the number of bank accounts accessed in each transaction. As the GPU has many more threads than the CPU both *PR-STM* and *GPU-STM* outperform *TinySTM* when the number of accessed accounts is low (below 16). As expected, when the transaction size increases the throughput of all three STMs drops because inter-transaction conflicts are now more likely. The sharpest drop in performance is witnessed in *GPU-STM* as the higher thread numbers exacerbate the degree of conflicts. In the results with 20 % read only transactions (Figs. 2(B) and (D)) throughput is marginally better. This is because fewer locks are acquired and so fewer conflicts occur.

Figures. 2(C) and (D) show normalised throughput instead of the absolute values shown in Figs. 2(A) and (B). This helps to differentiate the performance when the transaction size increases beyond 16 accounts, where the values are too close to read in absolute terms. Y-axes show the relative throughput of *PR-STM* and *TinySTM* if we treat *GPU-STM* as 100 %. With more accounts accessed we can see both *PR-STM* and *TinySTM* outperform *GPU-STM*. One possible reason for this is that our algorithm does not have to sort the local lock array at every read or write step (like *GPU-STM*) while the higher number of

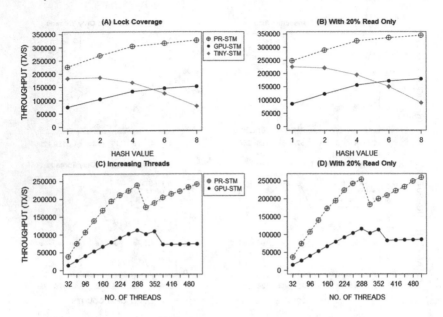

Fig. 3. Average throughput with increasing lock coverage and increased threads

threads enjoyed by *PR-STM* remains a benefit to performance rather than a hindrance.

4.2   STM Scalability

Figures. 3(A) and (B) show the degree of transaction throughput when the hash function is modified. The hash function determines the number of accounts covered by a single lock; the lower the hash value the less chance that threads will try to access the same lock when reading or writing to different shared data. Both the number of threads used and the transaction size were kept constant at 512(GPU)/8(CPU) and 128 respectively. Once again the Y axes show the throughput in transactions per second and the X-axes show the hash function value as the number of accounts covered by a single lock.

Figures 3(A) and (B) provide comparison between *PR-STM*, *GPU-STM* and *TinySTM* with different hash values. As the hash value increases the performance of *TinySTM* deteriorates due to the increased likelihood of false conflicts. Both *PR-STM* and *GPU-STM*, however, show increased throughput. This is because *PR-STM* and *GPU-STM* can both take advantage of reduced lock-querying (due to their lock-sets) and memory coalescing to reduce bus traffic when querying the status of locks held. In Fig. 3(B), with 20 % read only threads, performance is only slightly improved in all three techniques, but mostly in *TinySTM* which gains the most benefit from invisible reads.

In Figs. 3(C) and (D), we increase the number of threads. In these two graphs we only compare the performance of *PR-STM* and *GPU-STM* because

TinySTM is limited by the relatively small number of threads afforded by the CPU. Transaction throughput rises until 258 threads are used where inter-thread conflicts begin to occur at a substantial rate. Below 258 threads, the possibility of conflict is negligible because the high number of accounts used reduces the probability that threads will access the same account. As the number of threads increases, however, so too increases the rate of conflict and therefore the throughput decreases markedly. As thread numbers increase, however, *PR-STM* begins to improve once again, whereas *GPU-STM* levels out. The benefit of the work produced by extra threads is cancelled out by the overhead caused by inter-transactional contention. In Fig. 3(D) we can see that performance improves marginally with the introduction of 20 % read only threads. All other factors being equal, improvements in terms of read only transactions have little effect on the GPU.

5 Conclusion

In this paper we have presented *PR-STM*, a new scalable STM technique for the GPU which uses static thread ranking/priority to efficiently resolve contention for shared locks. We have demonstrated the performance of our approach against both GPU (*GPU-STM*) and CPU (*TinySTM*) software transactional memory libraries which, to our knowledge, is the first time such testing has been done. Results for transactional throughput and scalability demonstrate that our approach performs better than both *GPU-STM* and *TinySTM* in almost all cases.

We believe there exists much scope for expanding our approach. In the short-term we would like to enhance our Contention Management Policy to accommodate dynamic priorities and application semantics (this has been shown to provide substantial performance improvements [17,18]). In the long-term we would like to experiment with combining the GPU and the CPU within a heterogeneous transaction manager. The results suggest that the GPU is particularly effective at processing large numbers of short transactions, while the presence of read-only transactions provides only a small improvement to GPU performance. Further testing will allow us to formulate transaction allocation strategies, assigning work to either the CPU or the GPU based on the effectiveness of each processing element to execute that work.

References

1. Cederman, D., Tsigas, P., Chaudhry, M.T.: Towards a software transactional memory for graphics processors. In: EGPGV, pp. 121–129 (2010)
2. Dice, D., Shalev, O., Shavit, N.: Transactional locking II. In: Dolev, S. (ed.) DISC 2006. LNCS, vol. 4167, pp. 194–208. Springer, Heidelberg (2006)
3. Felber, P., Fetzer, C., Riegel, T.: Dynamic performance tuning of word-based software transactional memory. In: Proceedings of the 13th ACM SIGPLAN Symposium on Principles and Practice of Parallel Programming, pp. 237–246. ACM (2008)

4. Fung, W.W., Aamodt, T.M.: Energy efficient GPU transactional memory via space-time optimizations. In: Proceedings of the 46th Annual IEEE/ACM International Symposium on Microarchitecture, pp. 408–420. ACM (2013)

5. Fung, W.W., Singh, I., Brownsword, A., Aamodt, T.M.: Hardware transactional memory for GPU architectures. In: Proceedings of the 44th Annual IEEE/ACM International Symposium on Microarchitecture, pp. 296–307. ACM (2011)

6. Harris, T., Marlow, S., Peyton-Jones, S., Herlihy, M.: Composable memory transactions. In: Proceedings of the Tenth ACM SIGPLAN Symposium on Principles and Practice of Parallel Programming, pp. 48–60. ACM (2005)

7. Herlihy, M.: Wait-free synchronization. ACM Trans. Program. Lang. Syst. (TOPLAS) 13(1), 124–149 (1991)

8. Herlihy, M., Moss, J.E.B.: Transactional memory: architectural support for lock-free data structures, vol. 21. ACM (1993)

9. Holey, A., Zhai, A.: Lightweight software transactions on GPUs. In: 2014 43rd International Conference on Parallel Processing (ICPP), pp. 461–470. IEEE (2014)

10. Luebke, D., Harris, M., Govindaraju, N., Lefohn, A., Houston, M., Owens, J., Segal, M., Papakipos, M., Buck, I.: GPGPU: general-purpose computation on graphics hardware. In: Proceedings of the 2006 ACM/IEEE Conference on Supercomputing, p. 208. ACM (2006)

11. Nasre, R., Burtscher, M., Pingali, K.: Atomic-free irregular computations on GPUs. In: Proceedings of the 6th Workshop on General Purpose Processor Using Graphics Processing Units, pp. 96–107. ACM (2013)

12. Nasre, R., Burtscher, M., Pingali, K.: Morph algorithms on GPUs. In: ACM SIGPLAN Notices, vol. 48, pp. 147–156. ACM (2013)

13. Nvidia, C.: Compute unified device architecture programming guide (2007)

14. Nvidia, C.: Programming guide (2008)

15. Rajwar, R., Goodman, J.R.: Transactional lock-free execution of lock-based programs. ACM SIGOPS Oper. Syst. Rev. 36(5), 5–17 (2002)

16. Scherer III, W.N., Scott, M.L.: Advanced contention management for dynamic software transactional memory. In: Proceedings of the Twenty-fourth Annual ACM Symposium on Principles of Distributed Computing, pp. 240–248. ACM (2005)

17. Sharp, C., Blewitt, W., Morgan, G.: Resolving semantic conflicts in word based software transactional memory. In: Silva, F., Dutra, I., Santos Costa, V. (eds.) Euro-Par 2014 Parallel Processing. LNCS, vol. 8632, pp. 463–474. Springer, Heidelberg (2014)

18. Sharp, C., Morgan, G.: Hugh: a semantically aware universal construction for transactional memory systems. In: Wolf, F., Mohr, B., an Mey, D. (eds.) Euro-Par 2013. LNCS, vol. 8097, pp. 470–481. Springer, Heidelberg (2013)

19. Xu, Y., Wang, R., Goswami, N., Li, T., Gao, L., Qian, D.: Software transactional memory for GPU architectures. In: Proceedings of Annual IEEE/ACM International Symposium on Code Generation and Optimization, p. 1. ACM (2014)

Leveraging MPI-3 Shared-Memory Extensions for Efficient PGAS Runtime Systems

Huan Zhou[✉], Kamran Idrees, and José Gracia

High Performance Computing Center Stuttgart (HLRS),
University of Stuttgart, Stuttgart, Germany
zhou@hlrs.de

Abstract. The relaxed semantics and rich functionality of one-sided communication primitives of MPI-3 makes MPI an attractive candidate for the implementation of PGAS models. However, the performance of such implementation suffers from the fact, that current MPI RMA implementations typically have a large overhead when source and target of a communication request share a common, local physical memory. In this paper, we present an optimized PGAS-like runtime system which uses the new MPI-3 shared-memory extensions to serve intra-node communication requests and MPI-3 one-sided communication primitives to serve inter-node communication requests. The performance of our runtime system is evaluated on a Cray XC40 system through low-level communication benchmarks, a random-access benchmark and a stencil kernel. The results of the experiments demonstrate that the performance of our hybrid runtime system matches the performance of low-level RMA libraries for intra-node transfers, and that of MPI-3 for inter-node transfers.

Keywords: MPI · One-sided communication · Remote-memory access · RMA · Partitioned global address space · PGAS

1 Introduction

The Message Passing Interface (MPI, [7]) is the de-facto communication standard for distributed-memory parallel programming. One particular advantage for parallel programmers is the portability of MPI performance across systems with different underlying network hardware: While HPC hardware vendors and the MPI community spend considerable effort to optimize MPI implementations for the latest HPC network infrastructure, other alternative communication libraries typically do not have optimized support for a wide range of network hardware. With the advent of the remote-memory access (RMA, also referred to as one-sided communication) functionalities in MPI-2 [6] and the significant improvement of the RMA in MPI-3 [7], MPI has become an adequate communication backend for the implementation of partitioned global address space (PGAS) programming models [11].

DASH [4] is a C++ template library which implements a PGAS-like programming model. Unlike other PGAS models, DASH acknowledges the multi-level

© Springer-Verlag Berlin Heidelberg 2015
J.L. Träff et al. (Eds.): Euro-Par 2015, LNCS 9233, pp. 373–384, 2015.
DOI: 10.1007/978-3-662-48096-0_29

hierarchical or compositional nature of today's supercomputing systems, e.g.
cores, processors, nodes, racks, islands, full system, and thus does not classify
data into remote and local only, but allows for various degrees of remoteness. The
template library sits on top of a runtime system (DART), which is responsible
for providing services to the DASH library, including the definition of semantics
and the abstraction of the underlying hardware. In particular, DART provides
functions for the management of teams (a concept similar to MPI communicators), one-sided communications, collective operations, and global memory
management.

In an earlier paper [17], we have described DART-MPI, a portable implementation of the DASH runtime, that uses MPI-3 as low-level communication
substrate. There, we showed, that the overhead of DART-MPI RMA operations
on top of the corresponding MPI-3 operations is negligible in general. Most
other PGAS implementations however, do not use MPI as communication substrate; UPC [2] for instance is frequently based on GASNet [1], while GA [9]
uses ARMCI [8] as underlying communication substrate.

Originally, all the RMA operations in DART-MPI are substantially mapped
directly to the corresponding MPI-3 RMA operations. In particular, DART-MPI
invokes MPI RMA operations when source and target of a transfer reside on the
same node and share local, physical memory. Alternatively, one could do direct
load/store operations without additional copies in the runtime layer. In this
paper, the contributions we make on DART-MPI are threefold:

- We utilize the MPI-3 shared-memory extensions to enable direct memory
  access (memory sharing) for DART-MPI blocking operations for intra-node
  transfers. However, we turn to the MPI RMA operations when the non-
  blocking or inter-node data movements happen.
- We redefine the existing translation table to facilitate the reference to the
  DART-MPI collective global pointer when beginning with the shared memory
  window in mind.
- Using the low-level and application-level benchmarks, we show the improved
  performance achieved by embedding the shared-memory-related functionality
  into DART-MPI.

The rest of the paper is organized as follows: In Sect. 2, we present the background for our work. In Sect. 3, we describe the improved implementation of
DART-MPI and evaluate the performance of DART-MPI in Sect. 4. We summarize in Sect. 5.

2   Background

From the perspective of PGAS models, the recent MPI-3 standard [7] significantly improves the one-sided communication system. The relaxation of the
RMA semantics, the concretization of the memory consistency model, the introduction of new window types, fine-grained mechanisms for synchronization and

data movement, and atomic operations, make MPI-3 RMA attractive as back-end for PGAS implementations. Additionally, the results in Dinan et al. [3] indicate that the new MPI-3 RMA system has performance advantages over the MPI-2 interface. In this section, we briefly explain two new MPI-3 window types: *dynamically-allocated window* and *shared-memory window*, which will play a central role in understanding how to enable memory sharing within a node in DART-MPI. A more detailed description of the other new functionalities can be found in Hoefler et al. [5].

2.1 MPI Dynamically-Allocated Memory Window

A dynamically-allocated window is a new concept in MPI-3 that allows to arbitrarily grow and resize a given window by repeatedly attaching/detaching multiple, non-overlapping, user allocated memory regions to/from the associated window object.

The function *MPI_Win_create_dynamic* is called to generate a window object *d-win* without associating any initial memory block with it. User allocated memory is attached to *d-win*, and thus made available for RMA operations, by invoking the function *MPI_Win_attach*, and detached with *MPI_Win_detach*. Once memory regions are detached from *d-win*, they will not be the target of any MPI RMA operation on *d-win* unless they are re-attached. Notably, any local memory region may be attached and detached repeatedly, and multiple, but non-overlapping memory regions are allowed to be attached to the same window.

MPI_Get_address returns the address of the given memory and should be called to validate the RMA operations on *d-win*. This is due to the fact that the address of the target memory location is passed directly as window displacement parameter to the MPI RMA operations. Therefore, the target process is required to send the address of a certain memory location, that locals to it, to the origin process who inquires for it.

Noticeably, Potluri et al. [13] have published benchmark results which demonstrate that dynamically-allocated windows perform as good as the traditional static MPI-created windows in terms of put latency.

2.2 MPI Shared-Memory Window

The unified memory model, which is fully supported in MPI-3 in order to utilize the cache-coherence characteristics embodied in the modern hardware architectures, is a requirement for exposing the MPI shared-memory window.

To collectively allocate the shared memory region across all processes in a given communicator, MPI-3 defines a portable, shared-memory window allocation interface – *MPI_Win_allocate_shared* to generate a shared-memory allocated window object *shmem-win*. In addition, the communicator that the *shmem-win* associates with should be a *shared-memory capability* communicator, which means it is allowed to build a memory sharing region on top of this communicator. Therefore, the additional function *MPI_Comm_split_type*, as an extension of the function *MPI_Comm_split*, identifies sub-communicators on which the shared memory region can be created with the type of *MPI_COMM_TYPE_SHARED*. The function *MPI_Win_shared_query* is provided to query the base pointer to the memory on the target process. Coupled with the *shmem-win*, the locally-allocated memory can even be accessed by the MPI processes in the group of *shmem-win* with immediate load/store operations. Such access pattern can make data movements bypass the MPI layer and directly go through memory sharing, which brings in significant performance improvement.

3 The DART-MPI Implementation Design

In this section, we explain the approach of enabling the memory sharing option for the blocking RMA operations in DART-MPI and address the modifications and improvements that are made with respect to the existing DART-MPI.

There are two types of DART global memory, collective and non-collective [17]. The collective global memory, pointed to by a collective global pointer, is created and distributed across the given team. The non-collective global memory, pointed to by a non-collective global pointer, is only allocated in the global address space of the calling unit. We assume that all the following collective global memory blocks are allocated across team T consisting of P units.

3.1 Communication Hierarchy of the DART-MPI Blocking RMA Operations

To make the DART-MPI intra-node communication more efficient, we alter the existing implementation to let the DART-MPI blocking operations deal with the data locality explicitly. Note, that the DART-MPI non-blocking RMA interfaces do not yet support the memory sharing as described earlier in this paper.

In the team creation code, the team T is split into sub-teams on which it is possible to enable communication via sharing memory. We accomplish this by calling *MPI_Comm_split_type* with key *MPI_COMM_TYPE_SHARED*. In addition, a *d-win* is generated without any memory attached when team T is created, indicating one-to-one relationship is built between *d-win* and T. Such relationship is stored in an array named *dart_win_lists*. Therefore, the position of the team T in *teamlist* [17] can also be a perfect index into the array *dart_win_lists*. The *d-win* can potentially be utilized to complete all the data movements where the units are located in different sub-teams.

In the collective global memory allocation code, instead of allocating a block of memory from a memory pool that is reserved for T, we need to create a *shmem-win* spanning the memory of the specified size on each sub-team mentioned above. On top of that, each unit of the team T should attach the locally-allocated memory to the *d-win* explicitly to make them available for the units in the varying sub-teams. As the Fig. 1 shows, there are two overlapping windows sharing the same memory region for different purposes. On the one hand,

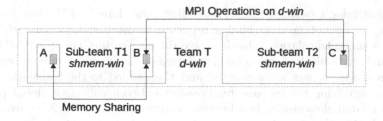

Fig. 1. Nesting of shared-memory window inside RMA window for blocking put/get operations

the units covered by the same *shmem-win* can communicate with each other via memory sharing (e.g., memcpy). On the other hand, the units located in different sub-teams should turn to the *d-win* for completing the remote accesses with MPI RMA operations. Note, that using shared-memory in the DART-MPI non-blocking RMA operations is anything but trivial as for instance the direct memcpy function itself is a blocking operation. Furthermore, the introduction of DMA copy engine could be a workaround to support asynchronous memory copying [16] for DART-MPI.

In the non-collective global memory allocation code, we provide two overlapping global windows, which indicates that all the DART-MPI non-collective allocations fall into two pre-defined global windows. One of the two windows is generated first spanning a large amount of shared memory region on the default communicator – *MPI_COMM_WORLD* [7] for intra-node communications, the other is then created with *MPI_Win_create* covering the above shared memory region to enable the message transferring across different nodes. As a result, these two windows share the same static shared memory region, and independently implement the data movements on them in an efficient manner.

3.2 DART-MPI Collective Global Pointer Dereference

In this section, we mainly explain the collective global pointer dereference of the updated DART-MPI since the non-collective global pointer basically continues to use the original dereference mechanism.

Besides the altered communication pattern, the meaning of the member *segid* in the global pointer is also re-specified for management convenience and data access efficiency. Therefore, the *segid* in the collective global pointer is no longer set to the related team ID but rather an increasing positive integer number, which can be used to determine any collective global block uniquely.

With the aid of the translation table [17], collective global pointer can get analyzed adequately. Thus it is critical for us to understand how the translation table reacts to the hierarchical communication pattern and the modification made in the global pointer, which also has an impact on the original collective global pointer deference method.

To be consistent with the modified definition of *segid* in global pointer, the key in the translation table is altered and the *segid* is utilized instead. The translation table is arranged in an ascending order based on the key *segid*. As a result, we do not need to bind a separate translation table to each team, instead a single translation table is active during the lifetime of a DART-MPI program. Once a block of collective global memory is created, a unique *segid* and the related *shmem-win* are generated and then added to the translation table together, signifying the one-one relationship between collective global pointer and the related *shmem-win*. In addition, according to the Sect. 2, we learn that after attaching the shared memory region onto the *d-win* locally, the routine *MPI_Get_address* should be invoked so as to collect the beginning address of the local shared memory region of each unit in team T. Thus, the translation table should also contain an array *disp-set* storing those separate addresses. As an example, when unit i in the team T is targeted, then the ith item in the related *disp-set* should be obtained and be utilized in the future to locate the target memory location in unit i. The offset returned in the generated collective global pointer is initialized to 0.

The location of target data is given by DART global pointer, which incorporates the information on the target unit, *segid* and a specific offset. For the collective global pointer, in the case of intra-node communications, we firstly query the appropriate *shmem-win* that covers the expected target location from the translation table according to the *segid*, then decode the location with offset. In the case of inter-node communications, we firstly query the *disp-set*, indicates the beginning address of the window segment of each unit in team T, from the translation table according to the *segid*, and then get the correct *d-win* from the array *dart_win_lists* and translate the absolute unit id to the relative unit id i in T, and finally access the remote data through MPI RMA operations, where the value of *offset+disp-set*[i] is passed as parameter *target_disp*.

4   Performance Evaluation

In the following, we evaluate the performance of DART-MPI using a set of benchmarks which includes low-level communication and application benchmarks. All the benchmarks are carried out on a Cray XC40 system named Hornet. Each compute node features two Intel Haswell E5-2680v3 2.5 GHZ processors and consists of 24 cores. The different compute nodes are interconnected through a Cray Aries network using Dragonfly topology. They use the Cray-MPI implementation of MPI-3.

Foremost, we are interested in the evaluation of the performance advantage of our DART-MPI, using MPI-3 shared-memory and RMA, over native MPI-3 RMA. As shown in a previous paper [17], the difference in performance of DART-MPI and MPI-3 RMA operations for non-local transfers is negligible. In that sense, MPI-3 can be seen as a proxy for the old DART-MPI. We will thus not show the latter explicitly in this paper. In addition, we compare DART-MPI with two important PGAS implementations: UPC and OpenSHMEM, which are both fully implemented and tuned on the Cray XC40 system. In all cases we use the Cray compiler, which also supports UPC (through the compiler flag *-h upc*)

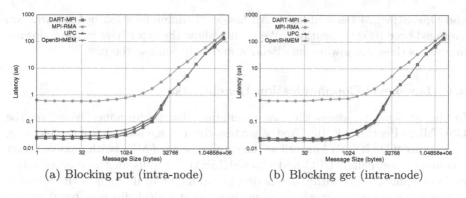

(a) Blocking put (intra-node)   (b) Blocking get (intra-node)

Fig. 2. Blocking put/get latency on 2 ranks/units

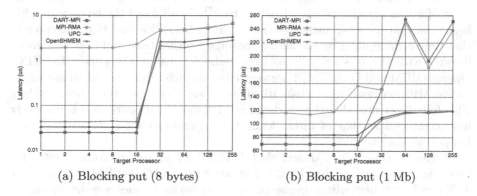

(a) Blocking put (8 bytes)   (b) Blocking put (1 Mb)

Fig. 3. Blocking put latency as a function of logically increasing distance between two involved ranks/units on 256 PEs

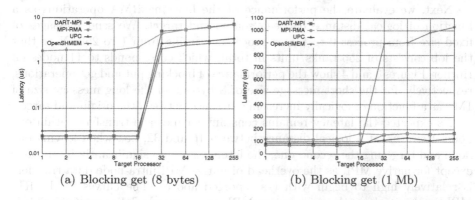

(a) Blocking get (8 bytes)   (b) Blocking get (1 Mb)

Fig. 4. Blocking get latency as a function of logically increasing distance between two involved ranks/units on 256 PEs

and OpenSHMEM (as a library). All low-level communication benchmarks are averaged over 10000 executions. We do not show the error bars in the following figures, as these are always small and would only confuse the plots.

4.1 Low-Level Communication Benchmarks

In this section, we assess the raw communication performance based on the OSU Micro Benchmark [10]. Firstly, we test the average latencies of the blocking operations of DART-MPI as well as the counterparts of MPI (with passive target communication calls), UPC and OpenSHMEM [12] only in the case of intra-node (communication within one node). Secondly, we evaluate how the blocking put and get operations perform when increasing logical distance between two involved processes for DART-MPI, MPI, UPC and OpenSHMEM.

Figure 2 shows the average latency of intra-node blocking put and get operations for message size ranging from 2^0 to 2^{21}. In all cases the latency roughly keeps constant for small messages (here < 1024 byte). Beyond that the completion time is dominated by the actual message transfer time and basically grows linearly with the message size as expected. Noticeably, the curves for UPC, OpenSHMEM and DART-MPI are very close to each other. For small messages, native MPI performs more than 10 times slower than the other three models. This fully illustrates that the overhead of MPI one-sided operations is relatively high compared to that of direct load/store operations when data movements happen within one node.

A careful comparison shows, that DART-MPI always performs better for blocking put operations than UPC (by about 20 %) and OpenSHMEM (by about 40 %), although such advantage becomes negligible as the message size increases. For blocking get operations, the variance between them is much lower in absolute terms, but the trend of curves seems to suggest that DART-MPI (and to a lesser extend, also UPC) performs slightly slower than OpenSHMEM.

Next, we evaluate the performance of the blocking RMA operations as a function of logical distance between source and target. We send messages of fixed size from process 0 to target processes varying from 1 to 255. Note that the job consists of 256 ranks/units in total, which corresponds to 11 nodes on Hornet. Figures 3 and 4 show the performance of blocking put and get operations, respectively, for the short message size of 8 bytes and the long message size of 1Mb as a function of logically increasing distance between the origin and target.

As expected the latency remains constant for message transfers within one node. However, at a logical distance between 16 and 32, i.e., when leaving one node and targeting the second one, the latency goes up significantly in all cases except for native MPI, as the overhead of native MPI intra-node data transfers is relatively high to begin with (as reported above). The curves for DART-MPI nearly sit above those for native MPI for inter-node data transfers. This is expected since DART-MPI falls back on MPI when communicating across nodes. Both, however, perform in general slightly worse than UPC and OpenSHMEM in latency for inter-node communications. An exception occurs when executing the

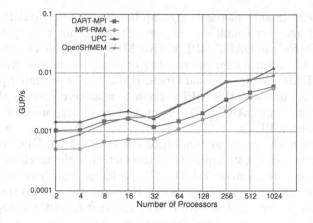

Fig. 5. Random Access performance comparison

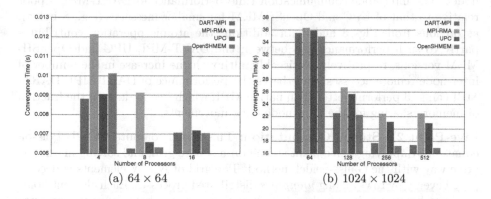

(a) 64×64 (b) 1024×1024

Fig. 6. Five-point stencil performance comparison

OpenSHMEM blocking get operation when transferring large messages; it performs 5 to 10 times worse than the other three models in latency. We do not have an explanation for such behavior, but the full data set we have seems to suggest that OpenSHMEM blocking get operations show relatively poor performance for large messages.

4.2 Application Benchmarks

In this section we present the results of two application benchmarks, namely Random Access and a stencil code kernel. All benchmarks were run on up to 1024 cores, i.e., 45 nodes on Hornet.

Random Access: The Random Access (RA) benchmark [14] is one of the HPC Challenge benchmarks developed for the HPCS program. It consists of concurrent, atomic updates of random elements of a distributed array by all ranks [15].

The general performance metric is giga-updates per second (GUPs). The messages involved are very small, i.e., 8 bytes. Figure 5 shows the performance in terms of GUPs for the DART-MPI, native MPI, UPC and OpenSHMEM versions of the RA benchmark for the number of processes varying from 2 to 1024. Interestingly, DART-MPI, UPC and OpenSHMEM achieve similar performance. The performance of the native MPI version is relatively poor in all cases, and the performance of the DART-MPI version suffers at large number of ranks due to the underlying MPI.

The relative performance evaluation of the DART-MPI, UPC and OpenSHMEM versions is complex stemming from the fact, that the blocking get, put and atomic operations are involved. DART-MPI performs slightly better than OpenSHMEM when RA runs on a single node. However, we can see there is a clear gap between the performance of DART-MPI and that of UPC and OpenSHMEM when the application is carried out across nodes. This is due to the fact that the amount of the inter-node remote accesses increases as the growing of the running nodes. The inter-node communication time performance of DART-MPI is poor relative to that of UPC and OpenSHMEM for smaller messages (e.g., 8 bytes), as obvious from Figs. 3 and 4. In addition, the atomic operation contributes partly to such performance gap between the DART-MPI, UPC and OpenSHMEM versions, respectively. Noticeably, although the increase in the number of inter-node remote accesses exacerbates the performance of DART-MPI, DART-MPI can still perform better than native MPI, which has to do with the fraction of memory sharing for the intra-node data movements.

Five-Point 2D Stencil Computation: This kernel computes the 2D Poisson equation by applying a five-point stencil on a square grid, and solving in an iterative way with the Gauss-Seidel method. The grid of $N \times N$ elements is decomposed evenly by rows among *numprocs* distributed processes. Each element holds a 4-byte floating point number. The kernel uses extra halo zones to exchange boundary elements between neighbors, A total of $4 \times N \times (2 \times numprocs - 2)$ bytes of data per iteration is transmitted using blocking put operations. With those halo data, all the inner grid cells can get updated successfully. We run the stencil kernel until convergence of solution. The time recorded in the benchmark includes the execution time of the Gauss-Seidel solver (local computation part) and communication time for halo exchange.

We run the five-point stencil benchmark for DART-MPI, MPI, UPC and OpenSHMEM versions on the grids of 64×64 elements and 1024×1024 elements respectively. Figure 6(a) shows comparison results of a 64×64 grid distributed across 4, 8 and 16 processes on a single node. We can see that the DART-MPI version always performs slightly better than the UPC version, when all the data movement happen within a single node. In addition, DART-MPI, UPC and OpenSHMEM outperform native MPI by $\sim 35\%$ for 16 processes.

The performance of the DART-MPI version degrades when there are data movements across nodes. Figure 6(b) shows benchmark results of a 1024×1024 grid for 64, 128, 256 and 512 processes. The convergence time of the DART-MPI and OpenSHMEM versions decreases as the number of processes involved is increased, which suggests that DART-MPI and OpenSHMEM are more scalable than native MPI and UPC from the perspective of this benchmark.

5   Conclusions

DART-MPI is the runtime system for the PGAS-like C++ template library DASH and built on top of MPI-3 one-sided communication primitives. In this paper we present an optimized design of DART-MPI which uses the new MPI-3 shared-memory extension for intra-node communications. In essence, we nest MPI-3 shared-memory windows inside RMA windows to do direct load/store operations for intra-node transfers, and MPI-3 one-sided communication operations on the RMA windows for inter-node transfers.

We expect that this optimization will improve the performance of DART-MPI for intra-node communication. To verify this claim, we run three classes of benchmarks, namely low-level put/get benchmarks, a Random Access benchmark and a stencil application kernel on the Cray XC40 system. We evaluate the performance of DART-MPI against that of native MPI. In addition, we compare DART-MPI to OpenSHMEM and UPC as two other PGAS-like programming models. The results of the evaluation demonstrate, first, that DART-MPI performs significantly faster than MPI RMA when messages are transmitted within a single node, i.e., that our optimization of DART-MPI leads to a better intra-node communication performance, second, that the comparison to Open-SHMEM and UPC show that the performance improvement that is brought by our optimization makes DART-MPI comparable with UPC and OpenSHMEM. Additionally, our performance evaluation also shows, that for some relevant operations – especially the inter-node RMA operations – DART-MPI still performs slower than the alternative PGAS approaches.

In this paper, we have only considered blocking RMA put and get operations. The current design of DART does not include an asynchronous progress engine, and therefore relies on other parts of the software stack to do progress as necessary for non-blocking operations. In particular, we rely on MPI for non-blocking RMA operations and thus see no benefit for non-blocking DART operations. An asynchronous progress engine which allows optimization of non-blocking intra-node transfers is a subject of further research.

Acknowledgments. The authors would like to thank Karl Fürlinger for fruitful discussion on the DASH runtime design. We gratefully acknowledge funding by the German Research Foundation (DFG) through the German Priority Programme 1648 Software for Exascale Computing (SPPEXA).

References

1. Bonachea, D., Jeong, J.: GASNet: A Portable High-Performance Communication Layer for Global Address-Space Languages. Technical report, CS258 Parallel Computer Architecture Project (2002)

2. Carlson, W., Draper, J., Culler, D., Yelick, K., Brooks, E., Warren., K.: Introduction to UPC and Language Specification. Technical report CCS-TR-99-157, IDA Center for Computing Sciences (1999)
3. Dinan, J., Balaji, P., Buntinas, D., Goodell, D., Gropp, W., Thakur, R.: An implementation and evaluation of the MPI 3.0 one-sided communication interface. In: Preprint ANL/MCS-P4014-0113. IEEE Computer Society (2013)
4. Fürlinger, K., et al.: DASH: data structures and algorithms with support for hierarchical locality. In: Lopes, L., et al. (eds.) Euro-Par 2014, Part II. LNCS, vol. 8806, pp. 542–552. Springer, Heidelberg (2014). http://dx.doi.org/10.1007/978-3-319-14313-2_46; http://dblp.uni-trier.de/rec/bib/conf/europar/Furlinger GGKTHIMMZ14
5. Hoefler, T., Dinan, J., Thakur, R., Barrett, B., Balaji, P., Gropp, W., Underwood, K.: Remote Memory Access Programming in MPI-3. Technical report, Argonne National Laboratory (2013)
6. MPI Forum: MPI: A Message-Passing Interface Standard. Version 2.2 (September 4th 2009), December 2009. http://www.mpi-forum.org
7. MPI Forum: MPI: A Message-Passing Interface Standard. Version 3.0 (September 21st 2012), September 2012. http://www.mpi-forum.org
8. Nieplocha, J., Carpenter, B.: ARMCI: A portable remote memory copy library for distributed array libraries and compiler run-time systems. Technical report (1999)
9. Nieplocha, J., Harrison, R.J., Littleeld, R.J.: Global arrays: a nonuniform memory access programming model for high-performance computers. J. Supercomputing 10, 169–189 (1996)
10. OSU Micro-Benchmarks (2014).http://mvapich.cse.ohio-state.edu/benchmarks/
11. Partitioned Global Address Space (2014). http://www.pgas.org/
12. Poole, S., Hernandez, O., Kuehn, J., Shipman, G., Curtis, A., Feind, K.: OpenSH-MEM - toward a unified RMA model. In: Padua, D. (ed.) Encyclopedia of Parallel Computing, pp. 1379–1391. Springer, US (2011)
13. Potluri, S., Sur, S., Bureddy, D., Panda, D.K.: Design and implementation of key proposed MPI-3 one-sided communication semantics on InfiniBand. In: Cotronis, Y., Danalis, A., Nikolopoulos, D.S., Dongarra, J. (eds.) EuroMPI 2011. LNCS, vol. 6960, pp. 321–324. Springer, Heidelberg (2011). http://dblp.uni-trier.de/db/conf/pvm/eurompi2011.html#PotluriSBP11; http://dx.doi.org/10.1007/978-3-642-24449-0_38; http://www.bibsonomy.org/bibtex/2b8d79bab12610e243ae48eceb 2905b91/dblp
14. RandomAccess GUPS (Giga Updates Per Second) (2013). http://icl.cs.utk.edu/projectsfiles/hpcc/RandomAccess/
15. Shamis, P., Venkata, M.G., Poole, S., Welch, A., Curtis, T.: Designing a high performance OpenSHMEM implementation using universal common communication substrate as a communication middleware. In: Poole, S., Hernandez, O., Shamis, P. (eds.) OpenSHMEM 2014. LNCS, vol. 8356, pp. 1–13. Springer, Heidelberg (2014)
16. Vaidyanathan, K., Chai, L., Huang, W., Panda, D.K.: Efficient asynchronous memory copy operations on multi-core systems and I/OAT. In: IEEE International Conference on Cluster Computing (2007)
17. Zhou, H., Mhedheb, Y., Idrees, K., Glass, C.W., Gracia, J., Fürlinger, K., Tao, J.: DART-MPI: an MPI-based implementation of a PGAS runtime system. In: PGAS 2014, 06–10 October 2014. http://dx.doi.org/10.1145/2676870.2676875

Multi- and Many-core Programming

A Practical Transactional Memory Interface

Shahar Timnat[1]([✉]), Maurice Herlihy[2], and Erez Petrank[1]

[1] Computer Science Department, Technion, Haifa, Israel
stimnat@cs.technion.ac.il
[2] Computer Science Department, Brown University,
Providence, USA

Abstract. Hardware transactional memory (HTM) is becoming widely available on modern platforms. However, software using HTM requires at least two carefully-coordinated code paths: one for transactions, and at least one for when transactions either fail, or are not supported at all. We present the MCMS interface that allows a simple design of fast concurrent data structures. MCMS-based code can execute fast when HTM support is provided, but it also executes well on platforms that do not support HTM, and it handles transaction failures as well. To demonstrate the advantage of such an abstraction, we designed MCMS-based linked-list and tree algorithms. The list algorithm outperforms all known lock-free linked-lists by a factor of up to X2.15. The tree algorithm builds on Ellen et al. [7] and outperforms it by a factor of up to X1.37. Both algorithms are considerably simpler than their lock-free counterparts.

1 Introduction

Transactional memory (TM) is becoming an increasingly central concept in parallel programming. Recently, Intel introduced the TSX extensions to the x86 architecture, which include RTM: an off-the-shelf hardware that supports hardware transactional memory. There are practical reasons for a developer to avoid using hardware transactional memory. First, HTM is only available for some of the computers in the market. Thus, a code that relies on HTM only suits a fraction of the available computers and must be accompanied with a different code base for the other platforms. Second, RTM transactions are "best effort" and are not guaranteed to succeed. Thus, to work with HTM, a *fall-back* path must also be provided and maintained, in case transactions repeatedly fail.

We propose a new programming discipline for highly-concurrent linearizable objects that takes advantage of HTM when it is available, and still performs reasonably (around X0.6) when it is not available. For this purpose, we suggest to encapsulate the HTM inside an intermediate level operation. The intermediate operation is compiled to an HTM implementation on platforms that support HTM, and to a non-transactional implementation otherwise. To a certain extent, our intermediate operation can even be implemented with an "out of the box" fall-back path for failing transactions. This fall-back path can be made lock-free, thus rendering our operation a valid alternative for designing lock-free operations.

© Springer-Verlag Berlin Heidelberg 2015
J.L. Träff et al. (Eds.): Euro-Par 2015, LNCS 9233, pp. 387–401, 2015.
DOI: 10.1007/978-3-662-48096-0_30

The intermediate operation we find best suited for this purpose is a slight variation of the well-known MCAS (Multi-word Compare And Swap) operation. The MCAS operation executes atomically on several shared memory addresses. Each address is associated with an *expected-value* and a *new-value*. An execution of MCAS succeeds and returns true iff the content of each specified address equals its expected value. In this case, the data in each address is replaced with the new value. If any of the specified addresses contains data that is different from the expected value, then false is returned and the content of the shared memory remains unchanged.

We propose an extended interface of MCAS called MCMS (Multiple Compare Multiple Swap), in which we also allow addresses to be compared without being swapped. The extension is functionally redundant, because, in effect, comparing an address without swapping it is identical to an MCAS in which this address' expected value equals its new value. However, when implementing the MCMS using transactional memory, it is ill-advised to write a new (identical) value to replace an old one. Such a replacement may cause unnecessary transaction aborts.

In order to study the usability of the MCMS operation, we designed two algorithms that use it. One for the linked-list data structure, and one for the binary search tree. The MCMS tree is almost a straightforward MCMS-based version of the lock-free binary search tree by Ellen et al. [7]. But interestingly, attempting to design a linked-list that exploits the MCMS operation yielded a new algorithm that is highly efficient. The main idea is to mark a deleted node in a different and useful manner. Instead of using a mark on the reference (like Harris [9]), or using a mark on the reference and additionally a backlink (like Fomitchev and Ruppert [8]), or using a separate mark field (like the lazy linked-list [11]), we mark a node deleted by setting its pointer to be a back-link, referencing the previous node in the list. This approach works excellently with transactions.[1]

We present three simple fall-back alternatives to enable progress in case RTM executions of MCMS repeatedly fail. The simplest way is to use locks, in a similar manner to *lock-elision* [14]. The second approach is to use CAS-based MCMS [10] as a fall-back. The third alternative is a copying scheme, where a new copy of the data structure is created upon demand to guarantee progress. Both the linked-list and tree algorithm outperform their lock-free alternatives when using either a lock-based fall-back path or a copying fall-back path. The list algorithm performs up to X2.15 faster than Harris's linked-list, and the tree algorithm performs up to X1.37 faster than the tree of Ellen et al. A fall-back path (that does not use transactions) is at times a bit faster (up to X1.1) and at times a bit slower than the lock-free alternatives, depending on the specific benchmark and configuration.

Another important advantage of programming with MCMS is that the resulting algorithms are considerably simpler to design and debug compared to

---

[1] This approach can also be used with locks. In fact, a lock-based version of this new algorithm outperforms all known linked-list implementations. However, the design of effective lock-based linked-lists is beyond the scope of this paper.

standard lock-free algorithms that build on the CAS operation. The stronger MCMS operation allows lock-free algorithms to be designed without requiring complicated "helping" mechanisms that facilitate lock-freedom.

2   Related Work

The search of means for simplifying the design of highly concurrent data structures, and in particular lock-free ones, has been long and it led to several important techniques and concepts. Transactional memory [12,16] is arguably the most general of these; a transaction can pack any arbitrary operation to be executed atomically. But the high efficacy comes with a cost. State of the art software implementations of transactional memory incur a high performance cost, while hardware support only spans across few platforms, and usually only provides "best-effort" progress guarantee (e.g., the widely available Haswell RTM).

MCAS [13] is another tool for simplifying the design of concurrent data structures. It may be viewed as a special case of a transaction. Several CAS-based software implementations of MCAS exist [10,17] with reasonable performance. A similar, yet more restrictive primitive is the recent LLX/SCX [3]. These primitives enable to atomically read several words, but write only a single word. Atomically with the single write, it also allows to *finalize* other words, which has the effect of blocking their value from ever changing again. A CAS-based software implementation of these primitives is more efficient than any available implementation of MCAS, and these primitives have been shown to be particularly useful for designing trees [4]. Yet, allowing only a single word to be written atomically can be too restrictive: our MCMS linked-list algorithm, which atomically modifies two different pointers, cannot be easily implemented this way.

Dragojevic and Harris explored another form of restricted transactions in [6]. They showed that by moving much of the "book keeping" responsibility to the user, and keeping transactions very small, almost all of the overhead of software transactional memory can be avoided. Using their restricted transactions is more complicated than using MCAS, and they did not explore hardware transactional memory.

Speculative lock elision [14] is a technique to replace a mutual exclusion lock with speculative execution (i.e., transaction). This way several threads may execute the critical section concurrently. If a read/write or a write/write collision occurs, the speculative execution is aborted and a lock is taken. [1] studies the interaction between transactions and locks and identifies several pitfalls. Locks that are well suited to work with transactions are proposed in [15]. Intel's TSX extension also includes support of Hardware Lock Elision (HLE). Our MCMS interface lends itself to lock-elision, and also has the potential to use other fallback paths, which could be lock-free.

3   The MCMS Operation

In this section we specify the MCMS interface, its semantics and implementation. The semantics of the MCMS interface are depicted in Fig. 1(left). The MCMS operation receives three parameters as input. The first parameter is an array of CAS descriptors to be executed atomically, where each CAS descriptor has an `address`, an `expected value`, and a `new value`. The second parameter, N, is the length of the array, and the last parameter C signifies the number of entries at the beginning of the array that should only be compared (but not swapped). We use a convention that the addresses that should only be compared and not swapped are placed at the beginning of the array. Their associated `new value` field is ignored.

3.1 Implementing MCMS with Hardware Transactional Memory

Intel Haswell Restricted Transactional Memory (RTM) introduces three new instructions: XBEGIN, XEND, XABORT. XBEGIN starts a transaction and receives a code location to which execution should branch in case of a transaction abort. XEND announces the end of a transaction, and XABORT forces an abort.

The implementation of MCMS, given in Fig. 1(right), is mostly straightforward. First, begin a transaction. Then check to see that all the addresses contain their expected value. If not, complete the transaction and return false. If all addresses hold the expected value, then write the new values, complete the transaction and return true. If the transaction aborts, restart from the beginning. However, before restarting, read all the addresses outside a transaction, and compare them to the expected value. If one of them has a value different than the expected value, return false.

This last phase of comparing after an abort is not mandatory, but has two advantages. The first is that in case the transaction failed because another thread wrote to one of the MCMS addresses, then it is possible for the MCMS to simply fail without requiring an additional transaction. The second advantage is that it handles a problem with page faults under RTM. A page fault causes a transaction to abort (without bringing the page). In such a case, simply retrying the transaction repeatedly can be futile, as the transaction will repeatedly fail without loading the page from the disk. Loading the addresses between transactions renders the possibility of repeated failures due to page faults virtually impossible.

3.2 Implementing MCMS Without TM Support

We also implemented the MCMS operation using the method of Harris et al. [10], including some optimizations suggested in that paper. As Harris's algorithm refers to MCAS, and not MCMS, we used identical expected value and new value for addresses that are only meant for comparison.

To execute an MCAS using Harris's algorithm, an object describing the MCAS operation is created. This descriptor holds an entry for each address that is to be CASed, and this entry holds the address, the expected value, and the desired new value. In addition, the MCAS descriptor holds a status field, which indicates one of three possible states: undecided, failed, and succeeded. After creating the descriptor, the target addresses are accessed one by one. For

The MCMS Semantics	HTM Implementation of the MCMS Operation
Atomically execute:	1: bool MCMS(CASDesc* descriptors, int N ,int C) {
1: bool MCMS (CASDesc* descriptors, int N, int C) {	2: while (true) {
2: for i in 1 to N: {	3: XBEGIN(retry); // an aborted transaction
3: if (*(descriptors[i].address) !=	// jumps to the retry label
descriptors[i].expected_val) {	4: for i in 1 to N: {
4: return false;	5: if(*(descriptors[i].address) !=
5: }	descriptors[i].expected_val) {
6: }	6: XEND();
7: for i in C+1 to N: {	7: return false; }}
8: *(descriptors[i].address) =	8: for i in C+1 to N: {
descriptors[i].new_val;	9: *(descriptors[i].address) =
9: }	descriptors[i].new_val; }
10: return true;	10: XEND();
11:}	11: return true;
	12: retry: // aborted transactions jump here
	13: for I in 1 to N: {
	14: if(*(descriptors[i].address) !=
	descriptors[i].expected_val) {
	15: return false; }}}}

Fig. 1. The MCMS semantics (left) and its HTM implementation (right)

each address, a CAS is used in an attempt to change the value from the expected value of the MCAS to a pointer that points to the MCAS descriptor. In fact, this is not done using a simple CAS, but a more evolved mechanism (named RDCSS in [10]) which also checks that the status field of the MCAS descriptor is still undecided. The implementation of RDCSS itself relies only on simple CAS operations, and is also described in [10].

If while executing the MCAS, an address that does not hold the expected value is found, then the status field is changed to failed, and any target address whose value was already changed from the expected value to a pointer to the MCAS descriptor is changed back to the old value using a simple CAS. If, on the other hand, all the addresses were successfully changed from the expected value to a pointer to the MCMS descriptor, then the status field is changed to succeeded, and all the target addresses are changed again, this time to hold the desired new value, using a simple CAS. The full details of [10] are considerably more complicated, and are not described here.

This MCAS algorithm burdens concurrent read executions. When a thread reads an address that is a part of an ongoing MCAS execution, it will see the pointer to the MCAS descriptor instead of the correct value (which is either the expected value or the new value) that should logically be stored in the address. Thus, every read execution must check that the read value is not a pointer to an MCAS descriptor, and if it is, it must first participate in completing the MCAS execution, and only afterwards return the (correct) value.

Our non-TM MCMS implementation is thus burdened with this complication. When the MCMS algorithm reads from an address that might be the target of an MCAS, it must be able to tell whether that memory holds regular data, or a special pointer to an MCAS descriptor. In our applications, we were able to steal the two least significant bits from target fields. For the list algorithm, each target field holds a pointer to another node, and regular pointer values have zero in those two bits. For the tree algorithm, each target field holds either a pointer or a binary flag, and we shift the flag value to the left by two bits.

4   The Linked-List Algorithm

We consider a sorted-list-based set of integers, similar to [8,9,18], supporting the INSERT, DELETE, and CONTAINS operations. Without locks, the main challenge when designing a linked-list is to prevent a node's next pointer from changing concurrently with (or after) the node's deletion. A node is typically deleted by changing its predecessor to point to its successor. This can be done by an atomic CAS, but such a CAS cannot by itself prevent an update to the deleted node's next pointer. For details, see [9].

Harris [9] solved this problem by partitioning the deletion of a node into two phases. In the first phase, the node's next pointer is *marked*, by setting a reserved bit on this pointer. This locks this pointer from ever changing again, but still allows it to be used to traverse the list. In the second phase, the node is physically removed by setting its predecessor to point to its successor. Harris uses the pointer least significant bit as the *mark bit*. This bit is typically unused, because the next pointer points to an aligned address.

Harris's mark bit is an elegant solution to the deletion problem, but Harris's algorithm still has some drawbacks. First, when a mark bit is used, traversing the list requires an additional masking operation to be done whenever reading a pointer. This operation poses an overhead on list traversals. Second, a thread that fails a CAS (due to contention) often restarts the list traversal from the list head. Fomitchev and Ruppert [8] suggested a remedy for the second drawback by introducing back-links into the linked-list. The back-link is an additional field in each node and it is written during the node's deletion.

Fomitchev and Ruppert used three additional fields in each node in excess of the obligatory key and next pointer fields. Those fields are: the mark bit (similar to Harris), another *flag bit* (also adjoined to the next pointer), and a back-link pointer. To delete a node, a thread first flags its predecessor, then marks the node to be deleted, then writes the back-link from the node to the predecessor, and finally physically removes the node (the same CAS that removes the node also clears the flag of the predecessor.) Due to the overhead of additional CASes, this list typically performs slower in practice compared to the list of Harris.

To illustrate the simplicity of the MCMS operation we present a new linked-list algorithm. The MCMS list is simpler, faster (if HTM is available), and does not use any additional fields on top of the key and next pointer fields. Similarly to Fomitchev and Ruppert, the MCMS list never needs to start searching from the head on a contention failure.

The crux of our algorithm is that it uses the atomic MCMS to atomically modify the node's next pointer to be a back-link simultaneously with deleting it from the list (see Fig. 2(b)). Thus the next pointer points to the next node while the node is in the list, and acts as a back-link once the node is deleted. Similar to [8,9,18] and others, we use a sentinel head node with a key of minus infinity, and a tail node with a key of infinity.

The algorithm is given in Fig. 2(a)(left), and is surprisingly simple. The SEARCH method receives three parameters, a key to search for, and pointers to pointers to the left and right nodes. When the search returns, the pointer fields serves as outputs. The left node is set to the last node with a key smaller than the given search key. The right node is set to the first node with a key equal to or greater than the search key. The left node parameter also serves as in input for the method, and indicates where to start the search from.

An invariant of the algorithm is that if a node A (which was already inserted to the list) points to node B, and B's key is greater than A's key, then both nodes are currently in the list. When node B is deleted, modifying its next pointer to point to A serves two purposes. First, it serves the purpose of the mark bit that ensures any concurrent operation that might try to modify B's next pointer will fail, which is vital to the correctness of the algorithm. Yet, without necessitating a masking operation before using the next pointer. Second, it establishes a back-link, which other threads might use to avoid the necessity of redoing the search from scratch. Yet, this back-link does not necessitate additional fields in the object, nor specific checks before following this back-link.

5 The Binary Search Tree Algorithm

We base our tree algorithm on the binary search tree of Ellen et al. [7] (this tree was shown in [5] to outperform both the lock-free skiplist Java implementation and the lock-based AVL tree of Bronson et al. [2]). Our tree is also a leaf oriented tree, meaning all the keys are stored in the leaves of the tree, and each internal node has exactly two children. However, in their original algorithm, each internal node stores a pointer to a designated *Info* object that stores all the information required to complete an operation. When a thread initiates an operation, it first searches the tree for appropriate location to apply it. Then it tests the internal node Info pointer to see whether there is already an ongoing operation, and helps such an operation if needed. Then it allocates an Info object describing the desired change, and attempts to atomically make the appropriate internal node points to this info object using a CAS. Then, it can proceed with the operation, being aware that it might get help from other threads in the process.

MCMS allows all changes to take place simultaneously. This saves the algorithm designer the need to maintain an Info object, and also boosts performance in the common case, in which an HTM successfully commits. Similarly to a list, a central challenge in a lock-free binary search tree is to ensure that pointers of an internal node will not be modified while (or after) the node is deleted (see [7] for details). For this purpose, in the MCMS tree algorithm, each internal node contains a mark bit (in addition to its key, and pointers to two children). The mark bit is in a separate field, not associated with any pointer. Leaf nodes contain only a key. Upon deleting an internal node, its mark bit is set.

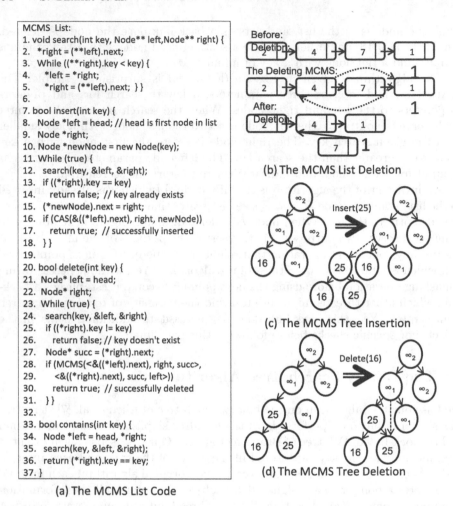

```
MCMS List:
1. void search(int key, Node** left,Node** right) {
2.   *right = (**left).next;
3.   While ((**right).key < key) {
4.     *left = *right;
5.     *right = (**left).next; } }
6.
7. bool insert(int key) {
8.   Node *left = head; // head is first node in list
9.   Node *right;
10.  Node *newNode = new Node(key);
11.  While (true) {
12.    search(key, &left, &right);
13.    if ((*right).key == key)
14.      return false; // key already exists
15.    (*newNode).next = right;
16.    if (CAS(&((*left).next), right, newNode))
17.      return true; // successfully inserted
18.  }}
19.
20. bool delete(int key) {
21.   Node* left = head;
22.   Node* right;
23.   While (true) {
24.     search(key, &left, &right)
25.     if ((*right).key != key)
26.       return false; // key doesn't exist
27.     Node* succ = (*right).next;
28.     if (MCMS(<&((*left).next), right, succ>,
29.       <&((*right).next), succ, left>))
30.       return true; // successfully deleted
31.   }}
32.
33. bool contains(int key) {
34.   Node *left = head, *right;
35.   search(key, &left, &right);
36.   return (*right).key == key;
37. }
```

(a) The MCMS List Code

(b) The MCMS List Deletion

(c) The MCMS Tree Insertion

(d) The MCMS Tree Deletion

Fig. 2. The list and tree algorithms

Each MCMS operation that changes pointers of a node also reads the mark bit and compares it to zero. If the bit is set, the MCMS will return false without changing the shared memory, guaranteeing that a deleted node's pointers are never mistakenly altered.

In order to avoid corner cases, we initialize the tree with two infinity keys, ∞_1 and ∞_2, such that $\infty_2 > \infty_1 >$ any other value. The root always has the value ∞_2 its right child is always ∞_2 and its left child is always ∞_1. This idea is borrowed from the original algorithm [7]. Both the INSERT and DELETE operations begin by calling the search method. The search method traverses the tree looking for the desired key, and returns a leaf (which will holds the desired key if the desired key is in the tree), its parent, and its grandparent.

To insert a key, replace the leaf returned by the search method with a subtree containing an internal node with two leaf children, one with the new desired key, and one with the key of the leaf being replaced (See Fig. 2(c)). An MCMS operation atomically executes this exchange while guaranteeing the parent is unmarked (hence, not deleted).

To delete a key, the grandparent pointer to the parent is replaced by a pointer to the deleted node's brother (See Fig. 2(d)), atomically with setting the parent mark bit on, marking it as deleted, and guarding against concurrent (or later) changes to its child pointers. An MCMS instruction also ensures that the grandparent is unmarked, and that the parent's child pointers retain their expected value during the deletion.

6   Fall-Back Execution for Failed Transactions

Formally, transactions are never guaranteed to commit successfully, and spurious failures may occur infinitely without any concrete reason. Our experimental results show that such repeated failures are not observed in practice. Nevertheless, we implemented several fall-back avenues that general algorithms using MCMS may benefit from, and we briefly overview them here. Each transaction is attempted several times before switching to a fall-back execution path. The number of retries is a parameter that can be tuned, denoted $MAX\_FAILURES$.

6.1   Using Locking for the Fall-Back Path

The idea of trying to execute a code snippet using a transaction, and take a lock if the transaction fails to commit, is known as *lock elision*. We add a single integer field, denoted *lock* to the data structure. In the HTM implementation of MCMS, before calling XEND the *lock* field is read, and compared to zero. If the lock is not zero, XABORT is called. This way, if any thread acquires the lock (by CASing it to one) all concurrent transactions will fail. If an MCMS operation fails to commit a transaction MAX_FAILURES times, the thread tries to obtain the *lock* by repeatedly trying to CAS it from 0 to 1 until successful. The MCMS is then executed safely. When complete, the thread sets the *lock* back to 0.

Our implementation of lock-elision is slightly different than that of traditional lock-elision. As described in Sect. 3.1, after each transaction abort we compare each address to its expected value, and thus in many cases we can return false after a failure without using any locking or transactions at all.

6.2   Non-Transactional MCMS Implementation as a Fall-Back Path

Another natural fall-back path alternative is to use the non-transactional MCMS implementation of Harris et al., described in Sect. 3.2. While this implementation was proposed for implementing the MCMS on a platform that does not support HTM, it may also be used as a fall-back when hardware transactions repeatedly fail. Several threads can execute this implementation of the MCMS operation concurrently. However, as mentioned in Sect. 3.2, during the execution of the MCMS operations, the target addresses temporarily store a pointer to a special operation descriptors instead of their "real" data. This requires a careful test for any read of the data structure, which unfortunately comes with a significant overhead.

We experimented with several different mechanisms to guarantee that each read of the data structure is safe. The first mechanism is to always execute the same read procedure that is applied when MCMS is implemented without TM, as described in [10]. The second alternative is to use transactions for the reads as well. Instead of doing a simple read, we can put the read in a transaction, and before executing the transaction XEND, read a lock field and abort if it does not equal zero. Each thread that executes a non-transactional MCMS increments the lock before starting it, and decrements the lock once the MCMS is completed. The reads can be packed into a transaction in different granularity. One may place each read in a different transaction and add a read of the lock field; but one may also pack all the reads up to an MCMS into a single transaction and add a single read of the lock. We tried a few granularities and found out that packing five reads into a transaction was experimentally optimal.

6.3 A Copying-Based Fall-Back Path

A third avenue for implementing a fall-back for failing transactions is copying-based. Again, a lock field is added. Additionally, a single global pointer which points to the data structure is added. When accessing the data structure an indirection is added: the external pointer is read, and the operation is applied to the data structure pointed by it. As usual, each HTM based MCMS operation compares the lock to zero before committing, and aborts if the lock is not zero.

Unlike previous solutions, in the copying fall-back implementation the lock is permanent, and the *current copy* of the data structure becomes immutable. After setting the lock to one, the thread creates a complete copy of the data structure, and applies the desired operation on that copy. Other threads that observes the lock is set act similarly. The new copy is associated with a new lock that is initiated to zero. Then, a CAS attempts an atomic change of the global pointer to point to the newly created copy instead of the original copy of the data structure (from which it copied the data). Afterwards, execution will continue as usual on the new copy, until the next time a thread will fail to commit a transaction MAX_FAILURES times.

7 Performance

In this section we present the performance of the different algorithms and variants discussed in this paper. In Figs. 3 and 4 we present the throughput of the list and tree algorithms compared against their lock-free counterparts. Each line in each chart represent a different variant of an algorithm. In the micro-benchmarks tested each thread executes either 50 % INSERT and 50 % DELETE operations, or 20 % INSERT, 10 % DELETE, and 70 % CONTAINS operations. The operation keys are integers that are chosen randomly and uniformly in a range of either 1–32, 1–1024, or 1–1048576. Before starting each test, a data structure is pre-filled to 50 % occupancy with randomly chosen keys from the appropriate range. Deleted nodes were not reclaimed. In addition to the reported results we also tested a work-load of a 100 % CONTAINS, and a work-load of 25 % INSERT, 25 % DELETE and 50 % CONTAINS We also tested a key range of 1–65536. The additional results are similar and are omitted from the figures for lack of space.

In all our experiments, we set the number of MAX_FAILURES to be 7. With this setting, we see MCMS operations that need to complete execution in the fallback path. Reducing this parameter to 6 causes a (slight) performance degradation in a few scenarios. We also tested the number of total MCMS transaction aborts, and the number of MCMS operations that were completed in the fall-back path, when valid. Higher MAX_FAILURES values yield similar performance, but with almost no executions in the fall-back path. This makes the measurements less informative, so 7 was chosen.

The measurements were taken on an Intel Haswell i7-4770, with 4 dual cores (overall 8 hardware threads) and 6 MB cache size, running Linux Suse. Haswell processors with more cores that support HTM are currently unavailable. The algorithms were written in C++ and compiled with GNU C++ compiler version 4.5.

In each chart we present nine algorithms. One for the original lock-free algorithm, which is either Harris's linked-list, or the binary search tree of Ellen et al. A line denoted *HTM MCMS* for the HTM based algorithm without any fall-back path. A line denoted *Software MCMS* for the algorithm in which MCMS is implemented without transactional memory, as described in Sect. 3.2. A line denoted *Locking* for the algorithm in which MCMS is implemented using HTM, and a locking fall-back path is used (Sect. 6.1). A line denoted *Software Read* for an HTM based implementation with a non-transactional based MCMS fall-back path (Sect. 6.2), where each read is executed as in Sect. 3.2. Three lines denoted *1-Read*, *5-Read*, *all-Read*, for HTM based implementations with a non-transactional based MCMS fall-back path (Sect. 6.2), where reads are executed inside transactions in different granularity. And a line denoted *Copying*, for an HTM based implementation with a copying based fall-back path (Sect. 6.3).

The fastest performing algorithm is always the HTM-based MCMS without any fall-back path. On a range of 1048576 available keys, this list algorithm outperforms Harris's by 30–60 %; on a range of 1024 available keys, it outperforms by 40–115 %, and on a range of 32 keys, it outperforms by 20–55 %. The tree algorithm outperforms the tree of Ellen et al. by 6–37 %. For both data structures the lock-based fall-back path adds very little overhead, and the corresponding algorithms trail behind the algorithms without the fall-back path by 1–5 %.

The copying fall-back path algorithm also performs excellently for the linked-list. On average, it performs the same as the lock-based algorithm, with a difference smaller than half a per cent. This makes the HTM MCMS algorithm with the copying fall-back path the fastest lock-free linked-list by a wide margin.

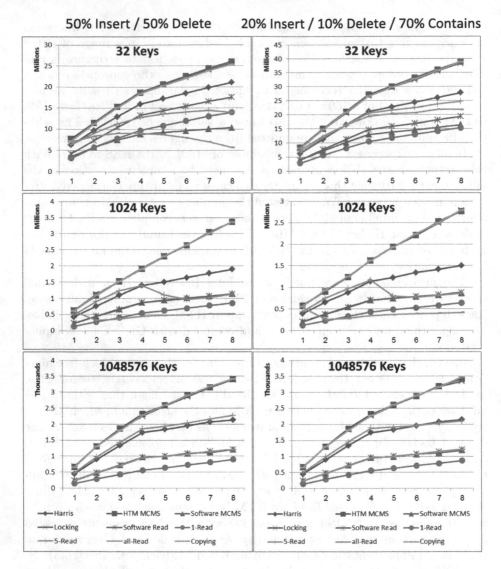

Fig. 3. MCMS-based lists vs. Harris's linked-list. The x-axis represents the number of threads. The y-axis represents the total number of operations executed per second (in millions for key ranges 32 and 1024, in thousands for key range 1048576.)

The copying tree algorithm is not as good, trailing behind the pure HTM algorithm by about 10 %. Yet this algorithm still beats the lock-free algorithm of Ellen et al. in all number of threads for all benchmarks, excluding, surprisingly, the benchmark of 100 % contains for 32 and 1024 available keys. This is surprising, because in this benchmark MCMS is not executed at all. We suspect that the reason is the fact that the search method of the copying based tree receives

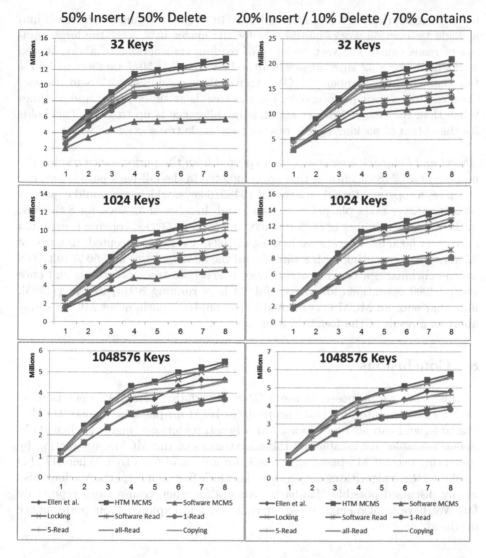

Fig. 4. MCMS-based trees vs. the BST of Ellen et al. The x-axis represents the number of threads. The y-axis represents millions of operations executed per second.

the root of the tree as an input parameter. In the pure HTM algorithm, the root is known at compile time to be final (never changed once it is allocated), which could allow the compiler to optimize its reading.

Using a CAS-based MCMS fall-back path does not work as well as the copying or the lock-based fall-back alternatives. For the list, packing five reads into a transaction yields reasonable performance, usually beating Harris's linked list for a lower number of threads and a larger range of keys (up 20 % faster), but trailing up to 40 % behind it for 8 threads in 32 or 1024 keys when the micro-benchmark is 50 % INSERTS and 50 % DELETES. Packing all the reads into a single transaction works quite badly for the longer lists, were the large number of reads causes the vast majority of reading transactions to abort. It also works badly for a 32 keys range when the benchmark is 50 % INSERTS and 50 % DELETE. The high number of MCMS transactions combined with read transactions results in poor performance. For the tree, is at times better and at times worse than the tree of Ellen et al., and the difference is up to 10 %. This holds for the option of packing all the reads into a single transaction as well.

Aborts and Fall-back Executions. As expected from the performance results, the number of MCMS executions that are completed in the fall-back path is low. For instance, a copying of a list or a tree of 1048576 keys, which one would expect to be costly, never takes place. On the other end, In a list of 32 keys, for 8 threads, in the micro-benchmark of 50 % INSERTS and 50 % DELETES, copying is executed once every 5000 list operations. In a list of 1024, it is never executed. In a tree of 32 keys when executing with 8 threads, on the 50 % INSERTS and 50 % DELETES micro-benchmark, a copying occurs once every 1730 tree operations, and once every 54000 operations for a tree of 1024 keys running 8 threads. In general, note that once an MCMS is executed in the fall-back path, other MCMS's may abort as a result of the *lock* field being set.

8   Conclusions

In this paper we proposed to use MCMS, a variation of MCAS operation, as an intermediate interface that encapsulates HTM on platforms where HTM is available, and can also be executed in a non-transactional manner when HTM is not available. We established the effectiveness of the MCMS abstraction by presenting two MCMS-based algorithms, for a list and for a tree. When HTM is available, these algorithms outperform their lock-free counterparts. We have also briefly discussed possible "fall-back" avenues for when transactions repeatedly fail. We have implemented these alternatives, and explored their performance overhead.

References

1. Bobba, J., Moore, K.E., Volos, H., Yen, L., Hill, M.D., Swift, M.M., Wood, D.A.: Performance pathologies in hardware transactional memory. In: 34th International Symposium on Computer Architecture (ISCA 2007), 9–13 June 2007, San Diego, California, USA, pp. 81–91 (2007)
2. Bronson, N.G., Casper, J., Chafi, H., Olukotun, K.: A practical concurrent binary search tree. In: PPOPP, pp. 257–268 (2010)
3. Brown, T., Ellen, F., Ruppert, E.: Pragmatic primitives for non-blocking data structures. In: PODC, pp. 13–22 (2013)
4. Brown, T., Ellen, F., Ruppert, E.: A general technique for non-blocking trees. In: PPOPP, pp. 329–342 (2014)

5. Brown, T., Helga, J.: Non-blocking k-ary search trees. In: Fernàndez Anta, A., Lipari, G., Roy, M. (eds.) OPODIS 2011. LNCS, vol. 7109, pp. 207–221. Springer, Heidelberg (2011)

6. Dragojevic, A., Harris, T.L.: STM in the small: trading generality for performance in software transactional memory. In: European Conference on Computer Systems, Proceedings of the Seventh EuroSys Conference 2012, EuroSys 2012, Bern, Switzerland, 10–13 April 2012, pp. 1–14 (2012)

7. Ellen, F., Fatourou, P., Ruppert, E., van Breugel, F.: Non-blocking binary search trees. In: Proceedings of the 29th Annual ACM Symposium on Principles of Distributed Computing, PODC 2010, Zurich, Switzerland, 25–28 July 2010, pp. 131–140 (2010)

8. Fomitchev, M., Ruppert, E.: Lock-free linked lists and skip lists. In: PODC 2004, pp. 50–59 (2004)

9. Harris, T.L.: A pragmatic implementation of non-blocking linked-lists. In: Welch, J.L. (ed.) DISC 2001. LNCS, vol. 2180, pp. 300–314. Springer, Heidelberg (2001)

10. Harris, T.L., Fraser, K., Pratt, I.A.: A practical multi-word compare-and-swap operation. In: Malkhi, D. (ed.) DISC 2002. LNCS, vol. 2508, pp. 265–279. Springer, Heidelberg (2002)

11. Heller, S., Herlihy, M., Luchangco, V., Moir, M., Scherer III, W.N., Shavit, N.: A lazy concurrent list-based set algorithm. In: Anderson, J.H., Prencipe, G., Wattenhofer, R. (eds.) OPODIS 2005. LNCS, vol. 3974, pp. 3–16. Springer, Heidelberg (2006)

12. Herlihy, M., Moss, J.E.B.: Transactional memory: architectural support for lock-free data structures. In: ISCA, pp. 289–300 (1993)

13. Israeli, A., Rappoport, L.: Disjoint-access-parallel implementations of strong shared memory primitives. In: PODC, pp. 151–160 (1994)

14. Rajwar, R., Goodman, J.R.: Speculative lock elision: enabling highly concurrent multithreaded execution. In: MICRO, pp. 294–305 (2001)

15. Rossbach, C.J., Hofmann, O.S., Porter, D.E., Ramadan, H.E., Aditya, B., Witchel, E.: TxLinux: using and managing hardware transactional memory in an operating system. In: Proceedings of the 21st ACM Symposium on Operating Systems Principles 2007, SOSP 2007, Stevenson, Washington, USA, 14–17 October 2007, pp. 87–102 (2007)

16. Shavit, N., Touitou, D.: Software transactional memory. Distrib. Comput. 10(2), 99–116 (1997)

17. Sundell, H.: Wait-free multi-word compare-and-swap using greedy helping and grabbing. Int. J. Parallel Prog. 39(6), 694–716 (2011)

18. Valois, J.D.: Implementing lock-free queues. In: Proceedings of 7th International Conference on Parallel and Distributed Computing Systems, pp. 64–69 (1994)

A Multicore Parallelization of Continuous Skyline Queries on Data Streams

Tiziano De Matteis, Salvatore Di Girolamo, and Gabriele Mencagli(✉)

Department of Computer Science, University of Pisa,
Largo B. Pontecorvo 3, 56127 Pisa, Italy
{dematteis,digirolamo,mencagli}@di.unipi.it

Abstract. Skyline queries are preference queries frequently used in multi-criteria decision making to retrieve interesting points from large datasets. They return the points whose attribute vector is not dominated by any other point. Over the last years, sequential and parallel implementations over static datasets have been proposed for multiprocessors and clusters. Recently, skyline queries have been computed over continuous data streams according to *sliding window* models. Although sequential algorithms have been proposed and analyzed in the past, few works targeting modern parallel architectures exist. This paper contributes to the literature by proposing a parallel implementation for window-based skylines targeting multicores. We describe our parallelization by focusing on the cooperation between parallel functionalities, optimizations of the reduce phase, and load-balancing strategies. Finally, we show experiments with different point distributions, arrival rates and window lengths.

Keywords: Continuous queries · Skyline queries · Sliding window · Parallel programming · Multicores

1 Introduction

Skyline queries are a particular class of preference queries that compute the set of Pareto-optimal points from a given set. They have become commonplace in real-time applications working on input data on-the-fly, such as network monitoring, sensor networks, stock market trading and social media. Usually, data are available in the form of *continuous streams* [1], i.e. sequences, possibly of unlimited length, of points (tuples) received from heterogeneous sources.

Most of the existing research works have focused on centralized [2] or parallel solutions [3,4] for traditional skyline queries over static datasets. Computing the skyline over data streams is more challenging [5]. Due to the unbounded stream length, the query is evaluated on substreams (*windows*) corresponding to equal-sized time intervals. Tuples enter the window at their arrival and expire after a fixed time interval called *window length* (denoted by T_w). In the literature a *lazy* algorithm and an *eager* variant [5] have been proposed to maintain window-based skylines with different features in terms of space and time efficiency.

© Springer-Verlag Berlin Heidelberg 2015
J.L. Träff et al. (Eds.): Euro-Par 2015, LNCS 9233, pp. 402–413, 2015.
DOI: 10.1007/978-3-662-48096-0_31

Parallel implementations of continuous skyline queries raise critical issues: *(i)* how to partition the window among a set of parallel Workers, and *(ii)* how to keep the partitions evenly sized in response to new point arrivals, pruning activities, and the expiration of old points. Existing works have only partially studied these problems. In [6] the authors have described an approach in which the computational load is moved from a centralized server to a set of data sites that interact with the server to notify changes in their local skyline. In [7] the authors have presented a parallel approach in the domain of uncertain streams, in which the associativity of the skyline operator does not hold. Both the approaches do not take into account any pruning phase of obsolete points, which is crucial to reduce memory occupancy at the expense of a harder load balancing.

In this paper we propose a parallelization of continuous skyline queries on multicores. We describe our parallelization as a *MAP* pattern with an asynchronous *reduce*. We study optimizations related to the reduce phase, and we show the effect of different load-balancing strategies. Then, we study the performance of our parallelization with different point distributions, arrival rates and window lengths. The results show good performance which proves the efficiency of our implementation and the effectiveness of our load-balancing strategy.

This paper is organized as follows. Section 2 describes related works. Section 3 introduces some prerequisites and a description of the parallelized sequential algorithm. Section 4 shows our parallelization which will be evaluated on a multicore architecture in Sect. 5. Finally, Sect. 6 concludes this paper.

2   Related Work

Skyline queries have been originally designed for static datasets by focusing on index structures to cope with high dimensional data (B-Trees, R-Trees, R*-Trees) [2]. Existing parallel solutions [3] share the idea of partitioning the datasets into regions processed in parallel and finally merging the results thanks to the associativity of the skyline operator.

On data streams a first work [8] has addressed n-of-N skyline queries, i.e. the skyline is computed over a count-based window of the last n received tuples (N is an upper bound to the window size). Time-based windows have been firstly used for continuous skyline queries in [9], with the algorithm *LookOut*. This solution does not perform any pruning strategy yielding to high memory occupancy. More recently in the work [5] the authors have proposed the *lazy* and the *eager* sequential algorithms for computing the skyline over streams with a time-based sliding-window semantics. The former method delays most of the computational work until the expiration of a skyline point. The latter, instead, performs a pre-computation phase at each new point arrival in order to minimize memory consumption at the expense of a higher processing burden.

Most of the previous approaches are centralized. Works proposing parallel solutions are [6,10]. In the first one a centralized server collaborates with intelligent data sites that notify the server of the changes affecting the global skyline. The role of data sites is to avoid sending useless data by reducing the bandwidth usage. A similar idea has been applied in [10] for continuous skylines over wireless sensor networks. Part of the logic is moved to the sensors that filter input data saving network bandwidth and energy. Parallel skyline queries over uncertain data streams (with imprecise stream elements) have been discussed in [7] by proposing a parallel implementation for multicores. This solution is highly dependent from the case of uncertain streams, with parallel servers maintaining skyline probabilities without performing pruning actions. This solution is different from our work, which focuses on time-based sliding-window skylines over certain data streams with the pruning of obsolete points.

3   Continuous Skyline Queries: Eager Algorithm

The goal of the skyline operator is to determine the points received in the last T_w time units that belong to the skyline set. Each point x is represented as a tuple of $d \geq 1$ attributes $x = \{x_1, x_2, \ldots, x_d\}$. Given two points x and y, we say that x *dominates* y (denoted by $x \prec y$) if and only if $\forall i \in [1, d]$ $x_i \leq y_i$ and $\exists j \mid x_j < y_j$. The skyline of a given set S is the subset of all the points not dominated by any other point in S. The output of the skyline operator is a stream of *skyline updates* expressed in the format (action, p, t), where *action* indicates whether point p enters (ADD) or exits (DEL) the skyline at the specified time t. The continuous skyline operator is characterized by three properties:

- *Point Maintenance*: if a new point x is not a skyline point at its arrival time, it cannot be discarded immediately because it could become a skyline point when all its dominators expire;
- *Point Expiration*: a skyline point x will be definitely removed from the system when it reaches its expiration time;
- *Pruning*: once a point x arrives, the older points dominated by it (*obsolete*) can be discarded since they will not be able to enter the skyline in the future.

The received points that cannot be pruned (*non-obsolete points*) must be stored in a data structure denoted by $\mathcal{DB}$. This data structure implements an abstract data type with the following operations: the *insertion* of a new point, the *removal* of an existing point, and the *search* of the critical dominator of a given point p (see Def. 1). Several implementations can be used. Common solutions are arrays and index structures for spatial searching such as R-trees and R*-trees [2,5].

     In this paper we study a parallelization of the *eager* algorithm [5]. This algorithm performs the pruning of obsolete points: only the points currently in the skyline and those points candidate to enter the skyline in the future are stored in $\mathcal{DB}$. This property comes at the expense of a larger computational effort w.r.t similar algorithms [6,7,10] such as the *lazy* variant which does not perform pruning. The eager algorithm is based on the following concept:

Definition 1. *The Skyline Influence Time of a point p (*SIT$_p$*) is the expiring time of the youngest point $r \in S$ dominating p (r is the critical dominator of p).*

The algorithm maintains an *event list* $\mathcal{EL}$. Two types of events are supported: *(i) skytime(p,t)* indicates that point p will enter the skyline at time t, *(ii) expire(p,t)* indicates the exit of point p from the skyline at time t. The rationale of the eager algorithm is to perform most of the work during the reception of a new point in order to update the event list correspondently. Then, the events are processed chronologically by emitting the changes in the skyline set through ADD and DEL updates transmitted onto the output stream of the computation.

At the reception of a new point p the algorithm executes the following steps:

1. *Pruning Phase*: all the points in $\mathcal{DB}$ dominated by p must be removed and their associated events cleared from $\mathcal{EL}$. If a removed point was part of the skyline, a DEL update is emitted onto the output stream;
2. *Insertion Phase*: the new point p is added to $\mathcal{DB}$;
3. *Search Phase*: the critical dominator r of p in $\mathcal{DB}$ must be found. If it exists, we add the event *skytime(p, t_r^{exp})* into $\mathcal{EL}$ where t_r^{exp} is the expiring time of r, i.e. $\mathtt{SIT}_p = t_r^{exp}$. Otherwise, if r does not exist, p becomes a skyline point immediately and we add the event *expire(p, t_p^{exp})* into the event list.

The algorithm processes the events by using an internal timer. When an event is triggered, there are two possibilities:

– in the case of a *skytime(p,t)* event the point p is added to the skyline and an ADD update is emitted. A new event *expire(p,t_p^{exp})* is added to $\mathcal{EL}$;
– in the case of an *expire* event the associated point (which is part of the skyline) is discarded from $\mathcal{DB}$ and its removal from the skyline is notified through a DEL update.

This behavior allows us to define an important property:

Lemma 1. *If a point p reaches its expiration time t_p^{exp} at that time the point is part of the skyline.*

Proof. By contradiction let suppose that a point r, which dominates p, exists and its expiration time is after the one of p. Since expiration times are defined as $t_r^{exp} = t_r^{arr} + T_w$ and $t_p^{exp} = t_p^{arr} + T_w$, this means that r has been received by the system after p ($t_r^{arr} > t_p^{arr}$). This is impossible because, in that case, being r younger than p and dominating it, p would have been pruned when r arrived. $\square$

Therefore, for each non-obsolete point p in $\mathcal{DB}$ there are two possible situations. If a new point r dominating p is received before the timer reaches $\mathtt{SIT}_p$, p is pruned and its skytime event cleared from $\mathcal{EL}$. Otherwise, when the internal timer reaches $\mathtt{SIT}_p$ the corresponding *skytime* event is executed, p enters the skyline and an ADD update is emitted. When point p reaches its expiration time, for Lemma 1 it is part of the skyline. The point is deleted and a DEL update is emitted. The expiration time of p matches the skyline influence time of the points critically dominated by it, that are exactly the ones that have to be inserted into the skyline as a consequence of p's expiration.

4   Parallelization Design

Our parallelization is based on the *data-parallel* paradigm. It is a composition of a *MAP* pattern with an asynchronous *reduce* phase. The data structures $\mathcal{DB}$ and $\mathcal{EL}$ are partitioned among a set of *Workers* interfaced with the input stream and the output stream through an *Emitter* and a *Collector* functionality.

The implementation targets shared-memory architectures such as modern multi/manycores. Emitter, Collector and Workers are implemented by standard POSIX threads. Threads cooperate by exchanging pointers to shared data structures through push and pop operations on shared queues. In our implementation we use the lock-free queues provided by the FastFlow library [11], which exhibit great performance on cache-coherent multi-core chips.

4.1   Implementation

In the following we describe in detail the functionalities of our implementation and their cooperation pattern. The parallelization is sketched in Fig. 1.

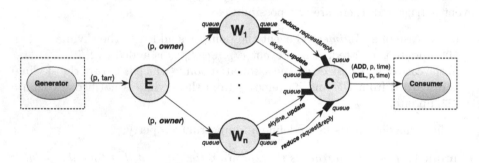

Fig. 1. Scheme of the parallel implementation: *Emitter* (E), *Worker* (W) and *Collector* (C) threads interacting through push and pop operations on FastFlow queues.

Emitter: the role of the Emitter is to interface the input stream (implemented by a TCP/IP socket) with the parallel computation. For each received point p the Emitter performs the following sequence of actions:

1. it assigns a timestamp t_p^{arr} according to the current system time;
2. it assigns the ownership of p to a specific Worker W_k, which will store p in its $\mathcal{DB}_k$ until the internal time reaches p's expiration time $t_p^{exp} = t_p^{arr} + T_w$;
3. p is multicasted to *all* the Workers. The Emitter performs a push operation on every input queue of the Workers. The message is the pair (p, k), where p is the tuple data structure and k is the index of the owner.

The role of the Emitter is critical for *load balancing*, i.e. to keep the size of the partitions of $\mathcal{DB}$ as similar as possible. To do that, the Emitter should implement clever *owner selection policies*. This aspect will be discussed in Sect. 4.2.

Workers: each Worker receives from the Emitter a stream of pairs (p, k). Any Worker W_i performs the following actions:

1. the pruning from its local partition $\mathcal{DB}_i$ all the points dominated by p; the private event list $\mathcal{EL}_i$ is cleared from the events related to the pruned points;
2. if a pruned point was in the skyline, a DEL update is generated;
3. W_i calculates the local SIT_p^i corresponding to the expiration time of the younger dominator of p in $\mathcal{DB}_i$. If p has no dominator in $\mathcal{DB}_i$ then SIT_p^i is zero. W_i sends the value of SIT_p^i to the Collector for the *reduce* phase;

After these actions all the Workers except the owner discard p, thus the owner has a very limited additional overhead. The reduce phase is necessary to determine the global value of $\mathtt{SIT}_p$, which is the maximum between the local $\mathtt{SIT}_p^i$ for all the partitions, i.e. $\mathtt{SIT}_p = \max_{i=1}^n\{\mathtt{SIT}_p^i\}$. Because of its fine-grained nature, the reduce is centralized in the Collector: C receives the values of $\mathtt{SIT}_p^i$ from the Workers, calculates the global $\mathtt{SIT}_p$ and sends it to the owner W_k that:

4. if $\mathtt{SIT}_p = 0$ p must be added to the skyline immediately: an $expire(p, t_p^{exp})$ event is added to $\mathcal{EL}_k$ and an ADD update is transmitted to the Collector. Otherwise, a $skytime(p, \mathtt{SIT}_p)$ event is added to $\mathcal{EL}_k$.

Workers are responsible for processing events in the correct order by producing skyline updates to the Collector. Each Worker has an internal notion of time that moves forward at each reception of a new point from the Emitter, i.e. when a point p is received, the current time is set equal to t_p^{arr}. Before starting the computation related to the received point, each Worker executes (unrolls) all the events in its $\mathcal{EL}_i$ with timestamp smaller than t_p^{arr}. ADD and DEL updates are transmitted to the Collector when *skytime* and *expire* events arise.

Collector: this thread receives two types of messages from the Workers:

- *reduce messages* with the local $\mathtt{SIT}_p^i$ of a point p from Worker W_i. Once all the $\mathtt{SIT}_p^i$ for $i = 1, \ldots, n$ have been received, the Collector computes $\max_{i=1}^n\{\mathtt{SIT}_p^i\}$ and sends this value *only* to the owner of point p;
- *skyline updates* need to be buffered by the Collector in order to transmit them onto the output stream by respecting the chronological order. To do that, the Collector buffers the updates and keeps them ordered by timestamp using a priority queue. The Collector maintains the timestamp of the last received update from each Worker (denoted by $lst\text{-}t_i$). All the buffered updates with timestamp smaller or equal than $\min_{i=1}^n\{lst\text{-}t_i\}$ can be safely transmitted onto the output stream of the computation.

4.2   Optimizations

In this section we discuss two optimizations: *(i)* we design an *asynchronous reduce* for the computation of the global SIT of each new point; *(ii)* we study proper *owner selection policies* to balance the workload among Workers.

Asynchronous Reduce: the value of the SIT of the last received point is the result of a reduce involving the Workers and the Collector threads. In the basic implementation the reduce is executed *synchronously*. The owner of the current point p cannot start the computation on the next point r until the reduce result is made available by the Collector.

According to the semantics of the eager algorithm the reduce can be performed *asynchronously*. Let the owner of the current point p be the Worker W_k. Instead of waiting the value SIT_p explicitly from the Collector, W_k can process subsequent points received from the Emitter while SIT_p is not available yet. For each successive point r the Worker W_k:

- searches the youngest dominator of r in its $\mathcal{DB}_k$: this operation uses the expire time of the stored points and their spatial coordinates, thus it is independent from SIT_p;
- all the points $v \in \mathcal{DB}_k$ such that $r \prec v$ can be pruned. If p is one of the pruned points, the value of SIT_p is no longer necessary.

In conclusion the asynchronous reduce works as follows:

1. when a new point is received by a Worker, whether it is the owner or not it participates in the reduce phase without waiting for the result;
2. each Worker waits for messages either from the Emitter (a new point) or from the Collector (reduce result);
3. when the reduce result is received from the Collector: *(i)* if the point has been pruned the SIT is ignored; *(ii)* otherwise, a new event (*skytime* or *expire*) is inserted into the event list of the owner according to the value of SIT (if it is equal or greater to zero, see Sect. 3).

This optimization leads to a significant improvement in the performance achieved by our implementation, as it will be shown in Sect. 5.

Owner Selection Policies: the ownership must be assigned in order to keep the partitions $\mathcal{DB}_1, \ldots, \mathcal{DB}_n$ evenly sized. This problem is particularly critical in continuous skyline queries, since the cardinality of the partitions can change significantly due to the variability of the arrival rate and the effect of the pruning.

In the literature a similar problem has been studied for skyline queries over static datasets. Local skylines are computed for each partition and then merged to define the global skyline. The partitions are usually determined using the spatial coordinates of points as in the *grid-based* and *angle-based* schemes proposed in [4]. In our case such approaches are not sufficiently effective: *(i)* in the case of points not uniformly distributed the partitions can have very different cardinalities; *(ii)* many skyline points can fall in few partitions, thus in our parallelization some Workers might provide a very marginal contribution to the skyline definition. In this paper we apply owner selection policies independent from the spatial coordinates of points. We consider four heuristics:

- *Round Robin* (RR): the ownership is interleaved among Workers, i.e. point x_j is assigned to Worker W_i such that $i = (j \mod n) + 1$;

- *On Demand* (OD): the ownership of a new point is assigned to the first Worker able to accommodate it in its input queue;
- *Least Loaded Worker* (LLW): each new point is assigned to the Worker with the smaller partition of $\mathcal{DB}$;
- *Least Loaded Worker* with *Ownership* (LLW+): this policy is an extension of LLW in which, in addition to the size of the partitions, the Emitter takes into account for each Worker the number of enqueued points for which it has been designated as the owner.

For the last two policies the Emitter must know the size of the partitions and the number of enqueued points owned by each Worker. We use shared counters between the Emitter/Workers threads, implemented as std :: atomic < int > of the standard C++ library with atomic increment/decrement operations.

Figure 2 shows a comparison on an Intel multicore composed of two Xeon Sandy Bridge E5-2650 CPUs for a total of 16 cores operating at 2 GHz with 32 GB or RAM. Each core has private L1d (32 KB) and L2 (256 KB) caches. Each CPU has a shared L3 cache of 20 MB. We use a configuration with 4.5 K non-obsolete points distributed in 12 partitions (one per Worker). We measure the difference between the biggest and the smallest partition, i.e. $\Delta = |\mathcal{DB}^{max}| - |\mathcal{DB}^{min}|$. We use five double precision floating-point numbers per point $(d = 5)$. Higher dimensionalities have minor effects on the results.

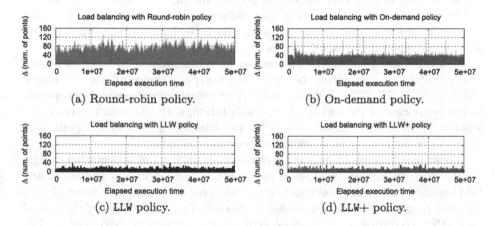

(a) Round-robin policy.   (b) On-demand policy.

(c) LLW policy.   (d) LLW+ policy.

Fig. 2. Load balancing results: independent distribution. Average window size of 4.4 K points. The same qualitative behavior is observed for the other point distributions.

The results show that the last two policies are able to produce partitions with very similar cardinalities over the execution. This is an expected result because the first two policies are independent from the actual load of the Workers. The best policy is LLW+. Numerically we have the following values $(\Delta^{avg} + \sigma^2)$: RR:64.02 + 229, OD:34.13 + 1791, LLW:3.15 + 4.28, LLW+:2.55 + 4.05. As we can observe: *(i)* load-aware policies are able to obtain smaller Δ^{avg} with a significantly lower variance; *(ii)* by taking into account the number of owned enqueued points, the LLW+ policy is able to achieve a 20 % improvement than LLW.

5   Experiments

In this section we study the performance of our parallelization on the Intel multicore. We use the gcc compiler version 4.8.1 with the $-$O3 optimization flag. We set the affinity of each thread on a different core. The maximum number of Workers is 12 in our machine, since we have four threads for the Generator, Emitter, Collector and Consumer. Mapping two threads onto the same core (hyperthreading) is not beneficial due to the aggressive busy-waiting synchronization performed by pop and push operations on the FastFlow queues [11].

Data Distribution and Memory Usage: the effect of the pruning depends on the spatial distribution of data. Analogously to existing works [5], we consider three point distributions: the *anticorrelated, correlated* and *independent* ones as shown in Fig. 3a for 2D points. In the correlated case a small set of points dominate the others and the pruning phase is very intensive. The anticorrelated case in on the opposite, with a large number of points that are part of the skyline set. The third one is an intermediate case with points uniformly distributed in the space. Fig. 3b shows the number of points maintained in $\mathcal{DB}$ with respect to the total number of points received per sliding window (denoted by $|\mathcal{W}|$). This number is given by the product between the arrival rate of the input stream and the window length, i.e. $|\mathcal{W}| = \lambda \times T_w$. The number of non-obsolete points is at least three orders of magnitude smaller than the number of received points. The pruning phase increases the processing time per tuple (all the dominated points must be identified and removed) but it greatly saves memory occupancy. In the worst case of the anticorrelated distribution, with 9M points received per window we need to maintain only $\sim$ 9K non-obsolete points in $\mathcal{DB}$ (with four doubles per point we need $\sim$ 280KB instead of $\sim$ 275MB).

These results have an important implication on the implementation design. Only a little portion of the received points needs to be stored by the algorithm. Furthermore, since our parallelization is a data-parallel solution, the set of non-obsolete points is partitioned among n Workers further decreasing the size of each $\mathcal{DB}_i$. According to [5,7], many existing applications of continuous skyline queries (e.g. analysis of social media such as Twitter, Facebook and so on) are executed with window lengths of few tens of seconds and arrival rates of several thousands of points/sec, leading to a total number of points per sliding window in the order of few millions of tuples. With these sizes, the $\{\mathcal{DB}_i\}_{i=1}^n$ data structures are implemented by *dynamic arrays* (usually one per dimension, to increase data locality in the cache hierarchy of multicores) without relying on additional index structures (e.g. R-tree and R*-trees) that are beneficial with larger datasets.

Effect of Asynchronous Reduce: we measure the benefit of the asynchronous reduce on throughput. Throughput is the average number of points processed

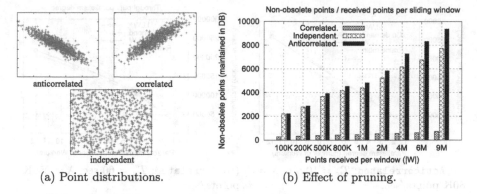

(a) Point distributions.   (b) Effect of pruning.

Fig. 3. Space distribution of points (anticorrelated, correlated and independent) and effect of the pruning on the number of stored points.

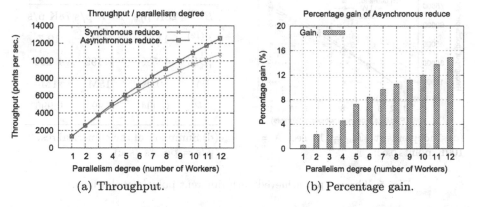

(a) Throughput.   (b) Percentage gain.

Fig. 4. Comparison between synchronous and asynchronous reduce. Scenario: $\lambda = 100\,K$ points/sec, $T_w = 20\,\text{s}$, independent distribution and LLW+ owner selection policy.

per second. With different configurations in terms of arrival rate and window length, we achieve an average gain between $(10 \div 20)\,\%$. Figure 4 shows a scenario with an arrival rate of $100\,K$ points/sec generated according to the independent distribution with a window length $T_w = 20\,\text{s}$. The average gain is of $\sim 10\,\%$ with a peak of $\sim 15\,\%$ with 12 Workers. As we can observe from Fig. 4b, the gain increases with the parallelism degree. The reason is that even the LLW+ policy is not able to produce perfectly equal partitions. With high parallelism degrees the partitions of $\mathcal{DB}$ are smaller and a slight difference in their cardinality has a negative effect (higher in percentage) on throughput. The asynchronous reduce is able to mitigate this slight load unbalance among Workers, by achieving better throughput compared with the synchronous reduce implementation.

Throughput and Scalability: we show the throughput and the best scalability achieved by our parallelization. For each distribution we use a different scenario in terms of arrival rate and window length. The results are shown in Fig. 5. For

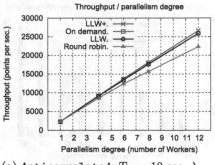

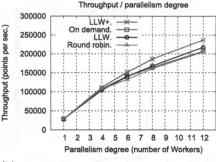

(a) **Anticorrelated:** $T_w = 10$ sec, $\lambda = 80K$ points/sec.

(b) **Correlated:** $T_w = 60$ sec, $\lambda = 250K$ points/sec.

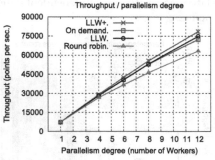

	Anticorr.	Corr.	Indep.
$\mathcal{B}^{(12)}$	28K p/s	237K p/s	78K p/s
$\mathcal{S}^{(12)}$	11.65	8.16	10.7
$\vert\mathcal{DB}\vert$	4,598	1,192	4,226
$\vert\mathcal{W}\vert$	800K	15M	1M
$\mathcal{P}$	0.994	0.999	0.996

(c) **Independent:** $T_w = 10$ sec, $\lambda = 100K$ points/sec.

(d) Summary of the numerical results (p/s = points /sec).

Fig. 5. Throughput achieved with different point distributions.

all the scenarios the maximum number of cores (12) is not sufficient to achieve the maximum throughput (equal to the arrival rate of the stream), hence we are able to study how the throughput increases up to the maximum number of physical cores of our machine. Figure 5d shows: the best throughput achieved with the highest parallelism degree ($\mathcal{B}^{(12)}$), the best scalability ($\mathcal{S}^{(12)}$) measured as the ratio between the throughput with 12 Workers and the one with just one single Worker thread, the number of non-obsolete points ($\vert\mathcal{DB}\vert$), the total number of points received per sliding window ($\vert\mathcal{W}\vert$), and the pruning probability $\mathcal{P}$. The best throughput and scalability results are reported only for the LLW+ policy. With the correlated distribution we achieve the lowest scalability. Although this scenario is characterized by the highest value of the arrival rate and window length, the number of non-obsolete points is small due to a very high pruning probability. In this case the computation is very fine grained and a slight difference in the cardinalities of the partitions (also of few units) prevents to achieve a near-optimal scalability also with the LLW+ policy and the asynchronous reduce. Near optimal results are achieved with the other two distributions.

6 Conclusions

This paper presented a *map-reduce* parallelization of the skyline operator on data streams, optimized with an asynchronous reduce phase and smart load balancing strategies. The experiments confirmed that the LLW+ policy is the best one, and near-optimal scalability can be achieved with the anticorrelated and independent distributions. The correlated case is the most challenging due to the very fine-grained nature of the computation, and deserves to be further investigated in the future with possible run-time mechanisms enabling dynamic adaptiveness to sustain highly variable input rates [12].

References

1. Babcock, B., Babu, S., Datar, M., Motwani, R., Widom, J.: Models and issues in data stream systems. In: Proceedings of the Twenty-First ACM SIGMOD-SIGACT-SIGART Symposium on Principles of Database Systems, PODS 2002, pp. 1–16. ACM, New York (2002)
2. Börzsönyi, S., Kossmann, D., Stocker, K.: The skyline operator. In: Proceedings of the 17th International Conference on Data Engineering, pp. 421–430. IEEE Computer Society, Washington, DC, USA (2001)
3. Im, H., Park, J., Park, S.: Parallel skyline computation on multicore architectures. Inf. Syst. **36**, 808–823 (2011)
4. Vlachou, A., Doulkeridis, C., Kotidis, Y.: Angle-based space partitioning for efficient parallel skyline computation. In: Proceedings of the 2008 ACM SIGMOD International Conference on Management of Data, SIGMOD 2008, pp. 227–238. ACM, New York (2008)
5. Tao, Y., Papadias, D.: Maintaining sliding window skylines on data streams. IEEE Trans. Knowl. Data Eng. **18**, 377–391 (2006)
6. Lu, H., Zhou, Y., Haustad, J.: Efficient and scalable continuous skyline monitoring in two-tier streaming settings. Inf. Syst. **38**, 68–81 (2013)
7. Li, X., Wang, Y., Li, X., Wang, Y.: Parallelizing skyline queries over uncertain data streams with sliding window partitioning and grid index. Knowl. Inf. Syst. **41**, 277–309 (2014)
8. Lin, X., Yuan, Y., Wang, W., Lu, H.: Stabbing the sky: efficient skyline computation over sliding windows. In: Proceedings of the 21st International Conference on Data Engineering, ICDE 2005, pp. 502–513 (2005)
9. Morse, M., Patel, J., Grosky, W.I.: Efficient continuous skyline computation. In: Proceedings of the 22nd International Conference on Data Engineering, ICDE 2006, pp. 108–108 (2006)
10. Xin, J., Wang, G., Chen, L., Zhang, X., Wang, Z.: Continuously maintaining sliding window skylines in a sensor network. In: Kotagiri, R., Radha Krishna, P., Mohania, M., Nantajeewarawat, E. (eds.) DASFAA 2007. LNCS, vol. 4443, pp. 509–521. Springer, Heidelberg (2007)
11. Aldinucci, M., Danelutto, M., Kilpatrick, P., Meneghin, M., Torquati, M.: An efficient unbounded lock-free queue for multi-core systems. In: Kaklamanis, C., Papatheodorou, T., Spirakis, P.G. (eds.) Euro-Par 2012. LNCS, vol. 7484, pp. 662–673. Springer, Heidelberg (2012)
12. Mencagli, G., Vanneschi, M.: Qos-control of structured parallel computations: a predictive control approach. In: 2013 IEEE 5th International Conference on Cloud Computing Technology and Science, pp. 296–303 (2011)

A Fast and Scalable Graph Coloring Algorithm for Multi-core and Many-core Architectures

Georgios Rokos[1]([✉]), Gerard Gorman[2], and Paul H.J. Kelly[1]

[1] Software Performance Optimisation Group, Department of Computing,
Imperial College London, South Kensington Campus, London SW7 2AZ, UK
{georgios.rokos09,p.kelly}@imperial.ac.uk
[2] Applied Modelling and Computation Group,
Department of Earth Science and Engineering, Imperial College London,
South Kensington Campus, London SW7 2AZ, UK
g.gorman@imperial.ac.uk

Abstract. Irregular computations on unstructured data are an important class of problems for parallel programming. Graph coloring is often an important preprocessing step, e.g. as a way to perform dependency analysis for safe parallel execution. The total run time of a coloring algorithm adds to the overall parallel overhead of the application whereas the number of colors used determines the amount of exposed parallelism. A fast and scalable coloring algorithm using as few colors as possible is vital for the overall parallel performance and scalability of many irregular applications that depend upon runtime dependency analysis.

Çatalyürek et al. have proposed a graph coloring algorithm which relies on speculative, local assignment of colors. In this paper we present an improved version which runs even more optimistically with less thread synchronization and reduced number of conflicts compared to Çatalyürek et al.'s algorithm. We show that the new technique scales better on multi-core and many-core systems and performs up to 1.5x faster than its predecessor on graphs with high-degree vertices, while keeping the number of colors at the same near-optimal levels.

Keywords: Graph coloring · Greedy coloring · First-fit coloring · Irregular data · Parallel graph algorithms · Shared-memory parallelism · Optimistic execution · Many-core architectures · Intel®Xeon Phi™

1 Introduction

Many modern applications are built around algorithms which operate on irregular data structures, usually in form of graphs. Graph coloring is an important preprocessing step, mainly as a means of guaranteeing safe parallel execution in a shared-memory environment but also in order to enforce neighborhood heuristics, *e.g.* avoid having adjacent graph edges collapse in sequence in graph coarsening [6]. Examples of such applications include iterative methods for sparse linear systems [14], sparse tiling [19,20], eigenvalue computation [16], preconditioners [12,18] and mesh adaptivity [7,10].

© Springer-Verlag Berlin Heidelberg 2015
J.L. Träff et al. (Eds.): Euro-Par 2015, LNCS 9233, pp. 414–425, 2015.
DOI: 10.1007/978-3-662-48096-0_32

Taking advantage of modern multi-core and many-core hardware requires not only algorithmic modifications to deal with data races but also consideration of scalability issues. The exposed parallelism of an irregular algorithm is directly dependent on the number of colors used. The lower this number, the more work-items are available for concurrent processing per color/independent set. Additionally, there is usually some thread synchronization or reduction before proceeding to the next independent set. A poor-quality coloring will only exaggerate the effects of thread synchronization on the parallel scalability of an application. Following this observation, it is obvious that a good coloring algorithm should be fast and scalable itself, so as to minimize its own contribution to the total execution time of the application, and use as few colors as possible.

The simplest graph coloring algorithm is the greedy one, commonly known as *First-Fit* (Sect. 2.1). There exist parallel versions for distributed-memory environments, but in this paper we focus on the intra-node, shared-memory case. Probably, the best known parallel algorithm is the one by Jones and Plassmann [13], which in turn is an improved version of the original *Maximal Independent Set* algorithm by Luby [15]. There also exists a modified version of Jones-Plassmann which uses multiple hashes to minimize thread synchronization [3]. A parallel greedy coloring algorithm based on speculative execution was introduced by Gebremedhin and Manne [9]. Çatalyürek *et al.* presented an improved version of the original speculative algorithm in [1] (Sect. 2.2). We took the latter one step further, devising a method which runs under an even more speculative scheme with less thread synchronization (Sect. 3), without compromising coloring quality.

It must be pointed out that First-Fit variants which use ordering heuristics were not considered here. Despite recent innovations by Hasenplaugh *et al.* [11], those variants take considerably longer to run than the plain greedy algorithm and in many cases do not achieve a sufficiently large improvement in the number of colors to justify their cost. Runtime of coloring for the purpose of dynamic dependency analysis becomes a serious consideration in problems like morph algorithms [17], which mutate graph topology in non-trivial ways and constantly invalidate existing colorings. In those cases, the graph has to be recolored in every iteration of the morph kernel, so coloring becomes a recurring cost rather than a one-off preprocessing step. As shown in [11], heuristic-based algorithms, although achieving some reduction in the number of colors, take 4x-11x longer to run and this would dominate the kernel's runtime. A notable example is the edge-swap kernel from our mesh adaptivity framework PRAgMaTIc[1] [10], in which coloring (using our fast method) already takes up 10 % of the total execution time.

The rest of this paper is organized as follows: In Sect. 2 we present the serial greedy coloring algorithm and its parellel implementation by Çatalyürek *et al.* We explain how the latter can be improved further, leading to our implementation which is described in Sect. 3 and evaluated against its predecessor in Sect. 4. Finally, we briefly explain why the class of optimistic coloring algorithms is unsuitable for SIMT-style parallel processing systems in Sect. 5 and conclude the paper in Sect. 6.

---

[1] https://github.com/meshadaptation/pragmatic.

2   Background

In this section we describe the greedy coloring algorithm and its parallel version proposed by Çatalyürek *et al.*

2.1   First-Fit Coloring

Coloring a graph with the minimal number of colors has been shown to be an NP-hard problem [8]. However, there exist heuristic algorithms which color a graph in polynomial time using relatively few colors, albeit not guaranteeing an optimal coloring. One of the most common polynomial coloring algorithms is *First-Fit*, also known as *greedy coloring*. In its sequential form, First-Fit visits every vertex and assigns the smallest color available, *i.e.* not already assigned to one of the vertex's neighbors. The procedure is summarized in Algorithm 1.

Algorithm 1. Sequential greedy coloring algorithm.

Input: $\mathcal{G}(V, E)$
for all vertices $V_i \in V$ **do**
    $\mathcal{C} \leftarrow \{$colors of all colored vertices $V_j \in adj(V_i)\}$
    $c(V_i) \leftarrow \{$smallest color $\notin \mathcal{C}\}$

It is easy to give an upper bound on the number of colors used by the greedy algorithm. Let us assume that the highest-degree vertex V_h in a graph has degree d, *i.e.* this vertex has d neighbors. In the worst case, each neighbor has been assigned a unique color; then one of the colors $\{1, 2, \ldots, d+1\}$ will be available to V_h (*i.e.* not already assigned to a neighbor). Therefore, the greedy algorithm can color a graph with at most $d + 1$ colors. In fact, experiments have shown that First-Fit can produce near-optimal colorings for many classes of graphs [4].

2.2   Optimistic Coloring

Gebremedhin and Manne introduced an optimistic approach to parallelizing the greedy graph coloring algorithm [9]. They described a fast and scalable version for shared-memory systems based on the principles of speculative (or optimistic) execution. The idea is that we can color all vertices in parallel using First-Fit without caring about race conditions at first (stage 1); this can lead to defective coloring, *i.e.* two adjacent vertices might get the same color. Defects can then be spotted in parallel (stage 2) and fixed by a single thread (stage 3).

Picking up where Gebremedhin and Manne left off, Çatalyürek *et al.* improved the original algorithm by removing the sequential conflict-resolution stage and applying the first two parallel stages iteratively. This work was presented in [1]. Each of the two phases, called *tentative coloring* phase and *conflict detection* phase respectively, is executed in parallel over a relevant set of vertices.

Like the original algorithm by Gebremedhin and Manne, the tentative coloring phase produces a pseudo-coloring of the graph, whereas in the conflict detection phase threads identify defectively colored vertices and append them into a list $\mathcal{L}$. Instead of resolving conflicts in $\mathcal{L}$ serially, $\mathcal{L}$ now forms the new set of vertices over which the next execution of the tentative coloring phase will iterate. This process is repeated until no conflicts are encountered.

Algorithm 2. The parallel graph coloring algorithm by Çatalyürek *et al.*

Input: $\mathcal{G}(V, E)$
$\mathcal{U} \leftarrow V$
while $\mathcal{U} \neq \emptyset$ **do**
    #pragma omp parallel for   ▷ Phase 1 - Tentative coloring (in parallel)
    for all vertices $V_i \in \mathcal{U}$ **do**   ▷ execute First-Fit
        $\mathcal{C} \leftarrow \{$colors of all colored vertices $V_j \in adj(V_i)\}$
        $c(V_i) \leftarrow \{$smallest color $\notin \mathcal{C}\}$
    #pragma omp barrier
    $\mathcal{L} \leftarrow \emptyset$ ▷ global list of defectively colored vertices
    #pragma omp parallel for   ▷ Phase 2 - Conflict detection (in parallel)
    for all vertices $V_i \in \mathcal{U}$ **do**
        if $\exists V_j \in adj(V_i), V_j > V_i : c(V_j) == c(V_i)$ **then**
            $\mathcal{L} \leftarrow \mathcal{L} \cup V_i$ ▷ mark V_i as defectively colored
    #pragma omp barrier
    $\mathcal{U} \leftarrow \mathcal{L}$ ▷ Vertices to be re-colored in the next round

---

Algorithm 2 summarizes this coloring method. As can be seen, there is no sequential part in the whole process. Additionally, speed does not come at the expense of coloring quality. The authors have demonstrated that this algorithm produces colorings using about the same number of colors as the serial greedy algorithm. However, there is still a source of sequentiality, namely the two thread synchronization points in every iteration of the while-loop. Synchronization can easily become a scalability barrier for high numbers of threads and should be minimized or eliminated if possible.

3   Implementation

Moving toward the direction of removing as much thread synchronization as possible, we improved the algorithm by Çatalyürek *et al.* by eliminating one of the two barriers inside the while-loop. This was achieved by merging the two parallel for-loops into a single parallel for-loop. We observed that when a vertex is found to be defective it can be re-colored immediately instead of deferring its re-coloring for the next round. Therefore, the tentative-coloring and conflict-detection phases can be combined into a single *detect-and-recolor* phase in which we inspect all vertices which were re-colored in the previous iteration of the while-loop. Doing so leaves only one thread synchronization point per round, as can be seen in Algorithm 3. This barrier guarantees that any changes committed by a thread are made visible system-wide before proceeding to the next round.

Algorithm 3. The improved parallel graph coloring technique.

Input: $\mathcal{G}(V, E)$
#pragma omp parallel for   ▷ perform tentative coloring on $\mathcal{G}$; round 0
for all vertices $V_i \in V$ **do**
 $\mathcal{C} \leftarrow \{\text{colors of all colored vertices } V_j \in adj(V_i)\}$
 $c(V_i) \leftarrow \{\text{smallest color} \notin \mathcal{C}\}$
#pragma omp barrier
$\mathcal{U}^0 \leftarrow V$ ▷ mark all vertices for inspection
$i \leftarrow 1$ ▷ round counter
while $\mathcal{U}^{i-1} \neq \emptyset$ **do**   ▷ ∃ vertices (re-)colored in the last round
 $\mathcal{L} \leftarrow \emptyset$ ▷ global list of defectively colored vertices
 #pragma omp parallel for
 for all vertices $V_i \in \mathcal{U}^{i-1}$ **do**
  if $\exists V_j \in adj(V_i), V_j > V_i : c(V_j) == c(V_i)$ **then** ▷ if they are (still) defective
   $\mathcal{C} \leftarrow \{\text{colors of all colored } V_j \in adj(V_i)\}$ ▷ re-color them
   $c(V_i) \leftarrow \{\text{smallest color} \notin \mathcal{C}\}$
   $\mathcal{L} \leftarrow \mathcal{L} \cup V_i$ ▷ V_i was re-colored in this round
 #pragma omp barrier
 $\mathcal{U}_i \leftarrow \mathcal{L}$ ▷ Vertices to be inspected in the next round
 $i \leftarrow i + 1$ ▷ proceed to the next round

---

4 Experimental Results

In order to evaluate our improved coloring method, henceforth referred to as *Reduced Synchronization Optimistic Coloring* (RSOC), and compare it to the previous state-of-the-art technique by Çatalyürek *et al.*, we ran a series of benchmarks using 2D and 3D meshes of triangular and tetrahedral elements respectively (commonly used in finite element and finite volume methods), alongside randomly generated graphs using the *R-MAT* graph generation algorithm [2]. Simplicial 2D/3D meshes are used in order to measure performance and scalability for our target application area [10], whereas RMAT graphs were used for consistency with the experimental methodology used in Çatalyürek *et al.*'s publication; the authors state that those RMAT graphs "are designed to represent instances posing varying levels of difficulty for the performance of multithreaded coloring algorithms" [1].

For the 2D case we have used a 2D anisotropic mesh (adapted to the requirements of some CFD problem) named `mesh2d`, which consists of $\approx 250k$ vertices. We also evaluate performance using two 3D meshes, taken from the University of Florida Sparse Matrix Collection [5]. `bmw3`$_2$ is a mesh modelling a BMW Series 3 car consisting of $\approx 227k$ vertices, whereas `pwtk` represents a pressurized wind tunnel and consists of $\approx 218k$ vertices. Finally, we generated three $16M$-vertex, $128M$-edge RMAT graphs, namely `RMAT-ER` (Erdős-Rényi), `RMAT-G` (Good) and `RMAT-B` (Bad), randomly shuffling vertex indices so as to reduce the benefits of data locality and large caches. For more information on those graphs the reader is referred to the original publication by Çatalyürek *et al.* [1].

The experiments were run on two systems: a dual-socket Intel®Xeon® E5-2650 system (Sandy Bridge, 2.00 GHz, 8 physical cores per socket, 2-way hyper-threading) running Red Hat®Enterprise Linux® Server release 6.4 (Santiago) and an Intel®Xeon Phi™ 5110P board (1.053 GHz, 60 physical cores, 4-way hyper-threading). Both versions of the code (intel64 and mic) were compiled with Intel®Composer XE 2013 SP1 and with the compiler flags -O3 -xAVX. The benchmarks were run using Intel®'s thread-core affinity support.

Table 1 shows the average execution time over 10 runs of both algorithms on the 2 systems, Intel®Xeon® and Intel®Xeon Phi™, using the 3 finite element/volume meshes and the 3 RMAT graphs. Rows preceded by "C" correspond to the algorithm by Çatalyürek et al., rows preceded by "R" pertain to the improved version. Timings for the meshes are given in milliseconds whereas for the RMAT graphs they are in seconds. As can be seen, RSOC performs faster than Çatalyürek et al. for every test graph on both platforms, while scaling better as the number of threads increases, especially on Intel®Xeon Phi™.

Table 1. Execution time of both algorithms on 2 different platforms, Intel®Xeon® and Intel®Xeon Phi™, with varying number of OpenMP threads and using the 3 finite element/volume meshes and the 3 RMAT graphs. Rows preceded by "C" correspond to the algorithm by Çatalyürek et al., rows preceded by "R" pertain to the improved version. Timings for the meshes are given in milliseconds whereas for the graphs they are in seconds.

		Intel®Xeon®						Intel®Xeon Phi™								
		Number of OpenMP threads						Number of OpenMP threads								
		1	2	4	8	16	32	1	2	4	8	15	30	60	120	240
mesh2d	C:	62.7	34.0	19.2	10.2	5.92	4.28	496	252	127	64.9	35.5	19.0	11.7	12.7	73.6
	R:	62.2	31.3	17.7	9.42	5.50	4.05	495	249	125	63.3	34.5	17.9	10.7	10.5	69.4
bmw3_2	C:	58.1	33.5	14.4	7.84	4.73	3.61	468	235	118	60.0	33.1	18.0	11.5	12.7	74.2
	R:	57.8	29.4	12.1	6.48	3.91	3.30	466	234	117	59.2	32.4	17.1	9.88	11.0	54.9
pwtk	C:	40.1	24.0	14.5	8.07	4.96	3.65	465	233	117	59.6	33.2	18.2	11.1	12.9	74.4
	R:	39.8	20.0	11.3	6.08	3.81	3.30	464	232	117	58.9	32.4	17.2	10.6	11.0	59.9
RMAT-ER	C:	6.11	3.21	1.82	1.09	0.79	0.85	196	97.8	48.9	24.6	13.0	6.41	3.16	1.64	0.94
	R:	6.09	3.20	1.81	1.08	0.78	0.85	196	98.0	49.0	24.7	13.1	6.43	3.16	1.64	0.95
RMAT-G	C:	6.10	3.18	1.82	1.08	0.77	0.81	195	97.1	48.6	24.3	12.9	6.34	3.12	1.62	0.93
	R:	6.07	3.17	1.81	1.07	0.77	0.81	195	97.3	48.7	24.4	13.0	6.38	3.13	1.63	0.93
RMAT-B	C:	5.47	2.86	1.62	0.93	0.65	0.64	189	94.1	46.7	23.5	12.3	6.08	3.12	1.90	1.49
	R:	5.46	2.83	1.60	0.92	0.64	0.63	189	94.0	46.9	23.5	12.4	6.02	2.95	1.60	1.00

Figures 1 and 2 show the relative speedup of RSOC over Çatalyürek et al. for all test graphs on Intel®Xeon® and Intel®Xeon Phi™, respectively, i.e. how much faster our implementation is than its predecessor for a given number of threads. With the exception of RMAT-ER and RMAT-G on which there is no difference in performance, the gap between the two algorithms widens as the number of threads increases, reaching a maximum value of 50 % on Intel®Xeon Phi™ for RMAT-B.

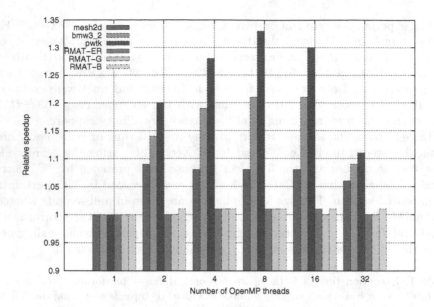

Fig. 1. Speedup of RSOC relative to Çatalyürek *et al.* as the number of threads increases on Intel®Xeon® E5-2650.

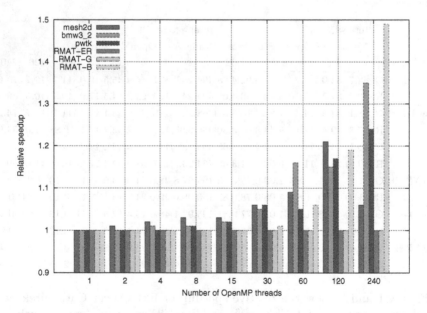

Fig. 2. Speedup of RSOC relative to Çatalyürek *et al.* as the number of threads increases on Intel®Xeon Phi™ 5110P.

Looking at the total number of coloring conflicts encountered throughout the execution of both algorithms as well as the number of iterations each algorithm needs in order to resolve them, we can identify an additional source of speedup for our algorithm (apart from the absence of one barrier). We will use the Intel®Xeon Phi™ system for this study, as it is the platform on which the most interesting results have been observed. Figures 3 and 4 depict the total number of conflicts for the three meshes and the RMAT graphs, respectively. When using few threads both algorithms produce about the same number of conflicts. However, moving to higher levels of parallelism reveals that RSOC results in much fewer defects in coloring for certain classes of graphs.

This observation can be explained as follows: In Çatalyürek *et al.* all threads synchronize before entering the conflict-resolution phase, which means that they enter that phase and start resolving conflicts at the very same time. Therefore, it is highly possible that two adjacent vertices with conflicting colors will be processed by two threads simultaneously, which leads once again to new defects. In our improved algorithm, on the other hand, a conflict is resolved as soon as it is discovered by a thread. The likelihood that another thread is recoloring a neighboring vertex at the same time is certainly lower than in Çatalyürek *et al.*

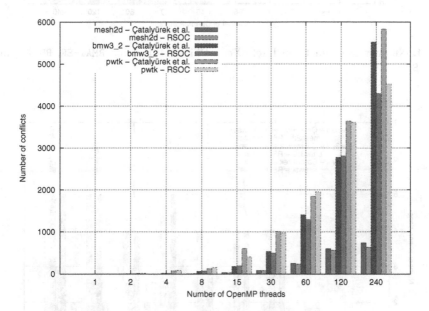

Fig. 3. Number of conflicts on Intel®Xeon Phi™ 5110P using `mesh2d`, `bmw3_2` and `pwtk`.

The reduced number of conflicts also results in fewer iterations of the algorithm, as can be seen in Figs. 5 and 6. Combined with the absence of one barrier from the while-loop, it is only expected that our new algorithm ultimately outperforms its predecessor. A nice property is that both algorithms produce colorings using the same number of colors, *i.e.* quality of coloring is not compromised by the higher execution speed.

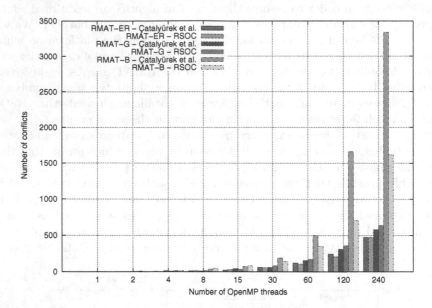

Fig. 4. Number of conflicts on Intel®Xeon Phi™ 5110P using RMAT-ER, RMAT-G and RMAT-B.

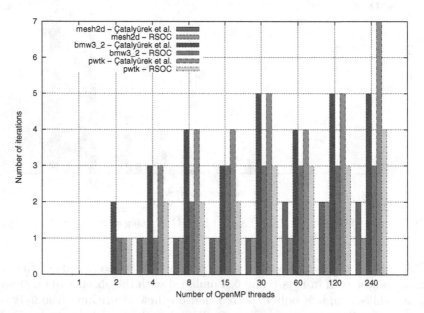

Fig. 5. Number of iterations on Intel®Xeon Phi™ 5110P using mesh2d, bmw3_2 and pwtk.

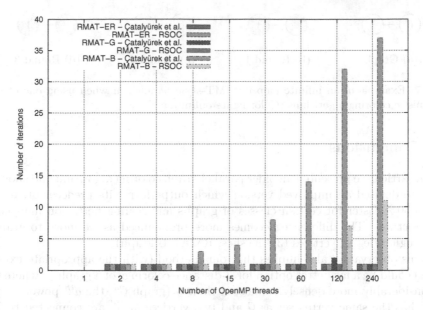

Fig. 6. Number of iterations on Intel® Xeon Phi™ 5110P using `RMAT-ER`, `RMAT-G` and `RMAT-B`.

5 SIMT Restrictions

Trying to run the optimistic coloring algorithms using CUDA on an Nvidia GPU revealed a potential weakness. Neither algorithm terminated; instead, threads spun forever in an infinite loop. This is due to the nature of SIMT-style multi-threading, in which the lockstep warp execution results in ties never being broken. An example of why these algorithms result in infinite loops in SIMT-style parallelism can be seen in Fig. 7, where we have a simple two-vertex graph and two threads, each processing one vertex (this scenario is likely to actually occur at a later iteration of the while-loop, where the global list of defects $\mathcal{L}$ is left with a few pairs of adjacent vertices). At the beginning (a), both vertices are uncolored. Each thread decides that the smallest color available for its own vertex is red. Both threads commit their decision at the same clock cycle, which results in the defective coloring shown in (b). In the next round the threads try to resolve the conflict and decide that the new smallest color available is green. The decision is committed at the same clock cycle, resulting once again in defects (c) and the process goes on forever.

Theoretically, this scenario is possible for CPUs as well, although the probability is extremely low. We believe that there will always be some randomness (*i.e.* lack of thread coordination) on CPUs which guarantees convergence of the optimistic algorithms. This randomness can also be "emulated" on GPUs by having a dynamic assignment of vertices to threads and making sure that two adjacent vertices are always processed by threads of different warps.

424   G. Rokos et al.

(a) Graph   (b) Round 1   (c) Round 2   (d) Round 3

Fig. 7. Example of an infinite loop in SIMT-style parallelism when using one of the optimistic coloring algorithms (Color figure online).

6   Conclusions

In this article we presented an older parallel graph coloring algorithm and showed how we devised an improved version which outperforms its predecessor, being up to 50 % faster for certain classes of graphs and scaling better on manycore architectures. The difference becomes more pronounced as we move to graphs with higher-degree vertices (3D meshes, RMAT-B graph).

This observation also implies that our method (with the appropriate extensions) could be a far better option for d-distance colorings of a graph $\mathcal{G}$, where $\mathcal{G}^d$ is considerably more densely connected than $\mathcal{G}$ (graph $\mathcal{G}^d$, the dth power graph of $\mathcal{G}$, has the same vertex set as $\mathcal{G}$ and two vertices in $\mathcal{G}^d$ are connected by an edge if and only if the same vertices are within distance d in $\mathcal{G}$).

Speed and scalability stem from two sources, (a) reduced number of conflicts which also results in fewer iterations and (b) reduced thread synchronization per iteration. Coloring quality remains at the same levels as in older parallel algorithms, which in turn are very close to the serial greedy algorithm, meaning that they produce near-optimal colorings for most classes of graphs.

Acknowledgments. The authors gratefully acknowledge funding from EPSRC grants EP/I00677X/1 and EP/L000407/1 supporting this work.

References

1. Çatalyürek, Ü.V., Feo, J., Gebremedhin, A.H., Halappanavar, M., Pothen, A.: Graph coloring algorithms for multi-core and massively multithreaded architectures. Parallel Comput. **38**(10–11), 576–594 (2012)
2. Chakrabarti, D., Faloutsos, C.: Graph mining: laws, generators, and algorithms. ACM Comput. Surv. **38**(1), 2 (2006)
3. Cohen, J., Castonguay, P.: Efficient Graph Matching and Coloring on the GPU. http://on-demand.gputechconf.com/gtc/2012/presentations/S0332-Efficient-Graph-Matching-and-Coloring-on-GPUs.pdf
4. Coleman, T., Moré, J.: Estimation of sparse Jacobian matrices and graph coloring problems. SIAM J. Numer. Anal. 20(1), 187–209 (1983). http://dx.doi.org/10.1137/0720013
5. Davis, T.A., Hu, Y.: The University of Florida sparse matrix collection. ACM Trans. Math. Softw. 38(1), 1:1–1:25, December 2011. http://doi.acm.org/10.1145/2049662.2049663
6. De Cougny, H., Shephard, M.S.: Parallel refinement and coarsening of tetrahedral meshes. Int. J. Numer. Meth. Eng. **46**(7), 1101–1125 (1999)

7. Freitag, L.F., Jones, M.T., Plassmann, P.E.: The scalability of mesh improvement algorithms. In: Algorithms for Parallel Processing IMA Volumes in Mathematics And Its Applications, pp. 185– 212. Springer-Verlag (1998)

8. Garey, M.R., Johnson, D.S.: Computers and Intractability: A Guide to the Theory of NP-Completeness. W.H. Freeman & Co., New York (1979)

9. Gebremedhin, A.H., Manne, F.: Scalable parallel graph coloring algorithms. Concurrency: Pract. Experience 12(12), 1131–1146 (2000). http://dx.doi.org/10.1002/1096-9128(200010)12:12<1131::AID-CPE528>3.0.CO;2-2

10. Gorman, G.J., Rokos, G., Southern, J., Kelly, P.H.J.: Thread-parallel anisotropic mesh adaptation. Accepted for Publication in Proceedings of the 4th Tetrahedron Workshop on Grid Generation for Numerical Computations (2015)

11. Hasenplaugh, W., Kaler, T., Schardl, T.B., Leiserson, C.E.: Ordering heuristics for parallel graph coloring. In: Proceedings of the 26th ACM Symposium on Parallelism in Algorithms and Architectures, SPAA 2014, pp. 166–177. ACM, New York (2014). http://doi.acm.org/10.1145/2612669.2612697

12. Hysom, D., Pothen, A.: A scalable parallel algorithm for incomplete factor preconditioning. SIAM J. Sci. Comput. 22(6), 2194–2215, June 2000. http://dx.doi.org/10.1137/S1064827500376193

13. Jones, M.T., Plassmann, P.E.: A parallel graph coloring heuristic. SIAM J. Sci. Comput **14**, 654–669 (1992)

14. Jones, M.T., Plassmann, P.E.: Scalable iterative solution of sparse linear systems. Parallel Comput. 20(5), 753–773, May 1994. http://dx.doi.org/10.1016/0167-8191(94)90004-3

15. Luby, M.: A simple parallel algorithm for the maximal independent set problem. In: Proceedings of the Seventeenth Annual ACM Symposium on Theory of Computing, STOC 1985, pp. 1–10. ACM, New York (1985). http://doi.acm.org/10.1145/22145.22146

16. Manne, F.: A parallel algorithm for computing the extremal eigenvalues of very large sparse matrices. In: Proceedings of the 4th International Workshop on Applied Parallel Computing, Large Scale Scientific and Industrial Problems, PARA 1998, pp. 332–336. Springer, London (1998). http://dl.acm.org/citation.cfm?id=645781.666669

17. Nasre, R., Burtscher, M., Pingali, K.: Morph algorithms on GPUs. In: Proceedings of the 18th ACM SIGPLAN Symposium on Principles and Practice of Parallel Programming, PPoPP 2013, pp. 147–156. ACM, New York (2013). http://iss.ices.utexas.edu/Publications/Papers/nasre13-ppopp.pdf

18. Saad, Y.: ILUM: a multi-elimination ILU preconditioner for general sparse matrices. SIAM J. Sci. Comput. 17(4), 830–847 (1996). http://dx.doi.org/10.1137/0917054

19. Strout, M.M., Carter, L., Ferrante, J., Freeman, J., Kreaseck, B.: Combining performance aspects of irregular gauss-seidel via sparse tiling. In: Pugh, B., Tseng, C.-W. (eds.) LCPC 2002. LNCS, vol. 2481, pp. 90–110. Springer, Heidelberg (2005)

20. Strout, M.M., Luporini, F., Krieger, C.D., Bertolli, C., Bercea, G.T., Olschanowsky, C., Ramanujam, J., Kelly, P.H.J.: Generalizing run-time tiling with the loop chain abstraction. In: Proceedings of the 28th IEEE International Parallel and Distributed Processing Symposium (IPDPS), May 2014

A Composable Deadlock-Free Approach to Object-Based Isolation

Shams Imam[✉], Jisheng Zhao, and Vivek Sarkar

Department of Computer Science, Rice University, Houston, USA
{shams,jisheng.zhao,vsarkar}@rice.edu

Abstract. A widely used principle in the design of concurrent programs is isolation – the property that a task can operate on shared data without interference from other tasks. In this paper, we introduce a new approach to object-based isolation that is guaranteed to be deadlock-free, while still retaining the rollback benefits of transactions. Further, our approach differentiates between read and write accesses in its concurrency control mechanisms. Finally, since the generality of our approach precludes the use of static ordering for deadlock avoidance, our runtime ensures deadlock-freedom by detecting and resolving deadlocks at runtime automatically, without involving the programmer.

Keywords: Object-Based isolation · Deadlock freedom · Lock composition · Read-Write locks · Delimited continuations

1 Introduction

Designing and implementing correct and efficient concurrent programs is a notoriously challenging task due to the possibility of data races. Programs must use concurrency control mechanisms to ensure that multiple threads of execution do not interfere with each other while sharing data in memory. One approach for enforcing mutual exclusion is to use critical sections that execute in isolation with respect to other *interfering* critical sections. Isolation is the property that a thread can access shared data without interference from other threads.

Threads use locks to guard the operations performed while the lock is held; this enforces isolation properties of a thread's guarded operations. The dominant concurrency control mechanism in high-level languages, such as Java and C#, are mutual-exclusion locks [2]. Parallel programming models (e.g. OpenMP 4.0 [20], Cilk [8]) also rely on locks for implementing mutual exclusion. In fact, there is comprehensive empirical evidence that programmers almost always use mutual-exclusion locks to enforce isolation properties [7]. Transactional memory offers a promising alternative to lock-based synchronization as a mechanism for isolation. A programmer can reason about the correctness of code within a transaction and need not worry about interactions with other concurrently executing transactions [14]. However, re-execution of conflicting transactions, and the logging of data accesses to prepare for the possibility of rollback, add overhead and often lead to poor performance even in the presence of moderate contention.

© Springer-Verlag Berlin Heidelberg 2015
J.L. Träff et al. (Eds.): Euro-Par 2015, LNCS 9233, pp. 426–437, 2015.
DOI: 10.1007/978-3-662-48096-0_33

The focus of this work is to provide a deadlock-free construct to support shared-exclusive object-based isolation in concurrent programs. When threads can not coordinate their accesses to shared data, deadlocks can occur while acquiring isolation privileges. When a deadlock can occur, a dynamically assigned low-priority thread is forced to roll back and release privilege(s) it is holding that is preventing a high-priority thread from making progress. Once released, this allows the high-priority thread to acquire the privilege and make progress. After the high-priority thread releases the conflicting privileges, the low-priority thread can resume execution. Our construct combines the features of transactions and shared-exclusive locks to resolve deadlocks and to minimize re-executions due to conflicts. It also enables promotion of shared privileges to exclusive privileges by rolling back part of the computation and re-executing it with an exclusive privilege.

In summary, the contributions of this paper are as follows:

- We introduce object-based isolation as a high-level construct for deadlock-free shared-exclusive mutual-exclusion.
- We describe an implementation approach for object-based isolation that resolves deadlocks at runtime, exploits the rollback benefits of transactions, and differentiates between read and write accesses in its concurrency control mechanisms.
- We compare the performance obtained by our implementation of object-based isolation with that of Java's **synchronized** statement, the regular and shared-exclusive locks available in the JDK [13], and with the Multiverse STM library [18].

2   Background and Motivating Example

Large multi-threaded programs that involve concurrency control via the use of multiple locks can be challenging to write. Deadlocks can occur when multiple threads need the same locks but obtain them in a different order. Always acquiring locks in a consistent order ensures that programs will not deadlock. But this can be challenging (or even impossible) to ensure as the dynamic dispatch capabilities or library composition features in many languages make it difficult to know a program's exact call graph structure at compile-time.

Using read-write (shared-exclusive) locks can significantly improve parallel performance if the protected data is read frequently and modified only occasionally. They can be acquired either for reading or for writing: multiple readers may hold the lock simultaneously, but writers must acquire exclusive ownership of the lock. Along with deadlocks, an issue while composing software components is the need to promote read privileges to write privileges and vice versa. Promoting (demoting) a write privilege to a read privilege carries no restrictions and can be supported trivially with reentrant behavior. However, promoting a read privilege to a write privilege is usually not permitted as doing so can lead to inconsistent behavior and is prone to deadlocks. As we will see in Sect. 3.3, our construct also supports promotion of read privileges to write privileges.

2.1 Motivating Example

Our motivating example is the classic bank transaction; a transaction must debit one account and credit another with a particular amount of money when legal to do so. For proper accounting, it is essential that either both operations succeed or neither operation succeeds. This means that both operations should be performed with transactional semantics to ensure the integrity of the system's state.

Listing 1.1. Classic bank transaction example using read-write locks.

```
 1 class BankTransactionRWLock {
 2   def trySafe(from, to, amount) {
 3     lock (from.readLock) {
 4       if from.balance() > amount
 5         transfer(from, to, amount)
 6         return true
 7       else
 8         return false
 9 } }
10   def transfer(from, to, amount) {
11     val low = min(from, to)
12     val high = max(from, to)
13     lock (low.writeLock) {
14       lock (high.writeLock) {
15         from.debit(amount)
16         to.credit(amount)
17 } } } }
```

Listing 1.2. Classic bank transaction example using transaction memory solution with **atomic** blocks.

```
 1 class BankTransactionAtomic {
 2   def trySafe(from, to, amount) {
 3     atomic {
 4       if from.balance() > amount
 5         transfer(from, to, amount)
 6         return true
 7       else
 8         return false
 9 } }
10   def transfer(from, to, amount) {
11     atomic {
12       from.debit(amount)
13       to.credit(amount)
14 } }
15 }
```

Listing 1.1 uses read-write locks to ensure fine-grained synchronization to increase concurrency. To avoid deadlocks, it uses ordering of the bank accounts to retrieve the locks (lines 11–12). However, composing of **trySafe** and **transfer** can still lead to deadlock since the locks individual instances can still be acquired out of order from multiple calls. In addition, deadlocks will also occur in systems that do not allow promotion of read privileges (in **trySafe()**) to write privileges (in **transfer()**).

Listing 1.2 displays the same example written using **atomic** blocks that offer software transactional memory (STM) support. Deadlock is not possible in this example as transactions never wait for one another; at least one transaction is guaranteed to succeed in the presence of conflicts. In STMs, a conflict occurs when two concurrent uncommitted transactions perform conflicting read or write operations on the same bank accounts. However, the likelihood of aborting due to intervening conflicting commits increases in longer running transactions or in write-heavy workloads, causing deterioration in performance.

3 Object-Based Isolation as a High-Level Construct for Concurrent Programming

In this section, we introduce Object-Based Isolation (OBI) as a high-level construct for concurrent programming. Our goal for OBI is to combine the programmability of scoped **synchronized** blocks with the efficiency of read-write locks

(RWLs) and the semantic guarantees of transactional execution (i.e. isolation, deadlock freedom, optimistic concurrency). As with locks, mutual exclusion is only guaranteed between instances of isolated statements; no such guarantees exist between isolated and non-isolated statements. Assuming that there are no data races between isolated and isolated/non-isolated statements, an isolated statement executing in parallel is guaranteed to produce the same answer (for the same input state) as when no other task/thread is executing at the same time [14]. As with transactions (but not with locks), the programmer is spared the burden of guaranteeing deadlock freedom – that burden is passed on to the implementation instead.

As we will see, our proposed isolated statement is scoped, and (unlike transactions) allows the user to specify a list of objects with read or write (R/W) modes for which isolation is desired. Two isolated statements are only guaranteed to execute in mutual-execution if they have a non-conflicting intersection in their shared-exclusive object sets. This allows isolated statements to execute critical sections that are guarded by explicitly specified objects, unlike in transactions where critical sections appear to be guarded globally leading to deadlock scenarios [16]. In transactional memory, a data access pattern with frequent writes to shared data will induce numerous aborts; such issues do not arise with isolated statements. isolated statements can be nested, and inner statements can add to the set of objects acquired. No total order is imposed on the nested isolated object list. This capability allows for the expression of "non-cautious" concurrency patterns[1] [21].

3.1   isolated Statements

Listing 1.3. Classic bank transaction example using isolated blocks with read and write privileges.

```
1  class BankTransactionIsolated {
2    def trySafe(from, to, amount) {
3      isolated(read(from)) {
4        if from.balance() > amount
5          transfer(from, to, amount)
6          return true
7        else
8          return false
9  } }
10   def transfer(from, to, amount) {
11     isolated(write(from), write(to)) {
12       from.debit(amount)
13       to.credit(amount)
14 } } }
```

The motivation for OBI is that there are many cases when the programmer knows the shared or exclusive mode for the set of objects that will be accessed in the body of an isolated statement. The specification of these modes in the isolated argument object set helps the runtime by explicitly stating the objects that need to be tracked. Listing 1.3 displays the bank transaction example from Sect. 2.1 using isolated statements. As with Java's synchronized construct, isolated is reentrant and scoped guaranteeing the absence of dangling unlock operations. Like RWLs, isolated statements can acquire (R/W) access privileges on the argument

---

[1] Cautious patterns require all reads to shared data to performed before mutations to any of them.

object. Unlike Java's RWLs, object sets in nested `isolated` blocks allow promotion of an object's access privilege from shared mode to exclusive mode (Sect. 3.3). For nested `isolated` constructs we follow open nested semantics [9], they do not enforce atomicity. Our prevention scheme (Sect. 3.4) avoids deadlock while acquiring privileges. While sequential composition of transactions to form a single, larger transaction can cause deadlocks [16], composition of `isolated` statements can never cause a deadlock.

3.2   Execution Mechanism

Since we allow free composition of `isolated` statements, we cannot guarantee an order in the acquisition of privileges by `isolated` statements. Similarly, it is impossible to prevent scenarios where a read privilege needs to be promoted to a write privilege. As mentioned in Sect. 2.1, both these behaviors are prone to deadlocks. As a result, our approach dynamically detects and resolves deadlocks by allowing instances of `isolated` statements to *abort* by rolling back and re-executing with possibly modified privileges when it is safer to do so.

Listing 1.4. Simple `Counter` that supports the *clone-merge* protocol. For simple data structures, these can be automated by a compiler.

```
1 class Counter(var value) {
2   def increment(amount) {
3     value += amount
4   }
5   def clone() {
6     return new Counter(value)
7   }
8   def merge(other: Counter) {
9     this.count = other.count;
10 } }
```

Roll backs during the execution of a thread can leave shared data in an inconsistent state. Two key observations help resolve this concern. Firstly, the inconsistency occurs only due to objects that were being modified, i.e. those objects executing with a write privilege. We resolve this issue by employing a *clone-merge* protocol where a clone of the object is created and used inside the body of the `isolated`. When the `isolated` statement completes successfully, this private clone is trivially merged back into the source object since only one `isolated` gets to run with write privileges. If an `isolated` statement aborts, the clone is not merged and discarded. Listing 1.4 displays a simple integer counter class that supports cloning and merging. Relying on the clone-merge protocol limits the applicability of our approach on classes for which the source code is not available and a clone method is cannot be generated automatically. The other approaches, such as transactional memory and locks, do not suffer from this limitation.

Secondly, we need a scheme to dynamically identify the target program points when a computation is rolled back. To address this concern, we use delimited continuations (DeCont) [6] to roll back the computation. Each `isolated` statement executes as a DeCont and the call stack is recursively unwound from nested `isolated` statements to a target `isolated` statement during rollback. Since our approach works on clones and only commits the results when successful, we can handle roll backs very easily. When re-executing an `isolated` statement, a new DeCont is created and executed.

With OBI, tracking every read and write is obviated as the programmer explicitly declares the read and write object sets. Unlike transactions where every mutated object is committed at the end of the transaction, only object sets opened in write mode are committed at the end of an `isolated` statement. We employ a pessimistic control policy [9], where `isolated` statements only execute their statements once they are guaranteed it is safe to do so. While the likelihood of intervening conflicting commits increases in longer running transactions, such situations do not arise with `isolated` statements. The guarantee relies on the use of read-write lock semantics where an `isolated` statement is forced to wait until it successfully acquires the desired read-write privilege.

In traditional transactions, a conflict is resolved by aborting and re-executing or delaying one of the conflicting transactions. Similarly in conflicting scenarios, at least one `isolated` statement aborts and re-executes later. However, the difference with transactions lies in the situations identified as conflicts. With our OBI, there are two scenarios that can cause conflicts. The first is when we dynamically detect that a nested `isolated` statement is attempting to acquire a write privilege for a previously acquired read privilege. The second is when `isolated` statements participate in a deadlock cycle while attempting to obtain a privilege as is possible in the bank transaction example.

3.3   Read-to-Write Promotion

It is not safe to simply promote a read privilege to a write privilege. Even if the write privileges are promoted serially without rollback, the invariants that were true while executing with read privileges may no longer hold due to intervening writes. To address this issue, we recursively roll back the computation to the outermost `isolated` statement that acquired the read privilege on the object. The privilege for that instance of the `isolated` statement is dynamically updated to a write privilege, and the statement re-executed. Listings 1.5 and 1.6 display an example of the transformation that happens dynamically at runtime before and after the read-to-write promotion, respectively. The read privilege for x in the outermost `isolated` on line 2 is promoted to a write, and the statements in lines 3 to 7 re-executed.

Listing 1.5. Snippet with nested `isolated` statements that require read-to-write promotion. Note that these promotions could occur across deeply nested blocks within different function calls.

```
1 isolated (write(w)) {
2   isolated (read(x)) {
3     isolated (read(y)) {
4       isolated (read(x)) {
5         isolated (write(x)) {
6           ...
7 } } } } }
```

Listing 1.6. Snippet with nested `isolated` statements after read-to-write promotion. Note that this promotion happens to the dynamic instance being executed and not to the static version of the code.

```
1 isolated (write(w)) {
2   isolated (write(x)) { //promoted
3     isolated (read(y)) {
4       isolated (read(x)) { //
            unchanged
5         isolated (write(x)) {
6           ...
7 } } } } }
```

3.4 Deadlock Resolution

While executing nested `isolated` statements, we rely on dynamically detecting and resolving deadlocks. We associate unique ids with threads to prioritize them; these priorities are used to resolve conflicts. When a thread acquires a read or write privilege on an object, the thread is registered as an owner of the privilege on the object. When another thread attempts to acquire the same privilege and fails, it compares its priority with the owner of the lock. If it has a lower priority, it aborts by rolling back its computation releasing any read or write privileges it had acquired. If the failed thread has a higher priority order, it re-attempts to acquire the lock. The lower priority thread will eventually release the lock, either by aborting as mentioned above (Sect. 3.2) or by completing successfully, and allow the higher priority thread to continue with its execution. This prioritization strategy introduces unfairness in its scheduling policy but allows livelocks to be ruled out in our `isolated` construct.

4 Implementation

In this section, we discuss our implementation of OBI presented in Sect. 3. Despite any productivity promises, an abstraction must be implementable in an efficient and scalable fashion for it to be accepted by programmers. The `isolated` construct must incur a sufficiently low overhead to be useful in practice, especially for small transactions. Our implementation [12] is a Java-based task-parallel runtime that supports `async-finish` style computations, though our ideas can also be implemented in other thread-based languages including C/C++. Our implementation conforms to the constraints imposed by a standard Java Virtual Machine (JVM). In particular, standard JVMs do not provide support for DeConts or for storing and restoring the stack. The DeConts created are thread independent and can be resumed on any worker thread.

We use an extended version of the open source bytecode weaver provided by the Kilim framework [23] to support DeConts. The Kilim bytecode weaver works by transforming the code of methods which can trigger rollback. It recognizes such methods by the presence of a `SuspendableException` exception in the method signature. It is important to note that no actual exceptions are thrown or caught which minimize the overhead of capturing and resuming continuations. Instead, the transformation performed is similar to a continuation passing style transformation, except that only methods that can suspend are transformed.

The runtime maintains a pool of custom RWLs, this pool can be extended to be one per user object. However, for ease of implementation we maintain a fixed size list and hash objects to one of the locks. When an `isolated` block requires a read or write privilege on an object, it hashes the object to a read-write lock and attempts to acquire the read or write privilege. During a deadlock or a read-to-write promotion conflict, the computation is rolled back by capturing the continuation. In other failed attempts, the task suspends and registers itself on a wait list and is resumed by moving itself into the work queue when the lock is available. Using continuations allows the worker thread to execute other ready tasks while suspended tasks are stored away in a separate queue.

5   Experimental Results

In this section, we present an experimental evaluation of the `isolated` construct introduced in this paper. We compare it against existing mutual-exclusion constructs available in the JDK - `synchronized` statement, JDK's ReentrantLock, and JDK's ReentrantReadWriteLock [13]. The JDK variants of the benchmarks were written to ensure there is no conflict (deadlock or read–to–write promotion) scenario during execution. We also compare our implementation on micro-benchmarks against the Multiverse library [18] whose STM implementation is based on [3]. We ran the benchmarks on four eight-core IBM POWER7 processors running at 3.8 GHz each. Each node contains 256 GB of RAM; the software stack includes IBM Java SDK Version 7. The JVM configuration flags used were (`-XX:-UseGCOverheadLimit -Xmx16384m -XX:+UseParallelGC -XX:+UseParallelOldGC`). Each benchmark was configured to run using 32 worker threads and run for thirty iterations in six separate JVM invocations. The arithmetic mean of the best fifty execution times (from the hundred and eighty iterations) are reported. Using the best execution time allows us to minimize the effects of JVM warm up, just-in-time compilation, and garbage collection.

5.1   Micro-Benchmarks

First, we compare the performance of the `isolated` construct on four microbenchmarks. The first microbenchmark uses Bank Transaction (BT) like those shown in Listings 1.1, 1.2, and 1.3. The second is an integer counter (CTR) microbenchmark where the increments to the counter are protected in mutual-exclusion blocks. The last two microbenchmarks are a concurrent read-write benchmarks on dictionary (CD) and sorted linked list (CSLL) data structures where the write percent is kept at 10 percent. The read and write operations in the CD benchmark takes $O(1)$ time while in the CSLL benchmark they take $O(N)$ time. All four lock variants perform similarly in BT, CTR, and CD as the critical section blocks are relatively short. The Multiverse STM version performs poorly compared to the other variants in the nested transactions BT benchmark. In CSLL, the critical section blocks take $O(N)$ time, hence the read-write lock version performs better than the reentrant lock version. The `synchronized` version performs better than the lock versions. The `isolated` version performs better as its use of continuations avoids blocking the worker threads allows all available read requests to be processed when there are no pending writes. The performance benefit comes from avoiding the need to context switch threads. Multiverse STM performs best on CSLL with a single transaction encapsulating the entire read or write operation (Fig. 1).

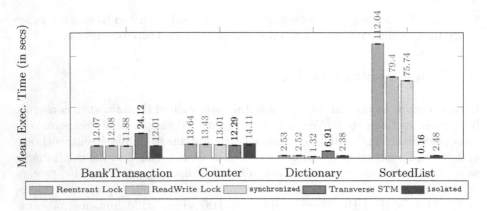

Fig. 1. Bank Transaction involves 6 million transactions on 8 thousand bank accounts. Counter includes 6 million increment operations each on 8 counter objects. The Dictionary benchmark 1 million operations with a write percent of 20 (split equal in put and remove) and remaining as read get operations. The SortedList benchmark 100 thousand operations with a write percent of 20 (split equal in add and remove) and remaining as read get operations. The y-axis represents program execution time, hence, smaller is better.

5.2 Macro-Benchmarks

We consider two larger benchmarks: Labyrinth and Parallel Breadth-First Search (BFS). The Labyrinth benchmark from the STAMP suite [17] is characterized by long transaction lengths, large read-sets, large write-sets, long transaction times,

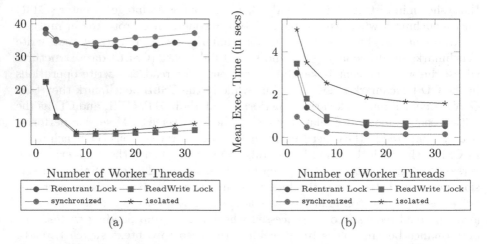

Fig. 2. Labyrinth (left) using the configuration 512 randomly generated inputs on dimension of $512 \times 512 \times 7$. Simple BFS (right) on a randomly generated connected graph with 500 thousand nodes and 5 million edges. The y-axis represents program execution time, hence, smaller is better.

and very high contention. The high contention causes the reentrant lock and synchronized versions to perform poorly with very low scalability. The read-write lock and isolated versions show improved performance as they allow multiple read requests to proceed in parallel. Simple BFS is a naive parallel implementation of the sequential BFS algorithm. In the BFS benchmark, the read-write lock, reentrant lock, and synchronized variants allocated one lock per graph node. The isolated version in our implementation shows higher overheads as it relies on the runtime to allocate a handful of locks (256 to be exact) and hashes on them (Fig. 2).

Note that the Java VM provides native support for synchronized statements and locks, but not for continuations. Our implementation of isolated uses DeConts without modifying the VM; the performance of our implementation would be greatly improved by using native support for DeConts in the VM. Work by Stadler et al. [24] to provide such native support in a Java VM reported over two orders magnitude speedup on micro-benchmarks compared to a bytecode transformation approach.

6   Related Work

Most of the state-of-art lock-free language constructs are based on transactional memory (TM) systems [10]. Both hardware transactional memory (HTM) [10] and software transactional memory (STM) [9] guarantee lock-free and deadlock avoidance by employing a rollback. By using TM, users can employ both coarse-grain and fine-grain parallelism, but have to pay for the overhead of rollback, especially for contention intensive (i.e. high conflict rate) critical sections. Recently, Aida [15] provides a high-level minimalistic programming model similar to Transactional Memory [10], with a single construct (async isolated) to define blocks of code to be executed concurrently and in isolation. Aida guarantees deadlock-freedom and livelock-freedom. Both STM and Aida need compiler support to instrument the memory accesses and enable the rollback mechanism.

Galois [19] is a runtime library-based approach, it provides library constructs called optimistic iterators for packaging optimistic parallelism as iterations over sets and for specifying the scheduling policy, and uses runtime scheme for detecting the conflicting shared data accesses and recovering from those unsafe access (i.e. rollback). Rajwar and Goodman based their technique on the observation that programmers often used coarse-grained locking to be sure "all bases are covered" and that programs can often run correctly even if the lock is never acquired [22]. Hence, the conservative locking strategies that programmers often use to ensure the correctness can frequently be elided dynamically, provided that one can detect and roll back concurrent updates that would have been prevented had the locking been performed. They built this work on speculative lock elision by automatically wrapping transactions around the critical sections of sequences of instructions detected at runtime as locks.

Lock inference [1,11] is a compiler-assisted approach to building efficient critical sections while also ensuring correctness. The basic idea is to employ compile-time analysis to identify the "really necessary" locks for the given critical section.

The efficiency depends on whether the static program analysis can precisely identify the lock set that should be applied to the critical section, i.e. in the presence of ambiguous object references a coarse-grain locking has to be chosen.

In this paper, we introduced the object-based isolation that is a runtime based mechanism provided to the user to efficiently build parallel application with guaranteed deadlock avoidance and livelock-freedom. The user interface is a language construct-like API, the advantage of this approach is that it provides the user a simple interface to build fine-grain locking based parallel applications, i.e. users can explicitly specifiy the mutual-excluded objects via our APIs. This is also a lightweight isolation support compared with Aida [15] and STM [10] which backups all objects within the language constructs specified scope. The user does not need to specify task scheduling strategies like Galois, our parallel runtime implicitly supports efficient scheduling mechanism (i.e. work-stealing).

Other approaches have exploited using lock-based implementation to improve the efficiency of STM. Ennals utilizes a hybrid policy where a pessimistic approach is used for write privileges, whereas an optimistic approach is used for read accesses [5]. Dice and Shavit used an optimistic control policy and only obtain locks before committing their writes, aborting the transaction if necessary [4]. Object-based isolation employs a pessimistic control policy for both read and write privileges (i.e. obtain the read or write privileges eagerly). In [5], deadlocks are detected while acquiring locks and a transaction can request another transaction to abort. [4] employs timeouts (for acquiring process) to abort a transaction and avoid deadlocks. Our approach does not require signaling the other task, a lower priority task cooperatively aborts its transaction to allow another task to make progress. The rollbacks of `isolated` statements happen only till the relevant outer boundary (for example, as shown in the example in Listing 1.6), unlike the above mentioned transaction approaches where the outermost transaction needs to be aborted.

7   Summary

We introduced a new composable approach to object-based isolation that is guaranteed to be deadlock-free, while still retaining the rollback benefits of transactions. Further, our approach differentiates between read and write accesses in its concurrency control mechanisms. Our construct incurs a cost for creating and merging clones which may, for some (large) data structures, require effort to implement efficiently by the programmer. We are currently exploring the possibility of implementing the `isolated` construct with native VM support to extract more performance. We, ambitiously, envision a scenario where the `synchronized` statement is replaced by the `isolated` construct semantics in modern programming languages.

Acknowledgments. We are very grateful to the anonymous reviewers, John Mellor-Crummey, Karthik Murthy, and Rishi Surendran for their insightful comments on early drafts that substantially improved the paper.

References

1. Cherem, S., Chilimbi, T.M., Gulwani, S.: Inferring locks for atomic sections. In: PLDI 2008, pp. 304–315 (2008)
2. Demsky, B., Lam, P.: Views: synthesizing fine-grained concurrency control. ACM Trans. Softw. Eng. Methodol. **22**(1), 4:1–4:33 (2013)
3. Dice, D., Shalev, O., Shavit, N.: Transactional locking II. In: Dolev, S. (ed.) DISC 2006. LNCS, vol. 4167, pp. 194–208. Springer, Heidelberg (2006)
4. Dice, D., Shavit, N.: Understanding tradeoffs in software transactional memory. In: CGO 2007, pp. 21–33. IEEE Computer Society, Washington (2007)
5. Ennals, R.: Software transactional memory should not be obstruction-Free. Technical report, Intel Research Cambridge (2006)
6. Felleisen, M.: The theory and practice of first-class prompts. In: POPL 1988, pp. 180–190 (1988)
7. Flanagan, C., Freund, S.N.: Atomizer: a dynamic atomicity checker for multithreaded programs. In: POPL 2004, pp. 256–267. ACM (2004)
8. Frigo, M., Leiserson, C.E., Randall, K.H.: The implementation of the Cilk-5 multithreaded language. In: PLDI 1998, pp. 212–223 (1998)
9. Harris, T., Larus, J., Rajwar, R.: Transactional Memory, 2nd edn. Morgan and Claypool Publishers, San Rafael (2010)
10. Herlihy, M., Moss, J.E.B.: Transactional memory: architectural support for lock-free data structures. In: ISCA 1993, pp. 289–300. ACM Press (1993)
11. Hicks, M., Foster, J.S., Pratikakis, P.: Lock inference for atomic sections. In: TRANSACT 2006, Ottawa, Canada, May 2006, pp. 95–102 (2006)
12. Imam, S., Sarkar, V.: Habanero-java library: a java 8 framework for multicore programming. In: PPPJ 2014, pp. 75–86. ACM (2014)
13. Lock (Java platform SE 7), September 2014. http://docs.oracle.com/javase/7/docs/api/java/util/concurrent/locks/Lock.html
14. Larus, J., Kozyrakis, C.: Transactional memory. Commun. ACM 51(7), 1364800, 80–88 (2008)
15. Lublinerman, R., Zhao, J., Budimlić, Z., Chaudhuri, S., Sarkar, V.: Delegated isolation. In: OOPSLA 2011, pp. 885–902 (2011)
16. Martin, M., Blundell, C., Lewis, E.: Subtleties of transactional memory atomicity semantics. IEEE Comput. Archit. Lett. **5**(2), 17–17 (2006)
17. Minh, C.C., Chung, J., Kozyrakis, C., Olukotun, K.: STAMP: stanford transactional applications for multi-processing. In: IISWC, pp. 35–46. IEEE (2008)
18. Multiverse: software transactional memory for Java and the JVM, April 2012. http://multiverse.codehaus.org/overview.html
19. Nguyen, D., Lenharth, A., Pingali, K.: A lightweight infrastructure for graph analytics. In: SOSP 2013, pp. 456–471. ACM (2013)
20. OpenMP API, version 4.0, July 2013. http://www.openmp.org/mp-documents/OpenMP4.0.0.pdf
21. Pingali, K., et al.: The tao of parallelism in algorithms. In: PLDI 2011, pp. 12–25. ACM (2011)
22. Rajwar, R., Goodman, J.R.: Speculative lock elision: enabling highly concurrent multithreaded execution. MICRO **34**, 294–305 (2001)
23. Srinivasan, S., Mycroft, A.: Kilim: isolation-typed actors for java. In: Vitek, J. (ed.) ECOOP 2008. LNCS, vol. 5142, pp. 104–128. Springer, Heidelberg (2008)
24. Stadler, L., Wimmer, C., Würthinger, T., Mössenböck, H., Rose, J.: Lazy continuations for java virtual machines. In: PPPJ 2009, pp. 143–152 (2009)

Scalable Data-Driven PageRank: Algorithms, System Issues, and Lessons Learned

Joyce Jiyoung Whang$^{(\boxtimes)}$, Andrew Lenharth,
Inderjit S. Dhillon, and Keshav Pingali

University of Texas at Austin, Austin, TX 78712, USA
{joyce,inderjit,pingali}@cs.utexas.edu
lenharth@ices.utexas.edu

Abstract. Large-scale network and graph analysis has received considerable attention recently. Graph mining techniques often involve an iterative algorithm, which can be implemented in a variety of ways. Using PageRank as a model problem, we look at three algorithm design axes: work activation, data access pattern, and scheduling. We investigate the impact of different algorithm design choices. Using these design axes, we design and test a variety of PageRank implementations finding that data-driven, push-based algorithms are able to achieve more than 28x the performance of standard PageRank implementations (e.g., those in GraphLab). The design choices affect both single-threaded performance as well as parallel scalability. The implementation lessons not only guide efficient implementations of many graph mining algorithms, but also provide a framework for designing new scalable algorithms.

Keywords: Scalable computing · Graph analytics · PageRank · Multithreaded programming · Data-driven algorithm

1 Introduction

Large-scale graph analysis has received considerable attention in both the machine learning and parallel programming communities. In machine learning, many different types of task-specific algorithms have been developed to deal with massive networks. In parallel computing, many different parallel programming models and systems have been proposed for both shared memory and distributed memory settings to ease implementation and manage parallel programs.

Recent research has observed that distributed graph analytics can have a significant slowdown over shared-memory implementations, that is, the increase in communication costs are not easily made up for by increase in aggregate processing power or memory bandwidth. Furthermore, a remarkable number of "large" graphs fit in the main memory of a shared memory machine; it is easy to fit graphs with tens of billions of edges on a large workstation-class machine. Given these factors, it is worth understanding how to efficiently parallelize graph analytics on shared-memory machines. A better understanding of how to implement

© Springer-Verlag Berlin Heidelberg 2015
J.L. Träff et al. (Eds.): Euro-Par 2015, LNCS 9233, pp. 438–450, 2015.
DOI: 10.1007/978-3-662-48096-0_34

fast shared-memory analytics both greatly reduces the costs and enables richer applications on commodity systems. Better implementation strategies also help distributed implementations, as they tend to use shared-memory abstractions within a host.

Many graph mining techniques usually involve iterative algorithms where local computations are repeatedly done at a set of nodes until a convergence criterion is satisfied. Let us define *active nodes* to be a set of nodes where computations should be performed. Based on how the active nodes are processed, we can broadly classify these iterative graph algorithms from three different points of view: work activation, data access pattern, and scheduling. In this paper, we present general approaches for designing scalable data-driven graph algorithms using a case study of the PageRank algorithm. In particular, using the three different algorithm design axes (i.e., work activation, data access pattern, and scheduling), we present eight different formulations and in-memory parallel implementations of PageRank algorithm. We show that by considering data-driven formulations, we can have more flexibility in processing the active nodes, which enables us to develop work-efficient algorithms. We focus our analysis on PageRank in this manuscript, but our approaches and formulations can be easily extended to other graph mining algorithms.

2   Work Activation

We first classify algorithms into two groups based on work activation: topology-driven and data-driven algorithms. In a topology-driven algorithm, active nodes are defined solely by the structure of a graph. For example, an algorithm which requires processing all the nodes at each iteration is referred to as a topology-driven algorithm. On the other hand, in a data-driven algorithm, the nodes are dynamically activated by their neighbors, i.e., the nodes become active or inactive in an unpredictable way. In many applications, data-driven algorithms can be more work-efficient than topology-driven algorithms because the former allows us to concentrate more on "hot spots" in a graph where more frequent updates are needed.

2.1   Topology-Driven PageRank

To explain the concepts in more detail, we now focus our discussion on PageRank which is a key technique in Web mining [4]. Given a graph $G = (\mathcal{V}, \mathcal{E})$ with a vertex set $\mathcal{V}$ and an edge set $\mathcal{E}$, let $\mathbf{x}$ denote a PageRank vector of size $|\mathcal{V}|$. Also, let us define $\mathcal{S}_v$ to be the set of incoming neighbors of node v, and $\mathcal{T}_v$ to be the set of outgoing neighbors of node v. Then, node v's PageRank, denoted by x_v, is iteratively computed by $x_v^{(k+1)} = \alpha \sum_{w \in \mathcal{S}_v} \frac{x_w^{(k)}}{|\mathcal{T}_w|} + (1 - \alpha)$, where $x_v^{(k)}$ denotes the k-th iterate, and α is a teleportation parameter ($0 < \alpha < 1$). Algorithm 1 presents this iteration, which is the traditional power method that can be used to compute PageRank. Given a user defined tolerance ϵ, the PageRank vector $\mathbf{x}$ is initialized to be $\mathbf{x} = (1 - \alpha)\mathbf{e}$ where $\mathbf{e}$ denotes the vector of all 1's. The PageRank values are repeatedly computed until the difference between $x_v^{(k)}$ and $x_v^{(k+1)}$ is smaller than ϵ for all the nodes. Since the Power method requires processing all the nodes at each round, it is a topology-driven algorithm.

Algorithm 1. Topology-driven PageRank

Input: graph $G = (\mathcal{V}, \mathcal{E})$, α, ϵ
Output: PageRank x
1: Initialize $\mathbf{x} = (1 - \alpha)\mathbf{e}$
2: **while** true **do**
3:     **for** $v \in \mathcal{V}$ **do**
4:         $x_v^{(k+1)} = \alpha \sum\limits_{w \in \mathcal{S}_v} \dfrac{x_w^{(k)}}{|\mathcal{T}_w|} + (1 - \alpha)$
5:         $\delta_v = |x_v^{(k+1)} - x_v^{(k)}|$
6:     **end for**
7:     **if** $\|\boldsymbol{\delta}\|_\infty < \epsilon$ **then**
8:         break;
9:     **end if**
10: **end while**
11: $\mathbf{x} = \dfrac{\mathbf{x}}{\|\mathbf{x}\|_1}$

Algorithm 2. Data-driven PageRank

Input: graph $G = (\mathcal{V}, \mathcal{E})$, α, ϵ
Output: PageRank x
1: Initialize $\mathbf{x} = (1 - \alpha)\mathbf{e}$
2: **for** $v \in \mathcal{V}$ **do**
3:     worklist.push(v)
4: **end for**
5: **while** !worklist.isEmpty **do**
6:     $v =$ worklist.pop()
7:     $x_v^{new} = \alpha \sum\limits_{w \in \mathcal{S}_v} \dfrac{x_w}{|\mathcal{T}_w|} + (1 - \alpha)$
8:     **if** $|x_v^{new} - x_v| \geq \epsilon$ **then**
9:         $x_v = x_v^{new}$
10:         **for** $w \in \mathcal{T}_v$ **do**
11:             **if** w is not in worklist **then**
12:                 worklist.push(w)
13:             **end if**
14:         **end for**
15:     **end if**
16: **end while**
17: $\mathbf{x} = \dfrac{\mathbf{x}}{\|\mathbf{x}\|_1}$

2.2   Basic Data-Driven PageRank

Instead of processing all the nodes in rounds, we can think of an algorithm which dynamically maintains a working set. Algorithm 2 shows a basic data-driven PageRank. Initially, the worklist is set to be the entire vertex set. The algorithm proceeds by picking a node from the worklist, computing the node's PageRank, and adding its outgoing neighbors to the worklist. To see the convergence of the data-driven PageRank, let us rewrite the problem in the form of a linear system. We define a row-stochastic matrix $\boldsymbol{P}$ to be $\boldsymbol{P} \equiv \boldsymbol{D}^{-1}\boldsymbol{A}$ where $\boldsymbol{A}$ is an adjacency matrix and $\boldsymbol{D}$ is the degree diagonal matrix. We assume that there is no self-loop in the graph. Then, the PageRank computation can be written as the linear system of $(\boldsymbol{I} - \alpha\boldsymbol{P}^T)\mathbf{x} = (1 - \alpha)\mathbf{e}$, and the residual is defined to be $\mathbf{r} = (1 - \alpha)\mathbf{e} - (\boldsymbol{I} - \alpha\boldsymbol{P}^T)\mathbf{x}$. In this setting, it has been shown in [9] that each local computation in Algorithm 2 decreases the residual. Indeed, when a node v's PageRank is updated, its residual r_v becomes zero, and $\alpha r_v/|\mathcal{T}_v|$ is added to each of its outgoing neighbors' residuals. Thus, we can show that Algorithm 2 converges, and on termination, it is guaranteed that the residual $\|\mathbf{r}\|_\infty < \epsilon$.

From the next section, we will focus on the data-driven formulation of PageRank, and build up various variations of the data-driven PageRank.

3   Data Access Pattern

Data access pattern (or memory access pattern) is an important factor one should consider for designing a scalable graph algorithm. When an active node is processed, there can be a particular data access pattern. For example, some algorithms require reading a value of an active node and updating its outgoing neighbors, whereas some algorithms require reading values from incoming neighbors of an active node and updating the active node's value. Based on these data

Algorithm 3. Pull-Push-based PageRank

Input: graph $G = (\mathcal{V}, \mathcal{E})$, α, ϵ
Output: PageRank $\mathbf{x}$
1: Initialize $\mathbf{x} = (1 - \alpha)\mathbf{e}$
2: Initialize $\mathbf{r} = 0$
3: **for** $v \in \mathcal{V}$ **do**
4:     **for** $w \in \mathcal{S}_v$ **do**
5:         $r_v = r_v + \dfrac{1}{|\mathcal{T}_w|}$
6:     **end for**
7:     $r_v = (1 - \alpha)\alpha r_v$
8: **end for**
9: **for** $v \in \mathcal{V}$ **do**
10:     worklist.push(v)
11: **end for**
12: **while** !worklist.isEmpty **do**
13:     v = worklist.pop()
14:     $x_v = \alpha \displaystyle\sum_{w \in \mathcal{S}_v} \dfrac{x_w}{|\mathcal{T}_w|} + (1 - \alpha)$
15:     **for** $w \in \mathcal{T}_v$ **do**
16:         $r_w^{old} = r_w$
17:         $r_w = r_w + \dfrac{r_v \alpha}{|\mathcal{T}_v|}$
18:         **if** $r_w \geq \epsilon$ and $r_w^{old} < \epsilon$ **then**
19:             worklist.push(w)
20:         **end if**
21:     **end for**
22:     $r_v = 0$
23: **end while**
24: $\mathbf{x} = \dfrac{\mathbf{x}}{\|\mathbf{x}\|_1}$

Algorithm 4. Push-based PageRank

Input: graph $G = (\mathcal{V}, \mathcal{E})$, α, ϵ
Output: PageRank $\mathbf{x}$
1: Initialize $\mathbf{x} = (1 - \alpha)\mathbf{e}$
2: Initialize $\mathbf{r} = 0$
3: **for** $v \in \mathcal{V}$ **do**
4:     **for** $w \in \mathcal{S}_v$ **do**
5:         $r_v = r_v + \dfrac{1}{|\mathcal{T}_w|}$
6:     **end for**
7:     $r_v = (1 - \alpha)\alpha r_v$
8: **end for**
9: **for** $v \in \mathcal{V}$ **do**
10:     worklist.push(v)
11: **end for**
12: **while** !worklist.isEmpty **do**
13:     v = worklist.pop()
14:     $x_v^{new} = x_v + r_v$
15:     **for** $w \in \mathcal{T}_v$ **do**
16:         $r_w^{old} = r_w$
17:         $r_w = r_w + \dfrac{r_v \alpha}{|\mathcal{T}_v|}$
18:         **if** $r_w \geq \epsilon$ and $r_w^{old} < \epsilon$ **then**
19:             worklist.push(w)
20:         **end if**
21:     **end for**
22:     $r_v = 0$
23: **end while**
24: $\mathbf{x} = \dfrac{\mathbf{x}}{\|\mathbf{x}\|_1}$

access patterns, we can classify algorithms into three categories: pull-based, pull-push-based, and push-based algorithms.

3.1 Pull-Based PageRank

In *pull-based* algorithms, an active node *pulls* (reads) its neighbors' values and updates its own value. Note that pull-based algorithms require more *read* operations than *write* operations in general because the *write* operation is only performed on the active node. In the PageRank example, Algorithms 1 and 2 are both pull-based algorithms because an active node pulls (reads) its incoming neighbors' PageRank values and updates its own PageRank.

3.2 Pull-Push-Based PageRank

In *pull-push-based* algorithms, an active node *pulls* (reads) its neighbors' values and also *pushes* (updates) its neighbors' values. When we consider the cost for processing an active node, pull-push-based algorithms might be more expensive than pull-based algorithms as they require both *read* and *write* operations on neighbors. However, in terms of information propagation, pull-push-based algorithms can have advantages because in pull-push-based algorithms, an active node can propagate information to its neighbors whereas in pull-based algorithms, an active node passively receives information from its neighbors.

Now, we transform the basic data-driven PageRank into a pull-push-based algorithm. Recall that in Algorithm 2, whenever a node's PageRank is updated, the residuals of its outgoing neighbors are increased. Thus, to guarantee that the maximum residual is smaller than ϵ, all the outgoing neighbors of an active node should be added to the worklist. However, if we explicitly compute and maintain the residuals, we do not need to add all the outgoing neighbors of an active node, instead, we only need to add the outgoing neighbors whose residuals are greater than or equal to ϵ. In this way, we can filter out some work in the worklist. In Algorithm 3, the initial residual $\mathbf{r}^{(0)}$ is computed by $\mathbf{r}^{(0)} = (1 - \alpha)\alpha \boldsymbol{P}^T \mathbf{e}$ (lines 3–8). For each active node, it pulls its incoming neighbors' PageRank values (line 14), and pushes residuals to its outgoing neighbors (line 17). Then, an outgoing neighbor w of the active node v is added to the worklist only if the updated residual r_w is greater than or equal to ϵ and its old residual is less than ϵ. The second condition allows us to avoid having duplicates in the worklist (i.e., we add a node to the worklist only when its residual crosses ϵ for the first time). In this algorithm, there is a trade-off between overhead for residual computations and filtering out work in the worklist. We empirically observe that in many cases, the benefit of filtering overcomes the overhead for residual computations.

3.3   Push-Based PageRank

In *push-based* algorithms, an active node updates its own value, and only *pushes* (updates) its neighbors' values. Compared to pull-based algorithms, push-based algorithms can be more costly in the sense that they require more *write* operations. However, push-based algorithms invoke more frequent updates, which might be helpful to achieve a faster information propagation over the network. Compared to pull-push-based algorithms, push-based algorithms can be more efficient because they only require *write* operations instead of *read & write* operations. To design a push-based PageRank, we need to notice that the $(k+1)$-th PageRank update of node v is equivalent to the sum of the k-th PageRank of v and its k-th residual. This can be derived from the linear system formulation which is discussed in Sect. 2.2. Thus, we can formulate a push-based PageRank as follows: for each active node v, its PageRank is updated by $x_v^{(k+1)} = x_v^{(k)} + r_v^{(k)}$. Algorithm 4 shows the full procedure. Note that the only difference between Algorithms 3 and 4 is line 14. In Algorithm 4, an active node updates its own PageRank and the residuals of its outgoing neighbors.

4   Scheduling

Task scheduling, the order in which tasks are executed, can be very important to graph algorithms [11]. For example, in a data-driven PageRank, we see that whenever a node v's PageRank is updated, the total residual is decreased at least by $r_v(1 - \alpha)$. This implies that if we process "large residual" nodes first, the algorithm might converge faster. Thus, we can define a node v's priority p_v to be the residual per unit work, i.e., $p_v = r_v/d_v$ where $d_v = |\mathcal{S}_v| + |\mathcal{T}_v|$

for the pull-push-based PageRank, and $d_v = |\mathcal{T}_v|$ in the push-based algorithm. Realizing the potential benefits in convergence requires priority scheduling. In priority scheduling, each task is assigned a value, the priority, and scheduled in increasing (or decreasing) order. More sophisticated schedulers allow modifying the priority of existing tasks, but this is an expensive operation not commonly supported in parallel systems. Practical priority schedulers have to trade off several factors: efficiency, communication (and thus scaling), priority fidelity, and set-semantics. In general, both priority fidelity and set-semantics require significant global knowledge and communication, thus are not scalable. To investigate the sensitivity of PageRank to different design choices in a priority scheduler, we use two different designs: one which favors priority fidelity but gives up set-semantics and one which preserves set-semantics at the expense of priority fidelity. We compare these with scalable non-priority schedulers to see if the improved convergence outweighs the increased cost of priority scheduling.

The first scheduler we use is the scalable, NUMA-aware OBIM priority scheduler [7]. This scheduler uses an approximate consensus protocol to inform a per-thread choice to search for stealable high-priority work or to operate on local near-high-priority work. Various underlying data-structures and stealing patterns are aware of the machine's memory topology and optimized to maximize information propagation while minimizing cache coherence cost. OBIM favors keeping all threads operating on high priority work and does not support either set-semantics or updating the priority of existing tasks. To handle this, tasks are created for PageRank every time a node's priority changes, potentially generating duplicate tasks in the scheduler. Tasks with outdated priorities are quickly filtered out at execution time (a process which takes only a few instructions).

The second scheduler we use is a bulk-synchronous priority scheduler. This scheduler operates in rounds. Each round, all items with priority above a threshold are executed. Generated tasks and unexecuted items are placed in the next round. The range and mean are computed for the tasks, allowing the threshold to be chosen for each round based on the distribution of priorities observed for that round. This organization makes allowing priority updates simple, priorities are recomputed every round. Further, set-semantics may be trivially maintained. However, to minimize the overhead of bulk-synchronous execution, each round must have sufficient work to amortize the barrier synchronization. This produces a schedule of tasks which may deviate noticeably from the user requested order.

We also consider FIFO- and LIFO-like schedules (parallel schedulers cannot both scale and preserve exact FIFO and LIFO order). It is obvious that a LIFO scheduler is generally bad for PageRank. Processing nodes after a single neighbor is visited will process the node once for each in-neighbor. FIFO schedulers provide time for a node to accumulate pending changes from many neighbors before being processed. We use a NUMA-aware scheduler, similar to that from Galois and QThreads, to do scalable, fast FIFO-like scheduling.

5   Related Work

Our approaches of considering three different algorithm design axes are mainly motivated by the Tao analysis [12] where the concepts of topology-driven and data-driven algorithms have been studied in the context of amorphous data-parallelism. While Tao analysis has been proposed for a general parallel programming framework, our analysis is geared more towards designing new scalable data mining algorithms.

For scalable parallel computing, many different types of parallel programming models have been proposed, e.g., Galois [10], Ligra [13], GraphLab [8], Priter [15], and Maiter [16]. Since PageRank is a popular benchmark for parallel programming models, various versions of PageRank have been implemented in different parallel platforms in a rather ad hoc manner. Also, in data mining communities, PageRank has been extensively studied, and many different approximate algorithms (e.g., [1,6]) have been developed over the years [3]. The Gauss–Seidel style update of PageRank is studied in [9], and parallel distributed PageRank also has been developed [5]. Our PageRank formulations can be considered as some variations of these previous studies. Our contribution in this paper is to systematically analyze and discuss various PageRank implementations in the perspective of designing scalable graph mining methodologies.

Even though we have focused our discussion on PageRank in this manuscript, our approaches can be easily extended to other data mining algorithms. For example, in semi-supervised learning, label propagation is a well-known method [2] which involves fairly similar computations as PageRank. We expect that our data-driven formulations can be applied to the label propagation method. Also, it has been shown that there is a close relationship between personalized PageRank and community detection [1,14]. So, parallel data-driven community detection can be another interesting application of our analysis.

6   Experimental Results

Experimental Setup. To see the performance and scaling sensitivity of PageRank to the design considerations in this paper, we implement a variety of PageRank algorithms, trying different scheduling and data access patterns. All implementations are written using the Galois System [10]. Table 1 summarizes the design choices for each implementation. Pseudo-code and more detailed discussions of each appear in previous sections. We also compare our results to a third-party baseline, namely GraphLab, varying such parameters as are available in that implementation. For all experiments, we use $\alpha = 0.85$, $\epsilon = 0.01$. We use a 4 socket Xeon E7-4860 running at 2.27 GHz with 10 cores per socket and 128 GB RAM. GraphLab was run in multi-threaded mode.

Datasets. We use four real-world networks, given in Table 2. Twitter and Friendster are social networks, and pld and sd1 are hyperlink graphs. These graphs range from about 600 million edges to 3.6 billion edges. These range in size for in-memory compressed sparse row representations from 2.7 GB to 14 GB for

Table 1. Summary of algorithm design choices

Algorithm	Activation	Access	Schedule
dd-push	Data-driven	Push	FIFOs w/ Stealing
dd-push-prs	Data-driven	Push	Bulk-sync Priority
dd-push-prt	Data-driven	Push	Async Priority
dd-pp-rsd	Data-driven	Pull-Push	FIFOs w/ Stealing
dd-pp-prs	Data-driven	Pull-Push	Bulk-sync Priority
dd-pp-prt	Data-driven	Pull-Push	Async Priority
dd-basic	Data-driven	Pull	FIFOs w/ Stealing
power-iter	Topology	Pull	Load Balancer

the directed graph. Most of the algorithms require tracking both in-edges and out-edges, making the effective in-memory size approximately twice as large.

Table 2. Input graphs

	# nodes	# edges	CSR size	Source
pld	39M	623M	2.7G	www.webdatacommons.org/hyperlinkgraph/
sd1	83M	1,937M	7.9G	www.webdatacommons.org/hyperlinkgraph/
Twitter	51M	3,228M	13G	www.twitter.mpi-sws.org/
Friendster	67M	3,623M	14G	www.archive.org/details/friendster-dataset-201107

Results. Figure 1 shows runtime, self-relative scalability, and speedup against the best single-threaded algorithm for the pld and twitter graphs. In Table 3, the final speedups are shown on the other inputs. We note that GraphLab ran out of memory for all but the smallest (pld) input. On pld, the serial GraphLab performance was approximately the same as the closest Galois implementation, power-iter, but GraphLab scaled significantly worse. Several broad patterns can be seen in the results. First, all data-driven implementations outperform topology implementation. The best data-driven PageRank implementation is 28x faster than GraphLab, and 10–20x faster than Galois power-iter, depending on the thread count. Second, push-only implementations outperform pull-push implementations which outperform a pure pull-based version. Finally, priority-scheduled versions scale better but perform worse than a fast, non-priority scheduler.

One surprising result is that pulling to compute PageRank and pushing residuals outperforms a pure pull-based version (dd-pp-* vs. dd-basic). The read-mostly nature of pull-based algorithms are generally more cache friendly. Push-based algorithms have a much larger write-set per iteration, and writes to common locations fundamentally do not scale. The extra cost of the pushes, however, is made up by a reduction in the number of tasks. Table 4 shows the number of

Table 3. Speedup on 40 threads relative to best serial on sd1 and friendster (frd)

	dd-push	dd-push-prs	dd-push-prt	dd-pp-rsd	dd-pp-prs	dd-pp-prt	dd-basic	power-iter
sd1	20.9	21.8	13.7	10.9	9.1	7.0	6.5	1.4
frd	18.5	17.1	9.0	14.7	11.5	6.2	9.2	6.1

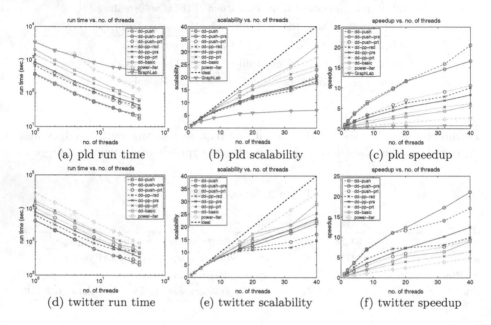

(a) pld run time   (b) pld scalability   (c) pld speedup

(d) twitter run time   (e) twitter scalability   (f) twitter speedup

Fig. 1. Runtime, scalability and speedup on pld and twitter graphs. Our data-driven, push-based PageRank achieves the best speedup.

completed tasks for each algorithm, and we see that pull-push methods (dd-pp-rsd) lead to 70–80% reduction in the number of tasks executed (compared to dd-basic). The pushing of residual allows a node to selectively activate a neighbor, and thus greatly reduces the total work performed (effectively, PageRanks are only computed when they are needed). On the other hand, the basic pull algorithm must unconditionally generate tasks for each of a node's neighbors when the node is updated. It is more understandable, though, that the push-only version outperforms all others. The pushing of residual is equivalent to the computation of PageRank deltas, thus, the pull can be eliminated, with no extra cost. This both reduces the number of edges inspected for every node, from in and out to just out, and reduces the total computation (instructions). Serially, a deterministic scheduler processes the same nodes, thus it does not save on total number of tasks, as can be seen in Table 4 rows for dd-push and dd-pp-rsd. The variation in those rows is due to the variation in scheduling order, especially at higher thread counts, though the variation is relatively minor.

Table 4. The number of completed tasks (unit: 10^6)

Threads	pld 1	40	sd1 1	40	Twitter 1	40	Friendster 1	40
dd-push	134	133	282	273	393	417	476	581
dd-push-prs	330	319	758	740	888	850	1076	1069
dd-push-prt	246	244	538	535	395	418	504	619
dd-pp-rsd	131	130	279	271	386	410	473	540
dd-pp-prs	311	303	712	716	963	835	1239	1212
dd-pp-prt	138	136	289	286	394	419	489	611
dd-basic	655	536	1029	896	1629	1526	1482	1356
power-iter	2606	2606	6716	6716	4297	4297	3104	3104

In Table 4, all reported numbers include all tasks (nodes) considered to make scheduling decisions. For *-prt methods, this includes the nodes which are duplicates in the worklist. For *-prs methods, this includes each round's examination of all the nodes in the worklist to pick the priority threshold. Priority scheduling favoring priority order, *-prt, shows the high cost of duplicate items in the worklist. This priority scheduler must insert duplicate tasks every time a node moves to a new priority bin. This means that many tasks are useless, they discover as their first action that there is nothing to do and complete. Figure 1 shows that this has a distinct time cost. Although filtering out duplicates is not expensive, the total work doing so is significant. Priority scheduling favoring set semantics, *-prs, also must examine a significant number of nodes to determine which tasks to pick at each scheduling round. We observe that the total number of nodes in the worklist decreases rapidly, making the working set after several rounds significantly smaller than the entire graph. This boost in locality helps offset the extra data accesses.

It is interesting to see that optimizing for cache behavior (pull-based) may not always be as effective as optimizing for pushing maximum information quickly (push-based). The push-only PageRank (dd-push-*) is entirely read-write access, while the pull-only version (dd-basic) does one write per node processed. In general, read-mostly access patterns are significantly more cache and coherence friendly. From this perspective, the pull-push versions, dd-pp-*, should be worst as they have the read set of the pull versions and the write set of the push versions. The extra writes are not just an alternate implementation of the PageRank update, but rather influence the scheduling of tasks. The extra writes weigh nodes, allowing nodes to only be processed when profitable. This improved scheduling makes up for the increased write load. Given the scheduling benefits of the residual push, it is easy to see that the push-only version is superior to the pull-push version as it reduces the memory load and work per iteration. We do note that when looking at the self-relative scalability of the implementations, the read-mostly algorithms, while slower, have better scalability than the push and pull-push variants.

Table 5. Runtime of different PageRank implementations on pld dataset

	GraphLab					Galois			
Threads	sync	async-fifo	async-qfifo	async-sweep	async-prt	power-iter	dd-basic	dd-pp-prt	dd-push
40	478 secs.	500 secs.	788 secs.	4,186 secs.	> 4 hrs.	132 secs.	62 secs.	58 secs.	17 secs.
32	496 secs.	580 secs.	804 secs.	5,162 secs.	> 4 hrs.	155 secs.	82 secs.	67 secs.	22 secs.
16	594 secs.	618 secs.	970 secs.	9,156 secs.	> 4 hrs.	299 secs.	140 secs.	118 secs.	36 secs.
8	845 secs.	898 secs.	1,292 secs.	> 4 hrs.	> 4 hrs.	510 secs.	269 secs.	193 secs.	53 secs.
1	3,332 secs.	5,194 secs.	5,098 secs.	> 4 hrs.	> 4 hrs.	3,650 secs.	2,004 secs.	1,415 secs.	355 secs

Third Party Comparison. Table 5 shows a comparison between our data-driven PageRank algorithms (implemented using Galois) and GraphLab's PageRank implementations when varying the scheduling on pld dataset. GraphLab supports different schedulers, though we find the simple synchronous one the best. We note that the GraphLab's asynchronous method refers to a Gauss–Seidel style solver, which still is a bulk-synchronous, topology-driven approach. The power-iter version (in Galois) is actually a classic synchronous implementation in this sense, but still notably faster. While GraphLab's topology-driven synchronous implementation has similar single threaded performance to the Galois topology-driven synchronous implementation, power-iter scales much better than GraphLab. Also, all the data-driven implementations (dd-*) are much faster than GraphLab's PageRank implementations.

7   Discussion

Priority scheduling needs some algorithmic margin to be competitive as it is more costly. While it is not surprising that priority scheduling is slower than simple scalable scheduling, this has some important consequences. First, the benefit is dependent on both algorithmic factors and input characteristics. When scheduling changes the asymptotic complexity of an algorithm, there can be huge margins available. In PageRank, there is a theoretical margin available, but it is relatively small. This limits the extra computation that can be spent on scheduling overhead without hurting performance. Secondly, the margin available depends on input characteristics. For many analytic algorithms, scheduling increases in importance as the diameter of the graph increases. Since PageRank is often run on power-law style graphs with low diameter, we expect a small margin available from priority scheduling.

Good priority schedulers can scale competitively with general purpose schedulers. We observe that multiple priority scheduler implementations scale well. We implement two very different styles of priority schedulers which pick different points in the design and feature space. This is encouraging as it leads us to believe that such richer semantic building blocks can be used by algorithm designers. PageRank updates priorities often, a use case which is hard to support efficiently and scalably. Even many high-performance, serial priority queues do not support this operation. Constructing a concurrent, scalable priority scheduler which maintains set semantics by adjusting priorities for existing items in the scheduler is an open question. The reason is simply one of global knowledge. Knowing whether to insert an item or whether it is already scheduled and thus only needs its priority adjusted requires global knowledge of the system. Maintaining and updating global knowledge concurrently in a NUMA system is rarely scalable. For scalability, practical implementations will contain multiple queues, meaning that not only does one need to track whether a task is scheduled, but on which queue the task is scheduled. The scheduler we produced for *-prs stores set semantics information by marking nodes in the graph and periodically rechecks priority. This essentially introduces latency between updating a priority and having the scheduler see the new priority. The amount of latency depends on how many iterations proceed before rechecking. This number determines the overhead of the scheduler.

8   Conclusions

Although PageRank is a simple graph analytic algorithm, there are many interesting implementation details one needs to consider to achieve a high-performance implementation. We show that data-driven implementations are significantly faster than traditional power iteration methods. PageRank has a simple vertex update equation. However, this update can be mapped to the graph in several ways, changing how and when information flows through the graph, which vary significantly in performance. Within this space, one can also profitably consider the order in which updates occur to maximize convergence speed. While we investigate these implementation variants for PageRank, seeing performance improvements of 28x over standard power iterations, these considerations can apply to many other convergence-based graph analytic algorithms.

Acknowledgments. This research was supported by NSF grants CCF-1117055 and CCF-1320746 to ID, and by NSF grants CNS-1111766 and XPS-1337281 to KP.

References

1. Andersen, R., Chung, F., Lang, K.: Local graph partitioning using PageRank vectors. In: FOCS, pp. 475–486 (2006)
2. Bengio, Y., Delalleau, O., Le Roux, N.: Label Propagation and Quadratic Criterion. MIT Press, Cambridge (2006)
3. Berkhin, P.: A survey on PageRank computing. Internet Math. **2**, 73–120 (2005)
4. Brin, S., Page, L.: The anatomy of a large-scale hypertextual web search engine. Comput. Network. ISDN Syst. **30**(1–7), 107–117 (1998)
5. Gleich, D.F., Zhukov, L., Berkhin, P.: Fast parallel PageRank: A linear system approach. Technical report YRL-2004-038, Yahoo! Research Labs (2004)
6. Jeh, G., Widom, J.: Scaling personalized web search. In: WWW, pp. 271–279 (2003)
7. Lenharth, A., Nguyen, D., Pingali, K.: Priority queues are not good concurrent priority schedulers. In: Träff, J.L., Hunold, S., Versaci, F. (eds.) Euro-Par 2015. LNCS, vol. 9233, pp. 209–221. Springer, Heidelberg (2015)

8. Low, Y., Bickson, D., Gonzalez, J., Guestrin, C., Kyrola, A., Hellerstein, J.M.: Distributed graphlab: a framework for machine learning and data mining in the cloud. In: VLDB Endowment, pp. 716–727 (2012)

9. McSherry, F.: A uniform approach to accelerated PageRank computation. In: WWW, pp. 575–582 (2005)

10. Nguyen, D., Lenharth, A., Pingali, K.: A lightweight infrastructure for graph analytics. In: SOSP, pp. 456–471 (2013)

11. Nguyen, D., Pingali, K.: Synthesizing concurrent schedulers for irregular algorithms. In: ASPLOS, pp. 333–344 (2011)

12. Pingali, K., Nguyen, D., Kulkarni, M., Burtscher, M., Hassaan, M.A., Kaleem, R., Lee, T.H., Lenharth, A., Manevich, R., Mndez-Lojo, M., Prountzos, D., Sui, X.: The Tao of parallelism in algorithms. In: PLDI, pp. 12–25 (2011)

13. Shun, J., Blelloch, G.E.: Ligra: a lightweight graph processing framework for shared memory. In: PPoPP, pp. 135–146 (2013)

14. Whang, J.J., Gleich, D., Dhillon, I.S.: Overlapping community detection using seed set expansion. In: CIKM, pp. 2099–2108 (2013)

15. Zhang, Y., Gao, Q., Gao, L., Wang, C.: Priter: a distributed framework for prioritizing iterative computations. IEEE Trans. Parallel Distrib. Syst. **24**(9), 1884–1893 (2013)

16. Zhang, Y., Gao, Q., Gao, L., Wang, C.: Maiter: an asynchronous graph processing framework for delta-based accumulative iterative computation. IEEE Trans. Parallel Distrib. Syst. **25**(8), 2091–2100 (2014)

How Many Threads will be too Many?
On the Scalability of OpenMP Implementations

Christian Iwainsky[1]([✉]), Sergei Shudler[2], Alexandru Calotoiu[2],
Alexandre Strube[3], Michael Knobloch[3], Christian Bischof[1], and Felix Wolf[1]

[1] Technische Universität Darmstadt, 64293 Darmstadt, Germany
{iwainsky,bischof}@sc.tu-darmstadt.de, wolf@cs.tu-darmstadt.de
[2] German Research School for Simulation Sciences, 52062 Aachen, Germany
{s.shudler,a.calotoiu}@grs-sim.de
[3] Forschungszentrum Jülich, 52425 Jülich, Germany
{a.strube,m.knobloch}@fz-juelich.de

Abstract. Exascale systems will exhibit much higher degrees of parallelism both in terms of the number of nodes and the number of cores per node. OpenMP is a widely used standard for exploiting parallelism on the level of individual nodes. Although successfully used on today's systems, it is unclear how well OpenMP implementations will scale to much higher numbers of threads. In this work, we apply automated performance modeling to examine the scalability of OpenMP constructs across different compilers and platforms. We ran tests on Intel Xeon multi-board, Intel Xeon Phi, and Blue Gene with compilers from GNU, IBM, Intel, and PGI. The resulting models reveal a number of scalability issues in implementations of OpenMP constructs and show unexpected differences between compilers.

Keywords: Performance modeling · OpenMP · Scalability

1 Introduction

In recent years, we saw a clear trend towards systems with more processing cores per node. All types of processors used in high-performance computing, including CPUs, GPUs, or accelerators such as Intel Xeon Phi, are nowadays either multicore or manycore processors. As a result of this trend, the degree of intra-node parallelism in supercomputers is on the rise. Before reaching exascale, it will still have to grow by one or two orders of magnitude [1]. However, this poses the question whether current implementations of multithreaded programming models can scale to the large number of threads this will entail.

In this paper, we try to answer this question for OpenMP, a mature and widely used API for multithreaded programming, and evaluate whether current implementations would scale to much larger numbers of threads. To this end, we adopt the automated performance-modeling method by Calotoiu et al. [2] and generate empirical scaling models of the most common OpenMP constructs.

© Springer-Verlag Berlin Heidelberg 2015
J.L. Träff et al. (Eds.): Euro-Par 2015, LNCS 9233, pp. 451–463, 2015.
DOI: 10.1007/978-3-662-48096-0_35

The method takes measurements of execution time or other metrics at smaller scales as input and produces human-readable growth functions as output which describe the behavior for larger scales. To capture the cost of individual OpenMP constructs, we extended the EPCC OpenMP micro-benchmark suite [3,4] and combined it with the modeling toolchain. We evaluated OpenMP implementations from GNU, IBM, Intel, and PGI on Xeon, Xeon Phi, and Blue Gene. Our main discoveries are:

- Previously unknown and potentially serious scalability limitations in implementations from GNU, IBM, and PGI
- Different behavioral classes depending on whether the number of threads is a power of two or not

Among all the evaluated compilers, the GNU compiler is the most problematic in terms of scalability.

The next section introduces the model generator we used to create the scaling models and how it was customized for our study. In Sect. 3, we explain the EPCC OpenMP benchmark suite along with our own extensions. Experimental results for selected OpenMP constructs with particularly noteworthy behavior are presented in Sect. 4. Then, we discuss related work in Sect. 5 and draw our conclusion in Sect. 6.

2   Model Generation

The approach underlying our study rests on the identification of *scalability bugs* using automated performance modeling [2]. A scalability bug is a part of a program whose scaling behavior is unintentionally poor, that is, much worse than expected. As computing hardware moves towards exascale, developers need early feedback on the scalability of their software design so that they can adapt it to the requirements of larger problem and machine sizes.

The input of the model generator is a set of performance measurements where only one relevant parameter, in our case the number of threads, is varied while all others are kept constant. The idea is to create functions that describe how a metric, such as the execution time, the number of floating point operations, or the number of bytes injected into the network, changes as the chosen parameter is modified. Depending on the availability of measurements, such models can be created for each function in a program or just one particular code region of interest.

When generating performance models, we exploit the observation that they are usually composed of a finite number n of terms, involving powers and logarithms of the parameter x of interest:

$$f(x) = \sum_{k=1}^{n} c_k \cdot x^{i_k} \cdot log_2^{j_k}(x)$$

This representation is, of course, not exhaustive, but works in most practical scenarios, since it is a consequence of how most computer algorithms are designed. We call it the *performance model normal form* (PMNF).

In this paper, we vary the number of threads t and model the time overhead of OpenMP constructs, i.e., the thread-management time lost in the OpenMP runtime system when executing certain constructs. While changes of the arithmetic intensity may restrict models of user code to specific segments of the domain of t [5], we believe that such effects do not have to be considered when judging the scalability of OpenMP runtime operations. Their critical resource is almost always the latency of memory accesses and, in particular, of cache coherence protocols. Moreover, our experience suggests that neither the sets I, J chosen from the set $\mathbb{Q}$ of rational numbers from which the exponents i_k and j_k are chosen nor the number of terms n have to be arbitrarily large or random to achieve a good fit. A possible assignment of all i_k and j_k in a PMNF expression is called a *model hypothesis*. Trying all hypotheses one by one, we find coefficients c_k with optimal fit. Then we apply cross-validation [6] to select the hypothesis with the best fit across all candidates.

For this study, we selected $n = 2$, $I = \left\{ 0, \frac{1}{4}, \frac{1}{3}, \frac{1}{2}, \frac{2}{3}, \frac{3}{4}, 1, \frac{5}{4}, \frac{4}{3}, \frac{3}{2}, \frac{5}{3}, \frac{7}{4}, 2 \right\}$, and $J = \{0, 1, 2\}$. Our choices for I and J reflect a range of behaviors, from perfect to poor scalability, in 39 shades (13 options for i times 3 for j). In the case of OpenMP constructs, we are not aware of any literature that specifies precise scalability expectations. This is why we operate under the not uncommon assumption that anything significantly worse than logarithmic is unacceptable on the path towards exascale. Given the jitter present in measurements of OpenMP constructs with their minuscule execution times, we only allow one active term plus a constant. Trying to model behaviors past the leading term is likely to capture only noise. Note that we are not trying to create accurate models for OpenMP constructs but rather want to draw the attention to unscalable behavior. Making accurate predictions for the execution times of OpenMP constructs at larger scales is beyond the scope of this work.

3   Benchmark Design

Our goal is to investigate the costs of individual OpenMP constructs for different compilers with a focus on the OpenMP runtime system, disregarding actual workloads. For this purpose, we define time-based metrics that characterize the behavior of OpenMP constructs and that can be further used as an input to the model generator. Because initial experiments indicated a high noise-to-measurement ratio on some of the target platforms, we filter the raw data to reduce noise and remove extreme outliers.

3.1   EPCC OpenMP Micro-Benchmarks

The EPCC OpenMP micro-benchmark suite [3,4] is an established and comprehensive collection of benchmarks that covers almost all OpenMP constructs. The micro-benchmarks compare the cost of the constructs by measuring the difference between a parallelized workload and the workload itself, while the workload per thread is kept constant. Multiple executions (inner repetitions) of a given OpenMP construct scale the cost of the construct for easier measurement and comparison with the reference workload. This inner measurement is again repeated multiple times (outer repetitions) to calculate the average and the standard deviation of the target construct. We modified the EPCC measurement system to directly interface with our model generator.

3.2 Custom Benchmarks

While the EPCC benchmarks are well-designed to capture the overhead of copying data environments, they are less suited to precisely capture synchronization overheads. Since they do not measure the costs of individual OpenMP constructs directly, the resulting timings are much more prone to noise. To measure the costs of OpenMP constructs in isolation, we therefore had to develop additional benchmarks, which are designed as follows: (i) compute local clock offsets between master and all the other threads; (ii) synchronize threads using adjusted window-based mechanism (see next sub-section); (iii) take a per-thread time stamp and call the OpenMP construct; (iv) take another per-thread time stamp directly after the construct, or in the case of `parallel` or `for`, directly in the construct. From these measurements, we then derive our metrics, providing information on minimum construct cost (first out - last in), average cost (average of end times - last in), etc. For example, in this way we can deduce the minimum time a barrier was active across all threads.

3.3 Window-Based Adjusted Synchronization Mechanism

The quality of our models depends on how accurately we can measure the timings of OpenMP constructs. All the threads should enter the construct at the same time, such that we have a uniform start time that does not depend on the particular construct being measured. A simple barrier synchronization is not enough, since the only guarantee it provides is that all threads will have arrived at the barrier before any thread leaves it. The solution, therefore, is to use a synchronization mechanism that forces all the threads to exit the synchronization construct at the same time. In this study, we use a variation of the window-based synchronization mechanism for MPI collective operations [7]. This mechanism forces the threads to wait until the agreed time-point is reached and only then allows them to enter the target construct.

The window-based synchronization mechanism assumes that all threads use the same clock. However, we discovered that this assumption does not apply to all test platforms equally. On some platforms, such as the BCS systems of RWTH Aachen University, which is described in Sect. 4.1, which consist of multiple motherboards, the high-precision timer used for our measurements was not well synchronized across all boards. Since we observed considerable clock skew, we had to calibrate clock offsets relative to the master thread using the cache coherency mechanisms as communication medium. This type of synchronization is similar to the NTP protocol [8].

4 Results

For the sake of brevity, we focus on a few very important OpenMP constructs: parallel, barrier, single, and for with all three schedule types (static, dynamic and guided) and the firstprivate modifier. Since our benchmarks consume a negligible amount of memory bandwidth, we can safely ignore bandwidth saturation effects. This also applies to the firstprivate measurement, which, in our case, uses a single eight-byte variable, which is sure to fit in the cache. We specified a chunk size of 16 for all loop schedules.

All models shown in the following sections depend on the number of threads as their sole parameter. Table 1 shows the performance models generated for the above-mentioned constructs together with their adjusted coefficient of determination as an indicator of model quality. Figures 2, 3 and 4 provide fit-comparisons between measurement and model. In general, we consider models with $\hat{R}^2 \geqslant 0.95$ valid descriptions of the observed behavior and define constructs with valid models of significantly faster than logarithmic growth to exhibit problematic scaling behavior.

4.1 Setup

We conducted our study on three different systems: (i) a node of the BCS cluster at RWTH Aachen University, (ii) an Intel Xeon Phi 7120 coprocessor, and (iii) a node of an IBM Blue Gene/Q system. The BCS cluster [9] is an Intel Xeon X7550-based hierarchical NUMA machine, where four boards with four sockets each are connected via the Bull Coherence Switch (BCS) to create a shared-memory domain of 128 physical cores. The Xeon Phi and the Blue Gene/Q node have 61 and 16 physical cores, respectively, with 4-way simultaneous multi-threading (SMT), i.e., four hardware threads per core. We used the GNU 4.9, IBM XL 12.1, Intel 15, and PGI 14 compilers. To reduce the effects of noise, we configured all benchmarks to generate at least 100 individual data points for each metric, i.e., we set the outer-repetitions of EPCC to 100 and compiled our own benchmarks with 100 internal repetitions after the warmup phase. We ran our benchmarks using numbers of threads that are either a power of two, multiples of eight, or a sequence between two and the number of physical cores of a single CPU. Each benchmark was executed in both spread or close configuration using OMP_PROC_BIND, with an additional binding to cores via OMP_PLACES="threads". Afterwards, we eliminated outliers by removing the 25 % best and 25 % worst values of a series. Since the close measurements were noisier than the spread measurements on Intel platforms and largely identical to spread measurements on Blue Gene, we exclusively focus on spread in this paper.

4.2 GNU 4.9, Intel 15, and PGI 14 Compilers on BCS

Parallel. We obtain a timestamp on the master thread just before entering the parallel construct and on each thread when it is ready for work in the parallel region. Then, we calculate the difference between the master timestamp before entering the construct and the average of all timestamps after entering the construct. We expect either close to constant behavior, e.g., if a thread pool is used, or logarithmic behavior otherwise, as one could ideally implement a tree-based thread-creation scheme.

Unfortunately, indiscriminately feeding data points for all thread counts into the model generator did not yield any meaningful models. A subsequent manual analysis of the available data showed separate trend functions for different subsets of the data: for powers of two and for multiples of 16 with and without an eight-thread offset. We call these classes $PO2$ $(t = 2^x)$, $EVEN$ $(t = 16x$ but $t \neq 2^x)$, and ODD $(t = 16x + 8$ but $t \neq 2^x)$ with $x \in \{0, 1, .., 7\}$. The effects observed for $EVEN$ and ODD are most likely the result of the multi-board hardware configuration of the BCS system. However, regardless of internal hardware boundaries, $PO2$ measurements consistently follow their characteristic pattern even if these thread counts are multiples of 16 with and without an eight-thread offset.

For example, as we can see in Figs. 2c and d, the behavior in the ODD case (half-circles) precludes the existence of a unifying simple model for the GNU compiler. Models for $EVEN$ have very low $\hat{R}^2$ and will not be considered. Note that the number of thread counts in EVEN is very small because many multiples of 16 are at the same time powers of two and, thus, belong to a different behavioral class. In the remainder of the paper, we therefore concentrate exclusively on $PO2$ and ODD. In contrast to GNU and PGI, the Intel compiler shows no observable differences between $PO2$ and ODD configurations. We therefore omit ODD models for Intel on BCS in Table 1 and Fig. 2.

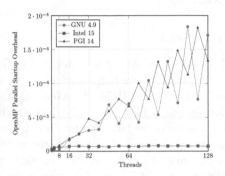

Fig. 1. Measurements of `parallel` on the BCS node in spread configuration. To make trends or their absence more visible, we the connected the measurement points with solid lines.

Obviously, not all compliers are sensitive to the machine architecture.

In Fig. 1, we see notable differences between GNU, Intel, and PGI compilers. Using the $PO2$ and ODD configurations, we obtain two separate models each for both the GNU and the PGI compiler (Fig. 2a). These four models show super-logarithmic scaling behavior. In contrast, the Intel compiler exhibits a uniform trend, but with low $\hat{R}^2$. The almost constant time visible in Fig. 1 for Intel suggests the use of some form of stand-by threads that can be cost-efficiently activated.

Barrier. We observe two different behavioral classes for the GNU compiler, while we observe similarly uniform behaviors for Intel and PGI (Fig. 2b). The $PO2$ implementation of GNU shows super-linear growth in contrast to its somewhat

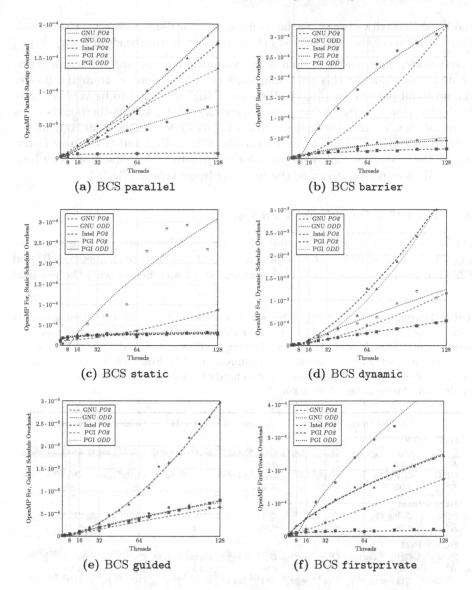

Fig. 2. Measurements (points) and models (lines) on the BCS node.

better-scaling *ODD* implementation. All but PGI *ODD* show worse-than-logarithmic growth, indicating that logarithmic implementations are possible.

Loop Schedules. For the `static` schedule (Fig. 2c), we expect constant overhead as no synchronization between threads is necessary and for `dynamic` (Fig. 2d) and `guided` (Fig. 2e) some thread-dependent growth for synchronizing the assignment of the remaining iterations. We obtained no acceptable *PO2* models for

Intel and PGI with `static`, as the model generator did not detect a clear trend; visual analysis of the data suggests close to constant overheads (Fig. 2c).

Firstprivate. This modifier requires the compiler to broadcast the values of one or more variables (in this particular case an 8-byte double) from the master thread to all participant threads. We expect this operation to be very sensitive to the hardware, as the latency between cores, sockets, and motherboards plays a crucial role. The Intel compiler exhibits logarithmic overheads for copying the data to each thread, whereas the overheads of both PGI and GNU grow faster. Again, the GNU compiler shows two clearly separable behaviors. Models for Intel and PGI show no sensitivity to the BCS hardware layout (Fig. 2f).

4.3   Intel 15 Compiler on Xeon Phi

On Xeon Phi, we expect less noise and more scalable OpenMP constructs. In Fig. 3a, we observe distinct behaviors for the first 2 to 61 threads, between 62 and 122 threads, and between 123 to 244 threads. This coincides with the physical

Table 1. Scaling models for the BCS node, XeonPhi, and Blue Gene/Q. Measurements with a † were generated using EPCC, measurements with ⋆ were generated using our supplemental benchmarks. Each row showing models is followed by a row with the corresponding adjusted coefficient of determination ($\hat{R}^2$). Since we are only interested in the scaling behavior and do not strive to predict the overhead in absolute terms, all models are shown in big O notation.

	Parallel Open⋆	Barrier⋆	Dynamic 16†	Static 16†	Guided 16†	Firstprivate†
BCS - GNU						
PO2	$\mathcal{O}(t^{1.25})$	$\mathcal{O}(t^{1.33}\log t)$	$\mathcal{O}(t^{1.25}\log t)$	$\mathcal{O}(t^{1.33}\log t)$	$\mathcal{O}(t^{0.75}\log t)$	$\mathcal{O}(t)$
$\hat{R}^2$	0.99	0.99	0.99	0.98	0.99	0.99
ODD	$\mathcal{O}(t^{0.67})$	$\mathcal{O}(t^{0.5})$	$\mathcal{O}(t^{0.67}\log t)$	$\mathcal{O}(t^{1.25}\log t)$	$\mathcal{O}(t^{0.5}\log t)$	$\mathcal{O}(t^{0.5}\log t)$
$\hat{R}^2$	0.95	0.93	0.96	0.94	0.93	0.98
BCS - Intel						
PO2	$\mathcal{O}(\log t)$	$\mathcal{O}(t^{0.25})$	$\mathcal{O}(t)$	$\mathcal{O}(\log t)$	$\mathcal{O}(t)$	$\mathcal{O}(\log t)$
$\hat{R}^2$	0.78	0.98	0.99	0.84	0.99	0.94
BCS - PGI						
PO2	$\mathcal{O}(t^{0.67}\log t)$	$\mathcal{O}(\log^2 t)$	$\mathcal{O}(t^{1.25}\log t)$	$\mathcal{O}(\log t)$	$\mathcal{O}(t^{1.67})$	$\mathcal{O}(t^{0.67})$
$\hat{R}^2$	0.99	0.95	0.99	0.62	0.99	0.99
ODD	$\mathcal{O}(t\log t)$	$\mathcal{O}(t^{0.5}\log t)$	$\mathcal{O}(t^{1.5}\log t)$	$\mathcal{O}(t^{2.5})$	$\mathcal{O}(t^{1.67})$	$\mathcal{O}(t^{0.5}\log t)$
$\hat{R}^2$	0.97	0.90	0.99	0.50	0.99	0.89
XeonPhi - Intel						
PO2	$\mathcal{O}(t^{0.67})$	$\mathcal{O}(t^{0.5})$	$\mathcal{O}(t^{0.25})$	$\mathcal{O}(t^{1.5})$	$\mathcal{O}(t)$	$\mathcal{O}(t^{0.67})$
$\hat{R}^2$	0.97	0.99	0.65	0.75	0.99	0.98
LINEAR	$\mathcal{O}(t^{0.67})$	$\mathcal{O}(t^{0.5})$	$\mathcal{O}(\log t)$	$\mathcal{O}(t^{2.33})$	$\mathcal{O}(t)$	$\mathcal{O}(t^{0.67})$
$\hat{R}^2$	0.95	0.94	0.55	0.30	0.99	0.96
8X	$\mathcal{O}(\log^2 t)$	$\mathcal{O}(\log t)$	$\mathcal{O}(t^{1.25}\log t)$	$\mathcal{O}(t^{0.75}\log t)$	$\mathcal{O}(t)$	$\mathcal{O}(\log^2 t)$
$\hat{R}^2$	0.95	0.86	0.92	0.70	0.99	0.94
Blue Gene/Q - IBM XL						
PO2	$\mathcal{O}(t^{1.25})$	$\mathcal{O}(t^{1.33}\log t)$	$\mathcal{O}(t^{2.33})$	$\mathcal{O}(t^{2.33})$	$\mathcal{O}(t^2)$	$\mathcal{O}(t^{1.25})$
$\hat{R}^2$	0.99	0.99	0.99	0.99	0.99	0.99

structure of the Xeon Phi, which has 61 cores supporting four hardware threads each. The first 122 threads show less spread in comparison with thread counts above 122. Because the erratic runtimes above 122 threads prevent the use of our model generator, we model the first two clusters only. We consider the first 2–61 threads in linear fashion, called *LINEAR*, and multiples of eight up to and including 120 threads, called *8X*. In addition, we also analyze powers of two up to and including 64 threads, again called *PO2*. All results are available in Table 1.

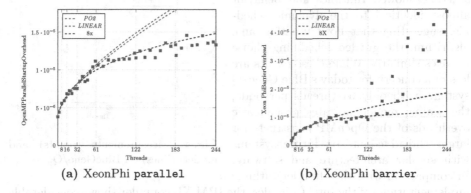

(a) XeonPhi `parallel`   (b) XeonPhi `barrier`

Fig. 3. Measurements (points) and models (lines) on XeonPhi.

Parallel. The *LINEAR* and *PO2* thread distributions have similar scalability models and closely model the first 61 threads. For thread counts beyond 61, the deviation becomes larger. The model derived from *8X* configurations captures the overall behavior of Xeon Phi thread creation quite well, including thread counts above 122. The erratic runtimes for thread counts above 122 (Fig. 3a) cannot be explained with our model normal form. When comparing the different configurations, models generated from *8X* base points seem to scale better.

Barrier. The behavior we observe is similar to the parallel construct. The *PO2*, *LINEAR* and *8X* configurations provide a good fit for their respective domains. The erratic behavior above 122 threads is even more dominant here, which is why again no models could be generated for this part of the domain (Fig. 3b). However, the measurements above 122 threads still suggest some undesirable performance effect, potentially resulting from Xeon Phi's internal network, something that is traditionally hard to model

4.4   IBM XL 12.1 Compiler on Blue Gene/Q

Blue Gene/Q nodes are single-socket systems without any explicit cache hierarchy. Analysis of our measurements showed very reliable data with very little noise and no indication of multiple algorithms or thread-count depended hardware scalability limitations. We therefore used only power-of-two configurations as input for our model generator.

Parallel and Barrier. Contrary to our expectations, either the IBM implementation of OpenMP or the Blue Gene/Q architecture exhibits problematic scaling behavior. We observe that metrics exhibit superlinear growth (see lower lines in Fig. 4). The model for the barrier exhibits similar behavior with just an order of magnitude lower overheads.

Loop Schedules. For `static` scheduling, which should have constant overhead, we detected non scalable growth. The `static` schedule showed runtimes and behavior almost identical to the dynamic schedule, suggesting that both use the same algorithm; the `guided` scheduling clause behaves similarly. While these results are less of a concern for today's Blue Gene/Q systems with only 64 threads per node, the scaling model indicates problematic overheads of the OpenMP constructs for larger thread counts on future systems with similar architecture and software. In comparison with the often logarithmic

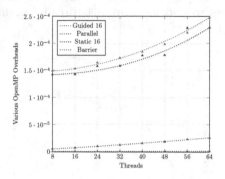

Fig. 4. Measurements (points) and models (lines) on BlueGene/Q.

implementations of the Intel Compiler, the IBM XL compiler shows considerable room for improvement.

5   Related Work

Performance models can provide important insights into application and systems. Manually-produced models were very effective in describing many qualities and characteristics of applications, systems, and even entire tool chains [10–12]. Recent work suggests to use source-code annotations [13] or specialized languages [14] to support developers in the creation of analytical performance models.

There are other automated modeling methods besides the one underlying our study. Many of these tools focus on learning the performance characteristics automatically using various machine-learning approaches [15]. Zhai et al. extrapolate single-node performance to complex parallel machines using a trace-driven network simulator [16], whereas Wu and Müller extrapolate traces to predict communications at larger scale [17]. Similar to our method, Carrington et al. extrapolate trace-based performance measurements using a set of canonical functions [18].

Several studies investigated the overheads of OpenMP constructs on various platforms [19–22]. Similar to our work, many of them used the EPCC OpenMP benchmark suite [4]. While they mainly concentrated on the implications the overhead of OpenMP may have on the scalability of scientific applications, our goal is to identify scalability issues in OpenMP implementations. One of the first performance evaluation of OpenMP on XeonPhi was performed by Cramer et al. [23]. Eichenberger and O'Brien evaluated the overhead of the OpenMP runtime on Blue Gene/Q [24].

6   Conclusion

In this work, we analyzed the scalability of OpenMP constructs using automatically generated empirical performance models. We conducted extensive evaluations of OpenMP implementations from Intel, GNU, PGI and IBM on Intel-based nodes as well as on IBM Blue Gene/Q nodes. In many cases, the behavior of OpenMP constructs deviated from our expectations and numerous scalability issues became apparent. We expected either logarithmic or constant growth of OpenMP overheads, but discovered mostly linear and super-linear growth. Neither of the evaluated compilers proved to be the best implementation in all situations. The Intel compiler showed the best absolute performance and scaling behavior for most of the metrics in our tests, but it was still surpassed by the PGI compiler on two occasions. Considering the increasing degree of intra-node parallelism, OpenMP compilers will have to tackle theses scalability issues in the future. Our benchmarking method is designed to support this process, as it can be used to continuously evaluate implementations as their scalability is improved.

Acknowledgment. This work was performed under the auspices of the DFG Priority Programme 1648 "Software for Exascale Computing" (SPPEXA). The authors thank Christian Terboven for the fruitful discussions on scalability expectations for OpenMP and for providing access to the BCS machine at RWTH Aachen University.

References

1. Stevens, R., et al.: Architectures and Technology for Extreme Scale Computing. Technical report, ASCR Scientific Grand Challenges Workshop Series, December 2009
2. Calotoiu, A., Hoefler, T., Poke, M., Wolf, F.: Using automated performance modeling to find scalability bugs in complex codes. In: Proceedings of the ACM/IEEE Conference on Supercomputing (SC 2013), p. 45 (2013)
3. Bull, J.M.: Measuring synchronisation and scheduling overheads in OpenMP. In: Proceedings of First European Workshop on OpenMP, pp. 99–105 (1999)
4. Bull, J.M., O'Neill, D.: A microbenchmark suite for OpenMP 2.0. ACM SIGARCH Comput. Archit. News **29**(5), 41–48 (2001)
5. Williams, S., Waterman, A., Patterson, D.: Roofline: an insightful visual performance model for multicore architectures. Commun. ACM **52**(4), 65–76 (2009)
6. Picard, R.R., Cook, R.D.: Cross-validation of regression models. J. Am. Stat. Assoc. **79**(387), 575–583 (1984)
7. Hoefler, T., Schneider, T., Lumsdaine, A.: Accurately measuring collective operations at massive scale. In: Proceedings of the IEEE International Parallel & Distributed Processing Symposium, IPDPS 2008, pp. 1–8 (2008)

8. Mills, D.L.: Internet time synchronization: the Network Time Protocol. IEEE Trans. Commun. **39**(10), 1482–1493 (1991)

9. Weyers, B., Terboven, C., Schmidl, D., Herber, J., Kuhlen, T.W., Müller, M.S., Hentschel, B.: Visualization of memory access behavior on hierarchical NUMA architectures. In: Proceedings of the First Workshop on Visual Performance Analysis, VPA 2014, Piscataway, NJ, USA, pp. 42–49. IEEE Press (2014)

10. Mathis, M.M., Amato, N.M., Adams, M.L.: A general performance model for parallel sweeps on orthogonal grids for particle transport calculations. Technical report, College Station, TX, USA (2000)

11. Pllana, S., Brandic, I., Benkner, S.: Performance modeling and prediction of parallel and distributed computing systems: a survey of the state of the art. In: Proceedings of the 1st International Conference on Complex, Intelligent and Software Intensive Systems (CISIS), pp. 279–284 (2007)

12. Petrini, F., Kerbyson, D.J., Pakin, S.: The case of the missing supercomputer performance: achieving optimal performance on the 8,192 processors of ASCI Q. In: Proceedings of the ACM/IEEE Conference on Supercomputing (SC 2003), p. 55 (2003)

13. Tallent, N.R., Hoisie, A.: Palm: easing the burden of analytical performance modeling. In: Proceedings of the International Conference on Supercomputing (ICS), pp. 221–230 (2014)

14. Spafford, K.L., Vetter, J.S.: Aspen: a domain specific language for performance modeling. In: Proceedings of the International Conference on High Performance Computing, Networking, Storage and Analysis. SC 2012, Los Alamitos, CA, USA, pp. 84:1–84:11. IEEE Computer Society Press (2012)

15. Lee, B.C., Brooks, D.M., de Supinski, B.R., Schulz, M., Singh, K., McKee, S.A.: Methods of inference and learning for performance modeling of parallel applications. In: Proceedings of the 12th ACM SIGPLAN Symposium on Principles and Practice of Parallel Programming (PPoPP 2007), pp. 249–258 (2007)

16. Zhai, J., Chen, W., Zheng, W.: PHANTOM: predicting performance of parallel applications on large-scale parallel machines using a single node. SIGPLAN Not. **45**(5), 305–314 (2010)

17. Wu, X., Mueller, F.: ScalaExtrap: trace-based communication extrapolation for SPMD programs. In: Proceedings of the 16th ACM Symposium on Principles and Practice of Parallel Programming (PPoPP 2011), pp. 113–122 (2011)

18. Carrington, L., Laurenzano, M., Tiwari, A.: Characterizing large-scale HPC applications through trace extrapolation. Parallel Process. Lett. **23**(4), 1340008 (2013). doi:10.1142/S0129626413400082

19. Fredrickson, N.R., Afsahi, A., Qian, Y.: Performance characteristics of OpenMP constructs, and application benchmarks on a large symmetric multiprocessor. In: Proceedings of the 17th Annual International Conference on Supercomputing, pp. 140–149. ACM (2003)

20. Fürlinger, K., Gerndt, M.: Analyzing overheads and scalability characteristics of OpenMP applications. In: Daydé, M., Palma, J.M.L.M., Coutinho, A.L.G.A., Pacitti, E., Lopes, J.C. (eds.) VECPAR 2006. LNCS, vol. 4395, pp. 39–51. Springer, Heidelberg (2007)

21. Liao, C., Liu, Z., Huang, L., Chapman, B.: Evaluating OpenMP on chip multithreading platforms. In: Mueller, M.S., Chapman, B.M., de Supinski, B.R., Malony, A.D., Voss, M. (eds.) IWOMP 2005/2006. LNCS, vol. 4315, pp. 178–190. Springer, Heidelberg (2008)

22. Bronevetsky, G., Gyllenhaal, J., de Supinski, B.R.: CLOMP: accurately character-
    izing OpenMP application overheads. In: Eigenmann, R., de Supinski, B.R. (eds.)
    IWOMP 2008. LNCS, vol. 5004, pp. 13–25. Springer, Heidelberg (2008)
23. Cramer, T., Schmidl, D., Klemm, M., an Mey, D.: OpenMP programming on
    Intel Xeon Phi coprocessors: an early performance comparison. In: Proceedings of
    the Many-core Applications Research Community (MARC) Symposium at RWTH
    Aachen University, pp. 38–44, November 2012
24. Eichenberger, A.E., O'Brien, K.: Experimenting with low-overhead OpenMP run-
    time on IBM Blue Gene/Q. IBM J. Res. Dev. **57**(1/2), 8–1 (2013)

Theory and Algorithms
for Parallel Computation

Efficient Nested Dissection for Multicore Architectures

Dominique LaSalle$^{(\boxtimes)}$ and George Karypis

Department of Computer Science and Engineering, University of Minnesota,
Minneapolis, MN 55455, USA
{lasalle,karypis}@cs.umn.edu

Abstract. Sparse matrices are common in scientific computing and
machine learning. By storing and processing only the non-zero elements
of a matrix containing mostly zeros, sparse matrix algorithms often
reduce computation and storage requirements of operations by an order
of complexity. The order of the rows and columns of the matrix can
have a significant impact on the efficiency of sparse direct methods. For
example, in a Cholesky decomposition, it is desirable to re-order the
input matrix so as to reduce the number of non-zeros in the factors. One
of the most effective methods for re-ordering is nested dissection, where
vertex separators are recursively found in the graph representation of
the matrix and are used to permute the rows and columns. In this work
we investigate the creation of vertex separators on shared memory parallel architectures and their use in nested dissection. We introduce a new
effective scheme for refining a vertex separator in parallel, and a specialized parallel task scheduling scheme for the nested dissection problem.
These algorithms have been implemented in the mt-Metis framework.
Our experiments show that mt-Metis is 1.5× faster than ParMetis while
producing orderings with 3.7 % fewer non-zeros and 14.0 % fewer operations.

1 Introduction

Sparse matrices are used in a variety of scientific computing and machine learning applications. Because sparse matrices do not store the zero-valued elements
which make up the majority of their entries, their use results in significant savings
of storage space as well as computation. Fill reducing orderings are permutations
on the input matrix which decrease the number of non-zero elements (fill-in) in
the output matrix of direct sparse methods [6]. For a Cholesky decomposition, we
want to find a re-ordering such that the Cholesky factor will have as little fill-in
as possible. One of the most effective methods for creating a fill reducing ordering is that of nested dissection [9,10]. In nested dissection, balanced minimum
vertex separators are recursively found in the graph representing the non-zero
pattern of the sparse matrix. The quality of the resulting ordering depends upon
being able to find small separators.

The problem of finding minimum size balanced vertex separators is known to
be NP-Hard [2]. Heuristic multilevel methods have been developed to find small

© Springer-Verlag Berlin Heidelberg 2015
J.L. Träff et al. (Eds.): Euro-Par 2015, LNCS 9233, pp. 467–478, 2015.
DOI: 10.1007/978-3-662-48096-0_36

vertex separators in near linear time [5,12,16,17]. Many of these approaches include scalable distributed memory algorithms. While these algorithms work well when each processor has its own memory hierarchy, their execution on modern multicore systems result in large degrees of memory contention and duplication. For generating edge separators, it has been shown that shared-memory parallel algorithms can result in significant runtime and memory usage reductions [4,5,19].

Vertex separators pose several additional challenges to parallelism beyond those of edge separators. Whereas most applications for edge separators demand that the partitioning be generated quickly and place only moderate importance on the quality of the separator, nested dissection places a much higher importance on quality. While the higher levels of recursion in nested dissection result in independent tasks, they are still bounded by memory bandwidth on multicore systems and are often unbalanced in their associated work. An effective approach must effectively balance these tasks while achieving high cache utilization.

In this paper, we present shared memory parallel algorithms for generating vertex separators and using those vertex separators to generate a fill reducing ordering via nested dissection in parallel. Our contributions build on the previous work for creating edge separators using the multilevel paradigm on shared memory architectures [19]. We adapt these algorithms for vertex separators and introduce a new method for refining a vertex separator in parallel while making minimal sacrifices in terms of separator size. We introduce specialized task scheduling to maximize cache efficiency for the nested dissection problem. We achieve up to 10× speedup on 16 cores, while producing orderings with only 1.0 % more fill-in and requiring only 0.7 % more operations than the serial ND-Metis. This is 1.5× faster, 3.7 % less fill-in, and 14.0 % fewer operations than ParMetis [16].

2   Definitions and Notation

In this work we deal with a simple undirected graph $G = (V, E)$, consisting of a set of vertices V, and a set of edges E. Each edge is composed of an unordered pair of vertices (i.e., $v, u \in V$).

We will denote the size of the vertex set by the scalar $n = |V|$, and the size of the edge set by the scalar $m = |E|$. Vertices and edges can have non-negative integer weights associated with them. The weight of a vertex v is denoted by $\eta(v)$, and the weight of an edge e is denoted by $\theta(e)$. If there are no weights associated with the edges, then their weights are assumed to be one. The *neighborhood* of a vertex v, that is the set of vertices adjacent to v, is denoted by $\Gamma(v)$.

A vertex separator is a set of vertices of the graph $S \subset V$, such that when removed it leaves two components A and B. Finding a vertex separator is often subject to a balance constraint, ϵ. That is, we want to minimize $|S|$ while satisfying:

$$2\frac{\max(|A|, |B|)}{|A| + |B|} \leq 1 + \epsilon.$$

3 Background

For over two decades multilevel methods have been used with great success for graph partitioning. These methods have been shown to be both extremely fast and produce results of high quality [11,15,21,23]. First, increasingly coarser graphs $G_1, \ldots, G_s$ are generated from the original graph G_0. This process is known as the *coarsening* phase. Next, in the *initial partitioning* phase, a partitioning of the coarsest graph G_s, is made via some direct partitioning algorithm (e.g., spectral bisection [22] or KL [18]). This initial solution is then projected through the multiple graph levels, and is refined at each level as the degrees of freedom are increased. This is known as the *uncoarsening* phase. Buluç et al. [3] provide a thorough overview of modern multilevel approaches to graph partitioning.

The use of threads to exploit shared memory parallelism has recently been used to decrease runtimes and memory usage compared to that of traditional parallel distributed memory codes. Chevalier and Pellegrini [5] presented PT-Scotch, a parallel partitioning library exploiting both shared and distributed memory parallelism. Threads are used to parallelize the coarsening phase, which provides significant speedup even with refinement and several other steps being performed serially. Çatalyürek et al. [4] similarly explored parallelizing the coarsening of hypergraphs via shared memory parallelism. LaSalle and Karypis [19] investigated methods for effectively parallelizing all three phases of the multilevel paradigm.

Originally proposed by George [9,10], nested dissection is a recursive algorithm for generating fill reducing orderings of sparse matrices. The algorithm works by recursively partitioning the graph representation of a symmetric sparse matrix via vertex separators, ordering the rows and columns with partition A first, B second, and S last. This new ordering can greatly reduce the required memory and number of computations for performing Cholesky factorization. Because at each level the vertex separators induce two disconnected components, A and B, parallelism can efficiently be extracted by ordering A and B in parallel.

As such, the creation of vertex separators for nested dissection can be parallelized by processing A and B independently. The popular parallel partitioning packages ParMetis [16] and PT-Scotch [5] both follow similar multilevel approaches to performing nested dissection. All p processors work cooperatively to create the first $\log p$ levels of separators in parallel, before each processor performs nested serial dissection on its subgraph.

4 Methods

This paper builds upon the previous work for multi-threaded multilevel graph partitioning [19]. We use the same parallelization and coarsening strategies. Each thread is assigned a set of vertices and their associated edges, and is responsible for the computations on them.

4.1   Coarsening

The coarsening phase consists of two steps: *matching* and *contraction*. During matching, each vertex is either paired with a neighbor vertex, or itself. During contraction, paired vertices are merged together to form coarse vertices in the next coarser graph G_{i+1}.

The matching scheme we use is known as Heavy Edge Matching (HEM) [16]. This prioritizes edges for matching across based on their weight. Then, in a matching vector M, the matches of vertices v and u are recorded, $M(v) = u$ and $M(u) = v$. As this matching is done without locks, it is possible for race conditions to exist in determining if a vertex is unmatched. To resolve this issue, the strategy proposed by Çatalyürek et al. [4] is used. Each thread re-iterates over its set of vertices, and any vertex for which $M(M(v)) \neq v$, is matched with itself ($M(v) = v$). Because the number of vertices is orders of magnitude greater than the number of threads, the number of broken matchings is extremely small.

Contraction is an inherently parallel process, as each coarse vertex in G_{i+1} can be independently constructed given G_i and M. This process of matching and contraction repeats until G_i is sufficiently small for the initial partitioning phase.

4.2   Vertex Separators

The generation of vertex separators differs from edge separators in the initial partitioning and uncoarsening phases.

Initial Separator Selection. A widely used method of generating a vertex separator from an edge separator is to find a vertex cover of the set of cut edges [22]. Because we apply refinement to the separator, we instead take all boundary vertices as the initial separator of the coarsest graph G_s, and let refinement thin the separator and possibly move it away from the boundary set of vertices. We repeat this process several times and select the minimum balanced separator. As these separators are generated and refined independently, the process in inherently parallel. As the input graph is the same across the generation of different separators, waiting until G_s is sufficiently small so as to fit into shared cache is desirable.

Separator Refinement. After the current separator is projected from G_i to G_{i-1}, it is refined. Refinement of a vertex separator consists of moving vertices from the separator S into either partition A or partition B. If a vertex being moved is connected to vertices on the opposite side of the separator, those vertices are then pulled into the separator. The reduction in separator size from moving vertex $v \in S$ to A is

$$gain = \eta(v) - \sum_{u \in \Gamma(v) \cap B} \eta(u). \tag{1}$$

FM Refinement: The Fidducia-Mattheyses refinement (FM) algorithm [7], as applied to the vertex separator problem [12], works as follows. First, priority queues for moving vertices out of the separator to either partition are initialized and filled with vertices in S. The priority of vertices in these queues is determined by Eq. (1). Vertices are selected from either priority queue in order of gain, except when one partition is overweight, in which case the vertex at the top of the priority queue for the lower weight partition is selected. Once a vertex is selected, it is moved out of the separator, and its neighbors in the opposite partition are pulled into the separator. If the neighbors being pulled into the separator have not been moved yet in this refinement pass, they are added to the priority queue. Once both priority queues are emptied, the best observed state is restored. To reduce runtime, this process is terminated early if a certain number of moves past the best state have been made. Keeping track of the best state and reverting to it, makes the FM algorithm inherently serial.

Greedy Refinement: The greedy algorithm moves vertices through the separator to one side at a time. This is done so that at any given moment, the current state of the separator is valid. First, the lowest weight side of the separator is selected as the side to which all moves will be made in the first pass. Then, each thread adds the vertices it owns that are part of the separator to its own priority queue, using Eq. (1) for the priority. Each thread makes a local copy the current partition weights which it uses to keep track of moves and enforce the balance constraint. These weights are periodically synchronized with the global weights as moves are made. While this makes it possible for refinement to violate the balance constraint if enough vertices are moved before partition weights are synchronized, it is unlikely as it is desirable for the balance constraint on vertex separators in nested dissection to be large [13]. In practice we have not observed Greedy refinement to cause imbalance.

Each thread then extracts vertices from its priority queue. If the vertex can be moved out of the separator without violating the balance constraint, and has a positive gain associated with it, it is moved. The neighboring vertices that the thread owns have their connectivity information updated and are added to the separator as applicable. Messages are sent to the threads owning the remote vertices to notify them of the move.

Once the queue is empty, or the gain associated with moving the top vertex is negative, the thread waits for the other threads to finish. The thread then reads its messages, and updates its vertices accordingly. Finally, the threads synchronize once more, and the process repeats with the other side selected. While efficient, this method often results in lower quality than the serial FM algorithm as it cannot break out of local minima.

Segmented FM Refinement: Because we want the improved quality that results from breaking out of local minima, one possible solution is to have threads perform FM on internal vertices (vertices which are not connected to vertices owned by another thread). We will refer to this approach as Segmented FM (SFM), which for these internal vertices works the same as the serial FM algorithm and allows us to break out of local minima in parallel. External vertices, those that have neighbors belonging to other threads, are prevented from moving out of the separator. This ensures that as long as each thread maintains a valid separator for its vertices, the global separator will also be valid. Each thread saves its best locally observed state, and independently reverts back to it at the end of each pass.

For this method to be effective, each thread must have a large number of internal vertices and few external vertices. To accomplish this, as a pre-processing step, we create a k-way edge separator of the graph using the method described in [19]. While this increases the runtime, it is a parallel step and scales well. Furthermore, this pre-partitioning improves data locality, which is particularly beneficial for nested dissection where we can use a single pre-partitioning for the entire process. We select a value for k that is several times larger than the number of threads and assign partitions to threads via hashing so that each thread owns vertices in several locations of the graph. This is done so that many of the threads will own vertices that will be part of the separator, and the work during refinement will be distributed across multiple threads. We found using a value of k that is five times the number of threads to be effective.

While this method allows us to find high quality local separators, the inability to move external vertices prevents the separator from moving significantly. For more than a few threads, this can have a significant impact on separator size as is shown in Sect. 6.

Greedy with Segmented FM Refinement: Both Greedy refinement and SFM refinement have their advantages and disadvantages. Greedy refinement's ability to move both internal and external vertices allows it to move the separator freely, but it cannot break out of local minima. SFM refinement can break out of local minima for a thread's internal vertices, however external vertices anchor the separator in place, limiting the improvement. As quality is one of our primary concerns, these disadvantages make both Greedy and SFM refinement unattractive options on their own.

For this reason, we investigated a hybrid refinement strategy by overlapping Greedy and SFM refinement passes. The first greedy pass thins the separator and moves it to a local minima. Next, the SFM pass moves the sections of the separator on internal vertices out of the local minima. The next Greedy pass then allows the external vertices to catch up with the moved internal ones. This process repeats until neither the Greedy pass nor the SFM pass move any vertices. This provides an effective refinement scheme that can break out of local minima and move external vertices in parallel, without leading to an invalid separator.

4.3   Nested Dissection

Our parallel nested dissection algorithm works as follows. First, the threads induce a vertex separator S cooperatively, and use this to split the graph into parts A and B. The threads then split into two groups, with one group recursing on A and the other recursing on B. This repeats until each thread group contains

Table 1. Graphs used in experiments

Graph	# Vertices	# Edges	Graph	# Vertices	# Edges
auto	448,695	3,314,611	delaunay_n24	16,777,216	50,331,601
NLR	4,163,763	12,487,976	large_fe	7,221,643	83,149,197
med_fe	1,752,854	20,552,976	nlpkkt240	27,993,600	373,239,376

only a single thread. Each thread then finds a vertex separator serially for its portion of the graph. It then spawns tasks for processing A and B, and adds them to the work pool. As threads pull tasks from the work pool, they continue to spawn new subtasks in this fashion. Once both A and B have been ordered, the ordering of G is computed by placing A first, B second, and S last. When $|A|$ is small enough, it is ordered via the Multiple Minimum Degree algorithm [20].

Task Scheduling. Splitting the recursive calls on the graph parts A and B into parallel tasks, allows us to dynamically balance the computational load. However, we need to effectively utilize the cache to overcome memory bandwidth restrictions. The task tree of nested dissection has several properties that we want to keep in mind when scheduling the tasks. (1) The lower a task is on the tree (the earlier it is generated), the larger the graph that is associated with it. (2) The graph associated with a given task is a subgraph of the graph associated with its parent's task, thus the best cache use is achieved by having a task processed immediately after its parent.

To maximize our cache use, we propose a task scheduling scheme specifically for the nested dissection problem, that takes advantages of these properties. Our scheduling scheme operates on two levels. Each thread maintains a local list of tasks that it generates. It processes the tasks in its list in Last-In First-Out order to ensure that whatever subgraph is currently cached is used by the next scheduled task as often as possible. When a thread runs out of tasks in its own list, it steals tasks from neighboring threads in First-in First-out order (the largest tasks). This not only ensures stolen tasks have enough work associated with them to achieve cache re-use, also ensures that the stolen tasks are the ones least likely to have their associated graph resident in another thread's cache. In Sect. 6.3 we compare this scheduling scheme against the generic scheme implemented in the OpenMP runtime.

5 Experimental Methodology

The experiments in this paper were run on a HP ProLiant BL280c G6 with 2x 8-core Xeon E5-2670 @ 2.6 GHz system with 64 GB of memory. We used Intel C Compiler, version 13.1, and the GNU GCC compiler 4.9.2. The algorithms evaluated here are implemented in mt-Metis 0.4.0, which is available from http://cs.umn.edu/~lasalle/mt-metis. We will refer to the new vertex separator and nested

Table 2. Size of vertex separators

	auto	NLR	med_fe	delaunay_n24	large_fe	nlpkkt240
FM (serial)	**2,133**	**1,811**	2,166	3,507	6,421	156,564
Greedy	2,277	1,918	2,281	4,167	6,717	148,665
SFM	2,985	2,264	5,882	4,302	12,430	262,243
Greedy+SFM	2,205	1,821	**2,071**	**3,492**	**6,024**	**146,523**

Table 3. Refinement time in seconds

	auto	NLR	med_fe	delaunay_n24	large_fe	nlpkkt240
FM (serial)	0.044	0.178	0.104	0.898	0.336	3.183
Greedy	0.048	0.091	0.071	0.130	0.181	1.251
SFM	**0.030**	**0.069**	0.068	**0.115**	0.185	**1.153**
Greedy+SFM	0.050	0.101	**0.062**	0.147	**0.134**	2.678

dissection functionality as mt-ND-Metis in the following experiments. For comparison, we also used Metis [16] version 5.1.0 (referred to in the experiments as ND-Metis) from http://cs.umn.edu/~metis, ParMetis [17] version 4.0.3 from http://cs.umn.edu/~metis, and PT-Scotch [5] version 6.0.3 from http://www.labri.fr/perso/pelegrin/scotch.

The results presented for vertex separators are the geometric means from 25 runs using different random seeds. The results presented for nested dissection are the geometric means from 10 runs using different random seeds.

Table 1 details the graphs used for evaluation in Sect. 6. We opted to use these graphs for varying sizes and domains. The auto, NLR, delaunay_n24, and nlpkkt240 graphs were obtained from the 10th DIMACS Implementation Challenge [1]. The graphs med_fe and large_fe are 3D finite element meshes used in physics simulations.

6   Results

6.1   Vertex Separators

Table 2 shows the effect on separator size of the different refinement schemes. We compare the three parallel methods run with 16 threads to that of serial FM. SFM refinement resulted in large separators compared to that of serial FM, due to its inability to move external vertices. Greedy refinement did much better, finding separators only 6.1 % larger than serial FM. The refinement scheme combining both Greedy and SFM refinement passes, produced separators of comparable size to FM, and for several graphs found slightly smaller separators on average. The number of external vertices that are prevented from being moved when trying to break out of a local minima in this scheme is quite small due to our pre-partitioning.

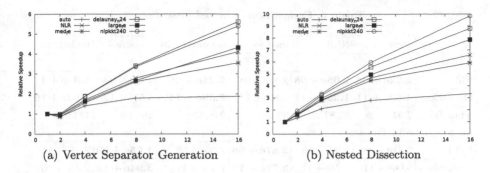

(a) Vertex Separator Generation   (b) Nested Dissection

Fig. 1. Strong scaling of mt-ND-Metis on 16 cores

Table 4. Improvement over OpenMP task scheduling

	auto	NLR	med_fe	delaunay_n24	large_fe	nlpkkt240
ICC OMP	68.9 %	38.3 %	48.7 %	30.4 %	39.9 %	25.9 %
GCC OMP	62.2 %	39.0 %	60.2 %	25.6 %	40.0 %	23.0 %

Table 3 shows the effect on runtime of the different refinement schemes. The runtime of serial FM is included for comparison against the other three refinement schemes run with 16 threads. None of the parallel refinement schemes exhibit significant speedup over FM consistently. There are two reasons for this. First, refinement operates on a small portion of the graph, and requires frequent synchronization. Second, the parallel refinement schemes make more passes before they settle on a separator. This also explains why the Greedy+SFM scheme is sometimes faster than the SFM and Greedy schemes. It performs more work per pass than either Greedy or SFM, but settles on a separator in fewer passes.

Figure 1a shows the strong scaling of mt-ND-Metis generating vertex separators using up to 16 cores. The time shown includes the cost of pre-partitioning the graph, which is why there is a slowdown observed between one and two threads. The speedup achieved is largely dependent upon the size of the graph, and how effectively the amount of work between synchronization points can hide the parallel overhead. Looking beyond two threads, the larger graphs achieve speedups nearing 6× overall. Discounting the pre-partitioning time, the largest and third largest graphs exhibit super linear scaling with speedups over 17×. This is due to improved locality that comes from the pre-partitioning, and the extra cache available on the second processor. This shows the importance of having a well distributed graph, even on shared memory architectures.

6.2   Task Scheduling

Table 4 shows the percent improvement of our nested dissection task scheduling scheme, over that of the implementation schemes provided by ICC [14] and

Table 5. Comparison of nested dissection

	auto	NLR	med_fe	delaunay_n24	large_fe	nlpkkt240
ND-Metis						
Fill-in	**2.22e + 08**	**2.05e + 08**	2.88e + 08	**7.24e + 08**	1.61e + 09	**1.98e + 11**
Operations	**4.53e + 11**	**1.25e + 11**	3.83e + 11	**7.39e + 11**	4.57e + 12	**1.93e + 16**
Time (s)	7.94	51.82	39.26	248.83	184.58	1148.52
mt-ND-Metis 16 Threads						
Fill-in	2.31e + 08	2.06e + 08	**2.87e + 08**	7.30e + 08	**1.55e + 09**	2.07e + 11
Operations	5.06e + 11	1.28e + 11	**3.71e + 11**	7.46e + 11	**3.94e + 12**	2.04e + 16
Time (s)	1.44	**4.67**	**4.44**	**17.85**	**16.34**	**93.80**
ParMetis 16 Processes						
Fill-in	2.29e + 08	2.13e + 08	3.10e + 08	7.58e + 08	1.60e + 09	2.17e + 11
Operations	4.94e + 11	1.52e + 11	4.98e + 11	9.40e + 11	4.51e + 12	2.30e + 16
Time (s)	1.60	6.21	6.43	29.52	31.17	169.84
PT-Scotch 16 Processes						
Fill-in	2.52e + 08	2.73e + 08	3.84e + 08	9.72e + 08	1.93e + 09	2.62e + 11
Operations	5.89e + 11	3.39e + 11	8.70e + 11	2.00e + 12	8.57e + 12	2.79e + 16
Time (s)	**1.12**	5.83	7.46	26.82	39.33	678.65

GCC [8]. Our scheme was on average 41.1 % faster than the ICC scheduler and 40.6 % faster than the GCC scheduler. This is because these schedulers are designed to handle tasks with varying properties, whereas our specialized scheduler takes advantage of the nature of the nested dissection task tree.

6.3 Nested Dissection

Figure 1b shows the strong scaling of mt-ND-Metis performing nested dissection. For the smallest graph, auto, the achieved speedup is limited to $3.3\times$, as the parallel overhead plays a significant role in the runtime. For the larger graphs, the different graph operations performed dominate the runtime and hide the parallel overhead. As a result, speedup of 6–$10\times$ is achieved on the other five graphs. We see a greater speedup here than on just vertex separators as the cost of performing nested dissection is significantly greater than that of creating a k-way edge separator, and better hide its added cost.

Table 5 compares the orderings of mt-ND-Metis with that of ND-Metis, ParMetis, and PT-Scotch, in terms of number of non-zeros in the Cholesky factor and the operations required to compute it. The runtimes to generate these orderings are also included (excluding I/O, but including preprocessing). Making efficient use of the multicore system, mt-ND-Metis was on average $1.5\times$ faster than the other two parallel methods, and $10.1\times$ faster than the serial ND-Metis. The number of operations required by orderings produced by mt-ND-Metis were only 0.7 % higher than those required by mt-ND-Metis, and 14.0 % lower than those required by ParMetis or PT-Scotch. The hybrid refinement of mt-ND-Metis enables these high quality results, close to that of ND-Metis. The high-speed parallel vertex separator generation during the low levels of the nested dissection tree coupled with the specialized task scheduling in the higher levels enables mt-ND-Metis to produce orderings the fastest for all datasets except the smallest.

7 Conclusion

In this work we presented new shared-memory parallel methods for producing minimal balanced vertex separators and fill reducing orderings of sparse matrices. Specifically, we introduced a new parallel refinement scheme that can break out of local minima. We also introduced a task scheduling scheme specifically designed for the nested dissection problem that outperforms OpenMP task schedulers by 40.8%. We implemented these algorithms in mt-ND-Metis, and show that produces orderings 1.5× faster than ParMetis [16] and PT-Scotch [5], and 10.1× faster than ND-Metis [16]. The orderings produced by mt-ND-Metis result in only 1.0% more fill-in and require only 0.7% more operations than those of ND-Metis.

Acknowledgment. This work was supported in part by NSF (IIS-0905220, OCI-1048018, CNS-1162405, IIS-1247632, IIP-1414153, IIS-1447788), Army Research Office (W911NF-14-1-0316), Intel Software and Services Group, and the Digital Technology Center at the University of Minnesota. Access to research and computing facilities was provided by the Digital Technology Center and the Minnesota Supercomputing Institute.

References

1. Bader, D.A., Meyerhenke, H., Sanders, P., Wagner, D. (eds.) Graph Partitioning and Graph Clustering - 10th DIMACS Implementation Challenge Workshop, Georgia Institute of Technology, Atlanta, GA, USA, 13–14 February 2012, Proceedings, volume 588 of Contemporary Mathematics. American Mathematical Society (2013)
2. Bui, T.N., Jones, C.: Finding good approximate vertex and edge partitions is NP-hard. Inf. Process. Lett. **42**(3), 153–159 (1992)
3. Buluç, A., Meyerhenke, H., Safro, I., Sanders, P., Schulz, C.: Recent advances in graph partitioning. CoRR, abs/1311.3144 (2013)
4. Çatalyürek, Ü.V., Deveci, M., Kaya, K., Ucar, B.: Multithreaded clustering for multi-level hypergraph partitioning. In: 2012 IEEE 26th International Parallel and Distributed Processing Symposium (IPDPS), pp. 848–859. IEEE (2012)
5. Chevalier, C., Pellegrini, F.: Pt-scotch: a tool for efficient parallel graph ordering. Parallel Comput. **34**(6), 318–331 (2008)
6. Davis, T.A.: Direct methods for sparse linear systems. SIAM **2**, 217 (2006)
7. Fiduccia, C.M., Mattheyses, R.M.: A linear-time heuristic for improving network partitions. In: 19th Conference on Design Automation, 1982, pp. 175–181, June 1982

8. Free Software Foundation. The GNU OpenMP Implementation (2014)
9. George, A.: Nested dissection of a regular finite element mesh. SIAM J. Numer. Anal. **10**(2), 345–363 (1973)
10. George, A., Liu, J.W.H.: An automatic nested dissection algorithm for irregular finite element problems. SIAM J. Numer. Anal. **15**(5), 1053–1069 (1978)
11. Hendrickson, B., Leland, R.: A multilevel algorithm for partitioning graphs. In: Proceedings of the 1995 ACM/IEEE Conference on Supercomputing (CDROM), Supercomputing 1995. ACM, New York (1995)
12. Hendrickson, B., Rothberg, E.: Effective sparse matrix ordering: just around the bend. In: Proceedings of the 8th SIAM Conference on Parallel Processing for Scientific Computing. Citeseer (1997)
13. Hendrickson, B., Rothberg, E.: Improving the run time and quality of nested dissection ordering. SIAM J. Sci. Comput. **20**(2), 468–489 (1998)
14. Intel. Intel OpenMP Runtine Library (2014)
15. Karypis, G., Kumar, V.: Multilevel graph partitioning schemes. ICPP **3**, 113–122 (1995)
16. Karypis, G., Kumar, V.: A fast and high quality multilevel scheme for partitioning irregular graphs. SIAM J. Sci. Comput. **20**(1), 359–392 (1998)
17. Karypis, G., Kumar, V.: A parallel algorithm for multilevel graph partitioning and sparse matrix ordering. J. Parallel Distrib. Comput. **48**(1), 71–95 (1998)
18. Kernighan, B.W., Lin, S.: An efficient heuristic procedure for partitioning graphs. Bell Syst. Tech. J. **49**(1), 291–307 (1970)
19. LaSalle, D., Karypis, G.: Multi-threaded graph partitioning. In: 2013 IEEE 27th International Symposium on Parallel and Distributed Processing (IPDPS), pp. 225–236. IEEE (2013)
20. Liu, J.W.H.: Modification of the minimum-degree algorithm by multiple elimination. ACM Trans. Math. Softw. (TOMS) **11**(2), 141–153 (1985)
21. Pellegrini, F., Roman, J.: Scotch: a software package for static mapping. In: Liddell, H., Colbrook, A., Hertzberger, Bob, Sloot, Peter M.A. (eds.) HPCN-Europe 1996. LNCS, vol. 1067, pp. 493–498. Springer, Heidelberg (1996)
22. Pothen, A., Simon, H.D., Liou, K.-P.: Partitioning sparse matrices with eigenvectors of graphs. SIAM J. Matrix Anal. Appl. **11**(3), 430–452 (1990)
23. Sanders, P., Schulz, C.: Engineering multilevel graph partitioning algorithms. In: Demetrescu, C., Halldrsson, M.M. (eds.) ESA 2011. LNCS, vol. 6942, pp. 469–480. Springer, Heidelberg (2011)

Scheduling Trees of Malleable Tasks for Sparse Linear Algebra

Abdou Guermouche[1], Loris Marchal[2(✉)], Bertrand Simon[2],
and Frédéric Vivien[2]

[1] University of Bordeaux and INRIA, 200 rue de la vieille Tour, Talence, France
abdou.guermouche@labri.fr
[2] CNRS, INRIA and University of Lyon, LIP, ENS Lyon, 46 allée d'Italie,
Lyon, France
{loris.marchal,bertrand.simon,frederic.vivien}@ens-lyon.fr

Abstract. Scientific workloads are often described by directed acyclic task graphs. This is in particular the case for multifrontal factorization of sparse matrices—the focus of this paper—whose task graph is structured as a tree of parallel tasks. Prasanna and Musicus [19,20] advocated using the concept of *malleable* tasks to model parallel tasks involved in matrix computations. In this powerful model each task is processed on a time-varying number of processors. Following Prasanna and Musicus, we consider malleable tasks whose speedup is p^α, where p is the fractional share of processors on which a task executes, and α ($0 < \alpha \le 1$) is a task-independent parameter. Firstly, we use actual experiments on multicore platforms to motivate the relevance of this model for our application. Then, we study the optimal time-minimizing allocation proposed by Prasanna and Musicus using optimal control theory. We greatly simplify their proofs by resorting only to pure scheduling arguments. Building on the insight gained thanks to these new proofs, we extend the study to distributed (homogeneous or heterogeneous) multicore platforms. We prove the NP-completeness of the corresponding scheduling problem, and we then propose some approximation algorithms.

1 Introduction

Parallel workloads are often modeled as directed acyclic task graphs, or DAGs, where nodes represent tasks and edges represent dependencies between tasks. Task graphs arise from many scientific domains, such as image processing, genomics, and geophysical simulations. In this paper, we focus on task graphs coming from sparse linear algebra, and especially from the factorization of sparse matrices using the multifrontal method. Liu [18] explains that the computational dependencies and requirements in Cholesky and LU factorization of sparse matrices using the multifrontal method can be modeled as a task tree, called the *assembly tree*. We therefore focus on dependencies that can be modeled as a tree.

This work was supported by the ANR SOLHAR project funded by the French National Research Agency.

© Springer-Verlag Berlin Heidelberg 2015
J.L. Träff et al. (Eds.): Euro-Par 2015, LNCS 9233, pp. 479–490, 2015.
DOI: 10.1007/978-3-662-48096-0_37

In the abundant existing literature, several variants of the task graph scheduling problem are addressed, depending on the ability to process a task in parallel: tasks are either *sequential* (not amenable to parallel processing), *rigid* (requesting a given number of processors), *moldable* (able to cope with any fixed number of processors) or even *malleable* (processed on a variable number of processors) in the terminology of Drozdowski [6, Chap. 25]. When considering moldable and malleable tasks, one has to define how the processing time of a task depends on the number of allocated processors. Under some general assumptions, Jansen and Zhang [14] derive a 3.29 approximation algorithm for arbitrary precedence constraints, which is improved in a 2.62 approximation in the particular case of a series-parallel precedence graph by Lepere et al. [16]. However, although polynomial, these algorithms relies on complex optimization techniques, which makes them difficult to implement in a practical setting.

In this study, we consider a special case of malleable tasks, where the speedup function of each task is p^α, where p is the number of processors allocated to the task, and $0 < \alpha \le 1$ is a global parameter. In particular, when the share of processors p_i allocated to a task T_i is constant, its processing time is given by L_i/p_i^α, where L_i is the sequential duration of T_i. The case $\alpha = 1$ represents the unrealistic case of a perfect linear speed-up, and we rather concentrate on the case $\alpha < 1$ which takes into consideration the cost of the parallelization. In particular $\alpha < 1$ accounts for the cost of intra-task communications, without having to decompose the tasks in smaller granularity sub-tasks with explicit communications, which would make the scheduling problem intractable. This model has been advocated by Prasanna and Musicus [20] for matrix operations, and we present some new motivation for this model in our context. As in [20], we also assume that it is possible to allocate non-integer shares of processors to tasks. This amounts to assume that processors can share their processing time among tasks. When task A is allocated 2.6 processors and task B 3.4 processors, one processor dedicates 60 % of its time to A and 40 % to B. Note that this is a realistic assumption, for example, when using modern task-based runtime systems such as StarPU [3], KAAPI [9], or PaRSEC [4]. This allows to simplify the scheduling problem and to derive optimal allocation algorithms.

Our objective is to minimize the total processing time of a tree of malleable tasks. Initially, we consider a homogeneous platform composed of p identical processors. To achieve our goal, we take advantage of two sources of parallelism: the *tree parallelism* which allows tasks independent from each others (such as siblings) to be processed concurrently, and the *task parallelism* which allows a task to be processed on several processors. A solution to this problem describes both in which order tasks are processed and which share of computing resources is allocated to each task.

In [19, 20], the same problem has been addressed by Prasanna and Musicus for series-parallel graphs (or SP-graphs). Such graphs are built recursively as series or parallel composition of two smaller SP-graphs. Trees can be seen as a special-case of series-parallel graphs, and thus, the optimal algorithm proposed in [19, 20] is also valid on trees. They use optimal control theory to derive general theorems for any strictly increasing speedup function. For the particular case of the speedup function p^α, Prasanna and Musicus prove some properties of the unique optimal schedule which allow to compute it efficiently. Their results are powerful (a simple optimal solution is proposed), but to obtain these results they had to transform the problem in a shape which is amenable to optimal control theory. Thus, their proofs do not provide any intuition on the underlying scheduling problem, yet it seems tractable using classic scheduling arguments.

In this paper, our contributions are the following:

- In Sect. 2, we show that the model of malleable tasks using the p^α speed-up function is justified in the context of sparse matrix factorization.
- In Sect. 4, we propose a new and simpler proof for the results of [19,20] on series-parallel graphs, using pure scheduling arguments.
- In Sect. 5, we extend the previous study on distributed memory machines, where tasks cannot be distributed across several distributed nodes. We provide NP-completeness results and approximation algorithms.

2   Validation of the Malleable Task Model

In this section, we evaluate the model proposed by Prasanna and Musicus in [19,20] for our target application. This model states that the instantaneous speedup of a task processed on p processors is p^α. Thus, the processing time of a task T_i of size L_i which is allocated a share of processors $p_i(t)$ at time t is equal to the smallest value C_i such that $\int_0^{C_i} (p_i(t))^\alpha \, dt \geq L_i$, where α is a task-independent constant. When the share of processors p_i is constant, $C_i = L_i/p_i^\alpha$. Our goal is (i) to find whether this formula well describes the evolution of the task processing time for various shares of processors and (ii) to check that different tasks of the same application have the same α parameter. We target a modern multicore platform composed of a set of nodes each including several multicore processors. For the purpose of this study we restrict ourselves to the single node case for which the communication cost will be less dominant. In this context, $p_i(t)$ denotes the number of *cores* dedicated to task T_i at time t.

We consider applications having a tree-shaped task graph constituted of parallel tasks. This kind of execution model can be met in sparse direct solvers where the matrix is first factorized before the actual solution is computed. For instance, either the multifrontal method [7] as implemented in MUMPS [1] or qr_mumps [5], or the supernodal approach as implemented in SuperLU [17] or in PaStiX [12], are based on tree-shaped task graphs (namely the assembly tree [2]). Each task in this tree is a partial factorization of a dense sub-matrix or of a sparse panel. In order to reach good performance, these factorizations are performed using tiled linear algebra routines (BLAS): the sub-matrix is decomposed into 2D tiles (or blocks), and optimized BLAS kernels are used to perform the necessary operations on each tile. Thus, each task can be seen as a task graph of smaller granularity sub-tasks.

As computing platforms evolve quickly and become more complex (e.g., because of the increasing use of accelerators such as GPUs or Xeon Phis),

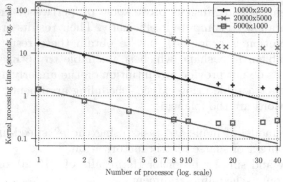

matrix	1D	2D
5000x1000	0.78	0.93
10000x2500	0.88	0.95
20000x5000	0.89	0.94

(b) Values of α

(a) Timings and model (lines) with 1D partitioning

Fig. 1. Timings and α values for qr_mumps frontal matrix factorization kernel

it becomes interesting to rely on an optimized dynamic runtime system to allocate and schedule tasks on computing resources. These runtime systems (such as StarPU [3], KAAPI [9], or PaRSEC [4]) are able to process a task on a prescribed subset of the computing cores that may evolve over time. This motivates the use of the malleable task model, where the share of processors allocated to a task vary with time. This approach has been recently used and evaluated [13] in the context of the qr_mumps solver using the StarPU runtime system.

In order to assess whether tasks used within sparse direct solvers fit the model introduced by Prasanna and Musicus in [20] we conducted an experimental study on several dense linear algebra tasks. We used a test platform composed of 4 Intel E7-4870 processors having 10 cores each clocked at 2.40 GHz and having 30 MB of L3 cache for a total of 40 cores. The platform is equipped with 1 TB of memory with uniform access. We considered dense operations which are representative of what can be met in sparse linear algebra computations, namely the standard frontal matrix factorization kernel used in the qr_mumps solver. We used either block-columns of size 32 (1D partitioning) or square blocks of size 256 (2D partitioning). All experiments were made using the StarPU runtime.

Figure 1(a) presents the timings obtained when processing the qr_mumps frontal matrix factorization kernel on a varying number of processors. The logarithmic scales show that the p^α speedup function models well the timings, except for small matrices when p is large. In those cases, there is not enough parallelism in tasks to exploit all available cores. We performed linear regressions on the portions where $p \leq 10$ to compute α for different task sizes (Fig. 1(b)). We performed the same test for 2D partitioning and computed the corresponding α values (using $p \leq 20$). We notice that the value of α does not vary significantly with the matrix size, which validates our model. The only notable exception is for the smallest matrix (5000×1000) with 1D partitioning: it is hard to efficiently use many cores for such small matrices. In all cases, when the number of processors is larger than a threshold the performance deteriorates and stalls. Our speedup model is only valid below this threshold, which threshold increases with the matrix size. This is not a problem as the allocation schemes developed in the next sections allocate large numbers of processors to large tasks at the top of the tree and smaller numbers of processors for smaller tasks. In other words, we produce allocations that always respect the validity thresholds of the model. Finally, note that the value of α depends on the parameters of the problem (type of factorization, partitioning, block size, etc.). It has to be determined for each kernel and each set of blocking parameters.

3   Model and Notations

We assume that the number of available computing resources may vary with time: $p(t)$ gives the (possibly rational) total number of processors available at time t, also called the processor profile. For the sake of simplicity, we consider that $p(t)$ is a step function. Although our study is motivated by an application running on a single multicore node (as outlined in the previous section), we use the term *processor* instead of *computing core* in the following sections for readability and consistency with the scheduling literature.

We consider an in-tree G of n malleable tasks $T_1, \ldots, T_n$. L_i denotes the length, that is the sequential processing time, of task T_i. As motivated in the previous section, we assume that the speedup function for a task allocated p processors is p^α, where $0 < \alpha \leq 1$ is a fixed parameter. A schedule $\mathcal{S}$ is a set of nonnegative piecewise continuous functions $\{p_i(t) \mid i \in I\}$ representing the time-varying share of processors allocated to each task. During a time interval Δ, the task T_i performs an amount of work equal to $\int_\Delta p_i(t)^\alpha \mathrm{d}t$. Then, T_i is completed when the total work performed is equal to its length L_i. The completion time of task T_i is thus the smallest value C_i such that $\int_0^{C_i} p_i(t)^\alpha dt \geq L_i$. We define $w_i(t)$ as the ratio of the work of the task T_i that is done during the time interval $[0, t]$: $w_i(t) = \int_0^t p_i(x)^\alpha \mathrm{d}x / L_i$. A schedule is a valid solution if and only if:

- it does not use more processors than available: $\forall t, \sum_{i \in I} p_i(t) \leq p(t)$;
- it completes all the tasks: $\exists \tau, \forall i \in I, \ w_i(\tau) = 1$;
- and it respects precedence constraints: $\forall i \in I, \forall t$, if $p_i(t) > 0$ then, $\forall j \in I$, if j is a child of i, $w_j(t) = 1$.

The makespan τ of a schedule is computed as $\min\{t \mid \forall i \, w_i(t) = 1\}$. Our objective is to construct a valid schedule with optimal, i.e., minimal, makespan.

Note that because of the speedup function p^α, the computations in the following sections will make a heavy use of the functions $f : x \mapsto x^\alpha$ and $g : x \mapsto x^{(1/\alpha)}$. We assume that we have at our disposal a polynomial time algorithm to compute both f and g. We are aware that this assumption is very likely to be wrong, as soon as $\alpha < 1$, since f and g produce irrational numbers. However, without these functions, it is not even possible to compute the makespan of a schedule in polynomial time and, hence, the problem is not in NP. Furthermore, this allows us to avoid the complexity due to number computations, and to concentrate on the most interesting combinatorial complexity, when proving NP-completeness results and providing approximation algorithms. In practice, any implementation of f and g with a reasonably good accuracy will be sufficient to perform all computations including the computation of makespans.

In the next section, following Prasanna and Musicus, we will not consider trees but more general graphs: *series-parallel graphs* (or SP graphs). An SP graph is recursively defined as a single task, the series composition of two SP graphs, or the parallel composition of two SP graphs. A tree can easily be transformed into an SP graph by joining the leaves according to its structure, the resulting graph is then called a *pseudo-tree*. We will use $(i \parallel j)$ to represent the parallel composition of tasks T_i and T_j and $(i \,;\, j)$ to represent their series composition. Thanks to the construction of pseudo-trees, an algorithm which solves the previous scheduling problem on SP-graphs also gives an optimal solution for trees.

4   Optimal Solution for Shared-Memory Platforms

The purpose of this section is to give a simpler proof of the results of [19,20] using only scheduling arguments. We consider an SP-graph to be scheduled on a shared-memory platform (each task can be distributed across the whole platform). We assume that $\alpha < 1$ and prove the uniqueness of the optimal schedule.

Our objective is to prove that any SP graph G is *equivalent* to a single task T_G of easily computable length: for any processor profile $p(t)$, graphs G and T_G have the same makespan. We prove that the ratio of processors allocated to any task T_i, defined by $r_i(t) = p_i(t)/p(t)$, is constant from the moment at which T_i is initiated to the moment at which it is terminated. We also prove that in an optimal schedule, the two subgraphs of a parallel composition terminate at the same time and each receives a constant total ratio of processors throughout its execution. We then prove that these properties imply that the optimal schedule is unique and obeys to a *flow conservation* property: the shares of processors allocated to two subgraphs of a series composition are equal. When considering a tree, this means that the whole schedule is defined by the ratios of processors allocated to the leaves. Then, all the children of a node T_i terminate at the same time, and its ratio is the sum of its children ratios.

We first need to define the length $\mathcal{L}_G$ associated to a graph G, which will be proved to be the length of the task T_G. Then, we state a few lemmas before proving the main theorem. We only present here sketches of the proofs, the detailed versions can be found in [10].

Definition 1. *We recursively define the length $\mathcal{L}_G$ associated to a SP graph G:*

$$\bullet\, \mathcal{L}_{T_i} = L_i \qquad\qquad \bullet\, \mathcal{L}_{G_1\,;\,G_2} = \mathcal{L}_{G_1} + \mathcal{L}_{G_2} \qquad\qquad \bullet\, \mathcal{L}_{G_1 \parallel G_2} = \left(\mathcal{L}_{G_1}^{1/\alpha} + \mathcal{L}_{G_2}^{1/\alpha} \right)^{\alpha}$$

Lemma 1. *An allocation minimizing the makespan uses all the processors at any time.*

We call a *clean interval* with regard to a schedule $\mathcal{S}$ an interval during which no task is completed in $\mathcal{S}$.

Lemma 2. *When the number of available processors is constant, any optimal schedule allocates a constant number of processors per task on any clean interval.*

Proof. By contradiction, we assume that there exists an optimal schedule $\mathcal{P}$ of makespan M, a task T_j and a clean interval $\Delta = [t_1, t_2]$ such that T_j is not allocated a constant number of processors on Δ. By definition of clean intervals, no task completes during Δ. $|\Delta| = t_2 - t_1$ denotes the duration of Δ, I the set of tasks that receive a non-empty share of processors during Δ, and p the constant number of available processors.

We want to show that there exists a valid schedule with a makespan smaller than M. To achieve this, we define an intermediate and not necessarily valid schedule $\mathcal{Q}$, which nevertheless respects the resource constraints (no more than p processors are used at time t). This schedule is equal to $\mathcal{P}$ except on Δ.

The constant share of processors allocated to task T_i on Δ in $\mathcal{Q}$ is defined by $q_i = \frac{1}{|\Delta|} \int_\Delta p_i(t)dt$. For all t, we have $\sum_{i \in I} p_i(t) = p$ because of Lemma 1. We get $\sum_{i \in I} q_i = p$. So $\mathcal{Q}$ respects the resource constraints. Let $W_i^\Delta(\mathcal{P})$ (resp. $W_i^\Delta(\mathcal{Q})$) denote the work done on T_i during Δ under schedule $\mathcal{P}$ (resp. $\mathcal{Q}$). We have

$$W_i^\Delta(\mathcal{P}) = \int_\Delta p_i(t)^\alpha dt = |\Delta| \int_{[0,1]} p_i(t_1 + t|\Delta|)^\alpha dt$$

$$W_i^\Delta(\mathcal{Q}) = \int_\Delta \left(\frac{1}{|\Delta|}\int_\Delta p_i(t)dt\right)^\alpha dx = |\Delta| \left(\int_{[0,1]} p_i(t_1 + t|\Delta|)dt\right)^\alpha$$

As $\alpha < 1$, the function $x \mapsto x^\alpha$ is concave and then, by Jensen inequality [11], $W_i^\Delta(\mathcal{P}) \leq W_i^\Delta(\mathcal{Q})$. Moreover, as $x \mapsto x^\alpha$ is *strictly* concave, this inequality is an equality if and only if the function $t \mapsto p_i(t_1 + t|\Delta|)$ is equal to a constant on $[0,1[$ except on a subset of $[0,1[$ of null measure [11]. Then, by definition, p_j is not constant on Δ, and cannot be made constant by modifications on a set of null measure. We thus have $W_j^\Delta(\mathcal{P}) < W_j^\Delta(\mathcal{Q})$. Therefore, T_j is allocated too many processors under $\mathcal{Q}$. It is then possible to distribute this surplus among the other tasks during Δ, so that the work done during Δ in $\mathcal{P}$ can be terminated earlier. This remark implies that there exists a valid schedule with a makespan smaller than M; hence, the contradiction.   □

We recall that $r_i(t) = p_i(t)/p(t)$ is the instantaneous ratio of processors allocated to a task T_i.

Lemma 3. *Let G be the parallel composition of two tasks, T_1 and T_2. If $p(t)$ is a step function, in any optimal schedule $r_1(t)$ is constant and equal to $\pi_1 = 1 \Big/ \left(1 + (L_2/L_1)^{1/\alpha}\right) = L_1^{1/\alpha} \Big/ \mathcal{L}_{1\|2}^{1/\alpha}$ up to the completion of G.*

Proof. First, we prove that $r_1(t)$ is constant on any optimal schedule.

We consider an optimal schedule $\mathcal{S}$, and two consecutive time intervals A and B such that $p(t)$ is constant and equal to p on A and q on B, and $\mathcal{S}$ does not complete before the end of B. Suppose also that $|A|p^\alpha = |B|q^\alpha$ (shorten one

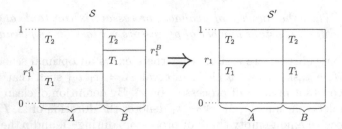

Fig. 2. Schedules $\mathcal{S}$ and $\mathcal{S}'$ on $A \cup B$. The abscissae represent the time and the ordinates the ratio of processing power

interval otherwise), where $-A-$ and $-B-$ are the durations of intervals A and B. By Lemma 2, $r_1(t)$ has constant values r_1^A on A and r_1^B on B. Suppose by contradiction that $r_1^A \neq r_1^B$.

We want to prove that $\mathcal{S}$ is not optimal, and so that we can do the same work as $\mathcal{S}$ does on $A \cup B$ in a smaller makespan. We set $r_1 = \left(r_1^A + r_1^B\right)/2$. We define the schedule $\mathcal{S}'$ as equal to $\mathcal{S}$ except on $A \cup B$ where the ratio allocated to T_1 is r_1 (see Fig. 2).

The work W_1 on task T_1 under $\mathcal{S}$ and W_1' under $\mathcal{S}'$ during $A \cup B$ are equal to:

$$W_1 = |A|p^\alpha \left(r_1^A\right)^\alpha + |B|q^\alpha \left(r_1^B\right)^\alpha \qquad W_1' = r_1^\alpha \left(|A|p^\alpha + |B|q^\alpha\right)$$

Then, with the concavity inequality and the fact that $|B|q^\alpha = |A|p^\alpha$, we can deduce that $W_1' > W_1$ and symmetrically that $W_2' > W_2$.

Therefore, $\mathcal{S}'$ performs strictly more work for each task during $A \cup B$ than $\mathcal{S}$. Thus, as in Lemma 2, $\mathcal{S}$ is not optimal. So $r_1(t)$ is constant in optimal schedules.

There remains to prove that in an optimal schedule $\mathcal{S}$, $r_1(t) = \pi_1$; hence, the optimal schedule is unique. As $p(t)$ is a step function, we define the sequences (A_k) and (p_k) such that A_k is the duration of the k-th step of the function $p(t)$ and $p(t) = p_k > 0$ on A_k. The sum of the durations of the A_k's is the makespan of $\mathcal{S}$. Then, if we note $V = \sum_k |A_k|p_k^\alpha$ and r_1 the value of $r_1(t)$, we have:

$$L_1 = \sum_k |A_k|r_1^\alpha p_k^\alpha = r_1^\alpha V \qquad \text{and} \qquad L_2 = \sum_k |A_k|(1 - r_1)^\alpha p_k^\alpha = (1 - r_1)^\alpha V$$

Then, $r_1 = 1/(1 + (L_2/L_1)^{1/\alpha}) = \pi_1$. $\qquad\square$

Lemma 4. *Let G be the parallel composition of tasks T_1 and T_2, with $p(t)$ a step function, and $\mathcal{S}$ an optimal schedule. Then, the makespan of G under $\mathcal{S}$ is equal to the makespan of the task T_G of length $\mathcal{L}_G = \mathcal{L}_{1\|2}$.*

Proof. We characterize $p(t)$ by the sequences (A_k) and (p_k) as in the proof of Lemma 3. We know by Lemma 3 that the share allocated to T_1 is constant and equal to $\pi_1 p_k$ on each interval A_k. Then, by summing the work done on each interval for both tasks, one can prove that they are completed simultaneously, and that this completion time is the same as that of task T_G under the same processor profile. $\qquad\square$

Theorem 1. *For every graph G, if $p(t)$ is a step function, G has the same optimal makespan as its equivalent task T_G of length $\mathcal{L}_G$ (computed as in Definition 1). Moreover, there is a unique optimal schedule, and it can be computed in polynomial time.*

Proof. In this proof, we only consider optimal schedules. Therefore, when the makespan of a graph is considered, this is implicitly its optimal makespan. We first remark that in any optimal schedule, as $p(t)$ is a step function and because of Lemma 2, only step functions are used to allocate processors to tasks, and so Lemma 4 can be applied on any subgraph of G without checking that the processor profile is also a step function for this subgraph. We now prove the result by induction on the structure of G.

- G is a single task. The result is immediate.
- G is the series composition of G_1 and G_2. By induction, G_1 (resp. G_2) has the same makespan as task T_{G_1} (resp. T_{G_2}) of length $\mathcal{L}_{G_1}$ (resp. $\mathcal{L}_{G_2}$) under any processor profile. Therefore, the makespan of G is equal to $\mathcal{L}_G = \mathcal{L}_{G_1\,;\,G_2} = \mathcal{L}_{G_1} + \mathcal{L}_{G_2}$. The unique optimal schedule of G under $p(t)$ processors is the concatenation of the optimal schedules of G_1 and G_2.
- G is the parallel composition of G_1 and G_2. By induction, G_1 (resp. G_2) has the same makespan as task T_{G_1} (resp. T_{G_2}) of length $\mathcal{L}_{G_1}$ (resp. $\mathcal{L}_{G_2}$) under any processor profile. Consider an optimal schedule S of G and let $p_1(t)$ be the processor profile allocated to G_1. Let $\tilde{S}$ be the schedule of $(T_{G_1} \parallel T_{G_2})$ that allocates $p_1(t)$ processors to T_{G_1}. $\tilde{S}$ is optimal and achieves the same makespan as S for G because T_{G_1} and G_1 (resp. T_{G_2} and G_2) have the same makespan under any processor profile. Then, by Lemma 4, $\tilde{S}$ (so S) achieves the same makespan as the optimal makespan of the task T_G of length $\mathcal{L}_{G_1\parallel G_2} = \mathcal{L}_G$. Moreover, by Lemma 3 applied on $(T_{G_1} \parallel T_{G_2})$, we have $p_1(t) = \pi_1 p(t)$. By induction, the unique optimal schedules of G_1 and G_2 under respectively $p_1(t)$ and $(p(t) - p_1(t))$ processors can be computed. Therefore, there is a unique optimal schedule of G under $p(t)$ processor: the parallel composition of these two schedules.

Therefore, there is a unique optimal schedule for G under $p(t)$. Moreover, it can be computed in polynomial time. We describe here the algorithm to compute the optimal schedule of a tree G, but it can be extended to treat SP-graphs. The length of the equivalent task of each subtree of G can be computed in polynomial time by a depth-first search of the tree (assuming that raising a number to the power α or $1/\alpha$ can be done in polynomial time). Hence, the ratios π_1 and π_2 for each parallel composition can also be computed in polynomial time. Finally, these ratios imply the computation in linear time of the ratios of the processor profile that should be allocated to each task after its children are completed, which describes the optimal schedule. □

5 Extensions to Distributed Memory

The objective of this section is to extend the previous results to the case where the computing platform is composed of several nodes with their own private memory. In order to avoid the large communication overhead of processing a task on cores distributed across several nodes, we forbid such a multi-node execution: the tasks of the tree can be distributed on the whole platform but each task has to be processed on a single node. We prove that this additional constraint, denoted by $\mathcal{R}$, renders the problem much more difficult. We concentrate first on platforms with two homogeneous nodes and then with two heterogeneous nodes.

5.1   Two Homogeneous Multicore Nodes

In this section, we consider a multicore platform composed of two equivalent nodes having the same number of computing cores p. We also assume that all the tasks T_i have the same speedup function p_i^α on both nodes. We first show that finding a schedule with minimum makespan is weakly NP-complete, even for independent tasks:

Theorem 2. *Given two homogenous nodes of p processors, n independent tasks of sizes $L_1, ..., L_n$ and a bound T, the problem of finding a schedule of the n tasks on the two nodes that respects $\mathcal{R}$, and whose makespan is not greater than T, is (weakly) NP-complete for all values of the α parameter defining the speedup function.*

The proof relies on the Partition problem, which is known to be weakly (i.e., binary) NP-complete [8], and uses tasks of length $L_i = a_i^\alpha$, where the a_i's are the numbers from the instance of the Partition problem. We recall that we assume that functions $x \mapsto x^\alpha$ and $x \mapsto x^{1/\alpha}$ can be computed in polynomial time. Details can be found in the companion research report [10].

We also provide a constant ratio approximation algorithm. We recall that a ρ-approximation provides on each instance a solution whose objective z is such that $z \le \rho z*$, where $z*$ is the optimal value of the objective on this instance.

Theorem 3. *There exists a polynomial time $\left(\frac{4}{3}\right)^\alpha$-approximation algorithm for the makespan minimization problem when scheduling a tree of malleable tasks on two homogenous nodes.*

Due to lack of space, we refer the interested reader to the companion research report for the complete description of the algorithm and proof [10]. The proof of the approximation ratio consists in comparing the proposed solution to the optimal solution on a single node made of $2p$ processors, denoted $\mathcal{S}_{\text{PM}}$. Such an optimal solution can be computed as proposed in the previous section, and is a lower bound on the optimal makespan on 2 nodes with p processors. The general picture of the proposed algorithm is the following. First, the root of the tree is arbitrarily allocated to the p processors of one of the two nodes. Then, the subtrees S_i's rooted at the root's children are considered. If none of these subtrees is allocated more than p processors in $\mathcal{S}_{\text{PM}}$, then we show how to "pack" the subtrees on the two nodes and bound the slow-down by $\left(\frac{4}{3}\right)^\alpha$. On the contrary, if one of the S_i's is allocated more than p processors in $\mathcal{S}_{\text{PM}}$, then we allocate p processors to its root, and recursively call the algorithm on its children and on the remaining subtrees.

5.2 Two Heterogeneous Multicore Nodes

We suppose here that the computing platform is made of two processors of different processing capabilities: the first one is made of p cores, while the second one includes q cores. We also assume that the parameter α of the speedup function is the same on both processors. As the problem gets more complicated, we concentrate here on n independent tasks, of lengths $L_1, ..., L_n$. Thanks to the homogenous case presented above, we already know that scheduling independent tasks on two nodes is NP-complete.

This problem is close to the SUBSET SUM problem. Given n numbers, the optimization version of SUBSET SUM considers a target K and aims at finding the subset with maximal sum smaller than or equal to K. There exists many approximation schemes for this problem. In particular, Kellerer et al. [15] propose a fully polynomial approximation scheme (FPTAS). Based on this result, an approximation scheme can be derived for our problem.

Theorem 4. *There exists an FPTAS for the problem of scheduling independent malleable tasks on two heterogeneous nodes, provided that, for each task, $L_i^{1/\alpha}$ is an integer.*

The proof is complex and detailed in [10]. The assumption on the $L_i^{1/\alpha}$s is needed to apply the FPTAS of SUBSET SUM, which is valid only on integers.

6 Conclusion

In this paper, we have studied how to schedule trees of malleable tasks whose speedup function on multicore platforms is p^α. We have first motivated the use of this model for sparse matrix factorizations by actual experiments. When using factorization kernels actually used in sparse solvers, we show that the speedup follows the p^α model for reasonable allocations. On the machine used for our tests, α is in the range 0.85–0.95. Then, we proposed a new proof of the optimal allocation derived by Prasanna and Musicus [19,20] for such trees on single node multicore platforms. Contrarily to the use of optimal control theory of the original proofs, our method relies only on pure scheduling arguments and gives more intuitions on the scheduling problem. Based on these proofs, we proposed several extensions for two multicore nodes: we prove the NP-completeness of the scheduling problem and propose a $\left(\frac{4}{3}\right)^\alpha$-approximation algorithm for a tree of malleable tasks on two homogeneous nodes, and an FPTAS for independent malleable tasks on two heterogeneous nodes.

The perspectives to extend this work follow two main directions. First, it would be interesting to extend the approximations proposed for the heterogeneous case to a number of nodes larger than two, and to more heterogeneous nodes, for which the value of α differs from one node to another. This is a promising model for the use of accelerators (such as GPU or Xeon Phi). The second direction concerns an actual implementation of the PM allocation scheme in a sparse solver.

References

1. Amestoy, P., Buttari, A., Duff, I.S., Guermouche, A., L'Excellent, J., Uçar, B.: Mumps. In: Padua, D.A. (ed.) Encyclopedia of Parallel Computing, pp. 1232–1238. Springer, USA (2011)
2. Ashcraft, C., Grimes, R.G., Lewis, J.G., Peyton, B.W., Simon, H.D.: Progress in sparse matrix methods for large linear systems on vector computers. Int. J. Supercomput. Appl. **1**(4), 10–30 (1987)
3. Augonnet, C., Thibault, S., Namyst, R., Wacrenier, P.A.: StarPU: a unified platform for task scheduling on heterogeneous multicore architectures. Concurrency Comput.: Prac. Experience **23**(2), 187–198 (2011)
4. Bosilca, G., Bouteiller, A., Danalis, A., Faverge, M., Herault, T., Dongarra, J.J.: PaRSEC: exploiting heterogeneity for enhancing scalability. Comput. Sci. Eng. **15**(6), 36–45 (2013)
5. Buttari, A.: Fine granularity sparse QR factorization for multicore based systems. In: International Confernece on Applied Parallel and Scientific Computing, pp. 226–236 (2012)
6. Drozdowski, M.: Scheduling parallel tasks - algorithms and complexity. In: Leung, J. (ed.) Handbook of Scheduling. Chapman and Hall/CRC, Boca Raton (2004)
7. Duff, I.S., Reid, J.K.: The multifrontal solution of indefinite sparse symmetric linear systems. ACM Trans. Math. Softw. **9**, 302–325 (1983)
8. Garey, M.R., Johnson, D.S.: Computers and Intractability: A Guide to the Theory of NP-Completeness. W.H. Freeman & Co., New York (1979)
9. Gautier, T., Besseron, X., Pigeon, L.: Kaapi: A thread scheduling runtime system for data flow computations on cluster of multi-processors. In: International Workshop on Parallel Symbolic Computation, pp. 15–23 (2007)
10. Guermouche, A., Marchal, L., Simon, B., Vivien, F.: Scheduling trees of malleable tasks for sparse linear algebra. Technical report, RR-8616, INRIA, October 2014
11. Hardy, G., Littlewood, J., Pólya, G.: Inequalities, Chap. 6.14. Cambridge Mathematical Library, Cambridge University Press, Cambridge (1952)
12. Hénon, P., Ramet, P., Roman, J.: PaStiX: a high-performance parallel direct solver for sparse symmetric definite systems. Parallel Comput. **28**(2), 301–321 (2002)
13. Hugo, A., Guermouche, A., Wacrenier, P.A., Namyst., R.: A runtime approach to dynamic resource allocation for sparse direct solvers. In: ICPP, pp. 481–490 (2014)
14. Jansen, K., Zhang, H.: Scheduling malleable tasks with precedence constraints. In: ACM Symposium on Parallelism in Algorithms and Architectures (SPAA), pp. 86–95 (2005)
15. Kellerer, H., Mansini, R., Pferschy, U., Speranza, M.G.: An efficient fully polynomial approximation scheme for the subset-sum problem. J. Comput. Syst. Sci. **66**(2), 349–370 (2003)
16. Lepère, R., Trystram, D., Woeginger, G.J.: Approximation algorithms for scheduling malleable tasks under precedence constraints. IJFCS **13**(4), 613–627 (2002)
17. Li, X.S.: An overview of SuperLU: algorithms, implementation, and user interface. ACM Trans. Math. Softw. **31**(3), 302–325 (2005)
18. Liu, J.W.H.: The role of elimination trees in sparse factorization. SIAM J. Matrix Anal. Appl. **11**(1), 134–172 (1990)
19. Prasanna, G.N.S., Musicus, B.R.: Generalized multiprocessor scheduling and applications to matrix computations. IEEE TPDS **7**(6), 650–664 (1996)
20. Prasanna, G.N.S., Musicus, B.R.: The optimal control approach to generalized multiprocessor scheduling. Algorithmica **15**(1), 17–49 (1996)

Elastic Tasks: Unifying Task Parallelism and SPMD Parallelism with an Adaptive Runtime

Alina Sbîrlea[1]([✉]), Kunal Agrawal[2], and Vivek Sarkar[1]

[1] Rice University, Houston, USA
alina@rice.edu
[2] Washington University in St. Louis, St. Louis, USA

Abstract. In this paper, we introduce *elastic tasks*, a new high-level parallel programming primitive that can be used to unify task parallelism and SPMD parallelism in a common adaptive scheduling framework. Elastic tasks are internally parallel tasks and can run on a single worker or expand to take over multiple workers. An elastic task can be an ordinary task or an SPMD region that must be executed by one or more workers simultaneously, in a tightly coupled manner.

This paper demonstrates the following benefits of elastic tasks: (1) they offer theoretical guarantees: in a work-stealing environment computations complete in expected time $O(W/P + S + E \lg P)$, where $E = \#$ of elastic tasks, $W =$ work, $S =$ span, $P = \#$ cores. (2) they offer performance benefits in practice by co-scheduling tightly coupled parallel/SPMD subcomputations within a single elastic task, and (3) they can adapt at runtime to the state of the application and work-load of the machine.

We also introduce ElastiJ — a runtime system that includes work-sharing and work-stealing scheduling algorithms to support computations with regular and elastic tasks. This scheduler dynamically decides the allocation for each elastic task in a non-centralized manner, and provides close to asymptotically optimal running times for computations with elastic tasks.

1 Introduction

As multicore machines become ubiquitous, *task parallelism* has emerged as a dominant paradigm for parallel programming. Many programming languages and libraries such as Cilk [10], Cilk Plus [1], Intel TBB [21], .Net Task Parallel Library [17], and Habanero-Java [5] support this paradigm, in which the programmer expresses the logical parallelism by specifying sequential tasks and their dependences, and a runtime scheduler maps the tasks on available processors.

SPMD parallelism [8] is an alternate paradigm for exploiting multicore parallelism, in which a fixed number of worker threads execute a single SPMD region. There is general agreement that SPMD parallelism can outperform task parallelism in certain cases, but task parallelism is more general than SPMD

© Springer-Verlag Berlin Heidelberg 2015
J.L. Träff et al. (Eds.): Euro-Par 2015, LNCS 9233, pp. 491–503, 2015.
DOI: 10.1007/978-3-662-48096-0_38

parallelism. There has even been work on compiler optimizations to automatically transform fork-join regions of code to SPMD regions for improved performance [7,18]. However, to the best of our knowledge, there has been no prior work that combines task parallelism and SPMD parallelism in a single adaptive runtime framework.

In this paper, we propose *elastic tasks*, a new primitive that helps bridge the gap between task parallelism and SPMD parallelism. An elastic task u is defined by: (1) $w(u)$ — the execution requirement (work) of u; and (2) $c(u)$ — the maximum number of workers (capacity) that task u can use. Elastic tasks are assumed to have linear scaling with $c(u)$ and to exhibit locality benefits from co-scheduling their internal parallelism, but they need not be data parallel. The user need only provide two additional parameters for u, both being an estimation rather than exact values: (1) the approximate length of the task on one worker as $w(u)$; and (2) the average parallelism of the task as $c(u)$. When an elastic task starts, it is assigned $a(u) \leq c(u)$ dedicated worker threads, which work on only this task until the task completes. An elastic task with $c(u) = 1$ is just like an ordinary task. An elastic task with $c(u) > 1$ is like an SPMD region which must be executed by one or more workers simultaneously in a tightly coupled manner.

We extend the work-sharing and work-stealing strategies [4] to handle computations with elastic tasks. We prove that the work-sharing scheduler completes a computation with work W and span S in $O(W/P + S + E)$ time, where E is the total number of elastic tasks. Similarly, the work-stealing scheduler completes the computation in $O(W/P + S + E \lg P)$ expected time.

Previous work, notably Wimmer and Träff [26] have considered a construct for mixed-mode parallelism, but, in their work, the number of workers assigned to a task is fixed, and user specified. In our scheduling strategy, if most workers are busy, then the elastic task is assigned fewer workers, since there is already ample parallelism in the rest of the program. If most workers are idle (or stealing), then it indicates a lack of parallelism and more workers are assigned to an elastic task. Finally, we are not aware of prior work that provides theoretical guarantees on the completion time for this form of combination of sequential and elastic tasks.

We have implemented a runtime system which implements elastic tasks, and include experimental results obtained from the work-stealing implementation.

In summary, the contributions of this paper are:

- the elastic task primitive, its definition, properties and requirements,
- theoretical proofs for the work-sharing and work-stealing runtimes,
- the ElastiJ runtime which executes computations with both sequential and elastic tasks and automatically decides the number of workers assigned to an elastic task,
- experimental results which indicate they provide locality benefits for certain computations and provide runtime adaptability.

The rest of the paper is organized as follows: Sect. 2 discusses the motivation for elastic tasks, Sect. 3 gives the theoretical proofs, Sect. 4 describes the implementation details of ElastiJ, Sect. 5 presents the experimental results, Sect. 6 discusses related work and finally Sect. 7 concludes.

2 Motivation for Elastic Tasks

2.1 Benefits of Elasticity

Given a computation expressible as an elastic task, we have a few other alternatives. First, we could create a *sequential task*. However, this can increase the critical path length (span) of the computation, thereby decreasing its parallelism.

Second, we could create an *inelastic task* where the programmer specifies the number of workers (say $m(u)$) which must execute node u (as in [26]). In this case, if the programmer accurately specifies $m(u)$ to be large, then the scheduler must find all these workers. If most workers are busy, the scheduler must either wait for a potentially long time (idle workers for long periods) or it must interrupt workers in the middle of their execution leading to large overheads. If the programmer artificially specifies $m(u)$ to be small to avoid this, then we are potentially wasting the internal parallelism of task u and decreasing the scalability of the overall computation, as with sequential tasks. Also, it is difficult to guarantee good performance theoretically for inelastic tasks.

Third, we could convert the task to a *task parallel computation* by dividing up the computation into independent tasks that need not be co-scheduled. This may be cumbersome if the different tasks need to communicate, since we must add a control synchronization point for every communication link. This also increases overheads; barriers within independently-scheduled tasks can be very inefficient. In addition, as discussed next, this transformation means that different iterations may be executed at very different times, leading to loss in locality.

2.2 Benefits of Co-Scheduling

Compared to sequential and inelastic tasks, with elastic tasks the programmer is only responsible for providing the capacity, not the precise number of workers. The runtime then adjusts the number of workers allocated to the task based on runtime conditions. Further we compare elastic tasks to task parallel computations.

Cache Locality on Multicores: Consider a loop in which all iterations access the same data. Using an elastic task forces all the iterations to be scheduled at the same time, so the shared data will be brought into the shared cache. Instead, had we converted this loop into a task parallel program, all the iterations would have been their own task, possibly scheduled at different times. Since other tasks that access other data may execute between different iterations of the loop, the shared data may have to be brought in multiple times leading to poor cache locality. We will show experimental results that validate this intuition in Sect. 5.

Locality on Future Architectures: While in this paper we show the importance of elastic tasks on multicores, we expect elastic tasks to become even more valuable for future extreme scale systems where collocation based on data sharing will be critical for performance. Additionally, an elastic task with data-parallel computations can also be automatically transformed into a GPU kernel using existing tools [3, 9, 16]. The adaptability of elastic tasks to task granularity also implies that applications can adjust to existing and future GPUs.

3   Theoretical Guarantees

We briefly state the theoretical guarantees proven in our technical report [22].

3.1   Model of Computation

Elastic tasks and normal sequential tasks are *processor oblivious* computations — the programmer expresses the logical parallelism and the *runtime scheduler* dynamically schedules and executes the computation on P worker threads.

The computation can be abstractly expressed as a computation DAG G; nodes are computation kernels and edges are dependences between nodes. A node is *ready* to execute when all its predecessors have been executed. Without loss of generality, we assume the maximum out-degree of any node ≤ 2. There are two types of nodes: *strands* — sequential chains of instructions and *elastic nodes*.

An elastic node u has the following properties: (1) Work $w(u)$ is its execution time on one worker. (2) Capacity $c(u)$ is its maximum internal parallelism. (3) Before an elastic node u can execute, the runtime scheduler must allocate it $1 \leq a(u)$ dedicated worker threads. Once u starts executing, these $a(u)$ workers can not work on anything else until u completes, and no other workers can work on u's work. (4) We assume that each elastic node provides linear speedup up to $c(u)$ workers and no speedup thereafter. When it is allocated $c(u)$ workers, we say that the node is *saturated*; otherwise we say that it is *unsaturated*.

As with traditional task parallel processor oblivious computations, we define two parameters for G. *Work* W is the sum of the computational requirements of all nodes or the execution time on one processor. *Span* is the weighted length of the longest path in the DAG where each node's weight is equal to its span. Span can also be seen as the execution time of the computation on an infinite number of processors. The parallelism of the program is defined as W/S and describes the maximum number of workers the computation can use effectively. Note that the execution time of the computation on P workers is at least $\max\{W/P, S\}$.

3.2   Theoretical Guarantees in a Work-Sharing Runtime

Theorem 1. *Given a computation graph with work W, span S, and E elastic nodes, the execution time of this computation on P workers using the work-sharing scheduler is $O(W/P + S + E)$.*

The above theorem states that the work-sharing scheduler provides linear speedup, and we prove this in the extended version of the paper [22].

3.3   Theoretical Guarantees in a Work-Stealing Runtime

Extending the Work-Stealing Scheduler with Elastic Nodes. In a regular work-stealing scheduler, a program is executed by P workers each having its own private deque of ready nodes. At any time, a worker p may have a node u **assigned** to it. When a worker finishes u, if p's deque is empty, then p becomes a thief, selects another worker p_1 as a **victim** at random and tries to steal from the top of p_1's deque. If p_1's deque is not empty and p gets a node, then the steal attempt is successful, otherwise p tries to steal again. Blumofe and Leiserson [4] prove that this randomized work-stealing scheduler finishes a computation with work W and span S in expected time $O(W/P + S)$ time on P worker threads.

For work-stealing schedulers with elastic nodes, a worker's assigned node may be a strand or an elastic node. The changes due to the elastic nodes affect what happens on steals and when a worker is assigned an elastic node:

1. If p picks up an elastic node u, p starts waiting on u, instead of starting execution.
2. When p is a thief, it randomly chooses a victim q. If q is waiting on an elastic node u, then u is also assigned to p and p also starts waiting on it. At this time $a(u)$ is incremented by 1. Otherwise, p steals the node at the top of q's deque; if the deque is empty then p tries again.
3. While u is waiting, its total waiting time $wait(u)$ is incremented by $a(u)$ in every time step.
4. An elastic node starts executing when either $a(u) = c(u)$ — the node is saturated; or its total wait time $wait(u) \geq w(u)$.
5. When an elastic node finishes executing, the worker that first enabled the elastic node enables its children. All other workers assigned to the elastic node start work stealing, as all their deques are empty at this time.

Analysis of Work-Stealing Scheduler

Theorem 2. *Given a computation graph with E elastic nodes, work W and span S, the expected execution time of this computation on P workers using the work-stealing scheduler is $O(W/P + S + E \lg P)$.*

If we compare this result to the result for computations without elastic nodes, we notice that the additional term is only $E \lg P$. This term is negligible for any computation where the number of elastic nodes is $O(T_1/P \lg P)$ — which implies that most elastic nodes have parallelism $\Omega(P)$ and at most $1/\lg P$ fraction of the work of the computation is contained in elastic nodes.

We mention that the constant factors hidden within the asymptotic bounds are not much larger than those hidden within the standard work-stealing bounds. An additional terms similar to $O(E \lg P)$ also appears in standard work-stealing if we consider the contention on the child counter (generally ignored).

In this section, without loss of generality, we assume that each strand is a unit time computation. A longer strand is simply expressed as a chain of unit time strands. We separately bound the types of steps that a worker can take at any time step. A worker could be working, waiting on an elastic node or stealing.

The total number of work-steps is at most W; and the total number of waiting steps is at most $W + PE$. Therefore, we need only bound the steal steps.

We classify steal attempts in three categories: (1) regular steal attempts occur when no elastic node is waiting and no unsaturated elastic node is executing. (2) waiting steal attempts are those that occur when some elastic node is waiting. (3) irregular steal attempts occur when some unsaturated elastic node is executing and no elastic node is waiting. We will bound the number of steal attempts in these three categories separately.

Intuition for the Analysis. We adopt a *potential function* argument similar to Arora et al.'s work-stealing analysis [2], henceforth referred to as ABP. In the ABP analysis, each ready node is assigned a potential that decreases geometrically with its distance from the start of the dag. For traditional work stealing, one can prove that most of the potential is in the ready nodes at the top of the deques. Therefore, $\Theta(P)$ random steal attempts suffice to process all the nodes on top of the deques. Therefore, one can prove that $O(PS)$ steal attempts are sufficient to reduce the potential to 0 in expectation. The ABP analysis does not directly apply to bounding the number of steal attempts for computations with elastic nodes because a steal may turn into a wait if the victim p has an assigned node u. Since u may contain most of the potential (particularly if p's deque is empty), and u cannot be stolen, steals are not longer effective in reducing the potential until u completes. Therefore, we must use a different argument to bound the steal attempts that occur while u is assigned to p.

Regular Steal Attempts: These occur when either a worker is assigned an elastic node (the normal ABP argument applies) or any elastic node that is assigned is saturated and is executing. We use a potential function argument very similar to the ABP argument, but on an augmented DAG in order to account for steal attempts that occur while a saturated elastic node is executing.

Waiting Steal Attempts: These occur when some elastic node (say u) is waiting — at this time, u is assigned to some worker(s), say p and p'. If any worker q tries to steal from p or p' during this time, then q also starts waiting on u and $a(u)$ increases by 1. Therefore, only a small number of steal attempts (in expectation) can occur before $a(u) = c(u)$ and u becomes saturated and stops waiting. We use this fact to bound the number of waiting steal attempts.

Irregular Steal Attempts: These occur when no elastic node is waiting and some unsaturated elastic node is executing. The analysis here is similar to the one we used to account for idle steps in the work-sharing scheduler (see [22]). Since this elastic node started executing without being saturated, it must have waited for at least $w(u)$ time — and during this time, all the workers not assigned to this elastic node were busy doing either work or waiting steal attempts. Therefore, any steal attempts by these workers can be amortized against these other steps.

The formal analysis can be found in the full technical report [22]. Below we provide the essential components that lead to the work-stealing bound.

Lemma 1. *Total number of regular steal attempts is $O(PS + P\lg(1/\epsilon))$ in expectation.*

Lemma 2. *There are $O(P\min\{\lg c(u), \lg P\})$ steal attempts in expectation while a particular elastic node u is waiting. Therefore, the expected number of waiting steal attempts over the entire computation is $O(PE\lg P)$.*

Lemma 3. *The total number of irregular steal attempts is at most $O(W + PE\lg P)$.*

Proof of Theorem 2: Combining Lemmas 1, 2 and 3 tells us that the total number of steal attempts over the entire computation is $O(W + PS + PE\lg P)$. In addition, we know that the total number of work steps and waiting steps is at most $O(W + PE)$. Therefore, if we add all types of steps and divide by P (since we have P worker threads and each take 1 step per unit time), we get the overall expected running time of $O(W/P + S + E\lg P)$.   □

4 Implementation Details

We created ElastiJ, a system that supports the creation and execution of elastic tasks. ElastiJ is build on top of the Habanero-Java library (HJlib) [14].

Elastic tasks are created using *asyncElastic*, a regular spawn call (*async* in HJlib) with two additional parameters: *work* - $w(u)$ and *capacity* - $c(u)$. The capacity of a task is the approximation of its average parallelism — for any task we can simply assume that it is the task's work ($w(u)$) divided by its critical path length (or span). The work $w(u)$ is the total running time of the task on 1 processor. Many tools exist to measure parallelism; e.g., for CilkPlus programs, Cilkview can be used to get $c(u)$. Two additional optional parameters: (*b(u)*, *e(u)*) can be used to describe the computation much like describing the iteration space for a loop. The runtime divides this range and assigns non-overlapping ranges to the workers executing the elastic node, similar to OpenMP's loop static scheduling [19], except that the number of workers is dynamic. For non-data-parallel computations these values can have a different meaning or simply not be used; e.g., in Sect. 5.2 we use Quicksort, where the partition phase - a computation that is not data parallel - is implemented as an elastic task.

ElastiJ uses a from-scratch work-sharing or work-stealing runtime implemented in Java. We use the work-stealing runtime in our results due to its better performance as shown in [10,12]. The runtime executes as described in Sect. 3.3, but the mechanism threads join an elastic task differs. The simplest approach is as follows: the first thread starts to wait $w(u)$, the second thread wakes up the first and both of them continue to wait for half of the remaining time, and so on. This approach causes a lot of overhead due to the several sleep and notify calls, in particular when many threads want to join at once. A better approach is for the first thread to wait $w(u)$ and store his wait start time. The second thread uses this wait time to compute how much the first thread already waited, and waits half of the remaining time, also storing the time he starts the wait. The process goes on until the last thread either saturates the task or has waited the remaining fraction of time and it wakes up all threads. This second approach has the advantage that each thread only goes to sleep once and is woken up once when it can start the work. However it also experiences a lot of overhead due to context-switching when the method wait is called. Since the waiting threads do not perform any work, a more efficient approach observed in practice is a bounded busy-wait approach. This third approach is the one we used in our experiments. In addition, the runtime uses as the total wait time a fraction of the full estimated work given to the task, in order to account for the constant factor in the theoretical proof, and thus offer competitive performance. The *asyncElastic* construct we propose also includes an implicit phaser [23] for all workers that join the task. The use of phasers instead of barriers can provide additional performance benefits [18].

5   Experimental Results

In this section, we use a series of benchmarks to demonstrate how elastic tasks perform in different scenarios. We first assess if elastic tasks have the potential to provide better locality using a synthetic micro-benchmark. Next, we use Quicksort and FFT algorithms to demonstrate that elastic tasks are easily integrated into task-parallel recursive programs and provide easy adaptability to task granularity. Finally, we evaluate the performance of ElastiJ using a set of single-level fork-join benchmarks from the IMSuite [13] set; we show little or no overhead from using elastic tasks and analyze their sensitivity to applications and parameters. The performance results were obtained on two platforms: (1) IBM POWER7: node with four eight-core POWER7 chips running at 3.86GHz, with 4 MB L3 cache per chip, and (2) Intel Westmere: node with 12 processor cores per node Intel Xeon X5660 running at 2.83 GHz.

5.1   Benefit from Locality

In Sect. 2, we described scenarios when elastic tasks give locality benefits. In this section, we evaluate this hypothesis by creating the following synthetic fork-join style application: the benchmark spawns n tasks of type ua in a single finish scope, where n is a multiple of the number of cores P. Each ua task accesses the same M elements of a vector A. Each ua task spawn P ub tasks, and each ub task accesses the same M elements of a different vector B. The capacity $c(u)$ of each elastic task is P, the maximum number of machine cores. All experiments in this section were obtained on the POWER7 (P=32). The program accepts a parameter to set the fraction α of ua tasks that are elastic tasks, and creates $n \times \alpha$ elastic tasks and $(1-\alpha) \times n$ regular tasks (strands). The program spawns α elastic tasks using *asyncElastic*, and $(1-\alpha)$ simulated elastic tasks using *async*. This simulation essentially means creating P regular tasks for each elastic task.

We expect a locality benefit due to the co-scheduling of the elastic tasks since all the workers executing the elastic task access the same array A. Therefore, it is likely that A will remain in the shared cache while this elastic task is executing. On the other hand, when we convert this elastic task into a normal task-parallel for-loop with P strands, these P strands may execute far apart in time — therefore, some of the ub tasks may pollute the cache in the meantime. The results below show this makes a difference when M is large enough to cause the ub tasks to evict part of the A data from L3 cache.

We run experiments by varying the fraction of elastic tasks: $0\% \leq \alpha \leq 100\%$ (0% means all tasks are regular tasks, while 100% means all tasks are elastic). All experiments report the average of the 20 best iterations over 3 runs, each with 30 iterations, to remove the JVM warm-up and variability between runs [11].

We set the size of the arrays to $M = 1,000,000$; with A being an array of integers this adds to 4MB of data. Note that we ignore the L1 and L2 caches, under the claim that the size chosen is large enough to ensure at least some evictions from L3 cache. The results of the experiments are shown in Fig. 1a. We notice that for elastic tasks the execution time remains essentially constant, while for regular tasks the performance is degrading as we increase their number. We ran an experiment with identical task size but with $M = 64.000$, and noticed constant performance when varying from 0–100% so the action of splitting the task cannot be the cause. We therefore go back to what we inferred and assume the data accessed by tasks ua is being invalidated by tasks ub. We use the $perf$ tool on the POWER7 to confirm this. Figure 1b plots the cache misses obtained by the $perf$ tool. We see that the number of cache misses increases up to $1.7\times$ when using regular tasks as opposed to elastic tasks.

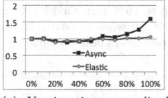
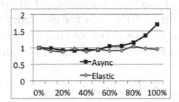

(a) Y-axis: time normalized w.r.t. 0%.

(b) Y-axis: cache misses normalized w.r.t. 0%.

Fig. 1. Microbenchmark comparing Elastic vs. Async task scheduling. X axis:% of elastic tasks.

We conclude that the use of elastic tasks should be used in a setting where their granularity amortizes the overhead of setting them up and that they can offer performance benefits due to improved locality.

5.2 Adaptability

We argue that elastic tasks provide the benefit that they integrate seamlessly with normal task parallelism which is suited to recursive algorithms. The quicksort algorithm is a recursive divide-and-conquer algorithm and can be easily expressed as a task-parallel program using async-finish or spawn-sync constructs. However, the divide step consists of a partition step. While partition can be expressed as a divide-and-conquer algorithm, that is a cumbersome implementation and many parallel implementations of quicksort simply use a sequential partition algorithm.

In this section, we evaluate the benefit of implementing the partition algorithm as an elastic task [25]. Note that the partition step is called at every level of recursion. The advantage of using elastic tasks for expressing it is that the number of workers assigned to this partition step is decided at runtime. At the shallow levels of the recursion tree where there is not much other work being done, the partition step will be automatically assigned more workers. At deeper levels of the tree, when there is already enough other parallel work available, the partition will execute mostly sequentially. Therefore, elastic tasks provide automatic adaptability without any intervention needed by the programmer.

In Fig. 2a, we compare elastic and async parallel implementations for quicksort with a parallel partition phase implemented with N asyncs, with N=# of machine cores, or as an elastic task. We present the results normalized w.r.t. the aync runs. In Fig. 2b, we compare two implementations of FFT, where the recombine phase is implemented either as a binary tree spawn using asyncs or as an elastic task. The data sets we use are 10^7 and 10^8 for quicksort, and 2^{22} and 2^{23} for FFT. For both quicksort and FFT we used a rough estimate for the work based on the array length; additional opportunities exist for auto-tuning the work based on the input, recursion depth, etc. We present results for both benchmarks on the POWER7 and the Westmere, by using the reporting the average of the best iterations out of 90 iterations, using 3 JVM invocations [11]. We get up to 70 % gain for quicksort and up to 16 % gain for FFT from using elastic tasks. We also note that the gains are larger when the data sizes increase a trend that we believe will lead to increased benefits in larger scale applications.

5.3   Sensitivity Analysis

We use 8 benchmarks from the IMSuite Benchmark Suite [13] to compare regular task spawning with the creation of elastic tasks. These benchmarks have a single-level fork-join structure, i.e., there is at most a single forAll loop active at a time,

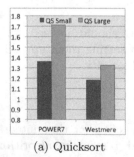

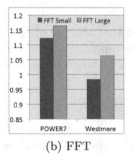

(a) Quicksort   (b) FFT

Fig. 2. Elastic task runs normalized over Async runs. >1 means elastic runs are better.

which means they do not offer any opportunity for benefits from elasticity. Our goal is to demonstrate on-par performance with regular work stealing (Async Finish primitives). We discover that elastic tasks can offer benefits even in this scenario due to their resilience to the theoretical assumptions and to the elastic task parameters. The benchmarks are: Bellman Ford, Byzantine Agreement, Dijkstra, General Leader Election, Maximum Independent Set, Vertex Coloring, k-Committee and Minimum Spanning Tree [13].

Figure 3 gives the results on the Westmere platforms (see the technical report [22] for full experimental analysis). Figure 3a shows better performance using elastic tasks for most benchmarks. The reason is that these benchmarks fail to scale linearly past 8 cores and our work estimation offers better performance by selecting fewer cores than the maximum. This means that elastic tasks can be used to tune applications even when the theoretical guarantee of linear scaling does not hold. So we looked into how sensitive the applications are to the API parameters, in particular the estimated work (restricting the capacity only limits parallelism so it makes no sense to restrict it). Figure 3b shows that the times are large for the W/10 case, which is expected, since a small estimation means not enough wait time for threads to join the task, thus wasting parallelism. Conversely, with W large we delay the computation, which leads to two combined causes for performance degradation: a longer wait time and a larger running time on 12 cores. Overall, the running time variation when W is varied is small and in many cases the added overhead is at most 10 %. In the few cases where the percentage-wise variation is larger, the absolute time is very small ([22]).

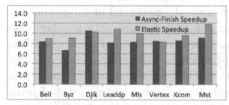

(a) Y axis: Speedup. Geomean=1.160.

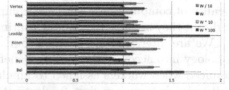

(b) X axis: Time normalized on the run using W.

Fig. 3. IMSuite results on Westmere. (a) The geomean is for elastic times normalized over Async runs (>1 if elastic runs are better).

We conclude our overall results with the following observations: (a) elastic tasks provide a common API for expressing task and SPMD parallelism and are straightforward and easy to use; (b) they can benefit from locality due to their coscheduling property; (c) they can be used to adapt the degree of parallelism for recursive benchmarks; (d) they can offer comparable performance with forall constructs, and are fairly resilient to the theoretical assumptions of elastic tasks and to the user-provided parameters.

6 Related Work

The closest related work is described as team-building [26] where programmers express inelastic tasks and the runtime allocates all workers. As mentioned in Sect. 1, our approach is quite distinct and we give theoretical proofs that our enhanced scheduler gives the same asymptotic bounds as regular work-stealing.

The problem of thread scheduling for locality improvements has been investigated in depth for work-stealing schedulers [6,12,20], both shared memory [12] and distributed [6,20]. ADAPT [15] proposes a framework implemented at OS level, which adapts the number of threads in a program, on machines where multiple programs concurrently. These works are orthogonal to elastic tasks.

A previous study [24] looked at a series of works which attempt to do coscheduling of tasks in general; this requires a coordinated effort which adds a lot of overhead in the absence of additional information. The authors formulate a mathematical model to analyze current approaches. Our work eases the challenge of coscheduling of tasks, when computations are expressible as an elastic task, and it can also be coupled with existing strategies. A more restrictive form of co-scheduling is gang scheduling, generally used for inelastic tasks.

7 Conclusions

In this paper we introduced the concept of elastic tasks, a construct that enables programmers to express adaptive parallel computations and rely on an elastic runtime to offer good performance from locality and load balancing. We proved that the work-stealing scheduler completes the computation in $O(W/P + S + E \lg P)$ expected time, where E is the total number of elastic tasks. We also showed practical results, that elastic tasks have the potential of improving the locality of computations, can yield comparable performance with regular tasks and that they are able to adapt at runtime, based on the load of the application.

We are interested in extending our approach to take more of the machine topology into account: the locality benefits of elastic tasks should be more pronounced when workers assigned to an elastic task share a certain level of proximity. As discussed in Sect. 2, elastic tasks are potentially useful for writing portable applications for heterogeneous machines that contain CPUs and GPUs and on distributed systems. Finally, elastic tasks have a potential to be useful for multiprogramming environments.

References

1. Agrawal, K., et al.: Executing task graphs using work-stealing. In: IPDPS 2010 (2010)
2. Arora, N.S., et al.: Thread scheduling for multiprogrammed multiprocessors. In: SPAA 1998 (1998)
3. Auerbach, J.S., Bacon, D.F., Cheng, P., Rabbah, R.M.: Lime: a java-compatible and synthesizable language for heterogeneous architectures. In: OOPSLA 2010 (2010)

4. Blumofe, R.D., Leiserson, C.E.: Scheduling multithreaded computations by work stealing. J. ACM **46**, 720–748 (1999)
5. Cavé, V., et al.: Habanero-java: the new adventures of old X10. In: PPPJ 2011 (2011)
6. Chen, Q., Guo, M., Guan, H.: Laws: locality-aware work-stealing for multi-socket multi-core architectures. In: ICS 2014 (2014)
7. Cytron, R., et al.: A compiler-assisted approach to SPMD execution. In: SC 1990 (1990)
8. Darema, F., George, D., Norton, V., Pfister, G.: A single-program-multiple-data computational model for EPEX/FORTRAN. Parallel Comput. **7**(1), 11–24 (1988)
9. ExascaleHabanero: Habanero C, https://wiki.rice.edu/confluence/display/HABANERO/Habanero-C
10. Frigo, M., et al.: The implementation of the Cilk-5 multithreaded lang. In: PLDI 1998 (1998)
11. Georges, A., et al.: Statistically rigorous java performance evaluation. In: OOPSLA 2007 (2007)
12. Guo, Y., et al.: SLAW: scalable locality-aware adaptive work-stealing scheduler. In: IPDPS 2010 (2010)
13. Gupta, S., Nandivada, V.K.: IMSuite: A Benchmark Suite for Simulating Distributed Algorithms. ArXiv e-prints, October 2013
14. Imam, S., Sarkar, V.: Habanero-java library: a java 8 framework for multicore programming. In: PPPJ 2014 (2014)
15. Kumar Pusukuri, K., et al.: Adapt: a framework for coscheduling multithreaded programs. ACM Trans. Archit. Code Optim. **9**, 45:1–45:24 (2013)
16. Luk, C.K., Hong, S., Kim, H.: Qilin: exploiting parallelism on heterogeneous multiprocessors with adaptive mapping. In: MICRO 2009 (2009)
17. Microsoft: "MSDN Magazine: Task Parallel Library", Accessed 11 September 2014. http://msdn.microsoft.com/en-us/magazine/cc163340.aspx
18. Nandivada, V.K., et al.: A transformation framework for optimizing task-parallel programs. ACM Trans. Program. Lang. Syst. **35**, 3:1–3:48 (2013)
19. OpenMP Architecture Review Board: The OpenMP API specification for parallel programming, version 4.0, July 2013
20. Paudel, J., Tardieu, O., Amaral, J.N.: On the merits of distributed work-stealing on selective locality-aware tasks. In: ICPP 2013 (2013)
21. Reinders, J.: Intel threading building blocks, 1st edn. O'Reilly and Associates Inc., Sebastopol (2007)
22. Sbirlea, A., et al.: Elastic Tasks: Unifying Task Parallelism and SPMD Parallelism with an Adaptive Runtime. Research Report TR15-02, Rice University (2015). http://engr.rice.edu/uploadedFiles/Tech_Reports/TR15-02_Elastic_Tasks.pdf
23. Shirako, J., Peixotto, D.M., Sarkar, V., Scherer, W.N.: Phasers: a unified deadlock-free construct for collective and point-to-point synchronization. In: ICS 2008 (2008)
24. Squillante, M.S., et al.: Modeling and analysis of dynamic coscheduling in parallel and distributed environments. In: SIGMETRICS 2002 (2002)
25. Tsigas, P., Zhang, Y.: A simple, fast parallel implementation of quicksort and its performance evaluation on sun enterprise 10000. In: PDP 2003 (2003)
26. Wimmer, M., Träff, J.L.: Work-stealing for mixed-mode parallelism by deterministic team-building. In: SPAA 2011 (2011)

Numerical Methods and Applications

Semi-discrete Matrix-Free Formulation of 3D Elastic Full Waveform Inversion Modeling

Stephen Moore[✉], Devi Sudheer Chunduri, Sergiy Zhuk, Tigran Tchrakian,
Ewout van den Berg, Albert Akhriev, Alberto Costa Nogueira Jr.,
Andrew Rawlinson, and Lior Horesh

IBM Research, Melbourne, Australia
stevemoore@au1.ibm.com

Abstract. Full waveform inversion (FWI) is an emerging subsurface imaging technique, used to locate oil and gas reservoirs. The key challenges that hinder its adoption by industry are both algorithmic and computational in nature, including storage, communication, and processing of large-scale data structures, which impose cardinal impediments upon computational scalability. In this work we will present a complete matrix-free algorithmic formulation of a 3D elastic time domain spectral element solver for both the forward and adjoint wave-fields as part of a greater cloud based FWI framework. We discuss computational optimisation (SIMD vectorisation, use of Many Integrated Core architectures, etc.) and present scaling results for two HPC systems, namely an IBM Blue Gene/Q and an Intel based system equipped with Xeon Phi coprocessors.

1 Introduction

In the field of exploration geophysics, Full Waveform Inversion (FWI) is regarded as the state-of-the-art seismic imaging technique. The goal of which is to detect and characterize subsurface geological structures such as ore minerals, hydrocarbons, geothermal reservoirs and aquifers. As the approach utilizes a comprehensive representation of the interaction between wave physics and subsurface properties, it offers unique advantages in terms of generality, fidelity, complexity, and robustness, and is hence capable of imaging arbitrarily heterogeneous compressional and shear wave velocity profiles of the subsurface constituents [1]. As a wavefield propagates through a medium of heterogeneous elastic properties, waves are reflected off different material regions in the subsurface. Data acquisition is performed by recording the response of the subsurface to excitation using an array of geophones deployed according to a predefined survey design [2].

By creating a computer model of the surveyed region (with a choice of subsurface material properties, or 'earth model') and assuming that a governing equation such as the acoustic or elastic wave equations are representative of the physics, a 'forward' simulation of the wavefield subject to the same excitation can be performed. From this simulation, synthetically generated seismograms

© Springer-Verlag Berlin Heidelberg 2015
J.L. Träff et al. (Eds.): Euro-Par 2015, LNCS 9233, pp. 507–518, 2015.
DOI: 10.1007/978-3-662-48096-0_39

can be created and the discrepancy between the experimental and computational seismograms can be assessed and used define an objective function in order to perform an inversion, minimising this descrepancy. At this point one may infer that the current a-posteriori subsurface estimate model is a sufficient approximation to reality, or alternatively, devise means to quantify uncertainty.

Two common approaches for the spatial discretization of a wave equation are the finite difference and spectral element methods (SEM), both of which generally use an explicit time marching scheme when solved in the time domain. The former technique is still the more common approach in the oil and gas industry, while the latter technique is more commonly related to the earthquake community, with much of the development in seismology performed by Komatitsch et al. [3,4] with the well known SPECFEM code. The advantages of the spectral element method lie in its applicability to unstructured meshes that can conform to a surface topology or subsurface structures, superior numerical dispersion properties, while still yeilding an efficient scalable algorithm. As such it has been used for large scale simulations [5] and incorporated the use of accelerators such as graphics processing units [6,7].

Our formulation is based heavily on the work of Komatitsch et al. and relies upon a high order spectral element discretization of the elastic wave equation and enables computation of the 'adjoint' wavefield, and consequently the gradient (or proximal function of which) of the objective function. The computational strategy privides a scalable algorithm based on a hybrid distributed-shared memory approach. The key contributions of the study are the investigation of computational optimisation including SIMD vectorisation and use of Many Integrated Core (MIC) architectures for two HPC systems, namely an IBM Blue Gene/Q and an Intel based system equipped with Xeon Phi coprocessors. This solver is one component of a greater effort aimed at the development of a cloud-based FWI framework.

2   Methods

The elastic wave equation [1] applied to a continuous solid is defined as

$$\rho \partial_{tt} u_i = \partial_{x_j} \sigma_{ij} + f_i \tag{1}$$

where $x \in \Omega \subset \mathbb{R}^3$ denotes a computational solid domain with boundary Γ, $t \in [0, T]$, $i, j \in [1, 2, 3]$, $\rho(x)$ is the mass density, $u(x, t)$ is the displacement vector field, $\sigma(x, t)$ is the stress tensor field, and $f(x, t)$ is a seismic source modeled in the form of a point source $f(x, t) = \theta(t)\delta(x - x_s)$ applied at x_s using a standard Ricker wavelet $\theta(t)$. Approximating the earth model with a linear isotropic relation, the stress tensor is related to displacement gradients as

$$\sigma_{ij} = \lambda \delta_{ij} \partial_{x_k} u_k + \mu \left(\partial_{x_i} u_j + \partial_{x_j} u_i \right) \tag{2}$$

where $\lambda(x)$ and $\mu(x)$ are the first and second *Lamé* parameters respectively. The elastic wave equation is subject to the standard initial conditions $u_i = \partial_t u_i = 0$, free surface boundary conditions $\sigma_{ij} n_j = 0$ and Clayton and Enquist absorbing boundary conditions $\sigma_{ij} n_j = -\rho v \partial_t u_i$ respectively, where n_j denotes the normal to the boundary Γ and v denotes the elastic wave speed. Using Galerkin projection with basis functions ψ, the weak form of the elastic wave equation is

$$\int_\Omega \psi \rho \partial_{tt} u_i d\Omega + \int_\Omega \partial_{x_j} \psi \sigma_{ij} d\Omega = \int_\Omega \psi f_i d\Omega + \int_\Gamma \psi \sigma_{ij} d\Gamma_j. \tag{3}$$

2.1 Discretization

Using the spectral element method for the spatial discretization, the computational domain is defined as a tesselation of N_e hexahedral elements (Fig. 1(c)) with the displacement field approximated as $u_i(x,t) \approx \psi_{pqr}(x) u_{i,pqr}(t)$, such that

$$\int_{\Omega^e} \psi_{abc} \rho \psi_{pqr} \partial_{tt} u_{i,pqr} d\Omega + \int_{\Gamma^e} \psi_{ab} \rho v \psi_{pq} \partial_t u_{i,pq} \, d\Gamma + \int_{\Omega^e} \partial_{x_j} \psi_{abc} \sigma_{ij} d\Omega = \int_{\Omega^e} \psi_{abc} f_i d\Omega \tag{4}$$

In this specific formulation the basis functions ψ_{pqr} are taken to be a tensor product of the family of Nth order Lagrange polynomials $\psi_{pqr} = \ell_p \ell_q \ell_r$ (Fig. 1(b)). After applying a geometric transformation to a reference element $\xi_i \in [-1, +1]$ (Fig. 1(a)), performing the integration with Gauss-Legendre-Lobatto (GLL) quadrature (Fig. 1(c)) [8], and then global assembly, gives the system of ODEs

$$\mathbf{M}(\mathbf{m})\ddot{\mathbf{u}} + \mathbf{C}(\mathbf{m})\dot{\mathbf{u}} + \mathbf{F}(\mathbf{m}, \mathbf{u}) = \mathbf{s}, \quad \text{s.t.} \quad \mathbf{u}(0) = \dot{\mathbf{u}}(0) = 0 \tag{5}$$

where $\mathbf{u}$ is the global set of displacements and $\mathbf{m}$ the global set of densities and Lamé parameters λ and μ defined for GLL points from all spectral elements in

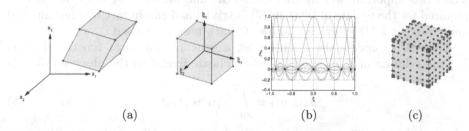

$$(a) \qquad\qquad\qquad (b) \qquad\qquad (c)$$

Fig. 1. Illustrations of (a) the transformation of a hexahedral element from x to ξ coordinates, (b) a family of 8th order Lagrange polynomials defined for $\xi_i \in [-1, +1]$, (c) an 8th order spectral element depicting the locations of the GLL quadrature/nodal points.

the grid. The mass M and damping C matrices, force $\mathbf{F}$ and source $\mathbf{s}$ vectors are given by

$$M = \sum_{e=1}^{N_e} \sum_{f,g,h=1}^{N+1} w_f w_g w_h \psi_{abc} \rho \psi_{pqr} \mathcal{J} \big|_{\xi_{1,f},\xi_{2,g},\xi_{3,h}}$$

$$C = \sum_{e=1}^{N_e} \sum_{f,g=1}^{N+1} w_f w_g \psi_{ab} \rho v_i \psi_{pq} \mathcal{J} \big|_{\xi_{1,f}\xi_{2,g}}$$

$$\mathbf{F} = \sum_{e=1}^{N_e} \sum_{f,g,h=1}^{N+1} w_f w_g w_h \partial_{\xi_k} \psi_{abc} \partial_{\xi_k} x_j \sigma_{ij,pqr} \mathcal{J} \big|_{\xi_{1,f},\xi_{2,g},\xi_{3,h}}$$

$$\mathbf{s} = \sum_{e=1}^{N_e} \sum_{f,g,h=1}^{N+1} w_f w_g w_h \psi_{abc} f_i \mathcal{J} \big|_{\xi_{1,f},\xi_{2,g},\xi_{3,h}} \tag{6}$$

where $\mathcal{J}$ defines the Jacobian of the transformation mapping to the reference element, and w_f denote the weights associated with the GLL quadrature. Due to the cardinal interpolation properties of the Lagrange polynomials $\ell_a(\xi_f) = \delta_{af}$ and the specific choice of GLL quadrature, the mass and damping matrices (which don't involve spatial derivatives of the Lagrange polynomials) are diagonal and hence trivially assembled and stored as 1D arrays. It is worthwhile mentioning that $\mathbf{F}(\mathbf{m}, \mathbf{u}) \equiv K(\mathbf{m})\mathbf{u}$ where K is the well known (sparse, but non-diagonal), stiffness matrix in solid mechanics, which linearly depends on $\mathbf{m}$. Finally, in order to perform the time integration, an explicit form of the Newmark Method [9] is used:

$$\mathbf{u}^{n+1} = \mathbf{u}^n + \Delta t \dot{\mathbf{u}}^n + \tfrac{1}{2}\Delta t^2 \ddot{\mathbf{u}}^n$$

$$\hat{\mathbf{u}}^{n+1} = \dot{\mathbf{u}}^n + \tfrac{1}{2}\Delta t^2 \ddot{\mathbf{u}}^{n+1}$$

$$\ddot{\mathbf{u}}^{n+1} = (M + \tfrac{1}{2}\Delta t C)^{-1} \left(\mathbf{s}^{n+1} - C\hat{\mathbf{u}}^{n+1} - \mathbf{F}(\mathbf{u}^{n+1}) \right)$$

$$\dot{\mathbf{u}}^{n+1} = \hat{\mathbf{u}}^{n+1} + \tfrac{1}{2}\Delta t^2 \ddot{\mathbf{u}}^{n+1} \tag{7}$$

where it is important to note that due to the diagonality of M and C the inverse required for the update of $\ddot{\mathbf{u}}^{n+1}$ in (7) is trivial and can in fact be precomputed and stored as a 1D array once M and C have been assembled.

In order to update the earth model, a generic data misfit functional relating the solution of the discrete forward elastic model to the observed data is defined as

$$J(\mathbf{u}, \mathbf{m}) = \int_0^T r(\mathbf{u}, \mathbf{m}, t) dt \tag{8}$$

where the $r(x) > 0$ if $x \neq 0$ is a noise model quantifying the error between observed and computed displacements at a number of sensor locations. Estimation of the earth model, $\mathbf{m}$, given the observed data by variational approaches (gradient descent or Quasi-Newton methods) requires the computation of $\partial_{\mathbf{m}} J$.

The latter is achieved by introducing the following adjoint equation

$$\ddot{\mathbf{a}}^T M - \dot{\mathbf{a}}^T C + \mathbf{a}^T K = \partial_u r, \quad \text{s.t.} \quad \mathbf{a}(T) = \dot{\mathbf{a}}(T) = 0. \tag{9}$$

By defining the system of first order ODEs

$$\dot{\boldsymbol{\beta}} = \left(\ddot{\mathbf{a}}^T \partial_{\mathbf{m}} M - \dot{\mathbf{a}}^T \partial_{\mathbf{m}} C + \mathbf{a}^T \partial_{\mathbf{m}} K\right) \mathbf{u} + \partial_{\mathbf{m}} r, \quad \text{s.t.} \quad \boldsymbol{\beta}(0) = 0, \tag{10}$$

then the gradient of the misfit functional is given by

$$\partial_{\mathbf{m}} J = \int_0^T \dot{\boldsymbol{\beta}} dt. \tag{11}$$

The key drawback of the approach for computing $\partial_{\mathbf{m}} J$ is that computation of $\dot{\boldsymbol{\beta}}$ requires the storage of either $\mathbf{u}$ or $\mathbf{a}$ in the memory, as the former is integrated forward in time and the latter is integrated backwards in time. Storage of either discrete wavefield at each GLL point at every time step in memory would prohibitively limit scalability. A number of techniques have been developed in order to address this problem [10], such as storing the forward solution only on boundary GLL points at each time step and then solving the elastic equation backward in time with the adjoint using this data as boundary conditions [11], or using some form of checkpoint strategy where the complete solution is stored periodically [12]. Our approach, is based heavily on a strategy from [10] where, in a first step, (5) is integrated forwards in time and the complete elastic wavefield $\mathbf{u}$, $\dot{\mathbf{u}}$, $\ddot{\mathbf{u}}$ is stored in memory at a series of checkpoint steps (Fig. 2). Then, in a second step, (9) and (10) are integrated backwards in time using the Newmark and Midpoint methods respectively. Between two checkpoints (5) is integrated forwards in time, and $\mathbf{u}$ is stored in memory at every time step between checkpoints such that the right hand side of (10) can be evaluated.

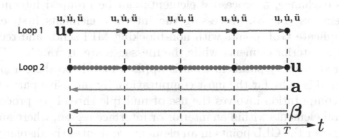

Fig. 2. An illustration of the checkpointing strategy used in the computation of the gradient. In the first loop $\mathbf{u}$ is integrated forward in time and at check points (black dots) $\mathbf{u}$, $\dot{\mathbf{u}}$, $\ddot{\mathbf{u}}$ are stored in memory. In the second loop these checkpoints are used to march $\mathbf{u}$ forward in time between two checkpoints where the entire displacement field is stored in memory at each time step (red dots). $\mathbf{a}$ and $\boldsymbol{\beta}$ are then integrated backwards in time from checkpoint to checkpoint allowing for $\boldsymbol{\beta}$ to be computed in (10) since all of the required data $\mathbf{u}$, $\mathbf{a}$, $\dot{\mathbf{a}}$, $\ddot{\mathbf{a}}$ is stored in memory (Color figure online).

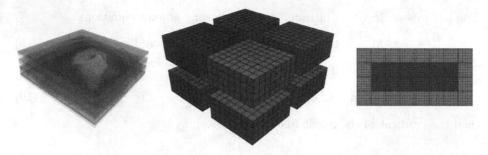

Fig. 3. An illustration of a computational domain (left) that is discretized into spectral elements and decomposed amongst multiple compute nodes (middle), where a given processes' portion of elements (right) are further separated into interior (blue) and interface (red) elements (Color figure online).

2.2 Parallel Implementation

The spectral element and Newmark discretization methods allow for a relatively simple explicit time marching scheme. The key contribution of this paper is focussed on the parallel implementation of this solver involves a hybrid distributed-shared memory approach implemented with MPI and OpenMP. The distributed memory aspect involves a standard domain decomposition approach where individual processes are responsible for the time marching over a unique subset of spectral elements (Fig. 3). This approach implies that GLL points shared by spectral elements on neighbouring processes will be duplicated and so when the forces $\mathbf{F}(\mathbf{m}, \mathbf{u})$ are assembled at each time step in the forward or adjoint solve, the forces need to be exchanged and summed between any processes that contain a duplicated GLL point. In order to hide the latency of this data exchange, a processes' elements can be grouped into interior and interface elements (Fig. 3), processing the interface elements first, exchanging forces on duplicate GLL points with non-blocking MPI sends and receives, and processing the interior elements while the messages are in transit.

The shared memory parallelization is applied mainly to the computation of the forces, as this is by far the most computationally intensive part of the algorithm. The computation involves the use of multiple threads to process the different spectral elements within an interior or interface region, where an OpenMP thread loops over the GLL points in an element, computes the displacement gradients and stresses at each GLL point, performs the integration, and updates the forces array, which is shared by all threads. The update involves a synchronized write to the memory, which is achieved using OpenMP locks by maintaining a lock for each shared GLL point; a more flexible and scalable approach compared to using either a critical or named critical sections. Pseudocode for the evalutation of the forces is presented in Algorithm 1.

```
for region=interface:interior
    #pragma omp for
    for e=1:N_e // in region
        for p,q,r=1:N+1 // each GLL point
            Compute displacement gradients
            Compute stresses
            Integrate
            omp_set_lock at GLL point pqr
                Update global forces array
            omp_unset_lock at GLL point pqr
        end
    end
    if region==interface
        MPI_Isend then MPI_Irecv forces on duplicate GLL points
    end
    MPI_WaitAll
end
```

Algorithm 1. Pseudocode for computation of forces at each time step.

2.3 Experimental Setup

Experiments were performed on two different systems, namely an IBM Blue Gene/Q and the Intel based 'Stampede' supercomputers. Each Blue Gene/Q compute node contains a 16 core 1.6 GHz A2 processor, with 16 GB of DDR3 memory. Each core supports four-way Symmetric Multithreading (SMT) and in our implementation uses 64 threads per node. Each core has a Quad Floating Point Unit (FPU) supporting 4-way double precision SIMD operations. The code was compiled with the IBM XLC compiler. The Stampede compute nodes contain two Intel Xeon E5-2680 8 core (Sandy Bridge) at 2.7 Ghz, one Intel Xeon Phi SE10P 61 core (Knights Corner) coprocessor at 1.09 GHz, and 32 GB of DRAM. The Sandy Bridge core has 256-bit vector registers and can be programmed using the 256-bit vector intrinsics. The Xeon Phi coprocessor is a Many Integrated Cor architecture, the basis of which is a light-weight x86 core with in-order instruction processing, coupled with heavy-weight 512bit SIMD registers and instructions. With these two features the Phi die can support 61 cores, and can execute 8 double precision SIMD instructions. The code was compiled and run using Intel Composer XE 2013 and Intel MPI Library 4.1.

The nature of the algorithm is such that most computations required at a GLL point, such as the displacement gradients in the ξ_i and x_i coordinates for example:

$$\frac{\partial u_i}{\partial \xi_1} = \sum_{f=1}^{N+1} \left(\frac{\partial \ell_f}{\partial \xi_1} u_i \right) \Big|_{\xi_{1,p}}, \qquad \frac{\partial u_i}{\partial x_1} = \frac{\partial u_i}{\partial \xi_1} \frac{\partial \xi_1}{\partial x_1} + \frac{\partial u_i}{\partial \xi_2} \frac{\partial \xi_2}{\partial x_1} + \frac{\partial u_i}{\partial \xi_3} \frac{\partial \xi_3}{\partial x_1} \qquad (12)$$

can be performed in a vectorizable fashion for $i \in [1, 2, 3]$, with similar expressions for displacement gradients in other directions, and with similar operations for the computation of stresses and the integration. Taking advantage of this fact we used the QPX intrinsics on Blue Gene/Q such as `vec_mul`, `vec_madd` for example, to perform multiply and multiply-add operations respectively, using 3 of the 4 available execution slots. Despite not using the full capacity of the floating point unit, this approach significantly improves performance without requiring development of a more complex algorithm. With the Sandy Bridge core the same approach is also used, but with the AVX intrinsics. With the MIC architecture on the other hand, the ability to perform 8 double precision SIMD instructions would mean that this approach would make far less efficient use of the SIMD registers. To test its full capacity a restriction was made to 7th order Lagrange polynomials in the discretization (hence $N+1=8$) and the algorithm for the computation of forces was restructured so that rather than vectorize the computation of quantities in $i \in [1, 2, 3]$, terms in the Lagrange polynomial $f \in [1-N+1]$ (12) were vectorized with KNC mutliply and a reduction instrinsic such as `_mm512_mul_pd` and `_mm512_reduce_add_pd` respectively.

3   Results and Discussion

To test the scalability of the solver, both strong and weak scaling runs were performed on each system for a simulation of the forward wavefield only, without checkpointing (since the nature of the algorithm means that the adjoint and β fields will scale in the same way) applied to the SEG/EAGE Salt Model (Fig. 3), where the subsurface material properties were interpolated onto a SEM grid of the equivalent domain. On each Blue Gene/Q compute node 1 MPI process was instantiated and multiple threads were instantiated on the 16 cores. To test the distributed memory parallelization, Figs. 4(a) and (b) present the speedup

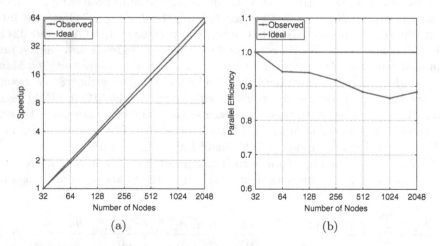

(a)   (b)

Fig. 4. Strong scaling results for the forward solver presenting (a) speedup and (b) parallel efficiency for an internode run, testing the distributed memory parallelization on Blue Gene/Q (Color figure online).

and parallel efficiency for a grid comprising approximately 5.5 billion degrees of freedom which is distributed over increasingly more compute nodes. As can be observed the solver scales well out to 2048 compute nodes (which is in fact two Blue Gene/Q 'racks'). To test the shared memory parallelization Figs. 5(a)–(b) present the speedup and parallel efficiency within a single compute node for a grid comprising approximately 6.4 million degrees of freedom. As can be observed the solver scales reasonably well to 16 threads per node. With 32 and 64 threads per node however, the hardware threading capability is being utilized, which shows an improvement but decreasing parallel efficiency, as expected. To test the weak scalability Fig. 6 presents the run time for a sample 500 time steps with grid portions comprising 6.4 million degrees of freedom per MPI process, implying that with 1024 compute nodes the total grid size comprises approximately 6.5 billion degrees of freedom. As can be observed the solver performs reasonably well requiring approximately 13 % greater run time for a grid approximately one thousand times larger. Figures 7(a) and (b) present the speedup and parallel efficiency for the grid comprising approximately 5.5 billion degrees of freedom on Stampede. As can be observed the solver scales reasonably well out to 512 compute nodes. The speedup on Stampede is less than that on Blue Gene/Q on for large node runs, the reason for which could be that the topology of nodes allocated on Stampede are in general irregular, whereas as on Blue Gene/Q the nodes allocated for a job have a structured topology resulting in good MPI communication performance.

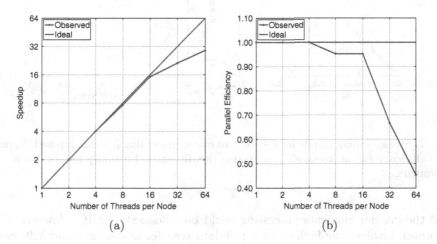

Fig. 5. Strong scaling results for the forward solver presenting (a) speedup and (b) parallel efficiency for an intranode run, testing the shared memory parallelization on Blue Gene/Q.

As previously mentioned, Stampede compute nodes are equipped with Intel Xeon Phi (MIC) accelerators. In general, there are two ways in which MIC accelerator could be used. Once a portion of the grid is allocated to a node, the elements in the domain could be distributed between host and MIC, for instance, the host operating on interface elements which involves MPI communication,

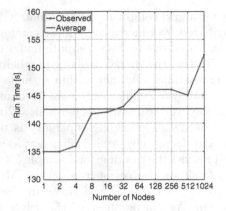

Fig. 6. Weak scaling results for the forward solver presenting the run time for 500 time steps on Blue Gene/Q (Color figure online).

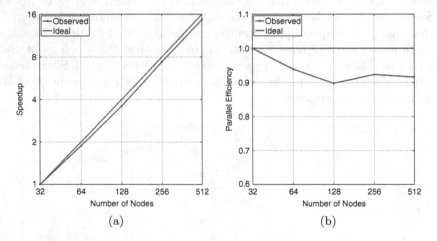

Fig. 7. Strong scaling results for the forward solver presenting (a) speedup and (b) parallel efficiency for an internode run, testing the distributed memory parallelization on Stampede.

and the interior elements processing could be offloaded to MIC. However, this approach involves the high overhead of data transfer across host and MIC each time step to update the displacement gradients and global force array. The other approach is to assign a portion of the grid to the MIC, and an MPI process running on each MIC. This could be accomplished using the symmetric MPI methodology between host and MIC. It becomes crucial in this approach to balance the compute load between CPU and MIC. Since the core computation part in the code involves irregular memory accesses, and hence poor last level cache locality, the memory access problem becomes even severe on MIC where a lot of threads compete for the memory interface controller. According to our

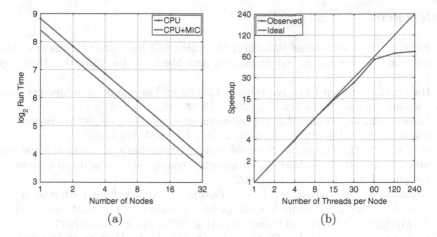

Fig. 8. Strong scaling results for the forward solver comparing CPU and symmetric CPU+MIC, presenting (a) runtime for an internode run testing the distributed memory parallelization and (b) speedup for a MIC intranode run testing the shared memory parallelization on Stampede.

experiments, we identified that on average, the code runs on a MIC (using 120 threads) 3 times slower than the host (using 16 cores). So, the approach used to balance the load is to have 3 MPI tasks run on the CPU each using 5 threads and 1 MPI task runs on the MIC. Figure 8(a) presents strong scaling results for both cases for a grid comprising approximately 115 million degrees of freedom, using only the host to run 3 MPI processes with 5 OpenMP threads per process, and additionally running 1 MPI task with 120 threads on the MIC. As the results show, using the MIC, results in around 34 % improvement in performance. To test the shared memory parallelization Fig. 8(b) presents the speedup within a MIC for a grid comprising approximately 32 million degrees of freedom. As can be observed the solver scales reasonably well to 60 threads per MIC. With 120 and 180 threads per MIC, the hardware threading capability (of which the MIC has support up to 4 hardware threads per core) are utilized, which show an improvement, but decreasing parallel efficiency. Since the code uses 512-bit vector intrinsics, and since the vector unit is shared across the threads in a core, there is no improvement when 240 threads are used.

4   Conclusions

A communication-avoiding, matrix-free formulation and parallelization strategy for a 3D elastic spectral element forward, adjoint, and gradient solver has been introduced. The proposed algorithmic framework requires minimal storage and communication and shows remarkable scalability on large computational domains. Future work will include the addition of the variational approach (using $\partial_m J$ to update the earth model and thereby completing the FWI algorithm) and integrating the solver with the cloud-based delivery model.

References

1. Fichtner, A.: Full Seismic Waveform Modelling and Inversion. Advances in Geophysical and Environmental Mechanics and Mathematics. Springer, Heidelberg (2010)
2. Haber, E., Van Den Doel, K., Horesh, L.: Optimal design of simultaneous source encoding. Inverse Prob. Sci. Eng. **23**, 1–18 (2014)
3. Komatitsch, D., Tromp, J.: Spectral-element simulations of global seismic wave propagation - i. validation. Geophys. J. Int. **149**, 390–412 (2002)
4. Komatitsch, D., Tromp, J.: Spectral-element simulations of global seismic wave propagation - ii. three-dimensional models, oceans, rotation and self-gravitation. Geophys. J. Int. **150**, 303–318 (2002)
5. Komatitsch, D., Tsuboi, S., Ji, C., Tromp, J.: A 14.6 billion degrees of freedom, 5 teraflops, 2.5 terabyte earthquake simulation on the earth simulator. In: ACM/IEEE Conference on Supercomputing, 2003, pp. 4–4, Nov 2003
6. Komatitsch, D., Erlebacher, G., Göddeke, D., Michéa, D.: High-order finite-element seismic wave propagation modeling with MPI on a large GPU cluster. J. Comput. Phys. **229**(20), 7692–7714 (2010)
7. Komatitsch, D.: Fluid-solid coupling on a cluster of GPU graphics cards for seismic wave propagation. Comptes Rendus Mécanique **339**(2–3), 125–135 (2011)
8. Parter, S.V.: On the legendre-gauss-lobatto points and weights. J. Sci. Comput. **14**(4), 347–355 (1999)
9. Kane, C., Marsden, J.E., Ortiz, M., West, M.: Variational integrators and the newmark algorithm for conservative and dissipative mechanical systems. Int. J. Numer. Methods Eng. **49**, 1295–1325 (1999)
10. Anderson, J.E., Tan, L., Wang, D.: Time-reversal checkpointing methods for rtm and fwi. Geophysics **77**(4), S93–S103 (2012)
11. Gauthier, O., Virieux, J., Tarantola, A.: Two-dimensional nonlinear inversion of seismic waveforms; numerical results. Geophysics **51**(7), 1387–1403 (1986)
12. Griewank, A., Walther, A.: Algorithm 799: revolve: an implementation of checkpointing for the reverse or adjoint mode of computational differentiation. ACM Trans. Math. Softw. **26**(1), 19–45 (2000)

10,000 Performance Models per Minute – Scalability of the UG4 Simulation Framework

Andreas Vogel[1]($\boxtimes$), Alexandru Calotoiu[2], Alexandre Strube[3],
Sebastian Reiter[1], Arne Nägel[1], Felix Wolf[4], and Gabriel Wittum[1]

[1] Goethe Universität Frankfurt, Frankfurt am Main, 60325 Frankfurt, Germany
vogel@gcsc.uni-frankfurt.de
[2] German Research School for Simulation Sciences, 52062 Aachen, Germany
[3] Forschungszentrum Jülich, 52425 Jülich, Germany
[4] Technische Universität Darmstadt, 64293 Darmstadt, Germany

Abstract. Numerically addressing scientific questions such as simulating drug diffusion through the human stratum corneum is a challenging task requiring complex codes and plenty of computational resources. The UG4 framework is used for such simulations, and though empirical tests have shown good scalability so far, its sheer size precludes analytical modeling of the entire code. We have developed a process which combines the power of our automated performance modeling method and the workflow manager JUBE to create insightful models for entire UG4 simulations. Examining three typical use cases, we identified and resolved a previously unknown latent scalability bottleneck. In collaboration with the code developers, we validated the performance expectations in each of the use cases, creating over 10,000 models in less than a minute, a feat previously impossible without our automation techniques.

1 Introduction

A broad variety of research questions in natural sciences is formulated in terms of partial differential equations. The range of applications reaches from classical continuum field descriptions - such as fluid dynamics, electromagnetism, or structure mechanics - over biological settings - e.g., drug diffusion through the human skin or computational neuroscience - to non-physical settings such as computational finance. Numerical simulations can be used to predict or compare with measured physical behavior and help to gain insight into the underlying physical processes. A software framework focusing on the grid-based solutions of these problems is UG4 [28].

Such simulation codes demand increased computational resources to perform larger and more refined simulations. Therefore, they must scale to the largest computing clusters to benefit from available computing power. However, code developers face two challenges: First, the source code is large, making manual analysis and optimization of the code time consuming and error prone. This creates a strong need for an automated workflow supporting scaling analysis.

© Springer-Verlag Berlin Heidelberg 2015
J.L. Träff et al. (Eds.): Euro-Par 2015, LNCS 9233, pp. 519–531, 2015.
DOI: 10.1007/978-3-662-48096-0_40

Second, code developers have to consume lots of computing resources for testing and can only run tests up to their currently available process counts. This requires a workflow that allows performance modeling using data from smaller process counts and hence offers the possibility to resolve performance bottlenecks at an early stage of code development. As a byproduct, the models for the resource consumption provide users with an estimate for the requirements of production runs.

We expanded the automated performance modeling approach by Calotoiu et al. [7] to meet the mentioned requirements. This approach creates performance models from a small number of test measurements with a small numbers of processes. The models are used to detect potential performance bottlenecks and to predict the resource consumption at larger core counts. We have combined this approach with the workflow manager JUBE [30] to facilitate the submission and collection of numerous test simulations that serve as inputs for the performance modeling approach. In this paper we focus on the applicability of our approach in realistic code development scenarios and show how scalability issues are detected.

We demonstrate the power of our automated performance modeling process by applying it to the software framework UG4. Given its approximately half a million lines of C++ code, manually modeling the performance of UG4 is practically impossible, which is why it provides a good example for the benefits of our approach. The major contributions of our work are:

- An automated modeling approach in combination with an automated workflow manager for a fast and streamlined detection of scalability issues.
- Demonstration of the tool chain by applying it to the large simulation framework UG4 focusing on human skin permeation simulations.
- Discussion of two performance issues detected by our approach.
- Validation of the UG4 scaling behavior.

The remainder of this paper is organized as follows. In Sect. 2, the UG4 simulation environment is presented, Sect. 3 outlines the modeling approach and Sect. 4 gives an overview on the benchmark environment JUBE. Then, in Sect. 5 we present three test cases where the tools are used in order to analyze the UG4 simulation code. Sections 6 and 7 are dedicated to related work and concluding remarks.

2   The UG4 Simulation Framework

The UG4 simulation framework (unstructured grids 4.0) [28] addresses the numerical solution of partial differential equations and is implemented as a C++ library. It uses grid-based discretization methods such as the finite element method or the vertex-centered finite volume method [6]. Complex physical geometries are resolved by hybrid, unstructured, adaptive, hierarchical grids in up to three space dimensions. In addition, a strong focus of the software framework is on efficient and highly scalable solvers, using algebraic and geometric multigrid methods. The framework is parallelized using MPI. To simplify the

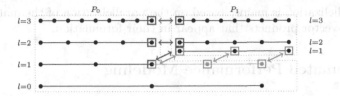

Fig. 1. Illustration for a 1d parallel multigrid hierarchy distributed onto two processes. Parallel copies are identified via horizontal (darker blue) and vertical interfaces (lighter blue) (Color figure online)

usage, a separate library called PCL (parallel communication layer) has been developed, which encapsulates the MPI calls and which provides lightweight structures for graph-based parallelization. A key feature of PCL is that parallel copies of objects are not identified by global IDs. Instead, containers, called *interfaces*, are used to store the parallel copies on each process in a well-defined order such that identification can be done by these interfaces in an efficient way [20,21,28].

A typical simulation run consists of several phases, each with its own character, especially with respect to parallelization. At first, a computing grid is required. In this specific work, we proceed as follows: A coarse grid describing the domain is loaded onto one process. The grid is refined, creating new levels of the multigrid hierarchy and after some refinements the finest grid level is distributed to empty processes, proceeding with the refinement in parallel. This process can be iterated, successively creating a tree structure of processes holding parts of the hierarchical grid. The grid refinement is mainly performed process-wise and communication is only needed at redistribution stages [20]. An illustration of the resulting hierarchy for a 1d distribution is shown in Fig. 1.

On the grid, the partial differential equations are discretized by assembling large sparse matrices and corresponding vectors based on the grid element contributions. Using only lower-dimensional parallel overlap (i.e., each full-dimensional element is present on exactly one process, but the lower-dimensional boundary has parallel copies on several processes), the assembly process can be performed by traversing the full-dimensional elements only and therefore it is an inherent parallel process. Given optimal load balancing, i.e., an equal distribution of the elements across the processes, perfect scalability is expected for the assembly.

The most difficult part, from a parallelization perspective, is the subsequent solution of the matrix equation. Since the algebraic structures are distributed, solvers naturally involve parallel communication. Multigrid methods are of optimal complexity (linear in the degrees of freedom) and thus a good candidate for weak scaling. They compute corrections iteratively to approximate the solution. On every level, simple iterative schemes, called *smoothers*, are applied and the problem is transferred to coarser grids in order to compute coarse corrections [6,13]. Our multigrid solver is based on the above-mentioned hierarchically distributed multigrid. Especially on coarser grid levels, where less computational work has to be done, fewer processes are involved in the solution algorithm. In addition, Krylov methods such as CG and BiCGStab are implemented [14].

Their parallelization is mainly based on the parallelization of the matrix-vector and vector-vector products that appear in their formulation.

3   Automated Performance Modeling

We developed an automatic performance-model generator [7, 8] for the purpose of simplifying the identification of scalability bottlenecks in complex codes. Our targets are *scalability bugs* defined as parts of a code that scale worse than expected. To this end, we create performance models for each part of the code at the level of function calls to better identify potential problems. Our focus is to create simple, easy to read, insightful models quickly, as opposed to detailed, precise models. In our studies, not only execution time is considered as a perfor-mance metric, but also requirements such as the number of bytes injected into the network or the number of floating-point operations are taken into account. This helps developers not only to uncover the existence of potential scalability bottlenecks, but also to explain their causes. For brevity, we will only present a short overview of the method.

When conducting a scalability study, our tool takes measurements of metrics (e.g., time, flops, bytes sent, ...) at different processor counts $\{p_1, \ldots, p_{max}\}$ for each individual program region (e.g., function call) as input. This is accomplished by instrumenting the application and generating parallel profiles at runtime, which are then analyzed post-mortem. Models describing the growth are gener-ated for each region, called *kernel*, and can be analyzed either in an interactive GUI, which displays a call tree of the application annotated with performance-model information, or in text form as a ranked list, ordered by either predicted execution time at a larger scale $p_t > p_{max}$, or asymptotic by behavior.

3.1   Model Generation

Our model generator rests on the observation that the models describing the behavior of parallel programs as a function of the number of processes are usu-ally finite combinations of terms composed of polynomials and logarithms. For practical purposes, models with two or three terms are often sufficient. The *per-formance model normal form* (PMNF) below describes our representation, which covers the practical cases encountered so far by virtue of the way that computer algorithms are designed.

$$f(p) = \sum_{k=1}^{n} c_k \cdot p^{i_k} \cdot log_2^{j_k}(p)$$

Moreover, the sets $I, J \subset \mathbb{Q}$ from which the exponents i_k and j_k are chosen from can be quite small and still allow a large number of different behaviors to be modeled. After creating the sets I and J and choosing n, all possible model assignments, called *model hypotheses*, can be tried and the best candidate is then selected via cross-validation [19].

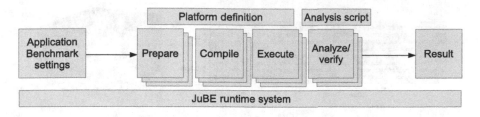

Fig. 2. JUBE workflow ([30])

3.2 Recursive Multigrid Extension

One of the core assumptions of our method is that a code will generate the same call tree for each of the different processor counts $\{p_1, \ldots, p_{max}\}$. This allows us to traverse the call tree and compare each individual function call and its behavior. However, within a weak scaling study, the number of grid levels increases with the process count. Since the multigrid algorithm is based on recursive calls for each grid level, the involved code kernels are visited recursively more often. This leads to a different call tree for different processor counts, which required us to develop a special method to be able to analyze multigrid applications. To handle this issue, we developed an extension to our method that compares the different performance measurements and creates a call tree containing only such kernels which are present in all measurements. The information of kernels which have to be removed is not lost, but rather added to the parent kernel of the one pruned from the call tree.

4 Automated Benchmarking Environment

The automated modeling of numerical software codes demands numerous experiments with varying execution parameters – such as process counts, used solvers, or physical parameters – and multiple repetitions, in order to ensure statistical significance. Configuring, compiling, running, verifying its correctness, and collecting results means a lot of administrative work and produces a large amount of data to be processed. Without a benchmarking environment, all these steps have to be performed manually. To facilitate all these tasks, Forschungszentrum Jülich provided and improved JUBE (Juelich Benchmarking Environment) [30], a script-based framework created to easily perform benchmark runs for different sets of parameters, execution sizes, compilation options, computer systems, and to evaluate the results thereafter.

Figure 2 shows the steps that are performed by JUBE in sequence: preparation, compilation, and execution, where each step might exist multiple times. Each of these steps can be adjusted to a given code or application by modifying XML-based setup scripts. The created runs can be verified and parsed by automatic pre- and post-processing scripts that filter out the desired information and store it in a more compact form for manual interpretation. With JUBE, it

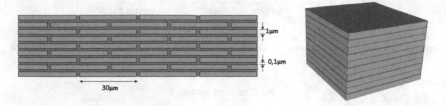

Fig. 3. Computing grids for the skin problem showing corneocytes (green) and lipid channels (red). Left: geometry ratios. Right: 3d grid for 10 layers of corneocytes (Color figure online)

is easy to create combinatorial runs of multiple parameters. For example, in a scaling experiment, one can simply specify multiple numbers of processes, different solver setups, and physical parameters. JUBE will create one experiment for each possible combination, submit all of them to the resource manager, collect all results, and display them together.

5 Results

Using the tools from Sects. 3 and 4, we analyze the UG4 code in three substudies: In the first two tests, we focus on modeling drug diffusion through the human skin. First, we analyze the code behavior under weak scaling, then we vary the diffusivity of the skin cells over several ranges of magnitude. In the third study, we compare two different types of solvers, again under weak scaling: the geometric multigrid solver and the unpreconditioned conjugate gradient (CG) method.

Drug Diffusion though the Human Skin. The outermost part of the epidermis (stratum corneum) consists of flattened, dead cells (corneocytes), that are surrounded by an inter-cellular lipid. The stratum corneum is the natural barrier to protect underlying tissue, but still allows for the throughput of certain concentrations (e.g., drugs, medicine). The latter process can be modeled by a diffusion process, in which the diffusion coefficient within the corneocytes differs from the one in the lipid. Different geometric representations of the stratum corneum have been used to compute the diffusional throughput [17].

In the following two studies, we use a brick-and-mortar model (Fig. 3). Assuming diffusion driven transport in the two subdomains $s \in \{cor, lip\}$ (corneocyte, lipid), the governing equation is given by

$$\partial_t c_s(t, \mathbf{x}) = \nabla \cdot (\mathbf{D}_s \nabla c_s(t, \mathbf{x})).$$

The diffusion coefficient $\mathbf{D}_s$ is assumed to be constant within each subdomain $s \in \{cor, lip\}$, but may differ between subdomains. For the scalability analysis, we compute the steady state of the concentration distribution.

As solver, we employ a geometric multigrid method, accelerated by an outer conjugate gradient method. The multigrid uses a damped Jacobi smoother, two

Table 1. Skin 3d study: Models for kernels creating MPI communicator groups (top), sparse matrix assembling, and multigrid (bottom). $|1 - R^2|$, the absolute difference between R^2 and the optimum scaled by 10^{-3}, which can be considered a normalized error, confirms the good quality of all models

	Time		Bytes sent	
Kernel	Model	$|1 - R^2|$	Model	$|1 - R^2|$
	time $= f(p)$ [ms]	$[10^{-3}]$	bytes $= f(p)$	$[10^{-3}]$
LoadUGScript → MPI_Allreduce	$9.33 + 0.91 \cdot \log p$	42.6	$4 \cdot \mathcal{O}(\text{MPI\_Allreduce})$	0.000
init_levels → MPI_Allreduce	$27.3 + 1.3 \cdot \log p^2$	19.6	$80.03 \cdot p \cdot \mathcal{O}(\text{MPI\_Allreduce})$	0.003
init_top_surface → MPI_Allreduce	$3.71 + 5.18 \cdot p^{1/4}$	9.88	$4 \cdot p \cdot \mathcal{O}(\text{MPI\_Allreduce})$	0.000

	Time		Invocations	
Kernel	Model	$|1 - R^2|$	Model	$|1 - R^2|$
	time $= f(p)$	$[10^{-3}]$	invocations $= f(p)$	$[10^{-3}]$
GMG → PreSmooth → jacobi	$1.89 \cdot 10^{-2} + 0.04 \cdot 10^{-2} \cdot \log p$	42.6	$70.6 + 1.4 \cdot \log p$	76.9
GMG → prolongate	$4.24 \cdot 10^{-2} + 0.10 \cdot 10^{-2} \cdot \log p$	84.4	$23.5 + 0.5 \cdot \log p$	76.9
assemble_linear	1.68	0	1	0

(resp. three) smoothing steps in 2d (resp. 3d), a V-cycle, and an LU base solver. The iterations are completed once an absolute residuum reduction of 10^{-10} is achieved. The main difficulty of this problem is the bad aspect ratio of the computational domain ($0.1\,\mu m$ vs. $30\,\mu m$ for the lipid channels). This is resolved by three (resp. five) steps of anisotropic refinement to enhance those ratios. Base solvers are applied at a level where ratios are satisfactory.

Weak-scaling Analysis of the 3d Skin Model. Using the 3d skin model described above, we fix the diffusion parameter to $\mathbf{D}_{cor} = 10^{-3}$. Table 1 shows models for a scalability issue we detected. In these kernels, we create MPI communicator groups for each level of the multigrid hierarchy, excluding processes from the group that do not own a grid part on the level. In order to inform every process on these memberships, we employ an MPI_Allreduce for an array of length p, resulting in a $p \cdot \mathcal{O}(\text{MPI\_Allreduce})$ dependency, that will lead to scalability issues for large process counts. In these kernels, we substituted MPI_Comm_split for MPI_Allreduce, also eliminating the linearly growing input. First tests do not show a significant improvement in runtime, however now the dependency is $\mathcal{O}(\text{MPI\_Comm\_split})$, whose scaling properties have been analyzed for exascale purposes [22]. Enhanced algorithms for MPI_Comm_split are known to scale with $\mathcal{O}(\log^2 p)$ [24].

Besides the above-mentioned issue, no further scalability bugs were detected, i.e., no kernel scales worse than logarithmically (see Table 1 for examples). The accumulated wallclock times for coarse-grain kernels (Fig. 4) show good scaling behavior, and bounded iteration counts are observed. Our empirical approach even reveals a rather small but apparent $\mathcal{O}(\log_2^2 p)$ dependent kernel during solver initialization where the matrix diagonal is communicated.

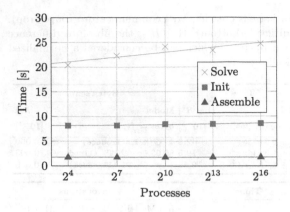

p	L	DoF	n_{gmg}
16	6	290,421	25
128	7	2,271,049	27
1024	8	17,961,489	29
8192	9	142,869,025	29
65536	10	1,139,670,081	29

Kernel	Model for time [s]
Solve	$19.75 + 0.32 \cdot \log_2 p$
Init	$8.17 + 0.002 \cdot \log_2^2 p$
Assemble	1.78

Fig. 4. Left: Measured wallclock times (marks) and models (lines) for the assembly, the multigrid solver initialization, and the solution of the skin 3d problem. Right, top: Number of grid refinements (L), degrees of freedom (DoF) and number of iterations of the solver (n_{gmg}). Right, bottom: Performance models for the kernels

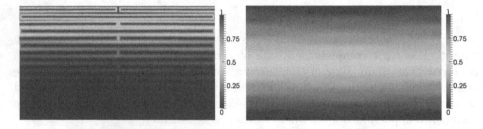

Fig. 5. Instationary (left) and stationary (right) solution for a 2d geometry

Varying the Diffusion Parameter. Our second substudy highlights the demand for a workflow manager. Biological case studies can require a variation of input parameters over 10 orders of magnitude. Combining this with 5–10 different process counts in scaling studies, several solver setups and repetitions for jitter reduction, easily hundreds of measurement runs have to be performed. We use the JUBE manager for this task. This allows us to easily schedule, collect, and analyze these runs. As an illustration, we present a study resembling results by Nägel et al. [17]: Fixing the lipid diffusion coefficient to $\mathbf{D}_{lip} = 1$, we vary the diffusion in the corneocytes in the range of $\mathbf{D}_{cor} = 10^2, 10^1, \ldots, 10^{-7}, 10^{-8}$. Figure 5

Table 2. Results of the parameter variation study of a 2d skin problem using 1024 MPI processes on 9 levels (43,476,225 DoFs)

$\mathbf{D}_{cor}$	10^2	10^1	10^0	10^{-1}	10^{-2}	10^{-3}	10^{-4}	10^{-5}	10^{-6}	10^{-7}	10^{-8}
$\mathbf{F}_{bot}$	$1.7e^1$	$9.4e^0$	$1.7e^0$	$1.9e^{-1}$	$2.1e^{-2}$	$3.1e^{-3}$	$1.0e^{-3}$	$8.0e^{-4}$	$7.8e^{-4}$	$7.7e^{-4}$	$7.7e^{-4}$
n_{iter}	27	26	26	26	26	26	25	25	25	25	25

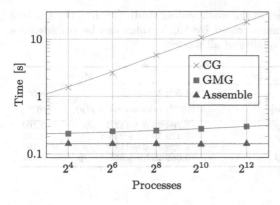

p	L	DoF	n_{cg}	n_{gmg}
16	7	66,049	524	14
64	8	263,169	1003	14
256	9	1,050,625	1977	13
1024	10	4,198,401	3875	13
4096	11	16,785,409	7588	13

Kernel	Model (time [s])
CG	$0.227 + 0.310 \cdot \sqrt{p}$
GMG	$0.219 + 0.0006 \cdot \log_2^2 p$
Assemble 0.1498	

Fig. 6. Left: Measured times (marks) and models (lines) for the assembling and solver execution for the conjugate gradient (CG) and multigrid (GMG) methods. Right, top: Number of grid refinements (L), degrees of freedom (DoF) and number of solver iterations (n_{cg}, n_{gmg}). Right, bottom: Performance models for the kernels

illustrates the solution at an early time step and the stationary case. The biologically interesting fluxes at the bottom of the domain, $\mathbf{F}_{bot} := \int_{\partial \Omega_{bot}} \nabla c \, dS$, and the iteration count for the multigrid solver are collected using JUBE (Table 2). The relatively constant iteration count over the whole range of physical parameters shows the robustness of the solver. The performance validation of the solver could have never been so thorough without the use of our automated process, allowing us to handle, analyze, and refine hundreds of experimental runs and to provide insights to developers as quickly as possible.

5.1   Analysis of Algebraic Solvers

This section demonstrates the usability of the presented approach to validate performance expectations. We analyze two solvers with known weak scaling properties: the nicely scaling multigrid method and the unpreconditioned conjugate gradient method with known weak-scaling issues. Our tests will confirm the theoretical expectations.

Weak Scaling Comparison of Multigrid and Conjugate Gradient. To allow a theoretical analysis, we choose a well known test problem: For the model equation $-\Delta c(\mathbf{x}) = f(\mathbf{x}), \mathbf{x} \in [0,1]^2$, discretized on a regular grid with mesh size h, it is known that the extreme eigenvalues of the resulting matrix are given by $\lambda_{min} = 8h^{-2}\sin^2(\pi h/2)$ and $\lambda_{max} = 8h^{-2}\cos^2(\pi h/2)$ and therefore, the condition number is given by $\kappa := \lambda_{max}/\lambda_{min} = \tan^{-2}(\pi h/2)$ [14]. For the CG method, it is known that the error reduction factor in each iteration step can be estimated by $\frac{\sqrt{\kappa}-1}{\sqrt{\kappa}+1}$ [14] and the number of iterations needed to achieve a prescribed reduction of the initial error by a factor of δ can be estimated by $n_{iter}(\delta) \leq \frac{1}{2}\sqrt{\kappa}\ln(\frac{2}{\delta})+1$. For the model problem under consideration and a fixed reduction factor δ, one can use the known condition number, the Taylor-series

Table 3. Models for CG solver kernels in the weak scaling study. $|1 - R^2|$, the absolute difference between R^2 and the optimum scaled by 10^{-3}, which can be considered a normalized error, confirms the good quality of all models

Kernel	Time		Invocations	
	Model	$|1 - R^2|$	Model	$|1 - R^2|$
	time = $f(p)$ [ms]	$[10^{-3}]$	invocations = $f(p)$	$[10^{-3}]$
CG → norm	$3.74 + 4.65 \cdot \sqrt{p}$	0.764	$75.6 + 117.7 \cdot \sqrt{p}$	0.102
CG → dotprod	$8.83 + 13.3 \cdot \sqrt{p}$	0.475	$149.2 + 235.4 \cdot \sqrt{p}$	0.102
CG → SparseMatrix_axpy	$96.3 \cdot \sqrt{p}$	0.398	$75.6 + 117.7 \cdot \sqrt{p}$	0.102
CG → VecScaleAdd	$13.7 + 22.3 \cdot \sqrt{p}$	0.088	$222.9 + 353.1 \cdot \sqrt{p}$	0.102

approximation of tan, and the fact that $\frac{1}{h}$ is proportional to $2^{n_{ref}}$, where n_{ref} is the number of refinements of the unit square, to estimate that the number of iterations $n_{iter} \sim \sqrt{\kappa} = \tan^{-1}(\pi h/2) \approx \frac{2}{\pi h} \sim \frac{1}{h} \sim 2^{n_{ref}}$ is related to the grid refinement and will increase roughly by a factor of two with each refinement. In contrast, for the multigrid method it is known that the reduction rate is independent of the mesh size and, thus, a constant number of iterations can be expected [13].

The multigrid results are equivalent to the skin tests. However, for the unpreconditioned conjugate gradient method, our empirical performance models reveal an $\mathcal{O}(\sqrt{p})$ dependency, expected via the explanation above. We increase the process count and work load by a factor of four under weak scaling. Ideally, a constant time is expected, but due to the increase by a factor of two for the iteration count, models as shown in Table 3 are observed. We emphasize that one invocation of matrix-vector or vector-vector products does scale and the increase is due to the iteration count increase. A remedy of this issue can not be achieved by implementation alone, but must be achieved by a change of the mathematical method, e.g., using multigrid. Figure 6 shows a wall-clock time comparison.

6   Related Work

Performance modeling has a long history. Manual models proved to be very effective in describing many qualities and characteristics of applications, systems, and even entire tool chains [5,18]. Recent approaches advocate source-code annotations [27] or specialized languages [25] to support developers in the creation of analytical performance models.

Various automated modeling methods exist. Many of these focus on learning the performance characteristics automatically using various machine-learning approaches [15]. Zhai et al. extrapolate single-node performance to complex parallel machines using a trace-driven network simulator [32], and Wu and Müller extrapolate traces to predict communications at larger scale [31]. Similar to our method, Carrington et al. extrapolate trace-based performance measurements using a set of canonical functions [9].

Numerous codes for the solution of partial differential equations exist, and several employ multigrid methods. There are a number of highly scalable geometric multigrid methods [4,12,23,26,29] and highly scalable algebraic multigrid [1–3]. Gahvari and Gropp model the performance of geometric [11] and algebraic multigrid methods [10]. Nägel et al. present an overview of how to treat skin permeation numerically [16].

7 Conclusion

UG4 is a framework with around half a million lines of code employed to solve problems such as drug diffusion through the human skin. With UG4, we have demonstrated the power of our performance modeling process as a fast and streamlined way to detect scalability bugs and validate performance expectations of simulation codes. The JUBE workflow manager vastly simplifies and accelerates the acquisition of performance measurements and our performance modeling method automates model creation. After removing a previously unknown performance bottleneck and validating the scalability of entire simulations, we can confidently claim that UG4 is ready for exascale.

Acknowledgment. Financial support from the DFG Priority Program 1648 *Software for Exascale Computing* (SPPEXA) is gratefully acknowledged. The authors also thank the Gauss Centre for Supercomputing (GCS) for providing computing time on the GCS share of the supercomputer JUQUEEN at Jülich Supercomputing Centre (JSC).

References

1. Baker, A., Falgout, R., Kolev, T., Yang, U.: Multigrid smoothers for ultra-parallel computing. SIAM J. Sci. Comput **33**, 2864–2887 (2011)
2. Baker, A.H., Falgout, R.D., Gamblin, T., Kolev, T.V., Schulz, M., Yang, U.M.: Scaling algebraic multigrid solvers: on the road to exascale. In: Competence in High Performance Computing 2010, pp. 215–226. Springer (2012)
3. Bastian, P., Blatt, M., Scheichl, R.: Algebraic multigrid for discontinuous galerkin discretizations of heterogeneous elliptic problems. Numer. Linear Algebra Appl. **19**(2), 367–388 (2012)
4. Bergen, B., Gradl, T., Rude, U., Hulsemann, F.: A massively parallel multigrid method for finite elements. Comput. Sci. Eng. **8**(6), 56–62 (2006)
5. Boyd, E.L., Azeem, W., Lee, H.H., Shih, T.P., Hung, S.H., Davidson, E.S.: A hierarchical approach to modeling and improving the performance of scientific applications on the KSR1. In: Proceedings of the International Conference on Parallel Processing (ICPP), pp. 188–192 (1994)
6. Braess, D.: Finite elements: Theory, Fast Solvers, and Applications in Solid Mechanics. Cambridge University Press, Cambridge (2001)
7. Calotoiu, A., Hoefler, T., Poke, M., Wolf, F.: Using automated performance modeling to find scalability bugs in complex codes. In: Proceedings of the ACM/IEEE Conference on Supercomputing (SC13). ACM, Denver, CO, USA, November 2013

8. Calotoiu, A., Hoefler, T., Wolf, F.: Mass-producing insightful performance models. In: Workshop on Modeling and Simulation of Systems and Applications. University of Washington, Seattle, Washington, August 2014
9. Carrington, L., Laurenzano, M., Tiwari, A.: Characterizing large-scale HPC applications through trace extrapolation. Parallel Process. Lett. **23**(4), 1340008 (2013)
10. Gahvari, H., Baker, A.H., Schulz, M., Yang, U.M., Jordan, K.E., Gropp, W.: Modeling the performance of an algebraic multigrid cycle on HPC platforms. In: Proceedings of the International Conference on Supercomputing, pp. 172–181. ACM (2011)
11. Gahvari, H., Gropp, W.: An introductory exascale feasibility study for FFTs and multigrid. In: International Symposium on Parallel and Distributed Processing (IPDPS), pp. 1–9. IEEE (2010)
12. Gmeiner, B., Köstler, H., Stürmer, M., Rüde, U.: Parallel multigrid on hierarchical hybrid grids: a performance study on current high performance computing clusters. Concurrency Comput. Pract. Experience **26**(1), 217–240 (2014)
13. Hackbusch, W.: Multi-grid Methods and Applications, vol. 4. Springer, Heidelberg (1985)
14. Hackbusch, W.: Iterative Solution of Large Sparse Systems of Equations. Springer, New York (1994)
15. Lee, B.C., Brooks, D.M., de Supinski, B.R., Schulz, M., Singh, K., McKee, S.A.: Methods of inference and learning for performance modeling of parallel applications. In: Proceedings of the 12th ACM SIGPLAN Symposium on Principles and Practice of Parallel Programming (PPoPP 2007), pp. 249–258 (2007)
16. Nägel, A., Heisig, M., Wittum, G.: Detailed modeling of skin penetration—an overview. Adv. Drug Deliv. Rev. **65**(2), 191–207 (2013)
17. Nägel, A., Heisig, M., Wittum, G.: A comparison of two- and three-dimensional models for the simulation of the permeability of human stratum corneum. Eur. J. Pharm. Biopharm. **72**(2), 332–338 (2009)
18. Petrini, F., Kerbyson, D.J., Pakin, S.: The case of the missing supercomputer performance: achieving optimal performance on the 8,192 processors of ASCI Q. In: Proceedings of the ACM/IEEE Conference on Supercomputing (SC 2003), p. 55 (2003)
19. Picard, R.R., Cook, R.D.: Cross-validation of regression models. J. Am. Statist. Assoc. **79**(387), 575–583 (1984)
20. Reiter, S.: Efficient algorithms and data structures for the realization of adaptive, hierarchical grids on massively parallel systems. Ph.D. thesis, University of Frankfurt, Germany (2014)
21. Reiter, S., Vogel, A., Heppner, I., Rupp, M., Wittum, G.: A massively parallel geometric multigrid solver on hierarchically distributed grids. Comp. Vis. Sci. **16**(4), 151–164 (2013)
22. Sack, P., Gropp, W.: A scalable MPI_Comm_split algorithm for exascale computing. In: Keller, R., Gabriel, E., Resch, M., Dongarra, J. (eds.) EuroMPI 2010. LNCS, vol. 6305, pp. 1–10. Springer, Heidelberg (2010)
23. Sampath, R., Biros, G.: A parallel geometric multigrid method for finite elements on octree meshes. SIAM J. Sci. Comput. **32**, 1361–1392 (2010)
24. Siebert, C., Wolf, F.: Parallel sorting with minimal data. In: Cotronis, Y., Danalis, A., Nikolopoulos, D.S., Dongarra, J. (eds.) EuroMPI 2011. LNCS, vol. 6960, pp. 170–177. Springer, Heidelberg (2011)

25. Spafford, K.L., Vetter, J.S.: Aspen: a domain specific language for performance modeling. In: Proceedings of the International Conference on High Performance Computing, Networking, Storage and Analysis, SC 2012, pp. 84:1–84:11. IEEE Computer Society Press, Los Alamitos (2012)

26. Sundar, H., Biros, G., Burstedde, C., Rudi, J., Ghattas, O., Stadler, G.: Parallel geometric-algebraic multigrid on unstructured forests of octrees. In: Proceedings of the International Conference on High Performance Computing, Networking, Storage and Analysis. p. 43. IEEE Computer Society Press (2012)

27. Tallent, N.R., Hoisie, A.: Palm: easing the burden of analytical performance modeling. In: Proceedings of the International Conference on Supercomputing (ICS), pp. 221–230 (2014)

28. Vogel, A., Reiter, S., Rupp, M., Nägel, A., Wittum, G.: UG 4: a novel flexible software system for simulating PDE based models on high performance computers. Comp. Vis. Sci. **16**(4), 165–179 (2013)

29. Williams, S., Lijewski, M., Almgren, A., Straalen, B.V., Carson, E., Knight, N., Demmel, J.: s-step Krylov subspace methods as bottom solvers for geometric multigrid. In: 28th International Parallel and Distributed Processing Symposium, pp. 1149–1158. IEEE (2014)

30. Wolf, F., Bischof, C., Hoefler, T., Mohr, B., Wittum, G., Calotoiu, A., Iwainsky, C., Strube, A., Vogel, A.: Catwalk: a quick development path for performance models. In: Lopes, L., et al. (eds.) Euro-Par 2014, Part II. LNCS, vol. 8806, pp. 589–600. Springer, Heidelberg (2014)

31. Wu, X., Mueller, F.: ScalaExtrap: trace-based communication extrapolation for SPMD programs. In: Proceedings of the 16th ACM Symposium on Principles and Practice of Parallel Programming (PPoPP 2011), pp. 113–122 (2011)

32. Zhai, J., Chen, W., Zheng, W.: Phantom: predicting performance of parallel applications on large-scale parallel machines using a single node. SIGPLAN Not. **45**(5), 305–314 (2010)

Exploiting Task-Based Parallelism
in Bayesian Uncertainty Quantification

Panagiotis E. Hadjidoukas[1]([✉]), Panagiotis Angelikopoulos[1], Lina Kulakova[1],
Costas Papadimitriou[2], and Petros Koumoutsakos[1]

[1] Computational Science and Engineering Laboratory, ETH Zürich,
Zurich, Switzerland
{phadjido,pangelik,kulina}@mavt.ethz.ch, petros@ethz.ch
[2] Department of Mechanical Engineering, University of Thessaly, Volos, Greece
costas@uth.gr

Abstract. We introduce a task-parallel framework for non-intrusive
Bayesian Uncertainty Quantification and Propagation of complex and
computationally demanding physical models on massively parallel computing architectures. The framework incorporates Laplace asymptotic
approximations and stochastic algorithms along with distributed numerical differentiation. Sampling is based on the Transitional Markov Chain
Monte Carlo algorithm and its variants while the optimization tasks associated with the asymptotic approximations are treated via the Covariance Matrix Adaptation Evolution Strategy. Exploitation of task-based
parallelism is based on a platform-agnostic adaptive load balancing
library that orchestrates scheduling of multiple physical model evaluations on computing platforms that range from multicore systems to
hybrid GPU clusters. Experimental results using representative applications demonstrate the flexibility and excellent scalability of the proposed
framework.

Keywords: Task-based parallelism · Bayesian uncertainty quantification

1 Introduction

Computational models for scientific and engineering problems are developed
based on the application of first principles, conservation laws and expert knowledge. Recent technological advances in sensing, measurement and imaging technologies provide an unprecedented opportunity to assist model development with
an abundance of data. Data driven model discovery and evaluation of their predictive capabilities as in the context of Uncertainty Quantification and Propagation (UQ+P) is currently a topic of renewed interest [1]. Fusing both expert
knowledge and experimental observations, Bayesian inference stands amongst
the prevalent UQ+P techniques. It is used for quantifying and calibrating uncertainty models, as well as propagating these uncertainties in engineering simulations to achieve updated robust predictions of system performance, reliability
and safety [2]. Common computational tools for performing Bayesian UQ+P

© Springer-Verlag Berlin Heidelberg 2015
J.L. Träff et al. (Eds.): Euro-Par 2015, LNCS 9233, pp. 532–544, 2015.
DOI: 10.1007/978-3-662-48096-0_41

include Laplace methods of asymptotic approximation [3] and stochastic algorithms such as Markov Chain Monte Carlo (MCMC) and its variants [4].

Bayesian UQ+P tools involve global optimization problems, sampling from probability distributions, as well as evaluating high dimensional integrals. The computational challenge of Bayesian tools is the large number of model evaluations required, specifically in cases of complex engineering models with high resources requirements and time to solution. The need for multiple model evaluations leads, on average, to long turn-around time for Bayesian analysis, limiting its applicability when swift decisions are needed as in e.g. the case of earthquake early warnings system [5]. The ability to efficiently harness available computational resources is paramount for the Bayesian UQ+P framework and defines its applicability in engineering problems. The situation can be improved by advancing the computational efficiency of the models and by developing efficient UQ+P algorithms and computational frameworks that exploit massively parallel computing architectures. The focus of this paper is the latter.

A small number of parallel software frameworks for uncertainty quantification studies are currently available to the scientific community, with a non-exhaustive list containing: DAKOTA [6], PSUADE [7] and QUESO [8]. The parallelization of these systems has been mostly based on MPI and either follows a master-worker approach or applies domain decomposition to construct processor groups where simulations are assigned for execution. Most systems exploit only one level of parallelism, otherwise they rely on cumbersome implementations that apply hard partitioning of processing units. In addition, they lack runtime support for asynchronous nested task-based parallelism and adaptive load balancing and they do not take into account heterogeneous computing architectures. Consequently, they cannot counteract the increasing number of sources of load imbalance, such as variable processing power and simulation time, hardware and software faults and the irregularity of UQ algorithms.

We present a Bayesian computational framework for UQ that aims to address the above mentioned issues. The framework is based on the TORC task-parallel library for clusters [9], which is designed to provide unified programming and runtime support for computing platforms that range from single-core systems to hybrid multicore-GPU clusters and heterogenous Grid based supercomputers. Within this framework, we implement population based MCMC methods, the Transitional Markov Chain Monte Carlo (TMCMC) [10], Approximate Bayesian Computational Subset-Simulation (ABC-SubSim) [11], while the Covariance Matrix Adaptation Evolution Strategy (CMA-ES) [12] is used as an optimization tool. Note that all the algorithms implemented have highly parallel task graphs and thus are ideally suited for distributed and parallel computing.

2   Bayesian Formulation

In the Bayesian framework [13], the uncertainty in a parameter set $\underline{\theta} \in R^n$ of a model class M simulating an engineering system is first quantified using a prior probability distribution function (PDF) $\pi(\underline{\theta}|M)$ and then updated using the

Bayes theorem to compute the posterior PDF $p(\underline{\theta}|D, M)$ based on available measurement data D as: $p(\underline{\theta}|D, M) = p(D|\underline{\theta}, M)\pi(\underline{\theta}|M)/p(D|M)$ where $p(D|\underline{\theta}, M)$ is the likelihood of observing the data from the model class and $p(D|M)$ is the evidence of the model class. Assuming that the model predictions $g(\underline{\theta}|M)$ and the measurement data $D = \{\hat{\underline{y}}\}$ satisfy $\hat{\underline{y}} = g(\underline{\theta}|M) + \underline{e}$, where the prediction error term $\underline{e}$, accounting for measurement, computational and modeling errors, is normally distributed with zero mean and covariance matrix Σ, the likelihood $p(D|\underline{\theta}, M)$ is given by [2] $p(D|\underline{\theta}, M) = |\Sigma(\underline{\theta})|^{-1/2}(2\pi)^{-n/2}\exp\left[-\frac{1}{2}J(\underline{\theta}; M)\right]$ where $J(\underline{\theta}; M) = [\hat{\underline{y}} - g(\underline{\theta}|M)]^T\Sigma^{-1}(\underline{\theta})[\hat{\underline{y}} - g(\underline{\theta}|M)]$, $|\cdot|$ denotes determinant, and the parameter set $\underline{\theta}$ is augmented to include parameters that are involved in the model structure of the correlation matrix Σ.

Bayesian computational tools include of stochastic algorithms and asymptotic approximations. Stochastic algorithms include variants of the MCMC technique [14] that are used to draw samples from the posterior PDF. TMCMC allows for the efficient execution of a large number of full system simulations on heterogeneous clusters/computers as described in Sect. 3, and can capture complex posterior PDFs. Using the Bayesian central limit theorem for large amounts of data, the posterior distribution of the model parameters can be asymptotically approximated by a Gaussian distribution centered at the most probable value $\hat{\underline{\theta}} = \mathrm{argmin}_{\theta} L(\underline{\theta}, M)$ of the model parameters, obtained by maximizing the posterior PDF $p(\underline{\theta}|D, M)$ or equivalently minimizing the function $L(\underline{\theta}; M) = -\ln p(\underline{\theta}|D, M) = \frac{1}{2}J(\underline{\theta}; M) - \ln \pi(\underline{\theta}|M)$ with covariance matrix equal to the inverse of the Hessian of the function $L(\underline{\theta}, M)$ evaluated at the most probable value $\hat{\underline{\theta}}$.

The asymptotic approximations for Bayesian model parameter and evidence estimation involve the solution of an optimization problem and the calculation of a single Hessian matrix [3]. Regarding the Hessian calculations, finite difference approximations of the gradient of the objective function scale up the computational effort by a factor proportional to the number of uncertain parameters. Computations can be performed in parallel since the derivatives of the objective function can be executed simultaneously, leaving the Time-to-Solution (TTS) independent of the number of uncertain parameters. Herein, numerical derivatives are calculated when needed fully in parallel using the non-intrusive adaptive parallel numerical differentiation library [15]. Evolution strategies are highly parallel and among several classes of evolution algorithms, CMA-ES [12] has been shown not only to to converge fast in particular when searching for a single global optimum, but to have an easily parallelizable task graph due to its generation based updating. Herein a task-parallel version of the CMA-ES is used to solve the single-objective optimization problems arising in Laplace asymptotic approximations.

In some cases the likelihood is hard to formulate (e.g. in case of stochastic model M) or hard to evaluate. ABC algorithms then are used to approximate the likelihood function $p(D|\underline{\theta}, M)$. A major difference of ABC algorithm as compared with standard Bayesian techniques is that it considers model parameters $\underline{\theta}$ and model outputs $\underline{x}$ as a pair of random variables and aims at evaluating the joint posterior distribution $p((\theta, \underline{x})|D, M)$. This can be done by applying

Bayes theorem and the chain rule: $p((\underline{\theta}, \underline{x})|D, M) \propto p((\underline{\theta}, \underline{x})|M)p(D|(\underline{\theta}, \underline{x}), M) = p(\underline{\theta}|M)p(\underline{x}|\underline{\theta}, M)p(D|(\underline{\theta}, \underline{x}), M)$. The function $p(D|(\underline{\theta}, \underline{x}), M)$ has a smaller discrepancy when the outcomes $\underline{x}$ are closer to the data D. ABC algorithms replace the equality with an approximation: $\underline{x} \approx D$. If $\underline{x}$ and D are from a high-dimensional space, we introduces a vector of summary statistics $\eta(\cdot)$ to facilitate an easier comparison. The discrepancy between data and model outcome is then given by $\rho(\eta(\underline{x}), \eta(D))$ where $\rho(\cdot, \cdot)$ is some metric. An approximate joint posterior is defined for a tolerance level δ as $p_\delta((\underline{\theta}, \underline{x})|D, M) \propto p(\underline{\theta}|M)p(\underline{x}|\underline{\theta}, M)p(\rho(\eta(\underline{x}), \eta(D)) \leq \delta|(\underline{\theta}, \underline{x}), M)$ where δ controls the quality of the posterior. Using the approximate posterior defined above, an ABC algorithm can evaluate the approximate joint posterior by simulating $\underline{\theta} \sim p(\underline{\theta}|M)$ and $\underline{x} \sim p(\underline{x}|\underline{\theta}, M)$ and accepting the generated pair $(\underline{\theta}, \underline{x})$ if $\rho(\eta(\underline{x}), \eta(D)) \leq \delta$.

3 Software and Runtime Environment

Aiming at support of both low-cost desktop machines and HPC environments from our Uncertainty Quantification and Optimization framework, we opted for a parallelization approach that:

– offers efficient exploitation of multilevel task-based parallelism
– provides ease of programming, hiding low-level parallelization details and thus facilitating algorithm development
– supports load balancing transparent to the user
– is highly portable and platform-agnostic, adapting automatically to the underlying hardware resources.

The Task-Parallel Library. In order to meet the above requirements, we based the parallel implementation of our tools on the TORC task-parallel library [9]. TORC provides a programming and runtime environment where parallel programs can be executed unaltered on both shared and distributed memory platforms. A TORC parallel application actually consists of multiple MPI processes that run on the cluster nodes and have one or multiple workers. Similarly to OpenMP, tasks are decoupled from the workers and thus the library allows for arbitrary nesting of tasks. Each worker continuously dispatches and executes tasks, submitted for execution to a set of priority queues. There is a single set of such queues in each MPI process and tasks are submitted to the queue that corresponds to the nesting level of parallelism they belong to. Task and data management are performed asynchronously and transparently to the user, by utilizing a server thread in each MPI process. The user can query the execution environment, e.g. number of workers, and specify the local or remote queue where each task will be submitted for execution. Due to the task stealing mechanism, idle workers can steal and execute tasks that have been submitted to a remote queue. An idle worker always try first to extract work from the lowest-level non-empty local queue. If there is no work available, it tries to steal tasks from the remote processes but starting from the highest-level queues. Therefore, the programmer is responsible for the task distribution policy: typically, this involves cyclic distribution of first-level tasks among the workers and local submission of inner-level tasks. Combined with task stealing, this policy favors stealing of coarse-grain tasks and local execution of deeper levels of parallelism. In the context of this work, task functions receive as input an evaluation point, i.e. a set of parameters, and return a value computed at that point. The function can either include source code supplied by the user or invoke an external simulation program. The injected user code can embrace intra-node parallelism expressed with OpenMP directives or TORC tasks. Launching of external software is based on the fork-exec system calls while input data and results are communicated through the local filesystem. We do not pose any restrictions on the external software, which can be sequential or parallel. If the execution time of simulations is not high enough to hide the overhead of the launching procedure, a proxy process is created at program initialization for each worker. This process remains active throughout program execution, minimizing the spawning overhead by running directly the simulations. In addition, a persistent communication path based on Unix-domain sockets is established between each worker-proxy pair, minimizing the communication overheads.

When the application is executed with one process and multiple workers, the library operates exclusively through hardware shared memory avoiding message passing. TORC has been successfully used to provide runtime support to OpenMP and extensions of it on clusters.

TMCMC. A brief sketch of the TMCMC algorithm [10] is depicted in Algorithm 1. At the initialization stage, the algorithm selects randomly C_1 points which will serve as starting points for the MCMC chains for the first generation of the algorithm. The posterior evaluation for each point can be performed in parallel, while each evaluation can require a fixed number (N_r) of simulations. If $N_r > 1$ then the initialization exhibits two levels of parallelism that can be fully exploited. Each generation (TMCMC stage) G involves the processing of C_G MCMC chains of variable length, according to the statistics for the set of accepted points produced by the previous generation. As chains do not perform the same number of steps, load imbalance is introduced in the algorithm. They are instantiated with tasks and distributed appropriately to the workers, trying to balance the total workload among them without relying exclusively on the task stealing mechanism of TORC. At each step of a chain, the algorithm requires a posterior evaluation, which in turn may involve multiple independent simulation runs that are submitted for asynchronous execution as tasks. This exploitation of second-level parallelism provides more effective utilization of hardware resources as the higher number of tasks increases concurrency, resulting in better load balancing and reduced idle time for the workers.

The task stealing mechanism is essential for the efficient management of the irregular task parallelism exhibited by TMCMC. This irregularity is attributed to the variable numbers of chains per generation and steps per chain. The complexity of dealing with this irregularity becomes significantly higher if the execution time of model evaluations varies. In many cases the execution time cannot be estimated

---

Algorithm 1. TMCMC

```
 1  Algorithm TMCMC()
        // Initialization
 2      θ = {}
 3      for each randomly selected starting point c = 1, ..., C₁ do
 4          Compute function value F(c) = Posterior (c);
 5          add c, F(c) to the set θ
 6      end
 7      compute statistics for the function values of the set θ
        // Main loop
 8      for each generation g = 2, ..., G do
 9          select Cg starting points from the set θ
10          θ = {}
11          for each chain c = 1, ..., Cg do
12              for each step s = 1, ..., Sc do
13                  propose next point p
14                  Compute function value F(c, s) = Posterior (p);
15                  accept/reject p, if accepted add it to the set θ
16              end
17          end
18          compute statistics for the function values of the set θ
19      end
20      return ;
21  Function Posterior(point p)
22      for t = 1, ..., Nr do
23          perform model evaluation M(p, t)
24      end
25      combine the results and compute F(p)
26      return F(p);
```

---

beforehand because it strongly depends on the input parameters of the search space where TMCMC is applied. Moreover, the execution time depends on the processing power of the underlying hardware, which can exhibit significant variability on computing environments that utilize heterogeneous nodes and hybrid computing architectures. TORC offers a programming and runtime environment where the irregular nested parallelism of TMCMC can be easily expressed and exploited at all possible levels, without making any assumption about the target hardware platform.

Subset Simulation for Approximate Bayesian Computational. Approximate Bayesian Computation Subset Simulation, *ABC-SubSim*, outlined in Algorithm 2, uses MCMC to efficiently generate conditional samples to gradually trace a rare event region. ABC-SubSim applies the idea of Subset Simulation to a special case of Approximate Bayesian Computation. The structure of ABC-SubSim is identical to that of TMCMC and differs in the following point: all MCMC chains in SubSim always perform the same predefined number of steps, in contrast to TMCMC where chain lengths are determined at runtime.

Asymptotic Approximation. The CMA-ES algorithm [12] includes, at each generation, a set of function evaluations that can be performed concurrently. The parallelization of CMA-ES using TORC is straightforward and involves the cyclic distribution of the tasks to the available workers. A second level

---

Algorithm 2. Subset Simulation

```
   // Initialization with Random Sampling from Prior
 1 z = {}
 2 for each randomly selected starting point c = 1, ..., C₁ do
 3 |    Compute function value F(c) = Prior (c);
 4 |    add c, F(c) to the set z
 5 end
 6 sort and keep the first a% of the set z, set discrepancy for next generation
   // Main loop
 7 for each generation g = 2, ..., G do
 8 |    select C_g starting points from the set θ
 9 |    z = {}
10 |    for each chain c = 1, ..., C_g do
11 |    |    for each step s = 1, ..., S do
12 |    |    |    accept/reject directions and propose next point p
13 |    |    |    Compute function value F(c, s) = Prior (p);
14 |    |    |    accept/reject p, if accepted add it to the set z, calculate acceptance rate ρ
15 |    |    end
16 |    end
17 |    sort and keep the first a% of the set z, set discrepancy for next generation, if ρ < 5 %
   |    then exit algorithm
18 end
```

---

of parallelism can be activated only if the objective function invokes multiple simulation runs, while load balancing issues arise on heterogeneous computing platforms or for variable execution time of simulation runs. The evaluation of the Hessian matrix is central to the Bayesian asymptotic approximation. This is normally provided as output of an optimization methodology (CMA-ES in our case). To select the appropriate differentiation step for each problem parameter, we first spawn tasks that compute partial derivatives for several differentiation steps. Then, we apply a Romberg extrapolation methodology to find the step with the most accurate result for each parameter and finally we compute the Hessian matrix. The multiple function evaluations introduce an additional level of task parallelism in the gradient and Hessian calculations, exploited by a parallel numerical differentiation module that has been also built on top of TORC.

4   Applications

In this section, we exemplify the key features and assess the parallel performance of our framework by performing UQ studies of representative applications. In particular, we compare the time to solution as well as the computational cost and PDF estimation efficiency for two engineering applications requiring significant computational resources. These applications exhibit significant TTS for a single posterior evaluation and target multi-core and hybrid CPU/GPU clusters. Furthermore, they demonstrate the coupling of third-party parallel scientific software into our framework.

4.1   TMCMC and CMA-ES on a GPU Cluster

We perform UQ+P in the most widely used MD model, that of water. We use a 5-site water model, TIP5P-E. The calibration data consist of the radial distribution function of oxygen-oxygen in bulk water and its experimental uncertainty. Each evaluation of a posterior sample requires two full MD-simulation run, with the MD-code GROMACS 5.0 compiled with hybrid CPU-GPU acceleration. The final posterior value is computed by applying a post-processing stage which invokes a Matlab script that processes the output of the simulation run. The prediction error matrix Σ can be decomposed into three contributions with elements $\Sigma_{ii} = \sigma_{exp}^2 + \sigma_{ens}^2 + \sigma_m^2$. We estimate the $\sigma_{ens}^2 \approx 0.005$. The experimental uncertainty contributions e^{exp} are known and finally, the additional model prediction error term σ_m^2 is left to be determined from the inference process [16]. The parameters $\left(\epsilon_{O-O}^{LJ}, \sigma_{O-O}^{LJ}\right)$ and q_O are the Lennard-Jones interaction parameters and charge interaction respectively. We use truncated Gaussian priors for the three parameters with mean values based on the literature values for TIP5P [17], with a standard deviation of 30 % of $\bar{\theta}_\pi$, whereas the hyperparameter follows a Gamma prior, that is $\sigma_m^2 \sim \Gamma(1.5, 0.25)$.

Results. We present the timings and the results of the calibration of the TIP5-P water model. We performed our simulations on 32 compute nodes of the Piz Daint Cray XC30 cluster at the Swiss National SuperComputing Center CSCS. Each node is equipped with an 8-core Intel Xeon E5-2670 processor and one NVIDIA Tesla K20X GPU. TORC is initialized with a single worker per node because each single posterior evaluation task fully utilizes a compute node by means of the hybrid CPU/GPU configuration of GROMACS. Posterior evaluations are invoked by a separate proxy server process that receives a set of parameters, invokes the GROMACS model executions, the Matlab-based post-processing phase and finally sends back the posterior value. This approach, depicted in Fig. 1, minimizes runtime overheads because the Matlab environment is initialized only once and, furthermore, it offers high flexibility and portability.

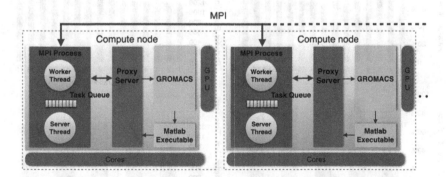

Fig. 1. Mapping of the parallel application on the compute nodes of the hybrid CPU/GPU cluster. The MPI application, the proxy server and the Matlab code run only on the cores while GROMACS is compiled with hybrid CPU/GPU configuration. To avoid initialization overheads, the Matlab code was compiled to a dynamic library and linked to the proxy process, replacing the Matlab executable depicted, for simplicity reasons, in the figure.

Each posterior evaluation requires between 17 and 21 min of wall clock-time in the above mentioned computing architecture. The variation of the mean time for completing each posterior evaluation is due to the different runtime for different initial parameters. The variance in the evaluation time and the maximum chain length are the main sources of load imbalance in this application. We address the first issue by using 256 samples per generation, i.e. 8x the number of workers, while we alleviate the second problem by sorting the chains according to their length and then evenly distributing the total workload to the available workers. The maximum chain length determines the lowest possible processing time for each generation and the maximum number of workers above which execution time does not improve and parallel efficiency is negatively affected.

Figure 2 (top, left) depicts the efficiency of TMCMC, while Fig. 2 (top, right) depicts how the time of a single posterior evaluation varies over a total of 15 generations. The above solutions, along with the stealing mechanism of TORC, minimize the idle time of workers and result in parallel efficiency higher than 97 % when every worker executes the same number of posterior evaluations. The lower efficiency ($\approx$88.4 %) for the 12th and 14th generation of TMCMC is attributed to the fact that the maximum chain length was equal to 9 for both cases, which imposes an upper limit of 88 % to the expected efficiency. Similar behavior is observed in Fig. 2 (bottom) for the parallel CMA-ES, where parallel efficiency and statistics for the evaluation time are reported every 10 generations. We notice that the measured parallel efficiency is equal to 90.1 % at the end of the 10th generation, which is due to the lower number of samples (64) per generation and the high variance of the evaluation time. This variance decreases as the algorithm evolves and the efficiency increases accordingly up to 97.4 %.

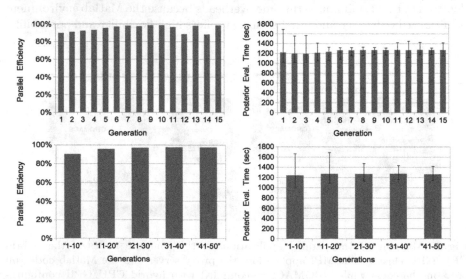

Fig. 2. Top: Parallel efficiency of TMCMC (left) and posterior evaluation time for the MD simulation (right). Bottom: Corresponding figures for CMA-ES.

Table 1. Computational effort of the MD calibration.

Method	Generations	Samples	Evaluations	TTS (hours)	Overall efficiency
TMCMC	14	256	3584	≈44.0	94.5 %
CMA-ES	50	64	3200	≈36.7	95.4 %

Table 2. Mean values and Coefficient of Variation of the posterior distribution of the model parameter, along with the LogEvidence values of each model class.

Class	$\bar{\epsilon}^{LJ}_{O-O}$	$u_{\epsilon^{LJ}_{O-O}}$	$\bar{\sigma}^{LJ}_{O-O}$	$u_{\sigma^{LJ}_{O-O}}$	$\bar{q}_O$	u_{q_O}	$\bar{\sigma}^2_m$	$u_{\sigma^2_m}$	LogEvidence
TMCMC	0.688	4.3 %	0.312	0.16 %	0.2417	0.76 %	0.00923	15.1 %	1401.34
CMA-ES	0.651	4.3 %	0.313	0.20 %	0.2392	0.81 %	0.01034	16.0 %	1414.21

The computational cost of the MD calibration with the two methods is presented in Table 1. The mean parameter estimates as well as their associated uncertainty are summarized in Table 2. The coefficient of variation u_θ of a parameter θ is defined as the sample standard deviation of that parameter over its estimated mean $\bar{\theta}$.

4.2   ABC-Subsim on a Multicore Cluster

As a stochastic model we took the calibration of the Lennard-Jones potential parameters for helium. To perform the calibration we used the data on the Boltzmann factor $f_B = \left\langle \exp\left(-\frac{H}{k_B T}\right)\right\rangle$ where H is the enthalpy of the system of helium atoms, T is the temperature of the system, k_B is the Boltzmann constant and $\langle \cdot \rangle$ denotes the ensemble average. The data was generated using the software LAMMPS for a system of 1000 atoms for 20 ns in the NPT ensemble with a timestep of 2fs. The system used for calibration consists of 1000 atoms and is equilibrated for 2ns, following a production run in the NPT ensemble for another 2ns with a 2fs timestep. We performed calibration with 2 different settings. 1) Assuming the resulting Boltzmann factor distribution was Gaussian, and a discrepancy function of: $\rho(x,y) = \sqrt{\left((\mu_x - \mu_y)/\mu_x\right)^2 + \left((\sigma_x - \sigma_y)/\sigma_x\right)^2}$. In the second setting the discrepancy is the given: $\rho(x,y) = D_{KL}(P\|Q)$ where D_{KL} is the Kullback-Leibler divergence, P is the data distribution, Q is the simulation outcome distribution of the Boltzmann factor.

Results. The algorithm runs a full molecular dynamic simulation for every parameter set and hence requires a significant amount of computational work. It also exhibits two levels of parallelism, as the Markov chains with different seeds can be processed in parallel while each single simulation can also run in parallel using the MPI version of LAMMPS.

The time to solution for each function evaluation varies with the given parameters, introducing load imbalance in the algorithm. We deal with this issue by submitting tasks with higher execution time first: we sort the samples according to the value of the σ parameter before distributing the corresponding function evaluation or Markov chain tasks to the workers. Moreover, we enhance this scheme with the task stealing of TORC.

We performed our simulations on 512 compute nodes of the Piz Daint cluster (4096 cores in total). TORC is initialized with two MPI workers per node and each LAMMPS simulation utilizes 4 cores in turn. The population size was set to be 15360 and the Markov chain length was equal to 5. The algorithm stops when the acceptance rate drops below 5%.

Table 3 summarizes the parallel performance of ABC-SubSim. Despite the high variance of the time for a single simulation run, we observed that the efficiency of the initialization phase (level 0) reaches 82% as 15360 function evaluations are distributed among the 1024 workers. The lower efficiency (70.5%) of Level 1 is attributed to the existence of chains with high accumulated running times and the small number of available chains that correspond to each worker (3072 chains in total, 3 chains per worker). As the algorithm evolves, the efficiency increases and reaches 92% for the last level, which exhibits a load imbalance of approximately 8% as computed by $(T_{max}-T_{avg})/T_{avg}$, where T_{max} and T_{avg} are the maximum and average time that the workers were busy during the processing of the specific level. The information about the prior and the posterior values of the parameters is given in Table 4.

Table 3. Detailed per-level performance results of ABC-SubSim on 512 nodes of Piz Daint. T_f shows the mean and standard deviation of the simulation times and T_w is the wall-clock time per generation, respectively. All the times are reported in seconds.

Level	T_f	T_w	Efficiency
0	82 ± 83	1497	81.8%
1	87 ± 57	1843	70.5%
2	68 ± 10	1237	81.9%
3	65 ± 6	1110	88.4%
4	66 ± 5	1078	92.2%

Table 4. Prior and posterior information of parameters of the Helium system in molecular LAMMPS units. The number of generations N_{gen} computed before the acceptance rate reached a threshold value of 5% and achieved tolerance levels δ for two models: M_G [Gaussian setting], M_{KL} [Kullback-Leibler setting]. Prior bounds $[\theta_l, \theta_r]$, mean values $\bar{\theta}$ and coefficients of variation u_θ of the Lennard-Jones parameters of Helium.

Model	$[\sigma_l, \sigma_r]$	$\bar{\sigma}$	u_σ	$[\epsilon_l, \epsilon_r]$	$\bar{\epsilon}$	u_ϵ	N_{gen}	δ
M_G	[0.1,0.8]	0.2452	11.5%	[0.01,1.0]	0.423	64.5%	4	3.40×10^{-3}
M_{KL}	[0.1,0.8]	0.2792	5.0%	[0.01,1.0]	0.117	15.4%	6	6.70×10^{-2}

5 Conclusions

We presented a computational framework for large scale Bayesian uncertainty quantification and stochastic optimization that can exploit massively parallel and hybrid (CPU/GPU) computing architectures. The framework incorporates several state-of-the-art stochastic algorithms for the computation of the likelihood that are capable of sampling from complex, multimodal posterior distribution functions. Built on top of the TORC task-parallel library, it offers straightforward extraction and exploitation of multilevel task-based parallelism in stochastic optimization and sampling algorithms. It targets both distributed and shared memory systems in a platform-agnostic way and provides transparent load balancing for efficient scheduling of multiple function evaluations. The Bayesian tools are written as clients upon the layer of the library and can be integrated with legacy codes as well as black-box system models, resulting in an easily extensible non-intrusive framework. The present framework aims to facilitate the implementation of UQ+P on engineering applications and harness the capabilities of contemporary and emerging HPC architectures. Current work includes the development of surrogate models and performance studies on the Intel Xeon Phi architecture.

Our open-source software can be downloaded from http://www.cse-lab.ethz. ch/software/Pi4U. We acknowledge computational time at the Swiss National Supercomputing Center CSCS under project number s448.

References

1. Owhadi, H., Scovel, C., Sullivan, T., McKerns, M., Ortiz, M.: Optimal uncertainty quantification. SIAM Rev. **55**(2), 271–345 (2013)
2. Beck, J.L., Yuen, K.V.: Model selection using response measurements: Bayesian probabilistic approach. J. Eng. Mech. **130**(2), 192–203 (2004)
3. Papadimitriou, C., Beck, J.L., Katafygiotis, L.S.: Asymptotic expansions for reliability and moments of uncertain systems. J. Eng. Mech. **123**(12), 1219–1229 (1997)
4. Chen, M.H., Shao, Q.M., Ibrahim, J.G.: Monte Carlo Methods in Bayesian Computation. Springer, New York (2000)
5. Wu, S., Beck, J.L., Heaton, T.H.: Earthquake probability-based automated decision-making framework for earthquake early warning applications. Comp. Aid. Civ. Infr. Eng. **28**, 737–752 (2013)
6. Adams, B., Bohnhoff, W., Dalbey, K., Eddy, J., Eldred, M., Gay, D., Haskell, K., Hough, P., Swiler, L.: DAKOTA, a multilevel parallel object-oriented framework for design optimization, parameter estimation, uncertainty quantification, and sensitivity analysis. Sandia Technical report (2013)
7. Lawrence Livermore National Laboratory. The PSUADE UQ project. http://computation.llnl.gov/casc/uncertainty_quantification/
8. Prudencio, E., Cheung, S.H.: Parallel adaptive multilevel sampling algorithms for the Bayesian analysis of mathematical models. Int. J. Unc. Quan. **2**(3), 215–237 (2012)
9. Hadjidoukas, P.E., Lappas, E., Dimakopoulos, V.V.: A runtime library for platform-independent task parallelism. In: 20th International Conference on Parallel, Distributed and Network-Based Processing, pp. 229–236 (2012)

10. Ching, J.Y., Chen, Y.C.: Transitional markov chain Monte Carlo method for Bayesian model updating, model class selection, and model averaging. J. Eng. Mech. **133**(7), 816–832 (2007)
11. Chiachio, M., Beck, J., Chiachio, J., Rus, G.: Approximate Bayesian computation by subset simulation. SIAM J. Sci. Comput. **36**, A1339–A1358 (2014)
12. Hansen, N., Muller, S.D., Koumoutsakos, P.: Reducing the time complexity of the derandomized evolution strategy with covariance matrix adaptation (CMA-ES). Evol. Comp. **11**(1), 1–18 (2003)
13. Beck, J.L., Katafygiotis, L.S.: Updating models and their uncertainties. I: Bayesian statistical framework. J. Eng. Mech. **124**(4), 455–461 (1998)
14. Galbally, D., Fidkowski, K., Willcox, K., Ghattas, O.: Non-linear model reduction for uncertainty quantification in large-scale inverse problems. Int. J. Num. Meth. Eng. **81**(12), 1581–1608 (2010)
15. Hadjidoukas, P.E., Angelikopoulos, P., Voglis, C., Papageorgiou, D.G., Lagaris, I.E.: NDL-v2.0: A new version of the numerical differentiation library for parallel architectures. Comput. Phys. Comm. **185**(7), 2217–2219 (2014)
16. Angelikopoulos, P., Papadimitriou, C., Koumoutsakos, P.: Data driven, predictive molecular dynamics for nanoscale flow simulations under uncertainty. J. Phys. Chem. B **117**(47), 14808–14816 (2013)
17. Rick, S.: A reoptimization of the five-site water potential (TIP5P) for use with Ewald sums. J. Chem. Phys. **120**, 6085–6093 (2004)

Parallelization of an Advection-Diffusion Problem Arising in Edge Plasma Physics Using Hybrid MPI/OpenMP Programming

Matthieu Kuhn[1]([⊠]), Guillaume Latu[2], Nicolas Crouseilles[3],
and Stéphane Genaud[1]

[1] ICube, University of Strasbourg, Strasbourg, France
matthieu.kuhn@inria.fr
[2] CEA, IRFM, 13108 Saint-Paul-lez-Durance, France
[3] INRIA Rennes, IPSO Project and IRMAR, University of Rennes 1, Rennes, France

Abstract. This work presents a hybrid MPI/OpenMP parallelization strategy for an advection-diffusion problem, arising in a scientific application simulating tokamak's edge plasma physics. This problem is the hotspot of the system of equations numerically solved by the application. As this part of the code is memory-bandwidth limited, we show the benefit of a parallel approach that increases the aggregated memory bandwidth in using multiple computing nodes. In addition, we designed some algorithms to limit the additional cost, induced by the needed extra inter nodal communications. The proposed solution allows to achieve good scalings on several nodes and to observe 70 % of relative efficiency on 512 cores. Also, the hybrid parallelization allows to consider larger domain sizes, unreachable on a single computing node.

Keywords: Hybrid MPI/OpenMP · Advection-Diffusion · Plasma physics

1 Introduction

In this work, we present a hybrid MPI/OpenMP parallelization strategy for an advection-diffusion problem, arising in a scientific application simulating toka-mak's edge plasma physics called Emedge3D. In a previous work (see [6]), we presented parallelization using OpenMP, but also several optimizations for a shared memory architecture. Enhancing this previous version is needed because of the memory-bound aspect of the application. Some optimizations were described that improved data access patterns, leading to better data locality. Even if one part of the code was successfully optimized with techniques such as loop tiling, the most consuming part of the code still suffered from a lack of performance on a 64-cores shared memory node. However, results were satisfying for a smaller node of 12 cores (bi-socket Intel X5675 @ 3.06 GHz).

M. Kuhn—Currently at INRIA Bordeaux Sud Ouest, HiePACS Project.

© Springer-Verlag Berlin Heidelberg 2015
J.L. Träff et al. (Eds.): Euro-Par 2015, LNCS 9233, pp. 545–557, 2015.
DOI: 10.1007/978-3-662-48096-0_42

Hence, we propose here to add a level of parallelism. To do so, we combine the OpenMP paradigm to the MPI standard to target distributed memory architectures. But, to achieve good efficiency, we show that several invasive modifications of the code have to be implemented. For example, considering 1D × 1D FFT versus 2D FFT routines divides the communication volume by a factor 2. Therefore, we consider in this paper an advection-diffusion equation. Even if it is a reduced problem compared to the model used in Emedge3D, the Poisson bracket (advection part) and the diffusion part (which is anisotropic) are the most challenging and time consuming ones in Emedge3D.

In this paper, we consider the unknown temperature $T = T(t, x, y, z)$, the operator $\nabla \cdot (A\nabla.)$ (where $\nabla = (\partial_x, \partial_y, \partial_z)$), and A a 3×3 matrix to be explicited. This operator is coupled with an advection operator $\{\phi, .\} = \partial_x \phi \partial_y. - \partial_y \phi \partial_x.$, also called Poisson bracket. We consider the equation

$$\partial_t T + \{\phi, T\} = \nabla \cdot (A\nabla T), \quad x, y, z \in [-1, 1], t \geq 0, \tag{1}$$

with periodic boundary conditions along y, z, Dirichlet boundary condition along x (classical in tokamak geometry) and ϕ the electric potential, assumed to be given here.

In the following, we first describe the advection-diffusion problem addressed in this work while providing the related work. Then, we present the numerical methods and our validation test case. After that, we detail the proposed parallel solutions to solve the advection-diffusion equation. Lastly, we give a performance analysis of the best known solution.

2   The Advection-Diffusion Problem

Advection-diffusion problems are widely used in physics models (see [2, 7]). Their numerical approximation often requires recent techniques (see [11] for example). However, most of the time, the diffusion operator is restricted to a 3D Laplacian, whereas several relevant applications requires an anisotropic diffusion.

The problem considered here is 3D in space and time-dependant. The advection part is 2D, in the plane (x, y), and consists in a Poisson bracket. The same operator can be found in Emedge3D's model (see [2]). For the diffusion part, the diffusion matrix A depends only on the spatial dimension x, corresponding to the radial direction in the SLAB geometry of Emedge3D.

As in Emedge3D, two kinds of discretization are considered to approximate spatial operators. First, a *semi-spectral* representation of 3D unknown is used to compute the diffusion part, in which y and z directions are expressed in the Fourier basis, and x in the real basis. Second, a representation in the full real space for the 3 directions is employed to compute the Poisson bracket. This kind of discretization is often encountered in nuclear fusion codes. As an illustration, we can cite GKV and GENE (see [8] and [4]), and also XTOR and JOREK (see [7] and [5]). These codes also try to take benefits of parallelization on both shared and distributed memory systems.

In Emedge3D, the execution time of a simulation is mostly driven by the pressure equation (see [2,3,9]), which is similar to Eq. (1). The next section aims to describe the numerical methods employed to solve the advection-diffusion problem given by the following equation:

$$\partial_t T + \{\phi, T\} = \nabla \cdot (A_x \nabla T) \text{ with } A_x = \begin{pmatrix} a(x) & 0 & 0 \\ 0 & b(x) & d(x) \\ 0 & d(x) & c(x) \end{pmatrix}. \tag{2}$$

3   Numerical Methods and Test Case

3.1   Spatial Discretization

This part deals with the spatial discretization used in the code. It presents first the numerical method to compute the advection and then the spatial scheme to solve the diffusion. These methods are extracted from Emedge3D.

The *advection term* is computed in the physical space (and not in semi-spectral representation) with a finite difference method. Indeed, when the Poisson bracket operator is explicited in semi-spectral representation, it leads to a convolution which has a quadratic computational complexity $\Theta(n^2)$ (assuming $n = N_y N_z$). This is why the discretization has to change by using FFT. Hence, it results in a more desirable linearithmic computational complexity $\Theta(n \log(n))$. This method is commonly used on nonlinear terms in case of a semi-spectral discretization (see [10]). An Arakawa scheme of order 2 (see [1]) is employed to compute this Poisson Bracket. This numerical method is often considered in the plasma physics community because of its robustness and conservation properties. This discretization induces the computation of a 2D stencil in the plane (x, y), the dimension z acts as a parameter. This spatial scheme has already been studied in one of our former work (see [6]).

The *diffusion operator* is characterized by the diffusion matrix A_x given by (2). As it only depends on the radial dimension x, it can be easily written in the semi-spectral form. Hence, the unknown T is expressed in the Fourier basis in the y and z directions. This implies manipulation of quantities of the form:

$$\hat{T}_{i,m,n} := \hat{T}(x_i, m, n) = \int_{\mathbb{R}} \int_{\mathbb{R}} T(x_i, y, z) exp(-i(my + nz)) dy \, dz,$$

where x_i stands for the grid points in the radial direction and (m, n) the Fourier mode. The diffusion operator is solved with a classical finite volume method of order 2 in the x direction, and spectral method in y and z directions:

$$\nabla \cdot (A_x \nabla \hat{T})_{|i,m,n} = a(x_{i+1/2}) \frac{\hat{T}_{i+1,m,n} - \hat{T}_{i,m,n}}{\Delta x^2} - a(x_{i-1/2}) \frac{\hat{T}_{i,m,n} - \hat{T}_{i-1,m,n}}{\Delta x^2}$$
$$- (b(x_i)m^2 + c(x_i)n^2 + 2d(x_i)mn)\hat{T}_{i,m,n},$$

where Δx denotes the spatial step in the direction x and $x_{i\pm1/2} = x_i \pm \Delta x/2$.

3.2   Temporal Discretization

The implemented time integration scheme uses an operator splitting between advection and diffusion terms. It is due to the different spatial discretizations employed to solve these operators. We denote by $T^k = T(t^k, x, y, z)$ the solution at time $t^k = k\Delta t$ in the direct representation, with Δt the time step; and $\hat{T}^k = \hat{T}(t^k, x, m, n)$ in the semi-spectral representation, where m (respectively n) stands for the mode number in the poloidal (respectively toroidal) direction. Hence, we first consider the advection $\partial_t T + \{\phi, T\} = 0$, that we decide to solve with a classical (explicit) Euler method $T^* = T^k + \Delta t \{\phi, T^k\}$.

The second step consists in solving the diffusion part $\partial_t \hat{T} = \nabla \cdot (A_x \nabla \hat{T})$. Recall the diffusion is solved in the semi-spectral space. Hence, the temporal scheme associated with the diffusion part is also applied in this representation. The Euler method to solve this part writes: $\hat{T}^{k+1} = \hat{T}^* + \Delta t \nabla \cdot (A_x \nabla \hat{T}^*)$.

Notice this scheme is referred as the Lie splitting, which is of first order. It can be upgraded to higher orders by using Strang splitting method. Also, as it is an explicit method, a stability condition is imposed on the value of Δt. The more restrictive stability condition comes from the diffusion operator. To bypass this limitation, it is possible to implement implicit or (well chosen) semi-implicit method (see [11] for example).

3.3   Analytical Test Case

This part gives a three dimensional analytical test case used to validate the numerical methods presented earlier and the parallelization implementations. The technique employed to construct our test case is called the Method of Manufactured Solution (MMS). The equation to solve is:

$$\partial_t T + \{\phi, T\} = \nabla \cdot (A_x \nabla T) + f, \tag{3}$$

where $\phi = \phi(x, y) = \cos(\pi x) \cos(\pi y)$ and $f = f(t, x, y, z)$ is a given source function added to perform the MMS. The solution we choose to reach for this test case writes:

$$T(t, x, y) = 1 + \sin(\pi x) \sin(\pi y) \sin(\pi z) e^{-t}, \tag{4}$$

where $x, y, z \in [-1, 1], t \geq 0$. For the matrix A_x, we consider the functions:

$$a(x) = (2 + \sin(\pi x)), b(x) = (2 + \sin(\pi x))^2,$$
$$c(x) = (2 + \cos(\pi x))^2, d(x) = (2 + \sin(\pi x))(2 + \cos(\pi x)).$$

Then, (4) is an analytical solution of (3) with the computed source term:

$$f(t, x, y, z) = -(T - 1) + \partial_x \phi \partial_x T - \partial_y \phi \partial_y T + b(x)\pi^2(T - 1) + c(x)\pi^2(T - 1)$$
$$- a'(x)\partial_x T - a(x)\partial_x^2 T - 2d(x)\partial_{y,z}^2 T.$$

4   Parallelization MPI/OpenMP

In this section, we first introduce the sequential algorithm description. Then, we explore the parallelization potential in the case of a distributed memory architecture. To finish, we present the OpenMP and the hybrid MPI/OpenMP parallelization of the code.

4.1   Sequential Algorithm

This part details the organization of the time loop in our simulation code, given by Algorithm 1. The algorithm for the advection-diffusion can be decomposed into 4 parts: the advection, the diffusion, the Fourier transforms and the transpositions of data in memory. In order to perform one temporal iteration, two arrays are used: $T_1[N_z, N_y, N_x]$ to store the value of the time evolutive temperature and $T_2[N_z, N_y, N_x]$ to store temporary results. In both arrays, data are in semi-spectral data representation. Here, the notation $T_1[z, y, x]$ refers to the value stored at position $z * (N_y * N_x) + y * (N_x) + x$, with N_d the number of points in direction d. As the advection source term f_{adv} and the diffusion one f_{diff} are known analytically, they are computed on the fly.

Discretization changes (real to semi-spectral and inverse) are encapsulated into the diffusion step. Hence, the diffusion step divides into three parts, detailed in Algorithms 2 and 3. Algorithm 2 consists in Fourier transforms in forward direction (from $\mathbb{R}$ to $\mathbb{C}$) in dimension y. In this Algorithm, $\text{buffer}_y[*]$ and $\text{buffer2}_y[*]$ are buffers of size N_y, used to store $(z, y = *, x)$ slices contiguously into the memory. This improves the temporal locality. The $*$ notation denotes an operation along all the points of the given dimension. Endly, notation $\hat{T}$ means that data are in semi-spectral representation ($\hat{T} \in \mathbb{C}$). Notice that storage dimensions order changes between input and output, going from $[z, y, x]$ to $[y, z, x]$. We compute this on the fly because the diffusion step and the FFT in z direction are in a same external loop on y.

Algorithm 3 details Fourier transforms in z direction and the diffusion computations. Here, the storage location $\text{buffer}_z[*]$ is an array of size N_z, used to

---

Algorithm 1. One time loop iteration

Input: $T_1 = T(t^n)$

Algorithm:

$T_2 \leftarrow \nabla \cdot (A_x \nabla T_1)$: Diffusion
$T_1 \leftarrow T_1 + \Delta t T_2$: Euler scheme
$T_1 \leftarrow T_1 + \Delta t f_{\text{diff}}^n$: Diffusion source
$T_2 \leftarrow \{\phi, T_1\}$: Advection operator
$T_1 \leftarrow T_1 - \Delta t T_2$: Euler scheme
$T_1 \leftarrow T_1 + \Delta t f_{\text{adv}}^n$: Advection source

Output : $T_1 = T(t^{n+1})$

Algorithm 2. FFT forward y

Input: $T_1[z, y, x] = T^n$
Algorithm:

for all z do
  for all x do
    $\text{buffer}_y[*] \leftarrow T_1[z, *, x]$
    $\text{buffer2}_y[*] \leftarrow \text{FFT}(\text{buffer}_y[*])$
    $\hat{T}_1[*, z, x] \leftarrow \text{buffer2}_y[*]$
  end for
end for

Output : $\hat{T}_1[y, z, x] = \hat{T}^n$

temporarily store Fourier representation along z direction. Notice that these FFT are also applied in-place, in order to maximize temporal locality on the buffer. Buffers $in_{xz}[x, *]$ and $out_{xz}[x, *]$ aim to store 2D (x, z) slices, $in_{xz}[x, *]$ for the input of the diffusion computation and $out_{xz}[x, *]$ for the output.

The backward Fourier transform on y dimension (from $\mathbb{C}$ to $\mathbb{R}$) is very similar to Algorithm 2 and is not presented here.

4.2 Parallelization Potential

For simplicity (implementation, readability and maintenance of the code done by the physicists), we choose to consider algorithms which do not need ghost cells between MPI processes.

The advection is solved in the direct representation (real space) of the unknown. It consists in a 2D stencil on variables x, y. The third direction z acts as a parameter here, and so it is a good candidate as parallelization axis. The diffusion part is solved in the semi-spectral representation of the unknown. It consists of a stencil in the x direction. Hence, it allows easier parallelization along y or z axes.

Between the two last operators, it seems natural to change the domain decomposition: arrays are parallelized with MPI along z for the advection and along y for the diffusion part. Moreover, another distribution change occurs at the same time to switch from semi-spectral to full real representation. It is computed via Discrete Fourier Transforms (DFT), with the FFTW3 library. These FFT act on the plane (y, z), corresponding to toroidal and poloidal directions of the tokamak geometry.

Table 1. Parallelization potential on distributed memory architectures. Dependencies include read statements (ghost cells not considered).

Step	Axe	Dependencies at (i, j, k)	Parallelization considered
Advection	x	$i - 1, i, i + 1$	no
	y	$j - 1, j, j + 1$	no
	z	k	yes
Diffusion	x	$i - 1, i, i + 1$	no
	y	j	yes
	z	k	yes
FFT 1D y	x	i	yes
	y	$j = *$	no
	z	k	yes
FFT 1D z	x	i	yes
	y	j	yes
	z	$k = *$	no

Instead of computing the FFT with the 2D functions proposed by the FFTW3 library (as in the Emedge3D code), we decide to compute FFT dimension by dimension (using 1D functions). It presents 3 major advantages:

- it operates on smaller data volumes, allowing more benefit from cache effects,
- it permits a larger set of possibilities for the parallelization on distributed memory architecture, as we will see afterwards,
- it does not imply a loss of performance in the sequential case (even if an additionnal transposition is needed). In particular, it allows to reuse data loads between FFT 1D and other parts of the algorithm.

Finally, as parallelization axes change between the different parts of the code, it remains to perform transpositions and redistributions of data, in order to have needed data locally on the computation node. These transpositions will depend on the chosen algorithm, and in particular on the way FFT are computed. Table 1 gives a summary of the last exposed parallelization possibilities.

4.3 OpenMP Parallel Version

Hereafter, an OpenMP parallel solution is introduced. Typically, the code consists in applying spatial operators compounded of loop nests of depth 3 (one

---

Algorithm 3. $\mathrm{FFT}^{\pm 1}$ z direction and diffusion

Input: $\hat{T}[y, z, x] = \hat{T}^n$

Algorithm:
for all y **do**
  for all x **do**
    $\mathrm{buffer}_z[*] \leftarrow \hat{T}[y, *, x]$
    $\mathrm{buffer}_z[*] \leftarrow \mathrm{FFT}(\mathrm{buffer}_z[*])$
    $\mathrm{in}_{xz}[x, *] \leftarrow \mathrm{buffer}_z[*]$
  end for
  for all x **do**
    $\mathrm{out}_{xz}[x, *] \leftarrow \mathrm{in}_{xz}[x, *] + \Delta t \nabla \cdot (A_x \nabla \mathrm{in}_{xz}[x, *])$
  end for
  for all x **do**
    $\mathrm{buffer}_z[*] \leftarrow \mathrm{out}_{xz}[x, *]$
    $\mathrm{buffer}_z[*] \leftarrow \mathrm{FFT}^{-1}(\mathrm{buffer}_z[*])$
    $\hat{T}[y, *, x] \leftarrow \mathrm{buffer}_z[*]$
  end for
end for

Output : $\hat{T}[y, z, x] = \hat{T}^n + \Delta t \nabla \cdot (A_x \nabla \hat{T}^n)$

Algorithm 4. Comms, $\mathrm{FFT}^{\pm 1}$ z direction and diffusion

Input: $\mathrm{Z\_dist}[y, z, x] = \hat{T}(t^n)$
Algorithm:
$\mathrm{pid} \leftarrow$ current process rank
for all y local to process pid **do**
  comm_{zy}: $\mathrm{Y\_dist}[y, *, *] \leftarrow \mathrm{Z\_dist}[y, *, *]$
  for all x **do**
    $\mathrm{buffer}_z[*] \leftarrow \mathrm{Y\_dist}[y, *, x]$
    $\mathrm{buffer}_z[*] \leftarrow \mathrm{FFT}(\mathrm{buffer}_z[*])$
    $\mathrm{in}_{xz}[x, *] \leftarrow \mathrm{buffer}_z[*]$
  end for
  for all x **do**
    $\mathrm{out}_{xz}[x, *] \leftarrow \mathrm{in}_{xz}[x, *] + \Delta t \nabla \cdot (A_x \nabla \mathrm{in}_{xz}[x, *])$
  end for
  for all x **do**
    $\mathrm{buffer}_z[*] \leftarrow \mathrm{out}_{xz}[x, *]$
    $\mathrm{buffer}_z[*] \leftarrow \mathrm{FFT}^{-1}(\mathrm{buffer}_z[*])$
    $\mathrm{Y\_dist}[y, *, x] \leftarrow \mathrm{buffer}_z[*]$
  end for
  comm_{yz}: $\mathrm{Z\_dist}[y, *, *] \leftarrow \mathrm{Y\_dist}[y, *, *]$
end for
Output : $\mathrm{Z\_dist}[y, z, x] = \hat{T}(t^n) + \Delta t \nabla \cdot (A_x \nabla \hat{T}(t^n))$

for each spatial dimension). The parallelization strategy resides in distributing the outermost loops. The clause `collapse(2)` is used in order to combine iterations of two successive loops. All steps are parallelized with OpenMP. Regarding the advection and the computations of the source terms, arrays are stored in order z, y and x (C-like notation). Parallelization occurs on z and y dimensions. Concerning the diffusion part, the FFT in y direction are parallelized along z axis too (see Algorithm 2). For the FFT part in z and the diffusion operator (see Algorithm 3), the parallelization directive is on the intermediate loops on dimension x. Notice the loops on dimension x can not be trivially merged, because of a Write/Read dependency between the FFT and the diffusion parts. However, as computations are coupled in a same y loop, the 2D slice computed for each y index is small enough to fit in cache (L3 or L2).

4.4   Hybrid MPI/OpenMP Parallel Version

This part proposes a hybrid MPI/OpenMP parallel version of the code that lowers the volume of communications.

The algorithm remains close to the OpenMP version, but with data and outermost spatial loops distributed on the MPI processes. Hence, there are two dimensions along which data are distributed. The first one is z direction. Data are stored in $[z, y, x]$ order, and 2D $[y, x]$ slices are uniformly distributed on the different processes. This distribution addresses the Arakawa method, the source terms computations and FFT on y dimension. The second one is y direction. This is the case for Algorithm 3, (FFT on z and diffusion). Indeed, to compute 1D FFT for direction z, each process must have all the points in that direction.

The two domain decompositions lead to two transposition steps implying communications. These communications are added to Algorithm 3, using non-blocking subroutines, in order to minimize communication overhead. Several versions have been tested, but only the fastest one is presented. The communications are performed within the y loop of Algorithm 3 as we will see afterwards.

Algorithm 4 gives the communication steps, coupled with the FFT in direction z and the diffusion operator. In this Algorithm, notation comm_{zy} corresponds to z to y transpose step (and inverse for comm_{yz}). Finally, Algorithm 5 describes how to transpose from a distribution in z to a distribution in y for one given index iy. The inverse transformation is not detailed as it is completely symmetric.

5   Performance Analysis

This section presents the numerical results and performances obtained for the algorithms detailed in Sect. 4. For each run, 10 temporal iterations were performed, with a $(N_x, N_y, N_z) = (256, 256, 128)$ grid for mono-node tests and both $(256, 256, 128)$ and $(1024, 1024, 512)$ for the multi-node case.

Tests were performed on two parallel computers: the Rheticus cluster based at Aix-Marseille University, France, compounded of 1152 cores organized in 96 nodes of 2 bi-socket X5675; and the Helios cluster based in Rokkasho, Japan at the International Fusion Energy Research Center, compounded of 2 bi-socket Xeon E5-2600 nodes. In terms of configuration, we used Intel compiler together with Open MPI version 1.6.3 and the FFTW3 library in version 3.3. Source codes were compiled with -O2 -axSSE4.2 flags.

Algorithm 5. Transpose $z \to y$: comm_{zy}

Input: Z_dist[NY,NZloc,NX],iy
Algorithm:
   pid ← current process rank
   for all process p ≠ pid **do**
      Irecv(Y_dist[iy,NZloc × p,NX]) from p
   end for
   for all process p ≠ pid **do**
      Isend(Z_dist[iy × p,NZloc,NX]) to p
   end for
   Wait for all communication to finish
Output: Y_dist[iy,NZ,NX]

In the following, programs performances are presented using notations: NCU the number of computing units (with NCU = NTH × NP), NTH the number of OpenMP threads, NP the number of MPI processes, t the execution time, SU the speedup relative to NCU, Eff% the relative efficiency, and Tot% the percentage of time relative to the total execution time.

Notice that the performance analysis does not take into account initialization and diagnostics execution times. When not specified, results are obtained with the Rheticus cluster. In a first part, results are presented for the OpenMP version, then the hybrid MPI/OpenMP version on only one node, and finally the hybrid MPI/OpenMP version on several nodes.

5.1   OpenMP Parallel Version

This part aims to evaluate the OpenMP parallelization of the code. Results are presented for the unique grid size $(N_x, N_y, N_z) = (256, 256, 128)$ as bigger tested sizes do not change speedup and efficiency results.

Table 2 shows results for 10 temporal iterations. With this parallel version, it is possible to reach a speedup of 7.7 using the 12 cores of the computing node, giving an efficiency of 64%. It can obviously be observed that the efficiency decreases when the number of used threads increases. The reason is that the needs of memory bandwidth resource

NCU	NTH	t(sec)	SU	Eff%	Tot%
1	1	8.76	1.00	100.0	100.0
4	4	2.54	3.44	85.9	100.0
8	8	1.50	5.85	73.1	100.0
12	12	1.14	7.68	64.0	100.0

Table 2. OpenMP: time loop.

increases together with the added cores, as we will see afterwards.

Tables 3 and 4 show performances for the main parts of the time loop (the diffusion and the advection). When increasing the number of threads for the advection part, one can see execution times, speedups and hence efficiency scale very well. On the contrary, the diffusion part still suffers from an efficiency degradation, lowering to 55.3% on the 12 cores of the node.

The diffusion part contains the one dimensional FFT computations in y and z directions. Let us have a look to the detail of computations inside the diffusion step. The times of Table 3 include times of Tables 5 and 6. They also contain the source term performance that is not explicited (although it shows nearly ideal scalings). Notice that Table 6 contains the diffusion operator computations together with the FFT in the z direction. The efficiency loss appears to be in the parts containing the FFT computations: for example, efficiency drops to 41.4 % for FFT on y on 12 threads. The FFT computations involve a high number of memory operations (*e.g.* data reorganizations between FFT), and hence increase the memory bandwidth requirements when adding computational cores.

Table 3. OpenMP: diffusion, source and fft 1D y and z.

NCU	NTH	t(sec)	SU	Eff%	Tot%
1	1	5.77	1.00	100.0	65.9
4	4	1.80	3.21	80.4	70.4
8	8	1.12	5.17	64.6	74.6
12	12	0.87	6.63	55.3	76.3

Table 4. OpenMP: advection.

NCU	NTH	t(sec)	SU	Eff%	Tot%
1	1	1.50	1.00	100.0	17.2
4	4	0.38	3.96	99.1	14.9
8	8	0.19	7.81	97.7	12.9
12	12	0.15	10.36	86.3	12.7

Table 5. OpenMP: fft 1D y.

NCU	NTH	t(sec)	SU	Eff%	Tot%
1	1	2.77	1.00	100.0	31.5
4	4	0.99	2.80	69.9	38.7
8	8	0.67	4.11	51.3	44.8
12	12	0.56	4.97	41.4	48.7

Table 6. OpenMP: diffusion and fft 1D z.

NCU	NTH	t(sec)	SU	Eff%	Tot%
1	1	1.38	1.00	100.0	15.7
4	4	0.40	3.46	86.4	15.6
8	8	0.24	5.77	72.1	16.0
12	12	0.18	7.76	64.7	15.6

5.2 Hybrid MPI/OpenMP Parallel Version

This part evaluates the multi-node version of the code presented in Sect. 4.4. This version aims to increase the number of computational nodes and the memory resource (bandwidth and space). This is particularly critical when attempting to reach targeted grid sizes. First, the deployment problem is addressed on one node (NTH and NP per node) in order to get the best mono-node performance.

Table 7 presents results for different couples (NTH, NP)[1] on one node. The best couple is $(3, 4)$, giving a 7.8 speedup on the 12 cores of the node. Also, computation times on the 12 cores are very similar to the OpenMP parallel version (see Table 2). This is surprising because this MPI version contains additional memory operations and overheads due to communications between processes.

Table 8 shows how performances scale on several nodes, using the previous (NTH, NP)=(3,4) per node deployment. The code was run on 12, 48, 96 and 192 computing units. On the 192 computing units, the code reaches a speedup of 81, leading to 42.4 % efficiency. To understand the loss of efficiency, each part of the code is also analyzed.

---

[1] Our code imposes NP as a power of 2.

Table 7. MPI/OpenMP: time loop.

NCU	NTH	NP	t(sec)	SU	Eff%	Tot%
1	1	1	8.87	1.00	100.0	100.0
12	3	4	1.14	7.79	64.9	100.0
12	6	2	1.28	6.92	57.7	100.0
12	12	1	1.43	6.21	51.7	100.0

Table 8. MPI/OpenMP: time loop.

NCU	NTH	NP	t(sec)	SU	Eff%	Tot%
1	1	1	8.87	1.00	100.0	100.0
12	3	4	1.13	7.84	65.3	100.0
48	3	16	0.31	28.32	59.0	100.0
96	3	32	0.19	46.40	48.3	100.0
192	3	64	0.17	81.37	42.4	100.0

The advection part (Arakawa scheme and source term) and the diffusion source term show very good efficiencies when increasing the number of nodes (close to 100 %). Table 9 shows performances for the FFT on the dimension y. Recall it does not include MPI communications. Whereas this part suffered from a limited efficiency in case of the OpenMP only parallelization (see Table 5), it is now able to reach a much better efficiency on the 192 computing units, reaching 81.8 %. Between 12 and 48 computing units (*i.e.* 1 and 4 nodes fully occupied), we observe a surlinear speedup due to positive cache effects: the volume of processed data per node is small enough to hold in the L3 cache.

Table 9. MPI/OpenMP: fft 1D y.

NCU	NTH	NP	t(sec)	SU	Eff%	Tot%
1	1	1	2.74	1.00	100.0	30.9
12	3	4	0.43	6.32	52.6	38.3
48	3	16	0.07	38.65	80.5	22.6
96	3	32	0.04	70.51	73.5	20.3
192	3	64	0.02	156.97	81.8	16.0

Table 10. MPI/OpenMP: comms, fft 1D z and diffusion.

NCU	NTH	NP	t(sec)	SU	Eff%	Tot%
1	1	1	1.46	1.00	100.0	16.4
12	3	4	0.30	4.77	39.7	27.0
48	3	16	0.14	10.07	21.0	46.2
96	3	32	0.10	14.34	14.9	53.2
192	3	64	0.07	21.86	11.4	61.1

Hence, it is the last part containing the communications which is responsible for the loss of efficiency. Indeed, Table 10 shows a drop in efficiencies due to the additional MPI communications needed to transpose data. Notice that this drop is particularly important between 1 and 4 processes (from 100 % to 39.7 %) because of the apparition of intranode communications and saturation of memory bandwidth, and again between 4 and 16 processes (from 39.7 % to 21 %) because of apparition of internode communications (involving the network). After 4 nodes, the drop of efficiency starts to become less stringent. Moreover, considering several nodes allows the user to handle bigger computational domains. This is the topic of the next Paragraph. The same study has been performed on the former presented machine Helios. Results are globally very close to those obtained on the Rheticus cluster, showing a speedup of 92 on 256 cores.

The bigger grid size $(1024, 1024, 512)$ targeted by Emedge3D implies the manipulation of 4 GB of memory per array. The no-MPI versions are not able to run: the memory requirements are to high to be handled by a unique node.

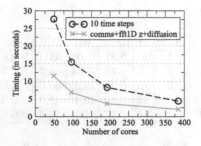 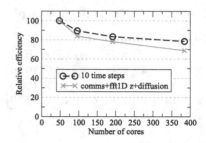

Each deployment uses 4 processes per node. The two last plots shows the timings (left) and efficiencies (right) for 10 time loop iterations (dashed line) and for the substep that includes communications (continuous line) as a function of the number of cores. They show a good scalability, leading to a relative efficiency of 78.5 % for 384 cores. On 768 cores, we do not expect dramatic loss of performance. Indeed, communication times diminish when adding cores and remain a fraction of the global execution time (comprised between 40 % and 50 %). This is because the reference time on 4 nodes already includes internodal communications. On Helios, the same $(1024, 1024, 512)$ grid size led to an efficiency of 70 % on 512 cores.

6   Conclusion

This work proposes a hybrid MPI/OpenMP parallelization strategy for an advection-diffusion problem relevant to the model simulated by Emedge3D, which is a dedicated code to study edge plasma physics in tokamaks.

The obtained parallel version allows to overcome the memory bandwith limitation, which was one of the main bottlenecks of Emedge3D. Indeed, considering additional nodes allows one to add memory resources that are needed when increasing the number of computing units. Plus, algorithm modifications (data organization in memory, FFT 1D in each direction) are particularly critical to reduce the amount of communications needed by the MPI version of the code. For a domain of size $(256, 256, 128)$, the parallel code is able to reach a speedup of 81 on 192 computing units. In addition to that, the code is also able to handle larger domain sizes, because adding nodes also increases available memory space. For example, it is able to handle grids of size $(1024, 1024, 512)$, leading to 4 GB for each 3D array, with an efficiency of 78.5 % on 384 cores.

As an immediate extension, tests could be performed on larger parallel systems, to see the evolution of the communications' scaling. Another axis is to couple this parallelization strategy with semi-implicit numerical method in order to increase the value of the time step Δt. Eventually, the integration of this parallelization strategy in Emedge3D code would enable to reach lower execution times and larger domain sizes.

Acknowledgements. The authors acknowledge the ANR (National Research Agency, project reference: ANR-10-BLAN-0940) and ERC Starting Grant Project GEOPARDI No. 279389 for financial supporting, the use of the Aix-Marseille University Computing Facility, and associated support services. The authors also express their acknowledgements to the IFERC for the access to Helios super-calculator. Finally, the authors thank the members of the research team PIIM of Aix-Marseille University for precious help.

References

1. Arakawa, A.: Computational design for long-term numerical integration of the equations of fluid motion: 2D incompressible flow. J. Comput. Phys. **1**(1), 119–143 (1966)
2. Beyer, N., et al.: Nonlinear dynamics of transport barrier relaxations in tokamak edge plasmas. Phys. Rev. Lett. **94**, 105001 (2005). http://link.aps.org/doi/10.1103/PhysRevLett.94.105001
3. Fuhr, G., et al.: Evidence from numerical simulations of transport-barrier relaxations in tokamak edge plasmas in the presence of electromagnetic fluctuations. Phys. Rev. Lett. **101**, 195001 (2008). http://link.aps.org/doi/10.1103/PhysRevLett.101.195001
4. Gorler, T., et al.: The global version of the gyrokinetic turbulence code GENE. J. Comput. Phys. **230**(18), 7053–7071 (2011). http://www.sciencedirect.com/science/article/pii/S0021999111003457
5. Huysmans, G., et al.: Non-linear MHD simulations of edge localized modes (ELMs). Plasma Phys. Controlled Fusion **51**(12), 124012 (2009)
6. Kuhn, M., et al.: Optimization and parallelization of Emedge3D on shared memory architecture. In: 2013 15th International Symposium on SYNASC, pp. 503–510. IEEE (2013)
7. Lütjens, H., Luciani, J.F.: The XTOR code for nonlinear 3D simulations of MHD instabilities in tokamak plasmas. J. Comput. Phys. **227**(14), 6944–6966 (2008)
8. Maeyama, S., et al.: Computation-Communication techniques for parallel spectral calculations in Gyrokinetic Vlasov simulations. Plasma Fusion Res. **8**, 1403150 (2013)
9. Monnier, A., et al.: Penetration of resonant magnetic perturbations at the tokamak edge. In: 38th EPS Conference on Plasma Physics (2011)
10. Orszag, S.A.: Transform method for the calculation of vector-coupled sums: application to the spectral form of the vorticity equation. J. Atmos. Sci. **27**(6), 890–895 (1970)
11. Zhang, Q., et al.: A fourth-order accurate finite-volume method with structured adaptive mesh refinement for solving the advection-diffusion equation. SIAM J. Sci. Comput. **34**(2), 179–201 (2012). http://dx.doi.org/10.1137/110820105

Behavioral Non-portability in Scientific Numeric Computing

Yijia Gu[1]($\boxtimes$), Thomas Wahl[1], Mahsa Bayati[2]($\boxtimes$), and Miriam Leeser[2]

[1] College of Computer and Information Science,
Northeastern University, Boston, USA
{guyijia,wahl}@ccs.neu.edu
[2] Department of Electrical and Computer Engineering,
Northeastern University, Boston, USA
{mbayati,mel}@coe.neu.edu

Abstract. The precise semantics of floating-point arithmetic programs depends on the execution platform, including the compiler and the target hardware. Platform dependencies are particularly pronounced for arithmetic-intensive parallel numeric programs and infringe on the highly desirable goal of software portability (which is nonetheless promised by heterogeneous computing frameworks like OpenCL): the same program run on the same inputs on different platforms often produces different results. Serious doubts on the portability of numeric applications arise when these differences are *behavioral*, i.e. when they lead to changes in the control flow of a program. In this paper we present an algorithm that takes a numeric procedure and determines an input that may lead to different *branching decisions* depending on how the arithmetic in the procedure is compiled. We illustrate the algorithm on a diverse set of examples, characteristic of scientific numeric computing, where control flow divergence actually occurs across different execution platforms.

1 Introduction

Many high performance computing applications make use of floating-point arithmetic. It is well known that floating-point expressions produce different results on different machines, due to lack of associativity, etc. Most practitioners assume that this affects only the last few bits of a computation, and can safely be ignored. In this paper, we present several examples where code run on different platforms on the *same* inputs can produce not just different results but different *control flow*. We use OpenCL as a programming language [9], which promises cross-platform portability. Yet, as our experiments show, this promise does in fact not guarantee portability of control flow.

All the computer hardware that we target complies with the IEEE 754–2008 standard [5]. The code generated to run on compliant hardware has several degrees of freedom. A compiler may reorder expressions, which affects the numerical values of the results. An example of such reordering is the use of *reductions*

Work supported by the US National Science Foundation grant CCF-1218075.

© Springer-Verlag Berlin Heidelberg 2015
J.L. Träff et al. (Eds.): Euro-Par 2015, LNCS 9233, pp. 558–569, 2015.
DOI: 10.1007/978-3-662-48096-0_43

to compute long sums by parallel threads. Further, the IEEE standard permits the use of a fused multiply-add (FMA) instruction (which contracts a multiplication followed by an addition into a singly-rounded operation) but gives no guidance on how a compiler should employ such an instruction (if it exists at all). In most applications, there are several *different, IEEE-compliant* ways for the compiler to implement an expression using FMA.

Using examples characteristic of floating-point computations in parallel computing, we demonstrate in this paper that the above vagaries of IEEE floating point can impact control flow in a platform-dependent way. We present an algorithm that, given a numeric procedure, determines an input that may lead to different branching decisions due to (fully IEEE compliant) expression reordering or the use/non-use of FMA instructions. Our two-stage algorithm first uses *symbolic execution* to determine inputs that make a given branching decision unreliable. It then examines such inputs for different ways of evaluating expressions.

Motivating Example: Ray Tracing. Consider the following C program, taken from http://www.cc.gatech.edu/~phlosoft/photon/. We have elided the code following the branching decision D > 0, since here we are merely interested in whether that code is executed at all, depending on the execution platform.

```
float dot3(float *a, float *b) {
return a[0] * b[0] + a[1] * b[1] + a[2] * b[2]; }

int raySphere(float *r, float *s, float radiusSq) {
float A = dot3(r,r);
float B = -2.0 * dot3(s,r);
float C = dot3(s,s) - radiusSq;
float D = B*B - 4*A*C;
if (D > 0)
  ...; }
```

This code employs well-known high school arithmetic. When "arithmetic" means floating point, however, the results are no longer so obvious: the computation of vector dot products in `dot3`, common in high performance libraries, depends on the compiler's choice to evaluate the sum left to right or vice versa, and whether to use FMA instructions and in which of several possible ways. For certain inputs, these choices translate into platform-dependent control flows across the `if` statement involving D. Such divergence is likely not accounted for and undesirable. In Sect. 2 we describe an algorithm to find such inputs. Our algorithm determines that, given the following inputs (trailing 0's omitted) to procedure `raySphere`, the NVIDIA Quadro 600 GPU computes a value $D_N \approx -3.56$, while an Intel 64-bit CPU computes $D_I \approx 4.55$; we observe $D_N \ll 0 \ll D_I$:

$$r = (-33.999900817871094, -54.0, -53.0); \quad radiusSq = 0.000000029802322;$$
$$s = (-33.370471954345703, -53.0, -52.01855468750).$$

Related Work. The scientific computing community has long been aware that floating point vagaries can affect a computation's output. Shewchuk shows how a near-zero determinant may cause flat-out incorrect results due to floating-point rounding errors [10]. Several works have demonstrated that rounding errors can cause the control flow of a floating-point program to differ from that of the corresponding idealistic real-arithmetic program [2,6]. Our technique is distinct in both motivational and technical aspects: (i) we compare the control flows on different floating-point platforms; (ii) instead of a purely dynamic (testing) approach, we use SMT technology to locate potentially problematic inputs.

2   Finding Inputs Witnessing Behavioral Non-portability

Motivated by the observations made in Sect. 1, the goal now is an algorithm that determines inputs to the given program that are likely to expose behavioral non-portability when the program is run on certain diverse execution platforms.

2.1   Problem Formulation

Behavioral non-portability is frequently caused by expressions whose floating-point semantics is dependent on the evaluation order, and on the use of hardware features such as fused multiply-add. We call such expressions *volatile* in this paper. These are expressions $<ve>$ defined by the following grammar:

$$
\begin{aligned}
<ve> \quad &:: \ <ve_{\oplus}> \ | \ <ve_{\otimes}> | \ <ve_{dot}> \ | \ <ve_{fma}> \\
<ve_{\oplus}> \quad &:: \ <e> \oplus \ \ldots \ \oplus <e> \\
<ve_{\otimes}> \quad &:: \ <e> \otimes \ \ldots \ \otimes <e> \\
<ve_{dot}> \quad &:: \ <e> \otimes <e> \oplus \ \ldots \ \oplus <e> \otimes <e> \\
<ve_{fma}> \quad &:: \ fma(<e>,<e>,<e>) \\
<e> \quad &:: \ c \ | \ var \ | <ve> \ | <e> < op > <e> \\
<op> \quad &:: \ \oplus \ | \ \ominus \ | \ \otimes \ | \ \oslash
\end{aligned}
$$

where c is a floating-point constant and *var* is a floating-point program variable. The semantics of $fma(x,y,z)$ is the term $(x \cdot y) \oplus z$, which represents the real value $x \cdot y + z$ followed by a single rounding step. Volatile expressions are *unparenthesized* sums, products, dot products, or FMA expressions over floating-point constants, variables, and other expressions.

Branch Point. We are interested in the effect of behavioral non-portability on the program control flow and, therefore, on conditional statements such as `if` statements and loops. We call such statements *branch points*. Each branch point refers to a conditional q, which is a Boolean-valued formula over atomic floating-point subformulas ψ of the (normalized) form

$$\psi :: X \rhd c, \quad \rhd \in \{\leq, \geq, >, <, ==\} \tag{1}$$

where c is a floating-point constant and X a floating-point valued expression.

We can now define the concept we are investigating in this paper. The value of the conditional q depends not only on the program input I, but also on platform parameters such as the availability of FMA and decisions made by the compiler about evaluating volatile expressions. We refer to an instantiation of such platform parameters as an *expression evaluation model* M. For example, a particular expression evaluation model might state that there is no FMA support, and that sums and products are evaluated left-to-right. An expression evaluation model therefore disambiguates among many of the common and IEEE-754 compliant ways expressions can be rendered by the compiler.

Let $q(I, M)$ denote the value of expression q for program inputs I (that cause q to be reached) and expression evaluation model M, and consider a program P.

Definition 1 (Control-Flow Instability). *Let q denote a Boolean-valued expression used as a conditional in program P. Input I is said to cause **control-flow instability** if there exist two evaluation models M_1 and M_2 such that*

$$q(I, M_1) \neq q(I, M_2). \tag{2}$$

Intuitively, input I is a candidate for causing program P to exhibit different control flows on different platforms, caused by different Boolean values of the conditional q, for the same input I, computed on those platforms. Control flow instabilities are likely undesirable. In the rest of this paper we describe an algorithm that, given program P and a branch point with conditional q, determines whether there exists an input that renders the control flow unstable. The algorithm *efficiently* searches through all possible inputs and evaluation models with the goal of finding I, M_1, M_2 such that $q(I, M_1)$ and $q(I, M_2)$ differ.

2.2   Detecting Behavioral Non-portability: Overview

Our algorithm for finding behavioral non-portability proceeds in two phases. Given is a program P with volatile expressions and a branch point, identified by the user to be of interest, with conditional q over atomic subformulas of the form $\psi_i :: X_i \rhd c_i$ (1). The first phase determines a *candidate input*, i.e. an input I_0 such that minor variations of I_0 cause q to flip. Numerically, this requires that there exists ψ_k in q such that X_k is close to c_k for input I_0. This phase is implemented using *symbolic execution*: we build a formula for the path leading from the program entry point to the conditional q. We change the comparison operator in q to an equality $=$ (or an approximate equality, see below) and solve the obtained path formula using a constraint solver.

In the second phase, the algorithm computes the *minimum and maximum* value of X_k for input I_0 and under all possible expression evaluation models. For two models that give rise to the minimum and maximum value, the chances are that the value of X_k is on either side of c_k, causing the conditional q to flip. The algorithmic challenge is to search among all these models efficiently.

Figure 1 shows our overall approach. We explain the details of each step in the following subsections.

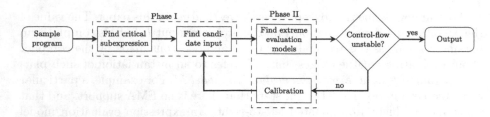

Fig. 1. Finding behavioral non-portability: overall approach

2.3   Phase I: Finding Candidate Input

Recall the form $\psi_i::X_i \rhd c_i$ (1) of the n atomic subformulas of q. Let $b_1, \ldots, b_n$ be fresh Boolean variables and $\bar{q}$ be the *Boolean skeleton* of q, i.e. the formula obtained from q by replacing each ψ_i by b_i. For a Boolean assignment A : $\{b_1, \ldots, b_n\} \rightarrow \{0, 1\}$, let $A|_{b_i \rightarrow v}$ denote A except that b_i is assigned value v.

Finding Critical Subexpression. A prerequisite for finding a candidate input is to identify a *critical subexpression* ψ_k in the conditional q: an index k and a Boolean assignment A_0 such that, under that assignment, flipping the value of ψ_k flips the value of q. We formalize this condition via the skeleton:

$$\bar{q}(A_0) \neq \bar{q}(A_0|_{b_k \rightarrow \neg b_k(A_0)}) \tag{3}$$

Algorithm 2.1 finds such an index k and a satisfying assignment A_0. In line 2, we use a SAT solver to check whether $\bar{q}(\ldots, b_k, \ldots) \veebar \bar{q}(\ldots, \neg b_k, \ldots)$ is satisfiable; $\veebar$ denotes exclusive-or.

Algorithm 2.1. Finding Critical Subexpression

   Input: Boolean formula $\bar{q}(b_1, \ldots, b_n)$
1 **for** $k = 1$ *to* n **do**
2   **if** $\bar{q}(\ldots, b_k, \ldots) \veebar \bar{q}(\ldots, \neg b_k, \ldots)$ *satisfiable* **then**
3   **return** *index k and sat. assignment*

Finding Candidate Input. In this step we generate, from the original C code, constraints whose solutions serve as possible candidate inputs I_0. We split the generated constraints into the following parts:

1. Path Constraint ϕ_{path}: this part symbolically encodes the execution path from the program entry point to the conditional q, following the appropriate branches at all intermediate program branch points.
2. Boolean Assignment Constraint ϕ_{assgn}: input I_0 must assign to all subexpressions ψ_i, for $i \neq k$, the same Boolean value as A_0 (determined in (3)) to b_i, and this should hold independently of the expression evaluation model M:

$$\forall M \; \forall i : \; i \neq k \Rightarrow \psi_i(I_0, M) = b_i(A_0) \tag{4}$$

Solving this constraint is very costly, not least due to the limited support for floating-point arithmetic in automated solvers. We therefore interpret (4) and other arithmetic constraints in this section over the *reals*. As a result, ϕ_{assgn} simplifies to

$$\forall i: \ i \neq k \Rightarrow \psi_i(I_0) = b_i(A_0) \tag{5}$$

since real arithmetic results do not depend on the evaluation model. A problem is of course that we lose precision: real results may not hold in floating-point arithmetic. However, the goal in Phase I is merely to determine an input I_0 that brings the conditional q *close* to the tipping point. The numerical differences caused by the interpretation of the code over $\mathbb{R}$ instead of over floating-point arithmetic will not affect this goal, as long as they are small. The solution will be made precise in Phase II of the algorithm.

3. Approximation Constraint ϕ_{appr}: the critical subexpression $\psi_k : X_k \rhd c_k$ must be unreliable, i.e.:
$$X_k(I_0) = c_k \pm \epsilon, \tag{6}$$

where ϵ is the smallest non-negative number that permits a solution to (6).

The total constraint for candidate inputs is then $\phi_{path} \wedge \phi_{assgn} \wedge \phi_{appr}$. As an example, given the raySphere program from Sect. 1 with the volatile expression $D = B \otimes B \ominus 4 \otimes A \otimes C$ and the conditional $D > 0$, we generate the *real-arithmetic* constraint $B \cdot B - 4 \cdot A \cdot C = 0$ and pass it to a suitable decision procedure for candidate input generation.

2.4   Phase II (a): Efficiently Searching Evaluation Models

Finding Extreme Evaluation Models. Given the candidate input I_0 that results in the conditional q to be unreliable, we now determine the minimum and maximum value of X, under any possible expression evaluation model that may reorder expressions and use FMA instructions. We first introduce algorithms $getMin_T$ and $getMax_T$ ($T \in \{\oplus, \otimes, dot, fma\}$) that compute these extreme values *in polynomial time* when X is a basic volatile expression. Later we extend these algorithms to handle general expressions.

Minimizing Volatile Sum: Given volatile expression $ve_\oplus = v_1 \oplus \ldots \oplus v_n$, where the v_i ($1 \leq i \leq n$) are floating-point constants, the goal is to efficiently determine $\min_M ve_\oplus(\boldsymbol{v}, M)$, i.e. $ve_\oplus$ minimized over all evaluation models M. To this end, consider the following array, for $1 \leq i \leq j \leq n$:

$$N[i,j] = \begin{cases} v_i & \text{if } i = j \\ \min_{i \leq k < j} \{N[i,k] \oplus N[k+1,j]\} & \text{if } i < j \end{cases} \tag{7}$$

We now claim that $N[1,n]$ is the quantity we are looking for:

Theorem 1. $N[1,n] = \min_M ve_\oplus(\boldsymbol{v}, M)$.

In order to prove this theorem, we strengthen it as follows:

Lemma 2. $N[i,j]$ *equals the minimum, over all possible orderings, of the floating-point sum of the numbers in the range $v_i, \ldots, v_j$.*

Proof. We induct over the quantity $j - i$. If $j - i = 0$, then $N[i,j] = v_i = v_j$, and the claim follows since there is only one element.

For the inductive step, assume that for all i', j' such that $j' - i' < j - i$, $N[i',j']$ is the minimum value of the sum of the elements $v_{i'}', \ldots, v_{j'}'$ (IH). Let k be one of the values that, in the definition of $N[i,j]$, gives rise to the minimum, i.e. $N[i,j] = N[i,k] \oplus N[k+1,j]$. Let further $N_o[i,j]$ be the sum for any fixed order o. We show that $N[i,j] \leq N_o[i,j]$.

The top-level $\oplus$ in the fixed-order sum $N_o[i,j]$ splits the sum from i to j into two sub-ranges i to l and $l+1$ to j, such that $i \leq l$ and $l+1 \leq j$. Thus:

$$
\begin{aligned}
N[i,j] &= N[i,k] \oplus N[k+1,j] &&\{ \text{ def. } k \text{ and def. } N[i,j] \ \} \\
&\leq N[i,l] \oplus N[l+1,j] &&\{ \text{ def. } k\text{: min sum in } N[i,j] \ \} \\
&= rd(N[i,l] + N[l+1,j]) &&\{ \text{ def. } \oplus \, (\, + \text{ denotes addition in } \mathbb{R} \ \} \\
&\leq rd(N_o[i,l] + N_o[l+1,j]) &&\{ \text{ IH: } l - i < j - i, j - (l+1) < j - i \ \} \\
&= N_o[i,l] \oplus N_o[l+1,j] &&\{ \text{ def. } \oplus \ \} \\
&= N_o[i,j] &&\{ \text{ def. } l \ \}.
\end{aligned}
$$

The second $\leq$ step exploits the monotonicity of the rounding function rd. $\square$

Value $\max_M ve_\oplus(\boldsymbol{v}, M)$ can be computed analogously. Both algorithms, denoted $getMin_\oplus$ and $getMax_\oplus$ in the sequel, can be implemented in $\mathcal{O}(n^3)$ time, by filling $N[i,j]$ "bottom-up". We use similar procedures $getMin_\otimes$ and $getMax_\otimes$ to minimize and maximize volatile products. In the following we describe how our method applies to the computation of extreme values for FMA expressions and volatile dot products, resulting in the four procedures $getMin_{\{fma|dot\}}$ and $getMax_{\{fma|dot\}}$. The correctness argument and the algorithmic complexity are the same as in the summation case and omitted.

Minimizing Volatile FMA: For an expression $ve_{fma} = fma(v_1, v_2, v_3)$, there are only two possible evaluation models, namely using or not using FMA. These two models can simply be compared against each other.

Minimizing Volatile Dot Product: Consider an expression $ve_{dot} = v_{11} \otimes v_{21} \oplus \ldots \oplus v_{1n} \otimes v_{2n}$ under an evaluation model that supports FMA. Here we need not only consider different ways of parenthesizing the expression, but also different ways of applying FMA. For example, for $n = 3$ the above expression can be evaluated in many different ways, among others the following:

$$
\begin{aligned}
&v_{11} \otimes v_{21} \oplus (v_{12} \otimes v_{22} \oplus v_{13} \otimes v_{23}) &&fma(v_{11}, v_{21}, v_{12} \otimes v_{22} \oplus v_{13} \otimes v_{23}) \\
&fma(v_{11}, v_{21}, fma(v_{13}, v_{23}, v_{12} \otimes v_{22})) &&fma(v_{13}, v_{23}, fma(v_{12}, v_{22}, v_{11} \otimes v_{21}))
\end{aligned}
$$

Our method can be used to compute the minimum over all different evaluation models. The following equations determine $\min_M ve_{dot}(\boldsymbol{v}, M)$ to be $N[1, n]$:

$$
N[i,j] = \begin{cases}
v_{1i} \otimes v_{2i} & \text{if } i = j \\
\min\{fma(v_{1i}, v_{2i}, N[i+1,j]), \\
\quad \min_{i<k<j-1}\{N[i,k] \oplus N[k+1,j]\}, \\
\quad fma(v_{1j}, v_{2j}, N[i,j-1])\} & \text{if } i < j
\end{cases}
$$

Minimizing General Volatile Expression: For an arbitrary floating-point expression e, we approximate the maximum and minimum values using *interval analysis* [4]. Interval bounds on floating-point expressions soundly propagate to sums, products, etc. as shown in Eq. (8) [7], where $[e]$ denotes an interval bound on expression e with lower and upper bounds $\downarrow e$ and $\uparrow e$:

$$
\begin{aligned}
[e_1 \oplus e_2] &= [\downarrow e_1 \oplus \downarrow e_2, \uparrow e_1 \oplus \uparrow e_2] \\
[e_1 \ominus e_2] &= [\downarrow e_1 \ominus \uparrow e_2, \uparrow e_1 \ominus \downarrow e_2] \\
[e_1 \otimes e_2] &= [\min(\downarrow e_1 \otimes \downarrow e_2, \downarrow e_1 \otimes \uparrow e_2, \uparrow e_1 \otimes \downarrow e_2, \uparrow e_1 \otimes \uparrow e_2), \\
&\qquad \max(\downarrow e_1 \otimes \downarrow e_2, \downarrow e_1 \otimes \uparrow e_2, \uparrow e_1 \otimes \downarrow e_2, \uparrow e_1 \otimes \uparrow e_2)] \\
[e_1 \oslash e_2] &= [e_1 \otimes [\tfrac{1}{\uparrow e_2}, \tfrac{1}{\downarrow e_2}]] \quad \text{if } 0 \notin [e_2] \\
[ve_T(e_1, \ldots, e_n)] &= getBound_T([e_1], \ldots, [e_n]) \quad (T \in \{\oplus, \otimes, dot, fma\})
\end{aligned}
\tag{8}
$$

Equation (8) suggests to find an interval for e under evaluation model variations by composing intervals for its subexpressions, computed recursively. In particular, function $getBound_T$ defined in Algorithm 2.2 computes an interval for volatile expression ve, given intervals for subexpressions e_i. The algorithm considers all 2^n combinations of lower/upper bound for expression e_i ($1 \leq i \leq n$), and call functions $getMin_T$ and $getMax_T$, which implement the min/max computations described earlier in this section. Note that at the "leaves" of the recursive descent the e_i's are constants, so $[e_i]$ degenerates to the single point. The loop in line 3 goes through **one** iteration in this case. For non-leaves, n is bounded by the code size of expressions in the program text.

Using (8) we can prove that $[\downarrow e, \uparrow e]$ contains the exact interval $[e^{\min}, e^{\max}]$.

Algorithm 2.2. $getBound_T$	**Algorithm 2.3.** Calibration
Input: $\{[e_1], [e_2], \ldots, [e_n]\}$	**Input:** constraint $\psi_k :: X_k \triangleright c_k$,
1 $\downarrow e = +\infty$ $\uparrow e = -\infty$	interval $[\downarrow X_k, \uparrow X_k]$ that
2 **for** $(v_1, \ldots, v_n) \in \{\downarrow e_1, \uparrow e_1\}$	does not contain c_k
$\times \ldots \times \{\downarrow e_n, \uparrow e_n\}$ **do**	**if** $c_k < \downarrow X_k$ **then**
3 $v_{min} = getMin_T(v_1, \ldots, v_n)$	$\epsilon = \downarrow X_k - c_k$ // $\epsilon > 0$
$v_{max} = getMax_T(v_1, \ldots, v_n)$	**else**
$\uparrow e = max(\uparrow e, v_{max})$	$\epsilon = \uparrow X_k - c_k$ // $\epsilon < 0$ $(\uparrow X_k < c_k)$
$\downarrow e = min(\downarrow e, v_{min})$	$\phi_{appr} := X_k(I_0) \approx c_k - \epsilon$
4 **return** $[\downarrow e, \uparrow e]$	

2.5 Phase II (b): Calibration

Given the conditional q over atomic subformulas $\psi_i::X_i \rhd c_i$, we use the above methods to compute an input I_0 and the interval $[\downarrow X_i, \uparrow X_i]$ ($1 \leq i \leq n$). We now check whether these results satisfy our requirements from Sect. 2.3: ϕ_{path}: given input I_0 the program follows the execution path that leads to the conditional q; ϕ_{assgn}: for $i \neq k$, ψ_i has the same Boolean value as A_0 assigns to b_i, for **both** bounds $\downarrow X_i$ and $\uparrow X_i$; ϕ_{appr}: the values of ψ_k for $X_k = \downarrow X_k$ and $X_k = \uparrow X_k$ differ: $\downarrow X_k \rhd c_k \neq \uparrow X_k \rhd c_k$.

If I_0 does not satisfy ϕ_{path} or ϕ_{assgn}, we ask the solver to generate a different input I_0, using a suitable blocking constraint. If I_0 and the interval fail ϕ_{appr}, we further distinguish the following cases: (a) the lower and upper bounds of X_k are the same: $\downarrow X_k = \uparrow X_k$. We deal with this as before by asking the solver for a new input; or (b) $\downarrow X_k \neq \uparrow X_k$ but the two bounds are on the same side of c_k: $\downarrow X_k \rhd c_k = \uparrow X_k \rhd c_k$. Here we employ a step-by-step calibration strategy shown in Algorithm 2.3. If, for example, $c_k < \downarrow X_k$, then the values returned by I_0 are slightly too large. We define ϵ to be the "error" $\downarrow X_k - c_k$ and adjust formula ϕ_{appr} to account for this error, by reducing the point of comparison c_k. We now repeat the process using the new set of constraints. In our experiments, we typically needed to go through 10–15 iterations of this calibration loop (see Fig. 1) if we were able to find an unstable input. The process is halted after some user-specified number of unsuccessful calibrations.

3 Empirical Results

We have vetted the algorithm described in Sect. 2 on several examples to generate inputs that may trigger control flow divergence. The examples are then executed on several different hardware platforms on these inputs, and the results are compared. The examples include the ray tracing code from Sect. 1, long summations, and molecular dynamics. More details are available at our website.[1]

Hardware Used in Comparisons. We target a range of different computer hardware for our experiments, including: (1) two different CPUs (Intel and AMD 64 bit processors), (2) an AMD Radeon 6550D GPU, and (3) three different NVIDIA GPUs (Quadro 600, Tesla C2075 and Tesla K20). All targets have OpenCL compilers, provided by each manufacturer, which were used to generate the results. All the target hardware is IEEE 754–2008 compliant. The Intel and AMD CPUs are 64 bits. Intel has FMA, but only in its multimedia instructions (AVX) which are not used in these experiments. The AMD processor does not have FMA. The three NVIDIA GPUs all have FMA instructions and the NVIDIA OpenCL compiler applies FMA aggressively. The AMD GPU does not have hardware FMA instructions.

---

[1] http://www.ccs.neu.edu/home/wahl/Research/FPA-Heterogeneous/Non-Portability.

Tool Specifics. We have implemented the algorithm on top of the KLEE symbolic analysis engine [3] with LLVM-2.9. We use the Z3 theorem prover [8], version 4.3.2, as KLEE's internal solver. The experiments are run on a Ubuntu 14.04.1 LTS machine with Intel Core-i7 3.10 GHz processor and 8 GB RAM. With the exception of the calls to Z3 for finding the candidate inputs, **the running time of our algorithm is negligible and in the tens of milliseconds**, which is why we omit performance details.

Code Instrumentation. We test our algorithm on the C code version of the examples. In the first step, we apply transformations to each program: we attach a **main** function that calls the tested program, and we annotate the symbolic variables and volatile expressions, so that our algorithm can detect these later.

For a conditional q in the execution path, there may exist multiple inputs that exhibit control flow instability. In our experiments we split the domain of each input variable into subintervals of length 0.01, and run our algorithm on each of these subintervals. For ray tracing, for example, this produced 408 sets of inputs over the range $[-50, 50]$ that cause control flow instability according to Definition 1.

3.1   Examples and Control Flow Divergence

Ray Tracing. The OpenCL ray tracing code was run with the 408 different sets of inputs generated by our algorithm to produce results where D is close to zero. Inputs provided were the three dimensions of the sphere: $s[0], s[1]$ and $s[2]$, the three dimensions of the ray, $r[0], r[1]$ and $r[2]$ and the *radiusSq*. All 408 input sets generated differences on different architectures. 45 of the 408 sets of inputs produce results that are on either side of zero for the comparison when the same code was run on different platforms.

Summation. Summations of floating-point values are common in scientific computing. We compare serial C code which accumulates a value to a register, and a reduction kernel, written in OpenCL which is the common way to implement long summation on a parallel architecture. The result of the sum is compared to a threshold, set to zero for these experiments.

We ran our OpenCL kernel for a sum of 32 values generated by the algorithm. We received 100 different sets of inputs from the algorithm, of which 58 gave us different results. Three sets of results are shown in Table 1. The reduction values differed from the serial summation, as expected. Most platforms produced the same results of the reduction sum except for the NVIDIA Tesla 2075, which produced different results. These differences are due to reordering. We were able to illustrate differences even with a short list of input values (32) where the range of these values is small ($[-1.05, 1]$). For practical applications where both the number of values and their range will be larger, we expect these differences to be more dramatic.

Table 1. Results for reduction sum (left) and MD (right)

Red Sum 1	Red Sum 2	Serial Sum
-4.6566E-8	-8.7544E-8	4.4936E-8
-5.9605E-8	-8.7544E-8	1.0547E-7
-5.9605E-8	-8.7544E-8	9.1502E-8

R1	R2
0.0	-2.3841858E-7
-2.3841858E-7	0.0

Molecular Dynamics. MD is a popular high performance computing application with many versions available that run on parallel processors and on GPUs [1]. MD is sensitive to drift in floating-point calculations due to the large number of time steps in simulation. Taufer et al. [11] show this and use a tuple of values to represent both the floating-point number and its error. Our experiments use open source code[2] to calculate the Lennard Jones potential energy of molecular systems. We specifically focus on the comparison with $rrCut$, a constant which specifies the cutoff distance (see Listing 1.1). Atoms further away than $rrCut$ are assumed to not affect the result.

```
/* Doubly-nested loop over atomic pairs */
...
    /* Computes the squared atomic distance */
        for (rr=0.0, k=0; k<3; k++) {
            dr[k] = r[j1][k] - r[j2][k];
            dr[k] = dr[k] - SignR(RegionH[k],dr[k]-RegionH[k])
                          - SignR(RegionH[k],dr[k]+RegionH[k]);
            rr = rr + dr[k]*dr[k]; }
/* Computes acceleration & potential within the cut-off distance */
if (rr < rrCut) { ... }
```

Listing 1.1. Molecular Dynamics

We implemented this code in OpenCL and ran it on our six target platforms. We set $rrCut$ to 2.25. The algorithm was used to generate inputs $r[j1][0]$, $r[j1][1]$, $r[j1][2]$, $r[j2][0]$, $r[j2][1]$, and $r[j2][2]$ that bring rr close to 2.25. It found twelve sets of values where this decision is on either side of $rrCut$. Table 1 shows the difference between 2.25 and the value rr. 6 sets of inputs produced one of these results and 6 sets produced the other. R1 results are produced by the two CPUs and the AMD GPU, none of which use FMA. The R2 results are produced on the NVIDIA GPUs, all of which use FMA. Note that MD simulations run for a long time, and the value of $rrCut$ affects the run time by determining how many calculations are done. Our algorithm can be used to help set $rrCut$ and thus reduce the overall run time.

4   Conclusions and Future Work

We have shown that floating-point instabilities can lead to different control flows in code, and have introduced an algorithm to find values that potentially exhibit

---

[2] http://cacs.usc.edu/education/cs596/src/md/.

such instability when code is run on the same inputs on different machines. Our algorithm can inform programmers whether their code has instabilities for certain ranges of input and parameter choices. For molecular dynamics, it can help improve run times by allowing an intelligent choice of cut off distance. In the future we plan to improve the usability of the algorithm and to apply it to more complicated examples.

References

1. Anderson, J.A., Lorenz, C.D., Travesset, A.: General purpose molecular dynamics simulations fully implemented on graphics processing units. J. Comput. Phys. **227**(10), 5342–5359 (2008)
2. Bao, T., Zhang, X.: On-the-fly detection of instability problems in floating-point program execution. SIGPLAN Not. **48**(10), 817–832 (2013). http://doi.acm.org/10.1145/2544173.2509526
3. Cadar, C., Dunbar, D., Engler, D.: Klee: unassisted and automatic generation of high-coverage tests for complex systems programs. In: Proceedings of the 8th USENIX Conference on Operating Systems Design and Implementation, OSDI 2008, pp. 209–224. USENIX Association, Berkeley (2008). http://dl.acm.org/citation.cfm?id=1855741.1855756
4. Hickey, T., Ju, Q., Van Emden, M.H.: Interval arithmetic: From principles to implementation. J. ACM **48**(5), 1038–1068 (2001). http://doi.acm.org/10.1145/502102.502106
5. Institute of Electrical and Electronics Engineers (IEEE): 754–2008 – IEEE standard for floating-point arithmetic, pp. 1–58. IEEE (2008)
6. Jzquel, F., Chesneaux, J.M.: Cadna: a library for estimating round-off error propagation. Comput. Phys. Commun. **178**(12), 933–955 (2008). www.sciencedirect.com/science/article/pii/S0010465508000775
7. Miné, A.: Relational abstract domains for the detection of floating-point run-time errors. In: Schmidt, D. (ed.) ESOP 2004. LNCS, vol. 2986, pp. 3–17. Springer, Heidelberg (2004)
8. de Moura, L., Bjørner, N.S.: Z3: An Efficient SMT Solver. In: Ramakrishnan, C.R., Rehof, J. (eds.) TACAS 2008. LNCS, vol. 4963, pp. 337–340. Springer, Heidelberg (2008)
9. Munshi, A.: The OpenCL Specification, version 1.2 (2012). https://www.khronos.org/registry/cl/specs/opencl-1.2.pdf
10. Shewchuk, J.R.: Robust adaptive floating-point geometric predicates. In: Proceedings of the Twelfth Annual Symposium on Computational Geometry, pp. 141–150. ACM (1996)
11. Taufer, M., Padron, O., Saponaro, P., Patel, S.: Improving numerical reproducibility and stability in large-scale numerical simulations on gpus. In: IEEE International Symposium on Parallel and Distributed Processing (IPDPS), 2010, pp. 1–9. IEEE (2010)

Accelerator Computing

Fast Parallel Suffix Array on the GPU

Leyuan Wang[1](✉), Sean Baxter[2], and John D. Owens[3]

[1] Department of Computer Science, University of California, Davis,
Davis, CA 95616, USA
leywang@ucdavis.edu
[2] D. E. Shaw Research, New York, NY 10036, USA
sean.baxter@deshawresearch.com
[3] Department of Electrical and Computer Engineering,
University of California, Davis, Davis, CA 95616, USA
jowens@ece.ucdavis.edu

Abstract. We implement two classes of suffix array construction algorithms on the GPU. The first, skew, makes algorithmic improvements to the previous work of Deo and Keely to achieve a speedup of 1.45 × over their work. The second, a hybrid skew and prefix-doubling implementation, is the first of its kind on the GPU and achieves a speedup of 2.3–4.4 × over Osipov's prefix-doubling and 2.4–7.9 × over our skew implementation on large datasets. Our implementations rely on two efficient parallel primitives, a merge and a segmented sort. We also demonstrate the effectiveness of our implementations in a Burrows-Wheeler transform and a parallel FM index for pattern searching.

Keywords: Suffix array · Parallel · GPU · Skew · Prefix-doubling · Burrows-wheeler transform · FM index

1 Introduction

The suffix array (SA) of a string is the sorted set of all suffixes of the string. This data structure is used in a broad spectrum of applications, including data compression, bioinformatics, and text indexing. The suffix array, along with its first construction algorithm, was introduced by Manber and Myers [11] as a more space- and cache-efficient, and simpler to construct alternative to suffix trees.

The straightforward way to generate a suffix array from a string is to simply sort all suffixes of that string using a comparison-based sorting algorithm. For a string of length n, this construction takes $\mathcal{O}(n \log n)$ suffix comparisons and each suffix comparison has time complexity $\mathcal{O}(n)$, so the total time needed is $\mathcal{O}(n^2 \log n)$. The key insight to develop a more efficient algorithm is to leverage the fact that suffixes are not arbitrary strings but related to each other.

The existing suffix array construction algorithms (SACAs) that leverage this property can be divided into three classes: prefix-doubling, recursive and induced copying. The first class of SACAs, prefix-doubling, sorts the suffixes of a string by their prefixes, the length of which is doubled every iteration. The idea was

© Springer-Verlag Berlin Heidelberg 2015
J.L. Träff et al. (Eds.): Euro-Par 2015, LNCS 9233, pp. 573–587, 2015.
DOI: 10.1007/978-3-662-48096-0_44

originally proposed by Karp et al. [7], first applied to suffix array construction by Manber and Myers [11] (MM), and later optimized by Larsson and Sadakane [8] (LS). LS is more efficient than MM, because it removes the unnecessary scanning of fully sorted suffixes from the previous pass. The second class of SACAs recursively sorts a subset of the suffixes, use the order of the sorted subset to infer the order of remaining subset, and finally merge the two sorted subsets to get the order of the entire set. The skew algorithm proposed by Kärkkäinen and Sanders [6] (KS) is a popular linear-time recursive algorithm. The final class of SACAs, induced copying, is non-recursive and uses already-sorted suffixes to quickly induce a complete order of the suffixes. Like the recursive formulation, their time complexity is $\mathcal{O}(n)$.

The recent explosion in data sizes and the emergence of commodity data-parallel processors motivate efficient parallel implementations of SACAs. In this paper, we focus on highly data-parallel SACAs that are suitable for implementation on devices such as many-core GPUs and multi-core CPUs. Because of their high arithmetic and memory throughput, these processors are well-suited for data-intensive computing tasks such as SACAs. However, parallelizing SACAs is a significant challenge.

Both Osipov [15] and Deo and Keely [2] have done seminal work on highly parallel SACAs on GPUs. Deo and Keely analyze the aforementioned three SACA classes and conclude that induced copying has numerous data dependencies and note a lack of parallel approaches to exploit this technique. Osipov concludes that prefix-doubling algorithms are more cost-efficient to implement on the GPU compared with the linear-time recursive skew approach, because the former only requires fast GPU radix sorting of (32-bit key, 32-bit value) pairs, while skew needs to sort large tuples by comparison-based sorting and merging. On the other hand, Deo and Keely conclude that skew is best suited for the GPU as all its phases can be readily mapped to a data-parallel architecture, while prefix-doubling has an irregular, data-dependent number of unsorted groups across phases, and the amount of work per group in each iteration is non-uniform.

Recently, Liu et al. [10] and Pantaleoni [16] have proposed scalable, space-efficient methods that exploit the sorting speed of modern GPUs for blockwise suffix sorting targeting bioinformatics applications to work specifically with large collections of relatively short DNA strings. Because the GPU has limited memory, Liu et al. focus on dividing the large inputs into several sets and sorting each set using a GPU-accelerated method while Pantaleoni solves the problem using insertion, with GPU sorting new blocks and CPU inserting the symbols into the external final result.

In this work, we address the parallel SACA problem by designing, implementing, and comparing two different formulations of SACAs on NVIDIA GPUs. We make three main contributions.

1. Our skew approach incorporates several optimizations that yield a speedup of 1.45x over Deo and Keely's implementation.

2. We also implement a hybrid non-recursive skew/prefix-doubling SACA that overcomes the parallelization challenges identified by Deo and Keely and performs much better than Osipov's plain prefix-doubling. Comparing our two implementations, we revisit Deo and Keely's conclusions on the most appropriate formulation for parallel SACAs, demonstrate that a recursive doubling-like formulation can be efficiently mapped to GPUs and that our hybrid implementation in general produces the fastest SACA implementation on GPUs. The speedup is as high as 12.76× over Deo and Keely's skew implementation, up to 4.4× over Osipov's parallel prefix-doubling, and 7.9× over our optimized skew implementation.
3. We integrate our hybrid implementation into our GPU implementation of the Burrows-Wheeler transform (BWT) and an FM index-based pattern search application.

2   Background and Preliminaries

We begin with the algorithmic background for the string algorithms we implemented. Section 2.1 provides the notation for suffix array construction that we use throughout the paper. Readers already familiar with the Burrows-Wheeler Transform (Sect. 2.2), the FM index (Sect. 2.3), and GPU terminology (Sect. 2.4) can skip to Sect. 3.

2.1   The Suffix Array

Consider an input string x of length $n \geq 1$ ending with a lexicographically smallest suffix (\$). We denote the suffix starting at position i (i.e., $x[i, \ldots, n-1]$) by *suffix i*. For convenience, let suffixes with starting position i where $i \bmod 3 \neq 0$ be S_{12}, suffixes with starting position j where $j \bmod 3 \equiv 0$ be S_0, and suffixes with starting position k where $k \bmod 3 \equiv 1$ be S_1.

The **suffix array** (SA) of x is defined as an $n + 1$ length array such that SA$[j]=i$ means "*suffix i* is the jth suffix of x in ascending lexicographical order". The **inverse suffix array** (ISA) is defined as follows:

$$ISA[i] = j \iff SA[j] = i$$

This implies that *suffix i* has rank j in lexicographic order. ISA is also called the *lexicographic ranks* of suffixes. For convenience, we denote the suffix array of S_{12} by SA$_{[12]}$ and that of S_0 as SA$_{[0]}$, correspondingly for the inverse suffix array, ISA$_{[12]}$ and ISA$_{[0]}$, and we denote the lexicographic ranks of S_1 by ISA$_{[1]}$.

Both algorithms we describe sort prefixes with increasing length $h \geq 1$. We will refer to this partial ordering as an h-order of suffixes. Suffixes that are equal under h-order are given the same rank, and put into the same h-group. If the sorting process is stable, h-groups with a larger h are refinements over their counterparts with a smaller h. Suffixes in a partial h-order are stored with their indexes in an approximate suffix array SA$_h$, and their ranks in ISA$_h$.

2.2   The Burrows-Wheeler Transform

The BWT of a string is generated by lexicographically sorting the cyclic shift of the string to form a string matrix and taking the last column of the matrix. The BWT groups repeated characters together by permuting the string; it is also reversible, which means the original string can be recovered. These two characteristics make BWT a popular choice for a compression pipeline stage (for instance, bzip2). It is directly related to the suffix array: the sorted rows in the matrix are essentially the sorted suffixes of the string and the first column of the matrix reflects a suffix array. The BWT of a string x can be computed from its SA as follows:

$$\text{BWT}[i] = \begin{cases} x[\text{SA}[i] - 1] & \text{if SA}[i] > 0 \\ \$ & \text{if SA}[i] = 0 \end{cases}$$

Table 1 shows an example of the SA, ISA and BWT of the input string "banana" as follows.

Table 1. SA, ISA and BWT for the example string "banana".

i	Suffix	Sorted suffix	SA$[i]$	ISA$[i]$	Sorted rotations	BWT$[i]$
0	banana\$	\$	6	4	\$banana	a
1	anana\$	a\$	5	3	a\$banan	n
2	nana\$	ana\$	3	6	ana\$ban	n
3	ana\$	anana\$	1	2	anana\$b	b
4	na\$	banana\$	0	5	banana\$	\$
5	a\$	na\$	4	1	na\$bana	a
6	\$	nana\$	2	0	nana\$ba	a

2.3   The FM Index

Proposed by Ferragina and Manzini [4], the FM (Full-text, Minute-space) index is a compressing and indexing method that allows compression of input text while still supporting fast arbitrary pattern searches. It is a lightweight *compressed suffix array* that combines the BWT and the suffix array data structure. The compressed index can be used to efficiently find the number of occurrences of a pattern from the text, as well as locate the position of each occurrence. The authors describe an algorithm called backward_search that calculates how many times a pattern occurs in BWT-compressed text without decompressing it. We refer the reader to the original paper [4] for further detail.

2.4   The Graphics Processor Unit (GPU)

In the following discussion we use NVIDIA CUDA terminology. Modern GPUs are massively parallel processors that support tens of thousands of hardware-scheduled threads running simultaneously. These threads are organized into blocks and the hardware schedules blocks of threads onto hardware cores. High-end NVIDIA GPUs have on the order of 16 streaming-processor (SP) cores, each of which contains 32-wide SIMD (single-instruction, multiple-data) units that run 32 threads in lockstep. GPUs also feature a memory hierarchy of per-thread registers, per-block shared memory, and off-chip global DRAM accessible to all threads. CUDA programs ("kernels") specify the number of blocks and threads per block under a SIMT (single-instruction, multiple-thread) programming model. Lindholm et al. [9] provides more detail on modern GPU hardware and Nickolls et al. [14] on the GPU programming model.

Efficient GPU programs have enough work per kernel to keep all hardware cores busy (load-balancing); strive to reduce thread divergence (when neighboring threads branch in different directions); aim to access memory in large contiguous chunks to maximize achieved memory bandwidth (coalescing); and minimize communication between CPU and GPU. Designing an SACA that achieves all of these goals is a significant challenge. We also prioritize using high-performance parallel algorithmic GPU primitives (e.g., scan, radix sort, compact, segmented sort) when applicable.

3   Algorithms and Analysis

We implement two fast parallel SACAs, skew (Sect. 3.1) and a skew/prefix-doubling hybrid (Sect. 3.2).

3.1   Parallel Skew Algorithm

Our first approach is implementing the skew algorithm using massively parallel kernels based on KS [6] and similar to the OpenCL implementation of Deo and Keely [2]. We compare our implementation of skew with Deo and Keely's in Fig. 1 and now describe several algorithmic optimizations over their work.

Both methods start by extracting S_{12} and S_0 from an input string (line 2) and launching a 3-step least significant digit (LSD) radix sort using Merrill and Grimshaw's approaches [12] to find the order of S_{12} based on their first triplets

```
 1 dk-SA (int* T, int* SA, int length)
 2 Initialize Mod12() // form triplet s12, s0
 3 RadixSort (s12) // LSD radix sort 1st char
 4 RadixSort (s12) // LSD radix sort 2nd char
 5 RadixSort (s12) // LSD radix sort 3rd char
 6 lexicRankOfTriplets (s12)
 7 if (!allUniqueRanks) then
 8     dk-SA () // Recurse
 9     storeUniqueRanks()
10 else
11     computeSAFromUniqueRank ()
12 RadixSort (ISA[1])
13 RadixSort (s0)
14 Merge (s0,s12)
```

```
 1 skew-SA (int* T, int* SA, int length)
 2 Initialize Mod12() // form triplet s12, s0
 3 RadixSort (s12) // LSD radix sort 1st char
 4 RadixSort (s12) // LSD radix sort 2nd char
 5 RadixSort (s12) // LSD radix sort 3rd char
 6 if (!allUniqueRanks) then
 7     lexicRankOfTriplets (s12)
 8     skew-SA ()// Recurse
 9     storeUniqueRanks()
10 Compact (ISA[12]) // compact out the order
      of ISA[1]
11 RadixSort (s0)
12 Merge (s0,s12)
```

Fig. 1. Left, Deo and Keely's skew implementation pseudocode; right, ours.

(line 3 to line 5). In the first iteration, each triplet is composed of the first three characters of each S_{12}. The ranks of the triplets are then used as the value for the key-value sort in the recursive iterations.

The ranks are computed by counting unique triplets. In practice, this is done by first comparing each triplet against its predecessor, storing a flag of 1 whenever they are unequal, and then doing a prefix-sum of the list of flags. We use the same flagging method as Deo and Keely to tell if S_{12} are fully sorted (line 6 right and line 7 left), but we do the prefix-sum only when the suffixes are not fully sorted instead of immediately after computing the flagging list (line 7 right and line 6 left). This change saves us from having to compute $SA_{[12]}$ from $ISA_{[12]}$ if we are at the end of the recursion and the suffixes are fully sorted (line 10 and 11 left). After the recursion, they continue to compute $SA_{[0]}$ by sorting S_0 with a 2-step LSD radix sort of (the first character of *suffix i*, rank of *suffix i* + 1) pairs where *suffix i* $\in S_0$ and thus *suffix i* + 1 $\in S_{12}$ whose rank is known from the previous steps (line 13 and 14 left). We use a faster one-step radix sort because the order of the ranks of S_1 (equivalent to $ISA_{[1]}$) can be filtered out from $ISA_{[12]}$ (result of line 7 right) using a compact operation (line 11 and 12 right).

The above optimizations allow our implementation to only use 2/3 of Deo and Keely's memory bandwidth in the recursive part, and 3 fewer memory transactions in the last round.

Finally, we optimize the merge step that combines the two sorted suffix arrays $SA_{[0]}$ and $SA_{[12]}$ while avoiding load-imbalance. Deo and Keely use the merge technique of Satish et al. [18], binary search, and memory locality optimizations of Davidson et al. [1]. Their work suffers from load-imbalance due to having two separate-sized lists being processed independently. Instead, we utilize vectorized sorted search to map threads and blocks to equally sized sections of each partition, which successfully avoids load-imbalance. This method is based on the Merge Path approach of Green et al. [5] and implemented as a merge primitive in the second author's *Modern GPU* library[1] and is described here for the first time in the literature.

The two keys to an efficient GPU merge operation are (1) dividing the two sorted inputs into independent chunks of equal sized work and (2) ensuring that the outputs of each of those chunks of work are contiguous in the final merged output. This contrasts with Deo and Keely's approach, where chunk size is not uniform. The key operation, then, is to identify the split points. The obvious way would require a two-dimensional search across both input arrays; Merge Path instead describes an elegant transformation to an one-dimensional search along a diagonal that connects the two input arrays.

Our implementation performs a two-part, hierarchical split: first dividing the entire input into equal-sized tiles that can be assigned to blocks, then dividing each tile into equal-sized subtiles that can be assigned to threads. The merge is completely parallel (not cooperative) between threads; its inputs are in shared

---

[1] Code is available at http://nvlabs.github.io/moderngpu and described in http://nvlabs.github.io/moderngpu/merge.html.

memory and its outputs are in registers. The result is a highly load-balanced, parallel-friendly implementation that achieves a throughput of greater than half the peak bandwidth of the GPU, compared to 12.1 % of the theoretical peak for the implementation by Green et al. [5].

3.2   Skew/Prefix-Doubling

Deo and Keely's work marked a significant milestone as the first implementation of a linear-time SACA skew on the GPU. However, skew on GPUs has two significant disadvantages:

1. As the skew formulation is recursive, we cannot parallelize across iterations.
2. At the end of each iteration, we may have sets of triplets that are fully sorted. However, to keep the algorithm recursive, we cannot declare these fully sorted suffixes complete and leave them out of further iterations; instead we must process them on every iteration, which results in a large amount of redundant work.

To address these two disadvantages, we turn to a combination of skew and prefix-doubling, which turns out to be a better fit for modern GPU architectures.

In our implementation, we still leverage our skew framework: we keep the first step of skew, which reduces the string size by a factor of 2/3, and the final skew merge stage, which is trivial. Only after the first step of skew do we transition to our non-recursive better-performing prefix-doubling implementation. In the first stage, we select all S_{12} suffixes, forming 3-character substrings, and do a 25-bit radix sort (25 bits for 3 chars from a constant alphabet in the range $[0\ldots255]$ plus a sentinel letter \$) on those substrings. Then we compute the ranks of S_{12} and assign the ranks into an inverse suffix array ($\mathrm{ISA}_{[12]}$). From now on, we work with suffixes in partially-sorted order rather than text order. In other words, after this initial radix sort, all suffixes with the same 3-character prefix are contiguous in our array (i.e., "Fun" is next to "Funicular") no matter where they appear in the original text.

Next, in our prefix-doubling step, we sort by ($\mathrm{ISA}[SA[i]+\delta]$, $\mathrm{ISA}[SA[i]+2\delta]$) pairs, where δ is the length of prefix which doubles in each iteration until all suffixes are in their own *segments*, which we define as a set of suffixes that are equal up to the current substring length. These are each given a rank (the index of the first element in the segment within the string). The rank of the segment next to the current one is used as the key for the next pass, and on each iteration, we double the length of the prefix. The key to high prefix-doubling performance is our ability to sort efficiently within segments, even though the number of segments and their sizes are non-uniform and are not known at compile time (this is the specific concern about prefix-doubling raised by Deo and Keely). We address this with an efficient *segmented sort* primitive, which we describe next. In our implementation, we also identify suffixes at the end of each iteration that are singletons in their own segments—their final positions in the suffix array are fixed, so we re-rank and compact them out of the working suffix array. This way, future iterations only need to consider suffixes whose final positions are not yet fixed.

Segmented Sort. The input to segmented sort is a contiguous list of segments with a variable number of unsorted items per segment; the output is the same list of segments but with items sorted within each segment. One way to solve this problem is to sort each segment one at a time, but it is likely on a highly parallel machine that many (or even most) segments will not have enough work to fill the machine. Another approach is to do a full sort over all items, but this is inefficient because it ignores the significant work that has already been completed in classifying the items into segments. We wish to both work on all segments simultaneously but still leverage the presence of segments. The challenge for an efficient *segmented sort* implementation is the variation in the size and number of segments. This method is implemented as a segmented-sort primitive in the second author's *Modern GPU* library[2] and is described here for the first time in the literature. An efficient segmented sort is the difference-maker in developing a competitive prefix-doubling implementation.

The core of our segmented sort implementation is merging, in the same style as the previously-described merge kernel. For illustrative purposes, consider a full merge sort of a single segment. We would begin by dividing the work into equal-sized blocks, sort each block of elements independently, then use our efficient merge to merge blocks of work together, starting with many small merges and concluding with one large merge. We have previously claimed that the most efficient way for us to merge is to use fixed-size blocks of work, which gives us straightforward parallelization and perfect load balancing.

How do we adapt such a merge in the presence of segments? We must respect the segmentation during the merge, and the way we do this is using a key insight: During a merge of two contiguous lists, *the only segment that is affected by the merge is one that spans the boundary between two blocks.* All other segments involved in this merge are copied without change from input to output. We illustrate this in Fig. 2.

The final optimization is early exit. The number of input boundaries is cut in half on each iteration, so once a segment no longer crosses an active input boundary, we can conclude that segment is fully sorted and mark it as inactive. A tile with no active segments is done with its work and can exit. Especially with a large number of small segments, this early-exit optimization dramatically decreases the number of passes over the data, the required memory bandwidth, and the overall runtime.

Comparison Against Plain Prefix-Doubling Implementation. Our hybrid prefix-doubling method has several optimizations over the pure prefix-doubling implementation by Osipov [15]. He modifies MM by replacing chunks of (32-bit key, 32-bit value) radix sort with a single (32-bit key, 64-bit value) radix sort. At the end of each iteration, he filters out fully-sorted suffixes to avoid unnecessary re-sorting, similar to LS. Throughout the implementation, he uses parallel primitives including prefix-sum, radix sort, random gather from and scatter to memory based on Merrill's *back40computing* library[3].

---

[2] Code is available at http://nvlabs.github.io/moderngpu and described in http://nvlabs.github.io/moderngpu/segsort.html.

[3] https://code.google.com/p/back40computing/.

$$
\begin{array}{cccccccccccccccc}
0 & 1 & 2 & 3 & 4 & 5 & 6 & 7 & 8 & 9 & 10 & 11 & 12 & 13 & 14 & 15
\end{array}
$$

$$
\underset{\wedge}{m}\; m\; i\; i\; \underset{\wedge}{s}\; s\; i\; i\; \underset{\wedge}{s}\; s\; i\; i\; \underset{\wedge}{p}\; p\; i\; i
$$

$$
(\,0\;\;1\;\;2\;\;3)\;|\,(4\;5\;6\;7)\,|\,(8\;9\;10\;11)\,|\,(12\;13\;14\;15)
$$

$$
(\underset{\wedge}{i}\; i\; m\; m)\,|\,(s\; \underset{\wedge}{i}\; i\; s)\,|\,(\underset{\wedge}{i}\; i\; s\; s)\,|\,(p\; \underset{\wedge}{i}\; i\; p)
$$

$$
(0\;\;1\;\;2\;\;3\;\,|\;4\;5\;6\;7)\,|\,(8\;9\;10\;11\;\,|\;12\;13\;14\;15)
$$

$$
(\underset{\wedge}{i}\; i\; m\; m\;|\;s\; \underset{\wedge}{i}\; i\; s)\,|\,(\underset{\wedge}{i}\; i\; p\; s\;|\;s\; \underset{\wedge}{i}\; i\; p)
$$

$$
\begin{array}{cccccccccccccccc}
0 & 1 & 2 & 3 & | & 4 & 5 & 6 & 7 & | & 8 & 9 & 10 & 11 & | & 12 & 13 & 14 & 15
\end{array}
$$

$$
\underset{\wedge}{i}\; i\; m\; m\;|\;\underset{\wedge}{s}\; i\; i\; s\;|\;\underset{\wedge}{i}\; i\; p\; s\;|\;s\; \underset{\wedge}{i}\; i\; p
$$

Fig. 2. Segmented Sort example. Consider an input string composed of 16 random characters grouped into four irregular segments (the first row). The head of each segment is marked with carets. First, we divide the characters equally into four blocks of four elements each, then launch four "blocksorts" to sort four inputs each while maintaining segment order. Next, we merge the first block with the second and the third block with the fourth. Note in the merge of the third and fourth blocks, two separate segments are involved, but only the first segment—the one that crosses the boundary between the two inputs—changes as a result of the segmented merge. Finally, there's one active input boundary left in the middle but with no segment crossing it, which means all segments are fully sorted and there's no need for further merging, so this is an early-exit. The final result is segments in the same order as the input, but sorted within each segment (the last row).

In our method, the first step of skew—a single pass of (32-bit key, 25-bit value) radix sort—is inexpensive and gives us a reduction ratio of 0.67. This is significantly better than Osipov's initial sorting of the first 4 characters. Also, our massively parallel *segmented sort* primitive has better locality than radix-sorting integer tuples across global memory. Furthermore, our induction step in the skew framework is cheaper than a radix sort when sorting the remaining 1/3 suffixes. Though we need an additional merge in the final step, our parallel merge primitive is quite efficient (see Sect. 3.1). We compare our approach with Osipov's pure prefix-doubling implementation in Fig. 3.

Skew vs. Prefix-Doubling. Skew with a difference cover modulo 3 is a "prefix tripling" technique[4], tripling the pace at which it samples its ranks each round. It is more efficient as a prefix-tripler than an integer alphabet sort, because the 2-integer segmented sort of prefix-doubling is certainly much faster than the 3-integer radix sort of skew. In its radix sort, skew uses the most significant digit simply to get the suffix back in its original segment, which comes for free with prefix-doubling's segmented sort. Furthermore, skew cannot drop fully-sorted suffixes, because it needs to transform their ranks into the new coordinate system

---

[4] A difference cover D modulo h, denoted by D_h, is a set of integers $i \in \{0, \ldots, h-1\}$ such that $i \equiv k - j \pmod{h}$ for some $j, k \in D_h$. For example, $\{1, 2\}$ is a difference cover modulo 3 and $\{1, 2, 4\}$ is a difference cover modulo 7.

1 Initialize SA$_4$ by sorting suffixes by their
   first 4 characters
2 Initialize ISA$_4[i]$ with the 4-rank of i =head
   of i's 4-group in SA$_4$
3 $size = n, h = 4$
4 while $size > 0$ do
5   Scan SA$_h$ and generate tuples
       (SA$_h[j] - h$, ISA$_h$[SA$_h[j]$ -
       h], ISA$_h$[SA$_h[j]$])
6   RadixSort tuples by 2nd component
       stably // contains SA$_{2h}$
7   Refine h-heads of h-groups // Re-rank
8   Update ISA$_{2h}$ // contains ISA$_{2h}$
9   Filter and Compact SA$_{2h}$
10     $size = size$ of SA$_{2h}$
11     $h = h * 2$

1 Initialize Mod12() // form triplets s12, s0
2 RadixSort (s12) // 25-bit radix sort on
   triplets s12
3 ComputeRanks ISA$_{[12]}$
4 $size = \frac{2}{3}n, h = 6$
5 while $size > 0$ do
6   SegmentedSort
       (ISA[SA[i]+h], ISA[SA[i]+2h])
7   Update ISA$_{2h}$ and Compact SA$_{2h}$
8      $size = size$ of SA$_{2h}$
9      $h = h * 2$
10 Compact (ISA$_{[12]}$) // compact out the
    order of ISA$_{[1]}$
11 RadixSort (s0)
12 Merge (s0,s12)

Fig. 3. Left, Osipov's parallel prefix-doubling description; right, our skew/prefix-doubling.

in which they will be sampled by the remaining unsorted suffixes. With prefix-doubling, suffixes are ranked in the same coordinate system (i.e., where they would be placed in the final sorted suffix array) throughout the computation, and since there is no need to re-rank fully-sorted suffixes, we can remove them from the problem.

For real-world texts, this makes prefix-doubling more efficient than skew. Skew has a solid reduction ratio of 0.67, regardless of the data. Prefix-doubling has a worst-case reduction ratio of 1.0 (if the pass fails to resolve any suffixes), but has a reduction ratio on real-world text that is usually favorable.

4 Experiments and Results

In this section we present a detailed experimental evaluation of our implementations of suffix array algorithms. For a more thorough comparison, we re-implement Deo and Keely's method using a current state-of-the-art radix sort primitive from Merrill's *CUB* library[5] merge primitive on an NVIDIA GPU using CUDA. For convenience, we call Deo and Keely's OpenCL parallel skew implementation on an AMD GPU *dk-amd-SA*, our CUDA implementation of Deo and Keely's approach *dk-nvidia-SA*, Osipov's parallel prefix-doubling *osipov-SA*, our parallel skew implementation *skew-SA*, and our parallel hybrid skew/prefix-doubling implementation *spd-SA*.

Our experimental setup is an Intel Core i7-3770K 3.5 GHz 4-core machine with 16 GB RAM and 8 MB L3 cache. We used an NVIDIA Tesla K20c GPU (launch date: November 2012; process: 28 nm; peak single-precision floating-point throughput: 3.524 TFLOPS; peak memory bandwidth: 208 GB/s). Deo and Keely's OpenCL implementation was on an AMD Radeon 7970 GPU (launch date: December 2011; process: 28 nm; peak single-precision floating-point throughput: 3.789 TFLOPS; peak memory bandwidth: 264 GB/s). The AMD GPU has slight peak performance advantages over the NVIDIA GPU we used,

---
[5] http://nvlabs.github.io/cub/.

but despite differences in programming environment and GPU architecture, we believe results from the two GPUs are directly comparable. We compiled and ran dk-nvidia-SA, skew-SA, spd-SA, and osipov-SA using CUDA 6.0 and Visual Studio 2010 on 64-bit Windows 7.

For evaluation, we use the same input datasets as Deo and Keely along with two larger datasets. The input strings range in size from 10 KB to 110 MB and are collected from the Calgary Corpus, Large Canterbury Corpus, Manzinis Corpus, Protein Corpus, and Silesia Corpus [13]. We compare the four GPU implementation results against Mori's highly tuned, OpenMP-assisted CPU implementation libdivsufsort 2.0.1 [13] based on induced copying on a 4-core PC, using its own internal runtime measurement, which excludes disk access time.

Figure 4 summarize our performance results and we make the following observations:

- On datasets of sufficient size (on the order of 1 MB for the skew implementations, smaller for spd-SA), all four GPU implementations are faster than the CPU baseline. Roughly speaking, the skew implementations are twice as fast as the CPU version, osipov-SA has a 4× speedup, and spd-SA's speedup ranges from 6× to 11×.
- Macroscopically, the fluctuations in the speedups of spd-SA and osipov-SA for the same datasets suggest that the behavior of our hybrid prefix-doubling spd-SA is similar to that of osipov-SA, and our skew-SA with dk-amd-SA and dk-nvidia-SA.
- spd-SA is 2.3× to 4.4× faster than osipov-SA.
- skew-SA is consistently 1.45× faster than dk-amd-SA and 1.1× faster than dk-nvidia-SA.
- Both prefix-doubling based GPU implementations outperform the three skew based methods on most datasets.

In general the performance of the GPU implementations track each other. The datasets with the highest speedups on GPUs are those with a non-uniform prefix distribution (e.g., *chr22dna*, which contains DNA sequences of only 4 different characters), whereas more uniformly distributed prefixes yield smaller speedups. The peaks of the speedup happen because the GPU implementations (especially our hybrid skew/prefix-doubling) are faster on non-uniform prefixes. For skew, a more uniform dataset results in more iterations in the recursive step, and thus takes longer time. For prefix-doubling, uniform datasets give us fewer segments for separation and thus result in less parallelism.

We take a closer look at two datasets for skew-SA and spd-SA. The first is a scalability test on increasing amounts of text data from the English Wikipedia dump "enwik8"[6], shown in Fig. 5 at left. In general, the larger the dataset, the higher the throughput; it takes an input size of many millions of characters for both approaches to reach the throughput asymptote. At 10 MB, skew-SA has a 2× speedup and spd-SA a 9× speedup over libdivsufsort.

---

[6] http://cs.fit.edu/~mmahoney/compression/textdata.html.

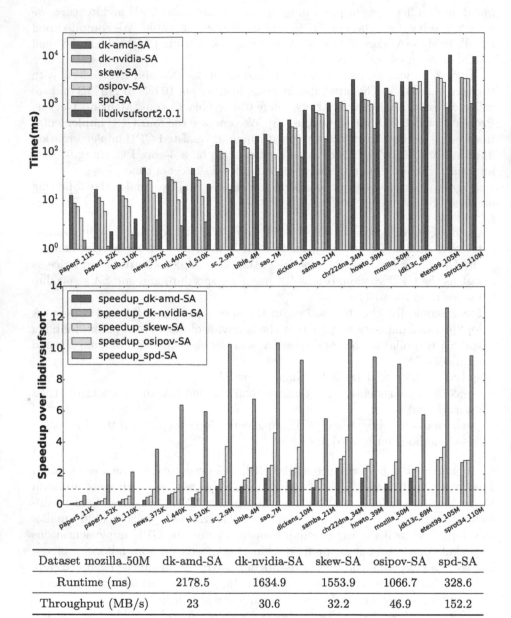

Dataset mozilla_50M	dk-amd-SA	dk-nvidia-SA	skew-SA	osipov-SA	spd-SA
Runtime (ms)	2178.5	1634.9	1553.9	1066.7	328.6
Throughput (MB/s)	23	30.6	32.2	46.9	152.2

Fig. 4. Runtimes (top) of five suffix array construction implementations over corpus datasets; the datasets are those chosen by Deo and Keely [2] in addition to two larger datasets for which we have no dk-amd-SA measurements. The CPU implementation libdivsufsort is the baseline for speedup comparisons (bottom). The five GPU implementations are dk-amd-SA, dk-nvidia-SA, osipov-SA, skew-SA, and spd-SA.

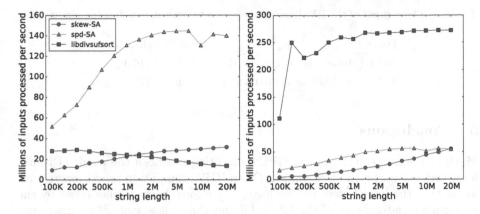

Fig. 5. Left, throughput on plain text "enwik8" as dataset size scales; right, throughput on a dataset consisting only of the repeated letter 'A', using the same legend as left graph.

The second is an artificial dataset composed of only the repeated single character 'A'. This is a pathologically bad case for prefix-doubling because (except for suffixes near the end of the string) every input position has an identical prefix on every iteration until the last one, so spd-SA cannot divide the prefixes into multiple segments—they all land in the same segment. Moreover, because those prefixes in that segment are lexicographically identical, they have worst-case sorting behavior. Skew's performance is much more predictable; although skew must recurse all the way to the base case and cannot finish early, it is not pathologically bad as with prefix-doubling. Nonetheless, except for very large inputs, spd-SA's performance still exceeds skew-SA's. Induced copying is much better suited for this dataset. For a 10 MB all-'A' input, libdivsufsort completes in 40 ms, compared with 224 ms for skew-SA and 196 ms for spd-SA.

Application Tools Implementation. The most recent release of the CUDA Data Parallel Primitives (CUDPP) Library[7] uses our optimized skew implementation in its parallel Burrows-Wheeler Transform (BWT) [17] and bzip2 data compression functions. As predicted, both gain significant speedups from replacing string sort with a suffix array algorithm [3]. We also implement our fast hybrid skew/prefix-doubling in a parallel BWT and use it as a partial step in implementing parallel FM index backward-search, along with CUB's DeviceHistogram routine and cudppMultiscan from CUDPP 2.2. We measured the performance of the parallel BWT and FM index based on our fast hybrid skew/prefix-doubling on "enwik8" and "chr22dna" datasets and show our results in Table 2.

---

[7] http://cudpp.github.io/.

Table 2. Throughput of the BWT and FM index's backward-search using our spd-SA.

Dataset	enwik8	chr22.dna
BWT (Millions of characters/s)	132.5	116.4
FM index (Millions of characters/s)	28.6	77

5   Conclusions

Much of the interesting work in GPU computing has been the result of brute-force techniques, judiciously applied. Often, GPU computing practitioners have found that the loss of efficiency by using brute force is more than offset by the performance advantages of the GPU. Of the three classes of suffix array construction algorithms, skew is perhaps the most suitable for brute-force methods, and was chosen by Deo and Keely, and ourselves when we began our work.

However, the maturation of GPU computing is leading to the development of elegant, efficient, load-balanced algorithmic building blocks that are designed for, and run well on the GPU. The merge and segmented sort implementations in this paper make the difference between an SACA that is uncompetitive vs. an SACA that is best in class. We expect that the next frontier in GPU SACAs will be tackling the third class of SACAs—induced copying. The research challenge is to determine whether the inherent algorithmic efficiency of their CPU implementation will translate into the GPU domain.

Acknowledgments. We thank to Yangzihao Wang for the initial implementation and good advice along the way. We would like to acknowledge Mrinal Deo for providing their paper's original data, Vitaly Osipov for sharing his paper's source code for comparision, and both Jason Mak and Carl Yang for feedback on early drafts of the paper. We appreciate the funding support of the National Science Foundation under grants OCI-1032859 and CCF-1017399, and UC Lab Fees Research Program Award 12-LR-238449.

References

1. Davidson, A., Tarjan, D., Garland, M., Owens, J.D.: Efficient parallel merge sort for fixed and variable length keys. In: Proceedings of Innovative Parallel Computing, InPar 2012 (2012)
2. Deo, M., Keely, S.: Parallel suffix array and least common prefix for the GPU. In: Proceedings of the 18th ACM SIGPLAN Symposium on Principles and Practice of Parallel Programming, PPoPP 2013, pp. 197–206 (2013)
3. Edwards, J.A., Vishkin, U.: Parallel algorithms for Burrows-Wheeler compression and decompression. Theor. Comput. Sci. **525**, 10–22 (2014)
4. Ferragina, P., Manzini, G.: Opportunistic data structures with applications. In: Proceedings of the 41st Annual Symposium on Foundations of Computer Science, FOCS 2000, pp. 390–398(2000)
5. Green, O., McColl, R., Bader, D.A.: GPU merge path: a GPU mergingalgorithm. In: Proceedings of the 26th ACM International Conference on Supercomputing, ICS 2012, pp. 331–340 (2012)

6. Kärkkäinen, J., Sanders, P.: Simple linear work suffix array construction. In: Proceedings of the 30th International Conference on Automata, Languages and Programming, ICALP 2003, pp. 943–955. Springer, Heidelberg (2003). http://dl.acm.org/citation.cfm?id=1759210.1759301

7. Karp, R.M., Miller, R.E., Rosenberg, A.L.: Rapid identification of repeated patterns in strings, trees and arrays. In: Proceedings of the Fourth Annual ACM Symposium on Theory of Computing STOC 1972, pp. 125–136 (1972)

8. Larsson, N.J., Sadakane, K.: Faster suffix sorting. Theor. Comput. Sci. **387**(3), 258–272 (2007)

9. Lindholm, E., Nickolls, J., Oberman, S., Montrym, J.: NVIDIA Tesla: a unified graphics and computing architecture. IEEE Micro **28**(2), 39–55 (2008)

10. Liu, C.M., Luo, R., Lam, T.W.: GPU-accelerated BWT construction for large collection of short reads (2014). arXiv preprint arXiv:1401.7457

11. Manber, U., Myers, G.: Suffix arrays: a new method for on-line string searches. In: Proceedings of the First Annual ACM-SIAM Symposium on Discrete Algorithms. pp. 319–327. SODA '90 (1990)

12. Merrill, D., Grimshaw, A.: Revisiting sorting for GPGPU stream architectures. Technical report CS2010-03, Department of Computer Science, University of Virginia (2010)

13. Mori, Y.: libdivsufsort, version 2.0.1 (2010). https://code.google.com/p/libdivsufsort/wiki/SACA_Benchmarks

14. Nickolls, J., Buck, I., Garland, M., Skadron, K.: Scalable parallel programming with CUDA. ACM Queue **6**, 40–53 (2008)

15. Osipov, V.: Parallel suffix array construction for shared memory architectures. In: Calderón-Benavides, L., González-Caro, C., Chávez, E., Ziviani, N. (eds.) SPIRE 2012. LNCS, vol. 7608, pp. 379–384. Springer, Heidelberg (2012)

16. Pantaleoni, J.: A massively parallel algorithm for constructing the BWT of large string sets, October 2014. arXiv.org abs/1410.0562(1410.0562v1)

17. Patel, R.A., Zhang, Y., Mak, J., Owens, J.D.: Parallel lossless data compression on the GPU. In: Proceedings of Innovative Parallel Computing (2012)

18. Satish, N., Harris, M., Garland, M.: Designing efficient sorting algorithms for manycore GPUs. In: Proceedings of the 23rd IEEE International Parallel and Distributed Processing Symposium (2009)

Effective Barrier Synchronization on Intel Xeon Phi Coprocessor

Andrey Rodchenko[✉], Andy Nisbet, Antoniu Pop, and Mikel Luján

School of Computer Science, The University of Manchester, Manchester, UK
{andrey.rodchenko,andy.nisbet,antoniu.pop,mikel.lujan}@manchester.ac.uk

Abstract. Barriers are a fundamental synchronization primitive, under-pinning the parallel execution models of many modern shared-memory parallel programming languages such as OpenMP, OpenCL or Cilk, and are one of the main challenges to scaling. State-of-the-art barrier synchronization algorithms differ in tradeoffs between critical path length, communication traffic patterns and memory footprint. In this paper, we evaluate the efficiency of five such algorithms on the Intel Xeon Phi coprocessor. In addition, we present a novel hybrid barrier implementation that exploits the topology, the memory hierarchy and streaming stores of the Xeon Phi architecture to achieve a $3\times$ lower overhead than the Intel OpenMP barrier implementation (ICC 14.0.0), thus outperforming, to the best of our knowledge, all other implementations, and which we evaluate on the CG and MG kernels from the NAS Parallel Benchmarks, the direct N-body simulation kernel and the EPCC barrier OpenMP microbenchmark. The optimized barriers presented in the paper are available at https://github.com/arodchen/cbarriers released as free software.

Keywords: Barrier synchronization · Scalability · Algorithms · Many-core architectures · Intel Xeon Phi

1 Introduction

Multi- and many-core systems have become the norm, and their efficient exploitation requires efficient and scalable synchronization mechanisms. Barriers are one of the fundamental synchronization primitives, underpinning the parallel execution models of many modern shared-memory parallel programming languages such as OpenMP, OpenCL or Cilk. The optimization of software barrier synchronization has been widely studied [2,7–9,12,18], yet no algorithm has proven optimal across the wide variety of parallel architectures. Indeed, each algorithm comes with its own set of tradeoffs with respect to communication complexity (volume) and patterns, length of the critical path, and memory footprint. For any given architecture, the optimal algorithm is largely dependent on factors such as the system's topology, the structure of the memory hierarchy, and the characteristics of the system interconnect.

© Springer-Verlag Berlin Heidelberg 2015
J.L. Träff et al. (Eds.): Euro-Par 2015, LNCS 9233, pp. 588–600, 2015.
DOI: 10.1007/978-3-662-48096-0_45

The focus of this paper is to analyze and optimize the efficiency of barrier synchronization on the Intel Xeon Phi coprocessor. Based on the Intel MIC (Many Integrated Core) Architecture, that provides a commodity off-the-shelf many-core system, the Xeon Phi has up to 61 cores, each 4-way multithreaded, for a maximum of 244 logical threads. At this scale, the efficiency of barrier synchronization is crucial for performance in synchronization intensive workloads.

Our **first contribution** is a thorough evaluation of the behavior of current state-of-the-art barrier algorithms, and an analysis of their tradeoffs for the memory hierarchy of Xeon Phi. We show that while the best algorithm depends on run-time conditions, a single statically chosen algorithm is only marginally outperformed in a small number of cases. Our **second contribution** is a novel and more efficient hybrid algorithm, mixing different (existing) barrier algorithms at different levels of granularity of synchronization, and optimized with *streaming store* instructions to write full cache lines, that eliminate a costly read-for-ownership cache coherency operation. We show that our hybrid approach outperforms all previous algorithms on the Intel Xeon Phi coprocessor.

Section 2 presents key features of the Xeon Phi and the resulting methodological constraints for experiments. Section 3 reviews the state-of-the-art barrier synchronization algorithms and their implementations. Our optimizations and our new hybrid synchronization scheme are presented in Sect. 4. Section 5 presents our experimental findings. Finally, Sect. 6 discusses previous work on Xeon Phi barrier optimization, and Sect. 7 summarizes our work. The optimized barriers presented in the paper are available at https://github.com/arodchen/cbarriers released under the Apache v2.0 free software license.

2 Intel Xeon Phi Coprocessor

We experimented on a 60-Core Xeon Phi 5110P with base frequency of 1.053GHz. Cores are in-order, 4-way SMT, using a bidirectional ring interconnect. Each core has 32 KB of L1 and 512 KB of L2 cache. The state of the distributed L2 cache is controlled by a distributed tag directory implementing the GOLS protocol [10]. The coherence of L1 and L2 caches is maintained by a modified MESI protocol. However the GOLS protocol makes it possible to emulate the *Owner* state, enabling a MOESI-like functionality. 8GB of GDDR5 RAM is accessed through 8 dual channel memory controllers connected through a ring interconnect interface.

The 512-bit SIMD instructions were used to optimize barrier synchronization in the *SIMD barrier* [4]. SIMD stores, also known as *streaming stores*, use a vector size matching that of a cache line. As a result, such store instructions do not need to issue a *read-for-ownership* request in the cache coherence protocol. Store instructions with the *no-read* hint can be either globally ordered (vmovnrap[d/s]), providing a *total store order* type consistency, or non globally ordered (vmovnrngoap[d/s]), leading to a weaker memory consistency.

The execution of HW threads can be paused, using the delay r32/r64 instruction, which forces the processor to halt the fetch and issue of further instructions for a parametric number of cycles. The pause instruction is not available.

3 Barrier Synchronization Algorithms

Many algorithms have been proposed for barrier synchronization. One of the simplest, and least scalable, is the *Sense-reversing centralized barrier*. It uses two global variables, a counter and a flag, and one thread-local flag called *sense*. The synchronization counter is initialized with the number of threads in the barrier, the global flag is set to `false` and all local sense flags are set to `true`. Upon reaching a barrier, each thread registers its arrival by atomically decrementing the counter, then waits while the value of the global flag is different from its local flag. The last thread to complete the atomic operation, when the counter reaches zero, re-initializes the counter, flips the global flag and its local flag. The other threads eventually perceive that the global sense has changed and pass the barrier, flipping their own flag. This technique, called *sense-reversing*, allows the reuse of the same barrier variables for the next synchronization round.

To reduce the contention on shared variables, the *combining-tree barrier* [18] organizes the participating threads in a tree, using an algorithm similar to a centralized barrier at each node of the tree: the last thread to decrement the synchronization counter of a node recursively proceeds to decrement the counter of its parent, while the other threads wait on node-level release flags for notification that the barrier has passed. It is also possible to use a global release flag, trading a shorter critical path for additional contention on the global flag.

Realizing that atomic operations were only necessary to reach a consensus on the arrival order of threads, Hensgen *et al.* [8] proposed the *static tournament barrier*. Instead of discriminating on arrival order, it relies on a statically determined thread, called *winner*, that will automatically progress to the next round once all other threads, the *losers*, have arrived at a given node of the tree. In this way, it is only necessary to determine whether all threads are accounted for, irrespectively of their arrival order, which does not require atomic operations. The initial version of the algorithm by Hensgen *et al.* [8] was later improved by Mellor-Crummey *et al.* [12] with a tree-based *Notification Phase* and sense-reversing to avoid re-initializing the barrier state. The *static f-way tournament* by Grunwald *et al.* [7] generalizes the static tournament approach, with an arbitrary number of participants per round. To avoid cases where a static winner arrives early and busy-waits on a location yet to be set by one or multiple losers, the *dynamic f-way tournament barrier* [7] lets the winner identify itself by checking the value of adjacent memory locations marked by other threads upon arrival.

A shortcoming shared by all previous algorithms is that they all require two phases: registration of threads arrival - *Registration Phase* and notification of threads arrival - *Notification Phase*. However, these phases can be merged, at the cost of additional communication, by providing each thread with sufficient information to locally decide when the barrier can be passed. The first instance of this class of barriers was the *butterfly barrier* [2]. When the number of threads participating in the barrier is not a power of 2, the *dissemination barrier* [8] can be a more efficient solution. In the dissemination barrier pattern, a thread i in round r notifies another thread $j = (i + 2^r) \bmod N$ by writing its local flag,

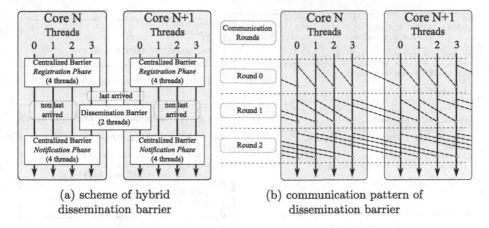

(a) scheme of hybrid
dissemination barrier

(b) communication pattern of
dissemination barrier

Fig. 1. Hybrid dissemination barrier rationale.

which is sense-reversed, to a dedicated memory location, where N is the number of threads, $i, j \in [0, N-1]$ and $r \in [0, \lfloor \log_2 N \rfloor]$. Each thread can proceed to the next round as soon as its notification variable is set to the appropriate value for the current round. In this way, synchronization is achieved in $\lceil \log_2 N \rceil$ rounds. The *f-way dissemination barrier* [9] is a generalized version, where each thread can notify f other threads in one round, requiring only $\lceil \log_{f+1} N \rceil$ rounds to complete. If $f = N - 1$, then it will be a broadcast barrier (all-to-all communication) requiring $N * (N - 1)$ notifications.

4 Hybrid Barrier

We came to the design of the hybrid barrier from the observation that, on systems with a hierarchical topology, different algorithms can be optimal for different levels in the hierarchy. As always, the objective is to minimize inter-core communication while exploiting the low cost of intra-core communication. During our preliminary evaluation, we observed that the most efficient algorithms were the dissemination barrier and the combining tree with arity 4. Figure 1b shows the communication patterns of a dissemination barrier. Evidently, each round contains at least one inter-core communication edge, which will be slower and will consequently determine the critical path for each round. We therefore propose to rely on the centralized sense-reversing barrier (equivalent to the combining tree with arity 4) for the intra-core phase, then revert to dissemination once a single thread remains per core. A similar approach was discussed by Cownie [5]. Figure 1a and Listing 1.1 show the scheme and pseudocode of the hybrid algorithm.

Busy-Waiting Amortization. Busy-waiting on the same memory location can have a negative impact on performance because of the increased memory traffic,

```
void                  /* Hybrid Barrier */
hb_wait( hb_Bar_t * hb, /* Shared Data  */
         tp_Data_t * tp)/* Thread Private Data */
{
  sr_Bar_t * srB = hb->srB[ tp->srBId ];
  int srBC = fetch_and_add( & (srB->count), -1);
  int tpsrBS = tp->srBSense;

  if ( srBC == 1 )
  { /* last thread inside core to arrive */
    /* call to dissemination barrier */
    dsmn_wait( hb->dsmnB, tp);
    mic_store( & (srB->count), srB->threadsNum);
    mic_store( & (srB->sense), tpsrBS);
  } else
  { /* non-last thread to arrive */
    while ( tpsrBS != srB->sense )
    {
      mic_pause( );
    }
  }
  mic_store( & (tp->srBSense), ! tpsrBS);
}
```

Listing 1.1. Hybrid barrier wait method.

```
inline static void
mic_pause( )
{
  _mm_delay_32( ARCH_MIC_DELAY);
}
```

Listing 1.2. Busy-waiting delay.

```
static inline void
mic_store( volatile void *addr, int data)
{
#if __use_streaming_stores
  _mm512i siVec =
    _mm512_set1_epi32( data);
  _mm512_storenr_ps( addr,
    _mm512_castsi512_ps( siVec));
#else
  *addr = data;
#endif
}
```

Listing 1.3. Utilization of streaming stores.

leaving less bandwidth to other threads. This effect was previously noted [1] and we empirically determined (see Sect. 5) the appropriate delay to amortize the impact of busy-waiting while balancing the additional latency this introduces for a thread to perceive a store operation. The delay can be introduced with the _mm_delay32 intrinsic, as shown in Listing 1.2, the parameter specifies the number of idle cycles.

Streaming Stores. Streaming stores can reduce barrier overhead [11] when storing notification values to flags in the *Notification Phase* or reinitializing counters in the combining tree or sense-reversing centralized barrier. Listing 1.3 details the implementation of the mic_store function. Note that, contrary to Caballero *et al.* [4], we use the *globally ordered* version of streaming stores; Sect. 5 presents the rationale for this.

5   Experimental Results

5.1   Benchmarks

EPCC OpenMP Microbenchmarks. We implemented a part of the EPCC OpenMP microbenchmark [3] evaluating the overhead of the standalone barrier primitive, which will be referred to as EPCC.

NAS Parallel Benchmarks. We chose the CG and MG kernels from the C versions [16] of the *NAS Parallel Benchmarks* (NASPB) [13] in order to evaluate the efficiency of barrier synchronization [4,15,17]. As the original inputs for these benchmarks lead to a low frequency of barrier synchronization, even using the smallest class S, which makes it difficult to observe barrier overhead, we

Table 1. Barrier frequency in NASPB for inputs Y and S.

NAS Parallel Benchmark Kernel	CG		MG	
Input Class	S	Y	S	Y
Frequency, 10^3 barriers per second	6.4	21.6	8.7	12.4

introduced our own input class Y for these 2 NASPB kernels. The frequencies of barrier synchronization in both classes S and Y are presented in Table 1. Class Y consists of inputs {na = 240; nonzer = 2; niter = 300; shiftY = 5.0} for CG and {problem_size = 16; nit = 800} for MG. We also added a `collapse(2)` clause to the relevant OpenMP parallel loops in the MG kernel, as suggested in [4], to increase the amount of parallelism which would otherwise not lead to a reasonable load balance. The `collapse` clause is used to specify that a loop nest is not only parallel on the first loop construct annotated, but also at a deeper level (parameter of the clause), which allows to collapse multiple loops into a single loop that is subsequently parallelized.

Direct N-body Simulation. We implemented a direct N-body simulation kernel to evaluate the efficiency of barrier synchronization in the task where synchronization cannot be relaxed. It was shown that using more relaxed synchronization constructs, like phasers, is more efficient than using barriers for CG and MG [17]. In the direct N-body simulation kernel we have implemented, each thread calculates the coordinates and velocities of a single particle, so that the frequency of barriers will be the highest. Coordinates and velocities of a single particle are stored within a private memory location which can fit into a single cache line. This kernel will be referenced as NBODY in the rest of the article.

To test our barrier implementations without interfering with the rest of the OpenMP implementation, we replaced the calls to the `__kmpc_barrier` function, which is the internal barrier function in the Intel OpenMP library, with a trampoline, `barrier_trampoline_`, that calls the function implementing the desired barrier algorithm.

5.2   Naming Convention and Methodology

For the remainder of this paper, the *geomean* overhead of a barrier (or execution time per barrier) is measured in our experiments on EPCC as the geometric mean of its overhead across the different thread counts; so $O_{geomean} = \sqrt[N]{\prod_{i=1}^{N} O_{n_i}}$, where N is the number of different thread counts, n_i is the number of threads in element i in the vector of different thread counts, and O_n is a barrier overhead for n participating threads. For CG, MG, and NBODY, we use execution time of a kernel instead of the overhead of a single barrier. On charts representing the geomean overhead (execution time), horizontal lines show the best (green, low horizontal line) and the worst (red, high horizontal line) geomean overhead respectively, calculated as geometric mean of the best and the worst barrier overheads for each number of threads amongst all algorithms.

The **best geomean overhead** represents the *practical lower bound of synchronization overhead*, which could be achieved given an oracle that predicts the best possible algorithm in every configuration. The performance of this **ideal meta-algorithm** shows the loss of performance resulting from using a single algorithm compared to the ideal performance that could (theoretically) be achieved by selecting algorithms dynamically with an oracle.

Individual barrier algorithms on the charts can be identified by their signatures. A signature uniquely identifies an algorithm by two 3–5 letter abbreviations and a number. The first abbreviation corresponds to the algorithm and its variations: **sr** - centralized sense-reversing barrier; **dsmn** - dissemination barrier; **dsmnH** - hybrid dissemination barrier; **ct** - combining tree barrier; **stn** - static tournament barrier; **dtn** - dynamic tournament barrier; **ls** - tree-based notification with local flags; **gs** - broadcast notification using a single global flag; **omp** - Intel OpenMP barrier.

The second part of the signature defines whether the waiting loops contained the *64-cycle delay* (which will be discussed below) - **pause**, or contained no delay - **spin**. This part is meaningless for Intel OpenMP barrier.

The last part is a **number** corresponding to the arity of the tree for tree algorithms, the number of ways for a *n-way* dissemination barrier and meaningless for the centralized sense-reversing barrier and Intel OpenMP barrier.

All of our experiments rely on a balanced strategy for thread mapping, mapping threads to cores with the least load first. This type of thread affinity is enabled in Intel OpenMP by setting the environment variable `KMP_AFFINITY` to `balanced`; the `KMP_LIBRARY` variable was set to `turnaround`; the `KMP_BLOCKTIME` variable was set to `infinite`; and the number of threads was controlled by setting the `OMP_NUM_THREADS` variable.

Each data point was obtained from 10 measurements and represented by a box plot. Unless otherwise indicated in a figure, the number of threads varies from 8 to 232 in increments of 8. The arities tested were: 2, 3, 4, 8, 16 and 32 for the combining tree barrier; 2, 3, 4 and 5 for the static tournament barrier; and 2, 3 and 4 for the dynamic tournament barrier.

5.3   Experimental Data and Discussion

Figure 2 shows the results for *geomean overhead* of barrier synchronization algorithms on EPCC, and Fig. 3 shows the results of the *ideal meta-algorithm* on EPCC.

Global Sense vs Local Sense. The overhead of tree barriers with global notification flag **gs** is much higher than that of barriers with a combining tree *Notification Phase* **ls** as can be seen on Fig. 2, where the fastest **gs** variant is close to 2× slower than the slowest **ls** variant.

It can be observed that a combining tree with global flag in *Notification Phase* has higher geomean overhead than a centralized sense-reversing barrier,

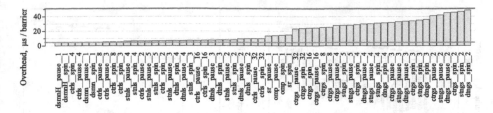

Fig. 2. Geomean overhead of barrier synchronization algorithms on EPCC.

and the higher the tree arity, the less the overhead. This indicates that another hybrid algorithm should be investigated: a single global counter for the *Registration Phase*, like in the centralized sense-reversing barrier, and a tree-based *Notification Phase*.

Delayed Busy-Waiting. As it can be seen from Fig. 2, where the geomean overhead for different algorithms follows increasing order, the same algorithm with delayed busy-waiting **pause** outperform the undelayed spinning variants **spin** in the majority of cases. Due to this fact, we did not consider undelayed busy-waiting in our further experiments.

Sizing the Delay for Spinning. To determine a suitable value (number of sleep cycles) to pass as parameter to the `delay` instruction conveniently provided on Xeon Phi, we evaluated delay values in the range from 0 to 128 cycles with step 8 on EPCC. Above 128 cycles, the performance starts to degrade as the delay introduces too much latency for waiting threads.

The best performance was obtained with a 64 cycle delay that was used in all subsequent experiments. In future studies, this parameter can be investigated further as it is likely to depend on runtime conditions, such as the level of contention on the interconnect.

Hybrid Barrier. Figures 2 and 3 show that the hybrid dissemination barrier is the closest to the ideal meta-algorithm on synthetic benchmarks. Indeed, as confirmed by the results presented in Fig. 4, the few instances where the hybrid barrier is not the most efficient in Fig. 3 only correspond to minor timing variability up to 60 threads, up to which point the algorithms have similar overhead. Above 72 threads, the hybrid barrier overhead is considerably lower than that of the dissemination barrier.

Streaming Stores. A non globally ordered streaming store is unordered in respect to other stores, meaning that other store instructions issued subsequently by the same thread can overtake it and become visible to other threads earlier. This relaxation of the memory ordering constraints makes it tempting to rely on this instruction for implementing barriers, as suggested by Cownie [5] and

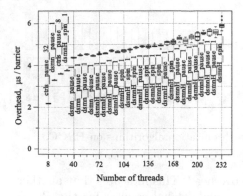

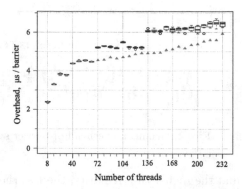

Fig. 3. Overhead of the ideal barrier synchronization meta-algorithm on EPCC.

Fig. 4. Dissemination barrier (black boxplots) compared to hybrid dissemination barrier (red triangles) (Color figure online).

implemented by Caballero *et al.* [4]. However, we observed 5 % less overhead on average for top performing barrier implementations on EPCC when using globally ordered streaming stores over both ordinary stores and non globally ordered streaming stores, having on average the same effect on barriers overhead.

Real-World Kernels. The most efficient barrier algorithms selected above were evaluated on the CG and MG kernels of the NAS Parallel Benchmarks and direct N-body simulation kernel. Our results are presented in Fig. 5. Hybrid dissemination barrier is superior over the other algorithms on CG and NBODY, while combining tree barrier with arities grater than 2 is slightly better than dissemination barrier on MG.

Effects of the Ring Interconnect. As discussed by Dolbeau [6], the address of the shared memory location used for communicating among threads may have a significant effect on latency, and therefore on barrier overhead. We observed the same behavior, induced by the ring interconnect and the distributed tag directories, on a centralized sense-reversing barrier. Figures 6a, b, and c show three sets of performance results obtained on EPCC for 1 to 60 threads. Within each experiment, the data for a given number of threads was obtained in a single execution, containing multiple iterations where the same memory locations are re-used to store synchronization variables. The only difference between the three experiments is the effective memory addresses allocated and used for the synchronization variables. It is apparent that the variability of performance results is negligible within a given set, but it is significant in-between sets. The graph in Fig. 6d shows the same benchmark, but for each thread count the benchmark was re-launched for every iteration, thus allocating different memory regions.

This variability is explained by the ring topology and the distributed tag directories. Indeed, in this configuration, each cache line is attributed a tag

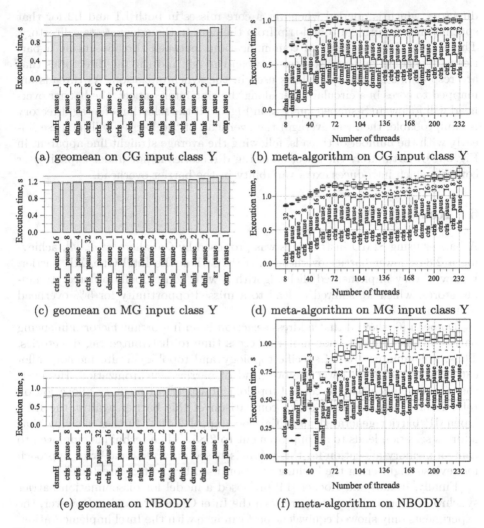

Fig. 5. Comparison of barrier synchronization algorithms on CG and MG kernels of NAS Parallel Benchmarks and direct N-body simulation kernel.

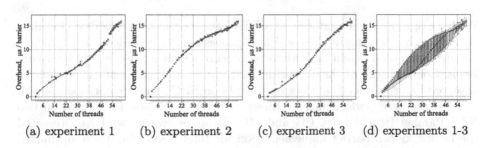

Fig. 6. Impact of non-uniform cache line access latency.

directory which is queried whenever a core misses in both L1 and L2 for that specific line, requiring a round-trip from the core to the adequate tag directory. This means that the delay of communications between threads during a barrier is dependent on the distances between threads and the tag directories that are responsible for the cache lines used in the synchronization. As threads are mapped to cores in a circular order along the ring interconnect, the barrier overhead will follow an S-shaped curve as in Fig. 6c. If the selection of a tag directory is equiprobable, then (on average) the overhead of the barrier will increase linearly with the number of threads, following the average straight line apparent in Fig. 6d. Unfortunately the selection of tag directories is not under explicit user control, which introduces extra variability in the barrier overhead.

6 Related Work

A barrier using SIMD instructions was proposed by Caballero *et al.* [4], achieving a 2.84× lower barrier overhead on EPCC than the Intel OpenMP barrier. However, they implemented their algorithm with non globally ordered streaming stores, which we showed to lead to a missed opportunity for 5 % overhead reduction.

Dolbeau [6] showed that address selection is an important factor influencing barrier overhead due to non-uniform access time to distributed tag directories. Thus, a combining tree of specific topology and topology-aware memory allocation would allow to lower the overhead of barrier synchronization. However, there is no explicit way to control topological aspects of memory allocation on Intel Xeon Phi systems. A direct comparison of this barrier against the Intel OpenMP barrier generated an initial speedup of 2.41×, further showing that address selection leads to an improvement to 2.85×. The technique employed to control memory allocation for this result is based on a trial-and-error approach for reverse-engineering the hashing function used by the tag directories.

Finally, Ramos and Hoefler [14] proposed a model for dissemination barrier synchronization and also compare with the Intel OpenMP barrier. However, the experiments only showed equivalent performance with the Intel implementation.

7 Conclusions

We have optimized the performance of five state-of-the-art barrier synchronization algorithms on the Intel Xeon Phi coprocessor and provided a novel hybrid variant based on different algorithms to synchronize at intra-core and inter-core levels. Comparing our hybrid algorithm with previous implementations, we have observed lower overheads in the experiments on EPCC barrier microbenchmark and an improved performance on direct N-body simulation kernel and on two NAS Parallel Benchmarks, CG and MG. In other words, we have presented the fastest known barrier implementation for Intel Xeon Phi. These optimized barriers are available at https://github.com/arodchen/cbarriers released as free software.

In addition, we have provided an analysis of key specificities of the Xeon Phi system, in particular characterizing: (1) the impact of the ring interconnect and distributed tag directories leading to non-uniform cache line access latencies; (2) the performance degradation that can result from spin-based synchronization with insufficient delay; and (3) the positive impact of using globally ordered streaming stores for fine grained synchronization.

Acknowledgements. This work is supported by EPSRC grants EP/M004880/1, DOME EP/J016330/1 and PAMELA EP/K008730/1. A. Rodchenko is funded by a Microsoft Research PhD Scholarship, A. Pop is funded by a Royal Academy of Engineering Research Fellowship and M. Luján is funded by a Royal Society University Research Fellowship. We also thank the anonymous reviewers for their constructive feedback.

References

1. Agarwal, A., Cherian, M.: Adaptive backoff synchronization techniques. In: Proceedings of the of the International Symposium on Computer Architecture, pp. 396–406 (1989)
2. Brooks III, E.D.: The butterfly barrier. Int. J. Parallel Program. **15**(4), 295–307 (1986)
3. Bull, J.M.: Measuring synchronisation and scheduling overheads in OpenMP. In: Proceedings of the First European Workshop on OpenMP, pp. 99–105 (1999)
4. Caballero, D., Duran, A., Martorell, X.: An OpenMP barrier usingSIMD instructions for Intel® Xeon Phi™ coprocessor. In: Rendell, A.P., Chapman, B.M., Müller, M.S. (eds.) IWOMP 2013. LNCS, vol. 8122, pp. 99–113. Springer, Heidelberg (2013)
5. Cownie, J.: Fastest possible barrier (Intel developer zone forum discussion) (2013). http://software.intel.com/en-us/forums/topic/392587. Last accessed 1-Jun-2015
6. Dolbeau, R.: Address selection for efficient barriers on the Intel Xeon Phi (2013). http://www.dolbeau.name/dolbeau/publications/barrierphi.pdf. Last accessed 1 Jun 2015
7. Grunwald, D., Vajracharya, S.: Efficient barriers for distributed shared memory computers. In: Proceedings of International Parallel Processing Symposium, pp. 604–608 (1994)
8. Hensgen, D., Finkel, R., Manber, U.: Two algorithms for barrier synchronization. Int. J. Parallel Program. **17**(1), 1–17 (1988)
9. Hoefler, T., Mehlan, T., Mietke, F., Rehm, W.: Fast barrier synchronization for InfiniBand. In: 20th International Parallel and Distributed Processing Symposium, p. 7 (2006)
10. Intel Xeon Phi coprocessor system software developers guide (2014). https://software.intel.com/sites/default/files/managed/09/07/xeon-phi-coprocessor-system-software-developers-guide.pdf. Last accessed 1 Jun 2015
11. Krishnaiyer, R., Kultursay, E., Chawla, P., Preis, S., Zvezdin, A., Saito, H.: Compiler-based data prefetching and streaming non-temporal store generation for the Intel Xeon Phi coprocessor. In: Workshop on Multithreaded Architectures and Applications published as 27th IEEE IPDPSW, pp. 1575–1586 (2013)

12. Mellor-Crummey, J.M., Scott, M.L.: Algorithms for scalable synchronization on shared-memory multiprocessors. ACM Trans. Comput. Syst. **9**(1), 21–65 (1991)
13. NAS parallel benchmarks. http://www.nas.nasa.gov/publications/npb.html. Last accessed 1 Jun 2015
14. Ramos, S., Hoefler, T.: Modeling communication in cache-coherent smp systems: A case-study with Xeon Phi. In: High-Performance Parallel and Distributed Computing 2013, pp. 97–108 (2013)
15. Sartori, J., Kumar, R.: Low-overhead, high-speed multi-core barrier synchronization. In: Proceedings of the 5th International Conference on High Performance and Embedded Architecture and Compilation, pp. 18–34 (2010)
16. Seo, S., Jo, G., Lee, J.: Performance characterization of the NAS parallel benchmarks in OpenCL. In: 2011 IEEE International Symposium on Workload Characterization, pp. 137–148 (2011)
17. Shirako, J., Peixotto, D.M., Sarkar, V., Scherer, W.N.: Phasers: A unified deadlock-free construct for collective and point-to-point synchronization. In: Proceedings of the 22nd International Conference on Supercomputing, pp. 277–288 (2008)
18. Yew, P.C., Tzeng, N.F., Lawrie, D.H.: Distributing hot-spot addressing in large-scale multiprocessors. IEEE Trans. Comput. **C–36**(4), 388–395 (1987)

High Performance Multi-GPU SpMV
for Multi-component PDE-Based Applications

Ahmad Abdelfattah[✉], Hatem Ltaief, and David Keyes

Division of Computer, Electrical, and Mathematical Sciences and Engineering,
Extreme Computing Research Center, King Abdullah University of Science
and Technology, Thuwal, Jeddah, KSA
{Ahmad.Ahmad,Hatem.Ltaief,David.Keyes}@kaust.edu.sa

Abstract. Leveraging optimization techniques (e.g., register blocking
and double buffering) introduced in the context of KBLAS, a Level 2
BLAS high performance library on GPUs, the authors implement dense
matrix-vector multiplications within a sparse-block structure. While
these optimizations are important for high performance dense kernel
executions, they are even more critical when dealing with sparse linear algebra operations. The most time-consuming phase of many multi-
component applications, such as models of reacting flows or petroleum
reservoirs, is the solution at each implicit time step of large, sparse spatially structured or unstructured linear systems. The standard method
is a preconditioned Krylov solver. The Sparse Matrix-Vector multiplication (SpMV) is, in turn, one of the most time-consuming operations
in such solvers. Because there is no data reuse of the elements of the
matrix within a single SpMV, kernel performance is limited by the speed
at which data can be transferred from memory to registers, making the
bus bandwidth the major bottleneck. On the other hand, in case of a
multi-species model, the resulting Jacobian has a dense block structure.
For contemporary petroleum reservoir simulations, the block size typically ranges from three to a few dozen among different models, and still
larger blocks are relevant within adaptively model-refined regions of the
domain, though generally the size of the blocks, related to the number
of conserved species, is constant over large regions within a given model.
This structure can be exploited beyond the convenience of a block compressed row data format, because it offers opportunities to hide the data
motion with useful computations. The new SpMV kernel outperforms
existing state-of-the-art implementations on single and multi-GPUs using
matrices with dense block structure representative of porous media applications with both structured and unstructured multi-component grids.

1 Introduction

Simulating the flow in porous media enables the petroleum industry to characterize the production potential of oil fields and to optimize their development. It is
also used in geological sequestration of carbon dioxide to mitigate anthropogenic

© Springer-Verlag Berlin Heidelberg 2015
J.L. Träff et al. (Eds.): Euro-Par 2015, LNCS 9233, pp. 601–612, 2015.
DOI: 10.1007/978-3-662-48096-0_46

climate change. The most time-consuming operation (up to 80 % of the total simulation time) in such simulations is the solution of large, sparse spatially structured or unstructured linear systems at each integration time step. The Sparse Matrix-Vector multiplication (SpMV) is the innermost computational kernel in such solvers and therefore, its performance impacts directly the solvers' overall performance. As opposed to more compute-intensive Level 3 BLAS kernels (e.g., matrix-matrix multiplication), the SpMV performance suffers from lack of data reuse and is thus limited by the speed at which data can be transferred from memory to registers. For the multi-species versions of the aforementioned applications and many others that drive investment in high performance, the resulting Jacobian has a dense block structure. For contemporary petroleum reservoir simulations, the block size typically ranges from three to a few dozen, and still larger blocks are relevant within adaptively model-refined regions of the domain. This structure can be exploited beyond the convenience of a block compressed row data format, because it offers opportunities to hide data motion with useful computations.

We leverage optimization techniques, such as register blocking and double buffering, introduced in the context of KBLAS [2], a Level 2 BLAS high performance library on GPUs, originally designed for dense matrix-vector multiplications. While these optimizations are important for high performance dense kernel executions, they are even more critical when dealing with sparse linear algebra operations, due to irregular memory accesses and low compute-intensity kernels. The new SpMV kernel outperforms existing state-of-the-art implementations on GPUs using matrices with dense multi-component blocks on structured-grid and random spatial block distributions. A multi-GPU SpMV interface allows simulation of larger problem sizes, while increasing the level of concurrency.

The reminder of the paper is organized as follows. Section 2 presents related work. Section 3 reviews the source of sparse with dense block Jacobian structure in mesh-based PDE applications. Section 4 describes the framework for a uniform design strategy for such matrices and presents its different features and functionalities. The implementation details of the high performance SpMV kernels are given in Sect. 5. Section 6 shows the SpMV performance results on GPUs and compares it against state-of-the-art high performance SpMV implementations with various data layouts. Section 7 illustrates the performance impact after integrating our SpMV kernel into a sparse iterative solver library and we conclude in Sect. 8.

2   Related Work

The literature is rich in contributions for GPU-accelerated SpMV. Bell and Garland [7] proposed SpMV implementations for several formats including Compressed Sparse Row (CSR), ELLPACK [14], and the Coordinate (COO) format. They also proposed HYB, which is a hybrid format that combines both the ELLPACK format with the COO format, in an effort to reduce the padding overhead of the ELLPACK format.

Monakov et al. [18] proposed a sliced version of the ELLPACK format, where each slice is separately stored in the ELLPACK format. Vázquez et al. [20] proposed the ELLPACK-R format that adds auxiliary information to avoid computing the extra padded zeros. Choi et al. [9] proposed a parameterized blocked version of the ELLPACK format that proves to be competitive for block-sparse matrices, although it is restricted to certain block sizes, and targets mainly Fermi generation GPUs. Kreutzer et al. [16] generalized the sliced ELLPACK format to the SELL-C-σ format [15], in an effort to provide a unified sparse storage format across different architectures. The SELL-C-σ format has been improved and optimized for GPUs by Antz et al. [3], by introducing some zero padding to satisfy the memory constraints of the GPU architecture, hence called the SELL-P format.

Ashari et al. [4] proposed an adaptive algorithm for SpMV using the CSR format (called ACSR), where additional metadata are used with the standard CSR format

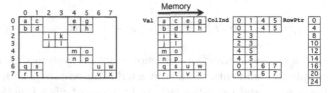

Fig. 1. The BSR format.

that help achieve better GPU utilization. ACSR is mainly proposed for adaptive graph applications, where the structure of the graph adjacency matrix changes frequently, thus making the preprocessing step a serious bottleneck.

We are mainly interested in the Blocked Sparse Row (BSR) format, which is the blocked version of the CSR format. It was first introduced for CPU architectures by Im et al. [11,12]. The BSR format targets sparse matrices that are naturally blocked, as shown in Fig. 1. It uses one integer per block to store its column index, as well as an integer to denote the start of every block row. In cases specific to structured grid problems, Godwin et al. [10] proposed a format called Column Diagonal Storage (CDS), which assigns only one integer for a group of blocks located at the same diagonal/off-diagonal. The work by Choi et al. [9] suggested GPU specific optimizations for the BSR format that were not enough to outperform the cuSPARSE HYB kernel [7]. They concluded that the BSR will be dominated by a reduction step that is affected by the number of blocks per block row. This work revisits the BSR formats and proposes some optimization techniques for a wide range of block sizes. The BSR format supports any structure of a block-sparse matrix.

Among all the aforementioned sparse formats, the cuSPARSE HYB format along with the SELL-P format usually achieve the best performance on the GPU across several matrices, as long as the matrix structure does not change during the simulation.

3   Multi-component Applications

Numerous applications result in sparse matrices of dense blocks, where the first nontrivial block size is 2 (e.g., streamfunction and vorticity in fluid dynamics) and the block size ranges up to hundreds in realistic contemporary applications that drive high performance computing (e.g., detailed kinetics models of hydrocarbon-air combustion). In the applications expressed as PDEs that motivate this work, the number of components is related to the number of fields defined over the domain. The blocks are square because each field (e.g., density, pressure, momentum, internal energy, concentration of a given species in a given phase in a given charge state) has its own conservation equation.

If the conservation equations were decoupled, all blocks would be diagonal and the data structures designed for this paper would not be relevant for high performance. However, most systems of conservation laws (see Eq. 1) couple the fields defined at each point through possibly several types of physical interdependencies.

$$\frac{\partial(\rho\phi_k)}{\partial t} + \nabla\cdot(\rho\mathbf{v}\phi_k) - \nabla\cdot(\mu_k\nabla\phi_k) = F_k(\phi_1, \phi_2, \cdots, \phi_K), \quad k = 1, 2, \cdots, K. \quad (1)$$

In the typical convection-diffusion-reaction system shown, the convection terms couple the momenta to all convected components. The momenta are products of density (ρ) and velocities ($\mathbf{v}$), and the density is a function of the mass fractions and thermodynamic state of all of the species ($\phi_1, \phi_2, \cdots, \phi_K$) in the system. The gradient operator acting on the density couples degrees of freedom across the grid points in the stencil, so the typical off-diagonal component of the off-diagonal blocks is nonzero. The diffusion terms couple the degrees of freedom to each other because the diffusion coefficients (μ_k) are also complex functions of the mass fractions and thermodynamic state at each point. Again, the gradient operator couples the degrees of freedom across the grid points in the stencil, so that the off-diagonal blocks are best regarded as fully dense. The structure of the reaction terms for the creation and consumption of each component (F_k) may lead to some exploitable sparsity within the diagonal blocks since not all components react with all others. However, the diagonal blocks are often factored as part of a block preconditioner to pre-scale the system and the blocks are best regarded as full in this case.

Equation 1 is a simplified schema of systems described by first principles in, e.g., [8] for porous media applications or [21] for reacting flows. In turn, such systems may be regarded as embedded in multiphysics applications for which computational modelers increasingly prefer fully implicit solvers [13] for reasons of numerical efficiency, stability, and/or robustness. Past generations of modelers lacking powerful high performance solvers have tended to employ operator splitting to solve such systems in a series of steps that leave behind first-order temporal splitting errors and potentially destabilizing mechanisms. Splitting also weakens temporal locality and arithmetic intensity. Contemporary high performance solver software allows such users to more fully exploit the inexpensive flops of a GPU and reduce expensive memory thrashing.

4   A Uniform Design Strategy for SpMV

We propose a uniform design
strategy for the SpMV kernel
based on the BSR format. Such
strategy builds on the same
design ideas used in the KBLAS
library [1,2].

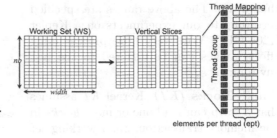

Fig. 2. Hierarchical register blocking.

**Hierarchical Register Block-
ing.** Using the BSR format, the
matrix is naturally described
using square dense *blocks* of
size $bs \times bs$, with no padding
assumed. We define the term *working set* to denote the minimum amount of
work assigned to a thread block (TB) at one time. A working set is generally
different from a *block*. A working set can be equivalent to: (1) one block, (2)
multiple adjacent blocks in the same block row, or (3) part of a block. The block
size bs drives how a working set is defined. A working set should always fit into
registers. Its dimensions are assumed to be $nb \times width$, where nb and $width$ are
two design parameters. A working set is always processed using a *thread array*.
In general, a TB consists of N_{ta} thread arrays ($N_{ta} \geq 1$). This allows a TB to
process multiple working sets concurrently. Each thread array is restructured
to $nb \times N_{tg}$ threads, where every nb threads are called a *thread group* (nb can
be any value, not necessarily a warp). A working set is further subdivided into
vertical slices. Each vertical slice is assigned to one thread group. A vertical slice
is further subdivided horizontally among threads in a thread group. As shown in
Fig. 2, each thread needs ept registers to store a segment of a row of the matrix.
The $width$ is equal to $N_{tg} \times ept$.

Double Buffering. The proposed strategy incorporates a double buffering
scheme in order to hide memory latency and overlap computation with data
prefetching. Each TB requires a storage large enough to fit at least two working
sets. Considering Fig. 2, each thread needs two independent buffers, each one is
ept in length.

5   High Performance Kernel Implementations

This section discusses how the aforementioned design ideas can be applied for
the SpMV kernel.

Dividing Block Size Range. We propose three kernels to divide the spectrum
of the block size. All kernels are available through the KSPARSE library[1]. Kernel
K1 can process small values of bs, strictly 2 through 5. Kernel *K2* is applicable
to medium *blocks* starting from 5 up to 45. Kernel *K3* is assigned for large *blocks*
starting from 45 and beyond.

---

[1] http://ecrc.kaust.edu.sa/Pages/ksparse.aspx.

These ranges are not strict, except for $K1$, which cannot be applied to blocks larger than 5×5. The above ranges are specified according to our experiments on a Kepler K20c GPU. With very little programming effort, ranges can be adapted to the test environment.

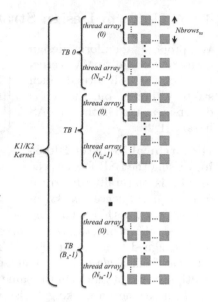

Small Blocks (K1). Kernel $K1$ assumes that a warp can read one or more *blocks* in one memory transaction. So, a working set spans multiple adjacent blocks in a block row. So $nb = bs$, but *width* is multiples of bs. Figure 3 shows the hierarchy of the overall kernel design, where thread arrays are strictly warps. Each warp is truncated to be fully divisible by bs^2, then restructured to $nb \times N_{tg}$ threads, where $N_{tg} = \lfloor \frac{32}{bs^2} \rfloor \times bs$. This restricts *ept* to be 1. A truncated warp can process $Nbrows_{ta}$ consecutive block rows

Fig. 3. $K1/K2$ structure.

($Nbrows_{ta} \geq 1$). If, for example, $bs = 3$, then a warp is truncated into 27 threads, that read 3 blocks at one memory transaction.

Medium Blocks (K2). The design of $K2$ is similar to $K1$ (Fig. 3), except that thread arrays are not strictly warps. $K2$ assumes that a working set is always equivalent to one block. This implies $nb = width = bs$. The value N_{tg} is in a tuning parameter $\leq nb$. Since $width = bs$, it is not always possible to subdivide the working set into vertical slices of the same width (e.g. consider $bs = 17$). Given a block size bs, and a number of thread groups $N_{tg} \leq bs$, we define, (1) $ept_{max} = \lceil \frac{bs}{N_{tg}} \rceil$, and (2) $threshold = (N_{tg} - (bs \mod N_{tg})) \mod N_{tg}$. To hold one block in registers, every thread needs at maximum ept_{max} registers. However, threads in thread groups $< threshold$ use only $ept_{max} - 1$ registers. This amount is different from the total register usage, which is decided solely by the compiler.

Large Blocks (K3). Since $K3$ targets very large blocks, each block can be subdivided into multiple working sets. Therefore, $K3$ uses multiple TBs to process a block. The dimensions of the working set are exposed as tuning parameters. Each group of $\lceil \frac{bs}{nb} \rceil$ TBs behave like a mini-grid of a dense GEMV kernel around every matrix block. Figure 4 shows the structure of the $K3$ grid. The next section presents the performance results of the proposed SpMV kernels.

6   Performance Results and Analysis

We denote an SpMV operation using the BSR format as BSRMV. The performance of KSPARSE is compared against the NVIDIA BSRMV kernel available in cuSPARSE. We also compare against the NVIDIA HYB format [7], and the SELL-P format [3] (which is based

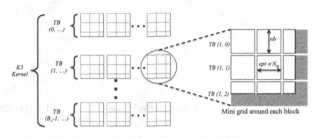

Fig. 4. *K3* structure.

on the SELL-C-σ format [15]). The two latter formats are known for their high performance and friendliness to GPU architectures. We consider only real matrices. Performance is shown for double precision. However, we emphasize that the same performance behavior, including speedups and achieved memory bandwidth, holds also for single precision. The online version of KSPARSE supports both single and double precisions.

System Setup. The performance test experiments are conducted on a system with 16-core Intel Xeon CPU E5-2650 (2.00 GHz) and four Tesla K20c GPU (ECC off). The system runs Ubuntu 14.04.1 LTS, CUDA driver version 340.32, and CUDA Toolkit 5.5. Through a set of bandwidth micro-benchmarks, the sustained memory performance is measured at 184.18 GB/s. This is 88.5 % from the theoretical memory bandwidth (208 GB/s). Results are properly averaged among multiple runs.

Matrix Test Suite. We use synthetically generated matrices using a matrix generator that produces two extreme cases for matrices with dense block substructure. The first is a structured matrix that has exactly seven block diagonals, which is typical for matrices arising from 3D scalar structured-grid problems from low-order finite differences. The second matrix type has a nonzero block main diagonal and otherwise random column placements of the remaining nonzero blocks per row. The number of non-zero blocks per block row is randomly generated between two input values to the generator. Sparsity is kept at least at 99.9 %. The number of rows/columns of the matrix is at least 1M, with at least 99.9 % sparsity. Figure 5 shows spy plots for sample structured and random matrices produced from our matrix generator. PDE applications on grids arising from low-order local discretizations of control volume or finite element type, unstructured by virtue of irregular domain geometry or adaptive refinement, lie between the structured and random cases. They tend to have superior regularity in the number of blocks per row and superior spatial locality relative to the random matrices. For space considerations, they are not considered herein.

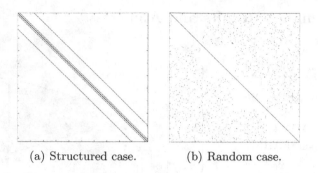

(a) Structured case.   (b) Random case.

Fig. 5. Spy plots for sample structured/random matrices.

Single GPU Performance. The single GPU performance is shown in Fig. 6. For structured matrices, the cuSPARSE-HYB and SELL-P kernels can exploit the structure and match or outperform KSPARSE for relatively small block sizes. As the block sizes gets bigger, KSPARSE can achieve up to 42 % and 49 % speedups against cuSPARSE-HYB and SELL-P respectively. Against cuSPARSE-BSR, and starting block sizes 6 and up, KSPARSE is between 1.34 × to 4.11 × faster. For the random case tests, KSPARSE outperform all other kernels in most cases, achieving speedups up to 2.15 ×, 1.52 ×, and 4.08 × against cuSPARSE-HYB, SELL-P, and cuSPARSE-BSR respectively. We note that the cuSPARSE-HYB kernel fails to run for some tests, where its memory footprint exceeds the GPU memory. **Multi-GPU Scaling.** A multi-GPU BSRMV can be broken down into individual calls to the single GPU BSRMV kernel, provided that matrix distribution among GPUs allows the local sparse submatrix to be individually described using the BSR format. As an example, we present the multi-GPU scaling when block rows and their respective column indices are assigned in a 1D cyclic manner among GPUs. The integer array that holds row pointers has to be reevaluated for each GPU. After building the local row pointer array, it is straightforward to launch a BSRMV kernel on each GPU. Figure 7 shows the double precision performance of KSPARSE for 1, 2, and 4 GPUs on the same node. The figure shows an almost linearly scaling performance. The only overhead of using multi-GPUs is a synchronization point to ensure that all GPUs are finished.

7   Impact on Sparse Iterative Solver

This section presents the impact of using KSPARSE on a sparse iterative solver based on GMRES [19]. The purpose of this part is to show the speedup achieved by using KSPARSE instead of cuSPARSE when calling the SpMV kernel based on the BSR format. Solver-related issues like implementation quality, convergence rate, and others are beyond the scope of this work. We use CUSP [6] as

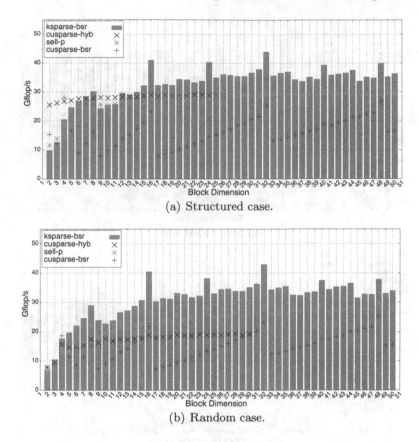

(a) Structured case.

(b) Random case.

Fig. 6. Single GPU performance.

the library implementing GMRES. This is an open-source C++ library that provides a high level template implementation of sparse linear solvers. CUSP is used by PETSc [5] within its GPU component [17]. We use an example implementation of GMRES from CUSP that uses a single GPU. We have added support for the BSR format inside CUSP. We show the GMRES execution time for a non-preconditioned system with at least a million unknowns. The solver stops at a residual norm of 10^{-5} or after reaching 1000 iterations. The solver is also set to restart every 50 iterations. We use synthetically generated structured matrices similar to Fig. 5(a). Figure 8 shows the execution time of GMRES. As expected from the SpMV performance, cuSPARSE achieves better execution time for GMRES using block sizes 2 and 4, achieving speedups up to 12 %. For block size 3, the KSPARSE-based solver almost matches its cuSPARSE counterpart. For block sizes 5 and up, the KSPARSE-based GMRES achieves speedups ranging 1.14 × to 2.62 ×, depending on the performance of the BSRMV kernel given a particular block size.

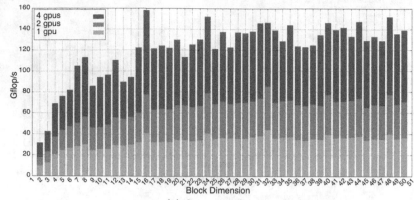

(a) Structured case.

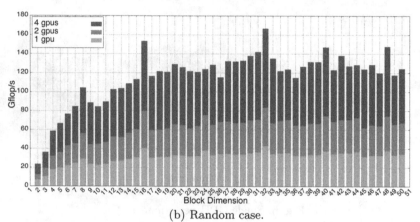

(b) Random case.

Fig. 7. Multi-GPU performance.

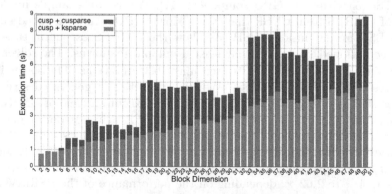

Fig. 8. Execution time of CUSP-GMRES.

8   Conclusion and Future Work

We have designed an SpMV kernel (part of the KSPARSE library) for solving large sparse structured or unstructured linear systems, in the context of applications that feature multi-component models, typified by contemporary porous media simulations, resulting in dense block Jacobian structure. Using a uniform design strategy based on hierarchical register blocking and double buffering optimization techniques, the new SpMV kernel outperforms existing state-of-the-art implementations on GPUs by achieving significant speedups using matrices with large dense block structure from applications with structured and unstructured multi-component grids. The proposed multi-GPU SpMV interface highlights an almost linearly scaling performance. Integrating our KSPARSE SpMV kernel into a sparse iterative solver library improves the overall performance up to 2.62 × speedup, as the block size increases. We plan to investigate the implementation of KSPARSE on distributed memory environments and to study the impact of high network interconnect linking remote GPUs on the overall iterative solver.

Acknowledgment. The support of Saudi Aramco through research project RGC/3/1438 is gratefully acknowledged. The authors would like also to thank NVIDIA for their support and generous hardware donations as well as Pascal Hénon from TOTAL S.A. for fruitful technical discussions.

References

1. KAUST BLAS. http://ecrc.kaust.edu.sa/Pages/Res-kblas.aspx
2. Abdelfattah, A., Keyes, D., Ltaief, H.: KBLAS: an optimized library for dense matrix-vector multiplication on GPU accelerators. ACM Trans. Math. Softw. (accepted subject to revision) (2014). http://arxiv.org/abs/1410.1726
3. Antz, H., Tomov, S., Dongarra, J.: Implementing a Sparse Matrix Vector Product for the SELL-C/SELL-C-σ formats on NVIDIA GPUs. Technical report (2014). http://www.icl.utk.edu/sites/icl/files/publications/2014/icl-utk-772-2014.pdf
4. Ashari, A., Sedaghati, N., Eisenlohr, J., Parthasarathy, S., Sadayappan, P.: Fast sparse matrix-vector multiplication on GPUs for graph applications. In: Proceedings of the International Conference for High Performance Computing, Networking, Storage and Analysis, SC 2014, pp. 781–792 (2014). http://dx.doi.org/10.1109/SC.2014.69
5. Balay, S., Abhyankar, S., Adams, M.F., Brown, J., Brune, P., Buschelman, K., Eijkhout, V., Gropp, W.D., Kaushik, D., Knepley, M.G., McInnes, L.C., Rupp, K., Smith, B.F., Zhang, H.: PETSc Web page (2014). http://www.mcs.anl.gov/petsc
6. Bell, N., Garland, M.: CUSP: Generic Parallel Algorithms for Sparse Matrix and Graph Computations. http://cusplibrary.github.io/
7. Bell, N., Garland, M.: Implementing sparse matrix-vector multiplication on throughput-oriented processors. In: Proceedings of the Conference on High Performance Computing Networking, Storage and Analysis, SC 2009, pp. 18:1–18:11. ACM, New York (2009). http://doi.acm.org/10.1145/1654059.1654078
8. Chen, Z., Huan, G., Ma, Y.: Computational Methods for Multiphase Flows in Porous Media. Society for Industrial and Applied Mathematics, Philadelphia (2006)

9. Choi, J.W., Singh, A., Vuduc, R.W.: Model-driven autotuning of sparse matrix-vector multiply on GPUs. In: Proceedings of the 15th ACM SIGPLAN Symposium on Principles and Practice of Parallel Programming, PPoPP 2010, pp. 115–126. ACM, New York (2010). http://doi.acm.org/10.1145/1693453.1693471

10. Godwin, J., Holewinski, J., Sadayappan, P.: High-performance sparse matrix-vector multiplication on GPUs for structured grid computations. In: Proceedings of the 5th Annual Workshop on General Purpose Processing with Graphics Processing Units, GPGPU-5, pp. 47–56. ACM, New York (2012). http://doi.acm.org/10.1145/2159430.2159436

11. Im, E.-J., Yelick, K.A.: Optimizing sparse matrix computations for register reuse in SPARSITY. In: Alexandrov, V.N., Dongarra, J., Juliano, B.A., Renner, R.S., Tan, C.J.K. (eds.) ICCS-ComputSci 2001. LNCS, vol. 2073, pp. 127–136. Springer, Heidelberg (2001). http://dx.doi.org/10.1007/3-540-45545-0_22

12. Im, E.J., Yelick, K., Vuduc, R.: Sparsity: optimization framework for sparse matrix kernels. Int. J. High Perform. Comput. Appl. **18**(1), 135–158 (2004). http://dx.doi.org/10.1177/1094342004041296

13. Keyes, D.E., McInnes, L.C., Woodward, C., Gropp, W.D., Myra, E., Pernice, M., Bell, J., Brown, J., Clo, A., Connors, J., Constantinescu, E., Estep, D., Evans, K., Farhat, C., Hakim, A., Hammond, G., Hansen, G., Hill, J., Isaac, T., Jiao, X., Jordan, K., Kaushik, D., Kaxiras, E., Koniges, A., Lee, K., Lott, A., Lu, Q., Magerlein, J., Maxwell, R., McCourt, M., Mehl, M., Pawlowski, R., Peters, A., Reynolds, D., Riviere, B., Rüde, U., Scheibe, T., Shadid, J., Sheehan, B., Shephard, M., Siegel, A., Smith, B., Tang, X., Wilson, C., Wohlmuth, B.: Multiphysics simulations: challenges and opportunities. Int. J. High Perform. Comput. Appl. **27**, 4–83 (2013)

14. Kincaid, D., Oppe, T., Young, D.: ITPACKV 2D User's Guide (1989). http://www.ma.utexas.edu/CNA/ITPACK/manuals/userv2d/

15. Kreutzer, M., Hager, G., Wellein, G., Fehske, H., Bishop, A.: A unified sparse matrix data format for efficient general sparse matrix-vector multiplication on modern processors with wide SIMD units. SIAM J. Sci. Comput. **36**(5), C401–C423 (2014). http://dx.doi.org/10.1137/130930352

16. Kreutzer, M., Hager, G., Wellein, G., Fehske, H., Basermann, A., Bishop, A.R.: Sparse matrix-vector multiplication on GPGPU clusters: a new storage format and a scalable implementation. In: Proceedings of the 2012 IEEE 26th International Parallel and Distributed Processing Symposium Workshops, IPDPSW 2012, pp. 1696–1702. IEEE Computer Society, Washington, DC (2012). http://dx.doi.org/10.1109/IPDPSW.2012.211

17. Minden, V., Smith, B., Knepley, M.: Preliminary implementation of petsc using gpus. In: Proceedings of the 2010 International Workshop of GPU Solutions to Multiscale Problems in Science and Engineering (2010)

18. Monakov, A., Lokhmotov, A., Avetisyan, A.: Automatically tuning sparse matrix-vector multiplication for GPU architectures. In: Patt, Y.N., Foglia, P., Duesterwald, E., Faraboschi, P., Martorell, X. (eds.) HiPEAC 2010. LNCS, vol. 5952, pp. 111–125. Springer, Heidelberg (2010). http://dx.doi.org/10.1007/978-3-642-11515-8_10

19. Saad, Y., Schultz, M.: GMRES: a generalized minimal residual algorithm for solving nonsymmetric linear systems. SIAM J. Sci. Stat. Comput. **7**(3), 856–869 (1986). http://dx.doi.org/10.1137/0907058

20. Vázquez, F., Fernández, J.J., Garzón, E.M.: A new approach for sparse matrix vector product on NVIDIA GPUs. Concurrency Comput. Pract. Experience **23**(8), 815–826 (2011). http://dx.doi.org/10.1002/cpe.1658

21. Williams, F.A.: Combustion Theory. Benjamin/Cummings, Menlo Park (1985)

Accelerating Lattice Boltzmann Applications with OpenACC

Enrico Calore[1], Jiri Kraus[2], Sebastiano Fabio Schifano[3]([✉]),
and Raffaele Tripiccione[1]

[1] Dip. di Fisica e Scienze Della Terra, Univ. di Ferrara and INFN, Ferrara, Italy
{calore,tripiccione}@fe.infn.it
[2] NVIDIA GmbH, Würselen, Germany
jkraus@nvidia.com
[3] Dip. di Matematica e Informatica, Univ. di Ferrara and INFN, Ferrara, Italy
schifano@fe.infn.it

Abstract. An increasingly large number of HPC systems rely on heterogeneous architectures combining traditional multi-core CPUs with
power efficient accelerators. Designing efficient applications for these systems has been troublesome in the past as accelerators could usually
be programmed only using specific programming languages – such as
CUDA – threatening maintainability, portability and correctness. Several
new programming environments try to tackle this problem; among them
OpenACC offers a high-level approach based on directives. In OpenACC,
one annotates existing C, C++ or Fortran codes with compiler *directive*
clauses to mark program regions to offload and run on accelerators and
to identify available parallelism. This approach directly addresses code
portability, leaving to compilers the support of each different accelerator,
but one has to carefully assess the relative costs of potentially portable
approach versus computing efficiency. In this paper we address precisely
this issue, using as a test-bench a massively parallel Lattice Boltzmann
code. We implement and optimize this multi-node code using OpenACC
and OpenMPI. We also compare performance with that of the same
algorithm written in CUDA, OpenCL and C for GPUs, Xeon-Phi and
traditional multi-core CPUs, and characterize through an accurate time
model its scaling behavior on a large cluster of GPUs.

Keywords: OpenACC · OpenMPI · Lattice Boltzmann methods ·
Accelerator computing · Performance analysis

1   Introduction and Background

Lattice Boltzmann (LB) methods are widely used in computational fluid dynamics, to simulate flows in two and three dimensions. From the computational point
of view, LB methods have a large degree of available parallelism so they are suitable for massively parallel systems.

Over the years, LB codes have been written and optimized for large clusters
of commodity CPUs [1], for application-specific machines [2–4] and even for

© Springer-Verlag Berlin Heidelberg 2015
J.L. Träff et al. (Eds.): Euro-Par 2015, LNCS 9233, pp. 613–624, 2015.
DOI: 10.1007/978-3-662-48096-0_47

FPGAs [5]. More recently work has focused on exploiting the parallelism of powerful traditional many-core processors [6], and of power-efficient accelerators such as GPUs [7,8] and Xeon-Phi processors [9].

As diversified HPC architectures emerge, it is becoming more and more important to have robust methodologies to port and maintain codes for several architectures. This need has sparked the development of frameworks, such as the *Open Computing Language* (OpenCL), able to compile codes efficiently for several accelerators. OpenCL is a low level approach: it usually obtains high performances at the price of substantial changes in the code and large human efforts, seriously posing a threat to code correctness and maintainability. Other approaches start to emerge, mainly based on directives: compilers generate offload-functions for accelerators, following "hints" provided by programmers as annotations to the original – C, C++ or Fortran – codes [12]. Examples along this direction are OpenACC [13] and OpenMP4 [14]. Other proposals, such as the Hybrid Multi-core Parallel Programming model (HMPP) proposed by CAPS, hiCUDA [15], OpenMPC [16] and StarSs [17] follow the same line. OpenACC today is considered the most promising approach. In many ways its structure is similar to OpenMP (Open Multi-Processing) [18]: both frameworks are directive based, but while OpenMP is more prescriptive, e.g. one maps work-loads explicitly using distribute constructs, OpenACC is more descriptive. Indeed, with OpenACC the programmer only specifies that a certain loop should run in parallel on the accelerator and leaves the exact mapping to the compiler. This approach leaves more freedom to the compiler and the associated runtime support, offering in principle more space for performance portability.

So far very few OpenACC implementations of LB codes have been described in literature: [19] focus on accelerating through OpenACC a part of a large CFD application optimized for CPU; several other works describe CUDA [21] or OpenCL [10,11] implementations; also scalability on GPU clusters has been rarely addressed [22]. In this paper we focus on the design and optimization of a multi-GPU LB code analyzing performances between a portable high level approach like OpenACC and lower level approaches like CUDA.

This paper is structured as follows: Sect. 2 gives a short overview of LB methods; Sect. 3 describes in details our OpenACC implementation, and Sect. 4 analyzes performance results and compares with similar codes written in CUDA, OpenCL and C for GPUs, Xeon-Phi accelerators and traditional multi-core CPUs.

2   Lattice Boltzmann Models

Lattice Boltzmann methods (LB) are widely used in computational fluid dynamics, to describe flows in two and three dimensions. LB methods [23] are discrete in position and momentum spaces; they are based on the synthetic dynamics of *populations* sitting at the sites of a discrete lattice. At each time step, populations hop from lattice-site to lattice-site and then incoming populations *collide* among one another, that is, they mix and their values change accordingly. Over the years, many different LB models have been devised, in 2 and 3 dimensions with different degrees of accuracy [24]. LB models in n dimensions with y populations are labeled as $DnQy$; in this paper, we consider a state-of-the-art $D2Q37$ model that correctly reproduces the thermo-hydrodynamical equations of motion of a fluid in two dimensions and automatically enforces the equation of state of a perfect gas ($p = \rho T$) [25, 26]; this model has been extensively used for large scale simulations of convective turbulence (see e.g., [27–29]).

From a computational point of view this physically very accurate LB scheme is more complex than simpler LB models; this translates into higher requirements in terms of storage (each lattice points has 37 populations), memory bandwidth and floating-point throughput (at each time step, ≈ 7600 double-precision floating point operations are performed per lattice point).

Populations ($f_l(\boldsymbol{x}, t)\ l = 1 \cdots 37$) are defined at the sites of a discrete and regular 2-D lattice; each $f_l(\boldsymbol{x}, t)$ has a given lattice velocity c_l; populations evolve in (discrete) time according to the following equation:

$$f_l(\boldsymbol{x}, t + \Delta t) = f_l(\boldsymbol{x} - \boldsymbol{c}_l \Delta t, t) - \frac{\Delta t}{\tau} \left(f_l(\boldsymbol{x} - \boldsymbol{c}_l \Delta t, t) - f_l^{(eq)} \right) \tag{1}$$

Macroscopic quantities, density ρ, velocity $\boldsymbol{u}$ and temperature T are defined in terms of the $f_l(x, t)$ and of the c_ls (D is the number of space dimensions):

$$\rho = \sum_l f_l, \quad \rho \boldsymbol{u} = \sum_l \boldsymbol{c}_l f_l, \quad D \rho T = \sum_l |\boldsymbol{c}_l - \boldsymbol{u}|^2 f_l; \tag{2}$$

the equilibrium distributions ($f_l^{(eq)}$) are known function of these macroscopic quantities [23], and τ is a suitably chosen relaxation time. In words, (1) stipulates that populations drift from lattice site to lattice site according to the value of their velocities (*propagation*) and, on arrival at point $\boldsymbol{x}$, they interact among one another and their values change accordingly (*collision*). One can show that, in suitable limiting cases and after appropriate renormalizations are applied, the evolution of the macroscopic variables defined in (2) obey the thermo-hydrodynamical equations of motion of the fluid.

An LB code takes an initial assignment of the populations, in accordance with a given initial condition at $t = 0$ on some spatial domain, and iterates (1) for all points in the domain and for as many time-steps as needed; boundary-conditions at the edges of the integration domain are enforced at each time-step by appropriately modifying population values at and close to the boundaries.

The LB approach offers a huge degree of easily identified parallelism. Indeed, (1) shows that the *propagation* step amounts to gathering the values of the fields f_l from neighboring sites, corresponding to populations drifting towards $\boldsymbol{x}$ with velocity c_l; the following step (*collision*) then performs all mathematical processing needed to compute the quantities in the r.h.s. of (1), for each point in the grid. One sees immediately from (1), that both steps above are fully uncorrelated for different points of the grid, so they can be executed in parallel according to any schedule, as long as step 1 precedes step 2 for all lattice points.

In practice, an LB code executes a loop over time steps, and at each iterations applies three kernels: `propagate`, `bc` and `collide`.

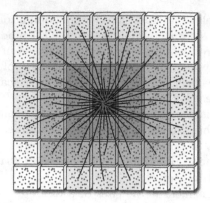 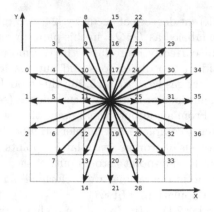

Fig. 1. Left: LB populations in the D2Q37 model, hopping to nearby sites during the **propagate** phase. Right: populations f_l are identified by an arbitrary label; for each l population data is stored contiguously in memory.

propagate moves populations across lattice sites according to the pattern of Fig. 1, collecting at each site all populations that will interact at the next phase (**collide**). In our model populations move up to three lattice sites per time step. Computer-wise, **propagate** moves blocks of memory locations allocated at sparse addresses, corresponding to populations of neighbor cells.

bc executes *after* propagation and adjusts populations at the edges of the lattice, enforcing appropriate boundary conditions (e.g., constant temperature and zero velocity at the top and bottom edges of the lattice). For the left and right edges, we usually apply periodic boundary conditions. This is conveniently done by adding *halo* columns at the edges of the lattice, where we copy the rightmost and leftmost columns (3 in our case) of the lattice before starting the **propagate** step. After this is done, points close to the boundaries are processed as those in the bulk.

collide performs all mathematical steps needed to compute the population values at each lattice site at the new time step, as per (1). Input data for this phase are the populations gathered by the previous **propagate** phase. This step is the most floating point intensive part of the code.

3   Implementation and Optimization of the D2Q37 Model

Our implementation uses CUDA-aware MPI and start one MPI rank per GPU to have GPU-to-GPU transfers transparently handled by the MPI library. The lattice is copied on the accelerator memory at the beginning of the loop over time-steps, and then all three kernels – **propagate**, **bc** and **collide** – run on the accelerator. Data is stored in memory in the Structure-of-Array (SoA) format scheme, where arrays of all populations are stored one after the other. This helps exploit data-parallelism and enables data-coalescing when accessing data needed by work-items executing in parallel. On each MPI-rank the physical lattice is

```
// processing of bulk
propagateBulk( f2, f1 ); // async execution on queue (1)
bcBulk( f2, f1 );        // async execution on queue (1)
collideInBulk( f2, f1 ); // async execution on queue (1)
// execution of pbc step
#pragma acc host_data use_device(f2) {
  for ( pp = 0; pp < 37; pp++ ) {
    MPI_Sendrecv ( &(f2[...]) , 3*NY, ... );
    MPI_Sendrecv ( &(f2[...]) , 3*NY, ... );
  } }
// processing of the three leftmost columns
propagateL( f2, f1 );    // async execution on queue (2)
bcL( f2, f1 );           // async execution on queue (2)
collideL( f1, f2 );      // async execution on queue (2)
// processing of the three rightmost columns
propagateR( f2, f1 );    // async execution on queue (3)
bcR( f2, f1 );           // async execution on queue (3)
collideR( f1, f2 );      // async execution on queue (3)
```

Fig. 2. Scheduling of operations started by the host at each time step. Kernels processing the lattice bulk run asynchronously on the accelerator, and overlap with MPI communications executed by the host.

surrounded by halo columns and rows: for a physical lattice of size $L_x \times L_y$, we allocate $NX \times NY$ points, with $NX = H_x + L_x + H_x$ and $NY = H_y + L_y + H_y$.

We split our 2-D physical lattice of size $L_x \times L_y$ on N accelerators along the X dimension; GPUs are connected in a ring-scheme and each one hosts a sub-lattice of $L_x/N \times L_y$ points. With this splitting, halo-columns are allocated at successive memory locations, so we do not need to gather halo data on contiguous buffers before communication. At the beginning of each time-step left- and right-halos are updated: we copy population data coming from the three adjoining physical columns of the neighbor nodes in the ring to the left and right *halos*. This is done by an MPI node-to-node communication step that we call *periodic boundary condition* (**pbc**). Once this is done, all remaining steps are local to each MPI-rank so they run in parallel.

At each iteration of the loop over time steps, each MPI-rank first update its halo columns using **pbc()**, and then runs in sequence **propagate()**, **bc()** and **collide()** on its local lattice.

As lattice data is stored in the SoA format, **pbc** exchanges 37 buffers, each of 3 columns, with its left and right neighbors. It executes a loop over the 37 populations and each iteration performs two MPI send-receive operations, respectively for the left and the right halo (see Fig. 2). On GPUs, we exploit *CUDA-aware* MPI features, available in the OpenMPI library and use data pointers referencing GPU-memory buffers as source and destination, making the code more compact and readable. In OpenACC this is controlled by the **#pragma acc host_data use_device(p)** clause, that maps a GPU memory pointer p into

```
inline void propagate (
  const data_t* restrict prv, data_t* restrict nxt ) {
  int ix, iy, site_i;
#pragma acc kernels present(prv) present(nxt)
#pragma acc loop gang independent
  for ( ix=HX; ix < (HX+SIZEX); ix++) {
#pragma acc loop vector independent
    for ( iy=HY; iy<(HY+SIZEY); iy++) {
      site_i = (ix*NY) + iy;
      nxt [       site_i] = prv [       site_i -3*NY +1];
      nxt [NX*NY+site_i] = prv [NX*NY+site_i -3*NY   ];
      ....
} } }
```

Fig. 3. OpenACC pragmas in the body of the `propagate()` function; pragmas before the loops instruct the compiler to generate corresponding accelerator kernel and configure the grid of threads and blocks.

host space, so it can be used as an argument of the MPI send and receive functions. Also, communications between GPUs are optimized in the library and implemented according to physical location of buffers and the capabilities of the devices involved, also enabling *peer-to-peer* and *GPUDirect RDMA* features. Figure 3 shows the code of the *propagate* function. For each lattice site we update the values of the populations, copying from the `prv` array onto the `nxt` array. The body of *propagate* is annotated with several OpenACC directives telling the compiler how to organize the kernel on the accelerator. `#pragma acc kernels present(prv) present(nxt)` tells the compiler to run the following instructions on the accelerator; it also carries the information that the `prv` and `nxt` arrays are already available on the accelerator memory, so no host-accelerator data transfer is needed; `#pragma acc loop gang independent` states that each iteration of the following loop (over the X-dimension) can be run by different gangs or block of threads; `#pragma acc loop vector independent` tells the compiler that iterations of the loop over Y-dimension can likewise be run as independent vectors of threads. Using these directives the compiler structures the thread-blocks and block-grids of the accelerator computation such that: one thread is associated to and processes one lattice-site; each thread-block processes a group of lattice sites lying along the Y-direction, and several blocks process sites along the X-direction. This allows to expose all available parallelism.

We split `bc()` in two kernels, processing the upper and lower boundaries. They run in parallel since there is no data dependencies among them. We have not further optimized this step because its computational cost is small compared to the other phases of the code.

The `collide()` kernel sweeps all lattice sites and computes the collisional function. The code has two outer loops over X and Y dimensions of the lattice, and several inner loops to compute temporary values. We have annotated the

Fig. 4. Profiling of one time step. pbc (yellow line marked as "MPI") and the kernels processing the bulk of the lattice (blue line marked as "Bulk") fully overlap (Color figure online).

outer loops as we did for `propagate()`, making each thread to process one lattice site. Inner loops are computed serially by the thread associated to each site.

Performance wise, `pbc()` is the most critical step of the code, since it involves node-to-node communications that can badly affect performance and scaling. We organize the code so node-to-node communications are (fully or partially) overlapped with the execution of other segments of the code. Generally speaking, `propagate`, `bc` and `collide` must execute one after the other, and they cannot start before `pbc` has completed. One easily sees however that this dependency does not apply to all sites of the lattice outside the three leftmost and rightmost border columns (we call this region the *bulk* of the lattice). The obvious conclusion is that processing of the bulk can proceed in parallel with the execution of `pbc`, while the sites on the three leftmost and rightmost columns are processed only after `pbc` has completed. OpenACC abstracts concurrent execution using queues; function definitions flagged by `#pragma acc async(n)` directive enqueue the corresponding kernels *asynchronously* on queue n, leaving the host free to perform other tasks concurrently. In our case, this happens for `propagateBulk`, `bcBulk` and `collideBulk`, which start on queue 1 (see Fig. 2), while the host concurrently executes the MPI transfers of `pbc`. After communications complete, the host starts three more kernels on two different queues (2 and 3) to process the right and left borders, so they can execute in parallel if sufficient resources on the accelerator are available. This structure allows to overlap `pbc` with all other steps of the code, most importantly with `collideBulk`, which is the most time consuming kernel, giving more opportunities to hide communication overheads when running on a large number of nodes.

Figure 4 shows the profiling of one time step on one GPU on a lattice of 1080 × 2048 points split across 24 GPUs. MPI communications started by `pbc` are internal (MemCopy DtoD), moving data between GPUs on the same host, or external (MemCopy DtoH and HtoD) moving data between GPUs on different hosts. The actual scheduling is as expected: both types of GPU-to-GPU communications fully overlap with `propagate`, `bc` and `collide` on the bulk.

4 Results and Conclusions

We start our performance analysis comparing OpenACC code with CUDA, OpenCL and C implementations of the same LB algorithm developed for NVIDIA

Table 1. Performance comparison between single (1CPU) and dual (2CPU) Intel 18-core CPUs (Haswell-v3 micro architecture), NVIDIA K40 GPUs and Intel Xeon-Phi 7120; the lattice size is 1920×2048 points. All quantities are defined in the text.

Code Version	Tesla K40			Xeon-Phi 7120	E5-2699-v3	
	CUDA	OCL	OACC	OCL	1CPU C	2CPU C
$T_{Pbc+Prop}$ [msec]	13.78	15.80	13.91	30.46	120.71	61.40
GB/s	168.91	147.33	167.37	76.42	19.53	37.91
$\mathcal{E}_p$	59 %	51 %	58 %	22 %	29 %	28 %
T_{Bc} [msec]	4.42	6.41	2.76	3.20	1.62	0.80
$T_{Collide}$ [msec]	39.86	136.93	78.65	72.79	136.24	67.95
$\mathcal{E}_c$	45 %	13 %	23 %	34 %	34 %	34 %
T_{WC}/iter [msec]	58.07	159.14	96.57	106.45	259.79	131.88
MLUPS	68	25	41	37	15	30

GPUs, Intel Xeon-Phi and Intel traditional multi-core CPUs. For OpenACC we have used PGI compiler version 14.10, while for GPUs we have used CUDA version 6.5, and for Xeon-Phi and multicore-CPUs the Intel compiler version 14.

We started with an early version for Intel commodity CPUs, using OpenMP to handle parallelism over all available cores (18 in this case) of each CPU, and controlling vectorization via intrinsics functions [30]. We then developed a CUDA version [20,21], optimized for Fermi and Kepler architectures, and an OpenCL version that we have run on NVIDIA and Intel Xeon-Phi accelerators [11,31].

Table 1 summarizes performance figures on a reference lattice of 1920×2048 sites. The first lines refer to the `propagate` kernel; we show the execution time, the effective bandwidth, and the efficiency $\mathcal{E}_p$ computed w.r.t. the peak memory bandwidth; the table then lists execution times of the `bc` function; For the `collide` kernel, we show the execution time and the efficiency $\mathcal{E}_c$ as a fraction of peak performance. Finally, we show the wall-clock execution time (WcT) and the corresponding *Millions Lattice UPdate per Second* (MLUPS) – counting the number of sites handled per second – of the full production-ready code. For `propagate`, which is strongly memory bound, the CUDA and OpenACC versions run at $\approx 60\%$ of peak, while the OpenCL version is 10 % slower. For the `collide` kernel – the most computationally intensive part of the code – the OpenACC code has an efficiency of 23 % while the CUDA version doubles this figure, running at 45 % of peak. The lower performance of the OpenACC code can likely be explained by latency overheads caused by two factors: (i) population values are used several times within the computation of the collide, and repeatedly read from global-memory; (ii) constant values like the coefficients of the Hermite polynomial expansion are stored on global memory. On the other hand the CUDA version [21] is more performing because explicit control with `cudaMemcpyToSymbol` allows to store constant values on low-latency constant-memory; OpenACC is not able to do that due to the large number of terms and their dependencies and then they are computed at run time. CUDA also uses

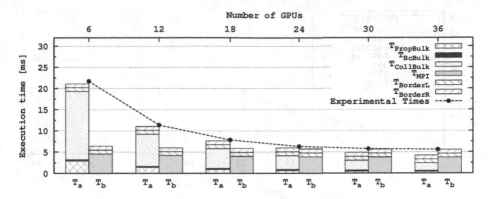

Fig. 5. T_a and T_b for the time model defined in the text on a lattice of 1080×5736 points as a function of the number of GPUs. The black points are the execution times of the code with all asynchronous steps enabled.

registers more efficiently, allowing to fully unroll inner loops, while on OpenACC this has a negative effect. A CUDA version which does not use these two optimizations matches the performance of the OpenACC code.

The OpenCL version is respectively 2X and 3X slower than OpenACC and CUDA. This reflects that the current version of the NVIDIA OpenCL driver does not optimize for the Kepler architecture (it can not exploit features introduced with the Kepler architecture, e.g. the capability to address 255 registers per thread) [11]. Comparing performances of our code across all architectures – CPUs, GPUs and Xeon-Phi accelerators – we see that on GPUs, using CUDA, `collide` runs $\approx 3.5X$ faster than on a single-CPU and $1.7X$ than on a dual-CPU using C, and $\approx 1.8X$ faster than the Xeon-Phi using OpenCL.

We now discuss in details the scaling behaviour of our implementation for a large number of GPUs. We model the execution time of the whole program as $T \approx \max\{T_a, T_b\}$, with T_a and T_b defined as:

$$T_a = T_{\text{bulk}} + T_{\text{borderL}} + T_{\text{borderR}}, \qquad T_b = T_{\text{MPI}} + T_{\text{borderL}} + T_{\text{borderR}}$$

and $T_{\text{bulk}}, T_{\text{borderL}}, T_{\text{borderR}}$ are respectively the sums of the execution times of `propagate`, `bc` and `collide` on the bulk, and on the left and right halos, while T_{MPI} refers to MPI communications.

This model is in good agreement with data measured on an Infiniband-interconnected cluster with 6 GPUs on each node: we first profile the execution time of each kernel and MPI communication running them in sequence, i.e. without any overlap, and then measure the execution time of the whole program with all asynchronous steps enabled. Figure 5 shows the values of T_a and T_b for a lattice of 1080×5736 points. The histograms show the times taken by each part of the code when running serially while the black dots show the time taken by the asynchronous code. For this choice of the lattice size, we see that $T \approx T_a$ up to 24 GPUs as communications are fully hidden behind the execution of the program on the bulk; as long as this condition holds, the code enjoys full

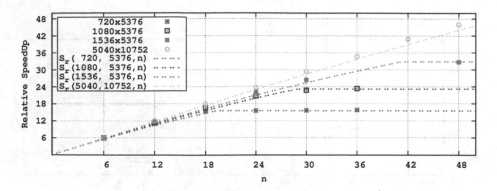

Fig. 6. Strong scaling behavior of the OpenACC code as a function of the number of GPUs (n) for several lattice sizes. Points are experimental data and dashed lines are the predictions of our timing model.

scalability. As we increase the number of GPUs (≥ 30) $T \approx T_b$, communications become the bottleneck and the scaling behavior necessarily degrades.

We further characterize the execution time assuming, to first approximation, that bulk processing is proportional to ($L_x \times L_y$), boundary conditions scale as L_x, and communication and borders processing scales as L_y; so, on n GPUs

$$T(L_x, L_y, n) = \max \left\{ \alpha \frac{L_x}{n} L_y + \beta \frac{L_x}{n}, \quad \gamma L_y \right\} + \delta L_y$$

We extract the parameters (α, β, γ and δ) from the profiling data of Fig. 5, and define the function $S_r(L_x, L_y, n) = \frac{T(L_x, L_y, 1)}{T(L_x, L_y, n)}$ to predict the relative speedup for any number of GPUs and any lattice size. Figure 6 shows the (strong) scaling behaviour of our code for several lattice sizes relevant for physics simulations; dots are measured values and dashed lines are plots of $S_r()$ for different values of L_x and L_y. Values of $S_r()$ are in good agreement with experimental data, and predict the number of GPUs for which the code does not scale any more. For large lattices (5040×10752) the code has an excellent scaling behavior up to 48 GPUs, slightly underestimated by our model as constants are calibrated on smaller lattices and then more sensitive to overheads.

In conclusion, we have successfully ported, tested and benchmarked a complete lattice Boltzmann code using OpenACC, and characterized its performances through an accurate time model. Our experience with OpenACC is very positive from the point of view of porting and programmability. The effort to port existing codes to OpenACC is reasonably limited and easy to handle; we started from an existing C version and marked through *pragmas* regions of code to offload and run on accelerators instructing the compiler to identify and exploit available parallelism. However, major changes in the structure of the code cannot be handled by compilers, so the overall organization must be (at least partially) aware of the target architectures; for example, in our case it is crucial to organize data as *Structure of Arrays* to allow to coalesce performance-critical memory accesses.

Concerning performance results, one is ready to accept that the use of a high level programming model trades better programmability with computing efficiency: we consider a performance drop of $\leq 20\%$ a satisfactory result. While the performance is not as good as we would like, we understand the reasons behind this gap and expect that compiler improvements will be able to narrow it. We believe that our analysis provides important feedbacks to help improve the performance of OpenACC. As an interim step, interoperability between OpenACC and CUDA allows to foster the high productivity of OpenACC and still get full performance by using CUDA for the most performance critical kernels.

Acknowledgements. This work was done in the framework of the COKA and Suma projects of INFN. We thank INFN-Pisa (Pisa, Italy), and the NVIDIA Jülich Application Lab (Jülich Supercomputer Center, Germany) for allowing us to use their computing systems.

References

1. Pohl, T., et al.: Performance evaluation of parallel large-scale lattice boltzmann applications on three supercomputing architectures. In: Proceedings of the Conference on Supercomputing (2004). doi:10.1109/SC.2004.37
2. Belletti, F., et al.: Multiphase lattice boltzmann on the cell broadband engine. Nuovo Cimento Soc. Ital. Fis., C **32**(2), 53–56 (2009). doi:10.1393/ncc/i2009-10379-6
3. Biferale, L., et al.: Lattice boltzmann fluid-dynamics on the QPACE supercomputer. Proc. Comp. Sci. **1**, 1075–1082 (2010). doi:10.1016/j.procs.2010.04.119
4. Pivanti, M., Mantovani, F., Schifano, S.F., Tripiccione, R., Zenesini, L.: An optimized lattice boltzmann code for bluegene/q. In: Wyrzykowski, R., Dongarra, J., Karczewski, K., Waśniewski, J. (eds.) PPAM 2013, Part II. LNCS, vol. 8385, pp. 385–394. Springer, Heidelberg (2014)
5. Sano, K., et al.: FPGA-based streaming computation for lattice boltzmann method. In: Proceedings of Field-Programmable Technology, pp. 233–236 (2007). doi:10.1109/FPT.2007.4439254
6. Biferale, L., et al.: Optimization of multi-phase compressible lattice boltzmann codes on massively parallel multi-core systems. Proc. Comp. Sci. **4**, 994–1003 (2011). doi:10.1016/j.procs.2011.04.105
7. Biferale, L., et al.: A multi-GPU implementation of a D2Q37 lattice boltzmann code. In: Wyrzykowski, R., Dongarra, J., Karczewski, K., Waśniewski, J. (eds.) PPAM 2011, Part I. LNCS, vol. 7203, pp. 640–650. Springer, Heidelberg (2012)
8. Bailey, P., et al.: Accelerating lattice Boltzmann fluid flow simulations using graphics processors. In: Proceedings of Parallel Processing, pp. 550–557 (2009). doi:10.1109/ICPP.2009.38
9. Crimi, G., et al.: Early experience on porting and running a lattice boltzmann code on the Xeon-phi co-processor. Proc. Comp. Sci. **18**, 551–560 (2013). doi:10.1016/j.procs.2013.05.219
10. McIntosh-Smith, S.N., Curran, D.: Evaluation of a performance portable lattice Boltzmann code using OpenCL. In: International Workshop on OpenCL (2014)
11. Calore, E., et al.: A portable OpenCL lattice boltzmann code for multi-and many-core processor architectures. Proc. Comp. Sci. **29**, 40–49 (2014). doi:10.1016/j.procs.2014.05.004

12. Wienke, S., Springer, P., Terboven, C., an Mey, D.: OpenACC — first experiences with real-world applications. In: Kaklamanis, C., Papatheodorou, T., Spirakis, P.G. (eds.) Euro-Par 2012. LNCS, vol. 7484, pp. 859–870. Springer, Heidelberg (2012)

13. OpenMP. http://www.openmp.org/mp-documents/OpenMP4.0.0.pdf

14. OpenACC directives for accelerators. http://www.openacc-standard.org/

15. Han, T., Abdelrahman, T.: hiCUDA: high-level GPGPU programming. IEEE Trans. Par. Distr. Syst. **22**(1), 78–90 (2011). doi:10.1109/TPDS.2010.62

16. Lee, S., Eigenmann, R.: OpenMPC: extended OpenMP programming and tuning for GPUs. In: Proceedings of SC, pp. 1–11 (2010). doi:10.1109/SC.2010.36

17. Ayguadé, E., et al.: Extending OpenMP to survive the heterogeneous multi-core era. Int. J. Parallel Prog. **38**(5–6), 440–459 (2010). doi:10.1007/s10766-010-0135-4

18. Wienke, S., Terboven, C., Beyer, J.C., Müller, M.S.: A pattern-based comparison of OpenACC and OpenMP for accelerator computing. In: Silva, F., Dutra, I., Santos Costa, V. (eds.) Euro-Par 2014. LNCS, vol. 8632, pp. 812–823. Springer, Heidelberg (2014)

19. Kraus, J., et al.: Accelerating a C++ CFD code with OpenACC. In: Proceedings of the First Workshop on Accelerator Programming Using Directives, pp. 47–54 (2014). doi:10.1109/WACCPD.2014.11

20. Biferale, L., et al.: An optimized D2Q37 lattice boltzmann code on GP-GPUs. Comput. Fluids **80**, 55–62 (2013). doi:10.1016/j.compfluid.2012.06.003

21. Kraus, J., et al.: Benchmarking GPUs with a parallel lattice-boltzmann code. In: Proceedings of Computer Architecture and High Performance Computing (SBAC-PAD), pp. 160–167 (2013). doi:10.1109/SBAC-PAD.2013.37

22. Obrecht, C., et al.: Scalable lattice boltzmann solvers for CUDA GPU clusters. Parallel Comput. **39**(6–7), 259–270 (2013). doi:10.1016/j.parco.2013.04.001

23. Succi, S.: The Lattice-Boltzmann Equation. Oxford University Press, Oxford (2001)

24. Aidun, C.K., Clausen, J.R.: Lattice-boltzmann method for complex flows. Annu. Rev. Fluid Mech. **42**(1), 439–472 (2010). doi:10.1146/annurev-fluid-121108-145519

25. Sbragaglia, M., et al.: Lattice boltzmann method with self-consistent thermo-hydrodynamic equilibria. J. Fluid Mech. **628**, 299–309 (2009). doi:10.1017/S002211200900665X

26. Scagliarini, A., et al.: Lattice boltzmann methods for thermal flows: continuum limit and applications to compressible Rayleigh-Taylor systems. Phys. Fluids **22**(5), 055101 (2010). doi:10.1063/1.3392774

27. Biferale, L., et al.: Second-order closure in stratified turbulence: simulations and modeling of bulk and entrainment regions. Phys. Rev. E **84**(1), 016305 (2011). doi:10.1103/PhysRevE.84.016305

28. Biferale, L., et al.: Reactive Rayleigh-Taylor systems: front propagation and non-stationarity. EPL (Europhys. Lett.) **94**(5), 54004 (2011). doi:10.1209/0295-5075/94/54004

29. Ripesi, L., et al.: Evolution of a double-front Rayleigh-Taylor system using a graphics-processing-unit-based high-resolution thermal lattice-Boltzmann model. Phys. Rev. E **89**(4) (2014). doi:10.1103/PhysRevE.89.043022

30. Mantovani, F., et al.: Performance issues on many-core processors: a D2Q37 lattice boltzmann scheme as a test-case. Comput. Fluids **88**, 743–752 (2013). doi:10.1016/j.compfluid.2013.05.014

31. Calore, E., Schifano, S.F., Tripiccione, R.: On portability, performance and scalability of an MPI OpenCL lattice boltzmann code. In: Lopes, L., et al. (eds.) Euro-Par 2014, Part II. LNCS, vol. 8806, pp. 438–449. Springer, Heidelberg (2014)

High-Performance and Scalable Design of MPI-3 RMA on Xeon Phi Clusters

Mingzhe Li[✉], Khaled Hamidouche, Xiaoyi Lu, Jian Lin,
and Dhabaleswar K. (DK) Panda

Department of Computer Science and Engineering,
The Ohio State University, Columbus, USA
{limin,hamidouc,luxi,linjia,panda}@cse.ohio-state.edu

Abstract. Intel Many Integrated Core (MIC) architectures have been
playing a key role in modern supercomputing systems due to the features of high performance and low power consumption. This makes them
become an attractive choice to accelerate HPC applications. MPI-3 RMA
is an important part of the MPI-3 standard. It provides one-sided semantics that reduce the synchronization overhead and allow overlapping of
communication with computation. This makes the RMA model the first
target for developing scalable applications with irregular communication patterns. However, an efficient runtime support for MPI-3 RMA
with simultaneous use of both processors and co-processors is still not
well exploited. In this paper, we propose high-performance and scalable
runtime-level designs for MPI-3 RMA involving both the host and Xeon
Phi processors. We incorporate our designs into the popular MVAPICH2
MPI library. To the best of our knowledge, this is the first research work
that proposes high-performance runtime designs for MPI-3 RMA on Intel
Xeon Phi clusters. Experimental evaluations indicate a reduction of 5X
in the uni-directional MPI_Put and MPI_Get latency for 4 MB messages between two Xeon Phis, compared to an out-of-the-box version
of MVAPICH2. Application evaluations in the symmetric mode show
performance improvements of 25 % at the scale of 1,024 processes.

1 Introduction

The emerging co-processors such as Intel Many Integrated Cores (MICs) [2] and
accelerators such as NVIDIA GPUs have been widely used to accelerate scientific applications. The features of high performance and low power consumption
per watt they offer have made them as key components in modern HPC systems. In the recent Top500 list [16] (November 2014), 75 systems in total are
using either accelerator or co-processor technology, including Tianhe-2, Titan,
and Stampede in the top 10 supercomputers. Networking technologies, such as
InfiniBand (IB) [1], have also rapidly evolved over the years to offer low latency

This research is supported in part by National Science Foundation grants #OCI-
1148371, #CCF-1213084 and #CNS-1419123.

© Springer-Verlag Berlin Heidelberg 2015
J.L. Träff et al. (Eds.): Euro-Par 2015, LNCS 9233, pp. 625–637, 2015.
DOI: 10.1007/978-3-662-48096-0_48

and high bandwidth communication to address the increasing communication requirements of current generation peta-scale applications.

Intel's Xeon Phi co-processor, based on the Many Integrated Core (MIC) architecture, packs up to 1 TFLOP of double precision performance in one chip. Several programming models, including MPI, OpenMP and others, used on multi-core architectures can run on Xeon Phi. So applications developed for multi-core systems could be easily ported to Xeon Phi. Xeon Phi also offers three usage modes for application developers: (1) Offload mode: It can be used as an accelerator to offload compute intensive regions of an application, using compiler directives. (2) Native mode: It can also be used in a many-core hosted mode to run applications. (3) Symmetric mode: It also offers a Symmetric mode where processes can be launched on both the co-processor and host.

Several scientific applications have already been successfully ported to leverage the compute power offered by Xeon Phi [7,8]. To maximize the performance of applications, several studies have optimized runtime systems for the send-recv based communication using new features available on Xeon Phi clusters. One-sided communication has been seen as a suitable model for Exascale Computing especially for applications with irregular communication patterns [5]. MPI-3 RMA provides one-sided semantics that reduce the synchronization overhead and allow overlapping of communication with computation. However, an efficient runtime support for MPI-3 RMA with simultaneous use of both processors and co-processors is still not well exploited.

To design a high-performance runtime for MPI-3 RMA, we need to cover window creation, communication and synchronization operations with existing and new channels available on Xeon Phi Clusters. For applications running in Native or Symmetric modes, different communication paths can be involved in MPI processes, such as Intra-MIC (MIC-MIC), Intra-Node (HOST-MIC), Inter-Node (HOST-MIC), Inter-Node (MIC-MIC), etc. To maximize the utilization of compute resources on MIC-based systems, it is imperative that all these operations are efficiently designed. In this work, we propose efficient and truly one-sided MPI-3 RMA designs to address the following important challenges:

- What are the bottlenecks involved in optimizing data transfers inside a node or across nodes with processor and co-processor?
- Can all the communication operations be implemented in a truly one-sided manner?
- What are the potential benefits of such a runtime design on the performance and scalability of parallel applications?

In this paper, we present a high-performance and scalable design of MPI-3 RMA on Intel Xeon Phi clusters. We also carry out a detailed analysis of our designs and evaluate them with various micro-benchmarks and applications. Our experimental evaluations show that our proposed design could reduce the unidirectional MPI_Put and MPI_Get latency for 4 MB messages from Xeon Phi to Xeon Phi by 5X. The design improves the performance of MPI-3 RMA based Graph500 by 25 % with 1,024 processes in symmetric mode. To the best of our knowledge, this is the first research work that proposes high-performance runtime designs for MPI-3 RMA on Intel Xeon Phi clusters.

2 Background

In this section, we briefly discuss MPI-3 RMA programming model. Later, we describe the communication channels available on Xeon Phi Clusters.

2.1 MPI-3 RMA

The MPI one-sided interface enables direct access to the memory of other processes through a window. Window is a memory region which can be accessed by processes in the same communicator. MPI-3 RMA introduces six communication routines to access windows. Synchronization modes provided by MPI-3 can be classified as passive (no explicit participation from the target) or active (involves both origin and target). All of these communication operations are non-blocking and are not guaranteed to complete, either locally or remotely, until a consequent synchronization operation (e.g. MPI_Win_unlock) occurs.

2.2 Communication Channels on Intel Xeon Phi Clusters

For processes running on MIC Clusters, there are three modes of inter-process communication: the shared-memory channel, the Symmetric Communication Interface (SCIF) channel, and the IB-verbs channel. SCIF is a socket-like API for communication between processes on the MIC and host within the same system [4]. The Intel Manycore Platform Software (MPSS) for MIC provides two ways of using IB verbs for communications on MIC clusters. A direct OFED communication stack is provided to support the Symmetric mode of communication on just the MIC or between the MIC and host. Alternatively, the MPSS also provides implementation of IB verbs over the SCIF API, called IB-SCIF, for intra-node communications. Our previous study showed that the current generation processor chipsets from Intel have a limited peak bandwidth when the HCA is directly accessing the accelerator memory. A Proxy-based approach is usually used to overcome this limitation [13]. Our work differentiates from previous design in that we implement MPI-3 RMA communications with truly one-sided schemes. Detailed description of the designs is presented in Sect. 3.3.

3 Proposed Designs

In this section, we present efficient MPI-3 RMA communication runtime designs for Intel MIC clusters. Figure 1 gives an overview of our proposed designs including window management, communication and synchronization operations.

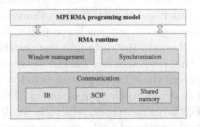

Fig. 1. Overview of MVAPICH2 MPI-3 RMA over Xeon Phi Clusters

3.1 Designs for Window Creation

In the window creation phase, each process discovers its neighbors and its location whether it is running on the MIC or HOST. The process with the lowest MPI rank of all running processes on the same MIC is assigned as the MIC leader process. The window is registered with the IB HCA and PCIe device to enable both IB verbs and SCIF communications. After registrations, all MPI processes call MPI_Allgather to get other processes' window information (window base, remote descriptor for IB network, remote offset for SCIF, etc.). Then, the MIC leader process sends all the window information to a helper process running on the host. The purpose of this helper process and this message exchange is mainly for the truly one-sided implementation which will be discussed in detail in later subsection. To provide high-performance one-sided communications, SCIF requires the source and target buffers to be 64-bit aligned. Thus, we align windows inside the library if the start address given by the user is not aligned. Further, as the registration is an expensive operation, we enhance the registration cache scheme used by MVAPICH2, to enable caching SCIF registration handlers. The whole procedure used for MPI_Win_allocate is shown in Algorithm 1. For a traditional window that is created by MPI_Win_create, each process needs to store address information of all other processes for data transfers. For newly introduced window routines in MPI-3 RMA, each process only needs to store per node address information instead of per process. The MPI-3 RMA window can also be implemented as a symmetric heap where the window base on all processes is the same. In this case, each process only needs to store one window address which can be used for all processes.

3.2 Designs for Intra-node Communication

In this subsection, we propose designs for the intra-node MIC-MIC, HOST-MIC and MIC-HOST communications. Here we focus on MPI_Get and MPI_Put operations.

Intra-node MIC-MIC Communication. For RMA communications operating on windows created by MPI_Win_create, the communication is implemented over the two-sided based shared memory channel. The origin process copies a header and the data into a shared memory region allocated during MPI_Init and the receiver process keeps polling for any incoming messages, detects the header and copies the data into the destination buffer. For RMA communications operating on a window backed by shared memory, the origin process could directly access the remote process window and finish the transfer by just one copy from the origin to the target buffer. These two designs work well for small messages. For large messages, relatively weak performance of single core on the MIC incurs high overhead with memcpy operation for data transfers. An alternative design is to use the SCIF channel to transfer large messages. The MPI_Put is mapped to *scif_writeto* which transfers the data from its source buffer to the target process's window. The MPI_Get is mapped to *scif_readfrom* to read the data from a target process's window into its own buffer.

Intra-node MIC-HOST and HOST-MIC Communication. There are two design alternatives for each of these two communication paths. One design is going through the native IB channel, and the other one is using the SCIF channel. We find that a single channel could perform the best for all message sizes, so we introduce a hybrid design which automatically chooses the best channel based on the communication pattern and message sizes. For small messages, the native IB channel always delivers better performance than the SCIF channel, so we use native IB channel for small messages in this scenario. For large message transfers, IB reads from the MIC memory will hit the bandwidth limitation introduced in [13]. This limitation adds significant overhead for MIC-HOST MPI_Put and HOST-MIC MPI_Get operations. To avoid this bottleneck, we take advantage of the SCIF channel for these two transfers. In our experiments, we find that SCIF transfers also deliver better bandwidth than HOST initialized IB transfers for large messages. So our design uses the low latency IB channel for small messages and the SCIF channel for large messages.

Algorithm 1. DETAILS OF MPI_WIN_ALLOCATE

---

1 /* MPI Process running on the HOST or MIC */
2 **if** *local_rank* = *0* **then**
3 | *shm_open(size)*
4 | *Bcast(node_comm, shm_hnd)*
5 **else**
6 | *Bcast(node_comm, shm_hnd)*
7 | *win_base* ← *mmap()*
8 **end**
9 *rkey* ← *ib_register(win_base)*
10 *scif_off* ← *scif_register(win_base)*
11 /* MPI processes exchange window info */
12 *Allgather(comm, {rkey, scif_off, win_base})*
13 **if** *on_mic* & *local_rank* = *0* **then**
14 | /* Send information to helper process */
15 | *Send(helper_process, {rkey, scif_off, win_base})*
16 **end**
17 /* Helper process running on Host */
18 *Recv({rkey, scif_off, win_base})*
19 **for** *k* = *0; k < node_size; k++* **do**
20 | *buffer.scif_off[k]* ← *scif_off[k]*
21 | *buffer.win_base[k]* ← *win_base[k]*
22 **end**

3.3   Designs for Inter-node Communication

In this subsection, we present design alternatives for inter-node MIC-MIC, HOST-MIC and MIC-HOST communications.

Inter-node MIC-MIC Communication. For small messages, the IB channel could be used for data exchange between MICs sitting on different nodes. For large data transfers between MICs, the IB transfer reading from a remote MIC will hit the same bandwidth limitation. To overcome this limitation, a two step based approach is proposed. The first step transfers the data from the MIC to the HOST, and then the HOST initializes IB transfers to the remote target in the second step. In order to achieve this two-step based transfer, we need to launch a helper process on the HOST to take care of the intermediate transfer. To implement this design in a truly one-sided manner, there are several challenges:

– Which communication channel should be used for each step?
– How can the helper process directly read/write from/to the window of MPI processes?
– How to avoid an active participation of the target process, to achieve best computation/communication overlap?

For the first step, we choose the SCIF channel that always performs the best for intra-node large message transfers. There are two alternative designs for the first step: (1) The MIC process sends the first handshake message to notify the helper process. The helper process responds with an intermediate address after receiving the notification. The real data transfer starts in the third step. (2) The other way is that the MIC process sends its source address and the SCIF offset together with the notification message. When the helper process receives the data, it could directly read the source buffer via the SCIF channel. In order to reduce the participation of the source and target to the minimum and thus achieve the best overlap, we choose the second way in our design. For the second step, we choose the IB channel to transfer data from the helper process to the remote target process. There are also two alternative designs here: (1) The helper process explicitly exchanges address and other window related information with the target process. In other words, this approach requires the participation of the target and an explicit synchronization during the data transfer. (2) The helper process stores all window related information during the window creation phase as indicated in Sect. 3.1. In this way, the helper process could directly access the remote target process window. With the objective of achieving a truly one-sided design and avoid a synchronization with the target process, our solution uses the second design.

In addition to ensure the one-sided semantics, the selected paths offer the best performance as they involve the DMA SCIF read initiation from the Host to the remote MIC. However, we still need to manage data transferred in each channel to get the peak bandwidth. Congestion in either channel will hurt the overall performance. To make the overall transfer work efficiently, we transfer

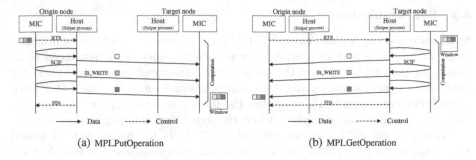

(a) MPI_PutOperation   (b) MPI_GetOperation

Fig. 2. Detailed designs of inter-node MIC-MIC communications

the data in a pipelined manner. The data is moved block by block from the
MIC process to the helper process via PCIe bus using SCIF and from the helper
process to the target process via the IB channel. As long as the helper process
receives one complete block from the MIC process, it issues RDMA write to the
remote target process. When the helper process finishes writing all blocks, it will
send a FIN message to the origin process. This two-step pipeline based design
is shown in Fig. 2(a) and (b).

Inter-node MIC-HOST and HOST-MIC Communication. For small
message transfers, the native IB channel always performs the best, so our design
takes advantage of the native IB channel for small messages. For large messages,
an MPI_Put from an MIC to a HOST or an MPI_Get from a HOST to an MIC
both will hit the bandwidth limitation if directly using the IB native channel. To
avoid this bottleneck, we use the same two-step pipeline based design to stage
the data to a helper process first, then initializing IB transfers. For the MIC-
HOST MPI_Get and HOST-MIC MPI_Put, we use direct IB channel transfers
for all message sizes.

3.4 Design for Atomic Operations

Since the IB HCA has already supported the *fetch_and_add* and *com-
pare_and_swap* operations with 64 bits element size, our first design takes advantage of this hardware feature. We use this feature for MPI atomic operation with
64 bits element size. This design only involves the origin process for the atomic
operations. For other message sizes which are not supported by the IB hardware,
MPI atomic operations are implemented over two-sided based communications.
When the origin process issues an atomic operation to the target process, it
sends out a packet including a header and the data to the target process. After
the target process receives the packet, it uses the kernel based atomic support
to do the operation and returns the final result to the origin process. We do not
need to consider the two-step based pipeline design here, since atomic operations
only involve small messages.

3.5 Synchronization

Synchronization operations ensure that window regions are ready to be accessed by other processes and all previous communication operations have been completed. In this work, we keep the same control messages and designs used for both active synchronization and passive synchronization in the Host. Our work extends current design by ensuring that the data transmission going through our proposed channels also completes when the synchronization operation returns. For transfers via SCIF channel, we call SCIF APIs to ensure that all issued SCIF operations have completed in synchronization routines. For transfers via the two-step based pipeline channel, we check the FIN message returned from the helper process to ensure that the data has been received by target process. Note that waiting for the FIN message involves only a memory polling which leads to the best performance.

4 Experimental Evaluation

In this section, we describe the experiments to evaluate the efficacy of the proposed design.

4.1 Experimental Setup

We use the TACC Stampede [15] system for experiments. Each Stampede node has a dual socket containing Intel Sandy Bridge (E5-2680) dual octa-core

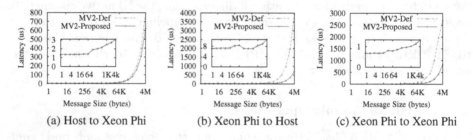

(a) Host to Xeon Phi   (b) Xeon Phi to Host   (c) Xeon Phi to Xeon Phi

Fig. 3. Intra-node put latency

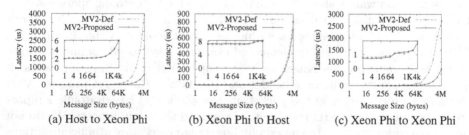

(a) Host to Xeon Phi   (b) Xeon Phi to Host   (c) Xeon Phi to Xeon Phi

Fig. 4. Intra-node get latency

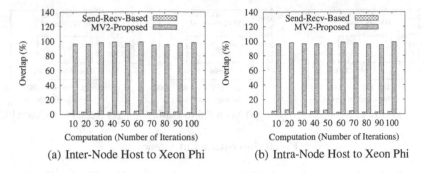

(a) Inter-Node Host to Xeon Phi   (b) Intra-Node Host to Xeon Phi

Fig. 5. Communication computation overlap evaluation

processors running at 2.70 GHz. It has 32 GB of memory, a SE10P (B0-KNC) coprocessor and a Mellanox IB FDR MT4099 HCA. The host processors are running CentOS release 6.3 (Final), with kernel version 2.6.32-431.17.1.el6.x86_64. The KNC runs MPSS 2.1.4346-16. The compiler suite used is Intel composer_xe_2013.2.146. Our designs are integrated in the popular MVAPICH2 [12] MPI library. We use OSU Micro-Benchmarks (OMB) 4.4 for evaluation performance of point-to-point communication. We then present evaluation using an RMA based LU kernel and MPI-3 RMA based Graph500 benchmark [9].

In this section, we first present experiments studying the impact of our designs for intra-node and inter-node communication on performance of point-to-point operations. 'MV2-Def' is the default version of MVAPICH2-MIC using the shared memory channel and native IB interface for MPI-3 RMA communication operations. 'MV2-Proposed' represents our proposed designs using the shared memory, SCIF and IB channels for inter-node and intra-node communications.

4.2   Micro-Benchmark Level Evaluation

We present the performance results of MPI_Put and MPI_Get uni-directional latency benchmarks in Figs. 3 and 4, respectively. For the intra-node MIC-MIC communication, MV2-Def uses the shared memory channel for all message sizes, whereas MV2-Proposed uses the shared memory channel for small messages and the SCIF channel for large messages. From the results, we see that the SCIF channel helps reduce the large message latency significantly. For the intra-node MIC-HOST MPI_Put and HOST-MIC MPI_Get results, MV2-Def uses IB channels for all message sizes, whereas our proposed design uses the IB channel for small messages and the SCIF channel for large messages. The HOST-MIC MPI_Get operation latency for 4 MB messages are 3949.6 and 721 μs respectively for MV2-Def and MV2-Proposed, which is a 5X reduction.

The Inter-node MPI_Put and MPI_Get performance results are presented in Figs. 6 and 7, respectively. For the inter-node MIC-HOST MPI_Put and HOST-MIC MPI_Get, MV2-Def uses the IB channel for all message sizes, which has overhead for large messages; MV2-Proposed uses the SCIF channel staging data from the MIC to the Host, then the HOST issues IB transfer to the

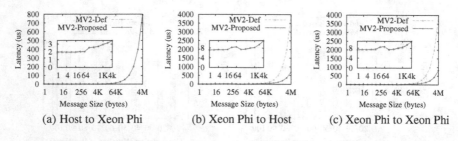

Fig. 6. Inter-node put latency

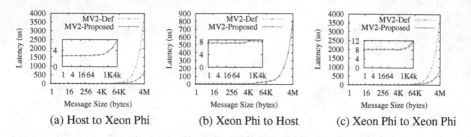

Fig. 7. Inter-node get latency

destination process. For the MIC-HOST MPI_Put of 4 MB message sizes, the latencies are 3947.9 and 700 μs for MV2-Def and MV2-Proposed, respectively, which is a 5X reduction. For the inter-node HOST-MIC MPI_Put and MIC-HOST MPI_Get, both MV2-Def and MV2-Proposed use direct IB transfer for all messages, because th Host initialized IB transfer doesn't have bandwidth limitation. For the inter-node MIC-MIC results, MV2-Def uses the IB channel for all message sizes, where MV2-Proposed uses two-step based transfers. That is why we also see big improvements in this case.

Figure 5 demonstrates the impact of the proposed design on communication computation overlap. The overlap benchmark is a two process test that measures the latency observed at the origin MPI process for MPI_Get and MPI_Win_flush on the window at the target process. During this time, the target process goes into a busy loop (mimicking computation) which is increased in each step. In Fig. 5, Send-recv-based means implementing communication over two-sided based designs, which involves both the origin and the target process in the communication. Our proposed design is a truly one-sided based implementation. By achieving near 98 % communication-computation overlap, the communication time of our proposed design is constant when the computation time increases, whereas the communication time keeps increases for the two-sided based design.

4.3   Application Level Evaluation

We use a modified version of the SPLASH LU benchmark written with MPI RMA to demonstrate the benefits of our proposed designs. This experiment

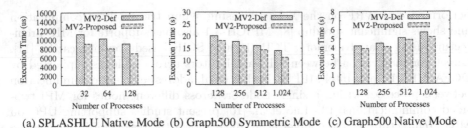

(a) SPLASHLU Native Mode (b) Graph500 Symmetric Mode (c) Graph500 Native Mode

Fig. 8. Application evaluations

uses 16 MPI processes per Xeon Phi in the native mode. The SPLASH LU benchmark does dense LU factorization. The dense 8192×8192 matrix is divided into blocks of size 128×128 each. Figure 8(a) shows the execution time of the benchmark for the proposed design from 32 to 128 processes. We observed that MV2-Proposed outperforms the MV2-Def by a factor of 24 % on 128 processes. The improvement seen by our design is due to the overlapping of the computation and communication time and efficient inter-node and intra-node Xeon Phi to Xeon Phi communication.

We also show the impact of our designs using an MPI-3 RMA based Graph500 benchmark [9] with processes running across MICs and hosts. In this experiment, we run 16 processes on each host and Xeon Phi. The results are presented in Fig. 8(b). We run the test with increasing number of processes on the MIC and Host from 128 to 1,024. We use scale 22 and edge factor 16 for the evaluation. We see that MV2-Proposed consistently delivers benefits compared to MV2-Def. The performance benefits come from our proposed design which optimizes all these communications. With 1,024 processes (512 on the host and 512 on the MIC), the execution times are 15.1 and 11.3 s, respectively, which is a 25 % improvement.

We then present the performance evaluation results of the same Graph500 benchmark for native mode. In this experiment, each node is running 16 Xeon Phi processes, and the total number of processes varies from 128 to 1,024. We present the BFS kernel time in Fig. 8(c). We can see that the proposed design performs better than MV2-Def at all system scales. MV2-Proposed performs better than MV2-Def because of two reasons: (1) The low latency and high bandwidth SCIF channel benefits intra-node large message sizes. (2) Our proposed two-step based design benefits inter-node data transfers. One thing we noticed was that the execution time increases with the increase in system size. This could mean that the Graph500 has some scalability limitations on native mode.

5   Related Work

Many researchers have explored different ways to utilize computing power of Xeon Phi. Currently, most explorations have tried to make use of the architecture's offload mode of computation [7]. Larry Meadow's work investigates the performance of WRF on the Xeon Phi using symmetric mode of computation and shows significant speedup [8]. MPICH-3.1 also has supports for MIC architecture using shared memory, TCP/IP, and SCIF based communication [11]. Direct communication between MIC accelerators across nodes is supported by DCFA-MPI [14] and Intel MPI [3]. Potluri et al. address efficient communication between processes within a single node or across different nodes for MPI two-sided communications [13]. Luo et al. [10] present studies supporting UPC on MIC architecture. Gerstenberger et al. have shown their work of implementing MPI-3 One-sided interface over RDMA networks with buffer-less protocols [6]. However, our work differentiates from previous work in that we propose truly one-sided and high-performance designs for MPI-3 RMA for symmetric and many-core hosted mode over InfiniBand networks.

6   Conclusion

In this work, we propose truly one-sided and high-performance designs for MPI-3 RMA on Intel Xeon Phi clusters. We present our designs for the window creation, communication and synchronization routines in MPI-3 RMA. We take advantage of Intel's low level communication API, SCIF, in addition to the standard communication channels like shared memory and IB verbs to efficiently support all possible data movement paths in the Native/Symmetric mode. Our proposed designs improve the point-to-point latency of intra-node and inter-node Xeon Phi to Xeon Phi uni-directional MPI_Put and MPI_Get by 5X compared to an out-of-the-box version of MVAPICH2-MIC. We also evaluate our designs with a SPLASH LU application kernel and MPI-3 RMA based Graph500. The MPI RMA based SPLASH LU benchmark indicates a reduction of 24 % at 128 processes with the native mode. The Graph500 benchmark shows improvements of up to 25 % improvement with 1,024 processes. As part of our future work, we plan to re-design MPI applications with MPI-3 RMA over Xeon Phi and evaluate the impact of our designs on a broader range of applications.

References

1. InfiniBand Trade Association, InfiniBand Architecture Specification, vol. 1, Release 1.0. http://www.infinibandta.com
2. Intel MIC Architecture. http://www.intel.com/content/www/us/en/processors/xeon/xeon-phi-detail.html
3. Intel MPI Library. http://software.intel.com/en-us/intel-mpi-library/
4. XEON-PHI Software Developer's Guide. http://www.intel.com/content/dam/www/public/us/en/documents/product-briefs/xeon-phi-software-developers-guide.pdf
5. Cantonnet, F., Yao, Y., Zahran, M., EI-Ghazawi, T.: Productivity analysis of the UPC language. In: 2010 IEEE International Symposium on Parallel & Distributed Processing (IPDPS), p. 254. IEEE (2004)
6. Gerstenberger, R., Besta, M., Hoefler, T.: Enabling highly-scalable remote memory access programming with MPI-3 one sided. In: Proceedings of the 2013 ACM/IEEE Conference on Supercomputing, SC 2013, Denver, Colorado, USA (2013)

7. Koesterke, L., Boisseau, J., Cazes, J., Milfeld, K., Stanzione, D.: Early experiences with the intel many integrated cores accelerated computing technology. In: Proceedings of the TeraGrid Conference: Extreme Digital Discovery (2012)
8. Meadows, L.: Experiments with WRF on intel many integrated core (intel MIC) architecture. In: Chapman, B.M., Massaioli, F., Müller, M.S., Rorro, M. (eds.) IWOMP 2012. LNCS, vol. 7312, pp. 130–139. Springer, Heidelberg (2012)
9. Li, M., Lu, X., Potluri, S., Hamidouche, K., Tomko, K., Panda, D.K.: 2014 IEEE International Conference on Scalable Graph500 Design with MPI-3 RMA. In: Cluster Computing (CLUSTER), Madrid, Spain (2014)
10. Luo, M., Li, M., Venkatesh, A., Lu, X., Panda, D.K.: UPC on MIC: early experiences with native and symmetric modes. In: 7th International Conference on PGAS Programming Models (PGAS) (2013)
11. MPICH:High-performance and Portable MPI. http://www.mpich.org/
12. Panda, D.K., Tomko, K., Schulz, K., Majumdar, A.: The MVAPICH project: evolution and sustainability of an open source production quality MPI library for HPC. In: Workshop on Sustainable Software for Science: Practice and Experiences, held in conjunction with Int'l Conference on Supercomputing (WSSPE) (2013)
13. Potluri, S., Bureddy, D., Hamidouche, K., Venkatesh, A., Kandalla, K., Subramoni, H., Panda, D.K.: MVAPICH-PRISM: a proxy-based communication framework using InfiniBand and SCIF for intel MIC clusters. In: International Conference for High Performance Computing, Networking, Storage and Analysis (SC) (2013)
14. Si, M., Ishikawa, Y.: An MPI library implementing direct communication for many-core based accelerators. In: 2012 SC Companion High Performance Computing, Networking, Storage and Analysis (SCC), pp. 1527–1528. IEEE (2012)
15. TACC Stampede Cluster. http://www.xsede.org/resources/overview
16. Top500 Supercomputing System. http://www.top500.org

Improving Performance of Convolutional Neural Networks by Separable Filters on GPU

Hao-Ping Kang[1] and Che-Rung Lee[2]([✉])

[1] Industrial Technology Research Institute of Taiwan, Hsinchu, Taiwan
HPKang@itri.org.tw
[2] National Tsing Hua University, Hsinchu 30013, Taiwan
cherung@cs.nthu.edu.tw

Abstract. Convolutional neural networks (CNNs) are one of the most successful deep architectures in machine learning. While they achieve superior recognition rate, the intensive computation of CNNs limits their applicability. In this paper, we propose a method based on separable filters to reduce the computational cost. By using Singular Value Decompositions (SVDs), a 2D filter in the CNNs can be approximated by the product of two 1D filters, and the 2D convolution can be computed via two consecutive 1D convolutions. We implemented a batched SVD routine on GPUs that can compute the SVD of multiple small matrices simultaneously, and three convolution methods using different memory spaces according to the filter size. Comparing to the state-of-art GPU implementations of CNNs, experimental results show that our methods can achieve up to 2.66 times speedup in the forward pass and up to 2.35 times speedup in the backward pass.

Keywords: Convolutional neural networks · Deep learning · Graphic processing units · Separable filters

1 Introduction

Deep learning has gained popularity recently in machine learning owing to its great recognition ability. The success of deep learning lies in its hierarchical features composition, which constructs features hierarchically from low levels to higher ones. By which, one can obtain more useful features for learning than that of "shallow learning". Architectures or models that utilize this concept are called *deep architectures*.

Among various deep architectures, convolutional neural networks (CNNs), proposed by LeCun et al. [16], achieve superior recognition ability, especially for images [26]. CNNs exploit the idea of hierarchical features composition by a sequence of convolutions and pooling operations, followed by classification operations such as logistic regressions [16,26] or SVMs [20,24]. Many industrial applications were built based on CNNs, for example, the face recognition systems of Google and Facebook [15,23], and the search engine of Baidu [10].

© Springer-Verlag Berlin Heidelberg 2015
J.L. Träff et al. (Eds.): Euro-Par 2015, LNCS 9233, pp. 638–649, 2015.
DOI: 10.1007/978-3-662-48096-0_49

One drawback of CNNs is their high computational cost. There are some approaches to accelerate the training speed. Glorot et al. used a biologically plausible activation function called rectified linear unit (ReLU), which converges faster than the commonly used sigmoid logistic and tanh activation functions [8]. Mamalet et al. proposed a method to combine the convolutions with the average pooling operations which leads to 1.6× speedup [18]. Mathieu et al. performed convolutions in Fourier domain through FFTs and achieve 3× speedup [19]. Cuda-convnet and Caffe drastically shortened the training time by using well-optimized GPU codes [1,13].

In this paper, we propose a method based on the *separable filters* to improve the performance convolution calculation on GPU. If a 2D filter is a rank 1 matrix of dimension $p \times q$, it can be decomposed into a product of two 1D filters [22], and the computation cost is decreased by a factor of $(pq/(p+q))$ theoretically. Many works have utilized this idea to accelerate the performance of CNNs, such as [5,12,17,21,25]. However, how to implement separable filters on GPU for better performance is still under investigation.

The implementation of separated filters on GPU requires two kernels. One is to decompose the separated filters and the other is to compute two 1D convolutions consecutively. We used singular value decomposition (SVD) to obtain the approximation and implemented a batched SVD kernel. For the computation of convolutions, we designed three implementations that use different memory spaces. The performance of those methods are varied for different filter sizes.

The contributions of this paper are summarized as follows:

- Design and implement batched SVD kernel on GPU.
- Design and implement GPU kernels to compute consecutive 1D filters.
- Analyze the performance and recognition accuracy of CNNs using approximate separable filters.

The rest of this paper is organized as follows. The notation and background knowledge including the architecture of CNNs in is introduced in Sect. 2. In Sect. 3, the SVD approximation algorithm and the proposed method are illustrated. In Sect. 4, the details of our GPU implementations are described. Experiment results are presented in Sect. 5. In Sect. 6, conclude and future work are given.

2 Background

2.1 Convolutional Neural Networks

Neural networks (NNs) are powerful models for machine learning due to their capability of learning nonlinear and complex mappings from input data to outputs. In [16], convolutional neural networks (CNNs) have been widely applied to image processing nowadays. CNNs perform a sequence of convolutions and pooling operations to extract features, which are then served as the input to classification operations such as logistic regressions and SVMs.

The convolution is an important operation in image processing field, which can be used to detect edges, to blur images, to sharpen details, etc. The convolution of two matrices $X \in \mathbb{R}^{m \times n}$ and $F \in \mathbb{R}^{p \times q}$ is $Y = X \otimes F$, where X is called the input and F is called the filter.

After convolutions, the pooling layer takes place. It summarizes a small subset of the input by taking their maximum or average. The outputs of the pooling layer are the features invariant to shifts because the same results will always be obtained no matter where the specific values are located in the pooling region.

CNNs construct deep architectures by stacking multiple stages, each of which consists of one convolutional layer and one pooling layer. There is an additional classification layer in the final stage, and the nonlinear activation functions are usually applied element-wisely between two stages [4].

2.2   Separable Filters

A 2D filter is separable if it can be expressed as an outer product of two vectors, so that a 2D convolution operation is equal to the combination of two 1D convolutions. The following proof is based on [22]. Let Y and X be $m \times n$ matrices and F be a $p \times q$ filter. By the definition of 2D convolution:

$$Y = X \otimes F,$$

$$y_{i,j} = \sum_{k=-\frac{p}{2}}^{\frac{p}{2}} \sum_{l=-\frac{q}{2}}^{\frac{q}{2}} x_{i+k,j+l} \cdot f_{k,l}, \tag{1}$$

where $x_{i,j} = 0$ for $i < 0, i \geq m$ and $j < 0, j \geq n$.

Suppose an $p \times q$ matrix $F = uv^T$, where u and v are vectors of length p and q respectively. The element $f_{k,l}$ in F can be expressed as

$$f_{k,l} = u_k \cdot v_l. \tag{2}$$

By substituting (2) into (1) we can get:

$$y_{i,j} = \sum_{k=-\frac{p}{2}}^{\frac{p}{2}} \sum_{l=-\frac{q}{2}}^{\frac{q}{2}} x_{i+k,j+l} \cdot f_{k,l} = \sum_{k=-\frac{p}{2}}^{\frac{p}{2}} \sum_{l=-\frac{q}{2}}^{\frac{q}{2}} x_{i+k,j+l} \cdot u_k \cdot v_l$$

$$= \sum_{k=-\frac{p}{2}}^{\frac{p}{2}} \underbrace{\left(\sum_{l=-\frac{q}{2}}^{\frac{q}{2}} x_{i+k,j+l} \cdot v_l \right)}_{\text{1D convolution with } X \text{ and } v} \cdot u_k. \tag{3}$$

Equation (3) first convolves X with v, and then convolves again with u. This equals to perform two 1D convolutions.

2.3   Singular Value Decomposition

In linear algebra, the singular value decomposition (SVD) is a decomposition of a matrix having the form:

$$A = U\Sigma V^T \tag{4}$$

where A is an $m \times n$ matrix and $m \geq n$, U is an $m \times m$ orthogonal matrix, V is an $n \times n$ orthogonal matrix, and Σ is an $m \times n$ diagonal matrix. The diagonal elements of Σ are called singular values and are sorted in the descending order. If A has rank r, the tailing $(n - r)$ entries are zeros. The m columns of U are the left singular vectors while the n columns of V are the right singular vectors.

The SVD can be used to obtain the low rank matrix approximation. Let Σ_k be a diagonal matrix that keeps the first k entries and zeros out the last $(r - k)$ entries in Σ. By multiplying Σ_k with U and V, we obtain a truncated matrix $A_k = U\Sigma_k V^T$. Let B be any matrix with rank k. It can be shown that

$$\|A - A_k\|_F \leq \|A - B\|_F,$$

where $\|\cdot\|_F$ denotes Frobenius norm of matrices. This shows that the error between A and A_k is smaller than the error between A and any other matrix B with rank k [6].

Alternatively, the SVD can be viewed as a weighted sum of rank 1 matrices. Let u_i and v_i be the i-th column of U and V respectively, and σ_i be the i-th entry along the diagonal of Σ. Equation (4) can be rewritten as $A = \sum_{i=1}^{r} \sigma_i u_i v_i^T$.

3   Algorithms

3.1   Filters Approximated by SVD

A 2D filter is separable into two 1D filters if it is a rank 1 matrix. But most 2D filters in CNNs are unlikely to be rank 1. As a result, we use the SVD decomposition to generate rank 1 matrices to approximate the filters, which is the well-known problem *low rank matrix approximation*. The common approaches to solve SVD are the Jacobi Algorithm and the Golub Kahan Algorithm [9], which are implemented in many LAPACK libraries [3,7]. Since we only interest in the rank 1 matrix approximation, the *Power Method* is used to decompose the matrix [9].

The power method is used to find the largest eigenvalue in magnitude and the corresponding eigenvector of a matrix. The power method performs refinements iteratively to approximate the largest eigenvalue in magnitude. The convergence rate is $\left|\frac{\lambda_1}{\lambda_0}\right|$, where λ_0 and λ_1 are the largest and the second largest eigenvalues in magnitude [9].

Let F be a $p \times p$ filter (assume all filters in CNNs are square.), and be decomposed into $F = U\Sigma V^T$. By pre-multiplying F^T to F, we obtain $F^T F = V\Sigma^2 V^T$, which can be applied through the power method to find the largest eigenvalue λ_0 and the corresponding eigenvector v_0, i.e. the singular value $\sigma_0 = \sqrt{\lambda_0}$, and the right singular vector. The left singular vector u_0 can be obtained by $u_0 = \frac{1}{\sigma_0} F v_0$. The algorithm is provided in Algorithms 1 and 2.

Algorithm 1. The Power Method

Input: Matrix A

Output: The largest eigenvalue in magnitude λ and the corresponding eigenvector v of A

1: Randomly initialize a vector b_0 such that $\|b_0\| = 1$
2: $k = 0$
3: **repeat**
4:     $k = k + 1$
5:     $u_k = Ab_{k-1}$
6:     $b_k = u_k / \|u_k\|$
7: **until** convergence
8: $v = b_k$
9: $\lambda = b_k^T A b_k$
10: **return** λ and v

Algorithm 2. Rank 1 Filter Approximation

Input: Filter F

Output: The largest singular value in magnitude σ and the right and the left singular vector v and u of F

1: $B = F^T F$
2: Compute Power Method: $[\lambda, v] = \texttt{PowerMethod}(B)$
3: $\sigma = \sqrt{\lambda}$
4: $u = \frac{1}{\sigma} F v$
5: **return** σ, v and u

3.2   CNNs Training Based on Separable Filters

The standard backpropagation algorithm consists of a forward pass and a backward pass. In the forward pass, it approximates 2D filters by two 1D filters as shown in Algorithm 2, and performs two 1D convolutions. In the backward pass, it reuses computed 1D filters to perform two 1D convolutions as well. The approximations are computed once in one batch (or mini-batch) iteration, and it is computed again when the filters (parameters) are updated.

To apply rotations to 1D filters, we have to flip the row filters in left/right direction and flip the column filters in up/down direction.

4   GPU Implementations

This section presents the GPU implementations based on `cuda-convnet`. Two major kernels are focused: batched SVDs and separable convolutions.

4.1   Batched SVDs

There are many GPU accelerated LAPACK libraries, such as `CULA` [11] and `MAGMA` [2], capable of computing SVDs. However, they are designed to parallelize over one problem with rather large size (more than 1000×1000). What needed in CNN is to solve many (several hundreds) but small (usually less than 15×15) SVDs simultaneously. Furthermore, we only need the largest singular value and the corresponding singular vectors. Other libraries do not meet those requirements.

We implemented the batched SVDs based on Algorithm 2 and assign each SVD problem to one block in the GPU. Some considerations relating to performance are addressed. First, there are several matrix-matrix and matrix-vector multiplications involved. Their data can be completely stored in the shared memory for fast computation because of their small dimensions. Second, in Algorithm 1, the number of iterations required for convergence are different among filters. It is unsatisfied that we have to wait for a few of the SVDs to converge while most of them are already finished. Therefore, in addition to the termination criterion stated in Algorithm 1, we set an upper limit for the number of iterations which stops the SVD computations no matter whether they are converged or not.

Third, the initialization of the vector b_0 in Algorithm 1 is an important factor for the convergence. A vector that is close to the eigenvector requires less iterations than those of a vector that is far from it. We can initialize b_0 to be the eigenvector in the previous batch iteration for fast convergence, since the eigenvector in this batch iteration is more close to that in the previous batch iteration than to a random vector.

4.2 Separable Convolutions

We implemented the separable convolutions by the tiling algorithm which proceeds as follows.

1. Divide the input into several small tiles to fit each of them into the fast but small memory.
2. Perform the convolutions in parallel.
3. Store the results to the destinations (the slow memory).

In the step 1, in addition to loading input data within the tile region, we have to load the "halo region" of the half of the filter size outside of the tile region. As can be seen in Fig. 1, the larger the filter size, the more the number of memory accesses are required. Therefore, we have implemented three versions which utilize different memory spaces according to their filter sizes: register-based method, one-pass method, and two-pass method.

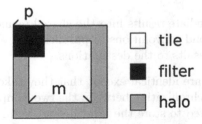

Fig. 1. An example illustrating the tile and the halo region.

Register-Based Method. For small filter, it is possible to load the whole data (the tile and the halo region) into the register file, which is the fastest but least memory and is only private to its thread. We load all data into the register file and let every thread perform convolutions in parallel. Because the register file cannot be indexed dynamically at runtime, we hardcode the filter sizes by using C++ templates, which allow the same code to be compiled for different sizes according to compile-time parameters. Below shows the partial code:

```
template<unsigned int filterSize> __global__ void conv(...)
...
if (filterSize>=3) ...//will be evaluated at compile time.
```

One-Pass Method. For larger filters, the whole data cannot fit into the register file and will cause the exceeding data be spilled into the slow memory. Thus, the one-pass method loads the data into the shared memory in which the data can be shared among the block. This method proceeds as follows.

1. Load all data into the shared memory.
2. Perform the first convolutions in parallel.
3. Store the intermediate results to the shared memory.
4. Wait until all threads are finished.
5. Perform the second convolutions with the intermediate results.
6. Store the final results to the destinations.

The above steps are similar to that of the register-based method. The major difference is the synchronization in the step 4. It has to wait all intermediate results are correctly stored in the shared memory because they are required for the second convolutions.

Two-Pass Method. In the one-pass method, a larger filter implies a larger halo region, which accounts for more memory accesses and the operation counts. The two-pass method solves this problem by breaking the computation in the one-pass method into two independent computations, which are

1. Computation 1:
   (a) Load data into the shared memory.
   (b) Perform the first convolutions in parallel.
   (c) Store the intermediate results to the slow memory.
2. Computation 2:
   (a) Load the intermediate results into the shared memory.
   (b) Perform the second convolutions in parallel.
   (c) Store the final results to the destinations.

The two computations are identical except that they take different input data. There is no explicit synchronization between the two computations and an additional memory is required to store the intermediate results. Figure 2 illustrates one-pass method and two-pass method pictorially.

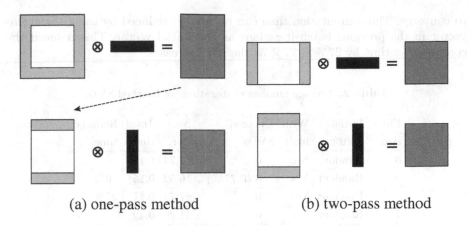

(a) one-pass method   (b) two-pass method

Fig. 2. Comparison of one-pass method and two-pass method.

Comparison of Three Implementations. Let the size of tile be $m \times m$ and the size of filter be $p \times p$. Table 1 compares the number of memory accesses and operation counts of three implementations of separable filter and the traditional 2D convolution.

Table 1. Comparison of memory accesses and operation counts of three implementations of separable filters and traditional 2D convolution.

Method	Memory access	Operation count
Register-based	$(m + p)^2 + m^2$	$2m^2p + mp^2$
One-pass	$(m + p)^2 + m^2$	$2m^2p + mp^2$
Two-pass	$2(m(m + p) + m^2)$	$2m^2p$
2D Convolution	$(m + p)^2 + m^2$	m^2p^2

5   Experiments

This section reports the evaluation results of the speed and the recognition accuracy for the proposed methods. All experiments were performed on the NVIDIA Tesla K20m GPU which has 5 GB memory and 2496 cores. Computation time is measured in milliseconds.

5.1   Evaluation of SVD Approximations

We report the computation time of our method by performing 1024 SVDs for different matrix sizes. We have set the relative error to be 10^{-6} and the max number of iterations to be to 100. As can be seen in Table 2, there are less than 20 % of the SVDs not converged under the limit. Without this limit, the computation time was increased because some SVDs required thousands of iterations to converge. The computation time can be further reduced by using the eigen-vector in the previous batch iterations as the initial vector. This reduced the computation time by 27 % ~ 77 % as the size increases.

Table 2. Average number of iterations of batched SVD.

Filter size	Initial vector	With limit	Unconv. SVDs	No. Iter.	Total time	Reduced time[%]
3	Random	No	0	17.74	0.15	
	Random	Yes	8 (0.77 %)	16.52	0.15	0 %
	Previous	Yes	0	7.74	0.11	27 %
7	Random	No	0	41.26	0.49	
	Random	Yes	56 (5.44 %)	39.08	0.36	27 %
	Previous	Yes	1 (0.02 %)	9.14	0.18	63 %
11	Random	No	0	62.85	0.86	
	Random	Yes	127 (12.37 %)	52.72	0.57	34 %
	Previous	Yes	25 (2.46 %)	10.89	0.23	73 %
15	Random	No	0	83.68	1.33	
	Random	Yes	204 (19.86 %)	62.22	0.91	32 %
	Previous	Yes	48 (4.63 %)	11.56	0.31	77 %

5.2   Evaluation of CNNs

We first compared the speed of our method with the original `cuda-convnet` and then compared the recognition accuracy.

Evaluation of Speed. The speed of the three implementations are compared with various filter sizes. For all experiments, we used 64 feature maps for both of the input and output. These settings are typical configurations in CNNs. The tile size is 16 × 16, which means each feature map has 16 tiles.

Figure 3 shows the computation time for the forward pass. For small filter sizes (less than 5), the register-based method is the fastest, but it slows down rapidly as the filter size increases. For the one-pass and the two-pass method, the computation time is increased more smoothly comparing to the register-based method. They are faster when the filter size is larger than 7. But overall, the separated filters methods are faster than `cuda-convnet`, which implements 2D convolutions. For the forward pass, the speedup is up to 2.66 times; and for the backward pass, the speedup is up to 2.35 times.

Evaluation of Recognition Accuracy. We evaluated the proposed method for image classification with the CIFAR-10 dataset [14]. CIFAR-10 consists of

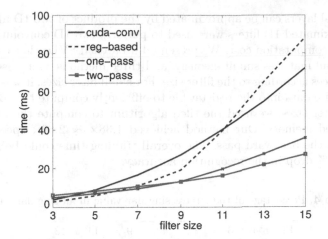

Fig. 3. Speed of the forward pass comparison with respect to the filter size.

60000 32 × 32 color images in 10 classes, with 6000 images per class. There are 50000 training images and 10000 testing images. The 10 classes are airplane, automobile, bird, cat, deer, dog, frog, horse, ship, and truck.

We construct two CNNs with different architectures. The first architecture (layers-18pct.cfg) consists of 3 convolutional layers, each of which followed by a pooling layer, and a logistic regression layer. All of the convolutional layers have filter size 5, and the input and output feature maps are 3 and 32, 32 and 32, 32 and 64 for the first, the second, and the third convolutional layer. The second architecture (layers-conv-local-11pct.cfg) consists of 4 convolutional layers, 2 pooling layers followed by the first 2 convolutional layers, and a logistic regression layer. The first 2 convolutional layers have filter size 5 and the last convolutional layers have filter size 3. The input and output feature maps are 3 and 64, 64 and 64, 64 and 64, 64 and 32 respectively. The experimental results are shown in the Table 3. Only slight accuracy degradation are observed when the sparable filter methods are used.

Table 3. Comparison of classification accuracy.

Architecture	Implementation	Accuracy (%)
3-layer	Our Method	81.07
CNN	cuda-convnet	81.25
4-layer	Our Method	87.42
CNN	cuda-convnet	88.71

6   Conclusion

In this paper, we proposed a performance improving method for training CNNs based on separable filters. First, by using the SVDs, the 2D filters in the convolutional layers can be approximated by the product of two 1D filters. Then, these approximated 1D filters were used to perform two 1D convolutions, which reduces the computation cost. We presented a batched SVDs that can compute multiple small matrices simultaneously, and three methods which used different memory spaces according to the filter size. For small filter sizes, it was possible to load the entire data into the register file to efficiently compute the convolutions. For large filter sizes, we used the tiled algorithm to compute the convolutions in the shared memory. Our method achieved $1.38\times \sim 2.66\times$ speedup in the forward and the backward pass. The overall training time could be reduced by 13 % with 1 % drop in the recognition accuracy.

Table 4. Percentage of the largest singular value in all singular values.

Filter size	3	5	7	9	11	13
$\dfrac{\sigma_1}{\sum_{i=1}^{n} \sigma_i}$	60 %	42 %	31 %	24 %	20 %	18 %

Because only the rank 1 filter approximations are used in our method, though a large speedup is achieved,the error also becomes large as the filter size increases. Table 4 shows the percentage of the largest singular values in the summation of all singular values for different filter sizes. In the future work, we will explore the higher rank filter approximation which can reduce the computation cost while sustain the recognition accuracy. One direction will be the use of multi-GPU in which multiple rank 1 filters are computed to form the full rank filters. Another direction is to combine the FFT method in [19] with our method.

References

1. cuda-convnet. https://code.google.com/p/cuda-convnet/
2. Agullo, E., Demmel, J., Dongarra, J., Hadri, B., Kurzak, J., Langou, J., Ltaief, H., Luszczek, P., Tomov, S.: Numerical linear algebra on emerging architectures: the plasma and magma projects. J. Phys: Conf. Ser. **180**, 012037 (2009). IOP Publishing
3. Anderson, E., Bai, Z., Bischof, C., Blackford, S., Demmel, J., Dongarra, J., Du Croz, J., Greenbaum, A., Hammarling, S., McKenney, A., Sorensen, D.: LAPACK Users' Guide, 3rd edn. Society for Industrial and Applied Mathematics, Philadelphia (1999)
4. Bouvrie, J.: Notes on convolutional neural networks (2006)
5. Denton, E., Zaremba, W., Bruna, J., LeCun, Y., Fergus., R.: Exploiting linear structure within convolutional networks for efficient evaluation. arXiv:1404.0736 (2014)
6. Eckart, C., Young, G.: The approximation of one matrix by another of lower rank. Psychometrika **1**(3), 211–218 (1936)
7. Galassi, M., et al.: GNU Scientific Library Reference Manual, 3rd edn
8. Glorot, X., Bordes, A., Bengio, Y.: Deep sparse rectifier networks. In: Proceedings of the 14th International Conference on Artificial Intelligence and Statistics. JMLR W&CP, vol. 15, pp. 315–323 (2011)

9. Golub, G.H., Van Loan, C.F.: Matrix computations, vol. 3. JHU Press, Baltimore (2012)

10. Hernandez, D.: "chinese google" unveils visual search engine powered by fake brains (2013). http://www.wired.com/2013/06/baidu-virtual-search/

11. Humphrey, J.R., Price, D.K., Spagnoli, K.E., Paolini, A.L., Kelmelis, E.J.: CULA: hybrid GPU accelerated linear algebra routines. In: SPIE Defense, Security, and Sensing. International Society for Optics and Photonics, p. 770502 (2010)

12. Jaderberg, M., Vedaldi, A., Zisserman, A.: Speeding up convolutional neural networks with low rank expansions. arXiv:1405.3866 [cs.CV] (2014)

13. Jia, Y.: Caffe: An open source convolutional architecture for fast feature embedding (2013). http://caffe.berkeleyvision.org/

14. Krizhevsky, A., Hinton, G.: Learning multiple layers of features from tiny images. Computer Science Department, University of Toronto, Technical report (2009)

15. Le, Q.V.: Building high-level features using large scale unsupervised learning. In: 2013 IEEE International Conference on Acoustics, Speech and Signal Processing (ICASSP), pp. 8595–8598. IEEE (2013)

16. LeCun, Y., Bottou, L., Bengio, Y., Haffner, P.: Gradient-based learning applied to document recognition. Proc. IEEE **86**(11), 2278–2324 (1998)

17. Mamalet, F., Garcia, C.: Simplifying ConvNets for fast learning. In: Villa, A.E.P., Duch, W., Érdi, P., Masulli, F., Palm, G. (eds.) ICANN 2012, Part II. LNCS, vol. 7553, pp. 58–65. Springer, Heidelberg (2012)

18. Mamalet, F., Garcia, C., et al.: Real-time video convolutional face finder on embedded platforms. EURASIP J. Embed. Syst. 2007 (2007)

19. Mathieu, M., Henaff, M., LeCun, Y.: Fast training of convolutional networks through ffts. arXiv preprint arXiv:1312.5851 (2013)

20. Nagi, J., Di Caro, G.A., Giusti, A., Nagi, F., Gambardella, L.M.: Convolutional neural support vector machines: hybrid visual pattern classifiers for multi-robot systems. In: 2012 11th International Conference on Machine Learning and Applications (ICMLA), vol. 1, pp. 27–32. IEEE (2012)

21. Rigamonti, R., Sironi, A., Lepetit, V., Fua., P.: Learning separable filters. In: IEEE Conference on Computer Vision and Pattern Recognition (CVPR), pp. 2754–2761 (2013)

22. Smith, S.W., et al.: The Scientist and Engineer's Guide to Digital Signal Processing. California Technical Publishing, San Diego (1997)

23. Taigman, Y., Yang, M., Ranzato, M., Wolf, L.: Deep-face: closing the gap to human-level performance in face verification. In: IEEE CVPR (2014)

24. Tang, Y.: Deep learning using linear support vector machines. In: Workshop on Challenges in Representation Learning. In: ICML (2013)

25. Vanhoucke, V., Senior, A., Mao, M.Z.: Improving the speed of neural networks on CPUs. In: Proceedings of Deep Learning and Unsupervised Feature Learning NIPS Workshop (2011)

26. Wan, L., Zeiler, M., Zhang, S., Cun, Y.L., Fergus, R.: Regularization of neural networks using dropconnect. In: Proceedings of the 30th International Conference on Machine Learning (ICML-13), pp. 1058–1066 (2013)

Iterative Sparse Triangular Solves
for Preconditioning

Hartwig Anzt[1]([⊠]), Edmond Chow[2], and Jack Dongarra[1]

[1] University of Tennessee, Knoxville, TN, USA
hanzt@icl.utk.edu, dongarra@eecs.utk.edu
[2] Georgia Institute of Technology, Atlanta, GA, USA
echow@cc.gatech.edu

Abstract. Sparse triangular solvers are typically parallelized using level-scheduling techniques, but parallel efficiency is poor on high-throughput architectures like GPUs. We propose using an iterative approach for solving sparse triangular systems when an approximation is suitable. This approach will not work for all problems, but can be successful for sparse triangular matrices arising from incomplete factorizations, where an approximate solution is acceptable. We demonstrate the performance gains that this approach can have on GPUs in the context of solving sparse linear systems with a preconditioned Krylov subspace method. We also illustrate the effect of using asynchronous iterations.

1 Introduction

Solves with sparse triangular matrices are difficult to parallelize efficiently, due to the often irregular structure of sparse matrices and the sequential nature of forward and backward substitution. The most common way to parallelize sparse triangular solves is to use a "level scheduling" technique [22]. A "level" consists of the unknowns that can be computed in parallel, given the dependency graph implied by the sparse matrix. The levels are processed in sequence until all the unknowns are computed. Depending on the sparse matrix, there may be a very large number of levels or not enough work within a level to efficiently utilize highly parallel architectures such as graphics processing units (GPUs).

In this paper, we investigate the approach of using an iterative method to solve sparse triangular systems. It is unconventional to apply iterative methods to triangular systems because such systems can be solved directly. However, due to high efficiency sparse-matrix vector product codes that have been vigorously developed in recent years, including on GPUs, iterations with sparse triangular matrices can be very fast compared to forward and backward substitution. In this paper, we use the Jacobi iterative method, although nonstationary methods and polynomial methods can also be used. Because triangular matrices are non-normal, the Jacobi method may diverge and cause overflow before converging, depending on the degree of non-normality of the matrix. However, for many types of sparse triangular matrices, such as the triangular parts of matrices

© Springer-Verlag Berlin Heidelberg 2015
J.L. Träff et al. (Eds.): Euro-Par 2015, LNCS 9233, pp. 650–661, 2015.
DOI: 10.1007/978-3-662-48096-0_50

from discretizations of partial differential equations, and from incomplete factorizations of these matrices, the triangular matrices have a degree of diagonal dominance that can avoid divergence of the Jacobi iterations. Thus, although Jacobi iterations will not work for all matrices, there are large, useful classes of matrices for which Jacobi iterations can be a viable approach for solving sparse triangular systems.

The iterative approach taken here is particularly applicable and competitive when only an approximate solution is sought, meaning, only a small number of Jacobi iterations are necessary. This is the situation when the triangular solves are used in preconditioned Krylov subspace methods for solving linear systems. Here, the triangular matrices themselves, such as from incomplete factorizations, are only approximations and approximate solves are acceptable when applying the preconditioner. By using approximate solves, the total number of iterations of the Krylov subspace method may be larger than when exact solves are used, but the total execution time may be much smaller.

We investigate the use of Jacobi iterations (also called sweeps in this paper) and a "block-asynchronous" variant to apply an incomplete LU (ILU) factorization preconditioner. The asynchronous variant does not synchronize the updates of variables within each sweep and may have improved convergence rate and execution time. When a fixed number of synchronous Jacobi sweeps are used, the operator is fixed, and standard Krylov subspace methods may be used. For the asynchronous variant, the operator is not fixed and therefore we use a flexible method, in particular, flexible GMRES (F-GMRES) [21] which we have implemented in the MAGMA [13] library for GPUs.

The acceleration of sparse triangular solves is the subject of much current research, e.g., [19], but almost all this research is based on the level scheduling idea [2,12,23]. Efficient implementations on state-of-the-art hardware still pose a challenge [14,15,26]. Another approach to parallelizing sparse triangular solves is to use partitioned inverses [1,20]. Here, a triangular matrix is written as a product of sparse triangular factors; each triangular solve is then a sequence of sparse matrix vector multiplications. The use of a sparse approximate inverse for a triangular matrix has been considered in [10,24], as well as the idea of approximating the inverse ILU factors via a truncated Neumann series [24,25]. The latter is similar to the idea of using Jacobi sweeps presented in this paper. The use of Jacobi sweeps for for sparse triangular solves was recommended in [6] for the Intel MIC architecture. Asynchronous iterations for these sweeps were not considered. The potential of replacing synchronous Jacobi with block-asynchronous Jacobi for more efficient use of the GPU hardware was investigated in [3] and applied to smoothers for geometric multigrid methods in [4].

This paper is organized as follows. Section 2 first provides some background and Sect. 3 gives details about the actual implementations for the methods we use for the experimental part (Sect. 4) in this paper. Section 4.1 describes our test environment, in Sect. 4.2 we compare the convergence of classical Jacobi and a block-asynchronous version when solving sparse triangular systems. For the latter, we investigate the effect of scheduling the GPU thread blocks consistently with the data dependency order in the triangular factors. We also compare the execution time with level-scheduling triangular solves. In Sect. 4.3 we investigate the impact of approximate triangular solves when used in preconditioned F-GMRES(50). We conclude in Sect. 5.

2   Background

2.1   Jacobi Method and Asynchronous Iteration

Classical relaxation methods like Jacobi or Gauss-Seidel are defined using a specific update order of the vector components and imply synchronization between the distinct iterations. The number of components that can be computed in parallel in an iteration depends on whether the update of a component uses only information from the previous iteration (Jacobi type) or also information from the current iteration (Gauss-Seidel type). Using newer information generally results in faster convergence. This however comes at the price of reduced parallelism: Gauss-Seidel is inherently sequential and requires a strict update order; for Jacobi, all components are updated simultaneously within one iteration. Asynchronous relaxation methods do not obey any update order. Instead they iterate the components in a nondeterministic fashion, always using the newest available values of the other components. The implied fine-grained parallelism and the lack of synchronization makes asynchronous methods attractive for GPUs, which themselves operate in an asynchronous-like fashion. At the same time, asynchronous iteration methods require the target matrix to have stronger properties to ensure convergence. For the asynchronous relaxation suitable for linear systems, a sufficient condition for convergence is given if the spectral radius of the positive iteration matrix, $\rho(|M|)$, is smaller than unity [11]. If this convergence condition is fulfilled, a block-asynchronous Jacobi iteration, where subsets of components are iterated in synchronous fashion and asynchronous updates are used in-between the subsets, also converges [5]. The Jacobi iteration for solving $Ax = b$ can be written as

$$x^{k+1} = D^{-1}\left(b - (A - D)x^k\right)$$
$$x^{k+1} = D^{-1}b + Mx^k \tag{1}$$

where D the diagonal part of A [5]. For the triangular systems that arise in the context of incomplete factorization preconditioning, we denote the iteration matrices as M_L and M_U for the lower and upper triangular, respectively. Let D_L and D_U be the diagonal parts of the triangular factors L and U, and let I be the identity matrix. For the diagonal of L being all ones,

$$M_L = D_L^{-1}\left(D_L - L\right) = I - L, \qquad M_U = D_U^{-1}\left(D_U - U\right) = I - D_U^{-1}U. \tag{2}$$

Hence, M_L is strictly lower triangular and M_U is strictly upper triangular, which implies that the spectral radius of both iteration matrices is zero. Therefore, the asynchronous method converges in the asymptotic sense for any triangular system [11].

2.2 Incomplete LU Preconditioning

An ILU factorization is the approximate factorization of a nonsingular sparse matrix A into the product of a sparse lower triangular matrix L and a sparse upper triangular matrix U, $A \approx LU$, where nonzeros or fill-in are only permitted in specified locations. The basic algorithm, called ILU(0), approximates the LU factorization by allowing only nonzero elements in L and U that are nonzero in A. In this case, the sparsity pattern of L and U matches the sparsity pattern of the system matrix A. The ILU factorization can also be computed efficiently in parallel on GPUs using a fine-grained parallel iterative algorithm [6,7].

3   Block-Asynchronous Jacobi on GPUs

If we allow Jacobi to use newer information in the component updates, the resulting asynchronous iteration can be realized in a single kernel that overwrites the iteration input vector with the updated values. The algorithm may be considered as block-asynchronous Jacobi as components handled by the same GPU thread block are updated simultaneously in Jacobi fashion, but the distinct thread blocks are executed asynchronously without enforcing a certain update order. Using newer information from remote components has the potential of improving the convergence, but carries the danger of degraded convergence if some components are updated several times in a row without using newer information about the other components [5].

The order in which the components are updated depends on the scheduling of the GPU thread blocks. GPUs use the concept of thread blocks to apply a kernel operation to data, and typically not all data is processed at the same time, but some thread blocks are scheduled before others [16]. The components handled by one GPU thread block are updated in parallel using the newest available information for the other components. Unfortunately, GPUs generally do not allow insight or modifications to the thread block execution order. However, backward-engineering experiments reveal that the thread blocks are usually scheduled in consecutive increasing order. With Gauss-Seidel converging usually faster than Jacobi, this motivates us to update the components in dependency order. For triangular matrices with a small bandwidth, i.e. the triangular factors arising from the RCM-reordered systems, this effect may be small. For matrix entries with a distance to the diagonal larger than the thread block size, updating in dependency order is equivalent to an Gauss-Seidel update, which would be equivalent to an exact substitution for this matrix component. For the lower triangular solve, updating the components in dependency order is equivalent to scheduling the thread blocks in consecutive increasing order. For the upper triangular solve, this scheduling order is against the dependency order, and faster convergence should be achieved by reversing the scheduling order. We investigate the effect of the thread block scheduling order in Sect. 4.2.

For classical (synchronous) Jacobi, the thread block scheduling has no impact, as no new information from the current iterate is used. This however implies, that the algorithm's implementation can not be realized in a single kernel overwriting the iteration input vector with its output (neglecting the case of the hardware parallelism being larger than the iteration vector length). Either separate input/output vectors have to be used, or the Jacobi is realized in two kernels where the first computes the sparse matrix vector product and the second performs the update.

4 Experimental Results

4.1 Test Environment

The experimental results were obtained using a Tesla K40 GPU (Kepler microarchitecture) with a theoretical peak performance of 1,682 GFlop/s (double precision). The 12 GB of GPU main memory, accessed at a theoretical bandwidth of 288 GB/s, was sufficiently large to hold all the matrices and all the vectors needed in the iteration process. Although all operations are handled by the accelerator, we mention for completeness that the host was being an Intel Xeon E5 processor (Sandy Bridge). The implementation of all GPU kernels is realized in CUDA [16], version 7.0 [18], using a thread block size of 128, NVIDIA's sparse matrix vector product was taken from the cuSPARSE library version 7.0 [17]. Double precision computations were used. To account for the non-deterministic properties of the asynchronous methods, the reported results are averaged over 50 runs.

Nonsymmetric test matrices were selected from the University of Florida sparse matrix collection (UFMC) [8], and are listed in Table 1. We also included a test matrix arising from a finite difference discretization of the Laplace operator in 3D with Dirichlet boundary conditions. A 27-point stencil was used on a $64 \times 64 \times 64$ mesh. Although this latter matrix is symmetric, we treat it as nonsymmetric in our experimental tests. The sparsity plots for all test matrices are given in Fig. 1.

Reverse Cuthill-McKee (RCM) ordering is well-known to reduce the matrix bandwidth and can produce more accurate incomplete factorization preconditioners [9]. Except for the DC test problem where RCM reordering fails to reduce the bandwidth, we consider all test matrices in RCM ordering (all matrices have symmetric structure). Note that we do not use multicolor orderings as these typically degrade the approximation properties of ILU preconditioners [9] although these orderings can enhance the parallelism for level scheduling.

Table 1. Test matrices.

	Name	Abbrev.	Description	Nonzeros n_z	Size n
UFMC	CHIPCOOL0	CHP	Convective thermal flow (FEM)	281,150	20,082
	DC1	DC	Circuit simulation matrix	766,396	116,835
	STOMACH	STO	3D electro-physical duodenum model	3,021,648	213,360
	VENKAT01	VEN	Unstructured 2D Euler solver (FEM)	1,717,792	62,424
	LAPLACE3D	LAP	3D Laplace problem (27-pt stencil)	6,859,000	262,144

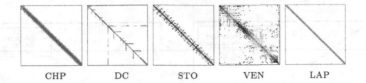

Fig. 1. Sparsity plots of test matrices listed in Table 1.

4.2 Sparse Triangular Solves

In this section, we report experimental results on convergence and performance when solving sparse triangular systems with relaxation methods. In these systems, the right-hand side is the vector of all ones, and the initial guess is the zero vector. Figures 2 and 3 show results for ILU(0) factors from two very different test problems, LAP and DC, respectively. In each figure, the top set of

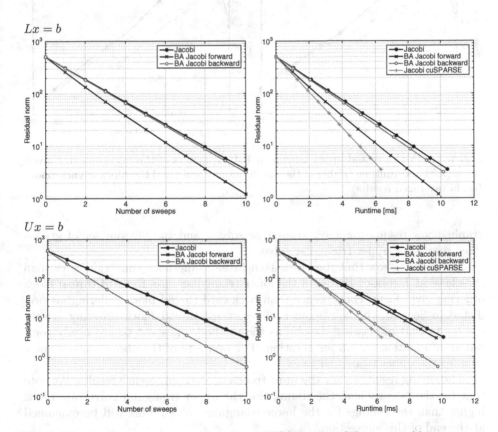

Fig. 2. For the lower and upper triangular ILU(0) factors of the LAP problem, convergence (left) and runtime (right) of the synchronous Jacobi and the block-asynchronous Jacobi (averaged results).

$Lx = b$

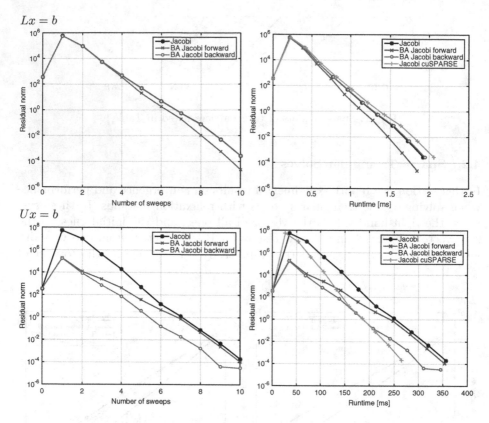

Fig. 3. For the lower and upper triangular ILU(0) factors of the DC problem, convergence (left) and runtime (right) of the synchronous Jacobi and the block-asynchronous Jacobi (averaged results).

graphs show results for lower triangular solves, and the bottom set of graphs show results for upper triangular solves.

The results show that the block-asynchronous methods converge faster than the classical Jacobi methods. In the lower triangular case, forward thread block ordering gives faster convergence than backward thread block ordering, as predicted in Sect. 3. The convergence of backward thread block ordering is very similar to that of classical Jacobi, as the method tends not to use newly computed information within an iteration. The opposite of the above statements is true for the upper triangular case.

The timing results follow the same trends as the convergence results. We note that for the DC problem, the timings for the upper triangular solves are much higher than the timings for the lower triangular solves. This will be explained at the end of this subsection.

The graphs also show results for a Jacobi implementation based on the sparse matrix vector product from NVIDIA's cuSPARSE library [17]. Naturally, the

Table 2. Runtime comparison [ms] between the exact triangular solve using the cuS-PARSE level-scheduling implementation and one Jacobi sweep.

Matrix	Factor	Exact triangular solve	Single Jacobi sweep
CHP	L	7.84	0.10
	U	7.07	0.10
DC	L	0.62	0.23
	U	4.65	26.57
STO	L	21.61	0.40
	U	24.16	0.37
VEN	L	17.49	0.23
	U	14.81	0.23
LAP	L	12.13	0.66
	U	11.57	0.65

optimization level of this routine is significantly higher than of our CUDA based implementations. In the end, the cuSPARSE based Jacobi is the overall winner in terms of runtime. However, from comparing the results of synchronous and block-asynchronous Jacobi, it can be deduced that applying the same level of optimization to the kernel for block-asynchronous iteration would make it superior also to the cuSPARSE based Jacobi. In the remainder of the paper we use the cuSPARSE based Jacobi implementation. There is no "asynchronous" sparse matrix vector product in cuSPARSE (which would give "approximate" and nondeterministic results) that we could use to implement a more efficient block-asynchronous Jacobi kernel.

Table 2 compares the runtime for exact sparse triangular solves from the NVIDIA cuSPARSE library to the runtime of one single Jacobi sweep. The data reveals that a Jacobi sweep typically costs a fraction of the total time for an exact sparse triangular solve using level scheduling (although multiple sweeps will generally be needed for an approximate solve). Only for the test case DC, which comes from circuit simulation modeling, one Jacobi sweep on the upper triangular system is more expensive than the level-scheduling exact solve. The reason for this is the structure of this matrix: very unbalanced lengths of rows in the upper triangular part of this matrix (see Fig. 1 for the DC matrix, where some rows have many more nonzeros than others) causes load imbalance in the GPU kernels. Performance could be improved by using a load balanced sparse matrix vector product kernel.

4.3 ILU-Preconditioned FGMRES

Figures 4 and 5 show the impact of replacing the exact triangular solves by approximate triangular solves in an ILU(0) preconditioned F-GMRES(50) solver. The left side of these figures relates the number of relaxation sweeps in the

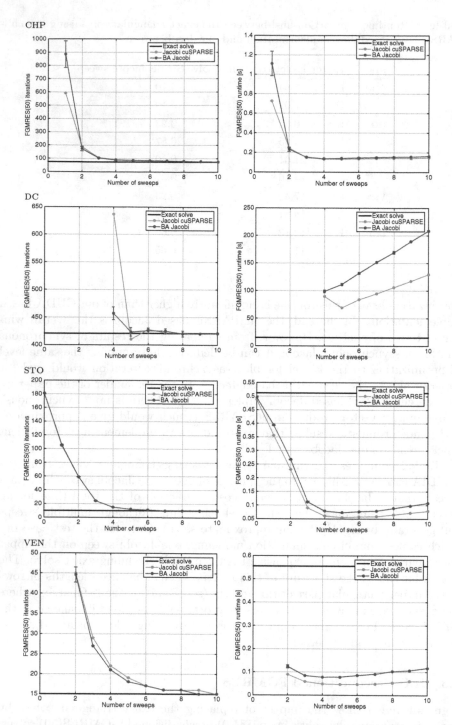

Fig. 4. F-GMRES(50) convergence (left) and runtime (right) when using either exact or approximate triangular solves for the test matrices from UFMC.

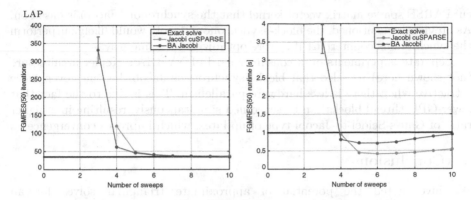

Fig. 5. F-GMRES(50) convergence (left) and runtime (right) when using either exact or approximate triangular solves for the LAP test case.

approximate triangular solve to the F-GMRES(50) iteration count. According to the convergence results on the triangular solves in the previous section, the block-asynchronous Jacobi algorithm schedules the thread blocks in dependency order. This is forward thread block scheduling when solving the lower triangular systems, and backward thread block scheduling when solving the upper triangular systems. In many cases, the faster convergence of the block-asynchronous Jacobi accounting for the dependency order compared to the synchronous Jacobi is reflected in the top level solver convergence: e.g., for CHP, VEN and LAP, the left-hand side plots show that on average, fewer F-GMRES(50) iterations are required for block-asynchronous Jacobi than for classical Jacobi. The error bars for block-asynchronous Jacobi indicate one standard deviation above and below the mean. They reveal that especially when using only few sweeps of block-asynchronous Jacobi, significant variation in the solver iterations may be expected. For systems with most entries close to the diagonal, the standard deviation is very small, and the iteration counts are almost identical to those using synchronous Jacobi. In general, few sweeps of the approximate triangular solve are sufficient to get the same F-GMRES(50) iteration count like when using exact triangular solves.

The right-hand side of Fig. 4 (respectively Fig. 5 for the LAP problem) relates the F-GMRES(50) convergence with respect to the runtime. Applying few sweeps of the relaxation method is usually less expensive than a level-scheduling exact solve, and can reduce the top-level solver execution time. In particular, the faster preconditioner application can compensate for a few additional iterations. Except for the DC problem (Fig. 4), where the sparse matrix vector product suffers from the unbalanced nonzero distribution, all problems benefit from replacing the level scheduling triangular solve by an approximate solve in the preconditioner application. We noticed that synchronous Jacobi usually requires a few additional F-GMRES(50) iterations. In terms of performance, synchronous Jacobi still beats block-asynchronous Jacobi. This is due to the performance of the cuSPARSE sparse matrix vector kernel that the synchronous Jacobi is based on. As previously mentioned, the block-asynchronous Jacobi would likely outperform the synchronous counterpart if it were optimized the same way.

Separate experiments on a consumer card of NVIDIA's Kepler architecture (not shown here) revealed that block-asynchronous Jacobi becomes even more attractive when there is less hardware parallelism. This is due to the fact that fewer GPU thread blocks can be scheduled simultaneously, resulting in a higher ratio of Gauss-Seidel-to-Jacobi-type of updates, which improves convergence.

5   Conclusions

We investigated the potential of approximate triangular solves for an incomplete LU factorization preconditioner on GPU accelerators, replacing the level-scheduled exact forward and backward substitutions with classical and block-asynchronous Jacobi iterations allowing for fine-grained parallelism. We analyzed the trade-off between convergence penalty caused by lower preconditioning accuracy and enhanced parallelism for several test matrices. We have shown that few sweeps of an iterative method are often sufficient to provide the same preconditioner quality as the top-level solver. Even if additional iterations are required by the approximate triangular solve, they are in many cases compensated by faster preconditioner application. Future research will focus on porting the approximate triangular solve to other hardware architectures, and investigating the potential of faster information propagation by adding local Jacobi sweeps for cached values for components handled by the same thread block, and using overlapping iteration blocks.

Acknowledgments. This material is based upon work supported by the U.S. Department of Energy Office of Science, Office of Advanced Scientific Computing Research, Applied Mathematics program under Award Numbers DE-SC-0012538 and DE-SC-0010042. Support from NVIDIA is also gratefully acknowledged.

References

1. Alvarado, F.L., Schreiber, R.: Optimal parallel solution of sparse triangular systems. SIAM J. Sci. Comput. **14**, 446–460 (1993)
2. Anderson, E.C., Saad, Y.: Solving sparse triangular systems on parallel computers. Intl. J. High Speed Comput. **1**, 73–96 (1989)
3. Anzt, H., Tomov, S., Dongarra, J., Heuveline, V.: A block-asynchronous relaxation method for graphics processing units. J. Parallel Distrib. Comput. **73**(12), 1613–1626 (2013)
4. Anzt, H., Tomov, S., Gates, M., Dongarra, J., Heuveline, V.: Block-asynchronous Multigrid Smoothers for GPU-accelerated Systems. In: ICCS. Procedia Computer Science, vol. 9, pp. 7–16. Elsevier (2012)
5. Anzt, H.: Asynchronous and Multiprecision Linear Solvers - Scalable and Fault-Tolerant Numerics for Energy Efficient High Performance Computing. Ph.D. thesis, Karlsruhe Institute of Technology, Institute for Applied and Numerical Mathematics, Nov 2012

6. Chow, E., Patel, A.: Fine-grained parallel incomplete LU factorization. SIAM J. Sci. Comput. **37**, C169–C193 (2015)
7. Chow, E., Anzt, H., Dongarra, J.: Asynchronous iterative algorithm for computing incomplete factorizations on GPUs. In: Kunkel, J.M., Ludwig, T. (eds.) ISC High Performance 2015. LNCS, vol. 9137, pp. 1–16. Springer, Heidelberg (2015)
8. Davis, T.A.: University of Florida Sparse Matrix Collection. na-digest 92 (1994)
9. Duff, I.S., Meurant, G.A.: The effect of ordering on preconditioned conjugate gradients. BIT **29**(4), 635–657 (1989)
10. Duin, A.C.N.V.: Scalable parallel preconditioning with the sparse approximate inverse of triangular matrices. SIAM J. Matrix Anal. Appl. **20**, 987–1006 (1996)
11. Frommer, A., Szyld, D.B.: On asynchronous iterations. J. Comput. Appl. Math. **123**, 201–216 (2000)
12. Hammond, S.W., Schreiber, R.: Efficient ICCG on a shared memory multiprocessor. Intl. J. High Speed Comput. **4**, 1–21 (1992)
13. Innovative Computing Lab: Software distribution of MAGMA version 1.6 (2015). http://icl.cs.utk.edu/magma/
14. Mayer, J.: Parallel algorithms for solving linear systems with sparse triangular matrices. Computing **86**(4), 291–312 (2009)
15. Naumov, M.: Parallel solution of sparse triangular linear systems in the preconditioned iterative methods on the GPU. Technical report NVR-2011-001, NVIDIA (2011)
16. NVIDIA Corporation: NVIDIA CUDA Compute Unified Device Architecture Programming Guide, 2.3.1 edn., August 2009
17. NVIDIA Corporation: CUSPARSE LIBRARY V7.0, March 2015
18. NVIDIA Corporation: NVIDIA CUDA TOOLKIT V7.0, March 2015
19. Park, J., Smelyanskiy, M., Sundaram, N., Dubey, P.: Sparsifying synchronization for high-performance shared-memory sparse triangular solver. In: Kunkel, J.M., Ludwig, T., Meuer, H.W. (eds.) ISC 2014. LNCS, vol. 8488, pp. 124–140. Springer, Heidelberg (2014)
20. Pothen, A., Alvarado, F.: A fast reordering algorithm for parallel sparse triangular solution. SIAM J. Sci. Statis. Comput. **13**(2), 645–653 (1992)
21. Saad, Y.: A flexible inner-outer preconditioned GMRES algorithm. SIAM J. Sci. Comput. **14**(2), 461–469 (1993)
22. Saad, Y.: Iterative Methods for Sparse Linear Systems. SIAM, Philadelphia (2003)
23. Saltz, J.H.: Aggregation methods for solving sparse triangular systems on multiprocessors. SIAM J. Sci. Stat. Comput. **11**, 123–144 (1990)
24. Tuma, M., Benzi, M.: A comparative study of sparse approximate inverse preconditioners. Appl. Numer. Math. **30**, 305–340 (1998)
25. van der Vorst, H.: A vectorizable variant of some ICCG methods. SIAM J. Sci. Statis. Comput. **3**(3), 350–356 (1982)
26. Wolf, M.M., Heroux, M.A., Boman, E.G.: Factors impacting performance of multithreaded sparse triangular solve. In: Daydé, M., Lopes, J.C., Marques, O., Palma, J.M.L.M. (eds.) VECPAR 2010. LNCS, vol. 6449, pp. 32–44. Springer, Heidelberg (2011)

Targeting the Parallella

Spiros N. Agathos, Alexandros Papadogiannakis,
and Vassilios V. Dimakopoulos[✉]

Department of Computer Science and Engineering,
University of Ioannina, P.O. Box 1186, 45110 Ioannina, Greece
{sagathos,apapadog,dimako}@cse.uoi.gr

Abstract. Heterogeneous computing involves the combined use of processing elements with different architectures and is widely considered a prerequisite in the quest for higher performance and lower power consumption. To support this trend, the OpenMP standard has been recently augmented with directives that target systems consisting of general-purpose hosts and accelerator devices that may execute portion of a unified application code. In this work we present the first implementation of the OpenMP 4.0 accelerator directives for the Parallella board, a very popular credit-card sized multicore system consisting of a dual-core ARM host processor and a distinct 16-core Epiphany co-processor. We discuss in detail the necessary compiler and runtime infrastructures of our prototype, both for the host and the co-processor sides.

1 Introduction

Multicore processing units have become the dominant elements of modern computing systems. Personal workstations pack multiple compute cores in a socket, while high performance supercomputers combine general purpose multicore CPUs with specialized accelerator devices such as GPGPUs, DSPs and application-specific FPGAs. As a result, modern system architectures present a mix of different processor and memory hierarchies within the same system. At the same time the building blocks of such heterogeneous computing nodes are designed for different workload scenarios; multicore CPUs perform best in coarse grained tasks, while accelerators reach their computational potential in large scale data and fine grained vector processing.

The real challenge is to provide programming models that enable the extraction of satisfactory performance while also keeping programmer productivity at high levels in application development. Programming models such as OpenCL and CUDA [10] provide very efficient albeit rather primitive mechanisms for an application to exploit the hardware capabilities of GPGPUs and other devices. In addition, the heterogeneity of the system architecture leads to heterogeneous programming styles, requiring different code bases for the host CPU and the accelerators.

S.N. Agathos is supported by the Greek State Scholarships Foundation (IKY).

© Springer-Verlag Berlin Heidelberg 2015
J.L. Träff et al. (Eds.): Euro-Par 2015, LNCS 9233, pp. 662–674, 2015.
DOI: 10.1007/978-3-662-48096-0_51

OpenMP, the de facto standard for shared-memory programming has been recently augmented with new directives that target arbitrary accelerator devices [17]. In the spirit of OpenACC [16], OpenMP 4.0 provides a higher level directive-based approach which allows the offloading of portions of the application code onto the processing elements of an attached accelerator, while the main part executes on the general-purpose host processor. What is important is that the application blends the host and the device code portions in a unified and seamless way, even if they refer to distinct address spaces.

The Parallella computer platform [5] is a recent and very popular credit card-sized multicore computer designed to be energy efficient and deliver high performance. It is an open source project and its processing power comes from a dual-core ARM CPU and a 16- or 64-core embedded accelerator, named Epiphany. The accelerator delivers up to 32 GFLOPS (102 GFLOPS, for the 64-core version) and is based on a 2D-mesh NoC of tiny, high performance, floating-point capable RISC cores with a shared global address space.

In this work we present the design and implementation of an OpenMP infrastructure for the Parallella board. It is the first OpenMP implementation for this particular system and also one of few OpenMP 4.0 implementations in general. We discuss both the compiler transformations and the runtime systems that provide the necessary support for the host and the device parts. Our implementation supports concurrent execution of multiple independent kernels. In addition it allows OpenMP directives within each offloaded kernel, supporting dynamic parallelism within the Epiphany.

The rest of the paper is organized as follows. In Sect. 1.1 we give an overview of related work. In Sect. 2 we present background material on the new OpenMP 4.0 device directives and summarize the Parallella board architecture along with its native programming models. We then describe our prototype implementation in detail in Sect. 3 while in Sect. 4 we present performance measurements. Section 5 concludes this work.

1.1 Related Work

Support for OpenMP 4.0 devices is fairly limited yet, both in the compiler side and the device side. In fact, the only commercial compiler that currently supports the **target** construct is the Intel ICC compiler and the only device it supports is the Xeon Phi [12]. Details of the offload procedure in the ICC compiler are given in [15].

Preliminary support for the OpenMP **target** construct is also available in the ROSE compiler. Chunhua et al. [13] discuss their experiences on implementing a prototype called HOMP on top of the ROSE compiler, which generates code for CUDA devices.

The GNU C Compiler has very recently added generic **target** support, designed to be tailored by device manufacturers, and combined with a runtime for the Intel Xeon Phi [1] accelerator. Bertolli et al. [7] propose a method to coordinate threads in an NVIDIA GPU using a single kernel as opposed to multiple kernels; they also discuss how their methods could be implemented as part of the LLVM compiler implementation of OpenMP 4.0. Finally, in [14] the authors present their implementation of OpenMP 4.0 on a TI Keystone II, where they use the DSP cores as devices to offload code to.

Regarding the Parallella board, higher-level parallel programming models are lacking. Offloading code to the Epiphany multicore chip is possible mainly through the native low-level eSDK [4] or using OpenCL as provided by the COPRTHR SDK [8]. The latter also provides a threading API similar to POSIX. Aaberge [3] analyzes the performance of Parallella and compares the two programming models, finding that generally the eSDK outperforms OpenCL. Finally, Varghese et al. [6] use the eSDK and raw assembly code to benchmark the Epiphany IV 64-core chip. They assess the effort required to extract good performance while noting the need for familiar, higher-level programming models.

2   Background

2.1   The OpenMP 4.0 Device Model

One of the goals of version 4.0 of the OpenMP API [17] is to provide a state of the art, platform-agnostic model for heterogeneous parallel programming. The extensions introduced since the previous version are designed to support multiple *devices* (for example accelerators, coprocessors, GPGPUs, etc.) without the need to create separate code bases for each device. The programmer simply marks portions of the (unified) source code to be offloaded to a particular device; the details of data and code allocations, mappings and movements are orchestrated by the compiler. The execution model is a host-centric one: program execution starts at the host processor (also considered a device) until one of the newly introduced constructs is met, which may cause the creation of data environment and the execution of a specified portion of code on a given device. The most important new directives are the *target*-related ones which mark the code and the data that are to be offloaded.

The **target** directive is used to transfer control flow to a device. The code in the associated structured block (kernel) is offloaded and executed directly on the device side, while the host task waits until the kernel finishes its execution. Each **target** directive may contain its own data environment which is initialized when the kernel starts and freed when the kernel ends its execution. In order to avoid repetitive creation and deletion of data environments, the **target data** directive allows the definition of a data environment which persists among successive kernel executions. Furthermore, the programmer can use the **target update** directive between successive kernel offloads to explicitly update the values of variables which are shared between the host and the device.

The memory for the data environment of a device is regarded as an autonomous extension of the OpenMP memory model. The data environment can be manipulated through **map** clauses within **target data** and **target** directives. These clauses determine how the specified variables are handled within the data environment. When an **alloc** map type is used an uninitialized variable is defined, whereas with a **to** map type the variable is additionally initialized from

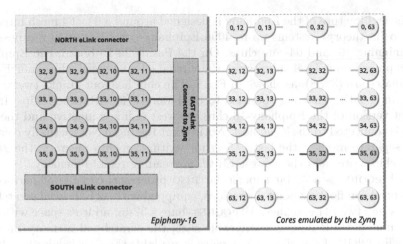

Fig. 1. The Epiphany mesh in a Parallella-16 board

the value of the corresponding host variable. If variable is mapped as `from` then an uninitialized device variable is defined; when the specified directive region finishes, the value of the device variable is copied back to the original host variable. If no type is specified or the type is `tofrom`, the variable is considered mapped as both `to` and `from`. Finally, the variables declared within `declare target` directives are also allocated in the global scope of the target device, and their lifetime equals the program execution time.

2.2   Parallella Board Overview

The Parallella-16 board [5] is an 18-core credit card sized computer and comes with standard peripheral ports such as USB, Ethernet, HDMI, GPIO, etc. The computational power of the $99 board comes from its two processing modules. The main (host) processor is a dual-core ARM Cortex A9 with 32 KiB L1 cache per core and 512KiB shared L2 cache, built within a Zynq 7010 or 7020 SoC. The other is an Epiphany 16-core chip which is used as a co-processor. The board has 1 GiB of DDR3 RAM, addressable by both the ARM CPU and the Epiphany. The former runs Linux OS and uses virtual addresses while the latter runs no OS and has a flat, unprotected memory map.

The Epiphany co-processor offers an impressive power efficiency that can reach up to 70 GFLOP/Watt, depending on the chip version. Two configurations of the Epiphany co-processor are currently available: the Epiphany-16 (with 16 cores and a 4×4 mesh NoC) and the Epiphany-64 (with 64 cores and an 8×8 mesh NoC). Although our discussion here holds for both versions, we refer mostly to the first one since it is widely available and is what our board contains. This particular chip is clocked at 600MHz and has a peak performance of approximately 25 GFLOPS (single-precision) with a maximum power dissipation of less than 2 Watt.

The architecture of the Epiphany is designed around a 64×64 mesh interconnect, so (in theory) systems up to 4096 Epiphany cores (eCORES) are possible, by combining 16- and 64-core chips. On the Parallella-16 board, the Epiphany chip is pinned on a 4×4 submesh of the virtual 64×64 mesh whose north-west coordinates are $(32, 8)$, as shown in Fig. 1. The chip has four eLinks (west, east, north and south), that may be used to interconnect it with other chips. In the current version of the Epiphany-16 chip the west eLink is inactive and the east eLink is connected to the Zynq host. Notice that the mesh NoC actually contains three separate meshes: the fast *cMesh* for writing on-chip memory, the *xMesh* for off-chip writes and the slowest *rMesh* for reading remote memory.

Each eCORE is a 32-bit superscalar RISC processor, capable of performing single-precision floating point operations, equipped with 32 KiB local scratchpad memory and two DMA engines. All eCOREs share a 32-bit address space with each one owning a 1MiB unique addressable slice; the scratchpad memory provides physically 32KiB of this slice. All memory is available through regular load/store instructions.

The Zynq, which is connected to the east eLink of the Epiphany, is perceived as the eastern part of the mesh. Based on the column-first routing scheme of the NoC, the Zynq can emulate the memory space of the cores in the 52 leftmost columns of the 64×64 virtual mesh, giving access to most of the board RAM to the Epiphany. A 32-MiB portion of the system RAM is left outside the Linux virtual memory manager area. From the Epiphany side it corresponds to the 32 cores located in coordinates from $(35, 32)$ to $(35, 63)$. This is designated as *shared memory* and is physically addressable by both the ARM and the Epiphany.

All common programming tools are available for the ARM host processor. For the Epiphany, the Epiphany Software Development Kit (eSDK) is available [4], which includes a C compiler and runtime libraries for both the host (eHAL) and the Epiphany (eLIB). A typical C program that utilizes the eSDK adheres to the following pattern: Initially the host executes some initializations and the sequential part of the application. Next, in order to offload code (kernel) to the co-processor it (a) initializes the Epiphany, (b) prepares the shared memory with all the data needed for the computation, (c) forms a workgroup of eCOREs and (d) triggers the execution of the kernel. All host-eCORE communication occurs through the shared memory.

3   Implementing OpenMP 4.0 on the Parallella

Our implementation is based on the OMPi OpenMP compiler [11]. OMPi is a lightweight OpenMP C infrastructure, composed of a source-to-source compiler and a flexible, modular runtime system. The input of the compiler consists of C code annotated with OpenMP pragmas and the output is an intermediate multithreaded code augmented with calls to the runtime system. A native compiler is used to generate the final executable. OMPi is an open source project that adheres to OpenMP V3.1 and targets general purpose SMPs and multicore platforms.

3.1   Compiling for the New Device Directives

The compiler has been extended to support the new OpenMP device model. In particular the input grammar has been modified to accommodate the new `target`-related directives. New nodes have been defined for the abstract syntax tree that represent the user code and new code generation routines have been introduced to produce the transformed code. The code generation phase now produces multiple output files, one for each different kernel (i.e. `target` region), plus the host code. The later contains the host part of the user program plus all kernels, since the host may be called to execute any of them, upon various runtime conditions. The kernel files are compiled using the eSDK tools.

When handling a `target data` directive, the compiler prepares a new data environment by injecting calls to the runtime system for each variable that appears in a `map` clause. The calls depend on the `map` type; specifically,

- For `alloc`-mapped variables, memory allocation calls are injected at the start of the construct block.
- For `to`-mapped variables, we additionally inject memory copy calls.
- `from`-mapped variables, are treated as `alloc` ones with additional calls to copy their values back to the original variable at the end of the construct block.
- For variables mapped as `tofrom`, we inject code as if the variable was both a `to`- and a `from`-mapped one.

The above calls are preceded by a runtime call to mark the beginning of a new data environment; this is needed because the runtime system has to track the nesting of `target`/`target data` constructs for each device so as to activate the appropriate data environment when offload time comes.

The `target` construct is more complex because it behaves like a `target data` construct while in addition it offloads and executes code on the device by actually transferring both the code and the data environment to/from the device. For its transformation *outlining* is used, in a manner similar to the `parallel` and `task` constructs: the associated construct block is moved to a new function (kernel) which will serve as the offloaded kernel, with a single argument which points to the necessary data environment. In its place, a runtime call to offload the outlined kernel is placed.

Before the actual outlining of the construct takes place, the construct block is analyzed in order to discover any variables used in the code which were created outside of the construct (i.e. in parent `target data` regions). These, combined with the ones explicitly marked by `map` clauses, form the complete data environment of the kernel function. Depending on the type of mapping, variables in the data environment will be created as local copies of the original variable, initialized or not, or as pointers to the shared memory. Variables already existing in a parent data environment are replaced by pointers to their storage. For the Parallella, all such variables are stored in the shared memory area. For `alloc`-mapped variables we simply create a local variable with the same name within the kernel. We treat `to`-mapped variables in the same way we treat *firstprivate* variables in a `task` construct; a snapshot of the original variable is created by allocating

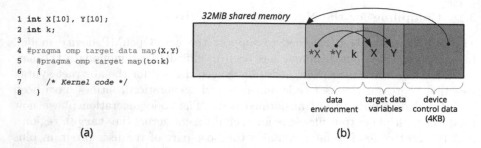

```
1  int X[10], Y[10];
2  int k;
3
4  #pragma omp target data map(X,Y)
5     #pragma omp target map(to:k)
6     {
7        /* Kernel code */
8     }
```

(a)   (b)

Fig. 2. Shared memory organization

space in the shared memory which is then initialized from the original variable. If the variable is of scalar type, a local variable is also defined within the kernel function and its value is copied from the shared memory in order to optimize access speed. No local copies are created for array types, due to the very stringent eCORE memory budget. The situation is similar for from-mapped variables. Here however, after the offload returns, the value is copied back from the shared memory to the original variable. Variables mapped as tofrom as well as variables which did not appear in any map clause are treated as if they appeared in a map(to:) clause with the extra copy-back steps of the from-mapped variables.

Finally, the target update directive is replaced by runtime calls to copy every variable in a from (or to) motion clause from (to) the shared memory to (from) the original host variable.

3.2 Runtime Architecture

At the host (Zynq) side the runtime system consists of two parts; the first is a full-fledged OpenMP runtime library, part of the regular OMPi infrastructure, necessary for supporting execution on the two ARM cores. The second part provides additional functionality, which is required for controlling and accessing the Epiphany device.

The communication between the Zynq and the eCOREs occurs through the shared memory portion of the system RAM as described earlier. The shared memory is divided in two sections, see Fig. 2(b). The first section is called Device Control Data (DCD) area, and it has a fixed size of 4KiB; it is used transparently by OMPi for kernel coordination and manipulation of parallel teams created within the Epiphany. The second part is used for storing the kernel data environments and part of the tasking infrastructure of the Epiphany OpenMP runtime described later. More specifically, during the preparation for offloading a kernel, a region is allocated to store the data environment of the kernel. This contains variables or pointers to variables which appeared in enclosing target or target data constructs and are not stored in the local memories of the eCOREs. An example is shown in Fig. 2(a). Variables X and Y in line 4 are annotated as tofrom. This causes a copy of each one to be created in the shared memory.

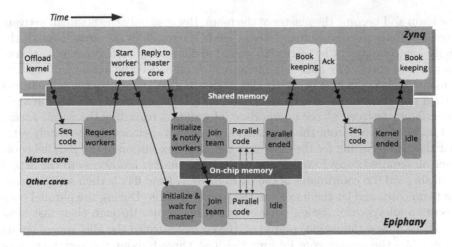

Fig. 3. Offloading a kernel containing dynamic parallelism

In line 5 the variable k is annotated as to and along with two pointers to X and Y form the data environment of the kernel. The beginning of the data environment is stored as a pointer in DCD, and is used by the kernel when starting its execution. All the above are stored at the higher end of the shared memory, leaving the lower end available for the programmer (e.g. for storing libraries which do not fit in the eCORE local memories).

In order to be able to control the eCOREs independently through eLIB calls, the initialization phase creates 16 workgroups, one for each of the available Epiphany's cores and puts them to the idle state for energy and thermal efficiency. For offloading a kernel, the first idle core is chosen and the precompiled object file is loaded to it for immediate execution. Because the current version of eHAL does not provide a way for an eCORE to notify directly the host for kernel completion, a special region of the DCD is designated to store special flags set by the eCOREs. The DCD infrastructure has a thread-safe design; this allows multiple host threads to offload multiple independent kernels concurrently onto the Epiphany.

3.3 OpenMP Within the Epiphany

The eCOREs do not execute any operating system and there is no provision for creating and handling dynamic parallelism (e.g. threads) within the Epiphany chip. In addition, the 32KiB local memory of each eCORE is quite limited, unable to handle sophisticated OpenMP runtime structures in addition to application data. As such, supporting OpenMP within the device side of the board is non-trivial.

The creation of a parallel team within an offloaded kernel is depicted graphically in Fig. 3. When a kernel is offloaded to a specific eCORE, the core executes its sequential part until a parallel region is encountered; the core will create a new team and become the master of the team. Because only the host can activate other Epiphany cores, the master core sends a request to the host through the device control data (DCD) section in shared memory, requesting the activation of a number of cores. The host-side thread which offloaded the kernel will activate as many cores as possible to satisfy the master request. A copy of the same kernel is then offloaded to the newly activated cores. The activated cores begin their execution by fetching all the appropriate information regarding the parallel team and its master core from the DCD section in shared memory. Immediately after that they spin waiting for the master to signal the execution of the parallel code. Once all required cores have been activated, the master has access to the actual team size and the coordinates of the team cores. A local flag is then set to release the team cores and let them execute the parallel region. During the parallel code execution all synchronization between the cores occurs through their fast local memories. When the region completes, the cores return to the idle, power saving state, while the master core informs the host thread about the termination of the parallel team. The host marks the idling cores as available for future use, and sends an acknowledgment to the master. The latter continues with the rest of kernel code.

We note that another, possibly faster, strategy for supporting dynamic parallelism would be to have all eCOREs loaded with the kernel(s) in advance and spin, waiting for the master to signal them which kernel to execute. However, this would increase power consumption dramatically and thus we did not pursue it further.

To support the OpenMP worksharing constructs (single, for, sections), the infrastructure originally designed for the host was trimmed down to a minimum so as to minimize its memory footprint; this is linked and offloaded with each kernel. The corresponding coordination among the participating eCOREs utilizes the structures stored in the local memory of the team's master core. This is possible because an eCORE can access any address in the Epiphany address space. In particular, while an eCORE may access its own scratchpad memory using *local* addresses (which range from 0_{16} to $7FFF_{16}$), its memory can also be globally accessed by all cores using its row and column coordinates: if r and c are the row and the column of a core, the start of its scratchpad memory is at address $r \times 4000000_{16} + c \times 1000000_{16}$. The mesh coordinates of the master core are available to all team cores through the DCD area in shared memory.

The eSDK libraries for the Epiphany provide mechanisms for locks and barriers between the eCOREs. Their implementation is highly optimized to exploit the fast cMesh subnetwork as much as possible. Because they assume that the synchronized cores belong to the same workgroup, we modified them in order to adhere with our multiple cooperating workgroup organization. Additionally the barrier was augmented with task execution extensions. Our prototype tasking infrastructure is based on a blocking shared queue stored in the local memory of the master eCORE. The corresponding task data environments are stored in the shared memory.

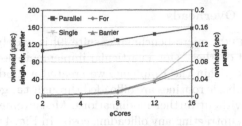

Table 1. Size of empty kernel (bytes)

Scenario	OMPi	eSDK
1 kernel	7092	2232
16-core team	10560	3084

Fig. 4. Overhead results of EPCC benchmark

4   Measurements

We have conducted a number of tests in order to measure the efficiency of our offloading mechanisms alongside the space and timing performance of the OpenMP runtime within the Epiphany accelerator. Our board is the Parallella-16 SKUA101020 and we use eSDK 5.13.9.10. The system runs Ubuntu 14.04 with kernel 3.12.0 armv7l GNU/Linux. GCC and e-GCC v.4.8.2 were used as back-end compilers for OMPi.

4.1   Memory Footprint

To examine the memory overhead of our Epiphany runtime, which gets linked with each offloaded kernel, we created a set of simple OpenMP programs. The kernels were compiled with "-O3 -funroll-loops" flags and we used the *e-size* tool of the eSDK to examine the produced ELF object files. The results are shown in Table 1. In the first scenario, one effectively empty kernel is offloaded, containing only a single assignment. It can be seen that OMPi incures a 4.5KiB overhead as compared to an identical kernel created using the native eLIB. Examining the ELF, it is seen that our runtime requires approximately 1KiB more for its internal data and another 3.5KiB for its runtime routines. In the second scenario we create a team of 16 cores running the previous trivial kernel; for OMPi this is accomplished through a **parallel** directive while for the eSDK program we create a workgroup of 16 cores which are synchronized using a barrier. While the data section remains constant, the additional offloaded runtime routines cause an increase in the text section; approximately 7KiB more than the corresponding native kernel are required. Additional functionality is offloaded if the kernel contains worksharing constructs and this accounts for another 3KiB approximately. All in all, OMPi was found to require 4–10KiB more than a similarly structured eSDK-based kernel. While this is certainly non-negligible, we note that (a) our prototype has not been optimized yet, (b) some portions could be moved to shared memory as a tradeoff between local memory space and speed and (c) the programmability gains are rather significant.

4.2 Overheads

The EPCC micro-benchmarks suite [9] is widely used to measure OpenMP construct overheads for a particular implementation. In order to measure OMPi overheads within the Epiphany, we created a modified version of the benchmarks. Their basic routines are offloaded through `target` directives and executed as kernels without further modifications. Measurements are taken from the host side, after subtracting any offloading costs. In Fig. 4 we present a sample of the results regarding the overheads of `parallel`, `for`, `single` and `barrier` constructs. The results are quite satisfactory, in all but the `parallel` construct. This is explained in part, because as described in Sect. 3.2, the formation of a dynamic team of cores incurs significant host-device communication, which includes additional kernel offloads. However, it should be stressed that offloading even an empty kernel has an overhead of at least 0.1 s, needed for resetting the core(s) that will execute it. Eliminating this cost, would require keeping all eCOREs active all the time, sacrificing power efficiency.

4.3 Mandelbrot Application

We tested OMPi using a simple version of the Mandelbrot deep zoom application which calculates a Mandelbrot set and zooms in and out up to 10500× at six predefined points. The whole frame by frame image is written directly to the frame buffer of the Parallella board (with a resolution of 1024 × 768), resulting in an impressive colorful video. The full traversal generates 204 frames per zoom point. The code for this application is one of the examples included with the eSDK in order to exhibit the real time performance possibilities of the Epiphany chip. Initially a host thread activates all 16 cores to execute the computation kernel. The kernel itself distributes the work statically among the cores; each core calculates the colors for a region of the image and writes the values to the frame buffer. At the end of each frame, all cores inform the host thread and wait to be synchronized. When all cores finish their caculations for the particular frame the host signals them to continue with the next one.

In order to utilize OpenMP, we unified the host and Epiphany code in a single file, moving the kernel code into a `target` region. Next, we removed all calls to eSDK and replaced them with OpenMP pragmas, and finally we removed the synchronization code, since this functionality is now carried out by a `barrier`. The generated kernel size was 11794 bytes; the original kernel was 4728 bytes, in comparison. The execution results are shown in Table 2. We give the total number of frames and the frame rate (i.e. the total number of frames divided by the execution time) for the original application and the OpenMP-based version. For comparison we also provide results of the application when the Zynq is used as the device that executes the kernels. In any given column, the differences between the frame rates is natural because of the variability of pixel calculations (darker pixels incur fewer computations).

As it can be easily seen, the original eSDK application performs from 8 % to 13 % better than the OpenMP-based one. We consider this as a very small

Table 2. Frames per second for the Mandelbrot deep zoom application (1024×768)

#frames	eSDK@Epiphany	OMPi@Epiphany	OMPi@Zynq
204	17.854	15.829	4.139
408	15.250	13.630	3.469
612	13.411	12.292	3.015
816	12.528	11.632	2.794
1020	13.330	12.304	2.997
1224	14.486	13.234	3.288

difference, given that our prototype is not yet highly optimized. Moreover, the OpenMP version, without any further modifications resulted in a total of 198 program lines, while the original required 301 lines of code. What is more important is that the programmability gains are huge. We achieved on average 90 % of the performance of the original application with a mere 5 OpenMP pragmas. Finally, notice that the Epiphany achieves up to 4× more frames per second as compared to the Zynq.

5   Conclusion and Future Work

We presented the design of the first OpenMP 4.0 infrastructure for the Parallella board. Our system treats the Epiphany-16 as an accelerator device, attached to a dual-core ARM host processor and allows the dynamic creation of parallel teams within the device itself. While not highly optimized yet, our prototype is able to support OpenMP 4.0 applications delivering performance up to 92 % of hand-written low-level eSDK code as observed for a particular application.

Currently, our prototype has a number of limitations which have to do with the handling of OpenMP internal control variables (ICVs) which are mostly lacking for the Epiphany. Another limitation is the lack of sophisticated management for the shared memory in the host runtime. The memory segments defined for kernel and tasking data environments are relinquished in the order they were allocated, which may cause unnecessary fragmentation. We are currently working on an improved allocator.

Our future work is concentrated mostly on two areas; first, optimize the current implementation and second, implement additional OpenMP functionality. For the former, we are working on minimizing both the memory footprint of the device runtime as well as its overheads for the OpenMP constructs. For the latter, our next target is the support of the new **teams** and **distribute** directives, which create a given number of thread teams within the accelerator, and divide loop iterations among them.

Acknowledgment. The authors would like to thank Adapteva for providing them with a Parallella-16 board through the Parallella University Program.

References

1. GCC 5 Release Series. https://www.gcc.gnu.org/gcc-5/changes.html
2. OpenMP/Clang. http://www.clang-omp.github.io/
3. Aaberge, T.: Analyzing the Performance of the Epiphany Processor. Master's thesis, Norwegian Univ. of Science and Technology, Aug 2014
4. Adapteva: Epiphany SDK reference Manual, Sept 2013
5. Adapteva: Parallella Reference Manual, Sept 2014
6. Varghese, A., Bob Edwards, G.M., Rendell, A.P.: Programming the adapteva epiphany 64-core network-on-chip coprocessor. In: Proceedings of the IPDPSW 2014, pp. 984–992. Phoenix, USA, Dec 2014
7. Chow, E., Anzt, H., Dongarra, J.: Asynchronous iterative algorithm for computing incomplete factorizations on GPUs. In: Kunkel, J.M., Ludwig, T. (eds.) ISC High Performance 2015. LNCS, vol. 9137, pp. 1–16. Springer, Heidelberg (2015)
8. Brown Deer Technology, LLC: COPRTHR API Reference (2014)
9. Bull, J.M.: Measuring Synchronisation and scheduling overheads in OpenMP. In: Proceedings of the 1st EWOMP, Lund, Sweden, pp. 99–105, Sept 1999
10. Kirk, D.B., Hwu, W.-M.W.: Programming Massively Parallel Processors. A Hands-on Approach, 2nd edn. Morgan Kaufmann, MA (2012)
11. Dimakopoulos, V.V., Leontiadis, E., Tzoumas, G.: A portable C compiler for OpenMP V. 2.0. In: Proceedings of the EWOMP 2003, Aachen, Germany, pp. 5–11, Sept 2003
12. Intel Corporation: User and Reference Guide for the Intel C++ Compiler 15.0, OpenMP* Support. https://software.intel.com/en-us/node/522679
13. Liao, C., Yan, Y., de Supinski, B.R., Quinlan, D.J., Chapman, B.: Early experiences with the OpenMP accelerator model. In: Rendell, A.P., Chapman, B.M., Müller, M.S. (eds.) IWOMP 2013. LNCS, vol. 8122, pp. 84–98. Springer, Heidelberg (2013)
14. Mitra, G., Stotzer, E., Jayaraj, A., Rendell, A.P.: Implementation and optimization of the OpenMP accelerator model for the TI keystone II architecture. In: DeRose, L., de Supinski, B.R., Olivier, S.L., Chapman, B.M., Müller, M.S. (eds.) IWOMP 2014. LNCS, vol. 8766, pp. 202–214. Springer, Heidelberg (2014)
15. Newburn, C.J., Deodhar, R., Dmitriev, S., Murty, R., Narayanaswamy, R., Wiegert, J., Chinchilla, F., McGuire, R.: Offload compiler runtime for the Intel® Xeon Phi^{TM} Coprocessor. In: Kunkel, J.M., Ludwig, T., Meuer, H.W. (eds.) ISC 2013. LNCS, vol. 7905, pp. 239–254. Springer, Heidelberg (2013)
16. OpenACC: The OpenACC Application Programming Interface Vesion 2.0, June 2013
17. OpenMP A.R.B.: OpenMP Application Program Interface V4.0, July 2013

Systematic Fusion of CUDA Kernels
for Iterative Sparse Linear System Solvers

José I. Aliaga[✉], Joaquín Pérez, and Enrique S. Quintana-Ortí

Dpto. de Ingeniería y Ciencia de Computadores,
Universitat Jaume I, 12071 Castellón, Spain
{aliaga,joaquin.perez,quintana}@uji.es

Abstract. We introduce a systematic analysis in order to fuse CUDA kernels arising in efficient iterative methods for the solution of sparse linear systems. Our procedure characterizes the input and output vectors of these methods, combining this information together with a dependency analysis, in order to decide which kernels to merge. The experiments on a recent NVIDIA "Kepler" GPU report significant gains, especially in energy consumption, for the fused implementations derived from the application of the methodology to three of the most popular Krylov subspace solvers with/without preconditioning.

Keywords: Graphics processors · CUDA · Sparse linear systems · Iterative solvers

1 Introduction

The solution of sparse linear systems [12] is an ubiquitous problem in ranking and search methodologies for the web, boundary value problems and finite element models for partial differential equations, economic modeling, and information retrieval, among others. The interest of these applications has given rise to a very large number of sophisticated sparse matrix storage layouts, libraries and algorithms for general-purpose processors (CPUs); see, e.g., [1,7,8,15]. NVIDIA also supports the solution of sparse linear systems on graphics processors (GPUs), via the libraries CUBLAS and cuSPARSE, which respectively contain (CUDA) GPU kernels operating on vectors and sparse matrices.

Despite the importance of energy consumption [9,11], few analyses of sparse linear algebra operations focus on this metric [3]. One particular source of energy inefficiency during the execution of an iterative solver [12] on a heterogeneous CPU-GPU server is that, when implemented via calls to the GPU kernels in CUBLAS/cuSPARSE, the CPU thread in control of the GPU repeatedly invokes fine-grain CUDA kernels of low cost and, therefore, short duration. Even if the solver avoids most data transfers between (the memories of) CPU and GPU, this continuous stream of kernel calls often prevents the CPU from entering an energy-efficient C-state. In [2] we introduced the *fusion of GPU kernels* as a

© Springer-Verlag Berlin Heidelberg 2015
J.L. Träff et al. (Eds.): Euro-Par 2015, LNCS 9233, pp. 675–686, 2015.
DOI: 10.1007/978-3-662-48096-0_52

means to avoid this power-hungry scenario, for the particular case of the conjugate gradient (CG) method [12]. The results in that work report significant energy gains combined with a slight improvement in performance on a platform equipped with an Intel i7-3770K plus an NVIDIA "Fermi" GTX480 board. In this paper we make the following major contributions:

- We evolve [2] into a systematic analysis of the fusion of GPU kernels arising in a representative collection of sparse linear solvers: CG, BiCG and BiCGStab [12], including Jacobi-based preconditioned versions of these.
- We include three alternative implementations (scalar CSR, 2-D vector CSR and ELL [6]) for the sparse matrix-vector multiplication (SpMV), with different properties/characterization which impact the possibilities of merging the corresponding solvers.
- We experimentally demonstrate the benefits of kernel fusion in a platform comprising an Intel Core i3770K plus an NVIDIA "Kepler" K20c GPU.

The rest of the paper is structured as follows. In Sect. 2 we briefly review related work on the fusion of GPU kernels. In Sect. 3 we present the iterative solvers targeted in our work, identifying the mathematical operations that are implemented as CUDA kernels. Furthermore, we provide a systematic characterization of these GPU kernels, defining the properties that allow the fusion of two (or more) kernels. Finally, in Sects. 4 and 5 we respectively evaluate the new merged iterative solvers and discuss the conclusions from this work.

2   Related Work

Kernel fusion has received considerable attention in the past as an optimization technique via, e.g., increased memory locality, lower overhead by eliminating multiple calls to kernels, and richer space for compiler optimizations. For brevity, we next discuss a few efforts that specifically target fusion of GPU kernels.

In [10] the authors analyze how to fuse several types of CUDA kernels (map, reduce, and combinations of these) corresponding to BLAS-1 and *dense* BLAS-2 operations. Our work specifically targets iterative solvers for sparse linear systems, and leads us to consider a richer set of operations, different from those in [10]. Furthermore, we break the implementation of reduction kernels into two stages so that one of them, which concentrates most of the computational work, can still be fused.

In [14] the authors study the fusion of CUDA kernels with the purpose of improving their power-energy efficiency by accommodating a higher and better balanced utilization of the GPU cores. Three classes of fusions are identified in their paper: "inner thread", "inner thread block", and "inter thread block", and their effects are *simulated* using two general benchmarks. Our fusions correspond to the first class as, for the type of operations arising in sparse linear algebra, this option yields a fair balance of the workload. Our approach differs in that we focus on the type of kernel fusions arising in sparse linear algebra, we provide a precise characterization of the kernels arising in this domain, and we offer experimental performance and energy results.

In [13] the authors propose the fusion of CUDA kernels arising in iterative sparse linear systems to improve performance, but only consider merging kernels that provide the same functionality and have no dependencies among them. The authors of [4] apply the techniques described in [2] to the iterative solution of sparse linear systems via BiCGStab. None of these works provides a systematic characterization of the GPU kernels and the conditions that allow their fusion.

3 Systematic Kernel Fusion for Sparse Iterative Solvers

3.1 Overview of Iterative Solvers for Sparse Linear Systems

Given a linear system $Ax = b$, where $A \in \mathbb{R}^{n \times n}$ is sparse, $b \in \mathbb{R}^n$ contains the independent terms, and $x \in \mathbb{R}^n$ is the sought-after solution, iterative projection methods based on Krylov subspaces, in combination with an appropriate preconditioner, often outperform the most efficient direct solvers available today in terms of memory consumption and execution time [12].

Concerning the computational effort of iterative Krylov subspace methods, in practical applications the cost of the iteration loop is dominated by one or two SPMV involving A. Given a sparse matrix A with n_z nonzero entries, in general the cost of the SPMV is roughly $2n_z$ floating-point arithmetic operations (flops). Additionally, the loop body contains several vector operations that require $O(n)$ flops each.

Figure 1 offers an algorithmic description of the preconditioned BiCG method. In general, we use Greek letters for scalars, lowercase for vectors and uppercase for matrices. There, the user-defined parameter $\tau_{\max}$ sets an upper bound on the relative residual for the computed approximation to the solution x_j, and (z_1, z_2) denotes the inner product (DOT) of vectors z_1, z_2. The method involves two SPMV as well as several BLAS-1 (vector) operations per iteration (AXPY, XPAY and DOT). The application of the Jacobi preconditioner matrix M requires an element-wise product of two vectors.

The preconditioned BiCG method in Fig. 1 contains all the GPU kernels that appear also in the preconditioned CG and BiCGStab. In the following section we characterize these kernels from the point of view of the type of access they perform to the data/results, we employ the preconditioned BiCG in order to present the systematic fusion of GPU kernels, and we generalize these principles to other variants of BiCG as well as other solvers.

3.2 Characterization of GPU Kernels for Sparse Iterative Solvers

A GPU kernel K performs a *mapped* access to a vector v if each thread of K accesses one of the elements of v, independently of other threads, and the global access is coalesced. We note that this property can be applied separately to the kernel input and output vectors. For the specific kernels identified in the sparse

$A \to M$	Compute Jacobi preconditioner
Initialize $r_0, r_0^*, p_0, p_0^*, x_0, \sigma_0, \tau_0; j := 0$	
while $(\tau_j > \tau_{\max})$	Loop for iterative solver
1. $v_j := A p_j$	1. SpMV
2. $\alpha_j := \sigma_j / (v_j, p_j^*)$	2. DOT
3. $x_{j+1} := x_j + \alpha_j p_j$	3. AXPY
4. $r_{j+1} := r_j - \alpha_j v_j$	4. AXPY
5. $z_j := M^{-1} r_{j+1}$	5. JPRED (Jacobi preconditioner)
6. $v_j^* := A^T p_j^*$	6. SpMV
7. $r_{j+1}^* := r_j^* - \alpha_j v_j^*$	7. AXPY
8. $z_j^* := M^{-1} r_{j+1}^*$	8. JPRED (Jacobi preconditioner)
9. $\zeta_j := (z_j, r_{j+1}^*)$	9. DOT
10. $\beta_j := \zeta_j / \sigma_j$	10. Scalar op
11. $\sigma_j = \zeta_j$	11. Scalar op
12. $p_{j+1} := z_j + \beta_j p_j$	12. XPAY (AXPY-like)
13. $p_{j+1}^* := z_j^* + \beta_j p_j^*$	13. XPAY (AXPY-like)
14. $\tau_{j+1} := \| r_{j+1} \|_2$	14. Vector 2-norm (DOT + sqrt)
$j := j + 1$	
endwhile	

Fig. 1. Algorithmic formulation of the preconditioned BiCG method.

Table 1. Types of access to the vector inputs/output of the GPU kernels.

Operation		Input vector(s)		Output vector
		x	y	y
AXPY	$y := \alpha x + y$	mapped	mapped	mapped
XPAY	$y := \alpha y + x$	mapped	mapped	mapped
DOT	$\alpha := x^T y = (x, y)$	mapped	mapped	unmapped
JPRED	$y := M^{-1} x$	–	mapped	mapped
SpMV scalar CSR	$y := Ax$	unmapped	–	mapped
SpMV vector CSR	$y := Ax$	unmapped	–	unmapped
SpMV ELL	$y := Ax$	unmapped	–	mapped

iterative solvers, we can then characterize their access types as shown in Table 1. For SpMV, we consider three well-known kernels/implementations [6]: *scalar* CSR, *vector* CSR and ELL.

3.3 Fusion of GPU Kernels

We first discuss two factors that may impact the performance that can be attained by merging two GPU kernels:

Grid dimensionality (1D, 2D or 3D). For kernels that operate on vectors, this parameter has little impact on the performance. Therefore, for simplicity, a practical approach is to enforce the same dimensionality for both kernels by, e.g., setting that to the highest one of the two kernels.

Grid dimensions (number of threads per block and number of blocks).
The approach here is, for simplicity, to enforce the same grid dimensions for both kernels, and to set the dimensions to the largest values employed by any of the two kernels. However, this must be done with care, as this parameter may have a real effect on the performance of the kernels.

Fusing kernels is targeted to improve performance and/or energy consumption, but obviously should produce the results of a non-fused execution. Let us elaborate now the properties that two GPU kernels, namely K_1 and K_2, must exhibit in order to participate in a fusion:

- In case K_1 and K_2 do not share any data (i.e., are independent), they can always be merged.
- Consider that K_1 produces an result or output vector v that is also an input for K_2, denoted hereafter as $K_1 \xrightarrow{v} K_2$. (That is, there exists a read-after-write or RAW data dependency between K_1 and K_2, dictated by the type and order of shared access to vector v.) For the type of (dependent) kernels arising in the sparse iterative solvers, the fusion is possible if K_1/K_2 perform a mapped access to the output/input vector v. This guarantees that *(i)* both kernels apply the same mapping of threads to the vector elements shared (exchanged) via registers; *(ii)* both kernels apply the same mapping of thread blocks to the vector elements shared (exchanged) via shared memory; and *(iii)* a global barrier is not necessary between the two kernels.

From the characterization in Table 1, we easily derive that AXPY, XPAY and JPRED can be always merged with any other dependent kernel (one or more of them) of the same sort (i.e., AXPY, XPAY and JPRED). Also, the scalar CSR and ELL versions of SPMV can be merged with any kernel of these three types that consumes the vector resulting from the product, i.e., SPMV (scalar CSR, ELL)$\xrightarrow{y}$ $K_2 \in \{$AXPY, XPAY, JPRED$\}$ can be merged; but $K_1 \in \{$AXPY, XPAY, JPRED$\}$ $\xrightarrow{y}$ SPMV cannot for any version of the sparse matrix-vector product.

The reduction kernel DOT is a special case that needs a tailored implementation so that it can be efficiently merged in $K_1 \xrightarrow{y}$ DOT. Concretely, in [2] we divided this kernel into two stages, say DOT$_{\text{ini}}$ and DOT$_{\text{fin}}$, with the first one being implemented as a GPU kernel which performs the costly element-wise products and subsequent reduction within a thread block, producing a partial result in the form of a temporary vector with one entry per block. This is followed by routine DOT$_{\text{fin}}$, which completes the operation by repeatedly reducing the contents of this vector into a single scalar via a sequence of calls to GPU kernels. The important aspect to note at this point is that, because the reduction proceeds within blocks, this initial stage of the reduction performs a mapped read of the input vectors, and therefore can be efficiently merged in the sequence $K_1 \in$ $\{$AXPY, XPAY, JPRED, SPMV$\}$ $\xrightarrow{y}$ DOT$_{\text{ini}}$. Routine DOT$_{\text{fin}}$ is in practice implemented as a sequence of GPU kernels with mapped/unmapped input/output; see [2]. In consequence, this collection of kernels cannot be merged into a single one themselves, and DOT$_{\text{fin}} \xrightarrow{y} K_2$ cannot be fused.

3.4 Fusions in BiCG

We next apply the previous fusion principles to the preconditioned BiCG with SpMV based on the scalar CSR or ELL format, and we summarize the results for the (2-D) vector CSR format and the non-preconditioned version.

The left-hand side graph in Fig. 2 identifies the dependencies (using arrows/ edges) between operations of the preconditioner BiCG, with the nodes and their numeric labels identifying the operations within the loop body of the solver; see Fig. 1. (For simplicity, we do not include the operations before the loop body or the dependencies between different iterations.) As argued earlier, the DOT operations (2, 9 and 14) are partitioned into two stages (a or b, corresponding respectively to kernel DOT$_{ini}$ and routine DOT$_{fin}$) in order to facilitate the fusion of the first part, if possible, with a previous kernel. The node colors distinguish between the four different operation types: SpMV, DOT, AXPY/XPAY and JPRED. The patterns on top and bottom of each node specify, respectively, the type of mapping for the input and output vector(s) of each operation. Concretely, the parallel lines correspond to a mapped operator and the chessboard pattern an unmapped one. Operations 10 and 11 are special cases as they only receive/produce (input/output) one scalar and are merged into a single node.

The right-hand side graph in Fig. 2 illustrates one specific fusion of kernels among the several possibilities dictated by the kernel dependencies and the mappings of the input/output vectors. The fusions are encircled by thick lines and

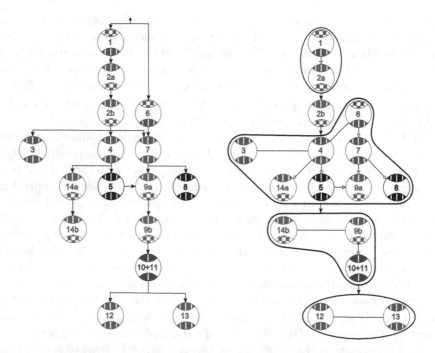

Fig. 2. Dependencies between GPU kernels and fusions (left and right, respectively) for the preconditioned BiCG solver with SpMV based on the scalar CSR or ELL format.

designate four macro-kernels: {1-2a}, {3-4-5-6-7-8-9a-14a}, {9b-10-11-14b}, {12-13}; plus a single-node (macro-)kernel: {2b}. The arrowless lines connect groups of independent kernels (e.g., 3 and 4). For simplicity, we do not include all the connections within a group. The arrows identify dependencies inside macro-kernels (e.g., from 4 to 5) and between them (e.g., from {1-2a} to {2b}).

Our fused version of the preconditioned BiCG, when SpMV employs the alternative vector CSR format (with unmapped input and output for SpMV), differs from that in Fig. 2 in that the two matrix-vector operations (kernels 1 and 6) are merged together; in addition, due to the unmapped output of kernel 1, kernel 2a becomes a single-node macro-kernel. The resulting macro-kernels are therefore: {1-6}, {2a}, {2b}, {3-4-5-7-8-9a-14a}, {9b-10-11-14b} and {12-13}. Also, for all variants of the BiCG solver (based on scalar CSR, vector CSR and ELL SpMV), the fusion graphs of their non-preconditioned counterparts simply differ in that kernels 5 and 8, corresponding to the application of the preconditioner, are not present.

These particular fusions were chosen following the fusion principles exposed in this section and some general performance guidelines:

- The fusions can be decided by performing a systematic analysis of each kernel, starting e.g. at 1, 2, etc., with those labeled with a higher number, taking into account the dependencies and the type of input/output (mapped or unmapped). In general, the strategy is to reduce as much as possible the total number of macro-kernels, in order to avoid the associated performance and energy overheads. For the preconditioned BiCG, the right-hand side graph in Fig. 2 presents the minimum number of macro-kernels due to the restrictions imposed by the unmapped output vectors of the three DOT operations (2a/b, 9a/b and 14a/b). We note that 10+11 could have been instead merged with {12-13} but we selected the first option for performance reasons.
- The dependencies between operations within the same macro-kernel specify a partial order for their execution. In principle, independent kernels are merged by integrating their instructions into a single code one after another. As an exception, for performance reasons, when the initial or final stages of two independent DOT operations are merged together into a single macro-kernel (e.g., 9a with 14a; and also 9b with 14b), their instructions are interleaved in the code. (Interleaving of multiple DOT operations was proposed in [4].)
- Alternatively, 6 can be merged with {1-2a}, but this option was discarded because, for the scalar CSR and ELL implementations of SpMV, the result attained lower performance.

3.5   Fusions in CG and BiCGStab

Figure 3 presents the fusion graphs for the preconditioned versions of CG and BiCGStab[1] when SpMV is based on the scalar CSR or ELL format. For the CG solver, the only difference when SpMV employs the vector CSR format

---

[1] For BiCGStab, nodes 7 and 12 of the graph actually embed two dependent operations of type AXPY/XPAY each. For brevity, they are represented with a single node each.

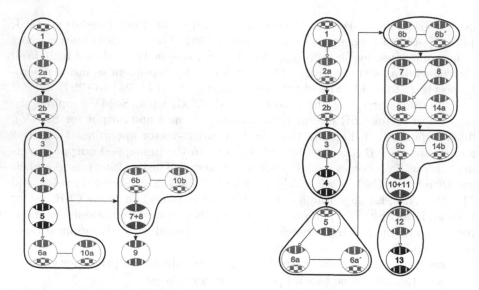

Fig. 3. Fusions of GPU kernels in the preconditioned CG and BiCGStab solvers (left and right, respectively) with SpMV based on the scalar CSR or ELL format. The colors of the nodes match those employed for the preconditioned BiCG solver, and identify the same four types of operations: SpMV, DOT, AXPY/XPAY and JPRED.

is that kernels 1 and 2a become two separate single-node macro-kernels. The same applies to the two SpMV in BiCGStab, i.e. kernels 1 and 5, which become an isolated macro-kernel each. As in the BiCG solver, the non-preconditioned versions of CG and BiCGStab differ in that the nodes corresponding to the preconditioner application (5 for the former and 4, 13 in the latter) disappear.

The graphs in Fig. 3 contain the minimum number of macro-kernels. Due to stricter dependencies of CG and BiCGStab compared with BiCG, the number of alternative fusions in the former two is reduced to instead joining 7+8 with 9 in CG, and 10+11 with 12–13 in BiCGStab.

In summary, the study of this collection of cases (three solvers, with and without preconditioner, and three different implementations of SpMV) exposes that, for the type of operations involved in these iterative solvers, the two stages of the DOT operations act as barriers (or synchronization points), enforcing a particular fusion/division of the macro-kernels.

4   Experimental Evaluation

In this section we evaluate the performance and energy gains of the merged solvers, comparing them with non-fused counterparts. For this purpose, we employ several sparse matrices from the University of Florida Matrix Collection (UFMC)[2] and a difference discretization of the 3D Laplace problem; see Table 2. The coefficient

---

[2] http://www.cise.ufl.edu/research/sparse/matrices/.

Table 2. Description and properties of the test matrices from the UFMC (left) and the 3D Laplace problem (right). In the matrix names, FEM_3DTH2 corresponds to the "FEM 3D nonlinear thermal problem".

Matrix	n_z	n	n_z/n
BMWCRA1_1	10,641,602	148,770	71.53
CRANKSEG_2	14,148,858	63,838	221.63
F1	26,837,113	343,791	78.06
INLINE_1	38,816,170	503,712	77.06
LDOOR	42,493,817	952,203	44.62
AUDIKW_1	77,651,847	943,645	82.28
FEM_3DTH2	3,489,300	147,900	23.59

Matrix	n_z	n	n_z/n
A100	6,940,000	1,000,000	6.94
A126	13,907,370	2,000,376	6.94
A159	27,986,067	4,019,679	6.94
A200	55,760,000	8,000,000	6.94
A252	111,640,032	16,003,001	6.94

matrix A for AUDIKW_1 and `inline_1` is too large to be stored in the ELL format and these combinations of matrix case/storage format are excluded from the evaluation. Moreover, A is unsymmetric for FEM_3DTH2 and, therefore, cannot be tackled via the CG solver. For all cases, the solution vector was chosen to have all entries equal 1, and the independent vector was set to $b = Ax$. The iterative solvers were initialized with the starting guess $x_0 = 0$. All experiments were done using IEEE single precision (SP) arithmetic. While the use of double precision (DP) arithmetic is in general mandatory for the solution of sparse linear systems, the use of mixed SP-DP in combination with iterative refinement leads to improved execution time and energy consumption when the target platform is a GPU accelerator [5].

The target architecture is a Linux server (CentOS release 6.2 with kernel 2.6.32) equipped with a single Intel Core i7-3770K CPU (3.5 GHz, four cores) and 16 Gbytes of DDR3 RAM, connected via a PCI-e 2.0 bus to an NVIDIA "Kepler" K20c GPU (compute capability 3.5, 706 MHz, 2,496 CUDA cores) with 5 GB of GDDR5 RAM integrated into the accelerator board. Power was collected using a *National Instruments* (NI) Data Acquisition System, composed of the NI9205 module and the NIcDAQ-9178 chassis, and plugged to the lines that connect the output of the power supply unit with motherboard and GPU.

In total, we evaluated CG, BiCG and BiCGStab, with and without preconditioning, using three different implementations of SPMV (scalar CSR, vector CSR and ELL), and five different versions of each solver:

- CUBLASL is a plain version of the solver implemented via calls to CUBLAS kernels from the legacy programming interface of this library, combined with *ad-hoc* implementations of SPMV. In this version, one or more scalars may be transferred between the main memory and the GPU memory address space each time a kernel is invoked and/or its execution is completed.
- CUBLASN is an evolved version of the previous implementation that, whenever possible, maintains the scalars in the GPU memory (via the new interface of CUBLAS), in order to avoid unnecessary communication/synchronization between CPU and GPU.
- CUDA replaces the CUBLAS (vector) kernels in the previous version by our *ad-hoc* implementations, including the two-stage DOT.
- MERGE applies the fusions described in Sect. 3.

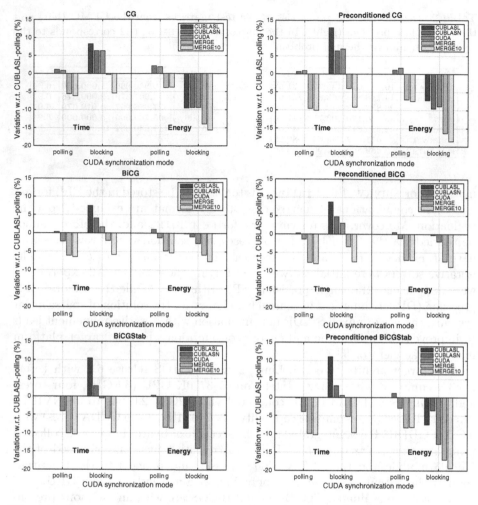

Fig. 4. Execution time and energy consumption for CG, BiCG and BiCGStab solvers (top, middle and bottom, resp.) without and with preconditioner (left and right, resp.).

- MERGE_10 applies the fusions as well and, in addition, only checks the convergence every 10 iterations of the solver, thus reducing the amount of synchronizations between CPU and GPU due to the evaluation of this test.

In review, there are 3 solvers, 2 preconditioning modes, 3 implementations of SpMV, and 5 versions of the solver; i.e., 90 combinations. Furthermore, we execute these configurations under the polling and blocking CUDA synchronization modes, and evaluate them for 12 test matrices (11 for CG), collecting the time and energy per iteration for each scenario. In order to reduce the number of results to show, *(i)* we report the variations in time/energy of the different implementations with respect to CUBLASL executed in polling mode; *(ii)* in addition, we summarize the results for the matrix test cases into a single average value, giving the same weight to all of matrix tests; and *(iii)* finally, we consider only the vector CSR implementation of SpMV for the UFMC cases and the ELL variant for the Laplace problems since our experiments showed that these are the best options from the point of view of performance.

With these considerations, Fig. 4 reports the time and energy variations for three solvers (CG, BiCG, BiCGStab) with/without preconditioning and five versions of each (CUBLASL, CUBLASN, CUDA, MERGE, MERGE_10), executed under two different synchronization modes (polling and blocking).

The first aspect to note is that all plots in Fig. 4 reflect the same qualitative trend, independently of the specific solver and whether or not the preconditioner is present. Let us consider, e.g., the top-left plot (CG solver without preconditioner). Compared with the baseline case (CUBLASL executed in polling mode), the two non-fused versions CUBLASN and CUDA only experience a slight increase in both time and energy (around 1 % and 2 %, resp.) when operating under the polling mode. For the alternative blocking mode, these versions present an appealing reduction of the energy consumption (above 9 %), but unfortunately this comes at the cost of a more visible performance penalty (a time increase superior to 6 %). The desired combination (reduction in both time and energy) is attained by the merged versions (MERGE and MERGE_10). Both algorithms report a decrease of execution time superior to 5 %, except for MERGE executed in blocking mode, for which the variation of time is negligible. The best combination is clearly MERGE_10, which combines this reduction of time with a remarkable decrease of energy consumption, superior to 15 %.

In general, the best option is to employ MERGE_10 executed in blocking mode. Compared with the baseline case, the reduction in time for all solvers and preconditioning modes is between 5.1 % and 10.2 %, while from the energy perspective the savings vary between 4.0 % and 20.0 %. Comparing MERGE_10 with the same implementation executed in polling mode, the blocking mode basically matches its performance (around the same execution time) while producing higher energy gains, especially for CG and BiCGStab.

5   Concluding Remarks

We have introduced and applied a systematic methodology to derive fused versions of three popular iterative solvers (with and without preconditoning) for sparse linear systems. An analysis of the type of access that the threads in charge of a kernel's execution perform on the kernel inputs and outputs, together with the observation of the data dependencies between kernels, determine the candidates to be fused. For performance and energy efficiency reasons, the general goal is to minimize the number of macro-kernels that results from the application of the fusions. From this point of view, we obtain reductions from $10 \rightarrow 5$, $13 \rightarrow 5$ and $14 \rightarrow 8$ for the preconditioned versions of CG, BiCG and BiCGStab, respectively. The gains are experimentally demonstrated on a recent CPU-GPU architecture, consisting of an Intel "Sandy-Bridge" multicore processor and an NVIDIA "Kepler" GPU. Compared with plain versions of the solvers based on CUBLAS and *ad-hoc* implementations of SpMV, the fused versions attain remarkable energy savings when executed in blocking mode. Furthermore, in general they match the performance of an execution of the same versions when executed in the performance-active but power-hungrier polling mode.

Acknowledgements. This research was supported by projects EU FP7 318793 (Exa2 Green) and TIN2011-23283 of the *Ministerio de Economía y Competitividad* and EU FEDER. We thank Hartwig Anzt from the University of Tennessee for his comments.

References

1. CSB library (2014), http://gauss.cs.ucsb.edu/aydin/csb/html/
2. Aliaga, J.I., Pérez, J., Quintana-Ortí, E.S., Anzt, H.: Reformulated conjugate gradient for the energy-aware solution of linear systems on GPUs. In: 42nd International Conference on Parallel Processing (ICPP), pp. 320–329 (2013)
3. Aliaga, J.I., et al.: Unveiling the performance-energy trade-off in iterative linear system solvers for multithreaded processors. Concurrency and Computation: Practice and Experience (2014, to appear)
4. Anzt, H., Sawyer, W., Tomov, S., Luszczek, P., Yamazaki, I., Dongarra, J.: Optimizing Krylov subspace solvers on graphics processing units. In: IEEE International Parallel Distributed Processing Symposium Workshops (IPDPSW), pp. 941–949 (2014)
5. Anzt, H., et al.: Analysis and optimization of power consumption in the iterative solution of sparse linear systems on multi-core and many-core platforms. In: International Green Computing Conference Workshops (IGCC), pp. 1–6 (2011)
6. Bell, N., Garland, M.: Efficient sparse matrix-vector multiplication on CUDA. NVIDIA Technical report NVR-2008-004, NVIDIA Corp., December 2008
7. Buluç, A., Williams, S., Oliker, L., Demmel, J.: Reduced-bandwidth multithreaded algorithms for sparse matrix-vector multiplication. In: IEEE International Parallel and Distributed Processing Symposium (IPDPS), pp. 721–733 (2011)
8. Choi, J.W., Singh, A., Vuduc, R.W.: Model-driven autotuning of sparse matrix-vector multiply on GPUs. In: ACM SIGPLAN Symposium Principles and Practice of Parallel Programming (PPoPP), vol. 45, pp. 115–126 (2010)
9. Duranton, M., et al.: HiPEAC vision 2015. High performance and embedded architecture and compilation (2015). http://www.hipeac.net/vision
10. Filipovic, J., Madzin, M., Fousek, J., Matyska, L.: Optimizing CUDA code by kernel fusion–application on BLAS. Computing Research Repository (CoRR) abs/1305.1183 (2013). http://arxiv.org/abs/1305.1183
11. Fuller, S.H., Millett, L.I.: The Future of Computing Performance: Game Over or Next Level? National Research Council of the National Academies (2011)
12. Saad, Y.: Iterative Methods for Sparse Linear Systems. SIAM, Philadelphia (2003)
13. Tabik, S., Ortega, G., Garzón, E.: Performance evaluation of kernel fusion BLAS routines on the GPU: iterative solvers as case study. J. Supercomputing **70**(2), 577–587 (2014)
14. Wang, G., Lin, Y., Yi, W.: Kernel fusion: An effective method for better power efficiency on multithreaded GPU. In: Green Computing and Communications (Green-Com), pp. 344–350 (2010)
15. Williams, S., Bell, N., Choi, J., Garland, M., Oliker, L., Vuduc, R.: Sparse matrix vector multiplication on multicore and accelerator systems. In: Kurzak, J., Bader, D.A., Dongarra, J. (eds.) Scientific Computing with Multicore Processors and Accelerators. CRC Press (2010)

Efficient Execution of Multiple CUDA Applications Using Transparent Suspend, Resume and Migration

Taichiro Suzuki[✉], Akira Nukada, and Satoshi Matsuoka

Tokyo Institute of Technology, Meguro, Japan
suzuki.t.cf@m.titech.ac.jp

Abstract. GPUs are now one of the mainstream high-performance processors, embodying rich sets of computational as well as bandwidth resources. However, an individual GPU application typically does not exploit the resources on a GPU in its entirety, and thus concurrent execution of multiple applications may be advantageous in terms of total execution time and energy, by multiplexing on less utilized resources. Although modern GPU features such as Hyper-Q allow such a concurrent execution, it is at the risk of causing device memory shortage, and thus crashing the application or even the entire node. Our Mobile CUDA realizes safe, concurrent execution of multiple, unmodified CUDA applications using a transparent checkpointing approach, and achieves both improved throughput and energy savings for a mix of applications exhibiting different GPU resource requirements on multiple GPUs. Performance evaluation using the Rodinia benchmark suite shows that Mobile CUDA reduces total execution time by 18.4 % and total energy by 5.5 % on mixed workloads.

1 Introduction

Graphics Processing Units (GPUs) are now mainstream processors for HPC workloads. Due to their origin in graphics processing, which is essentially embarrassingly parallel, a typical GPU architecture integrates many small SIMD cores for high floating-point performance as well as a large number of memory controllers for high memory bandwidth. Furthermore, they are also called many-core processors to express their generality beyond graphics processing. There are various general-purpose programming environments for GPUs, including NVIDIA CUDA [7], OpenCL and OpenACC, that are used to achieve application acceleration. Here we focus our attention on CUDA, although our proposal can be applied to other programming environments as well.

A given CUDA application normally utilizes only a limited portion of GPU's resources intensively. The usage depends on the characteristics of the application, usually its computational intensity. For example, N-body simulations and dense matrix multiplications are floating-point compute intensive, while most CFD applications generally require frequent memory accesses and high bandwidth,

© Springer-Verlag Berlin Heidelberg 2015
J.L. Träff et al. (Eds.): Euro-Par 2015, LNCS 9233, pp. 687–699, 2015.
DOI: 10.1007/978-3-662-48096-0_53

i.e. they are memory intensive. As such, if only a single CUDA application is running on a GPU, there are idle and wasted GPU resources during its execution.

Concurrent execution of multiple CUDA applications with different resource requirements could utilize the GPU resources more efficiently. Multiplexing the execution to maximize resource usage at a given time can result in increased throughput, reduction of execution time, and possibly reduction in energy consumption as well. However, there are several challenges with the naïve application of the scheme with respect to system safety; most seriously, since CUDA applications are programmed with the assumption of exclusive GPU usage, concurrent executions could cause shortages in device memory, terminating the application, and even possibly crashing the system. One could estimate the memory usage of each application with techniques such as test execution, but it could be expensive and moreover, there will be no guarantee that the application would not allocate more memory.

Our proposed Mobile CUDA is a computing environment that enables transparent, safe, and concurrent execution of multiple unmodified CUDA applications on multiple GPUs. Mobile CUDA is based on applying the swap-in and out checkpoint approach on each application in order to satisfy the capacity limit of device memory and maximize the opportunity of concurrent execution. Compared to previous work, our checkpoint implementation is more general, robust, and works on modern versions of CUDA runtime. Performance evaluation using the Rodinia benchmark suite [1] shows that Mobile CUDA successfully schedules applications with differing resource requirements without causing any errors, and reduces total execution time by 18.4 % and total energy by 5.5 % on mixed workloads.

2   Background

2.1   Concurrent Execution of Multiple CUDA Applications

Early incarnations of GPUs with so-called programmable shaders facilitated massive parallelism but did not support concurrent execution of multiple application codes. This changed in a limited fashion when NVIDIA introduced the G9X/GT200 series GPUs that allowed concurrent execution of one CUDA kernel and up to two PCI-Express data transfers using DMA controllers, making it possible to overlap data transfers with computation. The succeeding Fermi GPU architecture allowed concurrent execution of multiple CUDA kernels. However, this was restricted to kernels within the same CUDA application context and only a part of the kernels were executed concurrently. The follow-on Kepler GPU architecture finally allowed fully concurrent execution of multiple CUDA kernels from different CUDA applications, a feature which was called *Hyper-Q*.

2.2   Swap-in and -out Checkpointing of CUDA Applications

Given the Hyper-Q capability, we could now select and schedule a set of applications to run concurrently on a GPU that would maximize the resource usage and thus achieve higher throughput and reduced overall runtime. This entails that the scheduling and execution of multiple types of applications can be multiplexed on a single device. However, since the device memory usage of each GPU dynamically changes based on application activities, and there is no on-demand paging for current GPUs, we can select and run the set of applications that will maximize resource usage on the device within the bounds of device memory capacity. When we run out of device memory, we could suspend one or more applications with their data on device memory being saved to host memory in order to release the device memory. Such arbitrary swap-in and out of CUDA application is equivalent to checkpoint and restart in fault-tolerance and process migration. The question then is, how do we checkpoint CUDA applications?

In 2009, Takizawa et al. proposed CheCUDA [10], the first checkpoint and restart library for CUDA applications. CheCUDA was a system-level checkpoint based on BLCR [5]; although BLCR did not directly support CUDA applications because of its inability to save the state of GPU devices, they discovered that BLCR works if all CUDA contexts are destroyed at the time when checkpoint is being taken. After the BLCR checkpoint procedure has finished, CheCUDA restores all CUDA resources. In order to achieve this, CheCUDA employs virtual address for device memory by overriding the data types using class libraries. Since CheCUDA requires re-compilation of the application's source code, it cannot handle software in binary format, e.g. most commercial applications. In contrast, Mobile CUDA does not require source code re-compilation and thus does not suffer from such limitations.

NVCR [8] also checkpoints/restarts CUDA applications that use the CUDA driver API and works transparently without re-compilation of the source codes. In addition, NVCR inherently supported CUDA applications that use the CUDA runtime API, because in old versions of CUDA prior to CUDA 4.0, all the runtime API routines called the driver API internally to access the GPU. Similar to CheCUDA, NVCR also employs BLCR as an underlying checkpointing library, but uses another technique — *replay* of memory-related CUDA API calls — to restore the same addresses in the CUDA context, and it works transparently without modification to the application binaries. We inherit the same approach in Mobile CUDA, but now we have to handle the runtime API separately, a more difficult task as we see later. Also, we do not checkpoint the entire application process to storage, but rather leave it suspended in place and facilitate migration between multiple GPUs on the same machine.

3 Mobile CUDA

In general, the precise amount of device memory required to execute an application is unknown to application users until execution time, and moreover, the size of occupied device memory often fluctuates during the execution. CUDA 6.0 supports *unified memory* which enables on-demand paging between device memory and host memory, but the contents of the pages are merely mirrored between both memory spaces; so we are still faced with restrictions of device memory capacity.

Instead, Mobile CUDA constantly monitors the device memory usage of each CUDA application; if an application tries to allocate an additional device memory region larger than the remaining free memory size, it is suspended via checkpointing, that is, Mobile CUDA saves all GPU data onto host memory and releases all GPU resources. On the other hand, if a CUDA application releases a memory region or exits, other suspended CUDA applications could potentially restart execution. On systems with multiple GPU devices, CUDA applications may migrate and restart on another GPU device. By setting the LD_LIBRARY_PATH environment variable, CUDA applications load our MOCU library instead of NVIDIA's CUDA runtime library to allow for transparent checkpoint/migration. The CUDA runtime API calls are thus monitored and forwarded appropriately. The MOCU manager in turn collects the information such as device memory usage from the MOCU libraries, and is responsible for co-scheduling the CUDA applications to multiple GPUs given their memory constraints.

3.1 Checkpointing CUDA Applications

As mentioned, NVCR's replay technique is currently the only scheme that keeps device memory addresses exactly identical before and after the suspension of CUDA applications. Although Mobile CUDA principally employs the same techniques, there are various improvements and additions. Since the time NVCR was developed for the CUDA driver API 2.3 and 3.0, the implementation of CUDA runtime library changed significantly as noted above, and a set of new techniques are required to support the mainstream CUDA runtime API. In particular for the CUDA runtime API version 5.5 and above, it is impossible to clear the context using the CUDA driver API as was for NVCR; instead, a CUDA runtime API function call cudaDeviceReset needs to be called. Also, unlike with NVCR, suspended applications are not really suspended per second, but are blocked at recv() system call to wait until the GPU is re-assigned to that application. We will also outline the extensions we have made in the following subsections.

3.2 Device Memory Management

Mobile CUDA uses socket API calls for communication. To minimize the overhead, the MOCU library communicates with the MOCU manager only when the state of the CUDA application changes. This includes changes in the device memory usage level caused by allocation or release API calls of CUDA. In addition to such memory-related API calls, the device memory usage also changes when a CUDA context is created or destroyed on a device.

For low-level CUDA driver API, it is the responsibility of the application to first explicitly create a CUDA context. The context allocates at least 64 MB of device memory, along with device-side variables statically declared using the '__device__' keyword. For the CUDA runtime API, however, the CUDA context is implicitly created when the first resource allocation is attempted on the device. The MOCU library communicates with the MOCU manager at each CUDA

runtime API call until the MOCU manager detects the CUDA context of the
application; at this point, Mobile CUDA is fully initialized. After this, the MOCU
library only communicates at the CUDA runtime API calls relevant to device
memory allocation[1].

Whenever a CUDA application attempts to allocate device memory, the
MOCU library intercepts the call and first sends the requested device memory size to the MOCU manager and queries its availability. If available, the
MOCU library then calls the actual memory allocation API; otherwise, the
MOCU library suspends the application execution and the application is check-
pointed/swapped out to the host memory. When a CUDA application tries to
release device memory, the actual API call is made immediately and the size
of the released memory is sent to the MOCU manager. If a memory allocation
request from any of the suspended applications can be satisfied by any GPU as a
result of this, the MOCU manager can then (co-)schedule that application to that
GPU. MOCU manager may also swap-in an application if another application
is checkpointed/swapped out or terminates. In both cases, the MOCU manager
selects an application to resume. Currently this is prioritized by the order of
connection to the MOCU manager, but in future versions we will exploit the
co-scheduling efficiency aspect as experimented in Sect. 4.

```
__device__ float v[1024 * 1024];

__global__ void kernel(float *s) { ..... };

int main(int argc, char **argv) {
    float *p;
    cudaEvent_t s, e;

    cudaSetDevice(0);
    cudaEventCreate(&s);
    cudaEventCreate(&e);
    cudaMalloc((void **)&p, sizeof(float) * 1024 * 1024);
    ....
}
```

Fig. 1. A simplified code using the CUDA runtime API

Since multiple CUDA applications might allocate memory concurrently, the
MOCU manager manages "reserved memory size" and "allocated memory size"
for each application. The reserved memory size is the amount of memory that the
application wants to allocate. The MOCU library first sends this number to the
MOCU manager and asks if there is enough free memory. If the MOCU manager
knows that there is enough memory, it allows the MOCU library to allocate the
memory on the device. However, the actual allocation might fail or the actual
amount of allocated memory might exceed the requested memory (due to various

---

[1] In the current version of CUDA (6.5 as of this writing) the CUDA context is created
immediately at the first call to the runtime API, but this feature allows safeguarding
for future versions in which this assumption might change.

overheads). In any case, the MOCU library sends the result of the allocation to the MOCU manager. The MOCU manager then updates the "allocated memory size" variable to reflect the actual allocated memory size and resets the reserved memory size variable. The reason we need these two variables is the MOCU manager cannot know the actual amount of allocated memory at the request time. Moreover, two applications can concurrently request memory allocation. Thus, the reserved memory is for estimating the amount of memory used, and the allocated memory is for the actual allocated size. The MOCU Manager estimates the availability of device memory by using the NVIDIA Management Library (NVML), and allows allocation if available memory (=free memory size - reserved memory size) is greater than required memory (=requested memory size + 64 MB safety margin).

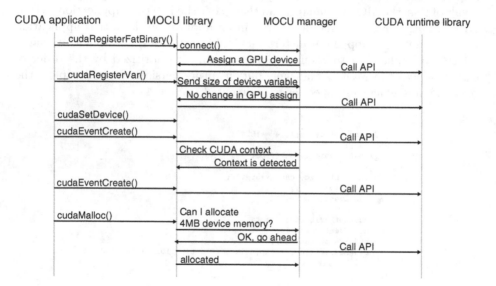

Fig. 2. MOCU library and MOCU manager

Figure 1 shows a simplified CUDA code while Fig. 2 describes how this code works with Mobile CUDA. As seen in Fig. 2, a CUDA application using the CUDA runtime API calls several internal CUDA commands before entering the main function.

Firstly, '__cudaRegisterFatBinary()' is called to register CUDA fat binaries. In this function, the MOCU library connects to the MOCU manager and asks for a GPU assignment. The MOCU manager chooses one of the GPU device with the lowest load (= number of processes). At the same time, 64 MB of memory is reserved on the device for the CUDA context. Since the sample code declares a device variable 'v', __cudaRegisterVar() is called to register each device variable. The MOCU library increases the reserved memory size by the variable size and sends the new size to the MOCU manager.

The application then enters the main function. Here, cudaSetDevice() actually does nothing because Mobile CUDA virtualizes the GPU devices and presents only one GPU to the application. Next, cudaEventCreate() is the first API call to allocate a GPU resource. After calling this function, the MOCU library asks the MOCU manager if the CUDA context exists or not. At this time, MOCU Manager detects the context and updates the allocated memory of the application with the reserved memory size. For the second call of cudaEventCreate(), MOCU library simply calls the actual API.

On call to cudaMalloc(), the MOCU library sends a 4 MB memory allocation request to the MOCU manager. The MOCU manager determines the availability of device memory and, if available, it allows the MOCU library to call the actual cudaMalloc(). If not available, the MOCU manager sends a suspend request to the MOCU library, and the application then releases all CUDA resources and waits until it could be assigned to any of the GPUs that can fulfill its memory requirement.

3.3 Mobile CUDA Optimizations

Mobile CUDA allows applications to use CUDA pinned memory which enables fast data transfer between host and device. Mobile CUDA also needs to transfer data for the swap-in and swap-out of CUDA applications, however we cannot use pinned memory for host-side buffer because pinned memory is related to the CUDA context, which will be destroyed. Due to this restriction, currently we are forced to using pageable host memory instead of CUDA pinned memory, causing possible performance overhead. One optimization implemented is that uninitialized memory regions will not be saved nor restored. This works efficiently, for example, when the application allocates multiple device memory regions and one of the allocations fails due to shortage of device memory.

Mobile CUDA limits the maximum number of CUDA applications running on each device. Running two applications concurrently may be much more beneficial than running each application exclusively. However, concurrently running six applications may not yield better performance than running five applications. Assigning many applications to a single device increases data movement between host and device, and the GPU resources will be quickly exhausted with only a few co-scheduled applications.

Mobile CUDA also can set a limit on the number of applications that can start execution. If a large number of applications connect to the MOCU manager, applications requiring a small amount of memory (small apps) will be more likely to get swapped in over those requesting larger memory (large apps). By limiting the number of the applications that can start, we reduce the probability of small apps preempting large apps.

4 Performance Evaluation

We performed a series of benchmarks to evaluate how much time and energy reduction we can achieve by using the Mobile CUDA. Table 1 shows the specification

Table 1. Specification of the system used in the performance evaluation

CPU	Intel Xeon CPU E5-2687W (3.10 GHz, 8 cores, Sandy Bridge EP) × 2
M/B	Supermicro X9DRG-QF (Intel C602 chipset, four PCI-E Gen3 x16 slots)
Memory	DDR3-1600 Registered ECC DIMM, 8 GB × 16
GPU	NVIDIA Tesla K20c (5 GB)
OS	CentOS 6.4 x86–64
CUDA	Version 5.5 (Driver 319.76)

of the system used in our performance evaluation. The system has four Kepler GPU devices with 5 GB device memory each, and 128 GB host memory. We used CUDA applications from the Rodinia benchmark suite [1]. Since these applications have short execution times with default launch parameters, we modified their command line arguments to increase data size, time steps or number of iterations as described in Table 2. The CUDA source code itself was not modified. Table 2 also shows new execution time and device memory usage of each application. Several Rodinia applications that did not provide a clear way to increase their workload/execution time were excluded from the evaluation.

Table 2. List of applications from Rodinia benchmark

Label	Application	Time [sec]	Memory [MB]	Command-line arguments
(1)	Back Propagation	78.30	201	./backprop 1000000
(2)	b+tree	59.23	83	./b+tree.out file ../../data/b+tree/mil.txt command ../../data/b+tree/command.txt
(3)	CFD Solver	65.57	92	./euler3d ../../data/cfd/missile.domn.0.2M
(4)	dwt2d	56.87	285	./dwt2d 192.bmp -d 4096 × 2048 -f -5 -l 3
(5)	gaussian	61.14	337	./gaussian -s 6000
(6)	HotSpot	67.39	64	./hotspot 512 2 1000000 ../../data/hotspot/temp_512 ../../data/hotspot/power_512 output.out
(7)	kmeans	37.42	194	./kmeans -o -i ../../data/kmeans/kdd_cup -l 1000
(8)	leukocyte	57.34	65	./leukocyte ../../data/leukocyte/testfile.avi 500
(9)	lud	71.49	1086	./lud_cuda ../../data/lud 16384.dat
(10)	Needleman-Wunsch	88.18	2110	./needle 16384 10
(11)	pathfinder	78.25	1988	./pathfinder 5000000 100 20
(12)	srad_v1	45.94	963	./srad 2000 2 1
(13)	srad_v2	56.88	3136	./srad 16384 8192 0 127 0 127 0.5 150
(14)	streamcluster	188.60	2200	./sc_gpu 10 20 256 2097152 2097152 1000 none output.txt 1

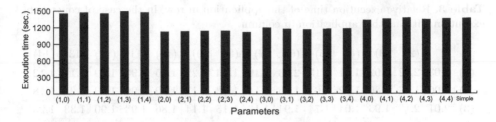

Fig. 3. Limiting parameters of Mobile CUDA and their execution time

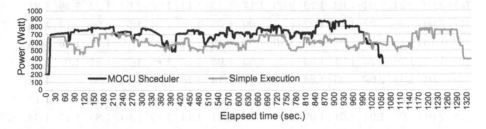

Fig. 4. Power consumption during the execution with and without Mobile CUDA

In total 14 applications were selected and each one executed five times in one benchmark round. We performed 10 such rounds with randomized order of applications in each round and averaged the total execution times. As the baseline, we used simple scheduling which assigns a single GPU exclusively to the application based on a first-come-first-serve policy.

The maximum number of active applications is defined as $\alpha \cdot p + \beta$, where p is the number of devices, α is the number of applications allowed to execute concurrently on one device, and β is the number of extra applications which are allowed to enter the out-of-order execution buffer. We evaluated the impact of choosing parameters α and β on the aggregated execution time as the first step. Parameter p is defined by the hardware set-up and equals 4 in our case.

Figure 3 shows the total execution time using Mobile CUDA, x-axis labels indicate parameters (α, β) and "simple" means normal execution. With Mobile CUDA, we launched all of the 70 application instances at the beginning, and many of them were blocked at the __cudaRegisterFatBinary() function in the MOCU library to wait for the response of the MOCU manager. On the other hand, the simple execution launched p applications on p devices. The overall execution time is mostly influenced by the choice of α. In case of $\alpha = 1$, Mobile CUDA has no advantage and has around 7% overhead. $\alpha = 2$ gives the best result, and $\alpha = 3$ is the second best. In the case of $\alpha = 4$, the execution time with Mobile CUDA is almost the same with the one of simple execution. We found $(\alpha, \beta) = (2, 4)$ to be the best combination of parameters that reduces the execution time by 18.4% and these values were used for the subsequent experiments.

Table 3. Relative execution time of the application in row, in the case of concurrent execution with another application in column.

	(1)	(2)	(3)	(4)	(5)	(6)	(7)	(8)	(9)	(10)	(11)	(12)	(13)	(14)
(1)	2.03	2.02	2.02	1.01	1.13	2.03	1.10	1.14	1.21	1.95	1.96	1.90	1.17	1.12
(2)	2.00	1.96	1.80	1.02	1.61	1.76	1.14	1.13	1.17	1.70	1.90	1.90	1.21	1.18
(3)	2.01	2.16	1.96	1.04	1.74	1.94	1.16	1.15	1.14	1.86	1.93	1.90	1.33	1.23
(4)	1.03	1.02	0.94	1.21	0.96	0.96	0.95	0.96	0.97	0.94	0.96	0.99	0.95	1.03
(5)	10.1	2.59	2.34	1.01	2.03	2.31	1.16	1.14	1.26	2.18	4.61	7.06	1.35	1.23
(6)	2.02	2.24	2.03	1.03	1.79	2.00	1.17	1.13	1.14	1.90	1.94	1.92	1.30	1.21
(7)	2.09	1.36	1.32	1.14	1.22	1.25	1.09	1.05	1.08	1.24	1.97	1.68	1.19	1.05
(8)	1.15	1.11	1.09	1.03	1.07	1.10	1.04	1.19	1.04	1.09	1.15	1.16	1.06	1.03
(9)	1.25	1.26	1.23	1.01	1.03	1.25	1.03	1.03	1.57	1.25	1.26	1.21	1.05	1.02
(10)	2.04	2.31	2.09	1.03	1.84	2.06	1.17	1.14	1.18	1.97	1.95	1.96	-	1.22
(11)	1.97	1.95	1.95	1.02	1.19	1.96	1.09	1.13	1.21	1.90	1.88	1.32	-	1.12
(12)	2.01	1.94	1.94	1.01	1.09	1.96	1.09	1.11	1.14	1.89	1.94	1.85	1.15	1.08
(13)	3.54	2.79	2.56	1.39	1.99	2.47	1.18	1.16	1.39	-	-	3.08	-	-
(14)	2.51	1.65	1.55	1.03	1.37	1.51	0.97	0.97	1.05	1.47	2.03	2.10	-	1.02

Figure 4 shows the power consumption during the execution with and without Mobile CUDA. We measured the AC Power of the machine using OMRON RC3008 in once per second frequency. Mobile CUDA increases power consumption which indicates that GPU resources are heavily utilized. But as the execution with Mobile CUDA completes earlier, the total energy consumption is reduced. The energy consumption for all 70 application instances was 775kJ with Mobile CUDA and 820kJ without Mobile CUDA, thus Mobile CUDA achieved 5.5 % reduction in overall energy consumption.

Table 3 shows the relative execution time of a given application when it is concurrently executed with another application. For example, when applications (1) and (10) are executed concurrently, application (1) takes 1.95x longer and application (10) takes 2.04x longer compared with the case when those applications are executed exclusively. The hyphens ('-') in the table indicate that it is impossible to execute the applications concurrently due to device memory capacity. Let a and b be the relative execution times of applications A and B, respectively, when executed concurrently. In this case, the relative processing speed of the GPU can be determined as $1/a + 1/b$. When this value is greater than 1.0, the concurrent execution is advantageous. Table 4 shows $1/a + 1/b$ for all application pairs from the benchmark.

Most values in Table 4 are above 1.0, which means the concurrent execution increases efficiency for those application pairs. Diagonal values correspond to the concurrent execution of instances of the same application. For the Back Propagation (1), Gaussian (5), and hotspot (6), it is evident that such execution is

Table 4. Relative processing speed of two applications executed concurrently

	(1)	(2)	(3)	(4)	(5)	(6)	(7)	(8)	(9)	(10)	(11)	(12)	(13)	(14)
(1)	0.98	1.00	1.62	1.96	0.98	0.99	1.39	1.75	1.62	1.00	1.02	1.02	1.14	1.29
(2)		1.02	1.02	1.96	1.01	1.01	1.61	1.78	1.65	1.02	1.04	1.21	1.18	1.45
(3)			1.02	2.02	1.00	1.01	1.62	1.79	1.69	1.02	1.03	1.04	1.14	1.46
(4)				1.66	2.03	2.02	1.93	2.02	2.03	2.03	2.02	2.00	1.78	1.94
(5)					0.99	0.99	1.68	1.81	1.77	1.00	1.06	1.06	1.24	1.54
(6)						1.00	1.66	1.79	1.67	1.01	1.03	1.03	1.17	1.49
(7)							1.86	1.91	1.90	1.66	1.42	1.51	1.69	1.98
(8)								1.68	1.93	1.80	1.76	1.77	1.81	2.01
(9)									1.27	1.65	1.61	1.70	1.67	1.93
(10)										1.01	1.04	1.04	-	1.50
(11)											1.06	1.07	-	1.38
(12)												1.08	1.19	1.41
(13)													-	-
(14)														1.97

inefficient. It can be explained by the fact that those applications have only one kernel and spend most of the time within it — concurrent executions of the same kernel does not give any advantage.

On the other hand, dwt2d (4), kmeans (7), srad_v2 (13), and streamcluster (14) require data transfers between host and device, so instances of these applications can be efficiently overlapped. Application srad_v1 (12) spends most of its execution time in kernels, however concurrent execution of this application's instances is efficient. That is because it has multiple kernels of different characteristics.

5   Related Work

Mobile CUDA environment essentially virtualizes GPU devices. There are other existing solutions for GPU virtualization, such as vCUDA [9] and GViM [4]. Both of them provide access to GPU devices from applications running on virtual machines but do not support concurrent execution.

Hyper-Q, pioneered in Kepler GPU, makes it easy to write pipelined GPU code. Many applications achieved speedups using Hyper-Q [6,11]. However, it is only applicable in the scope of a single application. Moreover, device memory usage has to be managed by the application code.

Endo et al., propose HHRT library [3] which enables swap-in and -out of data on GPU devices with small modification to the source code. However, HHRT has a different objective. Its aim is to hide data transfer latencies in a single MPI application, and it does not consider concurrent execution of multiple different applications as Mobile CUDA does.

rCUDA [2] virtualizes the GPUs on remote host as if they were local. Although it uses a similar API interception technology, its intentions are completely different, and does not allow co-scheduling of different CUDA processes beyond Hyper-Q. VGRIS [12] is a scheduling framework for VMs to share a single GPU in a paravirtualized environment. Although similar to Mobile CUDA in that there is a scheduling manager and GPU API calls are intercepted to allow for scheduling of processes, its application area is gaming, and thus focuses on rapid context switching of multiple gaming contexts, and does not allow for checkpointing as with Mobile CUDA.

6   Conclusion and Future Work

Performance of CUDA applications is generally bottlenecked by certain GPU resources, leaving other resources under-utilized. Concurrent execution of multiple CUDA applications can use GPU resources efficiently and reduce total execution time and energy, especially when those applications exhibit different demands for GPU resources and/or execution patterns. Such a concurrent execution scenario cannot be achieved by simply running applications simultaneously as it can cause GPU device memory shortage. To provide safe and concurrent execution transparently, we have proposed the Mobile CUDA computing environment. Based on the checkpointing approach, Mobile CUDA assigns GPU resources to CUDA applications to maximize the concurrency.

In order to suspend, resume and migrate unmodified CUDA applications, Mobile CUDA uses the MOCU manager, which is responsible for managing and scheduling all the GPU resources on the machine, and the MOCU library, which provides real-time API to the applications. By minimizing the communication between them, we achieved negligible overhead for using Mobile CUDA. In the performance evaluation using CUDA applications from Rodinia benchmark, we demonstrated that Mobile CUDA reduced the total execution time by 18.4%, and total energy consumption by 5.5%.

Future work includes the automatic, intelligent co-scheduling of applications with differing resource requirements onto the same GPU, dealing with device-level dynamic memory allocations when source is available, and possibly merging the features with HHRT.

Acknowledgments. This work was supported by JSPS KAKENHI Grant Number 23220003, JST-CREST (Research Area: Advanced Core Technologies for Big Data Integration), and NVIDIA CUDA Center of Excellence.

References

1. Che, S., Boyer, M., Meng, J., Tarjan, D., Sheaffer, J., Lee, S.H., Skadron, K.: Rodinia: a benchmark suite for heterogeneous computing. In: IEEE International Symposium on Workload Characterization 2009 (IISWC), pp. 44–54, October 2009

2. Duato, J., Pena, A.J., Silla, F., Mayo, R., Quintana-Orti, E.S.: Performance of CUDA virtualized remote GPUs in high performance clusters. In: Proceedings of ICPP 2011, pp. 365–374. IEEE Computer Society, Washington, DC (2011)

3. Endo, T., Jin, G.: Software technologies coping with memory hierarchy of GPGPU clusters for stencil computations. In: Proceedings of CLUSTER 2014, pp. 132–139 (2014)

4. Gupta, V., Gavrilovska, A., Schwan, K., Kharche, H., Tolia, N., Talwar, V., Ranganathan, P.: GViM: GPU-accelerated virtual machines. In: Proceedings of HPCVirt 2009, pp. 17–24. ACM, New York (2009)

5. Hargrove, P.H., Duell, J.C.: Berkeley lab checkpoint/restart (BLCR) for Linux clusters. J. Phys: Conf. Ser. **46**(1), 494 (2006)

6. Heinrich, H., Ziegenhein, P., Kamerling, C., Froening, H., Oelfke, U.: GPU-accelerated ray-tracing for real-time treatment planning. J. Phys: Conf. Ser. **489**, 012050 (2014). IOP Publishing

7. Lindholm, E., Nickolls, J., Oberman, S., Montrym, J.: NVIDIA tesla: a unified graphics and computing architecture. IEEE Micro **28**(2), 39–55 (2008)

8. Nukada, A., Takizawa, H., Matsuoka, S.: NVCR: a transparent checkpoint-restart library for NVIDIA CUDA. In: IPDPS 2011 Workshops and Phd Forum (IPDPSW), pp. 104–113, May 2011

9. Shi, L., Chen, H., Sun, J.: vCUDA: GPU accelerated high performance computing in virtual machines. In: Proceedings of IPDPS 2009, pp. 1–11. IEEE CS (2009)

10. Takizawa, H., Sato, K., Komatsu, K., Kobayashi, H.: CheCUDA: a checkpoint/restart tool for CUDA applications. In: Proceedings of PDCAT 2009 (UPDAS), pp. 408–413. IEEE CS (2009)

11. Wende, F., Steinke, T., Cordes, F.: Multi-threaded Kernel Offloading to GPGPU Using Hyper-Q on Kepler Architecture. Technical report 14–19, ZIB (2014)

12. Yu, M., Zhang, C., Qi, Z., Yao, J., Wang, Y., Guan, H.: VGRIS: virtualized GPU resource isolation and scheduling in cloud gaming. In: Proceedings of HPDC 2013, pp. 203–214. ACM, New York (2013)

Author Index

Printed in the United States
B... Bookmasters

Printed in the United States
By Bookmasters